"The original *How to Cook Everything* is the ONLY cookbook I use. Spine broken. Held together by rubber band. Spills everywhere. Handwritten notes on my recipes. Family recipes written into the blank pages. My kids play-fight about who will inherit the book. Thank you for your work and for sharing your gifts!"

—ALLISON MOIR-SMITH, MANCHESTER-BY-THE-SEA, MA

—————————

"I became a fan of yours with the publication of the first *How to Cook Everything*, which I then got my sons hooked on when they had kitchens of their own. Your yogurt biscuits, pancakes, and waffles are the only ones I make. Thank you for making people feel like they can cook, and cook well. You helped me become confident in the kitchen."

—MICHELLE ISKRA, CEDAR PARK, TX

—————————

"My grandmother introduced me to you when I was in high school, and I've carried *How to Cook Everything* with me to eight apartments in three countries so far. It's well worn and well used. I love it."

—JARED BAROL, WALNUT CREEK, CA

—————————

"I bought my first copy of *How to Cook Everything* at the home of some consulate or embassy staffer in Khartoum, Sudan circa 2001, where I was an enthusiastic early-twenties humanitarian far away from most of the food I knew growing up. From your book I learned that I could take risks, sub things in, and vary a basic recipe. I appreciate your dedication to demystifying the kitchen and making it possible for anyone who reads to follow your recipes and make a good meal. You've been a guide to me as I fed myself, as I served comfort food to friends in a tough setting, and as my family and I sit together to laugh and play around our table in our home."

—EMILY CHAMBERS SHARPE, CHARLOTTE, NC

How to
Cook
Everything®

Completely Revised Twentieth Anniversary Edition

How to Cook

Everything®

Mark Bittman

SIMPLE RECIPES FOR GREAT FOOD

Photography by Aya Brackett
Illustrations by Alan Witschonke

HOUGHTON MIFFLIN HARCOURT
Boston | New York | 2019

OTHER BOOKS BY MARK BITTMAN

How to Cook Everything Vegetarian

How to Cook Everything The Basics

How to Cook Everything Fast

How to Bake Everything

How to Grill Everything

Dinner for Everyone

Mark Bittman's Kitchen Matrix

VB6: Eat Vegan Before 6:00

The VB6 Cookbook

Food Matters

The Food Matters Cookbook

The Best Recipes in the World

Fish: The Complete Guide to Buying and Cooking

Leafy Greens

Mark Bittman's Kitchen Express

Mark Bittman's Quick and Easy Recipes from the *New York Times*

The Mini Minimalist

Jean-Georges: Cooking at Home with a Four-Star Chef

Simple to Spectacular

Copyright © 2019 by Double B Publishing, Inc.

Photography copyright © 2019 by Aya Brackett

Illustrations copyright © 1998, 2007, 2008, 2016, 2017, 2019 by Alan Witschonke

hmhbooks.com

Library of Congress Cataloging-in-Publication Data is available.

ISBN 978-1-328-54543-5
ISBN 978-0-358-30563-7 (special ed)
ISBN 978-1-328-54567-1 (ebk)

Book design by Toni Tajima
Food styling by Victoria Granof
Prop styling by Philippa Brathwaite

Printed in China
C&C 10 9 8 7 6 5 4 3 2 1

Contents

Acknowledgments vi
Introduction vii

Cooking Basics 1
What do you need to know—and own—to make great meals? Not much.

Spices, Herbs, Sauces, and Condiments 23
Here's a guide to seasoning, made easy.

Appetizers and Snacks 85
From no-cook to elaborate, here are finger foods, snacks, and knife-and-fork first courses.

Soups 135
These simple, fresh soups from around the world are surprisingly easy, with most ready in minutes, not hours.

Salads 181
Crisp, crunchy, colorful, and simply dressed—few meals are quicker to make.

Vegetables and Fruit 233
The ultimate lexicon of produce, from fresh to dried and frozen, including seaweed, nuts, and olives—with recipes.

Beans 385
Learn how to cook—and love—legumes, alone or in combination with vegetables, rice, meat, and seafood.

Rice and Other Grains 425
The huge world of grains, including and beyond rice, as main dishes and sides.

Pasta, Noodles, and Dumplings 473
From Italy to Asia, including sauces, shapes, and fresh and filled pastas.

Seafood 529
Conquer your fear of fish with a combination of master recipes and species-specific basics, plus advice on how to eat fish sustainably.

Poultry 591
Whether you start with parts, bone-in, bone-out, or whole birds, here's how to make America's favorite meat—and all poultry—taste delicious every time.

Meat 663
All you need to cook beef, pork, lamb, and veal, including international approaches.

Breakfast, Eggs, and Dairy 715
Nothing is more convenient for breakfast (and sometimes dinner): eggs, pancakes, waffles, cereal, and cheese.

Bread, Sandwiches, and Pizza 761
Get started on (or better at) making bread, whether yeasted or super-quick.

Desserts 825
Some new, some classic: cookies, cakes, frostings, sauces, pies, tarts, pastries, ice cream, and more.

More Ways to Navigate the Book 907
Converting Measurements 910
Index 911

Acknowledgments

My first reflex is to say that it feels impossible that I started working on *How to Cook Everything* in late 1994. In fact, like so many things in the past, it's both in a vivid way very like yesterday and in a vague, dreamy way like another lifetime, another person's life. I'm closing in on seventy, but then I was forty-four, and things were going well: My first book, *Fish*, at that point a twelve-year-old dream come true, had won a couple of awards; I was writing regularly for the *Times*, soon to become a columnist; I had agreed to write a book with Jean-Georges Vongerichten.

So it was one of those rare periods where both personally and professionally all was pretty much as I wanted it to be. And then this book came along—not my idea!—the biggest professional challenge imaginable. The idea was to rival *Joy of Cooking* and, other than that notion, there was no real plan. My thinking, such as it was, was to try to communicate in plain language everything I had learned how to cook up until then (I'd been cooking for twenty-five years at that point, so there was at least a foundation of sorts), while filling in whatever blanks there were (and there were plenty) with the help of friends and colleagues and mentors.

I was lucky—blessed—enough to have many of all of those, starting with my (now former) wife, Karen Baar; our children, Kate and Emma, who were girls then and are women now; my agent, Angela Miller; and a thankfully large number of people to whom I remain close, too many to start naming.

But naturally, twenty-five years later, the world, the book, and I have all changed, as have many of the people I hang with and rely on. Still, what was true then I say even more emphatically today: My gratitude extends to hundreds of people—chefs, cookbook writers, editors at all kinds of publications, publishers, producers, friends, relatives, casual acquaintances—who have shared a technique or dish, a kind or insightful word, an idea, an inspiration, and help and affection and thoughtfulness and at times even love. There are more of you to thank in less space than with the first edition. Please know that I appreciate everyone who has been generous with me throughout this journey.

Singling out people is difficult, but on this project it's important for me to acknowledge especially Daniel Meyer, Emily Stephenson, Mirella Blum, food stylist Victoria Granof and her team (Krystal Rack-Carter, Liza Meyers, Veronica Martinez, and Kristen Stangl), prop stylist Philippa Brathwaite (with help from Ryan Bourquin), photo tech Martyna Szczesna, and both Mark Kelly from Lodge and the folks at Workshop Studio. Aya Brackett, whom I love, is responsible for the amazing photography you see here; she is a star.

At my longtime publisher, I'm grateful to editor Stephanie Fletcher, who was fatefully and way more than symbolically (though I love the symbolism) helped through a few turns by the book's first editor, Pam Hoenig. Many thanks to Bruce Nichols and Deb Brody, as well as Marina Padakis Lowry, Melissa Lotfy, Toni Tajima, and Sari Kamin.

Somehow, Kerri Conan was not with me for the first edition of this book (and yet it got done!); she's been my right hand (well, left, really, 'cause for me that's more important) on every cookbook since, and corny as it is, I'll never be able to thank her enough. There's no aspect of this book that doesn't bear her mark.

As for love: Kat, Kateets, Buv, my boys Nick, Jeff, Holden . . . there's just nothing to say. Let's see what happens when this book turns fifty!

Mark Bittman
Glynwood, Spring 2019

Introduction

When *How to Cook Everything* came out more than two decades ago, friends and colleagues teased me about the promise of "everything" in the title. The publisher and I stood by the hyperbole, knowing that by offering instruction on core techniques and common ingredients, including hundreds of variations, and demonstrating how to make substitutions . . . the title was barely an exaggeration.

In the following years, I used the teaching of these skills and strategies to create a series that now includes *How to Cook Everything Vegetarian* (two editions!), *How to Cook Everything: The Basics*, *How to Cook Everything Fast*, *How to Bake Everything*, and *How to Grill Everything*.

Moving forward: This third edition of *How to Cook Everything*, again completely revised and updated, designed to satisfy home cooks hungry for photographs and streamlined content, remains my most important book. And this time around, I focus even more on the most important aspect of my cooking philosophy: flexibility.

I've had the good fortune to travel all over the country (and the world!), talking to people who cook regularly as well as to those who wish they cooked more, and I've discovered that one of the most important differences between those who enjoy cooking and those who treat it like a chore is the ability to be spontaneous. Following recipes to the letter works, but can only take you so far: With practice and increased confidence, you'll become more creative in the kitchen, personalizing food based on the seasonings you crave, the time of year, how much energy you've got, and—especially—what you see when you open the fridge.

Flexibility comes with knowledge and experience, the skills and strategies at the heart of this book. Let's talk about them one at a time.

Skills are the techniques outlined in Cooking Basics (starting on page 1) and detailed in the introduction to each chapter and major section. The recipe directions put these skills into practice. Though nothing in this book is especially complicated, I encourage you start with the simplest dishes, like the master recipes that appear in the beginning of each section. These basic formulas teach you how to poach chicken, for example, stir-fry any vegetable, or make a creamy soup. As you work through the section, the recipes expand on the skill to make dishes as complex or simple as you like. The more you cook through the book, the more you'll discover about your tastes, the best ingredients available near you, and how cooking works with your schedule and other passions. My job is to give you everything you need to make practicing new skills fun and delicious.

That's when the strategies come into play. The charts scattered throughout the book expand on the master recipes, giving you hundreds of ways to vary and customize the ingredients, seasonings, and techniques. Sometimes the changes are easy swaps; or maybe you mix and match among the columns. And as with all the How to Cook Everything books, almost every recipe—master or otherwise—is followed by variations.

As your skills improve, so will your drive to try new flavors and foods.

Soon you'll be adding your own ideas to your repertoire. There are about 2,000 recipes within these pages. When you combine skills and strategies, you really will be able to cook . . . Everything.

How to Use This Book

I set out to write a cookbook that was as much reference as recipe collection. And you'll use this new book the same way: Buy your ingredients, and there'll be a terrific recipe for them. Now there's likely to be a photo too, and a new, brighter, more accessible layout. This edition still has lots of chapters, sections, and subsections to organize material, including "lexicons" of the most important ingredients. Recipe names are as descriptive as possible. The number of servings follows: usually four generous portions, but some recipes (like breads, desserts, and beans) make more.

The Time entry estimates how long it takes to prepare, cook (if necessary), and serve. You might go slower or faster, but a 30-minute recipe shouldn't take even an inexperienced cook more than 45 minutes, and a long-braised meat won't be ready in under an hour.

Whenever applicable, icons (there are three: **F** **M** **V**) accompany recipes, often in combinations. **F** means fast: the recipe takes 30 minutes or less to prepare; **M** indicates that the dish can be made ahead—either in full or to a certain point—and stored for finishing or serving later (these are excellent dishes for entertaining); **V** means vegetarian: no meat, chicken, or fish in the recipe (though there may be some variations that add nonvegetarian ingredients).

The index is comprehensive and includes the names of variations and charts. If you know what you're looking for (fried chicken, brownies, the basics of tofu) or want to have all the recipes for a particular ingredient or technique at a glance, this is the fastest way to find them.

Cooking Basics

CHAPTER AT A GLANCE

What Ingredients Should I Buy? 2

What Equipment Do I Need? 3

What Techniques Do I Need to Know? 13

The Importance of Heat 16

Cooking is unlike any other activity, hobby, or sport. Getting started only takes a little basic knowledge—and I do mean basic. You don't need to be an expert or have fancy equipment or ingredients. You'll learn something new every time you go to the market or stand at the stove. As you become more comfortable in the kitchen, your skills and strategies will evolve and grow. Along the way there will be dramatic successes . . . and disappointing failures. But rarely will something be inedible. And tomorrow provides another opportunity to eat something you cook yourself.

This chapter is divided into ingredients, equipment, and techniques—the three building blocks of good cooking. Having the right ingredients handy means you can cook something delicious whenever the mood or craving strikes. With a few key tools, pots, and pans, you'll be able to make all the recipes in this book, and then some. Armed with these, you're ready to apply core techniques: cutting produce and meat, measuring and mixing ingredients, and controlling heat and doneness.

Whether you're a total newbie or looking to build on what you already know, here are the fundamentals, all in one place.

What Ingredients Should I Buy?

The food media—magazines, blogs, websites, television, and cookbooks—can be both inspiring and intimidating. You might think that having the best, priciest, hardest-to-track-down ingredients is the key to cooking.

My approach is simpler than that: You buy the best ingredients available and combine them in ways that make sense on any given day. An omelet made with farm-fresh eggs, a locally raised chicken roasted with fragrant olive oil, sliced tomatoes straight from the garden—these experiences cannot be duplicated with supermarket ingredients. But those ingredients are precious and rare and therefore unrealistic for most people to eat every day.

So shop at the farmers' market, corner vegetable stand, *and* the grocery store. When you can, order online to buy real foods (like grains, beans, and such) directly from the source or a reputable food retailer. Spend your money on the best ingredients you can afford, invest in some pantry staples, and skip the Himalayan pink salt and black truffles.

WHAT ABOUT ORGANIC?

Organic options are everywhere now, even in small supermarkets. So like many other people, I buy more organic animal foods and produce than I did twenty or even ten years ago. I also get lots of foods directly from their source, either at a farmers market or by shopping online. The choice is personal, financial, and yes, political. It becomes a cooking question when nutrition, freshness, and flavor are involved.

Here's what I continue to say and do: If you can garden—even just some herbs—go for it. Choose local vegetables from a conscientious farmer over organic vegetables from a multinational corporation. Buy the best food you can find when you can't find local. Avoid overly processed anything, organic or otherwise. And be flexible; there may be times when the best vegetable you can find is not only not local and not organic but might even be frozen.

THE BASICS OF FOOD SAFETY

Many food-borne illnesses can be prevented, and since food sickens millions of Americans each year, it's worth taking precautions. My kitchen is clean and I prepare and cook food properly. The recipes reflect this approach without being fanatical. Here are some details.

Begin by washing your hands frequently and keeping all food preparation surfaces and utensils clean; soap and hot water are fine. Wash cutting boards after using them, and don't prepare food directly on your counter unless you wash it as well. Never put cooked food on a plate, cutting board, or surface that previously held raw food. Change sponges frequently. Change your kitchen towel frequently also—at least once a day. Keep plenty of extras handy.

Make sure your refrigerator is at about 35°F (40°F is too warm), and your freezer at 0°F or lower. Thaw foods in the refrigerator or under cold running water. Don't leave cooked foods at room temperature forever; health departments recommend no longer than two hours, though in all honesty I often stretch that rule.

Many foods should be washed just before cooking or eating. For produce, rinse away visible dirt and (we hope) pesticide residue, bacteria, fungi, and by-products of handling either with water alone or with the help of a little mild soap if necessary. Fish, meat, and poultry generally need *not* be rinsed (assuming you're cooking them) and in fact doing so can spread germs around your sink—so if you do, clean up thoroughly afterward. Mollusks (clams, mussels, oysters) must be scrubbed really clean; shrimp can be peeled or not. Some seafood (squid, for example) have special cleaning techniques that are detailed in the appropriate chapter; the same is true for any vegetables that might not be obvious. And some people wash their eggs before cracking, especially if there's visible soiling on them.

Those are the easy parts; everything else requires judgment. Let me say from the outset that I do not obey many of the official recommendations and rules; there's little you can do about ingredients containing disease-causing bacteria except cook everything, every time, to well-done, and that's no way to live since it renders many ingredients inedible. The decision is ultimately yours.

Of common foods, cooked vegetables and grains—anything brought to a boil or steamed—are the safest; next comes cooked fish; then comes cooked meat other than hamburger; last come cooked chicken, eggs, hamburger, and raw vegetables, with which most concerns are associated. If you or someone in your family is at greater risk of serious food-borne illness—this includes infants, pregnant women, the elderly, and people with compromised immune systems—you should take every precaution possible. But this is a cookbook; if you have any questions at all about foods you should avoid for your health or safety, I suggest you speak with a doctor and a nutritionist.

For the rest of us, use common sense: Don't let your kitchen be a breeding ground for pathogens. Many experienced cooks and chefs are fanatical about cleanliness, and that's the best way to avoid food-related illness.

What Equipment Do I Need?

Sturdy, functional cookware need not be expensive. Bargains are out there, even with first-rate products, especially at a restaurant supply store or at clearance sales online. Upscale "culinary" stores are mostly for show, and big-box stores sell a lot of junk. Look for tools—and tableware—at tag sales and thrift stores; some of the most useful utensils are old-school anyway. And let your cooking style dictate how you expand your collection.

When you do buy new equipment, get a feel for the pieces—easier said than done now that so many of us shop virtually, though there are always the reviews and videos. Hold hand tools, check the movement and vibration of electric appliances, and compare the weights of different pans. Since the goal is to actually use the stuff, you should feel comfortable with everything you bring home.

Stocking Your Kitchen

With the following staples (listed in relative order of importance), all you need is a normal weekly shop for vegetables, fruit, meat, fish, milk, cheese, and other perishables to make anything in this book. (Many of these items are detailed elsewhere in the book too.)

INGREDIENT	DESCRIPTION	ESSENTIAL?
Olive oil	A multipurpose medium-flavor oil for cooking or drizzling is a good start. See page 184.	Yes. I cannot emphasize this enough.
Good-quality vegetable oil	See page 184 to figure out which oil is best for your cooking.	Yes
Salt and pepper	Kosher salt, and black peppercorns in a pepper mill, are my first choices. See page 26.	Yes
Vinegar	Have at least a few kinds; see page 186.	Yes
Soy sauce	Make sure it's fermented from grains, not just colored water with too much salt.	Yes. Since soy sauce delivers flavor like a milder, more natural bouillon, I put this high on my list.
Rice and other grains	Long- and short-grain rice, brown and white— as you like. And at least one other whole grain. See pages 428 and 452.	Yes. You can cook them ahead in bulk to reheat all week.
Pasta and other dry noodles	The Italian brands are still the best. Keep a few shapes in your pantry. See page 476.	Yes. The fastest dinners usually include pasta or noodles.
Beans	Dried and canned; frozen if you can find them. See page 386.	Yes
Spices	Whole spices are better than ground. See page 27.	Only you can decide which you'll use regularly. Buy only the amount you think you'll use in a year.
Flours and cornmeal	You can't bake—bread or anything—or make quite a few sauces without flour (whether wheat or otherwise).	Yes to the first for sure
Canned tomatoes	Spend the money for good-quality whole plum tomatoes.	Yes, definitely
Canned (or packaged) stock	See page 174.	Yes, unless you are very on top of making your own. Find a brand that tastes good and stock up.
Aromatic vegetables	Onions, garlic, shallots, celery, carrots, scallions, ginger, and fresh chiles	Yes on at least onions and garlic
Baking soda, baking powder, and cornstarch	Baking essentials	Yes on all except maybe cornstarch, which isn't used much in this book.
Dried mushrooms	I keep porcini and shiitake around; you could try more kinds too.	Yes. If you haven't cooked with them before, you will be shocked what they can do.

INGREDIENT	DESCRIPTION	ESSENTIAL?
Eggs	When they're fresh and the chickens raised with room to roam, the difference is remarkable. See page 716.	Yes
Parmesan cheese	You must get the real stuff, Parmigiano-Reggiano imported from Italy.	Yes
Nuts and seeds	Toasted nuts and seeds will do wonders for your cooking. See page 307.	Yes to at least one kind you like best.
Lemons and limes	Squeeze your own; always avoid bottled juice.	Yes. Either/or at the minimum.
Butter	Get the best you can find. The recipes here use unsalted. See page 751.	If you eat it regularly, yes. Keep some in the freezer if not.
Sweeteners	Sugar, honey, maple syrup	Yes to all three
Long-lasting vegetables and fruits	Including potatoes, sweet potatoes, carrots, cabbage, winter squash, apples, and oranges	Yes, especially in the winter
Condiments	Ketchup, mustard, salsa, mayonnaise, hot sauce. See the chapter beginning on page 23.	Yes, based on what you like; I use all these regularly.
Fish sauce	An increasingly common ingredient, necessary for Southeast Asian cooking	I think so.
Capers and anchovies	I love the salty, briny flavor they bring to Italian dishes. Get salt-packed if you can.	Not necessarily, but if you have them you'll use them.
Miso	White and yellow miso are mild, the red is quite strong. Experiment with what you like best.	Yes, especially if you like to experiment with different seasonings.
Sesame oil	Get the toasted stuff and keep it in the fridge.	If you like Chinese, Korean, or Japanese food, or eat a lot of grain bowls, then yes.
Bread crumbs	Fresh is always preferable; see page 801. Panko are a good alternative.	No, but I'd be lost without them.
Coconut milk	The reduced fat kind is fine, actually.	Not necessarily
Dried fruit	It keeps forever.	Nice to have for snacking, if not cooking.
Frozen vegetables	Definitely better than nothing. See page 237.	They're not essential until you're in a pinch; then they're crucial.
Fresh herbs	See page 46 for instructions on how to store them.	Parsley is essential, and you might think cilantro is too.
Wine	Red and white	No, but if you drink it, you should cook with it.

I recommend that you cook with the bare minimum of equipment for a while so that you can discover your preferences and prioritize accordingly.

THE BASICS OF KNIVES

A good knife is worth the investment, and it's better to buy fewer good quality blades than more junk. High-carbon stainless-steel alloy blades, which are what chefs and experienced home cook often use, are the best choice. Just know the different kinds of steel: High-carbon stainless steel is easiest to maintain and holds an edge; stainless steel is easy to maintain, but more difficult to get an edge; carbon-steel blades take an edge better, but dull more quickly and require drying and oiling. The handle may be wood or plastic, as long as it's durable and comfortable to hold. And don't be fooled by sets. Unless you're regularly butchering meat and fish, you only need the three knives below.

When you find the right knives, respect them: Start with good ones and keep them sharp; you'll know it's time to sharpen them when you have to use pressure to chop and slice. An electric sharpener is the best, easiest, and most expensive way to keep knife blades sharp. The alternatives are to learn to use a whetstone (not that difficult, and very effective, but time-consuming) or to take them to a hardware store to have them sharpened professionally for just a few bucks per knife. A steel is a handy tool for maintaining the edge of knives between sharpenings (see right). You should use it every few days, at least.

Correct washing and storage will keep your knives in good shape. Though you can put plastic-handled knives in the dishwasher, it's easy for them to get nicked there, so it's better to wash by hand. It's also a good idea to keep knives out of dish racks and other places where they might hurt someone. Professional kitchens have a rule I stick to at home: No knives in the sink.

Kitchen drawers are fine for storing knives if you buy inexpensive plastic guards to protect the blades (and your hands). Otherwise, invest in a wooden knife block or magnetic wall strip.

THE 3 KNIVES YOU MUST HAVE

You can accomplish nearly every basic cooking task with these knives.

1. CHEF'S KNIFE The all-purpose knife. An 8-inch blade is what most home cooks like; go to 10 inches if you have especially big hands and like the feel, or 6 inches if your hands are small. Make sure the handle feels good when you hold it; the grip is almost as important as the blade, and only you can judge whether it's a comfortable fit.

2. PARING KNIFE You can buy expensive paring knives, or pretty good ones that are so cheap you could almost consider them disposable. It's nice to have a couple in slightly varying styles. Use for peeling, trimming, and other precise tasks.

Using a Steel

Using a steel is an easy and effective way to keep knives sharp, but isn't a substitute for actual sharpening. The important thing is the angle you use it at, which should be between 15 and 20 degrees.

STEP 1 Pull one side of the knife toward you across the top of the steel, simultaneously sliding it from base to tip (your pulling hand will move in a diagonal motion).

STEP 2 Repeat with the other side across the bottom of the steel, always pulling toward you and trying to maintain a consistent angle.

3. LONG SERRATED KNIFE Sometimes called a bread knife. A must for bread and other baked goods; for splitting cakes into layers; for ripe tomatoes; and for large fruits or vegetables like melons and squash. They're trickier to sharpen, but the best ones hold their edges for many years.

THE BASICS OF POTS AND PANS

It's tempting to buy a full set of shiny new pots and pans. But your choices should be dictated by how you cook, not what a manufacturer can fit in a box. The pots you buy need to fit your style of cooking, and the foods you make. Look at them: Good pots and pans have their handles attached by rivets, and those handles are made of metal; wood and plastic can't go in the oven or broiler and are therefore useless.

Pans are made of all sorts of materials, and some materials require more care than others (see "Using and Caring for Pots and Pans," page 9). Here are your options, with my preferences up top. In all cases, those with an ovenproof handle are the most versatile.

STAINLESS STEEL This is a nonreactive metal, meaning you can cook anything in it, including foods high in acid, without worrying about discoloration or off-tastes. It's better to buy a few high-quality pots and pans—the kind with heavy bottoms where the steel encloses an aluminum or copper core to conduct heat well—than cheap, thin-bottomed cookware. Be willing to use some fat and properly heat them; not adding enough butter or oil will make food stick.

CAST IRON The old-school staple conducts heat nearly as well as stainless steel at a fraction of the cost of other materials, and is pretty much nonstick once it's properly seasoned. I now cook almost everything (except boiled foods) in well-seasoned cast iron. But cast iron is heavy, and the iron itself can react with acidic ingredients or porous vegetables (like eggplant) and discolor them. Enameled cast iron is a good solution since it's heavy enough to brown foods, and also nonreactive; but it can be expensive.

NONSTICK If you have concerns about the safety of using nonstick coatings—and you should, especially when cooking at high temperatures—read the labels carefully. There are some decent new alternatives like ceramic and other high-tech materials. But you never will get a deep brown crust in a nonstick pan. Consider sticking with cast iron.

BLACK OR CARBON STEEL This combines the best of stainless steel and cast iron, but requires some diligence to season and maintain. And like cast iron, you don't boil water in it.

Seasoning Cast Iron

Until a cast iron pan is seasoned with a combination of heat and fat, food will stick to it. You can now buy preseasoned cast iron, or you can season it yourself:

Heat the oven to 350°F and use a brush or towel to spread a tablespoon or so of vegetable oil (anything but canola) around the inside of the pan, sides and all. There should be no excess, but the entire surface should be shiny. Bake the pan for about an hour, then turn off the oven and leave it inside to cool. To maintain newly seasoned cast iron, it helps if you use the pan for sautéing or frying the first few times you cook in it. The more oil, the better.

Once the iron is seasoned, you can use a mildly abrasive scouring pad to wash it; mild soap is fine too. I dry my cast-iron skillet on the stovetop over low heat. When the water begins to evaporate, I wipe it out with a towel, use the towel to smear around a little oil, let it sit over the heat for a few more minutes, then wipe it out again. Proper care can avoid the need for major reseasoning, and even fix legacy and thrift-store cast iron (after you scrub off any existing rust).

Pots and Pans

These are the pans that you need to cook the recipes in this book, as well as select ovenware.

POT	DESCRIPTION	ESSENTIAL?
Large skillet	Cast iron or stainless steel, 12 inches across, 2–3 inches deep, with a lid. Sloped or straight sides both fine.	Yes
Large pot	4-quart is ideal. Must be nonreactive, flameproof, and ovenproof, with a lid. Doubles as vessel for boiling pasta.	Yes
Medium skillet	Cast iron or stainless steel, 8–10 inches across, for small-batch sautéing, frying, cooking eggs, and the like	Yes
Stockpot	6- to 8-quart stainless steel or heavy aluminum, with a lid	Maybe; nice as a backup for the large pot
Small or medium saucepan	1- or 2-quart, stainless steel or aluminum, with a lid	Yes to one or both
Double boiler	The best way to gently cook egg-based sauces and custards, melt chocolate, and keep gravies hot is over simmering water, not direct heat. There are special pots for this purpose though it's easy enough to rig your own.	Unless you plan on making a lot of hollandaise sauce and custards, there's no need to buy special equipment. Simply nest a heatproof mixing bowl over a saucepan of simmering water (without touching the water).
13 × 9-inch roasting pan	Metal if you're only going to have one; glass or ceramic is good for a second. Make sure it holds at least 12 cups.	Yes to at least one
Large rimmed baking sheet	Make sure it's heavy duty or your food will burn.	Yes, and you might as well buy two
Square pan	Either 8- or 9-inch is fine. Did you know this size holds half the volume of a 13 × 9-inch pan?	Yes. As versatile as a large skillet: You can use it for gratins and casseroles, baked pastas, quick breads, cakes, and small roasts.
Large gratin dish	Holds 2 quarts. Oval or square, no more than 3 inches deep. Glass, ceramic, or metal is fine.	Maybe; depends on how much you use your 13 × 9-inch pan, which is essentially the same size. Nice to have one glass or ceramic dish and one metal pan.
Standard loaf pan	Should be 8½ × 4½ × 3 inches; avoid glass	Yes if you like quick breads and/or meat loaf
Pie plate	9-inch is the standard. My recipes are almost always designed for standard depth, not deep-dish. One piece where glass is really nice.	If you bake even just one pie a year, yes

POT	DESCRIPTION	ESSENTIAL?
Cookie sheet	Not having rims makes it easier to transfer cookies, especially if you use a silicone mat too.	Essential for delicate cookies, otherwise a rimmed baking sheet is fine. If you bake a lot, get two.
9-inch round cake pan	For when you want to bake a layer cake. Nonstick is a nice option.	Yes if you like to bake, at least one set of 2 pans.
Specialty cake pans: springform, tube or Bundt pan, fluted tart pan	Look for 9-inch pans for all; make sure they're heavy-duty material to prevent scorching.	Yes for bakers, no for anyone else
Muffin tin	Standard 12-cup pan; jumbo and mini pans also available	You probably already know if you're the kind of person who likes to bake muffins and cupcakes. Otherwise, no; any muffin recipe can be converted to quick bread and baked in a loaf pan.
Ceramic cups or ramekins	6-ounce size is standard, and 8 is the right number to have.	Yes if you love to make desserts or if you like to use them to hold chopped ingredients before cooking
Wire rack	Make sure it fits in your roasting pan and baking sheets. Grid-style is most foolproof but more difficult to clean than those with simple parallel slats.	Yes for both cooling baked goods and roasting. Get several.
Oven thermometer	Hangs from an oven rack; analog readout shows actual temperature (may be different from oven setting)	Yes; unless your oven is regularly professionally calibrated, it can't hurt to have independent confirmation. Get one that is well reviewed.

ALUMINUM Another popular material for cookware but it must be anodized, a process that hardens the metal and makes it more durable and less reactive. Even though various cookware lines might look similar, quality and price can range wildly, so be sure the metal is thick, especially on the bottom.

CERAMIC AND GLASS Fine for oven-braising, gratins, and baking, but with rare exceptions, you can't use it on the stove. Don't even bother with glass pots and pans; they break when you least expect it, and they're worthless for anything but boiling water.

COPPER The inside should be coated with tin or stainless steel. Conducts heat perfectly, lasts forever, and looks incredible when polished, but it can be prohibitively expensive, often needs to be retinned after a while, and is time consuming to keep shiny (if that's your thing).

USING AND CARING FOR POTS AND PANS

Chefs will tell you to heat the pan dry, then add fat, heat that, then add the food. Sometimes I agree; other times these steps add a layer of fussiness when you could be

Kitchen Tools

A variety of tools can make kitchen tasks easier. Eventually you'll probably acquire as much kitchen stuff as your cabinets can hold. Here is a list to help you prioritize a bit.

TOOL	DESCRIPTION	ESSENTIAL?
Mixing bowls in multiple sizes	Preferably stainless steel and/or tempered glass (the most basic and functional materials); a nesting set is practical. Make sure one is bigger than you think you need.	Yes
Cutting board	Wood or plastic, your choice. Wood can be sanded clean; plastic can go in the dishwasher.	Absolutely. Get a few in different sizes so at least one is always dry. Designate one just for raw meat, fish, and poultry.
Wooden and stainless-steel spoons and spatulas	A couple of sizes and widths of each	Yes, a moderate assortment; include a slotted spoon for sure and a flexible spatula if you're a perfectionist.
Tongs	Spring-loaded rather than scissorlike or tension kinds	Yes. The single best item for turning foods.
Pot holders or mitts; kitchen towels	It doesn't matter what they look like; what's important is that they're easy to clean, and protect your hands from heat.	Yes
Measuring cups (liquid and dry), measuring spoons	Liquid measuring cups have a spout for pouring; dry-measure cups and measuring spoons have a flat rim to allow sweeping off the excess. Relatively inexpensive.	Yes. A 2-cup glass liquid measuring cup is a good place to start; if you have room, buy a 4-cup liquid measure too. Get two sets of spoons and dry-measure cups.
Colanders and strainers	Bowl- or basketlike devices with holes in them, for draining	Yes. From the get-go you need a large colander and a mid-sized fine-meshed strainer.
Cheese grater	An old-fashioned box grater is fine; invest in stainless steel to avoid rust. An ultrasharp Microplane is good for Parmesan and zest.	Yes to the box grater for sure; maybe to a Microplane. A rotary Microplane is a handy luxury for grating at the table.
Timer	Any kind—digital or dial.	Yes, especially if you don't want to dirty your phone. Keeping track of time—or not—can make or break a recipe.
Vegetable peeler	Sharpness and the handle grip are more important than the shape.	Yes. I lean toward the U-shaped ones you pull toward you. Straight peelers can go in both directions.
Instant-read thermometer	Thin, pointed metal shaft; head may have either digital or analog readout	For bread and meat, yes. Very handy for making sure foods are done. I absolutely depend on one when baking bread.

TOOL	DESCRIPTION	ESSENTIAL?
Salad spinner	A perforated basket with a lid and a mechanism to make the inner basket spin.	Yes. The best way to prepare all greens. Get the kind with a solid bowl so you can use it to store clean greens in the fridge, to prolong their life.
Potato masher	For quick, rough purées, usually right in the pot after cooking. The best have a disk with lots of holes; don't bother with the squiggly kind.	Yes, unless you're cool working slowly with a fork.
Kitchen scissors	Get ones you can take apart in order to wash them thoroughly.	Yes. Useful for butchering chicken. I also use them to cut cooked or raw greens right in the bowl.
Balloon whisk	For baking and for making sauces, beating eggs, and whipping cream	Yes. One medium-sized one with lots of wires is better than a cheap set of lesser quality.
Rolling pin	Get a straight wooden pin without ball bearings for the most control and versatility	You'll need one for pie and biscuit doughs, fresh pasta (if you don't have a machine), and dumplings.
Skewers	Nonround metal skewers are my first choice, so food doesn't spin around as easily. Wooden skewers are fine for crowds; flat ones are best	Yes if you like kebabs
Grilling utensils	Long-handled tongs, fork, brush, plus a wire brush for cleaning the grate.	Yes if you grill (obviously)
Mandoline	For evenly cutting paper-thin slices and fine shreds of vegetables. Very good plastic ones are now all over the place for less than 40 bucks.	Yes, since I love shaved vegetable salads, but not everyone would agree. And some food processors now have adjustable disks that do the same thing more efficiently.
Asian skimmers and spiders	Small wire baskets on long wooden sticks, or flat metal strainers; come in different sizes.	The best tool for deep-frying, but a metal slotted spoon works in a pinch.
Brushes	The new silicone ones are great because they don't leave bristles behind.	No; you can always smear with your hands or the back of a spoon. But they're nice to have.
Steaming basket	Expandable metal to fit different-sized pots, or silicone; cheap and convenient	If you steam often, yes. Otherwise you can rig a steamer using plates (see page 20)
Manual pasta machine	Hand-cranked rollers for thinning and cutting dough. A simple machine that won't set you back too much.	Yes if you have any interest at all in making pasta regularly.
Pizza stone, peel, and pizza cutter	All the tools you'd need to make pizza at home	For pizza enthusiasts only, though a wheel cutter is handy for other things too.

Appliances and Electric Gadgets

Here's a roundup of the extra electric gadgets that might make your kitchen life a little easier. (I'm assuming you have a fridge and a toaster, for example.)

APPLIANCE	DESCRIPTION	ESSENTIAL?
Food processor	Lightning-fast way to chop, slice, grate, and mix almost anything. There are very good ones available for less than $60. Get a large one that can handle at least 8 cups (preferably 12), for batter or dough.	If any appliance is essential, this is it. If you cook a lot, you will use it often.
Electric mixer	Either a stand mixer or a handheld mixer is fine.	For baking enthusiasts
Blender	Crucial for smoothies and blended drinks. Also for puréeing soups. An immersion blender, which you stick into a pot or bowl (see page 140), is helpful but not as versatile or powerful.	You can get away without one, but I use mine often.
Coffee/spice grinder	Small canister with a rotating blade and a cover; the best tool for grinding whole spices	Yes. Coffee drinkers probably already have one. But if you're going to grind whole spices at home at all—and you should—it's much easier with a designated grinder so spices don't compete with coffee grounds.
Ice cream maker	You might want to start with an inexpensive manual model with a container you freeze. Any machine is easier than churning by hand with ice and salt water.	Yes if you love to make ice cream.
Pressure cooker or multicooker	Pressure cookers can help you make soups and stews fast. New ones are completely safe and fool-proof.	Maybe. But the recipes here all describe conventional cooking.
Microwave	Good for reheating, melting butter, and taking the chill off foods; also good for "steaming" vegetables and fish.	No. I wouldn't rush out and buy one, but you probably have one already.
Scale	A small electric scale will set you back about $25 and prove invaluable in the kitchen.	For bakers, definitely.

chopping or doing other prep work. Note that nonstick pans should always be heated with something in them. The recipes provide direction.

As a general rule, I favor wooden spoons and spatulas to prevent scratching. But a metal spatula on a metal pan is often the only way to get desired results. With nonstick or enamel coatings you must use nonmetal utensils.

You can wash all materials in the dishwasher except cast iron and black steel, which are porous and will rust. But I usually clean pots and pans by hand after the dishes and glasses are out of the sink.

OVENWARE

You have three dependable ways to go for ovenware: metal (including metal pans coated with enamel), glass, and ceramic. If you're new to cooking, that's where I suggest you start, since they will be the most versatile and economical—even if there's nothing glamorous about taking metal pans to the table. You can always add prettier ovenware to your collection later.

Any metal pans except uncoated aluminum are fine for baking. These days you can find good, heavy, thick-gauge professional-style metal pans even in discount stores, and they're virtually indestructible. You can even heat them on top of the stove to deglaze the bottom or melt butter. The trick is to avoid thin pans that warp and bend when they're hot.

Glass or ceramic ovenware are more sensitive and should be used only in the oven; they can break or crack if heated or cooled too quickly.

What Techniques Do I Need to Know?

The process of learning to cook is rewarding, even when you hit bumps in the road. One of the joys of working in the kitchen is that not only do you learn from your mistakes, they never last long enough to haunt you. (And you can usually eat them anyway.)

Preparing food is as important as cooking it. So both stages are covered here, roughly in order of how you might tackle them. Vegetables need to be rinsed and trimmed, and sometimes dried. For meat, poultry, or fish, you need to trim excess fat (generally not all fat, just anything obvious you wouldn't want to bite into) and any inedible parts. Specific chapters and recipe directions provide all the details. And for information about food safety, see page 3.

THE BASICS OF CUTTING

I'm the opposite of fussy about slicing and dicing. But with a few simple knife skills, your food will cook evenly and look gorgeous.

Hold your knives however you feel most comfortable and secure. Some people "shake hands" with their chef's knife, but the way to hold one for maximum stability is illustrated on page 14.

Whether you're chopping an onion, mincing a clove of garlic, or cutting slices from a pork tenderloin to throw on the grill, you want all pieces to be approximately the same size and thickness so they cook in the same time. Here are the specific cuts mentioned in this book.

CHOPPING

This most basic cut results in three sizes: large chunks, chopped, and minced. For all of these, forget super-even cutting; you just want to get the job done and leave the pieces in relatively even sizes.

LARGE CHUNKS Pieces that are somewhat uneven, bite-sized or slightly bigger; you're just passing the food under the knife blade, without worrying much about being too precise. Use this cut for foods you'll purée or mash, or when the texture of the dish is intended to be rustic. Pieces can be as big as an inch in any direction.

CHOPPED Pieces from ½ to ¼ inch in size. In recipes where I don't specify size and just say "chopped," this is what I mean.

MINCED The tiniest bits you can manage: Once you get things chopped into small pieces, it's just a final burst of short, quick chops to get food to this stage. Mince when you want an almost invisible, textureless result with foods like garlic, ginger, shallots, chiles, lemongrass, and sometimes rosemary. I rarely call for mincing, but when I do, it's important.

One tip on chopping with a food processor: Don't overprocess. If you want to mince, use the pulse button, turning the machine on and off as many times as is necessary to get the texture you need. These are very powerful machines, capable of puréeing almost anything within seconds.

Using a Chef's Knife

STEP 1 You can hold a knife with your hand completely on the handle or with your first finger or two on the side of the blade. Use your other hand to hold the food on the cutting board.

STEP 2 For small pieces, put the tip of the blade on the surface and rock the knife up and down. Curl the fingers and thumb of your other hand, so your knuckles act as a guide.

STEP 3 When the pieces become very small and stable, put your free hand over the point of the blade for greater stability; use a rocking motion to chop or mince the food further.

Chopping

STEP 1 Cut the food into manageable, somewhat even-sized chunks.

STEP 2 Then chop it into smaller pieces.

STEP 3 Finally, if necessary, mince using a controlled rocking motion.

Slicing

For round vegetables like cucumbers or zucchini, just cut across.

Or cut into long strips.

Or on an angle, for attractive ovals.

To slice bread, use a serrated knife (aka a bread knife) with a sawing motion.

SLICING

To slice with a chef's knife, you still raise and press down, just with a little more precision. The goal is thick or thin slices of fairly uniform size. You can slice vegetables crosswise, lengthwise, or on the diagonal. The diagonal slice is probably most attractive and gives you the largest surface area for crisping, so it's nice to use for stir-fries.

Note that meat and poultry should be sliced against the grain; if raw, it's almost always easier to slice after freezing first for about 30 minutes. Spongy foods like bread and cake should be sliced using a serrated knife; grip the handle comfortably and use a gentle sawing motion. A mandoline is handy for getting even, thin slices, often called "shaved," and for cutting a volume of vegetables quickly. An adjustable slicing blade or slicing disk on a food processor does the same thing.

JULIENNE

Translation: Cut into sticks. They can be big like French fries or small like matchsticks. I don't call for julienne often, but it's an impressive cut and really not that tough—especially if you use a food processor or mandoline, both of which have attachments to make it a breeze. By hand, first make round foods—think of zucchini, as an example—stable on the cutting board by slicing a little off one side. Slice the food crosswise into whatever length you want the final julienne, then slice each segment lengthwise into planks. Stack the planks into piles of three or so, then slice them lengthwise into sticks the same thickness as the planks. (If you see a recipe elsewhere that calls for dice, simply cut the julienned pieces crosswise into cubes.)

PARING, CORING, PEELING, AND OTHER SPECIAL TASKS

Here you hold manageable pieces of food in one hand, a small paring knife in the other, and work in a controlled way without a cutting board; you might be coring and peeling an apple, for example, or trimming the eyes from a potato. Often these jobs involve pulling the paring knife toward you. If you're not confident working this way, stick to putting the food on a board and cutting downward, away from you.

THE BASICS OF MEASURING

All of the recipes in this book can be measured with cups and spoons, though I sometimes offer weights, too, when it might be easier, as when baking. Many experienced cooks eyeball everything, except when baking, and though I wouldn't advocate ignoring the measurements, with practice you'll get there. Think about this, for starters: Does it matter whether your stir-fry has a heaping cup or a shy cup of chopped carrots? One pound of carrots or 1 pound plus 2 ounces? However, when you bake breads, make desserts, or work with eggs in custards and desserts, you must measure carefully.

For liquids, set the liquid measuring cup (the transparent one with the pour spout) on the counter and fill it

---

Using a Mandoline

Japanese mandolines are inexpensive and incredibly efficient. To make perfectly thin slices, slide the vegetable over the blade—just watch your fingers.

to where you think the correct marking is. Then get down at eye level to the cup and double-check. Surface tension causes the liquid to look a little like a concave bubble, and the bottom "line" of that bubble should be even with the line on the cup. Add or pour off liquid until it is.

To measure dry ingredients, scoop them up with the dry measuring cup (the ones with a flat rim you can easily level) or use a spoon to put them in, heaping them a bit over the top, and sweep off the excess with the flat edge of a knife.

The Importance of Heat

Much of cooking is about heat. Whether you cook with gas or electricity or induction barely matters. What counts most when working with heat is your ability to trust your senses. Learn to smell when food is toasted or browned; listen for the sound of sizzling, simmering, and boiling vigorously. Learn to recognize physical signs of doneness like crisping around the edges, dryness, releasing from the pan or grill without sticking, or resistance when you press down on something.

Being observant puts you in control and gives you the confidence to use heat more assertively. You might worry about burning food, but assuming you don't put something on the stove then walk away, a greater concern is having enough heat for the technique you're using.

Food generally responds best when it comes into sudden contact with something hot. Whether you're plunging spaghetti into boiling water or a steak into an almost-smoking skillet, this heat impact is what will get you tender (not mushy) pasta and a crisp brown crust on the steak. Occasionally you might start with cold ingredients in a cold pan or a cold oven or a cold pot of water, but those exceptions are always noted.

THE 11 ESSENTIAL COOKING TECHNIQUES

Typically cooking is categorized by dry- versus wet-heat methods. Instead, I've organized this overview based on what's used in this book, in loose order from easiest (and most familiar) to more involved.

1. BOILING is one of the most straightforward and fundamental ways to cook. Put water in a pot (usually to about two-thirds full) and turn the heat to high. When bubbles vigorously break the surface, the water has reached a rolling boil. (This is what I refer to when I say

Making Julienne

STEP 1 The easiest way to cut even strips from a vegetable with rounded sides is to square it off first by removing thin slices.

STEP 2 It will sit flat so you can first it cut crosswise to the desired length, then into planks, and finally into sticks.

Using a Paring Knife

Before there were vegetable peelers, there were paring knives. As long as you're careful—peel toward you, using your thumb to counter the pressure of the knife—they work perfectly.

to bring a pot of water to a boil.) Then you usually add salt, and the food.

Boiling works well for many foods but is used most frequently for dry ingredients like pasta, rice, or legumes, which must absorb water to become edible. Many fresh vegetables are also surprisingly good boiled, as are fatty meats, chicken, or shellfish. To avoid bland, mushy food leached of nutrients, check the food frequently as it cooks. Residual heat will cause what's called "carry-over cooking," which you can stop by immediately shocking boiled food in ice water (see page 238), or at least by draining it in a colander under cold running water.

Simmering is when the liquid bubbles gently, just below the point of a rolling boil. *Poaching* describes cooking in an even more gently bubbling liquid— usually water, and less of it than you'd use to boil. See the recipes on pages 565 and 611.

2. STEAMING is when you suspend food to cook above— not in—boiling water. Since steam can superheat to more than 212°F (the temperature of boiling water), it's an excellent moist-heat method for quick-cooking vegetables, fish, dumplings, tofu, and custards. The color and texture can be better than when boiling, and you can avoid the need to shock the food after.

Measuring Dry Ingredients

To measure flour accurately, scoop the flour or use a spoon to overfill the measuring cup, then sweep the top evenly with the flat edge of a knife.

The pot you use should be large enough to hold the food comfortably and allow steam to circulate freely. Set the food on a surface—a metal or bamboo basket, or two plates—just above the water level (see "Ways to Rig a Steamer," page 20). Cover the pot and turn the heat to high. Once the water starts boiling, adjust the heat so that it bubbles steadily. As with boiling, check the food frequently so it doesn't overcook. Also check the pot to make sure it doesn't run dry, adding more water if necessary.

Microwaving in a covered, moist environment—a piece of fish or broccoli on a plate with a tablespoon or two of water, covered with a microwave-safe lid or clean paper towel, for example—is sort of like steaming and a good alternative.

3. SAUTÉING is the method of cooking food in a skillet or other shallow pan in a little oil or butter; the thin film of fat is the key. You can dredge the pieces of food in flour, bread crumbs, or seasonings before putting them in the pan, but it isn't necessary. The idea is to sizzle the food (some say you "surprise" it) to create a crust, so that it's browned (caramelized) outside and cooked through, tender, and moist inside.

You must follow a few rules: Make sure the fat is hot, almost smoking, before you add the food. (I sometimes make an exception when cooking aromatics like onions.) The food must be thin enough to cook through to the center; no more than 1 inch or so. And don't crowd the pan, or the food will steam and never brown. An inch or so between big pieces is fine; smaller pieces require less elbow room.

You should be able to hear the food sputtering as it cooks and see the fat bubbling around the edges as they brown. Don't try to move or turn the pieces until they release easily from the pan; that means a crust has formed and they're browned. You can adjust the heat and gently swirl the fat around if you like, but let the food itself be. Patience is key.

Searing is related to sautéing: You're browning the food on both sides—or all sides if it's thick—without the expectation of cooking it all the way through in one

process. Maybe you'll roast or braise it after searing, for example.

4. STIR-FRYING is like sautéing, except you keep things moving over high heat, and often work in batches to make sure each component is properly tender and browned. It's fast and easy and my favorite way to cook.

Forget what you've seen watching chefs stir-fry in restaurants or on TV; home stoves get nowhere near as hot as those in a restaurant. For starters, use a 12-inch skillet, not a wok. Otherwise the food will crowd the pan, the temperature will drop, and the food will end up steaming rather than browning. To compensate for the lack of fire power, I usually direct you to cook the vegetables and meat or other protein separately with some seasonings, transferring each batch out of the pan before doing the next. Then you return everything to the pan and make a sauce. The process still usually takes less than 15 minutes of active cooking—just enough time to cook a pot of rice.

Once you learn the technique, all the components—protein, vegetables, and seasonings—are interchangeable.

Ways to Rig a Steamer

STEP 1 You can use a collapsible metal steamer basket, which will work in any pot.

STEP 2 Or you can use a heatproof plate, slightly smaller than the pot. To raise it off the bottom of the pot, put it on an upside-down plate, a couple of small ramekins, a "raft" of sticks, or whatever else is heatproof and stable.

(See the discussion and basic recipe on page 242.) That means you can substitute ingredients more freely than with any other type of cooking. You can also vary the proportions in stir-fries. I usually figure a pound of meat for 4 servings, which puts an emphasis on vegetables. To cut back on the animal protein even more, drop the meat to 8 ounces and increase the amount of vegetables proportionally. And to adjust the protein up, just add more chicken or whatever and increase the seasonings and liquids—but don't cut back on the vegetables! Some components benefit from parboiling (see page 237); I'll direct you when necessary.

Most of my stir-fries include a teeny bit of sugar in the sauce; I consider it optional, although it's traditional throughout Asia. The sweetness helps balance acidity and the occasional spiciness, while working much like salt does to intensify the flavor.

5. ROASTING uses dry heat in a confined environment with good air circulation, to crisp and brown uncovered food on the outside while cooking it through. All you need is a big shallow pan and sometimes a little oil or butter. Two crucial points: The oven must be very hot, almost always over 400°F for all or some of the cooking time. The roasting pan can't be too crowded either; the hot air must be able to circulate so moisture in the food can evaporate easily. Otherwise, you're steaming or baking and you can forget about developing a browned crust.

6. BAKING is like roasting, but usually with moisture and at lower heat. Most foods that are baked are either a semiliquid or a fairly wet solid when they go in the oven; think of cake batter, custard, or bread dough. They may be solids surrounded by sauce, water, or other liquid, as in gratins, casseroles, or lasagne. As the heat from the oven warms whatever's in the pan, it causes the moisture to turn to steam and jump-starts all the other chemical reactions needed to raise the dough, melt the cheese, brown the crust, and so on. Delicate items like cakes are usually baked at a low temperature, like

325°F or 350°F. Breads, pizza, and other sturdy dishes take higher heat. Since ovens are notoriously untrustworthy, a thermometer placed near the food is an important tool; even a difference of 10 or 15 degrees can make a big difference.

7. BRAISING is a two-step cooking method: You first sear the ingredients, then add liquid to the pan, cover, and simmer. You can simmer in the oven, with low heat (300°F or lower) or on top of the stove. As the dish cooks, both the cooking liquid and the solid ingredients develop lots of flavor and a luxurious texture. Braising is often used to slow-cook tough pieces of meat—short ribs, brisket, veal shank, and so on—but you can also make delicious braised fish, chicken, and vegetables.

8. GRILLING OVER FIRE is the oldest cooking technique and still a favorite of modern humans. Now we use wood, charcoal, or gas to cook and flavor food with smoke and flame. There are two ways: direct-heat grilling, where you put the food on a grate right over a hot gas flame or charcoal to crisp, darken, and cook quickly; and indirect-heat grilling, with the food off to the side of the fire and the lid down, so the grill works like an oven and cooks food more slowly. Thick or large pieces are better off with indirect or a combination of both; that way the outside doesn't burn before the inside is done. Anything that's an inch or less thick is a good candidate for direct-heat grilling. *Barbecuing* isn't grilling, but actually slow-cooking with smoke.

With a gas grill, all you do is turn it on and wait for the grates to heat up. If you want to use indirect heat on a gas grill, simply turn a burner or two off and use that side for the food.

For a charcoal grill, I use lump charcoal and a chimney starter to get the fire going, but you can use briquettes if you like, and/or an electric starter. Stay away from lighter fluid, which you can taste even after it burns off. Once the charcoal is going, spread it out for direct grilling or pile it on one side for indirect grilling.

Generally, you want the coals to turn mostly white with ash before you start grilling. You're ready to sear when you can hold your hand right above the grate for only a second. For less intense grilling, you want to be able to hold your hand above the heat for 4 seconds or so. Adjust the distance of the grate from the fire if you can, or spread out the coals a bit. Or just wait. Otherwise the flames will flare up to kiss the grates periodically, and turn the food from pleasantly charred to burned. Be prepared to move things to the cooler parts of the grill as you cook.

9. BROILING is essentially upside-down indoor grilling. You get the same browning and even charring, though without grill marks. It's less work and, unless you use wood or wood chips when you grill, the flavor is about the same. It's also fast, which makes it one of my favorite cooking techniques. Most recipes in the book that use one of these techniques usually call for the other as an alternative.

Broil most foods about 4 inches away from the heat source. Thicker foods or toppings that burn easily benefit from what I call long-distance broiling, at about 6 inches from the source: After the food browns and cooks on one side, take it out and turn it over. Adjust the distance between the broiler rack and the heat as needed. As with grilling, you want a browned, crisp outside and moist, tender inside.

10. PAN-FRYING (also called shallow-frying) is halfway between sautéing and deep-frying. You put about ½ inch of oil in a skillet over medium-high heat. When it's hot, add the food so the pan isn't crowded. You've got to turn it to cook the other side, but because there's more fat than with sautéing, the crust develops easily, similar to deep-frying. As with sautéing, you can dredge the food in flour, or bread or batter it as for deep-frying. Or don't coat it at all.

Pan-frying works best for cooking thin slices (veal, chicken, eggplant, sole fillets, etc.), small pieces (meat chunks, scallops and shrimp, or thick-cut vegetables or fruits), and battered foods and fritters—whenever you want serious crisping but don't want the commitment of deep-frying.

11. DEEP-FRYING submerges food in hot oil to cook and brown it evenly. When it's done right, the result is crisp, moist, hot, and ethereal. (I'm sure I don't have to sell you on how good fried food can be.) Mostly, success depends on having enough good oil at the right temperature, usually 350°F or a bit higher.

Though deep-frying is easy, it's a bit of a production, so I consider it special-occasion cooking. But the rewards are worth the work, especially if you don't mind people hovering around the kitchen to get their food while it's at peak crispness. Use a large, deep, heavy-duty pot. The best oils are grapeseed (neutral and clean), peanut (especially for Asian-type dishes), and olive (best for European-type frying; just be careful not to overheat it).

Put at least 2 inches of oil into the pot (3 if there's room); there should be several inches left to allow the food and oil to rise without overflowing. Heat the oil over medium heat and use a candy or deep-frying thermometer to monitor the temperature (all deep-frying recipes give you a specific temperature). If you don't have a thermometer, put a piece of plain bread in the oil. It should bubble, float immediately to the top, and turn golden brown within 30 to 60 seconds. If it sinks and soaks up oil, turn up the heat a notch. If it doesn't sink

and turns brown too quickly, lower the heat a bit. Give the oil a few minutes to adjust, then test again.

While the oil heats, set up a way to drain the food as it comes out of the oil: either a towel-lined plate or a wire rack fitted over a rimmed baking sheet.

Allow plenty of room in the pot when frying, and work in batches if necessary. Gently turn the food with a slotted spoon or spider as it cooks so it browns evenly. If you're new to deep-frying, you might want to take a piece out when it looks done and cut it open. There should be a nice crisp crust surrounding a tender, just-done interior. Make sure the oil returns to the right temperature between each batch. After you transfer the fried food out of the oil to drain, sprinkle on some salt and let it cool only enough to eat without burning your mouth.

Overheating oil is dangerous. If you see the oil start to smoke, turn off the heat; carefully move the pot to a cool burner if using an electric stove. If the oil catches fire, don't put water on it or try to move the pot; both risk spreading the fire. Turn off the heat. If you can, slip a lid over the pan. If you have one, use a fire extinguisher suited for grease flames, or smother it with a cup or two of baking soda, flour, or sand. You should not deep-fry if you don't have any of these items at home.

Spices, Herbs, Sauces, and Condiments

CHAPTER AT A GLANCE

Salt and Pepper 26

Spices 27

Chiles, Peppers, and Chile Pastes 39

Herbs 46

Flavored Oils 52

Fresh (Uncooked) Sauces 55

Cooked Sauces 71

In the decades since I wrote the first two editions of this book, the American approach to flavoring food has changed dramatically. There's less butter, cream, and reduced stocks in our sauces; instead we depend on vinegars and oils. Bold and once-unfamiliar spices reflect our affinity for global cuisines. We take full advantage of all the fresh herbs now available year-round. And chiles are everywhere.

I still prefer to make most sauces and salsas, spice blends, herb mixtures, and condiments myself. But some high-quality store-bought versions are bound to be staples in your kitchen. I no longer believe most people want to make their own ketchup, for example. On the other hand, recipes for salsas, mustard, vinaigrette, and mayonnaise remain, along with many ways to vary them, and encouragement to give homemade a whirl. If you do buy the bottled kind, you'll have lots of ideas for customizing them.

These shifts strike at the core of how we cook, which is more sauce- and condiment-driven than ever before. When you combine contemporary seasonings with simply prepared proteins, vegetables, grains, and beans, the result is mix-and-match meal planning based on unfussy ingredients and remarkable flavors. That's why this chapter appears first. I've arranged the sections from most accessible ingredients—salt and pepper, followed by spices—to fresh staples (chiles and herbs) and finally to sauces that take anywhere from five minutes of work to a few hours. All will greatly improve the quality of your meals.

Many Ways to Use These Recipes

You can put the sauces and condiments in this chapter to work before, during, and after cooking to add flavor to the usual meat, poultry, fish, or vegetables, or something unexpected like eggs or tofu. Or think backwards and start with a favorite sauce recipe, then figure out what to eat it with.

RECIPE	MARINATING	BASTING	POACHING/ BRAISING	GARNISHING	DIPPING
Grainy Mustard		x		x	x
Chile Paste and variations	x	x		x	x
Red Curry Paste and variations	x	x	x		
Flavored Oil	x	x			x
Traditional Pesto and variations	x	x		x	x
Parsley (or Other Herb) Purée	x	x		x	x
Fresh salsas				x	x

 fast make ahead 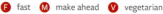 vegetarian

RECIPE	MARINATING	BASTING	POACHING/BRAISING	GARNISHING	DIPPING
Tahini Sauce and variations		x		x	x
Simplest Yogurt Sauce and variations	x	x		x	x
Raw Onion Chutney				x	
Cilantro-Mint Chutney	x	x		x	x
Coconut Chutney				x	x
Dried Fruit and Nut Chutney				x	x
Soy Dipping Sauce and Marinade and variations	x	x	x		x
Thai Chile Sauce		x		x	x
Ginger-Scallion Sauce and variations		x		x	x
Miso Dipping Sauce and variations		x		x	x
Miso-Carrot Sauce with Ginger		x		x	x
Homemade Mayo and variations		x		x	x
Real Ranch Dressing and variations	x	x		x	x
Reduction Sauce				x	x
Five-Minute Drizzle Sauce and variations				x	x
Salsa Roja or Verde and variations		x	x	x	x
Traditional Cranberry Sauce			x	x	
Barbecue Sauce		x	x	x	x
Peanut Sauce		x	x	x	x
Brown Butter		x		x	
Béchamel and 6 Other Creamy Sauces				x	
Hollandaise Sauce				x	

THE BASICS OF SALT AND PEPPER

For most of us, salt and pepper are fundamental, and often the only seasoning necessary. They're usually used together, and it's impossible to imagine cooking without them.

All salts are created naturally—in rock and bodies of water—but they're not all the same. Common table salt is mined, milled, refined, and "enhanced" with iodine and other ingredients into small, free-flowing grains. But consistency has a downside: the flavor of table salt is harsh and overly salty, with iodine the predominant mineral taste.

At the other end of the spectrum is an array of specialty salts, pulled from oceans or clay, with nuances of flavor and color I don't think are worth the expense. I primarily use kosher salt, and occasionally sea salt.

Salting food is a matter of personal taste, so I rarely specify quantities. The directions suggest when to season with salt—usually more than once during the process, and almost always at the end—and I always encourage you to taste as you go. I specify exact measurements in dishes where a precise amount of salt is crucial. When baking, use kosher salt; sea salt is less uniform and might have overpowering mineral flavors.

Pepper is native to India and now cultivated throughout the hot and humid regions of the world. This vine-growing fruit has been fought over, and for, throughout history—with good reason. The flavor is deep, sharp, smoky, slightly acidic, and pleasantly hot, a balance that cannot be duplicated with anything else. It's become ubiquitous, and its value can't be overstated.

I use black peppercorns (referred to as just "pepper" throughout the book) almost exclusively and grind them in a pepper mill as necessary. The most common kind is simply labeled "black pepper," though sometimes you can buy specialty varieties, known mostly by their region of origin. Whatever you choose, take a whiff if possible to make sure the aroma is complex and sharp without being acrid. Leave whatever black pepper—whole or ground—you'll need for a week or so handy on the counter and keep the rest in tightly sealed containers in a cool, dark place.

White peppercorns and pink peppercorns have less intense though similar flavors. Green peppercorns are best—but rare—fresh, where their mild fruity and grassy flavor is at its peak. They're packed in brine (refrigerate after opening) or dried. You must reconstitute the dried ones in hot water, like dried chiles or mushrooms. I hardly ever cook with any of these colors, though you might want to give one a try sometime.

Sichuan peppercorns aren't from the pepper vine, but are the flowers of a small tree. Sichuan pepper's flavor is unique and essential to Sichuan cooking; a flowery, slightly smoky aroma combines with a somewhat lemony-medicinal flavor, and a tongue-numbing, not-hot "spiciness" that feels almost like local anesthesia. This

A Word About Grinding Pepper (and Salt)

What you grind fresh doesn't taste at all like the same seasoning you shake from a container. But I'm not dogmatic about not using preground, especially salt, which can be a real pain to grind yourself, especially if it's wet enough to corrode common metal mills. It's more important that you taste and make adjustments as you cook, whatever form of salt and pepper is on your counter.

If you prefer the convenience of preground, one way to go is to grind your pepper—and salt, if you feel the need—in batches every week or so and keep them in opaque airtight containers. There are many types of pepper mills for table and kitchen grinding. Ideally you want a sturdy metal or wooden mill with a screw at the top or bottom to adjust the grind. Of course you can also grind pepper in a spice grinder (see "Toasting and Grinding Spices," page 27), or a mortar and pestle. Or simply crack peppercorns into large chunks with the flat side of a big knife or put them into a plastic bag and take a hammer to them.

 fast make ahead  vegetarian

is how Sichuan food can contain so many chiles without being overwhelmingly hot.

THE BASICS OF SPICES

I encourage you to buy spices from somewhere that specializes in them or at least sells them in bulk. That generally means Asian or Indian markets, gourmet shops, online, or by mail. You don't have to buy a lot, but you'll notice the difference from supermarket brands.

Whole spices are generally fresher than ground. You can also toast and grind them at the last minute, for maximum flavor. Most keep so well, for so long, you won't need to stock up more than once or twice a year. That said, the convenience of preground spices is alluring. When you just can't see toasting and grinding your own, buy the best you can find; like whole spices, good-quality ground spices are often available in bulk at natural food stores or online.

Sunlight, moisture, and heat are the enemies of all spices. Keep whole spices in tightly covered opaque containers or in jars in a dark place. The cooler, the better, though the refrigerator is too humid.

These are the most common spices for how we cook today. It's better to get an idea of how you cook and choose accordingly—if you love Middle Eastern food or Indian cooking, for example—than to go out and buy everything on this list at once. A comprehensive chart follows, including some spices that don't appear in this book; their descriptions might inspire you to explore on your own. For salt and pepper, see page 26. For mustard seeds, see page 35; for dried chiles, see the chart starting on page 41.

A note about garlic powder, which is probably conspicuous by its absence: I use fresh garlic, since it keeps for a long time and is one of the most important flavors in my cooking. Occasionally granulated garlic (*not* garlic salt) finds its way into a spice blend recipe that's designed for rubbing.

Toasting and Grinding Spices

Every spice benefits from a gentle warming that activates and releases their essential oils and makes them aromatic. "Gentle" is the operative word: direct heat burns them, resulting in a bitter taste.

Whenever possible, toast whole spices just before grinding. If they're big, like cinnamon sticks or nutmeg, break them up—with your fingers, the back of a knife, a hammer, the bottom of a pan, whatever. If they're encased in pods, like cardamom, lightly crush the pods to remove the seeds; discard the husks. Put a dry skillet over medium heat. Add the spices and cook, shaking the pan or stirring constantly with a wooden spoon, until they smell really good, just a minute or 2. Immediately remove them from the pan and let them cool a bit.

Whir the spice or spices in a coffee or spice grinder; purists use a mortar and pestle. Unplug the grinder, empty out the spices, then wipe it out as best you can. (If you're feeling really energetic, grind a little rice to a powder after removing the spices; the rice powder will remove the seasonings when you dump it out.) Store any extra ground spices you're not immediately using as you would whole ones. They'll stay potent for a few weeks.

Spice Mixtures

Spice mixtures are the easiest way to add multidimensional flavor with little extra work. Just think of the difference between adding cumin to a dish and adding chili or curry powder: One spice alone is fine; in combination with other seasonings it has the power to distinguish a unique complete dish. If you aren't already making your own spice mixes, I strongly encourage you to try a couple from this section.

Try spice mixtures as a last-minute dusting of flavor on already cooked foods. Or sauté them with aromatics at the beginning of cooking to provide a foundation before adding more ingredients. They also make terrific rubs to season seafood, poultry, meats, tofu, or vegetables before

(continued)

The Spice Lexicon

SPICE	DESCRIPTION	USES
Allspice Jamaica pepper; myrtle pepper; newspice; pimento	Berries of the aromatic evergreen pimento trees (not to be confused with pimientos, the peppers; see page 42). Small, hard, rough-skinned, they look like large peppercorns, smell a bit like a combination of cloves and nutmeg, and taste slightly peppery.	Ground, by the pinch; a little goes a long way. Particularly delicious with grains (bulgur, couscous, rice, polenta) and vegetables (beets, carrots, parsnips, winter squashes, sweet potatoes). Extremely useful in pies, puddings, gingerbread, some chocolate desserts.
Amchoor Amchur; green mango powder	Made from unripe green mangoes that are peeled, sliced, dried, and ground. Tangy sour taste; used much like lemon juice.	Sift if necessary to remove lumps. Used primarily in Indian cooking—curries, chutneys, pickles, and especially in the spice blend Chaat Masala (page 34).
Anise seeds Aniseed; sweet cumin	Tiny crescent-shaped greenish-brown seeds with a sweet licorice flavor. Star anise or fennel can usually fill in for these and vice versa.	Most common in desserts. Also work well in sweet and savory dishes with apples, cucumbers, carrots, turnips, cabbages; in fruit salads, salad dressings, pickles, stuffings, sauerkraut.
Annatto Achiote	Hard, triangular brick-colored seeds; sometimes available as prepared paste. Earthy or musky smell; slightly peppery but subtle taste. Traditionally used in Latin American dishes, mostly for color and a touch of nutty flavor.	Whole seeds usually heated with oil to color and flavor it; strained out before cooking. To grind, soak for 10 minutes in boiling water, drain, then grind with mortar and pestle or in spice grinder.
Asafetida Hing; devil's dung; stinking gum	Made from the dried resin of carrot family plants. Waxy brownish-black lumps; beige powder. Its unfortunate high-sulfur odor (like rotten garlic) can overcome your kitchen, but with a bit of cooking it transforms into a haunting flavor that smells a bit like onion. Powder is easier to use but generally less pure, so go for lump form if you can find it.	Indian cuisine primarily, especially vegetables, beans, potatoes, chutney, pickles, sauces; usually in spice mixtures like sambar powder. Very potent, so use only by the pinch. Try adding a tiny amount to plain boiled rice. To minimize the smell, double-pack powdered asafetida in a jar inside another jar. Lump will keep indefinitely; pulverize a bit just before use.
Caraway	Slender, ridged brown seeds from a parsley-related plant, with an anise-cumin flavor.	Traditionally used in rye bread; delicious in cabbage and potato dishes and other hearty soups and stews.
Cardamom	Whole pods may be green, brown-black, or whitish. Each contains about 10 brown-black, slightly sticky seeds with a rich spicy scent, a bit like ginger mixed with pine and lemon. Available as whole pods, "hulled" (just the seeds), and ground; ground is the least potent.	A staple in Middle Eastern and Indian cooking (a key ingredient in many spice mixtures); also used in pastries, especially in Scandinavia. Gently crush pods with the flat side of a knife to free seeds; grind or crush as required. (Sometimes pods are cooked whole, especially in braised dishes, where they soften.)
Celery seeds	Tiny tan seeds. Usually from lovage, a related plant with an intense celery flavor. Can be bitter.	A little goes a long way. Often used in pickling brines, cheese spreads, and salad dressings.

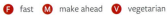

SPICE	DESCRIPTION	USES
Cinnamon Canela; Ceylon or Sri Lanka cinnamon	The aromatic bark of a tropical laurel tree. Cassia, cinnamon's less expensive cousin from a laurel tree native to China, often sold as cinnamon. Ground cinnamon is handy, though it's easy enough to grind sticks or use whole in liquids. Cassia is redder with a more bitter flavor, so it's better in savory dishes than sweet ones.	Use whole cinnamon sticks or pieces of cassia in soups, stews, chiles, curries; add to rice or other grains. True cinnamon is excellent in pastries, rice puddings, and other concoctions featuring sweet cream. Delicious paired with apples or in mulled cider.
Cloves	The unripe flower buds of an evergreen native to Southeast Asia. Pink when picked; dried to reddish brown, separated from their husks, then dried again. Whole cloves should be dark brown, oily, and fat, not shriveled. Sweet and warm aroma and piercing flavor.	Use cloves sparingly; remove whole cloves before serving (or at least warn people to look out for them!). To make this easier, wrap in cheesecloth or put in a tea ball. A pinch ground cloves is good in spice blends, batters and doughs, some pie fillings, stewed fruit.
Coriander	Seeds of the cilantro plant (see page 47). Small, round; color varies from pale green when fresh to light or dark brown when dried. Lemony flavor somewhat like cilantro leaves, but more nuanced, with hints of cumin, fennel, and even cloves.	Seeds can be cooked whole into dishes (and are quite pleasant to eat) or ground first. Most often used with other spices, especially cumin and cardamom; an important part of many spice mixtures or alone in Asian- and Latin American–style stews and soups.
Cumin Comino	The highly aromatic dried seed of a relative of parsley. Often confused with caraway, though they don't taste alike at all. If you find cumin bitter, seek out black cumin, which is more peppery and sweet; it can usually be found in Indian markets.	Like coriander, frequently included in spice mixtures (garam masala, kebsa, chili powder). Also used solo, especially in Latin American and Middle Eastern cooking.
Dill seeds	Light brown, oval, and flat. Stronger taste than the fresh herb.	Often used whole; occasionally ground. Excellent with cucumbers, radishes, potatoes, and sauces made with sour cream, yogurt, or mustard.
Fennel seeds Sweet cumin	From bulbless fennel, these seeds are small, pale greenish brown ovals with tiny ridges. Aromatic, warm, sweet taste reminiscent of licorice. Not as strong as anise, and a bit more useful.	Delicious in salad dressings, yogurt sauces, and pilafs. One of the five ingredients in Five-Spice Powder (page 35). In some curry powders; a popular flavor in India, Italy (think sausages), and southern France. An interesting addition to spice cookies, shortbread, quick breads.
Fenugreek (the leaves are *Methi*)	Distinctive small, rectangular, brownish-yellow seeds; very hard. Pungent aroma, faintly reminiscent of maple; earthy, somewhat bitter taste.	Used mainly in the cuisines of India and northern Africa in chutneys, dals (lentils), and curries. An essential ingredient in many curry powders. Especially good with eggplant and potatoes.
Ginger	Pungent, spicy, almost hot flavor. Yellowish tan and powdery when dried and ground. May be sliced and candied (crystallized), preserved in sugar syrup, or pickled.	Ground ginger is often used in sweets (cakes, cookies, quick breads); very convenient for spice mixtures. Candied and preserved ginger are delicious out of hand and can be used in cooking; you know pickled ginger from sushi.

(continued)

The Spice Lexicon (*continued*)

SPICE	DESCRIPTION	USES
Juniper berries	From the cones of the evergreen tree of the same name. The size of dried peas, blue-black in color. Very pungent taste like a mix of pine, fruit, and lemon peel; the dominant flavor in gin.	Use in moderation. Toasting brings out the aroma; crushing releases flavor. Or use whole in a cheese-cloth bag or tea ball, then remove before serving. Classic in stuffings, sauerkraut, sauces, and pickling.
Mace	The hard, lacy coating (aril) that covers the pod that contains the nutmeg kernel. Bright red when the fruit first opens; yellow brown after drying and pressing. Flavor very similar to nutmeg, though more bitter. Available in whole blades or ground. Nutmeg is almost always an adequate substitute.	Commonly used in cakes and other sweets; traditional in doughnuts and pumpkin pie. Add ground mace directly to savory dishes toward the end of cooking. Whole blades work in soups or stews as long as you remove them before serving.
Nigella	The teardrop-shaped seeds from a plant in the same family as buttercups. Look very similar to black sesame seeds. Taste like mild onions. Usually found whole in Middle Eastern and Indian grocery stores.	Seeds don't need to be toasted. Add a sprinkle as a savory finishing touch, especially on flatbreads and mild cheese.
Nutmeg	The egg-shaped kernel inside the seed of the fruit of a tropical evergreen tree. (Its covering is mace, above.) About 1 inch long. Dark brown; sometimes whitish, the result of being dusted with lime to discourage insects. (Wash this off before grating or grinding.) Sweet and warm; strong and slightly bitter. Available ground, but there's nothing quite like grating your own at the last minute.	Use sparingly: grate directly into the dish or break into pieces first (use a hammer); put the unused portion back in the jar or bag. Lovely in fruit dishes, custards, cakes, other sweets; also vegetables, especially spinach. Works well as a finishing touch to cream and cheese sauces.
Paprika Pimentón	Bright red-orange ground dried chile; anything turning brown is too old. Spicy-sweet aroma. Varying in heat from mild/sweet (usually from Hungary or increasingly California) to hot. Also smoked, called *pimentón* in Spanish (see page 42).	Use the same way as dried chile: delicious with grains, eggs, cheese, many vegetables, in soups, stews, sauces, rice, potato dishes. Ground mild chile (like ancho) can substitute for paprika with no problem.
Poppy seeds	From the same plant as opium; the pinhead-size seeds come from inside the flower's pods. Most of the seed we use in the U.S. are slate blue, but those used in India are usually smaller and yellow-white. Adds a nutty flavor and subtle crunch to foods. Available whole or crushed into a paste.	Used in Europe and the Middle East in or on sweets and baked goods. Good in salad dressings, fruit salads, with Eastern European–style noodle dishes. In India, poppy seeds are toasted, ground, and used to flavor and thicken curries. Paste is often a filling for strudel-type pastries and breads. Very finely ground almonds or almond paste is a good substitute.
Saffron Zafran; asafran	Expensive by the ounce, but you don't need much at any one time and it's worth having around. Be sure the source is reputable. Threads should be strong, long, and brilliant orange-red; don't bother with ground. Highly aromatic, warm, and spicy; slightly bitter taste. Gives food a distinctive and lovely yellow color and incomparable flavor.	Use sparingly (a good pinch is usually right); too much can give food a medicinal taste. Add threads directly to the dish or steep them in some of the cooking liquid or oil for a few minutes first. Used in many traditional breads and cakes, as well as rice (like Yellow Rice, page 436), pasta, cheese dishes. To approximate its color, use annatto or turmeric; but nothing tastes like saffron.

 fast make ahead **V** vegetarian

SPICE	DESCRIPTION	USES
Sesame seeds Benné	Small, flat, and oval with a pointed tip. Powerful nutty, somewhat sweet flavor, especially when toasted. (But pretoasted sesame seeds sometimes have an off flavor.) Available whole, as paste (tahini), or as sesame oil (see page 5). White (most common), red, and black varieties; also unhulled white seeds, which are slightly bitter and harder to digest.	An important flavoring in the cooking of China, Korea, Japan, India, the Middle East, and Europe. Toasting before use (see page 309) mellows the raw flavor (which is why they're perfect for sprinkling on cookies). Also delicious as a coating for fried foods, as a garnish, sprinkled into sauces, dressings, on salads. Store in the freezer to prevent them going rancid.
Star anise Chinese anise	The fruit of an evergreen tree native to China. Pods are a dark brown, eight-pointed star, about 1 inch in diameter, with seeds in each point. Perhaps the strangest-looking spice you'll ever buy and quite lovely. Licorice-like flavor, but botanically unrelated to anise.	Whole stars make an attractive garnish. If less than a whole star is required, break the star into individual points. Wrap the points in cheesecloth to remove them before serving. Use in soups, marinades, spice mixtures; part of Five-Spice Powder (page 35). Common in Vietnamese cooking, especially pho.
Sumac Summaq	Ground dried berries from a sumac plant. Usually found ground. Brick-red spice lends a bit of color.	Used as a souring agent (much like lemon) in the Middle East. Add to seasoning rubs; use as a final seasoning during the last few minutes of cooking. Use with grilled items, on salads, in dips like hummus or baba ghanoush.
Turmeric Indian saffron	A rhizome like ginger, but darker-skinned with thinner fingers and bright orange-red flesh. Increasingly available fresh. Ground is the most common form; its color is more golden than red.	Most frequently used dried and ground in spice blends. If you see it fresh, try adding to pickles (see page 228) or with ginger to stir-fries. Use sparingly; too much tastes bitter. Typical in Indian vegetarian cooking, especially dal; also good with rice and other grain dishes like couscous.
Vanilla beans	The seed pod of a climbing orchid, grown in tropical forests. The best are 4 to 5 inches long, dark chocolate brown, tough but pliant, and sometimes covered with white crystals (called *givre*—"frost"— in French). Inside, hundreds of tiny black seeds. Good vanilla is expensive, so be suspicious of cheap beans. Available in whole pods (superior) and extract (convenient, and fine for most uses).	It's usually best to split the pod lengthwise and scrape the seeds into a liquid, although you can steep pods whole in sauces or syrups. Make vanilla sugar by burying a couple of whole beans in a jar of sugar, which will absorb their aroma after a few days; replenish the sugar as you use it. Exceptional with chocolate and coffee. Used to flavor all kinds of desserts. Good with fruits: try poaching pears, apples, figs, or pineapple in a syrup flavored with vanilla. Surprisingly great with lobster. Wrap tightly in foil or seal in a glass jar and store in a cool place or the refrigerator.

grilling, broiling, or roasting: Sprinkle on the blend when you season with salt and pepper, adding a little oil if the food is lean, and use your hands to spread it evenly.

With all of these recipes, you can combine ground spices in the same quantities; the measurements will be close and the proportions will be the same. But if you start with whole spices (whenever practical) and toast and grind them yourself, the flavors are sharper.

Chili Powder

MAKES: About ¼ cup | TIME: 5 minutes

Do yourself and everyone you cook for a favor and toss out any taco seasoning or jarred chili powder tucked away in your spice rack. This mixture will blow anything you can buy out of the water.

    2 tablespoons ground ancho, New Mexico, or
       other dried mild chile (see page 41)
    ½ teaspoon cayenne, or to taste
    ½ teaspoon black peppercorns
    2 teaspoons cumin seeds
    2 teaspoons coriander seeds
    1 tablespoon dried Mexican oregano

1. Put all the ingredients in a small dry skillet over medium heat. Toast, shaking the pan occasionally, until the mixture is fragrant, 3 to 5 minutes.

2. Cool, then grind in a spice grinder until powdery. Store in a tightly covered container for up to several weeks.

Curry Powder

MAKES: About ¼ cup | TIME: 10 minutes

There is a wide and varied world of curry powders—a catchall term for spice blends used in Indian cooking—but this is my go-to. A mild and complex spice mix, perfect when you're looking for loads of flavor without heat. To crank up the chiles, try a pinch of cayenne for a pleasant tinge and build in more from there. The non-traditional addition of ground chipotle will add hot smokiness, while toasting and grinding one or two Thai chiles along with the other spices will bring nuanced flavors and bright color to the curry.

    ¼ cup coriander seeds
    2 tablespoons cumin seeds
    2 bay leaves
    1 3-inch cinnamon stick
       Seeds from 5 white cardamom pods
    3 whole cloves
    1 teaspoon black peppercorns
    ¼ teaspoon nutmeg pieces (see page 30)
    2 dried curry leaves (optional)
    1 teaspoon ground fenugreek

1. Put the coriander, cumin, bay leaves, cinnamon, cardamom seeds, cloves, peppercorns, nutmeg, and curry leaves if you're using them in a medium dry skillet over medium heat. Cook, shaking the pan occasionally, until lightly browned and fragrant, just a few minutes. For the last minute of cooking, add the fenugreek.

2. Cool, then grind in a spice grinder until powdery. Store in a tightly covered opaque container for up to several weeks.

 F fast   **M** make ahead **V** vegetarian

All the ingredients for
Curry Powder

Garam Masala

MAKES: About ¼ cup | **TIME:** 15 minutes

Literally meaning "warm mixture," this iconic North Indian blend is teak colored and redolent of baking spices, only more savory. Make small batches to use it quickly so it's as fresh as possible.

　　Seeds from 10 cardamom pods
1　3-inch cinnamon stick
1　teaspoon whole cloves
½　teaspoon nutmeg pieces (see page 30)
1　tablespoon cumin seeds
1　tablespoon fennel seeds

1. Put all the ingredients in a medium dry skillet over medium heat. Cook, shaking the pan occasionally, until lightly browned and fragrant, just a few minutes.
2. Cool, then grind to a fine powder in a spice grinder. Store in a tightly covered opaque container for up to several weeks.

Jerk Seasoning

MAKES: About ¼ cup | **TIME:** 5 minutes

In Jamaica, jerk seasoning is typically used as a rub or marinade for grilled chicken or pork. Nontraditional uses include marinating tofu, shrimp, sturdy vegetables like eggplant or potatoes, or even fruit destined for the grill, like pineapple.

1　tablespoon allspice berries
¼　teaspoon nutmeg pieces (see page 30)
1　teaspoon black peppercorns
2　teaspoons dried thyme
1　teaspoon cayenne, or to taste
1　tablespoon paprika

1　tablespoon sugar
2　tablespoons salt
2　teaspoons minced garlic
2　teaspoons minced fresh ginger or 2 teaspoons ground ginger

1. Put the allspice, nutmeg, peppercorns, and thyme in a spice grinder and grind to a fine powder.
2. Mix in the cayenne, paprika, sugar, salt, garlic, and ginger and use immediately. Or leave out the garlic and fresh ginger and store in a tightly covered container for up to several weeks, adding the ginger and garlic as you use the seasoning.

Chaat Masala

MAKES: About ½ cup | **TIME:** 5 minutes

Chaat masala is among my favorite spice blends, with an intense sourness that comes from amchoor, a powder made from dried mangoes that's available in Indian markets (where you'll also find asafetida). Traditionally used as a seasoning for raw or cooked vegetables or fruit, it's also good on plain rice, salads, beans, fresh cheeses like paneer or feta, and chicken or fish.

¼　cup amchoor
2　teaspoons ground cumin
2　teaspoons pepper
2　teaspoons ground coriander
2　teaspoon ground ginger
¼　teaspoon asafetida
¼　teaspoon cayenne
　　Pinch salt

Put all the ingredients in a tightly covered opaque container and shake or stir to combine. Use immediately or store for up to several weeks.

 fast make ahead vegetarian

Five-Spice Powder

MAKES: About ¼ cup | **TIME:** 5 minutes

Sichuan peppercorns make this spice blend unusual and unforgettable. Their unusual smoky, citrusy flavor with a "numbing" heat works perfectly in stir-fries, for spiced nuts, and even sprinkled on desserts like Butter Cookies (page 836) and Baked Custard (page 888). That said, black pepper is a fine stand-in.

1	tablespoon Sichuan peppercorns or black peppercorns
6	star anise pods
1½	teaspoons whole cloves
1	3-inch stick cinnamon
2	tablespoons fennel seeds

Put all the ingredients in a spice grinder and grind to a fine powder. Store in a tightly covered opaque container for up to several weeks.

Seaweed "Shake"

MAKES: About ¼ cup | **TIME:** 20 minutes

Not a smoothie, but an American translation for the ubiquitous family of Japanese seasonings that you sprinkle on food as a last-minute condiment—using either your fingers, a spoon, or some kind of big-holed shaker (thus the name). Sushi Rice (page 447) and Sushi Bowls (page 451) are good places to use it; so are bowls of broth with soba or udon noodles and fish, meat, or vegetables.

2	sheets nori
1	tablespoon sesame seeds
1	teaspoon salt, preferably sea salt Cayenne, to taste (optional)

1. If you're using untoasted nori, put a large dry skillet (preferably cast iron) over medium heat. When it's hot, put a nori sheet in the pan and toast until it turns slightly green, which will take only a few seconds. Turn and quickly toast on the other side. Transfer to a plate or rack cool and repeat with the other nori sheet.

2. Toast the sesame seeds in the pan (no need to let it cool if it's hot), stirring or swirling the pan constantly to keep them from burning. When they're fragrant and beginning to turn golden, after about a minute, put them in a small bowl, sprinkle with salt, and stir.

3. Whir the nori in a spice grinder for a few pulses, then add it to the sesame seeds. Stir in the cayenne if you're using it. Store, tightly covered, in a dark place for up to a week.

SHIITAKE SEAWEED "SHAKE" Chop 1 or 2 large dried shiitake mushroom caps and grind them in a spice grinder to make a powder. Add to the nori-sesame mixture in Step 3.

Mustard

The pungent mustard plant belongs to the same family as broccoli, cabbage, turnips, and—no surprise—horseradish (see page 298). We sometimes eat the greens (see page 307), though we're probably most familiar with the paste ground from the seeds—a spice used so much it has a chart of its own. Mustard seeds come in three varieties.

YELLOW AND WHITE MUSTARD SEEDS The largest of the mustard seeds, and the mildest. Their pleasant spiciness makes them good for everyday ground and prepared mustards, though I prefer them used in combination with other mustards or spices.

BROWN MUSTARD SEEDS The most pungent mustard, ranging from reddish to brown. The sharpest Chinese-, German-, and English-style mustards are all based on these.

BLACK MUSTARD SEEDS Indian cooking often features these slightly oblong seeds, which are sharp. In ground mustards they help add another dimension and deepen the color.

They can be used as a spice, or are commonly prepared in the ways listed below.

Grainy Mustard

MAKES: 1½ cups | TIME: 15 minutes, plus a day or two to soak the seeds

Like mayonnaise, homemade mustard is superior to almost anything you can buy, and is endlessly customizable—see the list that follows. Only it's easier. If you need mustard right away, grind the seeds in a spice grinder and slowly add the liquids until you get the consistency you want. It will be sharper and less subtle, but that's not always a bad thing.

> ¼ cup yellow mustard seeds (about 1½ ounces)
> ¼ cup brown or black mustard seeds
>   (about 1½ ounces)
> ½ cup red wine or water
> ½ cup sherry vinegar or malt vinegar, or any vinegar
>   with at least 5 percent acidity (see page 186)
>   Pinch salt

1. Put all the ingredients in a jar with a tight-fitting lid or other sealed glass or ceramic container. (Don't use metal; it will corrode.) Shake or stir, then let soak for a day or 2.

2. Put the mixture in a blender and purée for several minutes to grind, adding a little extra water as needed to keep the machine running. Stop and scrape the sides down once or twice and repeat. You'll never get the mustard as smooth as Dijon, but you can control the coarseness by how long you blend. Taste and add more salt if you like.

3. Return the mustard to the container and cover tightly. Store in a cool, dark place or refrigerate for up to several months. The mustard will be quite sharp at first, but it will thicken and mellow with time.

PICKLED MUSTARD SEEDS A surprising garnish that accomplishes the same heat: Use white wine or water in place of the red wine. Do not purée the mixture in Step 2; instead use as is, adding the whole seeds to dishes before, during, or after cooking.

14 WAYS TO FLAVOR GRAINY MUSTARD

Start with ½ cup mustard and stir in the following ingredients. Note that using fresh herbs, fruit, or vegetables will reduce the mustard's storage time to a week.

1. **Mustard Relish:** Add ½ cup chopped sweet pickle and ¼ cup each chopped red onion and red bell pepper.
2. **Tarragon Mustard:** Add 1 tablespoon chopped fresh tarragon.
3. **Rosemary Mustard:** Add 1 teaspoon chopped fresh rosemary.
4. **Tomato Mustard:** Add 1 tablespoon tomato paste.
5. **Honey Mustard:** Add 2 tablespoons honey.
6. **Horseradish Mustard:** Add 1 teaspoon freshly grated or prepared horseradish, or more to taste.
7. **Molasses Mustard:** Add 1 tablespoon molasses.
8. **Balsamic Mustard:** Add 1 to 2 tablespoons balsamic vinegar, to taste.
9. **Creole Mustard:** Add ¼ teaspoon cayenne, or more to taste.
10. **Roasted Garlic Mustard:** Add 2 or 3 cloves Roasted Garlic (page 294), mashed with a fork.
11. **Peach Mustard:** Add ¼ cup fresh peach purée (1 medium peach, peeled, pitted, sliced, and puréed or mashed with a fork).
12. **Mango Mustard:** Add ¼ cup fresh mango purée (½ medium mango, peeled, pitted, cubed, and puréed or mashed with a fork).

The Mustard Lexicon

NAME	DESCRIPTION	USES
Dry mustard	When seeds are ground very finely, the result is a powder or "flour."	The simplest mustard is made from this: Mix about ¼ cup with a sprinkle of salt and 1–2 teaspoons sugar. Stir in water, wine, or beer a little at a time until you get the desired consistency. It will be very strong, though the sugar rounds it out a bit. Chinese Mustard Dipping Sauce, below, is a little more sophisticated.
Dijon-style mustard	Smooth, pleasantly hot wine-based mustards modeled after those from Dijon, France. Since getting such a smooth grind with everyday kitchen equipment is impossible, you've simply got to buy it. American-made Grey Poupon is the most familiar brand; Maille (from France) is another good choice.	Use for salad dressings, sauces, and all-purpose smearing.
Coarsely ground, whole grain or stone-ground mustard	When bits of the seeds remain intact, the mustard has a slight crunch with an almost nutty flavor. This kind is easy to make at home; see the recipe on page 37.	Perfect for hearty dishes, next to a slab of corned beef, or whenever you want a more assertive flavor combined with texture.
Chinese mustard	A saucelike mustard, on the thin side and quite sharp. You can find it in Asian markets, well-stocked grocery stores, and of course Chinese restaurants. To make your own, just make a thinner version of the dry mustard recipe above.	To make delicious Chinese Mustard Dipping Sauce, add a little sesame oil and a splash of soy sauce; serve it with any dumplings (page 126), Fried Wontons or Egg Rolls (page 115) or deep-fried vegetables, like those on pages 111 to 115.
Prepared yellow mustard	A very mild version that gets its neon-yellow color from turmeric, not the mustard seeds	I don't bother with this. About the only thing it has going for it is its mildness, which isn't really a plus. Most contain extra ingredients you don't want anyway.
Wasabi	Natural fresh wasabi is a rhizome (a stem that grows underground, like ginger). It's bright green, with a heat that will clear your sinuses. It's now pretty easy to find ground dried wasabi. But mustard is the main ingredient of the prepared "wasabi" we use most often.	With sushi, of course, but adds a bite to anything that needs it
"Gourmet" mustards	Any of the above preparations with additions. They can range from outstanding to not-worth-the-price. You're better off making your own (see page 37).	Best for when the mustard will shine: simple sandwiches, as an accompaniment to meat, or in Cold Mustard Sauce (page 70)

13. **Brewhouse Mustard:** Instead of the red wine or water, use ½ cup strong-flavored beer, like stout, porter, bock, or dark or amber ale.
14. **Mock Mostarda:** For a shortcut to the fruity Italian sauce (usually served with rich meats), combine ½ cup mustard with ¼ cup orange marmalade or cherry or apricot preserves. Add 2 tablespoons cider vinegar.

THE BASICS OF CHILES AND PEPPERS

One of the most frequently used ingredients in this chapter is the chile in all forms—dried, fresh, chopped, whole, with seeds, without, processed, in paste. No wonder. Capsaicin, the thing that gives peppers their heat, releases "feel good" endorphins in the brain and chiles are high in vitamin C and contain some antioxidants. But really, the taste is what we love.

All chiles and peppers are in the same botanical family, capsicum. There are thousands of varieties, ranging from fingernail size to foot-long, from sunset orange to purplish green. They vary in terms of heat (some, like bell peppers, are not hot at all) and complexity of flavor, sometimes as much from individual pepper to pepper as from variety to variety. That variability can make things a bit unpredictable. Before I cook with chiles, I slice a tiny piece out of one and taste. Then I decide how much to use. Unless you like the thrill of chile roulette, you've got to have a nibble.

CHOOSING AND SUBSTITUTING CHILES

Sometimes I'm looking for a little background heat, in which case red chile flakes or ground cayenne are the easiest options. Sometimes, though, I want the full range of the sweet, fruity, and spicy flavors fresh or dried chiles can deliver, and I pay more attention.

My recipes call for a specific variety only when it really matters to a dish; usually the ingredient lists suggest a style and offer some suggestions. The following charts include substitutions. And you can always substitute dried chiles for fresh, and usually vice versa.

The bottom line, though, is this: Use what you like, what you can find, and as much as you think tastes good.

The chile and pepper lexicon that follows includes both fresh and dried, mild and sweet, in alphabetical order.

BUYING AND STORING CHILES

Look for firm, smooth fresh chiles with shiny skins and fresh-looking stems. Keep them in the fridge for a week to two, maybe even longer. For years I've been keeping small Thai chiles in the freezer; by the time I've finished chopping them, they've thawed.

Dried chiles that are still pliable are ideal—there's no need for them to be bone-dry—and they should never be dusty, dank, or moldy. When you get them home, put them in an airtight container and tuck them away in a dark corner of your pantry or spice shelf. Soak, grind, or crumble as needed.

For the sake of measurements, here are two general rules. Every square inch of chile flesh—not including seeds, pith, or the core—will yield about 1 tablespoon when chopped. One medium bell pepper—cored, seeded, and chopped—will yield about a cup.

WORKING WITH FRESH CHILES

Unless they're stuffed (see page 319), fresh chiles are almost always cut up before using, the hotter ones chopped or minced as small as you can manage; the size of the medium and mild ones (like poblanos or bell peppers) matters less. After handling any parts of hot chiles, wash your hands thoroughly to prevent burning your eyes later on.

Cook them with aromatic vegetables like onions, garlic, and ginger before adding them to other ingredients (or adding other ingredients to the aromatics), use them raw as a last-minute garnish, or add them anywhere in between.

WORKING WITH DRIED CHILES

The simplest way to use dried chiles is to add them whole. The only problem with this is that you have no idea what kind of heat level they will contribute to the dish. I've gotten some intense surprises this way.

MAKING CHILE POWDER Next easiest is to remove the stem—and the seeds and veins too if you want less heat—then toss them into a spice grinder and pulse until you get the desired texture. (Be careful when you open the lid; you don't want to inhale a lungful of chile.) Store as you would any other spice.

TOASTING DRIED CHILES Toasting dried chiles in a dry skillet over medium heat before using them is the best way to bring out their smoky flavor. It takes only a couple of minutes on each side. I usually bother with it only when the chile will be featured prominently.

SOAKING DRIED CHILES Especially for use in soups and stews, dried chiles are often soaked. Cover the chiles with boiling water and soak until they're soft and pliable, which may take as little as 15 minutes or as much as 30, depending on the age of the chiles. Then remove the seeds and veins. The flesh of some of the larger chiles will separate from the tough skins, so remove the skins too. Strain and save the soaking water (which can be very potent) if you want. Chop and use the chiles or purée them, and proceed with the recipe.

WORKING WITH MILD OR SWEET PEPPERS

Chiles are actually fruit, so maybe it's not surprising that some of the milder ones—referred to as peppers—can be quite sweet. Chopped or sliced, they are versatile both cooked and raw. The only thing you don't want to do is simmer them in liquid for too long; they'll turn bitter.

THE HEAT FACTOR

Scoville units are the most common way to measure the heat of chiles, but there are others. I don't find any of them useful since there is so much variation between peppers. There are, however, a few generalizations that are useful to know about: Small peppers tend to be hotter than large ones (with a few notable exceptions), while mature (red or orange) peppers pack a bigger wallop than green ones. And since the seeds and veins (the pith) are the hottest parts of the chile, any chile can be tamed (relatively) by removing them. Include some or all of these parts if you want to pump up the heat.

Please remember that chiles can burn, literally. If your hands are chapped or cut, chiles will irritate them. If you've got disposable gloves, use them. If not, every time you touch a chile, wash your hands with warm soapy water—twice is better than once—and be careful not to touch your eyes or any other tender area for a while.

And if your mouth is on fire, reach for something soothing and mild like milk, yogurt, plain bread, or crackers. It won't be an instant cure, but it should ease your suffering.

Chile Pastes

Like spice blends and rubs (see pages 27 and 32), chile pastes aren't exactly sauces, but are more commonly used as ingredients in dressings, sauces, and marinades and to smear on foods before grilling or roasting.

Chile Paste, Nine Ways

MAKES: About ½ cup | **TIME:** 45 minutes, largely unattended

Dried chiles, reconstituted and puréed, make a terrific paste. Take a look at the chart on page 41 to figure out the best chiles to achieve the right heat you're looking for. A combination will deliver more interesting flavor and be less incendiary than a single variety. The variations build on the all-chile base. If fresh herbs or aromatics are involved, use within a day or so for maximum freshness and oomph. Chile paste made with only dried seasonings will last for a couple of weeks.

(continued)

 fast make ahead vegetarian

The Chile and Pepper Lexicon

Like other produce, chiles and sweet peppers are now available in a dizzying array of heirloom and other varieties, even in supermarkets. So consider this list comprehensive but not exhaustive. Chiles are so interchangeable it hardly matters anyway. More important is the level of heat, which varies from each individual chile. In general green (immature peppers) are milder than red (fully ripe). But not always. Be prepared to taste while you're chopping them.

You should use rubber gloves if handling a lot of peppers or those that are super hot. Another option is to only handle the stem, using it to maneuver the chile during cutting. The smaller the fruit the trickier this can be. I almost always use the seeds since it's easier to just cut the whole thing. But they can be the hottest part, so if you want to remove them, grab the chile by the stem and cut downward lengthwise to separate a strip of the flesh from the seed core; roll the chile to another side and repeat until you're left with the seeds and the stem. Then chop the strips as finely as you want.

CHILE/PEPPER	DESCRIPTION	FORMS	SUBSTITUTIONS
Anaheim Chile colorado (when red)	Long and wide, somewhat flat. Green and red (mature). Medium to mild heat. Used for stuffing, grilling, roasting; egg dishes, mild salsas, sauces, dressings.	Fresh, or dried (see California below)	Poblano; New Mexico
Ancho	Compact, squarish, medium size. Almost purple or black. Medium to mild heat. Excellent dried mild chile, classic in mild chili powder.	Fresh (see Poblano on page 43) or dried	Pasilla; California
Banana peppers	Slightly larger than a jalapeño, and milder. Yellowish green. Don't confuse them with hot Hungarian wax peppers.	Fresh	
Bell peppers Sweet peppers; Holland peppers; also called by color: red, yellow, orange, green, or purple (which fades a little during cooking)	The ubiquitous sweet pepper: large, thick walled, and moister than chiles. Color ranges from shades of green (usually bitter, because immature) to pale or deep yellow, orange, red, or even purple. Crisp, with grassy or sweet flavor, depending on maturity.	Fresh	Try the specialty varieties of long sweet or mildly hot peppers–like Padron, Italian long peppers, or Corno di Toro
California	Longish and narrow, slightly flat. Rusty red color. Medium to mild heat.	Fresh (see Anaheim above) or dried	Ancho
Cascabel Chile bola or rattle chile (because seeds shake around inside)	Smooth skinned, puffy, like small brown Ping-Pong balls. Hot to medium. Deep, smoky flavor.	Fresh (rare) or dried	Chile de arbol
Cayenne Finger chile	Long, slightly gnarled, and slender. Green to red when mature. Very hot.	Fresh, or dried whole or ground	Thai; ground cayenne
Chile de arbol Red chile (see Thai on page 43)	Narrow; a couple of inches long. Unlike many dried chiles, these retain a bright reddish brown to almost orange color. Very hot to hot. Nice depth of flavor.	Fresh (less common) or dried	For dried, guajillo (milder); for fresh, jalapeño

(continued)

The Chile and Pepper Lexicon (continued)

CHILE/PEPPER	DESCRIPTION	FORMS	SUBSTITUTIONS
Chipotle Chile seco; smoked jalapeño	Dried: light to reddish brown. Canned, in adobo sauce: quite dark, almost purple. Very hot to hot. Flavor is incomparable: smoky, hot, and multifaceted. Gives rich smokiness to chilies, braises, cooked salsas. If using dried, grind and use judiciously as you would cayenne. Chopped or puréed, canned chipotles add body along with heat.	Dried or canned in adobo sauce	
Fresno	Like jalapeño but with thinner flesh. Usually red (mature), sometimes available green. Hot to medium.	Usually only fresh	Serrano; jalapeño
Guajillo	Flat; about an inch wide, a couple of inches long. Dark reddish brown with shiny, thick skin. Medium heat.	Fresh (rare) or dried	New Mexico; ancho
Habanero, dried	Small, roundish, very wrinkled. Reddish brown. Very hot. Use judiciously in chilies, soups, broths.	Dried; sometimes smoked and dried	Dried chipotle
Habanero, fresh Scotch bonnet (not technically the same, but virtually interchangeable)	Round and fairly small, like teeny bell peppers. Color ranges from neon green to yellow, gold, and orange, depending on maturity and variety. Very hot. Flavor is fruity and bright once you get past the fire.	Fresh	Nothing has the same complex flavor, or packs quite the same wallop.
Jalapeño	Sold green mostly, sometimes red. Flavor is slightly herbaceous and grassy. Hot to medium.	Fresh, or smoked and dried (see Chipotle above)	Serrano; chile de arbol
New Mexico Green chiles or red chiles (depending on maturity) Also known by where many are grown: Hatch	Similar to Anaheim, but pointed on both ends. Green and red (mature). Medium to mild heat. Fresh are used for stuffing, grilling, roasting, and puréeing into sauces and chilies.	Fresh or dried	For fresh, Anaheim; for dried, California
Paprika Hungarian paprika; Spanish paprika	Red. Mild; sometimes hot. Usually found ground in cans or jars in sweet or smoked varieties (especially Spanish).	Fresh (rare) or dried and ground	
Pasilla Chile negro	Very wrinkled, long, narrow. Almost black. Ranges from hot to mild, depending on variety.	Fresh (less common) or dried	New Mexico

 fast make ahead **V** vegetarian

CHILE/PEPPER	DESCRIPTION	FORMS	SUBSTITUTIONS
Pimiento	Narrower and slightly smaller than a bell pepper, with a pointed end. Red only. More intense, sweet flavor than bell.	More commonly found in jars, but sometimes you see fresh	
Piquin Piquín	Fingernail size and shape. Bright red; somewhat shiny skins. Very hot to hot. Very complex flavors.	Fresh (rare) or dried	Dried Thai chiles
Poblano	Like a smaller, flatter bell pepper. Usually very dark green or purple, sometimes red (mature). Medium to mild heat. Super for stuffing (you should peel first; see pages 318–319), grilling, and roasting.	Fresh, or dried (see Ancho on page 41)	Anaheim; New Mexico
Red chile flakes Crushed red pepper; dried red pepper; ground red pepper	Ubiquitous combination of seeds, bits of chile, and skin. Always red. Hot to medium. Sometimes suspended in oil. With supermarket kinds, assume a variety of chiles was used to achieve heat level specified by manufacturer. Use when you want to add plain old heat.		For more character, make your own: Crumble or grind any whole dried red chile, like Thai or serrano; for milder flavor, use California.
Serrano	Finger sized or smaller. Thin skinned. Green or red (mature). Hot.	Fresh or dried	Cayenne, Thai (use less), jalapeño (use more)
Shishito Guernika; padrón	Of Japanese or Spanish origin. Finger sized, slightly gnarled. Pale green. Delicious grilled or fried in a skillet with little or no oil, served with salt. Mild but occasionally you might get a hot one in the mix.	Only fresh	
Thai Thai bird (fresh); red chile (dried)	Pinky size or smaller. Green to red when mature. Very hot. Not the same as other small Asian or American varieties, but virtually interchangeable.	Fresh or dried; sometimes pickled	For fresh, cayenne; for dried, chile de arbol; Chinese chile
Thai, Giant	Basically a bigger Thai chile (see above). Hot.	Usually fresh only	Thai; jalapeño (use more)

Chile Paste, page 40

<pre>
  2 ounces any whole dried chiles
     (6 to 12, depending on size)
     Salt
  2 tablespoons good-quality vegetable oil
</pre>

1. Toast the chiles in a dry skillet over medium heat until fragrant, a minute or 2 on each side, then soak them in boiling water until soft, 15 to 30 minutes. Drain the chiles, saving the soaking liquid, and remove and discard the stems, seeds, and veins. (For a hotter paste, save some of the seeds.)

2. Put the chiles, any seeds you're using, and a pinch salt in a blender or food processor. Purée until smooth, adding a spoonful of soaking water at a time and stopping the machine to scrape down the sides as necessary, until it reaches the desired consistency.

3. Put the oil in a small skillet over medium-high heat. Cook the chile paste, stirring constantly, until deeply colored and fragrant, about 2 minutes. Just before using, taste and adjust the seasoning. Use immediately or refrigerate for up to 2 days.

MEXICAN-STYLE CHILE PASTE Use all guajillo or other dark chiles: In Step 2, purée in 1 teaspoon chopped garlic, 1 teaspoon ground cumin, and 2 tablespoons fresh epazote (see page 48), Mexican oregano, or oregano (or 2 teaspoons dried). Proceed with the recipe.

CHIPOTLE PASTE Hot. Hot. Hot: Use some or all dried chipotles. Or skip Step 1 and just use 1 small (7-ounce) can chipotles with their adobo sauce (about ⅓ cup).

THAI-STYLE CHILE PASTE Quite complex: Use 2 or 3 Thai chiles along with the mild chiles. In Step 2, purée in 1 inch lemongrass, peeled, trimmed, and chopped, and ¼ cup fresh cilantro or Thai basil.

VIETNAMESE-STYLE CHILE PASTE Use 2 or 3 Thai chiles along with the mild chiles. In Step 2, add 1 tablespoon chopped garlic and 2 tablespoons fish sauce,

2 tablespoons sugar, and ¼ cup fresh mint. After cooking, squeeze in the juice of 1 lime.

INDIAN-STYLE CHILE PASTE Useful if you want to add heat to Indian dishes: In Step 2, purée in 1 tablespoon garam masala (to make your own, see page 34), or more to taste.

HARISSA The flavor is quite complex: In Step 2, purée in 1 tablespoon ground coriander, 2 teaspoons ground cumin, and 1 teaspoon chopped garlic. Use olive oil instead of vegetable oil.

CHILE AND BLACK BEAN PASTE In Step 2, purée in 2 tablespoons fermented black beans. Omit the salt until you taste for seasoning in Step 3.

CHILE-GARLIC PASTE Much longer-lasting, and tangy from the vinegar: Use 1 cup dried red chiles; don't bother to toast and soak. Heat ½ cup cider vinegar until just boiling. Combine the chiles and vinegar in a blender with

7 Uses for Chile Pastes

1. Rub paste directly onto fish, poultry, or meat before cooking—any kind of cooking, not just grilling.

2. Toss a spoonful or two of any chile paste with simply cooked vegetables, pasta, or grains (along with a little butter or oil if you like).

3. To turn chile paste into a "real" sauce, heat a batch with ¼ cup or so of oil, butter, cream, stock, tomato sauce, or even water.

4. Stir chile paste directly into yogurt, sour cream, tahini, or mayonnaise for a quick chilled sauce.

5. Mix with a little olive or good-quality vegetable oil and brush on fish, chicken, meat, vegetables, or tofu as they come off the grill.

6. Stir a little into nut pastes for a spicy spread for toasted bread.

7. Smear a little on sandwiches (especially grilled cheese!). Or try it with peanut butter and be shocked.

¼ cup chopped garlic, 2 teaspoons sugar, and 1 teaspoon salt. Purée as directed, adding more vinegar if necessary to make a paste. Refrigerate for up to 3 weeks.

Red Curry Paste

MAKES: About ¾ cup | **TIME:** 25 minutes

The herbs and seasonings in here are intoxicating. Curry paste is almost always sautéed in oil—with or without aromatics—at the beginning of the recipe. Once it starts to color and become fragrant, you'll add liquid and other ingredients.

- 10 **Thai or other hot-to-medium dried red chiles, seeded, or to taste**
- 4 **dried lime leaves or fresh lime leaves, chopped, or 1 tablespoon grated lime zest**
- 1 **teaspoon coriander seeds**
- 1 **teaspoon cumin seeds**
- 2 **stalks lemongrass, peeled, trimmed, and chopped**
- 2 **shallots, cut into chunks**
- 1 **tablespoon chopped garlic**
- 1 **inch fresh ginger, cut into chunks**
- 2 **tablespoons cilantro roots (see page 47), rinsed well, or 3 tablespoons chopped cilantro stems**
- 3 **tablespoons good-quality vegetable oil**

1. Soak the chiles and dried lime leaves in warm water for about 15 minutes.

2. Put the coriander and cumin seeds in a small skillet over medium heat. Cook, shaking the pan occasionally, until lightly browned and fragrant, about 3 minutes. Cool, then grind to a powder in a spice grinder.

3. Drain the chiles (and lime leaves, if soaked); discard the soaking water. Transfer the chiles, lime leaves, coriander, cumin, lemongrass, shallots, garlic, ginger,

and cilantro to a blender or food processor. Grind to a paste, stopping the machine to scrape down the sides as necessary. Gradually add the oil while blending; you are looking for a fairly smooth, thick paste. Store in a tightly covered container and refrigerate for up to 2 weeks.

GREEN CURRY PASTE Substitute small fresh green chiles for the red chiles; if you can't find little ones use 1 or 2 jalapeño chiles. Add 1 tablespoon ground turmeric in Step 3.

RED OR GREEN CURRY SAUCE Put 2 tablespoons good-quality vegetable oil in a deep skillet over medium heat. Add ¼ cup Red or Green Curry Paste and cook, stirring constantly, until it becomes fragrant and the color deepens, about 2 minutes. Stir in 1½ cups coconut milk (to make your own, see page 372). Bring to a boil, reduce the heat a bit, and let it bubble gently until thickened, about 5 minutes. Stir in ½ cup chopped fresh Thai basil, mint, or cilantro if you like.

Herbs

The herbs in the following lexicon are the most common among hundreds. You no longer need to be a gardener to enjoy even the more obscure varieties; many are available in farmers' markets, international markets, and even the grocery store.

Though no herb is a direct substitute for any other, there are many situations in which you want simply the freshness that herbs provide. So you can often substitute parsley for basil, cilantro for mint, and so on, providing you don't expect the flavor to be the same. As always, taste a bite of the leaves and the food you're seasoning, then use your good judgment. If you don't have fresh herbs, it's usually better to just stick to salt and pepper and spices. Most dried herbs are a detriment; the rare exceptions appear below.

Fresh herbs should be stored in the refrigerator. Most need simply to be wrapped in damp towels and

The Herb Lexicon

HERB	DESCRIPTION	USES
Basil	Bright green Italian varieties with cupped leaves taste like licorice and cloves; smaller, slightly sturdier Thai basil is peppery and minty. Sold everywhere; easy to grow in warm weather.	Best raw or cooked only briefly. Use leaves whole or tear them (chop if you don't mind them turning black). Sharper-tasting edible flowers are gorgeous in salads.
Bay leaf Sweet bay; sweet laurel; bay laurel	Glossy, green, and sturdy when fresh; gray-green and brittle when dried. Flavor is subtle but multifaceted. Fresh are much stronger than dried, though both are good. The best whole dried leaves will always be quite fragrant and are preferable to ground. Sold everywhere. Laurel trees grow in warm climates.	In stocks, soups, sauces, and poaching liquids; to flavor vinegar; with roasts of all kinds—throw in a few leaves the next time you roast vegetables. Remove whole leaves from dishes before serving.
Chervil	Looks like smaller, lacy-leafed parsley. Anise-basil flavor. Easy to grow in not-too-hot climates, but so delicate you only really see it in farmers' markets or specialty stores.	So delicate it's best used raw or added at the end of cooking. Delicious in omelets, creamy or light sauces, salads, and with vegetables.
Chives	Mild onion flavor in bright green blades like grass but giant and hollow. Garlic chives have bigger, wider, and flatter leaves and a more garlicky taste. Fresh are sold everywhere; easy to grow.	Best raw or cooked only briefly. An assertive addition to soft cheese spreads and compound butters.
Cilantro Coriander; Chinese parsley; Mexican parsley	More tender than parsley but similar in appearance; lighter green and more serrate leaves. Aroma and flavor are distinctive and assertive (those who don't like it say it tastes soapy). The seeds are the spice coriander (see page 29). Sold everywhere and easy to grow; if you do, the flowers and green seeds are delicious.	Like basil and other soft herbs, best added at the last minute. Widely associated with Mexican, Thai, and Indian flavors. Unlike other herbs, you can—and should—eat the leaves and tender stems. Roots are excellent in stews, curry paste, or other long-cooked dishes.
Curry leaf	A flat, shiny leaf used in Indian and Southeast Asian cooking. Complex vegetal flavor, a little like cumin and eucalyptus. The curry plant is in the same family as citrus, thus the similarity to lime leaves. Can be purchased fresh or dried, which is a fine substitute.	Cook curry leaves in fat to draw out the complex flavors, then add them to stews, soups, or pilafs. Whole dried leaves should be removed (like bay leaves), but fresh leaves can be eaten.
Dill Dill weed	Blue-green feathery, tender leaves on long stalks. Familiar flavor. Sold in most supermarkets; easy to grow in not-too-hot weather.	Add at the end of cooking, as its flavor is diminished by heat (though tying stems in a bundle and cooking with stews imparts nice flavor). Super in dishes made with sour cream, yogurt, mustard; or tossed into green salad.

(continued)

The Herb Lexicon *(continued)*

HERB	DESCRIPTION	USES
Epazote Mexican tea; wormseed; pigweed	Bright green, narrow, jagged, pointed leaves with green stems, usually sold in bunches when fresh. Its powerful and unusual aroma and taste contribute a lot to Mexican dishes. Fresh leaves are better, but dried are acceptable and easier to find. Look in Mexican and Latin American markets, or grow as an annual.	Use chopped or whole fresh or dried leaves in small quantities. Traditionally used with beans and in some moles; good with corn and other summer vegetables, in quesadillas and scrambled eggs.
Lavender	Narrow gray-green leaves with long purple or pink flower spikes. The scent and flavor is minty and floral—you'll recognize it immediately. Can be grown as a perennial in any moderate climate.	Fresh leaves and flowers can be chopped and tossed into salads and fruit dishes or cooked in sauces, candies, and pastries. Great with roasted or grilled meat, especially lamb. Works well in infusions (see page 900).
Lemongrass Citronella root; sereh	A stiff, narrow stalk of overlapping fronds; like sugar cane or a tough scallion. Strong citrus flavor and aroma; think citronella candles. Sold in supermarkets and Asian markets. Easy to grow in warm climates, or as an annual in temperate zones.	Cut off woody tops and peel off tough outer layers; mince or pound white interior pieces to release flavor and aroma.
Lime leaves Makrut lime leaves	Tough, shiny green leaves. Very aromatic, with unusually floral and limy flavor. Fresh is best, though dried and frozen are good. Sold in most Asian markets; can be grown wherever citrus will grow.	In Southeast Asian dishes of all types. Chop or toss in whole leaves during cooking; use double the amount of dried leaves for fresh. Or substitute 1 teaspoon grated or chopped lime zest for each leaf.
Marjoram Sweet marjoram; knotted marjoram; wild marjoram	Light green, fuzzy, oval leaves on short, square stems. Often confused with oregano, but more nuanced. Sold in most supermarkets; an easy-to-grow perennial in most climates.	Add fresh toward the end of cooking. Wonderful with green salads, vinaigrettes, eggs, beans, all sorts of vegetables, and especially tomato sauces.
Mint	Bright green, wrinkled leaves (spearmint) or smooth ones (peppermint, other varieties) on square stems. Best fresh, though dried is the required option in certain dishes. Sold in most supermarkets; easy to grow (invasive, in fact).	Chop or crush fresh leaves to release their flavor. Traditional with peas or potatoes; goes well with many vegetables and fruits; perfect in yogurt-based sauces, chutneys, many Southeast Asian and Middle Eastern dishes. Ideal in herbal teas and cocktails.
Oregano Greek oregano; Mexican oregano; sometimes wild marjoram	Dark green, fuzzy, spade-shaped leaves on square stems. Stronger and spicier than marjoram. Fresh is infinitely better, but dried is acceptable. Sold in most supermarkets; an easy-to-grow perennial in most climates.	Fresh and dried can be cooked or used as a garnish in small amounts. In rare cases when specific varieties are listed, substitute whatever you can find. Good with tomatoes, cheeses, pizza, vegetables, beans, and vinaigrettes.

 fast make ahead **V** vegetarian

HERB	DESCRIPTION	USES
Parsley	Dark leaves with a pleasant grassy flavor, on crisp stems. There are two varieties: curly and flat-leaf (Italian) parsley; the latter is better, but it's not worth making a big deal about. Sold everywhere.	Use only fresh. Impossible to overstate its importance—used in just about everything: soups, salads, vinaigrettes, sauces, vegetables, eggs, pasta, and as a garnish. Its freshness is especially valuable in winter.
Rosemary	Grayish-green needles on woody branches. Crisp, piney aroma and flavor. Fresh rosemary is sold in nearly all supermarkets; easy to grow as a perennial in warmer climates or an annual elsewhere.	Wonderful with beans and roast meats, most vegetables, egg dishes, pasta, and breads. Woody branches make perfect skewers for broiling or grilling.
Sage	Soft, woolly, oval grayish-green or multi-colored leaves. Sharply flavored, slightly bitter, and very aromatic. Can be grown as a perennial almost anywhere.	Use fresh leaves whole or chopped. One of the most important herbs for Thanksgiving cooking. Wonderful with pork, chicken, beans, stuffings, breads, biscuits, and pasta.
Shiso Perilla; beefsteak plant	Flat bright green or reddish-purple heart-shaped leaves with a jagged edge. Combination of basil, mint, and cinnamon flavors. Sold fresh in many Asian (especially Japanese) and some Mexican markets; easy to grow inside or out (invasive, like mint; spreads like mad).	As you would use basil or mint. Traditionally served with sashimi and sushi, cucumbers, pickles, tempura; in salads, soups.
Tarragon	Narrow, lance-shaped, bright to dark green leaves, with strong, complex flavor and aroma, faintly licorice-like. Often sold in supermarkets; easily grown as a perennial in most climates.	Whole or chopped fresh leaves can be cooked; flavor is not at all tamed by heat, so use sparingly. Good with seafood, chicken, or eggs.
Thyme	A small shrub with tiny green or grayish-green leaves. Minty, lemony, and earthy. Fresh is more pungent and aromatic than dried, though dried is useful. Sold in supermarkets; easily grown as a perennial in most climates.	The classic French cooking herb, often used in long-simmering or braising recipes. Use fresh leaves and tips as a garnish, but very sparingly—its strong flavor easily overwhelms everything else. Perfect teamed with olive oil and garlic at the beginning of many sautés.

Traditional Pesto

slipped into a plastic bag. Put those with fragile leaves—like basil, chervil, dill, mint, and parsley—stem down in a jar of water (like flowers) with a plastic bag loosely covering the leaves; trim the bottoms and change the water every day.

The delicate stems of tender herbs like cilantro or parsley can be eaten, if you like. For herbs with tougher, more bitter stems (this is especially true of the strongest herbs like rosemary and oregano), simply strip the leaves as from thyme (see below).

Pesto, Herb Purées, and Herb Sauces

Vibrant green and intensely flavored, oil-based herb sauces scream freshness. They're easy too. They're obvious in summer, when herbs are abundant, but everyday supermarket parsley will bring welcome brightness to heavy dishes in the depths of winter. Whatever the season, use the best oil you can find and make sure there's no hint of rancidity before you begin.

Removing Leaves from Thyme

To remove the leaves from thyme or other fresh herbs, hold the top of the stem tightly with one hand and run your fingers downward to strip off the leaves.

Traditional Pesto

MAKES: About 1 cup | **TIME:** 10 minutes

 F M V

To get the authentic Genoese grandmother experience, try pulverizing pesto with a mortar and pestle. Otherwise a food processor is just fine. And note that big batches—topped with an extra layer of olive oil to maintain the color—are only worth making and freezing if you have a constant supply of basil from your garden. For basil you buy, make just one recipe, refrigerate it, and use within a week.

> 2 loosely packed cups fresh basil, rinsed and dried
> Salt
> ½ teaspoon chopped garlic, or more to taste
> 2 tablespoons pine nuts or chopped walnuts
> ½ cup olive oil, or more if needed
> ½ cup freshly grated Parmesan, pecorino Romano, or other hard cheese (optional)

1. Combine the basil, a pinch salt, the garlic, nuts, and about half the oil in a food processor or blender. Purée, stopping the machine to scrape down the sides as necessary and gradually adding the rest of the oil. Add more oil if you prefer a thinner mixture.

2. Store in an airtight container in the refrigerator for a week or in the freezer for several months. Stir in the cheese just before serving.

PESTO WITH BUTTER Toss this with pasta or rice or use it as you would Compound Butter (page 78); it's really quite special: Blend in 2 tablespoons softened butter along with the last bit of oil. Do not store this version.

MINT OR DILL PESTO Super on pasta or grilled fish, chicken, or vegetables: Substitute mint or dill for the basil; the garlic is optional. Use a good-quality vegetable oil instead of olive oil and omit the cheese. Finish, if you like, with a squeeze of lemon juice. Use within a day.

ARUGULA PESTO Terrific with grilled steak or vegetables or plain rice: Substitute arugula (tough stems removed) for the basil. Omit the cheese. Use within a day.

Parsley (or Other Herb) Purée

MAKES: About 1 cup | **TIME:** 10 minutes

This purée is for when you want the full-on taste of concentrated fresh herbs. Use it within a few days; there's no point in freezing it. Parsley is common enough that you can make it whenever the craving strikes, though there are lots of other options below.

    2   cups fresh parsley (thin stems are okay),
        rinsed and dried
        Salt
    ½   cup olive oil, or more if needed

1. Combine the parsley, a pinch salt, and about half the oil in a food processor or blender. Puree, stopping the machine to scrape down the sides as necessary and adding the rest of the oil gradually. Add a little more oil or some water if you prefer a thinner mixture.

2. Taste and add more salt if you'd like, then serve. Or transfer to an airtight container and refrigerate for up to a couple of days. Return the purée to room temperature to make it pourable again.

CILANTRO, DILL, BASIL, OR MINT PURÉE These are good for their straight herbaceous flavors; cilantro purée is terrific with grilled chicken, mint with lamb, and dill with vegetables or fish: Substitute any of these herbs (leaves only or leaves and very thin stems) for the parsley.

CHIMICHURRI Strong enough to stand up to grilled meat: Add 2 tablespoons or more chopped garlic, 2 tablespoons sherry vinegar or wine vinegar, and at

least 1 teaspoon red chile flakes before puréeing. To keep pourable, serve at room temperature.

ZHUG This spiced herb sauce is originally from Yemen, and an integral condiment in Israel and throughout the Middle East: Substitute cilantro for 1 cup of the parsley and reduce the oil to ¼ cup. In Step 1 add 2 or more chopped hot green chiles (like Thai bird or serrano), seeded if you like, 1 clove garlic, 2 teaspoons fresh lemon juice, ¾ teaspoon ground cumin, and ¼ teaspoon each ground coriander and ground cardamom. Process until smooth and pourable, adding water 1 tablespoon at a time if the mixture is too thick.

GREEN OLIVE MOJO Caribbean and intense: Reduce the olive oil to ¼ cup; add ¼ cup fresh lime juice, or more to taste. After puréeing, still in the food processor, pulse in 1 cup pitted green olives so they're in small bits but not puréed. Or chop the olives by hand and stir in at the start of Step 2.

CILANTRO SAUCE Even brighter: Replace the parsley with cilantro, add 1 teaspoon chopped garlic and 1 tablespoon lime juice.

THE BASICS OF FLAVORED OILS

Flavored oil is one of the remarkable cooking ingredients that is more than the sum of its parts. Use as a finishing oil to give anything an extra kick, in dressings, or even as a dip.

The first thing to consider is the oil itself: Do you want olive oil? Another flavorful oil like peanut or coconut oil? Or something neutral like grapeseed, sunflower, or safflower oils? This is a judgment call you make on a case-by-case basis, based on common sense and some knowledge of regional flavors: bundle together Mediterranean ingredients like rosemary and olive oil, for example, or tropical ones like coconut oil and lime. Whenever you're in doubt, reach for neutral oil; you can't go wrong flavoring it with ginger, chiles, garlic, or herbs. Just be sure to save your best olive oil for simple drizzling; it won't make a flavored oil noticeably better.

Infused oils can taste rancid after a while and even cause food poisoning. But you need not worry about this if you make the small batches (½ cup) that follow, just enough to store comfortably in the refrigerator and use within two weeks. Most oils will solidify in cold temperatures, but melt as soon as they warm up—or you can use them as a spread.

Use good, fresh ingredients. Over the years I've adjusted this advice to include making oils flavored with ground spices, though still not dried herbs. As long as you're careful to avoid burning them, you can have excellent results (see the chart below).

Flavored Oil

MAKES: ½ cup | **TIME:** 20 minutes, plus time to cool

The main recipe and the chart that follows are just outlines. Use whatever combinations you can imagine, and make special blends for your favorite dishes or meals. The amount of aromatics, herbs, or spices might change depending on whether they're fresh or dried,

11 Flavored Oil Combinations

Follow the directions for the recipe above, using these combinations or mixing and matching as you like.

OIL	FLAVORING A	FLAVORING B
Olive oil	Zest of 1 lemon, cut into strips	¼ cup fresh rosemary or thyme
Olive oil	Zest of 1 lime, cut into strips	1 tablespoon coriander seeds
Olive oil	Zest of ½ orange, cut into strips	1 tablespoon smoked paprika
Olive oil	1 tablespoon fennel seeds	¼ cup fresh marjoram, thyme, or a mixture
Olive oil	2 bay leaves	2 tablespoons chopped shallot
Good-quality vegetable oil	1 or more fresh red chiles, chopped	2 tablespoons chopped ginger
Good-quality vegetable oil	2 teaspoons mustard seeds	2 teaspoons cumin seeds
Good-quality vegetable oil	Zest of 1 lime, cut into strips	2 tablespoons chopped ginger
Coconut oil	Zest of 1 lime, cut into strips	2 tablespoons chopped lemongrass
Coconut oil	2 tablespoons chopped ginger	1 tablespoon coriander seeds
Olive or good-quality vegetable oil	2 tablespoons chopped garlic	1 tablespoon red chile flakes
Walnut or other nut oil like peanut, sesame, or almond	¼ cup chopped nuts; use the same as the oil	¼ cup chopped fresh parsley

Fresh fruit salsa: strawberry (top) and grape (bottom)

and how they've been stored. But in general, make it stronger than you think; If you make the oil too strong, you can always dilute the final result with more fresh oil.

- ¼ **cup washed and dried fresh herb: rosemary, thyme, bay leaves (dried are also fine), celery leaves, tarragon, marjoram, oregano, etc.**
  OR
- 1 **tablespoon whole spice: star anise, peppercorns, cloves, allspice, nutmeg pieces (see page 30), dried chiles (less if they're very hot), etc.**
  OR
- 2 **tablespoons aromatics: sliced garlic, fresh ginger or turmeric, shallots, scallions, or leeks, or a combination**
  Pinch salt
- ½ **cup olive oil or other good-quality oil**

1. Combine the ingredients in a small saucepan over low heat. Warm gently until the mixture sizzles then continue to cook, stirring occasionally, until the oil is very fragrant and the sizzling stops, another minute or 2 (or less for ground spices) or up to 10 minutes.

2. Remove from the heat, cool, then slowly pour into a clean bottle or other container through a fine mesh strainer. Refrigerate and use within a week. (There may be some sediment that will settle to the bottom.)

Fresh (Uncooked) Sauces

Perhaps the better word is "condiment," since a classically trained French chef would scoff at calling a bunch of chopped tomatoes, onions, chiles, and seasonings a "sauce." But salsas, chutneys, relishes, and Asian-style dipping sauces are easier to master and vary than classic French sauces based on butter and eggs. (See the chart on page 24 for more ways to use these sauces.)

Fresh Tomato or Fruit Salsa

MAKES: About 2 cups | **TIME:** 15 minutes

Salsa is America's favorite condiment for good reason, since you can use it for saucing meats, vegetables, eggs, or grains; dipping everything from crudités to dumplings; or serving the usual way with chips, tacos, and burritos. To take this chunky, pico de gallo–style recipe in a different direction, replace the tomatoes with a couple of cups fruit. Apples (especially tart green ones), peaches, pears, and plums are the obvious choices, but seeded grapes, pineapple, or even berries are all wonderful. Cooked salsas start on page 71.

- 2 **large ripe fresh tomatoes, cored and chopped (or see the headnote for fruit options; about 1½ cups)**
- ½ **large white onion or 3 or 4 scallions, chopped**
- 1 **teaspoon chopped garlic, or to taste**
  Chopped fresh chile (like jalapeño, Thai, or habanero), red chile flakes, or cayenne, to taste
- ½ **cup chopped fresh cilantro or parsley**
- 2 **tablespoons fresh lime juice or 1 tablespoon red wine vinegar**
  Salt and pepper

1. Combine everything but the salt and pepper in a medium bowl. Sprinkle with salt and pepper, then taste and adjust the seasoning.

2. If possible, let the flavors develop for 15 minutes or so before serving, but serve within a couple of hours.

PURÉED TOMATO OR FRUIT SALSA For more of a true sauce: Toss the finished salsa into a food processor and blend as smooth as you like.

Fresh Tomatillo Salsa

MAKES: About 2 cups | TIME: 10 minutes

Summer is the ideal season to make this, when tomatillos and poblanos are in season. In many areas you can find both in grocery stores year-round now, but in other regions the tomatillos may be a little harder to find. In those instances, try one of the variations, or use canned for a less-crunchy sauce.

- 2 medium poblano or other fresh mild green chiles
- 2 cups chopped husked tomatillos (about 1 pound)
- 3 scallions, chopped
- 2 teaspoons chopped garlic, or to taste
- ¼ cup chopped fresh cilantro
- 3 tablespoons fresh lime juice, or to taste
  Salt and pepper

1. Roast the chiles according to the directions on page 318, or leave raw. Either way, remove the stems and seeds from the chiles. Mince the chiles or pulse them a few times in a food processor.

2. Put the tomatillos, scallions, garlic, cilantro, and lime juice in a medium bowl with the chiles and stir to combine. Taste, adjust the seasoning, and if you have time, let sit for a few minutes for the flavors to blend before serving. Or refrigerate for up to a couple of hours (bring back to room temperature and adjust the seasoning before serving).

GREEN TOMATO SALSA Good in fall, when green tomatoes are plentiful and cheap: Substitute green tomatoes for the tomatillos.

GREEN CHILE SALSA Stronger: Replace the tomatillos with 2 cups chopped fresh mild green chiles, like more poblanos, or New Mexico. Increase the garlic to 2 tablespoons; substitute parsley for the cilantro and lemon juice for the lime.

PEPITA SALSA Nutty like mole, only faster: Replace half of the tomatillos with toasted pepitas (see pages 309 and 311). Serve immediately.

CORN SALSA Distinctive and delicious: Substitute corn kernels from Grilled Corn (page 252) for the tomatillos.

JÍCAMA SALSA Very crunchy: Replace the tomatillos with chopped peeled jícama and substitute minced fresh ginger for the garlic. Add 2 tablespoons chopped fresh mint leaves. Let sit for about 30 minutes before serving.

AVOCADO-TOMATILLO SALSA You'll want this on everything: Pit and peel 2 avocados and put everything in a food processor in Step 2; purée until smooth.

Tahini Sauce

MAKES: About 1 cup | TIME: 10 minutes

This is one of the easiest, best sauces you can have in your arsenal, and flavorful enough to please both carnivores and vegans.

- ½ cup tahini, or to more to taste
  Juice of 1 lemon, or more to taste
- 1 teaspoon chopped garlic, or more to taste
- ½ teaspoon ground cumin (optional)
  Salt and pepper

1. Put the tahini, ½ cup water, the lemon juice, garlic, and cumin if you're using it in a food processor, sprinkle with salt and pepper, and process until smooth. Or

12 More Fresh Salsas

Even more ways to get fresh, spicy flavor on the table in no time. Follow the directions for Fresh Tomato or Fruit Salsa on page 55 and eat the same ways, or with grilled meats, or stirred into grains.

NAME	MAIN INGREDIENT	SEASONINGS	SERVING DIRECTIONS
Chilean Salsa	2 large fresh ripe tomatoes, cored and chopped (about 1½ cups)	½ large white onion, chopped; 1 tablespoon chopped garlic; chopped fresh chile (like jalapeño), red chile flakes, or cayenne, to taste; ½ cup chopped fresh cilantro; 1 teaspoon chopped fresh oregano; 2 tablespoons olive oil; salt and pepper	Serve immediately.
Bean Salsa	2 large fresh ripe tomatoes, cored and chopped (about 1 ½ cups); 1 cup cooked black beans (see page 390)	½ large red onion, chopped; 1 teaspoon chopped garlic; chopped fresh chile (like jalapeño), red chile flakes, or cayenne, to taste; ½ cup chopped fresh cilantro; 1 teaspoon cumin; 2 tablespoons fresh lime juice or 1 tablespoon red wine vinegar; salt and pepper	Let sit for about 30 minutes to develop the flavor before serving.
Mexican Cheese Salsa	2 large fresh ripe tomatoes, cored and chopped (about 1½ cups); ½ cup crumbled queso fresco; ½ English cucumber, peeled and chopped	½ large white onion or 3 or 4 scallions, chopped; chopped fresh chile (like jalapeño), red chile flakes, or cayenne, to taste; ½ cup chopped fresh cilantro; 2 tablespoons fresh lime juice or 1 tablespoon red wine vinegar; salt and pepper	Serve immediately.
Papaya Salsa	2 cups firm but ripe papaya, cut into ½-inch chunks	½ cup chopped red onion; ½ cup chopped red, yellow, or green bell pepper; 2 tablespoons chopped fresh chile (like jalapeño or Thai), or red chile flakes or cayenne, to taste; ¼ cup chopped fresh cilantro; 3 tablespoons fresh lime juice; 1 tablespoon olive oil; salt and pepper	Let sit for 5 minutes, or refrigerate for up to a couple of hours (bring back to room temperature before serving).
Citrus Salsa	2 cups orange, lemon, and grapefruit segments (see page 378; alone or in combination)	½ cup chopped red onion; 2 tablespoons chopped fresh chile (like jalapeño or Thai), or red chile flakes or cayenne, to taste; ¼ cup chopped fresh cilantro; 3 tablespoons fresh lime juice; salt and pepper	Let sit for 5 minutes, or refrigerate for up to a couple of hours (bring back to room temperature before serving).

(continued)

12 More Fresh Salsas *(continued)*

NAME	MAIN INGREDIENT	SEASONINGS	SERVING DIRECTIONS
Summer Fruit Salsa	1 ripe tomato, chopped; 2 peaches, chopped; ¼ small cantaloupe, seeded, peeled and chopped	½ cup chopped red onion; ½ cup chopped red, yellow, or green bell pepper; 2 tablespoons chopped fresh chile (like jalapeño or Thai), or red chile flakes or cayenne, to taste; ¼ cup chopped fresh basil or mint; 3 tablespoons fresh lime juice; salt and pepper	Serve within 30 minutes.
Chipotle-Cherry Salsa	2 cups pitted sweet cherries (fresh or thawed frozen is fine), chopped	½ cup chopped red onion; ¼ chopped fresh cilantro; 3 tablespoons fresh lime juice; 1 tablespoon chopped chipotle chile in adobo; salt and pepper	Serve right away, or refrigerate for up to 2 days (bring back to room temperature before serving).
Radish Salsa	2 cups chopped radishes (like daikon, red, or a combination; about 1 pound); ½ English cucumber, peeled and diced	½ small red onion, chopped; 1 scallion, chopped; 1 teaspoon chopped garlic; 1 tablespoon chopped fresh chile (like jalapeño or Thai), or to taste; 2 tablespoons fresh lemon juice; ¼ cup chopped fresh cilantro; salt and pepper	Serve immediately or refrigerate for up to 1 day (bring back to room temperature before serving).
Cucumber Salsa, Thai Style	1½ cups chopped peeled and seeded cucumber; 1 medium carrot, chopped	1 shallot, chopped; 1 scallion, chopped; 1 tablespoon chopped fresh chile (like jalapeño or Thai), or to taste; 2 tablespoons fresh lime juice; 1 tablespoon rice vinegar; ¼ cup chopped fresh cilantro; salt and pepper	Serve immediately, or let "pickle" for a couple of hours in the fridge.
Green Papaya Salsa, Thai Style	2 cups peeled, seeded, and shredded green papaya	1 shallot, chopped; 1 tablespoon chopped fresh chile (like jalapeño or Thai), or to taste; 2 tablespoons fresh lime juice; 1 tablespoon rice vinegar; ¼ cup chopped fresh cilantro; salt and pepper	Serve immediately.
Watermelon Salsa	2 cups chopped, seeded watermelon	½ large red onion, chopped; 1 teaspoon chopped garlic; 1 tablespoon chopped fresh chile (like jalapeño), or red chile flakes or cayenne, to taste; ¼ cup chopped fresh mint; 3 tablespoons fresh lime juice; salt and pepper	Serve immediately.
Avocado-Cucumber Salsa	2 ripe avocados, pitted, peeled, and chopped; ½ English cucumber, peeled and chopped	½ cup chopped red onion; 2 tablespoons chopped fresh chile (like jalapeño), or red chile flakes or cayenne, to taste; ¼ chopped fresh cilantro; 3 tablespoons fresh lime juice; salt and pepper	Serve immediately.

 fast make ahead **V** vegetarian

mince the garlic instead of chopping it, and whisk everything together in a bowl.

2. Taste and adjust the seasoning, adding more lemon juice, tahini, water, or garlic as you like. Serve immediately or cover tightly and use within a day or so.

YOGURT TAHINI SAUCE Richer: Instead of water, use ½ cup yogurt (preferably whole milk).

COCONUT TAHINI SAUCE Perfect with grilled or broiled chicken or pork: Instead of water, use ½ cup coconut milk (to make your own, see page 372).

MINTY TAHINI SAUCE Add 1 cup chopped or minced fresh mint before processing or combining in Step 1.

ANCHOVY TAHINI SAUCE Lovely on Grilled Eggplant (page 252) or steamed asparagus (see page 262): Omit the salt. Add 1 or 2 anchovies before processing in Step 1. If whisking, first mash them in the bowl).

CHILE TAHINI SAUCE Omit the cumin and add 1 teaspoon any Chile Paste (page 40), or more to taste.

Simplest Yogurt Sauce

MAKES: 1 cup | **TIME:** 3 minutes

One of the greatest developments in American grocery stores over the last decade or so is the availability of good yogurt. By that I mean sour, rich, free of gelatin or pectin, and possibly even made with nonhomogenized milk. Since yogurt is practically a sauce in itself, be sure to buy the kind that only has dairy and cultures; then flavor it yourself. This isn't the place for Greek yogurt, though if you want a slightly thicker sauce, drain the yogurt for 15 minutes or so before starting (see page 752).

1 cup yogurt (preferably whole milk)
1 teaspoon minced garlic
   Salt and pepper
   Fresh lemon juice (optional)

1. Combine the yogurt with the garlic, a pinch salt, and a grind or two of pepper. Taste and adjust the seasoning, adding some lemon juice for tartness if necessary.

2. Serve immediately. Or refrigerate for up to a few hours (bring back to near room temperature before serving).

RAITA (CUCUMBER YOGURT SAUCE) The classic Indian yogurt sauce: Add about 1 cup cucumber, peeled if you like, seeded, and chopped (salted if necessary; see page 203), or seeded and chopped tomato, or any mixture of vegetables, like those you'd use in Chopped Salad (page 197).

BLUE CHEESE DRESSING Good made with sour cream or mayonnaise too: Omit the garlic. Add about ½ cup crumbled blue cheese (Roquefort, for example) along with a bit of fresh lemon juice.

8 ADDITIONS TO SIMPLEST YOGURT SAUCE

Try alone or in combination, tasting as you go.

1. ¼ cup chopped fresh herbs like mint, parsley, dill, cilantro, or basil, or 1 tablespoon chopped fresh tarragon or thyme
2. 1 tablespoon chopped shallot or scallion
3. 1 tablespoon (or more) good-quality olive oil
4. 1 tablespoon chopped or grated fresh ginger or candied ginger
5. Red chile flakes, cayenne, or chopped fresh chile (like jalapeño or Thai), to taste
6. A pinch ground cumin, curry powder, paprika, dry mustard, saffron, or other spice

Raita, a variation of Simplest Yogurt Sauce, page 59, made with chopped mixed vegetables

7. A spoonful of honey
8. Fresh lemon, lime, orange, or grapefruit juice, plus a teaspoon of the grated zest for more intensity

---

4 MORE USES FOR SIMPLEST YOGURT SAUCE

Any of the previous yogurt sauces can be used in myriad different ways. Here are some ideas beyond the chart on page 24:

1. As a salad dressing: thin with a little fresh lemon juice or sherry vinegar, plus olive oil
2. Alongside any simply grilled, broiled, roasted, steamed, or sautéed meat, fish, or poultry
3. Stirred into cooked rice or other grains for extra creaminess, body, flavor, and protein
4. Cooked on top of roasted vegetables, poultry, or meat as you might cheese; to avoid separation, brush or drizzle on top during the last 5 or 10 minutes of cooking

Coconut Chutney

MAKES: About 1 cup | TIME: 10 minutes

The appealing, chewy texture of this chutney makes it a welcome addition to dishes like Chicken Biryani (page 626) or Simplest Dal (page 409). You can achieve the same effect—and super-vibrant color and flavor—with grated carrots or beets in place of the coconut.

½ cup shredded coconut
1 inch fresh ginger, peeled if you'd like, and chopped, or 1 teaspoon ground ginger
1 small fresh hot green or red chile (like jalapeño or Thai), or red chile flakes, to taste
1 cup loosely packed cilantro (the tender sprigs with leaves)

¼ teaspoon ground cumin
2 tablespoons fresh lime juice
Pinch salt

1. Put the coconut, ginger, chile, cilantro, and cumin in a food processor or blender and pulse until finely ground.
2. Add the lime juice and salt and pulse again, until nearly but not quite smooth. Taste and adjust the seasoning. Serve at room temperature. Or refrigerate for up to a few hours (bring back to room temperature before serving).

Raw Onion Chutney

MAKES: About ¾ cup | TIME: 1 hour, largely unattended

An assertive classic from India that manages to taste great with just about anything, especially simply grilled or roasted fish, meat, or poultry or rice bowls. I like it on sandwiches, cheese boards, and avocado toast. Serve with lemon wedges and you're all set.

2 small to medium or 1 large red or Vidalia onions, quartered and thinly sliced or chopped
1 teaspoon salt, or more to taste
½ teaspoon coarsely cracked black peppercorns
¼ cup red wine vinegar
1 teaspoon paprika, or more to taste
Pinch cayenne, to taste (optional)
Pinch chaat masala (to make your own, see page 34), to taste (optional)

1. Separate the layers of the onion and combine with the salt, cracked pepper, vinegar, and paprika in a bowl. Let sit for an hour.
2. Stir in the cayenne and chaat masala if you're using them. Serve immediately. Or refrigerate for a day or 2 (bring back to room temperature for serving).

HOT OR MILD PEPPER CHUTNEY Replace the onions with 4 or 5 fresh hot red chiles, or use 1 medium red bell pepper or a combination of hot chiles and bell pepper for a milder version. Substitute 1 teaspoon chopped garlic for the peppercorns. Pulse everything in a food processor until coarsely chopped, but do not purée. You may refrigerate the chutney for about 2 weeks (bring back to room temperature before serving).

Cilantro-Mint Chutney

MAKES: 1½ cups | **TIME:** 15 minutes

This fresh, assertive combination pairs well with just about anything, from grilled meats to Samosas (page 116). You can make a great—although less complex version—with all just cilantro or mint, or for a completely different spin, Thai basil.

1½	cups firmly packed chopped fresh cilantro
½	cup firmly packed fresh mint
1 or 2	Thai or other fresh hot green chiles (seeded if you like), to taste, or red chile flakes, to taste
2	inches fresh ginger, peeled if you'd like and cut into chunks
½	red onion, quartered
1	teaspoon chopped garlic
¼	cup fresh lime juice
½	teaspoon salt, or more to taste

1. Combine the cilantro, mint, chiles, ginger, onion, and garlic in a food processor and pulse until finely ground.
2. Add the lime juice and salt and process until nearly smooth; you may need to add up to ¼ cup water to help the food processor get going. Taste and adjust the seasoning. Refrigerate for up to a day. Serve at room temperature.

CREAMY CILANTRO-MINT CHUTNEY This cools the whole thing down a bit: Add ½ cup or more good-quality yogurt or coconut milk; adjust the seasoning.

Dried Fruit and Nut Chutney

MAKES: About 1 cup | **TIME:** 15 minutes

My favorite use for this chutney is in sandwiches: with cheese on good whole grain bread, or mixed with chopped chicken and yogurt for chicken salad. Try any combination you like; just be sure to taste as you go and be prepared to adjust the seasonings. If the mixture is too bitter, add a little brown sugar, or if it's too dry, a bit of good-quality vegetable oil.

1	teaspoon cumin seeds
1	teaspoon coriander seeds
1	dried Thai or other small red chile, or to taste
1	cup roasted or raw unsalted pistachios or cashews
¾	cup dried fruit, like dates, apricots, raisins, cranberries, or cherries
½	teaspoon salt, or more to taste
½	teaspoon pepper, or more to taste
½	teaspoon chopped garlic

1. Toast the cumin and coriander seeds and the chile in a small dry skillet over medium heat, shaking the pan frequently until the seeds color slightly, about 5 minutes. Remove them from the pan and cool. (If the nuts are raw, you can toast them the same way.)
2. Combine all the ingredients in a blender or food processor. Process, stopping the machine to scrape down the sides as necessary, until coarsely ground—not as smooth as creamy peanut butter. Serve immediately. Or refrigerate for up to a week (bring back to room temperature before serving).

 F fast **M** make ahead **V** vegetarian

REAL GARLICKY NUT CHUTNEY If you want a chunky chutney, roughly chop the nuts and garlic by hand: Omit the dried fruit and use about 2 cups nuts. In Step 2, increase the garlic to 1 to 2 teaspoons.

Ginger-Scallion Sauce

MAKES: About 1 cup | **TIME:** 15 minutes

The amount of chopping required for this sauce is worth the effort, especially if you want fine bits. But I'll let you in on a secret: you can put the ginger, scallions, and garlic in a food processor and pulse until they're chopped, provided you don't purée them. I like this sauce with Steamed Dumplings (page 126), White Cut Chicken (page 637), Rice Porridge with Fresh Garnishes (page 155), Hot-and-Sour Soup (page 168), or any steamed or grilled fish.

- ¼ cup chopped fresh ginger
- ½ cup chopped scallions
- 1 teaspoon chopped garlic
- 1 teaspoon salt, or more to taste
- ½ cup good-quality vegetable oil

1. Mix the ginger, scallions, garlic, and salt together thoroughly in a heatproof bowl.
2. Heat the oil in a small saucepan or skillet over high heat until smoking. Carefully pour the oil over the ginger-scallion mixture and mix well. Serve hot or at room temperature. Or refrigerate for up to 3 days (bring back to room temperature before serving).

CHILE-SCALLION SAUCE A different kind of heat means you can use this with richer foods like grilled or roasted beef and pork. Add 3 tablespoons (or to taste) of your favorite chopped fresh chile (see the chart on page 41; either red or green is fine). Reduce the ginger to 1 tablespoon or omit it entirely if you'd like, and increase the garlic to 2 teaspoons.

Soy Dipping Sauce and Marinade

MAKES: About 1¼ cups | **TIME:** 15 minutes

The title only gives two uses—dipping and marinating—but this sauce is infinitely versatile. You can drizzle it over just about anything from Sushi Bowls (page 450) to noodles, or even use it as a salad dressing. If you don't have garlic, ginger, and/or scallions, you can still make a totally serviceable condiment.

- ½ cup soy sauce
- 2 tablespoons rice vinegar or sake
- 2 tablespoons sesame oil
- 1 tablespoon sugar
- 1 tablespoon chopped garlic
- 1 tablespoon chopped or grated fresh ginger
- ¼ cup chopped scallions

Combine all the ingredients and stir until the sugar is dissolved. Use immediately. Or refrigerate for up to 2 days (bring back to room temperature before serving).

SESAME-SOY DIPPING SAUCE AND MARINADE For richness and texture: Add ¼ cup toasted sesame seeds.

TAHINI SOY SAUCE Thicker and richer and terrific with anything grilled: Omit the ginger and scallions. Substitute ¼ cup honey for the vinegar and add 2 tablespoons tahini. Sprinkle with red chile flakes if you like.

SWEET-AND-SOUR SAUCE Omit the sesame oil. Increase the sugar to 2 tablespoons; increase the vinegar to 3 tablespoons. Cook briefly over low heat, stirring, to dissolve the sugar. Taste and add more vinegar or sugar if necessary. Cool before serving or use warm as a basting sauce for roasted, grilled, or broiled vegetables, fish, poultry, or meat. You can make this a hot-and-sour sauce by adding cayenne to taste.

 fast make ahead V vegetarian

SHORTCUT SWEET-AND-SOUR SAUCE Don't knock it until you've tried it: Omit the sugar and scallions and add ¼ cup ketchup. Use as a dipping sauce or as a final glaze for stir-fried shrimp, pork, or chicken.

Thai Chile Sauce

MAKES: About ½ cup | TIME: 5 minutes

One of the essential sauces of Thai cooking (called *nam prik*), this is perfect with grilled and charred meat, poultry, or vegetables. My version is tame and leaves room for adding many times more fresh chile, if that's your thing. But be sure to have a little extra of everything to make any adjustments you like.

- 2 tablespoons fresh lime juice
- 2 tablespoons fish sauce

Vinaigrette: Beyond Salad

I count vinaigrette as an all-purpose sauce and marinade. See page 188 for a master recipe and tons of flavoring options. Then here are some ideas beyond salad dressing:

1. Drizzle over chopped fruit, vegetables, or both and toss for an instant fresh salsa.
2. Serve as a dipping sauce for crudités, fritters, or other finger foods.
3. Use as a base to build other dressings or dips by adding mayonnaise, yogurt, sour cream, or tahini.
4. Drizzle or brush on plain roasted, broiled, grilled, or steamed vegetables toward the end of cooking or just before serving.
5. Ditto the above with fish, meat, poultry, or thickly sliced tofu.
6. Brush on thickly sliced bread before grilling or broiling.
7. Use as a condiment to drizzle on sandwiches.
8. Use sparingly as a bright garnish for soups and stews.

- 1 teaspoon minced garlic
- ¼ teaspoon minced fresh hot chile (like Thai or jalapeño), cayenne, or red chile flakes, or to taste
- 2 teaspoons sugar
- 1 tablespoon chopped dried shrimp (optional)
- 1 tablespoon shredded carrot (optional)

1. Combine all the ingredients and stir until the sugar dissolves.

2. Taste and adjust the seasonings as necessary. Let rest for a few minutes before serving. Or refrigerate for up to a day (bring back to room temperature before serving).

Miso Dipping Sauce

MAKES: About 1 cup | TIME: 15 minutes

Miso has become a much more popular way to add umami—the savoriness often called "the fifth basic taste"—to just about anything, not just Japanese food. I like this with sautéed greens, whole wheat pasta, roasted vegetables, and just about anything grilled. Choose a light miso like white or yellow for a subtler flavor, or red miso for a powerful punch.

- 6 tablespoons miso
- ¾ cup warm water or sake, or a mixture
- 1 teaspoon sugar
- 1 tablespoon mirin (or 1½ teaspoons honey mixed with 1½ teaspoons water) or white wine
- 1 tablespoon rice vinegar, or more to taste Salt

1. Put everything except the salt in a small bowl and whisk together. Taste and add more vinegar and salt if needed.

 fast make ahead 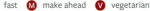 vegetarian

2. Serve immediately, warm or cold. To use warm, heat gently but do not boil. Or refrigerate for up to a week.

MISO-HERB DIPPING SAUCE Lots of bang for your buck: Use white miso and add ½ cup chopped fresh cilantro, basil, Thai basil, shiso, or mint (or a combination). Combine everything in the blender and purée until smooth.

MISO-CITRUS DIPPING SAUCE Brighter and fresher: Instead of the rice vinegar, add a tablespoon or two of fresh lemon, lime, orange, or tangerine juice. If you like, garnish with grated citrus zest.

MISO-SOY DIPPING SAUCE A no-brainer: Add a tablespoon or two of soy sauce to the main recipe or either of the preceding variations.

Miso-Carrot Sauce with Ginger

MAKES: About 1¼ cups | **TIME:** 15 minutes

This Japanese restaurant staple is great on so much more than iceberg lettuce. I like tossing some over chopped cabbage or kale to make a slaw, or drizzling over chickpeas or edamame. Or try it on Grilled Fish fillets or steaks (page 535).

¼	cup good-quality vegetable oil
¼	cup rice vinegar
3	tablespoons mild or sweet miso (like yellow or white)
1	tablespoon sesame oil
2	medium carrots, cut into chunks
1	inch fresh ginger, peeled if you'd like and cut into coins
	Salt and pepper

1. Combine the vegetable oil, vinegar, miso, sesame oil, carrots, and ginger in a food processor and pulse a few times to mince the carrots. Then let the machine run for a minute or so, until the mixture is chunky-smooth. (If you want it smoother, use a blender.)
2. Taste and adjust the seasoning. Serve immediately. Or transfer to an airtight container and refrigerate for up to several days.

MISO-CARROT SAUCE WITH CITRUS Wonderful in the winter, when you need all the brightness you can get: Omit the sesame oil. Replace the rice vinegar with any kind of orange juice, and add 1 teaspoon grated orange zest.

THE BASICS OF MAYONNAISE

For new cooks, reading that mayonnaise is easy to make at home can feel like a lie. But the first time you get it right—maybe even on your first attempt—you'll see it's not all smoke and mirrors. And then you'll have a sauce to work with that's infinitely better and more impressive than what the supermarket has to offer.

If you're worried about eating raw eggs—and I'm not going to argue with you—you can make mayonnaise with pasteurized eggs (though it's not my first choice), or try the sauce variation after the recipe.

DEMYSTIFYING MAYONNAISE

Mayonnaise is an emulsion, in which oil is dispersed in the water in eggs and vinegar or lemon juice through vigorous stirring, to produce a thick, pale yellow cream. A few basic seasonings balance the flavors. That's really all there is to it.

Homemade mayos go south when you add the oil too quickly or (less often) you add too much oil. To help you add the oil in a slow steady stream, you could put it in a squeeze bottle or a liquid measuring cup with a spout. Or use a teaspoon to add a few drops at a time. If you're using a food processor, note that many have

a small hole in the feed tube, put there specifically for this purpose; you put the oil in the tube and it drips out. (I have drilled holes in feed tubes without them, which also works.)

For general purposes, I like grapeseed oil best because of its neutral flavor, especially if I'm planning on adding other flavorings. Use olive oil if you want a particularly Mediterranean taste, which is often the case, especially with the Aïoli variation. But note that mayonnaise made with 100 percent olive oil tends to break more easily; go for a mix of grapeseed and olive. Asian ingredients go better with a mayonnaise made from grapeseed, corn, or—for a more pronounced flavor—peanut oil. For vinegar, I like sherry vinegar or white wine vinegar, but try lemon or even lime juice for a brighter flavor. All of these decisions should be based on how you plan to use the mayo.

TROUBLESHOOTING MAYONNAISE

If you're cautious, make sure your eggs and oil are roughly the same temperature, because fluctuations can cause some instability, though this is a really minor point. And despite what you may have heard, the direction in which you whisk does not matter.

If your mayonnaise doesn't emulsify on the first attempt, transfer the egg-oil mixture to a measuring cup with a spout and put a fresh egg yolk and more mustard in the bowl or machine. Begin again, adding the broken mayonnaise a few drops at a time, as you would the oil. Once all of that mixture has been added, you can begin to incorporate any remaining plain oil.

Homemade Mayonnaise

MAKES: 1 cup | **TIME:** 10 minutes

Do some experimenting and find the method—whisk, blender, food processor—that works for you. If you're adding something like chile paste or spices, you'll get

a smooth, even sauce no matter which method you use. If you want to make a chunkier sauce, like Tartar (page 70), whisk in the additions by hand.

- 1 egg yolk
- 2 teaspoons Dijon mustard
- 1 cup good-quality vegetable oil or olive oil
      Salt and pepper
- 1 tablespoon sherry vinegar, white wine vinegar, or fresh lemon juice

1. TO MAKE BY HAND: Put the yolk and mustard in a medium bowl. Beat together with a whisk. Begin to add the oil in dribbles as you beat, adding more as each amount is incorporated. You'll notice when a thick emulsion forms. Then you can add the remaining oil a little faster. Depending on how fast you beat, the whole process will take about 5 minutes.

TO MAKE BY MACHINE: Put the yolk and mustard in a blender or food processor and turn the machine on. While it's running, add the oil in a slow, steady stream. When an emulsion forms, you can add it a little faster (and scrape down the sides as necessary), until all the oil is incorporated.

2. Add salt and pepper, then stir in the vinegar. Taste and adjust the seasoning. Use immediately. Or refrigerate for about a week (less if adding fresh herbs or aromatics; see "13 Sauces to Make with Mayonnaise," page 70).

EGGLESS MAYONNAISE SAUCE A tad thinner than homemade mayo, but rich, creamy, and raw egg–free. It's perfect in salads or alongside simply cooked meat and fish; or drizzle judiciously on sandwiches. Replace the egg yolk with 2 tablespoons of the best mayo you can find. Halve the amount of oil and proceed by hand or machine as described above. The sauce will appear to separate a bit as you add oil; keep going and it will come together fine. Use plain or make adjustments as suggested on page 70.

13 Sauces to Make with Mayonnaise

Follow the directions for Homemade Mayonnaise and add the seasonings according to the directions.

NAME	SEASONINGS	DIRECTIONS
Aïoli Garlic Mayonnaise	3 to 8 cloves garlic; use ½ cup olive oil and ½ cup grapeseed oil	Using a machine: add the garlic with the yolk and mustard and purée. Whisking by hand: grate the garlic and add in Step 2.
Chile Mayonnaise	1 canned chipotle pepper or 1 or 2 dried mild chiles (like ancho) or 1 or 2 fresh chiles (like Thai), minced, or 1 tablespoon chile paste (see page 40); omit the mustard; use rice vinegar or lime juice	Using a machine: cut the chiles into chunks and purée with the yolk. Whisking by hand: mince the chiles and add in Step 2.
Green Sauce, French Style	1 sprig fresh tarragon, 10 sprigs watercress (tough stems removed), 10 chives, and leaves from 5 sprigs parsley	Use a machine. Add the herbs in Step 2. Process until not quite puréed but definitely green.
Cold Mustard Sauce	Up the mustard to 1 heaping tablespoon.	Thin the finished mayonnaise with a tablespoon or two of cream.
Saffron Mayonnaise	Pinch saffron; use lemon or lime juice in place of the vinegar	Crumble the saffron into the citrus juice and let sit for 10 minutes before proceeding with the recipe.
Tartar Sauce	Up the mustard to 1 heaping tablespoon; ¼ cup chopped sweet pickles or capers	Follow the directions; stir in the pickles by hand in Step 2.
Rémoulade	Use coarse-ground or whole grain mustard and increase to 2 tablespoons. Add ¼ cup chopped tender celery and celery leaves and 2 tablespoons chopped dill pickles. Season with hot sauce and lemon juice.	Omit the mustard in Step 1; stir it in with the seasonings in Step 2.
Thousand Island	¼ cup ketchup, 2 tablespoons chopped sweet pickles, 1 tablespoon minced onion	Stir the seasonings into the finished mayonnaise.
Soy Sauce Mayonnaise	2 tablespoons soy sauce	Add with the vinegar in Step 2.
Wasabi Mayonnaise	1 teaspoon or more wasabi powder	Add to the finished mayonnaise; taste and add more if you'd like.
Miso Mayonnaise	2 tablespoons white or yellow miso	Whisk it into the finished mayonnaise.
Spiced Mayonnaise	Up to 2 tablespoons any spice blend (see pages 32–35)	Add in Step 2.
Anchovy Mayonnaise	2 or 3 anchovies; omit the salt	Use a machine. Purée with the yolk in Step 1.

 fast make ahead 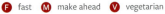 vegetarian

Real Ranch Dressing

MAKES: 2 cups | **TIME:** 10 minutes

The secret ingredient—buttermilk powder—is waiting for you in the baking aisle at the grocery store. You'll never use the bottled stuff again.

- 1 cup mayonnaise (to make your own, which is preferable, see page 69)
- 1 cup buttermilk
- ¼ cup buttermilk powder
  Salt and pepper
- ¼ cup chopped fresh chives or parsley (optional)

1. Put the mayonnaise, buttermilk, and buttermilk powder in a medium jar with a tight-fitting lid. Sprinkle with a little salt and lots of pepper. Add the chives or parsley if you like, put on the lid, and shake vigorously for 30 seconds or so.

2. Taste and adjust the seasoning. Use immediately or refrigerate for a few days. (It will keep longer if you don't add the fresh herbs.)

PARMESAN RANCH DRESSING A little more complex: Add 2 tablespoons grated Parmesan and cut back on the salt.

BACON RANCH DRESSING Undeniably delicious: Add ¼ cup or so crumbled crisply fried bacon.

GREEN GODDESS RANCH DRESSING Omit the optional herbs. Instead of mixing the ingredients in a jar, put everything in a food processor or blender along with 2 cups fresh mixed herb leaves (like mint, parsley, chives, basil, and/or chervil; you can include up to 2 tablespoons fresh oregano or thyme). Purée until bright green and smooth.

Cooked Sauces

This section ranges from near-spontaneous reductions to make-ahead sauces that keep for ages, like barbecue sauce. Some, like Dashi Dipping Sauce (page 76), weren't everyday sauces when I first wrote *How to Cook Everything*, but they certainly are now. And others, like the handful of classic French sauces, never seem to go out of style. For Fast Tomato Sauce and tons of variations, see page 478.

Salsa Roja

MAKES: About 2 cups | **TIME:** 45 to 50 minutes

This classic red Mexican salsa is more versatile than ketchup or mustard. Use it anywhere you want a bold, smoky, spicy flavor. The guajillo chiles here deliver all that with moderate heat. For a milder salsa, substitute ancho or other mild chiles. To crank up the heat, see the chile choices on page 41.

- 2 large guajillos or other medium-hot dried chiles, toasted, soaked, and cleaned (see page 40), soaking water reserved
- ¼ cup good-quality vegetable oil
- 2 large onions, chopped
- 1 tablespoon chopped garlic
- 2 pounds tomatoes, peeled, seeded, cored, and chopped, with their liquid (about 3 cups; canned are fine)
- 1 tablespoon sugar
  Salt and pepper
- ¼ cup chopped fresh cilantro
- 3 tablespoons fresh lime juice

1. Chop the chiles. Put the oil in a medium saucepan or deep skillet over medium-high heat. When it's hot, add

Salsa Roja, page 71

the chiles, onions, and garlic and cook, stirring occasionally, until the onions soften, about 5 minutes. Add the tomatoes, sugar, some salt, and plenty of pepper.

2. Adjust the heat so the mixture bubbles gently and cook, stirring occasionally, until the mixture has thickened and come together, about 20 minutes. If the salsa gets too thick, thin it with some of the reserved chile-soaking water or plain water.

3. Stir in the cilantro and lime juice. Taste and adjust the seasoning if necessary. Serve hot or at room temperature or refrigerate for up to 2 days.

RED ENCHILADA SAUCE Essential on Cheese Enchiladas (page 759): Use an immersion blender to purée the sauce in the pan. Or cool the mixture slightly, pour into a blender or food processor, and purée carefully.

CHARRED SALSA ROJA Cut the tomatoes and onions into thick slices and grill on both sides until charred, about 10 minutes total. Proceed with the recipe at Step 1; in Step 3, add 2 tablespoons or so chopped fresh mint along with the cilantro if you like.

SALSA SOFRITO Substitute Roasted Red (or yellow) Peppers (page 318) for the guajillos; replace the cilantro with a tablespoon or so chopped fresh oregano, and use red wine vinegar instead of the lime juice.

Salsa Verde

MAKES: About 2 cups | **TIME:** 40 minutes

I like cooked tomatillo salsa—or "green salsa"—with chips like everyone else, but it's at least as good with eggs and pork. You can change the proportions of chiles based on how hot or not-hot you like your salsa: Use another poblano in place of the serrano chiles for mild salsa or add as many hot chiles as you can handle; see the chart on page 41.

10 to 12	tomatillos, husked and rinsed
2	medium poblano or other fresh mild green chiles, roasted and cleaned (see page 318)
1 or 2	serrano or other fresh hot green chiles, roasted and cleaned (page 318; optional)
3	tablespoons good-quality vegetable oil
2	large onions, chopped
2	tablespoons chopped garlic
1	teaspoon Mexican or other oregano
1	cup vegetable stock (to make your own, see page 174) or water
	Salt and pepper
½	cup chopped fresh cilantro
¼	cup fresh lime juice

1. Heat the oven to 400°F. Put the tomatillos on a baking sheet and roast until the skins are lightly browned and blistered, about 20 minutes.

2. While the tomatillos are roasting, put the oil in a large deep skillet over medium heat. Add the onions and garlic and cook, stirring occasionally, until they are very soft and lightly browned, about 10 minutes.

3. Remove the tomatillos from the oven; when they're cool enough to handle, chop them with the chiles, saving their juices. Add the tomatillos and juices, chiles, oregano, stock, and a large pinch salt and pepper to the onions. Stir and bring to a low simmer. Cook, stirring occasionally, until the mixture thickens slightly, 10 to 15 minutes.

4. Stir in the cilantro and lime juice, taste, and adjust the seasoning. Serve at room temperature or refrigerate for up to 2 days.

GREEN ENCHILADA SALSA Use an immersion blender to purée the finished sauce in the pan. Or cool the mixture slightly, pour into a blender or food processor, and purée carefully.

GREEN CHILE SALSA Milder and simpler: Increase the chiles to 5 poblanos; omit the tomatillos and serranos. Decrease the stock to about ¼ cup, as needed. Proceed with Steps 1 through 3; then use an immersion blender to purée the salsa. Or cool the mixture slightly, pour into a blender or food processor, and purée carefully. Proceed with Step 4.

PUMPKIN SEED SAUCE Thick and with a toasted nut flavor like green mole, only much easier: Toast or roast 1 cup green pumpkin seeds (pepitas; see page 311) and pulse them several times in a food processor until chopped. Add them to the onion-garlic mixture in Step 2, along with 1 tablespoon chopped fresh epazote if you like. Proceed with the recipe.

SUPER-HOT CHILE-GARLIC SALSA Substitute 3 to 5 habaneros for the poblanos and serranos; omit the tomatillos, onion, oregano, and stock. Put the habaneros and garlic in a small skillet over medium heat. Cook, shaking the skillet occasionally, until the garlic and chiles are brown. Or loosely wrap the garlic and chiles in foil and roast in a 400°F oven, until they're soft, about 30 minutes. Stem and seed the chiles. Put the chiles, garlic, cilantro, and lime juice in a food processor or blender and purée until pasty.

Traditional Cranberry Sauce

MAKES: About 1 quart | TIME: 20 minutes, plus time to chill

 M V

The Thanksgiving accompaniment is often overwhelmingly sweet, but the sugar is what helps the cranberries gel and hold together. You can decrease the sugar; just know that the end result will be runnier.

    4 cups fresh cranberries (about 1 pound),
       picked over and rinsed, or frozen cranberries
    1½ cups sugar

1. Combine the cranberries and sugar with 2 cups water in a medium saucepan over medium-low heat. Cover and cook, stirring occasionally, until the berries are broken, 10 to 15 minutes.

2. Transfer to a bowl. Cool, then chill until you're ready to serve. The sauce can be refrigerated, covered, for up to a week.

FIRM CRANBERRY SAUCE OR CRANBERRY JELLY Increase the sugar to 2 cups. For sauce, proceed as directed. For jelly, cook for 5 minutes longer, stirring frequently. Pass through a strainer into a mold, bowl, or jelly jars. Cool, then chill until firm. Spoon out, or warm the container in hot water to turn the jelly out on a plate and then slice to serve.

CRANBERRY RELISH This isn't cooked, but it's handy to have all the cranberry options in one place: Reduce the sugar to ½ cup; zest 1 orange, then remove the pith and supreme the flesh (page 378). Combine the sugar, cranberries, orange segments, and zest in a food processor and pulse until chopped. Let sit for about 30 minutes before serving.

Barbecue Sauce

MAKES: About 3 cups | TIME: 20 minutes

 F M V

My go-to grilling sauce is ketchup-based and super-easy to make. To spin it in a Chinese barbecue direction, use the rice vinegar and soy sauce options. If you want to baste anything with it on the grill or in the oven, don't do so until the last few minutes of cooking, otherwise the sauce might burn.

    2 cups ketchup
    ½ cup dry red wine or water
    ¼ cup cider or rice vinegar
    1 tablespoon Worcestershire sauce or soy sauce
    1 tablespoon chili powder (to make your own,
       see page 32), or to taste
    1 tablespoon chopped onion
    1 teaspoon chopped garlic
       Salt and pepper

1. Combine all the ingredients except the salt and pepper in a small saucepan over medium-low heat. Cook, stirring occasionally, until the flavors have a chance to blend, about 10 minutes.

2. Taste and add salt and pepper if necessary. Use immediately or cool, cover, and refrigerate for up to a week.

CURRY BARBECUE SAUCE More fragrant: Add a teaspoon or more of curry powder (to make your own, see pages 32).

MUSTARDY BARBECUE SAUCE Reduce the vinegar to 2 tablespoons. Add ¼ cup Dijon or stone-ground mustard.

CHIPOTLE BARBECUE SAUCE Serious heat: In a small bowl, use a fork to mash to a paste 1 or 2 chopped canned chipotle chiles along with some of their adobo sauce. Add to the sauce in Step 1.

BOURBON BARBECUE SAUCE There's some woody complexity in this one: Replace the wine with ½ cup bourbon.

KOREAN-STYLE BARBECUE SAUCE Especially great with grilled beef—even burgers: Use soju or sake instead of the wine; choose rice vinegar and soy sauce. Omit the chili powder and increase the garlic to 1 tablespoon. Stir in 1 tablespoon gochujang (fermented chile paste), then taste to see if you want to add more.

Peanut Sauce

MAKES: 2 cups | TIME: 35 minutes

Make this Thai-style sauce your all-purpose go-to. It's great as a dip with vegetables or summer rolls (page 122), tossed with noodles or grains, used to baste or finish any grilled meat or vegetable, and as a salad dressing.

If you'd like to make it a little lighter, substitute stock or water for the coconut milk.

- 3 small dried red chiles (like Thai or piquin), seeded, or cayenne or red chile flakes, to taste
- 1 tablespoon chopped garlic
- 2 shallots, peeled
- 1 stalk lemongrass, white part only, peeled, trimmed, and thinly sliced (optional)
- 2 teaspoons ground turmeric
- 1 tablespoon good-quality vegetable oil
- 1 cup coconut milk (to make your own, see page 372)
- 1 tablespoon brown sugar
- 2 tablespoons soy sauce, or more to taste
- 2 tablespoons fresh lime juice
- ½ cup chopped roasted peanuts, or crunchy peanut butter
  Salt

1. Combine the chiles, garlic, shallots, lemongrass, and turmeric in a food processor and process until fairly smooth, stopping the machine to scrape down the sides as necessary.

2. Put the oil in a medium saucepan or skillet over medium heat. When it's hot, add the chile-garlic mixture and cook until fragrant, about 1 minute. Add the coconut milk, brown sugar, soy sauce, lime juice, and peanuts and whisk until combined. Simmer, stirring occasionally, until the sauce thickens, about 15 minutes. Taste and add a sprinkle of salt or a little more soy sauce if necessary. Serve immediately or refrigerate for up to a week (warm gently over very low heat or in a microwave before using if you'd like).

SOUTHERN-STYLE PEANUT SAUCE Peanut sauce, American style: Omit the chiles, lemongrass, turmeric, and soy sauce. You can mince the shallots and garlic by hand if you like, instead of using the food processor. Proceed with the recipe, but use cream instead of coconut milk and lemon juice instead of lime juice.

Teriyaki Sauce

MAKES: About 1 cup | TIME: 15 minutes

There's no reason to buy the gloopy, chemical-filled bottled kind when it's so simple to make at home. If you want to use it to marinate or baste raw meat or fish, set about half of the sauce aside ahead of time to pass at the table.

- ½ cup soy sauce
- ½ cup mirin (or ¼ cup honey mixed with ¼ cup water)
- 1 tablespoon minced or grated fresh ginger
- 1 teaspoon minced garlic
- ¼ cup chopped scallions

Combine the soy sauce and mirin in a small saucepan over medium-low heat. Cook until bubbling, about 2 minutes. Turn off the heat, stir in the ginger, garlic, and scallions. Use immediately or refrigerate for up to a day (and return to room temperature or reheat).

ROASTED GARLIC TERIYAKI SAUCE Increase the garlic to 2 cloves. Leave them whole and don't bother to peel. Wrap them in foil and roast in a 375°F oven until soft, about 20 minutes. Remove the skins from the garlic, mash the cloves into a paste, and add to the soy sauce and mirin.

Dashi Dipping Sauce

MAKES: About 1 cup | TIME: 5 minutes, plus time to cool

A mild sauce that's fast if you've made the dashi in advance. It's wonderful with Tempura (page 112) and soba noodles (page 520). Or for dipping raw vegetables like daikon, scallions, carrots, or lightly cooked and chilled snow peas or sugar snap peas.

- 1 cup Dashi (page 178)
- ¼ cup mirin (or 2 tablespoons honey or sugar mixed with 2 tablespoons water)
- 2 tablespoons soy sauce

1. In a small pot, combine all the ingredients and bring to a boil. Turn off the heat and let cool. Use immediately or cover and refrigerate for up to 3 days (and return to room temperature or reheat).

7 QUICK ADDITIONS TO DASHI DIPPING SAUCE

Once it's cooked, you can stir in almost anything. Use the amounts here as guidelines; you can really just add to taste.

1. **Ginger:** About 1 tablespoon grated fresh or 1 teaspoon ground
2. **Daikon:** About ¼ cup grated
3. **Wasabi:** About 1 tablespoon paste
4. **Sesame:** About 1 tablespoon toasted seeds (see page 307)
5. **Garlic:** About 1 teaspoon minced raw, or 1 tablespoon roasted (see page 294)
6. **Scallions or shallots:** About ¼ cup chopped
7. **Chile (see pages 39 and 41):** About 1 teaspoon minced fresh or ground dried

Butter Sauces

These classics fell out of style when we irrationally started to see butter as the enemy. Generally they're mild-tasting, valued for unsurpassed richness and creaminess. They're certainly not everyday sauces, but great for special occasions when you want something both satisfying and elegant.

Brown Butter, page 78

Compound Butter

Nothing more than butter mixed with a flavorful ingredient. I used to fuss with rolling compound butter into a tube in wax paper or plastic wrap to serve it in slices—and you can certainly try that—but it's much easier and just as good to serve it by the dollop. Use it as a finishing ingredient in sauces, toss with pasta or grains, or plop on top of grilled or broiled meats and vegetables so it melts and seasons at the same time. Or just spread on bread, crackers, or crudités.

To make compound butter, combine good-quality softened unsalted butter and your chosen seasonings; let your personal taste dictate the exact ratio. Start with 4 tablespoons (½ stick) butter and add a pinch salt and one or more of the following.

1. 2 tablespoons chopped scallion
2. 1 teaspoon grated citrus zest and 1 tablespoon of the fresh juice
3. 1 tablespoon capers, rinsed, and mashed with 1 teaspoon grated lemon zest
4. 1 teaspoon minced garlic
5. 2 tablespoons minced mixed fresh herbs like parsley, basil, cilantro, and/or dill
6. 2 teaspoons soy sauce
7. 1 or 2 (or more) mashed anchovies
8. 2 to 3 tablespoons minced dried shrimp
9. 2 pieces crisply cooked bacon, crumbled
10. About 3 tablespoons chopped cashews or other nuts, sautéed with a tablespoon or two of butter in a pan over medium-low heat until light golden

Brown Butter

MAKES: ¼ cup | TIME: 15 minutes

Browning butter gives it both color and a full spectrum of nutty, caramelized flavors. It takes only a few minutes, even with any of the additions in the variation and the list that follows. Serve over steamed or broiled fish or chicken, or toss it with noodles and Parmesan for a quick pasta. And the recipe is easy to double if you think you'll need more.

4 tablespoons (½ stick) unsalted butter

1. Put the butter in a small saucepan over medium heat. Stir, scraping down the sides with a rubber spatula, until the foam subsides and the butter turns brown and smells irresistible.
2. Turn off the heat. Keep warm until you're ready to use it, up to 15 minutes.

BLACK BUTTER SAUCE (BEURRE NOIR) One step further and more dramatic: Cook the brown butter until black

flecks start to form, another 2 to 3 minutes. Immediately drizzle the butter over whatever food you are serving, then turn the heat to medium and rinse the pan with 2 tablespoons sherry vinegar or white wine vinegar, swirling it and letting about half the liquid evaporate. Add 1 tablespoon drained capers if you like and ¼ cup chopped fresh parsley. Sprinkle with salt and pepper and drizzle over the food. Toss if necessary and serve.

---

5 SIMPLE ADDITIONS TO BROWN BUTTER

Stir in any of these during the last minute of cooking, when the butter is just about ready (this point is easy to recognize once you've made it a couple of times). If you want to use them in combination, increase the quantity of butter by 2 tablespoons for each additional ingredient.

1. **Finely ground nuts (¼ to ½ cup):** The usual ones, like hazelnuts, cashews, pistachios, walnuts, or almonds. But also macadamia nuts, sunflower or pumpkin seeds, or whole pine nuts

2. **Chopped fresh herbs:** A tablespoon or so of oregano, rosemary, sage, thyme, or tarragon; up to ¼ cup milder herbs like parsley, cilantro, mint, dill, or basil; or 1 fresh bay leaf
3. **Mustard:** Up to a tablespoon of either Dijon or whole grain, to taste, whisked in
4. **Vinegar:** About a tablespoon of sherry vinegar or balsamic vinegar, which will make a "broken" sauce rather than emulsifying into the butter
5. **Anchovies:** 2 or more mashed anchovies

Béchamel and 6 Other Creamy Sauces

MAKES: About 1½ cups | **TIME:** 10 to 20 minutes

The classic French thick and creamy white sauce is so versatile: Use it to "bind" pastas and noodles; layer it between thinly sliced vegetables or meats; spoon it judiciously under or over fish fillets or boneless chicken. Neither the main recipe nor any of the variations should be intimidating, even for new cooks. Since béchamel begins simply by cooking fat and flour (a mixture called a roux; see page 83), all of these sauces are virtually foolproof. The key to success is making sure that the flour actually cooks, otherwise it won't have any thickening power. You can carefully taste the flour to see if it's no longer raw if you're not sure.

To brighten any of these further, stir in 1 tablespoon or more prepared mustard, capers, or both during the last minute of cooking, or up to ¼ cup chopped fresh herbs or 1 tablespoon lemon juice after.

2	**tablespoons butter or olive oil**
2	**tablespoons all-purpose flour**
1 to 1½	**cups milk**
	Salt and pepper

1. Put the butter or oil in a small saucepan over medium-low heat. When the butter melts or the oil is hot, use a wire whisk to incorporate the flour. Turn the heat to low and cook, whisking constantly, until the mixture turns tan and smells like toast, about 3 minutes.

2. Stir in the milk a little bit at a time, whisking constantly to avoid lumps. When about a cup of the liquid has been stirred in, the mixture will be fairly thick. Add more milk a little at a time until the consistency is just a little thinner than you like, then cook, still over low heat, whisking occasionally, until the mixture thickens again.

3. Sprinkle with salt and pepper and serve immediately or keep warm for up to an hour, stirring occasionally, over gently simmering water or in a double boiler.

MORNAY (CHEESE) SAUCE Add ½ to 1 cup grated Emmental (Swiss), Gruyère, or other good melting cheese to the sauce after it has thickened.

BROWN SAUCE A pinch thyme is good here: In Step 1, cook the flour-fat mixture until brown, 3 to 5 minutes. Use beef, chicken, or vegetable stock (to make your own, see pages 176 and 174) in place of the milk.

VELOUTÉ (WHITE) SAUCE Use chicken, fish, or lobster stock in place of the milk.

SHALLOT SAUCE Cook ¼ cup chopped shallots, onion, or scallions, or 1 tablespoon chopped garlic, in butter until softened before adding the flour.

NUT SAUCE Cook 1 to 2 tablespoons pine nuts or other chopped nuts in the butter until lightly browned before adding the flour.

BEURRE NOISETTE SAUCE Cook the butter until it's brown before adding the flour (see page 78). This adds a distinctively nutty flavor.

Hollandaise Sauce

MAKES: About 1 cup | TIME: 10 minutes

The infamous brunch sauce that has many uses beyond Eggs Benedict (page 728). Try it spooned over steamed or poached fish, chicken, or vegetables—asparagus and broccoli are great. Hollandaise takes well to fresh herbs added at the end, like tarragon (a teaspoon), or dill or chervil (a tablespoon).

3	**egg yolks**
	Salt
6	**tablespoons (¾ stick) butter, softened**
1	**teaspoon fresh lemon juice**
	Pinch cayenne (optional)

1. Put the egg yolks, 2 tablespoons water, and a pinch salt in a small saucepan over very low heat. Cook, whisking constantly, until light, foamy, and slightly thickened, 3 to 5 minutes. If at any point during this process the yolks begin to curdle, immediately remove from the heat and continue to whisk for a minute before returning the pan to the stove.

2. Remove from the heat and add the butter a tablespoon or two at a time, whisking constantly to incorporate between each addition. Return to the heat and continue to whisk until the mixture is thick and bright yellow.

3. Add the lemon juice, then taste and adjust the seasoning (add the cayenne now if you're using it). Serve immediately, or if you like, you can keep the finished sauce warm over extremely low heat or (better) over very hot water for up to 30 minutes, whisking occasionally.

BLENDER HOLLANDAISE Melt the butter in a small saucepan over low heat or in the microwave; do not let it brown. Combine all the other ingredients in a blender and turn on the machine. Slowly drizzle in the butter; the mixture will thicken. Taste and add more lemon juice and/or other seasonings if necessary.

THE BASICS OF PAN SAUCES

After you roast or sauté something, you can build a sauce on what's left behind in the pan, the drippings and cooked bits known as the *fond*. (Turkey Gravy, page 649, is a perfect example.) Add some liquid (like stock, wine, cream, or water), then thicken it by boiling—or use it as is. Sometimes the "reduction" is finished with butter or cream. The result is a flavorful sauce that naturally enhances the food instead of being added as an entirely separate component.

The process is straightforward and foolproof:

DEGLAZE Once the meat, chicken, fish, or vegetables are done, remove them from the pan. Add about twice as much liquid as you would like sauce. Turn the heat to high (if you're working with a large roasting pan, put it over two burners) and stir, scraping the bottom of the pan to release any solids left from cooking.

REDUCE Keep the liquid bubbling vigorously until it is reduced by about half. If you'd like a smooth sauce, strain the solids out before proceeding.

ENRICH To finish the sauce, stir in some softened butter, Compound Butter (page 78), Flavored Oil (page 53), olive oil, or cream.

SEASON Taste and sprinkle with a little salt and pepper and some chopped herbs if you like and you've got them. To serve, you can pool the sauce underneath your food, pour a little on top, or pass it at the table.

Every reduction sauce is a variation on these simple steps. Some are thickened by adding flour to the fond before the liquid, or a cornstarch mixture after reducing (see page 83). Many are assertively seasoned. You change reduction sauces by making changes within the various stages. For example, when you heat the pan before deglazing, you might sauté a little garlic, shallot, or other aromatic. But basically, that's about it. Recipes for one true reduction and one shortcut follow, with plenty of ideas for more.

 fast make ahead **V** vegetarian

Five-Minute Drizzle Sauce

MAKES: ½ cup | **TIME:** 5 minutes

Nothing could be easier or more versatile. I'll start you off with the base recipe—a kind of warm vinaigrette—and a handful of variations, but no doubt you'll soon come up with even more ideas. See the list on page 82 for inspiration.

- ¼ cup olive oil or 4 tablespoons (½ stick) butter
- 1 tablespoon chopped onion, garlic, ginger, shallot, scallion, or lemongrass
- 2 tablespoons fresh lemon juice or mild vinegar like balsamic
  Salt and pepper

1. Put the oil or butter in a small saucepan over medium heat. When the oil is warm or the butter melted, add the onion and cook, stirring occasionally, until it softens, a minute or 2. Turn the heat down if it starts to color.

2. Stir in 2 tablespoons water and the lemon juice and sprinkle with some salt and pepper. Maintain the heat so it bubbles gently for a minute or 2. Taste, adjust the seasoning, and serve.

SESAME-SOY FIVE-MINUTE DRIZZLE SAUCE Replace the olive oil with 2 tablespoons each sesame oil and good-quality vegetable oil; replace the lemon juice with soy sauce. Add 1 tablespoon sesame seeds or chopped peanuts if you like in Step 1. Finish if you like by adding 2 tablespoons chopped fresh cilantro just before using.

MISO FIVE-MINUTE DRIZZLE SAUCE Scrap the whole main recipe and do this: Combine ½ cup miso, ¼ cup sugar, and ¼ cup mirin (or 2 tablespoons honey mixed with 2 tablespoons water) or sake (white wine or even water is okay too) in a small saucepan. Bring almost to a boil to dissolve the sugar, then just keep warm until you're ready to serve.

TEN-MINUTE DRIZZLE SAUCE Almost any high-quality juice works here—carrot, tomato, orange, or pomegranate, for example: Omit the lemon juice and water. In Step 2, stir in 1 cup fruit or vegetable juice instead. Bring to a boil and adjust the heat so it bubbles steadily. Cook, stirring occasionally, until the juice reduces by half and thickens almost to a syrup, about 5 minutes. Stir 2 tablespoons chopped fresh herbs if you like.

Reduction Sauce

MAKES: ½ cup | **TIME:** 10 minutes

Here's a sauce made in the same pan you just used to cook meat or vegetables. Keep your food warm in a low oven if necessary while you prepare the sauce. Or add the food back to the pan with the finished sauce and heat through for a minute or so.

- 1 tablespoon chopped shallot or onion
- ½ cup dry white wine (for fish, poultry, or vegetables) or red wine (for red meat)
- ½ cup chicken, beef, or vegetable stock (to make your own, see pages 174–178) or water, warmed
- 2 tablespoons cold butter, cut into bits
  Salt and pepper (optional)
  A few drops fresh lemon juice or vinegar (optional)
  Chopped fresh parsley for garnish

1. Spoon out all but 2 tablespoons of the fat in the pan; if there are dark juices, leave them. Turn the heat to high (if you're working with a large roasting pan, put it over two burners) and add the shallot and wine. Cook, stirring and scraping, until most of the wine has evaporated, the shallot is soft, and nothing is sticking to the pan.

2. Add the stock and cook briefly, stirring, until there is just under ½ cup liquid. Turn off the heat. Add the

4 Ways to Thicken a Sauce

I've got the same attitude about thickening sauces as I do about thickening soups: If you want them less watery—and sometimes you do—use less liquid or cook them a little longer. But here are some other ways you can add body and sheen to many of the cooked sauces.

1. **Puréeing:** Chunky sauces turn smooth and luxurious when puréed. An upright blender will give you the best results (always cool food to a safe temperature before putting it in a blender); an immersion blender is easier but not as powerful. A food processor or food mill will give you a little rougher texture.

2. **Enriching:** Adding cream, sour cream, yogurt, egg yolks, or small bits of very cold butter will add body to cooked sauces. But beware of excess heat: Cream and butter are relatively stable even if the sauce bubbles a bit, but boiling will curdle sauces made with yogurt or eggs. (Eggs are best tempered before being added to sauces: Stir a bit of the hot sauce into beaten eggs to warm them, then stir that mixture back into the sauce.)

3. **Starting with a roux:** A pan sauce made with roux is gravy. To make a roux, cook butter or oil and flour in equal proportion, stirring constantly, over medium heat, until the flour begins to toast. The darker you cook the roux, the deeper and nuttier the flavor; just be careful not to let it burn. You can cook the roux first and then whisk in a liquid like stock or milk (the technique used in Béchamel Sauce, page 79). Or you may add the cooked roux to an already simmering sauce. Either way, let the sauce cook for a few minutes to thicken fully.

4. **Adding cornstarch:** When you dissolve cornstarch in water or a bit of the sauce you want to thicken, the result is a cloudy mixture known as a slurry, and it works brilliantly. A general formula is 1 tablespoon cornstarch dissolved in ½ cup of liquid to thicken 2 to 4 cups sauce. Whisk it smooth with a fork or spoon, then incorporate into the sauce, which will thicken and get shiny as it is gently heated, without vigorously boiling. (You can use other starches, but cornstarch is most common.)

---

butter a little at a time, whisking well after each addition to incorporate it. Taste and sprinkle with salt, pepper, and/or lemon juice if necessary. Serve the sauce over or under the cooked food. Garnish with parsley right before serving.

LEMON-CAPER SAUCE Add 1 tablespoon or more chopped capers with the shallot and wine. Finish with at least 1 tablespoon fresh lemon juice, to taste.

GINGER REDUCTION SAUCE Replace the shallot with 1 tablespoon each chopped garlic, ginger, and scallion and cook until soft before adding the wine. Omit the butter; instead stir in 1 tablespoon soy sauce, fish sauce, or Worcestershire sauce. Finish with a few drops fresh lime juice. Garnish with chopped fresh cilantro.

MUSHROOM SAUCE Increase the shallot to 2 tablespoons, add 1 cup chopped fresh mushrooms, and cook until soft before adding the wine. Best with ¼ cup or more cream added at the last minute.

---

12 WAYS TO FLAVOR REDUCTION SAUCE

1. **Aromatic Reduction Sauce:** Add ½ cup or more chopped aromatic vegetables (onion, shallots, mushrooms, celery, carrot, or a combination) to the fat before adding the wine. Cook, stirring, until soft, then proceed with the recipe.

2. **Creamy Reduction Sauce:** Substitute cream for half or all of the stock.

3. **Boozy Reduction Sauce:** Substitute sherry, Madeira, port, vodka, bourbon, or vermouth for the wine.

   **F** fast **M** make ahead **V** vegetarian

4. **Herbed or Spiced Reduction Sauce:** Add chopped fresh herbs or ground spices at the beginning, the end, or both if you like. Those added at the beginning will be better incorporated; those added at the end will retain more of their flavor. Add them twice if you like.

5. **Piquant Reduction Sauce:** Add chopped anchovies, dried tomatoes, or olives along with the shallot.

6. **Tart Reduction Sauce:** Add 1 tablespoon or more fresh lemon juice or any vinegar, to taste, at the end of cooking.

7. **Tomato Reduction Sauce:** Add chopped or crushed tomatoes or tomato sauce in place of or in addition to some of the stock.

8. **Jammy Reduction Sauce:** Especially good with broiled meats. Whisk in 1 tablespoon or more marmalade or jam at the end of cooking.

9. **Dried Mushroom Reduction Sauce:** Add reconstituted dried mushrooms (see page 304) along with the shallot or onion. Use the mushroom-soaking liquid to replace some of the broth.

10. **Juicy Reduction Sauce:** Use fruit juice—especially orange, tomato, or anything fresh—in place of some of the stock or water.

11. **Mustardy Reduction Sauce:** Add prepared Dijon mustard or Grainy Mustard (page 37), along with some cream if you like, in place of or in addition to the oil or butter.

12. **Spicy Reduction Sauce:** After you pour off the excess fat in Step 1 but before you add the wine, stir in a tablespoon or so of any spice mixture, like curry powder, chili powder, or garam masala (to make your own, see pages 32–35) or any single ground spice. You can also stir in 2 to 3 tablespoons chopped or ground nuts at this point if you like. Cook and stir for about a minute, until just toasted. Then add the shallot and wine.

Appetizers and Snacks

CHAPTER AT A GLANCE

Quick Bites 87

Dips and Spreads 99

Sizzled Starters 109

Party Food 118

As dining becomes more casual, the ritual of individual servings organized in courses has all but disappeared. At restaurants, dishes often come to the table as they're ready and everyone happily shares. Family meals at home are served, well, family-style instead of plated. And for entertaining, it's common to have guests nibble their way from kitchen to living room to outside and back; if you do sit down, it's usually to pass platters around.

For this you can thank the small-plates trend, where you eat a tapas-like jumble of appetizers or snacks and call it dinner. Bites of many totally different things has undeniable appeal: It's a convivial way to enjoy a meal, and the variety can be more satisfying than bigger portions of the standard meat, potatoes, and vegetables.

To eat this way—which is also unfortunately dubbed "grazing"—you can't get hung up on definitions. These appetizers and snacks are what I consider classics, so they get special attention. But lots of recipes throughout the book can be nibbled as finger food, served with toothpicks, or plated for passing and sharing. (The lists on pages 96 and 132 will point you in the right direction to get started.)

I've organized the chapter into four sections, starting with the simplest and easiest recipes and working through to the more involved. There's something here for every occasion, and nothing is overly fussy. If you have 30 minutes or less, choose something from the first two sections; for golden, crisp deep-fried food, skip to Sizzled Starters, page 109. You can even go old-school and plan the meal around courses—just serve individual portions.

Whether you're entertaining one special person or a rowdy family gathering, this is the food that ensures everyone will have a good time, even the host.

THE BASICS OF APPETIZERS

My style of entertaining is almost always casual and low pressure. My secret: Serve as many room-temperature dishes as possible. You can do this by either preparing recipes ahead and pulling them from the fridge a little before guests arrive, or cooking things shortly before guests arrive and just not worrying if they're piping hot. (See the section on food safety on page 3.)

Choose dishes that provide some contrast of colors and textures. Generally you want there to be a common thread, though I'm even loose about that. The flavor profile might be the same—for example, you might go for a menu of all Japanese or all Mediterranean dishes. Or you might have a dumpling and fritter party, or serve an array of dips and dippers.

HOW TO SERVE APPETIZERS

Once that's all in place, here are some options for how to serve everything.

1. FAMILY-STYLE For casual sit-down dinners, offer an appetizer course; serve it on platters. The easiest option when hosting a sit-down dinner is to put any appetizers in the center of the table and let everyone help themselves. This works especially well for batches of fried foods as they come out of the oil.

2. ON A BUFFET Put foods and their accompanying condiments or sauces next to each other. Put plenty of napkins, plates, toothpicks, and other necessary utensils among the dishes, where they will be most handy. There's no law that says they all have to be at one end or other of the table.

3. SERVE AS YOU COOK This works especially well with fried foods or anything you want to be piping

 fast   make ahead   vegetarian

hot. (It also ensures you'll have some company in the kitchen!) Set up a place near the stove—but out of your way—and as bits come out of the hot fat or off the baking sheet, transfer them to a rack or platter (don't forget the final garnish or dipping sauce) and let people grab 'em as they're ready.

4. PASS AS YOU (OR SOMEONE ELSE) MINGLE Offer the sauce on the same plate and carry some extra napkins. If toothpicks are needed, put them in the food or carry them in a shot glass or small cup.

5. IN PLATED PORTIONS Working one course at a time, spread out individual serving plates on a work surface; have stacks of plates for the subsequent courses handy. Plate the components for the dish in an assembly-line fashion: Put all the main items on the plates first, then add the sauce, and finally garnish, instead of finishing one plate before turning to the next.

HOW MANY APPETIZERS TO COOK?

Serving sizes always depend on appetite and the amount of other food being served. That's particularly true for appetizers: A hungry television watcher can eat a couple of cups of nuts in thirty minutes with no problem. Put the same nuts out at a party with five other finger foods, and they'll be enough for ten people to nibble on.

With just a smidge of math, the serving sizes on these recipes will help you figure the right amount of food. For light snacking, figure one or two servings total per person. For eight people you might choose two dishes that each serve four and serve half-portions of both; or choose one dish and double it to serve eight. Then just multiply—dishes and servings—to serve more people a bigger and more filling array.

Quick Bites

I'm not saying these recipes are uncooked necessarily but when you do apply heat, the attention on your part

is minimal and the time goes fast. Besides being easy to pull together, they all require just one serving bowl or plate.

Roasted Nuts with Oil or Butter

MAKES: 4 to 6 servings | **TIME:** 15 minutes

Skip the oversalted canned nuts and impress your friends and family—with about 30 seconds of active work. Go with all one kind or combine; my go-tos are pecans, walnuts, almonds, pistachios, and cashews. I prefer to avoid premade mixes and buy the specific types of nuts I want in bulk whenever possible.

    2 cups (about 1 pound) unsalted shelled nuts
    2 tablespoons good-quality vegetable oil
       or melted butter
       Salt and pepper

Heat the oven to 450°F. Toss the nuts in a bowl with the oil and sprinkle with salt and pepper. Spread on a baking sheet and roast, shaking occasionally, until lightly browned, about 10 minutes. Cool before serving; they will crisp as they cool.

SAUTÉED BUTTERED NUTS Even better tasting: Put 4 tablespoons butter (½ stick) in a large skillet over medium-low heat. When the butter melts, add the nuts and cook, stirring, until lightly browned, about 10 minutes. Be patient; higher heat will burn the nuts. As they cook, season with salt and pepper. Cool before serving.

SPICED BUTTERED NUTS Real bar food: Add 1 teaspoon to 1 tablespoon of any spice mixture (pages 32 to 35), like chili or curry powder, to the mix. If roasting, toss the nuts with the spice at the beginning. If sautéing, add it to the butter as it heats.

DRY-ROASTED NUTS You avoid extra fat, but these are still infinitely better than nuts straight from a jar or can: Try to buy raw nuts. Heat the oven to 350°F. Run cold water over the nuts and put them, still wet, in one layer on a baking sheet. Sprinkle with coarse salt and put in the oven. Bake, without stirring, until they are light brown and fragrant, 10 to 15 minutes. Remove from the oven, cool slightly, and serve or hold at room temperature for up to a few hours.

ROASTED PUMPKIN, SQUASH, OR SUNFLOWER SEEDS
You can also use fresh pumpkin or squash seeds (see pages 309–311): Use the main recipe or any of the variations, baking at 350°F for about 30 minutes, tossing occasionally, until tan, or sautéing for about 5 minutes. Like nuts, they will crisp as they cool.

ROASTED BEANS WITH OIL Instead of the nuts, substitute cooked or canned chickpeas, soybeans, black beans, or any other legume you like: If you cooked the beans yourself, it's important that they're tender but still intact. Drain them well and pat dry with towels before starting the recipe. Lower the oven heat to 425°F and use olive or good-quality vegetable oil, not butter.

Caramelized Spiced Nuts

MAKES: 4 to 6 servings | **TIME:** 15 minutes

Sugar and bit of spice make these only slightly more involved than the roasted nuts in the preceding recipe and even more addictive. Use all one kind of nut or a combination. Add seeds to the mix if you like; sunflower, pumpkin, and sesame seeds all add flavor and texture.

> 2 **tablespoons good-quality vegetable oil**
> 2 **cups sugar**

> 2 **teaspoons garam masala (to make your own, see page 34)**
> ½ **teaspoon cayenne**
> 1 **teaspoon salt**
> 2 **cups (about 1 pound) unsalted shelled nuts (see the headnote)**

1. Heat the oven to 450°F. Grease a baking sheet with the oil. Put a large skillet over high heat and add 2 cups water and the sugar. Bring to a boil and stir in the garam masala, cayenne, salt, and nuts. Reduce the heat to medium and cook, stirring frequently, until the liquid is reduced to a syrup, 5 to 10 minutes.
2. Turn the heat to low. Remove the nuts with a slotted spoon, letting the excess syrup drain off a bit and spread the nuts on the baking sheet. Be sure to turn off the burner when you've finished.
3. Roast the nuts for 10 minutes, tossing once or twice with a spatula. Remove from the oven and let cool—the sugar coating will be very hot, so resist sampling for a few minutes! The sugar coating will harden as the nuts cool. Serve or store in an airtight container at room temperature for 2 or 3 days.

FIERY CARAMELIZED NUTS Substitute a tablespoon or more finely chopped canned chipotle chile with the adobo sauce for the garam masala.

ROSEMARY CARAMELIZED NUTS Substitute 1 tablespoon minced fresh rosemary for the garam masala.

MISO CARAMELIZED NUTS The miso flavor mellows after roasting. So go by your taste and the intensity you're using; see page 39 for more details. Omit the spices and wait to add salt. When the liquid has finished reducing in Step 1, remove from the heat and stir in up to 2 tablespoons any miso. Proceed with Step 2. As soon as you can safely taste a warm nut, decide if you want to toss in more miso or a little salt before transferring to a bowl.

 fast   make ahead  vegetarian

Popcorn

MAKES: 4 to 6 servings | TIME: About 10 minutes

If you depend on packages in the microwave, home-made stovetop popcorn is a revelation. It cooks twice as fast and takes brilliantly to real butter (instead of that terrible artificially butter-flavored oil), cheese, as well as many other seasonings; see "16 Flavor Boosters for Popcorn, Roasted Nuts, or Edamame" on page 91.

> 2 tablespoons good-quality vegetable oil
> ½ cup popping corn
> 4 tablespoons (½ stick) butter or ¼ cup olive oil (optional)
> Salt

1. Put the vegetable oil in a large pot (6 quarts or so) with a lid. Turn the heat to medium, add 3 kernels of the corn, and cover.

2. When the 3 kernels pop, remove the lid and add the remaining corn. Cover and shake the pot, holding the lid on. Cook, shaking the pot often, until the popping sound stops, after about 5 minutes. Meanwhile, melt the butter or gently warm the olive oil, if you're using it.

3. Turn the popcorn into a large bowl. Drizzle with the butter or olive oil, if using. Sprinkle with salt while tossing the popcorn. Serve immediately—popcorn is best hot.

SALTY-SWEET BUTTERED POPCORN Use the butter. Add 1 tablespoon superfine sugar to the butter as soon as it's melted and stir, then drizzle it over the popcorn and add the salt. Toss well, taste and add more sugar and/or salt if needed.

PARMESAN POPCORN You can use whatever cheese you like here, but Parmesan is the best: Sprinkle ¼ cup finely grated Parmesan (as fine as possible) over the hot popcorn and toss.

Edamame (or Any Bean) in Their Shells

MAKES: 4 servings | TIME: 5 minutes

A staple at Japanese restaurants, edamame are immature soybeans either in their pods or shelled, usually sold frozen. In their pods, they make terrific finger food for appetizers. To eat edamame from the pod the traditional way, put the whole pod in your mouth and pull it out, using your teeth to squeeze the beans into your mouth. It's also easy to shell them like peas, plucking them from the pods, and even easier to buy them frozen preshelled, though they're not as good.

> Salt
> 1 pound fresh or frozen edamame in their pods

1. Bring a large pot of water to a boil and salt it. Add the edamame, return to a boil, and cook until bright green, 3 to 5 minutes; drain. Or put them in a dish with a couple tablespoons of water, partially cover, and microwave for 3 to 5 minutes, depending on your microwave power.

2. Sprinkle with salt and any of the garnishes in the following list if you like. Serve hot, warm, or chilled, with an extra bowl for the empty pods.

SPICY STIR-FRIED EDAMAME Flash-cooking in a skillet with chiles gives the edamame a nice kick: Use either unshelled or shelled edamame. Put 1 tablespoon good-quality vegetable oil, 1 teaspoon sesame oil, the edamame, 2 tablespoons water, 3 or more Thai or other small hot fresh or dried chiles, 1 teaspoon Sichuan peppercorns (optional), and 1 teaspoon chopped garlic into a large skillet over high heat. Cover and cook, shaking the pan often, for about a minute. Remove the lid and stir-fry until softened, about 3 minutes longer. Sprinkle with salt and serve.

EDAMAME-STYLE SHELL BEANS When in season, fresh shell beans can be prepared and served like

edamame. And you don't need to peel each fava bean either; just eat their skin: Cook the beans in their shells until they're tender enough to pierce with a fork, anywhere from 10 to 45 minutes depending on the bean. Sprinkle with salt or any of the garnishes in the list above.

Marinated Olives

MAKES: 8 or more servings | **TIME:** 5 minutes, plus time to marinate

Like Roasted Nuts with Oil or Butter (page 87), this is an infinitely better homemade version of a store-bought item. They're so good, people assume there is some sort of trick to them; there's not. Just be sure to start with good olives (a few different kinds if possible; see page 313). For a slightly more involved version of this dish, see Sautéed Olives (page 313).

- 1 **pound olives (green, black, or a mixture, preferably imported from Greece, Italy, or Spain), pitted or not**
- 2 **tablespoons olive oil, or to taste**
- 4 **cloves garlic, crushed**
   Several sprigs fresh thyme or rosemary, or 1 tablespoon fresh chopped thyme or rosemary leaves, or 1 teaspoon dried thyme
- 2 **bay leaves (optional)**
- 1 **teaspoon red chile flakes (optional)**

Combine all the ingredients and transfer to a jar or serving bowl. You can serve these immediately, although they are better if they sit, covered and refrigerated, for a day or 2. They will keep, improving in flavor, for several weeks, but bring to room temperature before serving.

16 Flavor Boosters for Popcorn, Roasted Nuts, or Edamame

Just toss any of these thoroughly with the cooked popcorn, nuts, or edamame. Some are more potent than others, so be judicious (you don't want to use a tablespoon of cayenne, for example).

1. Chopped fresh herbs
2. Curry Powder (page 32)
3. Chili powder (to make your own, see page 32)
4. Chaat masala (to make your own, see page 34)
5. Five-spice powder (to make your own, see page 35)
6. Seaweed "Shake" or any of the variations (page 35)
7. Cayenne, paprika, or red chile flakes
8. Ground sumac or za'atar
9. Togarashi seasoning
10. Finely ground nuts
11. Toasted sesame seeds
12. Sesame oil
13. Soy sauce
14. Chile oil
15. Any grated citrus zest
16. Nutritional yeast (best for popcorn)

MARINATED OLIVES WITH CITRUS Great in the winter, when the bright acidity is welcome: Cut 1 lemon, orange, or grapefruit into wedges and add to the mixture. Remove the citrus before serving.

Deviled Eggs

MAKES: 4 servings | **TIME:** 5 minutes with precooked eggs

A wonderful old standard that can be varied in dozens of ways and infinitely scaled up. For lower-fat deviled eggs, replace the mayonnaise with yogurt. For a richer version, use sour cream or crème fraîche in place of the mayonnaise.

Top to bottom: Deviled Eggs (main recipe),
Pesto Deviled Eggs, Miso Deviled Eggs

4 Hard-Boiled Eggs (page 721)
   Salt
2 tablespoons mayonnaise (to make your
   own, see page 69)
1 teaspoon Dijon mustard, or to taste
¼ teaspoon cayenne, or to taste
   Paprika or chopped fresh parsley for garnish

1. Cool the eggs quickly and peel them. Halve them lengthwise with a small sharp knife. Carefully scoop out the yolks and put them in a small bowl.

2. Mash the yolks with some salt and the mayonnaise, mustard, and cayenne. Taste and adjust the seasoning. Spoon the filling back into the whites. (If you are making a lot of deviled eggs and want them to be especially attractive, use a pastry bag or zipper bag with a corner cut off to pipe the filling back into the whites.)

3. Sprinkle with paprika and serve or cover and chill, well wrapped, for up to 1 day before serving.

HERB-STUFFED EGGS Fresh looking and tasting: In Step 2, substitute 1 tablespoon olive oil for the mayonnaise. Add ¼ teaspoon minced garlic, 2 tablespoons chopped fresh parsley, 1 tablespoon drained and chopped capers (optional), and 1 teaspoon chopped fresh tarragon or 1 tablespoon chopped fresh basil. Garnish with parsley sprigs or chopped basil.

Deviled Eggs, 9 More Ways

Follow the main recipe, adjusting as described and tasting as you go. And who knew eggs could be such a good vehicle for leftovers? You might have to pile the filling a little high.

NAME	FAT	FLAVORINGS	GARNISH
Curried Deviled Eggs	Yogurt	1 teaspoon curry powder	Cayenne or paprika
Miso Deviled Eggs	Mayonnaise	1 teaspoon any miso; 1 teaspoon Dijon mustard	Toasted sesame seeds
Jalapeño Deviled Eggs	Sour cream	2 teaspoons or more minced jalapeño; ¼ teaspoon cumin	Chopped fresh cilantro
Pesto Deviled Eggs	Olive oil	1 tablespoon pesto (page 51) or any of the variations	Small basil leaves
Deviled Eggs with Shrimp, Lobster, or Crab	Mayonnaise	Up to ¼ cup chopped cooked shrimp, lobster, or crabmeat; 1 teaspoon mustard	Chopped fresh tarragon
Smoky Deviled Eggs	Sour cream	Up to ¼ cup crumbled cooked bacon, chorizo, or smoked sausage	Chopped fresh parsley
Deviled Eggs with Anchovies and Capers	Mayonnaise	2 or more mashed anchovies; 1 teaspoon chopped capers or olives; 1 teaspoon mustard	Chopped fresh parsley
Deviled Eggs with Feta	Olive oil	Up to ¼ cup crumbled feta	Chopped fresh dill
Parmesan Deviled Eggs	Softened butter	Up to ¼ cup grated Parmesan cheese; 1 teaspoon minced garlic	Lots of black pepper

Marinated Celery and Carrots, Chinese Style

MAKES: 4 appetizer or side-dish servings | TIME: 10 minutes, plus time to marinate

An easy and ultra-savory, crunchy little nibble. Next time you make this recipe, you'll want to double it. Or try substituting summer squash, daikon radish, or any other vegetables you like raw. See the first variation for more ideas.

    4 celery stalks
    4 carrots
    1 teaspoon salt
    1 tablespoon sugar
    2 tablespoons sesame oil
    2 tablespoons soy sauce
    2 teaspoons vinegar (preferably rice
       or cider vinegar)
    1 clove garlic, chopped
       Pinch cayenne (optional)

1. Cut the celery and carrots into 2-inch lengths, then into rough matchsticks. Mix with the salt and let sit for at least 10 minutes and up to an hour while you whisk together the remaining ingredients.

2. Rinse, drain, and pat the vegetables dry, then toss with the dressing. Serve or marinate in the refrigerator for up to a day and serve chilled or at room temperature.

ANY STURDY VEGETABLE, CHINESE STYLE Anything you don't want to eat raw works too: Cut 1 pound vegetables like broccoli or snow peas into bite-sized pieces. Instead of salting the vegetables in Step 1, whisk the salt into the dressing. Parboil and shock (see page 238) the vegetables. Use the same dressing.

"CARPACCIO"-STYLE VEGETABLES Especially impressive fanned out on a large platter: Omit the sesame oil, soy sauce, and vinegar. Peel 1 pound sturdy vegetables like carrots, kohlrabi, turnip, cauliflower, summer squash, celery, and/or beets. Slice the vegetables crosswise as thin as possible (a mandoline or food processor slicing blade is perfect for this). Toss with the salt and let marinate for at least 10 minutes or up to an hour. Scatter the vegetables in a thin layer, drizzle with olive oil and fresh lemon juice.

Bruschetta

MAKES: 4 servings | TIME: About 20 minutes

Grilled bread, doused with olive oil, scented with raw garlic, finished with coarse salt—what could be better? Add toppings from the list below and you have a classic starter. Use thick slices of Italian-style bread—or one of the home-baked European-style breads on pages 781 to 797—so that the outside gets crunchy while the inside stays moist.

      8 thick slices rustic bread
         Olive oil as needed
 1 to 4 cloves garlic, halved or crushed
         Salt and pepper

1. Turn on the broiler and position the rack about 4 inches below the heat, or prepare a charcoal or gas grill for low direct cooking. Brush both sides of the bread lightly with oil, then broil or grill, turning once, until lightly browned on both sides.

2. Rub one or both sides of the bread with garlic. Put the bread on a plate, then drizzle with oil (a tablespoon or so per slice is not too much) and sprinkle with salt and, if you like, pepper. Serve warm.

CROSTINI Like what Americans call "toast points" or the French call *croutons*, only Italian style: Cut the bread into thinner, smaller slices so you have 16 to 24. Brush them with oil and crisp them on a grill, under a broiler, or in a 400°F oven until golden on all sides. Rub them with garlic if you like and top them in any of the ways that follow.

BRUSCHETTA OR CROSTINI WITH PARMESAN For the broiler instead of the grill, this offers lots of bang for the buck: Omit the garlic, drizzle the bread with oil, and then sprinkle it with grated Parmesan; run under the broiler until the Parmesan just melts. Serve immediately.

BRUSCHETTA OR CROSTINI WITH TOMATOES AND BASIL
With good tomatoes, there's nothing better: Core about a pound of ripe tomatoes and squeeze most of the seeds out. Coarsely chop the tomatoes. If you have time, put them in a strainer for a few minutes to drain the excess water. When the bread is ready to cook, toss the tomatoes, about a cup of torn basil, a drizzle of oil, and a sprinkle of salt together in a bowl. Top the bread with the mixture after rubbing the garlic on the bread in Step 2, sprinkle with pepper, and serve.

---

25 TOPPINGS FOR BRUSCHETTA AND CROSTINI

1. Traditional Pesto (page 51)
2. Fresh Tomato or Fruit Salsa (page 55)
3. Any of the spreads in this chapter (starting on page 99)
4. Corn Salad with Avocado (page 201)
5. Any bean salad (pages 212 to 215)
6. Traditional Chicken Salad (page 223)
7. Crab Salad (page 223)
8. Seafood Salad, Mediterranean Style (page 227)
9. Virtually any puréed vegetable (see pages 240 to 242)
10. Sautéed Eggplant with Basil (page 290)
11. Braised Endive, Escarole, or Radicchio with Prosciutto (page 292)
12. Roasted Garlic (page 294)
13. Sautéed Mushrooms (page 306)
14. Caramelized Onions (page 315)
15. Spinach with Currants and Nuts (page 339)
16. Oven-Roasted Plum Tomatoes (page 347)
17. Oven-Baked Ratatouille (page 352)
18. White Bean Purée (page 392)
19. Beans and Tomatoes (page 396)
20. White Beans, Tuscan Style (page 402)
21. Beans and Greens (page 403)
22. Lentils, Six Ways (page 408)
23. Gravlax (page 550)
24. Sardines on the Grill (page 573)
25. Shredded Pork (page 697)

Marinated Mozzarella

MAKES: 8 servings | **TIME:** 20 minutes, plus time to rest

If you can find small mozzarella balls, by all means use them. Otherwise, cut a chunk of mozzarella into bite-sized pieces. In any case, fresh mozzarella delivers the best results since it absorbs the flavors so well.

 fast make ahead  vegetarian

5 Other Cheese and Marinade Combinations

NAME	CHEESE	MARINADE
Marinated Feta	Good-quality feta, cut into cubes	Vinaigrette (page 181); 2 tablespoons chopped fresh oregano or marjoram
Marinated Paneer	Cubed paneer or Fresh Cheese, The Easy Way (page 756)	Flavored Oil (page 53). Especially good with mustard seed–cumin seed combo on page 53
Marinated Ricotta Salata	Ricotta salata, crumbled	¼ cup Mint Pesto (page 51), thinned with olive oil
Marinated Queso Fresco	Queso fresco, crumbled, or Fresh Cheese, The Easy Way (page 756)	¼ cup Cilantro Sauce (page 52), thinned with ¼ cup good-quality olive oil
Marinated Goat Cheese	Whole logs or rounds of goat cheese; no more than 1 pound	Use the marinade in the main recipe, but use dill for the herb and squeeze the juice of 1 lemon over all.

¼ cup olive oil
¼ cup chopped fresh basil, parsley, or oregano
   or any combination
1 pound mozzarella, drained if packed in
   water and cut into bite-sized pieces if
   necessary
   Salt and pepper
   Red chile flakes, to taste

1. Combine the oil and basil; toss in a bowl with the mozzarella.
2. Taste and add salt and pepper and red chile flakes to taste. If possible, let stand for at least 30 minutes before serving.

Chickpea Flatbread

MAKES: 4 to 6 servings | **TIME:** 1 hour, plus time for the batter to rest
Ⓜ Ⓥ

Large tender breads made from bean flour are a classic snack throughout Provence and Liguria, where they are called *socca* and *farinata*, respectively. Fortunately, the batter is easy to make at home—and embellish with herbs or seasonings—and bake in a skillet.

1½ cups lukewarm water
1 cup chickpea flour
1 teaspoon salt
1 teaspoon pepper, or more to taste
4 tablespoons olive oil, plus more as needed
½ small yellow onion, thinly sliced (¼ to ½ cup, loosely packed; optional)
1 tablespoon chopped fresh rosemary (optional)

1. Combine the warm water, chickpea flour, salt, pepper, and 2 tablespoons of the oil in a medium bowl and whisk until smooth. (Lumps will inevitably form and dissolve as you stir.) Cover the bowl with a towel, and let the batter sit on the kitchen counter for at least a few minutes and as long as 12 hours. The batter will thicken a bit.
2. Heat the oven to 450°F. Put another 2 tablespoons of the oil in a large, well-seasoned cast-iron or nonstick skillet. Stir the onion and/or rosemary into the batter, if you're using them; the batter will still be a little thicker than it was originally. Pour the batter into the pan. Bake for about 15 minutes, until the pancake is firm and the edges set. Heat the broiler and brush the top with a little more oil if you like.
3. Put the pan a few inches away from the broiler for a minute or 2, just long enough to brown the pancake in places, but not long enough to color evenly or burn. Cut it into wedges or squares and serve hot or warm.

Shrimp Cocktail

MAKES: 4 servings | **TIME:** 20 minutes

One appetizer that never goes out of style. The sauce here is iconic, but you can spike the ketchup a million different ways, or skip it and serve the shrimp with Fresh Tomato or Fruit Salsa (page 55) or any sauce made with mayonnaise (see page 69). Adding slices of crisp raw vegetables like jícama, carrots, radishes, daikon, or chayote to the platter makes the shrimp go a little further.

1	pound jumbo shrimp
½	cup ketchup
1	teaspoon chili powder (to make your own, see page 32)
3	tablespoons fresh lemon juice
1	tablespoon Worcestershire sauce, or to taste
	Several drops Tabasco or other hot sauce
1	tablespoon prepared horseradish, or to taste
1	tablespoon minced onion (optional)
	Salt and pepper
	Iceberg lettuce (optional)

1. Put the shrimp a large pot over high heat with water to cover. Salt the water, and when it boils, reduce the heat to medium-low and cook just until the shrimp are pink all over, 3 to 5 minutes. Drain the shrimp and rinse them immediately in cold water until cool. Peel.

2. Combine all the other ingredients except the lettuce Taste and adjust the seasoning. If time allows, chill both the shrimp and the sauce.

3. Serve the shrimp, on a bed of lettuce if you like, with a bowl of sauce on the side.

SHRIMP LOUIE COCKTAIL Replace ¼ cup of the ketchup with mayonnaise (to make your own, see page 69). Replace the Worcestershire and horseradish with 2 tablespoons chopped dill pickles.

Dips and Spreads

You start with something creamy and rich and it hardly matters how you eat it. Usually dips are served in bowls with something alongside for the guests to do the action. The host might assemble spreads on crackers, bread, or sliced vegetables. To make a spread into a dip, thin it with sour cream, yogurt, heavy cream, or mayonnaise. To thicken nearly any dip for spreading, add more cream cheese or replace some of the sour cream with butter or cream cheese.

Many of the sauces and salsas in the "Spices, Herbs, Sauces, and Condiments" chapter can be used as dips or spreads too. And it's worth noting that refrigeration stiffens anything with a fair amount of fat or starch. So those benefit from sitting out to remove the chill for at least a few minutes before serving.

Classic Creamy Dip, Five Ways

MAKES: 6 to 8 servings | **TIME:** 10 minutes

Perhaps the easiest dip to make and customize. A few nuances: You can chop the vegetables in a food processor, as long as you don't purée them. If you go the cottage cheese route, purée it first to make it smooth, like the other options. You can also substitute mayonnaise (preferably homemade, page 69) for half the dairy.

1	cup chopped mixed raw vegetables, like seeded cucumber (see page 287), red or green bell pepper, carrot, and/or fresh or frozen peas
1	scallion, chopped
2	tablespoons chopped fresh dill or parsley
2	cups sour cream, Greek yogurt, or cottage cheese
	Salt and pepper
	Fresh lemon juice
	Milk (optional)
	Crackers, chips, crudités (see page 102), or Crostini (page 95) for serving

Mix the chopped vegetables with the scallion, herb, sour cream, and salt and pepper to taste. Add a little lemon juice, to taste. Thin with milk if necessary. Cover and refrigerate for up to a day. Serve with the accompaniments you like.

CARAMELIZED ONION DIP Easy and amazing: Omit the vegetables and scallion and use 1 cup Caramelized Onion (page 315), chopped, and ½ cup chopped parsley; you won't need the lemon juice.

BEET AND HORSERADISH DIP Use 1 cup shredded beets for the chopped vegetables and add 1 tablespoon or more prepared horseradish. Add Dijon mustard to taste to give this even more kick.

SMOKED SALMON OR TROUT DIP Also good with salmon or trout roe: Omit or include the vegetables and scallion, as you like. Add ½ cup (or a little more) flaked smoked trout or chopped smoked salmon. Choose dill for the herb. Lemon juice is a must here.

WATERCRESS OR ARUGULA DIP The pepperiness of these greens is fabulous in a dip: Omit the chopped vegetables. Add 1 cup trimmed, washed, well-dried, and chopped watercress or arugula.

Herbed Goat Cheese

MAKES: 6 to 8 servings | **TIME:** 10 minutes

The consistency here is somewhere between a dip and spread, so use it either way—with Crostini (page 95) or crudités (see page 102).

Other cheeses you can use: fresh ricotta or feta (you'll need to use a food processor in Step 1)

- 8 ounces fresh goat cheese
- 2 tablespoons heavy cream, sour cream, yogurt, or milk, or as needed

- ¼ teaspoon minced garlic, or to taste
- ½ cup chopped mixed fresh mild herbs like basil, parsley, chervil, dill, and/or chives
- 1 teaspoon chopped fresh tarragon or thyme
  Salt and pepper
- 1 tablespoon olive oil, or as needed

1. Mash the goat cheese and thin it with enough of the cream to make it spreadable or usable as a dip. You may need more or less depending on the density of the cheese and the consistency you prefer.
2. Stir in the garlic and herbs. Taste and add salt if necessary (some goat cheese is quite salty) and pepper to taste. Drizzle with the oil and serve, or refrigerate for up to several hours, then add the oil and serve chilled.

HONIED GOAT CHEESE Omit the herbs, garlic, and olive oil. After thinning in Step 1, stir in 2 tablespoons (or more) honey.

ROSEMARY-HONEY GOAT CHEESE Slightly sweet and lovely with any fresh or dried fruit: Omit the garlic, salt, and pepper. Use 2 tablespoons chopped fresh rosemary for the herb and as much honey as you like instead of oil.

GOAT CHEESE–STUFFED FIGS Terrific grilled: Thin the cheese as directed until spreadable. Omit the garlic and herbs. Taste and add salt if necessary. Halve 8 ripe fresh figs. Spread about 1 tablespoon of the cheese on the top of each fig half, pressing just enough so it adheres. Drizzle with a little olive oil, sprinkle with some pepper, and serve. Or refrigerate for up to an hour before garnishing and serving. To grill, just pop onto a not-too-hot grill, cheese side up, until the figs are warm.

FLAVORFUL CREAM CHEESE SPREAD Plenty of uses beyond bagels: Use cream cheese instead of goat cheese. Omit the garlic, herbs, and oil and add 4 ounces (about 1 cup) Roquefort, Maytag blue, or other good blue cheese. Add sour cream or yogurt as needed to get the desired consistency. Season with cayenne or hot sauce to taste, if you like.

Crudités

If you're going to put out crudités (cut-up raw vegetables), make sure they're more exciting and attractive than merely carrot and celery sticks. (To make those super-interesting, see Marinated Celery and Carrots, Chinese Style on page 95).

Preparing the vegetables: The best vegetables are always whatever is fresh. Beyond that, they must hold up to dip. Barely cooked asparagus spears are perfect, as are raw Belgian endive leaves. If they're not pleasant or edible when raw, then steam, roast, or grill them, or boil and shock them as described on page 238. And it's easier to pull together just one or two vegetables than it is to prep a whole array.

Keep the pieces large enough to pick up easily and dip without dipping your fingers too (very small pieces are annoying) or breaking the vegetable, but small or slender enough to pop into your mouth or bite easily; usually spears about ½ inch wide are just right. Broccoli and cauliflower florets work best with an inch or so of stem to hold onto. Core and seed bell peppers and slice them into roughly ½-inch-wide sticks.

Serving crudités: You can prepare all the components of a crudité platter, including the dip, in advance. Just store raw vegetables in ice water to keep them crisp, and lightly cooked vegetables in airtight containers; both will hold for a day or so. Drain raw vegetables well and put them on towels to dry thoroughly (dip doesn't stick to wet vegetables). Bring cooked vegetables to room temperature.

10 INTERESTING VEGETABLES TO USE AS CRUDITÉS

1. Real baby carrots (not the nubby kind sold in bags) with the green tops, tops trimmed to 1 inch, carrots peeled
2. Asparagus spears, trimmed and very lightly cooked so they're still crunchy and bright green
3. Green or wax beans, cooked until crisp-tender
4. Sugar snap peas, raw if very fresh or lightly cooked
5. Belgian endive leaves
6. Jícama, peeled and cut into sticks
7. Purple or other heirloom potatoes, cooked until just tender and cut into long wedges
8. Small new potatoes, cooked whole, then halved
9. Red or white radishes, whole or halved
10. Lightly cooked wedges of winter squash with edible skin like acorn or delicata

18 DIPS TO SERVE WITH CRUDITÉS

1. Traditional Pesto (page 51)
2. Parsley (or Other Herb) Purée (page 52)
3. Any Flavored Oil (page 53)
4. Tahini Sauce (page 56)
5. Simplest Yogurt Sauce (page 59)
6. Blue Cheese Dressing (page 59)
7. Creamy Cilantro-Mint Chutney (page 62)
8. Ginger-Scallion Sauce (page 64)
9. Miso Dipping Sauce (page 66)
10. Thai Chile Sauce (page 66)
11. Aioli or any mayonnaise-based sauce (page 70)
12. Green Goddess Ranch Dressing (page 71)
13. Real Ranch Dressing (page 71)
14. Peanut Sauce (page 75)
15. Any bean dip (starting on page 103)
16. Hummus (page 103)
17. Nearly any salad dressing, especially Vinaigrette (page 188)
18. Any well-seasoned vegetable purée (pages 240–242)

 fast make ahead vegetarian

ANCHOVY SPREAD A surprising hit, even for people who think they hate anchovies: Use 8 ounces cream cheese in place of the goat cheese. Omit the herbs. Add 4 mashed anchovy fillets or more to taste, along with the garlic and plenty of black pepper. Season with lemon juice instead of drizzling with oil.

Hummus

MAKES: 6 to 8 servings | **TIME:** 15 minutes with precooked chickpeas

Just because this Middle Eastern classic is now available in every supermarket in America doesn't mean you ever need to buy it. At home you can make it as garlicky, lemony, or spicy as you like (try it with smoked pimentón—see page 30—or other ground chile).

2   cups cooked or canned chickpeas (to cook your own, see page 407; reserve at least 1 cup cooking liquid)
½   cup tahini
¼   cup olive oil, plus more for garnish
2   cloves garlic, peeled, or more to taste
    Juice of 1 lemon, plus more as needed
1   tablespoon ground cumin or paprika, or to taste, plus a sprinkle for garnish
    Salt and pepper
    Chopped fresh parsley for garnish

1. Put the chickpeas, tahini, olive oil, garlic, and lemon juice, and 1 tablespoon cumin in a food processor (or a blender for even smoother hummus), sprinkle with salt and pepper, and begin to process. Add chickpea-cooking liquid or water as needed to produce a smooth purée.
2. Taste and adjust seasoning, adding more salt, pepper, or lemon juice as needed. (To make it thinner, add more cooking liquid, water, lemon juice, or olive oil.) Serve,

drizzled with olive oil and sprinkled with a bit of cumin or paprika and some parsley.

HERBED HUMMUS Brilliant and fresh: Put 1 cup loosely packed parsley, cilantro, and/or mint leaves (a mix is especially good) in the food processor first in Step 1.

MISO HUMMUS The perfect addition you didn't know you needed: Put ¼ cup white or yellow miso or 2 tablespoons red miso in the food processor first in Step 1.

SPICY HUMMUS Make this as hot as you like: Add ½ teaspoon paprika, ½ teaspoon cayenne (or to taste), and 2 tablespoons chopped dill to the food processor in Step 1.

Bean Dip

MAKES: At least 8 servings | **TIME:** 10 minutes with precooked beans

I used to think bean dip was made for tortilla chips; now I like it better with anything but, especially raw sliced vegetables. It's also great spread on toasted pita or other flatbread. If you don't feel like making Real Refried Beans, use 3 cups cooked—and lightly mashed—pinto beans and increase the seasoning as indicated in the chart that follows.

1   recipe Refried Beans (page 393)
    About 1 cup bean-cooking liquid or vegetable stock (to make your own, see page 174), as needed
½   cup chopped red bell pepper
¼   cup chopped scallions
½   cup peeled, seeded, and diced tomato (optional)
1   tablespoon chopped fresh chile (like jalapeño or Thai), or cayenne or hot sauce, to taste
1   teaspoon red wine vinegar or other vinegar
    Salt and pepper

1. Put all but 1 cup of the beans in a food processor or blender. Add enough liquid to start the purée.

2. Combine the remaining 1 cup beans with the puréed beans. Stir in the bell pepper, scallion, tomato if you're using it, chile, vinegar, and some salt and pepper. Taste and adjust the seasoning if necessary; thin with more liquid if necessary. Serve immediately or cover and refrigerate for up to 2 days; bring to room temperature or reheat gently before serving.

BEAN AND SALSA DIP Substitute 1½ cups Fresh Tomato or Fruit Salsa (page 55) or Fresh Tomatillo Salsa (page 56) for the bell pepper, onion, tomato, chile, and vinegar.

CREAMY BEAN DIP Use sour cream for a richer dip, yogurt for a tangy and lower-fat dip: Substitute sour cream or yogurt for the bean-cooking liquid or stock.

CHEESY BEAN DIP Easy-melting cheeses work best here; harder cheeses must be grated more finely: Prepare the bell pepper, scallions, tomato, and chile but don't add them to the dip. After Step 1, gently warm the beans over low heat. Stir in about ¾ cup grated cheese like Cotija, cheddar, or Monterey Jack until it's melted. Serve hot or warm, with the vegetables scattered on top.

8 More Bean Dips

Here are some combinations that work well. Follow the Bean Dip recipe or its variations, using 3 cups beans; only mash them a little before starting. To get the consistency you want, add bean-cooking liquid, stock, or water if a liquid isn't listed. For a smooth dip, purée any additions—like roasted red peppers or caramelized onions—with the beans.

BEANS (3 CUPS CANNED OR COOKED AND DRAINED)	FLAVORINGS	SEASONINGS (ALONG WITH SALT AND PEPPER)
Black beans	1½ cups chopped Roasted Red Peppers (page 318); 2 teaspoons chopped garlic	1 tablespoon ground coriander
Pink beans	1 cup chopped Caramelized Onions (page 315); ½ cup diced tomato	2 teaspoons smoked paprika
Red lentils or yellow split peas (no need to drain)	1 tablespoon each chopped fresh ginger and garlic; 1 cup yogurt	1 or 2 tablespoons chaat masala; ¼ cup chopped fresh cilantro
Lima beans	½ cup toasted pine nuts; ½ cup grated Parmesan; 2 teaspoons chopped garlic	1 cup chopped fresh basil
Edamame	½ cup white or yellow miso; ½ cup chopped scallions; 1 tablespoon chopped fresh ginger	2 tablespoons rice vinegar
Fava beans (green or mature)	1 tablespoon chopped garlic; ½ cup fruity olive oil	2 teaspoons grated lemon zest; 2 tablespoons lemon juice; lots of pepper
Black-eyed peas	2 teaspoons chopped garlic; ¼ cup chopped scallions	½ teaspoon cayenne, or to taste; ¼ cup chopped fresh cilantro
White beans	4 cloves Roasted Garlic (page 294), or more to taste; ¼ cup olive oil	1 teaspoon minced rosemary; 1 tablespoon lemon juice

 fast make ahead  vegetarian

Guacamole

MAKES: 6 to 8 servings | **TIME:** 10 minutes

At its core a combination of mashed avocado with a couple of crunchy, strong-tasting ingredients and some acidity, guacamole takes well to all sorts of variations and is justifiably popular as a sandwich ingredient. It's obviously a natural in tacos and burritos.

- 2 **large or 3 medium avocados, ripe**
- 1 **ripe tomato, cored and chopped (optional)**
- ¼ **cup chopped onion or shallot**
- ½ **teaspoon minced garlic, or to taste**
- 1 **seeded, minced serrano or jalapeño chile, or cayenne to taste (optional)**
- 1 **teaspoon (or to taste) chili powder (to make your own, see page 32) or any mild pure chile powder, to taste**
   Salt and pepper
- 1 **tablespoon fresh lime juice, or to taste**
   Chopped fresh cilantro for garnish

1. Halve the avocados, then pit and peel. Mash the pulp in a bowl with a fork or potato masher, and stir in the tomato (if you're using it), onion, garlic, chile (if you're using it), chili powder, salt and pepper to taste, and lime juice. Taste and adjust the seasoning as necessary.

2. Garnish with cilantro and serve. Or cover with plastic wrap, pressing down so there is no air trapped between the guacamole and the wrap, and refrigerate for up to 4 hours before garnishing and serving.

CRUNCHY CORN GUACAMOLE A nice twist: Add 1 cup corn kernels, preferably just stripped from the cobs (see page 283), but thawed frozen is acceptable. Garnish, if you like, with ¼ cup chopped toasted pumpkin seeds (see page 309).

"GUACASALSA" For salsa lovers, and very fast if you have salsa on hand: Add about 1 cup Fresh Tomatillo Salsa (page 56) or any of its variations; add all the other seasonings judiciously.

GUACAMOLE WITH FRUIT A great combination, especially with pomegranate seeds, pineapple, or apple: Add 1 cup Fresh Tomato or Fruit Salsa (page 55), using fruit.

AVOCADO-CRAB SPREAD OR DIP Chopped cooked shrimp also works here, or even lobster: Omit the garlic, chile, and cilantro. Substitute lemon juice for the lime juice. In Step 1, stir in 1 cup lump crabmeat. Use ¼ cup chopped fresh parsley for garnish, along with a tablespoon of chopped fresh tarragon if you like.

UN-AVOCADO GUACAMOLE Instead of the avocadoes, mash (or pulse in the food processor) 1 pound cooked and chopped asparagus, or thawed frozen or fresh cooked peas. Make sure they're super-tender. Add the other ingredients as you like.

Grilled or Roasted Eggplant Dip

MAKES: 6 to 8 servings | **TIME:** About 1 hour, largely unattended

There is nothing like grilled eggplant, and its smoky flavor makes a sensational dip; if you grill or roast a red pepper at the same time, so much the better. Serve with bread or crackers, or use as a sandwich spread.

- 2 **medium or 4 small eggplant (about 1 pound)**
- 1 **red bell pepper (optional)**
- ¼ **cup fresh lemon juice, or more as needed**
- ¼ **cup olive oil**
- ½ **teaspoon chopped garlic, or to taste**
   Salt and pepper
   Chopped fresh parsley for garnish

Grilled or Roasted
Eggplant Dip,
page 107

1. Turn on the broiler and position the rack about 4 inches below the heat, prepare a charcoal or gas grill for high direct cooking, or heat the oven to 500°F. Pierce the eggplant in several places with a thin knife or skewer. Grill or roast it, along with the pepper if you're using one, turning occasionally, until the eggplant and pepper collapse and their skins blacken, 15 to 30 minutes depending on size. Remove, wrap with foil, and let cool.

2. When the eggplant is cool enough to handle, unwrap it, make a cut in the skin (if it hasn't split on its own), scoop out the flesh, and chop it as finely as you can manage. Peel and core the pepper if you're using it (see page 319), then chop it. Mix the eggplant and pepper with the lemon juice, oil, and garlic, and sprinkle with salt and pepper. Taste and adjust the seasonings. Garnish with parsley and serve.

BABA GHANOUSH A little more elaborate: Omit the oil and bell pepper. While the eggplant is grilling or roasting, toast ½ cup pine nuts in a dry skillet over medium heat, shaking occasionally, just until they begin to brown. When the eggplant is cool, put it in a food processor with the pine nuts, lemon juice, garlic, pepper, and ⅓ cup tahini. Process until very smooth, adding a few teaspoons water or olive oil if necessary. Taste and add salt and/or more lemon juice or garlic to taste. Garnish with chopped fresh parsley and serve.

GRILLED OR ROASTED VEGETABLE DIP Works for carrots, parsnips, green beans, asparagus, Brussels sprouts, or winter squash: Trim and if necessary peel 1½ pounds of any vegetable mentioned. If you're roasting or using a grill pan, chop the vegetables; otherwise leave them whole. Toss with olive oil, salt, and pepper. Grill or roast, shaking the pan (or turning whole pieces) to cook them evenly, until they're quite tender. Purée in a food processor or blender with a little water and more olive oil.

Artichoke Dip

MAKES: 6 to 8 servings | **TIME:** 10 minutes

A lighter, potentially vegan version of the party favorite, which usually includes quite a bit of mayonnaise. You won't miss it. In a pinch you can use canned or jarred artichokes here, provided they're packed in brine, not marinade; drain and rinse them well.

- 1   thick slice day-old bread
- 1   cup warmed vegetable stock (page 174), milk, or water, plus more as needed
- 2   tablespoons olive oil, plus more if needed
- 1   cup shelled walnuts
- 2   cloves garlic, peeled, or to taste
- 8   ounces cooked artichoke hearts (about 4 large, see page 259; or use frozen)
- 1   tablespoon fresh lemon juice, or to taste
      Salt and pepper

7 Ways to Use Any Dip or Spread

1. On sandwiches or wraps, either alone or in combination with other ingredients

2. Thinned with a little of the pasta-cooking water if necessary and tossed with hot pasta for a quick sauce

3. As a topping for baked potatoes

4. Served alongside simply grilled or roasted meat, fish, or chicken

5. As a topping for Bruschetta or Crostini (page 95)

6. Spread or dolloped on top of pizza instead of a sauce

7. Alongside Corn Bread (page 769) or other quick or yeasted breads (pages 781–800)

Artichoke Dip, page 107

1. Put the bread in a bowl and saturate it with some of the stock. Squeeze the bread to drain off excess liquid. Put the bread in a food processor with the oil, nuts, and garlic. Process until the walnuts are ground. Then, with the machine running, pour in enough of the remaining liquid and more oil to form a creamy sauce.

2. Add the artichokes and pulse the machine until they are chopped and integrated but not puréed. Stir in the lemon juice and some salt and pepper. Serve right away or cover and refrigerate for up to 2 days.

PARMESAN ARTICHOKE DIP Still lighter than the usual mayonnaise-laden version: In Step 2, add ½ cup grated Parmesan cheese with the lemon juice. Transfer to a heatproof serving dish and run under the broiler until the top is browned in spots.

Tapenade

MAKES: 6 to 8 servings | TIME: 20 minutes

This Mediterranean spread is probably as old as olive oil. Tapanade is also a terrific seasoning to rub on meat, poultry, or fish that you're going to roast, grill, or broil.

1	pound black olives (preferably oil cured), pitted
3	tablespoons capers, rinsed if salted, drained if brined
6 to 8	anchovies, with some of their oil
1 or 2	cloves garlic, smashed
	About ½ cup olive oil, plus more if necessary
1	teaspoon fresh thyme (optional)
	Chopped fresh parsley for garnish (optional)

1. Combine the olives, capers, anchovies and their oil, and garlic in a food processor, along with a bit of the olive oil. Pulse the machine once or twice, then turn it on and add the remaining olive oil rather quickly; you don't want this purée to be too uniform, but rather rough, as it would be if you had the energy to use a mortar and pestle (which you can use if you prefer).

2. Stir in the thyme if you're using it, thin with more olive oil if necessary, garnish with parsley, and serve. Or cover and refrigerate for up to a month; bring back to room temperature before serving.

GREEN OLIVE TAPENADE A wedge or two of Preserved Lemon (page 375) is a nice addition here too, in addition to or in place of the anchovies: Substitute green olives for black. Add 1 teaspoon toasted and ground cumin seeds or ground cumin, or to taste.

DRIED TOMATO TAPENADE Powerful stuff, excellent used sparingly: Replace at least half or up to all of the olives with roughly chopped Oven-Dried Tomatoes (page 348) or store-bought dried tomatoes. Add 2 teaspoons chopped fresh thyme leaves or 1 teaspoon dried.

Sizzled Starters

Predinner or cocktail party snacks are the ideal times for fried foods: The cooking method guarantees small batches—so everyone gets a few indulgent bites fresh and hot from the oil. Or you can, of course, sit down to a plate of any of these. Just serve a salad or some simply cooked greens.

Frying requires your undivided attention, but not for long. Once you get a rhythm going (see "Deep-Frying," page 22), things proceed smoothly. Tortilla chips and plantain chips might be a good place to start. They require less than 2 minutes in the oil and never spatter, meaning you can produce a significant amount in 10 or 15 minutes. With a little practice you can easily work your way up to tempura and the like. Meanwhile, if you want a starter that resembles fried food but is easier, try good old Nachos (below right).

Fried Tortilla Chips

MAKES: 4 to 8 servings | **TIME:** 15 to 30 minutes

You can make tortilla chips at least as good as the ones at the neighborhood restaurant. Freshly made chips are especially delicious if you use good lard. Eat them as they are or use them to make nachos in the recipe at right.

Lard or good-quality vegetable oil
for deep-frying
12 corn tortillas, 6 or 8 inches in diameter
Salt

1. Put at least 2 inches of fat in a large pot over medium-high heat; bring to 350°F (see "Deep-Frying," page 22). The broader the vessel, the more chips you can cook at once, but the more oil you will use. (They cook very quickly, so don't worry if your pan is narrow.)
2. Stack the tortillas and cut them, pielike, into 6 or 8 wedges. Fry as many at once as will fit without crowding, turning if necessary. Total cooking time will be about 2 minutes; the chips should just begin to darken in color, not brown. Remove with tongs or a slotted spoon and drain on towels or paper bags. Sprinkle with salt and/or any of the suggestions in the list that follows and serve hot or at room temperature.

BAKED TORTILLA CHIPS Heat the oven to 400°F. Lightly brush or spray each tortilla on both sides with good-quality vegetable oil. Stack and cut as directed. Bake on a single layer on ungreased baking sheets, shaking once or twice, until just beginning to color, 6 to 10 minutes.

FRIED OR BAKED PITA CHIPS Instead of the tortillas, use six 8-inch pocket pitas. Separate the two sides by cutting into the fold around each circle with a sharp

knife. Follow the directions for stacking and cutting tortillas and fry or bake as described in the main recipe and variation. Check them frequently since the thickness of the bread—and whether you use white or whole wheat pitas—will affect the cooking time.

Nachos

MAKES: 6 to 8 servings | **TIME:** 30 minutes with premade tortilla chips

It's tempting to want to pile the chips as high as possible with toppings, but overloading quickly makes them soggy. To change things up, you could substitute Fried or Baked Pita Chips (at left) or Plantain Chips (page 111) for the tortilla chips. Or make a match of flavorful beans like Orange-Glazed Black Beans (page 395).

1½ cups drained or cooked or canned black, red, pink, or kidney beans

8 to 12	ounces tortilla chips (about 1 recipe Fried Tortilla Chips, page 110, or 1 big bag store-bought)
2	cups grated cheddar, Jack, or other mild cheese
½	cup hopped scallions
1 or 2	chopped jalapeño chiles
1	cup Fresh Tomato or Fruit Salsa (page 55) or Salsa Roja (page 71)
1	recipe Guacamole (optional)

1. Heat the oven to 375°F. Meanwhile, warm the beans if you're using them and sprinkle with salt and pepper. Spread the chips in one layer in a shallow pan with a rim, such as a pizza pan or a baking sheet. Top with the beans if using, then the cheese, and bake until the cheese melts, about 10 minutes.

2. Sprinkle with the scallion and/or jalapeño and serve immediately with bowls of salsa and guacamole if you like on the side.

---

8 IDEAS FOR TOPPING NACHOS

1. Chopped cilantro
2. Mexican crema or sour cream
3. Chopped tomato
4. Chopped red or white onion
5. Cooked ground beef, seasoned with chili powder (to make your own, see page 32)
6. Spicy Grilled or Broiled Shrimp (page 542)
7. Strips of Grilled or Broiled Boneless Chicken (page 599)
8. Shredded Pork (page 697)

Plantain Chips

MAKES: 4 servings | TIME: 15 minutes

Firm but ripe plantains make for a flavorful and lovely basket of chips, especially when fried in the traditional lard. Best served hot, simply sprinkled with salt, but not at all bad a few hours later. And they make an excellent base for nachos (page 110).

	Good-quality vegetable oil or lard for deep-frying
2	medium-ripe plantains (yellow-green; not green, yellow, or yellow-black), peeled (see page 323) Salt
1	lime, halved (optional)

1. Put at least 2 inches of oil in a large pot over medium-high heat; bring to 350°F (see "Deep-Frying," page 22). The broader the vessel, the more chips you can cook at once, but the more oil you will use. (They cook very quickly, so don't worry if your pan is narrow.)

2. While the oil is heating, use a mandoline set to almost the thinnest setting to shave the plantains, or slice as thin as you can by hand. Traditionally they're cut lengthwise, but you can make round or oval chips if you like.

3. Fry as many slices at once as will fit without crowding, turning if necessary. Total cooking time will be about 2 minutes; the chips should turn a deeper yellow but not brown. Remove with tongs or a slotted spoon and drain on towels or paper bags. Sprinkle with salt and squeeze some lime juice over all if you like, and serve as soon as you can.

BEET, YAM, OR OTHER VEGETABLE CHIPS The list includes carrots, parsnips, turnips, and taro. All gorgeous and sweet: Peel, then slice thinly on a mandoline. Cook and garnish as directed being extra careful not to burn them.

Vegetable Fritters

MAKES: 4 to 6 servings | TIME: 30 minutes without salting

You can make these Italian-style fritters with virtually any vegetable (see below, and the table on page 114).

Salting the raw vegetable usually improves texture, but it isn't essential. However, squeezing them dry is.

Other vegetables you can use: grated sweet potatoes, carrots, parsnips, winter squash, celery root, beets, turnips, rutabaga, or kohlrabi; sliced or chopped okra, chiles, bell peppers, mushrooms, green beans, or shelled fresh peas.

> About 1½ pounds zucchini, trimmed and grated (about 4 packed cups)
> Salt and pepper
> 1 egg
> ½ cup chopped fresh parsley
> ½ cup grated or roughly chopped Parmesan cheese
> 1 clove garlic, minced
> Pinch cayenne
> ½ cup bread crumbs, preferably fresh (page 801), or all-purpose flour
> Good-quality vegetable oil for deep-frying
> Lemon wedges for serving

1. If you like, put the zucchini in a colander, sprinkle with a large pinch salt and let sit for at least 30 minutes, preferably an hour, to drain; rinse.

2. Put the zucchini in a towel and wring to remove excess moisture. Beat the egg in a large bowl and add the zucchini, parsley, cheese, garlic, cayenne, and bread crumbs. Toss with a fork to combine thoroughly. If you didn't salt the zucchini in Step 1, add a pinch of salt to the mixture.

3. Put at least 2 inches of oil in a large pot over medium-high heat; bring to 350°F (see "Deep-Frying," page 22). If you're going to serve all the fritters at one time, heat the oven to 200°F. Working in batches, drop batter by the ¼-cup or large spoonful into the hot oil; you'll probably need to raise the heat to maintain the temperature.

4. Cook the fritters, turning once, until nicely browned on all sides, a total of 4 to 6 minutes per batch. Drain the fritters on towels. Serve them as they are done, or

keep them warm in the oven until all the batter is used. Sprinkle with additional salt if you like and serve with lemon wedges.

Tempura

MAKES: 6 to 8 servings | **TIME:** About 40 minutes

Some people eat this as dinner. And you certainly can. But I like it as finger food or a starter course, especially in Japanese-style meals.

> 1½ to 2 pounds assorted vegetables: zucchini, eggplant, winter squash, sweet potatoes, mushrooms, bell peppers, green beans, broccoli, cauliflower, leeks, onions
> 8 ounces seafood or chicken: firm white fish like cod or haddock, cut into chunks; 6 to 8 large shrimp, peeled and sliced in half lengthwise; or chicken tenders, cut into thin strips
> Good-quality vegetable oil for deep-frying
> 2½ cups all-purpose flour
> 3 egg yolks
> Soy Dipping Sauce and Marinade (page 64) or lemon wedges

1. Slice the vegetables and meat into big pieces about ½ inch thick, either lengthwise into sticks or crosswise into coins. Make the sauce.

2. When everything is ready, put at least 2 inches of oil in a large pot over medium-high heat; bring to 350°F (see "Deep-Frying," page 22). Combine 2 cups water and 2 cups ice; let sit for a minute, then measure 2 cups water from this. Beat lightly with 1½ cups of the flour and the egg yolks; the batter should be lumpy and quite thin.

3. Spread the remaining 1 cup flour in a shallow bowl. One piece at a time, dredge the vegetables and seafood or chicken in flour, then dip in the batter to coat; let excess batter drain off. Fry until golden and cooked

 fast make ahead vegetarian

7 More Vegetable Fritters

Follow the directions for Vegetable Fritters on page 111. Season the batter well with salt and pepper.

NAME	VEGETABLE	BINDER	SEASONINGS
Broccoli or Cauliflower Fritters	1½ pounds broccoli or cauliflower florets, boiled and shocked (see page 238), drained well, chopped	1 egg; ½ cup bread crumbs, preferably fresh (page 801), or all-purpose flour	½ cup chopped fresh parsley; ½ cup grated Parmesan cheese; 1 clove garlic, minced; pinch cayenne
Greens Fritters	1½ pounds chard, collards, spinach, watercress, Asian greens, or cabbage, boiled and shocked (see page 238), squeezed dry, chopped	1 egg; ½ cup bread crumbs, preferably fresh (page 801), or all-purpose flour	½ cup chopped fresh parsley; ½ cup grated Parmesan cheese; 1 clove garlic, minced; pinch cayenne
Celery Fritters	1½ pounds celery and celery leaves, chopped, raw or boiled and shocked if you like (see page 238)	1 egg; ½ cup bread crumbs, preferably fresh (page 801), or all-purpose flour	½ cup chopped fresh parsley; ½ cup grated Parmesan cheese; 1 clove garlic, minced
Bean Sprout Fritters	8 ounces bean sprouts, raw but drained well, chopped	1 egg; ½ cup panko or all-purpose flour	¼ cup chopped fresh cilantro; 1 tablespoon chopped fresh ginger; 1 chopped fresh chile (like Thai or jalapeño) or to taste
Cheesy Chayote Fritters	1½ pounds chayote, pitted, grated and used raw like zucchini	1 egg; ½ cup bread crumbs, preferably fresh (page 801), or all-purpose flour	½ cup crumbled queso freso; ¼ cup chopped fresh cilantro; 1 tablespoon chili powder
Corn Fritters	2 cups corn kernels (preferably fresh off the cob, but thawed frozen also work fine)	1 egg; ¾ cup cornmeal; ¼ cup all-purpose flour; 2 teaspoons baking powder; milk to thin batter if necessary	¼ cup chopped scallions; cayenne or hot sauce to taste
Eggplant Fritters	1½ pounds grilled or broiled eggplant (page 252), lightly mashed	1 egg; ½ cup bread crumbs, preferably fresh (page 801), or all-purpose flour	½ cup chopped fresh parsley; ½ cup grated Parmesan cheese; 1 tablespoon minced garlic; pinch cayenne

through, turning once if necessary, 3 to 7 minutes total, depending on the thickness and type of vegetable or protein. (The best way to check is to cut into a piece or two.) Drain on towels and serve immediately with the dipping sauce or lemon wedges.

EGGLESS VEGETABLE TEMPURA Club soda adds airiness to this two-ingredient batter and makes a nice light coating for delicate vegetables like thinly sliced eggplant or even leaves of spinach or chard: Omit the egg yolks and substitute well-chilled sparkling water for the ice water. Use rice flour if you prefer.

PAKORAS The batter-fried vegetables of India: Mix 1½ cups chickpea flour, 2 teaspoons baking powder, a pinch of cayenne, and salt and pepper. Pour in

 fast make ahead vegetarian

1½ cups warm water and let sit for at least 30 minutes or up to 24 hours. Season the batter with 1 tablespoon curry powder (to make your own, see pages 32). Dip the vegetables in the main recipe in this batter (you need not dredge in flour) and fry as directed. Serve with Cilantro-Mint Chutney (page 61), any of the recipes under Chile Paste, Nine Ways (page 40), any hot sauce, or lime wedges.

---

10 EXCELLENT DIPPING SAUCES FOR TEMPURA AND PAKORAS

For tempura:
1. A mixture of soy sauce and rice vinegar
2. Soy Dipping Sauce and Marinade (page 64)
3. Miso Dipping Sauce (page 66)
4. Wasabi Mayonnaise (page 70)
5. Dashi Dipping Sauce (page 76)

For pakoras:
1. Simplest Yogurt Sauce (page 59) or any of its variations
2. Coconut Chutney (page 62)
3. Cilantro-Mint Chutney (page 61)
4. Cilantro Purée (page 52)
5. Spiced Mayonnaise (page 70), made with curry powder (to make your own, see page 32).

Fried Wontons or Egg Rolls

MAKES: At least 36 wontons or 6 egg rolls (6 to 12 servings) | **TIME:** About 30 minutes

These are the easiest—and most foolproof—dumplings to shape and cook. They don't even spatter much, as long as the package is sealed well.

	Good-quality vegetable oil for deep-frying
1	cup ground or chopped pork or shrimp or a combination

¼	cup chopped scallions
½	cup finely shredded cabbage (preferably napa)
1	teaspoon chopped garlic
1	teaspoon minced or grated fresh ginger
¼	cup cored, seeded, and chopped red bell pepper
1	teaspoon soy sauce
1	teaspoon sesame oil
1	egg
	Salt and pepper
36 to 48	wonton skins or at least 6 egg roll wrappers (to make your own, see 509) Soy Dipping Sauce and Marinade (page 64)

1. Put at least 2 inches of vegetable oil in a large pot over medium-high heat; bring to 350°F (see "Deep-Frying," page 22). The broader the vessel, the more wontons or egg rolls you can cook at once, but the more oil you will use. (They cook very quickly, so don't worry if your pan is narrow.) Line one rimmed baking sheet with wax paper or parchment and another with towels.

Sealing Wontons

To make wontons, put a small amount of filling on a small square wrapper; brush the seam lightly (you can use your fingertip) with water, then press closed.

2. Combine the pork, scallions, cabbage, garlic, ginger, bell pepper, soy sauce, sesame oil, and egg, and season with salt and pepper. To fill the skins, put 1 to 2 rounded teaspoons of filling in the center of each skin; use more for egg rolls. Brush the edges lightly (you can use you fingertip) with water. Fold over to make a triangle for wontons; see the illustration on page 116 for egg roll and seal. Let rest on wax paper until you've filled all the skins or wrappers.

3. Working in batches to avoid overcrowding, put a few of the wontons or egg rolls in the hot oil, raising the heat to maintain the temperature if it drops. Cook, turning with a slotted spoon, until evenly browned, 3 or 4 minutes total for wontons, 5 to 10 minutes for egg rolls. Drain on the towels and serve immediately with the dipping sauce on the side.

VEGETARIAN WONTONS OR EGG ROLLS Omit the pork and/or shrimp. Add 1 cup crumbled tofu, 1 shredded carrot, and 4 or 5 chopped fresh or reconstituted dried shiitake mushrooms.

Potato-Filled Samosas

MAKES: 20 to 30 dumplings (5 to 10 servings) | **TIME:** At least 1 hour

An irresistible stuffed Indian dumpling made with a dough made rich and tangy with butter and yogurt. Take your pick: Cut the cold butter into the dough the traditional way, or use the less charming but more contemporary food processor. I serve samosas with the classic Indian restaurant pairings, Raw Onion Chutney (page 61) and Cilantro-Mint Chutney (page 61).

About 1½ pounds starchy potatoes
(1 large or 2 medium)

2 cups all-purpose flour, plus a little more as needed

Salt and pepper

8 tablespoons (1 stick) butter

2 tablespoons yogurt, sour cream, or buttermilk

About 4 tablespoons ice water

1 cup chopped onion

1 fresh chile like jalapeño or serrano, seeded and chopped, or cayenne to taste

Shaping Summer Rolls and Egg Rolls

STEP 1 Lay the wrapper with one point facing you. Put a large spoonful of filling about one-third of the way up, leaving a border on either side.

STEP 2 Fold up the bottom point.

STEP 3 Fold in the sides.

STEP 4 Roll up. Seal with a few drops of water.

 fast   make ahead    vegetarian

1 tablespoon chopped garlic

2 teaspoons minced or grated fresh ginger

1 tablespoon any curry powder (to make your own, see pages 32)

½ cup green peas (frozen are fine; thaw them in water to cover while you prepare the other ingredients)

Good-quality vegetable oil, as needed

1. Peel the potatoes and cut them into ½-inch cubes. Put them in a pot and add water to cover. Turn the heat to high and boil them until soft, 5 to 10 minutes. Drain.

2. Meanwhile, make the dough: Put the flour and 1 teaspoon salt in a food processor; pulse for a couple of seconds to blend. Cut 4 tablespoons butter into bits, add it to the flour, and turn on the machine; let it run until the butter and flour are combined. Add the yogurt and pulse a few times. Then, with the machine running, add ice water 1 tablespoon at a time through the feed tube. The instant the dough forms a ball, stop adding water. (To mix by hand, combine the flour and salt in a bowl. Rub the cold butter bits into the flour between your fingers very quickly; if the mixture begins to feel greasy, refrigerate it for a few minutes before proceeding. Then stir in the yogurt and water with a fork.) Turn the dough out onto a lightly floured surface and knead until smooth and elastic, about a minute. Cover with plastic wrap or a damp towel.

3. Put the remaining 4 tablespoons butter in a large skillet, preferably nonstick, and turn the heat to medium. Add the onion and chile and cook, stirring, until the onion softens, about 5 minutes. Add the garlic, ginger, and curry powder, sprinkle with salt and pepper, and cook, stirring, for about 2 minutes. Add the potatoes and peas (drained if they've been sitting in water), raise the heat a little, and cook, stirring frequently, until the potatoes begin to brown, about 10 minutes. Taste and adjust the seasoning if necessary; the mixture should be spicy but not fiery. Let cool while you roll out the dough.

4. Knead the dough for a few seconds, sprinkling it with a little flour if necessary. Break off a small piece of the

dough (you'll want to make 20 to 30 samosas, so judge accordingly) and roll it out on a lightly floured surface until it is a circle at least 3 inches in diameter. Make 5 or 6 circles, then fill them: Put 1 tablespoon or so filling in the center, then brush the edges lightly (you can use you fingertip) with water, fold over, and seal. Keep covered with a damp towel. Repeat until all the dough and filling are used up.

5. When you're about halfway through making the samosas, put at least 2 inches of oil in a large pot over medium-high and heat to 375°F (see "Deep-Frying," page 22). If you're going to serve all the samosas at one time, heat the oven to 200°F.

6. Fry the samosas a few at a time, turning if necessary, until they're golden brown on all sides and heated through, about 5 minutes. Drain on towels or paper bags and serve immediately, keep warm in the oven, or serve at room temperature (but within 1 hour or so).

BEEF- OR LAMB-FILLED SAMOSAS Reduce the potatoes to 12 ounces. To make the filling, heat 2 tablespoons butter in a large skillet over medium heat. Add the onion, chile, garlic, ginger, and curry as directed in Step 3. Add 12 ounces ground beef or lamb and cook, stirring, until the meat loses its color, about 5 minutes. Remove from the skillet with a slotted spoon, leaving all fat and other liquid in the pan. Stir ¼ cup chopped fresh cilantro into the filling and proceed to Step 4.

Filling and Forming Samosas

STEP 1 Put a small amount of filling on one side of the samosa dough.

STEP 2 Fold over, wet the edges, and pinch closed.

LENTIL-FILLED SAMOSAS Omit the potatoes, spices, and peas. For the filling, use half a recipe for Dal with Potatoes or Other Root Vegetables on page 410. Drain the peas, beans, or lentils very well before proceeding to Step 4.

BAKED SAMOSAS Works with the main recipe or any of the variations: Omit the frying oil. Heat the oven to 350°F. Lightly grease a baking sheet and bake the samosas until golden brown, 20 to 30 minutes.

Party Food

Some of the fanciest dishes I ever make are for friends and family on special occasions. The recipes in this section involve a little more work than the most of the others in this chapter, but celebrations are always worth it. Sometimes weeknight family dinners are too; there's nothing stopping you from making a meal from just one thing in this section.

In fact, that versatility is part of the appeal of what I consider party fare. All of these recipes work as plated or family-style first courses, on buffet spreads, as snacks, or passed as you mingle with guests. Some need adjustments for different kinds of gatherings: Some you can eat standing, with a small plate and a fork. Others, like Meatballs, Three Ways (page 127) can be served on toothpicks. Some, like Ceviche (page 132), can be served on chips or crackers. Finally, there are those you can skewer for easy handling, like Chicken or Pork Satay (page 130).

Cheese Fondue

MAKES: 8 to 10 servings | **TIME:** 25 minutes

You can make fondue even if you don't own a multi-piece set. Any enamel or ceramic-lined pot will do. Instead of the classic Swiss cheeses like Gruyère or Emmental (or Appenzeller, Fribourg, or Vacherin), any good melting cheese—like cheddar, Jack, Comté, or fontina—will work fine. Even the alcohol is flexible: Dry and acidic white wines are good for balancing the heaviness of the cheese, but beer, dry cider, and red wine are also nice. The classic dippers are cubes of crusty or hearty bread, cooked meat, and cut-up fruits and vegetables. (See "Crudités" on page 102 for some details about which should be cooked first.) In any case, be sure the vegetables are completely dry, or the fondue will not stick to them.

2 cups dry white wine, or a little more
1 large clove garlic, peeled and crushed (optional)
2 tablespoons cornstarch
1 pound Gruyère cheese, shredded (about 4 cups)
1 pound Emmental cheese, shredded (about 4 cups)

1. Combine the wine and garlic, if you're using it, in a large saucepan over medium heat and bring to a slow bubble. Whisk together the cornstarch and 1 tablespoon cold water in a small bowl.

2. Lower the heat, then gradually stir in the cheese a little at a time until it's melted and creamy; do not let the fondue boil. Whisk the cornstarch slurry again and then add to the fondue while stirring; cook until thick and creamy, another 5 minutes. If the fondue is too thick, add a little more wine and cook for another 3 minutes or so. Serve immediately and keep warm over a tea light, or gently reheat on the stove if it starts to thicken.

12 WAYS TO ADD MORE FLAVOR TO FONDUE

1. 1 cup chopped tomatoes
2. Pinch cayenne
3. Large pinch smoked paprika

4. Splash or two of Worcestershire sauce

5. 1 tablespoon chopped chipotle in adobo sauce, or to taste

6. 1 tablespoon chopped jalapeño or other fresh hot chile

7. 1 to 2 tablespoons prepared or freshly grated horseradish

8. ¼ cup or so prepared mustard, or 2 to 3 tablespoons Pickled Mustard Seeds (page 37)

9. ¼ cup Traditional Pesto (page 51), stirred in just before serving

10. 4 to 8 cloves Roasted Garlic (page 294), mashed

11. 2 to 3 ounces dried mushrooms, reconstituted (see page 304), or 1 cup finely chopped fresh

12. 1 cup minced Caramelized Onions (page 315)

Stuffed Mushrooms

MAKES: At least 6 servings | TIME: 30 minutes

The best use for plain-Jane button mushrooms, which have a fine shape for stuffing and benefit from a crisp, intensely flavored, cheesy filling.

    1 pound large button mushrooms
    1 egg
    ½ cup bread crumbs, preferably homemade (page 801)
    ½ cup grated Parmesan cheese
    ½ cup chopped fresh parsley
    1 teaspoon minced garlic
       Salt and pepper
       Olive oil as needed, plus more for greasing the baking sheet

1. Heat the oven to 400°F. Clean the mushrooms and trim off the bottoms of the stems. Remove the stems, taking care to leave the caps intact. Chop the stems and combine them with the egg, bread crumbs, cheese, parsley, and garlic and sprinkle with salt and pepper.

2. Stir enough oil into the mixture to make it shine—a tablespoon or two. Lightly grease a baking sheet with more oil. Stuff the mushroom caps with the stem mixture and put on the baking sheet, stuffed side up. Bake until lightly browned on top, about 15 minutes. Let cool a little, then serve hot or at room temperature, on toothpicks or with napkins.

10 MORE STUFFINGS FOR BUTTON MUSHROOMS

Fill the mushroom caps with any of these stuffings. Or if you've got leftovers, add a spoonful to the stuffing in the recipe:

1. Crumbled blue cheese, goat cheese, or feta cheese, with chopped nuts and/or fresh herbs if you like

2. Cooked crumbled sausage or chorizo, alone or added to the main recipe ingredients

3. Chopped raw or cooked shrimp, lobster, or crabmeat, alone or added to the main recipe ingredients

4. Classic Creamy Dip (page 99) or any of the variations—great with goat cheese

5. Herbed Goat Cheese (page 100)

6. Artichoke Dip (page 105)

7. Tapenade (page 109)

8. The raw meat stuffing from Fried Wontons or Egg Rolls (page 115) or Pot Stickers (page 124)

9. Meatballs, Three Ways (page 127); fill the caps with the raw meat mixture and bake until firm and no longer pink inside, 25 to 30 minutes

10. Risotto, Five Ways (page 440)

Stuffed Grape Leaves

MAKES: About 40 stuffed leaves (10 to 15 servings) | TIME: At least 1½ hours

This is a project, but a memorable one, especially if you begin with a visit to a grape arbor, as I did the first time

Lettuce Cups and Wraps

The idea to eat food in fresh, crisp lettuce leaves is undeniably fun and addictive. I usually let guests wrap their own, so I serve a plate piled high next to a bowl of whatever goes inside.

Iceberg, Bibb or Boston, endive, and radicchio are ideal, since they're naturally cupped like bowls to hold fillings; broad and sturdy green and red leaf lettuces are better for folding and rolling like burritos (see page 810). Romaine tends to break when you try to fold it.

The preparation is a snap: Cut the core out of head lettuce and pull off the leaves, being careful not to tear them. If you're preparing the lettuce in advance, keep it crisp by stacking the leaves in damp towels, then wrapping in plastic or closing in a plastic bag. They can be stored this way for a day or two.

Small diced or chopped foods make the best fillings (large pieces can crush or tear the lettuce); warm, hot, or heavily sauced food will wilt the lettuce.

And remember the garnishes: chopped scallions, fresh herbs, olives, capers, nuts, seeds, crumbled or grated cheese, a dollop of sour cream, yogurt, Guacamole (page 105), or any salsa or chutney (see pages 61 to 64), depending on the filling.

16 DISHES TO SPOON INTO LETTUCE CUPS AND WRAPS

Use at room temperature or lightly chilled, and chop into small pieces if necessary:

1. Basic Bean Salad (page 212)
2. Any chicken salad (page 221)
3. Grilled Beef Salad with Mint or any of its variations (page 223)
4. Stir-Fried Vegetables or any of its variations (page 244)
5. Any stir-fried shrimp dish (page 246)
6. Roasted Vegetables (page 247)
7. Stir-Fried Tofu with Snow Peas or Sugar Snap Peas (page 420)
8. Any rice pilaf (pages 431–437)
9. Any fried rice (pages 443–447)
10. Broiled Shrimp or Squid (page 534)
11. Deep-Fried Seafood (page 538)
12. Aromatic Poached Fish (page 565)
13. Any stir-fried chicken dish (pages 603–606)
14. Stir-Fried Beef with Green Peppers or Green Beans (page 671)
15. Any stir-fried beef dish (pages 671–672)
16. Any stir-fried pork dish (page 692)

I made these. More people live by wineries than ever before, so it's not too far-fetched to get fresh. You can also make these with cabbage or chard leaves prepared the same way, only parboiled for just a minute or 2. Bottled grape leaves have less flavor but are fine, too, and obviously more convenient.

Around 60 large grape leaves (fresh or a 2-pound jar; it's best to have backup, as some will tear)

2 tablespoons olive oil, plus more for garnish

1 cup chopped onion

¼ cup pine nuts

1 cup long-grain rice

1 teaspoon ground allspice

Salt and pepper

1½ cups chicken, beef, or vegetable stock (to make your own, see pages 174–178) or water, plus more for cooking the rolls

2 tablespoons chopped fresh mint or dill

¼ cup fresh lemon juice

1. If you're using fresh grape leaves, bring a large pot of water to a boil. Add a few to the pot at a time, and cook, stirring gently, until they're tender and pliable, usually about 5 minutes. Drain, then rinse under cold running water. (If you're using jarred leaves, rinse them well and separate them to drain.) Cut off the stems and

remove any hard veins near the base of the leaves. Pat dry with towels.

2. Put the oil in a large skillet over medium-high heat. When the oil is hot, add the onion and cook, stirring, until soft, 3 to 5 minutes. Add the pine nuts, rice, allspice, 1 teaspoon salt, and the stock. Reduce the heat so the liquid bubbles gently, cover, and cook until the rice is somewhat tender but still quite firm, 10 to 12 minutes. Transfer to a large bowl to cool. Check for salt and add lots of pepper, the mint, and 2 tablespoons lemon juice.

3. One at a time, put the grape leaves shiny side down on a work surface. Put 1 tablespoon or so of the rice mixture in the middle of the leaf. Fold over the stem end, then fold in the sides, like a burrito (see the illustration on page 810), and finally roll toward the tip, making a neat little package. Don't roll too tightly, as the rice will continue to expand during subsequent cooking.

4. Put the filled leaves seam-side down in a roasting pan or skillet (you can layer them if you like), add water (or even better, more stock) to come about halfway up the rolls, and weight with a heatproof plate. Adjust the heat so the liquid bubbles steadily, cover, and cook until most of the liquid is absorbed, about 30 minutes. Transfer the leaves to a platter and discard the liquid. Serve at room temperature, sprinkled with the remaining lemon juice and a drizzle of olive oil.

LAMB-STUFFED GRAPE LEAVES Cook 1 pound ground lamb in the skillet until no longer pink and remove with a slotted spoon and pour off all but about 2 tablespoons of the fat. Cook the onion until soft, then return the lamb to the pan with the nuts, spice, and salt and add ¾ cup rice and 1 cup stock. Proceed with the recipe from the rest of Step 2.

Spinach-Cheese Triangles

MAKES: About 40 triangles (10 to 20 servings) | **TIME:** About 1 hour

Ⓜ Ⓥ

This is one of those foods where the ratio of time spent making them to how fast they disappear is pretty stark. All the more reason to give them a try.

8	ounces cottage cheese or ricotta (about 1 cup)
1½	pounds fresh spinach, trimmed and well washed
2	tablespoons olive oil
1	cup chopped onion
½	cup chopped scallions
	Salt and pepper
	Pinch freshly grated nutmeg
3	eggs

Folding Spinach-Cheese Triangles

STEP 1 Spoon the filling onto one corner of the dough.

STEP 2 Fold over the corner to make a triangle.

STEP 3 Continue folding in triangles as you would a flag.

 fast   make ahead Ⓥ vegetarian

8   ounces feta cheese, crumbled (about 2 cups)
    ¼ cup chopped fresh dill
¼   cup chopped fresh parsley
1   pound phyllo dough (you probably won't need
    all of it), thawed in the refrigerator overnight
8   tablespoons (1 stick) butter, melted, or olive oil
1   cup bread crumbs, preferably fresh (page 801)

1. Put the cottage cheese or ricotta in a mesh sieve over a bowl to drain for at least 5 minutes. Steam or parboil the spinach until it wilts (see page 238). Drain, rinse under cold water, squeeze dry, and chop.

2. Put the 2 tablespoons oil in a medium skillet over medium heat. When it's hot, add the onion and scallions and cook, stirring, until softened, about 5 minutes. Stir in the spinach, a sprinkle of salt and pepper, and nutmeg.

3. Beat the eggs with the cheeses in a large bowl. Stir in the spinach mixture, dill, and parsley. Heat the oven to 350°F.

4. Unroll the phyllo sheets and cut half of them into thirds lengthwise. Cover the rest with a damp towel. Working with one strip at a time, brush lightly with butter or oil, then sprinkle lightly with bread crumbs. Put 1 heaping teaspoon of filling in one corner of the dough and fold the corner over to make a triangle. Continue to fold the phyllo, making triangles—as you learned to do with a flag. As each piece is finished, brush the top with melted butter and put on a baking sheet. If you need to use some from the remaining half, prepare and fill them as directed; otherwise re-wrap them and use them within a couple days.

5. When all the triangles are done, bake until evenly browned, about 20 minutes. Let rest for 5 to 10 minutes before serving. Serve warm or room temperature.

Vietnamese Summer Rolls

MAKES: 4 rolls (2 to 4 servings) | **TIME:** About 30 minutes

These are a perfect appetizer for putting out all the components and letting your guests make their own, assembly line-style; it's fun and it saves you the work. If you have leftover shrimp (or chicken or pork), you can make them in no time flat, especially once you've practiced on a batch or two.

1   small fresh chile, like Thai or serrano, chopped,
    or ½ teaspoon red chile flakes
1   tablespoon rice vinegar or other mild
    vinegar
1   tablespoon fish sauce or soy sauce
1   teaspoon sugar
1   tablespoon fresh lime juice
1   teaspoon chopped garlic
8   medium or large cooked shrimp, cooked,
    peeled, and halved lengthwise, or sliced
    cooked pork, beef, chicken, or tofu
1   cup grated or julienned carrot
1   cup bean sprouts
2   scallions, cut lengthwise into slivers
2   tablespoons chopped fresh mint
2   tablespoons chopped fresh cilantro
2   tablespoons chopped peanuts (salted are okay)
4   round sheets rice paper, 8 to 10 inches in
    diameter

1. Combine the chile, vinegar, fish sauce, sugar, lime juice, and garlic in a small bowl and stir to combine.

2. Line up the shrimp, carrot, bean sprouts, scallions, mint, cilantro, and peanuts on your work surface. Put out a wide, shallow bowl of hot water (110° to 120°F) and several clean kitchen towels.

3. Line a baking sheet with parchment. Put a sheet of rice paper into the water for about 10 seconds, just until pliable (don't let it become too soft; it will continue to soften as you work). Lay it on the towel. (You can soak a dozen or so in advance and stack them between towels if you'd like; refrigerate for up to 30 minutes before assembling.)

4. In the middle of the rice paper, lay 4 shrimp pieces and about a quarter each of the carrot, bean sprouts, scallions, mint, cilantro, and peanuts. Roll up the rice paper, keeping it fairly tight and folding in the ends to seal as you work.

(Like a burrito; see page 812.) Repeat this process until all the ingredients are used up. As you work, set the rolls on the parchment without stacking and drape with a damp towel. Serve halved or whole, with the dipping sauce.

Pot Stickers

MAKES: 24 dumplings (4 to 8 servings) | **TIME:** 30 to 45 minutes

M

Many cuisines have variations of these crisp-on-one-side dumplings: *gyoza* in Japan, *mandoo* in Korea, to name just two. The combination fry-steam cooking method is somewhat miraculous if you've never tried it. They may be filled with pork, shrimp or other shellfish, vegetables, or—as for mandoo—a mixture of kimchi and whatever else. So once you get the knack, you can have some fun with your own filling combinations. No matter what, they should be eaten immediately out of the pan.

- 8   ounces ground pork, chicken, or other meat (about 1 cup)
- ¼   cup chopped scallions
- 1   cup well-washed, chopped leek (white and light green parts only) or chopped napa cabbage or bok choy
- 1   teaspoon minced fresh ginger
- 1   teaspoon rice wine or dry sherry
- 1   teaspoon sugar
- 1   tablespoon soy sauce
- 1   tablespoon sesame oil
- 1   egg, lightly beaten
     Large pinch salt
- 1   teaspoon pepper
- 24 round dumpling skins (to make your own, see page 509)
     Good-quality vegetable oil, as needed
     Ginger-Scallion Sauce (page 64) for serving

1. Put the meat, scallions, leek, and ginger in a large bowl. Add the rice wine, sugar, soy sauce, sesame oil, egg, salt, and pepper and mix gently but thoroughly. Put about 1 heaping tablespoon of filling in the center of a wrapper, then moisten the edge of the wrapper with water and fold over to form a semicircle. Press the seam tightly to seal; it's best if there is no air trapped between the filling and wrapper. Put the dumplings up on a

Stuffing and Sealing Pot Stickers

STEP 1 To make half-moon pot stickers, put a small amount of filling in the middle of a wrapper. Brush the edges lightly (you can use you fingertip) with water.

STEP 2 Bring one edge of the wrapper over the filling to meet the other.

STEP 3 Secure the dumpling with the thumb of one hand, then press the edges closed.

lightly floured plate or wax paper. (At this point, you can cover the dumplings tightly and refrigerate for up to a day, or freeze for a couple of weeks; you can cook them from frozen in just a few extra minutes.)

2. Coat a large skillet with a thin layer of vegetable oil and turn the heat to medium-high. When the oil is hot, put the dumplings, one at a time, into the skillet, leaving space between them (you will probably have to cook in multiple batches). Turn the heat down to medium, then cover and cook for about 5 minutes. Add ½ cup water to the skillet, re-cover, and cook for another 2 minutes. Remove the lid, turn the heat to high, and cook until the water has evaporated, about 3 minutes. Remove the dumplings and serve right away with the dipping sauce.

STEAMED DUMPLINGS I like these lighter dumplings with Soy Dipping Sauce and Marinade (page 64). Works for the main recipe or the variation: Set up a steamer (to improvise, see page 20) in a covered pot. Lightly oil the steamer basket or plate to prevent sticking. Steam the dumplings in one or two batches for about 10 minutes per batch.

VEGETARIAN POT STICKERS OR GYOZA Substitute 8 ounces drained and mashed silken tofu for the meat. Reduce the quantity of leeks to ½ cup and add ¼ cup shredded napa cabbage, ¼ cup chopped fresh mushrooms, ¼ cup shredded carrot, and ¼ cup chopped walnuts to the filling. Use thinner store-bought gyoza skins if you can find them. Fill and cook as directed. (Note that if you use gyoza skins, the cooking time at each stage will be a little bit shorter.)

Bean and Cheese Empanadas

MAKES: 12 empanadas (4 to 12 servings) | **TIME:** About 1 hour with cooked beans

Beans, cheese, and sturdy vegetables are traditional empanada fillings, but you can use all sorts of other things; see the variations. Serve them hot or at room temperature, with any salsa you like (pages 55 to 58 and 71 to 74).

>   1½ cups all-purpose flour, plus a little more for dusting
>   ½ cup masa harina, finely ground cornmeal, or more all-purpose flour
>   1½ teaspoons baking powder
>   1 teaspoon salt
>   ½ cup plus 2 tablespoons lard or good-quality vegetable oil
>   ½ cup milk
>   2½ cups well-seasoned cooked beans, like Refried Beans (page 393)
>   1 cup grated or crumbled queso fresco, Monterey Jack, or Cotija cheese

1. Combine the flour, masa harina, baking powder, and salt in a food processor; pulse for about 5 seconds. With the machine running, add ½ cup of the lard through the feed tube and process for 10 seconds. With the machine still running, add just enough water for the dough to form a ball, about ½ cup. Don't add more water than necessary; the dough should be fairly dry. Turn the dough out onto a lightly floured surface and knead by hand until smooth, just a minute or so.

2. Divide the dough into 12 pieces, roll into balls, and wrap in plastic or cover with a damp towel and let rest for at least 20 minutes. (You can refrigerate the dough overnight; be sure to let it come to room temperature before proceeding.) On a well-floured surface, roll each piece into a 6-inch circle, adding flour as necessary.

3. Heat the oven to 450°F. Combine the remaining lard with the milk. Put about ¼ cup of the beans on a dough circle, followed by a sprinkle of cheese. Brush the edges lightly (you can use you fingertip) with water, then fold each circle over. Seal the seam and press with the tines of a fork to close. Put on an ungreased baking sheet and brush lightly with the milk mixture. Bake until the dough is golden brown, about 20 minutes. Serve immediately or at room temperature.

 fast   make ahead V vegetarian

CHORIZO AND CHEESE EMPANADAS Substitute 1 pound crumbled or chopped cooked chorizo for the beans.

SHREDDED PORK EMPANADAS Instead of the beans and cheese, use about 3 cups Shredded Pork (page 697) to fill the empanadas. Proceed with the recipe.

Meatballs, Three Ways

MAKES: 6 to 8 servings | **TIME:** About 40 minutes

These are the ideal party food because they can be rolled in advance then cooked in a matter of minutes, and need only toothpicks to serve. I've given you three flavor profiles and four ways to cook them, so you can use the recipe a dozen times and never repeat exactly the same flavors. Serve with Aioli (page 70) or Fast Tomato Sauce (page 478) as a dip, if you like.

Other ground meat you can use: pork, lamb, veal, turkey, chicken, or duck, or a combination.

>   1   thick slice or 2 thin slices white bread
>   ½   cup milk
>   1   pound ground sirloin or your own ground beef
>   (see page 686)
>   ½   cup chopped onion
>   ½   cup grated Parmesan cheese
>   ¼   cup chopped fresh parsley
>   Salt and pepper

1. Soak the bread in the milk until soggy, about 5 minutes. Squeeze the milk from the bread and combine the bread with the meat, onion, Parmesan, parsley, and some salt and pepper. Cook up a bite in the microwave or a skillet and adjust the seasoning if necessary—this step is worth it until you get the hang of how much salt to add. Shape into 1-inch meatballs, handling them as gently as possible.

2. Cook the meatballs one of three ways: gently drop into a large pot of simmering stock or water for 10

minutes; put on a lightly greased baking sheet and bake in a 350°F oven for 7 to 8 minutes; or working in batches, cook in 2 tablespoons hot olive oil in a large skillet for about 8 minutes, turning every couple of minutes. Serve hot or warm.

SPANISH-STYLE ALMOND MEATBALLS Serve with Saffron Mayonnaise (page 70) or Fast Tomato Sauce (page 478): Omit the bread and milk. Substitute bread crumbs for the Parmesan. In Step 1, whisk together ¼ cup roughly chopped almonds and 1 egg in a small bowl; add to the meat mixture and proceed.

MEATBALLS, VIETNAMESE STYLE Serve with Thai Chile Sauce (page 66) or Soy Dipping Sauce (page 64): Omit the bread and milk. Use ground pork instead of beef; scallion instead of onion; cooked white rice (short-grain or sticky) instead of the Parmesan; and cilantro instead of parsley. In Step 1, beat 1 egg in a large bowl and stir in the rice. Carefully combine the remaining ingredients into the egg mixture, along with 1 tablespoon chopped fresh ginger or garlic if you like.

SKEWERED AND GRILLED MEATBALLS, THREE WAYS You can add vegetables or shrimp to the skewers too: Prepare a charcoal or gas grill for hot indirect cooking. Prepare through the end of Step 1. Put 1 to 3 meatballs on a skewer (depending on whether you're adding anything else to the skewer), brush with oil, and put on the grill. Cook, rotating carefully to cook and brown all sides, about 4 minutes.

Chicken Wings

MAKES: 6 to 8 servings | **TIME:** About 1½ hours, largely unattended

These aren't quite the real-deal version credited to the Anchor Bar in—where else?—Buffalo. Those are a deep-fried, two-pan, stove-to-oven affair (with margarine as the secret ingredient, no less). This roasting technique

Chicken Wings, page 127

(which is essentially oven-frying) skips the oleo and is virtually foolproof, with many opportunities for variation.

¼ cup relatively mild hot sauce like Frank's RedHot, Crystal, Cholula, or Louisiana (Tabasco will be very hot, but you might want to add a dash)

4 tablespoons (½ stick) butter, melted

2 tablespoons sherry vinegar or white wine vinegar

1 tablespoon chopped garlic

3 pounds chicken wings, rinsed and patted dry, cut into 3 pieces each (see page 127), wing tips saved for stock

2 tablespoons good-quality vegetable oil

Salt and pepper

8 to 12 celery stalks, cut into sticks (optional)

1 cup Blue Cheese Dressing (page 59; optional)

1. Heat the oven to 375°F. Combine the hot sauce, butter, vinegar, and garlic in a small bowl.

2. Put the chicken wings in a large roasting pan, drizzle with the oil, and sprinkle liberally with salt and pepper. Toss to coat, then spread the wings out in a single layer. (It's okay if they're a little crowded; they'll shrink.) Roast the wings, undisturbed, until the bottom of the pan is coated with fat and the wings are beginning to brown, about 30 minutes. Use a spoon to baste the wings with the drippings, then carefully pour or spoon the fat out of the pan. If the wings are still sticking to the bottom of the pan, return them to the oven for another 5 or 10 minutes, until they release easily.

3. Turn the wings over, baste again, then carefully spoon out any remaining fat. Return the wings to the oven until nicely browned, another 20 minutes or so (again, they'll release easily from the pan when they're ready).

4. Raise the oven temperature to 450°F. Carefully pour off any accumulated fat, then drizzle the wings with the hot sauce mixture and toss to coat. Spread them back out into a single layer and return them to the oven. Roast, tossing once or twice, until crisp all over, about 10 minutes more. Serve hot or at room temperature, with the celery and blue cheese dressing for dipping if you like.

GRILLED WINGS This cooking technique works for the main recipe or any of the following variations: Prepare a charcoal or gas grill for hot indirect cooking. Cook the wings on the cool part of the grill until crisp and just cooked through, about 20 minutes. Remove the wings from the grill and toss them with the sauce in a large bowl until coated. Return them to the grill directly over the heat for a final browning and crisping.

HONEY MUSTARD CHICKEN WINGS Omit the hot sauce, vinegar, and garlic; combine the butter with ¼ cup Dijon mustard and 2 tablespoons honey. Proceed with the recipe, using this sauce to coat the wings in Step 4. Serve with lemon wedges.

SMOKY CHILE LIME CHICKEN WINGS Omit the hot sauce, vinegar, garlic, and butter. Make the sauce by combining ¼ cup olive oil with 2 tablespoons fresh lime juice, 1 teaspoon grated lime zest, 2 tablespoons chili powder (to make your own, see page 32), and 1 tablespoon smoked paprika. Proceed with the recipe from Step 2, using the sauce to coat the wings in Step 4. Garnish with lime wedges and cilantro and serve with Avocado-Tomatillo Salsa (page 56).

SPICY PEANUT CHICKEN WINGS Omit the hot sauce and vinegar and replace the butter with coconut milk (to make your own, see page 372). Make the sauce by combining the coconut milk and garlic with 2 tablespoons peanut butter and 1 tablespoon curry powder (to make your own, see page 32). Proceed with the recipe from Step 2, using this sauce to coat the wings in Step 4. Serve with Raita (page 59) for dipping.

LEMON-GARLIC WINGS Omit the hot sauce, vinegar, and butter. Make the sauce by combining ½ cup olive oil with 3 tablespoons lemon juice, the garlic, and plenty of pepper. Proceed with the recipe from Step 2, using the sauce to coat the wings in Step 4. Serve with herbed Yogurt Sauce variation (page 59) for dipping.

---

8 OTHER SAUCES TO USE ON WINGS

Use 1 cup of any of these sauces to toss with the cooked wings in Step 4:

1. ¼ cup any Chile Paste (page 40), or more to taste, thinned with ½ cup melted butter or olive oil
2. Red or Green Curry Sauce (page 46)
3. Simplest Yogurt Sauce (page 59) mixed with 1 tablespoon curry powder (to make your own, see page 39)
4. Soy Dipping Sauce and Marinade (page 64)
5. Thai Chile Sauce (page 66)
6. Miso Dipping Sauce or any of its variations (page 66)
7. Barbecue Sauce or any of its variations (page 74); Korean-Style Barbecue Sauce is especially good
8. Teriyaki Sauce (page 76)

Chicken or Pork Satay

MAKES: 10 skewers (5 to 10 servings) | TIME: 30 minutes to 24 hours, depending on marinating time

It's almost impossible to find a more perfect meat for outdoor gatherings. Wooden skewers are the way to go so guests can help themselves and walk around. Or if you're plating the satay, put a little Cucumber Salsa, Thai Style (page 58) on the side.

1½ pounds boneless, skinless chicken thighs or boneless pork shoulder or loin

¼ cup soy sauce
¼ cup fish sauce, or more soy sauce
1 teaspoon ground cumin
1 teaspoon ground coriander
1 tablespoon peanut butter or tahini
1 teaspoon minced fresh ginger
1 tablespoon minced garlic
1 tablespoon sugar
1 tablespoon fresh lime or lemon juice or rice vinegar

1. Freeze the meat for 15 to 30 minutes, only to firm it up. Meanwhile, combine the remaining ingredients with ½ cup water in a large shallow bowl.
2. Slice the meat ⅛ inch thick (the length matters not). Toss into the marinade and stir to coat. Let sit at room temperature for up to an hour, or cover and refrigerate for up to 24 hours.

13 Other Fish, Poultry, and Meat Dishes That Work as Appetizers

1. Any kebabs
2. Shrimp (or Crawfish) Boil, Louisiana Style (page 545)
3. Gravlax (page 550)
4. Fish Escabeche (page 564)
5. Fish Kebabs (page 566)
6. Seared Scallops with Pan Sauce (page 577)
7. Baked Clams with Wasabi Bread Crumbs (page 580)
8. Bare Bones Crab Cakes (page 585)
9. Chicken MarkNuggets (page 630)
10. Roast Quail with Honey, Cumin, and Orange Juice (page 660)
11. Slow-Roasted Spareribs or its variations (page 698)
12. Homemade Breakfast (or Any Other Meal) Sausage (page 703)
13. Tuna Salad (page 804)

 fast make ahead vegetarian

30 Other Dishes You Can Serve as Sit-Down Appetizers

Obviously, you can make small portions of almost any savory dish and call it an appetizer. And of course virtually any pasta or soup qualifies as well. These are some of my personal favorites to serve at the start of a meal.

1. Any vegetable soup (pages 137–150)
2. Any green salad (pages 197–198)
3. Any artichoke recipe (pages 258–262)
4. Beet Rösti with Rosemary or its variations (page 265)
5. Any leek recipe (pages 301–303)
6. Chiles Rellenos (page 319)
7. Crisp Pan-Fried Potatoes, Spanish Style (page 332)
8. Potato Rösti (page 332)
9. Rich Spinach Pie (page 339)
10. Zucchini Pancakes (page 343)
11. Pan-Fried Green and/or Red Tomatoes (page 347)
12. Crisp Vegetable Pancakes, Korean Style (page 355)
13. Any Bean Burger, Fritter, or Griddle Cake (pages 413–417)
14. Falafel (page 415)
15. Any risotto (pages 440–441)
16. Fried Rice Balls (page 441)
17. Any polenta (see pages 460–461)
18. Any pasta (see the chapter starting on page 473)
19. Deep-Fried Seafood (page 538)
20. Any shrimp dish, really (pages 541–547)
21. Fish Fritters (page 564)
22. Sardines on the Grill (page 573)
23. Steamed Clams, Mussels, or Other Shellfish (page 579)
24. Boiled or Steamed Crab or Lobster (page 584)
25. Sautéed Soft-Shell Crabs, Four Ways (page 587)
26. Octopus with Tomatoes and Red Wine (page 590)
27. Duck Confit (page 655)
28. Roast Quail with Honey, Cumin, and Orange Juice (page 660)
29. Grilled or Broiled Squab, Vietnamese Style (page 661)
30. Any quiche or baked custard (pages 732–736)

3. If you're going to use wooden skewers, soak them in water for a few minutes while the meat rests. When you're ready to cook, turn on the broiler and position the rack about 4 inches below the heat or prepare a charcoal or gas grill for hot direct cooking. Thread the meat onto skewers without crowding. Broil or grill, turning once or twice, until browned all over, a total of 5 to 8 minutes.

4. While the meat is cooking, bring the marinade to a boil and reduce it for 3 to 5 minutes. Serve the skewers hot, with a bowl of the sauce alongside for dipping.

Ceviche

MAKES: 4 to 8 servings | TIME: 30 minutes

A popular South American preparation that uses acid to "cook" raw seafood. Scallops alone are easy,

taste great, and are the safest shellfish to eat raw. Pristinely fresh fillets of your local white ocean fish are also lovely. Try cooked seafood if you prefer; it's like marinating poached or grilled shrimp, squid, or the scallops. Serve individual portions on a bed of salad greens or in lettuce cups (see page 121). For finger food all you need are a few Fried Tortilla Chips (page 110).

1 pound perfectly fresh sea scallops, tough adductor muscle removed if you like, cut into ¼-inch cubes, or a mixture of fish (see the headnote)
½ cup chopped red bell pepper
1 teaspoon grated lime zest
¼ cup fresh lime juice
Salt
Cayenne
Chopped fresh cilantro for garnish

 fast   make ahead   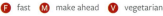 vegetarian

1. Toss together everything but the cilantro and let sit at room temperature for 15 minutes.

2. Taste, adjust the seasoning, and serve, garnished with the cilantro.

SASHIMI Use only extremely fresh ocean fish like sea bass or arctic char (for more information on sustainable fish, see page 531): Buy a 12-ounce fillet of very fresh fish, ideally in a piece of even thickness. Hold a very sharp, clean, narrow-bladed knife at a 45-degree angle to the fish and trim a triangle from one end of the fillet (you can chop this and serve it as tartar). Starting with that angled side, slice the fish, without sawing, into strips as thin as you can manage. Continue cutting slices until the slices become too short at the other end (chop the remainder too). If the fish sticks to the knife, rinse and dry the knife. Serve the slices immediately with soy sauce for dipping, and wasabi.

POKE Usually made with tuna but there are more sustainable options, too; see above variation. Expand this into a heartier starter or main course by adding cooked white or brown rice, avocado, or anything else you like: Cut 1 pound very fresh sushi-grade tuna or salmon into ½-inch cubes. Toss with ¼ cup Sesame-Soy Dipping Sauce and Marinade (page 64), ¼ cup chopped scallions, and 2 tablespoons chopped macadamia nuts (optional). Refrigerate for up to several hours. Garnish with crumbled toasted nori (see page 448) and serve with rice crackers.

Soups

CHAPTER AT A GLANCE

Vegetable Soups 137

Bean Soups 151

Grain Soups 154

Noodle Soups 157

Seafood Soups 161

Chicken Soups 164

Meat Soups 166

Stocks 171

Making homemade soup is only marginally more involved than throwing some stuff in a pot. It's almost impossible to mess up. And while it simmers away on the stove, the smell of home cooking wafting through the house, soup proves it can deliver all the drama of a full day in the kitchen with a fraction of the effort. Which is all good news, since soups are the most restorative, feel-good dishes in your repertoire.

Soups are "built" via a process that's rarely laborious or precise. My attitude toward measuring is more casual than with other dishes—there's lots of room to improvise based on what you've got handy (see page 140), and the timing is always flexible. Some recipes in this chapter take 30 minutes. Almost all can be made ahead and successfully reheated; others frontload your activity, then after some prep and assembly you let the ingredients do their thing for an hour or so while you go do yours.

I cannot deny that starting with homemade stock benefits every soup. (Stocks start on page 171.) But that doesn't mean you can't get excellent results with plain water (see "Using Water Instead of Stock" below). So please don't let lack of stock be a barrier to jumping into this chapter. Instead focus on how much you'll be enjoying the simple pleasure of really good soup.

Using Water Instead of Stock

All stocks are basically infused water. In the rare cases where you really need stock to do the trick, I say so, or only include stock as an option in the ingredient list. So you can use water in all the other soups, as long as you add sufficient aromatics and other flavorings—wine, extra vegetables, soy sauce, dried mushrooms, or herbs, for example—and cook the mixture long enough for a flavorful liquid to develop. It won't be quite as rich as with stock, but it will still be much better than anything dehydrated or canned.

THE BASICS OF BUILDING SOUPS

The recipes all include detailed, specific directions. Here are some considerations before you get started.

PREPARING FOODS FOR SOUP Cutting vegetables or other ingredients to about the same small-ish size allows them to all cook at the same pace to produce a soup that cooks quickly and is easy to eat.

HEATING STOCK (OR WATER) IN A SEPARATE POT BEFORE ADDING TO SOUP I used to advocate this as a way to save a few minutes—and it will—but then you've got another pot to wash. Your choice.

USING LEFTOVERS IN SOUP One of my first cooking teachers made cream-of-something-or-other almost every night with puréed leftover vegetables. Use any cooked food with a flavor that doesn't conflict with the basic seasonings of your soup: pasta, rice, bread, meat, fish, poultry, vegetables—even mashed potatoes—can contribute mightily.

PURÉEING SOUP The best tool to use is an immersion blender, which works right in the pot. Transferring the soup to an upright blender is second choice; just be careful to work in batches so the container is never filled more than halfway, to avoid the hot liquid bursting out of the top when you turn the machine

 fast make ahead **V** vegetarian

on. If the soup is too thick after puréeing, stir in some water, stock, or half-and-half to add flavor, enhance texture, and thin the soup all at the same time. If the results are too thin, see "Giving Soups More Body" on page 146.

STORING SOUP Most soups freeze brilliantly for a few months, so it's handy to double or even quadruple a recipe to save some for a rainy day. Some advice for those times you know you'll have leftovers: It's better to avoid freezing—or even refrigerating—a soup once you've added starches like rice and pasta, which continue to absorb liquid, even when cold; if possible store these foods separately and add them when reheating. Nor should you freeze soups based heavily on dairy; they're likely to curdle during reheating. They're fine to eat but might look a little funny.

Vegetable Soups

I purposefully made this category of hearty plant-based soups large and first in the chapter since they're the easiest to master. Plus you can always bulk them up with beans, fish, poultry, meat, or cheese. Using vegetable stock or water keeps them vegetarian or often vegan; for meatier undertones without actually using meat, try chicken or beef stock.

"Boiled Water"

MAKES: 4 servings | **TIME:** 20 minutes

Soup could not get any simpler than bread soaked in garlic broth. Whether you're a seasoned home cook or just learning, you'll make this recipe forever.

6 to 10   cloves garlic, lightly crushed
     1   bay leaf

        Salt and pepper
    ¼   cup olive oil
     4   thick slices French or Italian bread
        (slightly stale bread is fine)
    ½   cup grated Parmesan or pecorino Romano
        cheese
        Chopped fresh parsley for garnish

1. Combine 4 cups water with the garlic, bay leaf, and some salt and pepper in a large pot. Bring to a boil, cover partially, and turn the heat to very low. Let the liquid bubble gently for 15 minutes.

2. Meanwhile, put the oil in a large skillet over medium heat. When it's hot, brown the slices of bread in the oil, turning once, about 5 minutes total.

3. Put the bread in bowls and top with the cheese. Strain the soup into the bowls, garnish with parsley, and serve right away.

ROASTED GARLIC SOUP Substitute 10 or more cloves Roasted Garlic (page 294) for the crushed garlic. Or put the crushed garlic in the skillet with the oil and cook over medium-low heat until fragrant and just starting to color, about 4 minutes. Fish out the garlic, mince it, and add it to the pot in Step 1.

TOMATO-GARLIC SOUP Add 2 cups chopped tomatoes (canned is fine; don't drain) in Step 1. Don't strain the soup, but fish out the garlic and bay leaf before serving.

LIME-GARLIC-COCONUT SOUP Omit the oil, bread, and cheese. Juice and zest 2 limes. In Step 1, use one 14-ounce can coconut milk (or make your own; see page 372 and use about 1½ cups) and 3 cups of water, along with the lime zest. Omit Step 2. In Step 3, add the lime juice to the soup right before straining. If you like, ladle the soup over a small mound of cooked plain white rice, bean threads, or rice vermicelli. Garnish with cilantro instead of parsley.

Super-Easy 4-Ingredient Soups

The simplest soups need no recipe. Just work through the columns from left to right, adding the next ingredient after the previous becomes tender or cooks through. Taste and season with salt and pepper as you go.

SOUP	1	2	3	4	OPTIONAL ADD-INS
Miso Soup	4 cups Dashi (page 179) or water, hot but not boiling	1 tablespoon sesame oil	⅓ cup any miso, thinned with some of the dashi before adding	¼ cup chopped scallions; 1 cup sliced shiitake mushroom caps	4 ounces chopped soft or silken tofu; 1 cup rehydrated wakame or other seaweed (see page 336)
Potato and Leek Soup	4 cups chicken, beef, or vegetable stock (pages 174–178) or water, boiling	2 to 3 table-spoons butter	3 potatoes, any type, peeled and chopped	3 leeks, white and light green parts only, rinsed well and sliced	1½ cups drained canned or cooked chickpeas or white beans (page 390)
Egg Drop Soup	4 cups any stock (pages 174–180), at a slow bubble	1 tablespoon sesame oil	4 beaten eggs, slowly poured in while stir-ring so the eggs "scramble" in the stock	¼ cup chopped cilantro or scallion	1 tablespoon soy sauce, or more to taste
Stracciatella	4 cups Chicken Stock (page 176), at a slow bubble	1 tablespoon chopped garlic; 2 tablespoons olive oil	4 beaten eggs, slowly poured in while stir-ring so the eggs "scramble" in the stock	¾ cup grated Parmesan cheese	¼ cup chopped fresh basil or parsley
Wonton Soup	4 cups any stock (pages 174–180), boiling	1 tablespoon each minced gin-ger and sesame oil	2 cups sliced cab-bage or bok choy	12 to 24 freshly made or frozen wontons or gyoza	¼ cup chopped cilantro or scal-lion; 1 tablespoon soy sauce, or more to taste
Split Pea and Ham Soup	6 cups chicken stock (page 176), or water, boiling	½ cup each chopped carrot, celery, and onion	2 cups green split peas, rinsed and picked over; 1 smoked ham hock	2 tablespoons butter	Real or Cubed Croutons (page 799) for garnish
Beef and Barley Soup	8 cups beef or veal stock (page 176), boiling	2 tablespoons chopped garlic; 2 tablespoons olive oil	1 cup chopped carrot or parsnip; 1 cup pearled barley	8 ounces sirloin steak, chopped into small cubes	Worcestershire sauce, to taste

 F fast   **M** make ahead   **V** vegetarian

"Boiled Water," page 137

Cream of Mushroom Soup

MAKES: 4 servings | **TIME:** 30 minutes

This type of soup might be falling out of style, but I still love the rich, pure taste. The rice or potato makes the soup creamy and more substantial, but you could skip it. But even ¼ cup of cream is enough to lighten the color and smooth the texture of the puréed soup.

Other vegetables you can use: asparagus, fennel, celery, watercress, spinach, sorrel, cauliflower, broccoli, tomatoes, carrots, or more flavorful mushrooms like cremini or shiitake

	About 1 pound button mushrooms, trimmed and chopped
½	cup white rice, or 1 baking potato, peeled and cut into quarters
4	cups vegetable stock (to make your own, see page 174) or water
	Salt and pepper
¼ to 1	cup heavy cream or half-and-half
	Chopped fresh parsley or chives for garnish

1. Combine the mushrooms, rice, and stock in a large pot over medium-high heat. Bring to a boil, then adjust the heat so the mixture bubbles steadily. Cook until the vegetables are very tender, about 15 minutes.

2. Cool slightly, then purée through a food mill or with an upright or immersion blender. (At this point, you can refrigerate the soup, covered, for up to 2 days; reheat before proceeding.)

3. Return the soup to the pot and reheat over medium-low. Sprinkle with salt and pepper, then add the cream. Taste and adjust the seasoning. Heat through again, garnish, and serve right away.

ROBUST CREAM OF MUSHROOM SOUP A simple and noticeable improvement: Reduce the stock to 2 cups and soak 1 ounce dried porcini mushrooms in 2 cups boiling water. Add the reconstituted mushrooms (see page 304) along with their soaking water in Step 1.

Puréed Vegetable Soup Without Cream

MAKES: 4 servings | **TIME:** 45 minutes

To dress up a rustic vegetable soup to serve as a first course for a special occasion or fancy dinner, try puréeing it until velvety. Fibrous vegetables like celery might need to be strained, but that's simple enough. For this recipe, try carrots, squash, sweet potatoes, cauliflower, broccoli, Jerusalem artichokes, or peas.

Using an Immersion Blender

An immersion blender lets you purée soup right in the pot. Remove the pot from the heat. Hold the blender upright and make sure the blade is fully immersed to prevent splattering.

 fast make ahead  vegetarian

Soup on the Fly

Follow your gut, choosing an ingredient or two from each step. Taste as you go, season with salt and pepper as needed, and soon you'll have soup. To use raw Main Ingredients—like lentils, vegetables, or meat—let the soup boil until they're cooked through, up to 30 minutes.

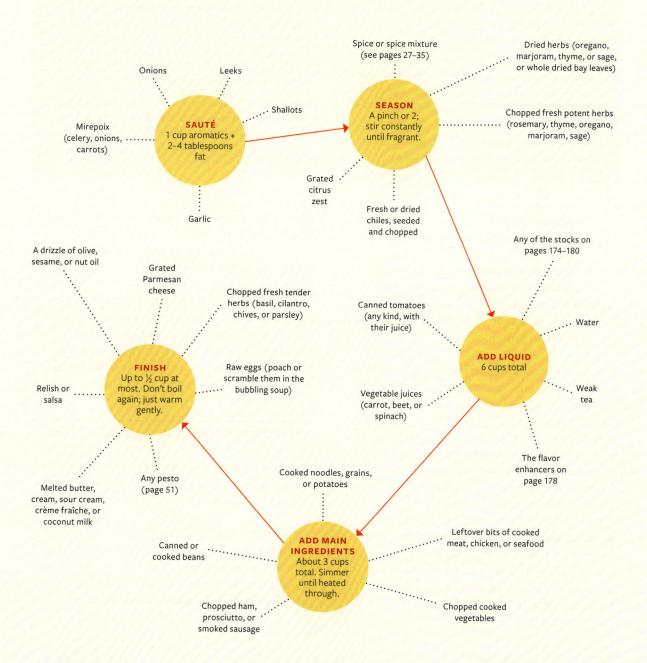

Onions

Leeks

Shallots

Mirepoix (celery, onions, carrots)

SAUTÉ
1 cup aromatics + 2–4 tablespoons fat

Garlic

Spice or spice mixture (see pages 27–35)

Dried herbs (oregano, marjoram, thyme, or sage, or whole dried bay leaves)

SEASON
A pinch or 2; stir constantly until fragrant.

Chopped fresh potent herbs (rosemary, thyme, oregano, marjoram, sage)

Grated citrus zest

Fresh or dried chiles, seeded and chopped

Any of the stocks on pages 174–180

A drizzle of olive, sesame, or nut oil

Grated Parmesan cheese

Chopped fresh tender herbs (basil, cilantro, chives, or parsley)

Canned tomatoes (any kind, with their juice)

Water

ADD LIQUID
6 cups total

FINISH
Up to ½ cup at most. Don't boil again; just warm gently.

Relish or salsa

Raw eggs (poach or scramble them in the bubbling soup)

Vegetable juices (carrot, beet, or spinach)

Weak tea

Melted butter, cream, sour cream, crème fraîche, or coconut milk

Any pesto (page 51)

Cooked noodles, grains, or potatoes

The flavor enhancers on page 178

Canned or cooked beans

ADD MAIN INGREDIENTS
About 3 cups total. Simmer until heated through.

Leftover bits of cooked meat, chicken, or seafood

Chopped ham, prosciutto, or smoked sausage

Chopped cooked vegetables

Cream of Something Soup (and a Note on Puréeing)

Take a look at Cream of Mushroom Soup (141) as an example, and follow the basic steps here:

1. Choose the vegetable or vegetables you want to become soup. For a nonvegetarian soup, note that poultry and meat aren't particularly appetizing puréed, but seafood is—as in lobster, shrimp, or crab bisque.

2. You can cook aromatics in a little oil or butter before adding the stock. Combine the stock, vegetables, and grains or potatoes (if using for thickness), and bring to a boil. Cook at a gentle bubble until the vegetables are quite tender.

3. Purée the soup. You can use various tools to purée your soup; The smoothest purées are done in a blender, in the pot with an immersion blender, or with a food mill; a food processor or ricer does a good job but doesn't get the soup velvety smooth. A potato masher or fork gives you the lumpiest results. For the ultimate smooth soup, you can pass the purée through a fine-meshed strainer, but the trade-off is that you'll strain out all the fiber and body.

4. Reheat and add enough cream to smooth the purée and lighten the soup, up to 1 or so cup; use water or stock to thin it further. Taste and adjust the seasoning, and garnish with fresh herbs. Serve right away or chill for a few hours and serve cold.

---

2 tablespoons butter
2 shallots or 1 small onion, chopped
1½ pounds vegetable (see headnote), sliced
6 cups vegetable stock (to make your own, see page 174) or water
   Salt and pepper
2 tablespoons chopped fresh parsley, mint, dill, or chives for garnish

1. Put the butter in a large pot over medium-high heat. When the butter is melted, add the shallots and vegetables. Cook until they start to soften but don't color, about 5 minutes.

2. Add the stock and bring it to a boil. Lower the heat so that the stock bubbles gently and cook, stirring occasionally, until it thickens slightly and the vegetables are fully tender, 10 to 15 minutes more.

3. Use an immersion blender to purée the soup in the pan. Or cool the mixture slightly and working in batches, pour it into a blender and purée carefully. Cool and refrigerate, covered, to serve it cold; it will keep for a day or so. Or reheat over low heat to serve hot. Taste and adjust the seasoning before serving either way. Serve garnished with chervil or parsley.

PURÉED TURNIP OR CELERY ROOT SOUP A bit of potato mellows out the flavor so it's not overpowering: Use 1 pound peeled and chopped turnips or celery root and 1 peeled and chopped all-purpose potato for the vegetables.

VICHYSSOISE A French classic that is especially great with homemade chicken stock: Reduce the stock to 4 cups and use 3 leeks, white and green parts only, rinsed well and sliced, and 3 all-purpose potatoes, peeled and chopped. Proceed with the recipe and serve cold, garnished with chopped chives.

---

7 TERRIFIC COMBINATIONS FOR PURÉED SOUPS

For times you want some kick, follow the recipe for Puréed Vegetable Soup Without Cream (page 141) with these combinations:

1. **Puréed Broccoli-Basil Soup:** Use chopped broccoli. Add ½ cup chopped fresh basil when you purée it. Garnish with a drizzle of olive oil and some shaved or grated Parmesan.

2. **Puréed Butternut Squash–Coconut Soup:** Use peeled and chopped butternut squash and

 **F** fast **M** make ahead **V** vegetarian

Puréed Vegetable Soup
Without Cream, page 140,
made with peas and
garnished with mint

substitute 2 cups coconut milk (to make your own, see page 372) for 2 cups of the stock. Add 2 tablespoons chopped garlic and 1½ tablespoons curry powder (to make your own, see page 32) in Step 1. Garnish with fried sliced shallots or garlic and chopped fresh cilantro.

3. **Puréed Roasted Red Pepper Soup:** Use 5 or 6 Roasted Red Peppers (page 318) and 1 large all-purpose potato, peeled and chopped, for the vegetable. Add 2 teaspoons smoked paprika and 1 tablespoon chopped garlic in Step 1. Garnish with chopped fresh parsley or cilantro.

4. **Puréed Winter Vegetable Soup:** Use equal parts peeled and chopped turnip, rutabaga, and parsnip for the vegetable. A small piece of fresh horseradish along with the other vegetables would be a welcome addition. Garnish with chopped fresh parsley or thyme.

5. **Puréed Sweet-and-Sour Beet Soup:** Use 12 ounces trimmed, peeled, and chopped beets and 12 ounces peeled and chopped all-purpose potato. Add 3 tablespoons good red wine vinegar, or to taste, when you purée it. Garnish with some crumbled goat cheese or a dollop of sour cream and chopped fresh chives.

6. **Puréed Carrot-Ginger Soup:** Use carrots. Add 1 tablespoon minced fresh ginger in Step 1. Season with soy sauce and sesame oil or drizzle a bit of cream or yogurt into each bowl before serving.

7. **Puréed Cauliflower-Saffron Soup:** Use chopped cauliflower. Add ¼ teaspoon saffron threads to Step 1 and 1 cup cream when you purée it. Garnish with pomegranate seeds or toasted pine nuts.

Tomato Soup

MAKES: 4 servings | **TIME:** 30 minutes

Many ways to go here: Tomato paste turns tomato soup into a year-round proposition since it improves mediocre fruit. Following the main recipe is a variation for the best summer tomatoes. Or see the variations for using fresh summer fruit or canned tomatoes, for add-ins, and for puréeing.

2	**tablespoons olive oil**
2	**tablespoons tomato paste**
1	**large onion, halved and sliced**
1	**carrot, chopped**
	Salt and pepper
3	**cups peeled, seeded, and chopped tomatoes (preferably plum; include their juices)**
1	**teaspoon chopped fresh thyme or ½ teaspoon dried**
2 to 3	**cups vegetable stock (to make your own, see page 174) or water**
1	**teaspoon sugar (optional)**
	Chopped fresh parsley or basil for garnish

1. Put the oil in a large pot over medium heat. When it's hot, add the tomato paste and let it cook for a minute, then add the onion and carrot. Sprinkle with salt and pepper and cook, stirring, until the vegetables begin to soften, about 5 minutes.

2. Add the tomatoes and thyme and cook, stirring occasionally, until the tomatoes break up, 10 to 15 minutes. Add the stock, stir, and bring to a boil, then adjust the heat so the mixture bubbles gently. Cook until the flavors meld, about 5 minutes. (At this point, you can refrigerate the soup, covered, for up to 2 days; reheat before proceeding.) Taste and adjust the seasoning; add the sugar to balance the acidity if you'd like. If the mixture is too thick, add a little more stock or water. Garnish with the herbs and serve right away.

SUMMERTIME FRESH TOMATO SOUP Excellent chilled: Omit the tomato paste. Increase the chopped tomatoes to 4 cups and use super-ripe, flavorful tomatoes in season.

WINTERTIME TOMATO SOUP Substitute 1 cup loosely packed dried tomatoes (about 2 ounces; preferably the kind not packed in oil) and 1 28-ounce can whole peeled

 fast   make ahead   vegetarian

tomatoes for the fresh tomatoes. Soak the dried tomatoes in 1 cup boiling water until softened. Remove the canned tomatoes from their juice and chop them. Add the reserved tomato juice with the tomato paste and cook until reduced by half, stirring frequently. Proceed with the recipe, adding the tomato soaking water along with the stock.

TOMATO-GARLIC SOUP Add 2 tablespoons chopped garlic or 8 to 10 cloves Roasted Garlic (page 294) along with the onion.

SMOOTH TOMATO SOUP Works for the main recipe and the above variations: Increase the tomato to 4 cups and reduce the stock to 1 cup. When the soup is done, purée it carefully in a blender, with an immersion blender, or through a food mill. Reheat, garnish (preferably with My Kind of Croutons, page 801), and serve.

TOMATO AND BREAD SOUP Brush both sides of 4 thick slices Italian or French bread (slightly stale is fine) with olive oil; broil or grill until nicely browned and crisp. Rub a large clove garlic on each slice of bread if you like. Break or cut the bread into pieces in the bowls and pour the finished soup over the top. Garnish with grated Parmesan.

Onion Soup

MAKES: 4 servings | TIME: About 1 hour

Despite what restaurants would have you think, onion soup is all about the incredible amount of flavor you can coax from onions and well-made stock—not about toast piled with gooey cheese. Though beef stock is often the base, I prefer a deep, rich vegetable stock with a few dried mushrooms added to the pot (page 174).

  4 large onions, peeled
  4 tablespoons (½ stick) butter
  5 cups vegetable stock (to make your own, see page 174) or water

  2 or 3 sprigs fresh thyme or a pinch dried
  2 or 3 sprigs fresh parsley
  1 bay leaf
  2 tablespoons cognac or other brandy (optional) Salt and pepper
  4 My Kind of Croutons (page 801), made with bread slices and butter (optional)
  1 cup grated Parmesan, Gruyère, or Emmental cheese (optional)

1. Halve the onions top to bottom and slice them as thinly as you can manage. Put the butter in a large pot over medium heat. When the butter melts, add the onions and cook, stirring occasionally, until very soft and beginning to brown, 30 to 45 minutes. Adjust the heat so they slowly turn into a melting mass and don't brown too fast. Don't rush.

2. Heat the oven to 400°F if you're using the croutons and cheese. Add the stock, raise the heat to medium-high, and bring to a boil. Adjust the heat so the mixture bubbles gently. Add the thyme, parsley, and bay leaf and the cognac if you're using it, sprinkle with salt and pepper, and cook, stirring occasionally, until the soup thickens a bit, about 15 minutes. Remove the bay leaf and herb sprigs. (At this point, you can refrigerate the soup, covered, for up to 2 days; reheat before proceeding.)

3. If you're using the croutons and cheese, put 4 ovenproof bowls in a roasting pan or on a sturdy cookie sheet. Put a crouton in each bowl, ladle over the soup, and top with cheese. Bake for 5 to 10 minutes, just long enough to melt the cheese. Serve immediately.

Corn Chowder

MAKES: 4 servings | TIME: About 1 hour

I know corn on the cob is available most of the year, but promise me you'll make this soup only in the summer, when the corn is as fresh and sweet as possible.

6 ears fresh corn
Salt and pepper
4 tablespoons (½ stick) butter or ¼ cup good-quality vegetable oil
½ cup chopped scallions
½ teaspoon sugar
¼ cup all-purpose flour
4 cups half-and-half or milk
My Kind of Croutons (page 801), made with Corn Bread (page 769) for garnish (optional)

1. Shuck the corn. Stand each ear up in a bowl and use a knife to cut off the kernels (see page 283). Put the corncobs and 2 cups water in a large pot with a tight-fitting lid over medium-high heat. Sprinkle with salt and pepper. Bring to a boil, then adjust the heat so the water bubbles gently. Cover and cook, stirring occasionally, until the water is cloudy, about 30 minutes. Leave the cobs in the pot until you are ready to make the soup, then discard them and save the broth.

Giving Soups More Body

I'd rather eat a thinner bowl of fresh-tasting soup than one thickened gratuitously with flour or cornstarch. But for those times when you want something a little heartier, here are the basic rules for making a good soup thicker.

Potato: If you're going to purée the soup after cooking, peel and dice an all-purpose or baking potato and add it at the same time as the stock or water. To thicken a chunky soup, mash cooked potatoes a bit with a fork first (leftover mashed potatoes will do the trick). A few minutes before serving, stir them into the pot until completely dissolved and heated through.

Pasta: Cooking small amounts of noodles in soup releases thickening starches. Be sure you have a little extra liquid and room in the pot to accommodate the noodles as they swell, and serve the soup immediately; the noodles will continue to absorb liquid and eventually turn to mush.

Grains: White rice is the obvious candidate, but any whole grain will do. To increase body and richness, add a small quantity of grain at the beginning of the recipe; cook until it's falling apart, then purée (or not).

Legumes: A flavorful way to thicken soup without using dairy, especially if you purée them first. White beans are the most versatile and creamy. Like grains, cooked legumes can be added to already-made soups as an afterthought, or cooked along with the other ingredients until tender, then puréed or mashed. Silken tofu puréed with the soup will thicken it quite a bit. And on occasion, I like to make a roux (see page 83) with chickpea flour.

Bread: If possible, use stale bread, which absorbs broth without disintegrating. Croutons are ideal, but bread crumbs work well too. And few things are simpler or more satisfying than slipping a piece of good toast into a bowl and pouring a ladleful of soup over it.

Butter: For unsurpassed velvety texture and heightened flavor, cut up a tablespoon or two of cold butter. When the soup is ready to serve, turn off the heat, add to the pot, and stir until melted.

Eggs: A convenient way to add both creaminess and richness to soup. You have two choices: Stir beaten eggs into bubbling soup and you'll get egg drop soup. The eggs scramble softly and remain visible, adding a distinct meatiness to many soups, especially brothy ones. Or use eggs strictly as a thickener: First beat a couple of yolks, whisk in about a cup of the hot soup, then gradually stir the yolk mixture back into the soup. Treated this way, the eggs add body to the soup with a smooth texture.

Nuts and seeds: A spoonful of peanut butter, tahini, or another type of nut butter adds distinctive flavor and body. Obviously use your judgment when to avoid clashing with the seasoning, or use cashew butter, which is pretty neutral.

 fast make ahead V vegetarian

2. Put the butter or oil in a large pot over medium-high heat. When the butter foams or the oil is hot, add the scallion and sugar and cook, stirring occasionally, until soft, about 1 minute. Lower the heat to medium and stir in the flour. Cook, stirring constantly with a whisk or a wooden spoon, until the mixture starts to turn golden and the flour smells toasted, just a couple of minutes. Add the milk and the reserved corncob broth and raise the heat to medium-high. Stir or whisk constantly until the roux is dissolved and the soup starts to thicken, about 2 minutes.

3. Stir in the corn kernels and any accumulated juices and bring to a boil, then adjust the heat so that the soup bubbles gently. Cook, stirring occasionally, until the corn is tender and the soup has thickened, 10 to 15 minutes. Taste, adjust the seasoning, and serve right away, garnished with croutons if you like.

ROASTED CORN CHOWDER Heat the oven to 400°F. Rub the shucked corn with a little olive oil. Sprinkle with salt and pepper and put on a rimmed baking sheet. Roast the corn, turning frequently, until the kernels start to brown, 15 to 25 minutes. When the corn is cool enough to handle, cut off the kernels and proceed with the recipe.

CHEESY CORN CHOWDER Prepare either the main recipes or the preceding variation through Step 2. In Step 3, along with the corn, add ½ cup grated cheese like Parmesan, sharp cheddar, or hard goat cheese.

Minestrone

MAKES: 4 to 6 servings | **TIME:** 45 to 60 minutes

I've written this recipe so that almost anything goes. You choose the mix of vegetables. Chop them fairly small—½-inch bits—for faster cooking and easy eating. Larger chunks make it a knife-fork-and-spoon affair. Nonvegetable add-ins might include the ends on prosciutto or other types of ham.

4	tablespoons olive oil
1	onion, chopped
1	carrot, chopped
1	celery stalk, peeled (see page 279) and chopped
½	cup chopped prosciutto or other ham (optional)
1½ to 2	cups hard vegetables like potatoes, winter squash, parsnips, or turnips, peeled if necessary and chopped
	Salt and pepper
6	cups vegetable stock (to make your own, see page 174) or water
1	cup peeled, seeded, and chopped tomato (canned is fine; include the juices)
1½ to 2	cups soft vegetables like green beans, cooked beans, zucchini or summer squash, or dark leafy greens like kale or collards, chopped
½	cup chopped fresh parsley
	Grated Parmesan cheese for garnish

1. Put 3 tablespoons of the oil into a large pot over medium heat. When it's hot, add the onion, carrot, and celery. Cook, stirring, until the vegetables soften, about 5 minutes. Add the ham if you're using it and cook, stirring, until golden, about 3 minutes more.

2. Add the hard vegetables and sprinkle with salt and pepper. Cook, stirring, for a minute or 2, then add the stock and the tomato; bring to a boil, then lower the heat so the mixture bubbles gently. Cook, stirring occasionally, until the vegetables are fairly soft and the tomato is broken up, about 15 minutes. (At this point, you can refrigerate the soup, covered, for up to 2 days; proceed to Step 3 and add the tender vegetables as the soup reheats.)

3. Add the soft vegetables and parsley and adjust the heat again so the mixture bubbles steadily. Cook until all the vegetables are very tender, 5 to 10 minutes. Taste and adjust the seasoning, add the remaining tablespoon oil, and serve right away. Pass the cheese at the table if you're using it.

PISTOU Pesto with a whole lot of garlic is traditional here: Stir in ½ cup or more of freshly made Traditional Pesto or any of its variations (page 51) just before serving.

PASTA E FAGIOLI (PASTA AND BEAN SOUP) Use about half as much of the hard and soft vegetables and add 2 cups cooked beans—kidney, white, borlotti, chickpeas, cannellini, or a mixture—with the soft vegetables. With them, add ½ to 1 cup small uncooked pasta like tubetti or larger pasta broken into bits. About 5 minutes before serving, stir in a teaspoon minced garlic or more, to taste.

RIBOLITTA (WHITE BEAN AND BREAD SOUP) Purée 1 cup cooked cannellini beans (drained canned beans are fine) with some of their cooking liquid (or water if using canned) into a thick paste. For each bowl, toast a thick slice of rustic Tuscan or other Italian bread and set in the bottom of the bowl. In Step 3, add the puréed beans to the bubbling soup. Thin with a little more water or stock if necessary. To serve, pour the hot soup over the bread and drizzle with a little olive oil.

MULLIGATAWNY (SPICY INDIAN VEGETABLE SOUP) Leave this chunky and brothy or purée it: Substitute good-quality vegetable oil for the olive oil. Omit the ham. Add 1 teaspoon each ground cumin and turmeric and cook with the onion in Step 1. Add 2 tablespoons curry powder (to make your own, see page 32) along with the soft vegetables. Substitute cilantro for the parsley and omit the Parmesan.

CABBAGE-AND-SOMETHING SOUP Take this in any number of directions, depending on what you've got: Substitute butter for 3 tablespoons of the oil. Omit the carrot and celery and sauté 1 pound shredded cabbage (about 1 small head) with the onion instead. With the stock, add 2 potatoes, peeled and chopped, and 1 tablespoon caraway seeds, or 2 cups sliced shitake mushrooms. Garnish with sautéed apples.

Frozen Vegetables in Soup

Yes you can—and should. Especially when they're going to cook for a long time. The frozen vegetables that work best in soups are: artichokes, broccoli, butternut squash, cauliflower, collards and kale, corn (except in the corn chowder on page 145), peas, and spinach. Stock a few bags in your freezer, complement them with fresh vegetables if possible, and you can put together a meal with little time and effort.

The rules for buying frozen vegetables in general are described on page 237. There are two good ways to use them in soup: Straight from the bag; you'll need to increase the cooking time to compensate for their chilling effect. Or to heighten the flavor you can cook the vegetables lightly in oil to thaw them before adding the liquid.

5 MORE TAKES ON MINESTRONE

The tomato is a given, but other vegetables are completely flexible.

1. **Summer Minestrone:** Use fresh corn kernels, zucchini or summer squash, and garnish with chopped fresh basil, mint, or thyme.
2. **Autumn Minestrone:** Use mostly cubes of butternut or other winter squash, and garnish with chopped fresh sage and chopped toasted hazelnuts.
3. **Green Minestrone:** Use peas, asparagus, green beans, and ¾ cup mixed chopped fresh herbs like parsley, basil, dill, mint, chervil, and chives.
4. **Spicy Chile Minestrone:** Use roasted, cleaned, and chopped poblanos (see page 43), minced jalapeño, a mix of potato, corn, and chayote or any summer squash, and cilantro. Garnish with crumbled queso fresco.
5. **Sausage and Lentil Minestrone:** Replace the prosciutto with 8 ounces hot or sweet Italian sausage, casings removed and crumbled; in place of the hard vegetables, add 1 cup brown or green lentils, rinsed and picked over.

 fast make ahead vegetarian

Pasta e Fagioli, back
left and right, and
Mulligatawny, front

Gazpacho, Fast and Simple

MAKES: 4 servings | **TIME:** About 20 minutes

What we Americans generally consider gazpacho is pretty close to what's eaten in Spain: tomatoes and cucumber, thickened with bread, then punched up with vinegar and garlic.

- 2 pounds tomatoes, roughly chopped, or 1 28-ounce can (include the juices)
- 1 cucumber, peeled, seeded if you like (see page 287), and chopped
- 2 or 3 slices bread, a day or two old, crusts removed, torn into small pieces
- ¼ cup olive oil, plus more for garnish
- 2 tablespoons sherry vinegar or red wine vinegar, or more to taste
- 1 teaspoon minced garlic
  Salt and pepper

1. Combine the tomatoes, cucumber, bread, oil, vinegar, and garlic with 1 cup water in a blender; process until smooth. If the gazpacho seems too thick, thin with additional water.

2. Taste and adjust the seasoning. Serve immediately, garnished with a drizzle of oil. Or refrigerate and serve within a couple of hours.

CHUNKY GAZPACHO Sort of like soupy salsa—in a good way: Chop the tomatoes, cucumber, and bread into as small pieces as you like, collecting all of the juices you can as you work. Toss together in a large bowl with the remaining ingredients and 1 cup water or dry white wine. Stir for a minute or 2 to combine thoroughly.

GAZPACHO, 7 MORE WAYS

Take the simple blend-and-serve formula from the main recipe—which is perfect for hot summer suppers—into some different directions. For the ingredient prep, peel, seed and chop everything as necessary, collecting any juices as you work.

1. **Spicy Gazpacho:** Use 2 pounds fresh tomatoes, or 1 28-ounce can (include the juices); 1 cucumber; 2 or 3 slices bread; ¼ cup olive oil; 1 teaspoon minced garlic. Garnish with minced fresh hot chiles (like jalapeño).

2. **Creamy Avocado Gazpacho:** Use 2 avocados, pitted and peeled; 2 cucumbers; 3 tablespoons fresh lemon juice; and 1 cup water. Garnish with chopped fresh mint and grated Parmesan.

3. **Grape Gazpacho:** Use 2 cucumbers; 1 pound green grapes; 1 thick slice bread; ½ cup toasted hazelnuts; 3 tablespoons olive oil; 2 tablespoons sherry vinegar; ½ small shallot; and 1 cup water. Garnish with chopped toasted hazelnuts and halved green grapes.

4. **Melon Gazpacho:** Use 2 pounds honeydew melon; 1 cucumber; 2 thick slices bread; ¼ cup olive oil; 2 tablespoons sherry vinegar; ½ small shallot; and 1 cup water. Garnish with chopped fresh mint and chopped toasted almonds.

5. **Strawberry Gazpacho:** Use 1 pound fresh tomatoes (include the juices); 1 pound ripe strawberries; 1 cucumber; 1 cup blanched almonds; ¼ cup olive oil; 1 tablespoon balsamic vinegar; 1 tablespoon fresh lemon juice; 1 clove garlic; and 1 cup water. Garnish with chopped fresh basil and grated Parmesan.

6. **Soy-Spiked Gazpacho:** Use 1½ pounds fresh tomatoes; 2 cucumbers; 2 thick slices bread; 2 tablespoons sesame oil; 2 tablespoons soy sauce; 2 tablespoons fresh lemon juice; and 1 cup water. Garnish with chopped scallions.

7. **Radish Gazpacho:** Use 1½ pounds fresh tomatoes; 8 ounces radishes; 1 cucumber; ¼ cup good-quality vegetable oil; 3 toasted tortillas; 2 tablespoons fresh lime juice; 1 jalapeño, or to taste; 1 clove garlic; a dash hot sauce; and 1 cup water. Garnish with chopped fresh cilantro and a dash of hot sauce.

 fast make ahead vegetarian

Bean Soups

Legumes provide an excellent foundation for satisfying soups. They also work as a thickener, as their starches release during cooking. And each bean adds its own distinct texture and taste, making for practically endless variety—without changing anything else in the recipe.

Some recipes here call for cooking raw beans in the soup pot, so their broth is integral to the soup; this is the most nutritious and flavorful option. Others add already-cooked beans. Whenever it's possible, the directions explain how to make the soup using either method.

I've suggested vegetable stock for all, although chicken or beef stocks are certainly options—as is the bean cooking liquid if you cooked the beans yourself. I'm not a fan of super-thick bean soups, but if that's what you're after, either decrease the amount of stock or water in these recipes by ½ cup or so or toss in another handful or two of beans.

7 Soups You Can Also Serve Cold

Chilled soups make a perfect start to a spicy meal in any season. And being able to make them ahead means they're ideal for entertaining. After you make the soup, let it cool a bit, then transfer it to a covered container and refrigerate until it's completely cold. This usually takes at least a couple of hours, so plan ahead.

1. Puréed Vegetable Soup Without Cream (page 140)
2. Vichyssoise (page 142)
3. Puréed Carrot-Ginger Soup (page 144)
4. Puréed Sweet-and-Sour Beet Soup (page 144)
5. Smooth Tomato Soup (page 145)
6. Summer Minestrone (page 148)
7. Green Minestrone (page 148)

Universal Bean Soup

MAKES: 4 servings | TIME: 1 to 2 hours, depending on the bean

Since no two types of beans are exactly the same, this soup is anything but monotonous. You also control how tender or intact the beans are—which in turn decides the level of creaminess—by monitoring their progress. The age of the beans (which you often have no way of knowing) will also affect their cooking time; another reason to check the soup frequently during cooking. Everything you need to know about the different beans starts on page 386. The other ingredients in the main recipe are minimal; see the list that follows for lots of ideas for adding vegetables, seasonings, and meat. And you can always serve bean soup with a spoonful of herb sauce, salsa, or chutney (see pages 51–64).

1½ cups dried beans, rinsed and picked over
6 cups vegetable stock (to make your own, see page 174) or water, or more as needed
1 onion, chopped
1 large carrot, chopped
1 celery stalk, chopped
2 bay leaves
1 teaspoon fresh thyme or pinch dried
Salt and pepper
Chopped fresh parsley for garnish

1. Put the beans in a large pot over medium-high heat. Add the stock, onion, carrot, celery, bay leaves, and thyme. Bring to a boil, then adjust the heat so the mixture bubbles gently. Cook, stirring and tasting occasionally, until the beans are soft or very soft, at least 1 hour; add more liquid as necessary so the mixture is soupy but not watery.

2. When the beans are very tender, sprinkle with salt and pepper. Taste and adjust the seasoning. If you like, you can purée some or all of the soup with an immersion blender or in a blender. (At this point, you can refrigerate the soup, covered, for up to 2 days; reheat before proceeding.) Serve right away, garnished with the parsley.

9 ADDITIONS TO UNIVERSAL BEAN SOUP

1. 1 or 2 mild chiles like anchos, stemmed and seeded. Add at the beginning of cooking.
2. A ham bone, 2 or 3 ham hocks, or about 8 ounces chopped bacon or pancetta. Add at the beginning of cooking.
3. 1 to 2 cups chopped potatoes, turnips, or other root vegetables. Add about 20 minutes before the end of cooking.
4. ½ cup or so any whole grain like brown rice, barley, or farro; reduce the beans by the same amount. Add at the beginning of cooking.
5. At least 1 tablespoon chopped garlic. Add with the aromatic vegetables.
6. About 2 cups chopped greens like kale or collards. Add during the last 5 minutes of cooking.
7. About 2 tablespoons butter, stirred in at the end of cooking.
8. Extra virgin olive oil, about 1 tablespoon per serving. Add at the table.
9. My Kind of Croutons (page 801). Put a couple in the bottom of each bowl before serving.

Smoky Black Bean Soup

MAKES: 4 servings | TIME: 30 minutes with cooked beans

For times when you want to use canned beans, adding just a few very flavorful ingredients helps make up for the lack of broth created by cooking beans yourself. This soup benefits from partial puréeing to make it thicker while retaining some texture. The variation explains how to convert the main recipe back to home-cooked black beans.

2 tablespoons good-quality vegetable oil
1 large or 2 small onions, chopped
1 tablespoon minced garlic
1 tablespoon chili powder (to make your own, see page 32)
1 chipotle chile, dried or canned in adobo (if using canned, use just a little bit of the adobo)
3 cups canned black beans, drained
4 cups vegetable stock (to make your own, see page 174) or water
   Salt and pepper
2 teaspoons fresh lime juice, or to taste
   Sour cream or yogurt for garnish
   Chopped fresh cilantro for garnish

1. Put the oil in a large pot over medium heat. When it's hot, add the onions and cook, stirring, until softened, about 5 minutes. Stir in the garlic and chili powder and cook, stirring, for another minute.
2. Add the chile, beans, and stock, and sprinkle with salt and pepper. Raise the heat to medium-high and bring the soup to a boil, then lower the heat so it bubbles gently. Cook, stirring occasionally, for about 10 minutes. Turn off the heat.
3. Purée some of the soup with an immersion blender or carefully in a blender. (At this point, you can cool and refrigerate the soup, covered, for up to 2 days; reheat gently before proceeding.)
4. Add the lime juice and stir; taste and adjust the seasoning. Serve right away, garnished with the sour cream and cilantro.

SMOKY BLACK BEAN SOUP, FROM SCRATCH Prepare a batch of black beans as described on page 390, but add an extra 3 cups water and be sure to cook them until they're falling apart. Drain the beans, reserving the cooking liquid. Measure out the 3 cups beans you need for this recipe and use the cooking liquid instead of vegetable stock.

Lentil Soup, Six Ways

MAKES: 4 servings | TIME: About 45 minutes

The difference between this soup and Simplest Dal (page 409) comes down to consistency. This includes more vegetables and is a little thinner but still creamy,

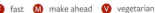   **F** fast **M** make ahead **V** vegetarian

Universal Bean Soup, page 151

and as you can see from the variations, it's endlessly versatile. Use any type of lentil you like (see page 408 for more info on lentils).

For even more ideas, see 9 Additions to Universal Bean Soup (page 152).

2 tablespoons olive oil
1 onion, chopped
1 carrot, chopped
1 celery stalk, chopped
1 cup dried lentils, rinsed and picked over
1 bay leaf
6 cups vegetable stock (to make your own, see page 174) or water
Salt and pepper

1. Put the oil in a large pot over medium heat. When it's hot, add the onion and cook, stirring frequently, until soft, just a minute or 2. Add the carrot and celery; cook and stir until they're brightly colored and hot, about 2 minutes.

2. Add the lentils, bay leaf, and stock, and sprinkle with pepper. Bring to a boil, then turn the heat to low and cook, stirring occasionally, until the lentils are tender, about 30 minutes. (At this point, you can cool and refrigerate the soup, covered, for up to 2 days; reheat gently.) Add more liquid if the soup is too thick. Just before serving, sprinkle with salt; taste and adjust the seasoning. Serve right away.

SPICED LENTIL SOUP Cumin, smoked paprika, chili powder, and curry powder all work great: Add 1 teaspoon spice before the lentils and cook, stirring, until fragrant, about 30 seconds. Proceed with the recipe.

LENTIL SOUP WITH LEMON AND DILL About a minute before serving, stir in 3 tablespoons fresh lemon juice and ½ cup chopped fresh dill, or to taste.

LENTIL SOUP WITH BACON Start by cooking about 4 ounces chopped bacon or pancetta in the soup pot until slightly crisp. Drain the fat, or leave it and omit the olive oil. Proceed with cooking the onion.

LENTIL SOUP WITH CARAMELIZED ONIONS Omit the onion. In Step 1, add ½ cup chopped Caramelized Onions (page 315) when the vegetables have softened. Add a tablespoon of cider or sherry vinegar with the stock, if you like.

LENTIL SOUP WITH HARISSA Add a tablespoon or two Harissa (page 45) with the lentils and stock.

Grain Soups

Whole grains work brilliantly as supporting actors in soup, contributing flavor—usually subtly—and body. Here, though, they're featured in leading roles.

Mushroom-Barley Soup, My New Way

MAKES: 4 servings | **TIME:** 1½ hours, largely unattended

I've changed how I make one of my favorite winter soups by using whole grain barley (also called "hulled") instead of the peeled form known as "pearled." The results are even more earthy and hearty, with a rich-tasting broth. You can substitute wheat or rye berries for the barley. Sweet potatoes, parsnips, or chard or other hearty greens are all welcome additions. And for faster versions, see the first two variations.

2 tablespoons olive oil
10 to 16 ounces fresh cremini or button mushrooms, halved if large and sliced
2 carrots, sliced
¾ cup hulled barley
Salt and pepper
½ ounce dried shiitake or porcini mushrooms, reconstituted (see page 304; optional)
1 bay leaf

 fast    make ahead   vegetarian

1. Put the oil in a large pot over medium-high heat. When oil is hot, add the fresh mushrooms and carrots and cook, stirring occasionally, until they begin to brown, about 10 minutes. Add the barley and continue to cook, stirring frequently, until it begins to toast, about 5 minutes. Sprinkle with a little salt and pepper.

2. Add the dried mushrooms if using, and 1 cup of their soaking liquid. Add the bay leaf and 6 cups water (5 cups if adding the mushroom soaking liquid). Bring to a boil, then lower the heat so the mixture bubbles gently. Cook until the barley is very tender, about an hour.

3. Taste and adjust the seasoning. (At this point, you can refrigerate the soup, covered, for up to a day; reheat before serving, adding a little more water to thin the soup if necessary.) Serve right away.

MORE TRADITIONAL MUSHROOM AND BARLEY SOUP
Substitute pearled barley for the whole grain and reduce the cooking time to 20 to 30 minutes.

MUSHROOM AND OTHER GRAIN SOUP Quinoa, steel-cut oats, and farro will all cook in about the same amount of time as the pearled barley variation above.

CHICKEN AND BARLEY SOUP Works for any of the above variations, too: Cook 12 ounces chopped boneless, skinless chicken thighs in the oil. Replace the mushrooms with 1 onion and 2 celery stalks, both chopped. Return the chicken to the pot in Step 2 when you add the water. Garnish with chopped fresh parsley.

Rice Porridge with Fresh Garnishes

MAKES: 4 to 6 servings | **TIME:** About 2½ hours

My version of *jook* or congee, the rice porridges known throughout China and southeast Asia. What's amazing is how a little bit of food becomes a meal: One cup of rice can satisfy up to six people, especially if you make one of the variations that follow. And with plenty of tasty garnishes—especially Ginger-Scallion Sauce (page 64)—it's wonderful stuff.

10	stemmed fresh or dried shiitake mushrooms, or a combination
1	cup short-grain rice, rinsed
1	teaspoon salt, or to taste
2	inches fresh ginger
	Soy sauce, to taste (optional)
	Sesame oil, to taste (optional)
½	cup chopped scallions for garnish
½	cup fresh cilantro for garnish
½	cup chopped roasted peanuts or cashews for garnish

1. If you're using dried shiitakes, cover them with boiling water and soak until pliable, about 30 minutes, then drain and slice them.

2. Put the rice in a large pot with 6 cups water and the salt. Bring to a boil over high heat, then adjust the heat so the mixture bubbles gently. Slice half the ginger and add it to the pot; mince the remaining ginger and set aside. Slice the mushrooms and add them to the pot.

3. Partially cover the pot and cook for about 2 hours, stirring occasionally to make sure the rice is not sticking to the bottom. The soup should have a porridgelike consistency, so if it becomes very thick too quickly, turn down the heat and stir in more water. When it's done, the rice will be soupy and creamy. Add the minced ginger and, if you're using them, soy sauce and/or sesame oil. Taste and adjust the seasonings. Serve hot, with whatever garnishes you choose.

RICE PORRIDGE WITH VEGETABLES During the last 30 minutes of cooking, add 4 cups chopped vegetables, like cabbage or spinach, carrots, fresh or frozen peas, or any combination of these. Be sure to add more water to keep the mixture soupy.

Rice Porridge with
Fresh Garnishes, page 155

RICE PORRIDGE WITH MEAT In Step 2, cut all the ginger into thin slivers. Add it, along with 8 ounces sliced sirloin, Chinese sausage, chicken breast, or lean pork, during the last 15 minutes of cooking.

RICE PORRIDGE WITH SEAFOOD In Step 2, during the last 30 minutes of cooking, add 4 ounces sliced squid; during the last 5 minutes of cooking, add 4 ounces peeled shrimp and 4 ounces firm white fish, skinned and sliced.

CREAMY WHOLE GRAINS WITH FRESH GARNISHES
Why not? Try farro, quinoa, steel-cut oats, cracked wheat, or even brown rice. Many will cook faster than short-grain rice. See the Lexicon on page 452 for some ideas about the cooking time. Otherwise the technique, variations, and garnishes are the same as the main recipe.

Noodle Soups

Usually the best way to make noodle soup is to add cooked noodles to the hot broth just before serving.

Undercook the noodles slightly so they don't turn to mush as you eat the hot soup. You can even cook them ahead if you like, then rinse them in cold water to stop the cooking and set them aside in a bowl of water; or use leftovers.

Then again, several recipes here ignore this principle and successfully cook the noodles right in the soup!

Noodles in Broth

MAKES: 4 servings | **TIME:** 30 minutes

This is one of the rare times you really must use home-made stock. The soup is so simple. But that doesn't mean it's boring; see the variations for great ways to layer in more ingredients. You can also use chicken or beef broth in the main recipe or any of the variations. Or if you decide to go with Asian noodles (see page 519), try Dashi (page 179).

10 Unexpected Soup and Grain Combinations

Cooked grains have the power to turn simple soups into dinner. This list will get you started. You can cook the grains in the soup; see the chart on page 452 for some ideas about cooking times and be sure to add enough extra water to keep the soup brothy. Or simply add cooked grains and heat them through at the end.

1. Tomato Soup (page 144) with couscous, steel-cut oats, or kasha
2. Onion Soup (page 145), with wild rice, cracked wheat, farro, or kasha
3. Corn Chowder (page 145) with millet, Israeli couscous, or long-grain white rice
4. Minestrone (page 147) with Arborio or short-grain brown rice, farro, or Israeli couscous
5. Universal Bean Soup (page 151) with bulgur, long-grain white rice, or cracked wheat
6. Lentil Soup, Six Ways (page 152) with couscous, freekeh, or wheat or rye berries
7. Lightning-Quick Fish Soup (page 161) with red or white rice, millet, or Israeli couscous
8. Basic Chicken Soup (page 164) with quinoa, millet, or hominy
9. Beef and Vegetable Soup (page 168) with wild rice, wheat berries, or barley
10. Lamb Soup, North African Style (page 171) with wheat berries, cracked wheat, or freekeh

8 ounces small pasta, like shells, orecchiette, orzo, or broken angel hair
   Salt and pepper
1 tablespoon olive oil
1 onion, halved and thinly sliced
1 carrot, chopped
1 celery stalk, chopped
6 cups vegetable stock (to make your own, see page 174)
¼ cup chopped fresh parsley for garnish
   Grated Parmesan cheese for garnish (optional)

1. Bring a large pot of water to a boil and salt it. Add the pasta and cook, stirring occasionally, until it's tender but not yet edible; there should still be some chew to it. Drain it and rinse in cold water until cool. (If you're cooking the pasta in advance by more than 30 minutes, hold the pasta in a bowl of cold water to cover.)

2. Put the oil in a large pot over medium-high heat. When it's hot, add the onion, carrot, and celery and cook until the vegetables are soft, about 10 minutes. Add the stock, sprinkle with salt and pepper, and bring to a boil.

3. Stir in the pasta and heat until it's cooked through, just a minute or 2. Taste and adjust the seasoning. Garnish with the parsley and the Parmesan if you're using it and serve right away.

CHICKEN AND NOODLES IN BROTH In Step 2, add 8 to 12 ounces cut-up boneless, skinless chicken (thighs are the most flavorful) to the pan before adding the stock; cook until opaque. Or add 8 ounces cooked and cut-up boneless, skinless chicken in Step 3 when you add the pasta. Garnish with chopped fresh celery leaves or chives.

PASTA AND PESTO SOUP Omit the onion, carrot, and celery if you like. Stir in ½ cup Traditional Pesto (page 51) just after the pasta.

PASTA AND CHICKPEAS IN BROTH If you've got it, use the cooking liquid from chickpeas instead of some of the stock. Add 1 tablespoon minced garlic and 2 teaspoons cumin seeds, if you like, in the last minute of cooking the vegetables. Add 2 cups drained cooked chickpeas (canned is fine) and 1 tablespoon chopped fresh rosemary (or 1 teaspoon dried), if you're using it, with the stock. Garnish with fresh cilantro if you used cumin, or parsley if you used rosemary.

FUSILLI AND ROASTED GARLIC SOUP Use fusilli or really any pasta. Add a head of Roasted Garlic (page 294), the cloves removed from the skins and mashed into a paste with a fork, to the softened vegetables just before adding the stock.

ORZO AND FRESH HERB SOUP WITH YOGURT Use orzo or other small pasta. Stir in ½ cup each minced fresh parsley, cilantro, chives, and mint just before serving, along with 1 cup yogurt, if you like. Be sure the soup isn't boiling when you add the yogurt.

CHINESE NOODLE SOUP WITH CABBAGE AND GINGER Use fresh or dried thin Chinese egg noodles. Substitute good-quality vegetable oil for the olive oil. Add 1 tablespoon each minced fresh ginger and garlic and 3 cups each chopped or shredded napa or green cabbage and bok choy with the vegetables. Garnish with chopped scallion and 1 teaspoon sesame oil.

Garlic Fideo Soup

MAKES: 4 servings | **TIME:** 30 minutes

You can't go wrong with a soup made of lots of fried garlic and noodles, and topped with fried bread crumbs. Chicken stock would work well if you have some handy.

 fast make ahead vegetarian

Garlic Fideo Soup, opposite

1 pound fideos, or capellini or other very thin pasta
¼ cup olive oil
¼ cup chopped garlic
   Salt and pepper
2 teaspoons sweet paprika (preferably pimentón; see page 30)
¼ cup chopped fresh parsley, cilantro, or epazote, plus 2 tablespoons for garnish
6½ cups vegetable stock (to make your own, see page 174) or water
½ cup Fried Bread Crumbs (page 801)

1. Put the noodles in a sturdy bag and whack them with a rolling pin or the back of a knife, breaking them into 1- to 2-inch pieces.

2. Put the oil in a large pot over medium-low heat. When it's hot, add the garlic and cook, stirring frequently, until soft and beginning to color, 5 to 8 minutes.

3. Raise the heat to medium-high. Add the noodles, sprinkle with salt and pepper, and cook, stirring almost constantly, until they darken, a minute or 2. They will probably not cook perfectly evenly—some will become darker than others—but avoid letting more than a few pieces blacken.

4. Add the paprika and ¼ cup parsley and stir for a minute to coat the noodles. Add the stock, taking care to loosen any noodles or garlic that might have stuck to the bottom of the pan. Cook, stirring occasionally, until the noodles are just tender, 8 to 10 minutes. Taste and adjust the seasoning. Serve right away, garnished with the remaining 2 tablespoons parsley and the bread crumbs.

Pho-Style Noodle Soup

MAKES: 4 main-course servings | TIME: About 1 hour

I can't call this traditional pho since I take liberties and the real deal is usually based on beef stock. But my interpretation is just as fortifying and comes together

quickly. Rice noodles are available everywhere now; the slightly wide, flat kind are the best.

8 cups beef, chicken, or vegetable stock (to make your own, see pages 174–178)
4 star anise pods
1 3-inch cinnamon stick
1 inch fresh ginger
1 onion, quartered (don't bother to peel)
4 whole cloves
1 pound rice sticks or rice vermicelli
12 ounces boneless, skinless chicken, or beef (preferably sirloin, tenderloin, or round), cut into thin slices
2 tablespoons fish sauce or soy sauce (or a little of both), or more to taste
   Pepper
   Sprigs of fresh cilantro, mint, and/or Thai basil for garnish
1 or 2 thinly sliced jalapeño chiles for garnish
3 limes, cut into wedges for garnish

1. Combine the stock, star anise, cinnamon, ginger, onion, and cloves in a large pot over high heat. When it boils, adjust the heat so it bubbles gently, and cover. Cook, undisturbed, for no less than 20 minutes, or up to an hour if you have the time. Strain and return to the pot.

2. Soak the noodles in hot water to cover until soft, 15 to 30 minutes. Rinse under cold water for a minute or so; drain, cover with cold water and let sit until you're ready to serve.

3. Bring the soup to a steady bubble; add the chicken and cook, stirring occasionally, until no longer raw, about 2 minutes. Add the fish sauce and plenty of pepper. Taste and adjust the seasoning, adding more fish sauce or soy sauce if you'd like.

4. Drain the noodles, run them under hot tap water, drain again, and shake to dry. Divide the noodles among 4 large bowls. Top with broth and meat. Serve with the garnishes on the side so everyone can add fresh herbs to their soup and season with chile and lime juice.

 fast   make ahead   V vegetarian

RICE NOODLE SOUP WITH PORK Infuse the broth as directed but cook for only 20 minutes. In Step 3, replace the chicken or beef with about 2 cups Spicy Braised Pork with Vietnamese Flavors (page 700), along with some of its liquid. Proceed with the recipe.

Seafood Soups

Unlike most soups, fish soups are usually best prepared at the last minute, because many fish and shellfish overcook quickly. You can often make the stock or base one day and finish the soup the next, but some are so easy you probably won't bother.

In fact, homemade fish stock isn't always essential. I've designed most of these recipes so you could use chicken or vegetable stock instead or, if necessary, water. What is important, as with all dishes containing fish, is freshness and an eye toward sustainability; see pages 530–531 for a discussion of this.

Lightning-Quick Fish Soup

MAKES: 4 servings | **TIME:** 20 minutes

The bright flavor of a sort-of-Spanish soup is a perfect light dinner with a salad and excellent loaf of bread. You can make it heartier by adding vegetables, rice, or pasta. If you have fish stock to use instead of water—or chicken or vegetable stock—all the better.

- 1 large onion, chopped
- 1 tablespoon minced garlic
- 1 teaspoon paprika
   Pinch saffron (optional)
- 2 tablespoons olive oil
- 1 cup peeled, seeded, and chopped tomatoes (canned is fine; include the juices)
   Salt and pepper

- 1½ pounds any white fish, cut into small chunks, or fish mixed with shelled seafood like clams, crab, shrimp, or scallops
   Chopped fresh parsley for garnish

1. Put the onion, garlic, paprika, saffron if you're using it, oil, tomatoes, and a sprinkle of salt and pepper in a large pot with 5 cups water and bring to a boil. Adjust the heat so the mixture bubbles steadily and cook stirring occasionally, until the tomatoes break down, about 5 minutes.

2. Add the fish and cook, stirring, until it's cooked through, about 5 minutes. Taste and adjust the seasoning. Serve right away, garnished with parsley.

LIGHTNING-QUICK FISH SOUP, CHINESE STYLE Use 6 cups water. Substitute 3 tablespoons soy sauce for the paprika, 2 teaspoons sesame oil and 4 teaspoons good-quality vegetable oil for the olive oil, and chopped bok choy or shredded cabbage for the tomatoes. Omit the saffron. Be sure to taste before adding salt. Garnish with chopped scallion.

LIGHTNING-QUICK FISH SOUP, FRENCH STYLE The saffron is essential: Substitute ½ cup dry white wine and ½ cup cream for 1 cup of the stock, and substitute ¼ teaspoon cayenne, or to taste, for the paprika. Add the cream when you add the fish in Step 2, and don't let the soup come to a rolling boil. Garnish with 2 tablespoons chopped fresh tarragon instead of parsley.

LIGHTNING-QUICK FISH SOUP, MEXICAN STYLE Omit the paprika and saffron and add a minced jalapeño or other fresh chile, to taste, along with the tomatoes. Add 3 tablespoons fresh lime juice or to taste. Garnish with cilantro instead of parsley.

LIGHTNING-QUICK FISH SOUP, THAI STYLE Great with shrimp: Omit the paprika and saffron, and add 1 tablespoon minced or grated fresh ginger and

1 tablespoon minced lemongrass. In Step 1, reduce the water to 4 cups. Add 1 tablespoon fish sauce, 3 tablespoons fresh lime juice, and 1 tablespoon Red or Green Curry Paste (page 46) when you add the tomatoes; make sure the paste completely dissolves. Add 1 cup coconut milk when you add the fish and cook the soup at a gentle bubble, not a full boil; it might take another minute or 2. Garnish with cilantro instead of parsley.

Bouillabaisse

MAKES: 8 servings | **TIME:** 1 hour

Perhaps the best-known fish stew, once humbly made from this and that and now often presented as something luxurious. I prefer the spirit of the original. So vary the recipe according to what you have, or what looks good at the market.

- 1 tablespoon olive oil
- 2 onions, chopped
- 1 navel or other orange
- 1 tablespoon fennel seeds
  Pinch saffron threads
- 1 dried chile, like Thai, or a pinch cayenne, to taste
- 2 cups chopped tomatoes (canned is fine; include the juices)
- 1 pound firm white fish, like cod or catfish, cut into 1-inch cubes
- 3 pounds clams or mussels (or a combination), scrubbed
- 1 pound scallops or peeled shrimp, cut into bite-sized pieces if necessary
- 1 pound fresh sole or other thin white fish, cut into 8 large pieces
- 1 tablespoon minced garlic
- ½ cup chopped fresh parsley

- 2 baguettes, sliced, for serving
- ½ cup Aioli or Saffron Mayonnaise (page 70) for serving (optional)

1. Put the oil in a large pot over medium heat. When it's hot, add the onions and cook, stirring occasionally, until softened, about 5 minutes. Meanwhile, use a vegetable peeler to strip the zest from the orange; save the orange itself for another use. Add the zest, fennel seeds, saffron, and chile and cook for about a minute.

2. Add the tomato and 3 cups water and bring to a boil. Adjust the heat so it bubbles steadily. Cook, stirring occasionally, until the mixture becomes saucy, 10 to 15 minutes. (At this point, you can cover the soup and refrigerate it for up to a day.)

3. Add the firm white fish and the clams or mussels and raise the heat to medium-high. When the mixture begins to boil, reduce the heat again so the soup bubbles gently. Cover and cook, undisturbed, until the fish is barely opaque, 5 to 10 minutes.

4. Add the scallops and thin white fish, stir gently, adjust the heat so the soup bubbles gently, and cover. Cook, without stirring, until the fish and seafood are just done (the pieces will be opaque and a thin-bladed knife will pierce them with little resistance), about 5 minutes. There should be some broth; if the soup is very thick, add a cup or so of hot water.

5. Stir in the garlic and cook for 1 minute more. Stir in the parsley and serve right away, with crusty bread and a dollop of mayonnaise if you're using it.

No-Holds-Barred Clam Chowder

MAKES: 4 servings | **TIME:** 30 minutes

I've spent much of my life in either New York City or New England, so both chowder styles are represented here. Your call on which is superior.

Lightning-Quick Fish Soup (bottom) and Lightning-Quick Fish Soup, Thai Style (top), page 161

4 to 6 slices good bacon (about 4 ounces), chopped

1 cup chopped onion

2 cups peeled and roughly chopped waxy or all-purpose potatoes

1 tablespoon fresh thyme or 1 teaspoon dried

24 littleneck or other hard-shell clams, shucked; about 1 pint shucked clams, cut up if very large

2 cups fish or chicken stock (to make your own, see pages 176–178), plus as much juice as you can salvage when shucking the clams

Salt and pepper

1 cup milk

1 cup cream or half-and-half

1 tablespoon butter

Chopped fresh parsley for garnish

1. Cook the bacon in a large pot over medium-high heat until crisp. Remove with a slotted spoon and let sit. Cook the onion, potatoes, and thyme in the bacon fat, stirring occasionally, until the onion softens, 5 to 10 minutes.

2. Add the stock and stir to scrape any browned bits from the bottom of the pot. Scatter the clams on top and bring to a boil. Cover and cook until the clams open, 3 to 5 minutes. Use tongs to transfer the clams to a bowl. Lower the heat to the liquid bubbles gently and cook, stirring once or twice until the potatoes are tender, about 10 minutes. When the clams are cool enough to handle remove the meat from the shells and add them to pot along with the bacon. (At this point, you can refrigerate the soup, covered, for up to 2 days; reheat before proceeding.)

3. Sprinkle with salt and pepper, then add the milk and cream. Adjust the heat so the soup barely bubbles; don't bring it to a rolling boil. Add the butter and let it melt on top of the chowder. Garnish and serve.

FISH CHOWDER Instead of the clams use 1 pound firm white fish like halibut or cod, cut into chunks. Add it after the potatoes are tender in Step 2.

MANHATTAN CLAM OR FISH CHOWDER Substitute 1 cup each chopped carrot and celery for the potatoes and 1 28-ounce can peeled tomatoes (you can use fresh— 3 cups or so), chopped, for the milk and cream. Add the tomatoes and their juices with the stock.

Chicken Soups

Ironically, few chicken soups contain much chicken, because if the stock is good enough, there's no need for it—the flavor is distilled into the golden liquid. But if you like to have something meaty to chew on, by all means add more chicken to your chicken soup.

Chicken Soup, Many Ways

MAKES: 4 servings | **TIME:** 30 minutes

This isn't meant to be an entire meal, but rather a light first course. To turn it into a hearty one-bowl lunch or dinner, double the amount of chicken and see the variations; or instead of the rice, cook thick noodles separately and add them to the pot just before serving. If you already have stock made, see the quick Chicken and Noodles in Broth (page 158).

6 cups chicken stock (to make your own, see page 176)

½ cup white rice

1 carrot, sliced

1 celery stalk, sliced

1 cup (or more) raw or cooked chopped boneless, skinless chicken

Salt and pepper
Chopped fresh parsley, dill, or cilantro
for garnish

1. Put the stock in a large pot over medium-high heat. When it is just about to boil, adjust the heat so that it bubbles steadily. Stir in the rice, carrot, and celery and cook, stirring occasionally, until they are all tender, about 20 minutes.

2. Stir in the chicken. If it is raw, cook until it is cooked through, another 5 to 8 minutes. If it is cooked, cook until it is hot, 2 or 3 minutes. Taste and adjust the seasoning. Serve right away, garnished with parsley.

CHICKEN SOUP WITH VEGETABLES Omit the rice, if you like, and add up to 1½ cups mixed vegetables like chopped carrots, celery, onion, turnip, parsnip, zucchini or yellow squash, or potato; sliced mushrooms; peas or corn kernels; and/or thinly shredded cabbage, bok choy, or greens. (The smaller the pieces are, the faster they'll cook.) Add the vegetables to the stock in order of their cooking times, starting with the harder, longer-cooking vegetables like carrots or potatoes.

CHICKEN SOUP WITH RICE, MEXICAN STYLE Omit the carrot and celery, if you like. Add 1 cup chopped tomatoes along with the chicken. Just before serving, add ½ cup chopped white onion and ¼ cup fresh lime juice, ½ cup chopped fresh cilantro, and minced jalapeños or other chiles (optional), all to taste.

CHICKEN SOUP WITH RICE, CHINESE STYLE Add 1 teaspoon each minced fresh ginger and garlic with the chicken. A cup or so green peas (frozen are fine; add at the last minute) or chopped mushrooms are a nice addition (added during the last few minutes of cooking). Season with a couple of tablespoons soy sauce and a lot of black pepper. Stir in 2 teaspoons sesame oil before serving.

CHIPOTLE CHICKEN SOUP Smoky tasting and a gorgeous shade of umber: Soak 4 to 6 dried chipotle chiles in just-boiled water to cover until soft, about 20 minutes; drain. Use a knife to slice open and scrape out all the seeds and remove the stems. Put the chiles, 2 cloves garlic, 2 tablespoons tomato paste, and 1 teaspoon dried oregano in a blender or food processor and purée; add only enough chicken stock from the soup to get the purée going. Add the chipotle paste to taste to the soup or pass it at the table.

CHICKEN SOUP, THAI STYLE Replace 4 cups of the stock with coconut milk (to make your own, see page 372). Omit the rice, onion, and carrot, and instead add 3 stalks lemongrass, cut into 2-inch lengths, 10 nickel-sized pieces ginger, 2 fresh chiles (preferably Thai), seeded and minced, and 1 cup sliced mushrooms. When the chicken is cooked through, add 3 tablespoons fish sauce, 3 tablespoons fresh lime juice, and 1 teaspoon sugar, and sprinkle with salt and pepper. Taste and adjust the seasoning and garnish with chopped fresh cilantro.

TORTILLA SOUP Grill or broil 2 fresh chiles, like serrano or jalapeño, and 1½ pounds tomatoes until charred, then peel and chop. Omit the rice, carrot, and celery. Shred the chicken after cooking, instead of chopping it. Cook 1 tablespoon sliced garlic and 1 large onion, sliced, in 2 tablespoons good-quality vegetable oil before adding the stock. At the end of cooking, stir in 1 to 2 cups tortilla chips and the juice of 1 lime. Taste and adjust the seasoning, then garnish with more tortilla chips, fresh cilantro, and chopped avocado.

Chicken Soup with Matzo Balls

MAKES: 6 servings | **TIME:** At least 2 hours

The classic version of the soup here can be built on by adding more vegetables, noodles, or cooked chicken meat. You can turn it into vegetable soup by using a meatless stock if you'd like, but this is one time water won't work. And taking the time to beat the egg whites separately will ensure the matzo balls are light and airy.

- 3 **eggs, separated**
- 6 to 9 **cups chicken stock (to make your own, see page 176)**
- ¼ **cup minced or grated onion (optional)**
- ¼ **cup rendered chicken fat or good-quality vegetable oil**
- ½ **teaspoon salt**
- ½ **teaspoon pepper**
  About 1 cup matzo meal
- 4 **carrots, cut into chunks**

1. Beat the egg yolks with ½ cup of the stock. Stir in the onion if you're using it, the fat, salt, and pepper. Add the matzo meal and stir to combine.

2. Beat the egg whites until stiff and fold them into the matzo mixture. The dough should be quite moist, barely stiff enough to make into balls. If it's too moist, add a little more matzo meal. Cover the dough and refrigerate for an hour.

3. When you're ready to cook, bring a large pot of water to a boil and salt it. (To cook the matzo balls directly in the stock, use the larger quantity of stock.) Using wet hands, shape the dough into balls about 1 inch in diameter. Meanwhile, bring the remaining stock to a boil, then reduce the heat so it bubbles steadily. Add the carrots and cook until just tender, about 20 minutes.

4. Adjust the heat so the water or soup bubbles gently, and cook the balls until expanded and set, about 30 minutes. Put them in soup bowls and ladle the stock and carrots over them. Serve right away.

CHICKEN SOUP WITH PASSATELLI A wonderful fresh "noodle" made from bread crumbs and cheese: Reduce the stock to 4 cups and omit the carrot. Bring it to a steady bubble. Mix together ⅓ cup Fresh Bread Crumbs (page 801), ¾ cup grated Parmesan, ⅛ teaspoon freshly grated nutmeg, ¼ cup chopped fresh parsley, and 2 eggs; it will form a soft, granular dough. Press the dough into the bubbling stock through a ricer (see illustration, page 519), a food mill fit with large holes, or a colander (using a large spoon); cook until the passatelli are tender but firm, about 2 minutes. Serve immediately with more grated Parmesan.

CHICKEN SOUP WITH BUTTER DUMPLINGS Use 6 cups stock and bring to a steady bubble. Whip 4 tablespoons (½ stick) butter until very soft, then beat in 2 eggs. Stir in ½ cup all-purpose flour, ¼ cup chopped fresh parsley, ¼ cup minced or grated onion, and a large pinch each salt and pepper. Add heated stock 1 tablespoon at a time, just until the batter is soft—not too loose or the dumplings will fall apart. Drop the batter by the teaspoonful into the bubbling stock. Cook until the dumplings are set, about 10 minutes, removing them as they are done. Serve immediately in the soup.

Meat Soups

Once you include rich and savory meat in soup—with or without the bones—it's hardly noticeable if you use water, unless you want to go all out and make beef stock. In fact, I'd go so far as to say: Save your chicken or vegetable stock for other soups where it will have more impact.

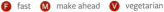 **F** fast **M** make ahead **V** vegetarian

Tortilla Soup (top) and Chicken Soup, Thai Style (bottom), both page 165

Beef and Vegetable Soup

MAKES: 4 to 6 servings | TIME: 1½ hours

Most meat soups are more like stews—see the meat chapter for those and the recipe on page 679 for a hybrid—but this is lighter, more brothy than stewy.

2	tablespoons good-quality vegetable oil
1	pound beef chuck or round, trimmed of surface fat and cut into ½-inch cubes
1	onion, chopped
6	cups beef or other stock (to make your own, see page 176) or water
2	parsnips or carrots, peeled and chopped
4	ounces celery root, peeled and chopped or 1 celery stalk, chopped
4	ounces butternut squash, peeled and chopped
2	sprigs fresh thyme or rosemary
1	bay leaf
½	cup green peas (frozen are fine)
	Salt and pepper
	Chopped fresh parsley or chives for garnish

1. Put the oil in a large pot over medium-high heat. When it's hot, add half the beef and brown the pieces on one side. Then stir, and cook until deeply browned all over, 5 to 10 minutes total. Remove pieces as they finish and repeat with the remaining meat. Pour off all but 2 tablespoons of the fat from the pan. Add the onion and cook until translucent, about 5 minutes.

2. Add the stock and bring to a boil; return the meat and any juices to the pot. Adjust the heat so the liquid bubbles steadily. Cover and cook, stirring once or twice, until the meat is tender, about 30 minutes.

3. Add the parsnips, celery root, squash, thyme, and bay leaf. Cook, stirring occasionally, until the meat and vegetables are tender, 30 to 40 minutes. (At this point, you can refrigerate the soup, covered, for 2 days; reheat gently before proceeding.) Fish out the thyme sprigs and bay leaf, stir in the peas, and sprinkle with salt and pepper. Taste and adjust the seasoning. Garnish with parsley and serve hot.

SPICY BEEF AND VEGETABLE SOUP Soak 2 dried cascabel, guajillo, or pasilla chiles in just-boiled water to cover; drain and use a knife to scrape out the seeds and remove the stems; chop and add to the cooked onion along with 1 tablespoon minced garlic. Strain and add the chile-soaking liquid (and reduce the amount of stock accordingly) for more kick. Garnish with fresh cilantro and serve with lime wedges.

BEEF AND MUSHROOM SOUP If you like, soak 1 ounce dried porcini or other dried mushrooms in 3 cups just-boiled water until soft, about 30 minutes. Lift the mushrooms out of the water and chop them. Strain the soaking liquid and add it to the soup with the chopped mushrooms; reduce the amount of stock by 3 cups. Or use 4 cups chopped fresh mushrooms, cooking them along with the onion in Step 1; it will take a few minutes longer.

Hot-and-Sour Soup

MAKES: 4 servings | TIME: 30 minutes

You may know this as a Chinese restaurant staple, but it's easy and fun to make at home too. The heat comes from lots of black pepper and the sourness from rice vinegar. This is perhaps the only instance where I consider cornstarch as an asset for the signature velvety texture, but you can skip it if you prefer.

8 ounces boneless pork shoulder or rib meat

3 teaspoons sesame oil

3 tablespoons soy sauce

3 tablespoons cornstarch

6 cups chicken stock (to make your own, see page 176) or water

1 teaspoon minced garlic

1 tablespoon minced fresh ginger

5 dried shiitake mushrooms, soaked in boiling water for at least 10 minutes

5 Chinese wood ear mushrooms, soaked in hot water for at least 10 minutes

8 ounces extra-firm tofu, cut into ½-inch cubes

¼ cup rice vinegar, or to taste

1 tablespoon pepper, or to taste

2 eggs, lightly beaten

¼ cup chopped fresh cilantro for garnish

½ cup chopped scallion for garnish

1. Thinly slice the pork against the grain, then cut the slices into strips. Whisk together 1 teaspoon of the oil with 1 tablespoon each of the soy sauce and cornstarch. Add the pork and stir to coat it well. Cover and let marinate while you prepare the soup.

2. Combine the stock with the garlic and ginger in a large pot and bring to a boil over medium-high heat. Drain the shiitake and cloud ear mushrooms, trim off any hard spots, cut into thin slices, and add to the stock. Adjust the heat so the stock bubbles steadily and cook for 5 minutes.

3. Bring the stock back to a boil. Add the pork and stir to make sure the pieces do not stick together. Cook until the meat loses its pinkness, about 3 minutes. Add the tofu, vinegar, pepper, and the remaining soy sauce. Adjust the heat again so the soup bubbles gently and cook, stirring once in a while, for 5 minutes.

4. Whisk the remaining cornstarch with ¼ cup cold water until smooth; stir this slurry into the soup until it thickens, about 1 minute. Continuing to stir, pour in the eggs in a slow stream. The eggs should form thin, almost transparent ribbons. Remove the soup from the heat and season with the remaining oil. Taste and adjust the seasoning. Garnish with the cilantro and scallion and serve.

VEGETARIAN HOT-AND-SOUR SOUP Omit the pork and add 8 ounces more tofu and 4 ounces shredded

19 Whole-Meal Soups

These recipes and variations are all filling and interesting enough to serve as a main course. For ideas about making additions and adjustments, see the lists that follow the recipes and the charts scattered throughout this chapter.

1. Tomato and Bread Soup (page 145)
2. Cheesy Corn Chowder (page 147)
3. Minestrone and its variations (pages 147–148)
4. Universal Bean Soup (page 151)
5. Smoky Black Bean Soup (page 152)
6. Lentil Soup (page 152)
7. Mushroom-Barley Soup, My New Way (page 154)
8. Rice Porridge with Fresh Garnishes (page 155)
9. Pasta and Chickpeas in Broth (page 158)
10. Chinese Noodle Soup with Cabbage and Ginger (page 158)
11. Pho-Style Noodle Soup (page 160)
12. Rice Noodle Soup with Pork (page 161)
13. Lightning-Quick Fish Soup (page 161)
14. No-Holds-Barred Clam or Fish Chowder (pages 162 or 164)
15. Bouillabaisse (page 162)
16. Chicken Soup, Many Ways (page 164)
17. Beef and Vegetable Soup (page 168)
18. Hot-and-Sour Soup (page 168)
19. Lamb Soup, North African Style (page 171)

 F fast M make ahead V vegetarian

bamboo shoots or water chestnuts. Instead of the chicken stock use good vegetable stock (to make your own, see page 174).

HOT-AND-SOUR SOUP WITH SHRIMP Make the vegetarian variation above, only instead of vegetable stock use Fish or Shrimp Stock if you'd like (pages 178–179). Before adding the cornstarch mixture in Step 4, stir in 8 ounces chopped large or medium peeled shrimp.

Lamb Soup, North African Style

MAKES: 4 servings | **TIME:** About 2 hours

A meaty lamb soup loaded with hearty vegetables remains popular around the world. Lamb stock is the traditional base, and this is a rare occasion to enjoy the unique taste so I encourage you to make a batch for this soup. But beef stock and boneless chuck might make more sense for you and that's fine, too.

- 1 tablespoon olive oil
- 1 pound boneless lamb (preferably from the shoulder or leg), trimmed of excess fat and cut into 1-inch cubes
   Salt and pepper
- 1 large leek, white and light green parts, chopped and rinsed well
- 2 carrots, cut into 1-inch chunks
- 1 teaspoon ground cumin
- ¼ teaspoon ground cinnamon
- ¼ teaspoon cayenne
- 8 cups lamb, beef, or chicken stock (to make your own, see page 176), water, or a combination
- 2 cups drained cooked or canned chickpeas, or uncooked lentils

- 2 cups chopped, seeded tomatoes (canned is fine; include the juices)
- 1 cup chopped fresh parsley
- 1 cup chopped fresh cilantro
- ½ lemon (optional)
   Yogurt for garnish

1. Put the oil in a large pot over medium-high heat. When the oil is hot, add the lamb, taking care not to crowd it (you may have to work in batches) and sprinkle with salt and pepper. Cook, turning as each side finishes, until the lamb is browned on all sides, 10 to 15 minutes total. As the pieces finish, remove them from the pot.

2. Add the leek and carrots to the fat and cook, stirring occasionally, until softened, 3 to 5 minutes. Add the cumin, cinnamon, and cayenne and cook, stirring constantly, until fragrant, about 1 minute. Add the stock, chickpeas or lentils, tomatoes, parsley, and cilantro. Return the lamb to the soup and stir.

3. Bring to a boil, then adjust the heat so the mixture bubbles gently. Skim any foam that rises to the top and cook, stirring occasionally, until the lamb and vegetables are tender, 50 to 60 minutes. Taste and adjust the seasoning. Add squeeze of lemon juice just before serving if you like. Garnish with a dollop of yogurt.

THE BASICS OF STOCK

Stock is the liquid that results from cooking foods in water, then straining them out. The solids may be vegetables, meat, fish, poultry, herbs, spices, or any combination.

Is stock essential for every soup? No. Will it improve almost any soup? Yes. Even the simplest vegetable stock—an onion, a carrot, a celery stalk, a few other scraps, cooked together for 20 minutes—can make a difference in most soups. And a grand, full-flavored chicken, meat, or fish stock is good enough to serve on its own. In fact, the popular "bone broths" are nothing more than stock cooked for hours—and sold at a quite a markup.

STOCK INGREDIENTS

The whole idea of a stock is to flavor water. The recipe might combine protein and aromatics or just include vegetables. Ingredients might be in dried, concentrated form. The stock might simmer for as little as 15 minutes or as much as several hours.

Onion, carrot, and celery find their way into most stockpots, but almost anything can substitute for the other ingredients—turkey for chicken; roasted meat and bones for raw. And similar vegetables are virtually interchangeable, in varying amounts and ratios.

With planning, stock need not be expensive: It's easy enough to start with bits of vegetables that you've frozen and saved over the course of weeks, the trimmings and ends from aromatics, and herb stems. Just avoid strong-tasting vegetables like broccoli and asparagus, and bitter ones like eggplant or bell pepper. Nor do you want to use anything inedible or spoiled.

The meaty raw bones of a single chicken, combined with a few vegetables, provide enough flavor for a pot of stock. Same thing with seafood in the shell, whole fish, or any other meat on the bone. Figure about a pound of bits and pieces per quart. So if you keep containers going in the freezer, you can use just about every butchering scrap except fat, chicken skin, and fish gills and innards.

Bones are an integral part of many stocks, since their components lend body to long-cooked stocks (again, the origin of "bone broth"). But a stock made only of bones tastes like bones rather than meat. Most raw bones are quite meaty, so that isn't so much of a problem. But if you are making a stock with leftovers and are using bones that have been completely stripped of meat, buy a few chicken wings, backs, or necks and add them along with the meat bones; you'll improve the flavor significantly.

Of course it's easier and arguably better to begin with fresh, whole ingredients. Take a carrot, an onion, a celery stalk, a whole chicken, some seasoning, and you can make three quarts of stock, enough for two or three batches of soup, or a batch of soup and a fantastic risotto. Keep the cooking time short and you can even make the soup and still have a chicken worth eating.

Anything you like to eat whole might be considered a candidate for the stockpot: a mild or hot fresh or dried chile; a few cloves garlic, which will become quite mellow; some dried mushrooms (almost always appropriate); herbs or herb trimmings. You know what you like.

STOCK-MAKING TECHNIQUES

BROWNING If you roast stock ingredients before adding water, you get a darker, more complex stock (see "How to Make Any Stock Darker and Richer" on page 178). Stocks that don't begin with browning are brighter and cleaner in flavor. So both ways are useful, depending on your taste and how you're going to use the stock.

STRAINING When you strain a stock—usually through a fine-meshed strainer, lined with cheesecloth if you like—you have two options: If you press on the vegetables and other ingredients, you intensify flavors. If you do not, your stock will be clearer. I opt for flavor, especially since making a stock perfectly clear requires extreme measures best left to the pros.

REDUCING The less water a stock contains, the more intense the flavor and the less room it takes to store. Concentrated stock, undiluted, makes a wonderful, low-fat flavor addition to stir-fries, sauces, and plain steamed vegetables. Remember, though, salt doesn't reduce, so if you're planning to reduce a stock by more than half, don't season it until you've boiled off the extra water.

To reduce stock, begin by straining and defatting it. Then boil it down, stirring now and then and watching to prevent burning, which can occur when the liquid becomes very thick. Be aware that reducing takes a while; reducing a gallon to a quart can take a half-hour or longer. To speed the process, use the widest pot you have, or divide the stock between two or more pots so more of the liquid is exposed to the air, which will help it evaporate more quickly.

REMOVING FAT There are two considerations about fat and stock. First, don't allow stocks to boil vigorously. Rapid boiling can so thoroughly disperse fat that it becomes difficult to remove it. This makes for a fattier stock (obviously), one that can taste greasy. To cook stock, bring it just to a boil, skim any foam that rises to the top, and then turn the heat down so it bubbles gently. On some stoves it helps to turn the heat down and partially cover the pan at the same time or move the pot partially off the heat. You cannot rush the process.

Removing the fat from the finished stock, however, is simple enough, if you make it a day or two before you need it. After cooking, strain the stock (see below) and let it cool just until the fat rises to the top. Refrigerate it; when the fat solidifies—as long as a day later, depending on the quantity of stock and the temperature of the storage place—skim it off with a big spoon and discard it (or if it's from chicken, duck, or pork, save it for cooking). If you don't want to wait that long, simply spoon off the liquid fat as it rises to the top during cooking, or use a degreasing pitcher.

STORING STOCK

The problem with homemade stock is it's so good that you eventually run out and have to make it again. The solution is cooking larger quantities at once—making big batches isn't much more difficult than making small ones—but storage can then become an issue.

Freezing stock is the most efficient method of long-term storage. Here you have a couple of options: One is to ladle or pour the stock into convenient-sized containers; 4-cup ones are usually good. (You can reuse plastic containers from yogurt and such.) Leave a little room for the liquid to expand as it freezes, and cover tightly.

Another option is to put the stock in zipper freezer bags (choose sizes you think you'll use most), lay them flat to freeze, then store upright.

Even more efficient: make stock concentrate. Boil the strained stock down to about half its original volume as described above. You can store the equivalent of 12 cups of stock in a couple ice cube trays. To use, just pop out a cube (it's actually best to pop them all out once they're frozen, then freeze the cubes in a tightly sealed container or plastic bag) and thaw it in a cup of boiling water. Or use the cubes on their own, without diluting, to make pan sauces or cook vegetables.

Frozen stock will keep for weeks or months, though it does deteriorate somewhat in flavor over time. If you remember you have it, however, it's unlikely to last that long. And the cycle will begin again.

PREPARED STOCK, CANNED OR BOXED STOCK, AND BOUILLON CUBES

High-quality prepared stocks are increasingly available from specialty stores and restaurant take-out counters. They cost a lot, so just make sure if you go this route, they're so good they're worth it.

Canned or boxed stock, whether chicken, beef, or vegetable, is usually worse than starting with water and a few vegetables and cooking for 10 minutes. I'd rather have a soup with slightly less flavor than one with lots of bad flavor. If you find a good packaged stock—I'm not saying it's impossible, just difficult—lay in a supply, because the recipe is rarely consistent. If you must buy packaged stock, however, here are some pointers:

- Low-sodium canned stock sometimes has more flavor than regular varieties. Sometimes, however, it tastes like water.

- I used to say that packaged stock can benefit from doctoring. But so will water, and it's almost free.

- As for bouillon cubes, forget them. You're always better off with water and a few vegetables.

Vegetable Stock

MAKES: About 12 cups | **TIME:** About 1 hour, somewhat unattended

Over the past decade or so, this has become my go-to stock. It's easier to make without any notice, and it works for most flavor profiles and diet preferences. To give it a little more depth, I like to add a splash of soy sauce. You can certainly use other vegetables. Just remember that whatever you add will flavor the stock. Avoid eggplant and bell peppers though; they only contribute bitterness.

4	large carrots, sliced
2	large onions, chopped (don't bother to peel)
1	large potato, sliced
2	celery stalks, chopped
5 or 6	cloves garlic (don't bother to peel)
10 to 20	button mushrooms, trimmed and halved or sliced
2	tomatoes, chopped (or use 1 cup canned tomatoes)
10 or 20	fresh parsley stems or sprigs
¼	cup soy sauce, plus more to taste
1	tablespoon black peppercorns

1. Combine all the ingredients in a large pot and add 14 cups water. Bring to a boil and adjust the heat so the mixture bubbles steadily but gently. Cook for about 30 minutes, or until the vegetables are very tender. (Longer is better if you have the time.)
2. Cool slightly, then strain, pressing on the vegetables to extract as much juice as possible. Taste and add more soy sauce if you'd like. Use immediately, refrigerate for up to 5 days, or freeze for up to 3 months.

MUSHROOM STOCK Use 1 carrot, 2 pounds mushrooms (this is the place to use all the shiitake stems you've

saved and frozen), and add ½ ounce dried shiitakes, porcini, or a combination.

Quickest Chicken Stock

MAKES: 12 cups | **TIME:** 40 to 60 minutes

This is my second-most-frequently used stock since it's a two-for-one deal: stock, plus poached chicken to use throughout the week. Just be aware that even though you're using a "wet" cooking method, the chicken breast can still dry out. More cooking is *not* better in this case.

> One 3- to 4-pound chicken
> 1 large onion, roughly chopped (don't bother to peel)
> 1 large carrot, roughly chopped
> 1 celery stalk, roughly chopped
> 1 bay leaf
> Several sprigs fresh parsley (optional)
> Salt and pepper

1. Cut the chicken up, if you like (see page 632); it will speed cooking. Put the chicken, onion, carrot, celery, bay leaf, and parsley in a large pot, add 14 cups water, and turn the heat to high.

2. Bring just to a boil, then lower the heat so the liquid sends up a few bubbles at a time. Cook, skimming any foam that accumulates, until the chicken is cooked through, 30 to 60 minutes, depending on the size of the chicken and whether it's cut up or whole.

3. Transfer the chicken to a bowl with a large fork. Cool the stock slightly, then strain, pressing on the solids to extract more liquid. Discard the remaining solids. When the chicken is cool enough to handle, remove the skin, remove the meat from the bones (discard the skin and bones), and store the meat to use in other recipes. Sprinkle with salt and pepper and taste and adjust the seasoning. Skim off any fat and use the

stock immediately. Or let cool, refrigerate, skim off any hardened fat from the surface, and use within 3 days or freeze for up to 3 months.

FULL-ON CHICKEN, TURKEY, OR DUCK STOCK Turkey or duck can be substituted for some or all of the chicken. And be aware that intensity of flavor can get expensive: Substitute 3 to 4 pounds chicken, turkey, or duck parts, preferably wings, thighs, and legs, for the whole chicken. Cook for at least 1 hour and up to 4 hours. Strain out and discard all the solids after pressing down on them.

Beef, Pork, Lamb, or Veal Stock

MAKES: About 14 cups | **TIME:** At least 3 hours, largely unattended

Meat stocks are less versatile than chicken or vegetable: Beef is the most useful option; I wouldn't make pork or lamb stock unless I had a specific use in mind. But they'll keep in the freezer for at least three months, so if you've got some meaty bones, go for it.

You can use chicken stock in a recipe if you don't have beef stock, but I'd rather use water than canned beef stock, which is essentially useless.

> 3 to 4 pounds meaty beef, pork, lamb, or veal bones, like shank, shin, tail, or short ribs
> 2 onions, chopped (don't bother to peel)
> 2 carrots, chopped
> 2 celery stalks, chopped
> 1 bay leaf
> At least 10 sprigs fresh parsley (optional)
> 1 teaspoon salt, plus more to taste
> 3 whole cloves
> 10 peppercorns

Beef Stock

How to Make Any Stock Darker and Richer

Roasting the ingredients—whether meat, poultry, or vegetables—before adding water yields a darker, more deeply flavored stock that's ideal for hearty soups, stews, braises, and rich gravies or sauces.

The technique is simple and universal: Heat the oven to 400°F. Put the ingredients in a roasting pan, drizzle with at least 2 tablespoons good-quality vegetable oil, and sprinkle with salt. Toss to coat evenly, then spread into a single layer. Roast, turning occasionally, until everything is well browned on all sides. Beef and veal bones will take the longest, 30 to 60 minutes, while thinly cut vegetables may take as little as 5 minutes.

Transfer the solids to the stockpot. Add some hot water to the browned bits in the pan (the *fond*), set it over two burners, and bring to a bubble, scraping up every last browned bit off the bottom. Pour this into the pot and proceed with the recipe.

Some other ingredients that will darken stock and make it richer:

Tomato paste: Mix it with the browned bits in the roasting pan, cooking and stirring until it turns a deep rust color. Then add the water.

Red wine: Add after removing the browned ingredients; stir it into the pan, scraping up the bits on the bottom. (You can also use it in combination with tomato paste, after cooking the paste a bit.) Once that's done, add the water as you normally would.

Garlic: Sometimes I put a whole head of garlic right into my stockpot, but once it's in I can't take it out, so I do it only when I'm making a relatively small amount and know that the garlic will be a welcome flavor.

Dried mushrooms: The distinctive flavor of mushrooms is almost always a fine addition, and I usually throw some directly into the stock as it's bubbling away. In fact, there's almost no reason not to do this, unless they're gritty; then reconstitute them separately as described on page 304 and add the strained soaking liquid to the stock. Use dried porcini (expensive) or dried shiitakes (cheap, especially when bought as black mushrooms in Chinese markets). The trimmings from fresh mushrooms are also good, of course.

1. Rinse the bones well under cold running water, then put them in a large stockpot. Add the onions, carrots, celery, bay leaf, parsley if you're using it, cloves and peppercorns. Add about 16 cups water, enough to cover by a couple of inches.

2. Bring just to a boil, then partially cover and adjust the heat so the mixture just barely bubbles. Cook, skimming off any foam that accumulates at the top, until the meat falls from the bones and the bones separate from one another, 2 to 3 hours.

3. Cool slightly, then strain, pressing on the solids to extract as much liquid as possible. Skim off any fat and use the stock immediately. Or let cool, refrigerate, skim off any hardened fat from the surface, and use within 4 or 5 days or freeze for up to 3 months.

Fish Stock

MAKES: About 4 cups | **TIME:** 40 minutes

I hope you're lucky enough to have a fishmonger close by, or at least a well-run fish counter in your local grocery store. You should be able to grab a few heads and skeletons for free. All you have to know is that usually you want white-fleshed fish, without their guts (which are strong tasting) or gills (which are bitter). Once you have those, you can make good fish stock in about half an hour.

- 1 onion, chopped (don't bother to peel)
- 1 carrot, roughly chopped
- 1 celery stalk, roughly chopped
- ½ cup dry white wine
- 1 pound bones and/or cleaned heads from white fish
- 1 bay leaf
- 1 teaspoon salt

1. Combine all the ingredients in a large pot and add 4 cups water. Bring just to a boil, then adjust the heat so the mixture just barely bubbles. Cook, stirring occasionally, until the mixture becomes cloudy and tastes like fish, about 30 minutes.

2. Cool slightly, then strain, pressing on the solids to extract as much juice as possible. Use immediately, refrigerate for up to 3 days, or freeze for up to a few weeks.

FULL-FLAVORED FISH STOCK Add 1 chopped tomato (canned is fine), 1 smashed clove garlic, a few sprigs fresh parsley, 2 slices lemon, and 3 or 4 peppercorns.

SHRIMP STOCK Omit the wine and bay leaf and use the shells from 1 to 2 pounds shrimp in place of the fish bones. Use ½ onion, sliced; ½ carrot, sliced; and ½ celery stalk, sliced. Increase the water to 4½ cups and cook for only 15 minutes in Step 1.

LOBSTER STOCK Use the ingredients from the shrimp variation, substituting the uncooked legs and shells from 1 to 2 pounds lobster. Cook for 15 minutes in Step 1.

Dashi

MAKES: 8 cups | **TIME:** 15 minutes

This subtle stock is one of the foundations of Japanese cooking. Even if the only two ingredients are difficult to track down, you're still in luck: Once you find them, they keep practically forever in your cupboard.

1 piece dried kelp (kombu), 4 to 6 inches long
½ to 1 cup dried bonito flakes

1. Combine the kelp and 8 cups water in a large pot over medium heat. Do not allow the mixture to come to a boil; as soon as it is about to, turn off the heat and remove the kelp (you can use it as a vegetable in stir-fries or salads if you like).

2. Immediately add the bonito flakes and stir. Let sit for a couple of minutes, then strain. Use the dashi immediately or refrigerate for up to 2 days.

VEGETARIAN DASHI Omit the bonito flakes and add 2 or 3 nickel-sized pieces ginger (don't bother to peel).

---

5 WAYS TO USE DASHI (BESIDES AS STOCK FOR SOUP)

1. Serve it chilled in small bowls for dipping cold soba or ramen noodles (page 522)
2. Substitute dashi for water when cooking rice.
3. Poach fish in dashi instead of water.
4. Reduce it to a glaze for dipping grilled shrimp.
5. Combine reduced dashi with miso to make a glaze for grilled chicken.

 fast make ahead  vegetarian

Salads

CHAPTER AT A GLANCE

Oil 182

Vinegar 183

Vinaigrettes 187

Green Salads 192

Vegetable Salads 199

Fruit Salads 210

Bean Salads 212

Grain Salads 215

Salads with Chicken, Meat, or Fish 221

Pickled Fruits and Vegetables 228

When I try to put my finger on the characteristic that tuna salad, dill pickles, and mixed greens have in common, the answer can only be "dressing."

Salads can be served chilled or at room temperature or even warm. You can toss them. Or just drizzle with dressing. Some might be a side dish or first—or second-to-last—course; others are full meals.

Maybe you assemble raw vegetables one day and use leftovers or precooked vegetables the next. But no matter what ingredients you choose, they wouldn't be salad without a tangy sauce that brings everything together. Even if that just means a few slices of fresh-from-the-garden tomato drizzled with oil and sprinkled with salt.

Maybe that's why I gravitate toward salads: They're improvisational and endlessly variable. The following pages offer salads for every season, craving, and schedule. This chapter runs the gamut from simple to big-deal, and though I've included a section on those that contain meat, poultry, or seafood, most are vegetable-driven. And yes, each includes a tangy dressing.

THE BASICS OF OIL

It's now been two decades since America nearly abandoned butter and began making the move away from trans fats to more healthy oils like olive oil. The no- or low-fat craze has never quite gone away, despite all evidence that sugar and fiberless carbs are more likely to make you fat. Thank goodness we're using oils not only for cooking and salad dressings, but for drizzling. And full-bodied first-press olive oils are thankfully now easy to find and afford for everyday cooking.

Some other oils are almost as good, whether used in cooking or raw. But before I run down my favorite oils, here's an overview to help you choose which to buy.

EXTRACTING AND REFINING OIL

There are a number of ways to coax oil from fruit (like olives), vegetables (corn), nuts (peanuts), legumes (soy), or seeds (grapes or rapeseed, which produces canola). Most oil seeds are first crushed, then washed in a solvent called hexane, then heated. These chemically extracted oils are common and cheap and should be avoided. Combine this information with The Oil Lexicon (see page 184) to figure out which oils are best for your cooking style and taste.

Cold-pressed oils, in which the seeds are put under intense pressure, are better; no hexane is used, and temperatures remain below 180°F. The result is oil with a distinct flavor that reminds you of its source. These oils are less stable than those that are chemically extracted, less tolerant of heat, and quicker to turn rancid, but you can easily deal with all these factors.

Expeller-pressed oils fall somewhere in between chemical extraction and cold pressing. They are pressed, not chemically extracted, though the process involves high heat. These retain some flavor and are relatively stable for cooking and storage; they're a good compromise.

The term *extra virgin* refers to the first cold pressing of the fruit (olive, coconut, avocado, and more). When I call for olive oil throughout the book, what I mean is extra virgin. This process was once done basically by hand, but is now done by machine. When I call for "good-quality vegetable oil" throughout the book, the oils I mean are labeled cold- or first-pressed fruit, nut, or vegetable oils. Soy oil and some seeds—canola and safflower, for example—are ones I avoid for their flavor and stickiness, though some people like them.

After oil is extracted, it may be refined further by heating or filtering to remove impurities and improve its shelf life. Refined oils can handle higher heat than their unrefined counterparts, but they don't have as much flavor. More-refined oils will generally be less cloudy, but once you find a brand you like, you'll know.

 F fast **M** make ahead **V** vegetarian

STORING OILS

When oil starts to turn rancid, it oxidizes, a process that converts some of its components into free radicals that ruin flavor and can be harmful to your health. Since cold-pressed oil spoils fastest, check it frequently. Then smell it before using it. You'll know when it's become rancid; if it has, toss it. To extend shelf life, keep the oil in a dark, cool place, preferably not in clear glass containers. Delicate and expensive finishing oils like those from walnuts, avocados, or hemp seeds and large quantities of olive oil should be stored in the refrigerator. If they solidify, just let them sit out for a few minutes until you can pour off what you need.

OILS, FATS, AND HEALTH

Oils contain saturated, monounsaturated, and/or polyunsaturated fats, usually in combination. Olive oil, for example, is the best known for being high in monounsaturated fats. Soy, seed, and vegetable oils tend to be high in polyunsaturated fats. Tropical oils like coconut and palm oil are mostly saturated fat, like animal fats.

There is debate about the right balance among these types of fats, but for most people it's enough to know that you should not overeat saturated fat, and should even watch your consumption of polyunsaturates. The bulk of the oil you eat should be monounsaturated.

Fortunately, the worst form of fat added to food, trans fat (or trans fatty acids, as it's also known), has been forbidden by regulation and is being phased out. For decades liquid vegetable oil, turned into a semisolid by a chemical process known as *hydrogenation*, was seen as a healthy and long-keeping alternative to butter. Until science proved otherwise. Solid shortening, margarine, commercial frying fats used for fast food, and processed baked goods were the most common sources of trans fat in our diets. These foods have now mostly been reformulated, and include saturated fats that are solid at room temperature. Butter and even lard are better-tasting and healthier alternatives than shortening or margarine. For vegans with pie or biscuit cravings, there are decent shortenings now made with specially formulated combinations of nonhydrogenated tropical oils that work quite well for baking.

About Heating Oil and Smoke Points

When oil is heated to a certain point, it will smoke; this temperature is called its "smoke point." Smoke points can vary from 225° to 450°F, depending on the type of oil and how it was processed. And if the oil is heated a little more it will eventually catch fire, which you obviously want to avoid. But oil heated to smoking also has off flavors and becomes less nutritious.

When cooking with any oil, watch the pan carefully and adjust the heat or move it off a hot burner as needed. For deep frying, you really should use a thermometer. For shallow-frying, stir-frying, or sautéing, knowing an oil's exact smoke point is helpful but almost impossible, even if you have a thermometer. Learn the visual cues: Oil becomes more fragrant as it heats up, and when it's ready for cooking the surface begins to ripple and shimmer, and looks thinner than it was in the bottle. Those are the signals that the oil is nearing its smoke point. Adding food automatically lowers the temperature of the oil, especially if your ingredients are cold.

THE BASICS OF VINEGAR

All vinegar provides acidity, which is valuable for balance and brightness. But only good-quality vinegars bring nuances of flavor beyond sharpness. Like wine or spirits, vinegar can be fermented from just about any fruit, vegetable, or grain.

Always store vinegar in nonreactive glass or ceramic containers, preferably with corks, or glass or lined-metal lids. Kept in a cool, dark place and used regularly, it will be gone before it ever goes bad. You might see a cloud of sediment drifting around the bottom of the bottle; that's called the mother and is harmless evidence of fermentation.

The recipes throughout the book reflect my first choice and often offer another option. But you should use what you like best and have handy. You can always start with less than what's called for in the ingredient list, then taste and adjust the quantity.

The Oil Lexicon

Oils are listed in order of preference and usefulness, though not too strictly because many oils are interchangeable.

OIL	TYPE OF FATS	DESCRIPTION	USES	SUBSTITUTES
Olive oil	Mostly monounsaturated	High-quality olive oils are readily available at a fair price. The best balance the fruity flavor of olives with a little acidity. They range from pale gold to radiant green. You can spend a fortune on them, but need not. The expensive stuff for last-minute drizzling is akin to fine wine; some brands, growing regions, and years are better than others. Don't bother with more refined or "lite" olive oils.	Dressings and cold sauces, sautéing, even some frying. Make Flavored Oil (page 53).	*Niente.* None. You've got to have it.
"Good-quality vegetable oil" (grapeseed, sunflower, safflower)	Mostly polyunsaturated	My go-to oils for high-heat cooking or when I want neutral flavor. Grapeseed oil has a velvety smoothness and often a green color that reminds me of olive oil; the others are a little nuttier and always golden. Buy minimally processed and refined kinds.	Sautéing, pan-frying, grilling, roasting	Any of these three are fine.
Peanut oil	Almost balanced: slightly more polyunsaturated than monounsaturated, and a teeny bit of saturated	I often use peanut oil for deep-frying since it can withstand high heat, a characteristic that also makes it ideal for stir-fry cooking. It has a distinctively peanutty flavor, perfect for many Chinese, Thai, or Vietnamese dishes. As with other oils, cold pressed is best.	Deep-frying, pan-frying, grilling, roasting, some baking	Good-quality vegetable oil, as listed above.
Sesame oil	Almost 50/50 mono- and polyunsaturated, with a little saturated	The toasted dark oil is what I mean by "sesame oil" throughout the book. It's the quintessential Asian condiment, full flavored with a distinctive sesame taste and aroma. A little goes a long way. You might see this seasoned with chile (hot oil), though I prefer to flavor it myself while I'm cooking, or by making Flavored Oil (page 53). If you're cooking with it, watch it well—it has a low smoke point.	Salads, dipping sauces, drizzling, seasoning	None, though toasted nut oils (below) come close.

OIL	TYPE OF FATS	DESCRIPTION	USES	SUBSTITUTES
Coconut oil	Just over 90% saturated fat, with monounsaturated and just a little polyunsaturated	An intensely flavored oil that's a darling of the health crowd, since it supposedly has the potential to raise metabolism despite the fact that it's nearly all saturated fat. It's solid at room temperature though, so it won't work for salads.	Sautéing, stir-frying, baking	Nothing has the same taste, but light sesame oil is good for added flavor, or peanut oil.
Nut oils	These vary: Almond and hazelnut contain predominantly monounsaturated fats; walnut is mostly polyunsaturated	Nut oils are super-flavorful, which makes them fun to use, especially on salads. Almond, walnut, and hazelnut are the most common; all are delicious. There are also roasted nut oils (check out pistachio oil if you see it), but their strong flavors limit their use.	Salads and drizzling; more-refined nut oils work well for low-heat cooking and baking	Fairly interchangeable within this category but otherwise utterly distinctive.
Not-so-everyday oils (apricot kernel, hemp seed, palm, avocado)	Varies depending on the oil, so read the labels	Apricot kernel oil is amazing for high-heat roasting and cooking. Avocado oil is tasty on salads. Hemp seed oil is nutty and rich and great as a garnish. Like coconut, palm oil is high in saturated fat, but has a more neutral flavor and works for high-heat cooking. Look for sustainable brands, as the palm oil industry has many environmental issues.	Varies, depending on the oil	These are one-of a kind, special-occasion oils.
Not recommended oils (mass-market "vegetable oils," soybean, corn, canola)	Varying combinations of mono- and polyunsaturated fats	The most common supermarket oils; if the bottle just says "vegetable oil," there's an excellent chance it's soybean oil, but check the fine print; it could be cottonseed, sunflower, or safflower oil, or a combination. Canola is made from rapeseeds, which are not edible; I find its flavor off-putting, though many people do not.	All-purpose, though I prefer other oils for everything	Buy "good-quality vegetable oil" (see above) whenever you can.

The Vinegar Lexicon

These are the kinds of vinegars I use most. I've included the percentage of acidity to help you make substitutions.

VINEGAR (ACIDITY)	DESCRIPTION	USES	SUBSTITUTES
Sherry vinegar (8%)	The best and most flavorful vinegar for the money, and increasingly available; the genuine stuff must say *vinagre de Jerez*. It is very acidic, so start by using less than you would of other vinegars or cut it with a little water.	Wherever you'd reach for balsamic, from salads to cooked dishes	White wine vinegar or champagne vinegar
Rice vinegar (4.5%)	A must-have for Japanese and other East Asian cooking, as well as light-tasting vinaigrettes. Being low in acid has its advantages.	Virtually any Asian-style salad, cooked dish, or sauce; anytime you want to use less oil/more vinegar) in a salad	No good ones, but in a pinch, white vinegar diluted with water; lemon juice
Balsamic vinegar (about 6%)	Some inexpensive balsamic has a pleasant flavor and is fine in salads. Just read the label and avoid distilled vinegar flavored with caramel syrup. *Aceto Balsamico Tradizionale di Modena* (real balsamic vinegar) is expensive, but if you want to upgrade to something rich and nuanced, look for one made from wine vinegar and aged at least a little while in wood barrels.	Vinaigrette (page 188); in Italy it's used for garnishing, glazing, and saucing meats or chicken; macerating fruit; even in pasta sauces	Sherry vinegar or Chinese black vinegar
Red wine vinegar (6%–7%)	Unless you're going to splurge on a good one from Spain or California, go with sherry vinegar.	Salads and cooked dishes, though remember it turns brown when cooked	Sherry vinegar
White wine vinegar; champagne vinegar; white balsamic vinegar (5%–7%)	Buy neither the cheapest nor the most expensive. Like white wine, white wine vinegar can be dull or delightful. Some is sold as "champagne vinegar," but few are actually made from Champagne; when they are, they're among the best.	Vinaigrettes; refrigerator (not preserved) pickles	White balsamic is a legit choice; rice vinegar; fresh citrus juice
Malt vinegar (4%–8%)	Made from malted grain, this actually tastes malty. Get real brewed malt vinegar—not a "nonbrewed condiment," which is nothing more than water, acetic acid, and caramel coloring.	Pickling; splashing on fried or roasted foods	Cider vinegar

 F fast **M** make ahead **V** vegetarian

VINEGAR (ACIDITY)	DESCRIPTION	USES	SUBSTITUTES
Chinese black vinegar (usually about 5% but may vary)	Made from glutinous rice, this has a delicious, almost haunting flavor. Look for one with *Zhenjiang*, *Zhejiang*, or *Chinkiang* on the label (the province in which it's traditionally made).	Stir-fries and cooked dishes like Simplest Fried Rice (page 444); as a dipping sauce or dressing by itself	A mixture of rice vinegar, soy sauce, and brown sugar (but it just won't be the same)
Cider vinegar (5%)	Made from apple cider, juice, or by-products of cider making; can have a distinct fruity flavor. The quality varies from flavored white vinegar to small-batch, imported, and domestic vinegars worthy of the best salads and vegetables.	The best make rich dressings and sauces; others are good for pickling, chutneys, glazes	White or malt vinegar
Cuisine-specific vinegars: cane, coconut, palm (acidities vary)	Cane and palm vinegars, which are often quite cloudy, are used throughout the Philippines. Coconut vinegar is used in Southeast Asia. They are slightly yeasty and bring a certain flavor to dishes that American vinegars can't provide.	Great for Adobo (page 616); chutneys; pickling; any Thai or Indian dishes	White or cider vinegar
White vinegar (distilled vinegar) (5%)	Acetic acid and water; no flavor, just acidity. Very, very inexpensive.	Pickling; acidulated water	Use for cleaning the house and choose another vinegar to eat.

The Mother of All Dressings: Vinaigrette

When you combine great olive oil, excellent vinegar, salt and pepper, garlic or shallot, and an herb or a little good mustard, you create an astonishingly delicious all-purpose sauce. The kind of thing chefs amaze people with—something you can make every day, serve with pride, and vary for the rest of your life. You can drizzle this mixture on everything from salad to grilled vegetables to cold grilled chicken or fish, grain bowls and noodles . . . anything, really.

The standard ratio is three parts oil to one part vinegar, but many people prefer more oil; a ratio of four to one can be quite nice, depending on how you use it. Adjust the ratio according to the strength of the components. You may prefer two parts oil to one part vinegar or something even a little sharper. And that's the key: Taste your vinaigrette, add a few drops of one or the other, then taste it some more.

Variations might swap out the oil or vinegar for additional flavors. You can skip the vinegar entirely and use citrus juice or even wine or sake. Spices, herbs, solid ingredients like tomatoes or chopped pickles, creamy ones like mustard or egg or roasted garlic—all of these are possible options. And best of all, even the most complicated vinaigrettes take no more than five minutes to make.

DEMYSTIFYING EMULSIFICATION

Novices may wonder how to turn these components into a creamy, cohesive dressing. The process itself is called *emulsification*: forcing oil and water to combine. Many vinaigrettes are emulsions, as is mayonnaise. It takes some energy to bring the two liquids together. Of course this need not be your energy; it can be electrical energy powering a blender, or you can choose a more relaxed approach and not worry about forming a perfect emulsion.

Bottled dressing, trust me—or read the long list of ingredients—is neither a convenience nor better than what you can make yourself in a jar. It's usually an emulsion of inferior oil (like soy or "vegetable") and liquid (often water, with some vinegar, especially in low-fat or "lite" dressings), seasonings (often artificial, or at least far from fresh), and preservatives.

I'm trying to convince you to make your own vinaigrette. Do it in a blender, by shaking the ingredients in a jar, by beating them with a fork or whisk, or with an immersion blender. Hand tools—like forks—won't emulsify much, though there's nothing wrong with that (or with a "broken vinaigrette," in which the oil and vinegar are barely combined), but for a creamy, rich emulsion,

just use a blender, which also has the advantages of puréeing whatever solids you're adding and producing a vinaigrette that will keep in the fridge for at least several days.

Vinaigrette

MAKES: About ¾ cup | **TIME:** 5 minutes

This is my baseline ratio of oil to acid to use when making a well-balanced vinaigrette. Using good wine vinegar—red or white—will result in a little less acidity. There are dozens of ways to change the flavors, as you can see from the chart that follows.

- ½ **cup olive oil**
- 3 **tablespoons sherry vinegar, or more to taste**
  Honey or sugar (optional)
- 1 **shallot, cut into chunks (optional)**
  Salt and pepper

1. Combine the oil and vinegar in a blender and turn the machine on; a creamy emulsion will form within 30 seconds. Taste and add more vinegar, if needed, a teaspoon or two at a time until it tastes balanced to you. If it's too acidic for your taste, add just a touch of honey or sugar and taste again. Keep adjusting until it tastes right.
2. Add the shallot and turn the machine on and off a few times until the shallot is chopped within the dressing. Taste, adjust the seasoning, and serve. (This is best made fresh but will keep, refrigerated, for a few days; bring it back to room temperature and whisk briefly before using.)

VINAIGRETTE IN A JAR The easiest way to make dressing works for the main recipe or any of the variations in the chart on page 190. Mince the shallot (or any additional ingredients). Put all the ingredients in a jar, seal it with a tight-fitting lid, and shake vigorously. Taste, adjust the seasoning, and reshake the dressing again just before serving.

5 More Salad Dressings

Generally these dressings are creamier, thicker, and richer than vinaigrette, so to prevent sogginess I suggest using them to top sturdy mixed greens right before serving rather than tossing the whole salad. Or thin them—with a little oil, heavy cream, milk, lemon juice, vinegar, or just water—to make them more dressing-like than dip-like. Here's where you'll find them.

1. Tahini Sauce (page 56)
2. Blue Cheese Dressing (page 59)
3. Miso-Carrot Sauce with Ginger (page 66)
4. Real Ranch Dressing (page 71)
5. Peanut Sauce (page 75)

 **F** fast **M** make ahead **V** vegetarian

From left to right: Herb, Fish Sauce, and Coconut-Curry Vinaigrettes (see variations on pages 190–191)

21 Variations on Vinaigrette

Simple additions or using different oils and vinegars—or citrus juices, with their lower acidity levels—can change vinaigrette dramatically. Use this chart to get you started with the most familiar flavor profiles, then mix and match components from around the chart and try your own ideas. For all, the methods remain the same as in the Vinaigrette recipe or variation on page 188.

VINAIGRETTE	OIL(S)	ACID	FLAVORINGS AND SEASONINGS (IN ADDITION TO SALT AND PEPPER)
Mustard or Honey Mustard Vinaigrette	½ cup olive oil	3 tablespoons or more good wine vinegar	1 heaping teaspoon any good mustard or about ½ teaspoon dry mustard, plus 1–2 tablespoons honey (optional)
Herb Vinaigrette	½ cup olive oil	3 tablespoons or more fresh lemon juice or good wine vinegar	¼ cup tender, milder fresh herbs like parsley, basil, or dill; 1 teaspoon stronger, tougher herbs like oregano, rosemary, tarragon, or thyme.
Creamy Vinaigrette	⅓ cup olive oil	3 tablespoons or more good white wine vinegar	3 tablespoons heavy cream, sour cream, yogurt, mayonnaise, or puréed silken tofu; 1 teaspoon Dijon mustard, or to taste; 1 small shallot, chopped
Parmesan Vinaigrette	⅓ cup olive oil	3 tablespoons fresh lemon juice or good wine vinegar	¼ cup grated Parmesan cheese. Or try Manchego with sherry vinegar.
Lemon or Lime Vinaigrette	½ cup olive oil	¼ cup or so fresh lemon or lime juice; 1 tablespoon warm water	Zest of 1 lemon or lime, grated or chopped (optional); lots of pepper
Soy Vinaigrette	½ cup good-quality vegetable oil; 1 teaspoon sesame oil, or to taste	3 tablespoons or more rice vinegar or lemon or lime juice	1 tablespoon soy sauce
Roasted Garlic Vinaigrette	½ cup olive oil	3 tablespoons or more balsamic vinegar	2 or more cloves roasted garlic (see page 294); 1 tablespoon honey
Bacon Vinaigrette	¼ cup olive oil; 2 tablespoons rendered bacon fat	3 tablespoons sherry or balsamic vinegar	1 large shallot, chopped; ¼ cup minced cooked bacon, stirred in just before using
Ginger Vinaigrette	½ cup good-quality vegetable oil	1 tablespoon sherry vinegar; 1 tablespoon lime juice; about 1 tablespoon warm water	1 inch fresh ginger, peeled and chopped; lots of pepper
Tomato-Basil Vinaigrette	½ cup olive oil	2 tablespoons or more good wine vinegar	¼ cup chopped seeded fresh tomato; 3 tablespoons chopped fresh basil

VINAIGRETTE	OIL(S)	ACID	FLAVORINGS AND SEASONINGS (IN ADDITION TO SALT AND PEPPER)
Nut Oil Vinaigrette	½ cup walnut, hazelnut, or other nut oil	3 tablespoons sherry vinegar	1 large shallot, chopped (optional)
Nutty Vinaigrette	½ cup olive oil	3 tablespoons sherry, balsamic, or good wine vinegar	¼ cup almonds, hazelnuts, pine nuts, pecans, or walnuts, ground in a food processor; 1 clove garlic
Maple Vinaigrette	½ cup olive oil	2 tablespoons cider, sherry, or white wine vinegar	1 tablespoon maple syrup, or to taste
Avocado Vinaigrette (discolors after an hour or so)	None	¼ cup or more fresh lime or lemon juice	½ avocado (mashed if using a jar); 1 teaspoon chopped garlic or 2 tablespoons chopped onion (optional)
Dried Fruit Vinaigrette	½ cup olive oil	3 tablespoons sherry, balsamic, or good wine vinegar	3 tablespoons dried fruit, chopped if necessary, soaked in the vinegar for 15 minutes; 1 small shallot, chopped
Roasted Pepper Vinaigrette	⅓ cup olive oil	3 or more tablespoons good wine or balsamic vinegar	½ Roasted Red Pepper (page 318), chopped
Anchovy-Caper Vinaigrette	½ cup olive oil	3 tablespoons good wine vinegar	4 anchovy fillets with a bit of their oil; 1 teaspoon capers with a bit of their brine; 2 tablespoons chopped fresh parsley
Coconut-Curry Vinaigrette	½ cup coconut milk	3 tablespoons or more rice vinegar or coconut vinegar	1 tablespoon curry powder
Miso Vinaigrette	3 tablespoons good-quality vegetable oil	3 tablespoons rice vinegar; 2 tablespoons warm water	3 tablespoons white or light miso; 1 tablespoon soy sauce
Pomegranate Molasses Vinaigrette	½ cup olive oil	1 tablespoon pomegranate molasses; 2 tablespoons or more warm water	1 or 2 teaspoons honey
Fish Sauce Vinaigrette	3 tablespoons good-quality vegetable oil	2 tablespoons rice vinegar plus 2 tablespoons lime juice	3 tablespoons fish sauce; 2 teaspoons sugar, 1 clove garlic; 1 small red chile (more or less), seeded

Green Salads

My baseline for green salads is one or more greens, drizzled with oil and a little lemon juice or vinegar and sprinkled with salt and pepper (see Simple Green Salad, page 194). Beyond that there are plenty of other directions to take them; I offer a few in this section. Be sure to see the list on page 196, "15 Ideas for Simple Green Salad."

THE BASICS OF SALAD GREENS

The difference between an average green salad and a great one is determined by just three things: the greens, the oil, and the vinegar. Even if you have good oil and vinegar, drizzle them on some tasteless old lettuce and all you have is terrible lettuce with good dressing.

Luckily, these days, good greens are easy to find. There are hundreds of edible leafy vegetables, each with a unique personality. They range from searing hot mustard to sweet and delicate butter lettuces. In between is a spectrum of flavors, colors, and textures as varied as that of the animal kingdom. That's all good news because it's more interesting to combine at least two or three—or even more.

Here's a brief primer on the common salad greens available from farmers' markets and specialty stores as well as the corner grocery. (Other greens are detailed in the Vegetables and Fruits chapter; see pages 280, 292, or 299). The next section provides some guidance about how to buy, prepare, and store them.

LETTUCES

There are four basic types: iceberg (the familiar light green head of crisp, super-mild leaves); romaine (another head, with long, crunchy leaves, still mild but with some bitterness); Boston (also known as butterhead; soft, well-defined heads with tender, only slightly bitter leaves); and loose-leaf (bunching or cutting lettuce, like green and red leaf; the biggest category of lettuces and the one whose leaves tend to be the most bitter. Sometimes you see the leaves intact, still in loosely formed heads.)

Don't sacrifice quality just because you want a specific mixture; buy what looks best and complements other ingredients. Romaine and Boston lettuces are fine alone, but their mildness can also offset stronger-tasting types. Iceberg—which is a little like eating water—needs more help. So it's good in combination with other vegetables as in a Chopped Salad (page 197), or broken into big wedges and used as a vehicle to show off dressing, like Real Ranch (page 71) or Blue Cheese Dressing (page 59). As the sturdiest of the group, loose-leaf lettuces stand up well to potent add-ins like nuts, cheese, or meats. And most lettuces are even tremendous grilled, braised, or thrown into soups—a nice way to get some mileage out of less-than-fresh leaves.

CHICORY AND ENDIVE

The range of flavors, textures, colors, and versatility of this huge group of greens—radicchio, Belgian endive, curly endive, escarole, frisée, and more obscure greens like Treviso and puntarella—is unmatched.

They're all sharp, crunchy vegetables that vary wildly in appearance but less so in taste and texture. Tight-headed bright red radicchio; long, leafy radicchio; thick-ribbed lettuce-looking escarole and chicory; smooth oval Belgian endive; and lacy, frilly frisée all feature a stark bitterness that is readily tamed by cooking or smoothed by olive oil. Most are super-crunchy, and some are very expensive.

Some people find these too bitter to use alone in salads; they're a piquant counterpoint when mixed with other greens. And I like them with fruit, especially citrus. Belgian endive can be served like celery, as a great edible scoop for dips and spreads. All of these greens are delicious braised (see page 247), stir-fried as described in Stir-Fried Vegetables (page 244), or brushed with olive oil, sprinkled with salt, and grilled (see Grilled Balsamic Radicchio, page 253).

 fast make ahead  vegetarian

ARUGULA, WATERCRESS, AND DANDELION GREENS

These dark green leaves fall on a spectrum of intensity: Dandelion greens—among the most vitamin-packed foods on the planet—are mild flavored when young, incomparably bitter when mature. Super-peppery cresses—now often sold with the roots intact to keep them fresh longer—deserve more attention than mere garnishing. Arugula (also called rocket or rucola) is the most interesting of the bunch. When mature, its distinctive spicy earthiness may be an acquired taste, but an easy one to adore. The much milder baby arugula is easier to find.

Arugula, lightly dressed with olive oil and lemon juice, is excellent warm, so it's perfect as a bed for anything grilled. (This is true for many greens, actually.) Watercress is also good on sandwiches and in soups or tossed with pasta. Dandelion greens can be eaten in salads when young but quickly become too bitter to eat raw and are then best when steamed or stir-fried with soy sauce or garlic and lemon. For more information and other recipes for cooking these greens, see pages 299 and 307.

MESCLUN

Mesclun, from the Niçoise dialect for "mixture," now describes virtually any combination of greens, herbs, and even edible flowers. Supermarket mesclun may not be as interesting as what you might pull together (especially if you're a gardener), but it's a convenient year-round staple, thanks to a special process called modified atmosphere packaging that keeps it fresh for a week. (The same is true of other prepackaged salads.) Once opened, however—or if you buy mesclun in bulk—use within a couple of days, before it turns even the slightest bit funky. Packaged greens are theoretically washed, but I rinse them anyway—until the water runs clear—and I recommend you do too.

THE OTHER GREENS

Some leafy greens don't easily fall into any of the previous categories. Ever-popular spinach (see page 338) is available everywhere in many forms. Mizuna (a spiky, sturdy green often used in mesclun) and tatsoi (a small-leafed member of the bok choy family) are becoming mainstream in America. Others like mâche, lamb's tongue, and their relatives are quite tender and fragile, with a small window of freshness.

Buying, Preparing, and Storing Salad Greens

Buying: In all cases, look for leaves without discoloration or wilting. For loose heads, try to peek inside and see how the center looks.

Trimming: For head and whole loose-leaf lettuces, first tear or cut out the core. (If the head is tight, you'll probably have to use a knife; or try bashing the bottom firmly on the counter to loosen it.) Trim away the outer round of leaves and any browned or wilted stems. Tear or cut into smaller pieces if you like.

Rinsing and Drying: A fast and easy process. Put the greens in a salad spinner or a colander inside a large pot or bowl. Fill the outer container with water and swirl the greens around. Now lift the salad spinner insert or colander out of the water. Pour the water out of the container. Repeat as necessary until the water contains no traces of sand. Then spin the greens or gently pat them dry with towels.

Storing: Rinsed, thoroughly dried salad greens are good to have on hand and often keep better than in the bag from the store. If you have a salad spinner, pour the water out of it after spinning and pop it into the fridge, greens and all. The remaining moisture and ventilated basket provide a good environment for keeping greens fresh for a couple of days or more. If you don't have a salad spinner, line a small plastic bag with clean towels, put the rinsed greens inside (taking care not to pack them too tightly), loosely tie the top, and refrigerate. For greens that come with roots, put them in a shallow container half-full of water and wrap the whole thing, container and all, in a plastic bag and refrigerate to create a mini tropical environment.

If you shop at farmers' markets, Asian grocers, or specialty stores, you'll run into all of these and more. Just treat them as you would any other lettuces or salad greens and try swapping them out for "assorted greens" in the recipes here. Almost all may also be lightly cooked—steamed, boiled and shocked, or stir-fried—though when they're young, fresh, and tender, raw is best.

Simple Green Salad

MAKES: 4 servings | **TIME:** 10 minutes

There's a reason green salad remains a staple side dish: It's fresh, quick, and easy. By changing the acid and the oil (see the chart on page 190) you can make one that complements any meal.

>   6   **cups torn assorted greens, like mesclun or any lettuce**
>   **About ⅓ cup olive oil**

About 2 tablespoons sherry vinegar, balsamic vinegar, or fresh lemon juice
Salt and pepper

Put the greens in a bowl and toss them with the oil, vinegar, a pinch of salt, and some pepper. Toss and taste. Adjust the seasoning and serve immediately.

GREEN SALAD WITH FRESH HERBS Use 5 cups assorted greens (mesclun or the like) and add about a cup of fresh parsley, dill, mint, or basil, or any combination. Use lemon juice as the acid, or replace the oil and acid with Lemon Vinaigrette (page 190) if you like.

WATERCRESS AND SESAME SALAD Use watercress for the greens; substitute Soy Vinaigrette (page 190) for the oil and vinegar. Sprinkle with toasted sesame seeds for garnish.

ENDIVE SALAD WITH NUT OIL VINAIGRETTE Substitute roughly chopped Belgian endive leaves for the assorted greens; add radicchio, watercress, and other

Rinsing Salad Greens

STEP 1 Plunge salad greens into a salad spinner filled with water or a colander set in a large pot or bowl; swirl the greens around, then lift the insert or colander and change the water, repeating as many times as necessary to remove all traces of grit.

STEP 2 If you have a salad spinner, spin the greens dry; otherwise, dry them in a towel.

STEP 3 Store, wrapped loosely in towels, in a semiclosed resealable plastic bag or the salad spinner.

 F fast   **M** make ahead   **V** vegetarian

strong-flavored greens if you like. Toss in about ½ cup toasted walnuts or hazelnuts (see page 309) and use Nut Oil Vinaigrette (page 191).

GREEK SALAD, SIMPLIFIED Add about ¼ cup chopped fresh mint or parsley (or a mix of both), about ⅓ cup crumbled feta cheese, and about ¼ cup pitted and roughly chopped black olives. Use lemon juice as the acid. You can also add chopped cucumber, tomatoes, and red onion for a less simplified salad.

15 IDEAS FOR SIMPLE GREEN SALAD

Choose one or at most two additions, to keep your salad simple. See the following recipes for heartier, more complicated salads.

1. Omit the oil or minimize the vinegar; either way, it'll still be good.
2. Substitute any good, flavorful oil like walnut, hazelnut, or sesame. Use less at first, because these are stronger than olive oil.
3. Add tomatoes, in quarters or eighths; you might want to remove their seeds first (see page 345), but it isn't essential. Or use halved cherry or grape tomatoes.
4. Add grated or shaved Parmesan cheese. This is probably the easiest upgrade you can make to many salads.
5. Add chopped vegetables; see Chopped Salad (page 197).
6. Add chopped pitted olives.
7. Add chopped shallot, onion, scallion, or leek, or just a little bit of minced garlic.
8. Add chopped or sliced Hard-Boiled Egg (page 721), or top with one or more Poached Eggs (page 725) or peeled Soft-Boiled Eggs (page 721).
9. Add crumbled blue cheese or any other cheese.
10. Add any toasted nuts or seeds, chopped if necessary.

11. Add sliced pears, apples, oranges, or other fruit.
12. Add about ¼ ounce seaweed, soaked and drained as in Sesame Seaweed Salad (page 209). Or add 1 sheet nori (laver), toasted briefly over a hot flame and crumbled as on page 448.
13. Add chopped Roasted Red Peppers (page 318; or yellow peppers), capers, or anchovies.
14. Use more intensely flavored greens: arugula, watercress, endive, radicchio, frisée, escarole.
15. Sprinkle with crumbled cooked bacon or top with anchovy fillets.

Caesar Salad

MAKES: 4 servings | **TIME:** 20 minutes

The essentials in a real Caesar salad are garlic, egg—which I like to coddle just a bit for texture—lemon juice, anchovies, and real Parmesan cheese. See the variation to turn the recipe into a satisfying lunch.

1	clove garlic, halved
2	eggs
2	tablespoons fresh lemon juice
6	tablespoons olive oil
2	tablespoons chopped anchovies, or to taste
	Dash Worcestershire sauce
	Salt and pepper
1	large or 2 small heads romaine lettuce, torn into pieces (about 6 cups)
	My Kind of Croutons (page 801)
½ to 1	cup grated Parmesan cheese

1. Rub the inside of a salad bowl with the garlic clove; discard the spent garlic.

2. Bring a small pot of water to a boil. Pierce a tiny hole in the broad end of each of the eggs with a pin or needle. Boil the eggs for 60 to 90 seconds; they will just begin to firm up. Crack them into the bowl, being sure to scoop out any white that clings to the shell.

3. Beat the eggs with a fork to combine. Gradually add the lemon juice, then the oil, beating constantly.

4. Stir in the anchovies and Worcestershire. Taste and add salt if needed and plenty of pepper. Add the lettuce and toss well. Top with the croutons and Parmesan, then toss again at the table. Serve immediately.

CHICKEN, SHRIMP, OR VEGETABLE CAESAR SALAD

Top the salad with slices of Grilled Boneless Chicken or Broiled Boneless Chicken (page 599), grilled or broiled shrimp (see page 534), or grilled or broiled vegetables (see page 251).

Chopped Salad

MAKES: 6 servings | **TIME:** 30 minutes

It's a stretch to call this a recipe—a formula is more like it. Include the optional meat for an easy dinner.

2	celery stalks (try to include some leaves), chopped
2	carrots, chopped
1	small-to-medium red onion, chopped
1	cucumber, peeled if necessary and seeded (see page 287), chopped
1	red or yellow bell pepper, cored, seeded, and chopped
1	cup chopped ham or cooked chicken (optional)
1	small head romaine lettuce, chopped (about 4 cups)
	Salt and pepper
½	cup or more Vinaigrette (page 188; made with 1 small clove garlic instead of shallot) or one of the variations (page 190)

1. Combine the celery, carrots, onion, cucumber, bell pepper, the meat if you're using it, and the lettuce in a bowl; sprinkle lightly with salt and pepper and toss.

2. Drizzle with the vinaigrette and toss to combine. Taste and adjust the seasoning. Serve immediately.

CHOPPED SALAD, SOUTHWEST STYLE Use avocado, jícama, tomatoes, and red or yellow bell pepper for the vegetables. Use Avocado Vinaigrette (page 191) for the dressing. Add chopped cooked chicken or shrimp if you like. Garnish with crumbled tortilla chips.

CHOPPED SALAD WITH COCONUT Use chopped tomatoes, steamed new potatoes, carrots, and chickpeas (rinsed and drained) for the vegetables, and Coconut-Curry Vinaigrette (page 191) or Creamy Cilantro-Mint Chutney (page 62) for the dressing. Garnish with toasted shredded coconut.

CHOPPED SALAD WITH PEANUT DRESSING Use carrots, scallions, shredded cabbage, and snow peas or sugar snap peas for the vegetables (with or without the lettuce). For the dressing, thin Peanut Sauce (page 75) with soy sauce, fresh lime juice, and/or water. Add chopped cooked chicken or cooked tofu (see pages 596 and 419). Garnish with fresh cilantro.

---

12 OTHER INGREDIENTS FOR CHOPPED SALAD

1. ½ bulb fennel, or so, trimmed and chopped

2. About 1 cup chopped haricots verts, or green or wax beans, boiled briefly and shocked (see page 238)

3. About 1 cup small chunks steamed waxy potatoes

4. ½ cup chopped radishes

5. About 1 cup peeled and chopped raw beets; use cooked if you prefer

6. About 1 cup corn kernels, cooked any way (grilled is excellent)

7. ½ cup grated or crumbled cheese, like Parmesan, blue cheese, or feta

8. ½ cup chopped pitted olives

9. ½ cup toasted nuts like almonds, pistachios, or peanuts, chopped into large pieces

10. 1 apple, cored and chopped

11. 1 cup cooked grain like farro, quinoa, or rice

12. 1 cup mixed fresh herbs like parsley, mint, dill, or cilantro

Warm Spicy Greens with Bacon and Eggs

MAKES: 4 servings | TIME: About 30 minutes

There's nothing reserved or subtle about this salad. Which sometimes is just what you want.

- 2 tablespoons olive oil
  About 8 ounces of the best slab bacon you can find, or pancetta, cut into ½-inch cubes
- 1 small shallot, chopped
- 4 cups torn dandelion or other bitter greens like mustard or turnip greens, watercress, or frisée
  About ¼ cup top-quality red wine vinegar
- 1 teaspoon Dijon mustard
  Salt and pepper
- 4 Poached Eggs (page 725), or peeled Medium-Boiled Eggs (page 721)

1. Put the oil in a skillet over medium heat. When the oil is hot, add the bacon and cook slowly until it's crisp all over, 10 minutes or more. Add the shallot and cook until softened, another minute or 2. Keep the bacon warm in the skillet.

2. Warm a salad bowl by filling it with hot water and letting it sit for a minute. Dry it and toss in the greens. Add the vinegar and mustard to the bacon and bring just to a boil, stirring. Pour the liquid and bacon over the greens, toss, and season to taste; it shouldn't need much salt. Top each portion with an egg and serve immediately.

WARM SPINACH SALAD WITH BACON AND EGGS
Substitute tender spinach leaves for the dandelion greens.

WARM KALE SALAD WITH BACON AND EGGS Substitute thinly sliced kale leaves for the dandelion greens.

SALADE LYONNAISE The French classic: Use frisée for the greens. Skip warming the salad bowl and boiling the vinaigrette; simply add the vinegar and mustard to the warm bacon. Toss the greens with the vinaigrette and serve immediately.

BLT SALAD Omit the shallots, if you prefer, and the eggs. Substitute any lettuce or salad greens for the dandelion; add 2 large fresh chopped tomatoes, and ½ cup crumbled blue cheese. Let the bacon cool in the pan after it's cooked. In Step 2, combine the lettuce, tomatoes, and cheese in an unheated salad bowl. Stir the vinegar and mustard into the bacon, then pour over the salad and toss; serve immediately.

Vegetable Salads

Many raw vegetables—tomatoes of course (actually a fruit) but also beets, carrots, artichokes, celery and celeriac, mushrooms, and others—make fantastic salads. Whether seriously crunchy or sublimely tender, subtly flavored or assertively strong, they stand up to bold dressings, which makes them more interesting than green salads. And many benefit from being made and marinated ahead, so it's okay to have leftovers.

Tomato, Mozzarella, and Basil Salad

MAKES: 4 servings | TIME: 5 to 15 minutes

I may sound like a broken record, but for salads as simple as this—it's barely more than the ingredients in the title—you must use the best ingredients possible, starting with seasonal tomatoes.

- 4 perfectly ripe tomatoes
  Salt and pepper
- 1 ball fresh mozzarella, cut into 8 slices
- 8 large fresh basil leaves
  Olive oil for drizzling

1. Core and cut the tomatoes into about ¼-inch-thick slices. If you like, lay them on a board and sprinkle them lightly with salt. Set the board at an angle so the liquid can drain into the sink, or into a bowl; it makes a refreshing drink.
2. Layer the tomatoes, mozzarella, and basil on a platter or 4 individual plates. Sprinkle with salt and pepper, drizzle with oil, and serve.

PEACH, MOZZARELLA, AND BASIL SALAD Substitute 2 perfectly ripe peaches, pitted and sliced, for the tomatoes.

MELON, FETA, AND MINT SALAD Use ¼ watermelon, seeded, peeled and sliced, 4 ounces sliced or crumbled feta, and ¼ cup fresh mint leaves. Drizzle with olive oil and sprinkle with salt and pepper.

Cherry Tomato Salad with Soy Sauce

MAKES: 4 servings | TIME: 15 to 30 minutes

Grape and cherry tomatoes are the only tomatoes worth eating all year round, and so this is the salad to satisfy your cravings until the summertime slicers are back in full swing. The combination of soy sauce and tomatoes is startlingly good, and letting the salad sit for 15 minutes tints the tomatoes with a deeply flavored mahogany glaze.

  2 tablespoons soy sauce, plus more to taste
     Pinch sugar

  2 teaspoons sesame oil
  4 cups cherry or grape tomatoes, stemmed and halved
  ½ cup whole fresh basil leaves, preferably Thai basil
     Pepper

1. Combine the soy sauce, sugar, and oil in a large bowl. Add the tomatoes and basil and sprinkle liberally with pepper. Stir gently to coat the tomatoes with dressing.
2. Let stand at room temperature for up to 15 minutes, stirring once or twice. Taste and add more soy sauce and pepper if you like. Serve.

Simple Radish or Jícama Salad

MAKES: 4 servings | TIME: 15 to 30 minutes

Super-crunchy radishes or jícama make a refreshing salsa-like salad to eat in warm weather, or a welcome companion for braised meats and heavy foods throughout the year. The lemon and lime juice mixture mimics the flavor of sour orange, common in Mexico but tough to find here. Try grapefruit juice for a less traditional, equally delicious dressing.

     About 12 ounces radishes, daikon, or jícama; peeled if necessary and sliced or chopped
  1 small white onion, chopped
     Salt and pepper
  2 tablespoons fresh lime juice, or to taste
  2 teaspoons fresh lemon juice
  2 tablespoons chopped fresh cilantro or parsley

1. If time allows, toss the radishes and onion with 1 tablespoon salt in a strainer and let sit for 15 minutes; rinse and pat dry with towels.

 fast   make ahead   vegetarian

2. Put the radishes and onion in a large bowl with some pepper (and salt if you didn't salt the radishes in Step 1), lime and lemon juices, and cilantro. Taste, adjust the seasoning, and serve immediately or refrigerate for up to an hour.

RADISH-CELERY-MINT SALAD A sweet addition: Substitute ½ cup chopped celery for the onion, olive oil for the lime juice, and orange juice for the lemon juice. Toss the radishes and celery with ½ cup chopped fresh mint instead of the cilantro and sprinkle with salt (if you haven't already salted them) and pepper. Drizzle with olive oil and orange juice, toss again, and serve.

CELERY-CUCUMBER-MINT SALAD More like chopped salad: Omit the radishes and onion and use ½ cup chopped celery and 1 English cucumber, peeled if you like and sliced. Substitute olive oil for the lime juice and ½ cup chopped fresh mint for the cilantro.

CELERY-PARSLEY-PARMESAN SALAD Omit the radishes and onion and use 2 cups chopped celery, and celery leaves instead of the herb. Replace the lime juice with olive oil and toss the salad with ¼ cup grated or shaved Parmesan cheese.

Corn Salad with Avocado

MAKES: 4 servings | **TIME:** 30 minutes

Usually I recommend frozen corn out of season, but not here. Instead seek out corn on the cob; even if it's mediocre, roasting will vastly improve the flavor. If you've got the freshest corn possible, skip Step 1, cut it from the cob and mix it raw with all the other ingredients in Step 2.

2	**tablespoons good-quality vegetable oil**
4 to 6	**ears corn, husked and the kernels removed (2 to 3 cups; see page 283)**

1	**small red onion, chopped**
½	**red bell pepper, cored, seeded, and chopped**
1	**teaspoon mild chile powder like ancho**
	Salt and pepper
1	**fresh tomato, cored, seeded, and chopped**
1	**ripe avocado, pitted, peeled, and chopped**
	Juice of 2 limes, or more to taste
	About ½ cup chopped fresh cilantro

1. Put the oil in a large skillet (cast iron is good here, but anything will do) and turn the heat to high. When the oil is very hot but not yet smoking, toss in the corn. Let it sit for a minute or so, then stir or shake the pan; brown the corn a bit, 3 to 5 minutes, then turn off the heat and stir in the onion, pepper, chile powder, salt, and pepper.

2. Cool for a few minutes, then toss with the tomato, avocado, lime juice, and cilantro. Taste, adjust the seasoning, and serve hot, warm, or at room temperature.

CORN SALAD WITH ARUGULA Omit the chile powder and cilantro and substitute 3 cups torn arugula leaves for the avocado and 2 tablespoons white wine vinegar for the lime juice.

CORN AND NOODLE SALAD WITH CHILE Add 1 teaspoon fish sauce to the dressing. Soak 8 ounces rice noodles in boiling water until soft (see page 520) then toss with the dressing. Omit the avocado and use 2 fresh chopped tomatoes. Substitute 2 chopped scallions for the onion. Replace the chile powder with 1 fresh chile, like Thai or serrano, sliced. Garnish with ½ cup chopped basil leaves.

CORN SALAD WITH TARRAGON Omit the chile powder and avocado. Substitute 2 tablespoons rice vinegar for the lime juice and 1 tablespoon chopped tarragon for the cilantro.

CORN SALAD WITH FETA AND MINT Omit the chile powder and lime juice and substitute 1 cup crumbled feta cheese for the avocado and mint for the cilantro. Add a sprinkle of any Vinaigrette (page 188).

Spicy No-Mayo Coleslaw

MAKES: 8 servings | **TIME:** 30 minutes

I like coleslaw on the spicy side, so I use plenty of Dijon mustard along with a little garlic and chile and some scallions. If this version sounds more like cabbage salad and you're worried you'll miss the mayonnaise, then use mayo instead of some or all of the oil.

- 2 **tablespoons Dijon mustard, or to taste**
- 2 **tablespoons sherry vinegar, red wine vinegar, or fresh lemon juice**
- 1 **small clove garlic, minced**
- 1 **tablespoon minced fresh chile like jalapeño or serrano, or to taste (optional)**
- ¼ **cup good-quality vegetable oil or olive oil**
- 6 **cups cored and shredded napa, savoy, green, and/or red cabbage**
- 1 **large red or yellow bell pepper, cored, seeded, and chopped**
- ⅓ **cup chopped scallions**
   Salt and pepper
- ¼ **cup chopped fresh parsley**

1. To make the dressing, whisk together the mustard, vinegar, garlic, and chile, if you're using it, in a large bowl. Add the oil a little at a time, whisking all the while.

2. Add the cabbage, bell pepper, and scallions and toss with the dressing. Sprinkle with salt and pepper and refrigerate until ready to serve. (It's best to let the slaw rest for an hour or so to allow the flavors to mellow; the cabbage will also soften a bit and exude some juice. You can let it sit longer, up to 24 hours if you like. Drain the slaw before continuing.) Just before serving, toss with the parsley.

To Salt or Not to Salt

The word *salad* comes from the Latin word for salt, so it's no surprise that the two concepts go hand in hand: salting vegetables, even briefly, can maximize their crispness and flavor by causing them to release their water. Specifically:

Cabbage: When slaws are made with salted cabbage, they are noticeably less watery and stay crisp and fresh for a few days longer. Put sliced cabbage in a colander, sprinkle with salt (about a tablespoon for 6 cups cabbage), and let sit. After about an hour, rinse and drain. For extra crispness, rinse, then wring dry in a towel after salting; if that's not your goal, just pat dry after rinsing.

Cucumbers: Ordinary cukes benefit a lot from salting. First peel, seed (see page 287), and slice them. Then use the same procedure as for cabbage.

Radishes: Sliced radishes may be salted like cabbage and cucumbers—they become milder and crisper—but only for an absolute maximum of 45 minutes, or they will become limp.

Tomatoes: Lightly salting tomatoes always improves their flavor and tightens their flesh, but they are fragile. Use less salt (about 1 teaspoon per pound) and leave them for only 15 minutes or so. Put salted chopped tomatoes in a colander (and set a bowl under it if you want to trap the tomato water for using in stocks or sauces). Sliced or wedged tomatoes work best put directly on towels before salting.

Onions: Onions become milder and crisper after salting, either directly or in a saltwater bath (about 1 tablespoon salt per 4 cups water). Let sit for a half hour or longer, then rinse and dry before using.

Kale: Treating raw kale this way makes it less tough and much tastier. Put chopped kale leaves in a colander and sprinkle with salt. "Massage" the salt into the leaves to start the process of breaking down the cell walls; let stand for up to an hour. Rinse and dry before dressing.

Salad greens: Avoid salting or dressing these in advance. You'll end up with a watery mess.

CABBAGE AND CARROT SLAW, MEXICAN STYLE Grate 2 carrots and use them instead of the bell pepper. Use fresh lime juice in place of the vinegar. Finish with cilantro if you like instead of the parsley.

APPLE SLAW Use carrots instead of bell pepper, as in the preceding variation. Use 1 onion, grated, in place of the scallions. Lemon juice or cider vinegar is the best choice of acid here. Shred or grate 2 small or 1 large Granny Smith apples or any tart, crisp, apple, and include them in the mix.

CUMIN-SCENTED CARROT SLAW Omit the mustard, use lemon juice, and add 1 teaspoon toasted cumin seeds to the dressing. Omit the cabbage and pepper. Shred or grate 1 pound carrots. Toss the carrots with the dressing and garnish with parsley or cilantro. Add ½ cup golden raisins if you like and toss again.

RED SLAW Use red cabbage and reduce the quantity to 3 cups; use red bell pepper and add about 1 pound red beets. Instead of the scallions, substitute a shallot or small red onion. Grate all the vegetables (a food processor is the handiest tool). Transfer the mixture to a cloth-lined strainer and press to extract as much liquid as possible before adding to the dressing in Step 2. Garnish with parsley if you like, but then the slaw won't be all red!

Fennel and Orange Salad

MAKES: 4 servings | **TIME:** 15 minutes

A classic, easy salad that seems fancy despite how simple it is to make.

1	**pound fennel (1 large or 2 small bulbs)**
3	**small sweet oranges or tangerines**
	Salt
1	**tablespoon fresh lime or lemon juice**
	Olive oil for drizzling

Composed Salads

"Composed salad" is a fussy name for arranging all the ingredients on a plate, then drizzling dressing on top. You can make individual composed salads or one big serving. All you need are greens and, say, at least three components that provide contrasting yet complementary textures, flavors, and colors. These can be cooked or raw, leftovers or specially prepared. Arrange them on the plate without fuss, then garnish with croutons, toasted nuts, or other crunchy tidbits. You can do all this a little in advance, but don't pour the dressing on top until right before serving.

1. Trim and core the fennel and cut it into thin slices, or shave it super-thin on a mandoline. Reserve some of the most tender fronds for garnish.
2. Squeeze the juice from one of the oranges, pour it over the fennel, add salt and lime juice, and let it sit for up to several hours while you prepare the other oranges.
3. Peel the remaining oranges and slice into wheels (see page 378); then slice into half moons and remove any pits and tough, fibrous material. Add the oranges and reserved fronds to the fennel, toss, and taste and adjust the seasoning. Serve drizzled with oil.

FENNEL, ORANGE, AND OLIVE SALAD Use lemon juice and parsley. Add ½ cup chopped pitted oil-cured, kalamata, or any green olives in Step 3.

RED ONION AND ORANGE SALAD Substitute 1 small red onion, thinly sliced, for the fennel and 1 teaspoon fresh rosemary or ½ teaspoon dried for the cilantro. Use 4 navel or Valencia oranges, but do not juice any of them; peel and slice them all. Omit the lime juice, drizzle with some olive oil and toss before serving.

CUCUMBER AND ORANGE SALAD Substitute thinly sliced cucumber for the fennel; peel and seed (see page 287) if you like. Use any of the herbs above, or try chives.

8 Shaved Vegetable Salads

Cut raw vegetables paper thin and you have an elegant "shaved" salad. A mandoline is an ideal tool—or easier still, use a food processor with an adjustable slicing disk on the lowest setting. Toss the shards with a little of the dressing, transfer to a serving platter—spread out on a big plate, it looks gorgeous—and garnish. Serve right away with the remaining dressing on the side. Just don't let any of these salads sit for more than 30 minutes, or they're apt to become soggy and watery.

SALAD	VEGETABLE	DRESSING	GARNISH
Celery Rémoulade	1 celery root, peeled and sliced	Creamy Vinaigrette (page 190) made with mayonnaise	Chopped fresh celery leaves or chives
Shaved Mushroom Salad	1 pound button mushrooms, sliced	Lemon Vinaigrette (page 190)	Shaved Parmesan cheese; chopped fresh parsley
Shaved Beet Salad	1 pound beets, peeled and sliced (golden beets make a lovely salad)	Pomegranate Molasses Vinaigrette (page 191)	Chopped toasted pistachios; chopped scallions
Shaved Kohlrabi Salad	1 pound kohlrabi, peeled and sliced	Ginger Vinaigrette (page 190)	Chopped fresh basil; toasted sesame seeds
Shaved Root Vegetable Salad	1 pound mixed root vegetables like parsnip, carrot, turnip, and/or rutabaga, peeled and sliced	Maple Vinaigrette (page 191)	Chopped fresh parsley
Shaved Asparagus Salad	1 pound asparagus, sliced	Miso Vinaigrette (page 191)	Chopped fresh cilantro
Shaved Zucchini Salad	1 pound small zucchini, sliced	Nut Oil Vinaigrette (page 191) with hazelnut oil	Chopped fresh mint; chopped toasted hazelnuts
Shaved Artichoke Salad	4 artichokes, trimmed, cleaned (see page 258), sliced	Lemon Vinaigrette (page 190)	Grated Parmesan cheese; chopped fresh parsley or basil

Cold Cooked and Dressed Greens

MAKES: 4 servings | **TIME:** 20 minutes

Inspired by a Greek dish called *horta*, I now serve all kinds of cooked greens this way, including leftovers. In addition to the dark greens listed below, it's also great with broccoli, broccoli raab, or Asian greens like *gai lan*.

Salt
1 to 2 **pounds dark leafy greens like kale, collards, chard, or spinach**
Several tablespoons olive oil
Pepper
2 **lemons, halved**

1. Bring a large pot of water to a boil and salt it. Trim the greens; remove and discard any stems thicker than ¼ inch. Rinse the greens well.

 fast   make ahead   V vegetarian

2. Cook the greens until tender, just a minute or 2 for spinach, up to 10 minutes or even longer for older, tougher greens. Drain them well in a colander and cool by running them under cold water.

3. Squeeze the greens as dry as you can manage. Chop them. (At this point, you can refrigerate them, covered, for up to a day, then bring to room temperature before proceeding.) Sprinkle with oil, salt, pepper, and a squeeze of lemon juice, then taste and adjust the seasoning. Serve with the remaining lemon.

COLD BOK CHOY AND GINGER SALAD Use bok choy or one of the other greens listed on page 206. Substitute 2 tablespoons grated fresh ginger, ¼ cup rice vinegar, and 1 teaspoon sesame oil, plus good-quality vegetable oil for the olive oil and lemons.

COLD ESCAROLE, GARLIC, AND PARMESAN SALAD Use escarole for the greens. Add 2 tablespoons chopped garlic. In Step 3, put ¼ cup olive oil in a large skillet over medium heat. When it's hot, add the garlic and cook until fragrant but not brown, about 30 seconds. Remove from the heat and stir in 3 tablespoons fresh lemon juice and a sprinkle of grated zest if you like. Toss the greens with the garlic-lemon mixture and ½ cup grated Parmesan cheese; sprinkle on salt and lots of pepper.

Potato Salad with Mustard Vinaigrette

MAKES: 4 servings | **TIME:** 30 minutes, plus time to cool

The best and simplest potato salad is made of just-boiled potatoes, dressed in a freshly made vinaigrette. They'll soak up some of the dressing while hot and get even better as they sit. If it's classic potato salad—with mayonnaise—you're after, see the first variation. Beyond the variations, see the list that follows for more suggestions.

1½ pounds waxy potatoes like red new potatoes or fingerling; or all-purpose like Yukon Gold; or even starchy baking potatoes are fine
Salt and pepper
½ cup chopped fresh parsley
¼ cup chopped scallions, or red or yellow onion
½ cup Mustard Vinaigrette (page 190) or any other vinaigrette (pages 188–191), plus more to taste

1. Peel the potatoes if you like, or rinse and scrub them well, then cut them into bite-sized pieces. Put them in a pot with enough water to cover and add a large pinch salt. Bring to a boil, then lower the heat so the water bubbles gently. Cook the potatoes until tender but still firm and not all mushy, 15 minutes or so, depending on the potato. Drain, rinse in cold water for just a minute, then drain again.

2. Toss the still-warm potatoes with the parsley and scallions. Add the vinaigrette until the mixture is as dressed as you like. Taste and adjust the seasoning, adding plenty of pepper. Serve as is, or refrigerate for an hour or so to chill the salad. (At this point, you can refrigerate the salad, covered, for up to a day.)

CLASSIC POTATO SALAD Omit the vinaigrette. Whisk together ½ cup mayonnaise (to make your own, see page 69) with 3 tablespoons sherry vinegar or white wine vinegar. (Mayonnaise flavored with herbs, garlic, mustard, or virtually any seasoning is fine—even an improvement here.) Taste and make sure there's enough salt. Proceed with the recipe, using the mayonnaise mixture as the dressing. Refrigerate for at least 4 hours and serve cold.

GRILLED POTATO SALAD Also good with sweet potatoes: Instead of boiling the potatoes, grill them according to the directions on page 253. While they are still warm, proceed with the recipe from Step 2.

ROASTED POTATO SALAD This works for the main recipe or the first variation (especially with flavored mayonnaise): Instead of boiling the potatoes, roast

Potato Salad with Mustard Vinaigrette, page 207

them according to the directions on page 329. While they are still warm, proceed with the recipe from Step 2.

17 SIMPLE ADDITIONS TO POTATO SALAD

You will probably need to add more dressing, depending on the ingredient.

1. Chopped fresh herbs, like chives, chervil, dill, oregano, rosemary, or sage, to taste
2. Chopped sweet or dill pickle
3. Chopped celery or fennel
4. Chopped red bell pepper, raw or roasted (page 318); or canned pimientos
5. Capers or chopped olives
6. Chopped shallots, raw or lightly cooked in olive oil
7. Cooked fresh peas, or thawed frozen
8. Chopped Hard-Boiled Egg (page 721)
9. Cayenne, smoked paprika, or chopped fresh chile (jalapeño, Thai, serrano, or habanero)
10. Curry powder (to make your own, see page 32) or other spice mixtures (start with a teaspoon)
11. Chopped or mashed anchovies
12. Crumbled cooked bacon or bits of ham or prosciutto
13. Grated hard cheese like Parmesan, cheddar, or Manchego, or crumbled feta, queso fresco, or ricotta salata
14. Sliced or grated radishes
15. Cooked and chopped greens like escarole or kale, or raw tender greens like spinach, arugula, or watercress
16. 1 tablespoon Dijon mustard or Pickled Mustard Seeds (page 37), mixed into the vinaigrette
17. Green beans, blanched, shocked (page 238), and chopped

Which Potato for Salads?

You—and I—almost always want low-starch waxy potatoes for salad, which keep their shape even after boiling. Waxy potatoes, often referred to as "new"— even when they're not freshly dug—have thin skins that may be red or tan (tan ones are called "white," though they're not even close). You might even see purple ones, which make stunning salads.

Starchy (baking) potatoes like Idaho or other russets work well, with a different effect. The breakdown of their starches gives the salad a little creaminess so it sticks together a bit. Their mealy texture can also be an asset, depending on your taste.

You can also use a so-called all-purpose potato like Yukon Gold, which will give you a firm potato whose exterior disintegrates just a little.

Sesame Seaweed Salad

MAKES: 4 servings | **TIME:** 20 minutes

If you're new to seaweed, buy a small package of mixed seaweeds (available at many natural food stores and most Japanese food stores) so you can get some variety and see what you like. Once you get more familiar with seaweed, you can use wakame, kelp, hijiki, or others, alone or in any combination you like. Then bulk up your stash; they'll keep for months in your pantry.

1 ounce assorted dried seaweeds, or all wakame
¼ cup chopped shallot, scallions, or red onion
2 tablespoons soy sauce, or to taste
1 tablespoon rice wine or other light vinegar, or to taste
1 tablespoon mirin or 1 teaspoon sugar, or to taste
1½ teaspoons sesame oil, or to taste
Pinch cayenne, or to taste
Salt (optional)
1 tablespoon toasted sesame seeds (see page 309)

1. Rinse the seaweed once and put in in a bowl with enough warm tap water to cover by at least

3 inches; soak until tender, 5 to 10 minutes or more. Drain and gently press the pieces to remove excess water. Pick through the seaweed to sort out any hard bits (there may be none) and chop or cut up with a sharp knife or scissors, if the pieces are large. Put in a bowl.

2. Toss with the shallot, soy sauce, vinegar, mirin, oil, cayenne, and salt if necessary; refrigerate for up to a day before serving. When you're ready, taste and adjust the seasonings. Serve, garnished with the sesame seeds.

MISO SEAWEED SALAD Omit the soy sauce, rice wine vinegar, mirin, sesame oil, and cayenne and use Miso Vinaigrette (page 191) instead.

---

12 ADDITIONS TO SESAME SEAWEED SALAD

You can add these singly or in combination.

1. 8 ounces to 1 pound cucumbers, peeled and seeded (see page 287) if necessary, thinly sliced, then salted and squeezed to remove excess water (see page 203)
2. Several radishes or a piece of daikon, peeled if necessary, thinly sliced, then salted and squeezed to remove excess water (page 203)
3. A tablespoon or two of Dashi (page 179) or Vegetarian Dashi
4. About 1 tablespoon grated fresh ginger, to taste
5. 1 fresh tomato, cored, peeled, seeded, and chopped
6. ½ to 1 cup peeled and chopped Granny Smith apple or Asian pear
7. ½ cup chopped nuts like walnuts, almonds, cashews, or pecans
8. ½ to 1 cup julienned or chopped carrot
9. ½ to 1 cup peeled and julienned or chopped jícama
10. A 2-ounce bundle of thin rice noodles (vermicelli), cooked (see page 520)
11. 1 avocado, pitted, peeled, and chopped
12. 1 cup shelled cooked edamame

Fruit Salads

As the recipes in this section prove, fruit salads aren't limited to breakfast or dessert, nor do they need to be sweet. In fact, savory fruit salads—that eat like salsa, only heartier—have some of the most interesting contrasts of flavor, and work beautifully alongside grilled and roasted fish, meat, or poultry. Or serve these on a bed of greens, rice, grains, or room-temperature noodles.

Green Papaya Salad

MAKES: 4 servings | **TIME:** 20 minutes

The fiery Northern Thai specialty that was once an anomaly here in the States—since unripe papaya was so hard to find—is now fortunately available in many restaurants. I crave it with any grilled meat, fish, or poultry, or even tofu. You should find green (unripe) papayas and long beans in Asian or Latin groceries, but you can also substitute Granny Smith apples for the papaya and use regular green beans.

- 1 green, unripe papaya, peeled and seeded
- 2 cloves garlic, lightly smashed
- 1 shallot, chopped
- 2 fresh chiles (preferably Thai), seeded and chopped
- 2 tablespoons fish sauce or soy sauce
- 3 tablespoons fresh lime juice
- 2 teaspoons sugar
- 6 ounces long beans, trimmed and cut into 1-inch lengths
- 1 small fresh tomato, cored and cut into eighths
- 2 tablespoons chopped dry-roasted peanuts
- ½ cup chopped fresh cilantro for garnish

1. Use a knife or the julienne disk of a food processor to cut the papaya into fine shreds.

2. Combine the garlic, shallot, and chiles on a cutting board and mince and press with the side of the

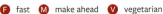

knife until pasty. Or as is traditional, use a mortar and pestle. Combine in a bowl with the papaya, fish sauce, lime juice, sugar, beans, and tomato and stir to combine.

3. Taste and adjust the seasoning; the mixture will be hot but may need more fish sauce, lime juice, and/or sugar. Garnish with peanuts and cilantro and serve.

Mixed Fruit Salad

MAKES: 4 servings | TIME: About 30 minutes

You don't need to follow the recipe to the letter—any combination of fruit will work, as long as it's ripe and delicious; there's no point in using fruit that has no flavor.

½ small cantaloupe or papaya, seeded, peeled, and cut into chunks

¼ small honeydew or 2 mangoes, seeded, peeled, and cut into chunks

½ pineapple, peeled, cored, and cut into chunks
   Grated zest and juice of 1 lemon

1 tablespoon sugar, or to taste

1 pint strawberries, hulled and halved

1 pint blueberries

1 pint blackberries

2 oranges, peeled and segmented (see page 378)

Put the melons, pineapple, lemon zest and juice, and sugar in a bowl and toss. Add the berries and oranges and toss gently, taking care not to crush the berries. Refrigerate until chilled if you like but serve within a few hours of mixing.

MIXED FRUIT SALAD WITH MINT Omit the sugar. Pick the leaves from 5 sprigs fresh mint. Combine ¼ cup Simple Syrup (page 859) and the mint stems in a small pot; bring to a boil, then turn off the heat and

steep until cool; discard the stems. Chop the mint leaves. Toss the fruit in the mint syrup along with the mint.

SALTY MIXED FRUIT SALAD Works with the main recipe or the following variation: Replace the sugar with 1 teaspoon coarse salt (Maldon is incredible). Just before serving, taste and add a little more salt and some pepper if you like.

MIXED FRUIT SALAD WITH COCONUT Great with tropical fruits like papaya, mango, and pineapple: Omit the sugar and add 2 tablespoons Simple Syrup (page 859), 2 tablespoons coconut milk (to make your own, see page 372), and ¼ cup shredded coconut. Toss with the fruit as in the main recipe.

Bean Salads

Undercooking the beans—just slightly, so they are barely tender inside and their skins remain intact—is the key to good texture here; see the section starting on page 389 for more detail. It's best to toss them gently with the dressing while they're still warm so the beans absorb all the dressing flavors. If you use canned beans, consider heating them gently first.

Basic Bean Salad

MAKES: 6 to 8 servings | TIME: 1½ to 3 hours, depending on the bean, largely unattended

The variables in this recipe are the seasonings and the choice of bean, which will impact only the cooking time. Note that I say "cooking time," not "opening-the-can time." Try this recipe first from scratch to see how good it can be. To substitute canned, halve the recipe and drain, rinse, and gently heat two 15-ounce cans of beans.

 fast   make ahead   vegetarian

The quantity here is enough to woo a small crowd or to keep in the fridge to eat over the course of several days, where it will only get better. Then add the parsley just before serving.

1 tablespoon red wine vinegar, other good vinegar, or fresh lemon juice, or to taste
2 to 4 tablespoons chopped red onion or shallot, to taste
Salt and pepper
¼ cup olive oil, plus more to taste
1 pound dried beans, split peas, or lentils, picked through, sorted, cooked by any method (see page 389) and drained, or 4 to 5 cups canned, gently heated and drained
¼ to ½ cup chopped fresh parsley

1. Stir the vinegar and onion together in a large bowl. Sprinkle with salt and pepper. Stir in the oil.
2. Add the beans to the dressing while they are still hot. Toss gently until the beans are coated with dressing, adding more oil if you like.
3. Let cool to room temperature or refrigerate, stirring once or twice to distribute the dressing. Taste, adjust the seasoning, and stir in the parsley just before serving.

10 SIMPLE LAST-MINUTE ADDITIONS TO BEAN SALADS

Depending on what you add, you may need more dressing and seasoning: For every extra tablespoon oil, add a teaspoon or so vinegar or fresh lemon juice; taste and up the salt, pepper, and spices accordingly.

1. Chopped fresh, dried, or oven-roasted (page 347) tomatoes
2. Chopped raw or roasted (page 318) bell peppers or chiles
3. Chopped or torn salad greens like romaine, mesclun, arugula, spinach, radicchio, or frisée
4. Chopped cooked vegetables like asparagus, kale, chard, spinach, watercress, broccoli, broccoli raab, bok choy, or green beans
5. Chopped cooked mushrooms
6. Grated, shaved, or cubed cheese like Parmesan, blue, feta, queso fresco, Jack, or cheddar
7. Crumbled or chopped crisp bacon or pancetta, or chorizo or other sausage
8. Chopped cooked shrimp or squid, or canned tuna
9. Any cooked grain (see page 450)
10. Traditional Pesto (page 51) or any other Herb Purée (page 52)

Warm Chickpea Salad with Arugula

MAKES: 4 side or 2 main-dish servings | TIME: 20 minutes with cooked chickpeas

Chickpeas are popular in salads throughout the Mediterranean and Middle East for good reason: Their distinctive, almost grain-like taste holds up well to aggressive seasoning, and they have a firm-outside-creamy-inside texture when cooked correctly. A spoonful of this makes the perfect side salad or appetizer, or add the hard-cooked egg and go for a bowlful as a light meal.

3 tablespoons olive oil
1 tablespoon chopped fresh ginger
1 tablespoon chopped garlic
½ teaspoon cumin seeds
Salt and pepper
1½ cups cooked or drained canned chickpeas
1 tablespoon white wine vinegar or fresh lemon juice
1 teaspoon honey
4 cups arugula leaves
1 small red onion, halved and thinly sliced
4 Hard-Boiled Eggs (page 721), peeled and quartered (optional)

10 Variations on Bean Salad

Use the bean quantities and instructions in Basic Bean Salad on page 212, but change the extras, seasonings, and garnishes and as described here. The specific beans in the first column are little more than a suggestion; try any cooked dried or canned beans you like.

SALAD	FLAVORINGS AND OTHER ADDITIONS	VINAIGRETTE OR OTHER DRESSING	GARNISH
Lentil Salad with Herbs	2–4 tablespoons chopped red onion or shallot; ½ cup chopped fresh parsley; ½ cup mixed chopped fresh chives, dill, basil, chervil; 1 tablespoon chopped fresh thyme, tarragon, or rosemary	Good wine vinegar or fresh lemon juice; olive oil	Thin slices of lemon
Chickpea Salad with Chutney	Any chutney (pages 61–64), ½ cup or more as needed to coat beans	None necessary	Something crunchy: toasted coconut, chopped scallion, or sliced radishes
Garlicky Red Bean Salad	2 tablespoons minced garlic, 2 tablespoons chopped red onion, shallot, or chives; or cloves from 1 head Roasted Garlic (page 294)	White wine vinegar; olive oil	1 teaspoon chopped fresh rosemary or ¼ cup chopped fresh basil
White Bean Salad, Tabbouleh Style	1 cup chopped fresh tomatoes; 1 cup peeled, seeded (see page 287), chopped cucumber; 3 tablespoons minced red onion	Fresh lemon juice; olive oil	1 cup mixed chopped fresh parsley and mint
Spicy Black Bean Salad	2 teaspoons minced garlic; ½ cup chopped red bell pepper; 1 cup pan-roasted corn kernels (for the method, see page 286) or plain fresh or frozen corn; 1 or 2 canned chipotle chiles, chopped with some adobo sauce	Red wine vinegar; olive oil	¼ cup each chopped fresh cilantro and scallions
Lemony Green Lentil Salad	1 lemon, peeled, chopped, and seeded; 1 tablespoon capers	Fresh lemon juice; olive oil	¼ cup chopped fresh chives, shallot, or red onion
Curried Black-Eyed Pea Salad	2 teaspoons each minced fresh ginger and garlic; 3 tablespoons chopped red onion; 1 tablespoon curry powder	Rice vinegar or fresh lemon juice; peanut oil	¼ cup or so chopped fresh cilantro
Three-Bean Salad	Use 1 cup kidney beans; 1½ cups cooked edamame or chickpeas; 1½ cups green or wax beans, trimmed, chopped into ½-inch pieces, cooked and shocked (see page 238); 2–4 tablespoons chopped red onion or shallot	Red or white wine vinegar or fresh lemon juice; olive oil	¼ cup or more chopped fresh chives or parsley
Gigante Salad with Pesto Dressing	¼ cup chopped dried tomatoes; 2 cups chopped spinach leaves	½ cup or more Traditional Pesto (page 51) thinned with lemon juice or white wine vinegar	Chopped toasted walnuts or pine nuts
Cannellini Salad with Balsamic Dressing	1 cup shredded radicchio and the white part of 1 large leek	2 tablespoons or more balsamic vinegar; ⅓ cup olive oil	2 tablespoons chopped fresh rosemary

 fast make ahead V vegetarian

1. Put the oil in a large skillet over medium heat. When the oil is hot, add the garlic, ginger, and cumin and cook, stirring constantly, until fragrant and the ginger and garlic are soft, 1 to 2 minutes. Sprinkle with salt and pepper, add the chickpeas, and stir until hot and coated in the oil and seasonings, about 3 minutes more.

2. Remove from the heat and stir in the vinegar, honey, and 1 tablespoon water. Mash a few of the chickpeas with the back of the spoon or a fork as you stir, to add texture to the dressing. Put the arugula and red onion in a large bowl and toss with the warm chickpeas and dressing. Taste and adjust the seasoning if necessary. Serve immediately, garnished with hard-boiled eggs if you like.

WHITE BEAN SALAD WITH TUNA Use cannellini beans instead of the chickpeas. Substitute grated lemon zest for the ginger, mustard seeds for the cumin, and use lemon juice instead of vinegar. Omit the honey. Add one 7-ounce can tuna (preferably packed in olive oil), drained, to the bowl along with the arugula (with or without the eggs).

Fava Bean and Mint Salad with Pecorino

MAKES: 4 servings | TIME: About 1 hour with unshucked beans

Ⓥ

This classic combination of fresh fava beans and mint signals spring in many parts of the world. If you like, add some of spring's other iconic produce: asparagus, artichokes, or fresh peas. Just make sure to increase the olive oil and lemon juice for each additional ingredient. If you can't find fresh favas—or don't feel like shelling and peeling them—try cleaned and frozen edamame, lima, or fava beans.

    3   tablespoons olive oil
    1   tablespoon fresh lemon juice

    3   pounds fresh fava beans, shucked, blanched,
        and shelled (see page 401; about 3 cups
        cleaned)
    1   cup fresh chopped mint
        Salt and pepper
    1   cup crumbled or shaved pecorino or Parmesan
        cheese
    1   tablespoon grated lemon zest for garnish

1. Whisk together the oil and lemon juice in a large bowl.

2. Add the fava beans and mint and sprinkle with salt and pepper; toss to coat. Toss with the pecorino, taste and adjust the seasoning, and serve, garnished with lemon zest.

Grain Salads

Like bean salads, dressed grains are versatile. They also provide the backbone of full-meal bowls: Toss them with raw or cooked greens or other vegetables. Top them with simply grilled chicken or fish, or maybe a fried egg. And like bean salads, you can make them days ahead for easy entertaining or everyday work or school lunches.

COOKING GRAINS FOR SALADS

I describe all my grain-cooking techniques in a designated chapter. For salads, I rely mostly on Cooking Grains, the Easy Way (page 450), rinsing after cooking to remove some of the starch and keep the grains separate.

In an ideal world, you would have time to prepare the grains right before using, undercook them slightly as you would beans, and dress them warm so they become tender and absorb flavor as they cool. Here's a more real-life approach: Whenever you cook grains, get in the habit of making extra and keeping some in the fridge. Then you'll always have the ingredients for last-minute salads at your fingertips. When using precooked grain, figure three times the quantity of raw kernels called for in the recipe.

Fava Bean and Mint Salad
with Pecorino, page 215

After making additions and tossing in dressing, I like to let chilled grains come to room temperature. That gives their starch a chance to relax, and the texture improves dramatically.

Rice Salad with Dried Apricots

MAKES: 4 servings | **TIME:** About 30 minutes

Basmati is the ideal rice for this sweet-and-savory concoction.

Other rice or grains you can use: any short- or long-grain brown rice, wild rice, wheat berries, pearled barley, couscous, quinoa

3 to 4	cups cooked rice (see page 430), preferably basmati, cooled
1	cup chopped dried apricots
½	cup slivered almonds, toasted (see page 309)
¼	cup chopped scallions
¼ to ½	cup Vinaigrette (page 188), made with white wine vinegar
1	tablespoon ground coriander
2	teaspoons ground ginger
1½	teaspoons cayenne
	Salt and pepper
½	cup chopped fresh cilantro

1. Put the rice, apricots, nuts, and scallions in a large bowl. Drizzle with vinaigrette and sprinkle with the coriander, ginger, cayenne, and salt and pepper. Use two big forks to combine, fluffing the rice and tossing gently to separate the grains. (You can refrigerate the salad at this point for up to a day; return it to room temperature before proceeding.)

2. Stir in the cilantro. Taste, adjust the seasoning, and add a little more dressing if necessary. Serve at room temperature.

RICE SALAD WITH GRAPEFRUIT AND PISTACHIOS

Instead of the dried apricots, peel and seed 2 small grapefruits and chop into bite-size pieces (or cut the segments into supremes as shown on page 378). Substitute pistachios for the almonds.

RICE SALAD WITH TOMATOES

Omit the almonds and spices. Substitute 1 cup halved cherry tomatoes for the apricots and ¼ cup thinly sliced red onions for the scallions. Toss the rice with 1 tablespoon minced garlic, and 2 to 4 chopped anchovy fillets (optional). Omit the cilantro and garnish with ½ cup grated Parmesan cheese. Serve within an hour.

WILD RICE SALAD WITH DRIED FRUIT AND PECANS

Use wild rice and substitute mixed dried cherries, cranberries, and/or blueberries for the dried apricots, and pecans for the almonds. Use parsley instead of cilantro.

WHEAT BERRY SALAD WITH APPLES AND WALNUTS

Use wheat berries instead of rice and Maple Vinaigrette (page 191) as the dressing. Substitute chopped or thinly sliced Granny Smith or Pink Lady apples for the dried apricots, and walnuts for the almonds. Omit the scallions and cilantro.

Tabbouleh

MAKES: 4 servings | **TIME:** 40 minutes

Fresh herbs, and lots of them, make the best tabbouleh. Ripe tomatoes pull some weight too. So really, this is the perfect salad alongside summertime grilled foods. The grain is important, however, and though bulgur is traditional, substituting other kinds keeps things interesting.

Other grains you can use: cooked cracked wheat, quinoa, millet, couscous, or short-grain rice (you may need extra dressing).

½ cup fine- or medium-grind bulgur
⅓ cup olive oil, or more as needed
¼ cup fresh lemon juice, or to taste
Salt and pepper
2 cups chopped fresh parsley (with small stems only)
1 cup chopped fresh mint
½ cup chopped scallions
4 fresh tomatoes, cored, seeded if you'd like, and chopped

1. Soak the bulgur in hot water to cover until tender, 15 to 30 minutes. Drain well, squeezing out as much of the water as possible. Toss the bulgur with the oil and lemon juice, and sprinkle with salt and pepper.

2. Just before you're ready to eat, add the parsley, mint, scallions, and tomatoes and toss gently. Taste, adjust the seasoning, and serve.

TABBOULEH WITH LOTS OF TOMATOES Reduce the parsley and mint to 1 cup and use 6 tomatoes.

Farro Salad with Cucumber and Yogurt-Dill Dressing

MAKES: 4 servings | TIME: 50 minutes

I used to make this cool, crunchy, and slightly chewy salad with pearled barley. Trust me, farro is way better, with a whole-grain heartiness that provides a counterpoint to the pleasant grassiness of the dressing.

Other grains you can use: brown rice, wheat berries, cracked wheat, Israeli couscous, pearled barley, or wild rice. Adjust the cooking time as necessary (see pages 452 to 455).

1 cup raw farro or 3 cups cooked
Salt and pepper
8 ounces cucumber (any kind), trimmed
3 or 4 scallions, chopped
2 tablespoons fresh lemon juice, or more to taste
2 tablespoons olive oil
1 cup Greek-style yogurt
½ cup chopped fresh dill

1. If you're starting with raw farro, rinse it and put it in a medium saucepan with water to cover by at least 2 inches. Add a large pinch salt and cook over medium-high heat, stirring occasionally, until the farro is tender, about 30 minutes from the time the water boils. Drain and spread on a plate to cool; if you're in a hurry, rinse it under cold water for a minute or so.

2. If you're using an English cucumber or other virtually seedless cucumber, simply chop it into bite-sized pieces. With seedy cucumbers, peel, halve them lengthwise, and scoop out the seeds before chopping (see page 287). Put the cucumber in a colander or strainer and sprinkle with about a tablespoon salt. Let sit for 20 minutes or so, then rinse, drain, and pat dry.

3. Toss together the farro, cucumber, and scallions in a salad bowl; sprinkle with pepper. Whisk together the lemon juice, oil, and yogurt. Toss this dressing with the salad, then taste and adjust the seasoning. Add the dill, toss all together, and serve.

FARRO AND CRESS SALAD Omit the scallions and yogurt. Add 3 cups trimmed watercress. Proceed with the recipe, adding the cress along with the herbs. Drizzle with more oil after serving.

FARRO SALAD WITH PEAS AND YOGURT-DILL DRESSING Instead of the cucumber, use 1½ cups cooked and shocked fresh or frozen peas (see page 238). Or use chopped raw snow peas or sugar snap peas.

FARRO SALAD WITH CUCUMBER AND SMOKED SALMON In Step 3, add 1 cup smoked salmon pieces to the salad and toss with the other ingredients. Serve with lemon wedges.

 fast  make ahead vegetarian

17 Picnic-Perfect Salads

With a little forethought, even tender green salads travel well; pack them and the dressing or other ingredients separately and toss on the spot. But most of the following salads can be finished at home and packed for an adventure—ideally in a container that protects them and the picnic basket—without loss of quality.

1. Tomato, Mozzarella, and Basil Salad (page 199), assemble on the spot
2. Simple Radish or Jícama Salad (page 200)
3. Cumin-Scented Carrot Slaw (page 205)
4. Fennel and Orange Salad (page 205)
5. Cold Cooked and Dressed Greens (page 206)
6. Any of the salads in the charts on pages 206, 214, and 224
7. Potato Salad with Mustard Vinaigrette (page 207)
8. Sesame Seaweed Salad (page 209)
9. Green Papaya Salad (page 210)
10. Basic Bean Salad (page 212)
11. Fava Bean and Mint Salad with Pecorino (page 215)
12. Rice Salad with Dried Apricots (page 217)
13. Tabbouleh (page 217)
14. Farro Salad with Cucumber and Yogurt-Dill Dressing (page 218)
15. Quinoa and Sweet Potato Salad (page 219)
16. Chicken Salad with Olive Oil and Fresh Herbs (page 221)
17. Seafood Salad, Mediterranean Style (page 227)

Quinoa and Sweet Potato Salad

MAKES: 4 servings | **TIME:** 40 minutes

You can add nearly anything to cooked quinoa and you'll have a good salad. But I like to take it in a slightly unusual direction and add stir-fried sweet potatoes, which add crunch and sweetness.

Other grains you can use: millet, bulgur, cracked wheat, couscous; any leftover cooked grain will work here too

1 cup raw quinoa or 3 cups cooked

4 tablespoons olive oil

1 pound sweet potatoes (1 large or 2 medium), peeled and grated

1 large shallot, minced

Salt and pepper

2 tablespoons sherry vinegar or white wine vinegar

1 red bell pepper, cored, seeded, and chopped

¼ cup chopped fresh chives or parsley for garnish

1. If you're starting with raw quinoa or other grain, cook it according to the directions on page 450. Drain if necessary and let cool a bit.

2. Put 2 tablespoons of the oil in a large skillet over medium-high heat. When it's hot, add the sweet potatoes and shallot, spreading them out as evenly as possible; sprinkle with salt and pepper. Cook, undisturbed, until the mixture sizzles and browns on the bottom, 3 to 5 minutes. Stir with a spatula to turn and separate the potatoes, then cook, stirring like that every 2 or 3 minutes, until they're just tender but not mushy. Transfer to a baking sheet and separate the pieces to cool quickly.

3. Whisk together the remaining oil and the vinegar in a large bowl with a sprinkle of salt and pepper. Add the sweet potatoes, quinoa, and bell pepper and toss with two forks, separating the ingredients as you coat them in the dressing. Taste, adjust the seasoning, and garnish with the chives. Serve at room temperature, or cover and refrigerate for up to a few hours.

SOUTHWESTERN MILLET AND SWEET POTATO SALAD
A little more punch, with the corny taste of the grain shining through: Substitute millet for the quinoa, lime juice for the vinegar, and cilantro for the chives. When you

Fattoush

assemble the salad in Step 3, add 1 avocado, peeled, pitted, and diced; ¼ cup toasted pepitas (pumpkin seeds; see page 311); and ¼ teaspoon cayenne or red chile flakes.

Fattoush

MAKES: 4 servings | **TIME:** 30 minutes

The trick to fattoush is to make sure the pita is very crisp. To turn this bread salad into a meal, spread a layer of Lentils, Moroccan Style (page 408) on a plate and put a mound of fattoush on top. Serve alone or garnished with greens; crumbled feta cheese is always a welcome garnish.

   Four 6-inch pita breads
   ¾ cup chopped fresh parsley, mint, or basil
      (preferably a mixture)
   1 large or 2 medium fresh tomatoes, cored
      and chopped
   1 cucumber, peeled, seeded if you like
      (see page 287), and roughly chopped
   1 red or yellow bell pepper, cored, seeded,
      and roughly chopped
      About ½ cup Vinaigrette (page 188),
      or olive oil and fresh lemon juice
      Salt and pepper

1. Heat the oven to 350°F. Cut the pitas like pies into 8 wedges each, put the pieces on a baking sheet, and toast in the oven, turning once or twice, until both sides are crisp and golden, about 15 minutes. Let cool. (You can store the pita wedges, tightly covered, for up to 2 days.)
2. Combine the mint, parsley, tomatoes, cucumber, and bell pepper in a large bowl, adding vinaigrette or olive oil and lemon juice to taste. Toss several times to coat. Break the pita wedges into the salad and toss gently again. Taste, adjust the seasoning, and serve.

CROUTON SALAD Substitute about 8 ounces crusty bread (stale is fine) or 8 ounces Dry-Baked Croutons

(page 803) for the pitas and 1 small red onion, halved and thinly sliced, for the bell pepper. Reduce the herbs to ½ cup chopped fresh basil and/or parsley and add 1 teaspoon minced garlic. Cut the bread into 1-inch cubes and toast like the pita. Proceed with the recipe.

GRILLED BREAD SALAD Make the preceding variation, but grill the bread on both sides on a charcoal or gas grill at medium-high heat, with the rack 4 inches from the heat source, 3 to 5 minutes total. Let cool a bit, cut roughly into large cubes, and add to the salad.

CORN BREAD SALAD Instead of the pita, oven-toast about 8 ounces cubed Corn Bread (about 3 cups, page 769). Reduce the herbs to ½ cup chopped fresh cilantro and add 1 teaspoon chili powder (to make your own, see page 32) and ½ cup chopped scallions.

Salads with Chicken, Meat, or Fish

Meal-sized salads are more popular—and varied—than when I wrote the first edition of this book. There are three ways to approach them: You can make the recipes and variations that follow. You can start with any salad from this chapter and add a simply grilled, roasted, or poached animal protein. Or you can make a dish to serve or toss with greens and dressing. (There are ideas to get you started on pages 223, 224, 225, and 227.)

Chicken Salad with Olive Oil and Fresh Herbs

MAKES: 4 to 6 servings | **TIME:** About an hour; 20 minutes with cooked chicken

Dark or white meat, or both—your choice. Leftover roast or grilled chicken is perfectly acceptable, and will add another dimension to the flavor. To cook for

Chicken Salad with
Olive Oil and Fresh
Herbs, page 221

this recipe, start with about 1½ pounds raw bone-in meat and see page 681 or 707 for a couple of cooking ideas; the meat will be more flavorful and moist when cooked on the bone. Serve the salad as is, on top of greens, or on cooked pasta or grains, or use it to fill sandwiches.

Other proteins you can use: salmon, shrimp, canned tuna, tofu.

    1   pound shredded or cubed roasted, grilled, or poached chicken meat
    3   tablespoons chopped shallot or red onion
    ¼   cup chopped pitted black olives
    1   tablespoon grated lemon zest
    3   tablespoons fresh lemon juice, plus more to taste
    ¼   cup olive oil, plus more to taste
    ½   cup chopped mixed fresh herbs like chives, parsley, chervil, dill, and/or basil
        Salt and pepper
4 to 6 cups torn assorted greens (optional)

1. Put the chicken, shallot, olives, and zest in a bowl and mix. (At this point, you can refrigerate the salad, covered, for a day; take out of the fridge 15 minutes or so before proceeding to take the chill off.)
2. Drizzle on the lemon juice and oil and sprinkle on the herbs and salt and pepper; mix again. Taste and adjust the seasoning. Use as is or arrange the greens on the plate(s) and top with the chicken salad.

TRADITIONAL CHICKEN SALAD Instead of the olives, add 1 tablespoon Dijon mustard and instead of the olive oil, use mayonnaise. Replace the herbs with 1 cup chopped celery. Add sliced almonds or chopped walnuts or pecans if you like.

LOBSTER SALAD Especially good with a pinch saffron stirred into the mayonnaise: Omit the olives; substitute mayonnaise (to make your own, see page 69) for the olive oil. Reduce the herbs to 1 tablespoon and chop them as fine as you can. (Try tarragon, which has an affinity for lobster.)

CRAB SALAD Omit the shallot, olives, and lemon zest. Use 8 ounces cooked crabmeat, picked through to remove any pieces of shell. Mix the crab with olive oil and lemon juice for the dressing or any flavored mayonnaise (see page 70). Toss with 4 cups torn assorted greens and serve.

Grilled Beef Salad with Mint

MAKES: 3 to 4 servings | **TIME:** 25 minutes

I never seem to get enough of this bright salad. Make it even heartier by serving over cooked rice noodles or bean threads.

Other proteins you can use: chicken, pork, shrimp.

12 Poultry Dishes That are Perfect on Greens

Almost any leftover or just-cooked poultry turns a salad into a meal. If the dishes are still hot or warm, the greens will soften and mingle with the juices, which can also be a nice touch.

1. Chicken or Pork Satay (page 130)
2. Broiled Boneless Chicken, including its grilled variation (page 596), or the variations in the chart on page 599
3. Simply Grilled or Broiled Chicken Parts (see the chart, too; pages 617–620)
4. Chicken MarkNuggets (page 630)
5. Simplest Whole Roast Chicken or its variations (pull the meat from the bones; page 633)
6. Chicken Under a Brick (page 641)
7. Grilled or Broiled Split Chicken (page 642)
8. Basic Roast Turkey Breast, on the Bone (page 650)
9. Roast Duck (page 654)
10. Fast "Roast" Duck, Chinese Style (page 654)
11. Duck Confit (page 655)
12. Grilled or Broiled Squab, Vietnamese Style (page 661)

10 More Fish, Chicken, or Meat Salads

Your choice: Toss the ingredients together and serve the salad alone (with crackers or toasted bread) or on a bed of greens. Or deconstruct the ingredients and present as a composed salad (see page 205). Any of these also make delicious sandwich or wrap fillings (see "The Basics of Sandwiches," page 803, and "Wraps," page 809).

SALAD	MEAT	VEGETABLES AND SEASONINGS	DRESSING AND GARNISHES
Chicken and Daikon Salad	3 cups shredded cooked chicken breast	2 cups peeled and grated daikon	Ginger Vinaigrette (page 190); 2 teaspoons each black and white sesame seeds, toasted, and chopped scallions
Pulled Pork and Mango Salad	2 cups shredded No-Work Smoked Pork Shoulder (page 695)	2 not-too-ripe mangoes, peeled and chopped; ½ small red onion, thinly sliced	Lime Vinaigrette (page 190); ½ cup or more chopped fresh cilantro
Steak and Roasted Pepper Salad	2 cups thinly sliced grilled or broiled steak (see page 670)	2 Roasted Red Peppers (page 318), cored, seeded, and chopped; 3 cups chopped radicchio; 1 cup crumbled Gorgonzola	Vinaigrette (page 188) made with balsamic vinegar; ½ cup chopped fresh chives or parsley
Pesto Shrimp Salad	1 pound peeled large (21–30 count) shrimp, grilled (see page 535) or steamed (see page 545)	1 cup chopped fresh tomatoes	¼ cup Traditional Pesto (page 51), thinned with olive oil or water
Curried Chicken Salad	4 cups chopped or shredded cooked chicken breast	½ cup peeled, chopped apple; ½ cup chopped cashews	3 tablespoons mayonnaise or yogurt, or to taste; 1 tablespoon curry powder; ¼ cup chopped fresh cilantro
Duck Salad with Dried Cherries	2 cups chopped or shredded cooked duck meat	½ cup dried cherries; ½ cup toasted hazelnuts (see page 309); 3 cups chopped frisée (optional)	Vinaigrette (page 188), made with sherry vinegar; ¼ cup chopped fresh chives or parsley
Beef and Avocado Salad	12 ounces beef tenderloin, grilled or broiled to medium-rare and cubed	1 avocado, pitted, peeled, cubed; 1 cup chopped fresh tomatoes; 1 red bell pepper, cored, seeded, chopped	Lime Vinaigrette (page 190); ½ cup chopped scallions
Buttermilk Chicken Salad with Corn Bread	3 cups chopped or shredded cooked chicken breast	1 cup crumbled Corn Bread (page 769) or My Kind of Croutons (page 801), made with Corn Bread; ½ cup dried cranberries	¼ cup Real Ranch Dressing (page 71) with 2 teaspoons chopped garlic; ½ cup toasted chopped pecans
Miso Salmon Salad with Snow Peas	3 cups flaked cooked salmon	1 cup thinly sliced snow peas	½ cup Miso Vinaigrette (page 191); ¼ cup chopped scallions
Spicy Pork Salad with Green Beans	2 cups chopped cooked pork tenderloin	1 cup chopped cooked green beans (see page 297); 1 cup shredded napa cabbage; 1 tablespoon chopped jalapeño or other fresh chile	¼ cup Soy Vinaigrette (page 190); ¼ cup chopped mint

F fast   M make ahead   V vegetarian

- 12 ounces beef tenderloin or sirloin
      Juice of 2 limes
- 1 tablespoon fish sauce or soy sauce
- ⅛ teaspoon cayenne, or to taste
- ½ teaspoon sugar
- 4 cups torn Boston or romaine lettuce leaves, mesclun, or any salad greens mixture
- 1 cup torn fresh mint
- ¼ cup chopped red onion
- 1 cucumber, peeled, seeded if you like (see page 287), and chopped

1. Prepare a charcoal or gas grill for medium direct cooking, or turn on the broiler and position the rack about 4 inches below the heat. Grill or broil the beef, turning once, until medium-rare, 5 to 10 minutes; transfer to a cutting board and let it cool.

2. Combine the lime juice, fish sauce, cayenne, and sugar with 1 tablespoon water in a large bowl—the mixture will be thin. Add the lettuce, mint, onion, cucumber and toss with the dressing to coat. Transfer the salad to a platter, reserving the remaining dressing in the bottom of the bowl.

3. Thinly slice the beef, reserving its juices; combine the juices with the remaining dressing. Put the slices of beef over the salad, drizzle with the dressing, and serve.

GRILLED CHICKEN SALAD WITH LEMONGRASS

Substitute boneless, skinless chicken breast or thighs for the beef. If you have time, marinate the raw chicken in the juice of 1 lime, 1 tablespoon soy sauce, ½ teaspoon sugar, and 2 tablespoons minced lemongrass for up to 30 minutes. Grill or broil, turning once, until cooked through, 5 to 15 minutes, depending on the cut. Proceed with the recipe, omitting the mint and adding 2 tablespoons minced lemongrass to the dressing.

GRILLED SHRIMP SALAD WITH CHILE AND BASIL

Substitute peeled large shrimp for the beef. If you have

time, marinate the shrimp in 2 tablespoons soy sauce, 1 tablespoon or more Chile-Garlic Paste (page 45), and 1 tablespoon chopped fresh Thai basil for up to 15 minutes. Grill or broil until pink, about 3 minutes. Proceed with the recipe, substituting torn Thai basil for the mint and 1 tablespoon Thai Chile Sauce (page 66) for the cayenne.

---

8 Meat Dishes to Serve on Greens

As with poultry, you can use any unsauced meat dish, hot or cold, to top a bed of greens.

1. Any of the steaks as described in Many Ways to Cook Steak (page 667), sliced
2. Grilled or Broiled Flank Steak (page 670)
3. Grilled Beef Kebabs with Lots of Vegetables or any of the kebabs on page 673
4. Grilled or Broiled Pork Chops (page 689)
5. Roasted Pork Tenderloin with Lots of Herbs or any of its variations (page 694)
6. Any of the hams as described in the sidebar on page 704
7. Roast Leg of Lamb, 5 Ways (page 709)
8. Grilled or Broiled Veal Chops (page 713)

Salade Niçoise

MAKES: 4 servings | **TIME:** 15 minutes

The Niçoise is French, but not fancy. The core components are lettuce, hard-boiled eggs, anchovies, black olives, tomatoes (if they're in season), and a garlic-spiked dressing. Most people add oil-packed tuna too. Other possible additions (and substitutes for tomatoes in winter) are cooked green beans, potatoes, artichoke hearts, raw or roasted bell pepper, capers, and basil.

6 cups torn assorted lettuces and other
   salad greens
2 Hard-Boiled Eggs (page 721), peeled and sliced
1 cup good black olives (preferably Niçoise
   or any oil-cured)
3 fresh tomatoes, cored, seeded if you'd like,
   and cut into wedges
6 anchovy fillets
2 cans tuna (preferably packed in olive oil),
   drained (optional)
2 tablespoons red wine vinegar, plus a little more
   if needed
   About ½ cup olive oil
   Salt and pepper
1 clove garlic, minced
1 small shallot, chopped
1 teaspoon Dijon mustard

1. Going in the order above, put the lettuce, eggs, olives, tomatoes, anchovies, and tuna, if you're using it, on a platter or in a shallow bowl, scattering or piling things as you like. Or—less attractive but easier to serve—toss all the ingredients together in a big bowl.

2. Put the vinegar, oil, salt and pepper, garlic, shallot, and mustard in a jar or small bowl. Shake or stir vigorously, taste and adjust the seasoning, and mix again. Pour over the salad and serve.

Seafood Salad, Mediterranean Style

MAKES: 4 servings | TIME: 30 minutes, plus time to chill

Another simply olive oil–dressed salad, only this time featuring poached fish and shellfish. Think of it as a fancy-ish shrimp cocktail. Vinegar is traditional in many places, but I prefer lots of lemon. Serve it over greens if you like, or on thick slices of grilled or toasted bread.

Salt and pepper
8 ounces firm white fish (see page 552),
   skinned and cut into ½-inch chunks
8 ounces shrimp, peeled
8 ounces sea scallops, cut in half if large
½ cup chopped fresh parsley
1 tablespoon brined capers with a little of
   their liquid, or to taste
1 shallot, chopped
¼ cup olive oil
2 lemons: 1 halved; 1 cut into wedges

1. Put about 1 inch water in a large skillet with a tight-fitting lid. Bring it to a boil and salt generously. Adjust the heat so the water is just barely bubbling and add the fish; 30 seconds later, add the shrimp and scallops.

2. Cover and turn off the heat; let the seafood sit in the water for about 10 minutes. Check a few pieces and

11 Seafood Dishes That Are Perfect on Greens

For an impressive light meal, cook some fish, put it on mixed salad greens, and dress with one of the vinaigrettes on page 190. Here are some possibilities.

1. Broiled Seafood (page 534)
2. Grilled Seafood (page 535)
3. Roasted Seafood (page 536)
4. Deep-Fried Seafood (pages 538)
5. Still the Simplest and Best Shrimp Dish (pages 542)
6. Fish Kebabs (page 566)
7. Roasted Tuna Steaks (page 567)
8. Sardines on the Grill (page 573)
9. Broiled or Grilled Scallops with Basil Stuffing (page 579)
10. Bare-Bones Crab Cakes (page 585)
11. Sautéed Soft-Shell Crabs, Four Ways (page 587)

make sure the centers are barely opaque. If any aren't, return the water to a gentle bubble, then turn off the heat; check again in a minute or 2. Drain the seafood (saving the liquid for pasta sauce or soup if you like), let cool, then chill. (At this point, you can refrigerate the seafood for up to 24 hours.)

3. Gently toss the seafood with the parsley, capers, shallot, oil, and salt and pepper. Squeeze in lemon juice and a little caper brine to taste. Taste, adjust the seasoning, and serve, garnished with the lemon wedges.

THE BASICS OF PICKLING FRUITS AND VEGETABLES

Pickling isn't simply an ancient means of food preservation—with its variety of salty, sour, sweet, and hot flavors, these intensely flavored foods are almost universally appealing. And almost anything, from cabbage to peppers to watermelon rind to hard-cooked eggs, can be pickled.

In America we usually associate the word *pickle* with cucumbers, but that's starting to change with the popularity of kimchi and other fermented foods.

Acidity can inhibit the growth of harmful microbes in food. There are two basic ways to get acid into foods: by directly using vinegar, or by salting, using straight salt or a saltwater brine. Vinegar penetrates by replacing the natural water in the food. Salting is a less direct and more complex process where the salt draws out the food's natural water and allows just enough good bacterial growth to produce lactic acid, which pickles the food. Salt is also used when pickling with vinegar, to draw out water and crisp the vegetables so the vinegar that permeates the vegetable or fruit remains undiluted.

Though vinegar and salt help create pickles, seasonings—spices, herbs, garlic, onions, and other aromatics—are often added as flavorings. Dill is a favorite with cucumbers in the United States, as are garlic, mustard, black peppercorns, and chiles or red chile flakes.

You can use any spice or herb you like; spice mixtures like five-spice powder or jerk seasoning add even more intensity. (To make your own, see pages 34 and 35.)

There are a few guidelines: Use the freshest foods for pickling; food that has blemishes or soft spots will start with more of the harmful microbes you want to avoid. Consider the size and density of the fruit or vegetable; smaller and softer pieces pickle more quickly than larger pieces. Think about timing—the pickles here can take anywhere from 20 minutes to several days to cure. If you want your pickles right away, go with the Quick-Pickled Vegetables (below). The Kosher and Three-Day Pickles (both on page 230) take two to three days.

Quick-Pickled Vegetables

MAKES: 4 to 8 servings | **TIME:** 1 hour or less

Salting vegetables, even for just 15 minutes, really changes their texture and flavor; they become both pliable and crunchy (see page 203). Of course, the thinner you slice the vegetables, the more quickly they will pickle.

Other vegetables you can use: shredded or sliced carrots, radish, jícama, or kohlrabi; thinly sliced celery, fennel, cabbage, onion

- 1 **pound cucumbers, zucchini, summer squash, or eggplant**
- 1 **tablespoon salt**
- ½ **teaspoon sugar**
- 1 **tablespoon chopped fresh dill or 1 teaspoon dill seeds**
- 1 **tablespoon cider vinegar**

1. Rinse the vegetables well, peel them if you like, and slice them as thin as possible (a mandoline or food processor is perfect for this). Put the vegetables in a colander and sprinkle them with the salt; toss well.

Gently rub the salt into the vegetables with your hands for a minute.

2. Put the colander in the sink or in a bowl for 15 to 30 minutes (cucumbers take less time than eggplant), tossing and squeezing every few minutes. When little or no more liquid comes out of the vegetable, rinse well in cold water, and drain. Transfer to a bowl.

3. Toss with the sugar, dill, and vinegar. Let sit for at least 10 minutes. Serve within a couple of hours.

SPICY QUICK-PICKLED VEGETABLES Use 1 pound Kirby cucumbers, sliced as thin as possible. Omit the sugar and dill. In Step 3 mix the cucumbers and vinegar with 3 to 4 tablespoons Chile-Garlic Paste (page 45), 1 teaspoon sugar, 2 tablespoons sesame oil, and 2 tablespoons soy sauce. Let the mixture sit for up to another 30 minutes before serving.

QUICK-PICKLED VEGETABLES, MEXICAN STYLE This makes a spicy garnish for tacos, rice, beans, and more: Use a mix of thinly sliced radishes, jícama, cucumber, and red onion. Substitute cilantro for the dill; add a thinly sliced jalapeño if you like, or habanero if you like it mouth-searingly hot; and use red wine vinegar.

QUICK-PICKLED CORN COINS WITH SICHUAN PEPPERCORNS Instead of the vegetables suggested, husk 4 ears corn. Carefully slice them crosswise through the cob into circles about ½ inch thick. Instead of the dill, crush 1 tablespoon Sichuan peppercorns with the flat side of a broad knife; use rice vinegar.

QUICK-PICKLED MANGO OR PAPAYA A perfect use for underripe mangoes or papaya, it easily moves between Indian, Southeast Asian, Latin, and Caribbean cuisines: Substitute thinly sliced or julienned still-firm mango or papaya for the vegetables, and cilantro, mint, or ginger for the dill.

QUICK-PICKLED RELISH Works for the main recipe or any of the variations: Instead of chopping the vegetables

or fruit, grate them; cut the corn off the cob. Let them sit after salting for just 5 to 10 minutes, depending on how watery they are. Proceed with the recipe.

Shortcut Kimchi

MAKES: 12 servings | **TIME:** About 3 hours, largely unattended

Once the best-known pickled cabbage in this country was sauerkraut, but kimchi is gaining popularity. Now this spicy Korean fermented staple is found jarred in supermarkets, and Asian markets usually offer several kinds. Making a quicker version at home is rewarding and gives you far more control over the level of spiciness.

Other vegetables you can use: all scallions (about 50 total, halved lengthwise), 2 to 3 pounds daikon, black radish, or turnip, peeled and shredded

1	head green, savoy, or napa cabbage (about 2 pounds), separated into leaves
	About ½ cup salt
20	scallions, roughly chopped, including most of the green parts
1	tablespoon *gochugaru* (Korean dried chile) or red chile flakes, or to taste
¼	cup soy sauce
¼	cup chopped garlic
3	tablespoons chopped fresh ginger
¼	cup sugar

1. Layer the cabbage leaves in a colander, sprinkling each layer with a little salt. Let sit over a bowl for at least 2 hours. When the cabbage is wilted, rinse and dry.

2. In a large bowl, mix together the scallions, chile flakes, soy sauce, garlic, and sugar. Roughly chop the cabbage and toss with the spice mixture. Let sit an hour before serving if you can, or refrigerate for up to a week; the kimchi will become stronger every day.

Kosher Pickles, the Right Way

MAKES: About 60 pickle quarters or 30 halves | TIME: 1 to 2 days, largely unattended

These remain my favorite pickles, and everyone I've ever made them for loves them too, which is good news since they only keep for about a week.

- ⅓ cup kosher salt
- 1 cup boiling water
- 2 pounds Kirby cucumbers, rinsed (scrub if spiny) and halved or quartered lengthwise
  At least 5 cloves garlic, crushed
- 1 large bunch fresh dill, preferably with flowers, 2 tablespoons dried dill and 1 teaspoon dill seeds, or 1 tablespoon coriander seeds

1. Combine the salt and boiling water in a large bowl; stir to dissolve the salt. Add a handful of ice cubes to cool the mixture, then add the cucumbers, garlic, and dill.

2. Add cold water to cover. Use a plate slightly smaller than the diameter of the bowl and a small weight to keep the cucumbers submerged. Set aside at room temperature.

3. Begin sampling the cucumbers after 4 hours if you've quartered them, 8 hours if you've halved them. In either case, it will probably take from 12 to 24 or even 48 hours for them to taste pickled enough to suit your taste.

4. When they are ready, transfer them to an airtight container and refrigerate them in the brine. The pickles will continue to ferment as they sit, more quickly at room temperature, more slowly in the refrigerator. They will keep well for up to a week.

Three-Day Pickles

MAKES: About 60 pickle quarters or 30 halves; 2 quarts sliced | TIME: 3 days, largely unattended

These are not the usual fermented dill pickle. Since they must be cured at a cold temperature, technically they qualify as "refrigerator pickles." This recipe calls for salt, sugar, and vinegar to create that sort of bread-and-butter-style, slightly sweet profile. The pickling spice adds layers of flavors that are warm (hot even, if you add more chiles) and quite delightful.

A word about some ingredients: Pickling spice is primarily mustard seeds and bay leaves, with some other warm seasonings in for good measure. It's now available everywhere, but if you have trouble finding it go for those two main components. A good-quality vinegar will be noticeable here. White wine or sherry vinegars are other options. And for an even more robust flavor, try turbinado sugar.

Other vegetables and fruit you can use: carrots, radishes, celery, fennel, kohlrabi, pearl onions, cauliflower, peppers, turnips, summer squash, eggplant, peaches, watermelon rind, spaghetti squash, beets

- 2 pounds Kirby cucumbers
- 6 tablespoons kosher salt
- 2 cups cider vinegar
- ¼ cup sugar
- ¼ cup pickling spice

1. Rinse the cucumbers well and scrub them if they're spiny. Halve or quarter them lengthwise or slice them. Put the cucumbers in a colander and sprinkle them with 2 tablespoons of the salt; toss well.

2. Let the colander sit in the sink or in a bowl until they "sweat," about 2 hours. Rinse the cucumbers, then pat them dry with towels. Put in a nonmetal bowl.

3. Put the remaining ¼ cup salt, the vinegar, sugar, and pickling spice, along with 2 cups water, in a pot over high heat. Bring to a boil, then remove from the heat and let cool for about 5 minutes. Pour the brine over the cucumbers and let cool to room temperature. (Add more vinegar or water in equal parts if the cucumbers are not covered.)

4. Transfer the cucumbers, brine, and spices to jars or containers; cover with airtight lids. Store in the refrigerator for at least 3 days, longer for stronger pickles. They will keep in their brine for up to 3 weeks. (Unlikely, but if at any point they start to smell funky or get foamy, discard them.)

PICKLED PEACHES, AFGHAN STYLE (*TERSHI*) Used like a condiment (great with rice dishes), these potent tangy-sweet pickles can be made with anything from peaches to tomatoes to eggplant: Substitute peeled, pitted, and sliced peaches for the cucumbers. Reduce the salt and sugar by half and use all cider vinegar to cover. Substitute 4 cloves garlic, crushed, 2 teaspoons dried mint, 2 teaspoons coriander seeds, and 1 tablespoon red chile flakes for the pickling spice. Skip Steps 1 and 2.

PICKLED WATERMELON RIND Instead of the cucumbers, use a 3-pound watermelon. Wash the outside well with soap and water. Cut open and remove the flesh (and seeds, if there are any); enjoy the fruit now or refrigerate for later. Cut the rind into manageable chunks and carefully remove the dark skin, leaving behind the white part and maybe a little bit of the remaining fruit. Cut the rinds into slices or chunks about 1 inch thick—you should have about 6 cups—and proceed with the recipe.

Vegetables and Fruit

CHAPTER AT A GLANCE

Buying and Handling Fresh Produce 234

Cooking Vegetables 236

The Vegetable Lexicon 258

The Nut and Seed Lexicon 310

Mixed Vegetable Dishes 352

Stuffed Vegetables 356

Cooking Fruit 359

The Fruit Lexicon 363

Turning the most basic skills loose on the wide and varied world of vegetables and fruits opens the door to cooking them all.

The key is knowing how to make substitutions. First up: general information for buying, storing, and preparing produce. The next section provides a set of master recipes, organized around the same core techniques in as Cooking Basics on pages 16 to 22.

But here the methods are spun specifically for vegetables, including additional methods for making purées and gratins, and followed in most cases by a master recipe that applies to a wide range of vegetables, and sometimes includes a small chart of variations for exploring different seasonings too.

After that, vegetables are explained individually in an alphabetized Lexicon; many entries offer a recipe or two—or three or four—specific to that food. A similar but smaller section for fruit follows.

I've divided vegetables and fruits according to the ways we usually think of them, even though the tomato, eggplant, winter and summer squashes, cucumber, and even corn are technically fruits. Similarly, rhubarb, though a vegetable, is usually cooked like a fruit, so you'll find it in that section.

The distinctions are only an organizing tool. Sweet fruit recipes largely stay where they belong, in Desserts. I hope that the savory treatments here like Grilled or Broiled Watermelon Steak (page 361) and Coconut-Fried Plantains (page 288), combined with "The Basics of Cooking Fruit" (see page 359), inspire you to enjoy fruit throughout the meal—just as you do vegetables.

THE BASICS OF BUYING AND HANDLING FRESH PRODUCE

Assuming you want produce to eat right away or soon, most of the vegetables you bring home should be slightly firm and most fruits slightly soft. Beyond that: Check for wrinkling, damage, or rotten spots and make sure the color is close to ideal. Give a sniff to confirm potency and ripeness—it should smell a little like how it tastes, even through the peel. I'm not saying you have to buy perfect produce—far from it—just be aware of what you're getting.

Pay attention to the little stickers to see where the produce came from, keeping in mind that miles traveled indicate the age of the fruits and vegetables and their stage of ripeness when harvested. Soon you'll naturally gravitate to what's seasonal locally or regionally, since what's grown closer to home will be freshest. Of course, that's easy to say in the American South or California. Elsewhere, eating seasonally means turning more frequently to root vegetables in the winter months, which I now crave on cold, dark days. And if you're interested in buying organic fruits and vegetables see "What About Organic?" on page 2.

Even though virtually all fresh produce is available year-round everywhere, you'll get better quality and support sustainable agricultural practices when you make seasonal choices. I try to be sensitive to this challenge by offering an "Other fruits/vegetables you can use" line for each item. And remember, frozen is an option (see "Don't Freeze Out Frozen" on page 237).

STORING FRESH PRODUCE

Once home, put the vegetables and fruits either where they will continue to ripen or will maintain their current state the longest. The vast majority of everyday vegetables—broccoli, cauliflower, cabbage, eggplant, mushrooms, lettuce, greens, green beans, carrots, celery,

 fast   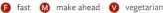 make ahead   V vegetarian

beets, radishes—last longest in the refrigerator. If there is visible moisture, remove them from plastic and keep them in bins; if they tend to dry out—like broccoli or carrots—keep them loosely wrapped. The sturdy ones will keep for a couple weeks; the tenderest might start getting funky in a day or two.

Most fruit is best left out at room temperature until ripe, with the exceptions of grapes, cherries, oranges, and apples. See "When to Refrigerate Fruits and Vegetables" below, for details on vegetables and fruits that should never be refrigerated or only be chilled after they ripen.

PREPARING FRESH PRODUCE

Wait until you're ready to use vegetables and fruit before rinsing them. While water helps remove both pesticide residues and other possible contaminants, it also washes away the plant's natural defenses against rotting, and storing moist produce can promote growth of mold or bacteria.

I rinse almost all fresh vegetables and fruits before cooking and eating. Even when the peel is inedible, it's a good idea; any bacteria or dirt on the outside can spread to the inside with handling. A soft scrubbing brush is perfect for potatoes you don't want to peel, cucumbers with little spines, and other, more rigorous jobs. You can also use a mildly abrasive dishwashing pad.

To rinse greens and other loose vegetables, put them in a salad spinner or a colander inside a large pot or the clean sink. Fill the vessel with water and swish the veggies around, then lift them out and let them drain in the colander, or transfer to a clean towel. Or for big fruits and vegetables like apples and tomatoes, simply run them under cold tap water, then drain and dry.

After rinsing, trim away ends, stems, cores, and seeds and peels as necessary. You're ready to get cooking. For details and illustrations about the common knife cuts see "The Basics of Cutting" starting on

When to Refrigerate Fruits and Vegetables

Most fruits and vegetables last longer when refrigerated. Here's a list of those that should *not* be, and instead left out to ripen properly. (There will be surprises in this list; that's to avoid mealiness.) Some things might be ready to eat before you are; so I've noted those you can move to the refrigerator after ripening. Then I usually try to let chilled fruit sit at room temperature before eating. Anything leftover should be refrigerated within a couple hours of cutting.

NEVER REFRIGERATE

Garlic
Onions (unless they're spring onions or scallions)
Peaches and nectarines
Plums
Potatoes
Sweet potatoes and yams
Tomatoes
Tropical tubers like taro, cassava, boniato, and malanga
Winter squash

OKAY TO REFRIGERATE WHEN RIPE

Apricots
Avocados
Bananas and plantains
Berries (try to eat within a day)
Figs
Grapefruit
Kiwis
Mangoes
Melons
Papayas
Pears
Persimmons
Pineapples

page 13. The Lexicon entries in this chapter include whatever you need to know for specific fruits and vegetables.

THE BASICS OF COOKING VEGETABLES

The main reason to cook a vegetable (or any food, really) is to improve its flavor and texture and to release nutrients that aren't available when it's raw. The way you apply heat will impact all those characteristics. For example, some cooking methods deepen flavor by caramelizing the natural sugar or starches during dry-heat methods like sautéing or roasting (usually with some fat), while moist-heat steaming and boiling brighten both taste and color.

By organizing this section by cooking technique—and including some master recipes and variation charts as examples—I hope both new and experienced cooks will become more comfortable preparing vegetables spontaneously, making substitutions based on availability and seasonality, and combining their own signature flavors and skills. But first, a little more background.

KEEPING THE NUTRIENTS IN VEGETABLES

Despite what enthusiasts of raw diets contend, cooking generally increases the bioavailability of the nutrients in vegetables. For example, the starch in potatoes is not absorbed by the stomach—and can cause gastric distress—unless the potatoes are cooked until just soft. And vegetables high in fiber and protein, like beans, benefit from some heat for the body to digest them efficiently.

Many vitamins, minerals, and other nutrients migrate out of the vegetables and into the surrounding liquid during cooking. Submerging vegetables for a long time in boiling water is the least nutritious way to cook them; steaming is a better alternative, especially if the vegetables remain above the steaming liquid or you can incorporate the steaming liquid into the dish.

The solution: Cook vegetables just enough to unlock the nutrients but not long enough to allow the bulk of them to escape. If you want the vegetables cooked beyond al dente for puréeing, mashing, or blending into soups or sauces, you might consider cooking them in a way that uses little or no water like roasting, stir-frying, or microwaving, or include the cooking liquid in the finished dish. And if you really love boiled vegetables, consider saving the cooking water and using it for soups or beverages.

CONTROLLING DONENESS IN VEGETABLES

Any vegetable—even those you usually eat raw, like lettuce—can be successfully cooked to any degree of tenderness. Your job is to know when to stop applying heat for a desired result. (See "What Does Crisp-Tender Mean?" on page 240 for one specific degree of doneness.)

It's easy: Try bending a vegetable slice or a single small whole one like a sugar snap pea or mushroom; the more flexible the vegetable, the shorter the cooking time, in general. Spinach will practically wilt if you breathe on it; thin asparagus tips or thinly sliced carrots require a bit more time on the heat. Thick asparagus stalks or chunks of carrots will take even longer. Slices you can't bend at all—like winter squash and root vegetables—are going to take much more cooking time to become tender.

Many vegetables can go from raw to mushy in a flash, especially when cut small. Though vegetables cooked until they're super-soft can be quite appealing, here are some tips to identify all the degrees of doneness long before that point:

- Watch for the color to brighten. Vegetables cooked al dente are even more vibrant than they are when raw. But they quickly peak and begin to look rinsed out as they start to soften:

- Check them frequently. Since most vegetables don't take long to cook, the color change will happen in an instant. There's no shame in poking around with a knife tip, toothpick, or skewer to gauge the tenderness. Every once in a while, grab a piece and taste. It's the only way you'll ever know for sure. Eventually you'll be able to do this by sight, smell, and a poke of your finger.

- Remember that vegetables—like other foods—continue to cook as they cool down. Remove them from the heat just before they reach the stage of doneness you want. (This will come easily with practice, trust me.)

- Take control of doneness by learning to "shock" vegetables by chilling them rapidly. This technique gets them ready ahead of time for finishing to perfect doneness at the last minute. (See "Shocking Vegetables," page 238.)

Vegetable Cooking Techniques

Here is a rundown of common ways to cook vegetables and control their doneness, starting with the fastest and easiest—including some master recipes and variation ideas.

MICROWAVING VEGETABLES

The microwave is good for steaming veggies with hardly any water at all, provided you know your machine well enough to pull them out before they overcook. Put vegetables on a plate or in a shallow bowl and sprinkle them with a few drops of water, then cover them loosely with a vented microwave cooking lid, a towel, or a heavy fitted glass lid. Set the time for a short interval (30 seconds at the most) and press the button. Repeat until the vegetables are a little less done than you want them, since they'll continue cooking out of the microwave. And be careful when you uncover them; the steam will be very hot.

Don't Freeze Out Frozen

All I am saying is give some frozen vegetables a chance. When you crave a pleasant flashback to summer, for example, pouring a bag of cut corn into a skillet of sizzling olive oil is going to get you there.

Frozen vegetables can be "fresher" (meaning brighter in color, more distinctive in flavor, and more consistently pleasing in texture) than their out-of-season produce-section counterparts. They can also be more convenient and are often less expensive. And since the quality of vegetables is pretty much preserved at the stage they're frozen, the nutritional value may be superior. Plus they're handy and easy to prepare—so you might eat vegetables more.

STEAMING VEGETABLES

Cooking vegetables above—not in—a small amount of gently bubbling water is fast and efficient and preserves water-soluble vitamins. (See Boiled or Steamed Vegetables on page 238.) This method is ideal for plain vegetables to either eat right away or marinate in a dressing as they cool. There's no need to buy a fancy vegetable steamer; a fold-up basket that fits in the bottom of a pot does the job, as does a metal colander or even, in a pinch, a heatproof plate (see "Ways to Rig a Steamer," page 20). Fill the steamer with vegetables, set it over an inch or so of water (see "Steaming," page 17), cover, and turn the heat to medium-high. Check frequently to prevent overcooking and to make sure there's still water in the bottom of the pot. To capture steamed vegetables when they're perfectly crisp-tender, shock them immediately in ice water (see page 238).

BOILING, PARBOILING, AND BLANCHING VEGETABLES

Simple and straightforward: Bring a large pot of water to a boil, salt it generously, and toss in whole or cut vegetables. Check them frequently and when they're just about as tender as you'd like, drain them—either by fishing them out with a strainer or slotted spoon or by pouring the vegetables and water into a colander to drain. As with steamed vegetables, shocking after boiling immediately stops the cooking, whether they're at crisp-tender or more well done for puréeing. ("Shocking Vegetables," below, tells you how.) And the term *parboiling* really means "partial boiling," in which vegetables are intentionally left underdone so they can finish cooking by another method.

Boiling or parboiling is also handy if you have different vegetables and each requires a different cooking time; you simply keep the water rolling and work in batches. If you're parboiling before cooking with another method—on the grill or in a stir-fry, for example—your goal is for all of them to finish cooking at the same time, so try to parboil each to the point where it is barely getting tender.

Blanching is the same process as parboiling, only the term can signify a different purpose. When you want to make a sharp-tasting vegetable, like garlic, onions, or shallots milder before further cooking, you can blanch it in a pot of bubbling liquid for a few minutes. (For a specific example, see Creamed Onions on page 316.) Water is the simplest, though you can also use milk, stock, wine, beer, or juice. The idea is not to make the vegetable soft but just to cook it long enough to take the bite out. Three to five minutes will do. It's worth noting that

the same technique, with the time reduced to 30 seconds or less, makes almost all fruits and vegetables—from peaches to tomatoes to garlic—easy to peel. (To confuse things a bit more, blanching is also used to soften meat or poultry before rendering fat and to help remove the skins from nuts.)

An easy and versatile recipe for all kinds of vegetables follows. Then see Parboiled or Steamed Vegetables in Butter or Oil on page 242 and "11 Ways to Jazz Up Simply Cooked Vegetables" on page 251 for ways to add more flavor to microwaved, steamed, or boiled vegetables.

Boiled or Steamed Vegetables

MAKES: 4 servings | **TIME:** 10 to 30 minutes

These are the two basic methods for cooking just about any vegetable, and they're more similar than different. Boiling leaves you with somewhat wet vegetables (sometimes desired); steaming is faster, since you don't have to wait for a pot of water to boil. The same vegetables will take about the same amount of actual cooking time to reach the same desired doneness. See the sidebar on shocking vegetables

Shocking Vegetables

After microwaving, steaming, or boiling vegetables, you can "shock" them to stop the cooking process and capture an exact degree of doneness—and their vibrant color. It's easy: Immediately plunge them into a bowl of ice water.

Shocking works brilliantly for virtually all vegetables; eggplant, bell and chile peppers, and mushrooms are the notable exceptions. It's terrific any time you want to cook vegetables for crudités (see page 102), partially cook them for a dish to finish later, or prepare multiple vegetables of differing cooking times for stir-fries, salads, or other dishes where some lingering crispness is desirable.

If you're shocking more than one type of vegetable for the same dish, work in batches, moving them through the

boiling or steaming process and into the ice water until you've done them all; there's no need to change the water in either the boiling pot or the shocking bath, though you will probably need to add ice to the bath.

Shocking greens—spinach, kale, escarole, and the like—has the added benefit of allowing you to remove extra moisture. Squeeze cooked, shocked, and drained greens tightly between your hands or press them against the strainer, then chop or cook according to the recipe.

After the cooked vegetables have been shocked and drained, use them right away or cover them tightly and refrigerate for a day or two before finishing or serving.

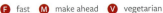

Shocking Boiled or
Steamed Vegetables

for the best way to stop the cooking process to finish later, or serve vegetables chilled in crudités or salads.

> **Salt**
> 1 to 2 **pounds vegetable of your choice, peeled, stemmed, seeded, and/or chopped as needed**
> **Fresh lemon juice, olive oil, butter, or any of the toppings from "11 Ways to Jazz Up Simply Cooked Vegetables" (page 251)**

Bring a large pot of water to a boil and salt it, or rig a steamer (see page 20). Add the vegetables to the water or the steaming basket and cook, checking frequently with the tip of a sharp knife, until they're either crisp-tender or tender. Drain, then serve, drizzled with lemon juice, oil, butter, or whatever you like. Or shock in ice water (see page 238), drain again, and use in stir-fries or sautés or to eat cold. You can refrigerate them to use later for up to a day; just pat them dry first.

GREENS Trim and rinse the greens. If the leaves and stems are pliable and can be eaten raw—like spinach, arugula, or watercress—that's a tender green. If the stems are as crisp as celery (more than ⅛ inch thick or so) and the leaves a little tough—like bok choy, chard, kale, or collards—it's best to separate the leaves from the stems (see the illustration on page 300) and give the stems a little head start. Add the stems or the stems and leaves to the pot and cook until bright green and tender, from 3 minutes for spinach to 10 for kale and collards. If you held back the leaves, add them when the stems are just about tender.

TENDER VEGETABLES like broccoli, cauliflower, green beans, asparagus, peas of any type, bok choy, corn, even eggplant (if you're careful not to overcook it). Cook until the vegetable is just tender, which will vary from about 3 minutes for peas to 7 for broccoli florets to 10 or 12 for broccoli stems and thick green beans. Keep in mind that the smaller the pieces, the quicker they will cook.

STURDY VEGETABLES like roots and tubers: A little different method, but this will work for potatoes, beets,

What Does Crisp-Tender Mean?

Applied to asparagus, green beans, broccoli, and more, "crisp-tender" describes a state where vegetables retain a subtle, pleasant crunch but are tender and moist enough to be pierced easily with a skewer or thin-bladed knife—or your teeth. When crisp-tender, vegetables like asparagus and broccoli will be flexible but not flopping over, and their color will be bright. You'll learn to assess crisp-tender doneness by sight after a while, but start by tasting the vegetable as it cooks.

turnips, radishes, winter squash, and anything rock hard. Peel the vegetable or not, as you prefer; leave whole if possible (or cut in big chunks) to minimize waterlogging. To boil, start by putting the vegetables in a pot with enough water to cover by at least 2 inches (or drop into the basket of a steamer). Bing the water to a boil and cook until the vegetable is quite tender and can be pierced easily with a skewer or thin-bladed knife, from 10 minutes (radishes, for example) to nearly an hour (large whole potatoes). If steaming, be sure to add water if necessary during cooking.

Puréed Vegetables

MAKES: 4 servings | **TIME:** 40 minutes

Puréed vegetables are luxurious, delicious, and simple. Root vegetables are best for puréeing since their starchiness lends a creamy texture, but almost anything can work, especially with enough fat. See the chart that follows for many more ideas.

Warm vegetable purées make an elegant bed for simply cooked fish, poultry, or meat. And at room temperature or chilled, they are excellent impromptu dips and spreads.

> **About 1½ pounds vegetables, one kind or a combination (see the chart on the next page)**

F fast   **M** make ahead   **V** vegetarian

10 More Vegetable Purées

VEGETABLE 2 pounds raw will give you 3 to 4 cups cooked and chopped	FAT 2 to 3 tablespoons	ENRICHMENT use as needed to reach desired consistency; about ½ cup	SEASONING 1 to 2 tablespoons, in addition to salt and pepper	GARNISH as much or as little as you like
Broccoli or Cauliflower Purée	Olive oil	Ricotta cheese	Pinch nutmeg	Grated Parmesan
Butternut Squash Purée	Good-quality vegetable oil	Coconut milk	Curry powder	Toasted shredded coconut
Puréed Carrots	Olive oil	Orange juice	Chopped fresh ginger	Grated orange zest
Puréed Chestnuts	Butter	Heavy cream or crème fraîche	Honey or maple syrup	Chopped roasted chestnuts (see page 283)
Corn Purée	Butter or olive oil	Sour cream	2 teaspoons chili powder	Queso fresco, chopped fresh tomato, chopped cilantro
Eggplant Purée	Olive oil	None needed; try 1 head Roasted Garlic (page 294)	Any Middle Eastern spice blend or a large pinch saffron	Chopped fresh parsley or mint
Puréed Peas	Melted butter	Heavy cream or half-and-half	Chopped fresh tarragon	A spoonful of Dijon mustard, stirred in
Pumpkin, Other Winter Squash, or Cassava Purée	Olive oil	Cooking liquid	Lots of garlic, roasted (page 294) or fried	Paprika or lots of pepper, a squeeze of lime juice
Puréed Bell Peppers or Mild Chiles	Olive oil	If needed, add more olive oil	None needed	Chopped fresh cilantro or red onion
Puréed Parsnips, Turnips, or Rutabagas	Melted butter or olive oil	Dab of sour cream	Chopped red onion	Chopped fresh parsley, chopped toasted nuts

Salt and pepper

2 tablespoons olive oil or butter, or more to taste

Chopped fresh parsley for garnish (optional)

1. Peel and trim the vegetables as necessary; cut them into roughly equal-sized pieces, 1 to 2 inches in diameter. Put the vegetables in a large pot with water to cover and add a large pinch of salt; or rig a steamer (see page 20) and put the vegetables in it above water. Bring to a boil and cook until the vegetables are tender, usually 5 to 15 minutes. You want the vegetables fully tender but not mushy.

2. Drain the vegetables well, reserving some of the cooking liquid. (At this point, you can refrigerate the vegetables, well wrapped or in a covered container, for up to 2 days before proceeding.) Cool the vegetables slightly and put them in a blender or food processor with as much of the cooking liquid as you need to get the machine going; purée until as smooth as you like. (You can also mash the vegetables with a large fork or potato masher or run them through a food mill set over a large bowl, adding the cooking liquid as needed.)

3. Add the oil or butter, and stir, then taste and adjust the seasoning, adding some pepper. Serve, keep warm, or cool and refrigerate for up to a day or 2; reheat them gently on the stove or in the microwave. Garnish with parsley before serving.

RICH VEGETABLE PURÉE Add up to ½ cup cream, sour cream, half-and-half, or milk when puréeing.

SAUTÉING VEGETABLES

I wish there were another word for sautéing, since it sounds much more intimidating than it is: nothing more than cooking food quickly in hot fat. Stir-frying is a subset of sautéing; see the following section. (And for more information on both, see pages 17 and 20 in Cooking Basics.)

The only potential downside is that you must check the vegetables frequently while sautéing and anticipate doneness, since they'll continue to cook even off the heat. The recipe that follows walks you through the process so you get the hang of what to look for. If you're comfortable boiling or steaming (or microwaving) vegetables—or want to prepare them in advance to finish easily at the last minute, then try the variation.

Sautéed Vegetables

MAKES: 4 servings | **TIME:** 5 minutes

The secret ingredient to perfect sautéed vegetables is often a little water. It's especially helpful if you're cooking hard vegetables like winter squashes.

2 tablespoons butter or olive oil, or more as needed
1 to 2 pounds the vegetable of your choice, peeled, stemmed, seeded, and/or chopped as needed
Salt
Pepper (optional)

1. Put the butter or oil in a large skillet over medium heat. When the butter foams or the oil is hot, add the vegetables and sprinkle with salt, and with pepper if you like.

2. Adjust the heat so the vegetables sizzle without burning, and cook, stirring occasionally, until their color turns vibrant, about 2 minutes.

3. Start tasting one of the smallest pieces. Quick-cooking vegetables like greens and snow peas might be tender. Sturdy vegetables and anything in between will require anywhere from a few minutes to 10 or 15 minutes more; adding water, 1 tablespoon at a time, helps prevent the vegetables from browning and can speed up cooking by creating steam. When the vegetables are just a little less tender than you ultimately want them, remove the pan from the heat, add a little more butter or oil if you like, taste and adjust the seasoning, and serve.

PARBOILED OR STEAMED VEGETABLES IN BUTTER OR OIL With a two-step process, you can cook vegetables perfectly at the last minute: Follow the recipe for boiling or steaming the vegetable of your choice on page 238, or see "Microwaving Vegetables" on page 237; make sure you cook it a little less tender than you ultimately want them. Shock the vegetables if you like (see page 238), and after draining, cover and refrigerate for up to 1 day. When you're ready to eat, follow the recipe above, but in Step 2 cook them just long enough to heat through, no more than a minute or 2.

STIR-FRYING VEGETABLES

Like sautéing, stir-frying is a stovetop technique that uses a little bit of fat in a broad-bottomed pan to cook

all kinds of vegetables quickly. There are a couple differences: With stir-frying you might choose to brown and sear the food before it has chance to overcook, and usually you make some kind of sauce in the pan simultaneously, or afterwards. And this method is versatile enough to cook multiple vegetables or add meat or other protein to get an entire meal on the table fast. For more detail on stir-frying, see page 20. Here are the basic points to get you started:

- The smaller you cut the food, the faster it will cook. That means grated vegetables like potatoes, beets, or squash can be stir-fried in several minutes.

- The list that follows outlines lots of options, but too many ingredients can crowd the pan, slow you down, and lead to overcooking and muddled flavors.

- Use the largest flat-bottomed skillet you have; stainless steel or well-seasoned cast iron is best, and high heat is essential. A wok is only good if you have a special deep burner designed to let gas flames lap up the sides.

- Stir almost constantly unless you want to promote searing and browning, in which case stir less frequently.

- For large pieces or vegetables that take a longer time to cook, you have three options: Parboil until tender and shock them; cut them small; or grate them.

- It's counterintuitive, but stir-frying in batches is faster than trying to overcrowd the pan, and the results are always superior. In the case of longer-cooking vegetables, you can stir-fry them first; using a little water or other liquid to create steam will speed things up. Transfer them to a plate, then add more fat and the quicker-cooking vegetables, or even meat. Repeat as necessary, then return everything to the pan to season and reheat.

- A little liquid is always valuable in stir-fries, whether it's water or something with more flavor like wine, stock, soy sauce, or fish sauce. It encourages vegetables to cook more quickly (see above and Sautéed Vegetables on page 242); at the end, liquid will keep ingredients from burning and will create a sauce.

Stir-Fried Vegetables

MAKES: 4 servings | **TIME:** 15 minutes

Stir-fries are among the best ways to use those odd bits of vegetables languishing in your fridge. Just remember: The smaller you cut them, the more quickly they'll become tender. And if you've got some stock handy, use that instead of some or all of the water.

1½	pounds quick-cooking vegetables like broccoli, sugar snap or snow peas, carrots, or asparagus
2	tablespoons good-quality vegetable oil
1	tablespoon chopped garlic
1	tablespoon chopped fresh ginger
½	cup chopped scallions or onion
	Salt and pepper
2	tablespoons soy sauce, plus more to taste
1	teaspoon sesame oil

1. Trim the vegetables and cut them into bite-sized pieces if necessary. Put a large skillet over medium-high heat for about 3 minutes to get hot. Add the oil, quickly followed by the garlic, ginger, and scallions. Cook, stirring constantly, for about 15 seconds, then add the vegetables and adjust the heat so they sizzle. Sprinkle with a little salt and pepper.

2. Cook, stirring frequently, until the vegetables are brightly colored but not quite as tender as you want them, 3 to 7 minutes, depending on the kind and how they're cut. Add ¼ cup water, the soy sauce, and sesame oil; stir and turn off the heat. Taste and

Stir-Fried Asparagus, front, and Curried Stir-Fried Potatoes, back, page 246

5 More Vegetable Stir-Fries

Start by heating 2 tablespoons good-quality vegetable oil in a large skillet, then add the ingredients in the order listed, cooking until crisp-tender before adding the next.

NAME	ADD FIRST	ADD SECOND	ADD LAST
Stir-Fried Asparagus	1 tablespoons minced garlic; 2 small dried chiles (optional)	1½ pounds asparagus, trimmed, peeled, and cut into 2-inch lengths (parboiled if thick; see page 237)	2 tablespoons water; 1 tablespoon soy sauce; 1 teaspoon sesame oil (optional)
Stir-Fried Bean Sprouts	1 pound bean sprouts (about 4 cups), trimmed if you like; 1 tablespoon each minced ginger and minced garlic	2 tablespoons any spice mixture like five-spice powder or curry powder	Squeeze of fresh lemon juice
Gingery Stir-Fried Broccoli and Shiitakes	1½ pounds broccoli, trimmed, stems cut into pieces no more than ⅛ inch thick; ½ pound sliced fresh shiitakes; 2 tablespoons chopped fresh ginger (all at the same time)	1 cup stock or mushroom soaking liquid (cook until the liquid evaporates)	2 tablespoons soy sauce
Curried Stir-Fried Potatoes	1 tablespoon cumin seeds; 1 small red onion, chopped; 1½ pounds all-purpose potatoes, peeled and grated (cook until the potatoes are lightly browned)	1 tablespoon garam masala; pinch cayenne; salt and pepper	¼ cup chopped fresh cilantro
Seaweed and Celery Stir-Fry	1 tablespoon minced garlic; 1 tablespoon minced ginger; ½ cup chopped scallions or onion	2 celery stalks, sliced; 1 ounce seaweed like arame, hijiki, dulse or wakame; soaked, drained, and sliced (if necessary); ¼ cup water	2 tablespoons soy sauce; 1 teaspoon sesame oil

adjust the seasoning. Serve or store covered in the refrigerator for up to a day to eat cold or at room temperature.

SHRIMP, CHICKEN, OR ANY MEAT AND VEGETABLE STIR-FRY Add 1 pound peeled shrimp or boneless, skinless chicken, pork (preferably shoulder), or beef (preferably sirloin), cut into thin strips and patted dry. In Step 1, make sure the skillet is very hot. Add the oil, then the meat, stir once or twice, and cook until it begins to brown, about a minute. Stir and cook until just done, another minute or so; remove from the pan.

Proceed with the recipe, adding more oil and water if needed. When the vegetables are almost as tender as you want them, return the shrimp, chicken, or meat to the pan to heat through. Increase the amounts of soy sauce and/or sesame oil, if you like.

TOFU AND VEGETABLE STIR-FRY Add 1 pound extra-firm tofu, chopped, and dried on towels. In Step 1, make sure the skillet is very hot. Add the oil, then the tofu, and cook, turning the pieces, until golden brown on all (or most) sides, about 5 minutes; remove from the pan. Proceed with the recipe, adding more oil or water if

F fast   **M** make ahead   **V** vegetarian

needed. When the vegetables are almost as tender as you want them, return the tofu to the pan to heat through. Increase the amounts of soy sauce and/or sesame oil, if you like.

STIR-FRIED VEGETABLES, VIETNAMESE STYLE Substitute onion for the scallion. In Step 1, add 2 dried hot red chiles or up to 1 teaspoon red chile flakes along with the garlic, ginger, and scallions; cook and stir an extra 15 seconds. After cooking the vegetables, add 1 tablespoon fish sauce with the soy sauce. Off the heat, squeeze in the juice from 1 lime. Garnish with chopped fresh cilantro or Thai basil before serving.

BRAISING VEGETABLES

A combination of sautéing and simmering, braising allows you to cook vegetables until they're fully tender—or even slightly mushy—and take advantage of all their flavor and nutrients since you eat the cooking liquid too. Root vegetables, cabbages, sturdy winter greens, and alliums (garlic, shallots, leeks, and onions) are all good candidates for braising. (For specific examples, see Braised Artichoke Hearts on page 261 or Leeks Braised in Oil or Butter, page 302.)

Begin with sautéing, described on page 242. After the vegetables have begun to turn golden (and to caramelize, if you like) in hot butter or oil, add enough liquid—stock, milk, juice, wine, or water—to come about halfway up the vegetables. Bring to a boil, then lower the heat so the liquid bubbles gently, or put the pot in a moderate oven (325° to 350°F). You can cover vegetables during braising, or leave them uncovered and add more liquid as needed to keep everything from drying out.

BRAISING AND GLAZING VEGETABLES

This valuable technique takes a little more attention than straight braising, but the approach is similar. See Braised and Glazed Radishes, Turnips, or Other Root Vegetable on page 334 for a specific example.

Follow these directions: Put oil or butter in a large skillet and turn the heat to medium. Sauté chopped or sliced garlic, onion, shallot, and/or ginger, or other aromatics if you like, for 30 seconds or so. Then add the vegetable—like carrots, broccoli, cauliflower, asparagus, or any root vegetable, sliced or chopped as you like—with a little water and a sprinkle of salt. The longer the vegetables need to cook, the more water you'll need, but generally ¼ to ½ cup will do.

Now cover the pan. Cook, uncovering only to stir occasionally and check the water level, until the vegetables are just tender, 5 to 15 minutes depending on the vegetable and how large the pieces are. The goal is to keep just enough water in the pan to steam the vegetables until they're cooked, without letting the pan go dry. To glaze, uncover and raise the heat to cook out virtually all the remaining water; the combination of the fat and the starches and sugars from the vegetables will create a glossy coating.

ROASTING VEGETABLES

The dry heat of roasting in a hot oven intensifies the flavor of vegetables by driving out their internal water. Depending on the vegetable, the results range from slightly chewy to completely tender on the inside and crisped on the outside, with good color. Roasting is a fine method for entertaining, because the results can be served right out of the oven or at room temperature.

Roasted Vegetables or Fruits

MAKES: 4 servings | **TIME:** About 1 hour

Something magical happens when vegetables are roasted: Their flavors concentrate, the texture becomes soft and a bit chewy, and the outside turns a beautiful golden brown, and sometimes charred in places. Just remember to give the pieces a little breathing room

7 Examples for Roasting and Seasoning Vegetables

Using the main recipe as a springboard, here are some specific variations for Roasted Vegetables, including a savory fruit.

NAME	VEGETABLE	FAT AND SEASONING	DIRECTIONS
Roasted Carrots with Cumin	1 to 1½ pounds baby carrots, green tops trimmed, or full-sized carrots, cut into sticks	3 tablespoons olive oil; salt and pepper; 2 teaspoons cumin seeds	Roast at 425°F until the carrots are tender and browning, about 25 minutes.
Roasted Brussels Sprouts with Garlic	1 pound Brussels sprouts, trimmed and halved	¼ cup olive oil; 5 cloves garlic, peeled; salt and pepper; 1 tablespoon balsamic vinegar for serving	For the crispest sprouts, put the oiled baking sheet in the oven as it heats to 450°F. Add the garlic and Brussels sprouts. Roast, stirring the pan once or twice, until the sprouts are tender and browned, about 30 minutes. Drizzle with the vinegar.
Roasted Cauliflower with Raisins and Vinaigrette	1 large head cauliflower, trimmed and separated into florets	3 tablespoons olive oil; salt and pepper; 2 Roasted Red Peppers (page 318), chopped; 2 tablespoons balsamic or sherry vinegar, or to taste	Roast the cauliflower at 400°F until just starting to soften and brown, about 15 minutes. Add the peppers and roast until browned, 10 minutes more. Stir in the vinegar.
Roasted Onion Halves	4 onions, peeled, halved around the equator	2 tablespoons olive oil; salt and pepper; 2 or 3 sprigs fresh thyme (optional)	Rub the onions with the oil. Roast cut side down at 400°F until starting to brown, about 20 minutes. Turn and brown on the other side.
Roasted Scallions	2 bunches scallions or spring onions, trimmed but with a lot of the greens remaining	2 tablespoons olive oil; salt and pepper; 1 or 2 limes; chopped fresh cilantro for garnish	Roast at 400°F until lightly browned and tender, about 20 minutes. Drizzle with the juice of 1 lime and mix, adding more lime juice if you like. Garnish with the cilantro.
Winter Squash Slices	1½ pounds winter squash, peeled if necessary and cut into ¼-inch-thick slices (if the skin is thin, don't bother to peel)	4 tablespoons olive oil or melted butter; salt and pepper	Toss the slices with 2 to 3 tablespoons of the oil, spread on the pan, then drizzle with another 2 to 3 tablespoons. Roast at 400°F until tender, 20 to 30 minutes.
Savory Roasted Apple Slices	1½ pounds apples, peeled if you like and cored, cut into wedges	4 tablespoons butter or olive oil; salt and ½ teaspoon cardamom	Toss the slices with the butter or oil and seasonings, spread on the pan, then roast at 400°F until tender, 10 to 20 minutes.

F fast   **M** make ahead   **V** vegetarian

in the pan; they'll shrink a bit but not much. You can always divide the vegetables between two or more pans, or roast in batches.

Seasoning with simple salt and pepper is fine. For more ideas, see the chart on page 248. The best time to add spices is during the last couple of minutes of cooking; fresh herbs should be tossed into the pan after the vegetables are out of the oven.

Vegetables and fruits you can use: apples, artichoke hearts (fresh, not canned; see page 258), asparagus, Brussels sprouts, carrots, cauliflower, celery root, eggplant (use extra oil), fennel, grapes, leeks, okra (trimmed but whole), onions, parsnips, potatoes, radishes, shallots (whole), summer or winter squash, sweet potatoes, yams, turnips, or rutabaga.

> 3 tablespoons olive oil, melted butter, or a mixture, plus more as needed
> 1½ to 2 pounds vegetables (one kind or a combination with similar cooking times), peeled, trimmed, seeded, and chopped or sliced as needed
> Salt and pepper

1. Heat the oven to 425°F while you prepare the vegetables. Drizzle half the oil on a roasting pan or baking sheet. Add the vegetables and drizzle with the remaining oil; sprinkle with salt and pepper. Stir, or if roasting vegetables that will fall apart with stirring like fennel, leeks, or onion slices, use a pastry brush to coat them with the oil.

2. Roast the vegetables undisturbed until they release easily from the pan, 5 to 15 minutes, depending on the sturdiness of the vegetable; then stir or toss with a spatula.

3. Continue roasting, stirring once or twice more, until the vegetables are tender and browned in places, another 10 to 50 minutes, again depending on the vegetable. If they're starting to burn, lower the temperature to 400°F and stir more frequently.

Taste and adjust the seasoning. Serve hot or at room temperature.

GRILLING OR BROILING VEGETABLES

When you expose the surface of vegetables to intense heat, the outside will cook much faster than the inside. So with grilling and broiling the goal is to balance that browning or charring outside with tenderness on the inside, while adding a smoky flavor.

Sturdy vegetables—eggplant, onions, mushrooms, squash, corn on the cob, and potatoes—are the most obvious candidates to grill or broil, though tomatoes, green beans, and asparagus work great too. Some small vegetables, like mushrooms and radishes, you can grill whole; other large ones, like cauliflower and eggplant, work as "steaks" when thickly sliced; others, like Brussels sprouts, cherry tomatoes, or onion wedges, are best cut into bite-sized pieces and skewered or tossed in a perforated grilling basket. To ensure perfect doneness, you can parboil vegetables that take a long time to cook—potatoes or winter squash, for example—and finish them on the grill with shorter-cooking vegetables.

Broiling is a good substitute, though you'll have just one heat source. Try to avoid overcrowding the pan so the vegetables brown in places; if necessary work in batches. The best thing about these cooking methods is that the vegetables are excellent warm or at room temperature, as well as hot, so it's okay if they sit for up to an hour before serving.

Coat the vegetables all over lightly with a little oil or a marinade and grill, or broil about 4 inches away from the heat source. You don't even need to parboil really hard vegetables like squash or potatoes; either slice them thin or grill them part of the time over indirect heat with the lid of the grill closed. Then move them over direct heat to finish browning. A master recipe and variation chart follow. There's information about building and lighting fires on page 21.

Grilled Vegetables

MAKES: 4 servings | **TIME:** 10 to 30 minutes

Grilling is the most fluid of all cooking techniques. This master recipe will help you learn how to control that variability—and have some fun, too—providing you use all your senses to pay attention to both the food and the flame. The point is that almost any vegetable can be successfully cooked on the grill. Just go with the flow: Keep a portion of the grill free of coals or gas flame to move things over to indirect heat whenever things start charring faster than you want them to.

Vegetables you can use: virtually everything except for leafy greens, though whole heads of romaine, radicchio, endive, escarole, or chicory are terrific. For some specific ideas, see "13 Recipes for Grilling Vegetables" on page 252.

> 1½   **pounds any vegetable, like eggplant, squash, peppers, onions, mushrooms, or a combination**
> 3   **tablespoons olive oil, plus more for drizzling**
>   **Salt and pepper**
>   **Lemon wedges for serving (optional)**

1. If you're using wooden skewers, soak them in water while you get the vegetables ready. Prepare a charcoal or gas grill for medium indirect cooking. Clean the grates; your vegetables will be less likely to stick.

2. Trim, peel, and seed the vegetables as necessary. Cut them into chunks no more than 1 inch thick; or leave the smaller vegetables whole. For potatoes, squash, or eggplant, slices are fine; they should be between ¼ and ½ inch thick, lengthwise or on the diagonal for smaller items like zucchini. For thin or fragile vegetables, thread them on skewers or use a grilling basket. Brush or drizzle them all over with the oil and sprinkle with salt and pepper.

3. Be prepared move the vegetables around as they cook. For sturdy or dense items like sliced potatoes or winter squash, start with the cool side of the grill over indirect heat. Then as the pieces become tender, move them over

direct heat to char the outsides. For pliable or small vegetables like sliced zucchini or peppers or mushrooms on skewers, start over direct heat; if they start to brown too quickly you can always move them to the cool side of the grill. If you're grilling a variety of vegetables, pull them off as they are done while the rest catch up. Some vegetables will be ready in just a few minutes; others will take up to 30.

4. Serve the vegetables hot, at room temperature, or chilled, with a drizzle of oil and lemon wedges if you like.

11 Ways to Jazz Up Simply Cooked Vegetables

Here are some quick last-minute additions that add punch to any kind of simply cooked vegetable. Sprinkle or drizzle, depending on the addition, then toss—or not. Saucing is always an excellent way to finish vegetables; browse through the sauces and condiments chapter for dozens of ideas.

1. Fresh lemon or lime juice
2. Chopped fresh herbs
3. Grated citrus zest
4. Chopped nuts
5. Toasted bread crumbs
6. Nut or seed oil like sesame, walnut, hazelnut, or pumpkin seed oil
7. Flavored Oil (page 53)
8. Compound Butter (page 78)
9. Spice mixtures, especially chili powder or chaat masala (to make your own, see pages 32 and 34)
10. Vinaigrette (page 188)
11. Any croutons (see page 801)

Broiled Vegetable Gratin

MAKES: 4 servings | **TIME:** 15 minutes with cooked vegetables

Using this broiler method, vegetable gratins are more about assembly than cooking. Start with boiled,

(continued)

13 Recipes for Grilling Vegetables

This chart walks you through the basics for grilling all sorts of vegetables, including some tips on how to punch up the flavor before serving.

VEGETABLE	PREPARATION	COOKING	SERVE WITH
Grilled Artichokes	Halve, remove chokes from large artichokes, or use baby artichokes or hearts (see page 258); parboil in salted water until just tender; shock (see page 238). Skewer baby artichokes and hearts. Brush with oil.	Grill over direct heat, turning occasionally, until browned and tender when pierced with a skewer or knife tip, about 10 minutes.	Aioli (page 70) or any other flavored mayo for dipping; Traditional Pesto (page 51) or its variations for topping
Grilled Asparagus	Trim but leave whole; brush or toss with oil.	Grill over direct heat, turning occasionally, just until the thick part can be pierced with a skewer or knife tip, 6 to 12 minutes.	Compound Butter (page 78) or Five-Minute Drizzle Sauce (page 81) for topping; or sprinkle with grated Parmesan
Grilled Chiles or Bell Peppers	Core and seed; halve or cut into wide strips and skewer; oil is optional.	Grill over direct heat, turning occasionally, until the skin is blistered, dark brown, and tender, 10 to 15 minutes.	Mint or Dill Pesto (page 51), Simplest Yogurt Sauce (page 59), or Creamy Cilantro-Mint Chutney (page 62)
Grilled Corn	Remove silk; keep the cobs in their husks or remove them. Oil is optional when husks are intact.	Grill over direct heat, turning occasionally, until some kernels char and others are lightly browned, 15 to 20 minutes with husks on, 5 to 10 with husks off.	Compound Butter (page 78) or Ginger-Scallion Sauce (page 64) for topping. Or sprinkle with chili powder or sumac.
Grilled Eggplant	Peel if you like; cut into ¼- to ½-inch-thick slices or 1½ inch cubes and skewer; brush with oil.	Grill over direct heat, turning occasionally, until browned and tender, 5 to 20 minutes.	Peanut Sauce (page 75) or Thai Chile Sauce (page 66) for topping; or sprinkle with Seaweed "Shake" (page 35).
Miso-Marinated Grilled Mushrooms	Remove stems from portobellos or shiitakes; trim small mushrooms; slice thickly, cut into cubes, leave whole, or skewer or use a grilling basket if small. Brush with oil.	Grill over direct heat, turning occasionally, until browned, juicy, and tender, 15 to 20 minutes.	Immediately toss the mushrooms in Miso Dipping Sauce (page 66) and serve hot, warm, or chilled.
Grilled Leeks Vinaigrette	Trim; rinse thoroughly; brush with olive oil.	Grill over direct heat, turning occasionally, until browned all over and very tender, 5 to 15 minutes.	Mustard Vinaigrette (page 190) to serve hot, or to marinate for up to an hour after grilling

 fast 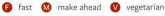 make ahead V vegetarian

VEGETABLE	PREPARATION	COOKING	SERVE WITH
Grilled Onions	Unpeeled and halved through the root end, or peeled and cut into wedges or ½-inch slices; brush with oil.	Grill over direct heat, turning once with a spatula to keep together, until browned and tender, about 15 minutes.	Any raw or cooked salsa (pages 55 or 71) or Teriyaki Sauce (page 76)
Grilled Potatoes or Sweet Potatoes	Use waxy red or white potatoes; parboil in salted water until just tender or start raw and cook longer; sweet potatoes don't need parboiling. Cut into long wedges or ½-inch slices; brush with oil.	Grill parboiled potatoes over direct heat, turning occasionally, until browned and fully tender, 5 to 10 minutes. Start raw or sweet potatoes over indirect heat, turning occasionally and moving over direct heat for brief spurts, until golden and very tender all the way through, 20 to 25 minutes.	Compound Butter (page 78), Barbecue Sauce (page 74), or Miso Dipping Sauce (page 66)
Grilled Balsamic Radicchio	Core; halve or quarter, depending on size; brush with olive oil.	Grill over direct heat, moving the pieces to the indirect side to prevent burning, just until the edges begin to crisp and char. Brush on 1 tablespoon brown sugar mixed with ¼ cup balsamic vinegar while grilling, taking extra care to prevent charring.	This makes a terrific warm salad; chop the radicchio and toss it with cooked pasta or rice, some more olive oil, and squeeze of lemon.
Grilled Squash or Zucchini	Trim; cut into ½-inch lengthwise slices or long diagonal slices; brush with oil.	Grill over direct heat, turning occasionally, until browned and tender, 10 to 15 minutes.	Cilantro, Dill, Basil, or Mint Purée (page 52) or Pepita Salsa (page 56)
Grilled Tomatoes	Use slightly green or not fully ripe tomatoes; halve, cut into ½-inch slices, or leave whole and skewer if small; brush with oil if cut.	Grill over direct heat, turning once, until browned but not falling apart, 5 to 10 minutes.	Traditional Pesto (page 51) or a variation, or Miso Five-Minute Drizzle Sauce (page 81)
Grilled Winter Squash	Use butternut, acorn, or pumpkin. Peel if you like; split and remove the seeds. Cut into 1-inch-thick slices or 1½-inch cubes and skewer; brush with oil.	Grill over indirect heat, turning occasionally, until very tender all the way through, 20 to 25 minutes; finish by browning over direct heat if you like.	Brown Butter (page 78) or Chile Tahini Sauce (page 59)

Braised Leeks au Gratin (top) and Tomato Gratin (bottom), page 256

steamed, roasted, grilled, or even sautéed vegetables; if needed, slice them, cut into wedges, or chop into bite-size chunks. Add a simple topping, and the results are easy and elegant. For something more involved, see the variation and the chart on page 256.

    2   tablespoons olive oil or butter, plus more
        for greasing the pan
4 to 6 cups any cooked vegetable (1½ to 2 pounds
        raw), sliced or chopped as desired
    1   cup grated Parmesan cheese
    ½   cup bread crumbs (preferably fresh; see page
        801)
        Salt and pepper

1. Turn on the broiler and position the rack about 4 inches below the heat. Grease a broad, shallow flameproof baking dish, or a rimmed baking sheet. Put the vegetables in the prepared dish, spreading them out a bit into an even layer. Sprinkle with salt and pepper if they're not already seasoned. Distribute the cheese and bread crumbs over all. Drizzle with the oil or dot with bits of butter, and sprinkle with salt and pepper.

2. Put the vegetables under the broiler and cook until the topping is golden brown, hot, and bubbly, which could be as little as 2 minutes but certainly no more than 10. Keep a close watch so it doesn't burn. Serve.

RICHER BROILED VEGETABLE GRATIN Use only enough butter or oil to grease the baking dish. Instead of the Parmesan make a recipe of Béchamel (page 79) and grate 1 cup Gruyère or other Swiss melting cheese. After spreading the vegetables into the prepared dish, cover the top with the sauce, then the cheese and breadcrumbs. Broil as directed and garnish with chopped parsley or chives if you'd like.

FRYING VEGETABLES

Messy, and you need a lot fat, but frying is popular for a reason, right? Whether you coat the vegetables or not,

you can pan-fry them in shallow oil (½ inch deep or so) or deep-fry in enough oil to submerge them (2 to 3 inches oil in a large pot).

TO PAN-FRY Put a large skillet over medium to medium-high heat and add the oil. It should be hot but not smoking before you add the vegetables (test a small piece first; the vegetable should sizzle immediately and vigorously). See Breaded and Fried Eggplant (or Any Other Vegetable) on page 288 for cutlets or flat slices cooked this way.

TO DEEP-FRY The oil should maintain a temperature between 350°F and 375°F, depending on the recipe (see "Deep-Frying," page 22). Be careful to allow enough room to add the vegetables without the oil overflowing. Work in small batches so the vegetables can properly crisp. The recipe that follows is a solid start; this method is actually pretty fast and easy.

Battered and Fried Vegetables

MAKES: 4 servings | TIME: 30 minutes

There are lots of ways to batter and deep-fry vegetables, but this is the most basic. You can use zucchini, eggplant, winter squash, sweet potatoes, mushrooms, bell peppers, green beans, broccoli, cauliflower, asparagus tips, onion rings, fennel, beets, or carrots. Hard vegetables like potatoes should be sliced no more than ¼ inch thick. Tender ones like zucchini and eggplant can be cut up to ½ inch thick. Small or thin vegetables like mushrooms or green beans should be left whole. These are great served with a dipping sauce. Or finish with kosher or sea salt and lemon wedges for last-minute squeezing.

9 Broiled Vegetable Gratins

Make impromptu gratins by using the following combos in the preceding recipe or variation—or mix and match

NAME	VEGETABLES	TOP WITH, THEN BROIL	GARNISH WITH
Asparagus or Green Bean and Gruyère Gratin	Steamed asparagus spears or whole green beans	The Béchamel and Gruyère as described in the variation. Instead of the bread crumbs, use ½ cup chopped hazelnuts or pecans.	A sprinkle of paprika
Winter Squash Gratin	Roasted winter squash, sliced or cut into wedges or chunks	The Béchamel and Gruyère as described in the variation. Instead of the bread crumbs, use ½ cup chopped nuts like walnuts or almonds.	1 teaspoon minced fresh sage
Spinach or Other Greens Gratin	Steamed spinach or other greens; whole leaves or ribbons	The Béchamel and bread crumbs as described in the variation, only use Parmesan instead of the Gruyère.	Lots of pepper and a sprinkle of nutmeg
Tomato Gratin	Fresh raw tomatoes, sliced crosswise	Follow the main recipe; instead of the Parmesan you can try any grated melting cheese like cheddar or asadero. Crumbled tortilla chips are a good switch from the crumbs.	Chopped fresh basil, dill, chives, or cilantro.
Sweet Potato Gratin	Roasted sweet potatoes, sliced or cut into wedges, or cooked and mashed (see page 344)	Instead of the Parmesan in the main recipe, dot on 1 cup softened cream cheese and sprinkle with ¼ cup turbinado sugar along with the bread crumbs	¼ cup chopped toasted hazelnuts or pecans
Baked Chard in Béchamel	Stalks from chard, cooked as in Boiled or Steamed Vegetables (page 238), drained and sliced	The Béchamel, Gruyère, and bread crumbs as described in the variation.	Pinch of nutmeg
Summer Squash and Salsa Gratin	Zucchini or yellow squash, halved or quartered lengthwise and grilled, roasted, or steamed	Drizzle the vegetables generously with olive oil and omit the bread crumbs. Instead of the Béchamel and Gruyère in the variation use 2 cups Salsa Roja or Salsa Verde (pages 71 and 73).	Crumbled queso fresco, chopped roasted pumpkin seeds, and chopped fresh cilantro
Scalloped Potatoes	Boiled or baked starchy or all-purpose potatoes, peeled if you like, thinly sliced crosswise	Instead of the Béchamel and cheese in the variation, use enough hot half-and-half to come most of the way up the potatoes; top with the bread crumbs.	Chopped fresh chives
Braised Leeks au Gratin	1 recipe Leeks Braised in Oil or Butter (page 302; omit the lemon juice)	The Béchamel as described in the variation; whisk in 1 tablespoon Dijon mustard at the end of cooking. And use Emmental cheese instead of the Gruyère.	A light sprinkle of chopped fresh tarragon

2 cups all-purpose flour
1 teaspoon baking powder
   Salt and pepper
1 egg
¾ cup beer or sparkling water
   Good-quality vegetable oil for frying
1½ to 2 pounds vegetables, prepared as described
   above

1. Mix 1 cup of the flour with the baking powder. Sprinkle with salt and pepper. Whisk in the egg and beer until just combined and the consistency of pancake batter. It's okay to have some lumps in the batter; you don't want to overmix. Put the remaining 1 cup flour in a shallow bowl or plate. Prepare all the vegetables as necessary and have them near the flour and batter. Line a baking sheet with towels or fit it with a wire rack.

2. Put at least 2 inches oil in a large pot over medium-high heat; bring to 350°F (see "Deep-Frying," page 22). Keep an eye on the temperature of the oil.

3. When the oil is ready, dredge one piece of food at a time lightly in the flour, dip into the batter to coat, and add to the oil. Don't crowd the vegetables; be prepared to work in batches. Cook, turning once if needed, until golden all over, 3 to 7 minutes. As the pieces finish

transfer them to the prepared pan to drain. Sprinkle with more salt and additional pepper if you like, and serve right away.

---

14 DIPPING SAUCES FOR BATTERED AND FRIED VEGETABLES

There are dozens of sauces that go well with this batter; here's where you'll find the standouts.

1. Traditional Pesto (page 51)
2. Parsley (or Other Herb) Purée (page 52)
3. Avocado-Tomatillo Salsa (page 56)
4. Simplest Yogurt Sauce (page 59)
5. Cilantro-Mint Chutney (page 62)
6. Soy Dipping Sauce and Marinade (page 64)
7. Miso Carrot Sauce with Ginger (page 67)
8. Aioli or almost any flavored mayonnaise (page 70)
9. Real Ranch Dressing (page 71)
10. Salsa Roja (page 71)
11. Salsa Verde (page 73)
12. Teriyaki Sauce (page 76)
13. Dashi Dipping Sauce (page 76)
14. Fast Tomato Sauce (without the pasta, page 478)

How to Add Meat, Fish, or Poultry to Almost Any Vegetable Dish

The easiest way to turn a vegetable side into a one-pot meal is to simply add pieces of cooked meat, fish, or poultry. You can break the protein into chunks, chop it, or shred it to enhance the overall texture. Obviously this is an excellent use for leftovers. Stir-fries and braises are easily adapted to this approach. Add the protein as the vegetables finish cooking; give them just long enough to heat through. Or cook the protein first, then remove it from the pan before proceeding.

Steaming is best for fast cooking proteins like fish, shellfish, and boneless chicken breasts. Put the pieces right on top of the vegetables in the steamer basket.

(Boiling meats and vegetables is desirable only when you plan on eating the cooking liquid too.)

Figure no more than 1 pound animal protein to convert the recipes in this chapter to a vegetable-forward main course. And you'll need to add a little fat: About 1 table-spoon oil for each pound of lean protein is enough for sautés, stir-fries, braising and glazing, and roasting. You might not even need that with fatty meat like sausage.

You'll probably need more water or stock when you add meat or poultry to braised or boiled dishes; with seafood you might not. So wait until the dish is almost done before adjusting the soupiness.

The Vegetable Lexicon

I've always been into vegetables, and now more than ever they form the foundation of my diet. So here is the information you need to cook most common vegetables many different ways; many are followed by recipes. Or you can put the general recipes at the beginning of this chapter to work on the vegetables you like best. And remember to check the index to access everything offered elsewhere.

That said, let's start at the beginning, and go A to Z.

ARTICHOKES AND CARDOONS

I just love 'em, even if they're a bit expensive and labor intensive. Artichokes are always worth it, especially the precious babies, which you can trim and eat whole, leaves and all, either raw and thinly sliced for salad, or quartered and sautéed in lots of olive oil. Cardoons, the celery-like, thistle family cousins to artichokes, have more open heads and can be cooked the same way.

PREPARING Whole artichokes: see the directions and illustrations below. Or quarter them as shown on page 259.

Artichoke hearts: You want the most tender interior, fully edible leaves, and the saucer-shaped firm bottom. Cut off the tops of the leaves then halve the artichoke lengthwise. Use a paring knife to peel the base; scrape out the choke with a spoon. Then cut away all the outside leaves. Leave in halves or quarter or cut into wedges.

Small or baby artichokes, if tender enough, can be eaten whole, but sometimes they benefit from removing the exterior leaves and trimming the tops of the rest. Otherwise, halve, quarter, or slice lengthwise. Remove the choke if necessary.

Canned and jarred artichoke hearts are already cooked. I'm not a fan, but you can add them to pastas or stir-fries—whole, chopped, or sliced—during the last few minutes of cooking. Always rinse them first to remove the brine or marinade, then squeeze and pat them dry.

Preparing Whole Artichokes

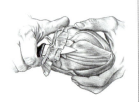

STEP 1 Peel off tough outer leaves.

STEP 2 Trim around the bottom of the artichoke.

STEP 3 If you want to cook only the heart, cut off the top half of the leaves, then trim off the remaining leaves until you're left with only the very pale ones.

STEP 4 Scoop out the choke if necessary. Put artichokes in acidulated water to keep them from browning. If you want to leave the artichoke whole but remove the choke, trim the leaves less, force them open, then scrape out the choke.

F fast   M make ahead   V vegetarian

Thaw and dry frozen artichoke hearts and use as you would fresh, but cut the cooking time roughly in half; they're already partially cooked.

Cardoons: Carefully strip off the spiny leaves and discard them. Use a knife to remove the tough fibers that run down the vegetable lengthwise (like celery), then chop into 2-inch pieces.

Raw artichokes and cardoons discolor very quickly when cut and darken quite a bit when cooked; rub with half a lemon or dip in water with a couple of tablespoons lemon juice or vinegar ("acidulated water") immediately after cutting to minimize darkening.

BEST COOKING METHODS steaming (whole, hearts, or cardoons), sautéing (baby artichokes and hearts), braising (baby artichokes and hearts, cardoons)

WHEN ARE THEY DONE? Whole artichokes are done when the outer leaves pull off easily and the meat in them is tender. Artichoke hearts are done when very tender; pierce with a skewer or thin-bladed knife to check, then taste to be sure. Cardoons should be tender enough to pierce easily with a skewer or thin-bladed knife.

OTHER VEGETABLES YOU CAN USE artichokes and cardoons are interchangeable in terms of flavor. There is no substitute for artichoke hearts, but you have lots of options for how to buy them.

Steamed Artichokes

MAKES: 4 servings | **TIME:** 45 minutes

The simplest and best way to cook artichokes is to steam them, since they don't become soggy. You can add some gentle seasonings to the pot if you like; tarragon or thyme, onion or garlic, lemon juice or vinegar are all good. Serve artichokes hot, at room temperature, or cold, with something for dipping.

> 4 large or 12 small artichokes
>   Melted butter, Vinaigrette (page 188),
>   mayonnaise (to make your own, see page 69), or
>   lemon wedges, olive oil, and salt for serving

1. Follow the illustrations on the previous page for preparing whole artichokes.

2. Rig a steamer (see page 20) and add the artichokes bottom up. Cover and cook until an outer leaf pulls away easily and its meat is tender, 20 to 40 minutes.

Quartering Artichokes

STEP 1 Use scissors or a sharp knife to cut the pointed tips from the top and outer leaves of the artichoke.

STEP 2 Cut the artichoke in half.

STEP 3 Cut it into quarters.

STEP 4 Scrape the fuzzy choke out of each quarter.

3. Drain them upside down for a minute or 2 longer before serving hot; store upside down if you plan to serve them later. Melted butter is best with hot artichokes; or serve at any temperature with vinaigrette, mayonnaise, or lemon juice and olive oil, and of course, salt.

Braised Artichoke Hearts

MAKES: 4 servings | **TIME:** 45 minutes

An artichoke dish that's just as good at room temperature as it is hot. If you double it, you'll have leftovers to slice and toss with pasta or rice, top pizzas, or mix into frittatas.

Other vegetables you can use: true baby artichokes (just trimmed) or small artichokes (trimmed and with the choke removed); chopped or sliced cardoons. Also excellent for winter squash: peel if you like, cut into 1- to 2-inch pieces, and start at Step 2.

    ½   cup fresh lemon juice (from 3 to 4 lemons)
        Salt and pepper
    6   large artichokes or about 3 cups frozen
        artichoke hearts (no need to thaw them
        first)
    3   tablespoons olive oil
    1   tablespoon minced garlic
        Chopped fresh parsley for garnish

1. If you're using whole artichokes, put the lemon juice in a bowl with ½ cup water and sprinkle with salt and pepper. Trim the artichokes down to the hearts as in the illustrations on page 258. As you finish each artichoke, cut the heart into thick slices; toss them with the lemon water.
2. Put the oil in a large skillet over medium heat. Add the garlic and cook, stirring frequently, until it softens, about a minute. Use a slotted spoon or tongs to transfer the artichokes to the pan; save the lemon water. If you're using frozen hearts, slice and add them. Mix the lemon

juice with ½ cup water, sprinkle with salt and pepper, and set aside.
3. Cook, stirring occasionally, until the artichokes begin to soften, about 5 minutes. Add the reserved lemon water, bring to a boil, and cover. Turn the heat down so it bubbles gently. Cook until tender, shaking the pan every now and then to toss the artichokes, about 10 minutes for fresh, 5 minutes for frozen.
4. Taste and adjust the seasoning. Serve hot or at room temperature; garnish with parsley just before serving.

ROASTED ARTICHOKE HEARTS Heat the oven to 425°F. In Step 2, increase the oil to ¼ cup, put it in a large ovenproof skillet or roasting pan, and set it in the oven. When the oil is hot, put the artichoke slices and garlic in the pan and toss to coat in the oil. (Save the lemon water.) Roast until the slices release from the pan, about 10 minutes, then turn them and continue roasting until tender, another 10 minutes. Transfer the artichokes from the pan to a serving platter and set the pan over medium-high heat. Add the lemon water and scrape up any brown bits from the bottom of the pan. Cook until the mixture thickens, about 3 minutes. Stir in the parsley, taste, and adjust the seasoning. Pour the sauce over the artichokes. Serve hot or at room temperature.

BRAISED ARTICHOKE HEARTS WITH POTATOES The potatoes will soak up most of the liquid, leaving you with a thick vegetable stew: Steam or boil 2 large waxy potatoes, then peel them and cut into large chunks; or use leftover potatoes. Increase the olive oil to ¼ cup and the garlic to 2 tablespoons. In Step 3, when you check the artichokes after the final cooking time, fold in the potatoes. Cover the pan again and cook just long enough for the potatoes to reheat.

BRAISED ARTICHOKE HEARTS WITH HAM, WINE, AND LEMON Substitute ½ cup white wine for the water. In Step 2, reduce the oil to 2 tablespoons and add 2 ounces chopped smoked ham, pancetta, or prosciutto. Cook the ham until the fat is rendered and the bits are beginning to crisp, then proceed with the recipe.

13 TERRIFIC STIR-INS FOR BRAISED ARTICHOKE HEARTS

Unless noted, add the following ingredients in Step 3 once the artichokes are fully tender.

1. Pitted green or black olives
2. Chopped dried fruit, especially golden raisins, currants, cherries, or apricots
3. Chopped nuts, especially walnuts, almonds, or hazelnuts
4. Herbs, especially chives, basil, tarragon, mint, or chervil
5. Arugula or spinach leaves
6. Oven-Dried or Oven-Roasted Plum Tomatoes (page 348 or 347) in slices or bits
7. Chopped fresh tomato, when you add the artichokes in Step 2
8. Crumbled cooked bacon or sausage
9. Virtually any Crouton (page 801)
10. Grated or crumbled cheese, especially Parmesan, feta, blue, or Fresh Cheese, the Easy Way (page 755)
11. Anchovies
12. Roasted Garlic (page 294)
13. Sherry vinegar, instead of the lemon juice

ASPARAGUS

The first signal that winter is over and green vegetables are on the way. They're available year-round from warmer climates, but true local or regional asparagus are worth the wait.

PREPARING Snap off the bottom of each spear; it will naturally break in the right place. I recommend peeling asparagus (use a vegetable peeler) to remove the fibrous skin from just below the tip to the base; this step isn't necessary if the spears are pencil thin.

BEST COOKING METHODS steaming, sautéing, roasting, grilling

WHEN ARE THEY DONE? When you can easily insert a skewer or thin-bladed knife into the thickest part of the stalk. Undercooked asparagus is crisp; overcooked asparagus is mushy.

OTHER VEGETABLES YOU CAN USE green or wax beans, sugar snap peas, broccoli raab

Steamed Asparagus Spears

MAKES: 4 servings | **TIME:** 15 minutes

Anything you can do with green beans or broccoli you can do with asparagus. (I love asparagus grilled; see page 252.) Otherwise, here are the most basic techniques. To partially cook asparagus ahead of time, use one of the methods here and cook until a smidge less tender than desired, then shock (see page 238), drain well, cover, and refrigerate for up to 2 days. Finish by heating the asparagus through with a little butter or olive oil, or try one of the ideas that follow.

1½ to 2 pounds asparagus, trimmed and peeled
Salt

Preparing Asparagus

Snap off the bottom of each stalk; they will usually separate naturally right where the woody part ends.

All but the thinnest asparagus are best when peeled.

 fast make ahead V vegetarian

1. Stand the asparagus in a tall pot with an inch of salted water on the bottom (it's nice, but hardly essential, to tie them in a bundle first).

2. Cover and bring the water to a boil. Cook just until the thick part of the stalks can be pierced with a knife. Start checking thin spears after a minute, thicker ones after 2 minutes. Remove from the water with tongs and serve.

BOILED ASPARAGUS Lay the asparagus spears in a skillet that can hold them without crowding, cover with salted water, cover the skillet, and turn the heat to high. When the water comes to a boil, cook and check for doneness as described in the main recipe. Immediately lift them from the water with tongs.

MICROWAVED ASPARAGUS Lay them in a microwave-safe plate or shallow bowl with about 2 tablespoons salted water. Cover with a microwave-safe lid and vent a corner. Microwave on high for 2 minutes, shake the container, and continue to microwave at 1-minute intervals just until the thick part of the stalks can be pierced with a knife.

---

10 WAYS TO SERVE STEAMED, BOILED, OR MICROWAVED ASPARAGUS

After cooking the asparagus, drain if necessary and serve in any of these ways, alone or in combination.

1. Drizzle with olive oil or melted butter; Brown Butter, page 78, is super. Any Compound Butter (page 78) or Flavored Oil (page 53) is also good.

2. Squeeze lemon or lime juice over it, or drizzle with vinegar.

3. Douse with any Vinaigrette (page 188).

4. Serve with a dollop of mayonnaise (to make your own, see page 69) or Hollandaise Sauce (page 81) alongside.

5. Top with chopped or finely crumbled Hard-Boiled Eggs (page 721).

6. Serve with a hefty topping of Sautéed Mushrooms (page 306).

7. Garnish with chopped Hard-Boiled Egg (page 721), toasted bread crumbs (see page 801), or chopped Roasted Red Peppers (page 318).

8. Wrap room-temperature or cold cooked spears in thin, narrow slices of prosciutto or other good ham.

9. Melt butter or warm olive oil in a small saucepan. Off the heat, stir in a big pinch minced fresh herbs like tarragon, chives, mint, or chervil. Drizzle over the asparagus.

10. While the spears are still hot, sprinkle with grated Parmesan cheese.

AVOCADOS

A fruit that has many uses beyond Guacamole (page 105) or smearing on toast, though it's almost never cooked, with the exception of grilling.

PREPARING Buy them still hard if you can and have patience; they're less likely to be bruised and over-ripe. They're ready to eat when they're uniformly slightly soft. Halve avocados lengthwise around the pit; twist apart the two halves; gently strike the pit with a knife and lift it out. Peel off the skin or scoop out the flesh with a spoon. If you want to store half, leave the pit intact, wrap tightly in plastic, and refrigerate.

Avocados discolor quickly when cut; sprinkle with lemon or lime juice immediately after cutting to minimize darkening.

BEST COOKING METHOD Best when sliced, mashed, or puréed and eaten raw; but can be peeled, then halved or quartered and lightly grilled.

WHEN ARE THEY DONE? Grilled, when lightly browned; but avocado needs no cooking

BEAN SPROUTS

Just about every bean, seed, or grain can be sprouted, but we most commonly see mung and soybean sprouts.

PREPARING Don't bother trimming them unless you see some funky bean kernels you want to pluck; just rinse and drain well.

BEST COOKING METHOD stir-frying (add at the last minute); some people like them raw in sandwiches or salads but I only do if they're marinated to soften a bit

WHEN ARE THEY DONE? When just heated through and still crunchy

OTHER VEGETABLES YOU CAN USE if it's bland crunch you're after, bamboo shoots or water chestnuts

BEETS AND BEET GREENS

Despite a reputation for muddiness, beets are actually one of the sweetest root vegetables you can find, especially some of the heirloom varieties. They also happen to have some of the best leafy greens on top.

PREPARING Scrub well; leave on an inch or so of the greens to minimize bleeding. If you're roasting or boiling the beets, peel them after cooking. Rinse the greens well and chop the stems.

BEST COOKING METHODS baking in foil, roasting, braising and glazing (beets); steaming, sautéing (greens and stems)

WHEN ARE THEY DONE? Beets: when tender all the way through; pierce with a skewer or thin-bladed knife to check. Slight overcooking is preferable to undercooking. Beet greens: when wilted, stems when tender.

OTHER VEGETABLES YOU CAN USE turnips (which also have great greens), rutabagas, carrots, parsnips

Beets Baked in Foil

MAKES: 4 servings | **TIME:** About 1 hour

This is the single best method for cooking beets, either to eat as is or use in another recipe. Since large beets

---

Preparing Avocados

STEP 1 Cut through the skin and flesh lengthwise to the pit, then rotate the avocado to cut all the way around it. Twist the halves apart.

STEP 2 A careful, swift, and not-too-forceful strike of the knife will implant it in the pit, which will then lift out easily.

STEP 3 Scoop out the flesh with a spoon.

F fast   **M** make ahead   **V** vegetarian

take longer to cook than small ones, try to buy beets that are roughly equal in size. And you don't have to roast them individually wrapped. If you're planning to use them all at once, right away, just put in a roasting pan or heavy skillet, cover, and proceed as directed.

Other vegetables you can use: turnips, rutabagas, other root vegetables.

4   large or 8 medium beets (1½ to 2 pounds)

1. Heat the oven to 400°F. Scrub the beets well and trim off any leaves. Wrap them individually in foil and put them on a cookie sheet or roasting pan.

2. Bake, undisturbed, until a skewer or thin-bladed knife can pierces one with little resistance (they may cook at different rates; remove each one when it is done), 45 to 90 minutes. Use in Parboiled or Steamed Vegetables in Butter or Oil (page 242) or any of the variations on Beets Done Simply or other recipes that call for cooked beets. Or store, refrigerated, for a couple of days before using.

Beet Rösti with Rosemary

MAKES: 4 servings | **TIME:** 20 minutes

One of my all-time favorite dishes is a caramelized savory cake, cut into wedges and served as a side. Thanks to chef Michael Romano, who shared this recipe with me 30 years ago. If you like, dust with any spice mixture (to make your own, see pages 27 to 35) just before serving.

Other vegetables you can use: carrots, parsnips, rutabagas, kohlrabi, sweet potatoes, turnips.

1½	**pounds beets**
1	**teaspoon chopped fresh rosemary**
1	**teaspoon salt**
¼	**cup all-purpose flour**
3	**tablespoons butter**

1. Trim the beets and peel them as you would potatoes. Grate them in a food processor or by hand. Put a medium-to-large nonstick skillet over medium heat.

2. Toss the grated beets in a bowl with the rosemary and salt, then add about half the flour; toss well, add the rest of the flour, then toss again.

3. Put 2 tablespoons of the butter in the skillet and cook until it foams. Scrape the beet mixture into the pan and press it down with a spatula to reach the edges. Adjust the heat so that the pancake sizzles without burning and cook until the bottom of the beet cake is crisped and releases, 6 to 8 minutes. Slide the cake out onto a plate, add the remaining tablespoon butter to the pan, and set it back over the heat.

4. Top the pancake with another plate, invert the two plates, and slide the cake back into the pan. (See page 332 for an illustration.) Continue to cook, adjusting the heat if necessary, until the second side is browned, another 6 to 8 minutes. Cut into wedges, sprinkle with more salt if you like, and serve.

BEET RÖSTI WITH PARMESAN Omit the rosemary if you prefer and add 1 cup grated Parmesan in Step 2.

CARROT AND ONION RÖSTI Substitute carrots for the beets. Grate 1 large onion and squeeze out the excess liquid. Proceed from Step 2.

BOK CHOY AND OTHER ASIAN GREENS
SHANGHAI BOK CHOY, BABY BOK CHOY, GAI LAN, TATSOI

The Cantonese word *choy* can be translated loosely as "cooking greens," and there's a slew of choy to choose from, especially at Asian markets. To keep things simple, only the most common are included here. Since you cook them all virtually the same way, what I like to do is grab a bunch of what looks best, even if it's not labeled, and take it home for dinner.

PREPARING Rinse and remove any damaged or yellowing leaves.

Beet Rösti with Rosemary,
page 265

Bok choy: cut off the root end and the inch or so above it; slice or chop as you like. If the stems are thick, separate them from the leaves and start cooking them for a couple of minutes before the leaves. Shanghai or baby bok choy can remain whole.

Gai lan: trim any dried-out or tough stems and separate the leaves from the stems, since the stems take longer to cook.

Tatsoi: cut the stems from the root end if they are still attached.

BEST COOKING METHODS steaming, sautéing, stir-frying

WHEN ARE THEY DONE? When the stems are tender but still crisp (especially gai lan) and the leaves are wilted

OTHER VEGETABLES YOU CAN USE These are interchangeable; cabbage, kale, or broccoli can replace any of them

Seared Baby Bok Choy with Bacon Vinaigrette

MAKES: 4 servings | **TIME:** 25 minutes

An unusual side dish that's lovely with a nice piece of salmon or other full-flavored fatty fish.

Other vegetables you can use: bok choy or other Asian greens; napa cabbage, cut lengthwise into long spears; endive, halved lengthwise; radicchio, quartered.

1½ to 2 **pounds Shanghai or baby bok choy, bottoms trimmed**
       Good-quality vegetable oil for cooking
       Salt and pepper
  4 **slices bacon, chopped**
  3 **tablespoons sherry vinegar or white wine vinegar**

1. Halve the bok choy lengthwise, rinse and put the cut side down on towels to drain.

2. Put a large skillet over medium-high heat. When it is hot, add 1 tablespoon oil and put some of the bok choy into the pan, cut side down (it will spatter, so be careful). Don't overcrowd the pan; there should be an inch of space between the pieces. Sprinkle with salt and pepper and cook, undisturbed, until the bottom is dark brown and slightly charred and the bok choy is crisp-tender, 3 to 5 minutes. Transfer the pieces, cut side up, to a serving plate and repeat with the remaining bok choy, adding more oil between batches.

3. When all the bok choy are done, return the skillet to medium-high heat and add the bacon. Cook, stirring occasionally and lowering the heat as necessary, until the bits are crisp and the fat is rendered, about 10 minutes.

4. Turn off the heat, remove the bacon with a slotted spoon, and add the vinegar and 1 tablespoon water to the fat in the skillet. Sprinkle with salt and a good amount of pepper. Bring the dressing to a boil so it thickens, just a minute or so, then turn off the heat and stir in the bacon. Taste and adjust the seasoning. Pour the hot dressing over the bok choy. Let sit for up to 5 minutes before serving.

SEARED BABY BOK CHOY WITH CHILE VINAIGRETTE
Substitute 1 or 2 tablespoons chopped fresh chiles like jalapeño or Thai for the bacon and rice vinegar for the sherry vinegar. Instead of Step 3, heat 3 tablespoons oil in the skillet and cook the chiles with 2 tablespoons each chopped ginger and garlic, stirring, for a couple minutes. Then add vinegar and proceed.

SEARED BABY BOK CHOY WITH BLACK VINEGAR
Sweet and smoky, Chinese black vinegar is available at most Asian markets: Follow the directions for the variation above but omit the chiles and use black vinegar instead of rice vinegar. Add a couple of teaspoons soy sauce just before dressing the bok choy.

Restaurant-Style Greens

MAKES: 4 servings | **TIME:** 15 minutes

The common bright-green stir-fry of Chinese restaurants, usually made with gai lan. It doesn't get much simpler.

Other vegetables you can use: broccoli raab, any other Asian green, collard greens, kale, broccoli.

1½	**pounds gai lan**
2	**tablespoons good-quality vegetable oil**
1	**tablespoon minced garlic (optional)**
¼	**cup oyster sauce**
	Salt and pepper

1. Separate the leaves and stems of the gai lan; cut the stems into 2-inch lengths.

2. Heat a large skillet over high heat for 3 or 4 minutes. Add the oil, wait a few seconds, then add the leaves and toss until they wilt, about 3 minutes. Transfer to a serving plate.

3. Add the stems, the garlic if you're using it, and about ⅓ cup water. Cook, tossing, until the stems are crisp-tender, adding a little more water to keep the pan from going dry, 3 to 5 minutes. Remove them with a slotted spoon and scatter them on top of the leaves. Add the oyster sauce to the liquid in the pan to heat, adding enough extra water so that the sauce coats the back of a spoon; taste and add some salt and pepper. Pour the sauce over the greens and serve.

RESTAURANT-STYLE GREENS WITH THICKENED SOY SAUCE Instead of the oyster sauce, make a slurry by whisking 2 teaspoons cornstarch into ¼ cup soy sauce.

BROCCOLI, BROCCOLINI, AND BROCCOLI RAAB

One of America's favorite vegetables (former president Bush notwithstanding) has two cousins that have been steadily gaining popularity too. Broccolini, a hybrid of broccoli and gai lan (see "Bok Choy and Other Asian Greens," page 265), is like a more delicate broccoli. Broccoli raab has slimmer, longer stalks, with more leaves than flowers, and a fairly bitter overall flavor.

PREPARING Broccoli: strip the stalk of leaves, if any (these are perfectly edible; cook along with the florets if you like). Cut off the dried-out end of the stalk and use a vegetable peeler or paring knife to peel the tough outer skin as best you can without going crazy. To peel with a paring knife, hold the broccoli upside down; grasp a bit of the skin right at the bottom between the paring knife and your thumb, and pull down to remove a strip of skin. Cut the stalk into equal-length pieces and break the head into florets.

Broccolini and broccoli raab: trim the dry ends of the stems. Pull off any yellowing or wilted leaves off the broccoli raab.

BEST COOKING METHODS steaming, microwaving, boiling, braising, braising and glazing, sautéing, stir-frying (broccoli); some people eat broccoli raw but I like it at least lightly cooked to take the edge off. Sautéing, stir-frying until tender, braising until quite soft (broccolini, broccoli raab). Parboil and shock all (see pages 237 and 238) to preserve the green color or for quicker cooking later.

WHEN ARE THEY DONE? The tenderness of broccoli (and its ilk) is a matter of taste. When bright green, it's still crisp and quite chewy; some people like it that way. Cook it another couple of minutes and it becomes tender; overcook it and it becomes mushy and begins to fall apart, which can also be excellent. Cook until a skewer or thin-bladed knife easily pierces the stalk. Regardless of method, it often makes sense to cook the stalks longer than the florets; just start them a minute or two earlier.

Broccoli raab is done when you can insert a skewer or thin-bladed knife into the thickest part of the stalk. Undercooked broccoli raab is too crisp; overcooked broccoli raab is mushy.

 fast make ahead vegetarian

OTHER VEGETABLES YOU CAN USE broccoli and cauliflower are almost always interchangeable, or use broccoflower, Romanesco, or broccoli raab. For broccoli raab and broccolini: broccoli, asparagus, gai lan, turnip or mustard greens

Crunchy Broccoli or Cauliflower

MAKES: 4 servings | **TIME:** 30 minutes

There are many ways to sauté vegetables with bread crumbs for added crispness, and they're all good. Since you'll still get the crunch wherever the bread crumbs land, it doesn't matter if they stick to the vegetables. But for the prettiest presentation, use the egg.

Other vegetables you can use: green beans, Brussels sprouts, broccolini, or broccoli raab.

> 1   **pound broccoli or cauliflower (about 1 head), trimmed, broken into florets of any size, parboiled and shocked (see pages 237 and 238), and patted dry**
>   **All-purpose flour for dredging (optional)**
> 2 or 3   **eggs, lightly beaten (optional)**
> 1   **cup bread crumbs (preferably fresh; see page 801) for dredging**
> 4   **tablespoons butter (½ stick) or olive oil**
>   **Salt and pepper**
>   **Chopped fresh parsley for garnish**
>   **Lemon wedges for serving (optional)**

1. If you're using the egg, roll each piece of broccoli or cauliflower in the flour, then dip in the egg, then in the bread crumbs. If you're not using the egg, just roll the pieces in the bread crumbs, patting to help them adhere.
2. Put the butter or oil in a large skillet over medium heat. When the butter foams or the oil is hot, add the broccoli or cauliflower, taking care not to crowd the pan; you might have to work in batches.

3. Sprinkle with salt and pepper. Cook, turning or tossing occasionally and adjusting the heat so the bread crumbs don't burn, until browned and tender, about 10 minutes. Taste and adjust the seasoning. Serve, garnished with parsley, and lemon wedges if you like.

CRUNCHY BROCCOLI OR CAULIFLOWER WITH ONION AND OLIVES Use olive oil; before cooking the broccoli or cauliflower, add 1 cup chopped onion (red is nice) to the pan; cook, stirring occasionally, until the onion softens, 3 to 5 minutes. Proceed as directed, then during the last two minutes of cooking add ½ to 1 cup pitted black olives (oil-cured are extra good here) and red chile flakes to taste.

CRUNCHY BROCCOLI OR CAULIFLOWER WITH GARLIC, VINEGAR, AND CAPERS Use olive oil; add 1 tablespoon chopped garlic along with the broccoli or cauliflower. Just as it's done, add 1 tablespoon red wine, sherry, or other vinegar and about a tablespoon of drained capers.

CRUNCHY BROCCOLI OR CAULIFLOWER WITH ALMONDS, RAISINS, AND SAFFRON In Step 3, when the broccoli or cauliflower is just beginning to turn golden, stir in a pinch saffron, ¼ cup chopped almonds, and ¼ cup golden raisins. Proceed with the recipe, cooking and stirring until everything is browned.

Broccoli Raab with Sausage and Grapes

MAKES: 4 servings | **TIME:** About 30 minutes

With the meat, this becomes a main course, a simple Italian classic and one of my favorites. Without the grapes and thinned with a little water or stock, it makes an amazing pasta sauce.

Other vegetables you can use: broccoli, broccolini, gai lan, turnip or mustard greens, asparagus, kale, collards. Substitute chopped apple for the grapes if you like.

Crunchy Cauliflower with Almonds, Raisins, and Saffron (left) and Crunchy Broccoli with Onion and Olives (right), page 269

1½ pounds broccoli raab, trimmed and cut up
1 pound sweet Italian sausages
2 or 3 cloves garlic, sliced
1½ cups seedless grapes (about 8 ounces)
Salt and pepper

1. Bring a large pot of water to boil and salt it. Prepare an ice bath for shocking (see page 238). Add the broccoli raab to the boiling water and cook, stirring once or twice, until it is bright green and beginning to get tender, about 3 minutes. Drain. Shock in the ice bath and drain again. At this point, you can refrigerate the broccoli raab, wrapped well or in a covered container, for up to 2 days.

2. Cook the sausages over medium heat in a large skillet, pricking them with a fork a few times and turning from time to time, until browned in places, 10 to 15 minutes.

3. Remove the sausages from the skillet (don't worry if it's not done) and cut into bite-sized pieces. Return to the skillet over medium heat; cook, turning occasionally, until all sides of the sausage are nicely browned, about 5 minutes more.

4. Squeeze the excess liquid from the broccoli raab; chop it coarsely. Add it to the skillet along with the garlic and cook, stirring occasionally, until it's fully tender and browned in places, 3 to 4 minutes. Add the grapes, sprinkle with salt pepper, and cook until the grapes are heated through. Taste and adjust the seasoning. Serve immediately.

BROCCOLI RAAB WITH GARLIC AND PECORINO
Omit the sausage, increase the garlic to 4 or 5 cloves, and substitute 1 cup grated pecorino cheese for the grapes. Skip Steps 2 and 3. Put 3 tablespoons olive oil in a large skillet over medium heat. When it is hot, add the garlic and cook for a minute before adding the broccoli raab. Toss with the pecorino just before serving.

BROCCOLI RAAB WITH ANCHOVIES Omit the sausage
and substitute 8 anchovies (rinsed if salt packed) for the grapes. Skip Steps 2 and 3. Put 3 tablespoons olive oil in a large skillet over medium heat. When it is hot, add the garlic and anchovies, and a pinch of red chile flakes if you like, and cook for about 2 minutes before adding the broccoli raab.

BRUSSELS SPROUTS
Believed to have been developed in Belgium (hence the name), these miniature cabbages are super when cooked properly.

PREPARING Trim the hard edge of the stem and remove any loose leaves. Cut, slice, or leave whole. Thinly slice raw Brussels sprouts for salad (a food processor makes this easy).

BEST COOKING METHODS roasting, sautéing, braising, grilling

WHEN ARE THEY DONE? When just tender enough to pierce easily with a skewer or thin-bladed knife; they tend to get bitter if overcooked.

OTHER VEGETABLES YOU CAN USE any cabbage, cut into 1- to 2-inch chunks

Sautéed Brussels Sprouts with Bacon

MAKES: 4 servings | **TIME:** 30 minutes

Perhaps the most delicious way to cook Brussels sprouts; their affinity for bacon is legendary.

Other vegetables you can use: shredded cabbage, green or wax beans; chicory or its relatives (see page 292).

6 ounces bacon, chopped
1 pound Brussels sprouts
Salt and pepper

1 tablespoon balsamic vinegar or fresh
lemon juice
1 tablespoon chopped fresh thyme (optional)

1. Put the bacon in a large skillet over medium-high heat. When the pan is hot, adjust the heat so it sizzles without burning; cook until crisp and the fat is rendered, 5 to 10 minutes.

2. Meanwhile, trim the hard edge of the stem from the Brussels sprouts, then cut each one into thin slices or shreds; you can do this on a mandoline, with the blade side of a box grater, the slicing attachment on a food processor, or with a knife. Or cut them into quarters.

3. Add the Brussels sprouts and ¼ cup water to the pan with the bacon; sprinkle with salt and pepper, turn the heat to medium, and cover. Cook, undisturbed, until nearly tender, about 5 minutes.

4. Uncover and raise the heat to medium-high. Cook, stirring occasionally, until any remaining water evaporates and the sprouts are fully tender, another 5 to 10 minutes. Stir in the vinegar and the thyme if you're using it. Serve hot.

SAUTÉED BRUSSELS SPROUTS WITH HAZELNUTS

Omit the bacon and skip Step 1. In Step 3, heat 3 tablespoons olive oil and add the sprouts. In Step 4, when the sprouts are tender, sprinkle with ½ cup chopped toasted hazelnuts and ¼ cup chopped fresh mint or dill instead of the thyme, along with the vinegar or lemon juice.

SAUTÉED BRUSSELS SPROUTS WITH CARAMELIZED

ONIONS Substitute 1 large onion, sliced, for the bacon. In Step 1, cook the onion in 2 tablespoons butter or olive oil until browned, then proceed with the recipe.

BURDOCK

The root of a thistle plant—and related to artichokes—burdock is sweet and earthy; in Japan, where it's most popular (and known as gobo), it's often braised with carrots or other vegetables.

PREPARING Scrub the dirt off the root just before using; peeling is optional. Trim and crush with the flat side of a large knife; and/or chop, slice, or shred.

Raw burdock discolors very quickly when cut; rub with half a lemon or dip in water with a couple of tablespoons lemon juice or vinegar ("acidulated water") immediately after cutting.

BEST COOKING METHODS braising, stir-frying, roasting

WHEN IS IT DONE? When either crisp-tender or soft enough to mash; in between is less interesting

OTHER VEGETABLES YOU CAN USE artichoke hearts and cardoons (similar flavor); carrots and celery

Quick-Braised Burdock and Carrots

MAKES: 4 servings | **TIME:** 15 minutes

If you've never tried burdock, this traditional Japanese dish is a nice introduction. Serve with plain white or brown rice, or for a less authentic—though delicious—approach, try tossing the finished dish with warm soba noodles.

Other vegetables you can use: potatoes, kohlrabi, parsnips, turnips, beets, or winter squash.

8 ounces burdock, chopped
Fresh lemon juice
1 tablespoon good-quality vegetable oil
2 teaspoons sesame oil
8 ounces carrot, chopped
2 tablespoons soy sauce
1½ tablespoons mirin, or 2¼ teaspoons honey mixed with 2¼ teaspoons water
1½ tablespoons sake or water
2 teaspoons sugar
2 teaspoons toasted sesame seeds (see page 309)

1. Immerse the burdock in a bowl of water with a squeeze of lemon juice so it doesn't discolor.

2. Put the vegetable and sesame oils in a large skillet over medium-high heat. Drain the burdock, add it to the pan, and cook, stirring, until it begins to soften, about 2 minutes.

3. Add the carrot and continue to cook and stir until the vegetables are just tender, about 2 minutes. Add the soy sauce, mirin, sake, sugar, and sesame seeds and cook until about half the liquid remains, 2 minutes more. Serve hot. Or store, covered, in the refrigerator for up to 2 days.

CABBAGE

GREEN CABBAGE, RED CABBAGE, SAVOY CABBAGE, NAPA CABBAGE (FOR CHINESE CABBAGE, SEE BOK CHOY)

Few vegetables are as versatile, inexpensive, and ubiquitous all over the world. And even though cabbages are technically leafy greens, they grow in tight, firm heads so they keep for weeks. You'll use them year-round, for sure.

PREPARING Trim the bottom to remove the first layer or two of exterior leaves. Then use a thin-bladed knife to remove the core: Cut a cone-shaped section out of the stem end wider than the area of the core and pull it out. To shred the head, cut the cabbage into quarters or eighths, depending on size, and cut crosswise into thin strips, or use a food processor or mandoline. Napa cabbage can be cut crosswise whole to shred it.

BEST COOKING METHODS boiling, sautéing, stir-frying, braising; also raw in salads and slaws, pickling or fermenting (see Shortcut Kimchi, page 229)

WHEN ARE THEY DONE? When crisp-tender to soft, but not mushy

OTHER VEGETABLES YOU CAN USE Brussels sprouts, collards, bok choy (especially for stir-frying)

Buttered Cabbage

MAKES: 4 servings | **TIME:** 20 minutes

Pretty delicious for a two-ingredient boiled vegetable dish. Serve with other relatively plain dishes, like Boiled Potatoes (page 326), Simplest Whole Roast Chicken, Unleashed (page 633), or Chickpeas in Their Own Broth (page 407). Or toss this with more butter or sour cream and piping-hot egg noodles.

Other vegetables you can use: Of course this is a basic vegetable preparation, but to keep it in the same spirit, think collards, kale, bok choy, and the like.

Salt and pepper
1 pound cabbage (about 20 leaves; savoy is best but any kind works)
2 to 4 tablespoons butter

1. Bring a large pot of water to a boil and salt it well. Chop the cabbage if you like. Put the butter in a small saucepan over medium-low heat and melt it; if you let it brown a little bit, so much the better. Sprinkle with salt and pepper.

2. When the water boils, add the cabbage and cook, stirring every now and then, until it's tender, about 5 minutes. Drain in a colander and shake to remove as much water as possible. Transfer to a serving bowl. Pour over the melted butter and toss gently. Taste and adjust the seasoning. Serve hot.

SPIKED BUTTERED CABBAGE When the butter is melting, add 2 tablespoons chopped garlic, ginger, or shallot, or as much minced hot fresh chile as you like. Proceed with the recipe.

MUSTARDY CABBAGE Tangy in a good way: Use 3 tablespoons olive oil instead of the butter. Put it in the saucepan in Step 1 along with 2 tablespoons Dijon or whole grain mustard and 1 teaspoon apple cider vinegar. Proceed with the recipe.

   **F** fast **M** make ahead **V** vegetarian

Sauerkraut with Juniper Berries

MAKES: 4 to 6 servings | **TIME:** 40 minutes

If possible, use homemade sauerkraut or prepared sauerkraut without preservatives; it's sold in bulk in specialty stores or in jars or bags at natural food stores. Substitute caraway seeds for the juniper berries if you can't get your hands on them.

Other vegetables you can use: shredded fresh cabbage.

2	tablespoons butter or good-quality vegetable oil
1	onion, sliced
1½ to 2	pounds sauerkraut, rinsed and drained
1	bay leaf
1	tablespoon juniper berries, crushed lightly with the side of a knife, or caraway seeds
1	cup chicken, beef, or vegetable stock (to make your own, see pages 174–178), or not-too-dry white wine

1. Put the butter or oil in a large skillet over medium heat. When the butter foams or the oil is hot, add the onion and cook, stirring, until it starts to soften, about 3 minutes.

2. Add the sauerkraut, bay leaf, juniper berries, and stock, and stir. Cook until some of the liquid bubbles away, 1 to 2 minutes. Cover, adjust the heat so it bubbles gently, and cook until the sauerkraut is tender, about 30 minutes. Serve hot or warm. Or refrigerate for up to several days; reheat gently before serving.

SAUERKRAUT WITH JUNIPER BERRIES AND HAM Add 8 ounces chopped or sliced cooked ham in Step 2 after the sauerkraut has cooked for about 15 minutes.

SAUERKRAUT WITH CABBAGE Less sharp but still cabbagey; works for the main recipe or the previous variation: Replace half the sauerkraut with shredded fresh green cabbage.

CARROTS

The most common of all root vegetables, carrots are cheap, versatile, and available year-round. Unless you

---

Coring and Shredding Cabbage

STEP 1 Cut a cone-shaped section from the bottom.

STEP 2 Pull out the core.

STEP 3 To shred a head of cabbage, first cut it into manageable pieces.

STEP 4 Cut thinly across the head. (You can also use a mandoline for this; see page 15.) If the shreds are too long, just cut across them.

buy actual baby carrots at a farmers' market or grow them yourself, so-called baby carrots are peeled and cut regular carrots packed into bags; they're undeniably convenient, though they dry out more quickly than whole carrots. Real baby carrots are simply small, whole carrots.

PREPARING Many carrots only need scrubbing. Remove the outer layer with a vegetable peeler if they seem tough or overly dirty. Trim off the greens and stems and the pointy ends. Chop, slice, or grate as you need.

BEST COOKING METHODS steaming, braising, braising and glazing, roasting, grilling

WHEN ARE THEY DONE? When tender but not mushy, unless you're going to purée them; then you want them quite soft. Taste and you'll know.

OTHER VEGETABLES YOU CAN USE parsnips, beets, turnips, celery root

Shredded Carrots with Chiles and Chives

MAKES: 4 servings | TIME: 10 minutes

Fast and fiery hot, this stir-fry is perfect next to or even piled on top of a piece of grilled meat, poultry, fish, or tofu.

Other vegetables you can use: potatoes, parsnips, turnips, daikon radish, jícama.

- 1 tablespoon good-quality vegetable oil
- 1 tablespoon sesame oil
- 1 pound carrots, shredded
- 1 tablespoon chopped fresh chile (like jalapeño or Thai), or red chile flakes or cayenne to taste

20 chives (preferably garlic chives), cut into 2-inch pieces
    Soy sauce to taste

1. Heat a large skillet over high heat for 3 or 4 minutes. Add the oils, wait a few seconds, then add the carrots. Cook, stirring constantly, for a minute.
2. Add the chile and cook, stirring occasionally, until the carrots are dry and beginning to brown, about 10 minutes. Add the chives and a dash soy sauce and stir quickly to mix. Taste and adjust the seasoning. Serve.

SHREDDED CURRIED CARROTS Use all good-quality vegetable oil. Add 1 tablespoon curry powder (to make your own, see page 32) along with the chiles. Substitute ¼ cup shredded coconut for the chives and salt for the soy sauce.

SHREDDED GINGERED CARROTS Instead of the chile and chives, use 2 tablespoons minced fresh ginger.

SHREDDED CUMIN CARROTS WITH GOLDEN RAISINS
Omit the sesame oil, chile, chives, and soy sauce. In Step 3, after the carrots are cooked, sprinkle with 2 teaspoons cumin and add ½ cup golden raisins; continue cooking and tossing until fragrant, just another minute. Squeeze with lemon juice just before serving.

Chopping a Carrot

STEP 1 Cut it in half lengthwise, then into quarters or, if necessary, smaller sections.

STEP 2 Cut across the sections, as small as you like.

F fast   M make ahead   V vegetarian

CAULIFLOWER

Even normal white cauliflower is striking looking, and cooler still are the orange or purple varieties, the chartreuse-colored broccoflower, and the outlandishly spiky, small, lime green variety called Romanesco.

PREPARING Remove the outer leaves and if necessary, scrape off any gray or brown spots. You can cook it whole or separate it into florets before cooking. To separate into florets, begin at the base of the head and cut florets from the core, one after the other. Then break or cut the florets into smaller pieces if you like and chop the core.

BEST COOKING METHODS steaming, braising and glazing, roasting, grilling

WHEN IS IT DONE? When just tender enough to pierce with a skewer or thin-bladed knife; intentionally overcooking is not a disaster however, since super soft cauliflower makes excellent sauces, soups, and purées.

OTHER VEGETABLES YOU CAN USE broccoli and cauliflower are almost always interchangeable

Basic Steamed Cauliflower

MAKES: 4 servings | **TIME:** About 30 minutes

With cauliflower, steaming or cooking in the microwave (see "Microwaving Vegetables," page 237) is generally better than boiling, since it's faster and less prone to waterlogging. If you're in a hurry, cut up the cauliflower first.

When you're done, you have several choices: Serve hot with butter or olive oil and/or lemon juice, and garnish with parsley. Or break the cauliflower into florets and try any of the ideas in "11 Ways to Jazz Up Simply Cooked Vegetables" (page 251).

1 head cauliflower (about 1½ pounds), trimmed

Put the cauliflower in a steamer above an inch or two of salted water. Turn the heat to high, cover, and cook until the cauliflower is just tender enough to be pierced with a thin-bladed knife. Check the pot occasionally to make sure there is still water in the bottom. Whole cauliflower will retain quite a bit of heat after cooking, so it should still be ever-so-slightly underdone when you remove it from the steamer. Total cooking time will be 12 to 25 minutes, depending on the size of the head.

Manchurian-Style Cauliflower

MAKES: 4 to 6 servings | **TIME:** 30 minutes

The sauce sounds crazy but the recipe—from my friend chef Suvir Saran—has inspired all sorts of spin-offs, including Stir-Fried Chicken with Ketchup (page 604). He says the dish is associated with the Chinatown in Kolkata (formerly Calcutta), where it's sold on the street, to be eaten off toothpicks.

Other vegetables you can use: broccoli.

  Good-quality vegetable oil for deep-frying
  and making the sauce
3 eggs
⅔ cup cornstarch
  Salt and pepper
1 large or 2 small heads cauliflower, trimmed
  and separated into florets
2 teaspoons minced garlic
1 cup ketchup
½ teaspoon cayenne, or to taste

1. Put at least 2 inches of oil in a large pot and turn the heat to medium-high; bring to 350°F (see "Deep-Frying," page 22). Line a baking sheet with towels.

2. Beat the eggs and cornstarch together until well blended in a bowl large enough to accommodate the cauliflower. Sprinkle the batter with 1 teaspoon each salt and pepper, then add the cauliflower. Use your hands to toss until the florets are coated evenly.

3. Working in batches, add the cauliflower to the pan a piece at a time without crowding; make sure the oil returns to 350°F between batches. Fry until the florets take on a pale, sandy color, with a little brown mottling, about 5 minutes; transfer with a slotted spoon to the towels to drain.

4. Put 1 tablespoon oil in a large skillet over medium heat and add the garlic. Cook, stirring constantly, until the garlic until fragrant but not colored, 1 to 2 minutes. Add the ketchup and cook, stirring, until the sauce bubbles, thickens, and starts to caramelize around the edges of the pan, about 5 minutes. Add the cayenne; taste and adjust the seasoning. Toss the cauliflower in the sauce until coated evenly and serve.

ROASTED CAULIFLOWER, MANCHURIAN STYLE Easier: Omit the eggs and cornstarch. Heat the oven to 400°F. Put the cauliflower in a large baking pan or rimmed baking sheet, drizzle with 2 tablespoons oil, and sprinkle with 1 teaspoon each salt and pepper. Toss until well coated. Roast, stirring once or twice, until the cauliflower is tender and golden, about 30 minutes. Prepare the sauce as described in Step 4 and proceed with the recipe.

CELERY AND CELERY ROOT

Celery is ubiquitous, but rarely cooked; when it is, it's always with something else, which is a shame. Celery root (also known as celeriac) has a mellower flavor and is better for long cooking methods. Celery root has knobby, gnarled skin with a slightly green tinge and a porous ivory interior. It can range from fist size to bulbs weighing more than 1 pound.

PREPARING Trim the leaves from the celery—reserve them for use as a garnish if you like—and cut off the bottom core or remove as many stalks as you need. String the celery if it's tough and very fibrous (see the illustration at right), or just cut it into whatever size pieces you need. Celery root must be peeled; use a sharp paring knife rather than a vegetable peeler and acknowledge from the outset that you will lose a good portion of the flesh. If more than a few minutes will pass between peeling the celery root and using it, you might drop it into acidulated water (1 tablespoon lemon juice or vinegar per cup water) to keep it from discoloring.

BEST COOKING METHODS braising (celery); boiling, sautéing, braising and glazing, roasting (celery root); both also excellent raw

WHEN ARE THEY DONE? Celery: when either just tender or super tender; taste a piece. Celery root should be soft.

OTHER VEGETABLES YOU CAN USE celery and fennel are almost always interchangeable for texture; for celery root: parsnips, kohlrabi, or turnips

Preparing Celery

STEP 1 Celery is usually best when its toughest "strings" are removed from the outer stalks. Grasp the end of the stalk between your thumb and a paring knife.

STEP 2 Pull the strings down the length of the stalk.

Pan-Roasted Celery Root with Rosemary Butter

MAKES: 4 servings | TIME: 40 minutes

This recipe is simple but full of flavor. Note the variation, which can double as a delicious dressing for turkey or other poultry.

Other vegetables you can use: parsnips, rutabaga, turnips, sweet potatoes, potatoes, carrots.

- 4 tablespoons (½ stick) unsalted butter
- 2 sprigs fresh rosemary, sage, or thyme, plus 1 teaspoon chopped fresh rosemary
- 2 cloves garlic, peeled
- 2 pounds celery root, trimmed, peeled, and chopped
   Salt and pepper

1. Put the butter in a large skillet over medium heat. When it foams, add the rosemary sprigs and garlic and let sizzle gently until fragrant, about 2 minutes. Adjust the heat as needed to prevent the rosemary from browning.
2. Add the celery root; it should be in a single layer with some space between pieces. Cook, stirring a few times, until the celery root is soft and golden brown on all or most sides, about 30 minutes. Remove the rosemary and garlic when they've browned.
3. Sprinkle with salt and pepper and the chopped rosemary and stir. Serve hot.

PAN-ROASTED CELERY ROOT AND CROUTONS

Add 1 recipe My Kind of Croutons (page 801) along with the chopped rosemary in Step 3. Serve immediately.

PAN-ROASTED CELERY ROOT WITH HAZELNUT BUTTER

Substitute ⅓ cup chopped hazelnuts for the chopped rosemary and sprigs. In Step 2, after about 15 minutes, when the celery root is beginning to brown, stir in the nuts. Garnish with chopped parsley if you like.

CHARD

SWISS CHARD, RAINBOW CHARD

Chard is beautiful regardless of color. It has dark green, sometimes ruffled leaves, and edible stems may be brightly colored crimson red, orange, fuchsia, yellow, or stark white.

PREPARING Rinse well and tear or chop the leaves. Some recipes direct you to strip the leaves from the thick stems, chop them separately, and give them a head start in the cooking process.

BEST COOKING METHODS steaming, braising, sautéing. Regardless of method, it often makes sense to cook thick stems longer than leaves; start them a minute or two earlier.

WHEN IS IT DONE? When the leaves are wilted and the stems tender

OTHER VEGETABLES YOU CAN USE chard and beet greens are almost always interchangeable; dandelion greens, turnip greens, spinach

Chard with Oranges and Shallots

MAKES: 4 servings | TIME: 25 minutes

A perfect winter dish with vibrant color and tangy sweet-sour flavor to perk up any braised dish it's served alongside. The skin of the orange or tangerine becomes almost candied and provides a nice chew, but if you'd rather not eat it, simply peel before chopping.

Other vegetables you can use: any chard, bok choy, kale, or cabbage. For the citrus, use kumquats (quartered) if available.

Chard with Oranges and Shallots

1 pound chard, trimmed
2 tablespoons olive oil
2 shallots, halved and sliced
2 tablespoons sugar
1 small orange or tangerine, seeded and coarsely chopped
2 tablespoons sherry vinegar
   Salt and pepper

1. Cut the stems out of the chard leaves. Cut the leaves into wide ribbons and slice the stems, on the diagonal if you like. Keep the leaves and stems separate.

2. Put the oil in a large skillet over medium heat. When it is hot, add the shallots and sugar and cook for a minute, then stir in the orange or tangerine and adjust the heat so the vegetables sizzle gently. Cook, stirring frequently, until everything is caramelized, about 10 minutes. Stir in the vinegar.

3. Return the heat to medium and stir in the chard stems. Cook, stirring occasionally, until they soften a bit, a minute or 2. Add the chard leaves, cover, and turn off the heat. Let the chard steam for 2 to 3 minutes. Uncover, stir, and re-cover the pan for another couple of minutes. Sprinkle with salt and lots of pepper. Serve hot, or within an hour or two at room temperature.

CHARD WITH OLIVES AND FETA Omit the sugar and orange. Substitute about ¼ cup pitted olives for the sherry vinegar. Add up to 1 cup crumbled feta cheese in Step 3 when you add the chard leaves.

CHESTNUTS
Sweet, starchy, and mealy, chestnuts have smooth shells, dark brown and rounded with a flattened side, and are sold fresh in their shells (the best way to get them) in the fall and early winter (or in jars or packages all year long). They look a little like nuts but eat more like a root vegetable.

PREPARING Chestnuts must be precooked, and their shells and skins removed. See the illustrations at right.

BEST COOKING METHODS After peeling: boiling if you're going to mash or purée them; roasting or grilling for eating out of hand, sautéing, or stir-frying

WHEN ARE THEY DONE? They're tender and edible when the shell is easily removed; or cook a little longer if you want to purée them.

Boiled Chestnuts

MAKES: 4 to 6 servings | TIME: About 30 minutes

You must peel chestnuts when they're hot, so beware you might "ooh" and "aah" as you handle them; use a thin towel to protect yourself a little. They need not be sizzling hot for the skins to slip off, but as you'll find out, the hotter, the better. If the skins start to stick a bit, reheat and try again.

1 pound chestnuts, flat side scored (see below)
   Salt

Put the chestnuts in a pot with lightly salted water to cover and bring to a boil. Turn off the heat after 3 or

Preparing Chestnuts

STEP 1 Before cooking a chestnut, score the flat side with a sharp knife, making an X.

STEP 2 After cooking, remove both outer shell and inner skin. If the peeling becomes difficult, reheat.

4 minutes. Remove a few chestnuts from the water at a time and use a sharp knife to cut off the outer and inner skins. You may need to cook the chestnuts longer out of the shell in some liquid to purée or mash, but otherwise they're ready to eat or use in other recipes.

GRILLED OR ROASTED CHESTNUTS Prepare a charcoal or gas grill for medium-hot direct cooking or turn the oven to 450°F. Put the chestnuts directly on the grill, in a perforated grilling basket, or on a sheet of foil with holes poked in it, or on a baking sheet if roasting. Grill with the lid closed, or roast, turning occasionally, until you can remove the shells easily, after about 15 minutes. Eat warm out of hand or use in other recipes.

CORN

One of our favorite vegetables, as it should be—originally known as maize, it's indigenous to the Americas and has been cultivated for thousands of years. When fresh it's used as a vegetable; dried, it acts more like a grain (see "Dried Corn," page 464). Fresh summer corn is excellent raw in salads, salsa, or as garnish. For other recipes, see Corn Fritters (page 114), Corn Salsa (page 56), and Corn Salad with Avocado (page 201).

PREPARING Shuck the corn just before cooking it. Always remove the silk from the ears before cooking, even if you're cooking in the husk: Peel back the husk, remove the silk, and fold the husk back over the corn. If you want kernels only, cut them from the cob with a knife.

BEST COOKING METHODS steaming, roasting, grilling, stir-frying

WHEN IS IT DONE? When it's hot; there's no point in cooking it any further

OTHER VEGETABLES YOU CAN USE for cooked corn kernels: green peas or green or wax beans; for raw corn kernels, diced jícama

Sort-of-Steamed Corn on the Cob

MAKES: 4 servings | **TIME:** 20 minutes or less

You don't have to submerge corn to cook it; piling it up in a couple inches water does a perfect job, and you avoid the hassle of bringing a huge pot of water to a boil.

> Salt and pepper
> 8 ears fresh corn, shucked
> Melted butter for serving (optional)

1. Bring an inch or two of water to a boil in a large pot. Add a large pinch salt and the corn; it's okay if some of the cobs sit in the water and some above it.
2. Cover and cook until the corn is just hot; start checking after 3 minutes. It could take as long as 10 minutes, depending on the power of your stove and the freshness of the corn.

Preparing Corn

To shuck corn, peel back the husk, take out the silk, then fold the husk back over the corn. This works well for grilling. For steaming or boiling, remove the husk and silk entirely.

When you want kernels only, stand the shucked corn on its end and use a sharp knife to cut the kernels from the cob.

3. Sprinkle the corn with salt and pepper, and if you like, drizzle with butter. Serve right away.

---

10 FLAVORINGS FOR HOT CORN

Use either alone or in combination. Coating the ear of corn with melted butter or olive oil first will help spices and nuts stick better.

1. Grated Parmesan or pecorino cheese or crumbled Cotija cheese
2. Fresh lemon or lime juice, especially with a few dashes hot sauce
3. Red chile flakes or cayenne
4. Chopped toasted pumpkin, sunflower, or sesame seeds
5. Chopped nuts like hazelnuts, almonds, cashews, or peanuts
6. Chopped fresh herbs like parsley, mint, chervil, cilantro, or chives
7. Any Compound Butter (page 78)—or simply more butter!
8. Any flavored mayonnaise (to make your own, see page 70)
9. Any spice mixture (to make your own, see pages 27–35), especially chaat masala or chili powder
10. Roasted Garlic (page 294), mashed

Creamed Corn

MAKES: 4 servings | TIME: 20 minutes

I said this 20 years ago and I'll say it again: If you've never made this with freshly shucked corn, you may pass out with pleasure. The cornstarch, which thickens the mixture and makes it more like the canned creamed corn some of us grew up with, is entirely optional—and honestly, I prefer it without.

6 ears fresh corn or 3 cups frozen corn kernels (no need to thaw)
3 tablespoons butter
1½ to 2 cups heavy cream or half-and-half
Salt and pepper
Cayenne (optional)
Sugar (optional)
1 tablespoon cornstarch (optional)
Chopped fresh parsley for garnish

1. If using fresh corn, shuck it and strip the kernels into a bowl (see page 283) to save the liquid.

2. Put the butter in a large skillet over medium heat. When the butter foams, add the corn and cook, stirring, for a minute or 2. Add 1½ cups cream and heat until it bubbles gently. Add a good pinch salt, some pepper, and a pinch cayenne if you like. Cook, stirring frequently, until the corn is tender, about 10 minutes.

3. Taste and add a little sugar if you like. Continue to cook until the mixture is thick, another few minutes. If you like it thicker, combine the cornstarch with a tablespoon cold water in a small bowl and whisk until smooth. Stir this slurry into the corn; the mixture will thicken almost immediately. Taste and adjust the seasoning. Garnish with parsley and serve.

CREAMED CORN WITH ONION Before adding the corn in Step 2, cook ½ cup chopped onion, stirring frequently, until quite tender but not browned, about 10 minutes. Proceed with the recipe.

CREAMED CORN WITH CHEESE, POSSIBLY GRATINÉED
Instead of the cornstarch slurry, add about a cup grated semihard cheese like sharp white cheddar or Manchego. If you like, sprinkle the top with Parmesan and fresh bread crumbs (see page 801) and run the pan under the broiler for a minute or 2.

CREAMED CORN WITH CLAMS OR OTHER SEAFOOD
Strange but wonderful: In Step 2, when you add the corn, stir in about 2 pounds well-scrubbed clams or

mussels in the shell; or 1 pound peeled shrimp, chunks of firm fish; or try a half dozen shucked and chopped oysters or a couple ounces chopped smoked salmon. Cover the pan and cook as directed, until the clams open and the corn is tender, about 10 minutes. Proceed with the recipe.

Pan-Roasted Corn with Cherry Tomatoes

MAKES: 4 to 6 servings | **TIME:** 20 minutes

At some point in the summer, you may get sick of gnawing on cobs and picking corn from your teeth. That's when you make this fast, easy, completely different spin. Browned like this, corn takes on a brand-new flavor. This is also lovely to use in Corn Salad with Avocado and its variations (page 201). The variations here make great fillings for tacos or tamales.

Other vegetables you can use: peas, chopped green beans or wax beans.

- 6 ears fresh corn, shucked
- 1 tablespoon olive oil
- 1 pint cherry or grape tomatoes
- 1 tablespoon chopped shallot or white or red onion
  Salt and pepper
- ¼ cup chopped fresh basil

1. Use a knife to strip the kernels from the corn (see page 283).

2. Put the oil in a large skillet over high heat. When it is hot, add the corn; let sit for a moment until the kernels begin to brown on the bottom, a minute or so.

3. Add the tomatoes and shallot and shake the pan to distribute everything evenly. Cook, undisturbed until the vegetables darken on the bottom without burning,

about another minute. Then shake the pan occasionally until the vegetables soften and the tomatoes collapse, 3 to 5 minutes.

4. Sprinkle with salt and pepper. Taste and adjust the seasoning, then stir in the basil. Serve hot or at room temperature.

PAN-ROASTED CORN WITH POBLANO CHILES Substitute 4 poblano or other mild fresh chiles, or Roasted Red Peppers (page 318), chopped, for the cherry tomatoes, and cilantro for the basil. Garnish with more cilantro and a sprinkle of fresh lime juice.

PAN-ROASTED CORN WITH STEWED TOMATOES What you make in winter: Substitute 3 cups frozen corn for the fresh. In Step 2, cook only the corn. When it browns, remove it from the pan with a slotted spoon and add 2 more tablespoons oil and 1 large onion, chopped; cook until the onion softens, about 3 minutes. Add 1 14-ounce can whole tomatoes and cook, stirring occasionally and breaking the tomatoes apart, until the mixture thickens, about 10 minutes Return the corn to the pan and proceed to Step 3. Use fresh basil, dill, or mint.

CUCUMBERS

Ubiquitous in salads, cucumbers—actually a fruit—come in many varieties, but these are the most common: the big cucumber with dark green skin in every grocery store; the long, slender hothouse or English cucumber or similar but tiny Persians; and the small, light green, nubby-skinned Kirby, most often used to make pickles.

PREPARING If you can only get waxed or oiled cucumbers, always remove the peel; otherwise peeling is optional. Halve the cucumber lengthwise and use a spoon to remove the seeds if they are large. Consider salting (see page 203) to remove excess water if you're looking for extra crispness or less bitterness, or if you'll be cooking the cucumber.

  **F** fast   **M** make ahead   **V** vegetarian

BEST COOKING METHODS best raw or pickled (see "The Basics of Pickling Fruits and Vegetables," page 228). Cucumbers are rarely cooked, though sautéing in butter or oil can be a nice change, especially if they're less than perfect.

WHEN ARE THEY DONE? When they're as crisp or tender as you want them; check frequently because they'll get tender fast.

OTHER VEGETABLES YOU CAN USE celery, jícama, fennel; almost any vegetable can be pickled

EGGPLANT

There are dozens of eggplant varieties, though the most common are big dark globes. The other shapes and varieties are worth seeking out at Asian or Italian groceries and farmers' markets. You can't cut them into big slices, but you can adapt most recipes for them.

PREPARING Trim the stem end. Peel if you like; if the eggplant is good, the skin is sometimes the best part. Slice it crosswise or lengthwise between ½ inch and 1 inch thick or cube it any size. Salting eggplant to remove bitterness is optional: slice or chop it, sprinkle

it liberally with salt, and let it rest in a colander for up to an hour; rinse, pat dry, and proceed with the recipe.

BEST COOKING METHODS roasting, grilling, broiling, sautéing, stir-frying

WHEN IS IT DONE? When it's tender, almost creamy, and there are no dry spots

Dry-Pan Eggplant

MAKES: 4 servings | **TIME:** 30 minutes

If you want to cook eggplant for later use, especially for stir-fries or salads, this is the technique. It uses no fat, turns the skin into a thin, crunchy, smoky delight, and makes the flesh creamy and tasty.

3 or 4	small to medium eggplant (preferably slender ones; 1¼ to 1½ pounds total), stems intact
	Salt and pepper (optional)
	Olive oil for serving (optional)
	Fresh lemon juice for serving (optional)

1. Put the eggplant in a skillet, preferably cast iron, over medium heat.
2. Cook, turning the eggplant as they blacken on each side and adjusting the heat so the skin darkens without burning, until the skin is blistered and black all over and the flesh collapses (you'll know when it happens), about 15 minutes.
3. Transfer to a cutting board (the stems won't be hot, so you can just pick them up that way) and slit them lengthwise. Let cool until you can handle them, then chop or purée for other recipes. Or sprinkle with salt and pepper, drizzle with olive oil and lemon juice if you like, and serve.

Preparing Cucumbers

STEP 1 First halve the cucumber vertically.

STEP 2 Then scrape out the seeds with a spoon if they're large or there are a lot of them.

Breaded and Fried Eggplant (or Any Other Vegetable)

MAKES: 4 servings | **TIME:** 1 hour

Though eggplant is the most familiar vegetable to bread and fry in an inch or so of oil, consider this the model for any vegetable you can slice into a large relatively flat piece or "cutlet." The breading delivers crispness—assuming you don't let the vegetables sit too long before eating—since it acts as a barrier to seal in moisture and keep out the fat. For an even richer taste, melt some butter in the pan along with the oil.

Other vegetables you can use: any winter or summer squash, large mushrooms, cauliflower, broccoli, green tomatoes.

4 or 5	small eggplants or 2 large (about 2 pounds), trimmed
	Salt and pepper
1	cup all-purpose flour
3	eggs, beaten
3	cups bread crumbs (preferably fresh; see page 801)
	Good-quality vegetable or olive oil for frying
	Chopped fresh parsley for garnish
	Lemon wedges for serving

1. Cut the eggplant lengthwise or crosswise into ½-inch-thick slices. Salt the slices if you're using large eggplant and time allows (see page 203). Put the flour, beaten eggs, and bread crumbs in separate plates or shallow bowls next to each other and have a baking sheet and stack of wax or parchment paper sheets ready. Sprinkle the eggs with salt and pepper.

2. Rinse and dry the eggplant if it was salted. One at a time, dredge the slices in the flour, then in the eggs to coat all over, and finally dredge in the bread crumbs, pressing just enough so they adhere. Put the eggplant on the baking sheet in single layers between sheets of wax paper; once it's all breaded, transfer the sheet to the refrigerator to chill for at least 10 minutes or up to 3 hours.

3. If you won't be serving the eggplant right away, heat the oven to 200°F. Line a baking sheet with towels. Put about ½ inch of oil in a large skillet over medium-high heat. When it is hot, put in a few of the eggplant slices; cook in batches as necessary, making sure not to crowd the pan and adding additional oil as needed. Use a spatula or tongs to turn the eggplant slices as soon as they're browned, then cook the other side; total cooking time will be about 5 minutes. As each piece is done, transfer it to the prepared pan to drain. If you're not serving right away, move them to an ovenproof platter and put it in the oven to keep warm.

4. Serve as soon as all the pieces are cooked, garnished with parsley and with lemon wedges on the side.

COCONUT-FRIED PLANTAINS Substitute 4 or 5 yellow to yellow-black plantains for the eggplant; peel (see page 323) and cut straight or on a diagonal into slices about ¼ inch thick. Replace half the bread crumbs with shredded coconut.

GRAIN-FRIED BUTTERNUT SQUASH Replacing part or all of the bread crumbs with ground whole grains adds a nutty flavor: Instead of the eggplant substitute about 2 pounds butternut squash, peeled, seeded, and sliced ½ inch thick. Coarsely grind about 3 cups rolled oats or barley in a food processor to use instead of the bread crumbs.

FRIED ONION RINGS, STREAMLINED Instead of the eggplant, substitute 2 large onions (any kind except sweet varieties like Vidalia or Walla Walla), sliced ½ inch thick, for the eggplant. Omit the bread crumbs and eggs. Separate the onion slices into rings; dredge the rings in seasoned flour. Fry until golden brown. (See page 255 for how to make more traditional battered onion rings.)

FRIED OKRA Omit the eggs. Mix 1 cup all-purpose flour, 1 cup cornmeal, and a pinch cayenne in a bowl and

sprinkle with salt and pepper. Trim 1½ pounds okra and halve vertically or slice. Mix with 2 cups buttermilk. Remove the okra from the buttermilk, dredge in the flour mixture (it's okay if it clumps a bit), and fry as described.

3 WAYS TO VARY ANY BREADED AND FRIED VEGETABLE

1. **Change the breading:** For the bread crumbs, use panko. Or replace up to half of the crumbs with cornmeal, unsweetened shredded coconut, chopped nuts or seeds, pulverized raw whole grains like rice, rolled oats, barley, or kasha (pulse in a food processor to grind any of these), or grated Parmesan cheese.
2. **Skip the breading:** Omit the eggs and bread crumbs and simply dredge the vegetable in flour or corn-meal before frying. Note that this works best for vegetables with a decent amount of moisture for the flour to stick to; hard vegetables like carrots or winter squash won't take a flour coating as well as onions or zucchini.
3. **Go eggless:** Instead of the eggs, use milk or buttermilk.

Sautéed Eggplant with Basil

MAKES: 4 servings | TIME: About 40 minutes without salting
V

It takes some time—and oil—to cook eggplant properly on the stove. The results are worth it: creamy and flavorful, like no other vegetable. Perfect alone or in rice or grain bowls, and dreamy with a fried egg on top.

Other vegetables you can use: zucchini or summer squash, though the results will not be as satisfying.

1½ to 2 **pounds eggplant (preferably small)**
    Salt and pepper

⅓ **cup olive oil, plus more as needed**
1 **tablespoon minced garlic**
½ **cup chopped or torn fresh basil**

1. Peel the eggplant if the skin is thick or the eggplant is less than perfectly firm. Cut it into ½-inch cubes. Salt them if the eggplant are large and time allows (see page 203).
2. Put the oil in a large skillet, preferably nonstick or cast iron, over medium heat. When it is hot, add the eggplant. Cook, stirring almost constantly, until the eggplant begins to release some of the oil it has absorbed, 5 to 10 minutes. Stir in the garlic.
3. Continue cooking, stirring frequently, until the eggplant is very tender, 20 to 30 minutes. Sprinkle with pepper, taste and adjust the seasoning, stir in the basil and serve.

SAUTÉED EGGPLANT WITH BASIL AND CHILES Substitute good-quality vegetable oil for the olive oil. Add 1 tablespoon or more chopped fresh chile (like jalapeño or Thai) or a pinch red chile flakes along with the garlic in Step 2. Sprinkle with fish sauce if you like before serving.

SAUTÉED EGGPLANT WITH GREENS Stick with me; it's that good: Use about 1 pound spinach, arugula, kale, collards, or any other fresh green; if you've got greens with sturdy stems, separate them from the leaves and chop everything roughly. You want 3 to 4 cups total. In Step 3, stems (if you've got them) should go in after the eggplant has cooked for about 15 minutes; sturdy leaves after about 20 minutes; tender greens like spinach should go in when the eggplant is tender. Add enough olive oil to keep the vegetables moist but not greasy. When everything is tender, stir in ½ cup grated Parmesan if you like. Taste and adjust the seasoning. Serve hot or at room temperature.

SAUTÉED EGGPLANT WITH WALNUTS Use butter instead of the olive oil if you like; omit the garlic and basil. Grind ½ cup walnuts in a food processor or chop finely by hand. In Step 3, stir in the walnuts instead of the garlic and add ½ cup cream if you like. Proceed with the recipe. Garnish with chopped fresh parsley.

5 ADDITIONS TO SAUTÉED EGGPLANT

Eggplant is so distinctive it can stand up to many different flavors. A lot of these can be used in combination.

1. Make the dish creamy with the addition of thick yogurt, which goes especially well with spices.
2. Make it more substantial by sautéing the eggplant with chopped tomatoes, sliced bell peppers, lots of onions, zucchini or other summer squash, chopped potato (which will take at least as long as the eggplant to cook), cauliflower, whole shallots, and so on. Any combination of these vegetables will make a simple ratatouille.
3. Make the dish crunchy by adding some fresh bread crumbs (see page 801) or a handful of toasted pine nuts, sunflower seeds, or any toasted nuts near the end of cooking.
4. Make it more fragrant with the addition of parsley, mint, cilantro, or other strong fresh herbs.
5. Make it sharper by increasing the amount of garlic; adding chiles, chili powder (to make your own, see page 32), or Chile Paste (page 40); capers or olives; or chopped scallion, shallot, or onion toward the end of cooking.

Curried Coconut Eggplant with Potatoes

MAKES: 6 to 8 servings | **TIME:** About 1 hour without salting

A big batch, easily halved but you'll be happy to pull leftovers out of the freezer. Serve this over basmati rice for a fantastic vegetarian meal, or add some animal protein (see "How to Add Meat, Fish, or Poultry to Almost Any Vegetable Dish," page 257).

Other vegetables you can use: green beans, summer squash, winter squash, okra, cauliflower, mushrooms.

2 pounds eggplant (2 or 3 large)
   Salt and pepper
1 tablespoon good-quality vegetable oil
1 teaspoon mustard seeds
½ teaspoon cayenne
½ teaspoon ground turmeric
2 teaspoons ground coriander
1 teaspoon ground cumin
1 tablespoon chopped fresh ginger
2 tablespoons sliced garlic
2 pounds fresh tomatoes, cored and chopped, or 1 28-ounce can whole or diced tomatoes, including the juices
1½ pounds potatoes (any kind), peeled and cut into ½-inch cubes
1½ cups coconut milk (to make your own, see page 372), stock (to make your own, see pages 174–180), or water, plus more if needed
2 tablespoons fresh lime juice
   Chopped fresh cilantro for garnish

1. Peel the eggplant if the skin is thick or the eggplant is less than perfectly firm. Cut it into ½-inch cubes and salt it if you like and time allows (see page 203). Rinse and pat dry with towels.
2. Put the oil and mustard seeds in a large skillet over medium heat; cook until the seeds begin to pop, about 2 minutes. Add the cayenne, turmeric, coriander, cumin, ginger, and garlic and cook, stirring occasionally, until the ginger and garlic soften, 3 to 5 minutes.
3. Add the tomatoes, potatoes, eggplant, and coconut milk and sprinkle with salt and pepper. Adjust the heat so the curry bubbles gently. Cover and cook, stirring once or twice, until the potatoes are nearly tender, about 30 minutes.
4. Uncover and turn the heat back up to medium; add more coconut milk or water if the mixture is dry. Cook, stirring occasionally, until both the eggplant and potatoes are very tender, about 15 minutes more. Stir in the lime juice, and taste and adjust the seasoning. Garnish with cilantro and serve.

CURRIED EGGPLANT, SOUTHEAST ASIAN STYLE
Substitute 2 to 3 tablespoons red or green curry paste (to make your own, see page 46) for all the spices, ginger, and garlic. If you like, use 8 ounces trimmed green beans and a sliced red bell pepper instead of, or in addition to, the potatoes.

ENDIVE, ESCAROLE, RADICCHIO, AND CHICORY
The important thing to know about these related but totally different greens is that everything in this group is bitter and leafy but firm and crisp. Endive can be white or shades of purple. Escarole is thick-leafed with light green-to-white shading. Chicory is similar-looking only with curlier leaves, and radicchio looks like a small red and white cabbage. All add good texture and structure to salads and are a real treat when cooked, which mellows their flavor.

PREPARING Trim and rinse as you would any lettuce (see page 193).

BEST COOKING METHODS sautéing, braising (endive, chicory, escarole); grilling (endive, radicchio)

WHEN ARE THEY DONE? When crisp-tender if sautéed or grilled; when soft but not mushy if braised

OTHER VEGETABLES YOU CAN USE Within this group, the varieties are interchangeable. For cooking, dandelion, turnip, mustard greens; when raw, any lettuce, arugula, watercress

Braised Endive, Escarole, or Radicchio with Prosciutto

MAKES: 4 servings | TIME: About 1 hour

Belgian endive, with its neat little shape, is perfect for braising whole or halved, but escarole and radicchio

taste just as good; I usually chop them into big piece first.

Other vegetables you can use: Brussels sprouts, cabbage, kale, chard, beet greens.

- 2 tablespoons olive oil
- 4 Belgian endives, trimmed, damaged leaves removed, or about 1 pound escarole or radicchio, chopped
- ¼ cup chopped prosciutto or other dry-cured ham
- ½ cup chicken, beef, or vegetable stock (to make your own, see pages 174–178) or water
  Salt and pepper
- 1 teaspoon fresh lemon juice or white wine vinegar

1. Put the oil in a medium to large nonstick skillet over medium heat. When it is hot, add the endives and cook, turning once or twice, until they begin to brown.
2. Add the ham, stock, and sprinkle with salt and pepper. Cover and cook over the lowest possible heat, turning occasionally, until very tender, about 45 minutes. Uncover and turn the heat up a bit to evaporate any remaining liquid.
3. Drizzle with lemon juice and serve.

BRAISED ENDIVE WITH ORANGE JUICE Substitute butter for the olive oil if you like and orange juice for the stock. Omit the prosciutto. Add 2 tablespoons brown sugar with the orange juice in Step 2, and omit the lemon juice.

FENNEL
The flavor of fresh fennel is way less intense than its cousin anise seeds, but even that still gives people pause. Give it a go: This celery-like vegetable—but with fewer fibrous strings—is wonderful served raw, braised alone, or combined with other vegetables.

PREPARING Trim off the stalks; reserve the fronds for garnish if you like. Cut off the hard bottom and slice the bulb vertically into quarters. Or after trimming, cut the bulb in half first, then slice lengthwise or crosswise.

BEST COOKING METHODS braising, roasting, sautéing

WHEN IS IT DONE? When tender enough to pierce easily with a skewer or thin-bladed knife

OTHER VEGETABLES YOU CAN USE Even though the flavor is different, celery and fennel are almost always interchangeable in recipes.

Fennel Baked in Stock

MAKES: 4 servings | **TIME:** About 1 hour, largely unattended

Ⓜ Ⓥ

Impossible to mess up: You throw the ingredients together, put the dish in the oven, and forget about it while you make the rest of the meal.

Other vegetables you can use: leeks, onions.

> 1 **large or 2 small fennel bulbs, trimmed and sliced (see above)**
> **About 2 cups any stock (to make your own, see pages 174–180)**

> 2 **tablespoons olive oil**
> **Salt and pepper**
> 1 **cup bread crumbs, preferably fresh (see page 801)**
> ½ **cup grated Parmesan cheese (optional)**
> **Chopped fresh parsley for garnish**

1. Heat the oven to 375°F. Put the fennel slices in a gratin dish or similar baking dish. Pour in enough stock to come to a depth of about ½ inch. Drizzle with the oil and sprinkle with salt and pepper. Top with the bread crumbs and the Parmesan if you're using it.

2. Bake, undisturbed, until the fennel is tender (a skewer or thin-bladed knife will pierce it with little or no resistance) and the top is nicely browned, 45 to 50 minutes. Add more liquid during baking if the dish gets dry. Serve right away or keep warm in the oven for up to 30 minutes. Garnish with parsley before serving.

FENNEL BAKED IN ORANGE JUICE Substitute 1 cup fresh orange juice for half the stock. Add 1 tablespoon chopped fresh thyme and/or ½ cup chopped almonds, hazelnuts, or pecans to the bread crumbs and omit the Parmesan.

Preparing Fennel

STEP 1 Trim the hard, hollow stalks from the top of the bulb and cut off the hard bottom. Save the feathery fronds for garnish if you like.

STEP 2 Slice the whole bulb vertically.

STEP 3 Alternatively, cut the bulb or quarters in half first.

STEP 4 Then slice lengthwise or crosswise.

FENNEL WITH ONIONS AND VINEGAR Add 1 onion, sliced, 1 tablespoon chopped garlic, and 2 tablespoons sherry vinegar or balsamic vinegar. Omit the bread crumbs and Parmesan.

OVEN-BRAISED CELERY You'll look at celery in a whole new light: Cut 1½ pounds celery into 2-inch pieces, reserving the leaves. Put the oil (or use butter) in a large ovenproof skillet over medium heat. When the oil is hot or the butter foams, add the celery and cook for 2 minutes. Add 1 cup stock and sprinkle with salt and pepper. Bring to a boil, then transfer the skillet to the oven. Cook until the celery is very tender, about 15 minutes. Garnish with the celery leaves.

GARLIC

Garlic is probably the most important vegetable in recorded history (really!) because of its universal value as a seasoning for all sorts of foods in virtually every cooking heritage. And if you shop at farmers' markets or specialty stores, or if you garden, you now have more of it to love. In addition to the cured heads available everywhere, try garlic scapes, the seed-and-flower stalks that shoot up from hard-neck varieties in early summer. They're bright green and mild tasting, and you can eat all but the toughest ends. And so-called green garlic—when the plants start to produce cloves underground but are either immature or not yet cured—has a fresh herbaceous taste that will remind you of leeks.

PREPARING Don't bother to peel garlic before roasting it whole; the cloves will slip easily from their skins when they're done. For raw garlic, peeling is easiest after half-smashing the clove with the flat side of a knife blade. For larger quantities, blanch the garlic (see page 237) for 30 seconds or toast it in a dry pan over medium heat, shaking the pan frequently, for about 5 minutes; either of these treatments will loosen the skin and make it easy to slip out the cloves. To chop large quantities, put whole cloves in a food processor. You can crush garlic through a press, but chopping is no more difficult and the flavor is more nuanced.

BEST COOKING METHODS roasting, sautéing, braising

WHEN IS IT DONE? Roasted: when very, very tender, almost mushy; the cloves will squeeze easily out of their skins. Sautéed or fried: It's up to you but generally the more you cook it—gently, without browning—the milder it becomes. Don't let it get darker than golden brown or it will be bitter.

OTHER VEGETABLES YOU CAN USE shallots, onions (but they just aren't the same)

Roasted Garlic

MAKES: 2 heads | **TIME:** About 1 hour, largely unattended

Mellow and delightful, roasted garlic works as a side dish, condiment, seasoning for oil or butter, or an ingredient in sauces and other dishes (see "8 Ways to Use Roasted Garlic," page 296, for ideas). I like to overkill the olive oil, because the oil itself—as long as it's stored

Crushing and Peeling Garlic

STEP 1 If you're peeling more than a few cloves, drop them into boiling water for 30 seconds and the skin will slip right off. To peel without blanching, crush the cloves lightly with the side of a large knife.

STEP 2 The skin will come off easily.

F fast   **M** make ahead   **V** vegetarian

in the fridge and used within a few days—is another terrific ingredient.

     2   **whole heads garlic**
     2   **tablespoons or more olive oil**
         Salt

1. Heat the oven to 375°F. Without getting too fussy or breaking the head apart, remove as much of the papery coating from the garlic as you can. Cut the top pointy part off each head to expose a bit of each clove.
2. Film a small baking dish with a little oil and add the garlic, cut side up. Drizzle with more oil and sprinkle with salt. Cover with foil and bake until the garlic is soft (you'll be able to pierce it easily with a skewer or thin-bladed knife), 40 minutes or longer. Use right away or refrigerate, covered, for up to several days.

FASTER ROASTED GARLIC If you're in a hurry: Break the heads into individual cloves, but do not peel them. Spread them in a pan, sprinkle with salt, and drizzle with oil. Bake, shaking the pan occasionally, until tender, 20 to 30 minutes.

---

8 WAYS TO USE ROASTED GARLIC

You could start and end like this: Spread it on bread and eat. But roasted garlic is so useful there's no reason to stop there.

1. Stir into any cooked sauce or soup in which you'd use garlic, usually toward the end of cooking.
2. Spread on any pizza (see pages 814–822) before adding other ingredients.
3. Add to any vegetable purée (see page 240) or Mashed Potatoes (page 329).
4. Add to Vinaigrette (page 188), mayonnaise (to make your own, see page 69), Traditional Pesto (page 51), Compound Butter (page 78), gravy, or almost any other sauce.
5. Add to cooked grain or legume dishes.

6. Toss with cooked vegetables.
7. Mash with olive oil or softened butter and spread on cooked meat, poultry, or hearty bread.
8. Mix with olive oil and butter and toss with hot pasta, using a little of the cooking water to make a sauce. Add chopped parsley, lots of black pepper, and some grated pecorino Romano to put it over the top.

GINGER

Spicy, aromatic, and essential in cuisines all over the world, this gnarled tropical plant is often called a root but is actually a rhizome—basically an underground stem. So it's more delicate than a true root.

PREPARING Scrape off the papery skin with the blunt side of a knife or the edge of a spoon, or peel with a vegetable peeler or paring knife, which are faster if less economical. If the skin is thin and moist enough, you don't even need to peel it. Grate the ginger (a Microplane is best), julienne and mince it, or cut it crosswise into coins.

BEST COOKING METHODS stir-frying, sautéing, adding to soups and braises; grating raw in salads; slicing for pickles

OTHER VEGETABLES YOU CAN USE galangal comes close, but it's hard to find. Fresh turmeric is increasingly available, and it's good, but more bitter and less sharp. Ground ginger tastes different (see page 29) but can work instead of fresh in long-cooked dishes or baked foods.

Pickled Ginger

MAKES: 4 servings | **TIME:** At least a day, largely unattended

Homemade pickled ginger is easy, keeps in the fridge for a couple of weeks, and is far better than the pink-tinted stuff, especially if you start with young, thin-skinned

ginger (which will turn pink!). Use as a condiment with Sushi Bowls (page 450), Sushi Rolls (page 448), and in sandwiches and salads of all kinds.

- 1 **large piece fresh ginger (about 4 ounces)**
- 1 **tablespoon salt**
- ¼ **cup rice vinegar, plus more as needed**
- 2 **tablespoons sugar, or more to taste**

1. Peel and slice the ginger as thin as you can manage, using a mandoline if you have one. Toss it with the salt and let sit for an hour. Rinse thoroughly, drain, and put in a 1-pint glass or ceramic container with a tight-fitting lid.

2. Combine the vinegar with ¼ cup water and the sugar in a small saucepan. Cook, stirring, over low heat until the sugar dissolves. Taste and add more sugar if you like. Cool slightly and add to the ginger. If the liquid does not cover the ginger, add more vinegar and water in equal parts. Cover and refrigerate.

3. You can eat the ginger within a day, though it will improve for several days and keep for up to a couple of weeks.

CITRUS-PICKLED GINGER Add the zest from 1 orange, lemon, or tangerine; 2 limes; or ½ grapefruit to the vinegar and sugar before heating in Step 2.

GREEN BEANS
STRING BEANS, WAX BEANS, LONG BEANS, HARICOTS VERTS

We're familiar with the common green bean; wax beans are identical except for their yellow color; long beans are originally Chinese (though now grown here too) and are anywhere from a foot to a yard long. Then there are the skinny, tender French haricots verts and the dozens of heirlooms that pop up among gardeners and farmers' markets in peak summer.

PREPARING Snap or cut off the stem end with a small knife or scissors; leave the bean whole or cut into any length you like. To French-cut larger beans, halve

them lengthwise. It's a lot of work with high payoff in both an appealing look—with the seeds exposed—and texture.

BEST COOKING METHODS steaming, boiling, microwaving, stir-frying, sautéing, roasting, braising

WHEN ARE THEY DONE? A matter of personal preference: crisp-tender, just tender, or meltingly soft

OTHER VEGETABLES YOU CAN USE asparagus, peas, broccoli

Slow-Cooked Green Beans

MAKES: 4 servings | **TIME:** About 1 hour

I learned to adapt the traditional Greek technique from the great cookbook author Paula Wolfert. "Overcooking" vegetables goes in and out of favor; these are always extraordinarily tender and delicious.

Other vegetables you can use: wax beans; broccoli and cauliflower are also incredible this way.

- 1½ **pounds green beans (the smaller the better), trimmed**
- ¼ **cup olive oil, plus more for drizzling**
- 1 **cup chopped onion**
- 1 **cup chopped tomatoes (or use 1 14-ounce can diced tomatoes, drained)**
  Salt and pepper
  Fresh lemon juice

1. Combine the green beans, oil, onion, tomato, a sprinkle of salt and pepper, and a squeeze of lemon juice in a large saucepan and bring to a boil. Adjust the heat so the mixture bubbles gently. Cover tightly and cook for 1 hour, checking every 15 minutes and adding a few tablespoons of water if the pan is dry. Longer cooking, up to 1 hour more, will not hurt a bit.

2. When the beans are very tender and all the liquid is absorbed, they are ready. (At this point, you can refrigerate the beans in a covered container for up to 2 days.) Serve hot or at room temperature, drizzled with a little more oil and a few more drops of lemon juice.

SLOW-COOKED GREEN BEANS WITH BACON Add 1 slice bacon, chopped, to the pot along with the beans.

GREEN BEANS WITH YOGURT AND DILL Omit the tomato. Cook as directed until the beans are tender but not meltingly so, only about 20 minutes. Uncover and boil off any excess cooking liquid. Remove from the heat, stir in 1 cup yogurt, ¼ cup chopped fresh dill, and some extra lemon juice; taste and adjust the seasoning. Serve warm or at room temperature, drizzled with more oil.

HORSERADISH

Though it's most often sold in a jar—sadly, often junked up with cream sauce or other additives—fresh horseradish is quite wonderful—and surprisingly mild and delicious when cooked. If you find a brand of prepared horseradish that's basically just pickled in vinegar that can be a pretty good substitute for fresh.

PREPARING Peel with a sharp paring knife, not a vegetable peeler, and acknowledge from the outset that you will lose some of the flesh; it's hard to peel. Grate for use as a condiment, or chop or slice it as needed. Beware: This will make you cry.

BEST COOKING METHODS boiling, braising; roasting, usually in combination with other vegetables

WHEN IS IT DONE? When it's soft

OTHER VEGETABLES YOU CAN USE Radish, parsnips, and celery root all lend their unique flavors to a dish; fresh horseradish can be cooked in any recipe calling for those vegetables, though it will almost always be spicier.

JERUSALEM ARTICHOKES

Not artichokes and not from Jerusalem, and often called "sunchokes," these are actually tubers from a sunflower native to North America. They're versatile and delicious, though I'm obligated to mention that Jerusalem artichokes contain a type of sugar, inulin, that can cause quite severe flatulence in people with sensitivity to it; you'll know soon enough whether you're among them. Cooking helps mitigate this issue a little.

PREPARING Peeling is optional; I prefer just to rinse and scrub well. Chop or slice as needed.

BEST COOKING METHODS sautéing; braising and glazing; shaved raw in salads but you've been warned; roasting or mashing with other vegetables like potatoes is a happy compromise

WHEN ARE THEY DONE? When quite tender; taste one

OTHER VEGETABLES YOU CAN USE raw or cooked: radish, jícama; cooked: parsnip, turnip, potato

Crisp-Cooked Jerusalem Artichokes

MAKES: 4 servings | TIME: About 30 minutes

For this recipe you definitely shouldn't bother peeling the Jerusalem artichokes; you'll lose half the flesh in the process and it's a total pain.

Other vegetables you can use: waxy potatoes.

1½	pounds Jerusalem artichokes
3 to 4	tablespoons olive oil
	Salt and pepper
1	tablespoon chopped garlic or shallot or
	¼ cup chopped onion
	Chopped fresh parsley for garnish
	Lemon wedges for serving

 fast  make ahead **V** vegetarian

1. Scrub the Jerusalem artichokes well, then trim off any hard or discolored spots. Slice about ⅛ inch thick.

2. Put the oil in a large skillet over medium heat. When it is hot, add the Jerusalem artichokes a few slices at a time, spreading them out around the pan; sprinkle with salt and pepper. Cook, stirring and turning occasionally and adjusting the heat so they sizzle without burning, until tender and just about brown, about 20 minutes.

3. Add the garlic and continue to cook until nicely browned and tender, about 5 minutes more. Taste and adjust the seasoning. Garnish with parsley and serve with lemon wedges.

JÍCAMA

The root of a tropical vine, jícama has a turniplike shape and light tan, thick, papery skin; the flesh is white, delicately sweet, and crisp, like raw potato or a crunchy pear only better, making it excellent for eating all sorts of ways.

PREPARING Peel with a vegetable peeler or paring knife, then chop, slice, or shred.

BEST COOKING METHODS best raw; broiling, sautéing, stir-frying are an interesting change

WHEN IS IT DONE? When just heated through and still crunchy

OTHER VEGETABLES YOU CAN USE radish, cucumber, water chestnuts

Broiled Jícama with Chile-Lime Glaze

MAKES: 4 servings | **TIME:** 15 minutes

A great introduction to this vegetable if you've never had it. Serve with grilled meat, poultry, or fish, or let it cool a bit, then toss in a green salad.

Other vegetables and fruits you can use: daikon radish, scallions, pineapple, celery root, water chestnuts.

- 1 **tablespoon good-quality vegetable oil**
  Juice and grated zest of 1 lime
- 1 **teaspoon chili powder (to make your own, see page 32)**
- 1 **teaspoon sugar (optional)**
  Salt
- 1 **pound jícama, peeled and cut into sticks like French fries**

1. Turn on the broiler and position the rack about 4 inches below the heat. Line a baking sheet with foil (for easier cleanup). Mix the oil, juice, zest, chili powder, sugar if you're using it, and a pinch salt in a large bowl. Add the jícama and toss until well coated.

2. Spread the jícama on the baking sheet in a single layer, leaving a bit of space between the sticks. Broil the jícama until it starts to brown, about 4 minutes on the first side. Turn and broil 2 minutes more on the other side. Serve hot or at room temperature.

KALE AND COLLARD GREENS

When I published the first edition of this book, kale and collards were a lot less universally popular, even though they're the prototypical dark, leafy cooking greens. Whether it's because they're healthy, delicious, or versatile, they've caught on in a big way and are now available in many varieties like green kale, red Russian kale, and lacinato (also known as black or Tuscan kale). Collards are essential in Southern cooking.

PREPARING If the stems are thick, strip the leaves, chop the stems, and start cooking the stems a couple of minutes before the leaves. To cut the leaves easily, stack a few, roll them up, then cut across the roll (see below).

BEST COOKING METHODS boiling, steaming, stir-frying, braising; adding to soups and stews. Raw kale is best when chopped or thinly sliced and "massaged" with a little salt to tenderize it (see page 203).

WHEN ARE THEY DONE? When the stems are tender enough to pierce easily with a skewer or thin-bladed knife, unless—and this is sometimes the case—you want the stems on the crunchy side. Note that collards take longer to become tender, but are also excellent a little shy of tender, as in the recipe that follows.

OTHER VEGETABLES YOU CAN USE cabbage, chard, beet greens, turnip greens

Flash-Cooked Kale or Collards with Lemon Juice

MAKES: 4 servings | **TIME:** 15 minutes

Sturdy greens can be just as good cooked quickly as they are when stewed for ages, as this recipe demonstrates.

Other vegetables you can use: any dark greens like turnip, mustard, or dandelion; shredded cabbage of any type.

1 to 1½ pounds kale or collards
      3 tablespoons olive oil
         Salt and pepper
⅓ to ½ cup fresh lemon juice, wine vinegar, or sherry vinegar

1. Separate the leaves from the stems of the kale or collards. Chop thin stems into 1-inch sections (save any thicker than ⅛ inch for another use); stack the leaves, roll them up like a cigar, and cut into thin strips (see illustration at right).

2. Put the oil in a large well-seasoned cast-iron or nonstick skillet over high heat. When the oil smokes, toss in the stems. Cook, stirring almost constantly, until they begin to brown, 3 to 5 minutes.

3. Add the leaves and continue to cook, stirring, until they wilt and begin to brown. Turn off the heat, season with salt and pepper, and add about ⅓ cup lemon juice. Taste, adjust the seasoning and vinegar, and serve hot or at room temperature.

FLASH-COOKED KALE OR COLLARDS WITH FETA AND TOMATO Add 1 cup seeded and chopped tomatoes (canned is fine; drain first) along with the leaves in Step 3. Substitute up to 1 cup crumbled feta cheese for the lemon juice.

FLASH-COOKED KALE OR COLLARDS WITH FERMENTED BLACK BEANS Use good-quality vegetable oil instead of the olive oil. Add 1 tablespoon sliced garlic and ¼ cup fermented black beans along with the leaves in Step 3. Substitute 2 tablespoons soy sauce for the lemon juice.

Preparing Leafy Greens with Thick Ribs

Remove the stems if they are very thick (cook them a little longer than the leaves). Cut on either side of them, at an angle.

The easiest way to cut ribbons is to roll large leaves and cut across the log. Then you can chop them by cutting the opposite direction.

 fast  make ahead V vegetarian

Collards or Kale with Tahini

MAKES: 4 servings | **TIME:** 20 minutes

This rich and filling dish is wonderful spooned over rice, especially basmati. It's okay if the sauce curdles a little bit.

Other vegetables you can use: broccoli raab, gai lan, beet greens, dandelion or turnip greens, chard, bok choy, tatsoi, cabbage, spinach.

- 1 **pound collards or kale**
- 3 **tablespoons tahini**
- 2 **tablespoons olive oil**
- 1 **tablespoon chopped garlic**
  Salt and pepper
- 2 **tablespoons fresh lemon juice**
  Chopped fresh mint for garnish (optional)

1. Trim the most fibrous ends from the collards and cut or tear the leaves from the stems. Chop the stems and leaves into bite-sized pieces, keeping them separate. Whisk the tahini with ¼ cup water in a small bowl until smooth.

2. Put the oil in a large skillet or pot over medium heat. When it is hot, add the garlic and stems and cook, stirring frequently, until the garlic turns golden but not brown, about 3 minutes. Add the leaves and ¼ cup water, and sprinkle with salt and pepper. Cover and cook, stirring occasionally, until the greens and stems are soft, 5 to 10 minutes.

3. Add the tahini mixture and continue to cook, uncovered, at a low bubble, stirring frequently, until the collards are very tender, at least 5 minutes more. Add more water if the pot looks dry; you want some sauce, but not soup. Remove from the heat and stir in the lemon juice. Taste and adjust the seasoning. Serve hot, warm, or at room temperature, garnished with mint if you like.

COLLARDS OR KALE WITH PEANUT SAUCE Substitute peanut butter for the tahini. Add 1 tablespoon chopped

fresh ginger with the stems if you like, and substitute lime juice for the lemon. Garnish with chopped fresh tomato if you like.

COLLARDS OR KALE WITH YOGURT Substitute ½ cup yogurt for the tahini, but add it with the lemon juice instead of in Step 1. Garnish with fresh dill or mint.

KOHLRABI

A funny-looking root—sometimes with a few leafy stems attached—with a sweet, slightly piquant flavor and crisp texture that can be treated as you would turnips in any recipe.

PREPARING Peeling is optional for small kohlrabi and recommended for large ones. Slice or chop as necessary.

BEST COOKING METHODS steaming, sautéing, roasting; raw: excellent sliced thin and served as a crudité or a crisp, fresh foil for charcuterie

WHEN IS IT DONE? When tender but still crisp (steamed or sautéed); when soft (roasted)

OTHER VEGETABLES YOU CAN USE turnips

LEEKS

Mild and sweet, silky when cooked, leeks have only one downside: their cost. If you're paying by the pound, make sure there is plenty of white on the stalk; you'll trim off most of the green.

PREPARING Rinse well; leeks usually contain sand between layers. The traditional process: Trim off the roots and any hard, dark-green leaves. Make a long vertical slit through the center of the leek, starting about 1 inch from the root end and cutting all the way to the green end. (Leaving the root end intact helps keep the leek from falling into pieces when you rinse it.) Rinse well, being sure to get the sand out from between the layers.

The easy way, which works only if you don't want the leeks whole: Trim, chop, and rinse in a salad spinner, as you would greens.

BEST COOKING METHODS sautéing, braising, roasting, grilling

WHEN ARE THEY DONE? When soft, almost melting

OTHER VEGETABLES YOU CAN USE onions, shallots, scallions

Leeks Braised in Oil or Butter

MAKES: 4 servings | **TIME:** 30 minutes

Perfect either as a side dish for simply roasted meats or fish, or as a first course. Better still, chop them up after cooking and toss them with egg noodles, rice, or grains. And note all the possibilities in the variations.

Other vegetables you can use: onions, shallots.

4	tablespoons olive oil or butter
3 or 4	leeks (about 1½ pounds), trimmed and cleaned
	Salt and pepper
½	cup any stock (to make your own, see pages 174–180) or water
	Fresh lemon juice
	Chopped fresh parsley for garnish

1. Put the oil or butter in a skillet or saucepan that will hold the leeks in one layer. Turn the heat to medium. When the oil is hot or the butter foams, add the leeks. Sprinkle with salt and pepper. Cook, turning once or twice, until they just begin to brown, about 5 minutes.

2. Add the stock and bring to a boil. Adjust the heat so the liquid bubbles gently, cover, and cook until the leeks are tender, about 20 minutes. If the leeks are still swimming in liquid, uncover, raise the heat, and boil some of it away, but allow the dish to remain moist.

3. Sprinkle about 1 tablespoon lemon juice over the leeks, then taste and adjust the seasoning. Serve hot, at room temperature, or cold, sprinkled with a little more lemon juice and garnished with parsley.

Preparing Leeks

STEP 1 Remove the tough dark-green leaves. Cut off the roots.

STEP 2 Slice the leek almost in half, just about to the root end.

STEP 3 Fan out the leaves and either rinse under cold running water or swish in a bowl. If you're chopping the leeks for cooking, rinse after chopping; it will be easier.

LEEKS BRAISED IN RED WINE Substitute red wine for the stock; add a sprig fresh thyme and a bay leaf along with the wine. Remove the bay leaf before serving.

BRAISED LEEKS WITH TOMATO Step 1 remains the same, but use oil, not butter. In Step 2, use 1 cup chopped tomatoes, preferably fresh, in place of the stock. Proceed with the recipe, finishing with lemon juice or vinaigrette.

BRAISED LEEKS WITH OLIVES Use olive oil. In Step 2, after the liquid comes to a boil, add about 1 cup black olives; oil cured are best (you can leave the pits in), but any will do and all are good. (You'll need less salt.)

BRAISED LEEKS WITH MUSTARD In Step 2, whisk 1 tablespoon Dijon mustard, or to taste into the stock before adding it.

Crisp Sautéed Leeks

MAKES: 4 servings | **TIME:** 30 minutes

In addition to the ideas for using cooked leeks in the previous recipe, these leeks make a dramatic garnish on top of fish or chicken. You must work in batches to get them to brown and crisp properly.

Other vegetables you can use: sliced shallots, red onion rings.

> 3 or 4 **leeks (about 1½ pounds), trimmed and cleaned**
> 3 **tablespoons good-quality vegetable oil**
> 2 **tablespoons sliced garlic**
> **Salt and pepper**

1. Cut the leeks into 3-inch lengths and then slice lengthwise into thin shreds. Pat dry thoroughly. Line a platter with towels.

2. Put a large skillet over medium-high heat. When it is hot, add 1 tablespoon of the oil and the garlic. Cook for just a few seconds until fragrant, then scatter about one-third of the leeks into the pan so as not to crowd the pieces. Raise the heat to high and sprinkle with salt and pepper.

3. When the leeks sizzle and brown, in a minute or 2, use a spatula to turn the leeks over and crisp the other sides. As they crisp, transfer the leeks to the prepared plate to drain. Repeat with the remaining leeks. Toss everything to distribute the garlic evenly. Serve as soon as possible.

SPICED CRISP LEEKS Immediately after frying, dust the leeks with a little five-spice powder, chaat masala, gram masala, or other fragrant spice mixture (to make your own, see pages 27–35).

MUSHROOMS

True wild mushrooms are a farmers' market treat; many varieties are now cultivated. Here's a brief primer on the mushrooms you're most likely to encounter.

BUTTON OR WHITE The most common and most bland cultivated variety. White to tan; thick caps and stems with gray to dark brown gills. Tender and brown when cooked.

CHANTERELLE WILD Delicious and usually expensive. Light to golden yellow; shaped like fat trumpets, with ruffle-edged caps. Flavor is earthy and nutty.

CREMINI (BABY BELLA) Immature cultivated portobello mushrooms. Tan, with dark brown gills; shaped like button mushrooms but more robust in flavor.

ENOKI A delicate Asian mushroom, often used as garnish. White with toothpick-sized stems and tiny round caps. Very mild in flavor; best used raw or barely cooked.

MOREL One of the treasures of cooking, this wild-only mushroom is available fresh in the spring and fall. White or brown, cone-shaped with a honeycomb-textured cap and hollow center. Wonderful, earthy flavor, both fresh and dried (you should have dried morels in your pantry). Make sure you rinse thoroughly, as they're usually sandy.

OYSTER Available wild and cultivated. White to dark gray, and sometimes pink or yellow. They grow in clusters with thick stems and a round or oval leaflike "cap." Mild mushroom flavor, slightly chewy texture.

PORCINI Dried porcini should be in every pantry; fresh are seasonal, and pretty pricey. They have the most robust and earthy flavor and the meatiest texture of all mushrooms. Very plump, tan to dark brown caps and fat, off-white stems when fresh. Buy dried porcini from a reputable purveyor in quantities of at least

4 ounces at a time; the ⅛-ounce packages often sold are rip-offs.

PORTOBELLO A supermarket staple. Tan to brown, with giant flat caps, thick stems, and dense, dark brown gills that darken whatever dish they're cooked with, so scrape them out first. The flavor is earthy. Excellent grilled.

SHIITAKE The most flavorful cultivated mushroom. Available fresh and dried. Flat tan caps with off-white gills and tough stems when fresh; brown with fatter-looking caps when dried (usually whole). Dried shiitakes, sold inexpensively in Chinese markets, where they may be called black mushrooms, are excellent for stock but have a rubbery though not unpleasant texture when reconstituted and cooked. Texture of fresh is meaty with a hearty, earthy flavor. Always remove stems when preparing; they're good in stock.

PREPARING You can brush or wipe them clean if you like, but I usually rinse fresh mushrooms as lightly as possible; they absorb water like a sponge if they sit in it. Either way, make sure you get any dirt out of hidden crevices. It's easier to trim some mushrooms before cleaning; morels are easiest to clean if you cut them in half lengthwise, but they don't look as nice afterward. Cut off any hard or dried-out spots, usually just the end of the stem. The stems of most mushrooms are perfectly edible. Clean the stems well, cut them in half if they're large, like portobello stems, and cook them with the caps.

To reconstitute dried mushrooms, see page 304.

BEST COOKING METHODS sautéing, stir-frying, roasting, grilling; raw if marinated

WHEN ARE THEY DONE? When tender, though you can cook them until they're crisp too.

OTHER VEGETABLES YOU CAN USE mushrooms are largely interchangeable, including reconstituted dried mushrooms. Otherwise there is no substitute.

Reconstituting Dried Mushrooms

A brief soak in boiling water and most dried mushrooms are ready to use, leaving you with a flavorful liquid as a bonus. Soak the mushrooms until they're soft, anywhere from 5 to 30 minutes; for very tough or thick mushrooms, you'll need to change the water if it gets cold before they're soft.

When they're tender, lift the mushrooms out of the soaking liquid with your hands or a slotted spoon. Carefully pour the soaking liquid into another container, leaving any grit in the bottom of the bowl. Use the liquid as stock in soups, stews, and sauces; it has intense mushroom flavor. Trim away any hard spots from the mushrooms, and use just as you would fresh.

Chinese dried shiitakes are a slightly different story. They must be soaked in boiling-hot water, you'll likely have to change the water once to get them soft, and they need to be trimmed assiduously. One way to deal with all of this is to cook them in stock or Dashi (page 179), then cool, trim, and use them; the process will enhance both stock and mushrooms.

 fast   make ahead V vegetarian

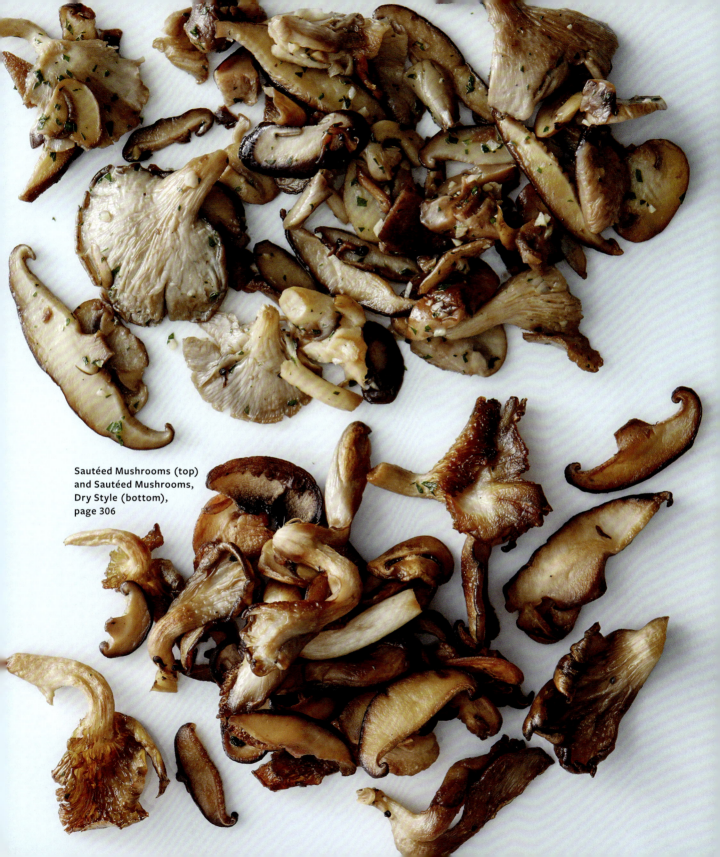

Sautéed Mushrooms (top)
and Sautéed Mushrooms,
Dry Style (bottom),
page 306

Sautéed Mushrooms

MAKES: 4 servings | **TIME:** About 20 minutes

On the spectrum of flavorful mushrooms, common button mushrooms rank low, even though the texture is pleasant. They're better when you combine them with some reconstituted dried mushrooms—preferably porcini—and maybe a handful of something more exotic like creminis or shiitakes. That said, even button mushrooms on their own are delicious cooked like this. Sautéed mushrooms are perfect on steak or chops, over rice or noodles, or tossed with steamed spinach or other greens.

> ¼   cup olive oil or butter (or a mixture)
> 1   pound fresh mushrooms (preferably an assortment), cleaned, trimmed, and sliced
>   A handful of dried porcini, reconstituted (see page 304; optional)
>   Salt and pepper
> ¼   cup dry white wine or water
> 1   teaspoon chopped garlic
> ¼   cup chopped fresh parsley

1. Put the oil in a large skillet over medium heat. When it is hot, add all the mushrooms, then sprinkle with salt and pepper. Cook, stirring occasionally, until tender, 10 to 15 minutes.

2. Add the wine and let it bubble away for a minute, then adjust the heat so it bubbles steadily. Add the garlic and parsley, stir, and cook until most of the liquid evaporates, about a minute. Taste and adjust the seasoning. Serve hot, warm, or at room temperature.

SAUTÉED MUSHROOMS, DRY STYLE Reduce the oil to 2 tablespoons; omit the white wine, garlic, and parsley. In Step 1, cover the skillet after adding the mushrooms and adjust the heat so the mushrooms sizzle without burning. Cook, undisturbed, for 5 minutes. Uncover and let the liquid from the mushrooms evaporate completely, another 5 minutes or so. Then continue to cook, stirring occasionally, until they're dry, shrunken, and as crisp as you like them, 5 to 15 minutes more.

SAUTÉED SHIITAKES WITH SOY SAUCE Use good-quality vegetable oil and fresh shiitake mushrooms if possible. Add a dried chile or two to the skillet along with the mushrooms and lots of pepper. Replace the wine with water and add 1 tablespoon soy sauce, or to taste, with the garlic. Finish with cilantro instead of parsley.

---

8 ADDITIONS TO SAUTÉED MUSHROOMS

1. Any chopped fresh herb you like, but especially chives (a handful), chervil (a handful), tarragon (a few fresh leaves or a pinch dried), or thyme (a teaspoon or so fresh), along with the garlic and parsley.

2. Finish with a teaspoon or more lemon juice or any vinegar (sherry vinegar is especially nice).

3. Substitute about ¼ cup chopped shallots, or about ½ cup chopped scallions or onion, for the garlic, cooking for 2 or 3 minutes longer after adding.

4. Instead of using oil, cook 2 ounces chopped bacon or pancetta until the fat is rendered; cook the mushrooms in the bacon fat.

5. Finish the dish with ½ to 1 cup heavy cream or sour cream; let it bubble very gently. This is best if you cook the mushrooms in butter from the start and use scallions in place of the garlic.

6. In the shiitake variation, stir in 1 tablespoon Chile Paste (page 40) or curry paste (to make your own, see page 46), or to taste, along with the garlic.

7. In the shiitake variation, stir in 1 tablespoon toasted sesame seeds (see page 309) with the garlic; finish with a teaspoon or more sesame oil.

8. In the dry-pan variation, marinate the mushrooms in any Vinaigrette (page 188) after cooking.

 fast   make ahead   vegetarian

MUSTARD, TURNIP, AND DANDELION GREENS

These are the so-called spicy greens: tender, peppery, and extraordinary when young; potent and potentially bitter and tough once mature. So when young, they're great raw; when old you gotta cook 'em.

PREPARING Rinse well; they're often sandy. Remove the stems if they're tough. Tear or chop the leaves.

BEST COOKING METHODS steaming, braising, sautéing

WHEN ARE THEY DONE? When wilted and tender

OTHER VEGETABLES YOU CAN USE mustard, turnip, and dandelion greens are interchangeable; broccoli raab, kale, collards, spinach; beet greens and chard will work as well

Spicy Greens with Double Garlic

MAKES: 4 servings | **TIME:** 15 minutes

The first batch of garlic mellows as it cooks with the greens; the second adds kick. In addition to the mustard, turnip, and dandelion greens listed above, you can use this recipe for broccoli raab, any Asian green (like bok choy, tatsoi, or gai lan), beet greens, chard, kale or collards, cabbage, or spinach.

1½	**pounds spicy greens (see the headnote)**
¼	**cup olive oil**
¼	**cup sliced garlic (about a whole head) plus 1 teaspoon minced garlic**
	Salt and pepper
½	**teaspoon red chile flakes, or to taste**
	Lemon wedges for serving

1. If the greens have thick stems, cut off the leaves; chop the leaves and stems and keep them separate (see page 300). If the stems are thin and pliable, chop everything together.

2. Put the oil in a large pot over medium-high heat. When it is hot, add the sliced garlic and thick stems, and sprinkle with salt and pepper. Cook, stirring frequently until the vegetables are tender, about 2 minutes. Add the red chile flakes and stir.

3. Add the greens and ½ cup water. Cover and cook until the greens are wilted and barely tender, 3 to 15 minutes.

4. Uncover the pot and continue to cook, stirring, until the liquid has mostly evaporated and the greens are quite tender, 1 to 5 minutes or more. If the pan is dry, add water, 1 tablespoon at a time. Taste and adjust the seasoning. Add the minced garlic and cook for 1 minute more. Serve hot, warm, or at room temperature, with lemon wedges.

SPICY GREENS WITH DOUBLE GINGER Instead of sliced garlic, use chopped fresh ginger; for the chopped garlic, mince or grate 1 teaspoon ginger.

COLLARDS WITH POT LIQUOR The classic; it will also work with cabbage: Separate the stems from the leaves as described in Step 1. Instead of the sliced and minced garlic, use about 2 tablespoons chopped, or mash the cloves from 1 head Roasted Garlic (page 294). In Step 3 increase the water to 1 cup and add 2 ham hocks, ½ cup cider vinegar, and ½ cup maple syrup to the pot. Adjust the heat so the mixture bubbles gently, cover, and cook, stirring once in a while and adding water to keep the mixture soupy, until the meat is falling of the bone and the greens are silky, about an hour. Remove the skin, fat, and meat from the ham hocks and chop the meat. Return the meat to the pot and add the red chile flakes. Skip Step 3 and serve hot in bowls with the cooking liquid.

NUTS AND SEEDS

As the interest in eating a more plant-based diet grows, nuts and seeds move from a snack toward a cooking ingredient. They're a good source of protein to be sure,

Spicy Greens with Double
Garlic, page 307

and in the bargain they add tremendous texture, flavor, and nutrients to many dishes.

PREPARING All kinds of good-quality nuts are available now. Make sure they're fresh; and ideally unsalted. I like to buy them in bulk, raw, and roast or toast and season them myself. In-shell nuts are usually fresher than shelled. To get at the meats, a nutcracker certainly makes things easier, but a hammer, mallet, or meat pounder works too. Covering them with a towel first minimizes the noise and mess. And some are just harder than others.

BEST COOKING METHODS Roasting: Heat the oven to 350°F. Spread the nuts or seeds in an even layer on a baking sheet. Bake until they are just starting to turn golden brown, 10 to 15 minutes, stirring every so often. Toasting in a dry pan on the stovetop is a good idea for the smallest seeds like sesame, poppy, or pepitas and for small quantities of larger nuts: Heat a pan over medium heat and add the nuts or seeds. Cook, shaking the pan and stirring often, until they're just starting to turn golden brown (pepitas will puff slightly), 5 to 10 minutes.

Whether roasting or toasting, immediately remove the cooked nuts or seeds from the pan and let cool. They will continue to cook for a bit afterward and will crisp as they cool.

Blanching nuts lets you remove the sometimes bitter skins. Roast or toast as above first if you like that flavor. Bring a pot of water to a boil, add the nuts, and turn off the heat. Let soak until you see the skins start to loosen, typically a couple minutes. Drain and pick out the skins. If the skins are stubborn, rub them in a towel until they loosen. (Note that the hazelnut skins are best removed by simply roasting and rubbing in a towel.)

Grinding: Nut meal and nut butter are easy to make. (Nut flour, finer than meal, requires special equipment.) All you need are nuts—raw, roasted, toasted, or blanched—and a food processor. Figure you'll end up

with about half the volume of the whole nuts. For meal, pulse the nuts in the food processor until they are finely ground and look like moist flour. Avoid overprocessing or the mixture will quickly turn into nut butter; if there are still larger bits of nut, either leave them in for texture or sift them out. If you see any bit of the meal clumping, stop processing; it's about to turn into butter. To make nut butter, just push the "on" button and stop it once the butter reaches the consistency you like; you can add some water if you want it to be on the thin side. Most nut butters are made from roasted nuts—the flavor is richer; raw or blanched nuts are milder. Refrigerate both meal and butter in airtight containers and use within a week or so.

10 Ways to Season Nut Butters

As long as you're grinding your own, you may as well customize the taste. Adding liquids or fresh ingredients like garlic or chiles will make the nut butter potentially thinner and more perishable, so keep it in the fridge. The following quantities are guidelines for about 1 cup butter; but really, add to taste.

1. **Salt:** ¼ teaspoon
2. **Sweetener:** 2 tablespoons sugar, brown sugar, honey, molasses, or maple syrup
3. **Spices:** ¼ teaspoon ground cinnamon, nutmeg, cloves, allspice, cardamom, coriander, cumin, or asafetida (to name a few) or any spice mixture (to make your own, see pages 27–35)
4. **Chile:** ¼ teaspoon cayenne, red chile flakes, or any chopped dried or fresh chile (see pages 39 and 40 for how to prepare), including chipotle chiles in adobo sauce
5. **Garlic:** 1 clove raw or 1 head roasted (page 294)
6. **Ginger:** about 1 tablespoon grated fresh or chopped candied
7. **Coconut:** 2 tablespoons of either milk or shredded
8. **Tamarind paste:** 1 to 2 teaspoons
9. **Vanilla:** 1 teaspoon
10. **Cocoa powder:** 2 tablespoons, any kind

The Nut and Seed Lexicon

Nuts and seeds—some of which are technically legumes—are more interchangeable than any other food. Often choosing which one to use is more a matter of what you have on hand than what's "right." Size only matters if cooking time is a factor; otherwise it's the flavor, color, and texture characteristics that count. As far as storage, I usually keep almonds, peanuts, pine nuts, pumpkin seeds (pepitas), sesame seeds, walnuts, and pecans in the freezer, which more than covers the basics. I buy other nuts and seeds in small quantities as I need them for specific uses. Chestnuts appear in their own section starting on page 282.

NUT	DESCRIPTION	FORMS
Almonds	Originally Middle Eastern, now from California and Spain. Sweet and delicate. Used in desserts and sweets; also for adding texture, richness, and light flavor to savory dishes.	Shelled and unshelled; blanched or skin-on; sliced, slivered; roasted and sometimes salted or otherwise flavored; processed into a paste (almond paste, marzipan); ground into flour, meal, or butter; pressed into oil; processed into milk
Brazil nuts	The majority are harvested in Amazon rainforests. Large, oblong, odd-shaped nut in a very hard dark brown shell, with meat more tender than crunchy.	Shelled and unshelled; roasted and sometimes salted
Cashews	Originally South American, now grown primarily in India. Shaped like fat commas; shells are toxic (they are related to poison ivy!) so always sold shelled. Super-rich and slightly sweet. Cooked, they soften a bit and acquire a somewhat meaty texture. Can be soaked in water and puréed for a dairy replacement for vegans.	Shelled; roasted and sometimes salted; ground into butter; processed into milk and vegan cheeses
Flaxseed Linseed	Small, shiny, flat, and nutty-flavored seeds that range in color from tan to dark brown. Their incredible nutritional profile includes lots of protein, fiber, and omega-3 fatty acids, but nutrients are less accessible when consumed whole.	Whole; ground into meal or flour; pressed into oil; sometimes processed into milk
Hazelnuts Filberts	Small round nuts; in their shells they resemble chestnuts, but smaller and lighter brown. Crunchy, with a mild nutty flavor (perfect with chocolate). Lower in fat than most nuts. The slightly bitter skins can be removed by rubbing the nuts between towels or your hands while still warm after roasting. Often used in European pastries.	Shelled and unshelled; blanched or skin-on; roasted and sometimes salted; ground into flour, meal, or butter; pressed into oil; processed made into milk
Macadamia nuts	Native to Australia, a rich, calorie-laden, high-fat nut. Medium-size, round, creamy white. Shells are almost impossibly hard.	Shelled; roasted and sometimes salted; pressed into oil
Peanuts Goober, groundnut	A native South American legume eaten like a nut. Virginia and Spanish are the two most common varieties; Spanish are smaller with a reddish brown papery skin.	Shelled and unshelled; oil- or dry-roasted and often salted or otherwise flavored; boiled; ground into butter; pressed into oil. Occasionally raw (in natural food stores), fresh (at farmers' markets, Chinese groceries, and online)

 F fast   M make ahead   V vegetarian

NUT	DESCRIPTION	FORMS
Pecans	Native to North America; used extensively in Southern cooking, like pecan pie. Similar to walnuts but flatter, with dark brown skins and a milder, sweeter buttery flavor.	Sometimes unshelled, more commonly shelled, in halves or pieces; roasted and sometimes salted
Pine nuts Pine kernel, Indian nut, pignoli	The seeds of various types of pine trees. These days China produces the most, though Native Americans have used them for centuries. Slightly golden, slender shape, with a delicate flavor. Commonly used in sweet baking and savory dishes like Traditional Pesto (page 51).	Shelled; raw or roasted
Pistachios	Originated in the Middle East; now California is the largest producer. A pretty green nut often sold in its split tan-colored shell, which cracks naturally as the nuts ripen.	Shelled and unshelled; roasted and sometimes salted or otherwise flavored; ground into a paste; pressed into gorgeous deep-green oil
Pumpkin and squash seeds Pepitas	The seeds of pumpkins or nearly any hard winter squash. Medium-size, oval with a point, flat, and ranging from green to tan to white. The flavor is like a cross between peanuts and sesame seeds. May be ground and used as a thickening and flavoring agent, as a coating like bread crumbs, tossed into salads, breads, muffins, or eaten out of hand. *Pepitas* is Spanish for "little seeds."	Fresh (right out of a pumpkin or squash) or dried; hulled or unhulled; roasted and sometimes salted; roasted and ground into butter; and pressed into oil
Soy nuts	Dried and roasted soybeans; small tan oval "nuts" (actually legumes) that are quite crunchy and loaded with protein. Eaten as a snack or tossed into salads, granola, or trail mix. (For more on soybeans, see page 388.)	Roasted and sometimes salted
Sunflower seeds	From the gigantic sunflower plant, native to North America. Used in baked goods like breads and muffins, on salads and other dishes as a crunchy and flavorful garnish.	Shelled and unshelled; roasted and often salted; processed into butter; pressed into oil
Walnuts	One of the most common and oldest known nuts, used almost everywhere. Shells are tan, round with a point, and ridged; nuts are fairly large and brain-shaped. They bring a rich, slightly bitter flavor to sweet and savory dishes. Less common black walnuts have harder shells and are even more flavorful.	Shelled and unshelled in pieces; ground into meal, flour or butter; pressed into oil

OKRA

Well-loved in the South and underappreciated elsewhere, okra is a green—or sometimes purple or crimson—pod with little round white seeds inside. Its polarizing sliminess also makes it useful for thickening stews.

PREPARING Rinse; cut off the stems. Chop or sliver okra before cooking if you like, but that releases the mucilaginous properties of okra's interior. Large pods must be cut into rounds no more than ½ inch thick, or they'll be too fibrous to enjoy.

BEST COOKING METHODS cut or whole: deep-frying, sautéing, stewing (either gently or for a long time; in between is problematic); whole: roasting, grilling

WHEN IS IT DONE? When tender and no longer viscous

OTHER VEGETABLES YOU CAN USE green or wax beans, asparagus (these won't have okra's thickening power)

Okra Gumbo with Spicy Sausage

MAKES: 4 servings | **TIME:** About an hour, largely unattended

Searing the okra first may not be traditional for gumbo, but it works. After that, there's little to do but let the pot bubble away. To serve this New Orleans style, pour a ladleful into a shallow soup bowl and nestle a scoop of plain white rice in the center. For a richer flavor and texture, try the variation made with roux.

Other vegetables you can use: green beans.

- 2 **tablespoons olive oil**
- 1 **pound spicy smoked sausage or kielbasa**
- 1 **large onion, halved and sliced**
  Salt and pepper
- 1 **pound okra, trimmed**
- 2 **tablespoons chopped garlic**

- 4 **cups chopped tomatoes (canned is fine; no need to drain)**
- 1 **tablespoon chopped fresh oregano (optional)**
  Chopped fresh parsley for garnish

1. Put 1 tablespoon of the oil in a large pot over medium-high heat. When it is hot, add the sausage, prick it with a fork a couple times, and cook until it's golden brown on all or most sides. Transfer the sausage to a cutting board.

2. Add the onion to the fat in the pot, sprinkle with salt and pepper, and cook, stirring frequently, until soft and turning golden, 2 to 3 minutes. Meanwhile, slice the sausage crosswise into rounds. Remove the cooked onions from the pot with a slotted spoon and set aside.

3. Add the remaining oil to the pot and stir in the okra. Cook, stirring occasionally, until it begins to brown a little. Add the garlic and cook for another minute or so, stirring once or twice. Return the sausage and onion to the pan and add the tomatoes along with 1 cup water. Sprinkle with salt and pepper.

4. Bring the gumbo to a boil, then lower the heat so it bubbles gently. Cook, uncovered, stirring every once in a while, until the okra is very tender and the broth has thickened, about 45 minutes. Stir in the oregano if you're using it. Taste and adjust the seasoning. Serve hot, garnished with parsley.

VEGETARIAN OKRA GUMBO Omit the sausage. Heat the oil in the pan, then skip directly to Step 2.

OKRA GUMBO WITH ROUX Use butter instead of oil if you like and increase the quantity to 5 tablespoons. Have ¼ cup flour ready. Follow the recipe through Step 2. In Step 3, add all of the remaining oil or butter (4 tablespoons) and turn the heat down to medium-low. Add the flour and cook, stirring almost constantly, until the roux darkens to the color of iced tea and becomes quite fragrant. This can take up to 15 minutes; lower the heat if it's sticking or darkening too much, too fast. Add the okra and continue cooking and stirring until the okra starts to soften, another 3 to 5 minutes. Proceed with the recipe.

OKRA GUMBO WITH SEAFOOD Use the main recipe or the preceding roux variation: Use peeled shrimp, scallops, shucked oysters or clams, or squid (alone or in combination) instead of the sausage. Skip Step 1 and don't add the seafood until the okra is just about done in Step 4. Add the seafood to the pot, cover, and keep the liquid bubbling for another 5 minutes or so, until the seafood is opaque but not overcooked.

OLIVES

Olives have been cultivated for millennia, and there are dozens of varieties and multiple curing methods in use today. Here are brief descriptions of the most common olives.

BLACK OR MISSION Most often pitted and canned—and nearly tasteless. Picked when unripe or green, they're cured in lye and then oxygenated, which turns them black.

CASTELVETRANO These bright green olives can now be found pretty easily, which is great for us. They're buttery, mellow, and a little sweet. They are grown in only one area of Sicily and are the most popular olive in Italy for snacking. They are picked when young and cured in a light brine.

KALAMATA Widely available, salty, and sometimes mushy, though not unpleasantly so. Dark brown, purple, or black. Picked when ripe or almost ripe, then cured in saltwater or red wine vinegar. A decent standby.

MANZANILLA OR SPANISH Big, green, rather crisp, and often stuffed with pimientos or garlic cloves. Usually picked young; cured in lye, then brined for 6 months to a year. Can be delicious.

MOROCCAN Also called oil- or dry-cured. Shriveled, shiny, and jet black. Picked ripe, then cured in oil or salt. These are an excellent staple, as they keep forever and can be plumped up by marinating in oil.

NIÇOISE From Nice, France. Dark red or brown, small, with a slightly sour flavor. Picked ripe, then cured in saltwater. Flavorful, but a lot of pit for a small bite.

PICHOLINE From France. Green, almond-shaped, and crisp. Picked green, then cured in saltwater or lime and wood ashes, finally brined, sometimes with citric acid to give them a tart flavor. Delicious.

PREPARING Remove the pit by slicing the flesh lengthwise and digging it out with your fingers, or crush with the side of a knife and pick out the pit, or use a pitter. It's also acceptable to leave the pit in; just be sure to warn your guests. If you like, you can reduce the saltiness by rinsing or soaking in water for 20 minutes or so or boiling for 30 seconds.

OTHER VEGETABLES YOU CAN USE caper berries, capers

Sautéed Olives

MAKES: 6 to 8 servings | **TIME:** 10 minutes

A quick and straightforward sauce, topping, appetizer, or side dish with loads of flavor. Olives don't need cooking, of course, but it makes them memorable.

- 3 tablespoons olive oil
- 2 cloves garlic, smashed
- 1 pound olives (preferably a combination of black and green), rinsed and pitted
- 2 sprigs fresh rosemary or marjoram or 4 sprigs fresh thyme
- 1 tablespoon red wine vinegar
  Salt and pepper

Put the oil in a large skillet over medium heat. When it is hot, add the garlic and cook for a minute. Add the olives and rosemary and cook, stirring occasionally, until fragrant and heated through, 4 to 5 minutes. Sprinkle with the vinegar and pepper; taste and adjust the seasoning. Serve hot, warm, or at room temperature.

SAUTÉED TOMATOES WITH OLIVES Just after adding the garlic, add 3 cups chopped tomatoes (canned is fine; drain first). Cook, stirring occasionally, until the tomato breaks up and the mixture comes together and thickens, about 10 minutes. Add the olives and rosemary and proceed with the recipe.

SAUTÉED OLIVES WITH CROUTONS Add 2 cups diced day-old bread and another tablespoon olive oil to the pan along with the garlic and cook, stirring often, until the bread browns and crisps, about 5 minutes. Proceed with the recipe.

ONIONS

YELLOW (SPANISH), WHITE, AND RED ONIONS, PEARL ONIONS, SCALLIONS (GREEN ONIONS), AND CIPOLLINE

After garlic, I count onions as the most useful and versatile vegetable, and one you probably always keep handy. The flavor and texture changes so much as they go from raw through the various stages of cooking, it's almost like they're multiple vegetables.

Cooking Onions

TIME	WHAT TO EXPECT
20 minutes	Ivory; softened; still oniony tasting
25 to 30 minutes	Golden; wilted; sweet, with a slight onion sharpness
40 to 45 minutes	Browned; starting to melt; onion flavor replaced with sweetness
60 minutes	Color of maple syrup; jamlike texture and flavor

PREPARING If you have a lot of onions to peel, drop them into boiling water for 30 seconds to 1 minute, drain, and rinse in cold water. See the illustrations for slicing and chopping onions below.

A properly sharpened knife also mitigates the amount of tear-inducing chemical released into the air. This substance, called lachrymator, combines with the moisture in your eyes to form a weak solution of sulfuric acid. No wonder it burns!

Leave the root end on onions you will cook whole; they'll stay together better.

Chopping Onions

STEP 1 Cut off both ends of the onion.

STEP 2 Make a small slit in the skin, just one layer down.

STEP 3 The skin will come off easily, along with the outer layer of flesh.

STEP 4 Cut the onion in half.

STEP 5 Make two or three cuts into the onion, parallel to the cutting board; don't cut all the way through.

F fast   **M** make ahead   **V** vegetarian

BEST COOKING METHODS caramelizing, roasting, grilling

WHEN ARE THEY DONE? The texture softens dramatically and the color darkens the longer they cook.

OTHER VEGETABLES YOU CAN USE shallots, and leeks and scallions in many cases

Caramelized Onions

MAKES: 4 servings | **TIME:** 25 to 60 minutes

"Cook until it's done" has never been a more accurate direction. You want a deeply colored "jam" that doesn't look—or taste—anything like the raw vegetable, but the time it takes to get there isn't fixed. Let the chart on the previous page provide some guidelines. Slicing the onions as thin as you can manage helps speed up the process. And you might as well make as much as your pan will hold; caramelized onions will keep for at least a week in the fridge.

Other vegetables you can use: pearl or cipollini onions (keep them whole; trim, blanch, and shock them to make peeling easier; see page 238).

STEP 6 Now make several cuts down through the top. Again, leave the onion intact at one end.

STEP 7 Cut across the onion.

1½ to 2 pounds onions (6 to 8), halved and sliced or chopped (5 to 6 cups)
2 tablespoons olive oil or butter, plus more as needed
Salt and pepper

1. Put the onions in a large skillet over medium heat. Cover and cook, stirring occasionally, until the onions are dry and almost sticking to the pan, about 20 minutes.
2. Stir in the oil or butter and a large pinch salt and turn the heat down so the onions sizzle gently. Cook, stirring occasionally, until the onions are done as you like them, adding just enough oil or butter to keep them from sticking without getting greasy. The cooking time will vary depending on how you want them. Taste and adjust the seasoning. Serve hot or at room temperature. Or refrigerate in an airtight container in the refrigerator for up to a week.

CARAMELIZED ONIONS WITH BACON OR PANCETTA
Substitute 4 ounces chopped bacon or pancetta for the olive oil, adding when you would the oil.

SWEETER CARAMELIZED ONIONS Good with hot, sour, or well-seasoned dishes: In Step 2, add 1 to 2 tablespoons brown sugar with the oil or butter and salt. Proceed with the recipe, lowering the heat as necessary to prevent sticking and burning.

SWEET-AND-SOUR CARAMELIZED ONIONS In Step 2, add ½ cup white wine with the oil or butter and salt; boil for a minute, then add ½ cup water, 3 tablespoons red or white wine vinegar, a bay leaf, and 2 teaspoons sugar. Cook at a steady bubble until the onions are very tender and the liquid is reduced significantly, about 30 minutes. Sprinkle with salt and pepper, garnish with parsley, and serve hot or room temperature.

CARAMELIZED SHALLOTS Peel 1½ pounds shallots; keep them whole. In Step 2, add 1 cup water and 1 tablespoon sugar with the oil or butter and salt and bring to a boil. Adjust the heat so the liquid bubbles steadily. Cook until the shallots are golden and very tender and the liquid has reduced to a syrup, about 30 minutes total.

10 USES FOR CARAMELIZED ONIONS

1. Thicken, color, and add subtle sweetness to soups and sauces.
2. Garnish grilled meats, poultry, seafood, or other savory foods.
3. Fill omelets, sandwiches, and burritos.
4. Stir into dips and spreads, or use as a spread by itself.
5. Toss with pasta or add to pasta sauce.
6. Top pizza, bread, or rolls before baking.
7. Fold into bread doughs and batters.
8. Use to flavor meat loaf, meatballs, or burgers.
9. Make Pissaladière (page 820).
10. Toss with plain noodles, pasta, rice, or whole grains.

Creamed Onions

MAKES: 4 servings | **TIME:** 30 minutes

A decadent and sort of old-fashioned dish that doesn't make it to the table often enough. You can use the results as a gravy or sauce for Mashed Potatoes (page 329) or pool a big spoonful on a plate and serve Roast Chicken Parts with Olive Oil or Butter (page 615) or Roast Pork with Garlic and Rosemary (page 695) on top. It's also classic at Thanksgiving.

Other vegetables you can use: pearl or cippolini onions, whole shallots, garlic cloves (you'll need lots, or cut the recipe in half).

> **Salt and pepper**
> 6 **onions (about 1½ pounds), trimmed and peeled**

1 **cup cream**
2 **tablespoons butter**
Pinch freshly grated nutmeg (optional)

1. Bring a large pot of water to a boil and salt it. Cut the onions crosswise into thick slices; there's no need to separate them into rings. Plunge the onions into the boiling water and cook for about a minute; drain well.
2. Put the cream and butter in a large skillet over medium heat. Add the onions and bring to a boil; cook, stirring occasionally, until the onions have absorbed a lot of the cream and the sauce is thick, about 5 minutes. Add a tiny bit of nutmeg if you like and sprinkle with pepper. Taste, adjust the seasoning, and serve hot.

CREAMED SPINACH Instead of the onions, use 1½ pounds trimmed spinach. In Step 1, after draining the spinach, cool it a bit or shock (see page 238), then squeeze dry and chop it. Proceed with the recipe.

CREAMED CARDOONS Instead of the onions, start with 2 pounds cardoons. Trim and hold them according to the directions on page 258. Proceed with the recipe.

CREAMED WHOLE SCALLIONS Trim any roots and just a bit of the greens from 1½ pounds scallions. Cook in Step 1 until tender and silky, about 5 minutes. Proceed with the recipe.

PARSNIPS

A longtime favorite in Europe, it's a shame that they're not more popular here. Parsnips are sweeter than carrots, and their slightly grassy, earthy flavor also helps distinguish between the two. But the differences are subtle to be sure.

PREPARING Just treat them as you would carrots. If large (more than 1 inch thick at the broad end), it's best—though not essential—to remove the woody core: Cut the thinner portion off and set it aside. Cut the

thick portion in half and dig out the core with the end of a vegetable peeler, a paring knife, or a sharp spoon; the procedure is neither difficult nor time consuming (which doesn't mean I always do it!).

BEST COOKING METHODS steaming, braising, braising and glazing, roasting, puréeing

WHEN ARE THEY DONE? When tender enough to pierce easily with a skewer or thin-bladed knife, but not mushy

OTHER VEGETABLES YOU CAN USE carrots

PEAS

Peas, which are pulses in the legume family, come in a variety of forms: shell peas (green or English peas), snow peas (mange-touts), sugar snap peas. Some must be removed from their inedible pods; others are entirely edible (pods and all); and many can be shelled and dried to be eaten as beans (think black-eyed peas and chickpeas—see page 387).

PREPARING You'll almost always use frozen peas for shell peas. They'll thaw quickly so there's usually no need to thaw them first, but if you do, put what you need in a strainer and run under cold water. Open

the pods of fresh shell peas at the seam and run your finger down the inside to release the peas. For snow peas and sugar snap peas, pinch the flower end of the pod and pull the string down toward the other end to remove it.

BEST COOKING METHODS steaming, quick-braising in butter, stir-frying; adding to rice or risotto

WHEN ARE THEY DONE? When they're hot and bright green, usually less than 5 minutes. Frozen peas heat through in just a minute or 2.

OTHER VEGETABLES YOU CAN USE green or wax beans, asparagus, edamame

Anything-Scented Peas

MAKES: 4 servings | **TIME:** 20 minutes

Peas have a delicate flavor that can be enhanced with just a touch of another ingredient, though subtlety is the key. A pinch of sugar makes the flavor more intense, the way salt does for other vegetables.

Other vegetables you can use: snow peas or sugar snap peas (about 1½ pounds).

2	**tablespoons butter or olive oil**
1	**tablespoon any seasoning from the list that follows**
2	**cups peas (frozen are fine; thaw first and drain well)**
	Salt
	Pinch sugar (optional)

1. Put the butter or oil in a large skillet over medium heat. When the butter is melted or the oil is hot, add the seasoning and cook, stirring constantly, until fragrant, just a minute or so.

Stringing a Pod Pea

For snow peas and sugar snap peas, pinch the flower end of the pea pod and pull the string down toward the other end to remove it.

2. Add the peas and cook, swirling the pan a bit to coat them in the pan juices, until heated through and softened a bit, 2 to 3 minutes. Taste, sprinkle with salt and a bit of sugar if you like, and serve hot or at room temperature.

PEAS WITH BACON, LETTUCE, AND MINT Substitute 4 ounces chopped bacon for the butter or oil. Chop 1 small onion, enough romaine lettuce hearts to make 2 cups, and ½ cup chopped fresh mint. In Step 1, render the fat from the bacon; remove the cooked bacon from the pan with a slotted spoon and reserve it. Cook the onion in the fat until soft and translucent, about 3 minutes. Add the peas and lettuce and proceed with the recipe. Sprinkle with the reserved bacon and mint before serving.

---

15 FLAVOR POSSIBILITIES FOR ANYTHING-SCENTED PEAS

1. Grated lemon, orange, or tangerine zest
2. Chopped light herbs like mint, tarragon, parsley, basil, chives, or chervil
3. Grated fresh ginger or chopped candied ginger
4. Black or white sesame seeds
5. Minced garlic
6. Fermented black beans
7. Shredded coconut and/or coconut milk
8. Chopped shallot
9. White wine or sake
10. Any miso paste
11. Chopped flowers, like thyme, lavender, rose petals, or anise hyssop
12. Curry powder; start with ½ teaspoon
13. Chopped reconstituted dried mushrooms (see page 304)
15. Traditional Pesto (page 51) or any other herb purée

PEA SHOOTS

The tender shoots and leaves of the pea plant are a sure sign of spring, the vine's new growth. Vibrant green in color, with a taste between that of fresh peas and spinach.

PREPARING Rinse well; trim away any dried-out stems or yellowing leaves.

BEST COOKING METHODS stir-frying, sautéing; only super-tender ones are good eaten raw

WHEN ARE THEY DONE? When just wilted, no more; they're usually perfect in just a couple of minutes

OTHER VEGETABLES YOU CAN USE spinach, snow peas, sugar snap peas, green peas

PEPPERS AND CHILES

For loads of info about both sweet peppers and hot chiles, see "The Basics of Chiles and Peppers," beginning on page 39.

Roasted Red Peppers

MAKES: 4 to 8 servings | TIME: 20 to 60 minutes

I roast peppers of all colors, and a combination is absolutely gorgeous. Sometimes chiles even find their way into the mix. Since red, yellow, purple, and orange peppers are fully ripe, they're sweeter than green, which is the color of all immature peppers. Green peppers have their own distinctive, more herbaceous taste. The goal is to blacken the skin; it doesn't matter how you get there. Some people even do them one or two at a time over an open stovetop flame. The only real work is peeling. Don't let that stop you: Roasted peppers keep for at least a week in the fridge and you'll eat them on everything; see the list that follows.

8   red or other bell peppers
    Salt
    Olive oil for drizzling

1. Heat the oven to 450°F or turn on the broiler and put the rack about 4 inches below the heat. Put the peppers in a foil-lined roasting pan. Roast or broil, turning the peppers as each side cooks, until they have blackened in spots and collapsed, 15 or 20 minutes in the broiler, up to an hour in the oven.

2. Transfer the peppers to a heatproof bowl and cover with the foil from the pan, or just bundle them up in the foil. When they're cool enough to handle, remove the skin, seeds, and stems with your fingers or a small knife; do this under running water to make it a little easier if you like. Unless you need them whole for some reason, don't worry if the peppers fall apart.

3. Serve the peppers right away. Or store in an airtight container in the refrigerator for up to a few days; bring back to room temperature before serving. When you're ready to serve, sprinkle with a bit of salt and drizzle with lots of olive oil.

ROASTED RED PEPPERS ON THE GRILL Prepare a charcoal or gas grill medium direct cooking. When the fire is hot, put the peppers directly over the heat. Grill, turning as each side blackens, until they collapse, about 15 minutes. Pick up from Step 2.

---

10 THINGS TO DO WITH ROASTED RED PEPPERS

1. Toss with chopped fresh or mashed roasted garlic.
2. Splash with balsamic or sherry vinegar.
3. Sprinkle with lots of chopped fresh herbs like parsley, mint, basil, or chervil or a little bit of oregano, thyme, or rosemary.
4. Sprinkle with grated Parmesan, Asiago, pecorino Romano, or Manchego cheese.
5. Use to fill sandwiches or top bruschetta, pizza, and salads.
6. Scramble with eggs.
7. Chop or purée to make a sauce or spread or to mix with other sauces, dressings, dips, and spreads.
8. Coarsely chop and use to flavor meat loaf, meatballs, or burgers.
9. Toss with sautéed onions and serve with grilled sausages.
10. Pulse in a food processor with garlic, nuts, and herbs to make a new spin on pesto. (With almonds and parsley, this is called romesco sauce.)

Chiles Rellenos

MAKES: 4 servings | **TIME:** 1 hour

The classic Mexican stuffed chile: The crisp coating is light, the chiles soft and yielding, and the cheese oozing. If time is an issue, make the chiles through Step 1, cover, and refrigerate until you're ready to batter and cook them.

4	large or 8 small poblano or other mild green fresh chiles
3	cups grated or shredded Chihuahua or Monterey Jack cheese
2	egg whites
½	cup all-purpose flour
½	teaspoon salt
1	cup beer or water
	Good-quality vegetable oil for deep-frying
	Green Enchilada Sauce or any other variation of Salsa Verde (page 73)
	Crumbled queso fresco for garnish

Chiles Rellenos

It helps to skewer the chiles closed after stuffing; break a wooden skewer in half if necessary.

1. Roast the chiles as directed on page 318; peel but leave the stems on. Cut a slit in one side and remove the seeds. Stuff the chiles with the grated cheese; use toothpicks or a long bamboo skewer to "sew" them shut; set aside.

2. Whip the egg whites until they hold soft peaks (see page 852). Whisk the flour, salt, and beer together in a medium bowl. It should have the consistency of thin pancake batter; adjust with more flour or beer as necessary. Gently fold the egg whites into the batter; some white streaks remaining are okay.

3. Put at least 3 inches oil in a large pot over medium-high heat; bring to 365°F (see "Deep-Frying," page 22). Line a baking sheet with towels.

4. Working in batches if necessary, carefully dip the stuffed chiles in the batter to coat and fry until crisp and golden brown on all sides, turning and rotating them once or twice, 3 to 5 minutes. Remove the chiles with a skimmer or slotted spoon; as they finish transfer to the towels to drain. Remove the picks or skewers and serve right away with the sauce, sprinkled with queso fresco.

GRILLED CHILES RELLENOS Omit the eggs, flour and beer. Prepare a charcoal or gas grill for medium direct cooking. Skip the roasting in Step 1. Cut a slit in one side of each chile, remove the seeds, and stuff. Brush with olive oil and grill, turning once or twice, until the skins are blistered and the flesh is tender. Serve right away; if anyone wants to remove the skins they can.

CHILES RELLENOS WITH MEAT OR POULTRY STUFFING
Substitute 1½ cups cooked ground beef, pork, or turkey for 1½ cups of the grated cheese; season as you like with salt, pepper, and a little chili powder (to make your own, see page 32). Or use chopped Spicy Braised Pork with Vietnamese Flavors (page 700), Braised Beef Brisket (page 684), shredded Simplest Whole Roast Chicken (page 633), or Shredded Pork (page 697).

CHILES RELLENOS WITH CORN AND PUMPKIN SEEDS
Substitute ¾ cup each fresh or frozen corn kernels and pumpkin seeds (pepitas) for 1½ cups of the grated cheese. Proceed with the recipe.

My Mom's Pan-Cooked Peppers and Onions

MAKES: 4 servings | **TIME:** 40 minutes

When I was growing up, once a week my mother would make us sandwiches of sautéed green peppers

Preparing Peppers

STEP 1 To core a pepper, first cut around the stem.

STEP 2 Then pull out the core; rinse to remove any remaining seeds.

STEP 3 Alternatively, cut the pepper in half, break out the core, and scrape out the seeds.

 fast make ahead **V** vegetarian

and onions, loads of each. Red Peppers are a sweeter option and its even better with mushrooms and herbs. For classic sausage, peppers, and onions, see page 704.

Other vegetables you can use: about 8 ounces any fresh chiles, mostly mild with a few hot.

- 4 tablespoons olive oil, butter, or a combination
- 2 or 3 bell or other sweet peppers (about 1 pound), cored, seeded, and cut into strips
- 2 medium-to-large onions, halved and sliced
- 1 cup trimmed and sliced shiitake or button mushrooms
  Salt and pepper
- 1 teaspoon fresh thyme or marjoram, or any fresh herb to taste plus more for garnish (optional)

1. Put the oil or butter in a large skillet over medium heat. When the oil is hot or the butter foams, add the peppers, onions, and mushrooms. Sprinkle with salt and pepper, stir in the thyme if you're using it, and cook, stirring occasionally and adjusting the heat so the vegetables cook without browning (at least not much), until very tender, at least 20 minutes.

2. Taste and adjust the seasoning. Garnish with more thyme if you like, and serve as a side dish or piled into rolls or baguettes.

PAN-COOKED PEPPERS WITH VINEGAR Excellent with Italian long peppers: Add a couple of tablespoons balsamic or good-quality red or white wine vinegar in the last couple minutes of cooking.

PAN-COOKED PEPPERS WITH PAPRIKA Substitute chopped tomato for the mushrooms. Omit the herbs if you prefer. Start cooking just the onions; sprinkle with 2 tablespoons paprika or 1 tablespoon smoked paprika; cover and cook for 5 minutes. Then add the peppers; cover and cook for another 5 minutes. Finally, add the tomato and cook for another 5 minutes.

Sprinkle with fresh lemon juice and serve hot or at room temperature.

PLANTAINS

The versatile plantain is a type of banana used much like a potato when starchy and green or as a sweet side dish when fully ripe and black. Unlike our familiar breakfast fruit, they are always cooked.

PREPARING Plantains require a special peeling technique. Begin by cutting off both tips of the fruit; then cut the plantain crosswise into several sections, unless the recipe directs otherwise. Make three vertical slits in the skin of each section, then peel off each piece of the skin (see page 323). Trim any remaining skin from the plantain with a paring knife.

BEST COOKING METHODS sautéing, pan-frying, deep-frying (green plantains); sautéing, braising, stewing, roasting, grilling (black ripe plantains)

WHEN ARE THEY DONE? When golden brown and slightly tender (green plantains); when caramelized and very soft (ripe plantains)

OTHER VEGETABLES OR FRUITS YOU CAN USE potato, yucca, boniato, taro, sweet potato, yam, green to green-yellow bananas, as long as they're not too ripe (for starchy green plantains); ripe bananas (for ripe plantains)

Sautéed Ripe Plantains

MAKES: 4 servings | **TIME:** 20 minutes

Sweet but appropriate as a side dish for simply grilled or roasted meat, poultry, or fish—and perfect with Baked Black Beans and Rice (page 410).

Other vegetables you can use: just-ripe bananas (yellow but with only a few black spots).

3 or 4 yellow-black or black plantains, peeled
2 tablespoons good-quality vegetable oil
   Salt and pepper
   Lime wedges

Cut the plantains into about 1-inch pieces. Put the oil in a large skillet over medium heat. When it is hot, add the plantains. Cook, turning as necessary and adjusting the heat so the plantains brown slowly without burning. Be especially careful as they near doneness; there is so much sugar in the plantains that they burn easily. (You may need to add a little more oil to keep them from sticking.) This will take 10 to 15 minutes. Serve hot or warm, sprinkled with salt, pepper, and lime juice.

GARLICKY SAUTÉED RIPE PLANTAINS When the plantains are almost as brown as you want them, add 2 tablespoons minced garlic and stir.

Fried Plantains

MAKES: 4 servings | **TIME:** 30 minutes

To me, these—commonly called tostones—need nothing more than salt and maybe a little lime juice, but

some people like them with hot sauce, Chile Paste (page 40), Fresh Tomato or Fruit Salsa (page 55), or another salsa.

2 green-to-yellow plantains or green bananas, peeled
   Good-quality vegetable oil for pan-frying
   Salt
   Lime wedges

1. Cut the plantains into ½-inch rounds. Cover the bottom of a large skillet with oil and turn the heat to medium. When the oil is hot, add the slices (you'll probably be able to do this in one batch) and sprinkle with salt. Brown lightly, then turn and brown the other side. Transfer to a plate as they finish. (At this point, you can set the plantains aside for an hour or two before proceeding with the recipe.)

2. When the plantain rounds have cooled a bit, put a few between two pieces of wax paper and pound with the side of your fist or the palm of your hand until they spread out and just about double in diameter. They will look squashed and might split a little around the edges, which is right. Repeat until they're all flattened. (At this point, you can set the plantains aside for another hour or two.)

Preparing Plantains

STEP 1 First, cut off and discard both ends.

STEP 2 Cut the plantain into several chunks.

STEP 3 Make three shallow vertical slits in each chunk.

STEP 4 Remove the peel in pieces. If any bits of peel cling to the flesh, remove them with a paring knife.

Fried Plantains, page 323

3. Line a platter with towels. Add more oil to the skillet to cover the bottom, turn the heat to medium, and again, brown the rounds on each side; this time you'll probably have to cook in batches. As they finish, transfer to the towels to drain. Sprinkle with salt and serve hot or warm with lime wedges.

POTATOES

All potatoes fall into one of three basic categories: starchy, waxy, or all-purpose.

STARCHY POTATOES These cook to a dry, fluffy, mealy texture that's ideal for baked, fried, and mashed potatoes, but not boiled—unless you want to exploit their crumbly quality in stews and soups, where their starch thickens and adds body. Russet potatoes, which include Idaho but are also grown elsewhere, are the archetypal starchy potato and are often called baking potatoes. They are large and oval-shaped with sandy-feeling, brown skin and off-white flesh.

WAXY POTATOES Sometimes called new or boiling potatoes, have a low starch content; their texture is moister, creamier, and firmer. They are typified by their smooth, thin skin, which may be a rosy-red or yellowish-white color, depending on variety. They hold their shape well during cooking and are ideal for boiling, steaming, and roasting.

ALL-PURPOSE POTATOES In between starchy and waxy potatoes. They're good mashed, fried, and baked, whenever you want potatoes with some fluffiness that don't fall apart easily; they contain too much starch to make them ideal for boiling. Yukon Gold potatoes are the classic all-purpose potato.

PREPARING Rinse. Peel if you like. Remove any eyes, dark spots, or greening. If the potato is largely green or has rot, discard it.

BEST COOKING METHODS baking, frying, mashing (starchy); boiling, steaming, roasting (waxy); frying, baking, mashing (all-purpose)

WHEN ARE THEY DONE? When a skewer or thin-bladed knife inserted into one meets almost no resistance

---

Using Potatoes in Recipes

It helps to know what type of potato works best in various recipes. Often it's a matter of preference: If you like the mealy and crumbly texture of starchy potatoes in potato salad, or the moist and creamy texture of mashed potatoes made from waxy potatoes, then go for it.

STARCHY POTATOES

- Potato and Leek Soup (page 138)
- Baked Potatoes (below)
- Mashed Potatoes (page 329)
- Scalloped Potatoes (page 256)
- French Fries (page 333)

WAXY POTATOES

- Potato and Leek Soup (page 138)
- Potato Salad with Mustard Vinaigrette (page 207)
- Boiled Potatoes or Steamed Potatoes (pages 326 and 327)
- Crisp Pan-Fried Potatoes (page 331)
- Oven-Roasted Potatoes (page 329)
- Scalloped Potatoes (page 256)

ALL-PURPOSE POTATOES

- Potato and Leek Soup (page 138)
- Potato Salad with Mustard Vinaigrette (page 207)
- Boiled Potatoes or Steamed Potatoes (pages 326 and 327)
- Potato Rösti (page 332)
- Scalloped Potatoes (page 256)

OTHER VEGETABLES YOU CAN USE sweet potato, taro, cassava, boniato, green plantains, or malanga

Baked Potatoes

MAKES: 4 servings | **TIME:** About 1 hour

Dry, fluffy, and wonderfully mealy baked potatoes are easy. Forget about wrapping them in foil or using the

microwave, because both techniques basically steam the potatoes and the results are inferior.

Other vegetables you can use: any whole root vegetable like rutabaga, turnip, or beet; large ones will take much longer. Though none will be as starchy and fluffy as potatoes they'll still be delicious.

    4 large starchy potatoes
       Salt and pepper

1. Heat the oven to 425°F. Scrub the potatoes well, especially if you plan to eat the skins. Use a skewer or thin-bladed knife to poke a hole or two in each potato.

2. Put the potatoes in the oven, right on the rack if you like or on a rimmed baking sheet. Bake until a skewer or thin-bladed knife inserted into one meets almost no resistance. You can turn them once during baking, though it's not necessary. Start checking after 45 minutes.

3. The potatoes will stay hot for a few minutes. To serve, cut a slit lengthwise into each about halfway into the flesh and pinch the ends toward the middle to fluff. Sprinkle with salt and pepper, then top however you like (see the list at right for some ideas). Or just serve plain.

SALTED BAKED POTATOES After scrubbing, dry well and rub each potato with about a teaspoon olive oil or butter. Rub each all over with a couple tablespoons salt. Bake on a rimmed baking sheet.

BAY- OR ROSEMARY-SCENTED BAKED POTATOES After scrubbing the potatoes, cut a deep slit lengthwise into each and rub all over the outside (and as much of the inside as you can) with salt and pepper . Put a couple of bay leaves or a sprig of fresh rosemary in each slit and drizzle with olive oil, then close them up and set them on a baking sheet. Smear some olive oil all over the skins and sprinkle with more salt and pepper. Bake as directed.

16 TOPPINGS FOR BAKED POTATOES

1. The classic: butter, sour cream, and/or chopped chives

2. Crumbled cooked bacon, sausage, or chorizo

3. Cottage cheese

4. A few dashes hot sauce

5. Ketchup

6. Worcestershire sauce

7. Goat cheese or cream cheese

8. Grated cheese like cheddar, Parmesan, Asiago, or Jack

9. Whipped cream (unsweetened and lightly salted or seasoned)

10. Olive oil or Flavored Oil (page 53)

11. Soy sauce or Soy Dipping Sauce and Marinade (page 64)

12. Aioli or other flavored mayonnaise (pages 70)

13. Any cooked salsa (pages 71–74), raw salsa (pages 55–58), or chutney (pages 61–64)

14. Barbecue sauce (to make your own, see page 74)

15. Any Vinaigrette (page 188) or variation, especially Mustard Vinaigrette

16. Any filling from "Building Hot Sandwiches" (page 810)

Boiled Potatoes

MAKES: 4 servings | TIME: About 30 minutes

You can boil or steam waxy and all-purpose potatoes, with wildly different results; see the descriptions on page 325. Peeling and/or cutting potatoes before boiling or steaming obviously speeds things up, but they can get a bit waterlogged—a tad less when steamed, but still.

    2 pounds waxy or all-purpose potatoes
       Salt

  **F** fast   **M** make ahead   **V** vegetarian

1. Peel the potatoes before cooking, if you like. If you're in a hurry, halve or quarter larger potatoes. Whether cut or whole, the idea is to have all the pieces about the same size. Put them in a large pot and cover with cold water. Add a large pinch salt and bring to a boil.

2. Keep the water rolling until the potatoes are done, anywhere from 15 to 30 minutes, depending on the size of the pieces and how tender you want them. They are done when a skewer or thin-bladed knife pierces one with almost no resistance.

3. Drain the potatoes well and let them dry out a bit. If peeling, give them an extra few minutes to cool enough to handle. See "The Many Ways to Flavor Mashed Potatoes" on page 330 for serving ideas; simply toss the ingredients with the warm potatoes. Or refrigerate, tightly covered, for up to 3 days. Reheat in the microwave or use in any recipe that calls for cooked potatoes.

STEAMED POTATOES These don't get waterlogged, and they retain more nutrients: Rig a steamer in a large pot (see page 20) with about an inch or so of water. Put the potatoes in the steamer. Sprinkle with a little salt if you like. Bring the water to a boil and steam for 15 to 30 minutes. Check the pot occasionally to make sure there is still water in the bottom.

Twice-Baked Potatoes

Bake the potatoes as on page 326. Let them cool a bit, cut in half lengthwise, and scoop the flesh into a large bowl, leaving the skins intact as a shell. Mash the flesh, adding other ingredients to jazz them up (see the list below), then pile the works back into the skins. Put them on a rimmed baking sheet and pop them back into a 400°F oven; most will take only 20 to 30 minutes to reheat. (Or you can put them in an airtight container and refrigerate them for up to a few hours first if you like.)

15 FILLINGS FOR TWICE-BAKED POTATOES

Mix and match as you like. Figure a total of up to ½ cup extra ingredients for each large potato; they won't hold much more.

1. Chopped fresh herbs (great with a little olive oil, butter, or sour cream)
2. Chopped olives, red chile flakes, chopped parsley, and olive oil
3. Grated hard cheese or mashed soft cheese like Brie, goat cheese, or cream cheese
4. Crumbled cooked bacon or sausage
5. Puréed or chopped cooked vegetables like eggplant, carrots, broccoli, or spinach, with lots of butter or olive oil
6. Any spice mixture (pages 27–35) or Chile Paste (page 40); best with a little butter, flavorful oil, or dairy or nondairy milk
7. Chopped shrimp with any pesto or herb purée (pages 51–52)
8. Any pesto or herb purée (pages 51–52)
9. Any chutney (pages 61–64)
10. Cold Mustard Sauce (page 70)
11. Salsa Roja (page 71)
12. Compound Butter (page 78)
13. Hollandaise Sauce (page 80)
14. Coconut milk (to make your own, see page 372) and curry powder, garam masala, or chaat masala (to make your own, see pages 32 and 34)
15. Fast Tomato Sauce (page 478)

Mashed Potatoes, opposite, and
Mashed Sweet Potatoes, page 344

Mashed Potatoes

MAKES: 4 servings | **TIME:** About 40 minutes

Ⓜ Ⓥ

Starchy potatoes make the fluffiest mash, but Yukon Gold or other all-purpose potatoes turn out well too, just with a little more body. If you like mashed potatoes with the peel, make sure you scrub them well before cooking. You have a few options for mashing tools; just keep the potatoes away from mixers, food processors, or blenders, which make them gummy.

Other keys to keeping mashed potatoes fluffy: Cook them whole, if possible; cook them with the peel on if possible (the peels will slip off easily after cooking—or you can include them, of course); refrain from poking them as they boil. All of these reduce the tendency of the spuds to absorb water, which makes them heavier.

Other vegetables you can use: any vegetable can be mashed (see "10 More Vegetable Purées," page 241); and sweet potatoes for sure.

- 2 **pounds starchy or all-purpose potatoes**
- 1 **cup milk, plus more if needed**
- 4 **tablespoons (½ stick) butter**
  Salt and pepper

1. Boil the potatoes according to the recipe on page 326. (The potatoes can be prepared to this point up to an hour in advance; leave them in a colander to drain and dry out a bit.)

2. While the potatoes are draining, wipe the pot dry and put it back on the stove over medium-low heat. Add the milk and butter and sprinkle with salt and pepper.

3. When the butter is almost melted, remove the pot from the heat. Peel the potatoes if you like and cut them into chunks if they're whole. For lumpy mashed potatoes, add them directly to the milk and mash with a fork or potato masher. For a super-light and puréed mash, rice the potatoes or run them through a food mill set over the pot. Return the pot to the heat and stir constantly with a wooden spoon to reach the desired consistency, adding more milk if necessary. Taste, adjust the seasoning, and serve right away.

MASHED BAKED POTATOES The drier texture means they'll soak up more milk and butter: Bake potatoes according to the recipe on page 325. Peel or not. Cut into cubes. Proceed with the recipe from Step 2, adding more milk and butter if you like.

"SMASHED" POTATOES Omit the milk. In Step 3, add the potatoes directly to the melted butter in the pan and mash with a fork or masher just enough to break them up a bit, leaving lots of lumps. Stir a few times, adding more butter if you like.

GARLICKY MASHED POTATOES Peel the cloves from 1 or 2 heads garlic—or even 3 if you're a fanatic—and boil them with the potatoes. If you want an stronger garlic flavor, add a teaspoon or up to a tablespoon minced garlic to the milk and butter.

BUTTERMILK MASHED POTATOES Tangy and fresh tasting: Instead of milk, use buttermilk.

JOËL ROBUCHON MASHED POTATOES In honor of one of the most famous French chefs, make this decadently buttery version at least once. Reduce the milk to ¼ cup; increase the butter to 1 pound (4 sticks), cut it into cubes, and refrigerate it until firm. In Step 2 don't add the milk and butter to the pot; pick up the recipe in Step 3 when you prepare the potatoes. Add them to the pot and mash and stir, adding in cubes of cold butter 1 at a time. When the butter is incorporated, add the milk and season with salt and pepper.

Oven-Roasted Potatoes

MAKES: 4 servings | **TIME:** About 1 hour

You can use any kind of potato in this recipe, with slightly different but always desirable results. Waxy

The Many Ways to Flavor Mashed Potatoes

Why stop at milk and butter? Mashed potatoes—or any plain-cooked potato, for that matter—provide a blank slate for all sorts of additions. Some you simply stir into the finished mash, while others require incorporating seasonings earlier in the process. You can mix and match as you like, but be careful not to fuse too many strong flavors.

Add to the butter as it melts in Step 2. Cook the aromatics for several minutes to soften them before adding the potatoes; heat the spices until fragrant, about a minute:

- Minced onion: up to ½ cup any kind
- Minced shallots: up to ¼ cup
- Minced garlic: 2 or more teaspoons, up to 2 tablespoons
- Roasted Garlic (page 294): 1 or more heads, peeled and mashed
- Minced or grated fresh ginger: 1 to 2 tablespoons
- Minced fresh chile (like jalapeño or Thai), or red chile flakes or cayenne, to taste
- Curry powder (to make your own, see page 32): 1 tablespoon or more
- Other spice mixture (to make your own, see pages 27–35): 1 to 2 tablespoons practically any kind
- Horseradish or wasabi, grated fresh or prepared: 2 tablespoons or more, to taste
- Chile Paste (page 40), to taste

Stir into the mashed potatoes as they heat (Step 3); reduce the milk to ½ cup (you can always add more later):

- Minced fresh light herbs like parsley, mint, chives, basil, or cilantro: up to 1 cup
- Grated cheese, virtually any that will melt, like Parmesan, Gruyère, cheddar, Jack, or Gouda: up to 1 cup
- Fresh goat cheese: up to 1 cup
- Cream cheese: up to 1 cup
- Sour cream: up to 1 cup
- Traditional Pesto or any herb purée (pages 51–52): up to 1 cup
- Miso: up to ½ cup any kind
- Chopped nuts: up to ½ cup any kind
- Chopped pitted olives: up to ½ cup

- Soy sauce: up to ¼ cup
- Ketchup (sounds crazy but it's delicious): about ½ cup
- Dijon or coarse-ground mustard: up to ¼ cup
- Crumbled cooked bacon or sausage: up to 1 cup any kind

Use to top mashed potatoes at the table:

- Any Five-Minute Drizzle Sauce (page 81)
- A dollop of sour cream and a sprinkle of chopped chives or other fresh herbs
- A drizzle of Flavored Oil (page 53)
- A ladleful of any Reduction Sauce (page 81)
- Creamed Onions (page 316) or any of the variations

8 OTHER VEGETABLES TO MASH ALONG WITH POTATOES

Replace up to half of the potatoes with any of the following vegetables. Add them to the potatoes while they boil, if you like, or cook them separately (roasted vegetables are especially nice) and mash them in later.

1. Cabbage or kale, cut into ribbons or chopped
2. Brussels sprouts, quartered
3. Celery root, turnips, or rutabagas, peeled and chopped
4. Carrots or parsnips, peeled and sliced or chopped
5. Peas (frozen are fine; no need to thaw them first), added to the butter and milk in Step 2
6. Winter squash like butternut or pumpkin, peeled, seeded, and chopped
7. Beets, peeled and chopped (they'll turn the mash fuchsia but taste delicious)
8. Cauliflower or broccoli florets, chopped

potatoes will form a crisp brown crust, and as long as you cook them long enough, a creamy interior; starchy varieties will darken more easily and turn very, very soft, without crisping as much. All-purpose potatoes crisp a little more but don't get very dark. Wait to add any additional seasonings—like chopped garlic or fresh herbs or ground spices—until the last time you turn them in Step 3.

Other vegetables you can use: any root vegetable, winter squash, tropical tuber.

> 2 tablespoons olive oil or melted butter,
>   plus more for the pan
> 2 pounds potatoes
>   Salt and pepper

1. Heat the oven to 400°F. Use a rimmed baking sheet big enough to hold all the potatoes in a single layer without overcrowding, or use two. Smear the pan with a thin layer of oil.

2. Scrub the potatoes; peel them if you like. Make sure they're fairly dry, and cut them into chunks of equal size, anywhere from 1 to 2 inches. Put them in the pan, drizzle with the oil, and toss gently to coat. Sprinkle with salt and pepper.

3. Roast undisturbed for 20 minutes before checking for the first time. If the potatoes release easily from the pan, stir them or turn the pieces over with tongs. If they look too dry and are sticking, drizzle with a little more oil and toss. Continue roasting, turning every 10 minutes or so, until crisp on the outside and tender inside, another 20 to 40 minutes, depending on the type of potato and how large the chunks are. The potatoes are done when a skewer or thin-bladed knife inserted into one meets almost no resistance.

4. Taste and adjust the seasoning. Serve hot, warm, or at room temperature.

OVEN-ROASTED "FRIES" Not as crisp as French Fries (page 333): Heat the oven and rinse the potatoes as in Steps 1 and 2. Peel the potatoes or not, then cut them into French fry–style sticks. Grease two baking sheets

or line them with parchment paper. Brush the potatoes with the oil and spread out on the baking sheets without crowding. Proceed with the recipe.

OVEN-ROASTED HASH BROWNS Increase the oil to 3 tablespoons. Heat the oven and rinse the potatoes as in Steps 1 and 2. Peel the potatoes, then grate them on the largest holes of a box grater or in a food processor with a shredding disk. Proceed with the recipe, resisting the urge to mess with the potatoes. Instead, when they're crisp on the bottom and tender on top, use a spatula to turn large portions and press them down a bit like diner hash browns; return them to the oven to crisp on the other side.

Crisp Pan-Fried Potatoes

MAKES: 4 servings | **TIME:** About 45 minutes

This technique delivers restaurant-style breakfast potatoes or "home fries," but you need waxy potatoes—the starchy kind will fall apart before they get crisp. And patience. If you're short on time, make the first variation.

Other vegetables you can use: beets, rutabagas, parsnips, carrots, though they won't get quite as crisp.

> 2 pounds waxy potatoes
> ¼ cup olive oil, good-quality vegetable oil;
>   or half butter, half oil; plus more if needed
>   Salt and pepper

1. Scrub the potatoes, and peel if you like. Cut them into 1-inch chunks. Put the oil in a large skillet, preferably nonstick or cast iron, over medium heat. When the oil is hot, add the potatoes. Cook, undisturbed, until they begin to brown around the edges and release from the pan, about 10 minutes.

2. Continue cooking, turning to brown all the sides without stirring too often. (This is the part that takes patience.) Add more oil if needed to prevent the potatoes from sticking. Adjust the heat so the potatoes sizzle gently without burning. They'll take up to 20 minutes more to cook.

3. When the potatoes are tender and golden, turn the heat up a bit to crisp them up. Sprinkle with salt and pepper and toss to coat. Taste and adjust the seasoning. Serve hot or at room temperature.

LAST-MINUTE CRISP PAN-FRIED POTATOES These are make-ahead and take less oil to cook; you can also make them from leftover boiled, steamed, or baked potatoes (pages 326, 327, and 325): After cutting the potatoes, boil them in salted water to cover until tender, 10 to 15 minutes. Drain, cool, cover, and refrigerate for up to 2 days. In Step 2, cook the potatoes over medium-high heat in 2 tablespoons of oil instead of ¼ cup. Proceed with the recipe, watching the potatoes more closely. They will crisp and turn brown in about half the time.

CRISP PAN-FRIED POTATOES, SPANISH STYLE (PATATAS BRAVAS) When the potatoes are ready, remove the skillet from the heat, sprinkle with 1 teaspoon smoked paprika and toss to coat. Serve the finished potatoes with a drizzle of Aioli (page 70) and hot sauce on the side.

Potato Rösti

MAKES: 4 servings | TIME: 20 minutes

A simple skillet cake is perhaps the quickest way to get potatoes on the table, even if you factor in the flipping technique.

Other vegetables you can use: beets or any other root vegetable; any winter squash.

- 2 **pounds all-purpose potatoes**
  Salt and pepper
- 2 **tablespoons olive oil or butter, plus more as needed**

1. Scrub the potatoes; peel them if you like. Grate or shred them in a food processor or by hand on a box grater. Drain in a colander or strainer, tossing and squeezing with a towel to extract as much water as possible. Transfer the potatoes to a bowl, sprinkle with plenty of salt and pepper, and toss to mix thoroughly.

2. Heat a large skillet, preferably nonstick or cast iron, over medium heat. Put the oil or butter in the skillet and heat until the oil is hot or the butter begins to brown. Spread the potatoes in the skillet in a nice circle, and press down with a spatula. Adjust the heat so the potatoes sizzle without burning and cook, shaking the pan occasionally, until the bottom of the potato cake is nicely crisp, 6 to 8 minutes.

3. Slide the cake out onto a plate, top with another plate, and invert the plates. Add a little more oil or butter to the pan and slide the cake back in (see the illustration below). Continue to cook, adjusting the heat if necessary, until the second side is browned, 5 to 10 minutes. Cut into wedges and serve hot or at room temperature.

LATKES Small patties are traditional, but if you're short on time, make one big pancake: Use starchy

Turning Potato Rösti or Any Large Vegetable Pancake

STEP 1 To turn this or any large pancake, slide the half-cooked cake onto a plate.

STEP 2 Cover with another plate, invert, and slide back into the pan.

potatoes, leave the skins of if you'd like, and grate 1 onion along with them. At the end of Step 1, mix in 2 lightly beaten eggs and 2 tablespoons plain bread crumbs or matzo meal. Use a good-quality vegetable oil for cooking. Proceed with the recipe, forming pancakes by spooning the batter into the hot oil or butter and adding more fat as necessary. Turn each pancake individually.

POTATO PANCAKES WITH SCALLIONS AND KIMCHI

At the end of Step 1, mix in 2 chopped scallions, ½ cup drained and chopped Shortcut Kimchi (page 229), and 1 egg. Proceed with the recipe, making one big pancake or whatever size you like. Serve with Soy Dipping Sauce and Marinade (page 64).

8 GARNISHES FOR POTATO RÖSTI OR LATKES

1. Sour cream or crème fraîche
2. Chopped chives or other fresh herbs like parsley, mint, dill, or chervil
3. Traditional Pesto or other herb purée (pages 51–52)
4. Any flavored mayonnaise (to make your own, see page 70)
5. Salsa Roja (page 71) or Salsa Verde (page 73)
6. Real Ranch Dressing (page 71)—outrageous, but excellent
7. Caramelized Onions (page 315) or any of the variations
8. Applesauce (to make your own, see page 364)

French Fries

MAKES: 4 servings | **TIME:** 30 minutes

You better double-fry French fries, or just don't bother. The fries will not only stay crisp longer, but the first step can be done well in advance, leaving you only a quick final fry right before serving. And that takes a lot of stress out of the recipe. Starchy potatoes are the only option here; waxy potatoes never quite crisp up right.

Other vegetables you can use: sweet potatoes, parsnips, celery root.

    2 pounds starchy potatoes
       Good-quality vegetable oil for deep-frying
       Salt and pepper

1. Scrub the potatoes; peel them if you like. Cut them any way you like—from shoestrings to big sticks—and dry them thoroughly.
2. Put at least 3 inches oil in a large pot on the stove and turn the heat to medium-high; heat to 300° to 325°F (see " Deep-Frying," page 22). Line a rimmed baking sheet with towels or fit it with a wire rack.
3. Fry the potatoes in batches, stirring occasionally and adjusting the temperature as necessary, until just tender and beginning to color slightly, 5 to 10 minutes, depending on the cut. Drain on the towels or wire rack. (At this point, you can set the potatoes aside for an hour or so before proceeding. Be sure to take the oil off the heat.)
4. Heat the oil again, this time to 350°F. Fry and drain the potatoes the same way, working in batches this time, until crisp and deeply colored, just a couple of minutes. Sprinkle with salt and pepper while still hot and serve right away.

POTATO CHIPS No prefrying necessary. You'll need a large, deep pot, and be prepared for the potatoes to absorb more oil. Use a mandoline (see page 15) or a sharp knife to cut the potatoes lengthwise for curls or crosswise for classic chips. You want the slices pretty thin, but not too wispy. Heat the oil to 350°F. Fry the chips in batches, using a slotted spoon or strainer to fish them out of the hot oil as they turn golden. Drain on towels or paper bags. Season while hot and serve.

RADISHES

There are so many choices: red, white, purple, French breakfast, black, daikon. The small, red varieties are the most common in supermarkets, but radishes come in a striking array of colors, shapes, and sizes. All taste sharp, to varying degree. Black radishes, for example, can be as hot as horseradish. And when the greens are in good shape, you can eat them, too.

PREPARING Trim; peel if you like (black radishes should always be peeled); slice or chop as necessary.

BEST COOKING METHODS sautéing in butter, braising and glazing; the tender greens, raw in salads; the sturdier greens, in stir-fries.

WHEN ARE THEY DONE? When crisp-tender to fully tender but not mushy

OTHER VEGETABLES YOU CAN USE jícama, water chestnuts (raw); turnips (cooked)

Braised and Glazed Radishes, Turnips, or Other Root Vegetable

MAKES: 4 servings | TIME: 30 minutes

An elegantly simple and wonderful way to prepare all kinds of vegetables. See the variations for many other ways to use the technique.

Other vegetables you can use: anything hard and fibrous, really—jícama, parsnips, celery root, waxy potatoes—but not vegetables that easily become mushy, like starchy potatoes or sweet potatoes).

- 2 tablespoons butter or olive oil
- 1 pound radishes, trimmed, or daikon, turnips, or rutabaga, peeled and cut into chunks

- ½ cup stock (to make your own, see pages 174–180), white wine, or water, plus more as needed
- Salt and pepper
- Fresh lemon juice (optional)
- Chopped fresh parsley for garnish

1. Combine the butter or oil, radishes, and stock in a large saucepan, sprinkle with salt and pepper, and bring to a boil. Cover and adjust the heat so the liquid bubbles gently. Cook until the radishes are tender, 15 to 20 minutes, checking once or twice and adding liquid as needed.

2. Uncover and raise the heat so the liquid bubbles aggressively. Cook off almost all the liquid so that the vegetable becomes glazed in the combination of butter or oil and pan juices. Taste and adjust the seasoning, and add a little lemon juice if you like. Garnish with parsley and serve.

BRAISED AND GLAZED RADISHES OR OTHER ROOT VEGETABLE WITH MISO Try this with daikon: In Step 1, add 1 tablespoon soy sauce. In Step 2, as the radishes become glazed, whisk together 2 tablespoons each any miso (white is mildest) and stock or water. Turn the heat under the radishes to a minimum, add the miso mixture, stir, and heat very gently for a minute or so before serving. Omit the lemon juice and parsley.

BRAISED AND GLAZED CARROTS Replace the radishes with 1 pound carrots, cut into 1-inch chunks. Garnish with dill, mint, or chervil.

BRAISED AND GLAZED BUTTERNUT SQUASH Use 1½ pounds butternut squash; peel and seed it, then cut into chunks. Use good-quality vegetable oil. Cook 1 tablespoon minced garlic in a large skillet for about a minute before adding the squash. Cook the squash until it begins to brown on one side, sprinkle with salt and pepper, and add ¼ cup stock or water. Cover and cook as directed in the main recipe. Garnish with chopped cilantro and serve with lime wedges.

 fast   make ahead   V vegetarian

BRAISED AND GLAZED BRUSSELS SPROUTS Combine 1 pound trimmed Brussels sprouts, 3 tablespoons butter or olive oil, and ½ cup stock in a large skillet. Bring to a boil then adjust the heat so the liquid bubbles gently. Cover and proceed with the recipe. Garnish with lots of pepper.

SEAWEED

Seaweed has become one of my favorite vegetables. It tastes like the ocean, for starters, and the textures are varied and interesting. It's also incredibly nutritious. Seaweed is almost always sold dry, which makes it ultra-convenient too. And it's not expensive when you remember that the volume and weight multiply during soaking.

PREPARING Arame, hijiki, kombu, wakame, and alaria: Use a damp towel to wipe kombu, but don't rinse. For all of these, soak in warm water until tender, 5 to 10 minutes; save the water for another use. Chop or slice as you like.

Use dulse straight out of the package or just give it a rinse in cold water.

Nori requires no soaking; cut it with scissors as needed. It's often toasted before use (see page 448).

Rinse and chop sea beans only if necessary.

BEST COOKING METHODS boiling and sautéing or stir-frying with other ingredients (arame, hijiki, alaria, and wakame); sautéing, stir-frying (dulse); steeping into Dashi (page 179), braising (kombu); parboiling for 30 seconds, then stir-frying or adding to a frittata, also good raw, as in slaws (sea beans)

WHEN IS IT DONE? When tender

OTHER VEGETABLES YOU CAN USE Most varieties of seaweed, with the exception of sea beans and kombu, are interchangeable. Substitute French-cut green beans (see page 297) for sea beans.

These are the most common seaweeds available in supermarkets, natural food stores, and, of course, Asian markets.

ARAME AND HIJIKI Different varieties but similar in look and use; both have slender, almost hairy strands. Arame is finer, milder, and lighter in color; hijiki is black, briny, and expands massively when rehydrated. Use in salads, soups, and stews or add to sautés or stir-fries.

DULSE Dark red, crumpled-looking, and relatively soft; sometimes sold as flakes. Can be eaten straight out of the package or added to salads, sandwiches, or soups.

KOMBU (KELP) A main ingredient in Dashi (page 179). Kelp contains a substance similar to MSG that enhances flavors. Best cooked with slow-cooked foods like beans, grains, soups, and stews. Sold in large, thick, hard, dark green pieces. Occasionally sold fresh on the West Coast.

NORI (LAVER) The familiar thin, shiny sheets used to wrap sushi. Deep greenish purple, almost black; brittle when dry, chewy when moistened. Nori dissolves in liquid. Has a mild, nutty flavor. It's excellent toasted (see Nori Chips, page 338).

SEA BEANS (SAMPHIRE, GLASSWORT) These small, delicate, thin green branches with nubby ends are lovely in salads, stir-fries, and egg dishes or chopped used as a garnish. Their flavor is as fresh and "sealike" as you can imagine, and the texture is crisp and delightful. If you see it fresh, buy it; when sold pickled, in jars, it's less exciting.

WAKAME AND ALARIA Used interchangeably; the former is harvested in Japan, the latter in North America. Both are dark green when dried and nearly transparent; they

Nori Chips, page 338

turn emerald green when rehydrated. Their flavor is mild, and they're nice in soups and stews or with grains or added to salads.

Nori Chips

MAKES: 2 to 4 servings | **TIME:** 5 minutes

Eat these straight as a snack, or mix with potato chips, popcorn (cooled, not hot), or Japanese rice crackers—or crumble over a bowl of steamed rice.

- 6 **sheets nori**
- 2 **tablespoons sesame oil**
  Salt

1. Put a skillet over medium-high heat. Brush one side of the nori with the oil and sprinkle with salt. Put a single nori sheet in the pan and toast it until it shrinks up, about 15 seconds; turn it over and toast the other side for 15 seconds. As they finish, stack the sheets on a plate.
2. Use scissors to cut the sheets into rectangular "chips." Serve right away or store in an airtight container and eat within a day or 2.

SHALLOTS

Related to onions and garlic botanically (all are alliums), but shallots have a milder, more nuanced flavor.

PREPARING Peel, slice, and chop them like onions. (See the illustrations on page 314.)

BEST COOKING METHODS sautéing, roasting; deep-frying for garnish when sliced thin

WHEN ARE THEY DONE? When tender and translucent

OTHER VEGETABLES YOU CAN USE scallions are closest; onions (especially red or white), leeks

SORREL

The flavor of these spinach-like leafy greens is deeply lemony (it's sometimes called sourgrass) and can be mild or intense, depending on the variety and maturity of the plant. And like spinach, it has a slight chalkiness when raw.

PREPARING Rinse well and trim any tough stems; no need to chop it unless you're using it raw.

BEST COOKING METHODS stirring into soups, stews, and braises; sautéing for omelets; puréeing and stirring with butter, cream, yogurt, or milk for a sublime sauce

WHEN IS IT DONE? When the leaves are melted and grayish green in color

OTHER VEGETABLES YOU CAN USE spinach, arugula, watercress; add a squeeze of lemon juice just before serving

SPINACH

Spinach is among the most convenient vegetables to prepare, especially in its prewashed, packaged form. But more important is where it's grown: Local is better. It's in season in spring and fall—spinach likes cool weather—but supermarkets carry it year-round.

PREPARING If it's in a bunch, either chop off all the stems (if you're in a hurry) or untie the bunch and pick off only the tough stems, leaving the tender ones attached. Rinse very thoroughly in several changes of water, especially if it was bunched, as there may be clumps of mud or sand between the leaves. After cooking squeeze it between your hands to extract as much water as possible, then chop or slice it if you'd like.

BEST COOKING METHODS steaming, sautéing

WHEN IS IT DONE? As soon as it wilts, though you can cook it longer if you like for extra tenderness; spinach cooked long and slow in butter is dreamy

OTHER VEGETABLES YOU CAN USE arugula, beet greens, chard

Spinach with Currants and Nuts

MAKES: 4 servings | TIME: 20 minutes

A Mediterranean classic, sweet from the currants or raisins, crunchy with nuts, and equally good hot or at room temperature.

Other vegetables you can use: almost any greens, chopped, though most will take a little longer time to cook than spinach; broccoli, cooked until quite tender.

- ¼ cup dried currants or raisins
- 1 pound spinach, trimmed of thick stems and well rinsed
- ¼ cup olive oil
- 1 teaspoon minced garlic (optional)
- ¼ cup pine nuts or chopped walnuts, briefly toasted (see page 309)
  Salt and pepper

1. Soak the currants in warm water for about 10 minutes while you clean and cook the spinach. Steam or parboil the spinach (see page 238) until tender, less than 5 minutes. Drain and let cool. When the spinach is cool enough to handle, squeeze all the excess moisture from it; chop it roughly.

2. Put the oil in a large skillet over medium heat. When the oil is hot, add the garlic, if you're using it,

and cook, stirring occasionally, until golden, about 3 minutes. Add the spinach and raise the heat to medium-high. Cook, stirring occasionally, for about 2 minutes.

3. Drain the currants and add them, along with the nuts. Reduce the heat to medium. Cook, stirring occasionally, until everything glistens, 3 to 4 minutes. Sprinkle with salt and pepper. Serve hot or at room temperature.

SPINACH WITH OVEN-ROASTED TOMATOES Omit the currants and nuts. Substitute 4 or so Oven-Roasted Plum Tomatoes (page 347), sliced or chopped as you like. Add the tomatoes when you would the currants in Step 3. Also add a handful of chopped pitted black olives, if you like.

SUSHI-STYLE SPINACH Omit the currants, garlic, and nuts, and skip Steps 2 and 3 entirely. Cool the cooked spinach; squeeze out excess moisture and chop it. Sprinkle the spinach with a little salt and 1 tablespoon soy sauce. Shape it into a 1-inch-thick log—if you have a bamboo sushi-rolling mat, use this to shape it. Cut the log into 1-inch-long slices; dip both ends of each slice into some toasted sesame seeds (see page 309) and arrange on a plate. Drizzle with a few drops of sesame oil; garnish with a tangle of bonito flakes, if you like, and serve right away. Or wait to garnish, cover and refrigerate for up to a day before serving.

Rich Spinach Pie

MAKES: 4 servings | TIME: 45 minutes

Vegetable pies are underrated. This one turns a familiar ingredient into a fancy side dish for an elegant dinner, or the main event for lunch or brunch. You can make it even more substantial by adding up to 1 cup cooked meat or seafood to the custard; shredded chicken, chopped shrimp or bacon, and crumbled sausage or ground beef are all good.

   Salt and pepper
2 pounds spinach, trimmed of thick stems and rinsed well
1 onion, chopped
3 eggs
1 teaspoon minced garlic
½ cup heavy cream or half-and-half
1 cup grated Parmesan cheese
1 recipe Savory Piecrust (page 869), prebaked (see page 867)
½ cup bread crumbs (preferably fresh; see page 801)
2 tablespoons butter, softened, or olive oil

1. Heat the oven to 375°F. Bring a large pot of water to a boil and salt it. Add the spinach and onion and cook for just about a minute, until the spinach wilts. Drain thoroughly and cool until you can handle it. Squeeze out as much of the water as you can. Chop the spinach and onion.

2. Beat the eggs in a medium bowl. Add the spinach and onion, garlic, eggs, cream, and about half the Parmesan. Mix well, then sprinkle with salt and pepper.

3. Pour the spinach mixture into the prepared piecrust and top with the remaining Parmesan, then the bread crumbs. Dot with butter or drizzle with oil. Bake until the filling is hot and set and the top is brown, about 20 minutes. If the top threatens to burn before the filling is set, lower the heat a bit. Serve hot, warm, or at room temperature.

SPINACH-FETA PIE Substitute 1 cup crumbled feta cheese for the Parmesan; mix in all the feta in Step 2.

SUMMER SQUASH
ZUCCHINI, YELLOW SQUASH, PATTYPAN (SCALLOPED), CHAYOTE (MIRLITON)

Beyond the commonplace yellow squash and zucchini, there is the flying saucer–shaped pattypan with its cute scalloped edge and vivid greens and yellows, and the pear-shaped gourd chayote, called mirliton in the South. And squash blossoms—sometimes with baby squash attached, sometimes not—are a rare treat.

PREPARING Yellow squash and zucchini: Trim the ends and slice or chop as you like. If the squash is flabby, salt it as you would cucumber (see page 203).

   Leave pattypans whole if tender enough, or halve.

   Chayote: peeling is optional. Halve the broad way through the stem end and remove the seed. Leave as halves or chop or slice as you like.

BEST COOKING METHODS steaming, sautéing, braising (chayote), roasting, frying, grilling; blossoms can be battered and deep-fried (see page 112)

WHEN ARE THEY DONE? When tender but not falling apart; pierce with a skewer or thin-bladed knife to check

OTHER VEGETABLES YOU CAN USE summer squashes are fairly interchangeable

Folding Vegetables in Parchment

Whether you use parchment paper or foil, crimp the edges of the package tightly to keep as much moisture inside as possible.

 fast   make ahead   vegetarian

Summer Squash and Herbs in Parchment

MAKES: 4 servings | TIME: 30 minutes

Baking in packages is like steaming—and when you open them, you've got a finished dish. The parchment seals in the moisture and heat so the vegetables cook in their juices and lose no flavor. Use a covered baking dish or individual covered crocks for very similar results.

Other vegetables you can use: chayote, mushrooms, broccoli, cauliflower, asparagus, sugar snap peas, snow peas, spinach, arugula, watercress.

½ small onion, sliced

12 ounces summer squash, trimmed and sliced ¼ inch thick

12 ounces zucchini, trimmed and sliced ¼ inch thick

2 sprigs fresh tarragon or basil

2 tablespoons olive oil or butter, plus more if you like
Salt and pepper
Lemon wedges

1. Heat the oven to 375°F. Cut parchment paper into 4 rectangles about 6 × 10 inches, fold in half crosswise to crease, then reopen. On one half of each rectangle, close to the crease, layer equal portions of the onion and squash, and half an herb sprig. Drizzle each with the olive oil or dot with the butter and sprinkle with salt and pepper.

2. Fold the parchment over the vegetables. Seal the packages by rolling the open edges together (see page 340). Put them on a baking sheet and bake until the squash is tender, about 20 minutes (test it with a toothpick or skewer). Transfer the packets to plates and serve with lemon wedges on the side. Warn your guests to be careful of the steam when opening the packets.

SUMMER SQUASH AND SHRIMP IN PARCHMENT Add 3 or 4 peeled large shrimp to each package.

5 More Vegetables in Parchment

NAME	VEGETABLES	AROMATICS	SEASONINGS
Steamed Fennel in Parchment	1½ pounds fennel, shaved	1 small red onion, sliced	2 teaspoons chopped orange zest
Tomatoes and Herbs in Parchment	1½ pounds fresh tomatoes, thickly sliced	1 leek, white part only, sliced	2 teaspoons chopped fresh marjoram, 3 tablespoons chopped olives
Spiced Peppers in Parchment	1½ pounds sliced mixed bell peppers (red, orange, yellow, and green)	1 small onion, sliced; 1 tablespoon chopped garlic	3 sprigs fresh cilantro, 1 teaspoon chili powder
Artichokes and Herbs in Parchment	4 large artichoke hearts (or 1 pound frozen), sliced	2 teaspoons chopped garlic (optional)	2 or 3 sprigs fresh basil or mint
Curried Butternut Squash in Parchment	1½ pounds peeled, seeded, and sliced butternut squash	2 tablespoons chopped fresh ginger	1 tablespoon curry powder, garam masala, or ground cumin, or a pinch saffron

SHIITAKES IN PARCHMENT Any fresh mushroom will also work here: Substitute 5 or 6 fresh shiso leaves for the tarragon if you like, sliced shiitake caps for the squash, and 2 teaspoons sesame oil for the olive oil. Add 1 teaspoon chopped fresh ginger or garlic too if you like.

Zucchini Pancakes

MAKES: 4 servings | **TIME:** At least 30 minutes

Zucchini is the main feature here; the batter just serves as binder.

Other vegetables you can use: turnips, winter squash, sweet potatoes, carrots, parsnips, beets, celery root (all peeled if necessary); sliced scallions; cooked, squeezed, and chopped spinach or other greens.

2	pounds zucchini or yellow squash
½	onion, grated
1	egg, lightly beaten
	About ¼ cup all-purpose flour or plain bread crumbs (preferably fresh; see page 801), plus more for dredging
½	cup grated Parmesan cheese
	Salt and pepper
4	tablespoons butter (½ stick) or olive oil

1. Grate the squash by hand with a box grater or the grating disk of a food processor. Mix the squash, onion, egg, ¼ cup flour, and Parmesan together and sprinkle with salt and pepper. Shape into 4 to 8 burger-shaped patties. Add more flour or bread crumbs if necessary to make a batter capable of holding its shape. If time allows, refrigerate for 1 hour to firm up the patties.
2. When you're ready to cook, put the butter or oil in a large skillet over medium-high heat. When the butter foams or the oil is hot, dredge the cakes in flour or bread crumbs and put in the skillet (if you've made 8, do this in 2 batches). Cook, turning once, until nicely browned on both sides, 10 to 15 minutes total depending on the thickness. Serve hot or room temperature.

SWEET POTATOES AND YAMS

There are so many more varieties of sweet potatoes and yams available now that it hardly matters what you call them, though they are different botanically. For eating, the most important distinctions are their colors, textures, and intensity of flavor. Neither is related to potatoes, and their flesh is quite different. Depending on the variety, the color of yams and sweet potatoes can range from ivory to golden to deep orange to nearly crimson. All have unsurpassed, slightly sweet creaminess, covered in skin in all stages of the sunset.

PREPARING Peel if the skins are thick or beat-up (though it is edible and delicious after roasting). Slice or chop as you like.

BEST COOKING METHODS baking, braising, roasting; cut small or grated and stir-fried

WHEN ARE THEY DONE? When tender enough to pierce easily with a fork

OTHER VEGETABLES YOU CAN USE potatoes, carrots, parsnips, winter squash, any tropical tuber

Baked Sweet Potatoes

MAKES: 4 servings | **TIME:** 1 hour or less

For basic use, sweet potatoes can be baked, boiled, steamed, or microwaved. Baked whole in their skin is the best way, in my opinion—especially if you're just going to eat them plain or with butter, or if you're using

them for mashing—but see what works best depending on how much time you have.

>   2   large or 4 medium sweet potatoes
>   (1½ to 2 pounds total)
>   Salt and pepper
>   Butter (optional)

Heat the oven to 425°F. Rinse the sweet potatoes and poke each with a skewer or thin-bladed knife in a few places. Put them in a foil-lined baking pan and bake, turning once, until very tender, about an hour. Serve hot, sprinkled with salt and pepper and, if you like, butter.

BOILED OR STEAMED SWEET POTATOES Peel the potatoes, cut into large chunks, and cook according to Just-Tender Boiled or Steamed Root Vegetables or Tubers (page 237). They'll probably take 20 minutes or less; don't overcook or they'll fall apart.

MICROWAVE-STEAMED SWEET POTATOES Peel the potatoes, cut into large chunks, and put on a plate or in a glass baking dish with a couple of tablespoons water, and a little butter if you like. Cover, vent to let steam escape, and microwave on high for at least 10 minutes, or until soft.

MASHED SWEET POTATOES Cook as described in the main recipe or either of the variations. Peel them if necessary and proceed with the recipe for Mashed Potatoes on page 329, starting with Step 2.

TOMATILLOS

A distant relative of the tomato, this green fruit is widely used in Mexican cooking. It's best when slightly firm and bright green. The tangy and herbaceous flesh turns yellow, more sour, and softer when overripe.

PREPARING Tear off the husks and rinse off the sticky resin. No need to core. Slice, chop, purée, or leave whole.

BEST COOKING METHODS raw; any way you'd cook tomatoes

WHEN ARE THEY DONE? From raw to cooked down into a pulp, and anywhere in between

OTHER VEGETABLES YOU CAN USE green tomatoes; in a pinch, fresh tomatoes

Stewed Tomatillos and Tomatoes

MAKES: 6 to 8 servings | TIME: About 1 hour, largely unattended

A winning combination. Tart tomatillos play the starring role in this stew, mellowed a bit by the sweetness of fresh tomatoes. Serve over rice, grits or polenta, or cooked hominy (see page 451). Or use as a poaching medium for eggs or chicken breasts.

Other vegetables you can use: all-green or not-quite-ripe tomatoes.

>   2   tablespoons olive oil, plus more for drizzling
>   1   large onion, chopped
>   1   bell pepper or 2 poblano chiles, cored, seeded, and chopped (see page 320)
>   2   cloves garlic, crushed
>   Salt and pepper
>   1½ pounds tomatillos, husked and rinsed
>   1   cup stock (to make your own, see 174–180), white wine, or water
>   1½ pounds fresh tomatoes, cut into large chunks
>   ½   cup chopped fresh cilantro

1. Put the oil in a large pot over medium-high heat. When it is hot, add the onion, bell pepper, and garlic and cook until the onion is soft and translucent, 5 to 10 minutes. Sprinkle with salt and pepper.
2. Add the tomatillos and cook until the skins start to break open, 10 to 15 minutes. Pour in the stock and stir.

Bring to a boil, then reduce the heat so the vegetables bubble gently. Cover and cook until the tomatillos are mostly dissolved, about 30 minutes. (At this point, you can cover and refrigerate for a day or two before proceeding.)

3. Return the heat to medium-high, and when the stew starts to bubble, stir in the tomatoes. Cook, stirring occasionally, until the tomatoes wilt but their skins remain intact. Stir in the cilantro, taste, and adjust the seasoning. Serve hot or at room temperature, drizzled with additional olive oil.

TOMATOES

Iconic tomatoes—the big, fat, red beefsteak kind—now share the limelight with a colorful array of heirloom varieties. Even cherry tomatoes now come in all different sizes and shapes. Tomatoes need hot sunny weather to thrive and just don't travel well. The vast majority of supermarket varieties—in season or not—are either picked green and ripened off the vine or grown in hothouses. Either way, the end result is the same: They're bland and not juicy enough. So in the off-season, I usually reach for canned tomatoes. During peak summer, I try to seek out those grown locally.

PREPARING See the illustrations below. Note that I've included directions for peeling, but the only time I ever bother anymore is when I want big pieces free of the tough skin, or a super-refined sauce. Otherwise I chop them small enough—or purée them before or after cooking—to retain all the tomato flavor.

BEST COOKING METHODS roasting, grilling or broiling, pan-frying; raw in sauce and salsa

WHEN ARE THEY DONE? Whenever you want them to be, from raw to cooked until just soft to a mushy sauce

OTHER VEGETABLES OR FRUITS YOU CAN USE tomatillos (beware: they're tangy!), pineapple, peaches, nectarines; watermelon (for raw tomatoes)

Preparing Tomatoes

STEP 1 First core the tomato. Cut a wedge right around the core and remove it.

STEP 2 To peel a tomato: Cut a small X in the flower (nonstem) end. Drop the tomato into boiling water and leave it until the skin begins to loosen, usually less than 30 seconds; then plunge into a bowl of ice water.

STEP 3 Remove the skin with a paring knife.

STEP 4 To seed a tomato: The easiest way, whether it's peeled or unpeeled, is to cut the tomato in half through its equator, then squeeze and shake out the seeds, or pop them out with your finger. Do this over a bowl if you want to strain and reserve the juice.

Pan-Fried Green and/or Red Tomatoes

MAKES: 4 servings | TIME: 20 minutes

A quick coating, rather than full-on breading, lets the tomatoes shine. There should be enough juiciness to help the crust stick, at least in spots. Just make sure the tomatoes aren't too ripe, or they will liquefy.

      3   tablespoons olive oil, or more as needed
2 or 3   large green, reddish-green, or greenish-red
         tomatoes, cored and cut crosswise into ½-inch-
         thick slices
         Plain bread crumbs (preferably fresh; see page
         801), cornmeal, or all-purpose flour for dredging
         Salt and pepper

1. Put the oil in a large skillet over medium-high heat. When the oil is hot, dredge the tomato slices, one at a time, in the bread crumbs and add them to the skillet; work in batches to avoid overcrowding.

2. Cook, adding a little more oil if needed to keep the slices sizzling. Sprinkle with salt and pepper as they cook. Turn when the first side is golden brown, then cook the other side; total cooking time will be less than 10 minutes. Repeat with the remaining tomatoes and serve hot or at room temperature.

Oven-Roasted Plum Tomatoes

MAKES: 4 servings | TIME: About 1 hour, largely unattended

Plum tomatoes (also known as Romas) have a high flesh-to-seed ratio; they are the kind used for canning and making sauces. Roasting even subpar supermarket plum tomatoes concentrates the flavor and eliminates mealiness. The results are gorgeous, and you can use them right away in sauces, as a garnish, in pilafs or soups, or in other vegetable dishes. Or store them, tightly covered, in the fridge for up to several days. You can also freeze them more or less indefinitely.

Other fruits or vegetables you can use: peaches, nectarines.

   2   tablespoons olive oil, plus more for the pan
   2   pounds plum tomatoes (about a dozen),
       cored and halved lengthwise
       Salt and pepper

1. Heat the oven to 375°F. Grease a large baking sheet or roasting pan with a little oil.

2. Scoop the seeds out of the tomatoes, if you like, and put the tomatoes on the pan cut side down. Drizzle or brush with 2 tablespoons oil and sprinkle with salt and pepper. Roast until they start to char a bit and shrivel, about 30 to 40 minutes; there's no need to turn them.

Heirloom Vegetables

As the name implies, heirloom varieties of fruits and vegetables—and other plants for that matter—were passed down from generation to generation by home gardeners who saved seeds or clippings. Once supermarkets became the primary place to buy produce, these varieties lost out to hybrids that were easier to pick, ship, store, and sell.

Even though heirlooms are back in style, and even sold in supermarkets, you have to seek them out—and be willing to pay for them. Generally they do taste better—often much, much better—than their mass-market cousins. You'll get the best from local farmstands and markets, growing them yourself (some simple searches will reveal online seed sources), or cozying up to someone with a green thumb.

OVEN-ROASTED WHOLE CHERRY TOMATOES
Concentrate their sweetness even more: Roast until they burst and start to char in spots, about 15 minutes.

OVEN-ROASTED CANNED PLUM TOMATOES How to turn a convenience food into something special and way more useful: Instead of the fresh tomatoes, drain a 28- or 35-ounce can whole plum tomatoes, reserving the juice for another use. Proceed with the recipe.

OVEN-ROASTED EVERYDAY TOMATOES Works for heirloom, beefsteak, or hothouse tomatoes, especially when you want to improve imperfect ones: Core the tomatoes and halve them around the equator instead of lengthwise. Squeeze out the seeds (see page 345). Cut the largest pieces in half again and proceed with the recipe.

OVEN-DRIED TOMATOES Omit the olive oil and salt and pepper. Heat the oven to 225°F. Set a wire rack on top of each of 2 rimmed baking sheets. Put the tomatoes on the racks cut side down. Put in the oven and forget about them for 2 hours. Rotate the baking sheets and continue to bake to desired doneness. If you just want to intensify the tomato flavor and use them immediately, they're done when still soft but somewhat shriveled, 2 to 3 hours total. If you want to keep them for a few days, they're done when shriveled and mostly dry, at least 4 hours total; refrigerate them in an airtight container. If you want to keep them for weeks, they're done when dark, shriveled, and dry, 6 or more hours total; and refrigerate or freeze in an airtight container.

TROPICAL TUBERS
TARO, CASSAVA (YUCA, MANIOC); BONIATO (BATATA); MALANGA (YAUTIA, TANNIA)
The tubers popular predominantly in Caribbean, South American, Polynesian, and West African cuisines, these are quite starchy, and are generally handled the way you would potatoes.

PREPARING Peel with a vegetable peeler, or for the tougher cassava, a paring knife. Note that some may be waxed, so they must be peeled, but otherwise peeling isn't necessary when you're baking others. You can chop, slice, or grate the flesh as you like. Raw boniato flesh discolors very quickly when peeled or cut and darkens quite a bit when cooked; immediately immerse in cold water after cutting and be sure to keep it covered with liquid while cooking to minimize darkening.

BEST COOKING METHODS Taro and malanga: boiling, frying. Cassava: baking, frying, braising. Boniato: boiling, baking.

WHEN ARE THEY DONE? When a skewer or thin-bladed knife inserted into one meets almost no resistance

OTHER VEGETABLES YOU CAN USE potatoes, sweet potatoes

TURNIPS AND RUTABAGAS
These cabbage-flavored root vegetables, also known as Swedes or yellow turnips, deserve a place in your repertoire even if you think you don't like them. They're versatile and easy to cook, and are perfect when you're tired of potatoes or carrots.

PREPARING Peel and leave whole (if small enough), or slice or chop as you like; rutabagas must be peeled with a paring knife because of their wax coating.

BEST COOKING METHODS boiling, braising and glazing; puréeing

WHEN ARE THEY DONE? When tender or very soft

OTHER VEGETABLES YOU CAN USE turnips and rutabagas are interchangeable; otherwise, parsnips, carrots, kohlrabi

 **F** fast **M** make ahead **V** vegetarian

WATER CHESTNUTS

This flat, small tuber from an Asian water plant might look a little like a chestnut but that's where the resemblance ends. It's mildly sweet and crunchy and is probably most familiar from its presence in Chinese restaurant stir-fries and fried rice. When fresh, they have a dark brown skin that covers the off-white, crisp flesh. Canned is always a decent option, since they're still a little crunchy.

PREPARING Peel (if fresh) and slice or chop as necessary.

BEST COOKING METHOD stir-frying, added at the last minute

WHEN IS IT DONE? When just heated through and still crunchy

WINTER SQUASH

The most noteworthy and accessible of the many varieties of so-called hard squashes are the butternut, acorn, pumpkin, spaghetti, delicata, kabocha, Hubbard, crookneck, and calabaza. You're bound to see others too.

PREPARING All get the same treatment. To peel, use a sturdy vegetable peeler or a paring knife for butternut if you're more comfortable; but for tougher, ridged squashes, set the squash on its flat end or cut off an end to create a flat, stable bottom. Use a sharp knife (the larger the squash, the larger the knife) and cut off slices of the skin starting from the top where the vegetable starts to curve, slicing down to the cutting board; cut off strips around the entire vegetable, then chop off the unpeeled ends. Split open and scoop out the seeds and stringy fiber; discard or roast the seeds (see page 309).

Spaghetti squash is a slightly different animal because its flesh is super-stringy. Though you can peel and prepare it as you would other winter squashes, it's best—and easiest—to cook it whole (see Roasted Whole Winter Squash, page 349), then split, remove the seeds, and scoop out the flesh.

BEST COOKING METHODS boiling or steaming, braising, braising and glazing, pan-frying, roasting; puréeing

WHEN ARE THEY DONE? When very tender and nicely browned (if pan-fried or roasted); when tender but not waterlogged (if boiled)

OTHER VEGETABLES YOU CAN USE except for spaghetti squash, winter squash are interchangeable; otherwise, sweet potatoes, yams, carrots, waxy potatoes

Roasted Whole Winter Squash

MAKES: 4 to 10 servings, depending on the size of the squash | TIME: 1 to 2 hours, depending on size, completely unattended

This is the easiest way to cook and extract the flesh from any winter squash, even the large, thick-skinned varieties like Hubbard and pumpkin. If the process of cutting apart a raw squash has ever seemed daunting

Peeling Winter Squash

With winter squash, waste is inevitable, so just hack away at the skin with a knife, carefully, in downward strokes. Most squash are simply too tough (and oddly shaped) for a vegetable peeler.

(or scary, given the knife or cleaver required), then oven roasting (or the first variation, steaming) whole squash will spare you that chore. Use cooked squash in purées, soups, or desserts.

Other vegetables you can use: eggplant; it will take a lot less time.

1   or more whole winter squash (1 to 8 pounds)

1. Heat the oven to 375°F. Rinse the squash. Use a thin-bladed, sharp knife, ice pick, or sturdy long-tined fork to poke several holes in the top of the squash around the stem.

2. Put the squash on a rimmed baking sheet or shallow roasting pan. Roast, undisturbed, for at least 30 minutes. When the sides start to soften and collapse, rotate or turn it to promote even cooking. Continue roasting until deeply colored and quite soft. Small squash will take 45 minutes or so, large ones up to 1½ hours.

3. Remove the squash from the oven and let it cool before handling. Halve and scoop out the seeds and stringy fiber. Then scoop out the flesh; discard the shell. Use right away or store, tightly covered, in the refrigerator for several days or in the freezer for several months.

WHOLE WINTER SQUASH, STEAMED Best for soups or other dishes where the added moisture can be beneficial: Prepare the squash as described in Step 1. Rig a steamer (see page 20) in a large pot with at least 1 inch of water. Put the squash on the steamer, stem up. Cover the pot and bring to a boil, then adjust the heat so the water bubbles vigorously. Check the pot every so often to make sure there's still water in the bottom; after a half-hour or so, turn the squash over if you can. Cooking time will be about the same as for roasting. When the squash is done, proceed with the recipe from Step 3.

ROASTED SQUASH PIECES IN THE SHELL Slightly faster, with most of your time spent preparing the squash: Heat the oven to 400°F. Cover a rimmed baking sheet or shallow roasting pan with foil. Cut and seed the squash

as directed on page 349. You should be left with squash halves or large pieces. Put the squash in the pan cut side down, and roast until it's starting to get tender, 20 to 30 minutes, depending on the variety. Turn the pieces over and roast until done, another 20 minutes or so. Let cool a bit, then scoop out the flesh.

Winter Squash Curry

MAKES: 4 servings | **TIME:** About 30 minutes

Preparing raw winter squash takes some practice, but since you'll want to make this otherwise-easy recipe all the time, you'll get a knack for it quickly.

Other vegetables you can use: any winter squash, potatoes, sweet potatoes, any root vegetable, eggplant, cauliflower, mushrooms, okra, peas, any summer squash, green or wax beans.

>   2   **tablespoons good-quality vegetable oil**
>   1   **onion, chopped**
>   1   **tablespoon curry powder (to make your own, see page 32)**
>   1   **tablespoon chopped fresh ginger**
>   1½ **pounds butternut or other winter squash, peeled and chopped**
>   1   **cup coconut milk, stock (to make your own, see page 372 or pages 174–180), or water**
>   **Salt and pepper**
>   **Chopped fresh cilantro for garnish**

1. Put the oil in a large pot over medium-high heat. When the oil is hot, add the onion and cook until softened, 3 to 5 minutes. Add the curry powder and ginger and cook until the onion just starts to brown, about 2 minutes more.

2. Add the squash and coconut milk and sprinkle with salt and pepper. Bring to a boil, cover, and adjust the heat so it bubbles steadily. Cook, stirring once or twice, until the squash is tender, about 20 minutes.

F fast   **M** make ahead   **V** vegetarian

Roasted Whole
Winter Squash,
page 349

Check the pot periodically and add a little more liquid to prevent the squash from sticking. If the squash is done and the mixture is still soupy, remove the lid and increase the heat so the liquid bubbles furiously; cook until it's thicker than stew. Taste and adjust the seasoning. Garnish with cilantro and serve hot or warm.

WINTER SQUASH, THAI STYLE Serve over Steamed Sticky Rice, Thai Style (page 430) or wide rice noodles: In Step 1, when you add the ginger, also add 1 chopped fresh chile, like jalapeño or Thai, red chile flakes, or cayenne, to taste. Stir in 2 tablespoons peanut butter along with the coconut milk.

WINTER SQUASH, AFGHAN STYLE Best with butternut, and don't skip the yogurt sauce here: Cook the onion until browned in Step 1. Substitute 1 teaspoon ground turmeric for the curry powder and garlic for the ginger; use stock or water. Proceed with the recipe. Serve drizzled with herbed yogurt sauce (see page 59, made with fresh or dried mint).

WINTER SQUASH WITH MIRIN Omit the curry powder, and instead of coconut milk use a ½ cup water, 3 tablespoons soy sauce, 3 tablespoons mirin (or 1½ tablespoons honey and 1½ tablespoons water), and a teaspoon of rice vinegar. Proceed with the recipe. Garnish with chopped scallion.

THE BASICS OF MIXED VEGETABLE DISHES

Most vegetables go quite well together, so I've only got a few rules for combining them. Try to stick to what's in season where you live. Pay attention to proportions—same-sized pieces cook at the same rates—and to the pliability test (see "Controlling Doneness in Vegetables," page 236). Hard vegetables take longer to cook than softer ones, of course. To compensate, either precook

the hard ones a bit or hold out the soft ones until near the end of the cooking time.

More is not necessarily better. Too many vegetables will muddy the flavor. Usually three or four vegetables per dish is just right. If you're looking for a "bigger" dish, see "How to Add Meat, Fish, or Poultry to Almost Any Vegetable Dish" (page 257), or toss the dish with noodles, beans, or cooked whole grains to turn it into a main course.

Oven-Baked Ratatouille

MAKES: 4 to 6 servings | **TIME:** about 1½ hours, largely unattended

The French classic country stew is simple no matter where you cook it: Combine vegetables, herbs, and olive oil, and soften them on the stove or in the oven. That's it. Longish, slow cooking and lots of good olive oil are important.

Other vegetables you can use: potatoes and mushrooms are the most common additions not already included here.

1½ to 2 **pounds eggplant (preferably small), sliced ½ inch thick, and salted if time allows (see page 203)**
½ **cup olive oil, plus more for garnish**
2 **large onions, sliced**
1 **pound zucchini, trimmed and cut into large chunks**
2 **red or yellow bell peppers, cored, seeded, and sliced**
4 **plum tomatoes, cored and chopped, or 2 large tomatoes (drained canned are fine) Fresh herbs like thyme, marjoram, rosemary, savory, basil, parsley, and/or chervil, plus more for garnish Salt and pepper**
10 **cloves garlic, halved**

 fast make ahead vegetarian

1. Heat the oven to 350°F. If you salted the eggplant, squeeze out excess liquid, then rinse and dry.

2. Film a baking dish or large ovenproof skillet with a couple of tablespoons of the oil. Make a layer of onion, followed by layers of eggplant, zucchini, peppers, tomatoes, herbs, a sprinkle of salt and pepper, and half the garlic (the order doesn't matter at all). Repeat. Drizzle with the remaining oil.

3. Bake, pressing down on the vegetables occasionally with a spatula, until they are all completely tender, about 1 hour. Garnish with more herbs, drizzle with a little more oil, and serve hot, at room temperature, or chilled.

STOVETOP MIXED VEGETABLES WITH OLIVE OIL

This requires a little more attention: Combine all the ingredients in the largest skillet you have; a broad saucepan will work too. Cook, stirring occasionally, over medium heat, adjusting the heat so the vegetable juices bubble gently and the vegetables cook without browning. Cooking will be just a little quicker, perhaps 45 minutes or so.

OVEN-BAKED OR STOVETOP MIXED VEGETABLES WITH

BEANS Works with the main recipe or variation above: Add about 2 cups drained cooked or canned cannellini beans or chickpeas to the vegetables before cooking. (Rinse them first if they're canned.)

Thai-Style Mixed Spicy Vegetables

MAKES: 4 servings | TIME: 30 minutes

Half stir-fry, half braise. This quick, thick stew can be varied drastically simply by choosing different vegetable combinations. If you like Thai-style curries, this is for

you. Serve with White Rice (page 430) or Sticky Rice (page 430).

3	tablespoons good-quality vegetable oil
1	large white onion, sliced
2	tablespoons chopped garlic
2	dried chiles, 1 minced seeded fresh chile, or 1 teaspoon Chile Paste (page 40) or Red or Green Curry Paste (page 46), or to taste
1½	pounds eggplant, zucchini, summer squash, or a combination, peeled as necessary and cut into 1½-inch chunks
1½	cups coconut milk (to make your own, see page 372)
3	lime leaves, chopped (preferably fresh; dried are okay), or the grated zest of 1 lime
3	tablespoons soy sauce or fish sauce
	Salt and pepper
	Lime wedges for garnish

1. Put the oil in a large skillet over medium-high heat. When it is hot, add the onion and cook, stirring occasionally, until it softens a bit, 3 to 5 minutes. Stir in the garlic and chiles, then the eggplant. If you're cooking a combination of eggplant and squash, which cooks faster, add the squash a little later to give the eggplant a head start. Cook, stirring occasionally and adjusting the heat as necessary so the vegetables cook quickly without burning, until they soften, 10 to 20 minutes.

2. Add the coconut milk and lime leaves and cook until the mixture has thickened, about 5 minutes. Add the soy sauce. Taste and add salt and pepper if necessary. Serve hot, with lime wedges.

INDIAN-STYLE MIXED SPICY VEGETABLES Reduce the
garlic to 2 teaspoons and add 1 tablespoon chopped fresh ginger at the same time. Use 2 fresh chiles, like serrano or jalapeño, seeded and chopped, instead of dried chiles. In Step 2, add 1½ teaspoons garam masala

  fast   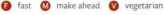 make ahead   V vegetarian

(to make your own, see page 34) and omit the lime leaves and soy sauce. Omit the lime wedges.

---

8 ADDITIONS TO THAI-STYLE MIXED SPICY VEGETABLES

1. 1 to 2 cups chopped fresh tomatoes (or 1 14-ounce can diced), after the eggplant begins to soften
2. 1 to 2 cups peeled and chopped potato (preferably a waxy variety), in addition to the eggplant, added at the same time. Or replace the eggplant with potatoes.
3. 1 to 2 cups peas, snow peas, or sugar snap peas, when the eggplant is just beginning to get tender
4. ½ to 1 cup chopped carrots or bell pepper, along with the onion
5. 1 tablespoon minced fresh ginger, along with the garlic and chile
6. ½ cup or more shredded fresh basil (preferably Thai), cilantro, mint or a combination, just before removing from the heat
7. About 1 pound boneless chicken, cut into thin shreds; chopped boneless pork (preferably from the shoulder—Boston butt or picnic); beef (preferably sirloin, cut across the grain); or peeled shrimp, in addition to the eggplant, at the same time. Or replace the eggplant with the protein.
8. 1 to 2 cups firm or extra-firm tofu (blotted dry, cut into ¼-inch cubes), just before adding the coconut milk

Crisp Vegetable Pancakes, Korean Style

MAKES: 6 to 8 servings | **TIME:** 45 minutes

When made with half rice flour, these big savory cakes are crisp on the outside, tender and chewy on the inside—and totally addictive. Serve the pancakes hot or at room temperature with Soy Dipping Sauce and Marinade (page 64), or a mixture of equal parts soy sauce and rice vinegar.

Other vegetables you can use: corn kernels, shredded cabbage, radishes.

2	eggs
1	cup all-purpose flour
1	cup rice flour
1	tablespoon good-quality vegetable oil, plus more for the pan
5	scallions, green parts only, cut into 3-inch pieces and shredded lengthwise
20	fresh chives (preferably garlic chives) or ½ cup chopped fresh cilantro
2	carrots, grated
1	small yellow squash or zucchini, grated

1. Lightly beat the eggs. Mix in the all-purpose flour, rice flour, oil, and 1½ cups water until smooth. Let the batter rest for at least 10 minutes, and up to an hour in the refrigerator. When you're ready to cook, stir the scallions, chives, carrots, and squash into the batter. Line a baking sheet with towels.

2. Heat a large nonstick skillet over medium-high heat and coat the bottom with oil. Ladle in one quarter of the batter and spread it out evenly into a circle. Adjust the heat so the pancake sizzles without burning. Cook until the bottom is browned, about 5 minutes. Turn the pancake and cook for another 5 minutes (see the illustration for turning rösti, page 332). Repeat with the remaining batter.

3. As each pancake finishes cooking, transfer it to the towels to drain. Cut into wedges and serve as soon as you can with a dipping sauce. (Or transfer them to a rack set in a rimmed baking sheet and keep them warm in a 200°F oven.)

CRISP KIMCHI PANCAKES Add about 1 cup chopped Shortcut Kimchi (page 229) to the batter.

SEAFOOD AND VEGETABLE PANCAKES, KOREAN STYLE
Add up to 2 cups sliced shrimp, squid, oysters, or mussels, precooked, shelled if necessary, alone or in combination. Reduce the vegetables by half. Proceed with the recipe, forming the pancakes so they're a bit thicker to hold the seafood.

THE BASICS OF STUFFED VEGETABLES

The best of two worlds: flavorful fillings in gorgeous edible vessels. Different vegetables require slightly different stuffing techniques; some of the most common are given here. But one general piece of advice: Resist the urge to overstuff.

To ensure that the vegetable will be tender and fully cooked, most require a bit of cooking—like boiling, steaming, or roasting—before filling. That way you decrease the final cooking time and prevent the stuffing from getting too dry. Since the vegetable will finish once it's filled, the idea it to precook until you can just barely stick a fork in it. The only exceptions are when your stuffing includes raw meat or fish, or raw grains, which

will take longer to cook, or when you're using quick-cooking vegetables such as tomatoes or bell peppers.

I usually finish cooking stuffed vegetables in a fairly hot oven; the browning adds a bit of richness. But steaming, braising, frying, grilling, and broiling also work well. This section will give you some ideas, and from there you can improvise a whole world of stuffed vegetables.

Tomatoes Stuffed with Sausage and Rice

MAKES: 4 or more servings | **TIME:** 50 minutes with cooked rice

When you stuff tomatoes with a raw filling and roast them for a relatively long time in a hot oven, you get maximum caramelization.

Other vegetables you can use: bell peppers, large mushrooms, small eggplant, and summer squash can be stuffed raw; chayote, onions, winter squash, cabbage, or any sturdy cooking green must be partially cooked before being stuffed. (See "6 More Stuffed Vegetables," page 358, for preparation instructions.)

How to Stuff Vegetables

When stuffing an eggplant—or any other vegetable—don't put in so much stuffing that it spills out.

Cut the bottom off the tomato if you like and hollow out the inside, removing the core. After filling, put the top back on, like a lid.

Or you can halve the tomato—lengthwise or on the equator—then scoop and fill.

Stuffing a cabbage or other leaf is much like making a burrito: Put a not-too-large amount of filling on the third closest to you and fold over that end. Fold in the sides, then roll it up.

 **F** fast **M** make ahead **V** vegetarian

Stuffed Onions, page 358

6 More Stuffed Vegetables

Figure 1½ pounds vegetables before trimming; you can always cut them into individual serving portions before or after filling. For the stuffing, make a full recipe from the suggestions that follow; you might have some extra. To improvise your own, 4 cups cooked filling is usually plenty.

VEGETABLE	PREPARATION	STUFFING IDEA	HOW TO COOK
Stuffed Eggplant	Peeling is optional. Halve lengthwise, or for large, thick eggplant, cut crosswise into 3-inch-thick cylinders; drizzle with olive oil and roast in a 350°F oven until tender. Scoop out a cavity for stuffing.	Crouton Salad (page 221) is excellent as a cooked filling.	Finish in a 375°F oven until the eggplant is very tender. Sprinkle with chopped fresh parsley or basil.
Stuffed Zucchini	Use fat, relatively straight zucchini or yellow squash. Halve lengthwise and scrape out the seeds.	Quinoa with Roasted Corn (page 458)	Bake in a 375°F oven until the zucchini is tender and the stuffing is hot, about 20 minutes.
Stuffed Acorn Squash	Halve the squash, scrape out the seeds, and rub the inside with olive oil or butter. Roast, cut-side down, in a 375°F oven for 25 minutes. Turn the squash over and fill.	Perfect for vegetarians during the holidays: Wild Rice Pilaf with Dried Fruit (page 468)	Finish in a 375°F oven until the flesh is tender, another 20 minutes or so. Garnish with chopped pecans and parsley.
Stuffed Cabbage or Kale	Use large, untorn leaves. Put them in a steamer above a couple of inches of salted water. Cover and cook until the leaves are just flexible enough to bend. Make a V cut in each leaf to remove the stem. Fill and wrap as shown on page 358.	Like vegetable kibbeh: Bulgur Pilaf with Lentils (page 458)	Put the rolls in the steamer (check that there is enough water) and steam until the leaves are tender, 10 to 15 minutes. Drizzle with olive oil or melt butter on top. Sprinkle with chopped fresh herbs.
Stuffed Onions	Halve unpeeled onions around their equator and put in a greased pan, cut-side down. Drizzle with melted butter and pour ¼ cup white wine or water over all. Bake in a 400°F oven until they're just tender, 15 to 20 minutes. Remove the inner layers of onion, and the skin if you like.	Chard with Olives and Feta (page 282).	Finish in a 375°F oven until the stuffing is hot and the onion is tender, about 20 minutes more. For an extra treat, cook some chopped bacon with fresh bread crumbs and sprinkle on top before serving.
Stuffed Peppers	Cut the tops off any color bell pepper and scoop out the seeds. Save the tops, if you like.	Mix Baked Black Beans and Rice Spanish Style (page 410) with a cup of grated mild melting cheese like mozzarella or Oaxaca.	Bake or grill the peppers until the cheese has melted and the outsides are browned in spots. Serve hot or warm with any salsa you like (see pages 55–58 or 71–74).

 F fast   **M** make ahead   **V** vegetarian

4 to 6	firm fresh tomatoes (about 6 ounces each)
8	ounces fresh sausage, removed from the casings if necessary
1	cup cooked white, basmati, brown, or wild rice or other cooked grain
1	tablespoon minced garlic (optional)
	Salt and pepper
½	cup olive oil
	Chopped fresh parsley or basil for garnish

1. Heat the oven to 450°F. Cut a ¼-inch slice from the flower end of each tomato (the bottom or opposite side of the stem end). Reserve these slices. Or halve the tomatoes lengthwise (see the illustrations on the previous page). Use a spoon to scoop out the insides of the tomatoes, leaving a wall about ¼ inch thick. Discard the woody core and seeds. Chop the pulp and mix it with the sausage, rice, garlic if you're using it, and sprinkle with salt and pepper.

2. Sprinkle the inside of the tomatoes with salt and pepper. Fill them with the sausage mixture, and replace the top slices. Spread ¼ cup of the oil in a shallow roasting pan that will allow for a little room between the tomatoes; put them in the pan. Sprinkle with salt and pepper.

3. Roast the tomatoes until they are shriveled and the sausage is cooked through, 30 to 40 minutes. An instant thermometer inserted into the middle of one of the tomatoes should read at least 165°F (or you can remove the top slice and peek inside; if not, continue roasting. Serve hot, warm, or at room temperature, drizzled with the remaining oil and garnished with parsley.

TOMATOES STUFFED WITH RICE AND CHEESE Substitute 1 cup grated Gruyère, Asiago, Manchego, Monterey Jack, or mozzarella cheese for the sausage.

QUICK STUFFED TOMATOES Halve the tomatoes, core, and scoop out the seeds. Omit the sausage and rice. Mix together ½ cup bread crumbs (preferably fresh; see page 801), ½ cup grated Parmesan, the garlic, salt and pepper,

and just enough olive oil to make it hold together. Fill the tomato halves with this. Proceed with the recipe and reduce the cooking time to 20 to 30 minutes, depending on the size of the tomato.

THE BASICS OF COOKING FRUIT

Cooked fruit can be incorporated into all sorts of dishes, not just desserts—for example, halved fruit on the grill, as well as spiced compotes, salsas, relishes, and chutneys. None of these, even the most complex, takes more than a few minutes to put together. It's also an excellent use of overripe, underripe, or even slightly damaged fruit.

Firmness is the best way to predict how long a fruit will take to cook. The least fibrous fruits (bananas, strawberries, papaya, and raspberries) cook fastest, while firmer fruit (pineapple, apple, and even citrus) will take far longer to become soft. Ideally, remove fruit from the heat before it's completely tender (use a fork, knife tip, toothpick, or skewer to judge tenderness).

Fruit is slightly more forgiving than vegetables when it comes to overcooking, since you generally eat it quite tender. That makes slow cooking like poaching, stewing, or roasting most appealing when you want to walk away from the stove. High-heat methods (grilling and sautéing) require more attention. And because fruit is naturally high in the sugar fructose, it will burn more easily if overheated. So cook fruit at a slightly lower temperature than you would vegetables, and keep an eye on it, stirring and turning as necessary.

For some ideas about how to season fruit before, during, and after cooking, see pages 361 and 363.

TO PEEL OR NOT TO PEEL?
Peeled fruit will cook through and lose its shape faster than unpeeled fruit, which might make you tend to cook fruit with its skin on. But if the flesh gets even slightly overdone, it tends to separate from the skin, especially during moist cooking like poaching and sautéing. Then

you're left with the worst of both textures: soft fruit and tough skin.

For every rule there's at least one exception, so try to use common sense: If the skin isn't edible—as in melons, mangoes, or papayas—peel the fruit before cooking. Leaving the edible skins on peaches, apples, plums, grapes, and pears during high-heat, fast-cook methods like grilling, broiling, or roasting helps hold the flesh together and improves color and flavor; to keep the skins from slipping off small fruits, just be careful not to overcook them. Virtually everything else should be peeled if at all practical.

Fruit-Cooking Techniques

Here's an overview of the methods for cooking fruit.

POACHING

Good candidates for poaching are pears, apples, pineapple, cherries, grapes, peaches and nectarines, plums, and quince. Dried fruit is also wonderful poached. It's best to poach fruit in seasoned juice, vinegar, or wine; water leaches out too much of the flavor.

Put the fruit in just enough liquid to cover it. Keep the liquid barely bubbling and cook, turning the fruit once or twice, until a toothpick or skewer pierces to the center with little resistance. A pear might take 20 minutes or so, while cherries will be done in less than 10. Let the fruit cool in the liquid so it absorbs as much flavor as possible, then remove. Serve with the poaching liquid-as-is, like a soup, or boil the liquid until it thickens into a syrupy sauce. Poached fruit keeps in the fridge for several days.

STEWING

Compote is a fancy name for stewed fruit, about the easiest thing in the world: Put cut fruit—either one kind or an assortment—into a pan with a tight-fitting lid. Sprinkle with a little sugar or other sweetener, or salt and pepper. Add a couple of tablespoons water or a more flavorful liquid, cover, and turn the heat to medium-low. Cook, stirring occasionally, until some of the juice is released and the fruit begins to soften, anywhere from 5 to 20 minutes depending on the fruit. Like poached fruit, this will keep in the fridge for several days.

In a pinch, you can microwave fruit as you would vegetables (see page 237), though it's really just as easy—and only slightly less fast—to stew it. You can also "stew" fruit without any cooking at all: See "Macerating and Seasoning Fruit" (page 363).

SAUTÉING

Set a large skillet over medium to medium-high heat. Swirl around a little oil or melt a pat of butter, just enough to coat the pan and the fruit; figure 1 to 2 tablespoons per pound. When the oil is hot or the butter melts, stir or toss the fruit around in the pan until it's cooked as firm or tender as you like. Add sweet or savory seasonings just as you would for vegetables (also see the chart and sidebar on pages 361 and 363 for more ideas). It's most common to sauté apples but pears, peaches, plums, apricots, figs, and even citrus segments are also terrific this way.

ROASTING

Any fruit you can sauté you can roast. As with vegetables, high, dry heat helps develop deep color and flavor. The only trick is to make sure the sugars in the fruit caramelize without burning. Set the oven between 325 and 350°F, a little lower than you would for vegetables. Grease a rimmed baking sheet or shallow roasting pan or line it with a piece of parchment paper (this makes cleanup much easier). Add whole or cut fruit, taking care not to overcrowd. Drizzle or brush with a little oil or melted butter and season as you like. Roast, checking occasionally and turning as necessary, until tender and golden, anywhere from 15 to 45 minutes depending on the fruit.

OVEN-DRYING

This make-ahead technique leaves fruit chewy and moist, or slightly crisp—you control the ultimate

 fast make ahead  vegetarian

9 Sweet and Savory Ways to Broil and Grill Fruit

FRUIT	PREPARATION	BROIL OR GRILL	SAUCE, SEASON, AND/OR SERVE
Broiled or Grilled Figs	Halve lengthwise. Brush with melted butter.	Broil or grill until browned and soft, or if topping with the cheese mixture, when the cheese has browned.	Mix honey, chopped fresh rosemary, and cream cheese or mascarpone and top the figs before or after broiling.
Broiled or Grilled Peaches or Nectarines	Halve; remove the pits. Fill cavities with about 1 teaspoon each butter and honey.	Broil until the edges just begin to brown, 3 to 5 minutes. Or omit the fillings and grill, cut side down, until just beginning to brown, 3 to 5 minutes.	Drizzle with more honey and sprinkle with pepper if you like.
Broiled Bananas	Peel, put in a flameproof baking dish, dot with butter, and sprinkle with sugar.	Broil until golden brown, about 10 minutes.	Squeeze a bit of lemon juice over the top just before serving.
Broiled or Grilled Citrus	Halve along the equator or cut into 1-inch-thick slices. Brush with oil or melted butter.	Grill over direct heat or broil, turning occasionally, until browned, 3 to 5 minutes.	Top with Chile Paste (page 40) or sprinkle with chopped fresh ginger.
Broiled or Grilled Mangoes	Peel; cut large slices or wedges off the pit. Brush with oil.	Grill over direct heat or broil, turning occasionally, until browned, 3 to 5 minutes.	Spoon on some Fresh Tomatillo Salsa (page 56), Cilantro Sauce (page 52), Cilantro-Mint Chutney (page 61), or Coconut Chutney (page 61).
Savory Broiled or Grilled Peaches or Nectarines	Halve or quarter. Brush with oil or melted butter.	Grill, cut side down, over direct heat or broil until browned, 2 to 3 minutes. Turn and cook the skin side for a minute or 2 if you like.	Smear with olive oil or Basil Purée (page 52). Off the grill, crumble blue or feta cheese on top.
Broiled or Grilled Pineapple	Peel and cut into slices, wedges, or 1½-inch cubes; skewer cubes. Brush with oil.	Grill over direct heat or broil, turning occasionally, until browned, 3 to 5 minutes.	Drizzle with Ginger-Scallion Sauce (page 64) or Soy Dipping Sauce and Marinade (page 64).
Broiled or Grilled Plums	Halve or quarter; skewer if you like. Brush with oil or melted butter.	Grill, cut-side down, over direct heat or broil until browned, 2 to 3 minutes.	Top with Simplest Yogurt Sauce (page 59), or Honey Mustard (page 37).
Grilled or Broiled Watermelon Steak	Cut into 2-inch-thick slices; remove seeds. Brush with oil; sprinkle with salt and pepper. Rub with ground dried chiles if you like.	Grill or broil until the flesh is lightly caramelized and dried out a bit, about 5 minutes on each side.	Sprinkle with chopped fresh rosemary; serve with lemon wedges. Omit the rosemary if you used chiles or chili powder.

Broiled Citrus and
Broiled Figs, page 361

Macerating and Seasoning Fruit

A simple technique that transforms the texture of fruit and leaves you with a little sauce in the process. Juicy fresh fruits like berries, citrus, and peaches often need only a sprinkle of sugar or salt to draw out their juices; others benefit from added liquid like simple syrup, fruit juice, vinegar, wine or brandy, or even water. Macerating is also a smart way to get some mileage out of less-than-perfect fruit.

Peel the fruit if the skin is tough or if you prefer it peeled. Chop or slice large or medium fruit; small fruit can be left whole. Mix together the fruit, the liquid, and whatever seasonings you're using—salt or sugar, fresh herbs, ground chiles, citrus zest, or warm spices like cinnamon or cardamom are all good in small quantities. Fresh fruit needs only about ½ cup liquid per pound of fruit, but dried fruit absorbs a good amount of liquid, so cover the fruit by an inch or even a little more; any extra liquid can have a second life as a flavorful cooking or deglazing liquid or mixer in beverages. Cover and set aside at room temperature, or in the refrigerator if the kitchen is warm, stirring every few hours.

Soft and juicy fresh fruit can take as little as 15 to 20 minutes to macerate; denser ones like apple and pineapple can take 3 to 4 hours; dried fruit requires 12 to 24 hours to soften fully. You want the fruit to be tender but not mushy.

Eat macerated fruit alone or with some cream, yogurt, or sour cream. Use it as a topping for pancakes, waffles, yogurt, or ice cream; as a filling for crêpes or blintzes; and as a garnish for simply cooked meat, fish, seafood, or chicken. Add to sauces and dressings. Puréed, it's a tasty addition to beverages like cocktails, tea, or smoothies.

texture—without the use of a special machine. See "Dried Fruit" (page 369) and Oven-Dried Tomatoes (page 348).

GRILLING OR BROILING

Broiled or grilled fruit teams beautifully with a green salad; complements the smokiness of grilled meats, seafood, or chicken; and works as an ingredient in salads; you can even use grilled fruit for making salsas. Sweet grilled fruit can be served with ice cream, sorbet, granita, rice pudding, or custard or next to cake or other drier desserts. Or use it to make grilled fruit pizza (see page 882).

Start with fruit that is ripe but still somewhat firm so it will hold together on the grill, the same kinds you would sauté or roast. Use a clean grill (very important!) and lower heat than you would for vegetables. Since most fruits are sugar-laden, they will char fairly quickly, in just a couple minutes in most cases. Give the fruit a good brushing with oil or melted butter before you put it on the grill, or else you'll be scraping it off. See "9 Sweet and Savory Ways to Broil and Grill Fruit" on page 361.

FRYING

With few exceptions, fruit should be breaded or battered before being deep-fried; coating the fruit not only protects it from overcooking but also helps control splattering. Flour and cornmeal—or a mixture of the two—are easy enough, though a batter creates wonderful fruit fritters. You can either pan-fry in shallow oil (½ inch deep or so; see page 21) or deep-fry in enough oil to submerge them (at least 3 inches of oil in a deep pot; see page 22). Then cook the fruit just as you would deep- or pan-fried vegetables.

The Fruit Lexicon

Turn the page for an alphabetical rundown of common fruits and what to do with them.

APPLES

There are thousands of varieties of apples in every shade of yellow, gold, red, and green, ranging from sweet to tart and mealy to crisp.

PREPARING Rinse and take a bite. Or peel and cut. To peel, start at the stem or flower end and work in strips up and down or around; a U-shaped peeler works best. Some people find it's easier to peel apples after cutting them into wedges.

To core, you have several options (see below): You can remove the core and leave the apple whole by digging into one end with a sturdy melon baller. You can either leave the stem intact for a nice presentation or work from that side if you want a flatter, more stable bottom. Or you can buy a slicer-corer, which will cut the apple into six or eight slices around the core in one swift motion. Or you can quarter the apple and dig out each piece of the core with a paring knife. There are even contraptions that hold the apple and spiral off the peel. Finally, you can just cut chunks of apple from around the core with a paring knife.

Apples brown quickly once peeled or cut. To prevent this, drop them into acidulated water (1 tablespoon lemon juice or vinegar per cup water) or white wine, or toss with lemon or lime juice.

OTHER FRUITS YOU CAN USE pears

Applesauce

MAKES: About 2 quarts | **TIME:** About 1 hour, largely unattended

A food processor is the easiest way to make smooth applesauce. The only question is whether you want flecks of skin in it or not. A food mill solves this dilemma deliciously since you can cook the apples with the skins on to lend both their flavor and color; the skins will be left behind during puréeing. Make as much as your time and the size of your pot allow by doubling or tripling the quantity. Applesauce freezes well and is handy when packed in small containers. See the list that follows for seasoning ideas.

Other fruits you can use: pears, cantaloupe.

> 5   **pounds apples (preferably a mixture of varieties)**
>   **Salt**

1. If you don't have a food mill, peel the apples or not as you prefer. Halve the apples, or quarter if they're very large; core. Put about ½ inch of water and a pinch of salt in a large pot. Add the apples. Cover and turn the heat to medium.
2. When the water boils, uncover the pot. Cook, stirring occasionally and adjusting the heat if the apples threaten to burn, until the apples break down and become mushy, at least 30 minutes. Let sit until cool enough to handle.
3. Working in batches, transfer the apples to a food processor and carefully pulse until it's the texture you like. Repeat with the remaining apples. Or if you have a food mill, pass the applesauce through it, discarding the solids that stay behind. To make applesauce without a machine, mash with a fork or potato masher. Serve warm. Or refrigerate for up to a week, or freeze for a couple months.

Coring an Apple

For whole baked or poached apples, use a melon baller and dig into either end, taking out a little at a time until the core has been removed. For the look of a whole apple, work from the flower end.

For other uses, cut the apple into quarters and remove the core with a paring knife, melon baller, or teaspoon.

 fast   make ahead   V vegetarian

CHERRY OR BERRY APPLESAUCE Replace up to 1 pound of the apples with pitted cherries, blueberries, raspberries, or cranberries. If using cranberries, plan on adding at least ¼ cup sugar in Step 1.

---

12 SWEET AND SAVORY SEASONINGS FOR APPLESAUCE

Just put any of the following ingredients into the pot or pan along with the apples. Start with a teaspoon or less, then taste after cooking and add more as needed.

1. Pepper
2. Ground cinnamon, cumin, coriander, caraway, or cardamom seeds
3. Chopped fresh chile like jalapeño or Thai, red chile flakes, or cayenne
4. Ground dried chipotle chiles, or minced canned with a little of their adobo sauce
5. Chopped fresh ginger or candied ginger (good with savory or sweet)
6. Granulated or brown sugar
7. Freshly grated nutmeg
8. Ground cloves or allspice
9. Any spice mixture (to make your own, see pages 27–35)
10. Roasted Garlic (page 294)
11. Minced fresh rosemary or thyme
12. Caramelized Onions (page 315) or any of the variations; start with ¼ cup

Sweet Sautéed Apples or Other Fruit

MAKES: 4 servings | **TIME:** 30 minutes

You can cook apples like a vegetable by sautéing or stir-frying. Or use the same technique to turn them into a

dessert, sort of a tarte Tatin without the crust. Serve the apples alone or with a scoop of vanilla ice cream or a dollop of Whipped Cream (page 854) or crème fraiche.

Other fruits you can use: pears, apricots, peaches, nectarines, plums, cherries, pineapple.

- 4 tablespoons (½ stick) unsalted butter
- 1½ pounds firm, crisp apples like Golden Delicious, peeled, cored, and cut into 8 or 10 pieces each
- ½ cup granulated or brown sugar
- ½ teaspoon ground cinnamon

1. Put the butter in a large skillet over medium heat. When the butter melts and foams, add the apples and stir. Adjust the heat so the apples sizzle gently and cook, stirring occasionally, until tender but not breaking apart, about 10 minutes.

2. Add the sugar and cinnamon and raise the heat so the apples brown without burning. Cook, stirring frequently, until the apples are tender and glazed, another 10 minutes or so. Serve hot or warm. (Or refrigerate in an airtight container for up to a week.)

SAVORY SAUTÉED APPLES OR OTHER FRUIT Perfect with pork chops or any roast pork, also in whole grain bowls or on Bruschetta or Crostini (page 95) for an autumn or winter twist: Use olive oil instead of butter if you like and omit the sugar. Season with salt and pepper. Instead of cinnamon use cumin, coriander, or curry powder.

Baked Apples

MAKES: 4 servings | **TIME:** About 1 hour

Go savory and use salt; go sweet and use sugar. Savory baked apples are excellent alongside pork, or with sour cream or yogurt; their sweet counterparts make

Common Apples

APPLE VARIETY	DESCRIPTION	FLAVOR AND TEXTURE	CATEGORY
Braeburn	Red with lighter flecks and a green tinge around the stem. Yellow flesh	Sweet, slightly tangy, juicy, crisp	All-purpose
Cortland	Red with bright green patches. White flesh that doesn't turn brown quickly	Sweet, juicy, tender	All-purpose
Empire	Red with lighter flecks and yellowish-green patches. Cream-colored flesh	Sweet-tart, juicy, very crisp; but can also be mushy	All-purpose
Fuji	Red with yellow and green mottling. Cream-colored flesh. Nothing special	Sweet, juicy, fairly crisp	Eating
Gala	Red with gold mottling. Light yellow flesh	Mild, sweet, crisp	Eating
Golden Delicious	Greenish-gold skin, sometimes with a blush of pink. Light yellow flesh	Full-flavored, sweet-tart, juicy, crisp	All-purpose
Granny Smith	Green with light flecks. White flesh	Tart to sweet-tart, juicy, very crisp; holds shape well when cooked	All-purpose
Honeycrisp	Small to huge. Bright red skin with golden streaks. Ivory flesh that doesn't brown fast	Super-sweet and, well, crisp, but with just enough tang for balance.	All-purpose
Ida Red	Large. Brilliant red. Light green flesh with a touch of pink	Sweet, juicy, firm; holds shape well when cooked	Cooking
Jonagold	Red with golden-yellow flecks and streaks of green. Light yellow flesh. Better than Golden Delicious but harder to find	Very sweet, juicy, crisp	All-purpose
Jonathan	Red with some bright yellow streaks. Off-white flesh. Doesn't bake well whole	Sweet-tart with a bit of spice, juicy, crisp	All-purpose
Macoun	Red with green patches and mottling. White flesh. A New England favorite, available late fall only	Very sweet, juicy, tender	Eating
McIntosh	Bright red with green patches. Off-white flesh	Sweet and crisp when very fresh; becomes mushy quickly	All-purpose
Opal	Bright yellow skin with a hint of rosiness; the insides are golden. Doesn't travel well so you might not see far beyond where they're grown	Tart and crisp, with tender, slightly mealy flesh	All-purpose
Pink Lady	Rosy pink and golden yellow. White flesh that doesn't turn brown quickly	Sweet-tart, juicy, very crisp; lots of flavor	All-purpose
Red Delicious	Dark red. Off-white flesh. The most common, but most often mealy	Sweet but not complex, often mealy	Eating
Rome	Bright red and round. Greenish flesh	Mildly tart and tender	Cooking

 fast  make ahead vegetarian

a simple dessert with cookies, ice cream, or whipped cream. Either way, serve them piping hot or at room temperature.

Other fruits you can use: any ripe firm pear, like Bosc.

> 4 **large round apples (preferably Cortland or Ida Red)**
> **About 1 cup water, sweet or dry white wine, or apple juice**
> **Salt (optional)**
> **Sugar (optional)**

1. Heat the oven to 350°F.

2. Core the apples (see illustrations on page 364), leaving the stem end intact, and peel the top half of each. Put in a baking dish and pour in the liquid to a depth of about ½ inch. If you're using salt, sprinkle some lightly all over. If you're using sugar, put about 1 teaspoon in the cavity of each apple and sprinkle another teaspoon or so on top.

3. Bake, uncovered, until the apples are very tender, about an hour. Baste occasionally with a spoon or brush, if you like. Serve warm or at room temperature. Or refrigerate for up to a day or 2; bring the apples back to room temperature before serving.

---

7 SIMPLE IDEAS FOR BAKED APPLES

1. Cream sugar or spices with 2 tablespoons unsalted butter before adding it.

2. Substitute maple syrup, honey, or brown sugar for the granulated sugar.

3. Add about ½ cup chopped nuts, shredded coconut, raisins, and/or chopped figs or dates to the sugar for filling.

4. Fill the apple cavities with jam after about 45 minutes of baking.

5. Fill the apple cavities with grated cheddar or crumbled blue cheese before baking, and use apple cider for the liquid.

6. Fill the apple cavities with crumbled sausage (removed from the casings) before baking.

7. Sprinkle the apples with Streusel Topping (page 221) after 30 minutes of baking.

APRICOTS

Good apricots are precious—sweet and tart, with silky skin and a dense but succulent interior. Get your hands on them and you're in for a real treat. But a perfectly ripe, juicy, and flavorful apricot is hard to find, even if you live where they're grown (now mostly California).

PREPARING Not much to it: tear or cut it in half and remove the pit. Or just bite into it. I don't bother to peel apricots but you can: Plunge them into boiling water for about 10 seconds, then slip off the skin. Soak or cook dried apricots in liquid to soften. Dried is the most accessible form to use in both sweet and savory dishes. Sauté fresh apricots along with the aromatics and let them melt away into the dish, or add dried at the last minute.

OTHER FRUITS YOU CAN USE peaches, nectarines; for dried apricots, any other soft dried fruit like raisins, prunes, dates

BANANAS

A tropical plant with hundreds of varieties including plantains (see page 322), the most familiar being the yellow Cavendish banana, sometimes called sweet or dessert banana. But there are also tiny finger bananas, red, and even blue varieties, all with varying flavors and sweetness.

PREPARING How ripe they are is a matter of personal preference. Peel and eat, or chop or slice as needed. Squeeze some lemon or lime juice over a freshly cut banana to prevent discoloring.

OTHER FRUITS YOU CAN USE There is no substitute for raw bananas; for cooking, use ripe plantains.

Baked Apples, page 365

Dried Fruit

Before the days of refrigeration and canning, drying fruit was the only way to preserve it. The process captures the optimal flavor and intensifies it, so dried fruit is often superior to its fresh counterpart. Several methods can be used to dry fruit, starting with the most primitive, sun-drying. The fruit may be halved or chopped, and just left out in the sun for several days.

More common drying methods include air-drying, a combination of air circulation and low heat that can be done in an oven, though it's best with a dehydrator; sugar-drying, by soaking or poaching fruit in a sugar syrup, followed by air-drying—think candied ginger; and frying like potato chips, best for high-starch, low-moisture fruits like bananas.

Regardless of the method, many commercially dried fruits are treated with sulfur dioxide before processing, a preservative that helps the fruit hold its color, flavor, and shape. If you're sensitive to sulfites—or can taste them—look for unsulfured dried fruits, which are now easy to find.

DRYING FRUIT AT HOME

Unless you have a dehydrator, oven-drying is your best option: It adds no extra sugar or fat; takes a few hours, but is mostly hands-off; and gives you plenty of control over the final product, which may be plump and chewy or shriveled and completely dry, depending on the size of the pieces and how long you dry them.

Small items like grapes, berries, and cherry tomatoes can be left whole; medium-size fruits, halved or sliced; large and/or very hard fruit like papaya, pineapple, and coconut must be sliced. Put the prepared fruit on a wire rack over a baking sheet, cut-side down where applicable, and bake in a 225°F oven for anywhere from 2 to 12 hours. Rotate the baking sheet every couple of hours. The fruit is done when it's as shriveled and dried as you like (see Oven-Dried Tomatoes on page 348 for descriptions).

In a dehydrator, the water is evaporated from fruit very slowly, with only a little heat. Most machines have a small electrical element in the base, a tower of racks, and a vent and ideally a fan on top. Depending on the fruit and how packed the dehydrator is, it can take more than 24 hours to dry fully, though as with oven-drying, you can stop the process at any point. Dehydrators are handy, especially if you have fruit trees or a vegetable garden.

Roasted Bananas

MAKES: 4 servings | TIME: 15 minutes

A fast and easy dessert or side dish to serve with pork chops and roasts or grilled fish, and one for which you will almost always have the ingredients on hand.

Other fruits you can use: ripe plantains.

- 4 bananas (ripe but not too soft), peeled and halved lengthwise
- 3 tablespoons unsalted butter
- 2 tablespoons sugar, or to taste (optional)
  Fresh lemon juice for serving

Heat the oven to 400°F. Put the bananas in a baking dish or roasting pan seeds side up, dot with the butter, and sprinkle with sugar if you're using it. Bake until golden brown, about 15 minutes. Squeeze a bit of lemon juice over the top just before serving.

SAUTÉED BANANAS Put the butter in a large skillet over medium-high heat. When the butter foams, add the banana halves and sprinkle with the sugar if you're using it. Cook, turning once, until golden and lightly brown on both sides, about 10 minutes. Transfer the bananas to a serving plate. Turn off the heat and squeeze in a bit of lemon juice or drizzle in some bourbon into the pan, scraping up any browned bits. Drizzle the pan sauce over the bananas and serve.

BERRIES

Hundreds of different berries grow all over the world on vines or bushes, ranging in color from white to blue to red, orange, yellow, or black. They might be sweet or tart and everything in between and, with the exception of the blueberry, cranberry, and a couple of less common varieties like gooseberries, they're very perishable. See the cranberry and cherry listings below and on page 374.

PREPARING Strawberries: see the illustration at right. Rinse and dry. Pull or cut off the leaves, then use a paring knife to dig out the stem and core.

Blueberries: Pick over, remove any stems, rinse, and dry.

Blackberries and raspberries: Rinse and dry very gently. I do not rinse wild berries as long as I'm sure of the source.

When in doubt, treat other berries like raspberries: gently.

OTHER FRUITS YOU CAN USE berries are fairly interchangeable when used raw, or use grapes or sweet cherries; blueberries, blackberries, and raspberries can substitute for one another in cooked dishes

Preparing Strawberries

First remove the leaves, then cut a cone-shaped wedge with a paring knife to remove the core.

CHERIMOYAS

Also known as the custard apple, a medium-size tropical fruit related to the soursop or guanabana, with green, leathery, scaled-looking skin and—at its best—a white, creamy, dreamy custardlike interior with a pineapple-banana flavor.

PREPARING Halve, remove the large seeds, and scoop out the flesh with a spoon. Eat raw.

CHERRIES

There are two types of cherries: sweet, and sour or tart. The former is best for eating out of hand, the latter for pie making and cooking. Sour cherries are often sold at farmers' markets and farmstands; they are typically smaller, brighter red, and rounder in shape than the sweet varieties and for many people are too tart to eat raw. They're great for pies and cobblers though, and frozen work just fine.

PREPARING Rinse and dry for eating out of hand. Remove the stem and pit for cooking. A cherry pitter (which also works for olives) is handy if you're going to pit a large number.

OTHER FRUITS YOU CAN USE fresh currants, dried cherries; for cooking: cranberries, blueberries

Stewed Cherries, Sweet or Savory

MAKES: 4 to 6 servings | **TIME:** About 30 minutes

Here's a simple treat: Go sweet and it's like cherry pie without the crust. Veer savory, and it's a lovely sauce for chicken or duck or any kind of game bird, pork, lamb, or juicy and rich steak. To make it savory, use stock or wine and add sugar just to taste, especially if you're using sour cherries; to make it sweet, use wine or water and add as much sugar as you like.

OTHER FRUITS YOU CAN USE apricots, cranberries, fresh currants, grapes, blueberries.

> 2 pounds cherries (preferably sour; thawed frozen are fine), pitted
> 1 cup water, red wine, or stock (see headnote)
> Sugar
> Salt and pepper (for savory)
> ¼ teaspoon ground cinnamon (for sweet; optional), or 1 sprig fresh thyme (for savory; optional)
> 1 tablespoon fresh lemon juice if using sweet cherries, or to taste
> 1 teaspoon chopped lemon zest (for sweet; optional)

1. Put the cherries and liquid in a medium saucepan over medium-high heat and cook, stirring occasionally, until the cherries are very tender, about 20 minutes.

2. Stir in the sugar, salt, pepper, and/or cinnamon if you're using them; taste and add more seasoning, including the lemon juice and zest if you like. Serve warm, at room temperature, or cold.

CHERRIES IN PORT, SWEET OR SAVORY Choose tawny or sweeter ruby as you prefer. Make either the sweet or savory version, but use port wine for the liquid. Port is sweet, so be sure to taste the cherries before adding any sugar.

CHERRIES JUBILEE Omit the cinnamon, lemon juice, and lemon zest. Proceed with the recipe, making it quite sweet. Dole out 4 to 6 servings vanilla or other ice cream. Add ¼ cup brandy (it must be at least 80 proof) to the cherries while still warm. Carefully touch with a match to ignite, then spoon the flaming cherries over the ice cream and serve.

COCONUT

This tropical fruit comes in many different forms: whole, shredded fresh, dried flakes, oil, water, milk, and flour. It's all good, as long as you buy the unsweetened kind.

PREPARING If you're starting with a whole coconut, drive the point of an ice pick, scissors blade, or corkscrew into its soft eye; drain out the water and drink or cook with it later. Put the coconut in a double layer of plastic grocery or trash bags. Go outside or wherever there is a concrete step or floor; slam the coconut into the concrete as many times as it takes to break it open. Come back into the kitchen and pry the pieces of meat out of the shell. Remove the brown skin. Chop, slice, or shred the white meat as you like.

BEST COOKING METHOD making fresh coconut milk; toasting; using in soups, braises, stir-fries, and for breading

WHEN IS IT DONE? When lightly golden brown

Toasting Coconut

An easy garnish or condiment. If you're using fresh coconut, grate it or slice it paper-thin. Heat a dry skillet over medium-low heat or put a rimmed baking sheet in a 350°F oven. When the pan is hot, spread the coconut in a single layer and cook until it darkens as much as you want, 5 to 10 minutes for dried or 15 to 20 minutes for fresh. Be sure to keep an eye on it and shake the pan occasionally; once it starts to turn, it goes fast.

Coconut Milk

MAKES: About 2 cups | **TIME:** 20 minutes

Though it's fine to use canned, homemade coconut milk is super-easy and much purer in both flavor and ingredients. All you need is unsweetened dried coconut, which is available in many supermarkets.

Coconut Milk

This recipe gives you a fairly thick milk, akin to canned. Thin it with water or repeat the process on the coconut again; the second pressing will be thinner.

1 cup unsweetened dried coconut meat

1. Combine the coconut with 2 cups very hot water in a blender. Pulse on and off quickly, then turn on the blender and let it work for 15 seconds or so; take care that the top of the blender stays in place. Let sit for a few minutes.

2. Pour the mixture through a fine-mesh strainer into a bowl, pressing to extract as much of the liquid as possible. Discard the solids. Use the milk right away. Or store, covered, in the refrigerator for up to a few days.

CRANBERRIES

Cranberries should be bright red, evenly round, and firm. They're too astringent to be eaten out of hand, so they're always cooked or combined with other ingredients.

PREPARING Pick over, rinse, and if necessary, dry.

OTHER FRUITS YOU CAN USE dried cranberries, sour cherries, fresh currants, blueberries

CURRANTS

Fresh currants are small berries that grow in clusters of brilliant red, purplish black, or white fruit. The most common dried currants are also known as Zante currants and are actually made from small grapes. Dried or fresh, currants are good in pies, jams, jellies, and other desserts. Fresh, they're also delicious with other fruits or served simply with some cream and sugar.

PREPARING Remove the stems, pick over, rinse, and if necessary, dry.

OTHER FRUITS YOU CAN USE cherries, raspberries, blueberries

DATES

More and more you see fresh dates from California. But it's most common to find them dried. Both ways are a delight—sticky-sweet, tender—and when fresh, they're even a little juicy.

PREPARING Remove the pits by slicing the fruit lengthwise and pulling the seed out by the tip.

OTHER FRUITS YOU CAN USE raisins, prunes, dried apricots or figs (though none are quite as sweet)

FIGS

When fresh and ripe, figs are supple, sweet, and wonderful. The delicate skin is soft and delicious, the interior flesh succulent, gorgeously white and pink, and loaded with tiny edible seeds. Dried, they are even sweeter, with a chewy, almost meaty texture.

PREPARING Rinse and eat fresh ones. Or sauté, roast, or grill them. Dried figs may be eaten, soaked, or cooked as any dried fruit.

OTHER FRUITS YOU CAN USE There is no substitute for fresh figs; for dried, nearly any dried fruit like raisins, prunes, apricots

GRAPES

There are two categories of grapes grown around the world: white (also called green) and black (often referred to as red). White grapes are actually green to greenish yellow, and black grapes range from reddish to the deepest of purple. Americans eat mostly seedless grapes—and raisins, which are of course dried grapes—but in fact, breeding out the seeds also breeds out much of the flavor. So varieties with seeds—muscat, Niagara, and Concord—are making a bit of a comeback.

PREPARING Pesticides are used heavily on grapes, so rinse them very well or consider buying organic.

 fast make ahead  vegetarian

OTHER FRUITS YOU CAN USE blueberries, cherries; also see Currants (page 374)

GRAPEFRUIT

West Indian in origin, now widely grown in Florida, Arizona, Texas, and California, there are two main types of grapefruit, white and red, differentiated more by the color of their flesh than their skin. Pomelo or shaddock and Ugli (aptly—if cruelly—named) are similar and may be treated the same as grapefruit.

PREPARING Halve the grapefruit through its equator, then cut down and around the inside sections, separating the flesh from the skin; eat with a spoon. Or peel and separate the segments as you would an orange; this is especially useful with smaller specimens.

OTHER FRUITS YOU CAN USE oranges, pomelos

KIWIS
CHINESE GOOSEBERRIES

A native Chinese fruit named after New Zealand's national bird (oddly, the fruit and the flightless bird do look somewhat similar), kiwis are soft, juicy, and sweet-tart when ripe, and more on the tart side (though not entirely bad) when not quite ripe enough.

PREPARING Peel—or not, if you don't mind the fuzz—and slice or cut into wedges. Or halve and scoop out the flesh with a spoon.

OTHER FRUITS YOU CAN USE star fruit, grapes, honeydew melon

KUMQUATS

Kumquats look like tiny oranges. The entire fruit is edible, and believe it or not it's the skin that's the best part: It's thin and sweet, while the flesh is heavily seeded and very tart.

PREPARING Rinse, dry, and use whole or slice, chop, or quarter, removing the seeds.

OTHER FRUITS YOU CAN USE oranges, tangerines

LEMONS AND LIMES

The most useful of kitchen fruits: a squirt of their juice or a sprinkle of zest can add just the right amount of acid and flavor to perfectly brighten and balance a dish, sauce, or beverage. The lemon is the essential fruit in European cooking, while the lime takes center stage in Asian and tropical cooking. It pays to keep some of each in your kitchen.

PREPARING Cut lengthwise into halves, quarters, wedges, or slices and remove any pits with the point of a knife. To juice, cut into halves through the equator.

There are a few ways to zest citrus; how you choose to do it should partly depend on how you'll use it. A zester is a nifty tool with small sharp-edged holes that cuts off long, thin strips of zest, which can then be minced; the strips are wonderful for garnishing when whole. Another method is to use a vegetable peeler or paring knife to remove the peel in ribbons. This technique inevitably brings part of the bitter white pith with it; to do a perfect job you should then lay the strips down on a cutting board and scrape the white part off with a paring knife, then slice or mince as you like. The easiest method is to use a sharp grater (like a Microplane), which results in tiny flecks of zest that are nearly undetectable in dishes except for their flavor.

OTHER FRUITS YOU CAN USE lemons and limes are more or less interchangeable

Preserved Lemons

MAKES: 1 quart | **TIME:** 20 minutes, plus 2 weeks to cure

A couple of recipes in this book call for preserved lemons, a salted condiment frequently used in Mediterranean stews. But they're tremendous in so many dishes:

Chopped up, you can add them to all sorts of pilafs and braised vegetable dishes. Or make a refreshing drink by muddling a couple of pieces in the bottom of a glass, then topping it off with ice and sparkling water.

3 pounds lemons (preferably unwaxed, otherwise scrubbed well)
About ¾ cup kosher salt
Half 3-inch cinnamon stick
2 or 3 whole cloves
1 star anise pod
2 or 3 black peppercorns
2 cardamom pods
1 bay leaf

1. Fill a clean quart-sized jar with a tight-fitting lid with boiling water; soak its lid in boiling water too. Let sit while you cut the lemons, then dump the water out.

2. Quarter the lemons lengthwise. Sprinkle a ¼-inch-deep layer of salt across the bottom of the jar. Nestle a layer of lemon quarters in the jar, sprinkle liberally with salt, then repeat, adding the cinnamon, cloves, star anise, peppercorns, cardamom, and bay leaf as you go. Stop when the jar is about three-quarters full. Squeeze the remaining lemons into the jar—seeds and all—so that the fruit is completely submerged in the lemon juice–and–salt brine. If you don't have enough lemons on hand, top off with more fresh juice no later than the following day.

3. Set the jar out on the counter; vigorously shake it once a day for 7 days. During this time it might start to bubble a little and the spices will swell back to their original size from before drying. (You'll be surprised at the size of the cloves!)

4. Put the jar in the refrigerator. Let the lemons continue to cure for another week before using. After that time, unscrew the lid. In a moment they should smell sweet and citrusy; an ammonia smell means they've gone bad somewhere along the line and you need to toss the batch. The lemons will keep for at least 2 months in the refrigerator, though you'll probably want to get into them sooner.

5. To use in stews, blanch the quartered lemons in unsalted boiling water for 10 seconds, just long enough to leach out a little of the salt. For salads or quick-cooked dishes, scrape the flesh away from the peel, discard the flesh, and blanch the peel in unsalted boiling water as above.

Peeling and Pitting a Mango, Version I

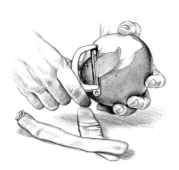

STEP 1 Peel, using a normal vegetable peeler or paring knife.

STEP 2 Cut the sides off, doing the best you can to work around the large oval pit.

STEP 3 Finally, chop the mango flesh with a knife.

 **F** fast **M** make ahead **V** vegetarian

LYCHEES

Native to southern China, lychees (or litchis) are small fruits with scaly, sometimes prickly inedible skin that protects the juicy white flesh, which in turn surrounds a shiny, brown inedible seed. The texture of lychees is like that of a fleshy grape, and the flavor is sweet and one-of-a-kind, though akin to that of cherries. Canned lychees are mostly just sugary sweet and not worth eating.

PREPARING Use the stem to break open the skin and gently peel it off; eat the fruit and spit out the seed.

OTHER FRUITS YOU CAN USE grapes; kiwi, star fruit (for a tropical flavor)

MANGOES

There are dozens of shapes, sizes, and colors of mango, from orange-size to melon-size; green to yellow, orange, or red; exceedingly tart to syrupy sweet. Both ripe and unripe mangoes are useful: unripe for chutney, pickling, and making amchoor (see page 28), and ripe for eating straight, making salsas, fruit salads, and cooking, especially on the grill. The small yellow Alfonso mangoes are, for my money, the best of the most commonly available.

PREPARING The method you choose will depend on your knife skills and your patience. (See the illustrations on page 376 and below.) The quick and messy way is to just peel off the skin—a vegetable peeler or paring knife makes quick work of it—and attack. For a neater presentation, trim a piece off the bottom end. Stand the fruit on a cutting board, trim off the skin with a sharp paring knife, then slice fruit from around the pit. For small pieces, cut the flesh off each side of the pit without peeling. Score the flesh in a cross-hatch pattern without cutting through the skin. Then turn each half inside out and cut away the cubes.

OTHER FRUITS YOU CAN USE papaya, cantaloupe or other fleshy orange melon, oranges

MELONS

Melons taste of summer, and the widest variety and most flavorful are at farmstands and farmers' markets in peak season. Selecting the right melon is part skill and part luck. You might ask for help from the farmer. Otherwise, start by smelling it; if it smells sweet and like a melon, that's a good start. For watermelons, slap the side and listen for a hollow sound.

Peeling and Pitting a Mango, Version II

STEP 1 Begin by cutting as much of the unpeeled mango off each side of the pit as you can.

STEP 2 Score the flesh with a paring knife.

STEP 3 Turn each mango piece inside out and slice off the cubes of flesh.

PREPARING Cut the melon in half and scrape out the seeds with a spoon; continue cutting it into quarters or slices. Use a paring knife to slice off the rind, if you like. A melon baller easily lets you scoop out spheres of melon. Or you can simply cut the flesh into pieces. Grated melon is good in yogurt sauces and raw salsas; just be sure to grate it over a bowl to save the juices.

Watermelons can be cut casually into wedges with seeds. But if you want to seed them, cut into wedges and slice off the top or "heart" to reveal the row of seeds. Remove them with the tines of a fork. Then cut to the desired size.

Allow a chilled melon to come to room temperature before serving; when it's chilled, the flavors are muted. Try serving with a squeeze of lemon or lime juice—it adds flavor to an underripe melon and complements a ripe one. A sprinkle of salt is an interesting change of pace (as is a dash of ground chile).

OTHER FRUITS YOU CAN USE melons are interchangeable with one another; papaya, mango, (sometimes) cucumber

ORANGES, MANDARINS, TANGERINES, AND SIMILAR CITRUS

There are three types of oranges: sweet (Valencia, navel, or temple), loose skinned (any Mandarin or tangerine), and bitter (Seville). Sweet and loose-skinned oranges are used for eating and juicing, while bitter ones are used only for making marmalades and other cooked products; we don't see them fresh too often in this country. Fortunately we do have more varieties of seedless and seed-in citrus available than ever before. Winter is a lot brighter than it used to be.

PREPARING Oranges are easiest to eat when cut into quarters or eighths. To peel, cut four or eight slits from top to bottom, through the skin but not into the flesh. Peel each of these off. Many oranges can be peeled with just your fingers. Or for neater segments or wheels, see the illustrations below.

OTHER FRUITS YOU CAN USE sweet and Mandarin oranges are interchangeable; lemon or lime juice can replace the acidic flavor of bitter oranges

Cutting Citrus Segments (Supremes) or Wheels

STEP 1 Before beginning to peel and segment citrus, cut a slice off both ends of the fruit so that it stands straight.

STEP 2 Cut as close to the pulp as possible, removing the skin in long strips.

STEP 3 Cut between the membranes to separate segments (also called "supremes").

STEP 4 Or cut across any peeled citrus fruit to make "wheels."

 F fast **M** make ahead **V** vegetarian

PAPAYAS

Grown in the tropical regions of the Americas and Asia, papaya is eaten both green (see Green Papaya Salad, page 210) and ripe, ideally with a sprinkle of lime. When ripe, papaya skin is golden yellow to deep orange; the flesh is soft, melonlike, deep orange to red, and the edible—though not very pleasant—seeds a shiny greenish gray.

PREPARING Rinse, peel, halve, and scoop out the seeds (to eat or not). Then slice or chop.

OTHER FRUITS YOU CAN USE mango, cantaloupe or other fleshy orange melons

PASSION FRUIT

Rare but worth seeking out. The flavor is quite tart but sensational, and the fragrance is wonderful too. I like to strain the pulp and blend it into sauces, juices, smoothies, and ice cream and sorbet bases. Ripe passion fruit will have a dimpled or slightly shriveled exterior.

PREPARING Halve and scoop out the flesh with a spoon. The seeds are edible, but for just the juice, use a fine-mesh strainer to separate them out; press to extract as much of the juice as possible.

OTHER FRUITS YOU CAN USE oranges, guavas, mangoes, pulsed in the food processor or blender (not the same, but reasonable)

PEACHES AND NECTARINES

They are nearly identical in shape and color, but peach skin has a soft fuzz and nectarine skin is smooth. Variations in color don't matter much, but there are two broad categories of peaches and nectarines based on how much the flesh clings to the pit: freestone and clingstone. Both are good; freestones are certainly easier to cut up.

Common Pears

PEAR VARIETY	DESCRIPTION	FLAVOR AND TEXTURE
Anjou	One of the most common varieties. Green and red types with a broad oval shape	Flesh is firm (good for poaching) and sweet but not spectacular
Asian	Round, apple-shaped. Yellow to russeted-gold	Flesh is crisp (and is best that way, which is unusual for a pear) and juicy, with a delicate apple-pear flavor
Bartlett	The most common variety and the only one used for commercial canning and drying. Bell-shaped and green when unripe, yellow with a red blush when ripe	Soft, sweet, juicy flesh; rarely impressive
Bosc	Somewhat tear-shaped with an elongated neck. Golden brown russet color. At its best, spectacular	Juicy flesh similar to Anjou but more aromatic
Comice	Squat pear shape with a stubby neck and stem. Green with a bronze blush. The best widely available pear	Very sweet, juicy, soft flesh. Wonderful fragrance
Packham	Imported in winter from the Southern Hemisphere. Fat, round, and a bit irregular in shape. Green to greenish yellow	Fairly sweet flesh; rarely great.
Seckel	Miniature and precious looking. Green with a deep red blush. The skin can be tough, but these are worth trying.	Spicy flavor. Lovely for poaching whole

Poached Pears with
Wine or Port Syrup

PREPARING Rinse, peel if you like, and eat. To pit, halve vertically; twist the halves, which will either come completely free of the pit (freestone) or leave a fair amount of flesh on the pit (clingstone). To peel, drop into boiling water for 10 to 30 seconds, just until the skin loosens; plunge into a bowl of ice water; remove the peel with your fingers and/or a paring knife.

OTHER FRUITS YOU CAN USE peaches and nectarines are interchangeable; apricots, plums, mangoes

PEARS

PREPARING Peeling is not necessary, but it's easy with a vegetable peeler. Core by slicing the pear into quarters, then cutting out the core with a paring knife; or halve it and dig out the core with a spoon. To keep the fruit whole, dig out the core from the blossom end with a paring knife. For varieties, see page 379

OTHER FRUITS YOU CAN USE apples

Poached Pears with Vanilla

MAKES: 4 servings | **TIME:** about 20 minutes, plus time to cool

Pears can be poached at any stage of ripeness, with added sugar making up for any lack of fully developed natural sugars. So even with an unripe pear, this becomes an impressive, light dessert.

Other fruits you can use: apples, apricots, peaches, nectarines, kumquats, pineapple.

2½	**cups sugar**
½	**vanilla bean, split lengthwise, or one 3-inch cinnamon stick**
4	**pears**

1. Combine the sugar and vanilla or cinnamon with 5 cups water in a medium saucepan (large enough to accommodate the pears) over high heat. Peel the pears,

leaving their stems on. Core them by digging into the blossom end with a melon baller, spoon, or paring knife.

2. Lower the pears into the boiling syrup and adjust the heat so that it bubbles gently. Cook, turning the pears every 5 minutes or so, until they meet little resistance when pierced with a skewer or thin-bladed knife, usually from 10 to 20 minutes. Turn off the heat and allow to cool in the liquid. (At this point, you can cover and refrigerate the pears for up to a day; bring to room temperature before serving.)

3. Transfer the pears to serving plates. Reduce the poaching liquid to a cup or less (this can also be stored for a day), then spoon a little over each pear before serving.

POACHED PEARS WITH GINGER AND STAR ANISE Add 3 star anise pods, 5 slices fresh ginger, and 2 whole cloves to the poaching syrup.

POACHED PEARS WITH WINE OR PORT SYRUP The flavor of the wine is dominant in the syrup so you can go sweet, fruity, or rich: For the poaching syrup use 1½ cups water, 2 cups red or white wine or port, ¾ cup sugar, one 3-inch cinnamon stick, and 1 lemon, sliced.

CINNAMON POACHED APPLES A nice alternative, and unexpected: Substitute apples for the pears and use the cinnamon stick instead of the vanilla bean.

PERSIMMONS

A vibrant orange fruit with either a juicy, jellylike interior or a crisp, applelike quality, depending on the variety. The heart-shaped, traditional Hachiya persimmon—that's the mushy one—is by far the most common and usually used for desserts. The squat Fuyu variety is gaining ground; it is excellent in salads or stir-fries.

PREPARING Ripe Hachiyas can be eaten out of hand (over a sink—they're messy). Or cut off the top and scoop out the flesh with a spoon. Remove the stem from a hard Fuyu and bite in or peel if you'd like and slice like an apple.

OTHER FRUITS YOU CAN USE There is no replacement for a Hachiya; apple or pear can replace a firm Fuyu, but only in terms of texture.

PINEAPPLE

One of the glories of nature, the pineapple is native to Central and South America and is grown throughout the tropics. Its prickly, diamond-patterned, spiny skin ranges from yellow to green to brownish red when ripe. The flesh is juicy, sweet-tart, and acidic. At its best, it's among the best-tasting fruits there is, especially when roasted, broiled, or grilled.

PREPARING There are a few ways to dismember a pineapple; my two favorites are illustrated below.

OTHER FRUITS YOU CAN USE oranges, grapefruit, kiwis, star fruit

PLUMS

Late summer is the time for plums, when the different varieties seem to hit stores and farmstands in waves. Ripe plums are quite soft, even oozing a sugary syrup—eat these right away—but avoid those that are mushy or split, or smell fermented. Underripe fruit is hard and sour; leave out at room temperature to ripen. Prunes (now mostly

Preparing a Pineapple, Two Ways

STEP 1 Cut off the top of the pineapple about an inch below the spikes, then slice off the other end as well.

STEP 2 Set the pineapple upright. Slice off the skin, working around the pineapple. If necessary, remove any eyes with a paring knife.

STEP 3 Cut the pineapple into round slices.

STEP 4 Cut out the core with a paring knife to make rings.

OR STEP 2 Alternatively, stand the pineapple up and quarter it.

STEP 3 Use a grapefruit knife to separate the fruit from the skin and a paring knife to dig out any eyes. Remove the core (the hard edge where the fruit comes to a point), slice, and serve.

F fast   **M** make ahead   **V** vegetarian

called "dried plums") are often your best bet if it's not peak growing season; they'll be different but delicious.

PREPARING Rinse and eat. You can peel them before cooking: drop into boiling water for about 10 seconds, or until the skins loosen, then peel with a paring knife. To rehydrate dried plums, soak them in boiling water until soft, up to an hour.

OTHER FRUITS YOU CAN USE apricots, peaches, nectarines

POMEGRANATE

An odd fruit in appearance and behavior that ranges from orange- to grapefruit-sized. Its exterior skin is speckled dark red and leathery, and the edible (and potassium-rich) seeds contained in inedible white pith are covered with a crisp and snappy ruby-red flesh. The seeds can be eaten whole or the juicy flesh sucked off and the seeds discarded; it's a matter of personal taste.

PREPARING Either halve or cut an inch or so into the top and pry open into segments. Breaking the segments apart can be done underwater; the bad seeds and inedible pith float to the top, the good seeds sink to the bottom, and the staining juice doesn't squirt all over. Or you can seed pomegranates in a plastic bag to contain the mess.

OTHER FRUITS YOU CAN USE cherries, fresh currants, raspberries

QUINCE

Quince, which is related to the apple, has been cultivated and cherished for its fragrance and fruity flavor since at least the time of ancient Rome. But it's almost always cooked—where it becomes dark pink—since it's virtually inedible when raw.

PREPARING Peel, quarter, and remove the core; the seeds are mildly poisonous—not enough to worry about, but don't eat them. Chop or slice as needed.

BEST COOKING METHODS braising, stewing

WHEN ARE THEY DONE? When very tender and easily pierced with a skewer or thin-bladed knife

OTHER FRUITS YOU CAN USE apples, pears

RHUBARB

Usually used as a fruit in sweet preparations (though not always; see Dal with Rhubarb, page 410), rhubarb on its own is actually extremely tart. You can take advantages of its tartness, or cook it with sugar or other sweet fruits, which is why we see it most often made into desserts, often paired with strawberries. Be aware that rhubarb leaves and roots are poisonous, though only mildly so.

PREPARING Although it's not entirely necessary, rhubarb is best if you string it. Grab one end between a paring knife and your thumb and pull straight down to remove the celerylike strings that run lengthwise through each stalk. See the illustrations on page 279.

BEST COOKING METHODS braising, stewing

WHEN IS IT DONE? When very tender and easily pierced with a skewer or thin-bladed knife

OTHER FRUITS YOU CAN USE cranberries, tart cherries, fresh currants

STAR FRUIT

Also known as carambola, a tropical fruit with five pointed ridges that, when sliced crosswise, create a pretty star shape. It's fragrant, juicy, and sweet-tart when perfectly ripe, but often the ones we get here in the U.S. fall short of that. The skin is edible; star fruit are best eaten raw in salads.

PREPARING Rinse, dry, and slice crosswise, the thinner the better.

OTHER FRUITS YOU CAN USE kiwi, orange segments, grapes

Beans

CHAPTER AT A GLANCE

The Basics of Beans 386

Recipes That Start with Cooked or Canned Beans 392

Beans in a Pot 400

Rice and Beans 410

Bean Burgers, Fritters, and Griddle Cakes 413

The Basics of Tofu 417

It's official: I eat beans at least as often as I do pasta. And you will too since they can take the lead in mains and sides, or sing backup as an ingredient in all sorts of other dishes.

Beans—a generic term used for peas, split peas, lentils, and other legumes and pulses—are low in fat and calories and a source of high-quality protein, fiber, and complex carbohydrates.

Dried, canned, or cooked and frozen, they're easy to store and keep for ages. They're an environmentally friendly part of plant-driven diets and even precious heirloom varieties are relatively inexpensive; common supermarket beans are around a buck a pound. Factor in tofu—essentially soybean cheese—and the only question is "How can I cook them?"

There are hundreds of varieties of dried beans, and virtually all can be treated in the same way. With canned, you exchange having fewer options for more spontaneity. To combine convenience with variety, cook a pot of plain beans regularly and use them like canned. The beginning of the chapter encourages you to do exactly that, by covering everything you need to know to buy, store, and cook dried beans. After those basics, it's your choice: Use either home-cooked or canned in the first section of recipes. The rest of the chapter takes you through beans simmered in pots with other ingredients, bean burgers and the like, and finally tofu.

THE BASICS OF BEANS

Beans, lentils, peas, and peanuts belong to the Leguminosae family of plants; thus the name "legumes." All produce their seeds in a pod; those seeds are what we eat. Green beans and snow peas—and others with edible pods—are usually referred to as vegetables, but they're still beans.

Legumes are easily dried and preserved for storage and future use, and have been for eons. Though you can happily find them in other forms (see "Fresh and Frozen Shell Beans" on page 401), most are sold dried and must be cooked for a relatively long time to rehydrate and become tender. Don't overthink the different techniques. The task is incredibly simple and I'll make things easy; there's plenty of flexibility.

BUYING AND STORING DRIED BEANS

Dried beans never really spoil but they do get old, which means they'll need more water and time to become soft; they'll also lose some nutrients and develop a musty taste. You have little way of knowing when beans were dried, though there are some visual clues. Avoid packages with a large percentage of broken beans, imperfect skins, or discoloration. Ideally, you should buy beans from a source that sells a lot and restocks them frequently. Since I wrote the first edition of this book, you can find locally raised and heirloom beans more easily—online, at farmers' markets, and in stores—and these will often be quite amazing.

Bean Math

Cook a pot of plain beans every week, I like to say. Here's how to calculate how much to make, depending on how you plan to use them in recipes: 1 pound dried beans yields 6 to 8 servings, depending on what other ingredients are involved. Since beans generally absorb three times their volume of water to become tender, to get an approximate cup count, measure the dry beans before cooking and multiply that by three. And since you might not finish them all in a week, for more about freezing leftovers, see "Storing Cooked Beans" on page 390.

 fast make ahead **V** vegetarian

The Bean Lexicon

Beans may have subtle differences in appearance, flavor, and texture, but they're easily interchangeable if you know how. To help you along, most recipes in this chapter include a list, "Other beans you can use." Take those as my best suggested substitutions. Which isn't to say others won't work; the results will just be more different. And I barely touch on heirloom varieties. This table will help you get a head start on anything you might find by comparing size and appearance. You'll soon discover your own favorites.

BEAN	DESCRIPTION	AVAILABLE FORMS
Adzuki beans Aduki	Small, oval, maroon, with a streak of white. Earthy and slightly sweet. Dense and creamy. Used in sweet dishes in East Asia.	Dried; canned; fresh; as sweet red bean paste
Anasazi beans Anastazi; Cave; New Mexico cave beans	Mottled with white and burgundy. Mild, sweet, and mealy	Dried; sometimes fresh
Black beans Turtle beans; frijoles negros	Medium-size, oval, deep black. Taste is rich and earthy, almost mushroom-like	Dried; frozen; canned. Don't confuse with Chinese fermented black beans, which are soybeans.
Black-eyed peas Cowpeas	Small, plump, ivory to beige, with a black spot. They cook relatively fast and absorb flavors well.	Dried; fresh; frozen; canned
Cannellini beans White kidney beans	Long, kidney-shaped, off-white. Nutty flavor and creamy consistency	Dried; canned
Chickpeas Garbanzo beans; ceci; channa dal; kabli channa	Acorn-shaped, tan or sometimes red or black. Robust, nutty flavor. They take a long time to cook and produce a rich cooking liquid.	Dried; fresh; frozen; canned
Cranberry beans Borlotti; Roman; Romano beans	Beautiful dried or fresh, off-white with bright to deep red dappling. Creamy texture. Similar in flavor to pinto beans; delicious fresh	Dried; fresh; sometimes frozen
Fava beans Broad; faba; haba; fève; horse; Windsor beans	Large, flattened, wide oval beans, light brown when mature and green (in or out of their pods) when young. Nutty and creamy when mature. Young, they're a bit sweet, and are usually eaten shucked and peeled, though when young you can grill or roast and eat the whole thing like big green beans.	Dried, get split favas, which are already peeled; fresh in the pod; frozen; canned
Flageolets	Small, kidney-shaped, green-tinged. Quick cooking with an herbal, fresh taste. Cook up creamy while maintaining their shape. Use in soups, stews (especially cassoulet in place of hard-to-find classic Tarbais beans) and salads.	Dried; fresh; canned
Gigantes Giant lima; great white, gigande; hija beans	Huge, off-white. Sweet, with potato-like texture. Popular in Greek, Spanish, and Japanese dishes.	Dried; canned, sometimes with tomato sauce
Great Northern beans	Large, oval all-purpose white beans	Dried; frozen; canned

(continued)

The Bean Lexicon (continued)

BEAN	DESCRIPTION	AVAILABLE FORMS
Kidney beans Red beans; frijoles rojos	Up to an inch long, shiny red, light red or pink, reddish brown, or white (see Cannellini beans). Hold their shape when cooked and absorb flavors well.	Dried; frozen; canned
Lentils	Tiny, thin-skinned, disk-shaped, and quick cooking. There are hundreds of varieties of lentils (see page 408).	Dried whole, sometimes peeled and split; canned
Lima beans Butter beans; butter peas	Flat, kidney-shaped, generally pale green when fresh, white when dried. Hearty texture and buttery flavor. The Christmas lima has pretty reddish-purple markings. When fresh, firm pods are best; bulging beans will be starchy. Baby lima beans cook fast.	Dried; fresh; frozen; canned
Mung beans Moong bean; green gram	A cousin to the urad bean. Small, pellet-shaped, green when whole, yellow when peeled and split. Slightly sweet.	Dried whole or peeled and split; fresh as sprouts
Navy beans Pea; Boston; Yankee beans	Small, round, plump, white, and very useful. Dense and mild flavored with a creamy consistency. Great for purées and baked beans.	Dried; frozen; canned
Peas, Dried Split peas; maquis peas; matar dal	Small and round. Green and yellow are nearly the same in all ways but color. Grown specifically for drying. When cooked, starchy and earthy.	Peeled and split, dried or canned
Pigeon peas Gandules; congo, goongoo, or gungo peas; toovar dal	Nearly round, with one side flattened; many colors: tan, black, brown, red, yellow, spotted. Sweet, a bit mealy.	Dried whole, sometimes peeled and split; fresh, frozen; canned
Pink beans Chili beans	Interchangeable with pintos. Slightly kidney-shaped, rounder, solidly pinkish tan. Common in the Caribbean.	Dried; canned
Pinto beans	Medium-size, oval, with a reddish tan and brown speckled exterior. Earthy and creamy. Used to make refried beans.	Dried; frozen; canned
Scarlet runner beans	A popular shell bean in the South. Black or dark purple with speckles. Fat and meaty. Keeps its shape when cooked. To enjoy fresh, pick when pods are less than 6 inches long.	Dried; fresh, if you grow your own
Soybeans Edamame	Round, small, yellow or black, and nutty. Edamame are immature soybeans: large, shiny, and usually green; a good substitute for fresh lima or fava beans	Hundreds of varieties, available dried, canned, sometimes fresh or frozen. Edamame are available fresh or frozen, in their pods or already shucked.
Urad beans Black gram	Indigenous to India. When sold whole, with skins on, known as black gram or black lentils. Called white lentils when sold split, which reveals the white interior. Available both with and without their skins. Used in dals.	Dried

 fast make ahead **V** vegetarian

Most beans are harvested late in summer, so the new crop is available in the fall. So each summer I try to finish all the beans I've accumulated during the course of the year; that way I know I'm not keeping any for longer than a year.

Store beans in a cool, dry place, making sure they are tightly sealed, either in their original packaging or—better—an airtight glass container. Freezing further dehydrates dried beans, so don't bother.

THE BASICS OF COOKING DRIED BEANS

Few foods are more variable to prepare and cook than beans. How much water beans absorb and the time it takes for them to become tender vary by the type, their age, the temperature of the cooking water, and how dry they were to begin with. Exact cooking times are virtually impossible to pinpoint.

Focus on what you can control: the *way* you cook them. Legumes are best cooked when they bubble gently in a covered pot, covered by a couple of inches of water. Beyond that, there are few guidelines.

PREPARING DRIED BEANS

Even though beans are cleaned and sorted before packaging, it's still worth rinsing and poking around for oddballs and stones before soaking or cooking. Put them in a colander and rinse well under running water, or fill the pot you plan to cook them in with water and dunk them a few times. Run your hands through the beans to pick out any that are discolored, shriveled, or broken, as well as any stray matter.

COOKING DRIED BEANS

After several decades regularly cooking beans I've honed my observations.

- You can soak beans or not, but I rarely do anymore. Soaking speeds cooking a little, so go ahead if you want. But don't let the fact that you didn't plan to cook

beans until the last minute stop you from cooking them at all. With a pressure cooker (see page 393), you can move beans from pantry to table in a half hour or so. Even without pressure cooking, almost all beans can soften completely by simmering on the stove in as little as an hour; lentils and split peas take 30 minutes or less.

- When you add salt has some impact on the outcome but not to the extent it's going to ruin anything. See "Cooking Beans, Your Way" (page 394).

- Though baking soda helps to break down the skin of beans and acid helps to keep skins intact, these additions are only necessary if manipulating the normal cooking process is important for some reason—and worth the slight difference in flavor. Again, see the sidebar on page 394.

- Don't boil beans vigorously in a lot of water like pasta, then dump them in a colander to drain. Bumping around will cause the skins to break before the beans become tender, leaving you with starchy soup. You want to create and keep a concentrated, flavorful, and nutritious cooking liquid to enhance whatever soup, stew, or stir-fry you're making.

Generally, I prefer beans on the creamy side—cooked until their skins burst and the insides begin melting into the cooking liquid—but there are times you might want firm beans: for a salad, pasta, or stir-fry, or just because you like them better that way. So taste the beans as they cook. When they're done the way you want them, take the pot off the heat.

Such imprecision serves the greater cause: You'll make beans more often if the method is simple. Rinse beans, put them in a pot, cover with cold water, and turn the heat on. In a few minutes the pot will come to a boil, you'll lower the heat so the beans bubble gently and slip on a lid. Then you walk away for a while, coming back to stir and taste once or twice and add more water and some salt toward the end of cooking. The timing varies, but little else changes except for ingredients you might add to the pot.

SERVING BEANS

Sometimes you drain beans before serving or using them in other recipes. Always save the cooking liquid to cover leftover beans or to enrich soups or stocks.

More often, though, you'll end up with beans as firm or tender as you like, with about an inch of cooking liquid on top, perfect for spooning like gravy with the beans. This extra liquid is also enough to cook some rice—or grains like quinoa, farro, barley, oat groats, or millet—during the last few minutes. Another no-brainer is creamy beans on toast: thick toast for something hearty, thin and crisp for a snack or appetizer (see Crostini, page 95).

Beans stir-fried, sautéed, or braised with vegetables are delicious, with or without meat, tossed with all kinds of noodles. Bean purées, once you thin them a bit, make excellent sauces, especially on pasta or under rich roasted meats or poultry; or you can add a spoonful to enrich soup. Beans also make excellent impromptu fillings for burritos, tacos, and enchiladas. And if you keep some firm-cooked beans handy, you'll always have a nice add-in for salads and other meals in bowls.

STORING COOKED BEANS

Once you get in the habit of cooking a pound or two of dried beans at a time, you'll almost never rely on canned. And the flavor and texture of both plain cooked beans and dried beans cooked in a pot with other ingredients improve with time and reheating.

To store cooked beans, let them cool in their liquid, then put them and their liquid in large airtight containers with tight-fitting lids. The recipes here typically call for 1½-cup increments, or store whatever size makes sense for how you will use them. Cover and refrigerate for up to 5 days or freeze for up to 6 months.

To reheat from the freezer, thaw for a day or so in the fridge, thaw in the microwave in 1–60-second bursts, or put the block of beans and liquid in a pan with a little water, cover, and turn the heat to low. Check occasionally to make sure they have enough water, but don't stir much or try to break up the ice block, or the beans will break into bits. Figure they'll take up to 30 minutes to thaw this way, depending on the size of the frozen block.

Simply Cooked Beans

MAKES: 6 to 8 servings (6 to 8 cups) | **TIME:** 30 minutes to 4 hours, largely unattended

When a recipe calls for cooked beans, this is it. Or check out the recipes for making beans using a pressure cooker or slow cooker (page 393).

> 1 **pound any dried beans, split peas, lentils, or peeled and split beans, rinsed and picked over**
> **Salt and pepper**

1. Put the beans in a large pot and cover with cold water by 2 to 3 inches. Add a large pinch salt if you want your beans to retain their shape. Bring the water to a boil, then reduce the heat so the liquid bubbles gently.

2. Cover and cook, stirring occasionally and checking the beans for doneness about every 15 minutes. Add more water, ½ cup at a time, to keep them covered by up to 2 inches. Adjust the heat to a gentle bubble after each addition.

3. When the beans start to get tender, add a sprinkle of pepper and, if you didn't earlier, a large pinch salt. As the beans get closer to being finished, they need to be covered with only an inch or 2 of water. Remove from the heat when the beans are done the way you like them; remember that they will continue to soften a little if left in the hot liquid. Taste and adjust the seasoning. Either use or cool and store (see "Storing Cooked Beans," page 390).

---

5 WAYS TO FLAVOR BEANS AS THEY COOK

Add any of the following ingredients to the pot, alone or in combination, when you start cooking the beans.

1. **Herbs or spices:** A bay leaf, a couple of whole cloves, some peppercorns, thyme sprigs, parsley leaves

and/or stems, chili powder (to make your own, see page 32), or other herbs and/or spices

2. **Aromatics:** An unpeeled onion, carrot, celery stalk, and/or 3 or 4 cloves garlic

3. **Stock:** Chicken, beef, or vegetable stock (to make your own, see pages 174–178), in place of all or part of the water

4. **Other liquid:** a cup or so beer, wine, coffee, tea, or juice

5. **Smoked meat:** a ham hock, pork chop, beef bone, or sausage; fish out after cooking, chop the meat, and stir it back into the beans.

Recipes that Start with Cooked or Canned Beans

The recipes and variations in this section include sides and main courses. In some you might build in more than a couple of ingredients, but all are dead simple. Start with plain cooked beans from the fridge or freezer—or from a can, in a pinch—and dinner will be on the table in 45 minutes or less.

USING CANNED BEANS

Canned beans, which are already cooked, take about 1 minute to prep: Open the can, drain and rinse the beans, and proceed. But there are some downsides:

- Although still quite inexpensive, they cost more per serving than dried beans.

- You lose all control over texture. Although many people like extremely soft beans, canned beans always come out of that way and that way only. You might find higher-quality canned—or pouch-packed—beans that aren't quite so overcooked, but they're even more expensive.

- Canned beans range in taste from decent to none: You'd be hard put to tell a canned black bean from a canned white bean with your eyes closed. And some have a decidedly metallic flavor.

- They're way more limited in variety than dried beans. You can buy much higher quality dried beans—grown locally and/or organically, heirloom, and so on.

I understand the convenience. If using canned beans is the difference between your cooking with and eating beans or not, then by all means do so. But my preference is to make a big batch of beans at my convenience, then freeze them in their cooking liquid in 1½-cup containers, as described on page 390 in "Storing Cooked Beans." This way I can thaw what I want (also see page 390) and pretend that I opened a can. (A 15-ounce can contains about 1½ cups.)

White Bean Purée

MAKES: 4 servings | **TIME:** 10 minutes with cooked beans

I almost always start home cooks with one of the most useful bean preparations there is—a mash, really—that works as a side dish, sauce, spread, or dip. Serve it with bread or pita chips, or carrot and celery sticks; pool under any grilled seafood, poultry, meat, or vegetables; or thin it a bit to use as a sauce for pasta or grains.

Other beans you can use: nearly any dried bean—cannellini, great Northern, favas, limas, chickpeas, pinto, kidney, most heirlooms, soybeans, black beans; lightly cooked fresh favas, edamame, limas.

  3 cups drained cooked or canned navy or other white beans (reserve the liquid if you cooked the beans yourself)
  3 tablespoons butter or olive oil
    Salt and pepper
    Chopped fresh parsley for garnish

1. Purée the beans in a food processor or blender, or with a food mill; or put them in a saucepan and use an immersion blender. Pulse, adding as much reserved

Making Beans in Machines

Both the slow cooker and pressure cooker can be a boon for beans. In both cases, you can walk away with no need to come back to lift a finger—or a lid.

Pressure-cooking is the only way to cook most dried beans in less than an hour, including the time it takes to pressurize the pot and then cool it enough to open. Many, like lentils and peas, are ready much faster, tender with no more than 10 minutes active cooking. And you never need to soak.

But the imprecision that makes cooking beans so easy creates a bit of a challenge with a pressure cooker, since you must release pressure to open the device and check the progress. You've got to estimate; usually half the expected time is a good start. Better machines come with some sort of bean guidance. If you overshoot, the beans might disintegrate; not terrible, since that will further thicken to cooking liquid. Adding salt at the start helps them keep their shape. And I like to quick release to minimize the threat of overcooking. Also be aware that the quantity you can cook is limited by the size of the machine. As long as you don't fill the pressure cooker more than half full of beans plus water, you'll be fine.

Slow-cooking beans is the ultimate hands-free experience. It's important that the beans remain covered with water the entire time, so increase the water until it covers the beans by at least 3 inches. (The device can be filled up to an inch or so from the top.) It's important to always use the "high" setting to make sure the beans cook at a safe temperature. Most beans take about 5 hours; lentils and split peas, including urad dal, should go for at least 2½ hours before you check them and might take another hour. After that you can keep them on the warm setting.

cooking liquid or water as you need to make a smooth but not watery purée.

2. Transfer the purée to a saucepan if it's not in one already, or to a microwave-safe dish. Add the butter and stir to combine. Heat gently until steaming hot. Taste and adjust the seasoning. Garnish with parsley and serve hot, warm, at room temperature, or even chilled.

ANY-BEAN PURÉE WITH ROASTED GARLIC Use favas, chickpeas, pintos, black-eyed peas, or soybeans: Add 15 to 20 cloves Roasted Garlic (page 294) in Step 1.

GARLICKY PURÉED BEANS A little lemon zest is good here too: Add 1 teaspoon or more minced garlic and a few fresh rosemary leaves or ½ teaspoon dried in Step 1.

PARMESAN PURÉED BEANS Or any cheese, really: Stir in up to ½ cup grated Parmesan in Step 2. Heat until the cheese melts, stirring frequently.

WHITE BEAN AND CELERY ROOT OR PARSNIP PURÉE
A terrific substitute for mashed potatoes: Add 1 cup cooked chopped celery root or parsnips in Step 1.

BLACK BEAN PURÉE WITH CHIPOTLES Spicy and smoky; perfect with Chiles Rellenos (page 319): Add 1 to 2 tablespoons chopped canned chipotle chiles in adobo sauce in Step 1. Garnish with cilantro.

RICHER, CREAMIER BEAN PURÉE For the main recipe or any of the variations—or your own combinations: When you thin the purée in Step 1, use up to 1 cup heavy cream or half-and-half instead of the cooking liquid or water.

Refried Beans

MAKES: 4 servings | **TIME:** 20 minutes with cooked beans

The traditional—and delicious—way to cook refried beans is with lard. Let's not argue about whether it's worse for you than butter or any other fat.

Other beans you can use: any red or pink beans. That said, this recipe offers a few options so you can choose.

Cooking Beans, Your Way

For Creamy Beans

- Don't add salt until the beans are tender. Adding salt to the water at the beginning will help the beans maintain their shape.
- Cook the beans at a more vigorous simmer, or cook them longer, until they start to break apart.
- When the beans are done, remove up to 1 cup, mash them, and return them to the pot. Or put an immersion blender in the pot and whirl it around once or twice.

For Creamy and Rich Beans

- Add 1 to 2 cups any milk to the beans toward the end of cooking. Dairy and nondairy are both fine; coconut is a lovely mix of rich and sweet. Butter or a flavorful oil like olive or a nut oil will have the same effect; add up to ¼ cup anytime during cooking. The same amount of lard or bacon fat puts the beans over the top.

For Beans That Keep Their Shape for Salads or Grain Bowls

- Add salt to the cooking water when you start.
- Don't cook the beans at more than a gentle simmer. If they boil, they'll bang against each other and break apart.
- Don't stir the beans any more than is necessary to keep them from burning on the bottom.
- Reverse-soak: Cook until they're not quite edible, then turn off the heat and let them soak in the hot liquid for up to an hour to finish cooking.
- Drain the beans (reserve the liquid for another use) and run them under cool water to stop cooking; shake the colander gently without stirring.

TO SOAK OR NOT TO SOAK

I cook beans from scratch every week, and it's been years since I've soaked them first. The only benefit to soaking is that it cuts the cooking time down somewhat. But beans are so low maintenance on the stove that letting them simmer for an hour or more is no big deal. (If you're really in a hurry or you want to slow-cook them, see "Making Beans in Machines," page 393.) However, if you prefer to soak, you have two options.

For the long-soak method: put the rinsed beans in a large bowl and cover with 2 to 3 inches of water. Let them soak for at least 8 hours and up to 12 hours at room temperature, or in the fridge if the kitchen is hot. Drain, put in the pot, cover with fresh water by 2 inches, add a pinch salt if you like, and simmer until tender.

For the quick-soak method: put the rinsed beans in a large pot and cover with 2 inches of water. Bring to a boil and keep the bubbling vigorous for 2 minutes. Remove from the heat, cover, and let the beans stand for up to 2 hours. Add more water to cover by 2 inches, add a pinch salt if you like, and cook until tender.

---

13 SIMPLE ADDITIONS TO COOKED BEANS

Add any of the following ingredients to cooked beans (the amounts assume around 3 cups cooked beans, 4 servings) or follow the procedures as described.

Stir into the hot beans before serving:

1. 2 tablespoons butter, olive oil, or sesame oil
2. ½ cup chopped fresh parsley, cilantro, mint, or basil
3. 2 tablespoons chopped fresh rosemary, tarragon, oregano, epazote, thyme, marjoram, or sage
4. 1 cup any cooked or uncooked sauce or chutney (see the sections starting on pages 55 and 71)
5. A tablespoon or so curry powder or any spice mixture (to make your own, see pages 27–35)
6. Soy, Worcestershire, or Tabasco sauce to taste
7. 1 or 2 tablespoons miso thinned with hot bean-cooking liquid, warmed gently with the beans

Stir into beans to serve at room temperature:

8. Up to ½ cup any Vinaigrette (page 188), or Simplest Yogurt Sauce (page 59)

Stir into beans when reheating:

9. Use stock (to make your own, see pages 174–180) or other flavorful liquid
10. Caramelized onion (see page 315)
11. Chopped leafy greens like kale or collards, cooked until soft
12. Peeled, seeded, and chopped tomato
13. A few slices bacon or pancetta, diced and cooked until crisp. Reheat the beans in the rendered fat and use the cooked bacon as a garnish

½ cup lard, bacon fat, or drippings from Mexican chorizo, 8 tablespoons (1 stick) butter, or ¼ cup good-quality vegetable oil

3 cups drained cooked or canned pinto, pink, or black beans (reserve the liquid if you cooked them yourself)

1 small onion, chopped

1 tablespoon ground cumin, or to taste

¼ teaspoon cayenne, or to taste
Salt and pepper
Chopped fresh cilantro for garnish

1. Put the fat in a large skillet over medium heat. When it is hot, add the beans. Mash with a large fork or potato masher until they're beginning to break up.

2. Add the onion, cumin, and cayenne and sprinkle with salt and pepper. Continue to cook and mash until the beans are more or less broken up (some remaining chunks are fine) and the onion is lightly cooked, about 5 minutes more. Thin with a little reserved cooking liquid or water to adjust the consistency. Taste and adjust the seasoning. Garnish with cilantro and serve.

---

8 ADDITIONS TO REFRIED BEANS

Add as much or as little of any of these at the beginning of Step 2 to cook them, or use for garnish.

1. Minced fresh or pickled chile
2. Chopped fresh cilantro
3. Minced fresh ginger or garlic
4. Chopped seeded tomato
5. Grated cheddar, Monterey Jack, or Chihuahua cheese, or crumbled queso fresco
6. Cooked rice
7. Crumbled cooked fresh or chopped smoked chorizo
8. Sour cream or crema

Orange-Glazed Black Beans

MAKES: 4 servings | TIME: 20 minutes with cooked beans

Beans often benefit from some acidity. The sweetness of oranges is perfect with black beans.

Other beans you can use: pinto or pink; black-eyed peas.

2 tablespoons olive oil

1 large onion, chopped

1 tablespoon minced garlic

1 cup fresh orange juice

3 cups drained cooked or canned black beans

1 tablespoon chili powder (to make your own, see page 32) or ground cumin

1 tablespoon honey
Salt and pepper

1. Put the oil in a large skillet over medium-high heat. Add the onion and cook, stirring occasionally, until soft, 3 to 5 minutes. Add the garlic and cook for about a minute. Add the orange juice, beans, chili powder, and honey. Sprinkle with salt and pepper.

2. Bring to a steady bubble and cook until the liquid is slightly reduced and thickened, about 15 minutes. Taste and adjust the seasoning. Serve hot. Or refrigerate for up to 3 days; reheat gently.

ORANGE-GLAZED BLACK BEANS WITH CRISP PORK
Cut 8 ounces boneless pork shoulder or sirloin into ½-inch pieces. Before you add the onion to the hot oil in Step 1, cook the pork, stirring frequently, until it's no longer pink and crisps in places, 5 to 10 minutes. Remove the pork with a slotted spoon and continue with the recipe from there, stirring the cooked pork back in at the end.

ORANGE-GLAZED BLACK BEANS WITH BACON This is good with tomatoes too: Cut up to 8 ounces bacon into 1-inch pieces and cook as directed in the variation above. Remove all but 2 tablespoons bacon fat from the pan, and omit the oil.

ORANGE–BLACK BEANS WITH CHIPOTLES The smoky heat of this seasoning paste melts into the beans: In Step 1, stir in a dollop of Chipotle Paste (page 45) along with the beans.

White Beans with Cabbage, Pasta, and Prosciutto

MAKES: 4 to 6 servings | TIME: 30 minutes

I used to think you needed chicken stock for richness, but water creates a potent cooking liquid when the ingredients have plenty of flavor. See the chart on page 397 for more ways to spin the concept.

- Salt and pepper
- 3 cups chopped cabbage, preferably savoy
- 8 ounces small pasta like cavatelli or orecchiette
- 2 tablespoons olive oil
- 2 cups chopped leeks, rinsed well
- 1 celery stalk, chopped
- 2 sprigs fresh thyme
- ¼ cup chopped prosciutto
- 3 cups drained cooked or canned cannellini or other white beans (reserve the liquid if you cooked them yourself)
- ½ cup grated Parmesan or pecorino Romano cheese, plus more for serving

1. Bring a large pot of water to a boil and salt it. Add the cabbage and cook until just tender, about 3 minutes; use a slotted spoon or small strainer to fish it out. Drain, shock if you like (see page 238), and let sit. When the water returns to a boil, add the pasta and cook until tender but firm; start checking after 7 minutes. Drain, reserving 1 cup of the cooking liquid.

2. Return the pot to medium heat (no need to rinse it) and add the oil. When it is hot, add the leeks and celery and cook, stirring occasionally until soft, 3 to 5 minutes. Add the thyme and prosciutto and stir until fragrant, just a minute or 2.

3. Add the beans and cabbage and sprinkle with salt and pepper. Add 1 cup of the reserved pasta or bean cooking liquid and cook, stirring once in a while, until the flavors blend and everything is hot, about 5 minutes more. If the mixture dries out, add a little liquid; it should be saucy but not soupy.

4. Return the pasta to the pot, sprinkle with the cheese, and toss to combine. Taste and adjust the seasoning. Serve, passing more cheese at the table.

Beans and Tomatoes

MAKES: 4 servings | TIME: 20 minutes with cooked beans

Totally rustic, especially if you leave the fresh tomatoes in big chunks. Serve these beans alongside roast or grilled meat, chicken, or fish; spoon over rice or thickly sliced bread; or toss with pasta or grains.

Other beans you can use: any white beans, the bigger the better.

- 3 tablespoons butter or olive oil
- ¼ cup chopped shallots or scallions
  Salt and pepper
- 1 tablespoon fresh thyme leaves or 1 teaspoon dried thyme
- 2 cups chopped fresh tomatoes, or 1 28-ounce can diced tomatoes
- 3 cups drained cooked or canned navy, lima, or butter beans (reserve the liquid if you cooked them yourself)
  Grated Parmesan cheese (optional)

1. Put the butter or oil in a large skillet over medium-high heat. When the butter is melted or the oil is hot,

Bean, Green, and Pasta Combos

Follow the recipe for White Beans with Cabbage, Pasta, and Prosciutto on page 396, mixing and matching the beans, greens, and pasta, and bonus ingredient as you like.

BEANS	GREENS	PASTA	BONUS INGREDIENT
Fava beans (mature or green)	Spinach	Rigatoni or radiatore	Omit the prosciutto. Start Step 2 by cooking 8 ounces ground lamb until no longer pink; season with ground cumin, cayenne, and cinnamon to taste.
Chickpeas	Chard	Linguine	A couple dozen or so clams or mussels. Add them instead of the prosciutto in Step 2, cover, and cook until they open, about 10 minutes; remove them from the shells before proceeding.
Cranberry beans	Radicchio and endive, mixed	Farfalle	Top each serving with a poached or fried egg.
Flageolets	Kale	Penne or ziti	Omit the prosciutto. Add bits of leftover roast chicken, turkey, pork, or duck (about 1 cup) with the liquid in Step 3.
Lentils	Escarole	Small shells	Omit or keep the prosciutto as you like. Start Step 2 by cooking 8 ounces crumbled Italian sausage.
Lima beans (any kind, but fresh are fantastic)	Napa or savoy cabbage	Large shells	Omit the prosciutto. Add 8 ounces uncooked peeled shrimp, cleaned squid, or fish fillets, cut into bite-sized pieces, with the liquid in Step 3.
Kidney beans	Collard greens	Macaroni	Use ham instead of prosciutto in Step 2.

add the shallots, sprinkle with salt and pepper, and cook, stirring occasionally, until soft, 3 to 5 minutes. Add the thyme and stir for about 30 seconds.

2. Add the tomatoes and adjust the heat so they release their liquid and bubble steadily. Cook, stirring occasionally, until the tomatoes break up and the liquid thickens, about 10 minutes. Add the beans and enough bean cooking liquid or water to make a slightly soupy mixture.

3. Raise the heat to medium-high. Cook, stirring, until the sauce is creamy, about 5 minutes. Taste and adjust the seasoning. Serve hot, topped with the Parmesan if you're using it. (Or refrigerate for several days or freeze for months; reheat gently.)

BEANS WITH TOMATILLOS AND HOMINY Pinto or black beans are good here; serve this with plenty of warm corn tortillas: Use fresh or canned tomatillos instead of the tomatoes and decrease the quantity of beans to 1½ cups. In Step 2, add 1½ cups drained canned or cooked hominy (see "Cooking Grains, the Easy Way," page 451). Instead of Parmesan, garnish with chopped fresh cilantro and a sprinkle of crumbled queso fresco.

RICH AND ELEGANT BEANS AND TOMATOES (OR BEANS WITH TOMATILLOS AND HOMINY) Start with dried beans and cook them as described on page 390, using 1 quart chicken or beef stock instead of the water; measure what you need from there and save the rest of the cooking liquid to use for soup. Peel and seed the tomatoes before adding them in Step 1.

Edamame with Fresh Tomatoes and Cilantro

MAKES: 4 servings | **TIME:** 25 minutes

I've adjusted this recipe so it's a summer stew, though it becomes a year-round dish if you use 1 28-ounce can diced tomatoes instead of fresh. You can also cook other vegetables in the sauce at the same time—try corn kernels, cubed eggplant or summer squash, whole green beans or okra, or cauliflower or broccoli florets.

Other fresh or frozen shell beans you can use: limas, favas, black-eyed peas.

2	tablespoons olive oil
1	small onion or 3 scallions, chopped
1	tablespoon minced garlic
1	teaspoon ground cumin
2	cups chopped fresh tomatoes
3	cups shelled edamame (fresh or frozen)
	Salt and pepper
¼	cup chopped fresh cilantro

1. Put the oil in a large skillet over medium-high heat. When it is hot, add the onion and garlic and cook, stirring occasionally, until soft, about 3 minutes.
2. Add the cumin and tomatoes and adjust the heat so the sauce bubbles gently. Cook, stirring occasionally until the tomatoes begin to break apart, about 10 minutes.
3. Stir in the edamame and sprinkle with salt and pepper. Cook until the edamame are tender, 5 to

> ## Edamame
> Edamame are immature soybeans, harvested at about 80 percent of their growth cycle. They're available both in the pod and shelled, usually frozen, though fresh beans are more and more common. Store fresh edamame in plastic bags in the fridge for up to a week. Frozen and well wrapped, the beans will keep for months.
>
> Rinse edamame just before cooking; use a brush to scrub some of the fuzz off the pods if you like. Since they're not dried, edamame cook much faster than mature fresh or frozen shell beans. (See page 90 for a simple recipe for salted boiled edamame.) You can use them like lima or fava beans too.

10 minutes. Taste and adjust the seasoning. Scatter the cilantro on top and serve.

EDAMAME WITH TOMATOES AND OLIVES Substitute 8 sliced pitted black olives for the cumin, and basil for the cilantro.

EDAMAME WITH GROUND PORK AND FRESH TOMATOES In Step 1, start by adding 8 ounces ground pork to the hot oil. Stir and cook, crumbling the meat as it browns, until it's crisp and cooked through, about 10 minutes. Remove the meat with a slotted spoon and pour off all but 2 tablespoons of the fat. Proceed with the recipe. In Step 3, add back the cooked pork when you add the edamame.

Stewed Chickpeas with Seared Chicken

MAKES: 4 servings | **TIME:** About 45 minutes with cooked chickpeas

Mediterranean seasonings make for a stew that once seemed exotic. I never tire of it. For a vegetarian version, see the first variation.

Other beans you can use: favas, lima beans.

1 tablespoon olive oil
4 large bone-in chicken thighs
   (about 2 pounds)
   Salt and pepper
1 large onion, chopped
1 celery stalk, chopped
1 carrot, chopped
2 tablespoons chopped garlic
2 teaspoons ground cumin
1 teaspoon ground coriander
3 cups drained cooked or canned
   chickpeas
1 28-ounce can diced tomatoes or
   3 cups chopped fresh tomatoes
¼ cup fresh parsley leaves for garnish

1. Heat the oven to 400°F. Put the oil in a large, deep skillet over medium-high heat. When it is hot, sprinkle the chicken with salt and pepper and cook, skin-side down, until the pieces are brown and release easily from the pan, about 5 minutes. Turn and brown the other side. Transfer the chicken to a rimmed baking sheet and put it in the oven.

2. Return the skillet to medium heat and add the onion, celery, carrot, and garlic; sprinkle with salt and pepper. Cook, stirring occasionally, until the vegetables soften, 5 to 10 minutes. Add the cumin and coriander and stir until fragrant, about 1 minute.

3. Add the chickpeas and tomatoes, bring to a gentle bubble, and cook, stirring occasionally, until the liquid thickens, about 10 minutes. Start checking the chicken; when it's ready, the juices will run clear if you make a small cut in the meat near the bone. Nestle the chicken pieces in the chickpeas and pour the pan juices over all. Taste and adjust the seasoning. Garnish with the parsley and serve.

STEWED CHICKPEAS WITH EGGPLANT OR ZUCCHINI
Omit the chicken and skip Step 1. Increase the oil to ¼ cup and cut 1 pound eggplant or zucchini into 1-inch pieces. In Step 2, cook the vegetable in the oil, stirring occasionally, until tender, 15 to 30 minutes. Remove and proceed with the recipe. Return the vegetable to the pot when the liquid thickens in Step 3.

CHICKPEA AND CHICKEN TAGINE Ideal with cooked couscous, barley, or bulgur: Omit the celery and carrot. In Step 1, don't bother to roast the chicken; instead transfer it to a plate. In Step 2, add ½ teaspoon ground cinnamon, ½ vanilla bean, and ½ cup raisins or chopped dates along with the spices. In Step 3, once the chickpeas and tomatoes are in the skillet, nestle in the chicken pieces and adjust the heat so the liquid bubbles gently. Cover the pan and cook until the chicken is very tender and no longer pink at the bone, 45 to 60 minutes.

Beans in a Pot

When you cook dried beans with a bunch of other stuff, they absorb all the flavors from the cooking liquid. These tend to be the satisfying dishes we closely associate with home and hearth, whether they're spiked with bits of vegetables or contain so much meat that the beans become a backdrop.

Whether the pot simmers on the stove or the oven, it never requires much attention. And all of these recipes reheat beautifully; just save the garnishes to add right before serving.

Baked Beans

MAKES: 6 to 8 servings | TIME: At least 4 hours, largely unattended
Ⓜ

I don't usually mess much with these. But when I want to, changes are easy; see "7 Ideas for Baked Beans" following the recipe.

Other beans you can use: red beans, lima beans.

1 **pound dried navy, pea, or other small white beans, rinsed and picked over**

8 **ounces salt pork or slab bacon**

½ **cup molasses, or to taste**

2 **teaspoons dry mustard or 2 tablespoons prepared mustard, or to taste**

Salt and pepper

1. Heat the oven to 300°F. Put the beans in a large pot and cover with cold water by 2 to 3 inches. Bring to a boil, then reduce the heat so the liquid bubbles gently. Cover and cook, stirring occasionally until they lose their dried look, about 20 minutes.

2. Cube or slice the pork and put it in a large ovenproof pot or deep baking dish. Drain off but reserve the bean cooking liquid. Stir the molasses and mustard into the beans and pour them over the pork. Pour on enough of the bean cooking liquid to cover the beans by about an inch; do not stir. Reserve the rest of the liquid.

3. Bake, uncovered and undisturbed, for an hour. Then start checking and stirring just the beans every half hour or so; you want the pork to remain on the bottom. Add more cooking liquid or water if necessary to keep the beans covered. After about 3 hours, taste and adjust the seasoning, adding salt and pepper, sweetener, and/or mustard as you like.

4. The beans may be fully tender; if not, keep checking every 15 minutes or so. When they're ready, scoop the pork up from the bottom and lay it on top of the beans. Raise the heat to 400°F and bake until the pork browns a bit and the beans are bubbling, about 10 minutes. You may turn and layer the meat across the top a couple more times; browning it all over darkens the color of the dish and adds flavor. Taste and adjust the seasoning. Serve hot. (Or refrigerate for several days or freeze for months; reheat gently.)

VEGETARIAN BAKED BEANS Less fat, but still really good: Omit the pork. In Step 2, spread 3 tablespoons softened butter or olive oil in the pot. Scatter 1 large or 2 medium onions, quartered, on top of the fat. Add 2 cups chopped tomatoes or 1 28-ounce can to the beans along with the molasses and mustard. Pour over the onions and tuck in a large piece of kombu, if you like, for extra flavor. Brown and stir the top layer of the beans as described for the meat in Step 4. Remove the kombu before serving; discard it or chop into pieces to stir back into the beans.

BAKED BEANS WITH A CRACKER CRUMB CRUST Works with the main recipe or the vegetarian version: After raising the oven temperature in Step 4, sprinkle the top of the beans with about 1½ cups crumbled saltines or bread crumbs (see page 801). Bake until the crust is golden, 20 to 30 minutes.

7 IDEAS FOR BAKED BEANS

1. Add ketchup to taste, or substitute sugar or maple syrup—or a combination—for the molasses.
2. Add Worcestershire, soy, or Tabasco sauce to taste.
3. Add an onion or two, quartered, and/or a few chunks of carrot in Step 2.
4. Substitute raw or smoked sausage, cut into chunks, for the pork.
5. Omit the meat and add 1 cup coconut milk (to make your own, see page 372) along with the cooking liquid.
6. Add 1 to 2 tablespoons curry powder, chili powder, or any other spice mixture you like (to make your own, see pages 27–35).
7. Add 4 cups beef, chicken, or vegetable stock (to make your own, see pages 174–178) after baking to make a big pot of soup.

White Beans, Tuscan Style

MAKES: 6 to 8 servings | TIME: 1 to 2 hours, largely unattended

To each his or her own: Encourage the beans to keep their shape, or cook them until they become supercreamy. Either way, serve these hot, warm, or at room temperature; toss with a bit of cooked small pasta like orecchiette, or greens like cabbage for lunch or dinner. These reheat perfectly too; just add a bit of water if the beans are dry, and wait to add the final dose of garlic and the olive oil in Step 3 if you can.

  1   **pound dried cannellini or other white beans, rinsed and picked over**
      Salt and pepper
 20   **fresh sage leaves or 1 tablespoon dried sage**
 10   **cloves garlic, peeled**
 ¼   **cup olive oil, or more to taste**
      Chopped fresh parsley for garnish

Mashed Beans

These are an excellent substitute for mashed potatoes and a perfect use for leftovers or even canned beans. Figure ⅓ cup liquid for every cup of beans; it can be milk, cream, sour cream, yogurt, stock, or water. Heat the beans in a medium pot with the liquid, then add a pat of butter or a couple of tablespoons olive oil. When the mixture starts steaming, remove from the heat and start mashing, either with a fork, against the side of the pot, or with a potato masher. Taste and add a sprinkle of salt and pepper, or whatever else you like from the list of seasoning possibilities for mashed potatoes on page 330. Add more liquid to reach the consistency you like.

1. Put the beans in a large pot with water to cover and bring to a boil. Add a pinch salt if you want the beans to keep their shape. Add the sage and 6 cloves of the garlic and lower the heat so the beans bubble gently but steadily. Cover and cook, stirring occasionally, until the beans begin to soften, about 20 minutes. If you haven't already, add salt and some pepper.
2. Continue to cook until the beans are very tender, anywhere from 30 minutes to an hour, depending on the bean. If the beans begin to dry out, add water ½ cup at a time.
3. Spoon off any extra cooking liquid, if necessary. Mince the remaining garlic and add it to the beans. Cook, stirring once or twice, until it mellows a bit, about 10 minutes. Taste and adjust the seasoning and stir in the oil. Garnish with parsley and serve, drizzled with more oil if you like. (Or refrigerate for several days or freeze for months; reheat gently.

WHITE BEANS AND SAUSAGE AND KALE While the beans cook in Step 1, chop about 8 ounces lacinato (Tuscan) kale and cut 2 or 3 links hot or sweet Italian sausage into bite-sized pieces. Brown the meat in a dry skillet over medium heat, stirring frequently. When it's no longer pink and has released most of its fat, add the kale and stir, scraping up any browned bits from the pan. Add to the beans at the start of Step 2.

 fast   make ahead   V vegetarian

WHITE BEANS AND SHRIMP An excellent combination and no more difficult than the basic recipe; also good tossed with leftover pasta and tomato sauce after cooking: Add about 1 pound peeled medium shrimp to the beans along with the minced garlic in Step 3.

Beans and Greens

MAKES: 4 servings | TIME: 1 to 2½ hours, depending on the bean

I never tire of this combination, especially since there are so many possible variations; be sure to see "Bean, Green, and Pasta Combos" on page 397 too.

Other beans you can use: any white or ivory bean, including soybeans.

Other greens you can use: escarole, romaine, any cabbage, mustard or turnip greens, kale or collards, spinach, bok choy, arugula, watercress.

- 1¼ cups dried white beans or chickpeas, rinsed and picked over
- 1 onion, unpeeled but root end trimmed
- 1 bay leaf
- 1 whole clove
  Salt and pepper
- 1 bunch (about 1½ pounds) broccoli raab or other greens
- 1 tablespoon minced garlic, or more to taste
- 2 tablespoons olive oil, or more to taste
- ½ cup grated Parmesan cheese, Bread Crumbs (page 801), or a combination for garnish

1. Put the beans in a large pot with water to cover by about 2 inches and bring to a boil. Cut a slit in the onion and insert the bay leaf, press in the clove, and drop the onion into the pot with a pinch salt. Adjust the heat so that the liquid bubbles gently. Cover and cook, stirring occasionally, until the beans begin to

soften, anywhere from 30 minutes to an hour, depending on the bean.

2. Sprinkle the beans generously with pepper. Continue to cook, stirring occasionally and adding water to keep them covered by about 1 inch, until the beans are tender but still intact, another 10 to 20 minutes.

3. If the stems of the greens are thick, remove the leaves and chop the stems and leaves separately. Otherwise just chop everything together. If you've got chopped stems, add them to the beans first and give them a 5-minute head start before adding the chopped leaves. Cover the pot again and cook, stirring occasionally until everything is tender, 10 to 30 minutes. For soupy beans, add more water, a little at a time.

4. Remove the onion and discard the bay leaf and clove; peel and chop the onion if you like and return it to the beans. About 3 minutes before serving, stir in the garlic and oil and taste and adjust the seasoning. Serve the beans and greens hot, garnished with the cheese and/or bread crumbs. (Or refrigerate for several days or freeze for months; reheat gently.)

BEANS AND GREENS WITH CANNED BEANS In Step 1, chop the onion and use the oil to cook it over medium-high heat until soft, 3 to 5 minutes. Drain and rinse 2 15-ounce cans beans; add them to the onion along with 2 cups water and the bay leaf and clove. When the water comes to a boil, pick up the recipe at Step 3.

Slow-Simmered Beef Chili

MAKES: 8 servings | TIME: 2 to 3 hours, largely unattended

Chili means different things to different people; this recipe and the chart that follows cover the highpoints. I've listed a couple of garnishes I like, but you might want to add grated cheese, pickled or fresh jalapeños, or sour cream. Serve with tortillas, crackers,

Slow-Simmered Beef Chili, page 403

chips, or rice, and hot sauce. For an all-meat, tomato-less Texas-style chili, see Beef Stew, 8 Ways on page 679.

2 tablespoons olive oil
1 pound boneless beef chuck, cut into bite-sized pieces
   Salt and pepper
1 large yellow or white onion, chopped
2 tablespoons chopped garlic
2 tablespoons ground ancho chile or Chili Powder (to make your own, see page 32)
1 teaspoon ground cumin
2 tablespoons chopped fresh oregano or 2 teaspoons dried oregano
1 28-ounce can diced tomatoes
1 pound dried pinto beans, rinsed and picked over
1 small red onion, minced, for garnish
   Chopped fresh cilantro for garnish

1. Put the oil in a large pot over medium-high heat. When it is hot, add the meat in a single layer (work in batches if the pan is crowded). Sprinkle with salt and pepper and cook until the pieces brown and release easily from the pan, about 5 minutes, then stir, and cook, stirring occasionally until the meat is well browned, another 5 to 10 minutes.

2. Add the yellow onion and garlic, sprinkle with a little more salt and pepper, and cook, stirring occasionally until the onion is soft, 3 to 5 minutes. Add the ground chile, cumin, and oregano and stir until fragrant, less than a minute. Add the tomatoes, scraping up any browned bits from the bottom of the pan.

3. Add the beans and enough water to cover by 2 inches. Bring to a boil, then lower the heat so the chili bubbles gently but steadily. Cover and cook, stirring once in a while and adding only enough water to keep the beans and meat covered by about an inch of liquid, until the beans and meat are very tender and the flavors have mellowed, at least an hour or up to 2.

4. If the chili is too soupy when the beans are tender, raise the heat, uncover the pot, and carefully let it bubble until thickened. Taste and adjust the seasoning. Serve hot, garnished with the red onion and cilantro. (Or refrigerate for several days or freeze for months; reheat gently.

FAST BEEF CHILI Use ground beef instead of chuck in Step 1. Replace the dried beans with 3 15-ounce cans pinto beans, drained and rinsed. When you add the beans in Step 3, cook only to heat them through; wait to add water until the chili thickens, as you might not need any.

Canned Cannellini Cassoulet

MAKES: 4 to 6 servings | **TIME:** 45 minutes

I've made cassoulet every possible way, from over-the-top (an all-day project) to nearly meatless (a pleasant surprise). This shortcut version borrows duck and sausage from tradition. See the list that follows for more ideas.

1 boneless duck breast (with skin if possible)
   Salt and pepper
1 Italian sausage
1 pound pork tenderloin, cut into 1-inch cubes
1 tablespoon olive oil
2 tablespoons chopped garlic
1 cup dry red wine, bean-cooking liquid, or water
1 28-ounce can diced tomatoes
2 15-ounce cans cannellini beans, drained
⅛ teaspoon cayenne, or to taste
2 tablespoons chopped fresh chives for garnish

1. If the duck has skin, cut a ½-inch crosshatch pattern into the, almost down to the fat layer. Sprinkle the breast all over with salt and pepper. Put the duck,

5 More Chilis, Slow or Fast

Follow the main recipe or variation above, making the following adjustments.

NAME	MEAT	SEASONINGS	BEAN	GARNISHES
White Chili	Boneless, skinless chicken thighs	Use 2 cups chopped fresh tomatillos or 1 28-ounce can instead of the tomatoes. Use 2 fresh poblanos, chopped, instead of the ground chile.	Cannellini or other white beans	Chopped parsley or basil
Pork and Black Bean Chili	Boneless pork shoulder	Use sage instead of oregano. Add 1 tablespoon grated orange zest to the spices in Step 2.	Black beans	Sliced scallions and fresh cilantro
Chickpea Chili with Lamb	Boneless lamb shoulder or leg	Reduce the ground chile to 1 tablespoon and add 1 teaspoon each ground coriander and cinnamon along with the cumin.	Chickpeas; they might take another 30 minutes to cook	Chopped fresh mint; keep the red onion
Vegetable Chili	Chop enough carrots, celery root, sweet potato, and kale for 1 cup each. Add them when the beans are tender in Step 3.	Keep the seasonings the same.	Use any bean you like	Chopped chives are perfect here
Tofu or Tempeh Chili	Crumble 1 pound tofu or tempeh into the hot oil in Step 1.	Keep the seasonings the same.	Lentils; reduce the cooking time to about 30 minutes	Sliced scallions and cilantro

skin-side down in a large pot over medium-high heat. Cook undisturbed until the skin browns and releases from the pan, 3 to 5 minutes. Turn the duck and brown the meat side until the inside is as pink as you like, another 3 minutes or so. Transfer to a shallow bowl.

2. Lower the heat to medium and add the sausage. Cook, turning occasionally, until the center is longer pink, 5 to 10 minutes. Transfer to the bowl with the duck and add the pork tenderloin to the pot. Sprinkle with salt and pepper and cook, stirring once or twice, until the pieces brown a bit but are still pink at the center, 3 to 5 minutes. Transfer to the bowl with the meat.

3. Add the olive oil and garlic to the pot and cook, stirring constantly until fragrant, about 30 seconds. Add the wine and stir to scrape any browned bits from the bottom of the pot. When it has almost bubbled away, add the tomatoes and adjust the heat so the sauce bubbles steadily. Cook, stirring once in a while until the tomatoes thicken, about 5 minutes.

4. Stir the beans into the pot along with the cayenne and again adjust the heat so the liquid once again bubbles steadily. Cook, stirring occasionally until the cassoulet thickens, another 5 to 10 minutes. Taste and adjust the seasonings, adding more cayenne if you'd like.

  **F** fast **M** make ahead **V** vegetarian

Slice the duck and sausage thickly and add all the meat to the stew, along with any accumulated juices. Stir once and serve right away, garnished with chives.

3 WAYS TO MAKE MORE AUTHENTIC CASSOULET

1. Start with dried beans—preferably flageolets or the utterly traditional *tarbaise*—cooked with a few sprigs of fresh thyme, ½ head of garlic, and a piece of salt pork or bacon.
2. If you can get duck confit, just brown it lightly on both sides, adding both it and its fat to the stew in place of the duck breast.
3. Finish the dish by topping the cassoulet with a layer of fresh bread crumbs (page 801) and transferring the pot to a 400°F oven. Bake until the topping browns and the stew is bubbly, about 20 minutes.

Chickpeas in Their Own Broth

MAKES: 4 servings | **TIME:** Up to 2 hours

Still my favorite way to eat chickpeas, provided—and this is important—I start with dried chickpeas. Canned won't cut it since the cooking liquid is half the dish and makes the whole thing delicious. Well, that and the bread crumb garnish.

1½	cups dried chickpeas, rinsed and picked over
1	tablespoon chopped garlic, or more to taste
	Salt and pepper
8	ounces (½ loaf) French or Italian bread (a day or two old, or oven dried)
½	cup olive oil
2	tablespoons chopped fresh parsley, plus more for garnish

1. Put the chickpeas and garlic in a large pot with enough water to cover by about 3 inches and bring to a boil; skim any foam from the surface. Adjust the heat so the liquid bubbles steadily, cover, and cook, stirring occasionally. Add water as necessary to keep the chickpeas covered by about 1 inch.
2. When the chickpeas are nearly tender, anywhere from 30 to 60 minutes, depending on the age of the chickpeas, add a large pinch salt and a sprinkle of pepper. Continue to cook, stirring occasionally and checking for doneness and water level every 10 minutes. The chickpeas should be quite tender but not turning to mush. (You can make the recipe up to this point, cover, and refrigerate for up to 3 days or freeze for several months.)
3. Cut the bread into chunks and pulse it in a food processor until the pieces are about the size of peas, but no smaller. Put ¼ cup of the oil in a large skillet over medium heat. Add the bread and a sprinkle of salt and cook, shaking the pan occasionally, until the crumbs are crisp and brown, 5 to 10 minutes. Add the parsley, stir a couple of times until combined, then remove from the heat.
4. Make sure the chickpeas and broth are steaming hot. Taste and adjust the seasoning. Serve in shallow bowls, drizzled with the remaining oil, sprinkled with the parsley bread crumbs and garnished with more parsley.

CHICKPEAS IN THEIR OWN BROTH WITH SMOKED CHORIZO Or in a pinch, dry salami: Just before serving the chickpeas, stir in about 4 ounces chopped smoked chorizo.

CHICKPEAS IN GINGERY COCONUT BROTH Excellent over sticky—or any—rice: Use ginger instead of garlic. After you salt the beans in Step 2, instead of adding more water, stir in about 1 cup coconut milk (to make your own, see page 372). Omit the bread crumbs, oil, and parsley. Garnish with lime wedges and chopped fresh cilantro or mint.

Lentils, Six Ways

MAKES: 4 servings | **TIME:** 45 minutes

Classics 20 years ago; classics now. I still say double the recipe, because the leftovers will keep in the fridge for a couple of days and reheat perfectly for lunch or a super-quick dinner. I also like to use them to poach eggs.

Other beans you can use: lentils de Puy, black lentils if you can find them.

- 2 tablespoons olive oil
- ½ onion, chopped
- 4 celery stalks (leaves included), chopped
- 1 carrot, chopped
  Salt and pepper
- 1 tablespoon chopped garlic
- 1 bay leaf
- ½ cup dry white wine
- 2½ cups chicken or vegetable stock (to make your own, see pages 174–178) or water
- 1½ cups dried brown lentils, rinsed and picked over
  Chopped fresh parsley for garnish

1. Put the oil in a large pot over medium-high heat. When it is hot, add the onion, celery, and carrot; sprinkle with salt and pepper. Cook, stirring occasionally, until the onion is soft, 5 to 10 minutes. Add the garlic and cook for another minute.

2. Add the bay leaf, wine, stock, and lentils and bring to a boil. Adjust the heat so the liquid bubbles gently. Cover and cook, stirring occasionally and adding water if necessary, until the lentils are tender but not falling apart, 20 to 30 minutes.

3. Sprinkle with salt and pepper and keep cooking until the lentils are as tender as you like; they should be saucy but not soupy. Taste, adjust the seasoning, and remove the bay leaf. Sprinkle with parsley and serve.

LENTILS, SPANISH STYLE Reduce the celery to 1 stalk. When you stir in the garlic in Step 1, add ½ teaspoon crumbled saffron threads or 1 tablespoon smoked paprika (pimentón). Use red wine or sherry instead of white wine.

LENTILS, MOROCCAN STYLE Warm with spices: Double the onion and omit the celery, carrot, and wine. In Step 1, when you stir in the garlic, add 1 teaspoon each ground turmeric, cinnamon, and cumin. Replace

---

Lentils

The fastest-cooking family of beans are also among the most versatile. Lentils are divided into three groups, each of which contains a number of varieties. Use this list to help you choose which to use in these recipes:

BROWN LENTILS

The common supermarket lentils fall into this category, as do others from around the world. Black varieties like beluga are in this group; they actually cook up sort of greenish gray. All tend to run large and slightly flat, and taste mildly earthy, sometimes nutty. During cooking they have a relatively large window between tender and falling apart, which makes them work in salads and stir-fries. But they really shine in soups and stews.

GREEN LENTILS

These are mostly the French green and Puy varieties. They have glossy, dark green to green-brown seed coats and hold up well in cooking, but generally take the longest to cook. They're the best for salads.

RED LENTILS

Actually, they're usually more yellow-to-orange than red. Many varieties are peeled and split and found by their Indian names: masoor (or masar) dal, or just plain dal. They cook in 15 minutes and fall apart when tender. Despite their being the world's most popular lentil, you may have to go to an Indian or Middle Eastern market to find all but the ubiquitous orange—so-called red—lentil.

1 cup of the stock with 1½ cups chopped fresh tomatoes. Garnish with chopped fresh cilantro.

LENTILS WITH ROASTED WINTER SQUASH Omit the celery and carrot. Peel and seed any medium-sized winter squash like acorn, butternut, kabocha, or turban and cut into 1- to 2-inch cubes (about 2 cups); toss in a bit of olive oil to coat and roast on a baking sheet in a 375°F oven until tender and caramelized. (See page 349 for more details on roasting squash.) Add the squash to the lentils at the start of Step 3.

LENTILS WITH PARSNIPS AND NUTMEG Celery root is another option: Replace the celery and carrot with about 2 cups chopped parsnips. Stir in ¼ cup cream during the last couple of minutes of cooking; sprinkle each serving with a pinch nutmeg.

LENTILS WITH LARDONS Bacon cubes, basically: Reduce the oil to 1 tablespoon. Cut 4 ounces slab bacon into small cubes. In Step 1, put the oil and bacon in the pot over medium heat. Cook, stirring occasionally, until the bacon crisps and browns, about 10 minutes. Remove the bacon with a slotted spoon, leaving the fat behind. Turn the heat to medium-high and proceed with the recipe. When the lentils are done, uncover the pot and boil off any excess liquid, stirring occasionally. Remove from the heat and stir in a teaspoon sherry vinegar; taste and adjust the seasoning. Serve, garnished with the bacon and parsley.

Simplest Dal

MAKES: 4 servings | TIME: 40 minutes, largely unattended

The iconic dish of India, made hundreds of ways with dozens of beans. It's almost always assertively spiced and rich with ghee (clarified butter) or oil. I've streamlined things so you can eat it more often. Dal is usually served hot or room temperature as a sauce but it's lovely cold, spread on toasted wedges of pita or other flatbreads; see below for more ideas.

Other beans you can use: brown lentils, yellow split peas, split mung beans without skins (moong dal).

- 1 cup dried red lentils, rinsed and picked over
- 2 tablespoons chopped fresh ginger
- 1 tablespoon chopped garlic
- 4 cardamom pods
- 1 tablespoon mustard seeds
- 2 whole cloves
- 1 ancho or other mild dried chile (optional)
   Salt and pepper
- 2 tablespoons cold butter or good-quality vegetable oil
   Chopped fresh cilantro for garnish

1. Put the lentils in a large saucepan with enough water to cover by about 1 inch. Add the ginger, garlic, cardamom, mustard, cloves, and chile if you're using it, along with a generous pinch pepper. Bring to a boil; adjust the heat so the liquid bubbles gently; cover.

How to Cook and Eat Dal

The word "dal" describes both the beans and the dishes made from them, and like pasta in Italy, specific beans are assigned to specific preparations. Exchanging other beans for the red lentils may not be strictly authentic, but it will result in delicious dishes, even if all you ever use are supermarket brown lentils.

I like both slightly soupy, slightly thick dal to pour over something else—usually rice—and "dry" dal, where the beans remain intact. Serve dal hot with cooked basmati or jasmine rice (see page 428), or hot or at room temperature with crudités (see page 102), Chapati (page 779), or Pita (page 798) for dipping. Soupy dal also makes an effective and creamy sauce for simply cooked fish, chicken, meat, or vegetables. Add more water, stock, cream, or coconut milk and it becomes soup.

2. Cook, stirring occasionally and adding water if needed to keep everything covered, until the lentils are tender, 25 to 30 minutes. Sprinkle with salt and cook, uncovered and stirring occasionally, to the desired thickness; the lentils should be saucy but not soupy.

3. Remove the cloves and, if you like, the cardamom pods; they're kind of fun to eat, though. Stir in the butter. Taste and adjust the seasoning. Serve garnished with cilantro.

DAL WITH RHUBARB The rhubarb almost dissolves into the lentils, leaving behind its trademark tartness and a slight blush of color: In Step 1, add 3 or 4 rhubarb stalks, strings removed (see page 279), chopped.

DAL WITH DAIKON Use jícama or any radish (the spicy black ones are incredible but can be incendiary): Peel and cut about 1 pound daikon into 1- to 2-inch pieces. Add in Step 1.

DAL WITH POTATOES OR OTHER ROOT VEGETABLES
The lentils are like a sauce for big pieces of vegetables. Potatoes are traditional but celery root, carrots, parsnips, rutabaga, turnips, sweet potatoes, even taro are all fair game: Peel and cut about 1 pound root vegetables into 2-inch pieces. Add in Step 1.

DAL WITH NUTS When you add the butter in Step 3, stir in ½ cup chopped pistachios or cashews.

Rice and Beans

Welcome to one of the world's most important culinary marriages. The combination provides good protein and doesn't take a lot of work. And you don't even really need a recipe: Take any well-seasoned bean dish, even leftovers, and serve it with any fluffy rice. Here are a handful of classics that are (mostly) cooked together.

Baked Black Beans and Rice

MAKES: 4 to 6 servings | TIME: About 2 hours, largely unattended

Moros y Cristianos—Moors and Christians—is one of the most dramatic-looking rice and bean dishes, popular throughout Spanish-speaking countries. The technique of puréeing some of the beans before adding the rice allows the bean flavor to penetrate every grain. The crisp crust that forms in the oven might be the best part.

- ¼ cup olive oil
- 1 onion, chopped
- 1 bell pepper (any color), chopped
- 1 tablespoon chopped garlic, or more to taste
  Salt and pepper
- ¾ cup dried black beans, rinsed and picked over
- 1½ cups long-grain rice
- 1 15-ounce can diced tomatoes or about 1 cup chopped fresh tomatoes
- ½ cup chopped fresh parsley or cilantro

1. Put the oil in a large ovenproof pot over medium heat. When it is hot, add the onion, bell pepper, and garlic. Sprinkle with salt and pepper and cook, stirring occasionally, until the vegetables are soft, about 5 minutes.

2. Add the beans and cover with about 2 inches of water. Bring to a boil, then turn the heat down to low so that the liquid bubbles gently. Cover loosely and cook, stirring occasionally and adding water if necessary, until the beans are half-done—softening on the outside but still tough in the middle—40 to 60 minutes, depending on the bean. Heat the oven to 350°F.

3. Use an immersion blender or a potato masher to mash (but not purée) half the beans in the pot. The mixture should be about the thickness of soup. If not, add some water.

4. Stir in the rice, tomatoes, and another sprinkle of salt and pepper. Transfer the pot to the oven and bake, uncovered, until the rice and beans are fully tender, up to an hour; start checking after 30 minutes. Add water

only if it starts to smell like toast starting to burn. Taste and adjust the seasoning. Sprinkle with the parsley, toss gently with a fork so as not to disturb the crust on the bottoms and sides, and serve.

BAKED COCONUT RICE AND KIDNEY BEANS Irresistible: Replace the bell pepper with 1 or 2 fresh hot chiles like jalapeño or serrano, the black beans with red kidney beans, and the tomatoes with a 14-ounce can or about 1½ cups homemade coconut milk (see page 372). Add 2 tablespoons chopped fresh ginger in Step 1. While the pot is in the oven, toast ¼ cup shredded coconut in a dry skillet over medium heat until golden; use that and cilantro for garnish.

Hoppin' John

MAKES: 4 to 6 servings | TIME: 1½ to 2 hours, largely unattended

You don't have to be from the South to appreciate the combination of smoked pork, black-eyed peas, and long-grain rice.

>   1 cup black-eyed or other dried whole peas,
>   rinsed and picked over
>   4 ounces slab bacon or smoked ham
>   1 large onion, chopped
>   1 4-inch sprig fresh rosemary, 2 sprigs fresh
>   thyme, or ½ teaspoon dried rosemary or thyme
>   1½ cups long-grain white rice
>   Salt and pepper

1. Put the peas in a medium pot with the bacon, onion, rosemary or thyme, and water to cover by about 2 inches. Bring to a boil, skim any foam from the surface, then reduce the heat so the liquid bubbles gently. Cover and cook until the peas are tender, up to an hour or more; start checking after 30 minutes.
2. Remove the sprigs if you used fresh herbs. Remove the bacon and cut it into bite-sized pieces, discarding

extremely fatty pieces if you like. The peas should be about the thickness of bean soup and plop, rather than pour, from a spoon. If not, add water to thin them, or gently boil to reduce the liquid. Add back the bacon.
3. Stir in the rice, sprinkle with salt and pepper, and adjust the heat so the liquid bubbles gentle. Cover and cook until the rice and beans are tender and the liquid has been absorbed, 15 to 20 minutes.
4. If there's still a lot of liquid, uncover the pot and let some bubble away. Re-cover the pot, remove it from the heat, and let sit for at least 5 or up to 15 minutes. Taste and adjust the seasoning, fluff with a fork, and serve.

Red Beans and Rice

MAKES: 6 to 8 servings | TIME: About 2 hours, largely unattended

The title neglects to mention the ham hocks—or the turkey in the variation—but they're in there. Unless you leave them out. In which case the recipe becomes vegan (see the other variation). You also have a choice about how to serve the rice: under the beans, or gumbo style, a scoop sitting like an island in the bowl of beans.

>   1 pound dried kidney or other red beans,
>   rinsed and picked over
>   2 meaty smoked ham hocks
>   1 large onion, chopped
>   1 green bell pepper, chopped
>   4 celery stalks, chopped
>   2 tablespoons minced garlic
>   4 bay leaves
>   ½ teaspoon ground allspice
>   Salt and pepper
>   1 recipe White Rice (page 430)
>   Tabasco or other hot sauce for serving

1. Put the beans in a large pot with the ham hocks, onion, bell pepper, celery, garlic, bay leaves, and allspice. Add enough water to cover by 3 inches. Bring to a boil

and skim any foam from the surface. Reduce the heat so the liquid bubbles gently; cover.

2. Cook, stirring once in a while and adding water ½ cup at a time to keep everything covered, until the beans are tender and starting to fall apart and the meat is falling off the bone, at least an hour. (You can prepare the recipe up to this point and refrigerate for up to several days or freeze for months.) Meanwhile, cook the rice.

3. Transfer the ham hocks to a shallow bowl. When they're cool enough to handle, pull the meat from the bones and shred it a bit; discard the bones and any skin and gristle. Return the meat to the pot and stir. Taste and adjust the seasoning. Serve over or under a scoop of rice, passing hot sauce at the table.

RED BEANS WITH SMOKED TURKEY AND RICE Instead of the ham hocks, use a smoked turkey drumstick.

VEGAN OR VEGETARIAN RED BEANS AND RICE Serve with brown rice for a little more heft: Omit the meat. Double the amounts of onion and bell pepper and add ¼ cup olive oil or 4 tablespoons butter in Step 1.

Bean Burgers, Fritters, and Griddle Cakes

I hate the term "meat substitute" so let's judge these for what they are: Delicious, crisp main dishes made with beans. Any can become appetizer finger food too. Just make them smaller and cook them for a little less time.

The Simplest Bean Burgers

MAKES: 4 servings | TIME: 20 minutes with cooked beans

Ⓜ Ⓕ Ⓥ

These are always the easiest and most versatile vegetarian burgers to make. Different beans give you slightly different results: Use chickpeas, and the patties are

golden brown and lovely; with black beans, much darker; with red, somewhere in between; and lentils deliver a pleasantly grainy texture.

> 2 **cups any drained cooked or canned bean or lentil (reserve the liquid if you cooked them yourself)**
> 1 **small onion, quartered**
> ½ **cup rolled oats (not instant)**
> 1 **tablespoon chili powder or any spice mixture of your choice (to make your own, see pages 27–35)**
>   **Salt and pepper**
>   **Olive oil or good-quality vegetable oil for frying**
>   **Buns or rolls and condiments (optional)**

1. Line a baking sheet with parchment or wax paper. Combine the beans, onion, oats, and chili powder in a food processor with some salt and pepper, and pulse until chunky but not puréed. Try pinching some between your fingers. If it doesn't hold together, add bean cooking liquid or water a teaspoon at a time until it does. Let the mixture sit for a few minutes. Taste and adjust the seasoning.

2. With wet hands, shape into four burgers about 1 inch thick, transferring them to the prepared pan as you work. Refrigerate the burgers, loosely covered, for up to several hours. Or wrap the mixture or the burgers tightly and refrigerate for a day or so or freeze for up to a month.

Shaping Bean Burgers

STEP 1 Gently form the mixture into a ball (it helps if your hands are wet), then . . .

STEP 2 . . . press—again, gently—into a burger.

3. Pour about ½ inch of oil in a large skillet (preferably cast-iron) and turn the heat to medium. When it is hot, add the burgers. Adjust the heat so the oil sizzles, and cook until the bottoms are brown and release easily, about 5 minutes; turn carefully and cook on the other side. The outsides should be crusted and the burgers firm when gently pressed. Serve on buns, if you like, with your preferred burger fixings.

BEAN-AND-CHEESE BURGERS Inside, not on top: Mix in ½ to 1 cup grated Parmesan, cheddar, Swiss, Jack, mozzarella, or other cheese before shaping.

BEAN-AND-SPINACH BURGERS Add a garlic clove when processing in Step 1. Cook 8 ounces spinach. Squeeze it dry in a towel and chop; you should have about 1 cup. Add it to the mixture after processing in Step 1 and proceed with the recipe.

Falafel

MAKES: 6 to 8 servings, about 24 balls | TIME: 1 hour, plus 24 hours to soak the beans

Most bean burgers and fritters are made from cooked beans, but for falafel they're just soaked. Serve the falafel in pita with lettuce, tomatoes, cucumbers, and other raw vegetables; on top of a green salad; or on their own, with Tahini Sauce (page 56) or any yogurt sauce (page 59) for dipping. Refrigerate leftovers in an airtight container for up to several days; reheat in a 350°F oven until hot and crisp, about 15 minutes.

Other beans you can use: dried lima beans.

- 1¾ cups dried chickpeas or 1 cup dried chickpeas plus ¾ cup dried split fava beans, rinsed and picked over
- 1 cup chopped fresh parsley or cilantro
- 2 cloves garlic, lightly crushed
- 1 small onion, quartered
- 1 tablespoon fresh lemon juice
- 1 tablespoon ground cumin
- 1 teaspoon ground coriander
- 1 scant teaspoon cayenne or 2 teaspoons mild pure chili powder
- 1 teaspoon salt
- ½ teaspoon pepper
- ½ teaspoon baking soda
  Good-quality vegetable oil for deep-frying

1. Put the chickpeas in a large bowl and cover with water by 3 to 4 inches. Soak at room temperature for 24 hours, checking once or twice to see if you need to add more water to keep the chickpeas covered. They will triple in volume as they soak.

2. Drain the chickpeas well and transfer them to a food processor with the parsley, garlic, onion, lemon juice, cumin, coriander, cayenne, salt, pepper, and baking soda. Pulse until almost smooth, scraping down the side of the bowl as necessary. Add 1 to 2 tablespoons water if necessary to allow the machine to do its work, but keep the mixture as dry as possible. Taste and adjust the seasoning, adding more cayenne if you like.

3. Put at least 2 inches of oil in a large pot. Turn the heat to medium-high, and bring the oil to about 350°F (a pinch of the dough will sizzle immediately). Line a baking sheet with towels or a wire rack. Heat the oven to 200°F.

4. Scoop out heaping tablespoons of the dough and shape them into balls or small patties between two spoons or with wet hands. Fry in batches, without crowding, and turning as necessary until browned on all sides; total cooking time will be less than 5 minutes. As they finish, transfer the falafel to the prepared pan to drain. Keep them warm in the oven if you like until they're all cooked. Serve hot or at room temperature.

BLACK-EYED PEA FRITTERS Street food in West Africa, and totally addictive: Replace the chickpeas and/or favas with black-eyed peas, the onion with ½ cup chopped scallions, the coriander with red chile flakes, and the cumin with minced fresh ginger.

INDIAN-STYLE SPLIT PEA FRITTERS Same process with some adjustments: Replace the chickpeas and/or fava beans with yellow or green split peas. Substitute cilantro for the parsley and instead of the onion add 1 tablespoon each chopped fresh ginger, garlic, and jalapeño chile. Add 1 teaspoon ground fenugreek if you've got it. Serve with lime wedges.

Bean Griddlecakes

MAKES: 4 servings | **TIME:** About 30 minutes

These are amazing. And you can use virtually any kind of cooked bean. Everything else you need to know is in the recipe and the lists that follow, so just cook these now.

- 2 cups drained cooked or canned beans (reserve the liquid if you cooked them yourself)
- 1 cup half-and-half or whole milk, plus more if needed
- 1 egg
- 2 tablespoons melted butter, olive oil, or good-quality vegetable oil, plus more for cooking
- 1 cup all-purpose flour
  Salt and pepper

1. Heat the oven to 200°F and line a rimmed baking sheet with a wire rack. Put a large skillet over medium-high heat or heat an electric griddle to 375°F. Put the beans in a large bowl and mash them roughly with a fork. Use the fork to stir in the half-and-half, egg, and melted butter. Stir until thoroughly combined.

2. Add the flour and sprinkle with salt and pepper, keeping in mind how well seasoned the beans were to begin with. Stir with the fork just enough to incorporate the flour, adding more half-and-half or reserved bean cooking liquid if necessary to achieve the consistency of thick pancake batter.

3. The skillet or griddle is ready when a drop of water dances on the surface. Working in batches, first brush with a little butter or oil. Spoon on about ⅓ cup batter at a time to form 3- or 4-inch griddle cakes. Cook until bubbles form on top and the cakes firm a bit, then turn and cook the other side until golden, about 4 minutes per side. As they finish, transfer the griddlecakes to the prepared pan and keep warm in the oven while you finish the others. Serve hot or at room temperature.

BEAN SPROUT GRIDDLECAKES Serve with soy sauce or one of the sauces on the following page: Instead of whole cooked beans, use 3 cups rinsed and drained mung or soybean sprouts; leave them whole. Use 2 tablespoons sesame oil instead of the butter or other oil in the batter, and add ½ cup sliced scallions if you like. Use a good-quality vegetable oil for cooking.

10 ADDITIONS TO BEAN GRIDDLECAKES

1. 2 tablespoons minced mild fresh herbs like parsley, mint, basil, chives, chervil, or cilantro
2. 2 teaspoons minced potent fresh herbs like rosemary, thyme, tarragon, oregano, or epazote
3. 2 teaspoons minced fresh or candied ginger
4. 1 teaspoon minced garlic
5. Up to ¼ cup chopped or sliced scallions or minced red onion
6. Minced fresh chile like jalapeño or Thai, red chile flakes or cayenne, to taste
7. 1 tablespoon any spice mixture like curry powder or chaat masala (to make your own, see pages 27–35)
8. Up to ¼ cup chopped nuts like almonds, walnuts, pecans, peanuts, or hazelnuts
9. Up to 1 cup corn kernels (frozen are fine; fresh are also fantastic added raw)
10. 4 ounces bacon or sausage, chopped and cooked until crisp

21 Main-Course Bean Dishes

With bread and salad, almost any bean dish can serve as a main course. But these are especially satisfying:

1. Orange-Glazed Black Beans with Crisp Pork (page 395)
2. White Beans with Cabbage, Pasta, and Prosciutto and its variations (page 396)
3. Beans and Tomatoes (page 396)
4. Beans with Tomatillos and Hominy (page 397)
5. Edamame with Fresh Tomatoes and Cilantro (page 398)
6. Edamame with Ground Pork and Fresh Tomatoes (page 398)
7. Stewed Chickpeas with Seared Chicken or any of its variations (page 398)
8. Baked Beans (page 400)
9. White Beans and Sausage and Kale or White Beans and Shrimp (pages 402–403)
10. Beans and Greens (page 403)
11. Slow-Simmered Beef Chili (page 403)
12. Canned Cannellini Cassoulet (page 405)
13. Chickpeas in Their Own Broth with Smoked Chorizo (page 407)
14. Lentils with Lardons (page 409)
15. Baked Black Beans and Rice or its variations (page 410)
16. Hoppin' John (page 412)
17. Red Beans and Rice or its variations (page 412)
18. Falafel and its variations (page 415)
19. Bean Griddlecakes and its variations (page 416)
20. Stir-Fried Tofu with Snow Peas or Sugar Snap Peas (page 420)
21. Braised Tofu with Eggplant and Shiitakes (page 425)

---

6 SAUCES FOR BEAN GRIDDLECAKES

1. Harissa (page 45)
2. Fresh Tomato or Fruit Salsa (page 55)
3. Fresh Tomatillo Salsa (page 56)
4. Sesame-Soy Dipping Sauce (page 64)
5. Miso Dipping Sauce (page 66)
6. Fast Tomato Sauce (page 478)

THE BASICS OF TOFU

Imagine fresh cheese made from soy milk. That's what tofu is; the process of coagulation, curds, and forming is very similar. This vegan food comes in all sorts of forms and shapes—some more processed than others—and is the most versatile food I know.

TYPES OF TOFU

Most all supermarkets carry refrigerated blocks of firm tofu and shelf-stable packaged silken tofu. Once you become an enthusiast—and you will—I encourage you to explore the many different kinds stocked in Asian markets. A lot of local and regional producers have popped up in the last few years, and their products are available at specialty stores and farmers' markets.

"REGULAR" TOFU (BRICK, MOMEN, OR CHINESE TOFU) The most familiar tofu, shaped in blocks that usually weigh about a pound, and sold sealed in plastic tubs with water or from an open tub. The texture is dense and crumbly; the firmness, determined by water content, may be soft, medium, firm, or extra-firm. The firm and extra-firm varieties hold their shape and are suitable for just about any cooking technique: stir-frying, baking, braising, grilling, or frying. Soft and medium tofu hold their shape when cut but not necessarily when cooked, so they're best served raw or used as thickeners, or blended to replace eggs or dairy.

SILKEN TOFU (KINUGOSHI OR JAPANESE TOFU) Also a rectangular block, and usually sold in aseptic boxes, silken tofu has the texture of custard and comes in soft, firm, and extra-firm varieties. It's an excellent thickener or replacement for eggs or dairy, and firm and extra-firm versions can be diced (or scooped) to slip into broths and soups, crumbled, deep-fried, or even gently stir-fried.

PRESSED OR EXTRA-FIRM TOFU Not to be confused with tofu you press yourself (see below). Tofu blocks are pressed under high pressure to form a very firm tofu with the density of Swiss cheese. Sometimes it's fried or seasoned after that, and is meant to be eaten as a snack. It's labeled a number of ways but is always brown and dense, and sold whole or cut into thin strips. Whole—and plain—it's ideal for stir-frying, marinating, and grilling; cut, it makes a delicious addition to soups or salads. Smoked tofu is similar in texture, with a stronger flavor. You'll also find various types of Chinese and Japanese styles of fried tofu, sold in different packaging.

TOFU SKINS (YUBA) Sold dried or fresh, in sheets or precut, this pleasantly chewy tofu is skimmed from the top of coagulated soy milk as it heats, much like the skin that forms on scalded cow's milk. You can use it like fresh pasta or egg noodles, or as a wrap for sushi rice or other savory and sweet fillings.

What about Tempeh?

Tempeh (pronounced TEM-pay) is based on fermented soybeans. So in that way it's more like soy sauce and miso, though you cook and eat it like tofu. It's high in protein and has a flavor that's yeasty, tangy (some might say sour), and heavy on the umami. Like blue cheese, tempeh isn't pretty: a lumpy, compressed cake of beans (and sometimes grains), usually less than an inch thick.

You can buy tempeh in most supermarkets, usually vacuum-sealed. Once you open the package, use it within a few days. It's good steamed, sliced and fried, braised, or baked. I like it best crumbled and crisped in a little hot oil like ground meat.

BUYING AND STORING TOFU

Tofu is best when fresh. Wet-packed firm supermarket tofu has an expiration date; once opened it can be refrigerated in fresh water, which should be changed daily, for a few days. Follow the same drill with bulk tofu from a tub of water or aseptic-boxed tofu once you open it. Spoiled tofu smells and/or tastes sour and the storing water becomes cloudy, though cloudy water alone does not mean the tofu is off. For longer storage, the best way is to freeze tofu in an airtight container for up to 3 months.

PREPARING TOFU

Though it's perfectly fine to simply drain tofu, pat it dry, and use it right away, you can easily change the texture before cooking, which also helps it absorb flavor from marinades and sauces.

Freezing changes the texture completely, creating a darker, firmer, chewier, and meatier block with a dry, spongy texture that's perfect for grilling, stir-frying, and braising. Drain the tofu and pat it dry; put it in an airtight container, and freeze for several hours or up to 3 months. For extra chew, cut tofu into cubes and dry them well before freezing. Allow enough time to thaw tofu and squeeze out all the water before slicing and cooking.

Squeezing Tofu

Put cut tofu between four layers of towels, weight evenly (about a pound is right; no more than two), and let sit for a few minutes, up to a half hour.

Squeezing a regular block of tofu to press out some of the liquid gives it a drier, firmer texture that makes it denser and easier to handle and cook (see page 418). Cut the tofu into two slabs, put the halves between towels, then top with a heavy cutting board, skillet, or similar weight so the tofu bulges at the sides slightly but doesn't crack. Let sit for up to 30 minutes, or as long as it takes you to prepare other ingredients.

Baked Tofu

MAKES: 4 or more servings | **TIME:** About 1 hour

Treated this way, tofu develops a crust on all sides, with an almost egglike interior. Cool, then slice or cube it, and you're ready for anything: sandwiches, salads, stir-fries, you name it. (See "14 Sauces for Any Simply Cooked Tofu," page 420.)

1 to 2   **pounds firm tofu, frozen, squeezed, or just patted dry**
      Salt

1. Heat the oven to 350°F. Pat the tofu dry with towels and rub with salt on all sides. Put in a small ovenproof skillet or baking pan.

2. Bake until the tofu forms a crust on the bottom and releases easily from the pan, about 30 minutes. Turn it over and bake until the other side and ends are as crisp and golden as you like, up to 30 minutes more. Use immediately or cool, wrap, and refrigerate for up to 3 days.

SOY-BAKED TOFU After patting the tofu dry, brush liberally with soy sauce. You may still want to sprinkle it with salt, but very lightly.

MISO-BAKED TOFU Thin a couple of tablespoons of any miso with sake, white wine, or water. After turning the tofu in Step 2, use this to brush or smear the tofu liberally.

TOFU CROUTONS OR STICKS Super-crisp for garnishing or snacking, or to add to stir-fries at the last minute: Line a baking sheet with parchment paper. Cut the tofu into 1-inch cubes or ½-inch-wide sticks like French fries. Spread them out in a single layer on the parchment and bake, undisturbed, until the tofu is crisp and golden all over, about 40 minutes.

Grilled or Broiled Tofu

MAKES: 4 to 6 servings | **TIME:** 30 minutes

It's not essential to freeze or press tofu before grilling or broiling, but it will make a big difference. You can use plain grilled tofu the same way you would use baked (see the headnote at left). To season it more assertively before cooking, try rubbing it as you would meat or poultry, with chili powder, jerk seasoning, curry powder, or five-spice powder (to make your own, see pages 27–35). Or serve it with one of the dipping sauces on pages 55–67.

1½ to 2   **pounds any tofu, frozen, squeezed, or just patted dry**
      Salt
      Good-quality vegetable as needed

1. Prepare a charcoal or gas grill for medium-high direct cooking or turn on the broiler and position the rack about 4 inches below the heat. If using wooden skewers, soak them for at least 30 minutes. Cut the tofu into large cubes and thread onto skewers or cut crosswise into 2 or more "steaks." Sprinkle the tofu with salt and rub or brush it with some oil.

2. Transfer the tofu to the grates directly over the flame or put it on a baking sheet under the broiler. Cook until it browns and crisps on one side, about 5 minutes, then turn and cook the other side. Serve right away, use in a stir-fry, or refrigerate for up to 3 days and eat cold.

BARBECUE- OR TERIYAKI-GLAZED TOFU In Step 2, brush the tofu liberally with any Barbecue Sauce (page 74) or Teriyaki Sauce (page 76) and continue to cook, turning and basting, until nicely browned. Serve immediately.

Stir-Fried Tofu with Snow Peas or Sugar Snap Peas

MAKES: 4 servings | **TIME:** 20 minutes

The best way to learn to love tofu is to cook it with lots of crisp vegetables. A ton of ginger and garlic help too. You can serve this with white or brown rice, of course. I also like it tossed with wide rice noodles. Whatever accompaniment you choose, get it ready before you start the stir-fry; this goes super-fast.

Other vegetables you can use: broccoli florets, chopped bok choy or asparagus, sliced carrots.

1½ to 2	pounds firm or extra-firm tofu, frozen, squeezed, or just patted dry
1	pound snow peas or sugar snap peas, trimmed
2	scallions
3	tablespoons good-quality vegetable oil
	Salt and pepper
2	tablespoons chopped garlic

2	tablespoons chopped fresh ginger (optional)
2	small dried chiles (optional)
2	tablespoons soy sauce, or to taste
1	tablespoon toasted sesame seeds (see page 309; optional)

1. Cut the tofu into cubes no bigger than 1-inch. Slice the peas in half lengthwise if you like (pretty, but not necessary). Trim and slice the scallions, keeping the white and green parts separate.
2. Put 2 tablespoons of the oil in a large skillet over medium-high heat. When it is hot, add the tofu in a single layer, sprinkle with salt and pepper, and cook, undisturbed, until the pieces brown on the bottom and release from the pan, about 5 minutes. Scrape them up with a spatula, toss, and let the tofu sizzle until they're crisp in places, just a couple of minutes more; transfer to a plate.
3. Add the remaining 1 tablespoon oil to the skillet and return it to high heat. Immediately add the scallion whites, garlic, and the ginger and chiles if you're using them and cook, stirring, for about 10 seconds. Add the peas and ½ cup water. Cook, stirring and scraping up any browned bits, until the peas turn bright green and most of the water has bubbled away, just a minute or 2. Add the tofu and soy sauce and remove from the heat. Stir in the scallion greens and the sesame seeds, if you're using them. Taste and adjust the seasoning and serve.

10 ADDITIONS TO ANY STIR-FRIED TOFU

You can build on Stir-Fried Tofu with Snow Peas or Sugar Snap Peas (page 420), or try other vegetables with any of these ideas:

1. Add up to 1 cup any cooked fish, seafood, poultry, or meat (shredded, sliced, chopped, or crumbled) with the tofu in Step 3. (You might need a little more liquid or oil.)
2. Add 2 teaspoons five-spice powder (to make your own, see page 35) and/or a few star anise pods with the tofu in Step 3. This is good with hoisin sauce; see below.
3. Add 1 medium-to-large tomato, halved, seeded, and chopped, along with the white parts of the scallions.
4. Add 1 cup bean sprouts, along with—or instead of—the scallion greens.
5. Add 1 tablespoon (or to taste) sugar, honey, or other sweetener, along with the scallion greens.
6. Add 1 tablespoon (or to taste) Chile Paste (page 40) or hoisin sauce, along with the soy sauce.
7. Add 1 tablespoon (or to taste) sesame oil, along with the garnish.
8. Add 2 tablespoons fermented black beans along with the water in Step 3.
9. Add 1 tablespoon grated orange, lime, or lemon zest along with the water in Step 3.
10. Add up to ½ cup chopped cashews or peanuts with the scallion whites and garlic in Step 3.

Braised Tofu with Eggplant and Shiitakes

MAKES: 4 servings | **TIME:** 30 minutes

I love this spicy, more-or-less traditional Sichuan dish for the contrasts: soft-cooked eggplant and tofu and crisp sautéed shiitakes.

Other vegetables you can use: green beans, baby bok choy, or zucchini (for the eggplant).

- 4 tablespoons good-quality vegetable oil
- 8 ounces shiitake mushrooms, stems removed, sliced
  Salt and pepper
- 1 tablespoon chopped garlic
- 1 tablespoon minced fresh ginger
- 1½ pounds eggplant, trimmed, cut into 1½-inch chunks, salted, rinsed, and dried if you like (see page 203)
- 1 tablespoon Chile Paste (page 40) or 1 teaspoon red chile flakes, or to taste
- 2 tablespoons soy sauce
- 1 pound tofu, frozen, squeezed, or just patted dry, and cut into ¼-inch cubes
- 1 tablespoon sesame oil
- 2 scallions, chopped, for garnish
- ¼ cup chopped fresh cilantro for garnish

1. Put 2 tablespoons of the vegetable oil in a large pot over medium-high heat. Add the shiitakes, sprinkle with salt and pepper, and cook, stirring occasionally, until the mushrooms release their liquid and become crisp, 10 to 15 minutes. Remove with a slotted spoon.

2. Add the remaining 2 tablespoons oil. When it is hot, add the garlic and ginger. Let them sizzle for about a minute, then add the eggplant and sprinkle again with salt if you didn't salt it earlier. Cook, stirring every minute or so, until it softens and browns in places, 5 to 10 minutes. Add the chile paste along with ½ cup water. Stir, scraping the bottom of the pan if necessary to release any stuck bits of eggplant. Cook until the eggplant is really tender, 10 to 15 minutes more, adding a little more liquid if necessary (unlikely but not impossible).

3. Stir in the soy sauce and tofu and cook, stirring occasionally, until the tofu is heated through, about 5 minutes; add more water it looks to dry. Add the sesame oil and reserved shiitakes, stir, and turn off

  **F** fast **M** make ahead **V** vegetarian

the heat. Taste and adjust the seasoning. Garnish with the scallions and cilantro and serve.

BRAISED TOFU WITH CHICKEN AND EGGPLANT

Omit the shiitakes. Cook 8 ounces sliced boneless, skinless chicken breast or thighs in Step 1 until no longer pink. Proceed with the recipe.

BRAISED TOFU WITH SPICY GROUND PORK

Omit the shiitakes and eggplant. Use 1 pound ground pork and cook as described in Step 1, breaking it up as it browns and crisps. Remove it from the pot and drain off all but 2 tablespoons of the fat before proceeding.

BRAISED TOFU WITH SHIITAKES AND BROCCOLI

Instead of the eggplant, trim 1½ pounds broccoli and cut into florets. In Step 2, after cooking the garlic and ginger, add the broccoli to the pot and proceed with the recipe; the broccoli cooking time will be a couple minutes faster than the eggplant so start checking after 3 minutes.

BRAISED TOFU WITH SHIITAKES AND GREEN BEANS

Instead of the eggplant, trim 1½ pounds green beans and cut into 1- or 2-inch pieces. In Step 2, after cooking the garlic and ginger, add the beans to the pot and proceed with the recipe. Garnish with chopped peanuts or cashews if you'd like.

Rice and Other Grains

CHAPTER AT A GLANCE

The Basics of Rice and Other Grains 426

The Rice Lexicon 428

Rice Recipes 430

Grain Recipes 451

The Grain Lexicon 452

Move over, oatmeal and grits. One of the biggest changes on supermarket shelves in the last decade is the abundance of whole grains. Even though we still enjoy white rice and a handful of other processed foods, more and more Americans are hip to whole grains as a solid source of protein, fiber, and the slow-burning energy provided by unrefined carbohydrates. And we're eating them at every meal.

It's obvious that if you stock whole grains in your pantry—where they keep for months—you'll eat them. As I do with beans, I encourage cooking a big batch of plain grains once a week (at least) to use as sides, in salads, or as the foundation of bowls and other mains. For that you're in luck: Both brown and white rice, and virtually all whole grains, cook the same way; start with the two basic recipes on pages 430 and 451.

Since white rice remains the gateway grain, this chapter starts there. But remember, brown rice is the whole form and provides an excellent transition to eating other grains; I explain an easy way to make the switch in any recipe on page 427. After rice come the other grains, starting with the quickest cooking. Both sections include details on the different kinds, and directions for substituting one for another. Along the way you'll learn to make everything from couscous—which is a pasta but cooks like a grain so appears here—to pilaf and sushi to risotto, polenta, and pozole.

THE BASICS OF RICE AND OTHER GRAINS

All parts of most grains are edible. Since almost all grains are grasses, they have the same basic composition: Working from the outside of the kernel inward, the external shell (if there is one) is known as the husk or hull, which must be removed before being eaten. Then comes the bran, very thin but tough layers that protect the interior components. The endosperm is next, which makes up the bulk of the grain and provides food for the core of the kernel, or germ.

MILLING

The steps it takes to remove parts of grains to make them edible or (by some standards) more palatable is called "milling." This general term describes processes that might happen all at once or in different stages. When only the hull is removed from a grain kernel and the bran and germ remain, it's called "brown," as in brown rice, or "whole," as in whole oats. Hulled kernels may then be cut into bits or ground, but they're still considered whole grains.

The less grains are milled, the higher they are in both nutrients and flavor, and the longer they take to cook. That's why white rice, pearled barley, rolled oats, and other heavily processed grains—which contain little more than the starch and protein in the endosperm—absorb water and become tender fast. They're also milder tasting. But with less fiber, micronutrients, and protein than whole or cracked whole grains, they're not as nutritious. And most people find the heartiness and rich flavor of whole grains quite satisfying.

BUYING AND STORING GRAINS

Now that many whole grains are easy to find, the question shifts to how to get your hands on the best quality and more unusual varieties. International or other specialty markets, natural food stores, and online

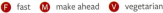 **F** fast   **M** make ahead   **V** vegetarian

sources should provide anything you want. And check your farmers' market for common foods like cornmeal, polenta, and rye and wheat berries, which are becoming more popular to grow and sell regionally.

Stored in a cool, dry place, white rice and other heavily milled products will keep well for at least a year. Brown rice and other whole grains are more sensitive; the natural oils in the bran and germ can turn rancid. Since you never know how long they've already been sitting on the store shelf, brown rice and other whole grains are best refrigerated or frozen if possible. (No need to thaw before use.) I try to buy relatively small amounts (a pound or less) of several kinds and use them within six months.

RINSING AND DRAINING

Grains are cleaned in the milling process, so you don't need to pick through them as you do beans. But because rice may have been coated with talc, quinoa may retain a bit of its natural saponin (a slightly bitter compound), and any grain may be gritty, I like to rinse them before cooking.

Swish grains in a strainer under cold running water or put them in the pot you're going to use, fill it with water, swirl the grains around, then pour off the water; repeat until the water is clear. You need not drain the grains well if you're just going to boil them, but you should if you're making pilaf, risotto, or similar dishes.

COOKING RICE AND OTHER GRAINS

The simplest way to prepare rice and grains is to boil them. I prefer using only the amount of water they will fully absorb while they become tender, but you can also cook them pasta-style in plenty of boiling water and drain them. Toasting in a dry skillet or sautéing in a skillet with a little oil or other fat can enhance the flavor and texture of grains, and of course you'll probably want to add other ingredients at least some times, but there's rarely anything more complicated than that.

Grains are dried, like most beans, which means they must be rehydrated to become edible. As grains absorb liquid, they swell, gaining volume. The amount of time this process and the accompanying cooking takes and the amount of liquid the grain needs to become fully cooked depend on six factors:

1. **The nature of the grain:** Larger takes longer, and some are just tougher than others.
2. **How dry the grain is:** Older grains are drier than those more recently milled.
3. **How many of its outer layers have been removed:** Brown rice has the bran; white rice does not.
4. **How much it has been milled:** Rolling or cutting oats exposes more surface area.
5. **Whether it has been precooked:** Kasha is toasted buckwheat, bulgur is precooked cracked wheat, and some rice is sold "converted" or parboiled. (You can also precook grains yourself; see page 450.)
6. **The cooking method:** Pressure cookers are faster than cooking in a pot on the stove; grains prepared in a slow cooker take much longer.

Once cooked, you can keep rice and grains warm and fluffy for up to 30 minutes or so. After fluffing, leave the lid on and set the pot over the lowest heat possible (the

Using Brown Rice in Recipes That Call for White Rice

To get the nutty, rich, toasted, satisfying taste and texture of brown rice in pilaf, paella, and even risotto, all you have to do is precook it. Start by bringing a large pot of salted water to a boil. Stir in the rice—long- or short-grain, whatever's called for in the recipe. Adjust the heat so that the water bubbles steadily. Don't stir again; just let it cook until the color lightens and the kernels begin to plump, about 12 minutes. Drain the rice thoroughly, then use it in the recipe instead of the raw white rice.

residual heat of a cooling electric burner is perfect for this) or wrap the pot in a towel. Leftover rice and grains will keep in the fridge for days, and grains store well in the freezer for months. So make double or even triple batches whenever possible.

The Rice Lexicon

There are thousands of varieties of rice; throw in the regional names for each variety and you've got a mass of confusion. In an effort to clear things up and make this information useful, I'll stick with the varieties that you're most likely to find in the United States, which is still a lot.

It helps to start with the big picture: the species and forms of rice. Indica (long-grain rice varieties), which produces fluffy and separated grains when cooked, is grown in warm, wet, mostly tropical regions, like Southeast Asia, India, Pakistan, and the southern United States. Japonica includes medium- and short-grain rices; there's not much of a difference between "medium" and "short" in this case. These kernels are sticky and moist when cooked. Japonica varieties are grown in more northern climates, like northern China, Japan, Korea, Europe, and California.

Within these two groups, grain length is the basic distinction used to describe the common forms rice takes, but it's not the only one. And the names applied to different rices can be confusing. Any rice can be "brown," for example—the term describes rice that has had only its inedible hull removed, leaving the bran and germ. All the fancy specialty colored rices—red, black, purple, etc.—are just brown rice with a different color bran. When you remove the bran and the germ, it goes from being brown—or whatever color—to white.

"Broken rice" describes kernels that have been purposely busted up into pieces, which helps them release more starch during cooking; it's used in the cooking of China and Southeast Asia. Converted and instant rice are processed products that have either been soaked and steamed before milling, or partially or fully cooked and then dried. The results are inferior to raw rices in every way: flavor, texture, and nutrition. Just avoid them.

LONG-GRAIN RICES

Generally, these are slender grains, at least three times longer than they are wide. When cooked, they're fluffy and separated.

SOUTHERN LONG-GRAIN RICE

VARIETIES AND FORMS Brown, white, converted, and instant.

DESCRIPTION The most common long-grain rice in the world, and the most widely grown rice in the United States. If a rice is labeled just "long-grain," it's most likely this.

BASMATI RICE

VARIETIES AND FORMS Brown and white.

DESCRIPTION The best-known and most aromatic rice of South Asia.

JASMINE RICE

VARIETIES AND FORMS Brown, white, and broken.

DESCRIPTION An aromatic rice with a sweet aroma, this Thai specialty is white in color, smooth, and slightly stickier than basmati, with a milder flavor.

AMERICAN AROMATICS

VARIETIES AND FORMS Texmati, Kasmati, Calmati, Jasmati, Della, Wild Pecan, Louisiana Pecan, Popcorn; brown and white.

DESCRIPTION Knockoffs of either basmati or jasmine, usually without the same intensity as their role models.

LONG-GRAIN STICKY RICES

VARIETIES AND FORMS Thai, sticky jasmine, glutinous, sweet, or khao niew (Laotian sticky rice); brown (called Thai black or purple, or black sticky rice) and white.

 fast  make ahead vegetarian

DESCRIPTION This is the stuff you know from Thai restaurants, and much different from plain long-grain white rice. (In Thailand and elsewhere, it's formed into small balls and eaten like bread.) To be sure you're getting real sticky rice, look for a Thai brand with long grains that may or may not be broken, or broken jasmine. Aromatic, with a sweet flavor and very sticky but firm texture.

RED RICES

VARIETIES AND FORMS California Red, Wehani, Himalayan Red, and more; brown.

DESCRIPTION Brown rices that, through breeding or accident, have red bran. They're usually more expensive than standard brown rice but not much different in flavor. Like all brown rices, these have a nuttier flavor, chewier texture, and longer cooking times than white rices.

SHORT- AND MEDIUM-GRAIN RICES

These Japonica rices have fat, round grains with a neutral flavor; they're sticky and moist when cooked. They're listed here from most commonly used and easiest to find to the more specialized.

COMMON SHORT- AND MEDIUM-GRAIN RICES

VARIETIES AND FORMS Many, from Calrose to Koshihikari; brown and white.

DESCRIPTION Often grown in California, the grains are glossy, sticky but firm, moist, and neutral in flavor. They are good, inexpensive substitutes for Arborio, Valencia, and other rarer short- and medium-grain rices. This is the rice associated with Southeast Asia and Japan, and is used for stuffings, mixed rice, and sushi.

RISOTTO RICES

VARIETIES AND FORMS Most commonly Arborio, but also Carnaroli, Vialone Nano, and more; brown (occasionally) and white.

DESCRIPTION Traditionally Italian-grown rices that are now also grown in California. They have a stark white center that remains firm as long as it's not overcooked, and starchy outer layers that absorb liquid and create that creamy risotto texture. Use common short- or medium-grain rice (see preceding description) as a substitute if you like.

PAELLA OR SPANISH RICES

VARIETIES AND FORMS Valencia, Bomba, Bahia, Granza; almost always white.

DESCRIPTION A medium-grain rice that produces a creamy texture similar to risotto, though the grains remain more separate. It has a neutral flavor that perfectly absorbs the flavors of the other ingredients in a dish.

AMERICAN BLACK, RED, AND MAHOGANY RICES

VARIETIES AND FORMS Available in various colors; often blended into mixtures.

DESCRIPTION American-grown specialty aromatic rices that have a nutty and somewhat spicy flavor. These hulled kernels are deeply hued and quite beautiful.

SHORT-GRAIN STICKY RICES

VARIETIES AND FORMS Chinese, Japanese, Korean, mochi, glutinous, sweet, waxy; brown and white.

DESCRIPTION Opaque and plump, with a slightly sweet flavor and sticky but firm texture. Often used in desserts and sweet dishes.

BHUTANESE RICE

DESCRIPTION A pretty, medium-grain red rice grown in the tiny high-altitude Himalayan country of Bhutan. Since some of the bran remains, it has a nutty, earthy flavor but cooks more quickly than other brown rices.

FORBIDDEN RICE; CHINA BLACK

DESCRIPTION Said to have been grown originally only for the Chinese emperor; prized for its black color, starchy texture, and earthy taste. Has a high visual impact; increasingly easy to find.

BAMBOO RICE

VARIETIES AND FORMS Also known as green rice; white rice infused with the extracted juice from bamboo (rich in the plant's chlorophyll).

DESCRIPTION A short grain white rice akin to other sushi rices, only with the addition of the bamboo, it takes on a light green tint and a slightly herbaceous flavor reminiscent of green tea. Cook as you would short grain white rice or sushi rice.

Rice Recipes

Beginning with the basic boiled and steamed rice and moving through pilafs and risotto into more involved and substantial recipes, these are all the techniques you need to cook all of the world's great rice dishes—and discover some of your own, too.

White Rice

MAKES: 4 servings | **TIME:** 20 to 30 minutes

The simple simmering method described in the main recipe and two variations—for brown and coconut rice—are the same. Only the time and the main components—rice and liquid—change. Let this model and the lexicon on page 428 inspire you to try many more of the different rices now available.

> 1½ **cups white rice**
> **Large pinch salt**

1. Put the rice in a medium saucepan with water to cover by about 1 inch. Add the salt and bring to a boil, then adjust the heat so the mixture boils steadily but not violently.

2. Cook without stirring until small craters appear in the surface, 10 to 15 minutes. When all visible moisture disappears (tip the pot to confirm that no water remains), cover and turn off the heat; let the rice sit for 5 minutes.

3. Fluff the rice with a fork. You can serve it now; it will be on the moist side, but fine. Or cover the pot again and let it sit with the heat off for at least 15 or up to 30 minutes to dry a bit before serving.

BROWN RICE In Step 2, cover the pot and cook for 30 to 40 minutes, checking occasionally to make sure the water is not being absorbed too quickly (you can add a little more water if necessary). When all the water has been absorbed, taste and see if the rice is tender or nearly so. If not, add about ½ cup more water, cover, and continue to cook; check every 5 minutes or so. When the rice is tender, proceed with Step 3.

COCONUT RICE Exceptional if you make your own coconut milk (see page 372), but still quite good with full- or reduced-fat canned. Best with short-grain rice: Instead of the water, use 1½ cups coconut milk and however much water you need to cover the rice by about 1 inch in Step 1. Add a bay leaf or a tablespoon minced fresh ginger if you like. Proceed with the recipe.

Steamed Sticky Rice

MAKES: 4 servings | **TIME:** 2 hours, with soaking time, largely unattended

In Thailand, among other places, sticky rice is eaten at just about every meal like bread. It has substance, flavor, and chew, and almost everyone who tries it loves it. All you need is the right kind of rice, cheesecloth, and some time. The rest is easy.

1½ cups sticky rice (broken jasmine is most common; see page 428)
Salt and pepper (optional)
Soy sauce (optional)

1. Rinse the rice, then soak it in water to cover for 1 to 24 hours. Rig a steamer (see page 20). Drain the rice, wrap it in cheesecloth, and put in the steamer above boiling water.

2. Steam until tender, adding more water to the steamer if necessary. about 30 minutes. (Just pull back the cloth to test a kernel.) It's almost impossible to overcook sticky rice, so you can keep it warm over low heat for up to an hour. Or remove the cheesecloth, wrap the bundle tightly in plastic, and refrigerate for up to several days; resteam the package in fresh cheesecloth until hot. Sprinkle with salt and pepper or soy sauce before serving, if you like.

SOUPED-UP STICKY RICE While the rice is steaming, toast ½ cup unsalted peanuts in a dry skillet over medium heat until fragrant, about 2 minutes. Chop the peanuts, then toss with ¼ cup chopped shallot or scallion, ¼ cup chopped fresh cilantro, 1 tablespoon soy sauce, and 2 teaspoons fresh lime juice. Toss with the cooked rice, then rewrap and steam or microwave for a few minutes to reheat.

THE BASICS OF RICE PILAF

Cooking rice in butter or oil before adding liquid and seasonings is a universal enhancement technique. Yellow rice is a form of pilaf, as is biryani (see Chicken Biryani, page 626) and, one could argue, jambalaya (page 437) and paella (page 435).

Much is up for grabs: You can use long- or short-grain rice; even brown rice is fair game, but the technique is slightly different (see page 427). Stock, wine, water, plain regular yogurt, or anything else you like can be the liquid. The herbs, spices, and solid ingredients can all be varied as you like.

One other thing that is really great about pilaf: It can be reheated successfully, either in the microwave or on the stove. Just add a little water first, cover, and warm using a low setting or low heat.

Rice pilafs; left to right: Rice
Pilaf, page 434; Rice Pilaf
with garam masala and cilantro;
Kimchi Rice, page 437

Rice Pilaf

MAKES: 4 servings | **TIME:** About 30 minutes, plus time to rest

Easy, fast, and reliable, pilaf has another bonus: Cooking it slightly in advance is not just possible, but desirable to help the flavors meld.

3 tablespoons butter or olive oil
1 onion, chopped
  Salt and pepper
1½ cups long-grain white rice, like basmati
2½ cups stock (to make your own, see pages 174–180) or water
  Chopped fresh parsley for garnish

1. Put the butter or oil in a large pot over medium heat. When the butter melts or the oil is hot, add the onion and sprinkle with salt and pepper. Cook, stirring, until the onion softens, about 5 minutes.

2. Add the rice and stir until the kernels are glossy and starting to color lightly, about 3 minutes. Add the stock, increase the heat, and bring to a boil. Reduce the heat so it bubbles gently but steadily, stir once or twice, then cover the pot.

3. Cook until most of the liquid is absorbed, about 15 minutes. Turn the heat to the absolute minimum and let sit for another 15 to 30 minutes. (If you have an electric stove, turn the heat off and let the pan sit on the burner.) Fluff with a fork, taste and adjust the seasoning, fluff again, then garnish and serve.

BAKED RICE PILAF Streamlines the process slightly and creates a little crust around the edge: Heat the oven to 350°F and be sure to use an ovenproof pot. Follow the recipe through Step 2, then transfer the pot to the oven; bake for 10 minutes. Remove from the oven, but leave on the lid. Let the rice rest for another 10 minutes before fluffing.

16 STIR-INS FOR RICE PILAF OR BAKED RICE PILAF

Stir in any of the following, alone or in combination, just after adding the rice in either Rice Pilaf or Baked Rice Pilaf (at left).

1. 1 cup seeded and chopped tomato (drained canned is fine)
2. ½ to 1 cup sliced fresh mushrooms like button or shiitake caps, or reconstituted dried porcini or shiitake mushrooms
3. 1 to 2 tablespoons minced fresh strong herbs like rosemary, thyme, oregano, or sage
4. 1 cup fresh or frozen lima beans, edamame, or chopped green beans or peas
5. 1 cup drained cooked or canned legumes like chickpeas, black-eyed peas, lentils, or pigeon peas
6. 2 tablespoons or more mashed Roasted Garlic (page 294) or 1 tablespoon minced raw garlic
7. ¼ cup Caramelized Onions (page 315)
8. Up to 1 cup cooked and crumbled bacon or sausage or chopped ham, or up to ½ cup other chopped cured meat like prosciutto, coppa, salami, or bresaola
9. Up to 1 cup (about 4 ounces) chopped cleaned squid, shrimp, or firm-fleshed fish like cod, snapper, or monkfish
10. Up to ½ cup (about 2 ounces) flaked smoked fish like salmon, trout, or mackerel
11. About ½ cup white or red wine; let it boil a bit before adding the stock
12. ½ cup chopped toasted nuts like almonds, pecans, walnuts, pine nuts, cashews, pistachios, peanuts, or hazelnuts
13. ¼ to ½ cup chopped dried fruit (especially good with nuts)
14. About 1 tablespoon minced or grated lemon, lime, or orange zest
15. 1 tablespoon cumin, coriander, mustard, or fennel seeds or 1 tablespoon ground spice mixture like

 **F** fast **M** make ahead **V** vegetarian

curry powder, garam masala, or five-spice (to make your own, see pages 27–35)

16. 1 cup chopped fresh mild herbs like parsley, basil, mint, dill, or chervil; stir in just before serving

Chicken Paella

MAKES: 4 servings | **TIME:** 45 minutes

Sometimes perceived as a major production, paella is nothing more than a combination of rice and something else—often a mixture of odds-and-ends pieces of seafood, chicken, meat, and vegetables. Everything about it can be simplified for weeknights, as in this recipe. Even the pan: A large ovenproof skillet is fine for developing everyone's favorite part: the crusty bits of rice at the bottom called *socarrat*.

3½ cups chicken or vegetable stock (to make your own, see pages 174–178) or water
Pinch saffron threads or 2 teaspoons smoked paprika
¼ cup olive oil
1 onion, chopped
2 tablespoons chopped garlic
Salt and pepper
2 cups short- or medium-grain rice, preferably paella rice (see page 429) or Arborio
1½ pounds boneless chicken thighs, cut into strips
Fresh parsley leaves for garnish

1. Heat the oven to 450°F. Warm the stock with the saffron or paprika in a saucepan. Put the oil in a large skillet over medium-high heat. When it is hot, add the onion and garlic, sprinkle with salt and pepper, and cook, stirring occasionally, until the onion softens, 3 to 5 minutes.
2. Add the rice and cook, stirring occasionally, until it's shiny, about a minute. Add the warm stock and stir to combine. Bring to a boil and cook without stirring for 3 minutes to let some of the liquid bubble away. Remove from the heat, scatter the chicken across the top of the mixture, and press down gently.
3. Put the pan in the oven and bake for 15 minutes. Check to see if the rice is dry and just tender. If not, return the pan to the oven for 5 minutes more. If the rice looks too dry at this point, but still isn't quite done,

17 Grain Dishes That Make Good Leftovers

These are all still good after a day or two in the fridge. (I include risotto even though few people will admit to eating risotto cold—just like pasta—because it's heresy to do so.) Reheat them gently, covered, on the stove or in the microwave. To serve them as salad, sprinkle with a little oil and vinegar or lemon juice, fluff with a fork, and let them sit for up to an hour to take the chill off.

1. Baked Black Beans and Rice (page 410)
2. Any Rice Pilaf (page 434)
3. Chicken Paella (page 435)
4. Shrimp Jambalaya or its variation (page 437)
5. Stuck-Pot Rice with Potato Crust (page 439)
6. Any Risotto (pages 440–441)
7. Any Fried Rice (pages 444–447)
8. Sautéed Cooked Grains (page 450)
9. Israeli Couscous Pilaf with Olives and its variations (page 457)
10. Bulgur Pilaf with Vermicelli and its variations (page 458)
11. Quinoa with Roasted Corn and its variations (page 458)
12. Polenta and its variations (page 460)
13. Kasha with Browned Onions and its variations (page 463)
14. Farro with Leeks, Cherry Tomatoes, and Basil (page 467)
15. Wild Rice Pilaf (especially the variations; pages 467–468)
16. Wheat Berries with Candied Walnuts (page 468)
17. Chipotle Pozole (page 469)

10 More Rice or Other Grain Pilafs

This chart is simple: just follow the main recipe, making substitutions as suggested in the columns. You can even substitute a different grain; just make sure to change the cooking time accordingly.

VARIATION	GRAIN	SAUTÉ IN STEP 1	ADJUSTMENTS IN STEP 2	GARNISHES
Herbed Pilaf	Basmati or other long-grain rice	Butter; chopped leek instead of onion	Use a 50/50 combination of water and white wine.	Add ½ cup chopped fresh herbs when you fluff in Step 3: parsley, basil, chives, mint, dill, or shiso, alone or in combination.
Red Rice (*Arroz Rojo*)	Basmati or other long-grain rice	Good-quality vegetable oil; red onion plus 1 tablespoon chopped garlic, 1 jalapeño chile, chopped	Add 1 cup chopped fresh or drained canned diced tomato with the stock.	Chopped fresh parsley or cilantro; a squeeze of lemon or lime juice.
Green Rice (*Arroz Verde*)	Basmati or other long-grain rice	Good-quality vegetable oil; the onion plus 1 tablespoon chopped garlic	Add 1 cup chopped tomatillos with the stock.	Chopped fresh parsley or cilantro; a squeeze of lemon or lime juice.
Yellow Rice	Any long- or short-grain white rice (short grain will take 5 to 10 minutes longer to cook)	Butter; the onion plus 1 chopped green or red bell pepper. When soft, add a pinch saffron threads and ⅛ teaspoon ground allspice.	Add 1 large fresh tomato, chopped, and 2 bay leaves with the liquid.	Add 1 cup fresh or thawed frozen peas when you fluff in Step 3. Garnish with chopped fresh parsley.
Pilaf with Currants and Pine Nuts	Basmati rice	Butter; the onion or chopped leeks	Add ¼ cup currants, raisins, or other chopped dried fruit; 2 tablespoons pine nuts or other chopped nuts; 1 teaspoon ground cumin; ½ teaspoon ground cinnamon.	Add 1 tablespoon grated lemon zest when you fluff in Step 3.
Brown Rice with Two Mushrooms	Brown basmati rice; cook an extra 25 to 30 minutes in Step 3 or parboil it as described on page 427.	Olive oil; the onion plus 1 pound shiitake mushrooms, caps only, sliced	Use mushroom stock if you like; add ⅓ cup chopped dried porcini with the stock.	Add 1 tablespoon chopped fresh thyme or oregano when you fluff in Step 3.
Rice-'n'-Noodles	¾ cup any long-grain white rice and about 4 ounces angel hair pasta, broken into 1-inch lengths	Olive oil or butter; the onion plus 1 tablespoon chopped garlic	Increase stock to 3 cups.	Chopped fresh parsley or basil.

 **F** fast   **M** make ahead   **V** vegetarian

VARIATION	GRAIN	SAUTÉ IN STEP 1	ADJUSTMENTS IN STEP 2	GARNISHES
Kimchi Rice	Any long-grain white rice	Sesame oil; 2 tablespoons chopped fresh ginger instead of onion	Omit salt; add ½ cup or more chopped kimchi, and soy sauce to taste.	Sliced scallions.
Pilaf with a Little Meat	Basmati rice	Butter or oil; the onion plus 1 tablespoon chopped garlic. Start by browning 8 ounces any ground meat (lamb and pork are my favorites), then adding the aromatics.	Add stock to meat mixture; bay leaves.	Chopped fresh parsley with anything; dill, mint, or parsley with lamb; basil or chives with chicken or other poultry.
Parmesan Rice	Any long-grain white rice	Butter or olive oil. Replace the onion with 1 tablespoon chopped garlic.	If you've got rinds from Parmesan cheese, add them with the water or stock.	Add ½ cup grated Parmesan cheese when you fluff in Step 3. Garnish with chopped fresh chives, basil, or parsley.

add a small amount of stock or water. When the rice is ready, turn off the oven and let it sit for at least 5 and up to 15 minutes.

4. Transfer the pan to the stove over high heat until the rice smells like toast and develops a crust without burning, just a minute or 2. Serve hot or at room temperature, garnished with parsley.

PAELLA WITH CHICKEN AND CHORIZO Cut 8 ounces Spanish chorizo or other spicy smoked sausage into small chunks. Tuck the sausage into the rice before transferring the pan to the oven.

SHRIMP (OR SQUID) PAELLA Substitute shelled large shrimp (or squid tentacles and bodies) for the chicken. Cut into pieces if you'd like and toss them in a little bit of olive oil; wait to add the shrimp (or squid) until Step 3,

when the rice is just a little less done than you ultimately want it. Scatter the pieces on top, sprinkle with salt, and return to the oven until the shrimp is pink (or the squid is white), 3 to 5 minutes.

Shrimp Jambalaya

MAKES: 8 servings | **TIME:** About 1 hour

In Louisiana, this often-improvised one-pot meal would be called a "red jambalaya" thanks to the tomatoes. For a "brown" interpretation, see the variation. Use medium-grain rice for a stickier dish, long-grain for fluffier. And if you can find tasso—a highly seasoned smoked ham classic in this dish—you're in for a treat.

Shrimp Jambalaya,
page 437

3 tablespoons olive oil

1 onion, chopped

1 large green bell pepper, cored, seeded, and chopped

2 celery stalks, chopped, plus some whole leaves reserved for garnish

4 ounces tasso or any ham, chopped (optional)
Salt and pepper

2 cups white rice (see headnote)

2 tablespoons chopped garlic

½ teaspoon cayenne, or to taste

1 tablespoon chopped fresh thyme or 1 teaspoon dried

2 cups seeded and chopped fresh tomato (or 1 28-ounce can diced tomatoes)

4 cups shrimp stock (to make your own, see page 179) or water

1½ pounds shrimp, peeled, cut into pieces if large

1. Put the oil in a large pot over medium heat. When it is hot, add the onion, bell pepper, celery, and tasso if you're using it. Sprinkle with salt and pepper and cook, stirring occasionally, until the onion softens and everything begins to brown, about 10 minutes.

2. Stir in the rice, garlic, cayenne, and thyme and stir for about a minute, until fragrant. Add the tomatoes and cook, stirring, until the pieces break up, about 5 minutes.

3. Add the stock. Bring to a boil, then lower the heat so the liquid bubbles gently. Cover and cook, stirring occasionally, until the rice is tender and the liquid just about absorbed, 15 to 20 minutes.

4. Add the shrimp and stir with a fork. Cover and cook until the shrimp are pink and opaque, 2 or 3 minutes. Fluff again, then cover and let rest off the heat for at least 10 and up to 20 minutes. Garnish and serve.

CHICKEN AND SAUSAGE JAMBALAYA This is called "brown jambalaya": Omit the ham, tomato, and shrimp. Use chicken stock or water and increase the quantity to 6 cups. In Step 1, add 8 ounces chopped andouille or other spicy smoked sausage to the vegetables. When everything starts to sizzle and brown, add 1 pound sliced boneless, skinless chicken thighs. When it starts to turn opaque, proceed with Step 2.

Stuck-Pot Rice with Potato Crust

MAKES: 4 to 6 servings | **TIME:** 1½ hours, largely unattended

Visualize a stovetop paella served upside down, the gorgeous crust sitting on top. Made with rice, potatoes, or anything else that browns and sticks to the bottom of a pot—and given the fact that the recipe actually directs that you simply walk away (you'll ruin it if you don't)—stuck-pot rice is one of the easiest ways to get an impressive rice dish on the table.

Use brown basmati rice here if you like. The kernels will be slightly less starchy than white basmati rice, but the flavor will be deep and delicious. And take the time to line the pot lid with a clean towel. This absorbs water so the condensation from the lid doesn't drip back into the rice.

Salt and pepper

1½ cups white or brown basmati rice

1 large or 2 small waxy potatoes like red or another thin-skinned variety

4 tablespoons butter or olive oil

1 fennel bulb, trimmed, halved lengthwise, and thinly sliced

1. Fill a large pot with a tight-fitting lid with water, bring to a boil, and salt it. Stir in the rice and return to a boil, then lower the heat so the water bubbles steadily. Cook until partially done—white rice for about 5 minutes, brown rice about 15 minutes. Meanwhile, peel the potato and cut crosswise into thin slices.

2. When the rice is ready, drain it in a strainer. Taste, add salt if necessary, and sprinkle with pepper. Wipe out the pot.

7 Main-Dish Rice Recipes Elsewhere in This Book

1. Baked Black Beans and Rice (page 410)
2. Hoppin' John (page 412)
3. Red Beans and Rice (page 412)
4. Shrimp and Rice, Japanese Style (page 546)
5. Arroz con Pollo (page 625)
6. Chicken Biryani (page 626)
7. Rice Pudding and its variations (page 895)

3. Put the butter or oil in the pot over medium-high heat. When the butter foams or the oil is hot, add the fennel, sprinkle with salt and pepper, and cook, stirring occasionally, until soft, about 2 minutes. Remove the pot from the heat and transfer the fennel to a bowl with a slotted spoon.

4. Add ¼ cup water to the pot. Cover the bottom with the potato slices, overlapping them a little if necessary. Spoon in half the rice, carefully spreading it evenly. Add a layer of the fennel, then the other half of the rice. Wrap a clean kitchen towel around the lid of the pot so that the corners are on top and won't fall anywhere near the burner and cover the pot. Turn the heat to medium-high. When you hear the water spattering, about 5 minutes, turn the heat down to very low. Cook, undisturbed, until the potatoes start to smell toasty—you will know—but not burned, about 45 minutes. Remove from the heat and let sit for another 5 minutes.

5. Remove the lid and the cloth and carefully turn the pot upside down over a large plate. If the potatoes come out in a single crust, terrific. If not, use a spatula to scrape the pieces out of the pan and put them on top of the rice. Serve immediately, sprinkled with a bit of salt and pepper if you like.

STUCK-POT RICE WITH PITA CRUST Like buttered toast: Omit the potato and fennel. If you like, use Caramelized Onions (page 315) between rice layers in Step 4. Use 1 large or 2 small pockets pitas, split so each become two thin circles; then tear them all into large pieces. Use the pita pieces to line the bottom of the pot in Step 4.

THE BASICS OF RISOTTO

Few dishes are more intuitive to vary once you learn the basic method. And few use leftovers more deliciously.

Start by ignoring whatever you've heard about the difficulty of making "real" risotto. If you can't find Aborio, Carnaroli, Vialone Nano, or any of the other Italian rices, use whatever short-grained white rice you can get your hands on.

Many people also have been scared off risotto by the claim that it must be stirred constantly. You do have to pay attention, but that doesn't mean constant stirring. Once you start the process, hang around the stove to check the moisture level every few minutes to avoid scorching. You can make a salad or vegetables, pour wine, or set the table.

The other hang-up I'm debunking is the liquid. Water is better than packaged or canned stock; you're going to be seasoning the risotto with an aromatic, cheese, and butter—at the very least. Using homemade stock will bring that flavor to the party, so you might consider it. Likewise heating the liquid before adding it is marginally helpful in terms of time. Some say it improves the way the rice develops its signature creaminess, but the difference is subtle, so don't bother if it seems like a hassle.

Just be careful not to overcook the rice. Handle risotto as you would pasta: Remove the rice from heat when there is still a tiny bit of crunch in the center of the kernels.

Risotto, Five Ways

MAKES: 4 to 6 servings | **TIME:** 45 minutes

If you don't have homemade stock on hand, I suggest simmering a carrot, an onion, a couple of celery stalks,

 **F** fast **M** make ahead vegetarian

and a garlic clove in water for 20 minutes, then strain and use that. If you must use straight water, up the other flavorings a bit.

6 cups chicken, beef, or vegetable stock (to make your own, see pages 174–178)
2 tablespoons olive oil
1 onion, chopped
    Large pinch saffron threads (optional)
1½ cups Arborio or other short- or medium-grain rice
    Salt and pepper
½ cup dry white wine or water
2 to 4 tablespoons softened butter
½ cup grated Parmesan cheese, or more to taste

1. Warm the stock in a saucepan if you'd like. Put the oil in a large pot over medium heat. When it is hot, add the onion and cook, stirring occasionally, until it softens, 3 to 5 minutes.

2. Add the saffron and rice and cook, stirring occasionally, until the rice is glossy and becoming translucent, 2 to 3 minutes. Add a little salt and pepper, then the wine. Stir and let the liquid bubble away.

3. Use a ladle to begin adding the stock, ½ cup or so at a time, stirring after each addition. When the stock has been absorbed, add more. (You might not need all of it.) The rice should be neither soupy nor dry. Keep the heat at medium to medium-high and stir frequently.

4. Begin tasting the rice after 20 minutes; you want it to be tender but still with a tiny bit of crunch—it could take as long as 30 minutes to reach this stage. When it does, stir in 2 tablespoons of the butter and at least ½ cup Parmesan. Taste, add more butter, cheese, salt, and/or pepper if you like, and serve immediately, passing additional Parmesan at the table.

RISOTTO ALLA MILANESE With a minor addition, still classic: Add ¼ cup chopped prosciutto—or beef bone marrow, if you can find it—along with the onion.

RISOTTO WITH THREE CHEESES Over the top: When you would ordinarily stir in the Parmesan, add equal amounts (¼ to ⅓ cup each) grated Parmesan, crumbled Gorgonzola or other creamy blue cheese, and shredded or chopped Fontina or other semisoft cheese. Other cheeses that will do well: cubed fresh mozzarella; Robiola; or any hard cheese like Grana Padano or pecorino Romano.

MUSHROOM RISOTTO Use Mushroom Stock (page 174); warm it in a medium saucepan and use it to soak ½ ounce dried porcini mushrooms until pliable, about 20 minutes. Remove them with a slotted spoon and chop. Instead of the onion, cook 1 pound sliced cremini mushrooms in Step 1 until they're dry and begin to color, 10 to 15 minutes. When you add the rice in Step 2, stir in 1 tablespoon chopped garlic and the reserved chopped porcini, then proceed with the recipe. When you add the stock, be careful to leave any grit from the porcini in the saucepan. Garnish with chopped fresh parsley or chives.

RISOTTO WITH SEAFOOD Use fish, shrimp, or lobster stock (to make your own, see page 179) according to the seafood you choose; use fish stock with a combination of seafood. Omit the cheese. In Step 4, when the rice is almost done, stir in 1 pound (total) of the following, alone or in combination: sliced cleaned squid; shelled chopped shrimp; shucked steamed mussels; thick firm fish fillets, cut into 1-inch chunks; scallops; shelled cooked lobster pieces; or lump crabmeat. Cook just until the raw seafood is opaque and firm or the cooked shellfish is heated through, Stir in the butter, taste and adjust the seasoning, and serve, garnished with chopped fresh chives.

Fried Rice Balls

MAKES: About 16 balls (4 main or 8 appetizer servings) | **TIME:** 30 minutes with cooked rice

A Roman treat and a fine use for cold simply cooked rice, especially risotto. Formally known as *supplì al telefono* because the stringy mozzarella center stretches

Risotto, Five Ways,
page 440 (main recipe)

when you bite through the center and is reminiscent of telephone wires. You can also make these bite-size to serve as appetizers (with tomato sauce for dipping) but I like to set them in a pool sauce and make a meal of them either with a big salad or sautéed spinach or kale on the side. (For a couple ideas using leftover rice, see the sidebar below.)

    2   cups cold cooked rice (preferably the main
        risotto recipe on page 440)
        Salt and pepper
    3   eggs
    3   ounces fresh mozzarella, chopped
    2   ounces prosciutto, chopped (optional)
    2   cups fresh bread crumbs (preferably
        homemade; to make your own, see page 801)
        Good-quality vegetable oil for deep-frying
    1   recipe Fast Tomato Sauce (page 478),
        optional for serving

1. Put the rice in a big bowl. If the rice isn't already seasoned, sprinkle with salt and pepper. Break one of the eggs into the rice and mix well. Use about ¼ cup of rice to form 16 balls. With your thumb, make a small indentation in the center of each ball, fill with a little mozzarella, plus a bit of prosciutto if you're using it, and seal the hole with the rice around it.

2. Line a plate with wax paper. Beat the remaining 2 eggs in a shallow bowl. Put the bread crumbs on a plate and sprinkle lightly with salt. Roll each ball in the eggs to coat, then dredge in the bread crumbs. Set the finished rice balls on the wax paper; you can cook them right away or refrigerate for up to a couple of hours.

3. When you're ready to cook, put at least 3 inches of oil in a large pot over medium heat; bring to 350°F (see "Deep-Frying," page 22). Line a rimmed baking sheet with towels.

4. Working in batches to avoid overcrowding, slide the balls into the oil with a slotted spoon. Fry until golden brown, turning as necessary, about 4 minutes. Transfer to the towels to drain and repeat with the remaining balls. Serve hot or at room temperature.

THE BASICS OF FRIED RICE

The best way to make fried rice is with leftover rice—or at least rice that's been cooked ahead and chilled.

Turning Leftover Rice and Other Grains into Griddle Cakes and Burgers

As cooked rice and grains cool, the starches help the kernels stick together in a way that makes them unpleasant to eat cold but ideal for turning the leftovers into cakes, patties, or burgers. You can start with rice that has been seasoned with herbs and spices but does not have any extra bits of ingredients mixed in or use plain rice. Here are some ideas to get you going on 4 servings.

Rice or Grain Griddlecakes: Beat 2 eggs in a large bowl until combined. Stir in 2 cups cooked rice or grains, ½ cup all-purpose flour, ½ teaspoon baking powder, and a pinch salt. If you want to add grated Parmesan cheese (up to ½ cup) or a spice blend like curry powder (between 1 and 2 teaspoons), stir it in, too. Let the mixture sit so the grains absorb some of the liquid. Form into thin, flat cakes and cook in butter or good-quality vegetable oil in a skillet or on a griddle as you would pancakes. Serve with Fast Tomato Sauce (page 478) or one of the raw or cooked sauces in beginning on page 55.

Rice- or Grain-Spiked Burgers: Try this with white or brown rice, bulgur, quinoa, or millet. Start with one of the meat or seafood burgers in this book; see the index to find them. Reduce the protein to 1 pound and add 1 cup cooked rice or grains along with all the other seasonings and ingredients. Shape and cook as you would the burgers.

(Chinese take-out rice is another option.) Warm, just-made rice inevitably clumps together, a lesson I learned in my early days at the stove. When cooked long-grain rice is chilled—even for a few hours, though a day or so is even better—it dries out, separates into individual grains, and is perfect for sizzling in some hot oil to get that signature crisp-but-not-too-crunchy texture.

Making fried rice is akin to making other stir-fries (see page 244). The choices of vegetables and other major ingredients are almost infinite. Use the first recipe as a model, the chart that follows for some ideas to expand your options, then forge your own path.

Simplest Fried Rice

MAKES: 4 servings | **TIME:** 20 minutes with cooked rice

The easiest fried rice dish, very fast, very easy, and very good. It's also an excellent way to use leftover rice. See the recipe at right if you're looking for something more complex or exciting.

- 4 tablespoons good-quality vegetable oil
- 1 red or green bell pepper, cored, seeded, and chopped
- 2 scallions, white and green parts sliced separately
  Salt and pepper
- 4 cups cooked white or brown long-grain rice (see page 430), chilled for at least a few hours
- 1 egg
- 2 tablespoons soy sauce, or to taste
- 1 tablespoon sesame oil

1. Put 2 tablespoons of the oil in a large skillet over medium-high heat. When it's hot, add the bell pepper and scallion whites, sprinkle with salt and pepper, and raise the heat to high. Cook, stirring occasionally, until the vegetables soften and brown in places, 3 to 5 minutes.

2. Remove the vegetables with a slotted spoon and swirl in the remaining 2 tablespoons oil. Immediately scatter the rice on top, separating the kernels with a spatula into an even layer. Cook, undisturbed, until the rice sputters and browns, about 2 minutes. Then stir, breaking up any lumps, until the rice is hot throughout and crisp in places, about 5 minutes. Crack in the egg and stir with a fork until it's scrambled and combined, about 2 minutes.

3. Return the vegetables to the skillet and add the soy sauce and sesame oil, and stir to combine. Taste and adjust the seasoning. Serve, garnished with the scallion greens.

Fried Rice with Shrimp and Pork

MAKES: 4 servings | **TIME:** 30 minutes

What you're getting the hang of here—by adding meat and seafood to fried rice—is moving things in and out of the pan so each component browns well. For bare-bones fried rice, see the recipe at left.

- 1 cup fresh or frozen peas
- 4 tablespoons peanut or good-quality vegetable oil
- 1 onion, chopped
- 1 red bell pepper, cored, seeded, and chopped
- 8 ounces boneless pork shoulder, Chinese sausage, or other pork, chopped
  Salt and pepper
- 8 ounces shrimp, peeled and chopped
- 1 tablespoon chopped garlic
- 1 tablespoon chopped fresh ginger
- 4 cups cooked white or brown long-grain rice (see page 430), chilled for at least a few hours

6 Simple Fried Rice Variations

Use the main recipe as your guide and change the ingredients as described here. For tips on different ways to eat eggs in fried rice and which oil is best, see the list on page 446, "5 Tips for Making the Best Fried Rice."

VARIATION	SUBSTITUTIONS IN STEP 1	CHANGES TO STEP 3
Fried Rice with Onion, Leeks, or Shallots	Replace bell pepper and scallion whites with 1 onion or 2 leeks or shallots, thinly sliced.	Add chopped cashews.
Fried Rice with Frozen Vegetables	Replace bell pepper and scallion whites with up to 1½ cups frozen peas, carrots, and/or corn.	Garnish with chopped fresh cilantro.
Chicken Curry Fried Rice	Replace bell pepper and scallion with whites with ½ onion, sliced. After it's soft, add 1 cup chopped cooked chicken and 1 tablespoon curry powder.	Garnish with chopped fresh cilantro and a squeeze of lime.
Fried Rice with Bok Choy and Ginger	Replace bell pepper and scallion whites with 2 cups chopped bok choy and 2 tablespoons chopped fresh ginger.	Use the scallion whites as well.
Fried Rice with Fried Eggs	Omit the scrambled egg and start by frying 4 eggs in the oil. Carefully transfer them to a plate before proceeding.	Top each serving with a fried egg; garnish with chopped fresh chives instead of scallion greens.
Fried Rice with Bacon and Chiles	Omit the bell pepper and scallion whites. Start by frying 4 slices chopped bacon, and 1 chopped onion in the oil until browned. Pour off all but 2 tablespoons fat from the pan before proceeding.	Garnish with chopped fresh hot red chiles (like Thai) and the scallion greens.

2 **eggs, lightly beaten (optional)**

¼ **cup rice wine, sherry, dry white wine, stock (to make your own, see pages 174–180) or water**

2 **tablespoons soy sauce**

1 **tablespoon sesame oil**

½ **cup chopped scallions or fresh cilantro**

1. If the peas are frozen, soak them in cold water to thaw while you begin cooking. Put 1 tablespoon of the oil in a large skillet over medium-high heat. When it's hot, add the onion and bell pepper and cook, stirring occasionally, until they soften and begin to brown, 5 to 10 minutes. Use a slotted spoon to transfer them to a bowl.

2. Return the pan to high heat, swirl in another tablespoon oil, and add the pork. Sprinkle with salt and

pepper and cook, stirring, until the pieces are browned in places and cooked through, about 3 minutes. Transfer to the bowl with the vegetables. Using the oil left in the pan, repeat with the shrimp, which will only take a minute or 2 to cook. Add them to the vegetables and pork.

3. Put the remaining 2 tablespoons oil in the skillet, followed by the garlic and ginger. About 15 seconds later, begin to add the rice, a bit at a time, breaking up any clumps with your fingers as you scatter it into the pan. When all the rice has been added, make a well in its center with a spoon and pour in the eggs if you're using them; scramble them a bit, then incorporate them into the rice.

4. Return the meat and vegetables to the pan and stir to mix them through. Add the rice wine and cook, stirring,

5 Tips for Making the Best Fried Rice

1. This is a good place to use peanut oil if you like a little stronger flavor.

2. If you're adding raw or cooked meat, poultry, or seafood, dice it into small pieces (½ inch or less) or use ground meat; cook it in a little hot oil after you remove any aromatics and before adding the rice; cook or heat it through.

3. No matter how much or how little garlic and ginger you use, they should be cooked in the oil for no more than 30 seconds before you add the rice, or their flavor will become too mild.

4. You can scramble eggs separately and cut them into the finished rice to keep them at their most distinctive.

Or beat them lightly, then stir them into the rice mix, in which case they will act as a pleasing thickening and bonding agent. Or—this is what I do—make a well in the finished rice and scramble them there, then mix them through, which retains their identity at least somewhat.

5. Some liquid in addition to the soy sauce might be necessary if the other ingredients are on the dry side; add it 1 tablespoon at a time as you stir. The most authentic choice is rice wine (which is sold at most Asian stores and keeps nearly forever), but sherry and white wine make decent substitutes. Stock is also good, and water works too, since there are already plenty of flavors in fried rice.

14 Super Additions or Substitutions for Fried Rice

The list of things you can add to fried rice basically fall into three categories: vegetables, protein, and seasonings.

VEGETABLES

1. At the last minute, stir in very tender vegetables that can be eaten raw, like watercress.
2. Cook those that will take about the same amount of time as the onion (scallion, shredded zucchini, corn kernels, etc.) with or instead of the onion.
3. Cut harder vegetables—broccoli, cauliflower, eggplant, potato, winter squash—into very tiny bits, so they will cook in just about the same amount of time as the onion. (This is a good place for leftover cooked vegetables, too.)
4. Tomatoes are a special case: Cut them into small wedges and add just after the rice; any sooner and you will have tomato sauce. Not that there's anything wrong with that, and if that's what you want, add the tomatoes when the onion is about half cooked.
5. You can also garnish with raw vegetables, like pickled cucumbers (see Quick-Pickled Vegetables, page 228), chopped cabbage, or tomato wedges.

PROTEIN

6. Add diced or ground meat (pork, beef, poultry, etc.), raw or cooked, as you would the pork (if raw) or

shrimp (if cooked) in the Fried Rice with Shrimp and Pork recipe.
7. Add chopped cleaned squid, or small or halved scallops with or instead of the shrimp in the recipe.
8. Any tofu—smoked, pressed, flavored, thawed frozen, you name it—is great in fried rice. Cut into small cubes and add as you would shrimp.
9. Hard-Boiled Egg (page 721) is another option, chopped or sliced and added right after the rice.

SEASONINGS

10. Stir in hoisin sauce or ketchup to taste.
11. Tear 10 to 15 big leaves basil (preferably Thai) and add at the last minute.
12. Stir in up to 2 teaspoons curry powder or almost any other spice mix (to make your own, see pages 27–35) just before you add the rice.
13. Seaweed "Shake" (page 35) is good, as are toasted sesame seeds (see page 309).
14. Add minced fresh chiles at the beginning, or any Chile Paste (pages 40–46) at the end.

 fast make ahead vegetarian

for about a minute. Add the soy sauce and sesame oil, then taste and add salt and pepper if necessary. Turn off the heat, stir in the scallions, and serve.

THE BASICS OF SUSHI

Making excellent sushi—which describes the rice, not the additional ingredients—at home is simple. You only need short-grain rice, rice vinegar, a few sheets of nori, and any additions you want, including leftovers.

Sushi comes in many forms: The simplest are sushi bowls (*chirashi*), a mound of seasoned sushi rice with the other ingredients scattered on top. Rolled sushi (*maki*) involves using a bamboo mat to wrap sheets of nori around the rice and filling. Finger sushi (*nigiri*) is sushi rice formed into a small rectangular brick and topped with whatever you choose; once you make Sushi Rice (page 447), you prepare some toppings and shape the pieces with your hands.

You can master all forms of sushi enough so that you'll be confident serving guests a platter of simply cut sushi rolls and finger pieces, an impressive and fairly easy party dish. But sushi doesn't have to be special-occasion food—a sushi bowl is one of the best ways ever to use small bits of leftover meat, seafood, vegetables, beans, and sauces. See "Improvising Sushi Bowls (Chirashi Sushi)" on page 451 to get started with possible ingredient combinations.

Sushi Rice

MAKES: About 4 cups (4 servings) | **TIME:** 40 minutes

Sushi rice can be served warm or at room temperature, but it cannot be made more than a couple of hours ahead or it will lose its great texture.

  1 **recipe White Rice or Brown Rice (page 430 or 427), made with short-grain or sushi rice**
  ¼ **cup rice vinegar**
  2 **tablespoons sugar**
  1 **teaspoon salt**

1. While the rice is cooking, combine the vinegar, sugar, and salt in a small saucepan over medium heat and cook, stirring, until the sugar dissolves, less than 5 minutes.

Rolling and Cutting Sushi Rolls

STEP 1 Put a square of toasted nori on a bamboo sushi-rolling mat; then press a bed of sushi rice onto it, ½ inch thick.

STEP 2 Put any filling you like about ½ inch from the edge nearest you. Do not overfill! (You will at first.)

STEP 3 Start rolling, tucking in the edge of the nori as you do so.

STEP 4 Keep rolling, as tightly as you can; you will soon get the hang of it.

STEP 5 Cut the roll into 1-inch lengths.

Put the saucepan in a bowl filled with ice and stir the vinegar mixture until cool.

2. When the rice is done, put it in a bowl with a volume more than twice that the rice—probably the largest bowl you have. Begin to toss the hot rice with a flat wooden paddle or spoon or a rubber spatula as if you were folding egg whites into a batter, but much faster and not quite as gently. While you're tossing, sprinkle the rice with the vinegar mixture; if the paddle becomes encrusted with rice, dip it in cold water, then shake off the water and proceed. The idea is to cool the rice quickly as it absorbs the vinegar.

3. Sushi rice will not keep for long, but if you cover it with a damp cloth, you can wait a couple of hours to proceed. Or eat it right away: see "Improvising Sushi Bowls (Chirashi Sushi)" (page 451) and Sushi Rolls (below).

Sushi Rolls

MAKES: 6 rolls | **TIME:** 40 minutes with prepared rice and filling

Use the items listed for Sushi Bowls on page 451 or your own ideas, but keep these points in mind: Sushi roll filling works best when it's cut into thin strips (julienned; see page 15) so you can set the pieces down the length of the roll. And overstuffing will get you in trouble during rolling. Think of the filling as a seasoning and the rice as the main component.

> 6   square sheets nori
> 2   tablespoons rice vinegar or other mild vinegar
> 1   recipe Sushi Rice (page 447), about 4 cups
>   Wasabi paste as needed
> 1   cup filling (see "10 Fillings for Sushi Rolls," right)
>   Pickled Ginger (page 296; optional)
>   Soy sauce (optional)

1. To toast the nori, hold the sheets with tongs one at a time over a medium-high flame for a few seconds, until they change color. If you have electric burners or an induction stove, run them under the broiler for 15 to 60 seconds on each side. Mix the vinegar with 1 cup water in a bowl (this is called "hand water").

2. Put a square of nori, shiny side down, on a bamboo rolling mat; make sure the slats are horizontal in front of you. Using your hands, spread it evenly with a ½-inch layer of sushi rice, leaving a 1-inch border on all sides; rinse your hands in the hand water as needed. (Although rolling is easy, you won't do it perfectly at first, so you might want to start with a slightly thinner layer of rice.) Smear the rice with a fingerful of wasabi (careful; it's hot), then put some filling (less than 3 tablespoons) along the edge closest to you.

3. Use the mat to tightly roll the nori around the rice, forming it into a log; you can unroll the mat at any time and check to see how things are going. (Follow the illustrations on page 450.) This takes a little bit of practice but is not at all difficult; you'll quickly get the hang of it. Slice the rolls into 1-inch sections and serve with pickled ginger and soy sauce, if you're using them.

10 FILLINGS FOR SUSHI ROLLS

Remember, keep the total quantity of fillings to less than 3 tablespoons; using one filling is usually helpful. Here are both traditional and nontraditional possibilities:

1. Avocado slices

2. Sushi-quality tuna, salmon, or other spanking-fresh raw fish, sliced or chopped

3. Simply cooked and chopped fish or seafood like poached and chilled shrimp or crabmeat, grilled fish, or even fried items like soft-shell crabs, clams, or oysters

4. Ceviche (page 132), chopped

5. Pickled vegetables, like Spicy Quick-Pickled Vegetables (page 228), cut into sticks

6. Shortcut Kimchi (page 229), chopped

 **F** fast   **M** make ahead   **V** vegetarian

7. Carrots, daikon, cucumber (peeled and seeded; see page 287), or scallions; cut into thin strips

8. Sautéed Mushrooms with Asian Flavors (page 306), preferably with sliced shiitakes

9. Cooked, squeezed, and chopped spinach, especially Sushi-Style Spinach (page 339)

10. Pan-Roasted Tuna Steaks (page 548), cut into strips

Grain Recipes

The information in the chart, combined with Cooking Grains, the Easy Way (below), provides all you need to know to make a plain batch of almost any grain. The rest of the chapter offers different techniques, ingredients, seasonings, and garnishes for specific dishes—most of which can be applied to many different grains. The specific grain recipes are organized from fastest-cooking grains to longest.

Cooking Grains, the Easy Way

MAKES: 3 to 4 cups (4 servings) | **TIME:** 10 minutes to more than 1 hour, depending on the grain

This process will allow you to cook almost any grain perfectly every time. (The most notable exceptions are bulgur, white or whole wheat couscous, and wild rice, which each has its own basic recipe in this chapter.) You really don't even have to measure anything other than the grain.

> 1 cup Israeli couscous, quinoa, barley (any type), oat groats, buckwheat groats, cracked wheat, dried hominy, rye berries, farro, or Kamut, or 1½ cups wheat berries
>
> Salt

1. Combine the grain with a large pinch salt and water to cover by about an inch in a medium saucepan. (Use 3 cups water for pearled barley, which predictably absorbs a more precise amount of water.) Bring to a boil, then adjust the heat so the liquid bubbles gently.

2. Cook, stirring occasionally, until the grain is tender. This will take as little as 7 or 8 minutes with Israeli couscous (for white and whole wheat couscous, see page 456) and as long as an hour or more for hulled barley, wheat berries, and other minimally milled grains. Hominy can take 2 hours or longer. Add boiling water as necessary to keep the grain covered, but—especially as the grain swells and begins to get tender—maintain just enough water in the pot to keep the grain from drying out.

3. The grain is done when it feels done; whole grains will always have some bite to them, but milled or cut grains will become mushy if overcooked, so be careful. Ideally, the water will all have been absorbed by about the same time the grain is tender, but if any water remains, drain the grain in a fine-mesh sieve.

4. To season the grain right away, see "8 Ways to Enhance Cooked Grains" (page 456) or Sautéed Cooked Grains (below). If you're storing this batch, toss with a fork to fluff the grains, then transfer to an airtight container and refrigerate for up to a week or freeze for up to several months.

Sautéed Cooked Grains

MAKES: 4 servings | **TIME:** About 10 minutes

I urge you to cook extra grains so you can store them in the refrigerator and reheat them with flavorings in a snap. Even if you do nothing more than warm them in olive oil, maybe with a little garlic, they'll be delicious.

(continued)

 fast   **make ahead**   **vegetarian**

Improvising Sushi Bowls (Chirashi Sushi)

Chirashi means scattered, and that's exactly what this is: various ingredients scattered over sushi rice. This will get you going on making your own. Pick any "Centerpiece"; slice the food into pieces as you like. Add an item or two from the "Vegetable(s)" list and finish with as much or as little "Sauce and/or Garnish" as you like. The only other advice I have is to match plain things, like pork chops, with more complicated sauces or garnishes, and vice versa; you don't want too many complicated components competing with one another. Once you get the hang of it, you'll be riffling through this book to make up your own combinations—or just improvising from your refrigerator.

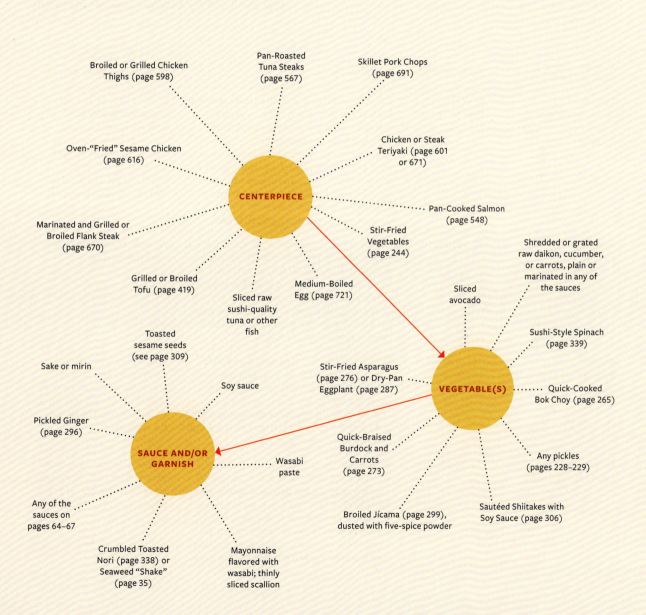

CENTERPIECE

- Broiled or Grilled Chicken Thighs (page 598)
- Pan-Roasted Tuna Steaks (page 567)
- Skillet Pork Chops (page 691)
- Oven-"Fried" Sesame Chicken (page 616)
- Chicken or Steak Teriyaki (page 601 or 671)
- Pan-Cooked Salmon (page 548)
- Marinated and Grilled or Broiled Flank Steak (page 670)
- Stir-Fried Vegetables (page 244)
- Grilled or Broiled Tofu (page 419)
- Medium-Boiled Egg (page 721)
- Sliced raw sushi-quality tuna or other fish

VEGETABLE(S)

- Sliced avocado
- Shredded or grated raw daikon, cucumber, or carrots, plain or marinated in any of the sauces
- Sushi-Style Spinach (page 339)
- Stir-Fried Asparagus (page 276) or Dry-Pan Eggplant (page 287)
- Quick-Cooked Bok Choy (page 265)
- Quick-Braised Burdock and Carrots (page 273)
- Any pickles (pages 228–229)
- Broiled Jícama (page 299), dusted with five-spice powder
- Sautéed Shiitakes with Soy Sauce (page 306)

SAUCE AND/OR GARNISH

- Toasted sesame seeds (see page 309)
- Sake or mirin
- Soy sauce
- Pickled Ginger (page 296)
- Wasabi paste
- Any of the sauces on pages 64–67
- Crumbled Toasted Nori (page 338) or Seaweed "Shake" (page 35)
- Mayonnaise flavored with wasabi; thinly sliced scallion

The Grain Lexicon

Grains have a lot in common—with each other and with rice—so despite their different characteristics, most are interchangeable to an extent that may surprise you. To help you try new kinds and make the best use of whatever you have on hand, I've included the line "Other grains you can use" in recipes that work with other options. The following table can help you determine how to adjust the cooking times if necessary.

The grains in this chart are organized first around cooking times, from shortest to longest, and second around what's most common and versatile (and my personal favorites). Cooking time can vary up to 10 minutes, depending on the age of the grain and how it was milled, the heat of your stove, and whether you like your grains chewy or fluffy. Use visual cues and taste to confirm desired doneness.

GRAIN/ALTERNATE NAME(S) OR TYPES	COOKING TIME	DESCRIPTION	FORMS AND VARIETIES
Couscous White; whole wheat; Israeli, Pearl, Fregula, Ptitim	5–15 minutes, depending on the type	Couscous is actually a small pasta traditional to Morocco that seems to be universally thought of as a grain. Usually made from semolina flour, sometimes in varying colors. Israeli couscous is extruded through a round mold and toasted, giving it a larger, pearl-like shape, nuttier flavor, and chewier texture; it's also more forgiving during cooking. Fregola, from Sardinia, is similar to couscous, deeply toasted to a golden brown.	Whole wheat couscous is available and very good. Israeli couscous is also known as super couscous, maftoul, or Israeli toasted pasta; there is a third, slightly larger variety often sold as Lebanese couscous.
Amaranth	10–15 minutes	Usually beige, though other varieties come in shades of tan and brown. Closely related to quinoa, it is tiny (1/32 inch) and round. Can be cooked like porridge, puffed like popcorn, or toasted and used as garnish. Its flavor is mildly nutty and malty. The cooked kernels get a bit sticky and rubbery if cooked too long, but retain a nice crunch.	Whole kernels most common; puffed is rare.
Bulgur Bulghur; burghul; bulger	10–20 minutes, depending on the grind	Wheat kernels, first steamed, then hulled, dried, and ground to varying degrees. Fine grind is ready to eat after soaking in hot water. Its nutty, mild flavor and fluffy, dry texture make it perfect for soaking up liquids and turning into salads. Often confused with cracked wheat (see page 454).	Available in fine, medium, coarse, and very coarse grinds, which are sometimes identified by numbers, from #1 for fine to #3 or #4 for the coarsest.
Rolled oats Old-fashioned oats	15–20 minutes	Whole oats are toasted, hulled, steamed, and flattened with giant rollers. The quick-cooking variety is cut before steaming and flattening; instant is cut, precooked, dried, steamed, then flattened. Stay away from the latter two if you want any flavor at all. Gluten-free but check the package to make sure it was processed in a gluten-free plant.	Raw or quick-cooking rolled oats, instant oats. Some are more heavily processed than others.

 fast make ahead **V** vegetarian

GRAIN/ALTERNATE NAME(S) OR TYPES	COOKING TIME	DESCRIPTION	FORMS AND VARIETIES
Teff Lovegrass	15–20 minutes	The smallest grain kernels in the world (less than 1/32 inch). Ivory, beige, dark brown, or deep purple-brown, depending on the variety. A staple in Ethiopia, with a mild, slightly sweet, nutty flavor. Cooked teff is soft and a little gummy. When ground into flour, it is used to make the Ethiopian bread injera.	Whole kernels
Quinoa Mother grain; supergrain	About 20 minutes	Pronounced KEEN-wa. Indigenous to the Andes, disk-shaped, and pinhead size (1/16 inch). White, red, or black. Different colors have very slight differences in taste and degree of crunch. Nutty and grassy in flavor, with a slightly crunchy but soft texture. Even plain, it's as good as grains get.	Whole kernels. Also made into flakes, which can be used like rolled oats
Pearled barley Peeled barley; polished barley	About 20 minutes	Barley that has been hulled, steamed, and polished (the bran removed). Creased, oval, dull white-and-tan grains that cook fairly quickly and have a creamy, chewy texture when cooked. A super rice alternative	This is the familiar barley sold everywhere and cooked much like rice. You may occasionally see barley flakes, which can be treated like rolled oats.
Cornmeal Grits (usually from white corn; sometimes from hominy); polenta	20–30 minutes	Yellow, white, occasionally blue or red dried corn kernels, ground to varying degrees. Fine grind (which is assumed unless otherwise stated) is usually used in baking or breading; medium grind is best for polenta; coarse makes a grittier polenta or grits (see page 462).	Fine, medium, and coarse grinds; water, stone, or steel ground. Water or stone grinding are more traditional methods and arguably superior to steel ground because the bran and germ remain intact. This makes cornmeal perishable, however, so be sure to store it in the fridge or freezer.
Oats Oat groats; whole oats; steel-cut; Scotch oats; Irish oats; porridge oats	20–45 minutes, depending on whether whole or cut	The whole oat kernel looks a lot like farro, has a nutty, sweet flavor, and is pleasantly chewy. When cut, oats cook relatively quickly and are often used for breakfast cereal. Whole oats take up to twice as long to cook.	Whole or cut kernels
Kasha Roasted buckwheat	20–30 minutes	Hulled and roasted buckwheat kernels, brown; triangular; and distinctively nutty. Traditionally toasted again at home, sometimes with egg, before liquid is added.	Whole kernels, cut, and ground

(continued)

The Grain Lexicon *(continued)*

GRAIN/ALTERNATE NAME(S) OR TYPES	COOKING TIME	DESCRIPTION	FORMS AND VARIETIES
Buckwheat groats Peeled buckwheat	20–30 minutes	Essentially raw kasha, buckwheat groats are hulled and crushed. Greenish tan, triangular, and fresher tasting than kasha—almost grassy.	Whole kernels; also rolled into flakes
Cracked wheat	20–30 minutes	Often confused with bulgur, cracked wheat is raw. It offers the same nutty wheat flavor as bulgur and wheat berries, but with a chewier, heartier texture than bulgur and quicker cooking time than wheat berries.	Fine, medium, and coarse kernels; most commonly available in medium grind
Freekeh Frikeh; farik	20–30 minutes	Very popular throughout the Middle East. It's roasted green wheat berries with the straw and chaff burned off; what's left is too moist to burn. Has a smoky taste and chewy texture. Has more protein than quinoa and twice as much fiber.	Whole kernels
Millet	20–30 minutes	Small, yellow, and beadlike, with a tiny spot at one end; you might recognize it from birdseed. Pleasant tasting, mildly nutty and cornlike. Cooks up fluffy.	Whole kernels are most common; meal is available too. Occasionally you may find puffed millet.
Farro Emmer	25–30 minutes	An ancient wheat-related grain, popular in early Rome, recently "rediscovered" in Tuscany. Tan and oval, not unlike "peeled" whole wheat in appearance. Has a nutty, wheaty flavor. Retains a chewy texture when cooked. With starch similar to short-grain rice, a nice whole grain substitute in risotto. Often confused with spelt (see page 455).	Whole (pearled and semi-pearled) and crushed or "cracked" kernels
Einkorn	30–40 minutes	An ancient form of wheat, first domesticated in what is now Turkey. Has never been cross-bred. Contains more protein, potassium, and beta-carotene than modern wheat, and is said to be a more easily digested alternative.	Whole kernels
Wild Rice	45–60 minutes	A marsh grass native to parts of Asia and the Great Lakes region, once a staple for many Native Americans. Long, narrow, deep-brown cylinder-shaped kernels that crack open to reveal their white interior when cooked.	Whole kernels. There is both farm-raised "wild" rice and truly wild rice, which tends to be less uniform in color, better tasting, and more expensive.

 fast make ahead  vegetarian

GRAIN/ALTERNATE NAME(S) OR TYPES	COOKING TIME	DESCRIPTION	FORMS AND VARIETIES
Hulled barley Whole barley; pot barley; Scotch barley	45–60 minutes	The least processed form of barley, with just the outer hull removed. Kernels are light brown, and oval with pointed ends. Takes longer to cook than pearled barley and has a chewier texture, but also a higher nutritional value.	Whole kernels and the slightly more processed Scotch or pot barley, which has more of the outer layers removed and is quicker cooking, less chewy, and somewhat less nutritious.
Sorghum	45–60 minutes	Part of the grass family; native to Australia, Africa, Asia, and Central America. Has a slightly sweet taste and chewy texture.	Whole kernels; popped sorghum (looks like mini popcorn)
Wheat berries Whole wheat	1–1½ hours	Second-largest grain crop in the world, after corn. Kernels with the bran and germ still intact. Light brown, rounded, oval kernels with a nutty flavor and very chewy texture.	Varieties are named for the traits of their hulls and the seasons they are grown in: hard red winter, hard white winter, soft white spring, etc. Whole, cracked wheat, and "peeled" wheat, which is slightly faster cooking. Flakes are also available and cook in about half the time.
Spelt	1–1½ hours	Cultivated for thousands of years, spelt is in the wheat family. Has a pleasant, mild flavor. Appearance is similar to brown rice, though plumper. Sometimes mistakenly labeled farro (see page 454).	Whole berries and flakes; flakes cook in about half the time.
Whole Rye Rye berries	1–1½ hours	Kernels with bran and germ still intact. The flavor is nutty, the texture firm.	Whole kernels and flakes; flakes cook in about half the time.
Kamut Khorasan	1–1½ hours	Pronounced KAH-moot. A modern breed of an ancient variety of wheat. Tan, with kernels two to three times larger than common wheat; also more nutritious, with a sweeter, more buttery flavor.	Whole berries and flakes; flakes cook in about half the time.
Hominy Pozole, Posole	2–4 hours; less if you soaked it first	A native American ingredient, hominy is corn that has been processed, usually with lime or lye, to remove the germ and bran. Looks like giant sweet corn kernels, only lighter; the flavor is uniquely corny. (Ground hominy is also known as hominy grits.)	Dried whole kernels, partially cooked whole kernels (*nixtamal*), canned, broken, or ground into grits (see page 462); there are yellow, white, red, and blue varieties.

3   tablespoons olive oil, butter, or a combination
1   teaspoon minced garlic
3 to 4   cups any cooked grain
     Salt and pepper

1. Put the oil and/or butter in a large skillet over medium heat. When the oil is hot or the butter foams, add the garlic and cook, stirring, until fragrant, about 1 minute.

2. Add the grain and cook, tossing frequently with a spatula to keep the kernels from sticking, until hot, 3 to 5 minutes. Sprinkle with salt and pepper; taste and adjust the seasoning. Serve.

COOKED GRAINS WITH TOASTED SPICE Before adding the grain in Step 2, stir in up to 1 tablespoon curry powder, chili powder, or virtually any spice mixture (to make your own, see pages 27–35), or 1 teaspoon of a single spice like ground cumin or smoked paprika.

COOKED GRAINS WITH CHILES Add 1 fresh chile like jalapeño or Thai, minced, ½ teaspoon red chile flakes, or cayenne to taste in Step 1 along with the garlic.

Simple White or Whole Wheat Couscous

MAKES: 4 servings | **TIME:** 5 to 15 minutes, depending on the type of couscous

Here's the go-to recipe for both white and whole wheat couscous. For Israeli couscous, which is larger, use Cooking Grains, the Easy Way (page 451). Like bulgur, couscous is best steeped rather than cooked. From there you can use it in soup, salad, or grain recipes, top it with stewed meats, seafood, or vegetables, or dress it simply as you would any plain-cooked grain.

1   cup white or whole wheat couscous
     Salt

1. Put the couscous in a medium saucepan with 1½ cups water and a generous pinch salt. Bring to a boil, then cover and remove from the heat.

2. Let white couscous steep for about 5 minutes, whole wheat for about 10. You can let them sit for up to 30 minutes or so, depending on how hot you want them. Fluff with a fork, taste and adjust the seasoning, and serve.

 fast   make ahead   V vegetarian

16 DISHES TO SERVE OVER COUSCOUS

Like polenta, couscous is best served with savory stews, whether meat or vegetable. Some ideas:

1. Sautéed Eggplant with Basil (page 290)
2. Winter Squash Curry (page 350)
3. Chickpeas in Their Own Broth (page 407)
4. Lentils, Six Ways (page 408)
5. The Simplest and Best Shrimp Dish (page 542)
6. Pan-Cooked Salmon (page 565)
7. Aromatic Poached Fish (page 565)
8. Stir-Fried Chicken with Ketchup (page 605)
9. Sauteed Chicken with Wine Sauce (page 607)
10. Curry-Poached Chicken (page 612)
11. Pheasant Stewed with Dried Fruits (page 662)
12. Beef Stew with Bacon or Beef Stew with Prunes (page 679)
13. Braised Pork with Coconut Milk and Carrots (page 700)
14. Lamb Stew with Cinnamon and Lemon (page 710)
15. Lamb Stew with Mushrooms (page 711)
16. Lamb Curry (page 711)

Israeli Couscous Pilaf with Black Olives

MAKES: 4 servings | **TIME:** 20 minutes

Israeli couscous—a round pasta also known as pearl couscous—is so forgiving: It won't turn to mush with too much liquid, it can be served hot or at room temperature, it reheats well, and it takes to all sorts of different ingredients. Oil-packed dried olives are sublime here, but use any kind you like, including green. And potent herbs like rosemary, sage or oregano are also lovely here; just reduce the quantity to 2 tablespoons.

2	tablespoons olive oil
1	small red onion, halved and thinly sliced
1½	cups Israeli couscous
1	tablespoon chopped garlic
⅓	cup black or green olives, pitted and chopped
1¾	cups chicken or vegetable stock (to make your own, see page 174–178) or water
¼	cup chopped fresh dill, basil, parsley, or mint (or a combination)
	Salt and pepper

1. Put the oil in a large skillet over medium-high heat. When it is hot, add the onion and cook, stirring occasionally, until the onion is soft and lightly browned in places, about 5 minutes. Add the couscous, garlic, and olives and cook until fragrant, another minute or 2.

2. Add the stock and bring to a boil. Lower the heat so it bubbles gently, cover, and cook until the liquid is absorbed and the couscous is al dente; start checking after 5 minutes. (To check for remaining liquid, just tip the pan.)

3. Add the herbs and fluff with a fork. Taste and add salt if it needs some and lots of black pepper. Serve hot or at room temperature.

ISRAELI COUSCOUS PILAF WITH SPINACH Omit the olives—or not—and the herbs. After cooking the couscous and garlic in Step 1, add 8 ounces fresh spinach, chopped, to the skillet and cook, stirring, until it releases its water and the pan is almost dry. Add the stock and proceed with the recipe.

Basic Bulgur

MAKES: 4 servings | **TIME:** Less than 30 minutes

Because bulgur is cracked wheat that's already partially cooked, it's so easy you don't need to cook it, just rehydrate it. It's light and fluffy, with a dry texture that's perfect for soaking up butter or oil, pan juices, dressings, and sauces.

1   **cup bulgur (any grind)**
2½   **cups boiling water**

1. Put the bulgur in a heatproof bowl and pour the boiling water over it. Stir once, cover with an inverted plate, and let sit.

2. Fine bulgur will be tender in 10 to 15 minutes, medium in 15 to 20 minutes, and coarse in 20 to 25. If any water remains when the bulgur is done, transfer the bulgur to a clean kitchen towel and squeeze gently to wring out excess water. Or put it in a fine-meshed strainer and press down on it. Season and serve as you like; see page 456 for ideas.

Bulgur Pilaf with Vermicelli

MAKES: 4 servings | **TIME:** 30 minutes

Combining grains with pasta is traditional in some cuisines but counterintuitive to Americans—unless you remember Rice-A-Roni. I love noodles with bulgur; the contrasts are delightful.

Other grains you can use: whole wheat, regular, or Israeli couscous.

4   **tablespoons butter or olive oil**
1   **large onions, chopped**
½   **cup vermicelli, broken into 2-inch or shorter lengths, or other, small pasta**
1   **cup fine- or medium-grind bulgur**
    Salt and pepper
1   **tablespoon tomato paste**
2¼   **cups chicken, beef, or vegetable stock (to make your own, see pages 174–178) or water**

2   **tablespoons chopped fresh dill or parsley**
1   **lemon, cut into wedges**

1. Put the butter or oil in a large skillet over medium heat. When the butter foams or the oil is hot, add the onion and cook, stirring frequently, until soft, about 5 minutes.

2. Add the vermicelli and bulgur and cook, stirring, until the pasta is lightly toasted, less than 2 minutes. Sprinkle with salt and pepper, add the tomato paste, and stir until it darkens, about 1 minute.

3. Add the stock and bring to a boil. Lower the heat so the liquid bubbles steadily, cover, and cook without opening the lid for 10 minutes. Turn off the heat and let the pilaf sit until the bulgur is tender, up to 15 minutes more. Taste and adjust the seasoning, then add the herb, fluff with a fork. Serve hot or at room temperature, with the lemon wedges.

BULGUR PILAF WITH VERMICELLI AND HOT SAUSAGE
In Step 1 reduce the butter or oil to 1 tablespoon and squeeze the meat from 2 hot Italian sausage links into the hot fat. Cook, stirring to break the clumps, until it's cooked through, then add the onion and proceed with the recipe.

BULGUR PILAF WITH LENTILS Omit the noodles. In Step 2 add 1 cup drained cooked lentils and 1 teaspoon ground cumin.

Quinoa with Roasted Corn

MAKES: 4 servings | **TIME:** About 1 hour, largely unattended

Unbeatable as a bed for grilled meat, poultry, seafood, or vegetables. Both the quinoa and corn have a pleasant subtle crunch.

Other grains you can use: cracked wheat, steel-cut oats, millet.

 fast   make ahead   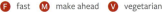 vegetarian

Quinoa with Roasted Corn

    2 tablespoons olive oil
1½ cups corn kernels (preferably fresh,
     cut from 2 or 3 ears), thawed if frozen
     Salt and pepper
    ¾ cup quinoa, well rinsed and drained
1½ cups chicken, beef, or vegetable stock
     (to make your own, see pages 174–178) or
     water
    2 tablespoons chopped fresh chives, cilantro,
     or chervil

1. Put the oil in a large skillet over medium-high heat. When it is hot, add the corn, sprinkle with salt and pepper, and cook, shaking the pan occasionally, until the corn begins to brown, 3 to 5 minutes.

2. Add the quinoa and stir. Cook, stirring occasionally, until the grains start popping and toasting, about 2 minutes. Add the stock and bring to a boil; lower the heat so the liquid bubbles gently, cover, and cook, undisturbed, for 15 minutes.

3. Test the quinoa for doneness. If the kernels are still a bit hard, make sure there's enough liquid to keep them moist, cover, and cook for another 5 minutes. When the quinoa is tender, add the herbs and fluff with a fork. Taste and adjust the seasoning, adding a few extra grinds of pepper. Serve hot or at room temperature.

ORANGE-SCENTED QUINOA WITH SHALLOTS AND DATES Omit the herbs. Replace the corn with 2 large shallots, chopped, and cook as directed in Step 1. Proceed with the recipe, adding ½ cup chopped pitted dates and 2 teaspoons grated orange zest when you fluff the quinoa in Step 3.

QUINOA WITH CARROTS Instead of the corn, grate 2 carrots and cook them as directed in Step 1. Proceed with the recipe, using cilantro for the herb.

QUINOA WITH GROUND PORK, GINGER, AND SOY SAUCE Omit the herbs. Replace the olive oil with 1 tablespoon good-quality vegetable oil. Instead of the corn, use 8 ounces ground pork and add 1 tablespoon minced fresh ginger; cook as directed in Step 1. When you add the stock, include 2 tablespoons soy sauce; wait to add any salt until the dish is finished. Garnish with ½ cup sliced scallions.

Polenta

MAKES: 4 servings | **TIME:** 20 minutes

Like risotto, the fuss about stirring is overblown, especially with this slurry method I've been using for a while now. You can serve it immediately while it's still soft, maybe with one of the toppings from the list that follows. Or pour it into a pan to set. See the variations for two options.

Other grains you can use: grits.

    1 cup medium or coarse cornmeal
    ½ cup milk (preferably whole)
     Salt and pepper
    ½ cup grated Parmesan cheese
    2 tablespoons butter or olive oil, or more

1. Put the polenta in a large pot with 1 cup water and whisk to form a smooth slurry. Whisk in the milk and a large pinch salt and set the pot over medium-high heat. Bring to a boil, then lower the heat to medium and cook, whisking frequently and adding more water a little at a time to prevent lumps and to keep the mixture somewhat soupy. Expect to add another 2½ to 3½ cups water before the polenta is ready.

2. The polenta will be tender in 15 to 30 minutes, depending on the grind. It will be thick and creamy, with just a little grittiness, and the mixture will pull away from the side of the pot when you stir. For soft polenta, you want a consistency about as thick as sour cream; for Grilled or Fried Polenta (see the variation), you want something approaching thick oatmeal. When the polenta is done, stir in the Parmesan and butter, and

taste and adjust the seasoning. Serve or use in one of the last two variations.

POLENTA WITH FRESH CORN When the polenta is almost ready, stir in the kernels stripped from 2 ears corn and cook for 1 minute more.

POLENTA GRATIN Immediately after cooking, spoon or pour the polenta into a buttered flameproof 13 × 9-inch baking dish. Top with about 1 cup grated Parmesan or pecorino Romano cheese and broil until the cheese melts and browns slightly. Use a spoon to serve hot or at room temperature.

GRILLED OR FRIED POLENTA Make sure the polenta is fairly thick when cooked. Omit the butter and cheese. Pour the cooked polenta into a greased 8- or 9-inch square pan. Let cool for at least 10 minutes or refrigerate overnight. Cut into 9 or 16 squares and carefully remove them. To grill, brush both sides with olive oil and cook over medium direct heat, turning once, until warmed and charred in places, about 10 minutes total. To fry, heat a thin film of olive oil in a large skillet over medium-high heat and, working in batches, cook the polenta until crisp on both sides, 5 to 10 minutes total.

---

14 DISHES TO SERVE ON TOP OF POLENTA

You can top a mound of soft polenta—or squares of Grilled or Fried Polenta—with almost any savory, liquid dish just as you would rice or other grains. Here are some ideas:

1. Sautéed Eggplant with Basil (page 290)
2. Braised Endive, Escarole, or Radicchio with Prosciutto (page 292)
3. Sautéed Mushrooms (page 306)
4. Oven-Baked Ratatouille (page 350)
5. Beans and Tomatoes (page 396)
6. Fast Tomato Sauce and any of its variations (page 478)
7. Still the Simplest and Best Shrimp Dish (page 542)
8. Fish Steamed Over Summer Vegetables (page 555)
9. Chicken Baked with Tomatoes (page 601)
10. Sautéed Chicken with Wine Sauce (page 609)
11. Beef Stew with Tomatoes and Porcini (page 680)
12. Braised Pork with White Wine and Celery Root (page 699)
13. Sausages with Peppers and Onions, or without sausages (page 704)
14. Lamb Shanks with Tomatoes and Olives and the Osso Buco (page 711)

Tamales

MAKES: 24 tamales | **TIME:** At least 2 hours, plus time to soak the husks

Tamales are work, and traditionally a group effort and opportunity to socialize. Whether you're alone or with friends, it's worth the labor (check out the One Big Naked Tamale variation for a quicker version).

Lard is traditional and results in an incomparable fluffy texture. Here's the best alternative: Freeze 1 cup olive oil until it solidifies, at least a couple of hours. Substitute this for the lard and work quickly to beat the baking powder and masa into it.

- 36 **dried corn husks**
- 2 **pounds fresh masa or 3½ cups masa harina**
- 2¼ **cups chicken stock (to make your own, see page 176), plus more as needed**
- 1 **cup lard, cubed**
- 1 **teaspoon salt**
- 1 **teaspoon baking powder**
- 1½ **cups Shredded Pork (page 697), shredded cooked chicken, or Refried Beans (page 393)**

1. Sort through the corn husks and make sure they're all clean. Soak in warm water for at least 3 hours or overnight. Drain, then separate the husks. Continue to soak in fresh water until you're ready to use them.

2. If you're using masa harina, add the stock a little at a time just until combined. Stop when the mixture is crumbly.

3. Beat the lard with the salt and baking powder in a stand mixer until fluffy. If you're using fresh masa, alternatively add the masa and stock, beating continuously. If you're using masa harina, add the masa harina mixture. Beat until the dough is light and fluffy, adding more stock if needed. The mixture is ready when a small ball of the dough floats in water.

4. Drain a husk and pat dry with towels. To form, fill, and secure the tamales, see the illustrations on the next page.

5. Rig a steamer (see page 20) in a large pot with the rack about 2 inches above the water. Stack the tamales, seam down, on the rack. Cover, bring the water to a gentle boil, and steam for about 45 minutes. Check from time to time and add more boiling water if the pot is getting dry. To test for doneness, remove one tamale and open the husk—the husk should come away easily and the dough should be firm. Serve hot or at room temperature.

ONE BIG NAKED TAMALE Also known as Tamale Pie: Omit the corn husks and skip Step 1. Heat the oven to 400°F. Grease a standard loaf pan, deep pie plate, or 10-inch springform cake pan wrapped on the outside with foil. Follow Steps 2 and Step 3. Put half the masa in the prepared pan, pressing it into an even layer. Top with the filling and the remaining dough. Cover the pan with foil and put in a large roasting pan; carefully pour boiling water into the roasting pan to come halfway up the tamale pan. Put the whole thing in the oven and bake until the masa is pulling away from the sides of the pan, about an hour. Let cool a bit, then turn the tamale out onto a platter. Cut into slices or wedges and serve.

10 DISHES THAT MAKE SUPER TAMALE FILLINGS

Debone any meat or poultry if necessary and chop or shred the ingredients into small pieces. Be careful not to overfill the tamales.

1. Raw fresh corn kernels, with or without a little crumbled queso fresco
2. Grated Asadero, Oaxaca, or Cotija cheese
3. Chopped grilled vegetables like eggplant, zucchini, tomatoes, chiles or bell peppers, or squash (see "Grilling or Broiling Vegetables," page 250)
4. Orange-Glazed Black Beans (page 395)
5. Slow-Simmered Beef Chili (page 403)
6. Broiled or Grilled Boneless Chicken Thighs, spicy (page 611)
7. Turkey Thighs in Almond Mole (page 652)
8. Braised Beef Brisket with Onions (page 684)
9. Roast Pork, Puerto Rican Style (page 695)
10. Carnitas or Shredded Pork (page 697)

Grits Gratin with Arugula and Garlic

MAKES: 4 to 6 servings | **TIME:** 45 minutes with cooked grits

You can—and should—cook and eat grits like polenta (see page 460). A light one-dish meal; as the garlicky arugula wilts, the slices of grits form a yummy golden crust akin to croutons.

Make the grits up to a day in advance, pour into a loaf pan or rimmed baking sheet, and let them set before proceeding.

Other grains you can use: coarse cornmeal.

    4 tablespoons olive oil, plus more for the pan
    4 cloves garlic, smashed
    5 ounces baby arugula
       Salt and pepper
    2 tablespoons balsamic vinegar

 fast   make ahead   vegetarian

1 recipe Polenta (page 460), made with grits and molded as described in the gratin variation
½ cup grated Parmesan cheese

1. Heat the oven to 400°F. Grease a shallow 2-quart gratin dish generously with oil.

2. Put 2 tablespoons of the oil in a large skillet over medium-low heat. When it is hot, add the garlic and cook, stirring occasionally, until it's soft, plump, and starting to color, about 10 minutes. Turn off the heat and add the arugula. Sprinkle with salt and pepper, toss gently once or twice, then spread the arugula and garlic in the prepared dish. Drizzle with the vinegar.

3. Turn the polenta out of its pan and cut into ½-inch-thick slices; sprinkle with salt and pepper. Carefully arrange the pieces on top of the arugula, overlapping them a little if necessary. Drizzle with the remaining 2 tablespoons oil and sprinkle with the cheese. Bake until the topping is golden and bubbling, 20 to 25 minutes. Serve, topped with lots of pepper.

GRITS GRATIN WITH ESCAROLE, GARLIC, AND LEMON
Instead of the arugula, use torn escarole leaves. Substitute fresh lemon juice for the vinegar.

GRITS GRATIN WITH ARUGULA, GARLIC, AND BACON
Chop 4 thick slices bacon. In Step 1, start by cooking the bacon over medium heat, stirring occasionally, until it renders some fat but isn't crisp, about 3 minutes. In Step 2, lower the heat, omit the oil, add the garlic, and proceed with the recipe.

Kasha with Browned Onions

MAKES: 4 servings | **TIME:** 30 minutes

There are two approaches to cooking this classic toasted buckwheat dish. Many people toss kasha with an egg before cooking, because it keeps the grains separate. But

Forming Tamales

STEP 1 For each tamale, drain a husk and pat dry with towels. Put the widest edge closer to you. Put 1 heaping tablespoon masa ½ inch from the widest edge of the husk, then use the back of the spoon to spread the masa into a 4 × 3-inch rectangle along the right edge of the husk, leaving at least ½ inch on each side.

STEP 2 Spoon 2 tablespoons filling lengthwise down the center of the masa rectangle. To wrap the tamales, fold the vertical edges over, bringing them over the dough in the filled center.

STEP 3 Fold up the tapered end (the wider end will remain open during steaming), and secure the tamale with kitchen string.

STEP 4 Repeat with the remaining masa and filling.

The Many Forms of Dried Corn

Fresh corn is pretty easy to understand: It's a grain we eat like a vegetable. But once dried—and sometimes treated to become more digestible—things get confusing.

Hominy: Dried whole corn kernels are soaked in lime (calcium hydroxide) before the hull is removed. See "The Grain Lexicon" (page 452) and Chipotle Pozole (page 469). Canned hominy is precooked and packed in brine, so drain and rinse it well before using.

Posole or Pozole: The Aztec name for hominy; also the name of any stew that features hominy and, usually, pork. The term for the liming process is *nixtamalization*.

Masa: The dough or paste made from grinding corn cooked with lime (*nixtamal*). When coarsely ground, it's used for tamales; when finely ground, it is the base for tortillas. You might be able to get a tortilla bakery to sell you some.

Masa Harina: This is masa dried into a convenient mix for making dough for tortillas, tamales, and other Mexican dishes. Its texture is somewhere between flour and fine cornmeal. Most supermarkets now carry masa harina; store for up to 6 months, preferably in the refrigerator.

Dried Corn: Dried without lime, not very common, and not nearly as tasty as hominy. Cook like any other whole grain; it takes at least an hour and maybe 2 to become tender.

Cornmeal: Ground dried corn without the lime treatment. See "The Grain Lexicon" (page 452) for details.

Corn Flour: Finely ground dried corn—finer than cornmeal—used in baking, usually in combination with wheat flour since it has no gluten and can be heavy.

Popcorn: The starch and water in dried kernels of this variety of corn are balanced in such a way that makes the hull explode under high heat. When heated in oil (see the recipe on page 90), popcorn is a classic snack. Boiled popcorn is edible, but not as good as either dried corn or hominy.

---

toasting it in oil accomplishes the same thing. Take your pick. (Without either, the kasha will become mushier, which is fine too.)

Other grains you can use: quinoa, steel-cut oats, farro.

- 2 onions, chopped
- 3 tablespoons good-quality vegetable oil
- 1 egg or 2 more tablespoons vegetable oil
- 1 cup kasha
   Salt and pepper
- 2 cups chicken, beef, or vegetable stock (to make your own, see pages 174–178) or water, warmed
- 1 tablespoons butter (optional)

1. Put the onions in a large skillet with a lid over medium heat. Cover and cook, undisturbed, until the onions are dry and beginning to stick to the pan, 10 to 15 minutes. Add 3 tablespoons oil, raise the heat to medium-high, and cook, stirring, until the onions are browned, another 10 minutes or so.

2. Meanwhile, if you're using the egg, beat it. Stir in the kasha and some salt and pepper. (If not, proceed to Step 3.) Transfer the mixture to a large skillet and set over medium-high heat. Cook, stirring, until the kasha smells like toast, about 3 minutes. Proceed to Step 4.

3. If you're using oil instead of egg, put the extra 2 tablespoons in a large skillet over medium-high heat. When it is hot, add the kasha, sprinkle with salt and pepper, and cook, stirring, until the kasha smells like toast, about 3 minutes.

4. Turn the heat down to a minimum, carefully add the stock, and stir once. Adjust the heat so the liquid bubbles steadily, cover, and cook until the liquid is absorbed, 10 to 15 minutes. Turn off the heat. Stir in the onions, and the butter if you're using it; taste, and adjust the seasoning. Fluff with a fork and serve hot or at room temperature.

KASHA WITH MUSHROOMS Replace the onions with 1 pound button or cremini mushrooms, chopped or sliced. In Step 1, heat the 3 tablespoons oil in a large skillet,

 fast make ahead **V** vegetarian

Grits Gratin with Arugula
and Garlic, page 462

then add the mushrooms; cook, stirring occasionally, until the mushrooms are browned and almost dry, about 10 minutes. Proceed with the recipe.

KASHA VARNISHKES These quantities will make enough to serve 6 to 8; halve the recipe if you want less: When you begin the onions, bring a large pot of water to a boil and salt it. When the kasha is just about done (or is already resting), cook 1 pound farfalle (bowtie) pasta until it's tender but not mushy and drain it, reserving some of the cooking water. Use a fork to toss the pasta with the kasha and onions, definitely adding some butter and enough of the reserved cooking water to make the dish a little creamy.

Cracked Wheat with Mustard

MAKES: 4 servings | TIME: About 20 minutes

The difference between savory, fluffy cracked wheat and breakfast porridge is basically a lot less water and a fork. And in this case a bistro flair that is perfect with roast chicken or grilled sausages.

Other grains you can use: quinoa, steel-cut oats, Israeli couscous.

- 2 tablespoons olive oil
- 1 cup cracked wheat (not bulgur)
  Salt and pepper
- ¼ cup dry white wine (optional)
- 2 teaspoons stone-ground mustard
- 1 tablespoon chopped fresh tarragon or
  2 tablespoons chopped fresh chives
- 1 tablespoon butter

1. Put the oil in a medium saucepan over medium-high heat. When it is hot, add the cracked wheat and sprinkle with salt and pepper. Cook, stirring frequently with a fork, until it smells like toast, about 2 minutes. Add the wine if you're using it, stir briefly to combine, and cook until it almost boils off, a minute or 2.

2. If you didn't add wine, add 1 cup water. If you did add wine, add ¾ cup water. Either way, stir again briefly with the fork, bring to a boil, cover, and reduce the heat to low. Cook, undisturbed, until the liquid is absorbed, about 15 minutes.

3. Lift the lid and use the fork to stir in the mustard, tarragon, and butter. Cover, turn the heat off, and let sit for at least 5 or up to 15 minutes. Taste and adjust the seasoning. Fluff one last time with the fork and serve.

Millet-Cauliflower Mash

MAKES: 4 servings | TIME: 45 minutes, largely unattended

A fluffy, golden mash that will stick to your ribs longer than a side of mashed potatoes. Virtually all the variations and additions you find there (page 330) will work with this too.

Other grains you can use: whole wheat couscous, quinoa, steel-cut oats.

- 2 tablespoons olive oil
- 1 cup millet
  Salt and pepper
- ½ head cauliflower, coarsely chopped
  (about 1½ cups)
- 3 cups chicken, beef, or vegetable stock (to make
  your own, see pages 174–178) or water
- 2 tablespoons butter, or more olive oil
- 1 head Roasted Garlic (page 294), squeezed from
  the skin (optional)

1. Put the oil in a large pot over medium heat. When it is hot, add the millet and stir constantly until it smells like toast, 2 to 3 minutes.

2. Sprinkle with salt and pepper and add the cauliflower and 2½ cups of the stock. Bring to a boil, then lower the heat so the liquid bubbles gently. Cover and cook, stirring occasionally, until the millet bursts, 30 to

40 minutes. Add a little more stock anytime the mixture looks too dry.

3. Remove from the heat and use an immersion blender to purée the millet and cauliflower in the pan. Or cool the mixture slightly, pour into a food processor and pulse to purée. Or put through a food mill, which will make the mash very fluffy. Return the mash to the pot, add the butter and the roasted garlic if you're using it, and reheat gently, stirring in the remaining stock if needed. Taste, adjust the seasoning, and serve.

CHEESY MILLET-CAULIFLOWER MASH After puréeing in Step 3, add 1 cup grated cheddar, Manchego, or Gruyère cheese to the mash, along with about ¼ cup milk and an additional pat of butter, if you like.

Farro with Leeks, Cherry Tomatoes, and Basil

MAKES: 4 servings | **TIME:** 40 minutes

The cherry tomatoes are abundant and perfectly softened in this dish, with the occasional farro kernel sticking to them here and there. The leeks add even more color and silkiness. Gorgeous.

Other grains you can use: kasha, buckwheat groats, millet, cracked wheat.

- 3 tablespoons olive oil or butter
- 1 large or 2 small leeks, sliced crosswise, rinsed well, and drained
  Salt and pepper
- 1 cup farro
- 1½ cups chicken or vegetable stock (to make your own, see pages 174–178) or water
- 1 pint cherry tomatoes, halved
- ½ cup chopped fresh basil

1. Put the oil or butter in a large skillet over medium heat. When the oil is hot or the butter foams, add

the leeks, sprinkle with salt and pepper, and cook, stirring occasionally, until they're quite soft, 5 to 10 minutes.

2. Add the farro, stock, and tomatoes. Bring to a boil, then reduce the heat so the liquid bubbles steadily. Cover and cook until the farro is tender and the liquid is absorbed, about 15 minutes. Tip the pan to see if liquid remains, if not and the farro isn't ready, add another ¼ cup stock or water and check in another 5 minutes. Add the basil and fluff with a fork. Taste and adjust the seasoning. Serve hot or at room temperature.

Wild Rice Pilaf

MAKES: 4 servings | **TIME:** 40 minutes

The cooking time for wild rice can vary, well, wildly. So if you want to combine it with other grains, like brown or white rice or quinoa, it's better to cook the other grain separately (see Cooking Grains, the Easy Way on page 451) and fluff them together at the end. This pilaf is a terrific Thanksgiving side; just double or triple the recipe, depending on the crowd.

- 2 tablespoons butter or olive oil
- 1 cup wild rice
- 3 cups chicken, beef, or vegetable stock (to make your own, see pages 174–178) or water
- 1 bay leaf
  Salt and pepper
  Chopped fresh parsley for garnish

1. Put the butter or oil in a large skillet over medium heat. When the butter melts or the oil is hot, add the wild rice and cook, stirring frequently, until fragrant and glossy, just a couple of minutes. Stir in the stock, bay leaf, and some salt and pepper and bring to a boil. Reduce the heat so the liquid bubbles steadily, cover, and cook undisturbed for 30 minutes.

2. Check the progress: The wild rice is done when the grains have puffed up—some may have burst—and are quite tender, regardless of whether the liquid has been absorbed. If the rice is not done, continue to cook, adding more liquid if necessary. If it is done, drain if necessary. Taste and adjust the seasoning and fluff with a fork. Garnish with parsley and serve.

WILD RICE WITH DRIED FRUIT When you fluff the wild rice in Step 2, stir in ½ cup chopped dried fruit like apricots, cherries, cranberries, mangoes, or apples. Put the lid back on for a minute or 2 to warm through and plump.

WILD RICE WITH CHESTNUTS Roast about 12 chestnuts (see page 283). Shell, peel, roughly chop, and stir into the rice just as it finishes cooking.

WILD RICE WITH ROASTED WINTER SQUASH Reduce the butter or oil to 1 tablespoon. Peel, seed, and cut into 1-inch chunks about 8 ounces butternut or other winter squash; roast as described on page 349 while the rice cooks. Add it to the pilaf just before fluffing in Step 2.

Wheat Berries with Candied Walnuts

MAKES: 4 servings | **TIME:** 45 minutes

Consider this a starter recipe for wheat berries, and vary the stir-ins freely. Olives, chopped cooked greens, or roasted vegetables, for example, can easily stand in for the nuts.

Other grains you can use (reduce the quantity to 1 cup): couscous, Israeli couscous, bulgur, quinoa, buckwheat groats, cracked wheat, wild rice, farro, hulled barley, spelt, rye berries, Kamut.

1½	cups wheat berries
½	cup packed brown sugar
1	tablespoon butter
¾	cup chopped walnuts
1	tablespoon chopped fresh thyme or 1 teaspoon dried
2	tablespoons olive oil
1	shallot or ½ medium onion, minced
	Salt and pepper

1. Put the wheat berries in a pot with water to cover by at least an inch. Bring a boil and cook until the kernels are tender, about 40 minutes. If you're using other grains, check the chart on page 452 for cooking times. Check periodically to make sure the water hasn't boiled off; add more water as needed.

2. While the wheat berries are cooking, put the sugar and butter in a large skillet over medium-low heat. Line a plate with parchment paper. When the sugar and butter begin to sizzle, stir and add the walnuts. Cook, stirring constantly, until they're coated and darkened, 3 to 5 minutes. Transfer the nuts to the parchment paper to cool. Clean the skillet.

3. Put the oil in the skillet over medium heat. When it is hot, add the shallot and cook, stirring occasionally, until soft, 3 to 5 minutes. Add the thyme and cook, stirring, for another minute. Turn off the heat.

 fast   make ahead   vegetarian

4. When the wheat berries are done, drain them well, and add to the skillet along with the walnuts. Taste and adjust the seasoning. Serve hot or at room temperature.

WHEAT BERRIES WITH CANDIED WALNUTS AND BUTTERNUT SQUASH Peel and seed about 8 ounces butternut squash. Cut the flesh into 1-inch cubes; you should have about 2 cups. In Step 3, cook the squash in the oil along with about ½ cup water until it's tender and the pan is almost dry, about 15 minutes. Add the shallot and another tablespoon oil, and use sage or rosemary instead of thyme, if you like. Proceed with the recipe.

Creamed Hominy

MAKES: 4 servings | TIME: About 20 minutes with cooked or canned hominy

Think of rich, old-fashioned creamed corn, only with more flavor and chew. Serve as a side dish with roasted, grilled, or simply pan-cooked meat or poultry.

Other cooked grains you can use: barley, farro, oat groats, millet.

> 3   cups cooked hominy (see Cooking Grains, the Easy Way, page 451) or canned, rinsed and well drained
> 1   cup heavy cream or half-and-half, plus more as needed
> 2   tablespoons butter
>   Salt and pepper

1. Put half the hominy in a food processor and pulse until the kernels are chopped but not puréed. Put the chopped and whole kernels and cream in a medium saucepan over medium-high heat. Bring to a boil, stirring occasionally, then adjust the heat so it bubbles gently.

2. Cover and cook, stirring occasionally, until the hominy is the consistency of thick soup, 5 to 10 minutes; add more cream if the mixture looks dry. Stir in the butter, sprinkle with salt and pepper, and serve.

CREAMED HOMINY AND KALE Use a large pot instead of a saucepan and increase the cream to 1½ cups. Cut 8 ounces lacinato kale crosswise into thin ribbons and add it to the pot in Step 1.

Chipotle Pozole

MAKES: At least 8 servings | TIME: 4½ to 5½ hours, largely unattended; 1½ hours with cooked hominy

A Mexican classic that's perfect for parties—this hearty pork and hominy stew can feed a crew, and everyone gets involved with the garnishing. Serve it with a stack of warm tortillas or Red, Green, or Yellow Rice (page 436), some roasted or grilled vegetables, and any or all of the garnishes on the list that follows.

The pozole can be made ahead through Step 2; just cool, cover, and store in the fridge for up to 2 days. Bring back to room temperature, then reheat before serving; the flavor will be better than if you served it immediately after making.

> 1½   cups dried hominy, or 4 cups cooked or canned hominy (liquid reserved if you cooked it yourself)
> 1½   pounds boneless pork shoulder, trimmed of excess fat and cut into 1-inch chunks
> 1   large onion, chopped
> 3   tablespoons chopped garlic
> 1   canned chipotle chile, mashed with 1 tablespoon of the adobo, or more to taste
> 2   tablespoons chopped fresh oregano or marjoram or 2 teaspoons dried
> 1   tablespoon ground cumin, or to taste
>   Salt and pepper

Chipotle Pozole, page 469

1. If you're using cooked or canned hominy, skip to Step 2. Put the dried hominy in a large pot with water to cover. Bring to a boil, then reduce the heat so the liquid bubbles gently. Cover and cook, stirring occasionally and adding water as necessary to keep the hominy covered, until the hominy has burst and is tender, 3 to 4 hours. Drain, reserving the liquid. Measure 4 cups and refrigerate any remaining hominy, covered, for up to several days, or freeze up to several months.

2. Combine the 4 cups hominy, pork, onion, garlic, chipotle and adobo, oregano, and cumin in a large pot. Add enough water or hominy-cooking liquid to cover by about an inch, and sprinkle with salt and pepper.

3. Bring to a boil, then adjust the heat so the liquid bubbles steadily but not violently. Cover and cook, stirring occasionally, until the pork is tender, about 1½ hours; add more cooking liquid or water if necessary. The pozole should be soupy.

4. Taste and adjust the seasoning, and add more mashed chile and adobo if you like; continue cooking for another 5 minutes or so. You can cool and refrigerate the pozole for up to several days; reheat gently before proceeding. Serve in bowls, garnished with any or all of the suggestions from the list that follows.

CHIPOTLE POZOLE WITH PUMPKIN SEEDS Toast 1 cup pepitas (green pumpkin seeds) in a small dry skillet over medium heat, shaking the pan frequently until the seeds pop and color slightly. Combine them with a bit of the pozole broth in a blender and process until smooth. Stir them into the stew in Step 3 and heat through.

10 GARNISHES FOR CHIPOTLE POZOLE

1. Chopped fresh cilantro
2. Crumbled queso fresco, farmer cheese, or goat cheese
3. Diced avocado
4. Crumbled cooked bacon or pork rinds
5. Chopped scallions, radishes, and/or cabbage
6. Lime wedges
7. Minced jalapeño or other fresh chile
8. Ground or crumbled guajillo or other dried chile
9. Any fresh or cooked salsa (pages 55–58 or 71–75) or hot sauce
10. Mexican crema or sour cream

Pasta, Noodles, and Dumplings

CHAPTER AT A GLANCE

The Basics of Dried Pasta 474

The Simplest Pastas 476

Pasta with Vegetables or Beans 482

Pasta with Dairy, Eggs, Seafood, or Meat 491

Baked Pasta 499

The Basics of Fresh Pasta 503

The Basics of Gnocchi and Other Dumplings 515

The Basics of Asian Noodles 519

Diet fads may come and go but noodles endure. Whether they take the form of Italian-style pastas, Asian-inspired stir-fries, or dough rolled or formed into dumplings, people always love them.

Dried pasta is a reliable and beloved pantry staple. It's the go-to dinner on the fly. Add dried Asian noodles to your larder and you can double your repertoire of fast-cooking meals.

When you're feeling more ambitious, try fresh pasta, which really isn't that difficult, even if ravioli or cannelloni are your goal. In between are the dumplings, mixed and dropped into boiling water then sauced and seasoned without much fuss. If you have a local Italian market or restaurant that sells fresh pasta, then yes, substitute it for the recipes in that section of the chapter. But otherwise, just use dried.

Perhaps most valuable in this chapter are the techniques and variations. Once you try a recipe or two, take a look at the lists of all the other recipes in the book you can turn into pastas and noodle stir-fries. You might not want to eat anything else.

THE BASICS OF DRIED PASTA

When people say "pasta," this is it: Italian-style round or flat strands, narrow or wide, and cut noodles of every conceivable shape and size. They're dried to the point of crackling, keep for many months in the pantry, and can go from package to table in less than 30 minutes, including the time it takes to boil a pot of water and make a simple sauce. Most are made from just flour and water; some include eggs.

Today there's a wide range of dried pasta options, from inexpensive (but fine) mass-produced brands to imports and small-batch domestic pastas that cost as much per pound as meat. Good pasta is harder to overcook and has a deeper, more appealing color than pastas of lesser quality, and a texture that grabs the sauce better. You don't know for sure you've got a quality pasta until

you cook it, but here are some clues: Buy pasta made from 100 percent durum wheat, specially ground into a flour known as semolina. The absolute best is made by extruding dough through brass dies; they are more porous than stainless steel and plastic and conduct a little bit of heat, which lightly toasts the outside of the noodle. Since this detail isn't always mentioned on the label, look for ivory-colored pasta with a coarse—not smooth—texture.

That said, you can substitute any kind of noodle in these recipes. See "What to Expect from Whole Wheat Pasta" on page 490 for more details. And if you've got gluten sensitivity, there are many widely available alternatives including noodles made from rice, cornmeal, quinoa, or starches. Pick one you like and make the sauce the same way. Just adjust the pasta cooking time, always starting to check well before the package directs.

COOKING PASTA

With a few exceptions—notably the one-pot technique starting on page 478—you must cook pasta in abundant water. Figure about a gallon per pound in a large pot. You should salt the water well, so it tastes like the sea; a fistful (a couple of tablespoons) is about right. It doesn't matter much when you add the salt to the water, but if you don't add enough, your pasta will be sticky and bland.

While the pasta cooks, adjust the heat to keep the water boiling, and stir frequently to separate the noodles and dislodge any sticking to the bottom of the pot. If you have problems, it's because you don't use enough water, don't salt enough, or don't stir enough. Adding oil to the water will not cure the problem, but it *will* prevent the sauce from properly coating the pasta.

 fast 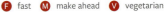 make ahead **V** vegetarian

If your pot is not deep enough for spaghetti or other long pastas, hold the noodles by one end and dunk the other. As the bunch softens, swirl the strands around until they bend enough for you to submerge the whole thing.

It's better to undercook than overcook. But it doesn't take much practice to get this right: As soon as the pasta starts to soften, taste it; it's done when a noodle retains a little bite but is no longer chalky. If you cut a piece in half, you should still see a little hard white bit in the center. At that point, get ready to drain; it will cook a little more as you sauce and toss it and get it on the table. The goal is for it to be al dente—literally "to the teeth."

Don't trust anyone's suggested pasta cooking times. It varies from box to box and even day to day. Cook by taste and you'll never go wrong. This holds true for every noodle you make, from fresh egg pasta made in your own kitchen, to gluten-free alternatives, to dried rice noodles from Thailand. The times given in this chapter indicate when you should start tasting.

DRAINING, SAUCING, AND TOSSING PASTA

Have a heated bowl ready, or finish pasta in the same pot you used to cook it. Pasta cools quickly and you want to eat it hot. You can easily warm a heatproof serving bowl or individual bowls by running them under hot tap water, then drying; or put them a 200°F oven while you're cooking.

Just before draining, remove about a cup of the pasta cooking water to thin the sauce later. Then drain the noodles quickly, but not thoroughly; the pasta should remain quite moist. Immediately combine the pasta and sauce. If the sauce is chunky and clumping up on the pasta instead of coating it evenly, thin it out with a little pasta cooking water, a tablespoon or so at a time, until you achieve the desired consistency. This technique is used by most home cooks in Italy. For even more flavor, replace the pasta cooking water with stock or water you used for cooking vegetables.

Toss quickly with tongs or a large spoon—or often both. Don't worry about solids collecting at the bottom of the bowl; you can scoop them over the pasta after you serve it. Taste and add salt and pepper, cheese, and/or garnish if called for, toss again, serve, and dig in.

CHOOSING PASTA SHAPES

I'm not one to let anything deter me from making pasta. "Use what you've got," I say. When you have a choice, here's how shape matters: Smooth, creamy, and butter- or oil-based sauces work well coating long strands or ribbons; so are sauces that include lots of liquid with some big pieces of seafood, meat, or vegetables. With a thick and chunky sauce, it's nice to use a cut noodle, like shells, farfalle, or orecchiette, that will catch the bits and pieces. Soup noodles should fit on a spoon, though angel hair or spaghetti is often good in broth, especially when broken into pieces.

Most recipes here offer a couple of suggestions in the ingredient list, whether the title indicates "pasta" in a general way or calls for something specific like linguine. But by all means, eat the shape of pasta that you like, even if it's not the exact kind called for in the recipe.

Pasta Math

I used to consider it suitable to split a pound of pasta with an equally hungry friend; this, however, is a large amount of food. Generally, I now think a pound of pasta serves three (fairly generously) to four, depending on the heartiness of the sauce and what else you're serving. As a side dish or appetizer you'll serve six with these recipes.

Over the last decade or so, I've also adopted a "more sauce, less pasta" philosophy with sauces that include vegetables, beans, eggs, dairy, seafood, poultry, and/or meat. You might try it too: Use 8 ounces pasta—or half the quantity in most of these recipes—with the same amount of sauce. This typically makes two main-course servings.

If you don't have a scale and want to only use a fraction of a package, I give you permission to eyeball it. Grabbing bundles of strands in both hands is effective, as is dumping cut pasta into a measuring cup and estimating that way.

Here are translations and descriptions of the most common shapes, organized from smallest to largest in each category.

LONG PASTA

Capelli d'angelo/capellini (angel hair): Very thin strands

Spaghetti/spaghettini: Round strands of varying thickness

Bucatini: Fat round strands with a hole through the center

Linguine: Narrow flat strands

Fettuccine: Wide flat strands

Tagliatelle: Wide ribbons, between fettuccine and pappardelle

Pappardelle: Very wide ribbons

Lasagne: Sheets or extra-wide ribbons, sometimes curled at the edges

CUT PASTA

Couscous: Teeny granules of pasta, cooked like grains (see page 452)

Pastina: teeny balls or other shapes (like stars); perfect for soup

Orzo: Shaped like grains of rice, only bigger

Ditalini: Short pencil-width tubes

Chifferi (go miti): The classic bent elbows

Orecchiette: Literally "little ears," small, thick saucer-shaped disks

Cavatelli: Small folded disks that look like tiny taco shells

Gemelli: Two thick strands of pasta twisted together

Trenette: Small three-sided tubes

Penne and ziti: Smallish narrow tubes; penne are cut on an angle while ziti are cut straight

Rigatoni: Large ribbed tubes, cut straight

Conchigliette and conchiglie: Seashells, small and large; good for stuffing

Cannelloni (manicotti): Very large tubes for stuffing; sometimes ribbed

Farfalle: What we call butterflies or bowties

Fusilli, rotini, and spiralini: Curlicues, corkscrews, and spirals with subtle differences

Radiatore: Short cylinders with circular rows of deep grooves for collecting sauce

The Simplest Pastas

Three techniques and three basic, unique sauces form the backbone of most pastas. So it makes sense to learn these recipes—the ones you'll probably use most often—first. This section starts with assertively seasoned olive oil tossed with cooked pasta. Next comes a master recipe and chart that builds on the handy one-pot method where you cook pasta and make the sauce at the same time. (See the list on page 477 for simple additions to either of these recipes.)

Then there's tomato sauce, which starts out simple and builds from there. There's more detail about how to choose tomatoes at the start of the recipe, which is then followed by more than a dozen variations.

Pasta with Garlic and Oil

MAKES: 4 servings | TIME: 30 minutes

Few midnight snacks are better than *aglio e olio*, the quintessential Roman pasta. And the whole thing comes together in the time it takes to pop a frozen pizza in the oven. Since olive oil is the backbone of the sauce, use a

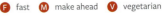

full-flavored one. Any pasta shape is fine here, though linguine is traditional. Cheese is not, however.

    Salt
⅓ cup olive oil, plus more as needed
2 tablespoons chopped garlic
    Red chile flakes (optional)
1 pound long, thin pasta like linguine or spaghetti, or any other pasta
½ cup chopped fresh parsley (optional)

1. Bring a large pot of water to a boil and salt it. Put the oil, garlic, red chile flakes to taste if you're using them, and a pinch salt in a small skillet or saucepan over medium-low heat. Let the garlic sizzle a bit, shaking the pan occasionally, until it turns golden, about 3 minutes. Turn off the heat if the pasta isn't ready.

2. Cook the pasta until it's tender but not mushy; start tasting after 5 minutes. When it's done, drain it, reserving about 1 cup of the cooking water; return the pasta to the pot.

3. Reheat the garlic and oil mixture briefly, if necessary. Drizzle the pasta with the sauce, adding some of the pasta cooking water or a little more oil if it seems dry. Toss, taste and adjust the seasoning, then toss with the parsley if you're using it.

PASTA WITH GARLIC, OIL, AND FRESH HERBS When the garlic oil is done, toss in up to 1 cup fresh herbs, a mixture of whatever you have on hand. You want some mild and some pungent. An example for proportions: ¼ cup chopped parsley, ¼ cup chopped basil or chervil, ¼ cup chopped mint or chives, and 2 tablespoons chopped tarragon, dill, thyme, or rosemary. The herbs will absorb all the oil, so in Step 3, when you toss it with the pasta, add more oil and some of the pasta cooking water.

PASTA WITH GARLIC, OIL, AND MASHED CHICKPEAS Good with cut pasta like ziti, penne, or shells: While you're cooking the pasta, add about 1 cup drained cooked or canned chickpeas to the garlic oil and mash a little with a fork as you warm them.

15 Additions to the Simplest Pastas

Some ingredients from the list below might be considered traditional in Italy, though you wouldn't combine more than two. Whatever you choose, add them to the sauce just before the final tossing and serving unless otherwise directed. Use your judgment about the quantity, keeping in mind that the noodles should remain the dominant component.

1. 2 ounces chopped pancetta or bacon, cooked in the hot oil or butter before adding other ingredients.

2. 4 or more anchovy fillets, mashed in the oil or butter as you cook the other ingredients.

3. Chopped fresh chiles like jalapeño, Thai, or serrano; cook them for a minute in the oil or butter with the other ingredients.

4. Black or green olives, pitted and chopped

5. Chopped fresh herbs

6. Dried tomatoes or dried porcini mushrooms (or both), cut into bits with scissors or, if not at all chewy, ground in a spice or coffee grinder

7. Roasted Garlic (page 294)

8. Fried shallots (see Crisp Sautéed Leeks, page 303)

9. Capers; cook them for a minute in the oil or butter with the other ingredients.

10. An unexpected spice blend like curry powder, garam masala, chili powder, or za'atar (to make your own, see pages 27–35), warmed in the oil before adding main ingredients.

11. Crumbled feta, blue, or fresh goat cheese

12. Frozen peas (no need to thaw; add them to the sauce just before you toss it with the pasta.

13. Grated lemon or orange zest

14. Fried Bread Crumbs (page 801)

15. Chopped Hard-Boiled Egg; or top each serving with a poached or fried egg (see pages 720 and 724)

PASTA WITH GARLIC, OIL, AND NUTS Use walnuts, almonds, hazelnuts, pecans, or pine nuts: Chop about ½ cup nuts in a food processor or finely by hand. In Step 1 make the sauce in a large skillet over medium heat; start with only the oil. When it is hot, add the nuts and cook, stirring frequently, until they start to toast and become fragrant, a minute or 2. Turn the heat to medium-low and stir in red chile flakes if you're using them, the garlic, and a large pinch salt. Proceed with the recipe from Step 2.

One-Pot Pasta with Butter and Parmesan

MAKES: 4 servings | **TIME:** 25 minutes

Instead of boiling pasta and making the sauce separately, you add liquid incrementally to toasted pasta until it's tender—yes, like risotto, which in fact can be mimicked quite effectively if you use orzo. The starch in thick orecchiette or shells encourages a creamy sauce; breaking long strands into thirds or fourths delivers more contrasting textures. The cooking time and absorption rate might vary a bit, so be sure to add the water a little at a time and check frequently for doneness.

> 4 tablespoons (½ stick) butter
> 1 small onion or large shallot, chopped
> 1 pound any pasta
> Salt and pepper
> ½ cup dry white wine or water
> 1 cup grated Parmesan cheese, plus more for serving

1. Put 2 tablespoons of the butter in a large pot over medium heat. When it is hot, add the onion and cook, stirring occasionally, until it softens, about 3 minutes. Add the pasta, raise the heat a bit, and cook, stirring

constantly, until it's glossy and smells toasty, about a minute. Add a little salt and pepper, then the wine, and stir.

2. Let the liquid bubble away. Begin to add water, ½ cup at a time, stirring after each addition. When the liquid is just about absorbed, add more. The noodles should be neither soupy nor dry. Keep the heat at medium to medium-high, stir frequently, and repeat as necessary.

3. Begin tasting the pasta 10 minutes after you added it; it should be tender but have some resistance when you bite. (It could take as long as 20 minutes to reach this stage.) When the pasta is ready, stir in the remaining butter and the Parmesan, adding a little more water if necessary to coat the noodles in sauce. Taste and adjust the seasoning. Serve right away, passing more Parmesan at the table.

ONE-POT PASTA WITH SPINACH, BUTTER, AND RICOTTA Reduce the Parmesan to ½ cup. When the pasta is just getting tender in Step 3 but still is too firm to eat, stir in 3 cups chopped spinach and 1 cup ricotta.

Fast Tomato Sauce, with or Without Pasta

MAKES: 4 servings (about 5 cups) | **TIME:** 20 minutes

Here you have many choices, starting with the tomatoes. Canned are by far the most convenient, and they're reliable all year long. Use whole if you want big chunks, diced for smaller pieces. In the summer, try fresh tomatoes for a real treat; the kind is less important than the ripeness—you want them downright squishy. I never peel or seed anymore, which are both a pain and reduce flavor. To avoid tough skins—and eliminate the task of chopping—pulse them in a food processor until as coarse or puréed as you like. And then consider making extra sauce and freezing the leftovers. You can thaw it slowly in the fridge, faster in the microwave, or heat gently in a covered pan, stirring occasionally to prevent sticking.

A-Little-Less-Simple One-Pot Pastas

Take the same basic idea, embellish every step of the way, and ratchet up the basic recipe to a whole different level.

VARIATION	STEP 1: SAUTÉ	STEP 2: ADD LIQUID	STEP 3: FINAL GARNISH
One-Pot Cacio e Pepe	Use olive oil instead of butter. Omit the onion and wine. Sauté 1 tablespoon black pepper in the hot oil for 30 seconds. Add the pasta.	Stick to water. For the cheese, combine 1 cup each grated Parmesan cheese and pecorino Romano. Use 1½ cups to toss with the pasta in the pot.	Sprinkle with the remaining cheese mixture. Offer more pepper at the table.
One-Pot Fettuccine Alfredo	Use fettuccine. Reduce the butter to 2 tablespoons and omit the onion and wine. Before starting, whisk 2 eggs with ½ cup cream and the Parmesan cheese. Melt the butter in the pot and proceed to Step 2.	Stick with water. When the pasta is cooked, add the cheese-egg-cream mixture and enough additional water to make a creamy sauce.	Pass more Parmesan cheese at the table.
One-Pot Pasta with Lemony Zucchini	Before starting, grate 1 pound zucchini on the large holes of a box and the zest of 2 lemons on the fine holes. Add them after toasting the pasta. Use lemon juice instead of the wine.	Use Chicken Stock (page 176).	Garnish the pasta by tossing in 2 tablespoons chopped fresh mint. Pass more Parmesan cheese at the table.
One-Pot Pasta with Mushrooms	Slice 1½ pounds cremini mushrooms; use 2 tablespoons sliced garlic instead of the onion. Start by cooking the mushrooms until they're crisp in places, about 10 minutes. Then continue.	Use Mushroom Stock (page 174). Reduce the cheese to ½ cup or skip it all together.	Garnish with 2 tablespoons chopped fresh parsley and pass some Parmesan cheese at the table.
One-Pot Pasta with Fava Beans	Start by boiling 1½ cups fresh shelled and peeled or frozen fava beans in the pot until soft; drain, reserving the liquid. Proceed with Step 1, using olive oil instead of the butter.	Use the reserved fava cooking liquid. Substitute 4 ounces (about 1 cup) crumbled goat cheese for the Parmesan. While the pasta cooks, mash the beans roughly with a fork; add them with the cheese.	Garnish with chopped fresh chives and pass Parmesan cheese at the table.
One-Pot Pasta with Spicy Shrimp, Crab, or Squid	Use either olive oil or butter, or a combination. When you cook the onion, add 1 or 2 chopped fresh hot red chiles like serrano or cayenne, or a pinch red chile flakes.	Use water, Shrimp Stock (page 179), or Fish Stock (page 178). Instead of the cheese, add 12 ounces chopped peeled shrimp, cleaned squid cut into rings (plus any tentacles), or lump crab meat. Cook until the seafood is opaque and heated through, just a minute or 2.	Omit the cheese. Garnish with chopped fresh basil and serve with lemon wedges.
One-Pot Pasta with Chicken and Fennel	Cut 12 ounces boneless, skinless chicken thighs into bite-sized pieces; brown on all sides in the butter before adding the onion.	Use Chicken Stock (page 176). When the pasta begins to soften, add 1 small fennel bulb, chopped.	Garnish with chopped fresh fennel fronds. Pass more Parmesan cheese at the table.

 F fast **M** make ahead **V** vegetarian

Salt and pepper

3 tablespoons olive oil or butter, plus more if needed

1 small onion, chopped

1 28-ounce and one 14-ounce can whole or diced tomatoes; or 2 pounds fresh tomatoes (see the headnote)

1 pound any dried pasta (optional)
Grated Parmesan cheese or pecorino Romano for serving (optional)
Chopped fresh parsley or basil for garnish (optional)

1. If you're serving pasta with this sauce, bring a large pot of water to a boil and salt it. Put the oil or butter in a large skillet over medium heat. When the oil is hot or the butter foams, add the onion and cook, stirring occasionally, until soft, 3 to 5 minutes. Add the tomatoes, sprinkle with salt and pepper, and bring to a boil.

2. Lower the heat to a gentle bubble. Cook, stirring and mashing the tomatoes occasionally with the back of the spoon, until they break down and the sauce comes together, 10 to 15 minutes. Taste and adjust the seasonings; keep warm. Or let cool, cover, and refrigerate for up to several days; reheat gently before serving.

3. If you're serving the pasta, cook it until tender but not mushy; start tasting after 5 minutes. When it's done, drain it, reserving 1 cup of the cooking water. Reheat the sauce if necessary. Toss the pasta with the sauce, adding a little more oil or some of the pasta cooking water if it seems dry. Taste and adjust the seasoning, then toss with cheese and parsley if you're using them.

16 SPINS ON FAST TOMATO SAUCE

Serving grated Parmesan cheese with any of these sauces is up to you.

1. **Garlicky Tomato Sauce:** Omit the onion. Using the flat side of a large knife, lightly smash 2 to 10 (or even more) cloves garlic and cook them in the oil or butter as described in Step 1. Proceed with the recipe. Garnish with parsley or basil.

2. **Puttanesca Sauce:** A Roman classic. Make the Garlicky Tomato Sauce above. When you add the garlic to the oil, stir in a few oil-packed anchovy fillets; mash them up a bit as you stir. Omit or reduce the salt. Add 2 tablespoons drained capers, red chile flakes to taste if you like, and ½ cup pitted black olives (the wrinkled oil-cured type, like Moroccan, taste best here). Then add the tomatoes. Garnish with chopped parsley or basil.

3. **Spicy Tomato Sauce:** Known as arrabbiata, this is one of those rare dishes in which garlic is browned intentionally; still, don't overcook it: Omit the onion. Cook about 2 tablespoons chopped garlic in the oil along with 3 to 5 small dried red chiles or ½ teaspoon red chile flakes, stirring, until the garlic is brown. Turn off the heat for a minute, add the tomatoes, and proceed. Remove the whole chiles before serving if you like. Garnish with parsley or basil.

4. **Tomato Sauce with Aromatic Vegetables:** Especially good puréed (see the last variation). Add ½ cup each chopped carrot and celery and 1 tablespoon chopped garlic along with the onion. Cook, stirring, until tender, about 10 minutes; add the tomatoes and proceed. Garnish with parsley or basil.

5. **Tomato Sauce with Wine:** Add ¼ cup dry white or red wine just before the tomatoes; let it bubble away for a moment before proceeding. Garnish with parsley or basil.

6. **Tomato Sauce with Bay Leaves:** Add 5 to 10 bay leaves and a small pinch (about ⅛ teaspoon) ground cinnamon before adding the tomatoes. Remove and discard the bay leaves before serving. Garnish with parsley or basil.

7. **Tomato-Mushroom Sauce:** Start by making Sautéed Mushrooms, Dry Style (page 306); remove them from the skillet. Continue with the recipe from the beginning of Step 1. Return the mushrooms to

the pan after you add the tomatoes. Garnish with chives or parsley.

8. **Tomato Sauce with Fresh Herbs:** Really delightful, especially in summer. Just before serving, add ¼ to ½ cup chopped fresh basil, parsley, dill, mint, or a combination. Or add 1 tablespoon (or more) chopped stronger herbs, like rosemary, oregano, marjoram, tarragon, or thyme

9. **Vegetable Tomato Sauce:** The vegetables must be tender before you add them to the tomatoes; this is nice puréed (see the last variation). After the tomatoes are cooked, add 1 cup of almost any cooked vegetable, chopped or sliced, like eggplant, zucchini, squash, fennel, celery, carrots, peppers, artichoke hearts, mushrooms, or cauliflower; grilled vegetables are ideal. Heat through. Garnish with parsley or basil.

10. **Tomato Pesto Sauce:** The fragrance at the table is awesome. Use as much or as little pesto as you like: After the sauce has finished cooking, stir in some Traditional Pesto or one of its variations (page 51). Or after tossing the pasta, top each serving with a spoonful of pesto. You might not need extra cheese.

11. **Red Pepper and Tomato Sauce:** For homemade Roasted Red Peppers, see page 318. Add 1 or more chopped roasted red peppers along with the tomatoes. Purée if you like (see the last variation). Garnish with parsley or basil.

12. **Creamy Vodka Sauce:** The alcohol is pleasantly sharp and balances the richness. Just before serving, stir in about ¼ cup vodka and ½ cup cream and cook just long enough to heat through without boiling.

13. **Tomatoey Tomato Sauce:** Stir about ¼ cup tomato paste into the onions just before adding the tomatoes. Garnish with parsley or basil.

14. **Oven-Roasted-Tomato Sauce:** Also great thinned with a little vegetable stock, wine, or water. Use Oven-Roasted Plum Tomatoes (page 347) or the canned tomato variation instead of canned or fresh tomatoes.

15. **Grilled-Tomato Sauce:** Cut the tomatoes into thick slices, or halves if they're small, and grill on both sides until browned, about 5 minutes total. When the tomatoes are cool enough to handle, chop or purée. Add 1 tablespoon chopped fresh oregano and about 1 tablespoon red wine vinegar after Step 1.

16. **Puréed Tomato Sauce:** Smooth and creamy. You can finish any sauce by passing it through a food mill or whizzing it in a blender or food processor (to avoid overflowing the container, cool the sauce slightly first and work in batches); add a little cream or ricotta cheese if you like.

Pasta with Vegetables or Beans

Vegetarian pastas make terrific light meals. You can either start from one of the recipes in this section or see the list on page 397 to use another dish—or leftovers—to toss with pasta as "sauce."

For the most flavorful results, cook aromatics, like onions, in oil or butter, add the vegetable, then cook until softer than you might usually eat them. Consider puréeing the simplest cooked vegetables for a smooth sauce before adding pasta, cheese, and garnishes. That covers almost all the options, but there are other techniques scattered among the recipes in this section.

Linguine with Raw Tomato Sauce

MAKES: About 4 servings | TIME: About 30 minutes

I love eating—and saying—*salsa cruda*, Italian for "raw sauce." In peak summer this fresh tomato sauce is unbeatable, and absurdly easy to make. You can also serve it alongside fried or grilled fish (or potato chips,

 fast make ahead **V** vegetarian

for that matter), on top of Polenta (page 460), or any-where you'd use a fresh salsa or relish.

Salt and pepper
2 cloves garlic, peeled
1½ pounds fresh tomatoes, chopped
2 tablespoons olive oil
¼ cup chopped fresh basil, or more to taste
1 pound linguine or other long pasta
Grated Parmesan cheese (optional)

1. Bring a large pot of water to a boil and salt it. Gently smash the garlic with the flat side of a wide knife.

2. Put the tomatoes, oil, some salt and pepper, the garlic, and some of the basil in a large shallow bowl. Mash together well, using a fork or potato masher, but do not purée. (At this point, you can let the sauce rest at room temperature for an hour or 2.)

3. Cook the pasta until it's tender but not mushy; start tasting after 5 minutes. When it's done, drain it, reserving ¼ cup of the cooking water. Add the pasta cooking water to the sauce to thin and warm it a bit. Remove the garlic. Toss the pasta with the sauce; taste and adjust the seasoning. Top with the remaining basil and serve, passing the Parmesan at the table if you're using it.

Pasta with Broccoli Raab

MAKES: About 4 servings | TIME: About 40 minutes

Using the same water to cook the broccoli raab as you do for the pasta saves cleaning a pot and makes things go a bit faster—and it adds a little flavor. For the best sauce—in the main recipe and the variations—go against your instincts and cook the vegetable until it's fully tender. You won't even need cheese. Trust me.

Salt and pepper
1½ ounds broccoli raab, cut into 1-inch pieces
¼ cup olive oil, or more as needed
2 tablespoons plus 1 teaspoon chopped garlic
1 pound penne, ziti, or other cut pasta

1. Bring a large pot of water to a boil and salt it. Boil the broccoli raab until it's fork-tender, about 5 minutes. Meanwhile, put the oil in a large skillet over medium-low heat. When it is hot, add the garlic and cook, stirring, until it begins to sizzle, about a minute; turn off the heat. Scoop the broccoli raab out of the water with a slotted spoon or small strainer and transfer it to the skillet. Keep the pot of water boiling.

2. Put the skillet over medium-high heat and cook, stirring and mashing the broccoli raab, until it's hot and quite soft, 10 to 15 minutes, adding some of the cooking water as needed to help soften the pieces. Keep warm.

3. Cook the pasta until it's tender but not mushy; start tasting after 5 minutes. When it's done, drain it, reserving about 1 cup of the cooking water. Add the pasta to the broccoli raab, tossing to combine and adding enough of the pasta cooking water to coat the noodles. Taste and add salt if necessary and lots of pepper, and serve.

PASTA WITH CAULIFLOWER OR BROCCOLI For a smoother, less bitter sauce, go this route: Use the tender stalks and florets of broccoli or cauliflower instead of the broccoli raab.

PASTA WITH GREENS Instead of the broccoli raab, use spinach, kale, collards, escarole, chard, mustard, or other greens. If the stems are thick, separate them from the leaves (see page 300) and chop into 1-inch lengths; chop the leaves. In Step 1, first cook the stems until tender, transfer to the skillet, then boil the leaves. Otherwise toss the whole greens in the boiling water.

PASTA WITH ASPARAGUS Soft-cooked asparagus makes a creamy, intensely flavored sauce: Instead of the broccoli raab, cut trimmed asparagus into 1-inch pieces.

 fast   make ahead    vegetarian

PASTA WITH BROCCOLI RAAB, CAULIFLOWER, BROCCOLI, GREENS, OR ASPARAGUS AND SAUSAGE Works for the main recipe or any of the variations: In Step 1, start by cutting 8 ounces hot or sweet Italian sausages into chunks. Reduce the oil to 2 tablespoons and cook the sausage in the oil until it's no longer pink, then add the garlic and proceed with the recipe, mashing and breaking up the sausage with the vegetables before adding the pasta.

Pasta with Mushrooms

MAKES: 4 servings | **TIME:** 30 minutes

Choose mushrooms you like—and if you can get can get your hand on fresh porcini or other truly wild varieties in season, I urge you to go for them.

Salt and pepper

1 pound any fresh mushrooms

⅓ cup olive oil, plus more for drizzling

1 tablespoon chopped garlic

1 pound dried cut pasta like rigatoni

¼ cup chopped fresh parsley

1. Bring a large pot of water to a boil and salt it. If you're using mushrooms with tough stems, remove them (and save for stock). Rinse the mushrooms quickly and cut into small chunks or thin slices.

2. Put the oil in a medium to large skillet over medium heat. When it is hot, add the mushrooms and sprinkle with salt and pepper. Raise the heat to medium-high and cook, stirring occasionally, until the mushrooms release their water and begin to sizzle, at least 10 minutes. Add the garlic, lower the heat a bit, and continue until the mushrooms and garlic are tender, another minute or 2. Turn off the heat.

27 Vegetable and Legume Dishes to Toss with Pasta

With this list your pasta repertoire has more than doubled. In all cases if, after saucing, you think the dish needs more moisture, while tossing add a little of the pasta cooking water or extra oil or butter—or both.

1. Broccoli Raab with Sausages and Grapes and its variations (page 239)
2. Braised celery (page 247)
3. Braised and Glazed Chestnuts (see page 247)
4. Braised Artichoke Hearts (page 261)
5. Braised Artichoke Hearts with Ham, Wine, and Lemon (page 261)
6. Crunchy Broccoli or Cauliflower with Onion and Olives (page 269)
7. Crunchy Broccoli or Cauliflower with Almonds, Raisins, and Saffron (page 269)
8. Sautéed Brussels Sprouts with Bacon (page 272)
9. Buttered Cabbage (page 274)
10. Shredded Carrots with Chiles and Chives (page 276)
11. Pan-Roasted Corn with Cherry Tomatoes and its variations (page 286)
12. Sautéed Eggplant with Basil and its variations (page 290)
13. Braised Endive, Escarole, or Radicchio with Prosciutto (page 292)
14. Slow-Cooked Green Beans (page 297)
15. Leeks Braised in Red Wine (page 303)
16. Caramelized Onions with Bacon or Pancetta (page 315)
17. Creamed Onions or Creamed Spinach (page 316)
18. Peas with Bacon, Lettuce, and Mint (page 318)
19. My Mom's Pan-Cooked Peppers and Onions (page 320)
20. Spinach with Currants and Nuts (page 339)
21. Oven-Roasted Plum Tomatoes (page 347)
22. Oven-Baked Ratatouille (page 352)
23. White Bean Purée (page 392)
24. Beans and Tomatoes (page 396)
25. White Beans, Tuscan Style (page 402)
26. Beans and Greens (page 403)
27. Chickpeas in Their Own Broth (page 407)

3. Cook the pasta until it's tender but not mushy; start tasting after 5 minutes. When it's ready, put the mushrooms over medium heat and drain the pasta, reserving 1 cup of the cooking water. Add the pasta to the mushrooms and toss together, adding enough of the pasta cooking water to coat the noodles with sauce. Taste and adjust the seasoning, toss with the parsley, and serve.

PASTA WITH FRESH AND DRIED MUSHROOMS As in any mushroom recipe, you can enhance the taste of ordinary button mushrooms by adding a portion of dried porcini: Soak ¼ to ½ cup dried porcini in hot water to cover until softened, about 10 minutes. Lift the reconstituted porcini out of the soaking liquid with your hands or a slotted spoon. Carefully pour the soaking liquid into another container, leaving any grit in the bottom of the bowl. Squeeze out excess moisture from the porcini, chop, and add in Step 2 along with the fresh mushrooms. In Step 3, use the mushroom soaking liquid to augment or replace the pasta cooking water.

Pasta with Fried Eggplant

YIELD: 4 servings | **TIME:** About 45 minutes

Sicilian *pasta alla Norma* has the most luxurious vegetable sauce I know. The pan-fried eggplant becomes silky, rich, and flavorful from olive oil. For a lighter version—which is also quite good—see the variation. And peel the eggplant if you must, but it's neither traditional nor necessary.

1½	**pounds eggplant**
	Salt and pepper
	Olive oil for frying (at least ½ cup)
2	**tablespoons chopped garlic**
3 or 4	**dried red chiles, or red chile flakes to taste**

1	**28-ounce can diced tomatoes, or 1½ pounds chopped fresh**
1	**tablespoon chopped fresh oregano or 1 teaspoon dried**
1	**pound long pasta**
½	**cup chopped fresh parsley or basil**
½	**cup grated ricotta salata or pecorino Romano**

1. Cut the eggplant crosswise into slices about ½ inch thick. Bring a large pot of water to boil and salt it.
2. Put about ½ inch oil in a large skillet over medium-high heat. When it is hot, add a layer of eggplant, careful not to overcrowd, and sprinkle with salt. Cook, turning once, until the eggplant is tender and browned on both sides, 5 to 10 minutes total; adjust the heat so the eggplant sizzles without smoking. As the slices finish, transfer them to a plate; don't drain on towels. Repeat with the remaining eggplant, adding more oil as needed.
3. When the eggplant is cooked, pour off all but about 2 tablespoons of the oil and set the pan over medium heat. Add the garlic and chiles, and cook, stirring constantly, until the garlic colors a little. Add the tomatoes and oregano, sprinkle with salt and pepper, and cook, stirring occasionally, until the tomatoes break down into a sauce, 10 to 15 minutes.
4. Cook the pasta until it's tender but not mushy; start tasting after 5 minutes. Cut the eggplant into strips and add to the tomato sauce. Drain the pasta, reserving 1 cup of the cooking water. Toss the pasta with the sauce, adding enough pasta cooking water to coat the noodles. Taste and adjust the seasoning, sprinkle with the parsley and cheese, and serve.

PASTA WITH ROASTED EGGPLANT Instead of slicing the eggplant, cut it into 1-inch cubes; roast according to the recipe on page 247. In Step 3, put 2 tablespoons olive oil in the skillet and proceed with the recipe. If the eggplant hasn't finished roasting by the time the rest of the sauce is done, turn off the heat under the tomatoes until you're ready to add the roasted eggplant.

Pasta with Corn, Zucchini, and Tomatoes

MAKES: 4 servings | **TIME:** 30 minutes

The best of summer in a bowl. Don't bother to make this other times of the year, but do be flexible about the type of tomato. Use whatever's ripest. And if you want to add cheese, try crumbling some feta or fresh goat cheese on top just before serving.

> Salt and pepper
> 4 tablespoons olive oil, or 2 tablespoons oil and 2 tablespoons butter
> 1 cup corn kernels (from 2 or 3 ears corn)
> 1 zucchini or summer squash, chopped
> 1 onion, chopped
> 1 tablespoon chopped garlic
> 1 tablespoon chopped fresh tarragon
> 8 ounces plum tomatoes, chopped (about 1¼ cups)
> 1 pound cut pasta, like penne, rigatoni, or fusilli

1. Bring a large pot of water to a boil and salt it. Put 2 tablespoons oil in a large skillet over medium-high heat. When it is hot, add the corn and sprinkle with salt and pepper. Cook, stirring occasionally, until the corn is dry and beginning to brown, about 5 minutes. Transfer it to a plate and return the pan to medium-high heat.

2. Add the remaining 2 tablespoons oil or the butter to the skillet along with the zucchini; sprinkle with salt and pepper. Cook, stirring occasionally, until the zucchini begins to brown, about 3 minutes. Add the onion and garlic and continue to cook, stirring occasionally, until the onion softens, about 3 minutes. Add the tarragon and cook for 30 seconds, then add the tomatoes and continue cooking the sauce over medium heat, stirring occasionally, while you cook the pasta.

3. Cook the pasta until it's tender but not mushy; start tasting after 5 minutes. When it's done, drain it, reserving 1 cup of the cooking water. Return the corn to the skillet. Toss the pasta with the sauce and corn, adding enough pasta cooking water to coat the noodles. Taste and adjust the seasoning, and serve.

Whole Wheat Farfalle with Roasted Sweet Potatoes

MAKES: About 4 servings | **TIME:** About 45 minutes

Hearty noodles meet hearty vegetables. All you need is a salad—or nothing.

> 4 tablespoons olive oil, plus more for greasing the pan
> 1 pound sweet potatoes, peeled and cut into 1-inch cubes
> Salt and pepper
> 1 tablespoon chopped garlic
> 1 pound whole wheat farfalle or other cut pasta
> ¼ cup chopped fresh parsley or chives
> 2 teaspoons red chile flakes, or to taste
> Grated Parmesan cheese for serving

1. Heat the oven to 400°F. Grease a large rimmed baking sheet with a little of the oil. The pan should be large enough to hold all the sweet potato cubes in a single layer without overcrowding; if not, use two pans.

2. Put the sweet potatoes in the pan, sprinkle generously with salt and pepper, and drizzle with 2 tablespoons of the oil; toss to coat. Roast the sweet potatoes until they brown on the bottom, about 15 minutes; scatter the garlic over the top, stir, and continue roasting until tender, another 15 to 20 minutes.

3. Meanwhile, bring a large pot of water to a boil and salt it. Cook the pasta until it's tender but not mushy; start tasting after 5 minutes. When it's done, drain it, reserving 1 cup of the cooking water. Toss the sweet potatoes with the parsley and red chile flakes, then return the pasta to the pot, add the sweet potatoes, and toss with the remaining oil, adding enough pasta

cooking water to coat the noodles. Taste and adjust the seasoning. Serve, passing cheese at the table.

WHOLE WHEAT PASTA WITH BROWNED CHICKEN
Substitute 1½ pounds boneless chicken (any parts, skinless or not), cut into chunks, for the sweet potatoes. Skip Steps 1 and 2. Put 2 tablespoons oil in a large skillet over medium-high heat. When it's hot, add the chicken, sprinkle with salt and pepper, and cook until browned and cooked through, stirring occasionally, about 8 minutes. Add the garlic and chile and stir until fragrant, about a minute. Proceed with Step 3, adding the parsley when you toss the pasta with the sauce.

WHOLE WHEAT PASTA WITH ROASTED WINTER SQUASH
Instead of sweet potatoes, use any winter squash; peel and seed it before cutting into 1-inch cubes. Add 1 tablespoon minced fresh rosemary or sage with the garlic in Step 2 if you like.

WHOLE WHEAT PASTA WITH CARROTS
Instead of the sweet potatoes, use carrots; peel them if you like and cut into 1-inch chunks. When you add the garlic in Step 2, add 1 teaspoon ground cumin if you like.

What to Expect from Whole Wheat Pasta

The nutty flavor and hearty texture of whole wheat pasta has undeniable appeal as a whole grain alternative to regular pasta. Ideally, whole wheat pasta should be flecked with bits of bran, and should cook from dry to tender without instantly turning to mush. You might have to try a couple brands to find one you like.

Whole wheat pasta may take a minute or two longer to cook, and you'll never get quite the same creaminess after saucing because the starch doesn't release the same way. But what you will get is a near-ideal vehicle for assertive sauces—especially nut sauces—and sauces that include big chunks of vegetables.

Pasta with Creamy Bean Sauce

MAKES: 4 servings | **TIME:** 30 minutes with cooked or canned beans

You've got to try this, even if you think it sounds a bit strange. The sauce is thick and comforting even without cheese—though some Parmesan or Pecorino Romano certainly ups the game. You can use any beans you like here; my favorites are listed below. And if they're homemade (see page 390), all the better, since the cooking liquid plays a role in the richness and creaminess of the sauce.

    Salt and pepper
 3 cups drained cooked or canned kidney or
    cannellini beans, or green lentils (reserve the
    liquid if you cooked the beans yourself)
 ¼ cup olive oil, plus more for drizzling
 2 tablespoons chopped garlic
 1 tablespoon chopped fresh thyme
 1 pound cut pasta like fusilli, rigatoni, or farfalle
    Grated pecorino Romano for serving (optional)

1. Bring a large pot of water to a boil and salt it. Purée the beans in a food processor or blender, scraping down the sides and adding just enough reserved bean cooking liquid or water to let the machine do its work.

2. Put the oil in a large skillet over medium heat. When it is hot, add the garlic and thyme and cook, stirring constantly, until fragrant, about a minute. Add the puréed beans, sprinkle with salt and pepper, and cook, stirring frequently, until bubbling; keep the sauce warm.

3. Cook the pasta until it's tender but not mushy; start tasting after 5 minutes. When it's done, drain it, reserving 1 cup of the cooking water. Toss the pasta with the sauce, adding enough pasta cooking water to coat the noodles. Taste and adjust the seasoning. Serve,

 fast make ahead **V** vegetarian

passing some olive oil for drizzling and cheese at the table if you're using it.

Pasta with Dairy, Eggs, Seafood, or Meat

Consider these—with sauces that include animal foods—the hearty pastas. That doesn't mean they're heavy, however. Butter, cheese, and cream are rich ingredients to be sure, so you don't need to use much to make a good sauce. Fish and shellfish bring the distinctive flavor of the sea to a bowl of pasta, while beef, pork, and cured meats turn noodles into dishes with some extra heft and bite.

Spaghetti with Pesto

MAKES: About 4 servings | TIME: 30 minutes

The cheese in pesto enriches this sauce, melting into the butter to become almost like cream. If you don't already have pesto on hand, you should still set the water to boil first. It's not going to take that long. You can also try a less traditional herb purée sauce (see page 52 for ideas).

  Salt and pepper
1 pound spaghetti, or maybe a fancy cut pasta
2 tablespoons butter
1 cup Traditional Pesto, made with the cheese (page 51)
  Grated Parmesan cheese for serving

1. Bring a large pot of water to a boil and salt it. Cook the pasta until it's tender but not mushy; start tasting after 5 minutes.
2. When the pasta is done, drain it, reserving 1 cup of the cooking water. Return the pasta to the pot with the

pesto and toss, adding enough pasta cooking water to coat the noodles. Taste and adjust the seasoning. Serve, passing cheese at the table.

Ziti with Creamy Gorgonzola Sauce and Fried Sage

MAKES: About 4 servings | TIME: 30 minutes

Start by choosing a blue cheese you like to nibble. Combine it with butter and cream and you'll have the richest sauce imaginable, even if it's not quite the prettiest. Besides Gorgonzola, other top-notch blue cheeses—think Stilton and Roquefort and the best domestic blues—work well here.

  Salt
2 tablespoons olive oil
  About a dozen fresh sage leaves
2 tablespoons butter
1 cup crumbled Gorgonzola or other good blue cheese (about 4 ounces)
½ cup heavy cream or half-and-half
1 pound ziti, penne, or other relatively large cut pasta
½ cup grated Parmesan cheese, plus more for serving

1. Bring a large pot of water to a boil and salt it. Line a small plate with towels. Put the oil in a large skillet over medium-high heat. When it is hot, put the sage leaves in the oil, flattening them out as much as possible. Cook, turning once, until the sage is crisp and lightly browned on both sides, a couple of minutes total. As they finish, transfer the leaves to the towels to drain. Don't bother to clean the pan.
2. Return the skillet to medium-low heat and add the butter. Crumble in the Gorgonzola and mash it with a fork or potato masher, gradually adding the cream. Don't worry about making it smooth; just make sure it is well

combined. Cook, stirring, until the sauce is steaming but not boiling; keep warm.

3. Cook the pasta until it's tender but not mushy; start tasting after 5 minutes. When it's done, drain it, reserving 1 cup of the cooking water. Add the pasta to the sauce and toss to combine, adding the Parmesan and enough of the pasta cooking water to coat the noodles. Taste and adjust the seasoning. Garnish with the sage leaves and serve, passing additional Parmesan at the table.

FARFALLE WITH MASCARPONE AND FRIED BASIL

Two simple substitutions make a totally different—milder, creamier—dish: Instead of the Gorgonzola, bring 6 ounces (¾ cup) mascarpone cheese to room temperature; reserve ¼ cup. In Step 1 fry whole basil leaves instead of sage. Garnish each serving with a spoonful of the reserved mascarpone, some basil, and lots of black pepper.

Linguine with Clams

MAKES: About 4 servings | TIME: 30 minutes

Instead of opening a can, let steam open your clams. Really, this amazing classic is just that easy, especially if you serve the clams in their shells, which is both dramatic and less work for you. To read more about clams, see page 575.

	Salt and pepper
4	tablespoons olive oil
3	pounds littleneck or other small hard-shell clams or cockles, scrubbed
1	tablespoon minced garlic
1	teaspoon red chile flakes, or to taste (optional)
1	pound linguine or other long pasta
	Chopped fresh parsley for garnish

1. Bring a large pot of water to a boil and salt it. Put 2 tablespoons of the oil in a large skillet over medium-high heat. When it's hot, add the clams, cover, and cook, gently shaking the skillet or stirring the clams occasionally, until the first few of them open, about 5 minutes.

2. Scatter the garlic and the red chile flakes, if you're using them, over the clams, re-cover, and cook, still shaking the pan occasionally, until almost all of the clams are open, about 3 minutes more. Turn off the heat and leave the skillet covered.

3. Meanwhile, cook the pasta until it's just becoming tender but is still white at the center; drain it, reserving 1 cup of the cooking water. Discard any clams that haven't opened. Sprinkle them with salt and pepper and drizzle with the remaining oil. Turn the heat to medium; add the pasta to the clams and cook, stirring, until the pasta is tender, a minute or 2, adding the some of the pasta cooking water if the mixture seems dry. Taste and adjust the seasoning. Garnish with the parsley and serve.

PASTA WITH RED CLAM SAUCE Just before adding the pasta to the clams, add about 1½ cups chopped fresh or canned tomatoes.

PASTA WITH CLAMS AND PESTO Prepare the clams as instructed. In Step 2, when the clams are almost all open, stir in 1 cup Traditional Pesto (page 51), then re-cover.

SORT-OF-SICHUAN NOODLES WITH CLAMS Prepare the clams as instructed, replacing the olive oil with 2 tablespoons each sesame oil and good-quality vegetable oil. In Step 2 add 2 teaspoons Sichuan peppercorns and 2 tablespoons fermented black beans along with the chiles. Garnish with scallions or cilantro.

PASTA WITH MUSSELS Works with the main recipe or any of the variations: Use 2 pounds mussels instead of the clams, and reduce the cooking time in Step 1 to about 3 minutes.

Sort-of-Sichuan Noodles
with Clams

14 Seafood, Meat, and Poultry Dishes That Work as Pasta Sauces

Make sure these dishes are piping hot before adding them to pasta. And if they seem soupy rather than saucy, drain off and reserve some of the liquid before tossing, then use the reserved liquid to moisten the pasta if you need to.

1. Bouillabaisse (page 162)
2. Sautéed Fish with Lemony Pan Sauce (page 537)
3. Sautéed Oysters with Lemony Pan Sauce (page 538)
4. Shrimp Scampi (page 542)
5. Seared Scallops with Cherry Tomatoes (page 577)
6. Steamed Clams, Mussels, or Other Shellfish (page 579)
7. Octopus with Tomatoes and Red Wine (page 590)
8. Chicken Baked with Tomatoes (page 601); cut them into chunks first
9. Sautéed Chicken with Wine Sauce (page 607); cut the chicken into strips or chunks first
10. Pepper Steak with Red Wine Sauce (page 671)
11. Braised Pork with Tomatoes and Fennel (page 700)
12. Sausage with Peppers and Onions (page 704); cut the sausage up if you like
13. Lamb Stew with Mushrooms (page 711)
14. Lamb Stew with Eggplant or Green Beans (page 711)

Penne with Tomato-Shrimp Sauce

MAKES: At least 4 servings | **TIME:** 30 minutes

A perennial favorite and all-purpose recipe, useful for almost any finfish or shellfish you have in the house; see the variations for a couple of suggestions.

Salt and pepper
3 tablespoons olive oil
1 small dried hot red chile, or red chile flakes to taste
2 cloves garlic, lightly smashed with the flat side of a knife
1 pound chopped seeded fresh tomatoes, or one 28-ounce can diced tomatoes
1 pound penne or other cut pasta
1 pound large shrimp, peeled and cut into chunks
½ cup chopped fresh parsley or basil

1. Bring a large pot of water to a boil and salt it. Put the oil in a large skillet over medium-high heat. When it is hot, add the chiles and garlic and cook, stirring, until the garlic turns brown (this is a somewhat strong-tasting sauce), about a minute.

2. Remove and discard the whole chile and garlic if you like, and add the tomatoes. Cook, stirring frequently, until the tomatoes begin to break down, about 5 minutes; add a good sprinkle of salt and pepper. Cook, stirring once or twice, until the tomatoes thicken into a sauce, about 5 minutes more, then turn off the heat. (At this point, you can refrigerate the sauce, covered, for a day or 2, or freeze for several weeks. Reheat before adding the shrimp.)

3. Cook the pasta until it is tender but not mushy; start tasting after 5 minutes. When the pasta begins to soften, stir the shrimp into the sauce and cook until the shrimp turn pink, a couple of minutes. When it's done, drain the pasta, reserving 1 cup of the cooking water. Toss it and the parsley with the sauce, adding enough pasta cooking water to coat the noodles. Taste and adjust the seasonings and serve.

PENNE WITH TOMATO-SQUID SAUCE Substitute squid for shrimp. Clean and rinse the squid if necessary, then cut it up (see the illustrations on page 589). Proceed

with the recipe, adding the squid as described in Step 3. Cook until opaque, about 2 minutes, careful not to overcook; immediately add the pasta.

PENNE WITH TOMATO-TUNA SAUCE Instead of the shrimp use 2 4- or 5-ounce cans tuna (packed in olive oil). In Step 3, stir the tuna into the sauce, breaking it into flakes. Add 2 tablespoons capers along with the pasta.

Pasta with Sardines

MAKES: 4 servings | TIME: 30 minutes with canned sardines

By all means, if you have the time and energy to grill or broil fresh sardines, and then remove the bones—go for it (see the variation). But good-quality canned sardines, packed in olive oil, are surprisingly excellent here.

	Salt and pepper
¼	cup currants
¼	cup pine nuts
¼	cup olive oil
1	large onion, chopped
1	pound bucatini, or cut pasta like penne or farfalle
4	3.75-ounce cans sardines packed in olive oil
1	teaspoon grated lemon zest
½	cup chopped fresh parsley, plus more for garnish

1. Bring a large pot of water to a boil and salt it. Soak the currants in warm water to cover. Toast the pine nuts in a large dry skillet over medium heat, shaking the pan occasionally, until lightly browned, just a few minutes; then remove them.

2. Return the skillet to medium heat and add the oil. When it is hot, add the onion and cook, stirring occasionally, until softened, about 5 minutes; sprinkle

with salt and pepper. Cook the pasta until it's tender but not mushy; start tasting after 5 minutes.

3. Meanwhile, drain the currants and add them to the skillet along with all but a tablespoon of the pine nuts, the sardines with their oil, and the lemon zest. Cook, stirring gently, until heated through, a couple of minutes. Cover and keep warm until the pasta is ready.

4. When the pasta is done, drain it, reserving 1 cup of the cooking water. Add the pasta to the sardine sauce along with the parsley, adding enough of the pasta cooking water to coat the noodles. Taste and adjust the seasoning. Serve garnished with parsley and the remaining pine nuts.

PASTA WITH FRESH SARDINES Substitute fresh sardines for canned: Grill or broil about 1½ pounds fresh sardines according to the directions on pages 573 to 574. When cool enough to handle, remove the bones, trying to leave the flesh in big pieces. Add them in Step 3, along with 3 tablespoons olive oil.

PASTA WITH RADICCHIO, PINE NUTS, AND CURRANTS A piquant vegetarian option, using the same technique: Instead of sardines, trim about 1 pound radicchio and cut it into thin ribbons. Use orange instead of lemon juice. In Step 3, add the radicchio to the onion with the currants, pine nuts, and orange zest.

Spaghetti with Meat Sauce

MAKES: 4 servings, with about 2 cups leftover sauce | TIME: About 3 hours, largely unattended

This fairly traditional Bolognese sauce or *ragù* doesn't require much in the way of work, but it does require occasional attention over the course of a morning or afternoon. Since this sauce freezes so well—and to make the time well spent—you'll have enough sauce leftover

1. Put the oil in a large skillet over medium-low heat. When it is hot, add the onion, carrot, celery, and bacon. Cook, stirring occasionally, until the vegetables are tender, about 10 minutes.

2. Add the ground meats, sprinkle with salt and pepper, and cook, stirring and breaking up any clumps, until all traces of red are gone, about 5 minutes. Add the wine, bring to a boil, and cook, stirring occasionally, until most of the liquid has evaporated, about 5 minutes.

3. Crush the tomatoes with a fork or your hands and add them to the skillet along with the stock. Adjust the heat so the sauce bubbles gently and cook, stirring occasionally to break up the tomatoes and meat, until the mixture thickens and develops a uniform texture, 1½ to 2 hours. (At this point, you can refrigerate the sauce for a day or 2, or freeze it for several months. Reheat before proceeding.)

4. Bring a large pot of water to a boil and salt it. Add the cream to the sauce and cook at a gentle bubble, stirring occasionally, until it's incorporated, 20 to 30 minutes. Taste and adjust the seasoning.

5. Cook the pasta until it's tender but not mushy; start tasting after 5 minutes. When it's done, drain it, reserving about 1 cup of the cooking water and return the pasta to the pot. Toss the pasta with half the sauce, adding enough of the pasta cooking water to coat the noodles. Serve right away, passing the Parmesan at the table.

to freeze for another meal. (Or double the amount of pasta and feed eight easily.)

2 tablespoons olive oil
1 small onion, chopped
1 carrot, chopped
1 celery stalk, chopped
2 ounces bacon or pancetta, chopped
8 ounces lean ground beef
8 ounces lean ground pork
Salt and pepper
¾ cup dry white wine or juice from the tomatoes
2 28-ounce cans whole plum tomatoes, drained; reserve the juice if you're using it instead of wine
1 cup beef or chicken stock (to make your own, see pages 174–178)
1 cup heavy cream, half-and-half, or milk
1 pound spaghetti or any long or cut pasta
Grated Parmesan cheese for serving

Pasta with Pancetta and Pecorino

MAKES: 3 to 6 servings | **TIME:** 30 minutes

You can generate a lot of flavor from bits of crisp-cooked meat and grated sharp cheese, as demonstrated with this recipe and its variations. The most common meat for these pastas is pancetta (salted, cured, and rolled pork belly), now available at almost all Italian delis and

Spaghetti with
Meat Sauce,
page 495

many supermarkets, but you can also use bacon (which will be smoky)—or even better if you can find it, guanciale, which is cured pig's jowl.

Salt and pepper
2 tablespoons olive oil, plus more as needed
4 ounces pancetta, guanciale, or bacon, chopped
1 pound linguine or other long pasta
½ cup grated pecorino Romano, plus more to taste

1. Bring a large pot of water to a boil and salt it. Put the oil and pancetta in a medium skillet over medium heat. Cook, stirring occasionally, until the pancetta is crisp and browned, about 10 minutes. Turn off the heat.

2. Cook the pasta until it's tender but not mushy; start tasting after 5 minutes. When it's done, drain it, reserving 1 cup of the cooking water.

3. Add the pasta to the pancetta along with the cheese. Toss, adding enough of the pasta cooking water to coat the noodles. Taste and adjust the seasonings; sprinkle generously with black pepper. Add more cheese if you like, and serve.

PASTA CARBONARA Basically pasta with bacon and eggs: While the pasta is cooking, warm a large bowl and beat 3 eggs in it. Stir in about ½ cup grated Parmesan cheese and the crisped pancetta and juices from the skillet. When the pasta is done, drain it and immediately toss with the egg mixture. If the mixture is dry (unlikely), add a little pasta cooking water. Add plenty of pepper and more Parmesan to taste, and serve right away.

PASTA ALL'AMATRICIANA The balance of sweet onion, salty bacon, and acidic tomatoes is incredible: After Step 1, remove the pancetta with a slotted spoon and, in the juices left behind, cook 1 sliced onion over medium heat, stirring occasionally, until quite soft, about 10 minutes. Stir in one 28-ounce can diced tomatoes, or about 2 cups chopped fresh tomatoes. Add the reserved pancetta and cook, stirring occasionally, while you cook the pasta, then proceed with the recipe.

Pasta with Sausage

MAKES: 4 servings | **TIME:** 30 minutes

A simply made pasta, dominated by the flavor and texture of crumbled sausage.

Salt and pepper
2 tablespoons butter
8 ounces sweet or hot Italian sausage
1 pound ziti or other cut pasta
½ cup grated Parmesan cheese, plus more for serving

1. Bring a large pot of water to a boil and salt it. Put the butter in a large skillet over medium heat. As it melts, squeeze the sausage from its casings into the pan; break the meat into ½-inch or smaller bits. Add ¼ cup water and adjust the heat so that the mixture bubbles gently, adding a little more water if necessary, until the sausage is cooked through and tender, about 5 minutes.

2. Meanwhile, cook the pasta until it's tender but not mushy; start tasting after 5 minutes. When it's done, drain it, reserving about 1 cup of the cooking water. Toss the pasta and cheese with the sausage, adding enough of the pasta cooking water to coat the noodles. Taste and adjust the seasoning. Serve, passing more Parmesan at the table.

PASTA WITH SAUSAGE AND GREENS Use escarole, broccoli raab, arugula, spinach, kale, or chicory: Fill a large bowl with ice water. Once the pasta water comes to a boil, add 1 pound washed, trimmed greens and blanch them for no more than a minute (only 20 seconds for spinach or arugula). Fish them out with a slotted spoon, spider, or strainer and immediately plunge into the ice water. When cool, squeeze dry and roughly chop. Return the water to a boil and proceed with the recipe, adding the cooked greens to the sausage along with the water in Step 1.

F fast   M make ahead   V vegetarian

Baked Pasta

Some of the best dishes for entertaining fall into this category, since baked pastas are all precooked and assembled and can hang out in the fridge or freezer for a while. They're also gooey and rich and, yes, I'll say it: comforting. All you need with any of these is a salad or simply cooked vegetable and maybe some rustic bread.

Baked Ziti with Mushrooms

MAKES: 4 to 6 servings | **TIME:** About 1 hour

A lot like lasagne, only without the layering. Be sure not to overcook the pasta; it should be too tough to actually eat when you mix it with the sauce, which will make it perfect after baking.

	Salt and pepper
3	**tablespoons olive oil or butter, plus more for the baking dish**
1	**pound any mushrooms, preferably mixed with about 1 cup reconstituted dried porcini (see page 304)**
1	**large onion, chopped**
1	**tablespoon minced garlic**
1	**28-ounce can whole plum tomatoes**
1	**pound ziti or other large cut pasta**
8	**ounces mozzarella (preferably fresh), chopped**
1	**cup grated Parmesan cheese**

1. Bring a large pot of water to a boil and salt it. If you'll be baking the pasta right away, heat the oven to 400°F. Grease a 13 × 9-inch baking dish.

2. Put the oil or butter in a large skillet over medium-high heat. When the oil is hot or the butter foams, add the mushrooms and cook, stirring occasionally, until they soften, release their water, and then begin to dry, 5 to 10 minutes. Add the onion and garlic and sprinkle with salt and pepper. Lower the heat to medium and continue to cook, stirring occasionally, until the onions are soft, about 2 minutes.

3. Break up the tomatoes with a fork or your hands, add them to the skillet, and stir. Bring to a boil, then adjust the heat so the sauce bubbles gently and cook, stirring occasionally and mashing the tomatoes more, until the sauce thickens slightly but is still a little watery, about 5 minutes. Turn off the heat.

4. Cook the pasta until it's just starting to soften but is still too hard to eat. Drain, but don't shake the colander; allow some water to cling to the noodles. Toss the pasta with the sauce and about half the mozzarella. Spoon the pasta mixture into the prepared baking dish. Top with the remaining mozzarella and the Parmesan. (You can prepare the pasta to this point, wrap it tightly, and refrigerate for up to a couple days; take it out about an hour before proceeding. Or freeze for up to a month; put it in the cold oven and figure the pasta will take about 90 minutes to thaw and reheat.) Transfer to the oven and bake until the top is browned and the cheese is bubbly, 20 to 30 minutes.

BAKED ZITI WITH RICOTTA Stir up to 1 cup ricotta cheese into the sauce right before adding the pasta. Or nestle dollops of ricotta in the pasta after you put it in the baking dish.

BAKED ZITI WITH SAUSAGE Instead of the mushrooms, cook 8 ounces chopped hot or sweet Italian sausage in Step 1. Stir occasionally until it begins to brown, 5 to 10 minutes. Add the onion and garlic and proceed with the recipe.

Baked Macaroni and Cheese

MAKES: 4 to 6 servings | **TIME:** About 45 minutes

One of the most popular recipes in the original *How to Cook Everything*, which I attribute to too many people growing up with the mac and cheese that comes from

Baked Macaroni and
Cheese, page 499

a box. The real thing is rich, filling, delicious, and dead easy. You can change the type of cheese you use: Try blue cheese, goat cheese, smoked Gouda, or even mascarpone. Or mix in about ½ cup crisp-cooked chunks of thick-cut bacon or pancetta.

Salt and pepper
4 tablespoons (½ stick) butter
2½ cups milk (low-fat is fine)
2 bay leaves
1 pound elbow, shell, ziti, or other cut pasta
3 tablespoons all-purpose flour
1½ cups grated cheese like sharp cheddar or Emmental
½ cup grated Parmesan cheese
¾ cup bread crumbs (preferably fresh; see page 801)

1. Heat the oven to 400°F. Bring a large pot of water to a boil and salt it. Grease a 13 × 9-inch baking pan with 1 tablespoon of the butter.

2. Heat the milk with the bay leaves in a medium saucepan over medium-low heat. When small bubbles appear along the sides, after about 5 minutes, turn off the heat and let stand. Cook the pasta until it's just starting to soften but is still too hard to eat. Drain, rinse it quickly under cold water to stop the cooking, drain again, and put in a large bowl.

3. Melt the remaining 3 tablespoons butter in a large saucepan over medium-low heat. When it foams, add the flour and cook, stirring, until the mixture browns, about 5 minutes. Remove and discard the bay leaves and add about ¼ cup of the milk to the hot roux, stirring with a wire whisk all the while. As soon as the mixture becomes smooth, add a little more milk, and continue to do so until all the milk is added and the mixture is thick and smooth. Add the cheddar or Emmental and stir until it melts.

4. Pour the sauce over the pasta, toss in the Parmesan, and taste and adjust the seasoning, adding some pepper. Transfer the pasta to the prepared pan. (You can make the recipe to this point, cover, and refrigerate for up to a day; return to room temperature before proceeding.)

Sprinkle the bread crumbs on top of the pasta and bake until bubbling and the crumbs turn brown, 15 to 20 minutes. Serve piping hot.

SHORTCUT MACARONI AND CHEESE The ingredients are layered and cooked together so it's less creamy and a little more crusty, but still really good: In Step 1, butter the baking pan with an extra 1 to 2 tablespoons butter. Skip Step 3; instead layer in one-third of the pasta in the prepared pan, sprinkle with half of the flour, fleck with half of the butter, cover with about ½ cup of the grated cheeses, pour half of the heated milk over the top, and sprinkle with salt and pepper. Repeat the layers, using up the remaining flour, butter, and milk. Top with the remaining pasta, cheeses, and the bread crumbs. Bake until bubbling and browned on top, about 30 minutes.

RICH MACARONI AND CHEESE Reduce the milk to ¾ cup. Omit the bay leaves, 3 tablespoons of the butter, and all of the flour; don't heat the milk. Substitute 1½ cups (about 6 ounces) mascarpone for the cheddar. Cook the pasta as directed. Skip Step 3; instead, mix together the milk, mascarpone, and Parmesan in a large bowl. Add the cooked pasta and the sage, sprinkle with salt and pepper, and combine. Proceed with Step 4.

MACARONI AND CHILE CHEESE For a spicy dish, use a hotter chile or add 1 tablespoon chopped chipotle chile with adobo sauce: Use 2 cups grated Jack or cheddar cheese and omit the Parmesan. Add 2 medium poblano or other mild green fresh chiles, roasted, cleaned, and chopped (see page 318) and about ¼ cup chopped fresh cilantro, and use crumbled tortilla chips instead of the bread crumbs. Proceed with the recipe, stirring the chiles and cilantro into the pasta in Step 4, then top with the crumbled chips.

6 GREAT MAC-AND-CHEESE COMBOS

Any pasta will work with any of the cheeses, so mix these up as you like. Some drier hard cheeses, like

Parmesan, Asiago, Manchego, and some pecorinos, are best when combined with softer cheeses; similarly, very strong cheeses are best paired with mild cheeses. Try:

1. Pasta shells with ½ cup cream cheese and 1½ cups grated pecorino cheese
2. Fusilli or corkscrews with 1½ cups grated smoked Gouda or mozzarella and ½ cup Parmesan cheese
3. Wagon wheels with 1½ cups crumbled goat cheese and ½ cup grated pecorino Romano or Parmesan cheese
4. Rotini or spirals with 1 cup crumbled Gorgonzola and 1 cup grated Bel Paese or fontina cheese
5. Tube pastas like penne, rigatoni, and ziti with 1 cup grated Manchego and 1 cup grated Jack
6. Orecchiette with 1 cup ricotta and 1 cup grated Parmesan or pecorino cheese

Meaty Lasagne

MAKES: 6 to 8 servings | **TIME:** 45 minutes with prepared sauces and pasta (or up to several hours start-to-finish)

Spinach pasta is traditional in Bolognese-style lasagne, but really, use any kind of noodle you like here, including whole wheat. If you're making fresh pasta, increase the flour in that recipe to 3 cups; the dough will be stiffer, easier to handle, and will hold up during baking.

You can make all the components of this recipe in advance. I help you with the timing and assembly here, but if you freeze anything it's up to you to have everything thawed, properly seasoned, and ready to go before beginning assembly.

  1 recipe Meat Sauce (page 495; without the spaghetti)
    Salt and pepper
    Softened butter or olive oil for greasing the pan

  1 recipe Fresh Spinach Pasta (page 508) or other fresh pasta, or 1 pound dried lasagne noodles
  1 recipe Béchamel Sauce (page 79; about 1½ cups)
1½ cups grated Parmesan cheese

1. Prepare or reheat the meat sauce and keep it warm. When you're ready to assemble the lasagne, bring at least 5 quarts water to a boil in a large pot and salt it. Grease a 13 × 9-inch baking pan with the butter or oil. If you're using homemade fresh pasta, roll it out to 13 inches long. You will need to cut the noodles so that they fit reasonably snugly into the pan.

2. Cook the noodles a few at a time; keep them underdone (if they're fresh, this means about a minute; about 3 minutes for dried noodles that are pliable but still white at the center). Drain carefully in a colander, then lay flat on clean kitchen towels. Prepare the béchamel sauce if you have not done so already. Heat the oven to 400°F if you'll be baking the lasagne right away.

3. Spread about ½ cup meat sauce over the bottom of the pan and add a layer of noodles, touching but not overlapping. Trim any overhanging edges. Cover the noodles with about one-quarter each of the béchamel, meat sauce, and Parmesan, then a light sprinkle of black pepper. Layer noodles, béchamel, meat sauce, Parmesan, and pepper 3 more times, ending with Parmesan. (At this point, you can wrap the lasagne well and refrigerate it for a day, or freeze for a month; thaw in the refrigerator for a day before proceeding.)

4. Bake until the lasagne is bubbly around the edges and steaming hot in the center, 30 to 60 minutes, depending on how cold it was going into the oven. Remove from the oven and let rest for 5 minutes before cutting into squares and serving.

VEGETARIAN LASAGNE Substitute 3 cups Mushroom Sauce (page 82) or any vegetarian tomato sauce for the Meat Sauce.

MEATY LASAGNE, ITALIAN-AMERICAN STYLE Omit the béchamel. Over each layer of noodles, spread about

1 cup ricotta, thinned if necessary, with some of the sauce. Top the ricotta with meat sauce, the meat sauce with about 1 cup grated mozzarella, and the mozzarella with a sprinkle of Parmesan.

THE BASICS OF FRESH PASTA

Two basic doughs—one flour and egg, the other flour and water—form the backbone of all fresh noodles: pasta, ravioli, gnocchi, dumplings, even spaetzle. The differences are how you shape, sauce, or decide to fill them. This first section focuses on Italian-style pastas but includes variations to make fresh Asian-style noodles too, with recipes that range from rich and eggy to eggless to bright and herby; they're all pretty much classic in both noodle-making traditions.

BASIC PASTA-MAKING TECHNIQUES

You can make fresh pasta by kneading and rolling the dough by hand, but it's far easier to combine and "knead" the ingredients in a food processor, then finish it with a pasta-rolling machine.

For literally handmade pasta, pile your flour on a smooth, clean work surface (for Fresh Egg Pasta) or in a large bowl (for Fresh Eggless Pasta) and create a well in the middle of the flour. Put the eggs or liquids into this well, then use a fork or wooden spoon to incorporate the flour. Once a dough begins to form, use your hands to fully incorporate the remaining flour. It'll be messy at first but should start to come together within a couple of minutes. It's at this point, when the dough is still shaggy, that you want to add more liquid (water or olive oil) or flour in small amounts. You'll know which to add by the look and feel of the dough; if it's mushy and sticking to your hands, you need more flour; if it's not coming together, but separating into dried-out-looking pieces, you need more liquid.

From this point it's a matter of kneading, and although it takes some energy, it's much faster and easier than kneading bread dough. Form the dough into a ball, then sprinkle it and the work surface with flour.

Use the heel of your hand to push into the middle of the dough, fold the dough over, rotate it 90 degrees, and push into it again. Continue kneading until the dough is completely smooth, somewhat skinlike, with some elasticity (if you pull off a piece, it should stretch a bit before breaking; if it breaks off immediately, keep kneading). If the dough is sticking to your hands or the work surface, sprinkle it with flour; it doesn't need to be drowning in flour—just enough to keep it from sticking.

The food processor is not for purists but I like it, and the end result is the same—or nearly the same—as handmade. Put the flour and salt in the processor's work bowl and pulse it a couple of times; add the egg (if you're using it) and a bit of the liquid you're using and turn the machine on. Gradually add the rest of the liquid(s) until the dough forms a ball.

With either method, you must let the dough rest for at least 30 minutes before rolling it out. Then knead the dough by hand (see above) or sprinkle it with enough flour so it doesn't stick and use a pasta-rolling machine to knead it. To knead using a pasta roller, set the rollers to the thickest setting and work the dough through several times, folding it over after each pass. Slowly work your way down to about the middle setting. Let the dough rest again.

Basic Pasta-Making Techniques

To make the pasta by hand, first make a well in the mound of flour and break the eggs into it.

To knead the dough, use the heel of your hand to push into the middle of the dough, fold the dough over, rotate it 90 degrees, and push into it again.

Using a Manual Pasta Machine

STEP 1 Begin by putting a piece of dough through the thickest setting, usually #1.

STEP 2 Decrease the distance between the two rollers, making the strip of dough progressively thinner. Note that as the dough becomes longer, it will become more fragile. Dust with flour between rollings if necessary.

Cutting Pasta

STEP 1 To make any broad noodle, sprinkle the pasta sheet lightly with cornmeal or flour, roll it loosely, and cut across the roll at the desired width.

STEP 2 Sprinkle with more cornmeal and leave the noodles in a tangle (short term) or hang individually to dry if not using right away.

USING A MANUAL PASTA-ROLLING MACHINE

If fresh pasta is something you make—or intend to make—regularly, a reliable pasta-rolling machine is essential. Though you can roll pasta without one: Just use a rolling pin, roll from the center, out and keep flouring and turning the dough. But a machine will cut your rolling time by at least half, and most come with a cutter attachment, which will also save you time and give you beautifully cut pasta. These machines are simple to use, easy to maintain, and worth the investment.

1. Secure the machine to a sturdy counter or tabletop, making sure the crank handle has clearance and there is surface area on both sides of the machine.

2. Sprinkle the machine and surrounding surfaces with flour and set the rollers to their thickest setting (most machines use sequential numbers to indicate settings, but some use letters or tick marks).

3. Dust the portion of dough with flour and pass it through the machine. Add more flour if the dough sticks. Repeat passing the dough through the machine.

4. Decrease the separation of the rollers by one notch and pass the dough through again; continue decreasing the thickness one notch at a time and rolling the dough. If the dough tears or sticks, ball it up and start over.

5. When you get to the thinnest setting, cut the sheet of pasta in half so it's a more manageable length. Roll the sheet through twice more; it's now ready for cutting, stuffing, or freezing.

6. To clean the machine, use a clean, dry pastry or paint brush to brush off the flour. Use a dinner knife to scrape off any bits of dough stuck to the rollers, and wipe off the exterior with a damp towel. Do not wash; any flour in it will gum up and the gears may rust.

 **F** fast **M** make ahead **V** vegetarian

Using Other Flours in Fresh Pasta

This chart is a quick reference for using alternative flours in any of the fresh pasta recipes.

Two important considerations: Flours that contain little or no gluten, like buckwheat, cannot make the same kind of chewy, tender pasta that all-purpose flour does. It's the gluten in flour that enables the dough to be rolled thin and hold its shape when boiled. The other factor is flavor. Buckwheat and whole wheat must be combined with all-purpose flour or the pasta will be too bitter.

FLOUR	EFFECT ON TEXTURE AND FLAVOR	QUANTITY TO USE IN RECIPE
Semolina	Pleasant grittiness, but that grainy texture makes it trickier to handle	2 cups semolina
Whole wheat	Nuttier flavor and more fiber, but dough will be stiffer and less elastic	1 cup whole wheat and 1 cup all-purpose flour
Buckwheat (finely ground)	Delicate texture and flavor, but dough tears more easily	1½ cups buckwheat and ½ cup all-purpose flour
Whole durum wheat	Excellent taste and handling results, but tough to find	2 cups whole wheat durum flour

CUTTING PASTA

Cutting the pasta into shapes is really fun, and these can be just about anything (even maltagliati—"badly cut"—is traditional; cook the scraps as you would any fresh pasta, or add them to a soup or broth). Use the machine's cutting attachment for long, flat fettuccine or tagliatelle, and your knife or a pasta or pizza cutter, or fluted pastry wheel for other shapes and sizes (see "Free-Form Pasta," page 507).

To hand-cut fettuccine, pappardelle, lasagne, or other ribbonlike pasta, dust the sheet of pasta with flour, loosely roll it lengthwise, and cut the roll crosswise as wide or narrow as you like. So the cut pasta doesn't stick together, you can toss it with a bit more flour or fine cornmeal. You can leave the noodles in a tangle if you'll be cooking them shortly, or hang them individually to dry (on a pasta-drying rack if you have one, but you can also use the backs of chairs or clothes hangers) if not using right away. Homemade fresh pasta is best used the day it is cut.

Fresh Egg Pasta

MAKES: 4 servings (about 1 pound) | **TIME:** At least 1 hour, somewhat unattended

From the Emilia-Romagna region in Italy comes a rich, golden pasta, colored by egg yolks. Because this recipe contains a good amount of egg, the dough is moist and forgiving—a benefit if you're a beginner.

- 2 **cups all-purpose flour, plus more as needed**
- 1 **teaspoon salt**
- 2 **whole eggs**
- 3 **egg yolks**

1. WITH A FOOD PROCESSOR: Put the flour and salt in the work bowl and pulse once or twice. Add the eggs and yolks all at once and turn the machine on. Process just until a ball begins to form, about 30 seconds. Add a few drops of water if the dough is dry and grainy; add a tablespoon of flour if the dough sticks to the side of the bowl.

Fresh Egg Pasta, page 505,
made with all-purpose
flour (left) and Pizzocheri
(right)

BY HAND: Combine 1½ cups of the flour and the salt on a counter or large board. Make a well in the middle. Put the eggs and yolks into this well. Beat the eggs with a fork, gradually incorporating the flour, a little at a time. When it becomes too hard to stir with the fork, use your hands. When all the flour on the surface has been mixed in, knead the dough, pushing it against the counter and folding it repeatedly, until it is not at all sticky and has become quite stiff. Add only small amounts of the remaining flour during kneading, if you absolutely need it.

2. Sprinkle the dough with a little flour and cover with plastic wrap or a kitchen towel; let it rest for about 30 minutes. (At this point, you can refrigerate the dough, wrapped in plastic, until you're ready to roll it out, up to 24 hours.)

3. Clean your hands and clamp a pasta machine to the counter; sprinkle the work surface lightly with flour. Cut off about one-third of the dough; keep the rest wrapped in plastic or covered with a towel while you work. Roll the dough lightly in flour and use your hands to flatten it into a rectangle about the width of the machine. Set the machine to its thickest setting and crank the dough through. If it sticks, dust it with a little more flour. Repeat. Set the machine to its next-thinnest setting and repeat. Each time, if the pasta sticks, sprinkle it with a little more flour, and each time put the dough through the machine twice.

4. Continue to work your way down—or up, as the case may be; each machine is numbered differently—through the numbers. If at any point the dough tears badly, bunch it together and start again; you will quickly get the hang of it. Use as much flour as you need to, but in small amounts each time.

5. Pass the dough through the machine's thinnest setting; if this fails, pass it through the next-thicker one. Repeat two more times (by this time it will be going quickly), then flour the dough lightly, cover it, and get it out of the way. Repeat the process with the remaining dough.

6. Cut each sheet into rectangles roughly 16 inches long; trim the ends to make it neat. At this point the dough is ready to be used. You can leave it as sheets to make lasagne or stuffed pasta, cut the sheets with a sharp knife to make noodles, or pass the dough through the machine once more, this time using the desired cutting attachment. Cook right away, or hang the strands to dry for up to a couple of hours.

7. To cook the noodles, drop them into boiling salted water; they'll be done when tender, in less than 3 minutes, probably less than 2. Sauce them immediately and serve.

PIZZOCHERI The robust buckwheat pasta of northeastern Italy. It's more fragile to work with, but a treat to eat: Use 1½ cups fine buckwheat flour and ½ cup all-purpose flour. Roll and cut as wide as

Free-Form Pasta

Cut pasta is gorgeous, but free-form pasta, which ranges in shape and size from small pinches of dough to fat ribbons or whatever you like, is also appealing and equally traditional. To avoid rolling dough altogether, check out Spaetzle (page 519).

Pasta grattata: Literally "grated dough," the simplest fresh pasta, usually served in the broth in which it's cooked. Use either Fresh Egg Pasta or Fresh Eggless Pasta dough; let it rest in the refrigerator for at least 30 minutes. Using the largest holes on a box grater, grate the dough while still very cold; keep the pasta shreds as separate as possible. Cook as you would any fresh pasta.

Pasta handkerchiefs: Roll either Fresh Egg Pasta or Fresh Eggless Pasta dough and cut it into squares no larger than 4 inches across; cook as you would any fresh pasta.

Wide pasta ribbons: Think lasagne, but narrower. Roll either Fresh Egg Pasta or Fresh Eggless Pasta dough and cut it into ribbons as wide as you like; cook as you would any fresh pasta.

tagliatelle, but the finished noodles should be about 3 inches long.

CHINESE-STYLE EGG NOODLES The recipe remains the same, so you roll the dough as thin as possible. Then cut the noodles either up to an inch wide or very narrow, in shorter strands than you would Italian pasta.

HERBED FRESH PASTA Use 3 whole eggs and omit the extra yolks. Add 1 tablespoon chopped fresh sage, 1 teaspoon chopped fresh rosemary or thyme, or ¼ cup chopped fresh basil, chervil, or parsley (or minced if mixing by hand) when you add the eggs. If using basil, chervil, or parsley, to keep the dough from sticking during kneading, you may need to add about ¼ cup more flour.

FRESH SPINACH PASTA Deep color; subtle spinach flavor: Use 3 whole eggs and omit the extra yolks. Stem, rinse, and steam 8 ounces fresh spinach, or thaw 4 ounces frozen spinach. Drain, squeeze to get as much water out as possible, and chop (or mince if mixing by hand). Add the spinach with the eggs, making sure to break up any clumps when mixing. To keep the dough from sticking during kneading, you may need to add about ½ cup more flour.

ORANGE PASTA Neutral-tasting but a stunner: Use 3 whole eggs and omit the extra yolks. Add 2 tablespoons tomato paste when you add the eggs. Make sure everything gets thoroughly mixed. To keep the dough from sticking during kneading, you may need to add a little extra flour.

FUCHSIA PASTA Brilliantly hued: Use 3 whole eggs and omit the extra yolks. Bake 8 ounces beets as in Beets Baked in Foil (page 264). When cool enough to handle, peel, chop, and purée in a food processor until smooth. Squeeze out any excess moisture using cheesecloth. Add ½ cup of the well-drained purée with the eggs. To keep the dough from sticking during kneading, you might need to add up to an additional 1 cup flour.

5 OTHER FLAVORED PASTAS

There are many add-ins that will bring a touch of flavor and color to fresh pasta dough. Serve black pepper pasta with Spicy Tomato Sauce (page 481); saffron, mushroom, and herb pastas (page 508) are lovely with a simple, rich sauce like Brown Butter (page 78) or Reduction Sauce (page 81); toss the tomato and roasted garlic versions with olive oil and lots of Parmesan or pecorino.

1. **Black Pepper Pasta:** Freshly grind about a tablespoon black pepper into the flour.
2. **Saffron Pasta:** Steep a large pinch crumbled saffron threads in a couple of tablespoons hot water; add along with the eggs in Fresh Egg Pasta (page 505) or with the hot water in Fresh Eggless Pasta (page 508). You may need a little more flour to compensate for the extra liquid.
3. **Mushroom Pasta:** Grind dried mushrooms to a fine powder in a clean coffee or spice grinder and add to the flour; you want a tablespoon or 2 powder. Porcini are excellent.
4. **Tomato Pasta:** Use completely dry tomatoes (see Oven-Dried Tomatoes, page 348). Grind them to a fine powder in a clean coffee or spice grinder and add to the flour; you want a tablespoon or 2 powder.
5. **Roasted Garlic Pasta:** Mash several cloves Roasted Garlic (page 294) to a smooth paste; add along with the eggs in Fresh Egg Pasta (page 505) or hot water in Fresh Eggless Pasta (below), making sure to mix the garlic in very well. You may need to add more flour to compensate for the extra liquid in the garlic.

Fresh Eggless Pasta

MAKES: 4 servings (about 1 pound) | **TIME:** At least 1 hour, somewhat unattended

Just as simple and almost as easy to work with as the egg pasta, though less rich.

   fast   make ahead   vegetarian

2 **cups all-purpose flour, plus more as needed**

1 **teaspoon salt**

2 **tablespoons butter, softened, or olive oil**

1. WITH A FOOD PROCESSOR: Put the flour and salt in the container and pulse once or twice. Turn the machine on and add ½ cup hot water and the butter or oil through the feed tube. Process just until a ball begins to form, about 30 seconds. Add a few drops of water if the dough is dry and grainy; add a tablespoon flour if the dough sticks to the side of the bowl.

BY HAND: Combine the flour and salt on a counter or large board. Make a well in the middle. Put the butter or oil in this well, along with about ½ cup hot water. Beat the butter and water with a fork, gradually incorporating a little of the flour at a time. When it becomes too hard to stir with the fork, use your hands. When all the flour has been mixed in, knead the dough, pushing it against the counter and folding it repeatedly until it is not at all sticky and is quite stiff. Add water ½ teaspoon at a time if the mixture is dry and not coming together; add flour if it is sticky.

2. Sprinkle the dough with a little flour and cover with plastic wrap or a cloth; let it rest for about 30 minutes. (At this point, you can refrigerate the dough, wrapped in plastic, until you're ready to roll it out, up to 24 hours.) Clean your hands, then follow Steps 3 through 8 in the Fresh Egg Pasta recipe (page 505) for rolling, cutting, and cooking.

ASIAN-STYLE DUMPLING WRAPPERS Omit the butter and add more water, a little at a time, to reach the consistency described. Rest the dough as directed. Knead the dough for a minute, then cut it into 4 pieces. On a lightly floured surface, roll each piece into a 1-inch log, then cut into 1-inch pieces and roll each one out from the center to form a 4-inch round or square, adding a bit more flour if necessary. (You can also roll sheets of dough with a pasta-rolling machine, then cut it into the desired shapes; see page 504.) Use immediately or dust with flour, stack, wrap tightly, and refrigerate for up to a couple of days or freeze for up to 2 weeks. For filling ideas, see page 513.

THE BASICS OF STUFFED PASTA

In Italy alone there are dozens of different types of stuffed pastas, from simple rolls to complex folds. I'm focusing on a few basics: ravioli (squares), tortellini (folded loops), and cannelloni (large open-ended tubes), which can all be stuffed with any of the fillings that appear in the following recipes.

Making Dumpling or Wonton Skins and Egg Roll Wrappers

STEP 1 Make the dough for Asian-Style Dumpling Wrappers (above). On a lightly floured surface, roll the dough into a log about 1 inch wide.

STEP 2 Cut the log into 1-inch pieces.

STEP 3 Roll each piece out from the center to form a thin 4-inch circle or square, adding a bit of flour if necessary.

STEP 4 To make larger egg roll wrappers, roll the log into a rectangle, no more than ¼ inch thick.

STEP 5 Cut into 4-inch squares.

Though it's not ideal, you can freeze stuffed pasta to cook another time. Once it's made, dust with cornmeal and freeze on a baking sheet for a few hours to keep the pieces separate. Then seal in zipper bags and store in the freezer for up to a couple of months.

STUFFING PASTA

Your choice: If you like a moist, gooey stuffing, stuff the pasta with a soft cheese like ricotta; adding a sharper-tasting cheese like goat or sheep's milk cheese gives more character. For contrasting texture, mix in chopped herbs, vegetables, or nuts. For a drier filling, start with bread crumbs, or chopped or puréed vegetables.

SERVING STUFFED PASTA

Once the labor-intensive rolling and stuffing is done, cooking and saucing is fast. Generally, if the stuffing is well contained, as with ravioli or tortellini, you boil and sauce them like any other pasta. Or if you like, you can boil, then sauté in a butter or oil sauce (like herbed

Brown Butter; see page 79) to develop a crust on one side, then finish the sauce with some pasta cooking water and grated cheese.

If the pasta is loosely stuffed, as with cannelloni, it's best baked directly in the sauce (see Spinach-Cheese Cannelloni, page 514). And small stuffed pasta like tortellini can be cooked and served in broth and brothy soups.

Butternut Squash Pansotti

MAKES: 4 servings (about 60 pansotti) | TIME: 2 hours (or less than an hour with cooked squash and prepared pasta sheets)

It takes only one fold to create these triangular packages—perfect for beginners, and anytime you don't want to fuss. Serve in Brown Butter (page 78) with sage or rosemary leaves, or the sauce from Pasta with Garlic and Oil or any of the variations (page 476). Or make the sauce from One-Pot Pasta with Butter and Parmesan (page 478) or any of its variations (see page 480) in a large skillet and toss the cooked pansotti with it along with some of the pasta cooking water until coated.

- 2 cups roasted butternut squash (see page 349)
- ½ cup grated Parmesan cheese
- ½ teaspoon freshly grated nutmeg
  Salt and pepper
- 2 eggs
  Cornmeal or all-purpose flour for dusting
- 1 recipe Fresh Egg Pasta (page 505) or Fresh Eggless Pasta (page 508), rolled out into sheets and kept moist under plastic wrap or a kitchen towel

1. Purée the squash, preferably by passing it through a food mill or ricer. Put it in a bowl with the Parmesan, nutmeg, and some salt and pepper and mix; taste and

Meat Tortellini, page 514

adjust the seasoning, adding more nutmeg if you'd like. Beat in the eggs.

2. Lightly dust the work surface with cornmeal or flour. Working with a few sheets at a time, cut the pasta dough so that it is 4 to 5 inches wide, then cut into 2- to 2½-inch squares. Brush the dough very lightly with water so it will stick together when you shape the pansotti. Put a rounded teaspoon of stuffing on each square and fold in half to make a triangle, pressing tightly to seal the edges. Put the pansotti on baking sheets, dusting them with cornmeal and keeping them separate, until you're ready to cook. (At this point, you can loosely wrap and refrigerate the pansotti on the pans for up to a day. Or freeze them for 24 hours, then transfer them to airtight containers for up to 3 months.)

3. Bring a large pot of water to a boil and salt it. Cook the pansotti, 30 or so at a time, until they rise to the surface, which will take just a few minutes. Drain, sauce, and serve right away.

SWEET POTATO PANSOTTI Wonderful boiled and sautéed with olive oil and pecans or walnuts (for the technique, see Pasta with Garlic, Oil, and Nuts, page 478): Substitute cooked sweet potato for the butternut squash and omit the sugar.

CHESTNUT PANSOTTI Perfect with the sauce from One-Pot Pasta with Butter and Parmesan (page 478): Substitute crumbled peeled cooked chestnuts (see page 282) for the butternut squash. Add 3 tablespoons minced shallot or onion if you like, and mix in with the eggs.

Spinach-Ricotta Ravioli

MAKES: 4 to 6 servings (about 40 ravioli) | **TIME:** About 1 hour with prepared pasta sheets

The most recognizable stuffed pasta. Serve it with Fast Tomato Sauce (page 478), Traditional Pesto (page 51), or the sauce from One-Pot Fettuccine Alfredo (page 480).

1	egg
1½	cups ricotta, drained in a strainer for a few minutes
1	cup grated Parmesan cheese
1	cup cooked fresh spinach (about 8 ounces raw), squeezed dry and chopped
¼	cup chopped fresh parsley
1	teaspoon minced garlic
¼	teaspoon freshly grated nutmeg
	Salt
	Cornmeal or all- purpose flour for dusting
1	recipe Fresh Egg Pasta (page 505) or Fresh Eggless Pasta (page 508), rolled out into sheets and kept moist under plastic wrap or a kitchen towel

1. Put the egg, ricotta, Parmesan, spinach, parsley, garlic, nutmeg, and Parmesan in a bowl and mix well. (At this point, you can refrigerate the stuffing, covered, for up to a day.)

2. Put a little water in a small bowl and lightly dust the work surface with cornmeal or flour. Cut each pasta sheet lengthwise into 4-inch-wide strips. Drop heaping teaspoons of the stuffing at about 1½-inch intervals, about

Making Cannelloni

To make cannelloni, put a small amount of filling about an inch up from the shorter end (nearest you), spreading it almost but not quite to the sides; then roll up.

28 Dishes for Stuffing Pasta

From caramelized onions to mashed favas. Drain off excess liquids and mash, crumble, or finely chop large pieces as you like. Then use as filling for any of the recipes in this section.

1. Puréed Vegetables (page 240)
2. Roasted Artichoke Hearts (page 261)
3. Crunchy Broccoli or Cauliflower (page 268)
4. Broccoli Raab with Garlic and Pecorino (page 272)
5. Sauerkraut and Cabbage (page 275)
6. Chard with Olives and Feta (page 282)
7. Sautéed Eggplant with Basil (page 290)
8. Roasted Garlic (page 294), peeled and roughly mashed
9. Sautéed Mushrooms (page 306)
10. Caramelized Onions (page 315)
11. Anything-Scented Peas (page 317)
12. Spinach with Currants and Nuts (page 339)
13. Baked Sweet Potatoes (page 343)
14. Oven-Roasted Plum Tomatoes (page 347)
15. Roasted Whole Winter Squash and its variations (page 349)
16. White Beans, Tuscan Style (page 402)
17. Broiled Fish Fillets (and a Lot Else) (page 534)
18. Roasted Shrimp (page 537)
19. Salmon Roasted in Butter (page 549)
20. Steamed Clams or Mussels (page 579)
21. Sautéed Chicken with Wine Sauce (page 607)
22. Breaded Chicken Cutlets (page 608)
23. Carbonnade (page 680)
24. Braised Beef Brisket (page 684)
25. Braised Pork with White Wine and Celery Root (page 699)
26. Italian-Style Sausage, Sweet or Hot (page 703)
27. Lamb Stew with Cinnamon and Lemon (page 710)
28. Shortcut Ricotta (page 758)

1 inch from one long edge of a strip (that is, about 3 inches from the other edge). Dampen the edges with a little water (the tip of your finger is a fine tool for this), then fold the dough over onto itself, pressing with your fingers to seal. Trim the dough with a sharp knife or fluted pasta cutter, then cut into individual ravioli. (You can prepare the ravioli up to this point in advance; dust with cornmeal or flour, cover loosely with plastic wrap, and refrigerate for up to a day. Or cover tightly and freeze; transfer to zipper bags when frozen, and keep for up to a couple months.)

3. Bring a large pot of water to a boil and salt it. Cook the ravioli, 20 to 30 at a time, until they rise to the surface, which will take just a few minutes. Drain, sauce, and serve immediately.

RICOTTA AND HERB RAVIOLI Substitute 1 cup chopped mild fresh herbs like basil, parsley, chives, chervil, mint, or dill for the spinach.

CHEESE RAVIOLI Herbed Fresh Pasta (page 508) is really nice here: Substitute bread crumbs, preferably fresh (see page 801) for the spinach. For stronger flavor, use a sharper cheese, like aged pecorino, to replace some of the Parmesan.

SPINACH RAVIOLI Or use chard, kale, or dandelion greens: Increase the spinach to 2 cups and add ¼ cup chopped fresh herbs like sage, chervil, basil, fresh fennel fronds, or a mixture. Omit the egg and ricotta.

MUSHROOM-CHEESE RAVIOLI Use any kind of mushrooms you like: Substitute ¾ cup Sautéed Mushrooms (page 306) for the spinach and reduce the ricotta to 1¼ cups. Drain the mushrooms and finely chop.

SPINACH-CHEESE CANNELLONI Make Fast Tomato Sauce (page 478). Heat the oven to 375°F. Cut the pasta sheets into rectangles about 4×6 inches, boil them until they soften a little, 1 to 2 minutes, then drain. Working with one piece at a time, use a tablespoon to dollop a line of filling along the short side, about an inch from the edge; roll the pasta into a tube. Spread a thin layer of sauce in a 13-×9-inch baking dish and add the cannelloni, side by side in a single layer. Cover with the remaining sauce, sprinkle with grated Parmesan, and bake until bubbling, about 20 minutes.

Meat Tortellini

MAKES: 4 to 6 servings (50 to 60 tortellini) | **TIME:** About 2 hours with prepared pasta sheets

Since they're small and have multiple folds, tortellini can be a little tricky to make the first time. You can make them bigger if you like—and call them tortelloni—or use this filling to make ravioli, which are easier. Serve in a flavorful broth or with Fast Tomato Sauce (page 478) or any of the sauces from One-Pot Pasta with Butter and Parmesan and its variations (page 478).

Making Tortellini

STEP 1 On a counter dusted lightly with cornmeal or flour, cut fresh pasta dough so it is 4 to 5 inches wide. Cut into 2- to 2½-inch squares.

STEP 2 Brush the dough very lightly with water.

STEP 3 Place a small mound of filling on each square.

STEP 4 Fold into a triangle, pressing tightly to seal the edges.

STEP 5 Fold the widest point toward the filling.

STEP 6 Pick up the triangle and press the two bottom points together. Place your finger inside the ring and fold over the top of the dough inside the circle. Press to seal. Keep the tortellini separate until you are ready to cook.

F fast **M** make ahead **V** vegetarian

- 2 tablespoons olive oil
- 1 pound ground meat (preferably a mixture of beef, veal, and pork or pork sausage)
- 1 cup red wine or beef or chicken stock (to make your own, see page 176), plus more if needed
  Salt and pepper
- 1 teaspoon minced garlic
- ¼ cup chopped prosciutto or other ham (optional)
- ½ cup chopped fresh parsley
- ½ cup grated Parmesan cheese
- 1 egg
  Bread crumbs (preferably fresh; see page 801), if needed
  Cornmeal or all-purpose flour for dusting
- 1 recipe Fresh Egg Pasta (page 505) or Fresh Eggless Pasta (page 508), rolled out into sheets and kept moist under plastic wrap or a kitchen towel

1. Put the oil in a large skillet over medium heat. When it is hot, add the meat and cook, stirring and breaking up any lumps, until it's no longer pink, about 10 minutes. Add the wine and sprinkle with salt and pepper. Adjust the heat so the liquid barely bubbles and cook, stirring occasionally and adding more liquid if the pan becomes dry, until the meat is tender and the filling thickened, about 45 minutes.
2. Add the garlic and the prosciutto if you're using it and cook, stirring occasionally, until the garlic softens, about 5 minutes. Remove from the heat and cool completely. Add the parsley, Parmesan, and egg and stir until thoroughly combined. If the mixture is liquidy, stir in some bread crumbs. (At this point, you can refrigerate the filling, covered, for up to a day.)
3. Lightly dust the work surface with cornmeal or flour. Cut the pasta dough so that it is 4 to 5 inches wide, then cut into 2- to 2½-inch squares.
4. Brush the dough lightly with water so it will stick together when you shape the tortellini. Put a rounded teaspoon of stuffing on each square and fold into a triangle, pressing tightly to seal the edges. Fold the widest point toward the stuffing, then pick up the

triangle and press the two bottom points together. Put your finger inside the newly formed ring and fold over the top of the dough inside the circle. Press to seal. Keep the tortellini separate on cornmeal- or flour-dusted baking sheets until you're ready to cook. (At this point, you can dust the tortellini with flour, cover loosely with plastic wrap, and refrigerate for up to a day. Or cover tightly and freeze; transfer them to zipper bags once frozen and keep for up to 3 months.)
5. Bring a large pot of water to a boil and salt it. Cook the tortellini, 30 or so at a time, until they rise to the surface, which will take just a few minutes. Drain, sauce, and serve right away.

CHEESE TORTELLINI Omit the olive oil, ground meat, wine, garlic, and ham, and skip Steps 1 and 2. Instead, drain 1 pound ricotta cheese in a strainer for a few minutes and combine it with the parsley, Parmesan, and egg and add a pinch nutmeg; sprinkle with a little salt and pepper. Use this mixture to fill the tortellini.

SEAFOOD TORTELLINI Substitute skinless white fish fillets like flounder or cod, peeled shrimp, or cooked lobster or crabmeat for the ground meat. Omit the wine, garlic, prosciutto, and Parmesan. Cook raw seafood by steaming (see page 558), poaching or boiling (see page 550), or sautéing (see page 537). Chop or flake the seafood and mix it with the parsley, egg, 3 tablespoons minced shallot or onion, a sprinkle of salt, and a pinch cayenne instead of black pepper. Add bread crumbs only if absolutely necessary. Use this mixture to fill the tortellini.

THE BASICS OF GNOCCHI AND OTHER DUMPLINGS

Gnocchi (pronounced, kind of, NYO-kee) are easy-to-make Italian dumplings. The basic formula combines cooked potatoes, flour, and sometimes an egg; they're then boiled and sauced like pasta. The starch in the potatoes is mostly what holds gnocchi together, so use baking potatoes (see page 325).

You can also make dumplings from spinach, sweet potatoes or other roots and tubers, fresh cheeses, or ground grains like semolina or cornmeal. Most of the recipes in this section are Italian, but Spaetzle (page 518) hails from Alsace. For Asian dumplings and wontons, see the Appetizers chapter.

GNOCCHI TECHNIQUE

Making the lightest gnocchi requires a dough that combines potato and flour, with gentle mixing. The first time you make them you'll probably use a bit too much flour and overmix the dough, but don't be discouraged if your gnocchi aren't delicate and fluffy. You'll improve with each batch and get to the point where it's easy enough to make gnocchi for lunch.

Indenting the gnocchi with your finger or rolling them over a fork, cheese grater, or special gnocchi board is optional, but the texture helps them grab the sauce. To indent the dumplings, flour your thumb and roll it over the gnocchi. Using the fork, grater, or board takes some practice; use your thumb to roll the gnocchi over the tines or ridges—your thumb will simultaneously indent the opposite side.

TIPS FOR MAKING GREAT GNOCCHI

- Use freshly cooked potatoes; leftover baked or mashed potatoes are better for croquettes.

- Add the flour in small amounts so you don't add too much.

- Mix and then knead the dough gently; you're trying to not overdevelop the gluten.

- Keep your work surface well floured so the gnocchi don't stick.

- Roll the logs out quickly and don't worry too much about getting them perfectly even, which may overwork the dough. They're supposed to look handmade!

- Test-cook a piece of the dough just as it comes together; it may be closer to ready than you think.

Making Gnocchi

STEP 1 Start by rolling a piece of the dough into a log. Use flour as needed to prevent sticking, but try to keep it to a minimum.

STEP 2 Cut the dough into approximately 1-inch lengths.

STEP 3 Roll each of the sections off the back of a fork to give it the characteristic ridges.

F fast M make ahead V vegetarian

Pan-cooking or roasting cooked gnocchi, or baking them with a premade sauce, adds color, richness, and flavor.

To sauté: Put a couple of tablespoons olive oil or butter in a skillet over high heat; when the oil is hot or the butter foams, add a layer of cooked gnocchi, careful not to overcrowd the pan. Cook, shaking the pan occasionally, until they brown in places, 5 to 10 minutes.

To roast: Heat the oven to 450°F. Toss the cooked gnocchi with 3 tablespoons olive oil or melted butter and put on a rimmed baking sheet; roast, shaking the pan to roll the gnocchi every couple of minutes, until all the sides are golden, 5 to 10 minutes.

To bake them in a sauce: Heat the oven to 425°F. Grease a 2-quart gratin or other baking dish and add the gnocchi. Spoon on a sauce like Fast Tomato Sauce (page 478) or the sauce from Spaghetti with Meat Sauce (page 495), or toss them in melted butter and sprinkle with cheese (or other topping; see "14 Seafood, Meat, and Poultry Dishes That Work as Pasta Sauces," page 494). Bake until the sauce is bubbling and hot, 10 to 15 minutes, depending on the size of the dish.

Potato Gnocchi

MAKES: 4 servings | **TIME:** 1½ hours

The classic recipe, with variations. Whenever you add ingredients to gnocchi dough, they won't be quite as ethereal, but will still be fluffy and flavorful. For the sauce, I suggest simple butter or a tomato sauce—with Parmesan of course. Or once you get into making these, you can explore using some of the other pasta sauces in this chapter.

- 1 **pound starchy potatoes, scrubbed**
  Salt and pepper
- 1 **cup all-purpose flour, plus more as needed**
- ¼ **cup butter or 1 recipe any Tomato Sauce**
  (pages 478–482)
  Grated Parmesan cheese to taste

1. Put the potatoes in a large pot with salted water to cover. Bring to a boil, adjust the heat so the water bubbles steadily, and cook until the potatoes are quite tender, about 45 minutes. Drain and peel—use a pot holder or kitchen towel to hold the potatoes and peel with a small knife; it will be easy. Rinse the pot, fill it again with salted water, and bring to a boil.

2. Use a fork, potato masher, or ricer to mash or rice the potatoes in a bowl. Sprinkle with salt and pepper. Add about ½ cup of the flour and stir; add more flour until the mixture forms a dough you can handle. Knead on a lightly floured work surface for a minute or so. Pinch off a small piece of the dough and boil it to make sure it will hold its shape; if it does not, knead in a bit more flour. The idea is to get a dough with as little additional flour and kneading as possible.

3. Roll a piece of the dough into a rope about ½ inch thick, then cut the rope into 1-inch lengths; traditionally, you would spin each of these pieces off the tines of a fork to score it lightly. As each one is ready, put it on a sheet of wax paper dusted with flour; do not allow them to touch.

4. Melt the butter (or heat the sauce) in a large skillet and keep warm. Add the gnocchi to the boiling water a few at a time; stir. You will need to work in a couple of batches so they aren't too crowded in the pot. A minute after they rise to the surface, the gnocchi are done; transfer them to the sauce with a slotted spoon. Toss with the sauce and some Parmesan cheese to coat and eat within a few minutes; these do not keep well.

HERB GNOCCHI Fold ½ cup chopped fresh herbs like basil, parsley, mint, dill, chives, or chervil into the mashed potatoes.

SPINACH GNOCCHI Stem, wash, and steam 10 ounces fresh spinach (see page 339), or thaw 5 ounces frozen spinach. For either, drain, squeeze (get as much water out as possible), and chop it as fine as you can manage. Add it to the potatoes along with the flour; add a pinch nutmeg if you like.

SWEET POTATO OR BUTTERNUT SQUASH GNOCCHI Substitute sweet potatoes or butternut squash for the potatoes. It's best to roast or steam sweet potatoes or squash, because they will absorb too much water if boiled. If you're using butternut squash, add an egg and mix it in with the mashed squash; you will likely need more flour too.

Gnudi with Noodles

MAKES: About 4 servings | **TIME:** 45 minutes

You don't pronounce g in *gnudi*, so the translation from Italian is more obvious. These are "naked" ravioli—the stuffing is cooked like dumplings, separate from the pasta. The recipe here includes a simple butter-cheese sauce but you can also use any of the tomato sauces on pages 478 to 482.

- 1 pound ground meat (preferably half veal and half pork, but you can use any combination you like)
- 1 egg
- ¼ cup grated Parmesan cheese, plus more for serving
- ¼ cup chopped fresh parsley
- ¼ cup chopped onion
  Salt and pepper
- 1 pound pappardelle or other fresh or dried pasta
- 4 tablespoons (½ stick) butter
- 20 fresh sage leaves

1. Put the meat in a bowl with the egg, cheese, parsley, onion, and a sprinkle of salt and pepper. Mix well but do not knead. Form into tiny round dumplings about ½ inch

in diameter, and put on a rimmed baking sheet. Refrigerate until you're ready to cook, for up to several hours. When you're ready, bring a large pot of water to a boil and salt it.

2. Heat the oven to 200°F and have a baking dish handy. Working in batches, cook the dumplings in the boiling water until they're firm and float to the surface, about 5 minutes. As they finish, transfer them to the baking dish with a slotted spoon. Put them in the oven to keep warm.

3. Cook the pasta in the same water until tender but not mushy; start tasting after 5 minutes. Meanwhile, put the butter in a large skillet over medium heat; when it foams, add the sage and cook, stirring frequently, until the butter and sage leaves are light brown, about 5 minutes.

4. Drain the pasta, reserving about 1 cup of the cooking water, then toss it with the sage-butter sauce, adding enough of the pasta cooking water to coat the noodles. Top with the gnudi and serve, passing grated Parmesan at the table.

VEGETARIAN RAVIOLI NUDI Substitute 1 cup bread crumbs, preferably fresh (see page 801), for the meat. Add another egg and increase the Parmesan to ¾ cup and the parsley to ½ cup. Allow the bread crumb mixture to rest for at least 10 minutes before shaping into balls. Proceed with the recipe, cooking the dumplings until they rise to the surface, about 3 minutes.

Spaetzle

MAKES: 4 servings | **TIME:** 30 minutes

Half noodle, half dumpling, spaetzle are made from a pancake-like batter that's dropped into gently boiling water. They might be seasoned and served plain with butter, sautéed and sauced, or added to broth or soup.

There are many techniques for dropping the batter into the water—with a spaetzle maker (it looks like a grater without sharp edges, with an attachment that slides across the top), through a colander, or simply dropping it from a spoon, as I do.

Salt and pepper

2 cups all-purpose flour

3 eggs

1 cup milk, plus more if needed

2 tablespoons butter or olive oil, plus more
   as necessary

   Chopped fresh parsley or chives for garnish

1. Bring a large pot of water to a boil and salt it. Have a large bowl of ice water ready. Combine the flour with ½ teaspoon pepper (or more to taste) and a large pinch salt in a large bowl. Beat the eggs and milk together in a separate bowl and stir into the flour. If necessary, add a little more milk to make a batter about the consistency of pancake batter.

2. Scoop about a tablespoon of the batter and drop it into the boiling water; small pieces may break off, but the batter should remain largely intact and form an uneven disk. Spoon in one-third to one-fourth of the batter, depending on the size of your pot. When the spaetzle rise to the top, which will take just a few minutes—you may have to loosen them from the bottom, but they'll float right up—cook for about another minute, then transfer with a slotted spoon or strainer to the bowl of ice water. Repeat until all the batter is used.

3. Drain the spaetzle. (At this point, you can toss them with a bit of oil and refrigerate, covered, for up to a day.) Put 2 tablespoons of the butter or oil in a large skillet over medium-high heat. When the butter foams or the oil is hot, add the spaetzle in a single layer, working in batches. Cook, shaking the pan and stirring until the dumplings are brown in places, just a couple minutes. Remove from the pan, add more butter or oil if necessary and repeat with the remaining spaetzle. Serve hot, garnished with parsley.

HERB SPAETZLE A mix of parsley, chervil, chives, and tarragon is lovely: Stir about 1 cup chopped fresh herbs into the batter.

ALSATIAN MAC AND CHEESE Heat the oven to 400°F. Make a batch of Mornay (Cheese) Sauce (page 79) and keep it warm. Grease a 13 × 9-inch baking pan or similar gratin dish with butter. After draining the spaetzle, spread them in the prepared pan and spoon on enough sauce to coat them completely. Sprinkle the top with ¾ cup fresh bread crumbs (see page 801) and bake until bubbling, 15 to 20 minutes.

THE BASICS OF ASIAN NOODLES

The assortment of Asian noodles now widely available is even more exciting than it was when I wrote the previous edition of this book. To the novice, though, it can be overwhelming.

Wheat-based Asian noodles are practically identical to their European counterparts. Others—made from

Making Spaetzle or Passatelli

Use the back of a spoon or a ladle to press the dough through the holes of a colander, letting the dough fall right into the bubbling liquid. Or use a ricer or food mill with large holes.

rice, mung beans, sweet potatoes, or other starches—are radically different in every way. To help you make sense of it all, here's a rundown of the varieties you're likely to encounter, along with preparation tips and cooking times.

CHINESE EGG NOODLES

Long, thin golden noodles made with wheat flour; round or flat; fresh or dried. The fresh noodles cook quickly, in about 3 minutes, or you can add them to hot soup to cook. Dried take a little longer, about 5 minutes (timing depends on the thickness of the noodle, of course); leave them slightly undercooked if you are adding them to soup or stir-frying them.

CHINESE WHEAT NOODLES

Long and thin, either round or flat; fresh or dried. They are typically white or light yellow and are made of wheat, water, and salt. Boil the dried noodles for about 5 minutes and the fresh for roughly half that time. Again, cooking time depends on the thickness of the noodle.

RICE STICKS, RICE VERMICELLI

White, translucent rice noodles, most often from Southeast Asia, ranging in thickness from angel hair (vermicelli) to spaghetti to greater than ¼ inch. Soak in boiling water until softened, 5 to 30 minutes, depending on the thickness. Then drain and hold in a bowl of tap water until you're ready to heat in soup or stir-fry.

UDON

Round, square, or flat wheat noodles from Japan, available in a range of thicknesses and lengths; usually dried but may be fresh. Most typically served in soups and stews, though you can also use them in braised dishes or serve them cold. Boil fresh or dried noodles for a few minutes, until just tender (dried take a bit longer, of course).

SOBA

Long, thin, flat Japanese noodles made from a combination of buckwheat and wheat flour; distinctively nutty. Light beige to brownish gray; sometimes green tea is added,

tinting them green. Most often dried, but you may see fresh. Boil dried noodles for 5 to 7 minutes, fresh for 2 to 4.

SOMEN

White, round, ultra-thin all-wheat noodles from Japan that cook in just a couple of minutes. Best in soups.

RAMEN AND SAIMIN

Long, slender, off-white wheat Japanese noodles that appear either crinkled in brick form or as rods; fresh, dried, frozen, or instant. The instant variety is typically deep-fried to remove moisture before being dried and packaged. Saimin is similar but made with egg. When fresh, boil ramen for just a couple of minutes; dried takes around 5.

BEAN THREADS

Also known as mung bean threads, cellophane noodles, glass noodles, or spring rain noodles, these long, slender, translucent noodles made from mung bean starch are usually sold in 2-ounce bundles. To prepare, soak the noodles in hot or boiling water until tender, 5 to 15 minutes; use kitchen scissors to cut them into manageable pieces if necessary. If you're adding them to soup or deep-frying them, don't bother to soak. You can also prepare the noodles by boiling them for a minute or 2, then draining.

TOFU SKINS (YUBA), TOFU NOODLES

These narrow, flat, beige noodles are made by skimming off the skin that forms on soy milk as it heats. Tofu skins are fabulous in salads, soups, and stir-fries and are available fresh, frozen, and dried. To use fresh tofu noodles, simply rinse and pat dry; thaw frozen noodles in the fridge, then treat as fresh. Soak dried noodles in warm water for about 15 minutes, then rinse and drain.

YAM NOODLES, SHIRATAKI

Like bean threads, these are translucent and made from a vegetable starch. They're made in Japan and Southeast Asia and come in several different varieties and colors, including fresh noodles, which cook like fresh pasta or

Cold Soba Noodles with
Dipping Sauce, page 522

tofu skins. Dried noodles should be soaked in boiling water until pliable, anywhere from 5 to 15 minutes. Drain and use them in soups, salads, and stir-fries.

Cold Asian Noodles

These two recipes aren't at all like American refrigerated pasta salads. They're noodles eaten at room temperature, with maybe some cold ingredients. The difference is subtle but you'll love them both.

Cold Soba Noodles with Dipping Sauce

MAKES: 4 small servings | TIME: 30 minutes

There's nothing like this dish in summer. So savory, yet so refreshing. It's the perfect light meal.

	Salt
1	cup Dashi (page 179) or chicken stock (to make your own, see page 176)
¼	cup soy sauce
2	tablespoons mirin, or 1 tablespoon honey mixed with 1 tablespoon water
12	ounces dried soba noodles
3	tablespoons minced scallion
2	tablespoons toasted sesame seeds (see page 309)
1	teaspoon finely grated or minced fresh ginger

1. Bring a large pot of water to a boil and salt it. Meanwhile, combine the dashi, soy sauce, and mirin; taste and add a little more soy sauce if it's not flavorful enough. Divide the sauce among small dipping bowls.
2. Cook the noodles until tender but not mushy; start checking after 3 minutes. Drain and rinse quickly under cold running water until cold. Drain well. Serve the noodles with the scallions, sesame seeds, and ginger scattered on top, with the sauce on the side.

COLD SOBA NOODLES WITH SHIITAKES Remove the stems from 8 ounces fresh shiitake mushrooms; slice the mushrooms thin. When the noodles are ready, drop the mushrooms into the boiling water with the noodles, stir, then drain and cool both together. Serve as described in Step 2.

Cold Noodles with Sesame or Peanut Sauce

MAKES: 2 main-course or 4 side-dish or appetizer servings | TIME: 30 minutes

Some things never change, like this perennially crowd-pleasing easy starter or side. To make it a meal, add firm tofu cubes or cooked edamame. Or top each serving with a few slices of grilled, roasted, or poached chicken, or grilled large shrimp.

	Salt and pepper
1	medium or 2 small cucumbers
12	ounces fresh Chinese egg noodles or long pasta like linguine
½	cup tahini, peanut butter, or a combination
3	tablespoons soy sauce, or to taste
2	tablespoons sesame oil
2	tablespoons sugar
1	tablespoon rice vinegar, white wine vinegar, or other vinegar
1	teaspoon minced fresh ginger (optional)
	Hot sauce
	At least ½ cup chopped scallions for garnish

1. Bring a large pot of water to a boil and salt it. Peel the cucumbers, cut them in half lengthwise, and scoop out the seeds with a spoon (see page 287). Cut the cucumbers into thin sticks.
2. Cook the noodles until tender but not mushy; start tasting after 5 minutes. Meanwhile, whisk together the tahini, soy sauce, sesame oil, sugar, vinegar, ginger if

 fast make ahead **V** vegetarian

you're using it, ½ teaspoon pepper, and hot sauce to taste in a large bowl. Thin the sauce with hot water until it's about the consistency of heavy cream; you will need ¼ to ½ cup water. Stir in the cucumber. When the noodles are done, drain, rinse under cold water, and drain again.

3. Toss the noodles with the sauce and cucumbers. Taste and adjust the seasoning, garnish with the scallions, and serve.

SPICY COLD NOODLES WITH PORK In Step 2, omit the tahini and hot sauce. Instead use 2 teaspoons or more Chile Paste (page 40), to taste, and an extra tablespoon rice vinegar and ½ cup hot water (or a little more) in Step 2. In Step 3, toss about 8 ounces thinly sliced roasted or grilled pork or smoked ham with the noodles and sauce. Garnish with bean sprouts, chopped cilantro, sliced scallions, and/or chopped radishes as you like.

Stir-Fried Asian Noodles

Cooking Asian noodles is a lot more like Italian-style pasta than you might think. There's a little less sauce maybe, and the timing and movement of ingredients in and out of the pan is more like a stir-fry, but the results are always a terrific combination of textures and flavors. And the components are super easy to vary—see "Improvising Noodle Bowls" on page 529.

Pad Thai

MAKES: 4 servings | **TIME:** 30 minutes

Easy to make at home—easier than you thought—and better than most pad Thai you've had in restaurants. Just make sure you have everything on hand and prepared before you start stir-frying, because it goes pretty fast once the heat is on.

12 ounces dried flat ¼-inch-wide rice noodles

5 tablespoons good-quality vegetable oil

3 eggs, lightly beaten

4 cloves garlic, minced

4 ounces small shrimp, peeled

4 ounces pressed tofu (see page 418), or extra-firm tofu prepared by any of the methods on pages 418–419 or blotted dry and sliced

2 scallions, cut into 1-inch lengths

1 cup bean sprouts, rinsed and trimmed

2 tablespoons fish sauce

2 teaspoons tamarind paste or ketchup

2 teaspoons sugar

½ cup chopped peanuts

½ cup chopped fresh cilantro

2 small fresh green chiles (preferably Thai), seeded and sliced (optional)

2 limes, cut into wedges

1. Put the noodles in a heatproof bowl and pour boiling water over them to cover. Soak until softened, at least 15 minutes; drain, reserving about 1 cup of the soaking water. Fill the bowl with cold water, and return the noodles to the bowl.

2. Put 2 tablespoons of the oil in a large skillet over medium heat. When it is hot, add the eggs and scramble quickly for about a minute with a fork almost flat against the bottom of the pan; you're aiming for a thin egg crêpe. Cook just until set. Transfer the crêpe to a cutting board and cut into ¼-inch-wide strips.

3. Raise the heat to high and add the remaining 3 tablespoons oil. When it is hot, add the garlic and shrimp and cook, stirring occasionally, until the shrimp turn pink, about 2 minutes. Transfer the shrimp and garlic to a plate with a slotted spoon. Add the tofu, scallions, and half of the bean sprouts to the oil and cook, stirring occasionally until the vegetables are soft and the tofu is heated through, 3 to 5 minutes. Transfer to the plate with the shrimp.

4. Put the drained noodles, fish sauce, tamarind, and sugar in the pan and cook, stirring occasionally and adding a little of the reserved soaking water, until the noodles are heated through and coated. Add the shrimp, garlic, stir-fried tofu mixture, and eggs, and toss once or twice.

5. Top with the peanuts, cilantro, chiles, and remaining bean sprouts and serve with the lime wedges.

VEGETARIAN PAD THAI Omit the shrimp and increase the tofu to 8 ounces. Substitute soy sauce for the fish sauce.

Stir-Fried Noodles with Meat and Vegetables

MAKES: 4 servings | TIME: 30 minutes

Lo mein—as we usually call it—is the model for stir-fried noodles. The best cuts of meat to use are beef sirloin strip, pork shoulder (Boston butt or fresh ham), and chicken breast or thigh. The meat will be easier to slice thin if you freeze it for 30 to 60 minutes first. Tofu is also a good option, especially pressed tofu or a block that you've had time to freeze, thaw, and squeeze (see pages 418–419).

> 12 **ounces beef, chicken, pork, shrimp, or tofu (see the headnote)**
>
> 2 **tablespoons soy sauce**
> **Salt**
>
> 12 **ounces fresh Chinese egg noodles, or about 8 ounces dried Chinese wheat noodles or spaghetti**
>
> 3 **tablespoons peanut or good-quality vegetable oil**
>
> 1 **large onion, thinly sliced**
>
> 1 **pound broccoli florets or asparagus, chopped**
>
> 1 **red bell pepper, cored, seeded, and cut into thin strips**
>
> 2 **tablespoons chopped garlic**
>
> 1 **tablespoon chopped fresh ginger**
>
> ½ **cup unsalted cashews, roughly chopped**

1. Cut the meat, shrimp, or tofu into thin strips about 2 inches long and ½ inch wide. Toss with the soy sauce in a small bowl and let sit.

2. Bring a large pot of water to a boil and salt it. Cook the noodles until tender but not mushy; start tasting fresh noodles after a minute, dried after 5 minutes. Drain, reserving about 1 cup of the cooking water. Quickly rinse the noodles under cold water. Toss with 1 tablespoon of the oil to prevent sticking, and let them sit in the colander.

3. Put another tablespoon of the oil in a large skillet over medium-high heat. When it is hot, add the onion and cook, stirring frequently, until it begins to brown, about 5 minutes. Add the broccoli and bell pepper and cook, stirring occasionally, until the broccoli is crisp-tender, 5 to 8 minutes. Add the garlic and ginger and cook for 1 minute, stirring almost constantly. Remove the vegetables from the pan.

4. Add the remaining tablespoon oil to the skillet and turn the heat to high. Drain the meat, reserving the soy sauce. Add the meat to the pan, and cook, stirring occasionally, until caramelized, a minute or 2. Add the reserved soy sauce along with ½ cup of the noodle cooking water and stir. Add the noodles and vegetables and toss to combine. Taste and adjust the seasoning. Heat until steaming, then serve, sprinkled with the nuts.

STIR-FRIED UDON NOODLES Great with pork and shiitake mushrooms but, here, too, any meat or vegetables can be used: Substitute udon noodles for the egg noodles and 3 sliced scallions for the onion. Omit the garlic, ginger, and cashews. Garnish with ¼ cup bonito flakes if you like.

Glass Noodles with Vegetables and Meat

MAKES: 4 servings | TIME: About 1 hour

Classic Korean *japchae* is seen more often in restaurants than homes, but it's easy to make. Since the noodles are best at room temperature, you can make the components up to an hour in advance. Substitute peeled

Glass Noodles with
Vegetables and Meat

shrimp, salmon fillets, or boneless chicken thighs for the meat, or use tofu slices for a vegetarian version.

Salt and pepper

2 tablespoons good-quality vegetable oil, plus more if needed

1 tablespoons sesame oil, plus more if needed

8 ounces boneless beef sirloin, cut into bite-size pieces

2 carrots, julienned or minced

1 large onion, thinly sliced and separated into rings

12 scallions, roughly chopped

5 ounces fresh spinach

8 ounces mushrooms, trimmed (preferably a mixture of oyster, shiitake, and enoki)

2 tablespoons chopped garlic

8 ounces Korean sweet potato vermicelli or bean threads

2 tablespoons soy sauce, plus more to taste

¼ cup pine nuts, lightly toasted (see page 309)

¼ cup sesame seeds, lightly toasted (see page 309)

1. Bring a large pot of water to a boil and salt it. Put 2 tablespoons of the vegetable oil and 1 tablespoon of the sesame oil in a large skillet over medium-high heat. When they're hot, add the meat, sprinkle with salt and pepper, and cook, stirring occasionally, until browned, 5 to 10 minutes. Transfer with a slotted spoon to a very large bowl. Cook the carrots in the same skillet, stirring occasionally, until they lose their crunch, about 3 minutes. Add to the meat.

2. Return the pan to medium-high heat and add the onion; cook, stirring occasionally, until it begins to brown, about 5 minutes. Transfer to the bowl with the carrots and meat. Raise the heat to high and add the scallions. Cook, stirring, until they soften, 2 to 3 minutes. Add to the bowl.

3. Add a little more vegetable and sesame oils to the skillet if necessary and stir-fry the spinach over medium heat until it softens a little, a couple of minutes. Sprinkle with a little salt and add it to the bowl. Add the mushrooms and garlic to the pan and cook, stirring occasionally, until they soften, about 5 minutes. Add to the bowl.

4. Add the noodles to the boiling water and turn off the heat. Let them soak, stirring a couple times, until the noodles are tender but not mushy; start tasting after 3 minutes. Drain the noodles and add them to the bowl, along with the soy sauce. Toss until thoroughly combined, adding salt, pepper, and more sesame oil and/or soy sauce to taste. Garnish with the pine nuts and sesame seeds and serve at room temperature.

17 Dishes to Toss with Asian Noodles

1. Any Stir-Fried Vegetables (page 244)
2. Seared Baby Bok Choy with Chile Vinaigrette (page 267)
3. Seared Baby Bok Choy with Black Vinegar (page 267)
4. Restaurant-Style Greens with Thickened Soy Sauce (page 268)
5. Quick-Braised Burdock and Carrots (page 273)
6. Winter Squash Curry, Thai Style (page 350)
7. Thai-Style Mixed Spicy Vegetables (page 354)
8. Shrimp and Scallion Stir-Fry and its variations (page 543)
9. Squid with Chiles and Greens (page 588)
10. Chicken Teriyaki (page 601)
11. Stir-Fried Chicken with Broccoli or Cauliflower and its variations (page 603)
12. Stir-Fried Chicken with Ketchup (page 605)
13. Stir-Fried Beef with Green Peppers or Green Beans (page 671)
14. Sichuan Steak with Plum Wine Sauce (slice it first; page 671)
15. See "Improvising Meaty Stir-Fries" (page 672)
16. Stir-Fried Pork with Bok Choy and its variations (page 692)
17. Spicy Braised Pork with Vietnamese Flavors (page 700)

 fast make ahead V vegetarian

Improvising Noodle Bowls

Use this mix-and-match graphic to assemble vibrant noodle bowls that combine all sorts of ingredients and textures, whether you cook the components specifically for the bowl, or use whatever's in your fridge.

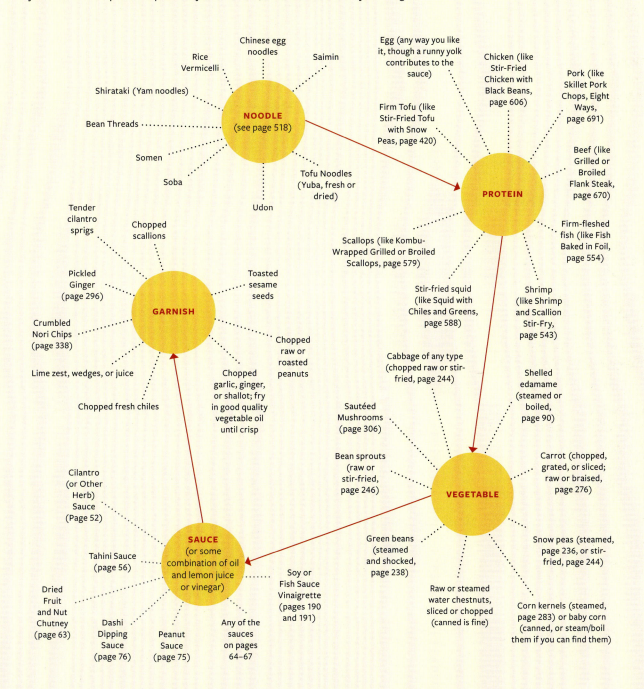

NOODLE (see page 518)

- Rice Vermicelli
- Chinese egg noodles
- Saimin
- Shirataki (Yam noodles)
- Bean Threads
- Somen
- Soba
- Udon
- Tofu Noodles (Yuba, fresh or dried)

PROTEIN

- Egg (any way you like it, though a runny yolk contributes to the sauce)
- Chicken (like Stir-Fried Chicken with Black Beans, page 606)
- Pork (like Skillet Pork Chops, Eight Ways, page 691)
- Firm Tofu (like Stir-Fried Tofu with Snow Peas, page 420)
- Beef (like Grilled or Broiled Flank Steak, page 670)
- Firm-fleshed fish (like Fish Baked in Foil, page 554)
- Scallops (like Kombu-Wrapped Grilled or Broiled Scallops, page 579)
- Stir-fried squid (like Squid with Chiles and Greens, page 588)
- Shrimp (like Shrimp and Scallion Stir-Fry, page 543)

GARNISH

- Tender cilantro sprigs
- Chopped scallions
- Toasted sesame seeds
- Pickled Ginger (page 296)
- Crumbled Nori Chips (page 338)
- Lime zest, wedges, or juice
- Chopped raw or roasted peanuts
- Chopped fresh chiles
- Chopped garlic, ginger, or shallot; fry in good quality vegetable oil until crisp

VEGETABLE

- Cabbage of any type (chopped raw or stir-fried, page 244)
- Shelled edamame (steamed or boiled, page 90)
- Carrot (chopped, grated, or sliced; raw or braised; page 276)
- Sautéed Mushrooms (page 306)
- Bean sprouts (raw or stir-fried, page 246)
- Green beans (steamed and shocked, page 238)
- Snow peas (steamed, page 236, or stir-fried, page 244)
- Raw or steamed water chestnuts, sliced or chopped (canned is fine)
- Corn kernels (steamed, page 283) or baby corn (canned, or steam/boil them if you can find them)

SAUCE (or some combination of oil and lemon juice or vinegar)

- Cilantro (or Other Herb) Sauce (Page 52)
- Tahini Sauce (page 56)
- Dried Fruit and Nut Chutney (page 63)
- Dashi Dipping Sauce (page 76)
- Peanut Sauce (page 75)
- Any of the sauces on pages 64–67
- Soy or Fish Sauce Vinaigrette (pages 190 and 191)

Seafood

CHAPTER AT A GLANCE

The Basics (and Flexibility) of Cooking Seafood 530

Shrimp 541

Salmon and Trout 547

Thick Fish Fillets and Steaks 552

Thin Fish Fillets 567

Whole Fish 569

Scallops, Clams, Mussels, and Oysters 574

Crab and Lobster 580

Squid and Octopus 588

I'm a longtime fish fan and my goal for eating seafood has remained the same over the years: Buy it right, cook it simply. The cooking is still dead easy—maybe even easier now, since my recipes are more flexible than they were two decades ago. Everything about buying seafood, however, has changed. The globalization of harvesting and farming has created a situation that puts the sustainability of some species and resources into question.

I now choose fish with an open mind, rather than a rigid plan. I buy the most sustainable, seasonal fillets, steaks, whole fish, or shellfish available at any given time and then pick a simple cooking method. Or for those times I'm craving a cooking method—like grilling when the weather is good, or a crisp bite of something fried—I start there and work backward to the fish.

Either way, I always win: The variety of flavors among available seafood is still fantastic; the cooking time is ridiculously fast, usually from less than 1 minute to maybe 10 minutes; and seafood will always be a healthy source of animal protein. The difference is that species is no longer the driving factor. This approach ensures freshness, economy, and sensitivity to the environment while allowing me to eat as much seafood as I want.

To encourage you to do the same, the organization, information, and recipes in this new edition also reflect flexibility and simplicity. The sections on different fish and shellfish group species that are cooked and eaten in a similar way, starting with the most popular and moving into less common kinds you may have never tried. My hope is to encourage you to explore the full range of what's available, sustainable, and convenient. Even if you don't live by a coastline.

The master recipes and variations at the beginning of this chapter demonstrate just how interchangeable different species really are. From grilling and broiling to sautéing and deep-frying, all the techniques are covered. And throughout, I'll show you the many ways to season fish—from simple salt, pepper, and maybe a little lemon to the judicious use of assertive flavorings.

The Basics (and Flexibility) of Cooking Seafood

There's tremendous freedom in being flexible about cooking seafood. The considerations are relatively basic and intuitive: The sturdiness and thickness of fillets and steaks is the best way to determine how to cook them; the darker the fish or shellfish, and the more assertive the flavor, the better it takes to strong seasonings.

The recipes here will walk you through the rest, starting with the first handful, which are organized by essential techniques. When you build confidence in the basics—rather than trying to master an entire fish vocabulary and repertoire of recipes—cooking seafood will always be enjoyable. As the chapter progresses, the recipes become more specific, though none are difficult. And I usually offer alternatives. But first you've got to get some seafood home and ready to cook.

BUYING SEAFOOD

Choosing what to buy starts with finding a source you trust. That can be your local supermarket, a fish store, or the farmers' market—any or all. If protecting the environment is important to you—as it is to me—then you'll start by seeking out the most sustainable seafood available in your area. You'll have many options; the sidebar on page 531 provides more detail. Beyond that, here's my quick, no-nonsense course in supermarket fish shopping.

 fast make ahead  vegetarian

- Avoid fish counters that smell or look dirty.

- Steer clear of prewrapped fish. It might be good, and there's nothing intrinsically wrong with it, but it's difficult to smell or otherwise evaluate.

- Lobster, crab, whole clams, oysters, and mussels must be alive when sold. Lobsters and crabs should be quite lively; if they seem tired, move on. The muscles of live mollusks make it difficult to pry their shells apart, so this is a good test. When mollusks are shucked and separated from their guts—as scallops usually are, and oysters frequently are—they can be frozen or packed in brine for longer shelf life. In this case, smell them if possible.

- Shrimp are almost always shipped frozen, and thawed before sale. It's better to buy them still frozen. The price might be lower, and you can control how and when they're thawed. The best way to thaw shrimp is in the refrigerator (which takes a while) or under cold running water (which is fast); avoid trying to speed things up with warm water.

- A few fish counters butcher whole fish, which is a treat, especially if you can make special requests. But most finfish comes precut in fillets and steaks. The surface of fillets and steaks should be bright, clear, and reflective—almost translucent. There should be no cracking or gaping between flakes, nor any dryness. The color should be consistent with the type of fish. For example, pearly white fish should not have spots of pink, which are usually bruises, or browning, which indicates spoilage. Creamy or ivory-colored fish should have no areas of deep red or brown. It's easy enough to get to know the ideal appearance of your favorite fish and reject any that doesn't meet your standard, but it's just as important to know the warning signs for fish in general.

- Fresh whole fish will smell sweet or salty, not "fishy." The best look alive, as if they just came out of the water, starting with clear, shining eyes. Lift the gills behind the head and peek inside; they should be red. The skin will be bright and reflective, with an undamaged layer of scales (if they haven't been removed already) and no browning. The flesh should feel be firm to a gentle touch.

Trust your instincts. If your supermarket fishmonger won't let you smell the fish but it passes the appearance tests, try buying it, then opening the package on the spot, and if the smell is at all off, hand it right back. If you're reluctant to do that, take any fish that doesn't meet your expectations when you unwrap it back to the supermarket for an exchange or a refund. Demand quality.

I've limited the number of recipes that call for the least sustainable species, and always offer alternatives. You can no longer make blanket assumptions about farmed versus wild: I still avoid farmed salmon and shrimp, for example, though cultivated catfish, mussels, and oysters can be excellent options for both flavor and the environment. But to get a handle on all this you'll have to do some research. The most prominent authority, the Seafood Watch run by the Monterey Bay Aquarium, updates frequently and is accessible on mobile devices. See https://www.seafood watch.org/.

PREPARING SEAFOOD

I will always stand by this statement: Fish and shellfish are the fastest and easiest animal protein to cook. You sprinkle them with salt and pepper, expose them to heat, give them a turn (or not, if fragile), garnish with lemon wedges, and you're ready to eat.

There are more details within the other sections throughout the chapter, and I give a range of time and visual cues in each recipe and variation. But here's some general guidance to help you get cooking.

- Fish are often characterized anatomically by whether they're flat (like flounder or halibut) or round (like salmon or snapper). For cooking, that's less important than the thickness of the piece of fish and whether or not it's still on the bone.

- Fillets are boneless pieces cut lengthwise from either side of the fish's backbone. They may be the whole side or cut into smaller portions, with or without the skin attached. See page 553 for details.

- Clams, mussels, and oysters must be scrubbed clean.

How Much Fish to Make?

In general, figure about 1½ pounds of any cleaned boneless seafood—fish fillets, scallops, squid, whatever—will serve four people generously. You can cook fillets whole and serve them family style or divide among individual plates, or cut them into portions before cooking. Whole fish is a little trickier: Fish of about a pound should feed one person, but as they grow in size there's more meat to bone, so a 2-pounder will feed two or three people, and a 4-pounder will feed at least six. Small fish like sardines have minimal bones so 2 pounds usually feeds four to six. For mollusks and shellfish where the shells are significant—mussels, clams, lobster, crab, oysters— you can either count them to determine how much to buy based on their size, or figure at least a pound per person for thin-shelled mussels or up to twice that for the biggest clams. In all cases the recipes provide guidance.

- Fillets and steaks should patted dry; rinse them first if you like. You can leave the skin on or remove it (see page 548). If the scales have been removed, the skin of some species (like salmon or snapper) is good to eat, especially crisped. When the skin is too rubbery to eat or the scales are still on, leaving the skin on for cooking will protect the flesh against drying out, and then you can easily remove it before serving.

- A steak is a cross-section of a fish, and may include both sides, whatever bones there are in the cross-cut, and (usually) the skin. See page 553 for details.

- To keep the skin and flesh from sticking during cooking, you need a thin layer of fat and a lot of patience. Whether you're grilling or cooking in a pan, make sure the surface is well greased and hot. Then you wait, letting the fish sizzle away undisturbed until it releases easily; if it's burning, you have permission to lower the heat or move it. Then turn the fish and let it alone again until it is cooked through. A broad, flexible spatula is a big help for maneuvering the fish.

- Whole fish should be gilled, gutted, and scaled. Usually the fishmonger will do that for you, but you can do it yourself if you like or must; see page 571.

- You can cook fish to varying degrees of doneness, though the window between the stages is smaller for fish than meats; thin fish fillets are fully cooked moments after hitting the heat. Unless you're eating it raw or nearly so, you want to pull fish from the heat when the flesh just starts to turn opaque and flakes or pierces easily without being dry.

- For seasoning ideas, see the sidebar on page 539.

 fast make ahead 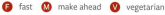 vegetarian

Broiled Seafood (thin fish fillets), page 534

Broiled Seafood

MAKES: 4 servings | **TIME:** About 20 minutes

Broiling is the easiest way to cook all but the largest cuts of seafood. The main recipe starts with the quickest cooking, thin fish fillets; see the variations for other cuts and seafood. The key is to preheat the broiler and the pan. You can use a carbon steel or stainless-steel pan, a large flameproof skillet, or a rimmed baking sheet. Or use the broiler pan without its liner, if that's the best fit.

> 3   tablespoons olive oil
> 1½ pounds thin fish fillets (see the list on
>   page 568)
>   Salt and pepper
>   Chopped fresh parsley for garnish (optional)
>   Lemon wedges for serving

1. Turn on the broiler to high and position the rack as close to the heat source as possible—3 or 4 inches is good and 2 inches is not too close. Put a sturdy pan on the rack and heat it for about 5 minutes.

2. When it's hot, carefully remove the pan and pour in the olive oil. Lay the fillets flat in the pan and sprinkle with salt and pepper. (If your pan won't hold all the fish comfortably, work in batches, transferring the first fillets to warmed plates or a heated platter before proceeding.) Time under the broiler will be 90 seconds to 2 minutes, rarely more. Do not turn the fillets; they're delicate, and anyway it's not necessary. The fish is ready when it becomes opaque and the tip of a thin-bladed knife flakes the thickest part easily.

3. Carefully remove the fillets with a spatula. Repeat with the rest of the fillets, if necessary. Sprinkle with parsley if you like, and pour the pan juices over all. Serve with the lemon.

BROILED SHRIMP OR SQUID Good for peeled shrimp or cleaned squid cut into rings and tentacles: While the pan is heating, coat the shrimp or squid in the olive oil, along with a sprinkle of salt and pepper. Spread in the pan and broil, shaking the pan once or twice, until the seafood turns opaque, about 3 minutes.

BROILED THICK FISH FILLETS OR STEAKS (INCLUDING SALMON; SEE THE LISTS ON PAGES 552 AND 553) Shoot for pieces about 1 inch thick. Make sure fillet skin is scaled. While the pan is heating, brush or rub the fish with some of the olive oil and sprinkle with salt and pepper. When the pan is hot, put the fish in the pan; if you're planning to serve the fillet with the skin, put it skin side down. Drizzle with the remaining oil. Broil, carefully turning sturdy fish once when it's firm and opaque around the edges; more delicate pieces require no turning. Total cooking time should be no more than 10 minutes. To check for doneness, see the directions in Step 2.

BROILED WHOLE FISH Works best with fish under 3 pounds; you can cook as many as will fit in the pan without crowding: Make sure the fish are gilled, gutted, and scaled. While the pan is heating, coat the fish in the olive oil and sprinkle with salt and pepper; get some inside the cavity too. Broil, turning once, until the skin blisters and chars a bit and the flesh is opaque and just flaking, 5 to 10 minutes per side, depending on the thickness.

BROILED SCALLOPS While the pan is heating, coat the scallops in the olive oil and sprinkle with salt and pepper. Broil, turning the scallops once, until they're opaque almost all the way through, but still a little underdone at the center, 3 to 8 minutes total depending on the thickness. If they're of uneven sizes, check occasionally and remove the smaller ones from the pan as they finish.

BROILED SOFT-SHELL CRABS OR LOBSTER Clean the crabs as described on page 582; prepare lobsters as illustrated on page 584. Cut lobsters in half and remove the head sac. You can leave the coral and tomalley in the body (see page 583) or remove and reserve them for

 fast   make ahead Ⓥ vegetarian

sauces. Heat the pan as in Step 1; rub or brush the crabs or lobster with oil and sprinkle with salt and pepper. Broil the crabs, turning once, until they're firm to the touch and change color, 3 to 4 minutes per side. Start lobster cut side up and turn once, about 5 minutes on each side; the meat should be just opaque at the center.

BROILED OCTOPUS Boil the octopus in seasoned water until it's fork-tender or if it's already cooked, thaw it in the refrigerator before proceeding (see page 588). Cut the body into thick slices and the tentacles into chunks. Heat the pan as in Step 1. Toss the octopus with the oil and sprinkle with salt and pepper. Broil, turning the pieces a few times, until crisped and browned on most sides, 5 to 10 minutes.

Grilled Seafood

MAKES: 4 servings | **TIME:** 40 minutes

Many fillets, regardless of their thickness, are simply too delicate to grill. The exceptions are sturdy, large-flake fish like salmon, striped bass, halibut, blackfish, and grouper. Fish steaks are more foolproof. And whole fish, regardless of their size, are also good. You can always use a grilling basket—nice but not absolutely necessary—to keep fish from falling apart as you turn and maneuver them. Most important: Make sure the grill is clean and that both the fish and the grates are well oiled. Shellfish is more forgiving; see the variations.

    1½ pounds thick, sturdy fish fillets or steaks
         (see pages 552 and 553)
    3   tablespoons olive oil
        Salt and pepper
        Lemon wedges for serving

1. Prepare a charcoal or gas grill for hot direct cooking; make sure the grates are clean. Drizzle the fish with the olive oil on both sides and sprinkle with salt and pepper.

6 Ways to Serve Simply Cooked Fish

1. On green salads, or as a salad, dressed with Vinaigrette (page 188) or mayonnaise (to make your own, see page 69)
2. In sandwiches, tacos, or burritos, or on top of Bruschetta (page 95)
3. Tossed in Simplest Fried Rice (page 444)
4. On top of Sushi Bowls (see page 451) or inside Sushi Rolls (page 448)
5. On a bed of cooked vegetables or other foods (see the sidebar on page 560)
6. Scrambled with eggs or as an ingredient in omelets or frittatas

2. Put the fish directly over the fire, close the lid, and grill until the fish is firm and releases easily from the grate, 3 to 5 minutes. Turn, close the lid, and grill until the flesh is firm and opaque at the center but still juicy, and a thin-bladed knife passes through it easily, 1 to 3 minutes more. Serve with the lemon.

GRILLED SHRIMP OR SQUID Use peeled or shell-on shrimp, or cleaned squid cut into rings and tentacles, or left whole. A grilling basket is helpful here, or thread shrimp or whole squid onto skewers. Prepare the fire and seafood and proceed with the recipe. They'll cook much more quickly, so be ready to shake the pan or turn them as soon as they begin to turn opaque, just a minute or 2. When they're opaque at the center, pull them off the heat quickly; squid might only take another minute, shrimp up to 3 minutes, depending on the size.

GRILLED SCALLOPS For easiest handling, thread the scallops onto two parallel skewers so the flat sides will sit directly on the grates: Prepare the fire and scallops and proceed with the recipe. Grill, turning once, until the scallops are browned in spots and the centers are still ever so slightly translucent, 3 to 5 minutes per side.

GRILLED WHOLE FISH The same method works for large or small fish; figure 3 pounds total will easily serve 4. Make sure the fish are gilled, gutted, and scaled. If grilling one large fish, make 3 or 4 parallel diagonal slashes on each side of the fish, down to the bone. Prepare the fire and fish and proceed with the recipe. Small fish will take just a couple of minutes per side; one large fish will take 5 to 8 minutes per side. If the skin ever starts to look dry, brush with additional oil. To check for doneness, peek down to the bottom of the gashes; the meat should be white.

GRILLED CLAMS OR MUSSELS Both are awesome drizzled with a vinaigrette (see page 188) or simply melted butter: Prepare the fire as described in Step 1. No need to oil or season the shellfish. Put the whole clams or mussels directly over the fire with the flatter shell facing up. Close the lid and cook, without turning, until the shells open, 3 to 5 minutes. As they're done, transfer them to a bowl, careful to save any juices in the bottom shell. Sprinkle with salt and pepper and gently toss before serving.

GRILLED OYSTERS, TWO WAYS Have about 1 cup barbecue sauce ready, if you like, and melt 8 tablespoons (1 stick) butter. Prepare the fire as described in Step 1. No need to oil or season the oysters. Put them directly over the fire with the flatter shell facing up. Close the lid and cook, without turning, until the shells open enough to vent some steam, just a couple of minutes. Transfer the oysters to a rimmed baking sheet in a single layer, careful to save any juices in the bottom shell. When they're cool enough to handle, carefully pop the top shell off with an oyster knife. You can either serve the oysters as they are, lightly poached with their juices, drizzled with melted butter. Or dab them with barbecue sauce and butter and return them to the grill, shell down, cover, and cook until browned, 2 to 3 minutes.

GRILLED OCTOPUS Fantastic dressed and served as a warm salad over greens: Boil the octopus in seasoned water until it's fork-tender (see page 590). The amount of time is unpredictable, but this can be done up to a day in advance. Cut the body into thick slices and the tentacles into chunks. Skewer the pieces if you like. Prepare the fire and octopus and proceed with the recipe. Grill, turning a few times, until crisped and browned on most sides, 5 to 10 minutes total.

Roasted Seafood

MAKES: 4 servings | **TIME:** 30 to 45 minutes, depending on thickness

The best tool for this job is a large rimmed baking sheet. Provided you don't overcook the seafood, results

  fast   make ahead   V vegetarian

are lightly golden and crusted on the outside and juicy inside. Tartar Sauce (page 70) and lemon wedges are always good companions here, or serve with any of the salsas on pages 55–58 or 71–74.

- 1½ pounds large, thick fish fillets like salmon, halibut, or tuna, or steaks of any size (see pages 552 and 553)
  Salt and pepper
- 3 tablespoons olive oil
- 2 tablespoons chopped fresh parsley or chives for garnish

1. Heat the oven to 450°F. Put the fish in a rimmed baking sheet, rub on all sides with the oil, and sprinkle with salt and pepper. Spread it out in a single layer, skin side down if using fillets, even if the skin has been removed.
2. Roast until the fish is firm and juicy and barely opaque inside; a thin-bladed knife will pass through it fairly easily. You can turn thick steaks or fillets once they release easily from the pan. Fillets or steaks 1 inch thick will take 5 or 10 minutes total, much thicker pieces up to 20 to 30 minutes; start checking after 15 minutes. Serve the fish hot or at room temperature, garnished with the herb.

ROASTED SHRIMP OR SQUID Ready in a flash: Use peeled or shell-on shrimp or cleaned squid, whole or cut into rings and tentacles. Prepare the seafood as described in Step 1. In Step 2, start checking after 2 minutes; if the shrimp or squid isn't ready, shake the pan and test again every minute or 2. You want it to be just opaque at the center but not at all dry or rubbery.

ROASTED SCALLOPS Prepare the scallops as described in Step 1, spreading them in a single layer, flat side down. No need to turn them. They'll take 3 to 10 minutes to become barely opaque at the center, depending on the size.

ROASTED WHOLE FISH Works for small and large fish: Cut 3 or 4 parallel diagonal gashes in both sides of the fish, almost down to the bone. In Step 1, you'll probably need an extra tablespoon or 2 or oil to coat; sprinkle the inside and outside with salt and pepper. Roast the fish until it releases easily from the pan and the skin on top is crisp, 5 to 20 minutes, depending on the size, then turn and repeat until it's done as described in Step 2.

CLAM, MUSSEL, OR OYSTER PAN ROAST Use a large roasting pan. Spread the mollusks across the bottom, sprinkle with salt and pepper, drizzle with the oil, and pour ½ cup each water and white wine (or all water) over all. Roast, shaking the pan once or twice, until the shells start to open, 10 to 30 minutes, depending on the size of the mollusks. As the mollusks are ready, transfer them to warmed serving bowls and return the pan to the oven, adding with a splash more liquid if the pan becomes dry. When all have opened, pour the pan juices over them.

Sautéed Fish with Lemony Pan Sauce

MAKES: 4 servings | **TIME:** 20 minutes

The classic technique of lightly flouring fish and sautéing it in butter, known as "meunière," is traditionally applied to sole but works equally well for any thin fillets. Note that you must work in two batches, because you shouldn't crowd too many fillets in the pan at once. The whole process still only takes only a few minutes per batch.

- 1½ pounds thin fish fillets (see page 568), cut into 4 portions
  Salt and pepper
- 1 cup all-purpose flour
- 2 tablespoons olive oil
- 4 tablespoons (½ stick) butter
- ¼ cup fresh lemon juice
- ¼ cup chopped fresh parsley

1. Put ovenproof dinner plates or a serving platter in a 200°F oven to warm. Sprinkle the fillets with salt and pepper. Put the flour in a shallow bowl.

2. Heat a large skillet over medium-high heat for 2 to 3 minutes. Add 1 tablespoon of the oil and 1 tablespoon of the butter. When the butter foams, dredge one of the fillets in the flour, shaking off any excess, and add it to the pan. Repeat with another fillet. Adjust the heat so the fish sizzles, and cook until the fillets are golden on the bottom and release easily, 2 to 3 minutes. Turn and cook on the other side, just until the fish flakes when poked with a fork but is still juicy inside.

Transfer the fish to the warm plates or platter and put in the oven. Wipe out the pan with a towel and repeat with the remaining tablespoon oil, 1 tablespoon of the butter, and the remaining fillets. Once they're done, don't bother to wipe out the skillet again unless the flour is burned.

3. Lower the heat to medium and add the remaining 2 tablespoons butter to the pan. Cook until the butter foams, a minute or 2. Add the lemon juice and ¼ cup water and cook, stirring and scraping the bottom of the pan, until the sauce bubbles and thickens, another minute or 2. Stir in the parsley, taste and add a little salt if you'd like, pour the sauce over the fillets, and serve.

SAUTÉED THICK FISH FILLETS WITH LEMONY PAN SAUCE
Salmon, halibut, and cod are especially nice like this, and so is catfish: In Step 2, cook the fillets for 3 to 5 minutes per side. Any thick fillet will still be firm and juicy when done, and will have turned opaque inside; a thin-bladed knife will pass through it fairly easily.

SAUTÉED OYSTERS WITH LEMONY PAN SAUCE Figure about a pound of shucked oysters (at least 1 pint, drained) to serve 4: You should be able to fit them all in the skillet comfortably in one batch, so use all the oil and 2 tablespoons of the butter in Step 2. Cook the oysters until just opaque around the edges, 1 to 2 minutes per side. They will still be a little underdone in the center. After you make the sauce in Step 3, return the oysters to the skillet, remove from the heat, and toss

until coated. Serve, drizzling with the remaining sauce from the pan on top.

SAUTÉED OYSTERS WITH CREAM Dreamy over thickly slice challah or brioche: Figure about a pound of shucked oysters (1 pint, drained) to serve 4: You should be able to fit them all in the skillet comfortably in one batch, so use all the oil and 2 tablespoons butter in Step 2. Cook the oysters until just opaque on the outside, 1 to 2 minutes per side. They will still be a little underdone in the center. To make the sauce in Step 3, substitute 1 cup cream for the remaining butter, lemon juice, and water; omit the parsley. After removing the oysters, add the cream to the skillet, stir to scrape up any browned bits, and let it thicken a bit. Return the oysters to the pan, remove from the heat, and toss them until coated. Serve, drizzling the sauce on top.

Deep-Fried Seafood

MAKES: 4 servings | **TIME:** 30 minutes

The crisp, light breading in this recipe has been my go-to since I began cooking. It works for shrimp, clams, oysters, squid, very small fish, and sturdy fillets—catfish is classic. As with all deep-frying, make sure the oil is properly heated, and avoid overcrowding the pot.

Whatever seafood you choose, make sure everything is patted dry before dredging. I like to cut squid bodies into rings (if they're not already) and include the tentacles. Peeled large shrimp and shucked oysters, mussels, and clams are worth the extra work.

Good-quality vegetable oil, as needed
1½ pounds skinned fish fillets, whole or cut into chunks; or shelled and cleaned squid, shrimp, oysters, or clams
Salt and pepper
1 cup all-purpose flour
1 cup cornstarch
Lemon wedges for serving

 fast   make ahead   vegetarian

How to Season Simply Cooked Fish

The simple recipes at the beginning of this chapter demonstrate that butter and/or oil, salt, pepper, and the occasional lemon wedge are all you need to serve delicious seafood. But you can up the seasoning before or after cooking. Seafood can take it; just use a light hand on thin, delicate fish.

FLAVORING SEAFOOD BEFORE COOKING

Dry Seasoning: ground individual spices, a blend, or cracked whole spice seeds; combine a pinch or 2 with salt and pepper and gently rub all over seafood before cooking.

Wet Seasoning: Best for dry-heat methods like broiling, grilling, or roasting. It's neither necessary nor beneficial to let seafood sit in a marinade for more than 30 minutes; instead, mix flavorings with a little bit of fat to help them adhere. Start by mixing a pinch or 2 of ground individual spices, a blend, or cracked whole spice seeds with salt and pepper in a small bowl, or use a spoonful of flavorful purée like miso or chile paste, or chopped fresh herbs. Stir in up to ¼ cup any oil, yogurt, mayonnaise, or coconut milk. Spread it all over the seafood before cooking.

For poaching: Season the water more generously; when frying, season the seafood or the batter or breading with a dry seasoning above.

16 WAYS TO FLAVOR SEAFOOD AFTER COOKING

Most seafood is complemented by salty, sweet, sour, or even bitter ingredients. The trick is to rely on complexity rather than intensity. The following ideas work for seafood cooked by any technique, though fried and sautéed seafood usually pair best with something acidic to balance their richness. And if there's already a pan sauce or some braising or steaming liquid, you won't need much else.

1. Seaweed "Shake" (page 35)
2. Virtually any fresh or cooked salsa (see pages 55–58 and 71–74)
3. Any Yogurt Sauce (page 59)
4. Any chutney (pages 61–62)
5. Ginger-Scallion Sauce (page 64)
6. Thai Chile Sauce (page 66)
7. Miso Dipping Sauce (page 66)
8. Mayonnaise (page 69), especially the flavored versions
9. Barbecue sauce (to make your own, see page 74), especially with shrimp
10. Teriyaki Sauce (page 76)
11. Compound Butter (see page 78)
12. Brown Butter (page 78)
13. Velouté (White) Sauce (page 79)
14. Virtually any Five-Minute Drizzle Sauce (page 81)
15. Any Vinaigrette (pages 188–191)
16. Fast Tomato Sauce and most of its variations (page 479)

1. Line a rimmed baking sheet with towels or fit it with a wire rack. Heat the oven to 200°F. Put 2 to 3 inches of oil in a large pot over medium-high heat; bring to 350°F (see "Deep-Frying," page 22). Meanwhile, season the seafood with salt and pepper, and combine the flour and cornstarch in a bowl.

2. When the oil is hot, start dredging the seafood lightly in the flour-cornstarch mixture, tapping to remove excess, then add the pieces slowly to the oil without crowding. Cook in batches, adjusting the heat as necessary so the temperature remains nearly constant.

3. Fry, turning once or twice, until the seafood is lightly browned and cooked through; a skewer or thin-bladed knife will pass through each piece with little resistance. This should take no longer than 5 minutes total, unless your pieces are large or extra-thick. Remove with a slotted spoon and drain on the prepared baking sheet. Repeat with the remaining seafood. Sprinkle with additional salt if you like and serve with lemon wedges.

Deep-Fried Seafood, page 538

DEEP-FRIED SEAFOOD WITH A THICKER CRUST Before beginning, soak the fish in 1 quart buttermilk for up to an hour at room temperature or several hours in the fridge. Lift the pieces from the buttermilk and let some of the liquid drip off then dredge as directed in Step 2, but press the flour mixture into the buttermilk on the fish to create a thick coating; you will probably need another ½ cup or so flour-cornstarch mixture to do the job. Shake off the excess and proceed with the recipe. Cooking time might increase by a minute or 2.

SPICED OR HERBED DEEP-FRIED SEAFOOD Use with either the light or thick breading: Spike the flour mixture with 2 tablespoons black pepper, a pinch cayenne, or any spice blend (to make your own, see pages 32–35), or 2 tablespoons chopped fresh herbs like parsley, dill, or chives.

---

6 OTHER COATINGS FOR DEEP-FRIED SEAFOOD

1. A mix of half cornmeal and half flour
2. Finely crushed saltine cracker crumbs
3. Unsweetened shredded coconut, substituted for no more than half the flour
4. Tempura batter (page 112)
5. Beer batter (see page 319)
6. Bread crumbs, preferably fresh (see page 801) or panko; dip the seafood in beaten egg or milk first to help them stick

Shrimp

Shrimp is still the most popular noncanned seafood in America. I prefer sustainably caught wild shrimp from the Atlantic or Pacific Oceans or the Gulf of Mexico. The flavor is more like the sea and therefore better to my taste—even including the slight iodine taste in somewhat rare brown shrimp. I recognize, however, that most people only have access to farmed. Just make sure it's been raised responsibly—check with your fishmonger or Monterey Bay Aquarium's Seafood Watch.

Since shrimp doesn't keep long after harvesting, almost all are frozen before sale, which means when you see them thawed, they're not necessarily freshly caught. Unless you have access to shrimp that are truly local, buying frozen shrimp gives you better quality and the flexibility of thawing them yourself. Once home, frozen shrimp retain their quality for a month or more.

Some frozen shrimp are sold in blocks of 5 pounds (or 2 kilos, slightly less than that), but usually they're IQF (individually quick frozen) and packed in bags of 2 pounds or 1 kilo. These are super-convenient, because you can take, say, six shrimp out of the freezer, leaving the rest frozen. If you have time, thaw shrimp in the refrigerator for about 24 hours; if you're in a hurry, in a bowl of cold water. Partially thawing a block to cut it in half, then refreezing the rest for later use, while not ideal, is still preferable to buying thawed shrimp.

Small, medium, large, extra-large, jumbo, and other size classifications are subjective and relative, but that's the most common way they're sold. The standardized distinctions are calculated by number of shrimp per pound: 16/20 means sixteen to twenty in a pound; U-15 means fewer than fifteen will make a pound, and so on. I look for shell-on shrimp sized between fifteen and thirty per pound—medium or large, usually. They tend to have the best combination of flavor, ease of peeling, and value. If you just can't bear peeling them yourself—which isn't too much work since I don't usually bother to devein them—buy shrimp already shelled. (To make the most of the shells, see the stock on page 179.)

Recognizing doneness with shrimp is easy but might require some poking and peeking. They aren't always cooked through when the outside turns pink—larger shrimp can take a little longer. Just look inside: The flesh should be opaque at the thickest part but not at all dry or stringy.

I include crawfish (also called crayfish) in this section. Although many devotees believe them to be not only different from shrimp but superior, I find the two generally interchangeable in all ways except peeling, which is more tedious for crawfish. You can also use squid (with the bodies cut into rings and the tentacles left whole) or small scallops (see page 574) in virtually all of these recipes.

Still the Simplest and Best Shrimp Dish

MAKES: 4 servings | **TIME:** About 30 minutes

Excuse the superlatives; this spin on a spicy Spanish tapa remains my favorite, and everyone I serve it to loves it too. It's good with bread, over rice, tossed with pasta, or stuffed into tacos.

Other seafood you can use: similar-sized scallops (or larger, though they'll take longer to cook).

⅓	cup olive oil, or more as needed
3 or 4	large cloves garlic, cut into slivers
1½	pounds peeled large shrimp, patted dry
1½	teaspoons hot paprika

1   **teaspoon ground cumin**
    Salt and pepper
    Chopped fresh parsley for garnish

1. Put the olive oil in a large skillet over low heat. There should be enough oil to cover the bottom of the pan by about ⅛ inch; don't skimp. Add the garlic and cook, stirring, until it turns golden, a few minutes.

2. Raise the heat to medium-high and add the shrimp, paprika, cumin, and salt and pepper. Stir to combine and continue to cook, shaking the pan to turn the shrimp once or twice, until they're just opaque at the center and the mixture is bubbly, 3 to 5 minutes. Garnish with the parsley and serve hot or at room temperature.

SMOKY SHRIMP Use smoked paprika instead of some or all of the hot paprika.

SHRIMP SCAMPI Substitute butter for half the oil. In Step 2, omit the cumin and paprika; sprinkle with salt and pepper. Don't disturb the shrimp until they sear on one side; then shake the pan. When they're done, stir in 2 tablespoons each lemon juice and dry sherry, white wine, or water, and ¼ cup chopped fresh parsley.

Preparing Shrimp

STEP 1 To peel shrimp, grasp the feelers on the underside and pull the shell away from the meat.

STEP 2 Deveining is optional. Should you choose to devein, make a shallow cut on the back side of the shrimp, then pull out the long, black threadlike vein.

STEP 3 To butterfly shrimp, cut most of the way through the back of the shrimp.

STEP 4 Then open it up.

 fast   make ahead   vegetarian

GARLIC SHRIMP WITH TOMATOES AND CILANTRO Omit the cumin and paprika and double the amount of garlic. Dice 4 plum tomatoes; substitute fresh cilantro for the parsley. In Step 2, scatter the tomatoes in the skillet with the shrimp; cooking time will increase by a couple of minutes. Garnish with the cilantro.

Shrimp and Scallion Stir-Fry

MAKES: 4 servings | **TIME:** 30 minutes

Time for a master recipe with lots of ideas; see the variations that follow. This one is so versatile you can even use it for other seafood. You don't have to serve this on rice; it could also go well with any type of Asian noodle (see "Asian Noodles," page 519), as used in a Noodle Bowl (see page 527).

Other protein you can use: squid rings and tentacles; scallops (large ones might take longer to cook); thinly sliced boneless beef sirloin, or pork or lamb shoulder; cut-up boneless chicken thighs; firm tofu cubes.

- 1 batch White Rice (page 430) or Brown Rice (page 430)
- 2 bunches scallions (about 6 ounces total), trimmed
- 3 tablespoons good-quality vegetable oil
- 1½ pounds peeled medium shrimp, or cleaned, prepared squid
  Salt
- 2 cloves garlic, sliced
  Juice of 1 lemon

1. Start cooking the rice so it's ready when the shrimp are. Cut apart the green and white parts of the scallions. Split the whites lengthwise and cut into 1-inch pieces; chop the greens. Put 2 tablespoons of the oil in a large skillet over high heat. When it's hot, add the shrimp and a large pinch salt and cook, stirring only occasionally, until the shrimp are uniformly pink, 3 to 5 minutes.

Transfer the shrimp to a bowl with a slotted spoon, leaving behind as much oil as possible.

2. Turn the heat to medium-high and add the scallion whites and garlic. Cook, stirring occasionally, until they're brown in places and fragrant, about 3 minutes. Transfer the aromatics to the bowl with a slotted spoon. If the rice isn't ready yet, remove the skillet from the heat until the rice is done.

3. Return the skillet to medium-high heat and add the remaining 1 tablespoon oil. When it's hot, add half of the scallion greens and cook, stirring constantly, until they're coated, less than a minute. Add ½ cup water, bring to a boil, and let it bubble until the scallions are soft, about 1 minute.

4. Return the shrimp, scallion whites, and garlic to the skillet and add the lemon juice. Taste and adjust the seasoning. Serve with the rice, garnished with the remaining scallion greens.

SHRIMP AND SNOW PEA STIR-FRY Use only 1 bunch scallions. Proceed with Steps 1 and 2. In Step 3, first stir-fry 8 ounces snow peas until crisp-tender, about 3 minutes, then add half the scallion greens and proceed. Replace the lemon juice with lime juice. Garnish with a handful of tender cilantro sprigs as well as the scallion greens.

SHRIMP AND ASPARAGUS STIR-FRY Omit the scallions; increase the garlic in Step 2 to 3 or 4 cloves. In Step 3, stir-fry 1 pound asparagus, cut into 1- to 2-inch lengths, until crisp-tender, 3 to 5 minutes. Add the water and proceed. Garnish with 2 tablespoons chopped fresh mint.

SHRIMP STIR-FRY WITH SCALLION PURÉE Cut 2 extra bunches scallions into 2-inch lengths. Proceed with Step 1. In Step 2, first cook the extra scallions until soft. Remove from the pan and purée with half the garlic, adding water as needed to make the mixture smooth. Proceed with the scallion whites and remaining garlic. In Step 3, add the purée to the cooked scallion greens and garlic and proceed with the recipe. Replace the

Shrimp and Scallion Stir-Fry (top), page 543; Shrimp and Bok Choy Stir-Fry with Water Chestnuts

lemon juice with lime juice. Garnish with chopped Thai basil as well as the scallion greens.

SHRIMP AND CABBAGE STIR-FRY WITH FERMENTED BLACK BEANS

Use only 2 scallions; thinly slice them. Marinate the shrimp for a few minutes in a mixture of ½ teaspoon sugar, 1 tablespoon soy sauce, the garlic, 1 teaspoon salt, and 1 teaspoon sesame oil. Add the marinade to the pan with the shrimp in Step 1. Combine 2 tablespoons fermented black beans and ¼ cup dry sherry, white wine, or water in a small bowl. Skip Step 2. In Step 3, omit the scallions. Stir-fry 1 tablespoon minced fresh ginger and 12 ounces cabbage, chopped (about 3 cups) until the cabbage is lightly browned in places. Increase the water to ¾ cup and let it bubble for a minute or 2. Replace the lemon juice with rice vinegar and add the soaked black beans and their liquid. Garnish with the scallions.

SHRIMP AND BOK CHOY STIR-FRY WITH WATER CHESTNUTS

Omit the scallions. Marinate the shrimp for a few minutes in a mixture of ½ teaspoon sugar, 1 tablespoon soy sauce, the sliced garlic, 1 teaspoon salt, and 1 teaspoon sesame oil. Add the marinade to the pan with the shrimp. In Step 2, replace the scallion whites with 1 onion, thinly sliced. In Step 3, stir-fry 1 tablespoon minced fresh ginger, 12 ounces bok choy, chopped (about 3 cups), and 1 cup sliced peeled water chestnuts until crisp-tender, 3 to 5 minutes. Proceed with the recipe. Garnish with 1 tablespoon toasted sesame seeds.

SHRIMP AND CASHEW STIR-FRY

Marinate the shrimp for a few minutes in a mixture of ½ teaspoon sugar, 1 tablespoon soy sauce, the sliced garlic, 1 teaspoon salt, and 1 teaspoon sesame oil. Add the marinade to the pan with the shrimp. Add 4 ounces bean sprouts along with the scallion whites. In Step 3, add 1 tablespoon minced fresh ginger and ½ cup cashews to the cooked scallion greens and garlic. Replace the lemon juice with lime juice. Garnish with lime wedges and chopped cilantro as well as the scallion greens.

SHRIMP STIR-FRY WITH COCONUT CURRY

Sprinkle the shrimp lightly with 2 teaspoons curry powder as they cook. In Step 2, stir 1 teaspoon curry powder into the scallion whites. Add 1 tablespoon minced or grated fresh ginger to the softened scallion greens and cook until fragrant. Add 1½ cups coconut milk and cook until the sauce has thickened somewhat, another 5 to 10 minutes. Return the shrimp to the pan and cook until warmed through, less than a minute. Garnish with ¼ cup chopped peanuts and a large handful of tender cilantro sprigs, as well as the scallion greens.

CHILE SHRIMP WITH CELERY

Omit the scallions. Slice 8 celery stalks and chop as many celery leaves as you can; keep them separate. In a blender, purée the garlic, 2 inches peeled fresh ginger, 1 shallot, and 4 small fresh hot red chiles with enough water to make a paste. In Step 1, cook the paste in the oil for 30 seconds, then add the shrimp and celery stalks and cook stirring, until the shrimp is opaque and the celery softens, about 3 minutes. Skip Step 3. In Step 4, omit the lemon juice; stir 2 tablespoons each lime juice, fish sauce, soy sauce, and water, and a pinch sugar into the chile sauce, and add the celery. Garnish with a small chopped cucumber.

Shrimp or Crawfish Boil, Louisiana Style

MAKES: 4 to 6 servings | **TIME:** 30 minutes, plus time to cool

It's traditional to serve the shell-on seafood and big pieces of vegetables (see the variation) dumped from the pot down the center of a newspaper-covered table, punctuated with bottles of hot sauce and maybe a couple of bowls of a creamy condiment like rémoulade or tartar sauce. Everyone eats with their hands and gets a chunk of French bread and a cup of the savory cooking water for dipping.

About 6 quarts water, fish stock, or shrimp stock (to make your own, see pages 178–179)

4 bay leaves

2 teaspoons dried thyme or several sprigs fresh thyme

1 tablespoon black peppercorns

4 cloves garlic, crushed

1 tablespoon coriander seeds

3 whole cloves

4 small dried hot red chiles
Salt and pepper

4 pounds whole shrimp or crawfish
Tabasco or other hot sauce for serving
Lemon wedges for serving

1 recipe Aioli (page 70), Rémoulade (page 70), or Tartar Sauce (page 70) for dipping (optional)

1. Bring the liquid to a boil in a large pot and add the bay leaves, thyme, peppercorns, garlic, coriander, cloves, chiles, and plenty of salt. Adjust the heat so it bubbles gently, and cook until the garlic is soft and the broth is fragrant, about 10 minutes.

2. Return the broth to a boil, then add the shrimp or crawfish. Cook, stirring once or twice, until the seafood is almost opaque at the center (to be sure break into a couple pieces) about 5 minutes. Turn off the heat and cover; let the seafood sit for a few minutes in the liquid.

3. Remove the seafood with a strainer, sprinkle with more salt, and serve, passing hot sauce, lemon wedges, and creamy sauce at the table.

SHRIMP OR CRAWFISH BOIL WITH VEGETABLES More of a meal: In Step 1, add 1½ pounds waxy potatoes and 1 pound onions, all cut into large chunks if they're bigger than eggs. Boil with the seasonings until just beginning to get tender, about 10 minutes. When you add the seafood in Step 2, add 4 to 6 ears shucked corn (cut in half, if you like). Proceed with the recipe.

Shrimp and Rice, Japanese Style

MAKES: 4 servings | TIME: 40 minutes

Based on the classic dish known as *kayaku gohan*, this all-shrimp version might remind you of paella, but with a different technique. It's even better if you start by making dashi, which only takes 10 minutes.

Other protein you can use: squid (rings and tentacles); any thick fish fillets, salmon fillets or steaks, or virtually any combination of seafood; sliced boneless chicken thighs.

2 tablespoons good-quality vegetable oil

8 fresh shiitake mushroom caps or dried shiitakes, soaked in hot water until soft, sliced

1 onion, chopped

1¾ cups short-grain white rice

4 cups Dashi (page 179) or water, plus more as needed

2 tablespoons soy sauce, plus more to taste

1 tablespoon mirin, or 1½ teaspoons honey mixed with 1½ teaspoons water

1 pound large or medium shrimp, peeled and cut into small pieces

1 cup fresh or frozen peas, or chopped snow peas
Salt (optional)

1. Put the oil in a large pot over medium-high heat. When it's hot, add the mushrooms and onion, and cook, stirring occasionally, until they're soft and brown in places, about 10 minutes.

2. Reduce the heat to medium and add the rice; stir to combine. Add the dashi, soy sauce, and mirin. Stir, adjust the heat so it bubbles gently, and cover. Cook until the rice is almost fully tender, about 15 minutes.

3. When you remove the cover, the mixture should still be a little soupy (add a little dashi or water if it's dried out). Stir in the shrimp and peas, then raise the heat a bit and cook, stirring occasionally, until the rice is tender, the shrimp cooked, and the mixture is still

 fast make ahead 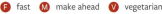 vegetarian

moist but not soupy, 3 to 5 minutes. Taste and adjust the seasoning, then serve.

Shrimp Burgers or Sliders

MAKES: 4 servings | **TIME:** 90 minutes

The best alternative burgers have superior flavor and interesting texture. This two-step food processor method consistently delivers both. Since shrimp contain natural gelatin, the burgers can take lots of add-ins without falling apart, so you can either grill these burgers or cook 'em in a pan. To change the seasonings, omit and substitute as you like, maintaining no more than the quantities of vegetables and herbs listed in the main recipe. Try small amounts of stronger herbs—tarragon, mint, basil, or parsley; a tablespoon or two of chile paste (page 40) or a spice mixture (pages 27–35) is always good, especially curry powder.

Other seafood you can use: scallops or salmon.

- 1 large clove garlic, peeled
- 1 dried or fresh chile, seeded, or more to taste
- 1 inch fresh ginger, roughly chopped
- 1½ pounds shrimp, peeled
- ¼ cup chopped scallions
- ¼ cup chopped red or yellow bell pepper
  Salt and pepper
- ½ cup fresh cilantro leaves, or to taste
  Good-quality vegetable oil as needed
- 2 limes, halved
- 4 large or 8 small rolls or buns (brioche, hamburger, Hawaiian, or potato), toasted
  Lettuce, ketchup, mayonnaise, and/or other toppings for serving

1. If you'll be grilling, prepare a charcoal or gas grill for medium direct cooking; make sure the grates are clean.
2. Combine the garlic, chile, ginger, and a third of the shrimp in a food processor and process to a purée, stopping the machine to scrape down the sides of the

container as necessary. Add the remaining shrimp along with the scallions, bell pepper, salt and pepper, and the cilantro and pulse as many times as is necessary to chop the shrimp and vegetables, but not too finely. Shape the mixture into 4 burgers about 1 inch thick. Or make 8 smaller burgers for sliders. Put the burgers on a plate and refrigerate for 15 to 20 minutes to firm up.
3. Brush the grill and the burgers with oil, put the burgers on the grate over the fire, and close the lid. If you're pan-cooking the burgers, now is the time to heat the pan: Put a thin film of oil in a large skillet over medium heat; when it's hot, add the burgers. Cook undisturbed until a crust appears on the bottom and the burgers release easily with a spatula, about 5 minutes. Turn and cook until opaque throughout, 3 to 4 minutes on the other side (nick with a sharp knife to take a peek). Squeeze the juice from the limes over the burgers and serve on the buns with the desired toppings.

Salmon and Trout

After shrimp and canned tuna, salmon is the most popular seafood in America. And though it cooks like other thick fish fillets and steaks, its distinctive richness—and different types and sources—warrant special attention.

All Atlantic salmon now—that is, the species is called "Atlantic" regardless of which ocean it comes from—is farmed. It's not bad, eating-wise—it has a lot of fat, so it's easy to cook well—but there are serious concerns about the impact raising it has on the environment, as there are with most kinds of aquaculture.

Use wild Pacific salmon if at all possible. King (aka Chinook) and sockeye—which is in general leaner and much redder—are best, even if you have to buy it frozen. Coho is also good; chum is not bad; pink (or humpy) is usually canned. Buying fresh wild salmon—most of which comes from Alaska—will be occasional and expensive.

Intentionally deceptive or well-intentioned but ignorant purveyors might not always have reliable information. In order to find the best sustainable sources—there are some responsible farms, but you need to seek them out—be prepared to ask questions; check for current recommendations online (see page 531). Then you'll also be able to determine when you find a trustworthy fish market.

Full-service fish markets and good supermarket counters scale their fish—a bonus, since salmon skin is delicious, especially when crisp. If you buy some that still have scales, you have three choices: Remove the scales yourself, which, for whole fish or fillets, isn't difficult (see page 571). Skin the raw fish, also quite easy to do (see below). Or cook the fish with the scales on and discard the skin with the scales before serving, which is easiest. As a plus, the scales give added protection against overcooking.

All cooking methods work for salmon. The key is to avoid overcooking. I prefer salmon cooked to what might be called medium-rare to medium, with a well-cooked exterior and a fairly red, moist center. You might like it more well-done and pink. I use a knife tip to peek at the center. The fish will continue cooking after it has been removed from the heat, so stop just before the salmon reaches the point you'd consider it done.

Trout—which is almost always available farmed in fresh water, unless you are (or know) a fisherman—is similar to salmon in terms of flake but smaller and not as fatty. Some varieties of trout—steelhead, Arctic char, and orange-fleshed rainbow trout—look and eat a little like salmon, only milder. Use trout in any salmon recipe here, knowing it will probably cook faster. You can also use trout in any recipe for whole fish or thin fillets.

Pan-Cooked Salmon

MAKES: 4 servings | TIME: 20 minutes

Salt and pepper is the only seasoning you need here. For sauce ideas, see the list that follows.

Skinning a Fillet

STEP 1 Use any long, thin, sharp knife to cut a small piece from the tail end, at an angle, to expose the skin.

STEP 2 Grasp the exposed piece of skin (use a towel to get a grip if necessary) and insert the knife between skin and flesh, angled slightly toward the skin.

STEP 3 Run the knife up the entire length of the fillet.

Other seafood you can use: 4 trout fillets (you'll probably have to work in two batches, but they cook more quickly).

    2   tablespoons olive or good-quality vegetable oil
    4   salmon fillets (1½ pounds), skinned if you like,
        pin bones removed (see below)
        Salt and pepper
        Lemon or lime wedges for serving

1. Put a large skillet, preferably cast iron, over medium heat to get hot. Add the oil and swirl to coat the pan. Sprinkle the fish with salt and pepper. Add the fish, skin side down (even if the skin has been removed) and raise the heat to medium-high.

2. Cook until the fillets release easily, 3 to 5 minutes. Turn the salmon and cook to reach the desired stage of doneness, 2 to 5 minutes more (use a knife tip to peek inside). If you're going to eat the skin, serve the fillets with that side up. Serve with the lemon on the side.

Removing Pin Bones

STEP 1 Fillets of many fish, no matter how skillfully cut from the whole fish, may contain long bones along their center that must be removed by hand. Feel with your fingers to see if your fillet contains pin bones.

STEP 2 Remove them with a needle-nose pliers or similar tool.

10 SAUCES FOR PAN-COOKED SALMON

Spoon the sauce over the fillets just before serving.

1. Fresh Tomato or Fruit Salsa (page 55) or Fresh Tomatillo Salsa (page 56)
2. Tahini Sauce (page 56)
3. Simplest Yogurt Sauce (page 59)
4. Cilantro-Mint Chutney (page 62)
5. Soy Dipping Sauce and Marinade (page 64)
6. Miso-Carrot Sauce with Ginger (page 67)
7. Tartar Sauce (page 70)
8. Compound Butter (see page 78)
9. Any Five-Minute Drizzle Sauce (page 81)
10. Virtually any Vinaigrette (pages 188–191)

Salmon Roasted in Butter

MAKES: 6 to 8 servings | **TIME:** 25 minutes

It might seem like overkill to roast a rich fish in butter. But you won't think so after you try a bite. You can use olive oil or coconut oil instead, and change up the herbs as you like.

Other seafood you can use: trout; scallops (adjust the cooking time depending on their size).

    4   tablespoons (½ stick) butter
    1   2- to 3-pound salmon fillet (skin-on
        and scaled is nice), pin bones removed
        (see left)
        Salt and pepper
        Chopped fresh parsley for garnish

1. Heat the oven to 475°F. Melt the butter in a large rimmed baking sheet, either on top of the stove or in the oven, until the foam subsides. Sprinkle the salmon all over with salt and pepper.

2. Put the salmon in the butter, skin side up (even if the skin has been removed), and put the pan in the

Cold Poached Salmon with Dill Sauce; shown with quick-pickled cucumbers, page 228

oven. Roast until the fish releases from the pan, about 5 minutes. Use two spatulas to carefully turn the fillet, in one piece if possible.

3. Carefully spoon some of the butter over the top and continue roasting until the salmon is done a little less than you ultimately want it, 3 to 8 minutes more. To check, peek between the thickest flakes with a thin-bladed knife. Sprinkle with a little more salt if you like, garnish with parsley, and serve, pouring any pan drippings over the fish.

SALMON ROASTED WITH HERBS Omit the parsley garnish. In Step 1, use all olive oil or half oil and half butter. In a small bowl, combine 2 tablespoons minced shallot with 2 to 4 tablespoons fresh chopped herbs; tarragon, parsley, chervil, basil, dill, and thyme, or a combination are all lovely. After turning the salmon in Step 1, scatter the herb mixture over the fish; proceed as directed.

SALMON ROASTED WITH MISO BUTTER Omit the parsley. In Step 1, use 2 tablespoons of the butter for the pan and combine the remaining 2 tablespoons butter with 3 tablespoons white or yellow miso in a small bowl. After turning the salmon in Step 1, dot the top with bits of the miso butter and finish cooking.

Cold Poached Salmon with Dill Sauce

MAKES: 6 to 8 servings | **TIME:** 30 minutes, plus time to chill

Salmon cooked this way is so versatile for salads, sandwiches, Sushi Bowls (see page 451), and other quick dishes. My favorite sauce is a dill mayonnaise spiked with mustard. Or use any of the sauces listed after Pan-Cooked Salmon, on page 549.

 1 **2-pound salmon fillet, skin on and scaled, pin bones removed (see page 549)**

 1 **heaping tablespoon salt, plus more as needed**
 ¾ **cup mayonnaise (to make your own, see page 69)**
 3 **tablespoons chopped fresh dill**
 2 **tablespoons lemon juice**
 1 **tablespoon Dijon mustard**

1. Put the salmon skin side down in a large skillet with enough cold water to cover it. Sprinkle with the salt and bring to a boil. Immediately remove from the heat, cover, and let the salmon sit in the hot water until it's done as you like it. Start checking after 10 minutes by peeking with a thin-bladed knife at the thickest part.

2. Lift the fillet (skin and all) from the liquid with two spatulas, letting as much water fall back into the skillet as possible. Put the fillet on a rimmed baking sheet, skin down. When cool, cover tightly and refrigerate until cold, a couple hours or up to a day.

3. About an hour or 2 before serving, combine the mayonnaise, dill, lemon juice, and mustard in a small bowl. Add a little salt if you like, and refrigerate until you're ready to serve.

4. To serve the salmon, cut it crosswise into portions and lift the slices from the skin with a spatula. Pass the sauce at the table.

COLD POACHED TROUT WITH DILL SAUCE Use 1 large or up to 3 small whole trout or 4 to 6 trout fillets. Start checking them for doneness after steeping for 5 minutes at the end of Step 1. Proceed with Step 3.

Gravlax

MAKES: 4 to 6 main-course servings, more as an appetizer | **TIME:** 20 minutes, plus at least a day to cure

Why buy lox when your own cured fish is so easy to make? Use the good stuff here: King or sockeye salmon in season are ideal; the fish must be spanking fresh. With roasted potatoes and a salad, this is a luxurious meal. Or serve it with some condiments like mustard, crème fraîche, capers, and lemon slices and thinly sliced rye bread for lunch or as an appetizer. Gravlax keeps for several days after curing, and though it's not ideal (the texture softens), you can freeze it for a few weeks.

    1 1½-pound salmon fillet, skin on and scaled, pin bones removed (see page 549)
    ½ cup salt, plus more for seasoning
    1 cup sugar
    1 bunch fresh dill, chopped (including the stems is fine)

1. Put the salmon, skin side down, on a large piece of plastic wrap.

2. Mix the salt, sugar, and dill. Pack the salt mixture onto the salmon flesh, making sure it's completely covered, and putting a thicker layer on the thickest part of the fillet. Wrap the fillet tightly and put it on a rimmed baking sheet or large plate. Refrigerate until the flesh is darkened and firm, some liquid has leeched out, and a sharp, thin-bladed knife inserted into the thickest part of the fish meets some resistance, 24 to 36 hours.

3. Unwrap the salmon and rinse off the salt mixture. Pat dry with towels. Refrigerate in an airtight container for up to a couple days. When you're ready to serve, slice thinly, holding the knife at a slight angle.

Thick Fish Fillets and Steaks

Anything that's at least an inch thick falls into this category, the biggest in the chapter. Sometimes thick fillets come from the same fish found on the list of thin fish fillets (see page 568)—they're just cut from larger fish—and others are from fish that produce only thick fillets. So you'll see overlap in these lists. There's more detail about fish steaks starting on page 553, but almost all the recipes in this section work for both thick fillets and steaks.

Many of these fillets can—and should—be sold with their skin removed; steaks will always have a band of skin around the outside. You decide if you want to eat the skin or not. To cut fillets and steaks from whole fish, see the illustrations on pages 553 and 554.

TESTING DONENESS OF FISH FILLETS AND STEAKS

These pieces may be thick, but they still cook relatively quickly: Figure 8 to 10 minutes total per inch of thickness with most cooking methods. There is, of course, some variation based on the nature of the individual fish, so the only way to know is to check for sensory cues like tenderness, dryness, ease of flaking, opacity, and translucence. First, insert a thin-bladed knife or a skewer into the thickest part. If it penetrates with little or no resistance, the fish is done, or nearly so.

Use the same blade to gently open the fish at its thickest part and peek inside—a flashlight can be helpful here if your kitchen light is not direct. Once it's opaque throughout, the fish is completely done. If you stop cooking just before this point—when a bit of translucence remains—the fish will finish cooking on the way to the table. This judgment will come easily with practice.

Thick fish fillets and steaks cook quickly, but not in a flash, so you can broil and even roast them long enough to assure browning. The sturdiest—those marked with ■ in the following list—can stand up to turning on a grill without falling apart.

	Atlantic pollock (also known as Boston blue)
■	Blackfish
■	Carp
	Catfish
	Cod (including salt cod)
■	Grouper
■	Monkfish (see page 559)
	Orange
	Pacific pollock (also known as Alaskan pollock)
■	Red snapper and other snappers
■	Rockfish of any type
	Sablefish (also known as black cod)
	Sea trout (also known as weakfish)
	Seabass

 fast   make ahead    vegetarian

- Striped bass
- Sturgeon
- Tilefish
- Turbot
  Whiting (also known as hake)

FISH STEAKS

You just don't see fish steaks as much as you used to. Some—like swordfish and tuna—are available but expensive and often not sustainably fished. Other fish—like salmon and cod—are more commonly sold in fillets so you have to look or ask for them. All the species I've cooked as steaks are in the list that follows, which I share with the hopes that you'll be encouraged to try them when you have a chance.

Those that are boneless are marked with a ▨, and some have a more delicate texture (marked with a ☐). All can be grilled—and are excellent that way—though you still must avoid overcooking to prevent them from falling apart or becoming dry.

FISH FREQUENTLY CUT INTO STEAKS

- ☐ Bluefish: strong flavored; a good sometime substitute for tuna
- ☐ Cod: more delicate than halibut, but a good substitute
    Grouper: sturdy, firm-textured steak

Halibut: classic white steak, mild flavored and fairly sturdy
- ☐ Mackerel: strong flavored
- ☐ Mahi-mahi: in a class by itself; fairly sturdy, fairly strong flavored
- ☐ Mako: almost-tough flesh, mild flavored
- ☐ Monkfish: not a true steak, and scarce; see page 559
- ☐ Sturgeon
- ☐ Swordfish: classic, though in limited supply
- ☐ Tilefish: not common; mild; somewhere between cod and halibut in texture
- ☐ Tuna: look for sustainable options

WHEN ARE STEAKS DONE?

The same guidelines apply to steaks as do for thick fish fillets (see page 552), with some exceptions. The uniform thickness of steaks means they usually cook evenly. Be aware, though, that some of these fish, most notably swordfish and tuna, have a much more interesting texture and flavor when they're cooked only to medium or even medium-rare than when cooked to well-done. Some, like halibut and cod, become downright dry if they're overcooked. Sturgeon and mako are on the tough side if they're either under- or overdone. And the darker fish like bluefish and mackerel turn grayish white when they're done.

Filleting Fish

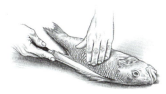

STEP 1 Lay the fish on its side and cut all the way down its back, just to one side of the top fin.

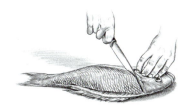

STEP 2 Make a deep vertical incision just below the gills, from the top of the fish to the bottom.

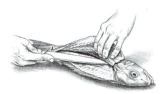

STEP 3 Cut over the backbone and the ribs, right down through the belly flap, to release the fillet. Repeat on the other side of the fish.

Fish Fillets or Steaks Baked in Foil

MAKES: 4 servings | **TIME:** 40 minutes

Cooking fish in a sealed package is an act of faith, but this method always works. The individual portions are lovely, especially if you use parchment paper (see the illustration with the summer squash recipe on page 340). Either way, you can assemble the dish up to several hours in advance and refrigerate it until you're ready to cook, which makes this an excellent dish for entertaining.

  4 **6-ounce thick fish fillets or steaks (see page 552 or 553)**
  ¼ **cup olive oil**
     Salt and pepper
  1 **tablespoon chopped garlic**
  ¼ **cup chopped fresh parsley or basil leaves**
     Lemon wedges for serving

1. Cut 4 sheets of foil or parchment paper, each about 18 inches long (you will be making 4 packages). Rub a piece of fish with some of the olive oil, season it with salt and pepper, and center it on a piece of foil. Sprinkle with garlic and parsley. Fold the foil over the fish, crimping the edges as tightly as possible. Repeat to make the remaining packages. (You can refrigerate the packages until you're ready to cook, no more than 6 hours later.)

2. Put a rimmed baking sheet in the oven and heat it to 400°F. Put the packages in the hot pan and bake for 15 minutes total, or about 8 minutes from the time you can hear the packages sizzling. Remove from the oven and let sit for a couple of minutes before carefully cutting open the packages. Transfer the fish to each plate with a spatula, remove any skins if you'd like, pour the juices over all, and serve with lemon wedges.

FISH BAKED IN FOIL WITH VEGETABLES Before adding the fish, put 1 or 2 of the following on the foil of each package, being careful not to overload: 1 chopped plum tomato; a few pitted black olives; some capers; 1 or 2 very thinly sliced small waxy potatoes; a thinly sliced whole lemon; several fennel slices; several slices from the white part of a leek.

WHOLE FISH BAKED IN FOIL A 3- to 4-pound fish is ideal, or use 2 to 4 smaller fish and share: Cut the foil or parchment big enough to entirely wrap the whole fish; you may need one piece under a large fish and another to cover it. Follow the recipe, adding more oil, garlic, or herbs, depending on the size of your fish. Bake for 15 minutes for small individual fish; 20 to 25 minutes for larger fish. I like to serve the fish whole, with the skin still on, and let everyone pick what they like off the bones.

Cutting Fish Steaks

STEP 1 Mark the fish by scoring it lightly with a knife to ensure you'll cut even steaks.

STEP 2 With most fish, the backbone is so thick that you'll need a little help to get the knife through; use a meat mallet or an ordinary rubber or wooden mallet.

Oven-"Fried" Fish Fillets

MAKES: 4 servings | **TIME:** 25 minutes

This is a retro recipe that lives on because it's both easy and tasty. You can use thin fillets here—just be careful handling them; they'll cook in about half the time. For

 fast   make ahead   Ⓥ vegetarian

more ideas about how to vary this recipe, see the list that follows, and "How to Season Simply Cooked Fish" (page 539).

1½ pounds thick fish fillets (see page 552), cut into 4 pieces
1½ cups buttermilk, yogurt, or milk
1 cup bread crumbs, preferably fresh (see page 801)
   Salt and pepper
4 tablespoons melted butter or olive oil
   Lemon wedges for serving
   Tartar Sauce (page 70) for serving (optional)

1. Soak the fillets in the buttermilk while you heat the oven to 450°F with the rack in the highest position. Put the bread crumbs on a plate and sprinkle with salt and pepper.
2. Drizzle about half of the butter or oil over a large rimmed baking sheet. When the oven is hot, pull a piece of fish from the marinade and let it drain a bit. Dredge the still-wet fish in the bread crumbs, patting them to make sure they adhere to both sides, then lay it in the pan. Repeat with the remaining pieces. Drizzle with the remaining butter or oil.
3. Bake for 8 to 15 minutes, depending on the thickness. The fish will be crisp on the outside, opaque on the inside, and firm when done; test with a thin-bladed knife. Serve right away with lemon wedges and some tartar sauce if you like.

OVEN-"FRIED" FISH STICKS OR NUGGETS The real deal, and kids love 'em: Cut the fillets into finger-length rectangles or squares of relatively equal size. Proceed with the recipe, reducing the cooking time by a minute or 2. Serve with ketchup if you like.

---

6 WAYS TO VARY OVEN-"FRIED" FISH FILLETS, STICKS, OR NUGGETS

1. Use cornmeal or a mixture of half flour and half cornmeal instead of the bread crumbs.

2. Use finely ground unsweetened coconut instead of bread crumbs.
3. Use crushed good-quality cereals like puffed rice or corn flakes.
4. Use crushed saltine or whole-wheat crackers instead of bread crumbs.
5. Skip the soak; rub the fillets with freshly squeezed lime juice and dredge them in flour spiked with a little chili powder (to make your own, see page 32).
6. Skip the soak; smear the fillets with miso thinned with a little white wine or sake and dredge them in panko.

Fish Steamed over Summer Vegetables

MAKES: 4 servings | **TIME:** 30 to 40 minutes

Versatile and foolproof, this "ratatouille-plus" recipe provides both fish and side dish in one fell swoop. The idea is to give the vegetables—whichever you choose—a head start in a hot skillet, then use them as a bed to steam sturdy fillets, steaks, or even a whole fish (which might take just a couple of minutes longer). The chart that follows has even more ideas.

4 tablespoons olive oil
1 onion, chopped
1 tablespoon chopped garlic
   Salt and pepper
1 zucchini, cut into 1-inch chunks
1 eggplant, peeled if you like, cut into 1-inch chunks
1 red bell pepper, cut into 1-inch chunks
1 pound tomatoes, chopped
1 tablespoon fresh chopped thyme or oregano
½ cup pitted black olives
1½ pounds thick fish fillets or steaks (see page 552 or 553), cut into 4 portions, one 3- to 4-pound whole fish, or four 1-pound whole fish
1 cup chopped fresh basil

(continued)

Left to right: fish Steamed over Summer Vegetables, Fish Steamed over Autumn Vegetables, Fish Steamed over Fennel, pages 555–558

Fish Steamed over Something

Follow the main recipe, using the onion and garlic unless otherwise noted, but replacing the fat, vegetables, and basil, and adding a liquid instead of the tomatoes. Whichever combination you choose, the goal is to let the vegetables soften and the sauce thicken but not quite come together. That way, when you lay on the fish everything finishes cooking together.

VARIATION	FAT	VEGETABLES	ADDED LIQUID	FINISHING FLAVORS
Fish Steamed over Autumn Vegetables	Olive oil	2 pounds total before trimming and/or peeling: butternut squash; leeks; peeled roasted chestnuts; Brussels sprouts	¼ cup or more apple cider or water	¼ cup chopped hazelnuts
Fish Steamed over Spring Vegetables	Butter	1½ pounds total before trimming: shelled fresh or frozen peas; scallions, cut into chunks; fresh spinach leaves; asparagus spears	½ cup cream	¼ cup chopped fresh mint
Fish Steamed over Potatoes	Butter	1½ pounds red potatoes, fingerlings, or other waxy potatoes, cut into ¼-inch-thick slices	1 cup milk	¼ cup chopped fresh chives
Fish Steamed over Greens	Olive oil	1½ pounds kale, collards, bok choy, cabbage, or spinach; trimmed and chopped. Some won't take more than a couple of minutes to soften.	¼ cup water or cream	¼ cup chopped black olives and hot red pepper flakes to taste
Fish Steamed over Fennel	Olive oil	Omit the garlic. Trim and thinly slice 1 pound fennel; chop and reserve the most feathery fronds.	¼ cup fresh orange juice	Garnish with the reserved fennel fronds.
Fish Steamed over Artichokes	Olive oil	Omit the garlic and onion. Trim, clean, and thinly slice 4 large artichoke hearts or 1½ pounds baby artichokes (see page 258). Cook until just tender, about 3 minutes.	2 tablespoons each water and lemon juice	Garnish with chopped fresh chervil, dill, or chives.
Fish Steamed over Gingered Sweet Potatoes	1 tablespoon sesame oil and 2 tablespoons good-quality vegetable oil	Omit the garlic and onion. Use 1½ pounds grated sweet potatoes and 2 tablespoons grated fresh ginger.	2 tablespoons each water and fresh lemon juice	Garnish with 2 sliced scallions.
Fish Steamed over Beans	Butter or olive oil	3 cups frozen lima or fava beans or edamame	¼ cup water	Garnish with chopped chives; serve with lemon wedges.

 **F** fast **M** make ahead **V** vegetarian

1. Put 2 tablespoons of the oil in a large skillet over medium-high heat. When it's hot, add the onion and garlic and sprinkle with salt and pepper. Cook, stirring occasionally, until the vegetables begin to soften, about 3 minutes.

2. Add the zucchini, eggplant, bell pepper, and more salt and pepper. Adjust the heat so the vegetables sizzle, and cook, stirring occasionally, until the eggplant is fork-tender, 10 to 15 minutes. Add the tomatoes, thyme, and olives and cook, stirring occasionally, until the tomatoes begin to break up, 5 minutes or so. Taste and adjust the seasoning.

3. Cut the fillets to fit the skillet if necessary. Lay the fish on top of the vegetables. Sprinkle with salt and pepper, and adjust the heat so the vegetables bubble steadily. Cover and cook the thinnest fillets for 5 minutes, thick fillets or steaks about twice that long or a few even longer; small whole fish should take about 15 minutes, a large one might take as long as 30 minutes. To check for doneness, insert a thin-bladed knife into the fish at its thickest point; it should meet little resistance, and the inside should be almost opaque. Transfer the fish to plates or a platter. (If you'd like, remove the skins and bones from large whole fish first serve as is.) Stir the basil into the vegetables, taste, and adjust the seasoning. To serve, spoon the vegetables around the fish and drizzle with the remaining olive oil.

What Happened to Monkfish?

Previous editions of this book included recipes and notes for cooking monkfish (which is really the monkfish tail, an irregular, tapered triangle that has firm, nonflaky flesh and a chewy texture). Over the years monkfish has become vulnerable to overfishing. What's more, the tail—and, secondarily, the liver, which is considered a delicacy—are usually harvested at sea and the rest of the fish is wasted. There are some sustainable fisheries, but it's important to recognize that most of the world's monkfish is not sustainably harvested.

Caramel Fish Fillets

MAKES: 4 servings | TIME: 30 minutes

The once-unusual technique from Vietnam is now almost commonplace. Here fish is poached in melted sugar, which miraculously becomes a not-too-sweet sauce. Serve over simply cooked white long-grain rice (page 430) or Steamed Sticky Rice (page 430).

Other protein you can use: shrimp; scallops; thinly sliced or cubed pork shoulder or boneless chicken thighs; beef sirloin; tofu cubes.

1	cup sugar
½	cup fish sauce, plus more to taste
3 or 4	shallots, sliced
1	teaspoon black pepper, or more to taste
	Juice of 2 limes, plus more to taste
1½	pounds thick fish fillets (see page 552)
	Chopped fresh cilantro for garnish

1. Put a large skillet over medium heat and add the sugar and 2 tablespoons water. Cook, occasionally shaking the pan gently, until the sugar liquefies and begins to bubble, about 5 minutes. When the sugar is all melted, cook without stirring until it darkens to resemble honey, another minute or so; remove from the heat.

2. Mix the fish sauce with ½ cup water. Carefully, at arm's length to avoid getting splattered, add this to the melted sugar. Return the pan to medium-high heat and cook, stirring constantly, until the caramel melts into the liquid, 1 to 2 minutes. Lower the heat to medium, add the shallots and cook, stirring occasionally, until they soften, about 5 minutes.

3. Add the pepper and lime juice, then lay the fish in the sauce. If the sauce does not reach at least halfway up the fish, add some water. Adjust the heat so the sauce bubbles. Cover and cook until the fish is done, 5 to 10 minutes; a thin-bladed knife inserted into the center will meet little resistance. Taste and add more fish sauce, lime juice, or pepper if necessary. Garnish with cilantro, and serve with the sauce poured on top of the fillets.

Curried Fish

MAKES: 4 servings | TIME: 45 minutes

Fish braises quickly and easily. In order for the pieces to keep intact, they have to be pretty big, even whole. So for stews like this curry, use sturdier thick fillets (see page 552), fish steaks (see page 553), or small whole fish. Be sure to check out the variations: One is for two different Thai-style curries; the other is for something totally different—fish braised with herbs and cream.

  1 cup all-purpose flour
1½ pounds sturdy, thick fish fillets or steaks, skinned if you'd like and cut into 2-inch chunks
      Salt and pepper
  3 tablespoons good-quality vegetable oil, plus more as needed
  1 large onion, halved and sliced
  2 tablespoons curry powder or garam masala (to make your own, see pages 32–34)
1½ cups coconut milk (to make your own, see page 372)
  2 tablespoons fresh lemon juice
      Chopped fresh cilantro for garnish
      Chopped pistachios for garnish

1. Put the flour in a shallow bowl. Sprinkle the fish with salt and pepper and toss it in the flour until lightly coated.

2. Put the oil in a large skillet over medium-high heat. When it's hot (a pinch of flour will sizzle), shake the excess flour from several pieces of fish and add them to the pan. Work in batches to avoid crowding, and adjust the heat so the fish sizzles. Cook, turning as necessary to brown the fish on all sides, 3 to 5 minutes total. As the pieces finish, transfer them to a plate with a slotted spoon. Repeat with the remaining fish, adding more oil if needed.

3. Spoon off all but 1 tablespoon of the oil and lower the heat to medium. Add the onion and cook, stirring occasionally, until it's soft and brown in places, about 10 minutes. Stir in the curry powder, sprinkle with a bit more salt and pepper, and cook, stirring constantly until fragrant, about a minute.

4. Add the coconut milk and ½ cup water to the skillet and adjust the heat so the sauce bubbles steadily. Cook, stirring once or twice, until it thickens, about 3 minutes. Return the fish to the skillet and cook, stirring gently to coat the pieces in the sauce, until the fish is opaque at the center, 3 to 5 minutes; test with a thin-bladed knife. Add the lemon juice, taste, and adjust the seasoning. Garnish with the cilantro and nuts, and serve.

THAI-STYLE RED OR GREEN CURRIED FISH Substitute ¼ cup Red or Green Curry Paste (page 46) for the curry powder. Use 6 to 8 scallions instead of the onion. Substitute 2 tablespoons fish sauce for the lemon juice. Proceed with the recipe, garnishing with a combination of mint and basil (preferably Thai basil) and peanuts instead of the cilantro and pistachios. Serve with lime wedges.

 fast   make ahead   vegetarian

FISH WITH CREAMY HERB SAUCE Use butter instead of the oil; omit the curry powder, onion, and coconut milk. Before beginning, purée 1 cup mixed mild herbs—like dill, chives, chervil, parsley, or mint—with 1 cup white wine and 1 cup cream. Proceed with the recipe, simmering the herb sauce for a few minutes in Step 4 before returning the fish to the pan.

Skate or Other Fish with Brown Butter, Honey, and Capers

MAKES: 4 servings | **TIME:** 20 minutes

Sometimes you can find skate; sometimes you can't. Fortunately when you can, it's almost always skinned, freed from its cartilage, and ready to cook. Just make sure the fish looks and smells utterly fresh. And when the stars don't align, just use any thick fish fillet or steak for this recipe—even salmon. And thin fillets can work too; just cut the cooking time about in half. The impressive pan sauce is too good not to eat on something.

- 1   cup all-purpose flour
     Salt and pepper
- 3   tablespoons olive oil
- 2   skate wing fillets (about 1½ pounds total) or thick fish fillets or steaks, skinned if you'd like
- 4   tablespoons (½ stick) butter
- ¼   cup honey
- 2   tablespoons drained capers, or to taste
- 2   tablespoons white or red wine vinegar
     Chopped fresh parsley for garnish

1. Heat the oven to 200°F. Put a large skillet over medium-high heat. While it's heating, put the flour in a shallow bowl and sprinkle with salt and pepper. Put the oil in the skillet; when it's hot, dredge one of the skate

fillets in the flour, shake to remove the excess, and add it to the pan.

2. Cook until the fish is browned and releases from the pan, 3 to 5 minutes, then turn. Repeat on the second side, cooking until it's firm to the touch and opaque at the thickest part, another 3 minutes or so. Transfer the skate to an ovenproof plate, put in the oven, and repeat with the remaining fillet.

3. Reduce the heat to medium and wipe out the pan if the flour looks burned. Add the butter and honey to the skillet and cook, stirring occasionally, until bubbly and brown, about 2 minutes. Add the capers and swirl them around, then pour the sauce over the fish. Immediately add the vinegar to the pan to deglaze any browned bits from the bottom, swirl it around, and pour it over the fish, too. Garnish with parsley and serve right away.

Deep-Fried Fish with Twice-Fried Ginger, Garlic, or Shallots

MAKES: 4 servings | **TIME:** 30 minutes

I learned to make this dish with ginger but have decided that garlic and shallots are equally good. Yes, it's a lot of aromatics. And yes, there's movement in and out of the hot oil. But if you're going to deep-fry, you may as well do it up right.

- Good-quality vegetable oil for deep-frying
- 1½ pounds thick fish fillets or steaks (see pages 552 and 553), skinned if you'd like, and cut into large chunks
     Salt and black pepper
- 1   cup all-purpose flour
- 1   cup cornstarch
- 8   ounces ginger, garlic, or shallots, peeled, trimmed, and thinly sliced or chopped (about ¾ cup)
- 4   scallions, cut into 2-inch lengths

 fast   make ahead   vegetarian

1 tablespoon soy sauce or fish sauce
Fresh tender cilantro sprigs for garnish

1. Heat the oven to 200°F. Put 2 to 3 inches of oil in a large pot over medium heat; bring to 350°F (see "Deep-Frying," page 22). Line a plate with towels and fit a wire rack in a rimmed baking sheet. Sprinkle the fish with salt and pepper. Combine the flour and cornstarch in a bowl.

2. When the oil is hot, fry the ginger, garlic, or shallots, stirring gently with a slotted spoon or small strainer just until lightly browned, 3 to 10 minutes, depending on which you're using and how you cut it. Adjust the heat as needed so the temperature remains nearly constant. Transfer to the towels with an Asian skimmer or slotted spoon and let drain.

3. Dredge the fish in the flour mixture, tapping to remove the excess. Add a few pieces slowly to the oil. Work in batches to avoid crowding, and adjust the heat as necessary so the temperature remains nearly constant. Fry, turning once or twice, until the fish is lightly browned and cooked through (a skewer or thin-bladed knife will pass through each chunk with little resistance), 3 to 5 minutes. As the pieces finish, transfer them to the wire rack and put the pan in the oven. Repeat with the remaining fish.

4. Deep-fry the scallions for 15 seconds. Remove with a slotted spoon and drain on the towels. Refry the ginger for about 30 seconds, then remove and drain. Put the fish on a platter and scatter the ginger, garlic, or shallots and scallions on top; drizzle with the soy sauce or fish sauce, garnish with the cilantro, and serve.

Mackerel Simmered in Soy Sauce

MAKES: 4 servings | **TIME:** 20 minutes

There are a handful of thick fish fillets and steaks that are a special case, since their flesh is dark, oily, and quite flavorful. Mackerel is the most common but others

that fall into this category are shad, bluefish, bonito, mullet, king or Spanish mackerel, and pompano. Make sure the fish is in good shape: Even more than most fish, mackerel is best eaten when it is super-fresh. Its quality deteriorates rapidly once the fish is out of water, and it does not freeze well. If none of this sounds appealing to you, try one of the options listed below instead. You won't be disappointed.

Other seafood you can use: any thick or thin fish fillet or steak; whole cleaned sardines; boiled octopus (see page 590).

1	recipe White Rice (page 430)
¾	cup soy sauce
½	cup sake, dry sherry, or water
1	tablespoon sugar, plus more to taste
3	tablespoons rice or white wine vinegar
1	inch peeled fresh ginger, thinly sliced
5 or 6	cloves garlic, smashed
1½	pounds mackerel fillets (preferably skin on) or mackerel steaks
	Grated fresh ginger, lemon zest, or both for garnish

1. Start the rice. Mix the soy sauce, sake, sugar, vinegar, ginger, garlic, and ¾ cup water together in a large skillet. Bring to a boil and adjust the heat so it bubbles gently, and cook until it thickens a bit, about 5 minutes.

2. Add the fish skin side down, cover, and simmer until the fish is cooked through, 5 to 10 minutes. The fish is done when the flesh turns opaque and a thin-bladed knife inserted into the thickest part meets little resistance. If it's ready, spoon a serving of fish and some sauce onto a mound of white rice; garnish and serve.

SAKE-SIMMERED FISH Lighter and perfect for delicate-flavored fish: Reduce the soy sauce to 2 tablespoons and increase the sake to 1¼ cups. Proceed with the recipe, adding a sprinkle of salt and pepper to the simmering liquid if you like.

Escabeche

MAKES: 4 servings | TIME: 45 minutes, plus time to cool

In this recipe, the fish is floured and lightly fried *before* marinating, then served at room temperature. The results are flavorful, unusual, and excellent for parties or picnics since it's one of the rare fish dishes that you can—and should—make well in advance.

1	cup all-purpose flour
¾	cup olive oil
1½	pounds thick fish fillets (see page 552), skinned
	Salt and pepper
10	cloves garlic, smashed
2	bay leaves
5	sprigs fresh thyme or 1 teaspoon dried
½	teaspoon cayenne, or to taste
1	cup red wine vinegar or other vinegar
1	cup dry red wine

1. Put the flour in a shallow bowl. Put ½ cup of the oil in a large skillet over medium-high heat. When it's hot, sprinkle the fish with salt and pepper and dredge it in the flour mixture, tapping to remove the excess; add a few pieces slowly to the oil. Work in batches to avoid crowding, and adjust the heat as necessary so the fish sizzles. Cook until the fillets release from the pan, 3 to 5 minutes, then turn and cook the other side until the fish is opaque at the center, another minute or 2. As they finish, transfer the fillets to a shallow glass or ceramic baking dish; they can overlap slightly. Repeat with the remaining fish.

2. Let the pan cool and wipe it out. Add the remaining oil and set it over medium heat. When it's hot, add the garlic and cook, stirring occasionally, until it begins to turn golden. Add the bay leaves, thyme, and cayenne and stir. Add the vinegar, bring to a boil, and simmer for a minute. Add the wine, bring back to a boil, and simmer until it almost evaporates, about 5 minutes. Add 1 cup water, bring back to a boil, and cook quickly to reduce the mixture to about half its volume, about 15 minutes.

3. Pour the liquid over the fish. Let cool to room temperature and serve. Or cover and refrigerate; the escabeche will be good for at least a couple of days. Bring back to room temperature before serving.

Fish Fritters

MAKES: 4 main-dish or 6 to 8 appetizer servings | TIME: 30 minutes

Few dishes are as versatile as fritters, and few fritters are as wonderful as those made with fish. It doesn't matter whether the seafood is raw or cooked, as long as you finely chop or flake it and combine it thoroughly with the other ingredients.

Other seafood you can use: shrimp; crawfish; scallops; shucked clams, mussels, or oysters; shelled crab or lobster.

1	pound raw or cooked thick or thin fish fillets or steaks, skinned (see page 548), bones removed if necessary (see page 549)
1	small onion, chopped
2	cloves garlic, minced
	Salt and pepper
	Cayenne pepper to taste (optional)
1	cup all-purpose flour
2	eggs
½	cup chopped fresh parsley or cilantro
	Good-quality vegetable oil, for deep frying
	Lime wedges for serving

1. Heat the oven to 200°F. Chop the fish with a knife. If it's cooked, shred it with your fingers; if it's raw, keep chopping until it's finely chopped. Combine it in a bowl with the onion and garlic, sprinkle with salt and pepper and a little cayenne, and stir gently but thoroughly to combine.

2. Add the flour and stir a few times, then beat in the eggs one at a time. Add about ½ cup water and stir, then continue to add water (up to another ¼ cup) until a batter forms—it should be a bit thicker than pancake batter, but not much. Stir in the herb and let sit.

3. Fit a rimmed baking sheet with a wire rack. Put 2 to 3 inches oil in a large pot over medium heat and bring to 350°F. (See "Deep-Frying," page 22.) When it's the right temperature, a drop of the batter will sizzle energetically but not violently. Working in batches to avoid crowding, gently drop spoonfuls of the batter into the oil and fry, turning once, until golden brown, about 5 minutes total.

4. Transfer the fritters to the rack to drain and keep them warm in the oven while you repeat with the remaining batter. Sprinkle with more salt if you like and serve with lime wedges.

INDIAN-STYLE FRITTERS You can also use shrimp or squid here: Add 1 teaspoon ground cumin and 1 teaspoon ground turmeric to the batter. Substitute 2 fresh hot green chiles, seeded and minced, for the parsley.

Aromatic Poached Fish

MAKES: 4 servings | **TIME:** 30 minutes

When you add a generous amount of the classic seasoning vegetables (known as *mirepoix*) to the poaching liquid in this recipe, they provide a bed for cooking the fish and leave you with a built-in garnish and super-flavorful broth. Serve this hot in a shallow bowl with lots of good bread, boiled potatoes, or plain rice to soak up the cooking liquid. Or cool in the liquid and serve just the fish, chilled, with Saffron Mayonnaise or Green Sauce, French Style (page 70) or Lemon Vinaigrette (page 190). This is also an excellent way to cook fish for salads.

    3   tablespoons butter
    2   carrots, chopped
    2   onions, chopped
    2   celery stalks, chopped
    1   tablespoon chopped garlic
        Salt and pepper

    1½ pounds thick fish fillets or steaks (see page 552
        or 553), skinned if you'd like
        About 2 cups fish, chicken, or vegetable stock
        (to make your own, see pages 174–179), or
        water

1. Put the butter in a large skillet over medium heat. When it foams, add the carrots, onions, celery, and garlic, sprinkle with salt and pepper, and cook, stirring occasionally, until the vegetables soften, 5 to 10 minutes.

2. Put the fish on top of the vegetables and add enough liquid to come just up to the top, not over it. Sprinkle with salt if you're using water. Bring to a boil, then remove from the heat and cover. Start checking the fish after about 10 minutes: a thin-bladed knife inserted between bone and flesh should reveal little or no translucence. Remove the fish with a slotted spoon and taste and adjust the seasoning of the broth. Serve as described in the headnote.

POACHED WHOLE FISH You will need a large, deep skillet or a roasting pan set over 2 burners, depending on the size of your fish: Double or triple the other ingredients as necessary, in proportion to the size of the fish. Follow the recipe through Step 1, cooking the vegetables just until soft. Put the fish on top, add enough liquid to come to the top without submerging the fish, and bring to a boil. Remove from the heat and cover; if the pan you're using doesn't have a lid, cover with aluminum foil. Large whole fish will take up to 30 minutes to cook; smaller ones will take 15 to 20 minutes.

---

4 OTHER LIQUIDS FOR POACHING FISH

1. Red or white wine, or sake (cut with some water if you'd like)

2. A mixture of ½ cup soy sauce and 1½ cups water

3. Half orange juice and half water

4. Half coconut milk (to make your own, see page 372) and half water

Fish Kebabs

MAKES: 4 servings | TIME: 45 minutes

A versatile recipe for grilled fish on skewers, brushed with a quick herb paste after cooking. Toss some vegetables on the grill at the same time and you have a full meal.

Other seafood you can use: scallops; shrimp; raw lobster chunks; whole cleaned squid (cut the cooking time in half).

- 1½ pounds thick fish fillets or steaks (see page 552 or 553) skinned if you'd like and bones removed if necessary, cut into large chunks
- ⅓ cup olive oil, plus more for brushing
  Salt and pepper
- 2 cloves garlic, peeled
- 1 tablespoon chopped fresh oregano, rosemary, lavender, or thyme
- ¼ cup chopped fresh parsley, plus more for garnish
  Juice of 1 lemon

1. The fish will be easier to turn if you use 2 skewers per kebab. If you're using wooden skewers, soak them in water for at least 15 minutes. Prepare a charcoal or gas grill for hot direct cooking; make sure the grates are clean. Thread the fish onto skewers to make 4 large or 8 small kebabs. Brush the fish with a little oil and sprinkle with salt and pepper.

2. Chop the garlic and herbs as fine as possible and combine them with ⅓ cup oil and salt and pepper, mashing and stirring with a fork into a rough purée. (A mortar and pestle or a small food processor is ideal, but you can easily do this by hand.) Stir in the lemon juice.

3. Put the fish over the fire and cook until it releases easily, 2 to 3 minutes. Turn and repeat with the other side until the fish is done but not dry; a thin-bladed knife inserted into the center should meet only a little resistance. Right before removing from the fire, brush the kebabs with the herb sauce. Serve garnished with a little more parsley.

Halibut Steaks with Creamy Saffron Sauce

MAKES: 4 servings | TIME: 30 minutes

You can use the yogurt sauce in this recipe with any simply cooked seafood, though I especially like it this way, with a delicate-tasting fish like halibut, gently cooked in lots of butter.

Other seafood you can use: any fish steak listed on page 553; any thick fish fillet on page 552; scallops; shrimp.

- 1 cup yogurt (preferably whole milk)
  Salt and pepper
  Small pinch cayenne
- 1 shallot, minced
- ½ teaspoon saffron threads
- 1½ pounds halibut steaks or thick fillets, skinned and cut into 2 or 4 pieces
- 4 tablespoons butter
  Juice of ½ lemon, or more to taste

1. In a small bowl, whisk the yogurt with salt and pepper, the cayenne, and the shallot. Rub the saffron between your fingers to crush it, then stir it into the yogurt mixture. Let sit for about 20 minutes, or cover and refrigerate for up to 2 hours.

2. Sprinkle the halibut with salt and pepper. Put the butter in a large skillet over medium heat. When it foams, add the fish and cook gently, turning once or twice, until a thin-bladed knife meets little resistance when inserted into the thickest part; this will generally take less than 10 minutes total. Just before serving, add the lemon juice to the sauce, then taste and adjust the seasoning. Serve the fish hot, warm, or at room temperature, with first the butter from the pan and then some yogurt sauce spooned over it.

HALIBUT STEAKS WITH SOUR CREAM-CHIVE SAUCE
Instead of the yogurt use half or all sour cream in Step 1. Replace the cayenne, shallot, and saffron with ⅓ cup minced fresh chives.

 fast make ahead vegetarian

Pan-Roasted Tuna or Other Fish Steaks

MAKES: 4 servings | TIME: 20 minutes

Assuming you can get your hands on extremely fresh, sustainably harvested tuna from a reliable source (it is possible; see the sidebar on page 531), then this is the way to prepare it. Cook the fish to rare or medium-rare and slice it thin for Sushi Rolls (page 448), Sushi Bowls (see page 451), salads, or a sashimi-style appetizer (page 133). And if you can't do all that, choose another fish, cook it all the way through if you like, and eat it in one piece as you would beef steak or a chop.

Other fish you can use: steaks or fillets of salmon, tuna, or halibut; swordfish.

1½ pounds tuna steak
    Salt and pepper
2 tablespoons olive oil

1. Heat the oven to 500°F. Cut the fish into manageable pieces if it's not already, and sprinkle with salt and pepper. Put a large ovenproof skillet over high heat and add the olive oil. When it's hot, add the fish. Cook until the bottom is browned and releases easily, 3 to 5 minutes, then turn the pieces and transfer the pan to the oven.

2. When the fish is done as you want it—anywhere from 3 minutes for rare to 10 minutes for cooked through (a thin-bladed knife will meet little resistance when inserted into the center), transfer it to a plate, along with any pan juices. Serve whole, cut in half, or thinly slice and serve fanned out on a platter or individual plates so the interior is face up.

SESAME-CRUSTED PAN-ROASTED TUNA OR OTHER FISH STEAKS Instead of olive oil, use good-quality vegetable oil. Press about ¼ cup sesame seeds into all sides of the tuna and proceed with the recipe.

Canned Fish

Seafood from a can—or a pouch—accounts for about a quarter of all fish and shellfish consumed in the United States. And given the challenges of buying fresh fish, I'm not surprised by the growing popularity of canned fresh or smoked anchovies, crab, clams, salmon, sardines, oysters, kippers, and mackerel, all packed in tins—or better still, jars. Even chefs are cooking with them.

On the plus side, canned fish is undeniably convenient, since it's there in your pantry, ready when you are. I use anchovies and tuna in all sorts of pasta sauces. Smoked oysters are terrific in scrambled eggs, and any of these make excellent spreads and snacks. On the other hand, I prefer to cook with fresh crab and clams, though if you don't have good access to good fresh seafood, canned can be an acceptable alternative.

Sometimes the fish in cans are underutilized species, like sardines and mackerel; often they're expensive commodities (crab and sockeye salmon). So if you care about sustainability, pay attention to the labels and do some homework (see page 531 for the most comprehensive source). And be sure to look for cans that aren't lined with the plastic that contains BPA (bisphenol A, a potential toxin). That's usually on the label now too.

Thin Fish Fillets

What the fillets in this group have in common is the way they cook: lightning fast. The fish on the list below fall loosely into two groups: They're thinner fillets from the thick fish listed on page 552; or they're cut from species that are naturally small or thin-fleshed.

All thin fillets cook very quickly and overcook just as fast. A ¼-inch-thick fillet can cook through in 2 minutes. Obviously you've got to watch them, and poke and peek often, as always looking for sensory cues. How do you know when they're done?

- For thinner fillets, less than ½ inch thick: By the time the outside of these fillets is opaque, the inside is nearly done. This is absolutely true if you turn the fish during cooking, as you do on the stovetop. But in the broiler or oven, you won't even need to turn the fish, so look for external opacity as a sign of internal doneness.

- For fillets between ½ and 1 inch thick: You can roughly estimate doneness by timing. About 8 minutes total is the longest you want to cook any fillet under 1 inch thick. Take a peek between the flakes of the fish. If most of the translucence is gone and the fish can just barely be separated into flakes—but isn't at all yet dry—it's done.

- For mixed fillets, with thick and thin parts: When the thinnest part flakes, the thicker part is done. When the thicker part flakes, it's overcooked.

All fillets continue to cook after you take them off the heat, so remember that fish fully cooked in the kitchen will likely be slightly overcooked at the table. Not a disaster: After a couple of times you'll have the experience to anticipate doneness.

The texture of the thin fillets on this list can range from extremely delicate to somewhat sturdy. All of the sturdier ones (marked with ■) can be substituted in the recipes for the more delicate ones; not vice versa though. Beyond the recipes here, see the sidebar on page 539 for more ways to prepare thin fish fillets.

- ■ Catfish
- ■ Dogfish (also known as Cape shark)
  Flatfish of any type: flounder, fluke, sole, dab, plaice
  Haddock (likely to have skin on, but it's edible)
  Large- or small-mouthed bass (freshwater)
  Pickerel (freshwater)
  Pike (freshwater)
  Ocean perch
- ■ Red snapper or other snappers
- ■ Rockfish of any type
- ■ Seabass
  Tilapia (see the sidebar at left)
  Trout (freshwater)
  Sea trout (also known as weakfish)
- ■ Wolffish (also known as ocean catfish; delicious but hard to get)
  Whiting (also known as hake)

Crisp Sesame Fish Fillets

MAKES: 4 servings | **TIME:** 20 minutes

Similar to the Sautéed Fish with Lemony Pan Sauce on page 537, but even crisper with the addition of a crunchy coating. I usually serve these with Steamed Sticky Rice (page 430) and Ginger-Scallion Sauce (page 64) or Soy Dipping Sauce and Marinade (page 64) for drizzling.

Other fish you can use: skate fillets (which may take a little longer to cook).

1½ pounds thin fish fillets (see above), cut into
    4 portions
    Salt and pepper

 fast   make ahead   V vegetarian

1 cup sesame seeds

1 tablespoon sesame oil

2 tablespoons butter or good-quality vegetable oil, plus more as needed

Chopped fresh parsley, cilantro, or mint for garnish

Lemon or lime wedges for serving

1. Put ovenproof dinner plates or a serving platter in a 200°F oven to warm. Sprinkle the fillets with salt and pepper. Put the sesame seeds in a shallow bowl.

2. Put a large skillet over medium-high heat for 2 or 3 minutes. Add the sesame oil and butter. When the butter foams, dredge one of the fillets in the sesame seeds, pressing them gently into the fish, then shake off any excess. Add it to the pan and repeat with another fillet. Adjust the heat so the fish sizzles and cook until the fillets are golden on the bottom and release easily, 2 to 3 minutes. Turn and repeat on the

other side, cooking just until the fish is opaque but is still juicy inside.

3. Transfer the fish to the warm plates or platter and put in the oven. Repeat with the other fillets, adding more butter to the pan if necessary. Garnish with the herb and serve with lemon or lime wedges.

CRISP NUT-CRUSTED FISH Almonds, hazelnuts, peanuts, pecans, or pistachios—all good: Substitute olive oil for the sesame oil or use butter. Omit the sesame seeds; grind 1 cup nuts to a fine powder (a food processor or blender will do the trick). Proceed with the recipe, using the nuts to dredge the fish. Garnish with parsley and serve with lemon wedges.

10 Other Recipes for Thin Fish Fillets

The cooking time will vary in direct proportion to how thick the pieces are—so check for doneness early and often. Their variations usually work well too.

1. Broiled Seafood using thin fillets (page 534)
2. Sautéed Fish with Lemony Pan Sauce (page 537)
3. Oven-"Fried" Fish Fillets (page 554)
4. Fish Steamed over Summer Vegetables (page 555)
5. Skate or Other Fish with Brown Butter, Honey, and Capers (page 562)
6. Mackerel Simmered in Soy Sauce (page 563)
7. Fish Fritters (page 564)
8. Halibut Steaks with Creamy Saffron Sauce (page 566)
9. Quick-Braised Fish Fillets in Black Bean Sauce (page 570)
10. Pan-Fried Trout Fillets With or Without Bacon and Onions (page 573)

Whole Fish

Okay, I know not everyone likes to cook whole fish. Maybe the sight of it freaks you out, or you don't have a pan big enough. Though I prefer the whole thing—and the "cheeks" are considered a delicacy—both problems are often solved by having the fishmonger remove the head and tail as part of the general cleaning and scaling. See page 571 if you want to learn to do the preparation yourself.

Whole trout is almost always easy to find. Sardines are getting easier. You might run across options like bass, carp, grouper, tilapia (not my favorite—see page 568), snapper, rockfish, or mackerel. And the best fish counters will order what you want.

The benefits of whole fish are flavor and texture—and for some of us, yes, presentation. Plus you get a bit bigger window for doneness since you're essentially cooking two pieces of fish stacked on top of each other. The whole fish recipes and variations in this section help with the timing, but if you want to use whole fish for some of the other recipes in this chapter, you can guestimate on your own by doubling the cooking time for the corresponding fillets, then add a couple minutes to account for the bones.

Quick-Braised Whole Fish in Black Bean Sauce

MAKES: 4 servings | TIME: 30 minutes

A classic Chinese preparation that's really quite easy. Or try the variation for fillets if you're skittish. Serve this over plain white or brown rice (page 430), with Spicy Quick-Pickled Vegetables or Quick-Pickled Corn Coins with Sichuan Peppercorns (page 229), or steamed vegetables. After buying gutted (cleaned) fish, see the illustrations on the next page for scaling and removing fins and gills.

- 5 tablespoons good-quality vegetable oil
- ¼ cup fermented black beans
- ¼ cup rice wine, dry sherry, or water
- 2 cups all-purpose flour
- 1 3-pound whole fish (see page 569), gilled, gutted, and scaled
  Salt and pepper
- 1 tablespoon chopped fresh ginger
- 1 tablespoon chopped garlic
- 4 scallions, chopped
- 1 large onion, halved and sliced
- 2 cups chopped tomatoes (a 15-ounce can diced tomatoes is fine)
  Soy sauce to taste

1. Put 3 tablespoons of the oil in large skillet over medium-high heat. Soak the beans in the wine. Mix the flour in a shallow bowl with enough water to make a batter the consistency of sour cream. Cut 3 or 4 parallel diagonal gashes in each side of the fish, all the way down

to the bone; sprinkle the fish inside and out with salt and pepper.

2. Coat the fish on both sides with the batter. When the oil is hot (a pinch of flour tossed into it will sizzle), add the fish. Cook until the bottom browns and releases easily from the pan, about 3 minutes, turn the fish and cook the second side for another 3 minutes, then transfer it to a plate. Turn off the heat and let the pan cool down a bit, then discard the oil and wipe out the pan.

3. Put 2 tablespoons fresh oil in the pan and turn the heat to high. When it's hot, add the ginger, garlic, and scallions and cook, stirring until fragrant, about 30 seconds. Add the onion and cook, stirring almost constantly, until it begins to soften, about 2 minutes. Turn the heat down to medium and add the tomatoes and the beans with their soaking liquid; cook, stirring occasionally, for about 5 minutes, just until the tomatoes begin to release some juice.

4. Return the fish to the skillet, cover, and cook until done, 10 to 15 minutes more; a thin-bladed knife inserted into the center will meet little resistance and the thickest part will be opaque. Taste and add soy sauce if the dish isn't salty enough; serve the fish whole, drizzled with the sauce.

QUICK-BRAISED FISH FILLETS IN BLACK BEAN SAUCE
Use any of the sturdy thick or thin fillets listed on pages 552 or 553, or try large scallops, shrimp, or whole or sliced squid. Start with about 1½ pounds seafood. Depending on their thickness, the cooking time for fillets in Step 2 will be 1 to 2 minutes per side, and 1 to 5 minutes in Step 4. For scallops, shrimp, or squid, it will be 2 minutes per side and just a minute or so for the final rewarming in Step 4.

Scaling Fish

Use a spoon or dull knife to scrape the scales from the gutted (cleaned) fish, and always work from the tail up toward the head.

Removing Fins

Like the gills, fins are best tackled with scissors. Note that they are removed only for appearance, and may be left on whole fish during cooking if you prefer.

Removing Gills

STEP 1 Use scissors to remove the gills, taking care not to cut yourself; gills are sharp.

STEP 2 Cut the gills on both sides from where they attach to the body.

STEP 3 Remove and discard—gills are too bitter to use for stock.

Removing Heads and Tails

STEP 1 To remove the head, make a cut right behind the gill covers to guide the knife.

STEP 2 Use a mallet to pound the knife through the backbone, if necessary.

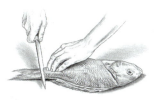

STEP 3 I do not recommend removing the tail unless your cooking method requires it or your pan is too short to hold the whole fish. If you must, however, simply use a sharp, heavy knife to cut right through the tail.

Pan-Fried Whole Trout with Bacon and Red Onions

MAKES: 2 servings | **TIME:** 45 minutes

Always and forever campfire food, made at home.

Other fish you can use: salmon; any thick fillets or steaks (see pages 552 or 553); whole sardines (which will cook in half the time).

    4 thick slices bacon
    1 large red onion, thinly sliced
    2 trout (about 12 ounces each), gutted and scaled
       (see page 571)
       Salt and pepper
    1 cup cornmeal
    ½ cup beer (a strong ale is good) or water
       Chopped fresh parsley for garnish

1. Line a plate with towels. Put the bacon in a large skillet, preferably cast iron, over medium heat. Cook, turning several times, until it begins to get crisp, about 5 minutes. Transfer to the towels to drain.

2. Immediately add the onion to the hot bacon fat and cook, stirring occasionally, until softened and starting to turn golden, about 5 minutes, then transfer with a slotted spoon from the pan to a bowl. Roughly chop the bacon and add it to the onion.

3. Rinse and dry the fish and sprinkle them with salt and pepper. Dredge the fish in the cornmeal, patting the sides to make sure it adheres. Put both whole fish in the pan and raise the heat to high. Cook, turning once, until the coating browns on both sides and the interior turns white and opaque, 8 to 12 minutes total. Transfer to a platter.

4. Turn the heat under the skillet to medium-low and add the beer, scraping up any browned bits that have stuck to the pan. Let the beer bubble and thicken a bit, then return the onion and bacon to the pan. Cook, stirring frequently until the sauce thickens. Taste and adjust the seasoning, adding lots of black pepper. Spoon the bacon, onions, and pan sauce over the fish, garnish with parsley, and serve.

PAN-FRIED TROUT WITHOUT BACON AND ONIONS
Simpler and faster: Omit the bacon, onions, and beer. Skip Steps 1 and 2. Instead, melt 4 tablespoons (½ stick) butter or heat ¼ cup olive oil in the skillet. When the butter foams or the oil is hot, dredge the fish in cornmeal and proceed with Step 3. Skip Step 4; instead, serve the trout right away with Tartar Sauce (page 70) and lots of lemon wedges.

PAN-FRIED TROUT FILLETS WITH OR WITHOUT BACON AND ONIONS For the main recipe or the first variation: Use 4 boneless trout fillets, skinned or skin-on as you like. In Step 3, cook the fillets in two batches, starting with the skin side down and adding more oil in between if the pan looks dry. They'll cook in about half the time. Then proceed.

Sardines on the Grill

MAKES: 4 servings | **TIME:** 45 minutes

Fresh sardines are widely beloved in Europe. They're easily broiled (the recipe on page 534 will show you how), but since we don't see them too often in the United States, this slightly special treatment (which works only with oily, skin-on whole fish) is a real treat, leaving them dried and crisp, with a smoky flavor.

Sardines are often sold gutted, with their heads on. If they are not gutted, make a lengthwise slit into the belly of each, and scoop out the innards with your fingers. Rinse and dry well. In addition to lemon, Aioli (page 70) and a sliced baguette will take you right to the Mediterranean.

Other fish you can use: whole mackerel (will take longer to cook).

    2 pounds large sardines, gutted, with heads on
       Olive oil for brushing
       Salt and pepper
       Chopped fresh parsley for garnish
       Lemon wedges for serving

1. Prepare a charcoal or gas grill for medium indirect cooking; make sure the grates are clean. Brush the fish inside and out with oil; sprinkle with salt and pepper.

2. Put the sardines on the cooler side of the grill, side by side, without crowding. Cover and cook for about 10 minutes before checking. If the sardines are opaque and firmed up a bit, carefully move them directly over the heat to crisp the skin on both sides, about a minute on each side. If they're not quite ready, cover and cook for a few more minutes before crisping. Garnish with parsley and serve with lemon wedges.

Scallops, Clams, Mussels, and Oysters

This group of shellfish are all bivalve mollusks, meaning the meat is enclosed in two shells. They're among the tastiest sea creatures that exist. Clams and oysters, of course, are often eaten raw (mussels are not), though clams are equally good cooked. To me, oysters are best raw, though I'm not against cooking them.

Buying in-shell mollusks is easy, since they must be alive and fresh to stay tightly closed. If they are open a little, then they should close quickly when tapped lightly; otherwise pass them up. Dead mollusks smell pretty bad, so it's unlikely you'll be fooled. (Scallops are a special case; see below.)

Never store clams, mussels, or oysters in sealed plastic or plastic bags, or in water; they'll die. Just keep them in a bowl in the refrigerator, where they will remain alive for several days—in the old days, oysters were kept alive in barrels for months.

Though they have different flavors, textures, and appearances, clams, mussels, and oysters can all be prepared the same way: You cook them in their shell until they open, or shuck them to remove them from their shells and cook them as you would other seafood. And like other seafood, they become firm and opaque when they're ready.

SCALLOPS

The creamy and almost translucent scallop is easy to cook, delicious, wonderfully textured—as long as it's not overcooked—and widely available. And it's almost always sold out of its shell. All of this makes it the most accessible mollusk, though it's usually pricey.

Scallops are often sold with their tendon, a stark white strip of gristle that attaches the muscle to the shell. If you're cooking just a few scallops, or making ceviche, or have a little extra time, just strip it off with your fingers. It's not necessary but this tendon is pretty chewy.

Sometimes scallops are soaked in phosphates, which cause them to absorb water and lose flavor; these are called "wet" scallops. Always buy scallops from someone you trust and let him or her know that you want unsoaked ("dry") scallops.

Shucking Clams

STEP 1 To open a clam, you must use a blunt, fairly thick knife; there is a knife made specifically for this purpose (called, not surprisingly, a clam knife), and it's worth having for this chore. Hold the clam in your cupped hand and wedge the edge of the knife into the clam's shell opposite the hinge. Once you get it in there, the clam will give up all resistance.

STEP 2 Run the knife along the shell and open up the clam. Try to keep as much liquor inside the shell as you can. Detach the meat from the shell and serve.

  F fast **M** make ahead **V** vegetarian

Sea scallops, with a flavor that ranges from mild to quite briny, are harvested year-round. They are the biggest type, at least an inch thick and twice that in diameter; some range to several ounces, but most weigh ½ ounce or so.

Bay scallops are caught in the winter months in a small area between Long Island and Cape Cod, and sometimes farmed in other regions and countries. These are the most expensive—and the best—scallops. Cork shaped and about the size of pretzel nuggets, they are slightly darker in color than other scallops. If you're not paying top dollar, you're not buying real bay scallops. Farmed versions from China and elsewhere are much less expensive and not nearly as good.

Calico scallops are little, inexpensive scallops found off the Atlantic and Gulf coasts and in Central and South America. They're shucked by blasting the shells with a hit of steam. Of course, this partially cooks them, further contributing to their tendency toward toughness. Calicos run to 200 or even 300 scallops per pound, although larger ones are also harvested, and passed off as bays.

For all scallops, avoid overcooking; you want their interior to remain creamy, not stringy or dry.

CLAMS

Clams range from little (littlenecks and Manilas) to sea clams that weigh hundreds of pounds; they may be hard (littlenecks, cherrystones, or the huge quahogs) or soft (steamers, razor clams, and other clams with fragile shells). The biggest and toughest are chopped into bits to be made into chowder. The choicest—essentially the smallest—are sold live and are great raw or briefly cooked.

Clams are dug all year, but since it's easier to dig in the summer months, they may be more plentiful and less expensive at that time. Commercially harvested clams are shipped with a certification tag, which you can ask to see when you buy them. Eating raw clams may be risky since they can harbor bacteria that is killed by cooking, so if you want to go that route know your source and talk to the fishmonger about their safety.

Steamers and other soft-shell clams (which are hard to find anywhere but at their source) usually contain large quantities of sand, and you must wash them well before cooking (soft-shells are never eaten raw). Hard-shells require little more than scrubbing their shells with a stiff brush under running water. To shuck them for serving raw or cooking out of the shell, see the illustrated steps that follow. Hard-shells are also nice lightly steamed like mussels, especially the smaller ones. I pry open the ones that stay closed to see what's going on inside; you'll see and smell if they should be discarded. The freshest clams need only lemon; sauces are superfluous.

MUSSELS

Mussels are usually less expensive than clams, and can be heavenly. They come from Maine to New Zealand, to the Pacific Northwest to Mexico. I prefer wild to cultivated mussels, but definite strides have been made in farming them, so I don't fuss much about it. And farmed mussels are cleaner and require only thorough rinsing.

In fact, the only disadvantage to wild mussels lies in cleaning them. If you have the time, let them sit in a pot under slowly running cold water for 30 minutes or so. Then scrub them thoroughly, discarding any with broken shells, those whose shells remain open after being

Removing a Mussel Beard

Most mussels have a beard, a small amount of weedy looking growth extending from their flat side. Pull or cut it off just before cooking.

tapped lightly, and those that seem unusually heavy—chances are they're filled with mud. As you clean them, pull or scrape off the "beard" (a weedy-looking growth that emerges from the side of the shell) from each one.

OYSTERS

Oysters are safe to eat year-round, but because of their spawning cycle they really are better in cooler months whose names contain an *R*. The very best oysters are harvested in winter, when the water is coldest.

There are five major species of oysters seen in the United States: the familiar Atlantic (*Crassostrea virginica*), known for its brininess, and grown all along the Atlantic and Gulf coasts; the Pacific (*Crassostrea gigas*), known for its wildly scalloped shell and fruity flavors; the Belon or European flat (*Ostrea edulis*), a round, metallic-tasting, flat-shelled oyster grown in Western Europe and in Maine; the Olympia (*Ostrea lurida*), the half-dollar-sized oyster indigenous to the Northwest and grown only there; and the kumamoto, a Japanese variety (*Crassostrea sikamea*, a subvariety of the Pacific) that's become popular on the West Coast.

Within each species, there are nicknames: The Atlantic is not only called the Eastern, but is casually referred to by many of its places of harvesting, especially Bluepoint, Wellfleet, and Apalachicola; the European is known as the flat (*plat* in French); and the Pacific, which is also grown in Europe, is sometimes called a Portuguese (*Portugaise*), from a now-extinct species that once made up the majority of oysters grown in Europe.

Nomenclature is confusing but important, because each species is markedly different from the others. Even within a species, the differences between a northern and a southern oyster can be profound, because much of the distinctive flavor of any oyster comes from its habitat. If you eat oysters on the half-shell, learn to recognize your favorite; I strongly believe that the best oysters come from the coldest waters, so I look for those. If you're cooking oysters, the differences are not as important.

Shucking Oysters

STEP 1 You can use an oyster knife, a punch can opener, or any sturdy (but preferably not-sharp) knife to open an oyster. The danger is in the knife slipping, so protect your hand with a towel or glove. Place the oyster, cupped shell down, on a flat surface and insert the knife into the hinge. Press and wiggle and twist the knife in there until the oyster pops.

STEP 2 Twist off the top shell, trying to keep as much juice inside as possible. Detach the meat from the shell and serve.

BUYING AND SERVING RAW OYSTERS

Buying oysters for cooking is easy; you can use ones that have been shucked, packaged, and marked with a sell-by date. But for oysters on the half-shell, you first have to determine which oyster you like, and then make sure the shells are undamaged and shut tight. To clean them, just scrub the shells thoroughly with a not-too-stiff brush. There's never any sand inside.

Shucking is the truly difficult part; illustrations follow, but you can also ask your fishmonger to do it for you. Keep opened oysters on a bed of crushed ice and serve them within a couple of hours.

To serve oysters on the half-shell, use any condiment you like. I prefer nothing at all, or at most a squeeze of lemon. But many people like pepper, Tabasco sauce, horseradish, or cocktail sauce (see Shrimp Cocktail, page 99). Another possibility is a flavored vinegar called mignonette: Combine 1 teaspoon coarsely ground black pepper, 1 tablespoon minced shallot, and ½ cup good-quality champagne vinegar or white wine vinegar.

 fast make ahead vegetarian

Seared Scallops with Pan Sauce

MAKES: 4 servings | TIME: About 15 minutes

The secret to simple and perfectly cooked scallops comes to life with this go-to recipe.

Other seafood you can use: shrimp; squid (cook for half the time); any thick fish fillets or steaks from the lists on pages 552 or 553 (which take a little longer to cook).

- 2 tablespoons butter
- 2 tablespoons olive oil
- 1 teaspoon minced garlic
- 1½ pounds scallops (preferably sea or bay)
- Salt and pepper
- Juice of 1 lemon
- 1 tablespoon chopped fresh chives

1. Heat a large skillet over medium-high heat for 3 or 4 minutes. Add the butter and olive oil, garlic. When the butter foams, about 30 seconds, add the scallops, a few at a time if they're big. Work in batches if necessary to avoid overcrowding the pan; there should be at least 1 inch between the scallops. Sprinkle them with salt and pepper as they cook.

2. Turn the scallops as they brown and release from the pan; allow about 1 minute per side for scallops less than an inch thick, and 3 minutes for those well over an inch. They're ready when the center is still slightly translucent, but overdone when they start to split and look dry. Check with a thin-bladed knife. Transfer them to a bowl as they finish. Repeat until you've cooked all the scallops.

3. Add the lemon juice to the pan along with a tablespoon or 2 water, scraping up any brown bits, and cook until the liquid is reduced to a glaze, 1 to 2 minutes. Return the scallops to the skillet, along with any juices that have accumulated. Add the chives and stir to coat with the sauce and heat through, 1 to 2 minutes. Serve right away.

BUTTER-BASTED SCALLOPS Omit the chives. In Step 1, heat the skillet over medium heat for only 2 minutes; use 4 tablespoons (½ stick) butter and omit the oil, and add all the scallops at one time. Don't brown them; keep the heat at medium and cook them on both sides until opaque, 5 to 8 minutes total, depending on their size. As the scallops cook, tip the pan slightly and spoon some of the butter over their tops. Finish as directed in Steps 2 and 3, stirring in another tablespoon or 2 butter when you return the scallops to the skillet. There's no need to garnish.

SEARED SCALLOPS WITH CHERRY TOMATOES Omit the lemon juice and chives. Halve 8 ounces cherry tomatoes. In Step 3, before returning the scallops to the skillet, add the tomatoes to the sauce and cook just long enough for them to wrinkle a bit and release their juice, about 2 minutes. Garnish with chopped fresh basil or mint.

SEARED SCALLOPS WITH GINGER AND SOY Use 2 chopped scallions instead of the chives. In Step 1, use ¼ cup good-quality vegetable oil instead of the butter and olive oil. Add 2 tablespoons minced or grated fresh ginger instead of the garlic. In Step 3, in addition to the lemon juice and water, stir in 1 tablespoon soy sauce and 1 tablespoon dry sherry or white wine. When you return the scallops to the skillet, add the scallions and 2 teaspoons sesame oil.

SEARED SCALLOPS WITH WHITE WINE In Step 3, replace the lemon juice and water with 1 cup dry white wine (a really good one would not be wasted here) and cook, stirring and scraping the pan with a wooden spoon, until the wine is reduced by more than half and is syrupy and thick, about 3 minutes.

SEARED SCALLOPS WITH RED WINE Don't knock it until you try it: Follow the white wine variation above but use a fruity but dry red wine. When the sauce is reduced and syrupy, add 1 tablespoon chopped fresh thyme or oregano and a generous pinch of black pepper before serving.

Broiled or Grilled Scallops with Basil Stuffing

MAKES: 4 servings | **TIME:** 30 minutes

One of my all-time favorite recipes. Even though it's super-easy to split and fill scallops, the results are guaranteed to impress.

Other seafood you can use: large shrimp (split lengthwise for stuffing).

½	cup fresh basil leaves
2	cloves garlic, peeled
⅓	cup plus 1 tablespoon olive oil
	Salt and pepper
1½	pounds large sea scallops
	Lemon wedges for serving

1. Chop the basil and garlic together on a cutting board as fine as you can manage, almost a purée (a mini food processor or mortar and pestle will help you here). Transfer to a small bowl and mix in 1 tablespoon of the oil and some salt and pepper.

2. Make a deep horizontal slit in the side of each scallop, but don't cut all the way through. Fill each scallop with about ½ teaspoon of the basil paste. Pour the remaining oil onto a plate or pan and turn the scallops in it. Let them sit while you turn on the broiler and position the rack about 4 inches below the heat or prepare a charcoal or gas grill for hot direct cooking; make sure the grates are clean.

3. Remove the scallops from the oil and put them under the broiler or on the grill (don't pour the remaining oil over them, as it will catch fire) and cover. Broil or grill, turning once, until golden all over and the stuffing is warm, 2 to 3 minutes per side, no more. Serve hot or at room temperature, with lemon wedges.

BROILED OR GRILLED SCALLOPS WITH THAI BASIL STUFFING Use Thai basil and substitute good-quality vegetable oil for the olive oil; use 2 teaspoons fish sauce instead of salt. When you make the paste in Step 1, stir in about 1 tablespoon minced fresh chile (like jalapeño or Thai) or a pinch hot red pepper flakes, and a pinch of sugar. Garnish with lime wedges instead of lemon.

BROILED OR GRILLED SCALLOPS WITH MISO STUFFING Omit the basil and garlic and substitute good-quality vegetable oil for the olive oil. Make a paste of ½ cup white or yellow miso with 2 tablespoons mirin (or 1 tablespoon each honey and water), a light sprinkle of salt, a pinch cayenne, and 1 tablespoon oil. Proceed from Step 2.

BROILED OR GRILLED FISH STEAKS WITH THREE DIFFERENT STUFFINGS Works for any steak thicker than 1 inch and any of the fillings: Use 4 fish steaks, about 6 ounces each. Cut a pocket in the side of each steak with a small sharp knife, as described for the scallops; don't cut all the way through. Proceed with the recipe, increasing the cooking time by up to 5 minutes per side so that the interior begins to flake but isn't quite opaque.

Steamed Clams or Mussels

MAKES: 4 servings | **TIME:** 15 minutes

The most common method for cooking clams and mussels also works for shrimp (see the variation). In all cases, steaming leaves you with rendered juices that are excellent as they are or easily enhanced with spice pastes, herbs, condiments, or other flavorings; see "How to Season Simply Cooked Fish" (page 539).

5	pounds clams (like littlenecks) or 4 pounds mussels, well scrubbed
1	cup white wine, water, or a mixture
	Salt and pepper
	Lemon wedges for serving
	Melted butter for dipping (optional)

1. Put the clams or mussels in a large pot. Pour the wine over all and sprinkle with salt and pepper. Cover, bring to a boil, then reduce the heat to maintain a steady bubble; you'll hear it and see some steam escaping.

2. Cook, undisturbed, for 5 minutes, then lift the lid to check the progress. If the majority of shells haven't opened, cover again and give them a couple more minutes. When they're all open, spoon off the clams and some of the cooking liquid, leaving behind any grit and serve with lemon wedges and little bowls of melted butter, if you like.

PEEL-AND-EAT STEAMED SHRIMP Use 2 pounds shrimp in their shells; if they're frozen, thaw them under cold running water for a couple minutes. Check after 3 minutes of steaming. When they're just turning pink, but still slightly translucent inside, remove from the heat. Give the pan a couple good stirs, then serve.

Baked Clams with Wasabi Bread Crumbs

MAKES: 4 main-dish or 8 appetizer servings | TIME: About 1 hour

Clams Casino are baked stuffed clams—ubiquitous but often mediocre. These are far more interesting and just as easy. Serve with Cold Soba Noodles with Dipping Sauce (page 522) and thick tomato slices and you have a meal. Or pass them at your next gathering for something dressed to impress.

Other seafood you can use: shucked mussels or oysters on the half-shell (adjust the quantity to the number of people you are serving).

24	clams, well scrubbed
2	tablespoons sesame oil
2	cups panko
2	teaspoons wasabi powder, or to taste
2	tablespoons chopped fresh chives
¼	cup soy sauce, or to taste
	Salt and pepper
	Lemon wedges for serving

1. Heat the oven to 450°F. Shuck the clams, reserving half the shells and as much of the liquor as possible (see page 576). If you're not confident about shucking, steam the clams lightly, removing them the second their shells begin to open. You can also microwave them, removing them the second they begin opening. Then shuck the clams, still preserving as much of their liquor as possible.) Chop the clams; I suggest by hand, but you can use a mini food processor if you are careful not to overprocess.

2. Heat the oil in a medium skillet over medium heat. Add the panko and cook, stirring, just until the crumbs begin to brown a bit. Add the wasabi and cook, stirring, until fragrant, just a minute or 2. Remove from the heat and stir in the chives. Add the reserved clam liquor and the soy sauce, a little at a time, to moisten the mixture. Fold in the clam meat. Taste and add more wasabi, soy, or a sprinkle of salt and pepper as needed.

3. Fill the reserved shells with this stuffing. Put them on a baking sheet or roasting pan, and bake until the stuffing is bubbling and lightly browned but not dry, about 10 minutes. Serve hot or warm, with lemon wedges.

Crab and Lobster

Crabs and lobster are treasured crustaceans, with sweet, delicious, chewy meat that is best left pretty much alone.

CRAB

Crabs are sold live, cooked, or frozen. All forms can be cooked (or reheated) by simple boiling. You need only put live crabs in a large pot of boiling water; if they have been cooked before freezing, submerge them in boiling water just long enough to heat through or even better, steam them above water (see page 20).

Crabs also taste good cold. So you can even just thaw frozen cooked king crab legs slowly in the refrigerator and serve them with any mayonnaise (to make your own, see page 69) or Cold Mustard Sauce (page 70)

6 Ways to Vary Steamed Clams or Mussels

Before putting the clams or mussels in the pot, heat the fat and cook the aromatics until fragrant. Then add the seafood, pour in the liquid, and add the stir-ins. Garnish as indicated (or not).

VARIATION	FAT	AROMATICS	LIQUID	STIR-INS	GARNISH
Steamed Clams or Mussels with Tomatoes	2 tablespoons olive oil	2 tablespoons chopped garlic	1 cup chopped tomatoes (partially drained canned is fine)	A sprig of fresh thyme or a couple of bay leaves	Chopped fresh parsley or basil and Fried Bread Crumbs (page 801, optional)
Steamed Clams or Mussels, French Style	2 tablespoons butter	2 or 3 shallots, chopped; 1 tablespoon chopped garlic (optional)	Dry white or fruity red wine	½ cup cream	Chopped fresh chervil or parsley
Soy-Steamed Clams or Mussels	2 tablespoons good-quality vegetable oil	¼ cup chopped scallion; 1 tablespoon chopped fresh ginger	2 tablespoons soy sauce; ½ cup sake or water	Minced fresh chiles (like Thai or serrano) or hot red pepper flakes, to taste	Chopped shiso leaves (optional)
Steamed Clams or Mussels, Thai Style	2 tablespoons good-quality vegetable oil	2 stalks lemongrass, trimmed, smashed, and roughly chopped; 1 or 2 fresh or dried hot red chiles	Juice of 1 lime; ½ cup water	1 tablespoon fish sauce; ½ cup chopped fresh Thai basil	Thai basil and lime wedges
Steamed Clams or Mussels with Something Meaty	Cook 2 ounces chopped bacon, ham, prosciutto, or spicy sausage, in 1 tablespoon olive oil until crisp. Drain off some fat, if you like.	1 small yellow or ½ sweet onion, chopped	½ cup white wine, ale, or water		Chopped fresh parsley or chives
Steamed Clams or Mussels in Curry Broth	2 tablespoons butter or good-quality vegetable oil	2 tablespoons chopped fresh ginger, minced; 2 tablespoons curry powder	1 cup coconut milk	1 cup peas or diced carrot or 2 cups parboiled potato (optional)	Chopped fresh cilantro

for an eating experience you couldn't duplicate if you worked for two hours.

Once crabs are cooked and shelled, they flesh is commonly referred to as lump crab meat. Whether you're buying it frozen, refrigerated, or canned or jarred, you should always run your fingers through it to look and feel for any cartilage or bone bits. It only takes a couple minutes.

Here are the most common types:

DUNGENESS CRAB There's nothing better than this Pacific crab, which runs 3 to 4 pounds and tastes more like lobster than the other crabs. It's almost always cooked and refrigerated for local sales, or frozen for shipping immediately after the catch. It's sold whole and is easy to eat but precious.

BLUE CRAB The familiar 4- to 6-inch blue crustacean, often with red claw tips. Close to where they're caught, you can usually buy them live. They're also cooked and picked from the shell so that the meat can be sold refrigerated or frozen throughout the country. When sold as picked meat, claw meat is best; lump means large pieces from the body, and flake means smaller pieces. Fresh blue crabmeat is expensive but incredibly convenient and wonderfully flavorful; with a squirt of lemon, it's celestial. Or toss it with some mild mayonnaise (to make your own, see page 69) to make a simple crab salad. Frozen, canned, and pasteurized "fresh" crabmeat never have the same taste and texture as freshly caught and cooked, but those of good quality are still worth eating.

Cleaning Soft-Shell Crabs

Cleaning live soft-shelled crabs (which kills them) is a messy job, not for the squeamish. Use a sharp knife or scissors to cut off the face, then scrape underneath both sides of the shell flap to remove the gills. Finally, if you want to remove the last bit of tough shell, pull off the apron, which looks like a *T* on the male and a bell on the female: Lift the tab on the underside and clean underneath the leathery coat of armor.

ROCK CRAB Similar in size and shape to blue crab, with a harder shell. Good eating; treat it like blue crab.

SOFT-SHELL CRAB Spring brings one of the best treats of all to fish counters: the live soft-shell crab. This strange delight is nothing more than a plain old blue crab, caught just after it has molted (shed its hard outer shell). Once out of the water, the crabs will not form new shells. But they live for only a couple of days and are therefore either shipped by air for immediate sale or cleaned (which kills them) and frozen. When you get live soft-shell crabs home, you have three choices: Clean them (if your fishmonger has not done this for you after purchase) and cook them right away; refrigerate and clean right before cooking (which will give you a day to think about what to do with them, but no longer than that); or clean and freeze. Though soft-shells freeze fairly well, this last option is a bit wasteful since frozen soft-shell crabs are available year-round.

KING CRAB The largest crab, which may weigh 25 pounds and have a 6-foot claw-span. This northwestern (mostly Alaskan) delicacy is not available fresh in other parts of the country; the crabs are cooked, dismembered, and frozen. Sometimes the legs are split, which is nice because it makes eating them so easy. But that's not difficult, in any case. Two or three legs make a good serving.

STONE CRAB The recyclable crab of Florida: Claws are broken off by fishermen and the crab is returned to the water, where it generates another limb. (It's illegal to be in possession of whole crabs.) It has a very hard shell, which is usually cracked with a small wooden mallet; it's usually sold cooked. Serve cold with Cold Mustard Sauce (page 70).

SURIMI Not crab at all, but rather a processed blend of fish, sugar, and other ingredients, sometimes made to look like crab; it's sold as "crabstick" or "imitation crab." Unless the label says crabmeat—and unless it's expensive—it probably isn't.

F fast   **M** make ahead   **V** vegetarian

LOBSTER

A fresh lobster, properly cooked, makes even butter superfluous. Buying can be the hard part; as a friend who sells lobster for a living says, "Just because it's alive doesn't mean it's fresh." When you're buying a lobster, make sure its claws are pegged or banded, and lift it; if it doesn't flip its tail and kick its legs, look for another. Tired lobsters are not fresh.

In the summer, lobsters—like crabs—discard their old shells and grow new ones as they get bigger. But soft-shell lobsters ("shedders") have a smaller meat-to-shell ratio than hard-shells, and they tend to be filled with water. Some people believe that soft-shells have sweeter meat—and indeed, some are terrific—but I prefer hard shells. You can tell the difference with a little squeeze— soft shells yield to pressure.

Then there's size to consider. Lobsters grow slowly and have been overfished for decades. Consequently, there are more "chickens" (1-pounders), "eighths" (1⅛ pounds), and "quarters" (1¼ pounds) than there are larger lobsters. But in my experience, two people sharing a 3-pound lobster will get more meat of higher quality than if each has his or her own 1½-pound lobster. There's less work, less waste, and more meat hidden in those out-of-the-way places.

Should you boil or steam? If you're cooking one batch of lobsters—whatever fits in your pot—steam them in a basket above simmering water. It's easier and, because the lobsters will absorb less water, far less messy. But since lobsters (mostly the shells) flavor the cooking water as they cook, the cooking liquid can in turn flavor the lobsters and it makes a lovely broth. So if you're cooking a bunch, go ahead and boil them. As for other cooking methods (once you're bored with steaming or boiling), grilling, stir-frying, roasting, and broiling are all good options.

To kill a lobster before cooking (which you must do before any cooking method other than steaming or boiling), use a sturdy, thin-bladed knife to poke a hole behind the lobster's eyes, right at the "crosshairs." It's also good to do this after boiling, to drain out the water that's accumulated in the beast. As an added refinement, you might also crack the claws (with a nutcracker, small hammer, or the back of a chef's knife) and split the tail before taking the lobster to the table. All of this is illustrated on page 584. For eating instructions, see page 586.

There are few parts of a lobster that you can't eat. If you split the lobster for grilling, you can remove and discard the head sac before cooking. You can also remove the tomalley (the pale green, liverlike organ) and in female lobsters, the coral (the very dark green unfertilized eggs, which turn bright red after cooking) to use raw in sauces. Otherwise, just remove the head sac after boiling.

How to Eat Crab

STEP 1 Twist off the claws and break them open with a mallet or nutcracker to pick and suck out the meat.

STEP 2 Break off the apron, then pull off the top shell. Rub off the feathery gills.

STEP 3 Break the body in two; then break each piece in two. Go to work, picking and sucking that meat out.

Finally, there is the spiny or rock lobster, from Florida and the Caribbean or even California. These lobsters and their related species are available worldwide, and it is their tails that are frozen to become the ubiquitous "lobster tails." With no claws, these babies are far simpler to eat than northern lobsters. They're not bad and can be used in any recipe for lobster, shrimp, or crawfish.

Boiled or Steamed Crab or Lobster

MAKES: 2 to 4 servings | **TIME:** 10 minutes

Put a dozen blue crabs—or a 3-pound lobster—in front of people, and you'll be amazed at how much they can eat. It's important the water be seriously salted: You can cook in seawater, which is nice if you can get it; you can add seaweed, which is charming (and makes a terrific seasoning); or you can use a fistful of salt, as most of us do. To get at the meat in crabs and lobster, see the illustrations on pages 583 and 586. For serving ideas see the list on page 585.

Handful of salt (or a big pinch if steaming)
6 to 12 **live blue or rock crabs, or 1 or 2 lobsters (about 3 pounds)**

1. Fill the largest pot you have halfway with water if you're boiling, just an inch or so if you're steaming (then rig it with a steamer as described on page 20). Salt it and bring to a boil. Using tongs, put the crabs or lobsters in the pot one by one.

2. Count cooking time from when the water returns to a boil: Cook crabs for about 5 minutes, or until red; lobster for about 8 minutes for its first pound and then an additional 3 to 4 minutes per pound above that. (For example, a 3-pounder should boil for 15 to 20 minutes.) The foolproof way to check doneness—essential with larger lobsters—is to insert an instant-read thermometer into the tail meat by sliding it in between the underside of the body and the tail joint; lobster is done at 140°F.

Preparing Lobster for Cooking

STEP 1 Before grilling, broiling, or stir-frying, plunge a knife right into the "crosshairs" behind the eyes to kill the lobster (see page 583) or parboil it for just a couple of minutes.

STEP 2 Cut in half through the head and down through the tail.

STEP 3 Your final product will look like this. Hack it up with or without the shell or leave as is.

 fast make ahead  vegetarian

3. Drain the seafood in a colander for a few minutes, reserving the liquid for another use if you like, and serve immediately, cool to eat later, or remove the meat from the shells to use for another recipe. If you want to drain the water accumulated in the lobster shell, use a sturdy, thin-bladed knife to poke a hole in the crosshairs right behind the eyes, then drain.

SPICY CRAB OR LOBSTER BOIL For every gallon of well-salted water in your pot, add 2 onions, roughly chopped; 2 celery stalks, roughly chopped; the juice of 2 limes or ¼ cup white wine vinegar; 1 tablespoon fresh thyme leaves or 1 teaspoon dried thyme; 1 teaspoon ground allspice; 2 dried or fresh hot chiles or 1 teaspoon cayenne; 1 tablespoon paprika; and 1 teaspoon freshly ground black pepper. Bring to a boil and let bubble for 15 minutes before adding the crustaceans and cooking as directed.

STEAMED COOKED CRABS OR KING CRAB LEGS This is a good way to heat frozen cooked crabs—or raw. Use a very big pot and make sure there's enough liquid to fill about an inch in the bottom. Rig a steamer (see page 20)

to keep the crab above the water. Put the crabs or legs in the steamer, cover, and bring to a boil. Check after 5 minutes; raw crab is done when the shell is reddish pink and the flesh hot throughout, flaky but still juicy. If not, keep cooking for another couple of minutes. You can cook frozen raw king crab legs straight from the freezer; just allow a minute or 2 more time. Frozen cooked crabs need only to be cooked long enough to thaw and get hot.

Bare-Bones Crab Cakes

MAKES: 4 servings | **TIME:** 20 minutes, plus time to chill

I don't mess around much with the crab-to-crumb ratio in my crab cakes recipe. But I try to stay loose on the flavorings. To the basic recipe below, I might add a little bit of finely chopped red bell pepper or scallion, or maybe some parsley or dill, to the crabmeat, or a pinch of curry powder to the dredging flour. Or I'll just make it as is, so the crab is kept front and center. And if you want to serve these as appetizers or a first course, form 8 or 12 cakes and cook them in two batches.

Other seafood you can use: cooked lobster; cooked fish fillets or steaks (see the variation).

- 1 **pound fresh lump crabmeat (3 cups), picked over for cartilage**
- 1 **egg**
- ¼ **cup mayonnaise (to make your own, see page 69)**
- 1 **tablespoon Dijon mustard**
  Salt and pepper
- 2 **tablespoons bread crumbs (preferably fresh; see page 801) or cracker crumbs, or as needed**
- 1 **cup all-purpose flour**
- 2 **tablespoons olive oil**
- 2 **tablespoons butter, or more oil**
  Lemon wedges and/or Tartar Sauce (page 70) for serving

9 Things to Serve with Any Simply Cooked Crab or Lobster

Go basic or go big. Or go nothing. But since people like what they like, it's best to offer some choices for dipping or drizzling.

1. Clarified butter (see page 752), or just melted butter
2. Freshly squeezed lemon juice
3. Some of the cooking broth (strained or spooned out of the pot to avoid grit)
4. Ginger-Scallion Sauce (page 64)
5. Any herb sauce (pages 51 to 52)
6. Soy Dipping Sauce and Marinade (page 64)
7. Thai Chile Sauce (page 66)
8. Miso Dipping Sauce (page 66)
9. Any of the flavored mayonnaises on page 70 (best with cold crab or lobster)

1. Mix together the crabmeat, egg, mayonnaise, mustard, and salt and pepper. Add enough bread crumbs to bind the mixture just enough to form into cakes; start with 2 tablespoons and use more if you need it. (Try pinching some in your palm to see if the mixture holds together.) To taste and adjust the seasoning, cook a spoonful of the mixture if you'd like.

2. Refrigerate the mixture until you're ready to cook. It will be easier to shape if you refrigerate it for 30 minutes or more, but it's ready to go when you finish mixing.

3. Season the flour with salt and pepper. Shape the crabmeat mixture into four 1-inch-thick cakes. Put a large skillet over medium-high heat for 2 or 3 minutes. Add the oil and butter and heat until the butter foam

How to Eat Lobster

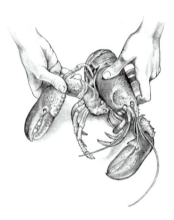

STEP 1 Twist the claws to remove them; they will come off easily.

STEP 2 Use a nutcracker to split their shells and a pick to pull out the meat.

STEP 3 Twist the lobster in half to separate the tail from the body.

STEP 4 Cut through the soft side of the tail.

STEP 5 Crack it open like a shrimp to remove the tail meat.

STEP 6 Cut through the underside of the front part of the body to extract the meat there.

 fast  make ahead V vegetarian

subsides. Dredge each cake in the flour and cook, adjusting the heat so the edges sizzle, until the bottoms brown and release easily, about 5 minutes. Gently turn the cakes and cook on the second side, another 3 to 5 minutes. Serve with lemon wedges and/or tartar sauce.

BARE-BONES FISH CAKES There is no better way to use leftover simply cooked fish. Salmon, halibut, cod—anything works, really: Use your fingers to break whatever pieces you have into shreds and small chunks, being careful not to turn it to mush. Substitute the fish for the crab in Step 1 and proceed with the recipe.

Sautéed Soft-Shell Crabs, Four Ways

MAKES: 4 servings | **TIME:** 30 minutes

Soft-shell crabs contain so much moisture that they're just about impossible to overcook, and they cook so quickly they're difficult to undercook. Plus they have built-in crispness from the shell (which is delicious) and a sweet, briny flavor. So they need no further adornment, especially if you make the buttery variation. But you can always make a Five-Minute Drizzle Sauce (page 81); transfer the crabs to a 200°F oven and use the same pan. If the crabs you bought haven't been cleaned, see the cleaning directions on page 582.

Other protein you can use: shrimp; boneless chicken breasts or thighs (cook them about twice as long).

- 2 **eggs**
- 2 **cups milk**
- 1 **cup cornmeal**
- 1 **cup all-purpose flour**
- ½ **teaspoon cayenne, or more to taste**
   Salt

Good-quality vegetable oil, as needed
4 **large soft-shell crabs, cleaned**
   Lemon wedges for serving

1. Beat the eggs and milk together in a bowl. Combine the cornmeal, flour, cayenne, and a large pinch salt on a plate. Put about ¼ inch of oil in a large skillet over medium heat.

2. When the oil is hot—a pinch of flour will sizzle—one by one dip the crabs in the egg mixture, then dredge in the cornmeal mixture and shake to remove the excess. Put in the skillet; adjust the heat so the crabs sizzle but the breading isn't burning.

3. Cook until the bottoms brown and release easily, 3 to 5 minutes. Turn the crabs and brown the other side, about 3 minutes more; the crabs will be quite firm when they're fully cooked. Sprinkle with a little more salt if you like and serve with lemon wedges.

SIMPLEST SAUTÉED SOFT-SHELL CRABS Omit the egg, milk, and cornmeal. In Step 2, when the oil is hot, dredge the crabs in the seasoned flour, shake a bit to remove the excess, proceed with the recipe.

BREADED SAUTÉED SOFT-SHELL CRABS Omit the cornmeal and use 1 cup bread crumbs—panko is nice, or fresh bread crumbs (see page 801)—or fine cracker crumbs. In Step 1, set up the seasoned flour in one bowl, the egg mixture in another, and the crumbs in another. When the oil is hot, dredge the crabs first in the flour, then in the egg mixture, then in the crumbs, patting them to make them adhere. Proceed with the recipe.

BUTTERY SAUTÉED SOFT-SHELL CRABS Instead of the cornmeal, use all flour for dredging. Replace the oil with butter; you could use as much as 8 tablespoons (1 stick). In Step 2, heat it until it foams, and proceed with the recipe. After you remove the crabs, add 2 tablespoons fresh chopped parsley and the juice from 1 lemon to the pan; heat the sauce until steaming, then pour it over the crabs when you serve them.

21 Seafood Recipes Elsewhere in This Book

1. Shrimp Cocktail (page 99)
2. Smoked Salmon or Trout Dip (page 100)
3. Anchovy Spread (page 103)
4. Tempura (page 112)
5. Fried Wontons or Egg Rolls (page 115)
6. Vietnamese Summer Rolls (page 123)
7. Ceviche (page 132)
8. Rice Porridge with Seafood (page 157)
9. The seafood soups on pages 161–164
10. Lobster Salad (page 223)
11. Crab Salad (page 223)
12. Pesto Shrimp Salad (page 224)
13. Miso Salmon Salad with Snow Peas (page 224)
14. Salade Niçoise (page 225)
15. Grilled Shrimp Salad with Chile and Basil (page 225)
16. Seafood Salad, Mediterranean Style (page 227)
17. Shrimp, Chicken, or Any Meat and Vegetable Stir-Fry (page 246)
18. Okra Gumbo with Seafood (page 313)
19. Summer Squash and Shrimp in Parchment (page 341)
20. Shrimp (or Squid) Paella (page 437)
21. Shrimp Jambalaya (page 437)

cleaned fresh squid; if you need to clean it yourself, see the illustrations at right.

Cooking squid is all about speed; like scallops and shrimp, it's almost impossible to undercook. When I was learning about squid, the old-timers would say, "Cook it for 2 minutes or 2 hours," and that advice is just about right. From hitting the heat to turning opaque—a sign that it's done—squid usually takes no more than a couple of minutes.

After that, it becomes tough, and then it takes long cooking in liquid for it to become tender again. In braised dishes, after 30 to 60 minutes of cooking toughness is no longer a concern, but the meat goes from pleasantly chewy to super tender.

Most octopus is cleaned and frozen at sea; thaw it in the refrigerator or in cold water.

Nearly everyone will tell you that octopus must be "tenderized" before cooking, and nearly everyone has some odd method of doing so—dipping it into boiling water three times, kneading it with grated radish, or hurling it against a stand of rocks (or, more likely, the kitchen sink). The reality is that some octopus are more tender than others—generally, smaller ones are more tender than larger, but not always—so I don't tenderize it; instead, I cook it until it's fork-tender, however long that takes.

Squid and Octopus

Both of these cephalopods (the word means that their feet grow out of their heads) are increasingly popular, but still mostly only in restaurants. It's a shame; they're not hard to cook, they're relatively inexpensive, and they're among the mildest, best-flavored seafood.

Like shrimp, squid freezes well and can be thawed and refrozen with little loss of flavor or texture. Frozen squid, typically cleaned before freezing, is available in supermarkets all over the country, frequently for just a few dollars a pound. Fresh squid should be purple to white, not brown, with a clean, sweet smell (spoiled squid smells particularly foul). Increasingly you can buy

Squid with Chiles and Greens

MAKES: 4 servings | **TIME:** 20 minutes

Squid freezes so well and cooks so fast that this dish can easily become a pantry staple for weeknights. As with most stir-fries, just about all the ingredients can be varied. Serve with Steamed Sticky Rice (page 430) or over rice noodles.

Other seafood you can use: shrimp and squid are virtually interchangeable in stir-fries. See the recipe and variations on pages 543–545.

Other vegetables you can use: any cooking green like pea shoots, cabbage, watercress, or spinach; chopped

  fast   M make ahead   V vegetarian

carrots, or parsnips for a nice all-white dish; chopped bell peppers. You can add a little chopped fresh Thai basil or mint at the end if you're not using greens.

- 1 **pound greens like collards, kale, arugula, or dandelion**
- 3 **tablespoons good-quality vegetable oil**
- 1 **chopped jalapeño or other fresh chile, or to taste, or several dried hot chiles**
- 1 **tablespoon chopped garlic**
- 1½ **pounds cleaned squid, cut into rings and tentacles (see below)**
   Salt

1. Remove the leaves of the greens from the stems, chop them both, and keep them separate.

2. Put 1 tablespoon of the oil in a large skillet over high heat. When it's hot, add the green stems, chile, and garlic and stir until fragrant and sizzling, about a minute. Add the green leaves and cook, stirring almost constantly, until they soften and release their water, 2 to 3 minutes. Transfer the greens and their liquid to a bowl.

3. Return the skillet to high heat and add the remaining oil. When it's hot, add the squid and a large pinch of salt and cook, stirring almost constantly, until the squid becomes opaque, about 2 minutes. Remove from the

Cleaning Squid

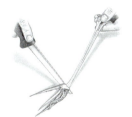

STEP 1 A whole, uncleaned squid.

STEP 2 Pull off the tentacles and head; they'll come out in one piece.

STEP 3 Reach inside the body, pull out and discard the hard, plasticlike quill.

STEP 4 Cut the tentacles from the head and discard the head and the hard, ball-shaped beak inside it.

STEP 5 You may remove any longish tentacles if you find them offensive, although they're perfectly edible.

STEP 6 Peel off the skin from the body, using a knife if necessary although your fingernails will likely be enough.

STEP 7 You can also submerge the squid in a bowl of water, which may make skinning it easier.

STEP 8 To make squid rings, cut across the cleaned body.

heat and return the greens (and liquid) to the pan and stir. Taste, adjust the seasoning, and serve right away.

Octopus with Tomatoes and Red Wine

MAKES: 4 servings, plus extra octopus for another dish | **TIME:** 2 to 3 hours, largely unattended

Most of the prep time in this recipe is for the simmering of the octopus in Step 1, a technique that tenderizes it for finishing with other cooking methods. Since the simmering time can be unpredictable, I suggest doing that part at least a few hours—or up to a couple of days—in advance so the pre-cooking doesn't throw off your timing on the rest of the recipe. I always freeze some of the cooked octopus in a little of the cooking liquid to use for something else. (It keeps for a couple of months. See the recipe for mackerel on page 563 for ideas.) For a bigger dish, serve as a pasta sauce or stir in Crisp Pan-Fried Potatoes (page 331) at the last moment.

1	2- to 3-pound octopus, cleaned and rinsed
3	cloves garlic, smashed, plus 1 tablespoon minced garlic
1	bay leaf
3	tablespoons olive oil
1	large onion, chopped
1	teaspoon fresh thyme leaves or ½ teaspoon dried
10	fennel seeds
3	medium tomatoes, cored and cut into chunks, or 6 to 8 canned plum tomatoes, drained
2	cups dry red wine
	Salt and pepper
½	cup chopped fresh parsley or basil leaves

1. To boil the octopus: Put it in a large pot with the smashed garlic, bay leaf, and water to cover. Bring to a rolling boil, lower the heat so the liquid bubbles gently, and cook, stirring once in a while, until the octopus is tender, 1 hour or more. Poke the thickest part with a sharp, thin-bladed knife or large fork; the octopus is ready when it can be pierced fairly easily. Drain the octopus in a colander over a bowl, reserving the liquid and discarding the bay leaf.

2. Cut about half the octopus into bite-sized pieces. Freeze the rest in an airtight container for another use, covered with about half the cooking liquid. Return the remaining liquid to the pot; raise the heat to high and reduce until about 1 cup remains, 15 to 20 minutes.

3. Put the oil in a large skillet over medium-high heat. When it's hot, add the octopus and cook, stirring, until it begins to brown, about 5 minutes. Add the onion and lower the heat to medium. Cook and stir until the onion softens, 2 or 3 minutes.

4. Add the thyme, fennel seeds, and tomatoes and stir. Cook for 1 minute, then add the wine. Bring to a boil, and cook, stirring occasionally until the sauce thickens, about 2 minutes. Add the reduced octopus cooking liquid, bring to a boil, then adjust the heat so the braising liquid bubbles gently.

5. Cook until the liquid thickens into a sauce, about 20 minutes. (Raise the heat if the octopus is very tender but too much liquid remains.) Add the minced garlic, stir, and cook until it softens, another couple minutes. Add half the herbs, stir, and taste and adjust the seasoning. Garnish with the remaining herbs and serve.

 F fast  **M** make ahead **V** vegetarian

Poultry

CHAPTER AT A GLANCE

Buying Chicken 592

Boneless Chicken 594

Chicken Parts 613

Fried Chicken 627

Whole Chicken 631

Whole Turkey 643

Turkey Parts 650

Duck and Goose 653

Other Whole Birds 658

How we buy and cook chicken has changed dramatically since the first edition of this book. The alternatives to mass-produced poultry are easier to find, even in supermarkets. Often there's little need to butcher these high-quality birds; boneless cuts—including thighs—are quite common.

All this is good news. Thigh meat (my favorite cut) is as convenient as the ubiquitous (and usually huge) boneless breasts. Wings are available by the pound and usually come separated. And most importantly, more people are cooking poultry that's been raised in ways that are better for the animals, for us, and for the environment.

What hasn't changed is the versatility of poultry, especially chicken. You can cook it with virtually every technique; its mild taste takes to a world of seasonings. Or you can simply brown and crisp it: Roast chicken with no more than olive oil or butter, salt, and pepper (page 633) is a near-universal favorite. To emphasize all the possibilities, this edition includes more charts and lists so you can customize the recipes and satisfy any craving.

After some basic information to help you sort through the confusion of buying chicken, the recipes are organized by the most common, easiest ways to cook it—boneless, bone-in parts, then whole birds—covering the many methods from poaching to grilling. The rest of the chapter is devoted to preparing turkey, duck, other small birds, and rabbit.

THE BASICS OF BUYING CHICKEN

The choice of whole birds and assortment of cuts has become a potentially mind-boggling spectrum that's easy to navigate with a little knowledge of labeling standards. At one end are the mass-produced, commercially fed, bred-to-be-big-breasted chickens; at the other are those raised in small flocks on small farms with plenty of room to roam. In between are lots of options to bridge the gap of price, quality, and convenience.

It's worth repeating that no one is getting rich selling a chicken for $15 or even $20, and that this represents something like the true cost of raising one and bringing it to market. Only you can prioritize what characteristics are most important, though I suggest you try to avoid chicken meat from animals that were given antibiotics as a way to help them put on weight quickly. Since the government forbids the use of growth hormones for poultry, keeping the birds "healthy" in crowded conditions with antibiotics is far too common. But the practice is increasingly being linked to antibiotic resistance in humans.

The following section will help you ask questions and make choices.

TYPES OF CHICKEN
STORE, NATIONAL, AND LARGE REGIONAL BRANDS
Since uniformity of size and a universally mild (I'd say bland) taste are the most valued commercial characteristics, these are essentially the same birds raised on the same large-scale farms by the same methods, just packaged with different labels. They're the least expensive chickens, but they also have the least flavor and, frequently, a watery texture. Some supermarket birds might be dubbed "premium"—but this isn't an officially recognized or regulated distinction.

If you cannot jump up the quality ladder, for whatever reason—availability, budget, or someone else did the shopping—choose a cooking method that will develop a crust or crisp the skin, often by adding butter or oil, and season the chicken assertively.

NATURAL A meaningless term. Thanks to bad federal government policy, just about every chicken qualifies to be labeled natural, even those raised with a heavy dose of antibiotics. In fact, other than the USDA's green organic and the looser definition of "Free Range" (see below), other labels are certified by the producer or third parties. This honor system is actually called "truthfulness in labeling" if you can believe it.

KOSHER AND HALAL Mostly, you're going to have to live in or near a big city to have these options, which indicate that the chicken has been raised, slaughtered, and processed according to Jewish or Islamic law, respectively. Though the standards don't officially evaluate quality, they do signal that someone has been paying attention. Sometimes the breeds are better and the (literally ancient) processing methods often result in excellent texture and flavor. They're often sold frozen, which is not ideal, but it's still better than the previous two options. More expensive too, about the same price as organic or locally raised chicken, but these could be the better option all around. The only way to know is to try a kosher or halal chicken sometime.

FREE RANGE Again, using this term alone to judge quality is iffy, since the people who sell chickens under this label need only to prove to the federal government that the birds spent *some* time with access to the outdoors. How long and in how much space—and what they were fed—depends as much on the good will of the producer as anything else. That said, odds are you'll find better-tasting chickens under this label. In my experience, some are tough but flavorful, so be careful not to overcook, or use them for braised recipes.

ORGANIC To be certified organic and receive the USDA's seal, chickens must be produced under specific conditions that assure the birds have at least some mobility, do not receive antibiotics or other drugs, and eat only organic, non-GMO (genetically modified organism) feed. Being organic doesn't guarantee the chicken will taste better (or be free of salmonella), though it is the only way you can know for sure that it was raised somewhat decently and fed well.

SPECIALTY OR LOCALLY RAISED Usually the most expensive and highest-quality chickens. In this category, I count imported chickens (which I never bother with) and locally raised. Often they're American "heritage" birds, those breeds that are not generally suited to the demands of large-scale farming but are valued by small farmers for both flavor and texture. Specialty birds may or may not be organic. I highly recommend seeking out locally raised chickens at farmers' markets, natural food stores, or directly from the producer. And ask questions!

FRESH VERSUS FROZEN CHICKENS

Chicken freezes well. So well that most whole birds and parts have been frozen at some point. Provided they were thawed slowly under cold refrigeration, you can buy previously frozen birds with confidence. In fact, frozen rock solid is frequently what you get from farmers markets and other local or specialty producers.

The only way to know if what you're buying has been previously frozen is to ask (assuming the source is trustworthy). To freeze—or refreeze—chicken, remove it from the package and rewrap tightly in two layers of plastic, or slip the original container in a freezer bag. Whole birds tend to keep better, and as long as you use the chicken within a month or two, you probably won't notice any difference.

CHICKEN SIZE AND AGE

Years ago chickens were labeled according to weight, sex, and age. Now it's one size range fits all. Occasionally you might see something labeled "fryer" or "broiler" (anything under 4 pounds or so) or "roasting chicken" (anything larger). Specialty birds might still be called "hens" or older, tougher "stewing chicken," which is best used for stock or braised in a dish like Coq au Vin (page 624). Capons are larger, neutered male birds that have a lot of flavor; they roast and braise well, though you rarely see them anymore.

CHICKEN SAFETY AND DONENESS

First, it's important to avoid cross contamination. That's when surfaces, utensils, vessels, and cleaning cloths and sponges that came into contact with raw meat—and potential pathogens—are then used to handle cooked meat. This also applies to marinades: To serve as a sauce, reserve some before you add the meat to the rest, to be sure you have some that never came into contact with the raw chicken.

The potential for cross contamination has prompted the USDA and food safety experts to recommend against rinsing chicken, since doing so can splatter raw juices around the sink and on to the counter. I rarely bother with the fuss of rinsing, but if you do, be sure to scrub everything down immediately afterwards. See "The Basics of Food Safety" on page 3 for a general discussion.

Chicken can harbor a couple of different pathogens, notably the potentially harmful bacteria salmonella, which are killed by cooking chicken until it is fully done. The easiest and surest way to reliably judge this is to use an instant-read thermometer: Poke it into the breast in two or three places (don't touch the bone), then into the thigh (again, avoiding the bone) if you're cooking a whole bird, in between the thigh and leg. The USDA currently recommends an internal temperature of 165°F in all these places.

Like all meat, chicken continues to cook after you take it off the heat; this is called carryover cooking. So here's my compromise for the best flavor and texture: To avoid overcooking, I remove chicken when the temperature is a little below the "safe" level and let the chicken rest for 5 or 10 minutes—basically the time it takes to finish pulling together the rest of the meal—during which the temperature continues to rise. And I've never had a problem.

If you want chicken that tastes its best, pull it off the heat at 155°F; if you want to be completely sure the chicken is absolutely safe, take it off the heat at 165°F. If you want some sort of balance between the two, remove the bird at around 160°F.

You can also check for doneness visually, by making a small cut in any section, right down to the bone. You should see no red whatsoever. Again, if you want to be really sure, wait until the meat is no longer pink at the bone.

THE BASICS OF BONELESS (SKINLESS) CHICKEN

Boneless, skinless chicken breasts are standard weeknight fare for many Americans, for obvious reasons: They cook in minutes and take to a wide range of techniques and seasonings. Their main problem is that overcooking leaves them tough and dry.

Boneless, skinless thighs have some advantages: They are more flavorful, since dark meat contains more fat. And they're more tolerant of slight overcooking for the same reason. They're now almost as widely available as boneless breasts, and are ideal for stir-frying and grilling, either whole or as kebabs.

Since the vast majority of boneless chicken sold in America is also skinless, from now on I'll assume boneless also means skinless unless otherwise described. I usually take the extra step of blotting boneless chicken pieces dry before grilling, broiling, roasting, or sautéing. Reducing the amount of moisture on the surfaces will promote searing instead of steaming, and help them develop flavor that the skin would normally provide. You've also got to use enough fat to keep them from sticking.

Since these cuts cook quickly, check frequently to avoid overcooking; the recipes give you a range of times. With thin cuts, nicking with a knife to check the color is more reliable than a thermometer. But to get an accurate reading, slide the probe in from the end, rather than down from the top, and insert it into the thickest part of the cutlet. Breasts or thighs are ready to come off the heat between 155° and 165°F (see page 593). I remove them from the heat when the inside is still a little pink, and still juicy. Though technically you can't see through raw chicken obviously—or fish or meat—it's a common cue to refer to cooked chicken or fish as "opaque," meaning it loses that translucent look of rawness.

Cutting your own boneless pieces from a whole bird is rewarding work and leaves you a carcass for stock or soup. (See the illustrations on pages 597 and 614). It's usually cheaper, too, though of course it will never be as

 fast 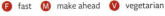 make ahead vegetarian

Customizing Poultry Recipes

I often refer to chicken—especially boneless breasts—as a blank canvas, since their own flavor is so mild. In case the variations and lists that follow most recipes still leave you wanting more ideas, here are other ways to transform simply prepared chicken. Choose the seasoning that hits all the notes you want. Or mix and match from different columns. (For more about umami, see page 66.) In some cases, the cooking time for the additions will vary depending on what you add. With your judgment and a live-and-learn attitude, everything will be just fine.

FOR FRESHNESS

- Squeeze with lemon juice before cooking or serve with lemon wedges.
- Add chopped fresh herbs to the seasonings before cooking, and/or garnish with herbs.
- Include fresh chopped tomatoes in stir-fried, sautéed, or poached recipes.
- Add quick-cooking vegetables like frozen peas or corn, radishes, or tender greens at the very end of cooking.
- Garnish with chopped scallions.
- Serve with any Herb Purée (page 52) or Fresh Salsa (pages 55–58).
- Top with any Yogurt Sauce (page 59).

FOR UMAMI

- Season the chicken with smoked paprika before cooking.
- Add fermented black beans to the cooking liquid or a stir-fry.
- At the beginning of cooking, add reconstituted dried mushrooms (see page 304); include some of the liquid if you like.
- Garnish with toasted seeds or nuts (see page 309).
- Baste the poultry with soy sauce while cooking.
- Just before serving, stir 1 tablespoon or more dark or light miso into the cooking liquid or sauce.
- Include a piece of kombu seaweed in any poached, boiled, or braised dish.

FOR SPICE

- Baste with any Chile Paste (page 40).
- Serve with Hot or Mild Pepper Chutney (page 62).
- Marinate in Thai Chile Sauce (page 66).
- Season with any spice mix (pages 27–35) before cooking.
- Add a few tablespoons Red Curry Paste or Green Curry Paste (page 46) to the cooking liquid; or thin the paste with about ¼ cup coconut milk and use to baste.
- Throw a whole dried chile or two into the mix at the beginning of cooking (smoked ones add another dimension).
- Baste chicken with Dijon mustard during cooking, or add coarse mustard to the liquid in braised or poached dishes.

FOR A ONE-DISH MEAL

- Add up to 1½ pounds any chopped vegetable to braised or roasted dishes; you might need to increase the cooking time.
- Add up to 1½ cups any raw grain to poached or braised dishes; you might need to increase the cooking time.
- Add up to 3 cups drained cooked beans (see page 390) to any recipe toward the end of cooking.
- Poach poultry in chicken or vegetable stock with up to 1½ pounds chopped vegetables.
- Poach poultry in "Boiled Water" or any of its variations (page 137).
- Put the meat and sauce on a big mound of raw spinach or chopped kale and spoon the cooking juices over all.
- Toast thickly sliced bread and serve the chicken and pan juices on top. Even bone-in pieces are fine; you just have to work a little harder.

convenient as buying the meat already boned, which is the whole idea.

Now that most boneless chicken is sold in individual pieces, the specific terms for the different formats have less meaning than they did even with the last update to this book. But knowing them can be helpful, especially when determining portion size.

A *chicken breast* technically describes the whole breast, two sides joined by a breastbone. So the single lobes currently sold as breasts are usually halves or what were once called *fillets* (unless you stumble onto a place that still sells them attached). To get *cutlets*, you'd take one breast and make it even thinner by halving the piece horizontally with the knife parallel to the cutting board, or flatten it with a meat pounder or the side of your fist. Boneless thighs also now qualify as cutlets. You can also buy boneless chicken *tenders* (short for tenderloins), the thin strip of white meat between the breasts and rib bones. (Remove any remaining tough pieces of tendon before cooking.)

The weights of pieces can vary wildly depending on the source and type of chicken. The largest supermarket breasts can weigh 12 ounces or more each; those from heritage birds weigh more like 6 to 8 ounces each. Thighs range between 4 and 8 ounces each. The recipes are usually based on weight and assume you cut or slice the meat for cooking as described, or as you like for serving. In cases where it's important to have intact portions of boneless chicken, the number of pieces and size are specified.

Broiled or Grilled Boneless Chicken

Broiling pairs a convenience ingredient with a convenient cooking method. You can, of course, grill boneless chicken if you have the equipment and the time; if you're firing up the grill anyway, I give instructions. For the rest of the time, broil them fairly close to the heat source, or heat up a cast-iron grill pan and cook on the stovetop. Whatever technique you choose, the idea is to brown the outside before the inside dries out and toughens.

Any of these recipes can also be used for turkey cutlets—or veal or pork. Most work equally as well with boneless thighs as with breasts; the results are just different. When it matters, I tell you which is preferred. To try it on your own, remember you'll have to increase the cooking time somewhat for thighs, to around 6 to 8 minutes per side.

Broiled Boneless Chicken

MAKES: 4 servings | **TIME:** 20 minutes

This basic dish shows how good home cooking can be with little effort. Though boneless chicken is excellent grilled, I almost prefer them broiled, since the seasonings stay with the meat instead of dripping onto the fire. It's also more accessible for most people. For poultry recipes that focus on grilling, see the section starting on page 617.

1½	pounds boneless white-meat chicken (breasts or tenders), pounded to uniform thickness if necessary, and blotted dry
3	tablespoons olive oil
3 or 4	cloves garlic, sliced (optional)
	Salt and pepper
½	lemon
	Chopped parsley for garnish (optional)

1. Put the chicken on a rimmed baking sheet or broiler pan. Toss with the oil, and the garlic if you're using it. Sprinkle with salt and pepper. If you like, cover and set aside for an hour or so to marinate.

2. Turn on the broiler and position the rack about 4 inches below the heat source.

Sectioning and Boning Chicken Legs

STEP 1 To cut the leg-thigh piece in two, simply find the joint where they meet and cut through it with a sharp knife. You'll know when you've found it because the knife will not hit bone.

STEP 2 To bone the thigh, cut the meat away from the thick center bone on the meat (nonskin) side.

STEP 3 Continue to cut until the bone is nearly free.

STEP 4 Cut the bone from the remaining meat and remove the skin.

Boning Chicken Breasts

 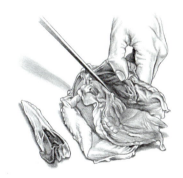 

STEP 1 Use a sharp, thin-bladed knife (usually called a boning knife) and cut as close to the bone as you can on the breastbone (not rib) side.

STEP 2 Continue to cut the meat away from the bone, keeping the knife blade just about parallel to the bone.

STEP 3 When the meat is almost detached, make the final cut. Trim the boneless breast of any pieces of tendon and, if you like, remove the skin.

3. Broil the chicken, turning once, no more than 3 or 4 minutes per side. To check for doneness, cut into a piece with a thin-bladed knife; the center should be white or slightly pink. Sprinkle with lemon juice and, if you like, parsley. Serve hot or at room temperature.

GRILLED BONELESS CHICKEN Put the chicken on a plate and toss with the oil, garlic if you're using it, and salt and pepper and let it marinate for up to an hour if you have time. Prepare a charcoal or gas grill for hot direct cooking; make sure the grates are clean. Grill the chicken until it releases easily, about 3 minutes, then turn and cook the other side until the inside is done as described in the main recipe. Move the chicken to the edges of the grill if it's cooking too fast or causing flare-ups.

BROILED OR GRILLED BONELESS CHICKEN THIGHS
Works with the main recipe, variation above, or any in the chart that follows: Substitute boneless chicken thighs for the breasts. Adjust the cooking time to 7 to 10 minutes per side, depending on their thickness.

Why Pound Chicken?

This extra step isn't meant to be fussy or make your life harder. In fact, it achieves the opposite. Whether you're working with cutlets—a slightly old-fashioned term for a thin slice of meat, in this case a halved chicken breast (see page 596)—or are using whole chicken breasts, pounding them prevents any thinner parts from overcooking before the thicker parts are done. It also cuts down on cooking time and tenderizes the meat.

I don't usually advocate for single-use kitchen tools, but a disk-shaped meat pounder is a good one. You'll find plenty of uses in the meat chapter too (starting on page 663). And you can use it to crush nuts, garlic, or a bag of ice. But even just pressing down on the chicken with the heel of your hand will flatten it enough to make a difference.

Chicken Escabeche

MAKES: 4 servings | **TIME:** 20 minutes if eaten immediately or up to 6 hours if marinated

With escabeche you cook, then marinate. Breast and thigh meat both work perfectly here; if you mix them, remember the thighs take longer to cook. You can use any Vinaigrette (page 188) instead of the garlicky variation listed here, and you can also use other herbs instead of parsley.

Other protein you can use: boneless pork or veal loin; Grilled or Broiled Tofu (page 419).

- 1½ pounds boneless chicken (breasts, tenders, or thighs), pounded to uniform thickness if necessary
- 2 tablespoons olive oil
- ½ cup Roasted Garlic Vinaigrette (page 190)
  Chopped fresh parsley for garnish

1. Turn on the broiler and position the rack about 4 inches below the heat. Rub the chicken with the oil and broil until cooked through, 3 to 10 minutes per side, depending on the cut and its thickness. (Thighs will take the longest.) Make a small cut and check; the center should be no longer raw but still juicy. Meanwhile, gently warm the vinaigrette in a small saucepan over medium-low heat.

2. Transfer the chicken to a serving platter; pour the vinaigrette over it. Serve right away, garnished with parsley. Or cover and marinate in the refrigerator for 1 to 6 hours, then serve cold or at room temperature, garnished with parsley.

GRILLED CHICKEN ESCABECHE Prepare a charcoal or gas grill for hot direct cooking and proceed with the recipe. Move the chicken to the edges of the grill if it's cooking too fast or causing flare-ups.

CHICKEN ESCABECHE WITH WHITE WINE MARINADE
Broil or grill the chicken as you like: Instead of the

Broiled or Grilled Boneless Chicken, 10 Ways

Starting with the main recipe for Broiled or Grilled Boneless Chicken as your guide, replace the olive oil and garlic with the fats and seasonings listed; instead of the lemon and parsley, garnish and serve as suggested.

VARIATION	FAT	SEASONING	GARNISHING AND SERVING
Mediterranean Broiled or Grilled Boneless Chicken	Olive oil	1 tablespoon cracked or ground pepper; 1 tablespoon ground coriander; 1 tablespoon chopped garlic	Garnish with chopped fresh oregano if you like. Serve with Baked Sweet Potatoes (page 343) or Chickpea Flatbread (page 97).
Spiced Broiled or Grilled Boneless Chicken	Olive oil	2 tablespoons curry powder, five-spice powder, or any other spice mixture	Garnish with chopped fresh parsley or cilantro. Serve with Dry-Pan Eggplant (page 287), drizzled with any Yogurt Sauce (page 59).
Broiled or Grilled Boneless Chicken, North African Style	Olive oil (just 2 tablespoons)	2 tablespoons honey; 1 tablespoon dry sherry (or dry white wine, fresh orange juice, or water); 1 tablespoon ground cumin; and the garlic	Serve with Collards or Kale with Tahini (page 301) or Simple White or Whole Wheat Couscous (page 456).
Broiled or Grilled Boneless Chicken with Thyme and Mustard	Melted butter	2 teaspoons chopped fresh thyme; 1 tablespoon Dijon mustard	Serve with any Broiled Vegetable Gratin (page 251) and Slow-Cooked Green Beans (page 297).
Curried Broiled or Grilled Boneless Chicken	Yogurt	1 tablespoon curry powder	Serve with basmati rice (page 430) and any Yogurt Sauce (page 59).
Parmesan Broiled or Grilled Boneless Chicken	Mayonnaise	2 tablespoons fresh lemon juice; 1 tablespoon grated lemon zest; 2 tablespoons grated Parmesan cheese; go easy on the salt	Serve with any pasta with Fast Tomato Sauce (page 478), or on top of a big bowl of mixed greens with a drizzle of Vinaigrette (page 188).
Broiled or Grilled Boneless Chicken with Vietnamese Flavors	Good-quality vegetable oil	2 tablespoons fresh lime juice; 1 tablespoon fish sauce; 1 tablespoon chopped garlic; 1 teaspoon sugar	Serve with Green Papaya Salad (page 210) and plain bean threads or rice vermicelli.
Broiled or Grilled Boneless Chicken with Thai Flavors	Coconut milk	1 tablespoon peanut butter; a pinch red chile flakes or cayenne	Garnish with slices of raw carrot, bell pepper, and scallion. Serve with bean threads or rice vermicelli, tossed with Thai Chile Sauce (page 66).
Rosemary Broiled or Grilled Boneless Chicken	Olive oil	2 tablespoons fresh lemon juice; 1 tablespoon chopped fresh rosemary	Serve with Oven-Roasted Potatoes (page 329) or Steamed Asparagus Spears (page 262).
Miso Broiled or Grilled Boneless Chicken	1 tablespoon sesame oil; 2 tablespoons good-quality vegetable oil	2 tablespoons any miso paste; 2 tablespoons ground walnuts; go easy on the salt	Serve with Cold Soba Noodles with Dipping Sauce (page 522), sliced cucumber, and tomato.

vinaigrette, combine 1 cup fruity, sweet white wine like riesling; 1 cup water; ½ cup white wine vinegar, white balsamic, or sherry vinegar; 1 tablespoon chopped garlic, and 1 thinly sliced onion in a small saucepan. Bring the mixture to a boil and adjust the heat so it bubbles gently. Cook until the onion is soft, about 5 minutes. Proceed with the recipe from Step 2. Garnish with chopped fresh oregano.

Chicken Teriyaki

MAKES: 4 servings | **TIME:** About 20 minutes

Caramelized and sweet; no wonder many Americans love it. Serve with plain short-grain brown or white rice (page 430).

Other proteins you can use: boneless turkey thighs, pork chops, tuna steaks, sirloin steaks.

- ⅓ **cup soy sauce**
- ⅓ **cup sake, white wine, or water**
- ⅓ **cup mirin, or 3 tablespoons honey mixed with 3 tablespoons water**
- 2 **tablespoons sugar**
- 2 **teaspoons grated lemon zest**
- 1½ **pounds boneless chicken thighs**

1. Turn on the broiler and position the rack about 4 inches below the heat. Combine the soy sauce, sake, mirin, and sugar in a medium saucepan, and bring to a boil. Lower the heat so the sauce bubbles steadily and cook, stirring once or twice, until it thickens. Stir in the lemon zest and remove from the heat; pour off half the sauce and reserve for serving.

2. Broil the chicken, basting frequently with the remaining sauce and turning the chicken every 2 or 3 minutes, until browned all over and cooked through, 10 to 15 minutes. Make a small cut and check; the center should be no longer raw but still juicy. Give the meat one

final baste and serve hot or at room temperature with the reserved sauce.

GRILLED CHICKEN TERIYAKI A little smokier: Prepare a moderate charcoal or gas grill for medium direct cooking (make sure the grates are clean) and proceed with the recipe. Move the chicken to the edge of the grill if it's cooking too fast or causing flare-ups.

STIR-FRIED CHICKEN TERIYAKI Toss this with boiled soba or udon noodles (page 520): Cut the chicken into strips about 1-inch wide. Heat a large skillet over medium-high heat for about 2 minutes. Swirl in 1 tablespoon good-quality vegetable oil, then add the chicken. Cook until the pieces brown on one side, about 3 minutes; transfer to a plate. Turn the heat to medium. Add ¼ cup water, followed by the sake, mirin, sugar, soy sauce, and zest. Stir to combine, then return the chicken to the pan. Cook, turning the chicken occasionally in the sauce, until the liquid thickens and glazes the chicken. Taste and add a little salt if you like and serve.

Baked Boneless Chicken

The best oven-cooked boneless chicken is baked with a little liquid and fat, so these recipes fall somewhere in between braising and roasting. Rather than browned and crisp, the results are moist, flavorful—and foolproof.

Chicken Baked with Tomatoes

MAKES: 4 servings | **TIME:** 40 minutes

Scented with cumin and coriander, this has a Moroccan feel to it but is no more difficult than putting together the simplest tomato sauce.

Other proteins you can use: any relatively thin boneless cuts of pork or veal loin; thinly sliced turkey breast.

¼ cup chopped fresh parsley or cilantro, plus more for garnish
1 tablespoon chopped garlic
    Pinch cayenne
1 tablespoon ground cumin
1 teaspoon ground coriander
    Salt and pepper
1½ pounds boneless chicken (breasts, tenders, or thighs), pounded to uniform thickness if necessary
2 tablespoons olive oil
2 cups chopped tomato (drained canned is fine)

1. Heat the oven to 400°F. Mix together the parsley, garlic, cayenne, half of the cumin, and the coriander and a pinch each salt and pepper; rub this all over the chicken.

2. Mix the remaining cumin with the oil and tomatoes and a pinch each salt and pepper. Spread half in a roasting pan. Put the chicken on top, then spread the remaining tomato mixture over it. Bake, basting once or twice with pan juices, until the chicken is tender and cooked through, 15 to 20 minutes (or more for thighs). To check make a small cut; the center should be no longer raw but still juicy. Garnish with parsley or cilantro and serve hot or warm.

HERB-BAKED CHICKEN Light and fresh: Omit the garlic, cayenne, cumin, and coriander. Increase the parsley to ½ cup and combine with ¼ cup chopped dill or chervil and 1 tablespoon chopped tarragon if you like. Set aside a few tablespoons of the herb mixture for garnish, and use the rest to coat the chicken in Step 1. Proceed with the recipe, using butter instead of the olive oil if you like; substitute 1 cup chicken or vegetable stock (to make your own, see pages 176 or 174) for the tomatoes.

Chicken Baked with Tomatoes, 4 Other Ways

The amount of chicken and cooking directions stay the same, but the flavor possibilities can be easily changed.

NAME	SEASONING	LIQUID	GARNISH
Turkish-Style Baked Chicken	1 tablespoon ground cumin; 1 teaspoon ground cinnamon; 1 teaspoon ground allspice; olive oil, salt and pepper	2 cups chopped tomatoes (drained canned are fine) with 2 bay leaves	Chopped fresh mint or parsley
Spicy Fennel Baked Chicken	¼ cup chopped fresh parsley; 1 tablespoon chopped garlic; olive oil or butter, salt and pepper	2 cups chopped tomatoes (drained canned are fine); 1 teaspoon fennel seeds; ½ teaspoon red chile flakes, or to taste	Chopped fresh parsley and toasted bread crumbs
Spanish-Style Baked Chicken	¼ cup chopped fresh parsley; 2 tablespoons chopped garlic; 2 teaspoons smoked paprika; olive oil, salt and pepper	1½ cups chopped tomatoes (drained canned are fine); ½ cup dry white wine	Chopped fresh parsley
Thai Curry Baked Chicken	1 tablespoon Red Curry Paste or Green Curry Paste (page 46)	1 cup coconut milk	Chopped fresh cilantro and lime wedges

 **F** fast **M** make ahead **V** vegetarian

STIR-FRIED CHICKEN

Grilling, broiling, and baking are great for chicken parts. But if you don't mind some chopping or slicing, you might consider mastering the recipes in this section first, especially if you like to improvise. Stir-frying is the quickest way to get a weeknight dinner on the table, since you use one pan for both meat and vegetables.

Boneless breasts and thighs are both fine here, cut into smaller pieces; you can also stir-fry chicken wings (see page 618) and eat them with your fingers. And be sure to check out other stir-fry recipes in the book and cook them with chicken. For more about the mechanics of stir-frying and making substitutions, see page 20.

Stir-Fried Chicken with Broccoli or Cauliflower

MAKES: 4 servings, with rice | **TIME:** 20 to 30 minutes

This is the model recipe for making stir-fried chicken with firm vegetables, those that must be parboiled before stir-frying. The extra step sometimes saves time and always helps you pinpoint doneness. But if you want to cook everything in one pan, cut the broccoli into small bits (½ inch or so) and start the recipe at Step 2.

  Salt and pepper
2 cups broccoli or cauliflower florets and stems, cut into bite-sized pieces
4 tablespoons good-quality vegetable oil
2 tablespoons chopped garlic
2 tablespoons grated or chopped fresh ginger
1 onion, sliced
½ cup chopped scallions, plus more for garnish
1 pound boneless chicken breasts or thighs, cut into ½- to ¾-inch chunks or thin slices and blotted dry
1 teaspoon sugar (optional)

2 tablespoons soy sauce
½ cup chicken or vegetable stock (to make your own, see pages 176 or 174), white wine, or water

1. Bring a large pot of water to a boil, salt it, and cook the broccoli until it just loses its rawness, 2 to 3 minutes. Drain and run under cold water to stop the cooking.

2. Put a large skillet over high heat. Add 2 tablespoons of the oil, swirl it around, and immediately add 1 tablespoon each of the garlic and ginger. Cook for 15 seconds, stirring constantly, then add the onion and cook, stirring, for 2 minutes. Add the broccoli and scallions and cook, stirring occasionally, until the broccoli becomes tender but not at all mushy, about 5 minutes.

3. Turn the heat down to medium and remove the vegetables. Add the remaining oil to the pan, then the remaining garlic and ginger. Stir, then add the chicken. Raise the heat to high, stir the chicken once, and let it sit for 1 minute before stirring again. Continue cooking, stirring occasionally, until the chicken has lost its pink color, 3 to 5 minutes.

4. Return the vegetables to the pan and toss once or twice. Add the sugar if you're using it, then the soy sauce; toss again. Sprinkle with salt and pepper, then add the stock. Cook, stirring and scraping the bottom of the pan, until the liquid is reduced slightly and you've scraped up all the bits of chicken, about 30 seconds. Garnish with scallions and serve.

13 SIMPLE ADDITIONS TO STIR-FRIED CHICKEN

You can throw almost anything you like into a stir-fry. These are some of my favorites; some require a trip to an Asian market, but many will be in your pantry.

1. Add 1 tablespoon or more of hoisin, plum, oyster, or ground bean sauce with the soy sauce.
2. Add ½ teaspoon or more Vietnamese-Style Chile Paste (page 45) or Chile and Black Bean Paste (page 45).

Stir-Fried Chicken with
Cabbage, page 606

3. Add 1 tablespoon sesame oil with the soy sauce. A tablespoon or so of toasted sesame seeds (see page 309) is also good, alone or with the oil.

4. While the chicken cooks in Step 1, sprinkle it with 1 tablespoon curry powder or five-spice powder (to make your own, see page 35).

5. Toss in ½ to 1 cup raw or roasted cashews or peanuts when you return the vegetables to the pan.

6. Omit the stock or water and add ½ cup or more coconut milk (to make your own, see page 372) along with the soy sauce.

7. Add 1 cup chopped fresh tomatoes when you return the vegetables to the pan.

8. Replace half or all the soy sauce with fish sauce, fresh lime juice, or vinegar.

9. Add 1 cup mung bean sprouts when you return the vegetables to the pan.

10. Add ½ cup chopped shallots with the chicken; omit the onion or scallions if you like.

11. Use snow peas, mushrooms, or other quick-cooking vegetables, alone or in combination, in addition to or instead of other vegetables.

12. Add a handful of dried chiles with the vegetables or 1 fresh chile, sliced and seeded if you like, when you return the vegetables to the pan. (Don't eat the dried chiles.)

13. In addition to the stock or water, add 1 tablespoon rice wine or dry sherry for the sauce.

Stir-Fried Chicken with Ketchup

MAKES: 4 servings | TIME: 20 minutes

Once you try cooking with ketchup (I'm betting you'll love it), play around some: Cook peanuts with the chicken, toss some slivered scallions in at the end (the color contrast is brilliant), or substitute soy sauce for the salt.

Other proteins you can use: squid, shrimp.

1½ pounds boneless, skinless chicken breasts or thighs, cut into bite-size chunks and blotted dry
½ cup cornstarch, rice flour, or all-purpose flour, or more as needed
4 tablespoons good-quality vegetable oil
   Salt and pepper
2 tablespoons sliced garlic
½ teaspoon cayenne, or to taste
1 cup ketchup
   Chopped fresh cilantro for garnish

1. Toss the chicken with cornstarch so that it is lightly dusted. Put 2 tablespoons of the oil in a large skillet, preferably nonstick, over high heat. When the oil just begins to smoke, shake off any excess cornstarch and add the chicken in one layer. Sprinkle with salt and pepper.

2. Cook, undisturbed, until the chicken browns on one side, then toss and cook until almost done; smaller pieces will take 5 minutes total, larger pieces about 10. Transfer to a plate. Turn off the heat and let the pan cool for a moment.

3. Add the remaining oil to the pan and turn the heat to medium-high. Add the garlic and cayenne and cook, stirring, for about 2 minutes. Add the ketchup and stir; cook until it bubbles, then darkens slightly, about a minute. Return the chicken to the pan and stir to coat with the sauce. Taste and adjust the seasoning. Serve, garnished with cilantro.

STIR-FRIED TOFU WITH KETCHUP Instead of the chicken, use 1½ pounds firm or extra-firm tofu, cut into 8 slices and lightly squeezed (see page 418). Proceed with the recipe. (It will need to cook for only about 5 minutes total in Step 2.)

Sautéed Boneless Chicken

This traditional pan-cooking method is ideal for chicken—you end up with something elegant even on a weeknight. Boneless breasts are the classic cut but

Stir-Fried Chicken, 6 Ways

As in the recipe above, use 1 pound boneless, skinless chicken breasts or thighs and good-quality vegetable oil. Add the aromatics and vegetables in Step 2 and the extras and sauce in Step 4. If the pan seems dry when you make the sauce, add water 1 tablespoon at a time.

NAME	AROMATICS	VEGETABLES	EXTRAS	SAUCE
Stir-Fried Chicken with Black Beans	2 tablespoons chopped garlic; 1 tablespoon chopped ginger; 1 cup sliced onion	¼ cup chopped scallions, plus more for garnish	2 tablespoons fermented black beans soaked in 2 tablespoons rice wine, dry sherry, or white wine	1 teaspoon sugar (optional); 2 tablespoons soy sauce; 1 tablespoon sesame oil
Stir-Fried Chicken with Mushrooms	2 tablespoons chopped garlic; 1 leek, rinsed thoroughly and chopped	8 ounces fresh mushrooms, sliced	½ ounce dried shiitake mushrooms, reconstituted and drained (see page 304)	2 tablespoons soy sauce; 2 tablespoons rice wine, dry sherry, or white wine
Stir-Fried Chicken with Basil and Chiles, Thai Style	2 tablespoons chopped garlic; 1 tablespoon chopped ginger; 2 cups sliced onion	¼ cup chopped scallion; 1 cup shredded fresh basil, plus more for garnish	2 or 3 chopped fresh chiles like jalapeño or serrano, or to taste, or dried chiles, red chile flakes, or cayenne to taste	1 teaspoon sugar (optional); 1 tablespoon fish sauce
Stir-Fried Chicken with Greens	2 tablespoons chopped ginger; 1 tablespoon chopped garlic; 1 cup sliced onion	3 cups chopped kale or Chinese greens like water spinach	2 tablespoons toasted sesame seeds (see page 309) for garnish	2 tablespoons soy sauce; 1 tablespoon sesame oil
Stir-Fried Chicken with Cabbage	2 tablespoons chopped garlic; 1 tablespoon chopped ginger	2 cups shredded green cabbage		2 tablespoons soy sauce; ½ cup chicken stock or water
Stir-Fried Chicken with Orange and Chiles	2 tablespoons chopped garlic; 2 tablespoons chopped ginger; 20 dried small red chiles, like Thai; zest of 2 oranges, left in strips (Don't eat the chiles and oranges.)			¼ cup orange juice, 2 tablespoons soy sauce

 fast make ahead **V** vegetarian

thighs work well if you pour off any excess fat after cooking so the dish doesn't become greasy. They're a little chewier and less refined, though that's often a positive for me. Other substitutes include inch-thick sliced turkey breast, pork, or veal; fish fillets; or even thin beef steaks.

A little bit of extra fat is required to brown boneless, skinless chicken properly during sautéing. If you want to use less fat, well okay: The chicken will still be moist and tender, but the pieces may stick to the pan and cook unevenly, and you can forget about the crunchy crust.

You've also got to use a skillet large enough to give the pieces space to sizzle. Make sure that the skillet is good and hot—not quite smoking—before you add the fat. Then wait a few seconds for the fat to heat before cooking (oil will shimmer and sizzle when you add a pinch of flour; the foam of butter will subside and begin to color). This will both prevent sticking and brown the meat properly. The chicken will signal when it's time to turn it by releasing easily from the pan; peek underneath to confirm it's well browned. You can't walk away from the stove for too long, but you also don't need to fuss. (For more general information about sautéing, see page 17.)

Sautéed Chicken with Wine Sauce

MAKES: 4 servings | **TIME:** 25 minutes

Spend an additional 5 minutes in front of the stove and you get a flavorful reduction sauce to pour over the chicken and any starch or vegetable you serve with it. (See "The Basics of Pan Sauces," page 80.)

Other proteins you can use: boneless pork loin chops; turkey or veal cutlets.

1½ **pounds boneless chicken (breasts, tenders, or thighs), pounded to an even thickness if necessary, and blotted dry**

Salt and pepper
1 **cup all-purpose flour**
2 **tablespoons olive oil**
3 **tablespoons butter, or more olive oil**
½ **cup dry white wine**
½ **cup chicken or vegetable stock (to make your own, see page 176 or 174) or water**
¼ **cup chopped fresh parsley, plus more for garnish**

1. Heat the oven to 200°F. Put a large skillet over medium-high heat for 2 to 3 minutes. Meanwhile, sprinkle the chicken with salt and pepper and put the flour on a plate.

2. Add the oil and 2 tablespoons butter or 2 tablespoons more oil to the skillet and swirl it around. When it is hot—a pinch of flour will sizzle—dredge a piece of the chicken in the flour, pressing to coat evenly. Shake it gently so that excess coating falls off. Add the chicken piece to the pan, then move on to the next one. (Don't be tempted to dredge in advance and add all the pieces at once; the coating will become soggy, and the heat in the pan will drop too quickly.)

3. Cook the chicken, regulating the heat if necessary so that there is a constant sizzle but no burning. After 2 minutes, rotate the chicken (don't turn it yet) so that the pieces at the outside edges are moved toward the center and vice versa. When the pieces are brown, after 3 to 4 minutes, turn them over.

4. Cook the second side until the chicken is firm to the touch, 3 to 4 minutes. (Make a small cut and check; the center should be no longer raw but still juicy. It's better to be slightly underdone than overdone.) As the pieces are done, transfer them to a heatproof platter and put it in the oven.

5. Return the pan to medium-high heat and add the wine. Let it bubble away, stirring and scraping the bottom of the pan, until it is reduced by half, about 2 minutes. Add the stock and cook, stirring, until the sauce is slightly thickened and a bit syrupy, another 2 or 3 minutes. (If you want just a little bit of sauce, cook longer; if you want more, cook a little less.)

6. Add the remaining 1 tablespoon butter or oil (if you're not using butter) and swirl the pan around until the butter melts; if you're using olive oil, stir vigorously with the back of a spoon. Add any juices that have accumulated around the cooked chicken, along with the parsley. Stir, taste, and adjust the seasoning. Spoon the sauce over the chicken, garnish with more parsley, and serve.

SAUTÉED CHICKEN WITH CREAM SAUCE Classic and rich: In Step 4, after removing the chicken, cook ¼ cup chopped shallots in the remaining fat over medium heat, stirring, until soft, about 5 minutes. Raise the heat to medium-high and continue with the recipe. After you add the wine and stock and reduce the sauce, turn off the heat, wait 30 seconds, then stir in 1 cup cream. Turn the heat to low; reheat, stirring, but do not boil. Spoon some of this sauce over the chicken and garnish with chopped parsley or a sprinkle of paprika. Pass the remaining sauce at the table.

12 SIMPLE SPINS ON SAUTÉED CHICKEN WITH WINE SAUCE

1. Add 1 to 2 tablespoons capers or pitted chopped olives along with the stock.

2. Add 1 teaspoon to 2 tablespoons any chopped fresh herb instead of the parsley; use chives, dill, basil, chervil, or cilantro for garnish.

3. Add 1 or 2 bay leaves with the wine; remove them before serving.

4. Cook 2 tablespoons chopped shallot, scallion, or onion or 1 teaspoon chopped garlic in the fat remaining in the pan for 1 minute, stirring, just before adding the wine. Add 1 tablespoon chopped anchovy if you like.

5. Add 1 tablespoon fresh lemon or orange juice after swirling in the butter or oil at the end. Add 1 teaspoon to 1 tablespoon grated lemon or orange (or grapefruit) zest at the same time, if you like.

6. Add ½ cup or more peeled, seeded, and diced tomato along with the stock. Especially great with

1 tablespoon balsamic vinegar stirred in just before adding the butter or oil at the end.

7. Cook ½ cup chopped fresh mushrooms in the fat remaining in the pan for 1 minute, stirring, just before adding the wine. Or use ¼ cup chopped reconstituted dried mushrooms (see page 304).

8. Stir in 1 teaspoon to 1 tablespoon Dijon or other mustard after swirling in the butter or oil at the end.

9. Add up to ½ cup Caramelized Onions (page 315) when you add the stock.

10. Use butter and increase the amount in the final addition to as much as 4 tablespoons (½ stick). This butter should be cold and cut into small bits, and incorporated a little at a time to make a smooth sauce.

11. Add 2 ounces chopped pancetta or bacon to the pan after removing the chicken; omit the last 1 tablespoon butter or oil.

12. Don't dredge the chicken in flour. Simply rub with salt and pepper or a little of any spice blend (to make your own, see pages 27–35) and cook directly in the hot butter or oil. If you crank up the heat a little bit, you'll get a nice brown crust with tender, juicy insides; reduce the cooking time accordingly.

Breaded Chicken Cutlets

MAKES: About 4 servings | **TIME:** 20 minutes

Some things, like thin boneless chicken coated with bread crumbs and pan-fried, never go out of style. Given good chicken, some pounding, attentive cooking, and a squeeze of lemon, these are brilliant as is—especially thighs, which are worth trying for sure. You can turn them into Chicken Parmigiana or use the same technique with eggplant (see the variations).

Other proteins you can use: any cutlets, ideally cut thinly from the leg or shoulder—pork, veal, or turkey.

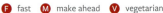 **F** fast **M** make ahead **V** vegetarian

1½ **pounds boneless chicken (breasts, tenders, or thighs)**
   Salt and pepper
1 **cup all-purpose flour**
2 **eggs**
2 **cups bread crumbs (preferably fresh; see page 801) or panko**
¼ **cup olive oil, plus more as needed**
   Lemon wedges for serving

1. Heat the oven to 200°F. Fit a wire rack in a rimmed baking sheet and put it in the oven.

2. If you're using breasts, spread them out flat side down on a cutting board and carefully slice through the meat parallel to the work surface so you split each breast in half horizontally. Working with one cutlet at a time, cover with a piece of plastic and flatten the chicken evenly with a pounder, a heavy skillet, or your hand until it's about ½ inch thick. Repeat with the remaining breasts and pat them dry with towels and sprinkle with salt and pepper. If you're using tenders or thighs, just pound them.

3. Put a large skillet over medium-high heat for 2 to 3 minutes. Put the flour, eggs, and bread crumbs on separate plates or shallow bowls next to each other. Sprinkle the eggs with salt and pepper and beat them with a fork until blended.

4. Pour the oil into the skillet and swirl it around. The oil should be hot but not smoking—a pinch of flour will sizzle. Dredge a piece of chicken on both sides first in the flour, then in the eggs, and finally in the bread crumbs, pressing to coat evenly. Shake it gently so that excess crumbs fall off. Add the chicken piece to the pan, then move on to the next one. (Don't be tempted to dredge in advance and add all the pieces at once; the coating will become soggy, and the heat in the pan will drop too quickly.)

5. Cook the chicken, adding a little oil and regulating the heat if necessary so that it sizzles without burning. When the pieces release, after about 2 minutes, rotate the chicken (don't turn it yet) so that the pieces at the outside edges are moved toward the center and vice versa.

6. Cook until the breading browns and crisps on the bottom, 3 to 5 minutes, or a couple minutes longer for thighs, depending on their thickness, then turn. Repeat on the second side, rotating and adjusting the heat as necessary until the chicken is firm to the touch and no longer pink inside. As the pieces finish, transfer them to the prepared pan and keep warm in the oven for up to 10 minutes. Serve hot with lemon wedges.

CHICKEN PARMIGIANA Use this method for veal parmigiana, too, using cutlets you can buy or cut yourself: Before cooking the chicken, make a recipe of Fast Tomato Sauce (page 478). Heat the oven to 400°F. Spread about ½ cup sauce in a 9 × 13-inch baking dish. As the chicken finishes, nestle the pieces in the sauce, then top them all with about 1 cup sauce. Keep the remaining sauce warm. Sprinkle 1½ cups coarsely grated Parmesan or mozzarella (or a combination) over all. Bake until the cheese melts and the sauce is bubbly, 10 to 15 minutes. Top with a tablespoon or two chopped fresh parsley or oregano and serve with the extra sauce on the side.

EGGPLANT PARMIGIANA Follow the directions in the variation above. Only instead of chicken, slice 2 pounds large eggplant lengthwise into ½-inch slices and use them for the cutlets in Steps 3 and 4 instead of the chicken; the cooking time will be almost the same.

6 MORE WAYS TO VARY BREADED CHICKEN CUTLETS

1. Add ¼ cup grated Parmesan cheese to the bread crumbs.
2. Add spices to the flour, like 1 tablespoon chili powder, curry powder, five-spice powder (to make your own, see page 35), or ground cumin. Use good-quality vegetable oil instead of olive oil and garnish with lime wedges.
3. Use unsweetened coconut flakes instead of half the bread crumbs; use good-quality vegetable oil instead of olive oil.

Naked Chicken Enchiladas,
page 612

4. Marinate the chicken breasts in buttermilk or yogurt, any Vinaigrette (page 188), or coconut milk (to make your own, see page 372) for up to a few hours before dredging and cooking. Be sure to scrape off as much of the marinade as you can before proceeding.
5. Add up to ¼ cup chopped fresh herbs like parsley, cilantro, chives, or a combination, or about a table-spoon chopped fresh rosemary or thyme, to the bread crumbs.
6. When you beat the eggs, add 1 to 2 tablespoons Dijon mustard.

POACHED BONELESS CHICKEN

Of all the techniques given for boneless chicken, this is probably the most forgiving. Since the chicken is cooked in liquid from start to finish, you have a little more latitude in timing, although severe overcooking will, ironically, result in dry chicken—all the juices leach into the pot—so don't wander too far. All of these dishes create enough sauce to use on a side dish of rice, noodles, polenta, potatoes, or bread.

Poached Boneless Chicken Breasts or Thighs

MAKES: 4 servings | TIME: 30 minutes

A recipe that that must be served with good bread, or at least a soup spoon to get every drop of sauce. Poached boneless thighs are the less traditional choice, with results that are richer and pleasantly chewy. Double the quantities and you'll have plenty of chicken for sand-wiches and salads throughout the week.

Other proteins to use: any cutlets—pork, veal, or turkey.

  4 tablespoons butter or olive oil
  2 leeks, washed well and chopped, including some of the light green part, or 1 onion, chopped
  ½ cup dry white wine or water

  ½ cup chicken or vegetable stock (to make your own, see pages 176 or 174) or water
  2 bay leaves
  1½ pounds boneless chicken breasts, tenders, or thighs
     Salt and pepper
     Chopped fresh parsley for garnish

1. Put 2 tablespoons of the butter or oil in a large skillet over medium heat. When the butter foams or the oil is hot, add the leeks and cook, stirring occa-sionally, until soft, about 5 minutes. Add the wine, stock, and bay leaves; bring to a boil and cook for a minute or 2.
2. Add the chicken in a single layer and adjust the heat so the liquid bubbles gently. Cover and cook, undisturbed, until the center of the breasts are opaque or only slightly pink, 5 to 6 minutes for breasts, 3 to 4 minutes for tenders, and 7 to 9 minutes for thighs. Remove the chicken from the liquid and keep warm.
3. Bring the liquid to a boil and cook, stirring occasionally, until about ¾ cup remains, 5 to 10 minutes. Turn heat to medium-low and add the remaining butter or oil, a bit at a time. If you're using oil, add it gradually, stirring vigorously with the back of a spoon.
4. Taste and adjust the seasoning. Return the chicken to the sauce to heat through. Remove the bay leaves, garnish with parsley, and serve.

POACHED BONELESS CHICKEN BREASTS OR THIGHS WITH LEMON SAUCE More or less traditional Provençal: Omit the bay leaves and use 2 teaspoons chopped fresh tarragon or thyme, or 1 teaspoon dried. Before adding the extra butter in Step 3, add 2 tablespoons fresh lemon juice.

---

8 MORE ADDITIONS TO CHICKEN POACHING LIQUID

1. Use ½ cup cream instead of the wine; add it with the chicken and avoid vigorous boiling.

Poached Boneless Chicken Breasts or Thighs, 5 Ways

Thin any of the sauces (except the Flavored Oil) with a splash of water if necessary to prevent scorching.

NAME	POACHING LIQUID	GARNISH WITH	SERVE WITH
Naked Chicken Enchiladas	Red Enchilada Sauce (page 73) or Green Enchilada Sauce (page 73)	Chopped scallions	Tortillas and Refried Beans (page 393)
Spiced Tomato Poached Chicken	Spicy Tomato Sauce (page 481)	Chopped fresh cilantro	Baked Rice Pilaf (page 434)
Curry-Poached Chicken	Red or Green Curry Sauce (page 46)	Lime wedges	Steamed Sticky Rice (page 430), White Rice (page 430); or Brown Rice (page 430)
Oil-Poached Chicken	1 cup olive oil; cook twice as long over low heat to prevent browning	Any chopped fresh herb and lemon wedges	Fresh bread or Baked Rice and White Beans, Tuscan Style (page 402)
Not-Quite Chicken Parmesan	Fast Tomato Sauce (page 478) or any of its variations	Grated Parmesan cheese and toasted bread crumbs, preferably homemade (see page 801)	Buttered spaghetti or other long pasta

2. Replace the stock or water and all or some of the wine with any vegetable juice.

3. Add 1 cup chopped fresh tomato with the liquid.

4. Replace the leeks with 1 large shallot, sliced.

5. Omit the leeks and use 2 tablespoons sliced ginger, 2 tablespoons sliced garlic, and 4 scallions, chopped. Use all chicken stock (page 176) or water for the poaching liquid and replace the bay leaves with 1 fresh chile, like serrano or jalapeño, halved. Add 2 tablespoons soy sauce and go easy on the salt.

6. Add ½ ounce dried mushrooms, reconstituted and drained (see page 304) with the liquid and bay leaves.

7. Replace the bay leaves with 1 sprig fresh rosemary.

8. Replace the wine with balsamic, sherry, or rice vinegar.

Boneless Chicken in Packages with Orange

MAKES: 4 servings | **TIME:** 1 hour

This method—traditionally called cooking *en papillote*—is simple and foolproof, using either parchment paper or aluminum foil to wrap the chicken and its seasonings. It's also impressive to serve the packages at the table.

Other proteins you can use in this recipe: any cutlets—pork, veal, or turkey.

> 2 oranges
> 4 small boneless chicken breasts (about 1½ pounds)
> Salt and pepper

 fast   make ahead  vegetarian

12 fresh basil leaves, or 4 sprigs fresh chervil,
    parsley, or cilantro
    About 2 tablespoons olive oil

1. Cut the ends off each orange, and use a knife to remove the zest, pith, and outer membrane, cutting as close to the flesh as possible. Cut the oranges into wheels (see the illustrations on page 378).

2. Tear off two 1-foot-square pieces of aluminum foil or parchment paper and put one on top of the other. Put a chicken breast on the foil; top with a sprinkle of salt and pepper and one quarter each of the orange slices and basil; add a drizzle of oil. Seal the package (see illustration on page 340) and repeat with the rest of the ingredients. (At this point, you can refrigerate the packages or dish for up to 4 hours before proceeding.)

3. Heat the oven to 450°F. Put the packages in a large baking dish and bake for about 20 minutes. Carefully cut through a package and nick into the chicken; the knife should meet with little resistance and when you peek, the meat will show very little or no hint of pink. (Sorry, there is no other way until you get a feel for this technique.) If not, return the packages to the oven for another 5 minutes. To serve, transfer the packages to shallow bowls to be opened at the table.

THE BASICS OF CHICKEN PARTS

Cut-up chicken is by far the most popular way to buy bone-in parts. It's more convenient than hacking up a raw bird. Plus, you have options: Mix and match parts or buy all the same. Or cut a whole chicken into eight pieces—two legs, two thighs, two breast halves, and two wings. The last option will save you money and give you trimmings for the stockpot. If you're buying farmers' market birds, which often only come whole, practice butchering with the illustrations on page 614.

The assortment of parts you use can change depending on the occasion, the preferences of your guests, or the cooking method. Using parts instead of whole chickens has another advantage too: Since more of the seasoning comes into direct contact with the meat and skin, it has more impact.

Whatever you choose, the recipes in this section are easily varied. For guaranteed juiciness, use all dark meat. Breasts are milder and more tender but prone to overcooking, so check them frequently, especially when using a mix of parts. You can improve the odds of everything finishing at the same time by starting the thighs and legs first and by keeping them in the hottest part of the pan. Then after 5 minutes or so add the breasts and wings. Or remove the breasts as soon as they're done, even if the legs have a few minutes more to go. When measured with an instant-read thermometer, the safest range for both breasts and thighs is between 155° and 165°F (see "Chicken Safety and Doneness," page 593).

ROAST CHICKEN PARTS

I've come to appreciate the appeal of roasting chicken parts. They may not come to the table with as much drama as a whole bird, but they cook considerably faster and there's no carving. And you can pretty much count on even browning and crisp skin, as long as the heat is high enough and there's room between the pieces.

I often roast all dark meat—legs and thighs either alone or in combination. They remain moist even if you overcook them slightly, and give you the crunchiest skin. If you buy leg-thigh quarters, separate them with a simple cut, illustrated on page 614—you'll also reduce the cooking time by about 10 minutes. The recipes also work with cut-up whole chicken; just make sure to separate the legs from the thighs if they're not already in two pieces so they'll cook almost as quickly as the breast pieces; even then, you may want to remove the breasts a little early to keep them from drying out.

Butchering Chicken

STEP 1 Use a knife or sharp kitchen scissors. Cut through the breast near, rather than through, the wing joint. This serves two purposes: It's easier—you don't have to locate the exact spot of the joint—and it gives you a much meatier wing at little sacrifice to the breast.

STEP 2 Hold up one of the legs by its end and slice the skin between the breast and leg; it's easy to see.

STEP 3 Find the joint where the thigh meets the carcass and cut through it.

STEP 4 Pop the back off the breast; the carcass will break in half quite easily.

STEP 5 Cut the back away from the breast. (Save the back, wing tips, and any other scraps for stock.)

STEP 6 Cut the breast in half; what's illustrated here is cutting lengthwise, but you can cut across the breast as well. You can also cut it into three or four pieces instead of two.

STEP 7 Find the joint connecting the leg and thigh and cut through it, if you like.

STEP 8 Find the joint connecting the main wing sections and cut through it if you like. Cut off the wing tips (they have virtually no meat) and reserve for stock.

F fast   **M** make ahead   **V** vegetarian

Roast Chicken Parts with Olive Oil or Butter

MAKES: 4 to 6 servings | **TIME:** 40 minutes

The simplest chicken recipe there is, and perhaps the easiest too. Add the herbs suggested here if you like or see the flavoring ideas that follow. This is the kind of dish you'll never get tired of, because you can change the direction every time you make it.

> 4 tablespoons olive oil or butter
> 3 to 4 pounds bone-in chicken parts (1 whole chicken, cut up, or any combination of pieces)
> Salt and pepper
> ½ cup any chopped mild fresh herb like parsley, dill, or basil, or a combination (optional)

1. Heat the oven to 450°F. Put the oil in a roasting pan large enough to hold the chicken pieces in one layer and put it in the oven for a couple of minutes, until hot. Add the chicken and carefully turn it a couple of times in the oil, leaving it skin side up. Sprinkle with salt and pepper and return the pan to the oven.

2. After the chicken has cooked for 15 minutes, sprinkle on one quarter of the herb, if you're using it, and turn the pieces. Sprinkle on another quarter of the herb and roast for another 10 minutes.

3. Turn the chicken over (now skin side up again), add another quarter of the herb, and cook until the chicken is done (you'll see clear juices if you make a small cut in the meat near the bone), another 5 to 15 minutes. Skim excess fat from the pan juices if necessary. Serve with some of the juices spooned over the chicken and garnished with the remaining herb.

Roast Chicken Parts with Olive Oil or Butter, Unleashed

Keep the quantities loose. Choose one addition or a combination at multiple steps.

ADDITIONS IN STEP 1

- A few sprigs of a strong herb like thyme, sage, oregano, or rosemary
- Several cloves garlic (20 wouldn't be too many), smashed
- A cup or so chopped onion, shallots, or leeks
- Rub the chicken with about ½ cup Traditional Pesto (page 51) or other Herb Puree (page 52)
- 2 or 3 lemons, halved (oranges and limes are good too); when the chicken is done, squeeze the hot juice over it
- Use Compound Butter (page 78), Flavored Oil (page 53), or Vinaigrette (page 188) at the beginning Step 1 or as a basting sauce during cooking

ADDITIONS IN STEP 2

- A cup or so sliced fresh mushrooms
- Use good-quality vegetable oil in Step 1; add several slices of ginger and garlic; garnish with scallions and/or cilantro in Step 3

- Stir a couple of tablespoons of any curry powder into a cup of yogurt or coconut milk; spoon or brush it on as a basting sauce during cooking
- 2 cups chopped broccoli, cauliflower, zucchini, or bell pepper
- 2 cups fresh or frozen corn kernels (great with oregano added in Step 1)
- A lot of hot dried hot chiles; a couple of toasted, soaked, and chopped dried milder chiles; or both

ADDITIONS IN STEP 3

- 1 pint cherry tomatoes; pitted black olives
- A cup or so Tomato Sauce with Fresh Herbs (page 482; use dill)
- Stir a dollop of whole grain mustard into the pan juices when the chicken is done
- Stir in a cup of any Fresh Salsa (starting on page 55)
- Garnish the chicken with 2 tablespoons sesame seeds
- After turning, sprinkle with ¼ cup bread crumbs (preferably homemade; see page 801)

Oven "Fried" Chicken

MAKES: 4 servings | TIME: 50 minutes

The best way to get the crunch of traditional fried chicken without the fat and mess of deep-frying. Remove the skin for a lower-fat version or use boneless, skinless breasts or thighs; they won't take quite as long to cook. If you don't have buttermilk, substitute an egg beaten with a tablespoon of water and the seasonings to coat the chicken.

Other protein you can use: bone-in or boneless pork chops.

1	cup buttermilk
1	teaspoon paprika (optional)
½	teaspoon cayenne, or to taste, or pepper
1½	teaspoons salt
3 to 4	pounds bone-in chicken parts (1 whole chicken, cut up, or any combination of pieces)
2	cups bread crumbs (preferably fresh; see page 801) or panko
	Good-quality vegetable oil, as needed

1. Heat the oven to 400°F. Mix the buttermilk, paprika, cayenne, and salt in a large bowl. Add the chicken, mix well, and let it soak for a few minutes. Meanwhile, put the bread crumbs on a plate or in a shallow dish. Brush a baking sheet with the oil.

2. Remove the chicken pieces from the bowl 1 piece at a time and coat in the bread crumbs; press the chicken into the crumbs to help them stick. Put the coated chicken on the oiled baking sheet, skin side up, leaving at least an inch between pieces. Bake until the exterior is golden brown and the chicken cooked through, 30 to 40 minutes. To check for doneness, cut into a piece with a thin-bladed knife; the center should be no longer raw but still juicy, and you'll see clear juices run out. Serve hot or at room temperature.

OVEN "FRIED" PARMESAN-HERB CHICKEN A mixture is best but you can also use a single herb: Replace 1 cup of the bread crumbs with ½ cup grated Parmesan and ½ cup chopped fresh herbs, the bulk of which should be a mild kind like parsley, chives, basil, and/or dill; include up to 2 tablespoons hardier herbs like thyme, rosemary, marjoram, and/or sage. Or skip the mild herbs and use 2 tablespoons of the hardier kind.

OVEN "FRIED" SESAME CHICKEN Substitute ½ cup sesame seeds for half the bread crumbs. Serve with Soy Dipping Sauce and Marinade (page 64) or any soy-based sauce.

Chicken Adobo

MAKES: 4 servings | TIME: About 1¼ hours

This Philippine classic has been called the best chicken dish in the world by a number of my friends and readers. It's braised first, then roasted, grilled, or broiled. The poaching liquid is then reduced to make a sauce to pass at the table for both the chicken and white rice, its natural accompaniment. Use a brand of soy sauce you know to not be too salty, as the flavors will concentrate.

Other protein you can use: bone-in or boneless pork chops.

1	cup soy sauce
½	cup white or rice vinegar
1	tablespoon chopped garlic
2	bay leaves
½	teaspoon pepper
1½	cups coconut milk (to make your own, see page 372)
3 to 4	pounds bone-in chicken parts (1 whole chicken, cut up, or any combination of pieces)

1. Combine the soy sauce, vinegar, garlic, bay leaves, pepper, 1 cup water, and ¾ cup of the coconut milk in a covered skillet or saucepan large enough to hold the chicken in one layer. Bring to a boil over high heat. Add the chicken. Reduce the heat to medium-low and cook, covered, turning the chicken once or twice, until it's almost done, about 20 minutes. (At this point, you can refrigerate the chicken in the liquid for up to a day before proceeding; skim the fat before reheating.)

2. Heat the oven to 450°F, turn on the broiler and position the rack about 4 inches below the heat, or prepare a charcoal or gas grill for hot indirect cooking (make sure the grates are clean). Remove the chicken pieces from the liquid and dry them gently with towels. Add the remaining ¾ cup coconut milk to the sauce and boil over high heat until it is reduced to about 1 cup; discard the bay leaves and keep the sauce warm.

3. Roast, broil, or grill the chicken, turning and rotating as necessary, until the pieces are brown, crisp, and heated through, 10 to 15 minutes total; roasting might take a little longer. Serve the chicken with the sauce.

GRILLED OR BROILED CHICKEN PARTS

Any of these recipes can be cooked either way, but read the detailed instructions that follow before proceeding. And although I love grilling, sometimes it's just not possible, while broiling almost always is.

Note that most grilled and broiled chicken dishes are as good at room temperature as they are hot, which makes them perfect for picnics, potlucks, or anytime you don't want to rush.

GRILLING CHICKEN PARTS The key to grilling chicken parts is to melt the fat and crisp the skin without letting the drips fall onto the heat source. When it does, the fire will flare up and potentially scorch the chicken before it cooks on the inside. The solution is to grill using a two-level fire for indirect cooking.

Start a charcoal fire or get the gas grill going with both hot and cool sides; see page 21 for more about indirect grilling.

Grilled chicken parts are done when firm and browned; if you have any doubts about doneness, cut into one alongside the bone. The juices should run clear. It effects the presentation a bit, but it's better than raw chicken. Or use a thermometer (see page 10). With experience, you'll be able to judge doneness by appearance and feel alone.

If you like more char and you're willing to take your time and keep an eye on things, you can grill chicken parts over direct heat in an uncovered grill, whether using wood, hardwood charcoal, briquettes, or gas. Don't build too hot a fire and keep some part of the grill cool—don't have any fire under it at all—so you can move the pieces over should any of them cause flare-ups. Start the chicken skin side down and be prepared to move and rotate the pieces frequently.

BROILING CHICKEN PARTS Cooking chicken indoors under an electric or gas broiler is like grilling with direct heat. Think of broiling as upside-down grilling: Start with the skin side down and broil, checking frequently to make sure the pieces don't burn, until they're nearly done, about 15 minutes, then turn and cook until the skin is browned, another 5 minutes or so. If a lot of fat starts to collect in the pan, spoon or pour some of it off.

If the pieces need a few more minutes, turn them skin side down again and cook until done and the juices by the bone run clear. Turn the pieces one more time and broil them skin side up for a minute or so to ensure the skin is crisp.

Simply Grilled or Broiled Chicken Parts

MAKES: 4 servings | **TIME:** 20 minutes

This basic recipe begins with chicken and simple seasonings. The other recipes in the chart that follows are not much more complicated, but you have plenty of options.

> 3 to 4 pounds bone-in chicken parts (1 whole chicken, cut up, or any combination of pieces)
> Salt and pepper
> Olive oil
> Lemon wedges for serving

1. Prepare a charcoal or gas grill for hot indirect cooking (make sure the grates are clean) or turn on the broiler and position the rack about 6 inches below the heat. Sprinkle the chicken with salt and pepper and brush or toss with some olive oil.

The Special Case of Chicken Wings

Dozens of recipes in this chapter can be adapted for chicken wings, which are a unique combination of white meat and dark. If you butcher your own chickens, you can cut a little into the breast when removing the wings, giving them an extra hunk of breast meat.

For quicker cooking and neater eating, cut the wing in three pieces before cooking (see page 614). Freeze the wing tips for making stock and use the two-boned middle section (all dark meat) and the drumstick-like upper wing—often sold as a "drumette"—in any of these recipes. They both take about the same amount of time to cook.

I lean toward broiling, grilling, and stir-frying for chicken wings, and here's why: Broiling and grilling are fast and easy and give consistently good results. Stir-frying, while a bit trickier, is fun, saucy, and worth the finesse. Roasting to crisp and season the skin requires some attention, but is good for feeding a crowd. Braising, simmering, or any other method of cooking wings with liquid isn't great because the wings have a relatively large amount of skin and both the wings and cooking liquid become gummy.

There's an appetizer recipe for Chicken Wings on page 127; here too is a list of other chicken recipes that also work well with wings. Just note that they will cook up to twice as fast as bone-in breasts or legs. And after the main recipe that follows, be sure to see "Simply Grilled or Broiled Chicken Parts, 9 Ways" on page 617 and "Ideas for Seasoning Any Grilled or Broiled Chicken" on page 621.

10 OF THE BEST RECIPES FOR CHICKEN WINGS

1. Chicken Escabeche or its variations (page 598)
2. Chicken Teriyaki (page 601)
3. Stir-Fried Chicken with Ketchup (page 605)
4. Roast Chicken Parts with Olive Oil or Butter and the variations in the sidebar that follows (page 615)
5. Simply Grilled or Broiled Chicken Parts (page 617) and the variations in the table that follows (page 620)
6. Grilled or Broiled Chicken, Japanese Style and its variations (below)
7. Arroz con Pollo (page 625)
8. My New Favorite Fried Chicken (page 628) with any spice rub (pages 32–35)
9. Chicken MarkNuggets and its variations (page 630)
10. Grilled or Broiled Split Chicken or its variation (page 642)

---

2. TO GRILL: When the fire is ready, start the chicken skin side up on the cool side of the grill. After some of the fat has been rendered, about 10 minutes, turn the chicken; if the fire flares up, move the chicken to an even cooler part of the fire or turn it so the skin side is up again. When the skin has lost its raw look and most of the fat has been rendered, another 20 to 30 minutes total, it's safe to move the chicken directly over the fire. Cook, turning occasionally, until both sides are browned and the flesh is firm and cooked through, 5 to 15 minutes longer, depending on the piece. To check for doneness, cut into a piece close to the bone; the juices should run clear.

TO BROIL: Line a roasting pan with foil to help cleanup if you like. Start with the skin side down and broil, making sure the meat does not burn, until it's nearly done, about 15 minutes, then turn and cook until the skin is brown, 5 to 15 minutes longer. To check for doneness, cut into a piece close to the bone; the juices should run clear.

3. Serve hot or at room temperature, with lemon wedges.

Grilled or Broiled Chicken, Japanese Style

MAKES: 4 servings | **TIME:** 45 minutes, plus time to marinate

If you like that slightly sweet, soy-saucy crunch of grilled Japanese food, this recipe is for you.

 fast make ahead **V** vegetarian

Simply Grilled Chicken
Parts, page 617

Simply Grilled or Broiled Chicken Parts, 9 Ways

In Step 1, season as described below and finish as described in the Garnishing and Serving column.

VARIATION	SEASONING	GARNISHING AND SERVING
Grilled or Broiled Chicken with Mustard	Combine 2 tablespoons olive oil with ½ cup Dijon mustard, 1 tablespoon fresh lemon juice, and salt and pepper. Reserve ¼ cup. Use the rest to coat the chicken in Step 1.	Immediately after grilling, brush with the reserved mustard sauce.
Grilled or Broiled Chicken with Lemon and Herbs	Put a bit of fresh herb (sage, tarragon, basil, rosemary, thyme) between the skin and the meat; chop the same herb for garnish. In addition to olive oil, salt, and pepper, rub the chicken all over with fresh lemon juice.	Garnish with the reserved chopped herbs and lemon wedges.
Grilled or Broiled Chicken with Cilantro and Lime	Combine 2 tablespoons olive oil, 2 tablespoons chopped fresh cilantro, 1 tablespoon fresh lime juice, 1 tablespoon chopped shallot or onion, ¼ teaspoon cayenne, salt, and pepper. Baste with this mixture in Step 2.	Garnish with chopped fresh cilantro and lime wedges.
Grilled or Broiled Chicken with Citrus	Combine 2 tablespoons olive oil, the zest and juice of 1 lemon, orange or ½ grapefruit, salt, and pepper. Baste with this mixture in Step 2.	Serve with lemon, orange, or grapefruit wedges.
Grilled or Broiled Chicken with Smoky Maple Syrup Glaze	Combine 2 tablespoons olive oil, ¼ cup maple syrup, ½ teaspoon smoked paprika, salt, and pepper. Baste with this mixture in Step 2.	Garnish with lots of chopped fresh chives.
Grilled or Broiled Chicken with Soy Glaze	Combine 1 tablespoon each good-quality vegetable oil and sesame oil with ¼ cup soy sauce. Baste with this mixture in Step 2.	Garnish with lots of chopped fresh cilantro and/or scallions.
Grilled or Broiled Chicken with Peanut Sauce	Make a batch of Peanut Sauce (page 75). Use this mixture for basting in Step 2.	Garnish with chopped fresh cilantro or Thai basil and lime wedges.
Shortcut Jerk Chicken	Mix 1–2 tablespoons Jerk Seasoning (page 34) with 2 tablespoons good-quality vegetable oil; baste with this mixture in Step 2.	Scatter several lemon wedges around the chicken.
Curried Grilled Chicken	Mix ½ cup coconut milk with 2 tablespoons curry powder; baste with this mixture in Step 2.	Garnish with toasted coconut flakes (page 372).

 fast   make ahead   V vegetarian

- ¼ **cup soy sauce**
- 2 **tablespoons sake or dry white wine**
- 2 **tablespoons mirin, or 1 tablespoon honey mixed with 1 tablespoon water**
- 3 **scallions, chopped**
- 1 **tablespoon chopped garlic**
- 1 **tablespoon chopped fresh ginger**
- 3 to 4 **pounds bone-in chicken parts (1 whole chicken, cut up, or any combination of pieces)**
- **Good-quality vegetable oil for brushing**
- **Lemon wedges for serving**

1. Mix the soy sauce, sake, mirin, scallions, garlic, ginger, and chicken pieces together in a large baking dish or heavy plastic bag. Cover or seal the bag and refrigerate for at least 2 hours and as long as overnight, turning the chicken occasionally.

2. When you're ready to cook, prepare a charcoal or gas grill for hot indirect cooking (make sure the grates are clean) or turn on the broiler and position the rack about 6 inches below the heat. Drain the chicken and discard the marinade.

3. TO GRILL: When the fire is ready, start the chicken skin side up on the cool side of the grill, brushing it with some oil. After some of the fat has been rendered, about 10 minutes, turn the chicken; if the fire flares up, move the chicken to an even cooler part of the grill or turn it so the skin side is up again. When the skin has lost its raw look and most of the fat has been rendered, after about 20 minutes total, it's safe to move the chicken directly over the fire. Cook, turning occasionally, until both sides are browned and the flesh is firm and cooked through, 5 to 15 minutes longer, depending on the cut. To check for doneness, cut into a piece close to the bone; the juices should run clear.

TO BROIL: Line a roasting pan with foil to help cleanup if you like. Start with the skin side down and broil, making sure the meat does not burn, until it's nearly done, about 15 minutes, then turn and cook until the meat is done and the skin is browned, 5 to 15 minutes longer. To check for doneness, cut into a piece close to the bone; the juices should run clear.

4. Serve hot, warm, or at room temperature, with the lemon wedges.

GRILLED OR BROILED CHICKEN, THAI STYLE Minor adjustments make a huge difference in flavor: Use fish sauce instead of the soy sauce; omit the sake, scallions, and ginger. Add to the marinade 2 tablespoons minced lemongrass (the tender core only), 1 tablespoon

Ideas for Seasoning Any Grilled or Broiled Chicken

Before grilling, rub with a couple of tablespoons of:
- Chili Powder (to make your own, see page 32)
- Curry Powder (to make your own, see page 32)
- Garam Masala (to make your own, see page 34)
- Jerk Seasoning (to make your own, see page 34)
- Red Curry Paste or Green Curry Paste (to make your own, see page 46)

During grilling, brush with a cup or so of:
- Any Chile Paste (page 40)
- Traditional Pesto (page 51) or any other pesto or Herb Purée (page 52)
- Simplest Yogurt Sauce (page 59)
- Any Barbecue Sauce (to make your own, see page 74)
- Teriyaki Sauce or its variation (page 76)
- Compound Butter (see page 78)

After grilling, serve with one recipe of:
- Any Chile Paste (page 40)
- Traditional Pesto (page 51) or any other pesto or Herb Purée (page 52)
- Any Fresh Tomato or Fruit Salsa (page 55)
- Simplest Yogurt Sauce or any variation (page 59)
- Any Chutney (pages 61–62)
- Soy Dipping Sauce and Marinade (page 64)
- Ginger-Scallion Sauce or its variation (page 64)
- Miso Dipping Sauce (page 66)
- Salsa Roja (page 71) or Salsa Verde (page 73)
- Barbecue Sauce (page 74)
- Teriyaki Sauce (page 76)
- Any Five-Minute Drizzle Sauce (page 81)

coriander seeds, and a full teaspoon of ground black pepper. Garnish with lime instead of lemon.

GRILLED OR BROILED CHICKEN, VIETNAMESE STYLE

Use fish sauce instead of the soy sauce, lime juice instead of the sake, and sugar instead of the mirin. Omit the scallions, garlic, and ginger. Season the chicken very generously with black pepper. Garnish with chopped fresh cilantro or Thai basil and mint.

BRAISED CHICKEN PARTS

These are fast, flavorful, one-pot chicken dinners. Recipes like these develop more flavor and texture when they begin with browning the chicken, but it's a step you can consider optional. The added flavor is nice, but browning takes time and energy and makes a bit of a mess, and when you add liquid and cover the pan to finish the cooking, the skin softens again. And many people don't eat it anyway. A good compromise is to sear just the skin side of each piece.

For these recipes you need a large (at least 12 inches), deep skillet or large, heavy-bottomed pot, so all the chicken will fit comfortably in one layer. Since there's so much sauce, serve these dishes with plain rice (page 430), polenta (page 460), mashed potatoes (page 329), or plenty of crusty bread.

Chicken and Lentils

MAKES: 4 servings | **TIME:** 1 hour, largely unattended

A spicy, North African–style dish that comes together in one pot. Using chickpeas (see the variation) is a little more work but worth the effort when you have extra time and want a little more bite.

- ¼ cup olive oil
- 3 to 4 pounds bone-in chicken parts (1 whole chicken, cut up, or any combination of pieces)
- 1 large or 2 small onions, sliced
- 1 tablespoon chopped garlic
- 1 tablespoon chopped or grated fresh ginger, or 1 teaspoon ground ginger
- 1 cup chopped tomatoes (canned is fine; don't bother to drain)
- 1 teaspoon ground coriander
  Salt and pepper
- 1 large bunch fresh cilantro or parsley, tied into a bundle with kitchen string
- 2 3-inch cinnamon sticks
- 1 cup brown or green lentils, washed and picked over

1. Put the oil in a large skillet or large pot over medium-high heat. When it's hot, add the chicken skin side down and brown it well, rotating and turning the pieces as necessary; browning will take 10 to 15 minutes. (You can skip this step if you like, as noted at right; heat only 1 tablespoon oil and go directly to cooking the onions in Step 2.)

2. When the chicken is browned, transfer it to a platter and turn the heat down to medium. Pour or spoon off all but 1 tablespoon of the fat. Add the onions,

 fast   make ahead   vegetarian

garlic, ginger, tomatoes, coriander, a sprinkle of salt and pepper, 4 cups water, the cilantro, cinnamon, and lentils. Adjust the heat so the liquid bubbles gently but steadily, cover, and cook for about 30 minutes, until the lentils are almost tender.

3. Remove and discard the herb bundle and cinnamon sticks and return the chicken to the pan skin side up, along with any juices that accumulated. Cover and continue to let the liquid bubble gently until the chicken is cooked through, another 10 to 20 minutes; the chicken is done when an instant-read thermometer inserted into the thickest part of a thigh reads between 155° and 165°F. Taste and adjust the seasoning, and serve. (At this point, you can let the dish sit for a few hours, or cover and refrigerate for up to a day before reheating and serving; you may have to add a little water to thin the sauce a bit.)

CHICKEN AND CHICKPEAS If you must, use canned, though it's so much better (and not that much work) to start with dried: Follow the method for cooking beans on page 390, cooking the chickpeas to the point where they would be ready to salt, just barely tender. Use about 2 cups cooked chickpeas and a little of their cooking liquid instead of lentils; add them with the chicken in Step 3. (Save the remaining chickpeas and their liquid for another use.)

CHICKEN AND RICE

It's amazing how many wonderful and iconic dishes from around the world are made with little more than two ingredients. From fragrant, beguiling chicken biryani to the more austere but no less enjoyable arroz con pollo, the combination always results in richly seasoned rice and succulent chicken. You're basically braising the chicken and the rice, but instead of resulting in a sauce, the liquid is soaked up by a delicious grain. All you need is a salad or vegetable to round out the meal.

I suggest what rice to use in the recipe, but you can always try others you like. In general, use long-grain like basmati if you want separate, super-fragrant grains and short-grain if you want a clumpier, more substantial-feeling dish. (For a detailed rundown of your options, see the lexicon on page 428).

Coq au Vin

MAKES: 4 servings | **TIME:** About 40 minutes

The French home-style standard, deliciously dark and rich, without too much fuss. If you happen upon an older laying hen—the traditional chicken for these types of rustic dishes—good for you: The flavor will be lovely; just cook it a while longer to get tender.

1	ounce dried porcini mushrooms
4	ounces slab bacon, cut into ¼-inch pieces
3 to 4	pounds bone-in chicken parts (1 whole chicken, cut up, or any combination of pieces)
20	pearl onions, peeled, or 1 large onion, sliced
8	ounces button mushrooms, trimmed and cut into chunks
6	cloves garlic, peeled
	Salt and pepper
2	cups chicken stock (to make your own, see page 176)

2　cups pinot noir or other dry, fruity red wine
　2　bay leaves
　　　Several sprigs fresh thyme
　　　Several sprigs fresh parsley
　2　tablespoons butter
　　　Chopped fresh parsley for garnish

1. Soak the porcini mushrooms in hot water to cover while you proceed with the recipe. Put the bacon in a large pot. Cook over medium-high heat, stirring occasionally, until the bacon gives up its fat and becomes brown and crisp, about 10 minutes. Add the chicken, skin side down, and cook, rotating and turning the pieces as necessary; browning will take 10 to 15 minutes. After about 5 minutes, add the garlic and sprinkle the chicken with salt and pepper.

2. Transfer the chicken to a plate and pour or spoon off all but 2 tablespoons of the fat. Add the onions and button mushrooms, and cook, stirring occasionally, until the vegetables soften, about 3 minutes. Add the stock, wine, bay leaves, thyme, and parsley, scraping up any browned bits from the bottom of the pot. Return the chicken to the pot and adjust the heat so that the liquid bubbles gently but steadily.

3. Cover and cook until the chicken is tender and cooked through, about 20 minutes. The breast pieces will finish cooking first; they're done when an instant-read thermometer inserted into the thickest part reads between 155° and 165°F. Remove the breast pieces, transfer them to a platter, and keep them warm while the leg pieces finish. Check the leg pieces the same way. Transfer the remaining chicken to the platter.

4. Lift the porcini out of the soaking water and add them to the pot. If you like, strain the soaking water and add that too. Turn the heat to high and boil until the sauce is reduced by about three-quarters and becomes fairly thick. Lower the heat, stir in the butter, and return the chicken to the pan, just to reheat a bit and coat with the sauce. (You can make the dish ahead to this point and refrigerate for up to a day; reheat gently.) Taste and adjust the seasoning, remove the bay leaves, garnish with parsley, and serve.

Arroz con Pollo

MAKES: 4 servings | **TIME:** About 1 hour

There are as many ways to make this as there are to make fried chicken. This version is stripped to the bare essentials: onion, chicken, rice. For bells and whistles, see "7 Ingredients to Add to Arroz con Pollo" on page 626. Stock makes the best cooking liquid but water is fine, because as it simmers with the chicken it makes a flavorful broth for the rice to soak up.

Saffron is customary to tint everything yellow and lend a haunting flavor, but optional. Other options include a pinch turmeric or ground annatto or a few drops annatto oil, which are more about color than flavor. I also like smoked paprika, which is about both. Take your pick.

　　　2　tablespoons olive oil
　3 to 4　pounds bone-in chicken parts (1 whole chicken, cut up, or any combination of pieces)
　　　　　Salt and pepper
　　　1　large or 2 small onions, sliced
　　1½　cups short-grain white rice
　　　　　Pinch saffron threads or turmeric (optional)
　　　3　cups chicken or vegetable stock (to make your own, see pages 176 or 174), or water
　　　　　Chopped fresh parsley for garnish
　　　　　Lemon or lime wedges for serving

1. Put the oil in a large skillet over medium-high heat. When it's hot, add the chicken skin side down. Sprinkle with salt and pepper and cook until the pieces release easily from the pan and are lightly browned, 5 to 10 minutes. Remove them from the pan.

2. Pour off all but 2 tablespoons of the fat. Add the onions and sprinkle with salt and pepper. Cook, stirring occasionally, until they're softened and translucent, 5 to 10 minutes. Add the rice and stir until it's coated with fat, a minute or two. Sprinkle with the saffron if you're using it. Stir in the stock. Nestle the chicken pieces into the rice and pour over any juices that accumulated. Bring to a boil, then adjust the heat so that the liquid bubbles gently but steadily.

3. Cover and cook until all the liquid has been absorbed and the chicken is cooked through, about 20 minutes; the chicken is done when an instant-read thermometer inserted into the thickest part of a thigh reads between 155° and 165°F. (At this point, you can keep the dish warm over very low heat for another 15 minutes; it will retain its heat for 15 minutes beyond that.) Garnish with parsley and serve with lemon wedges.

---

7 INGREDIENTS TO ADD TO ARROZ CON POLLO

1. After removing the chicken pieces at the end of Step 1, render about 4 ounces bacon, cut into small cubes, in the skillet. Remove it with a slotted spoon when crisp. Proceed with Step 2, and cook the onions and rice in the remaining fat as directed. Sprinkle the bacon on top before serving.
2. Add 2 tablespoons chopped garlic to the onions in Step 2.
3. Add 1 chopped red bell pepper or a mix of red and green to the onions in Step 2.
4. Add 1 chopped fresh tomato or about 1 cup canned to the rice in Step 2, just before adding back the chicken.
5. Add pinch ground allspice and a bay leaf to the onions in Step 2. Remove the bay leaf before serving.
6. Tuck 1 cup fresh or frozen peas into the rice in Step 3, about 5 minutes before the dish is finished.
7. During the last 5 minutes of cooking, scatter 2 cups chopped fresh spinach or watercress on top of the simmering dish to let it soften. Stir it into the rice with a fork before serving.

Chicken Biryani

MAKES: 4 servings | **TIME:** About 1 hour

The prince of chicken-and-rice dishes, simply magnificent but easy enough for a weeknight. You must use a fair amount of butter, and preferably good spices: cardamom in the pod, whole cloves, a cinnamon stick, and real saffron. Remember to remove the whole spices before serving; biting down on a whole clove is especially unpleasant.

4	**tablespoons (½ stick) butter**
1	**large or 2 small onions, sliced**
	Salt and pepper
1	**large pinch saffron threads**
10	**cardamom pods**
5	**whole cloves**
	One 3-inch cinnamon stick
2	**tablespoons chopped fresh ginger**
1½	**cups basmati rice**
3	**cups chicken stock (to make your own, see page 176) or water**
3 to 4	**pounds bone-in chicken parts (1 whole chicken, cut up, or any combination of pieces)**
¼	**cup slivered blanched almonds (optional)**

1. Put 2 tablespoons of the butter in a large pot over medium-high heat. When it melts and foams add the onions, sprinkle with salt and pepper, and cook, stirring occasionally, until the onions soften but aren't browned, 5 to 10 minutes. Add the saffron, cardamom, cloves, cinnamon, and ginger and stir for another minute.

2. Add the rice and cook, stirring occasionally, until it's glossy, 2 to 3 minutes. Add the stock, chicken, and more salt and pepper and bring to a boil; adjust the heat so that the liquid bubbles gently but steadily.

3. Cover and cook, undisturbed, until the chicken and rice are both tender and the liquid has been absorbed, about 25 minutes. The chicken is done when an instant-read thermometer inserted into the thickest part of a thigh reads between 155° and 165°F. If either chicken or rice is not quite done, add a little—no more than ½ cup—boiling water, re-cover, and cook for another 5 minutes before checking again. When the chicken and rice are done, turn the heat off and re-cover.

4. Meanwhile, melt the remaining 2 tablespoons butter in a small skillet over medium heat. Add the almonds

 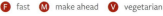

if you're using them and brown them very lightly, about 3 minutes; if you're not using them, simply melt the butter. Pour this over the biryani, sprinkle with a bit more salt, and re-cover; let rest for another 2 or 3 minutes. (At this point, you can put the dish in a 200°F oven for up to 30 minutes to keep it warm without sacrificing quality.) Take the pot to the table, uncover, and serve.

THE BASICS OF FRIED CHICKEN

For a simple dish like fried chicken, the right technique makes all the difference between good food and great food.

First, some fried chicken definitions: *Pan-frying* (also known as shallow frying) is usually done in a large skillet in about an inch of oil; *deep-frying*, where the food is submerged during cooking, requires about 3 inches of oil in a large pot. Both the recipes here call for deep-frying, though the temperatures of the oil and the processes are different.

A good-quality vegetable oil works well for frying pretty much anything, though I sometimes like to pan-fry in olive oil if I want that distinctive flavor. (There is a myth that olive oil is not suitable for frying; on the contrary, it works well at even moderately high temperatures.) Some people swear by lard, so if you can find good rendered pork fat—not always an easy task—and convince people that they won't drop dead after one bite, give it a try. (They won't, and they'll thank you for the delectable chicken.)

Use a large deep pot, work carefully, and add one piece of chicken at time, and splattering should be minimal. I no longer recommend covering the pot during cooking—you just end up steaming the meat; plus uncovered, the pieces will form a better crust. It helps if the pot isn't too crowded; plan on frying in batches.

Getting rid of the oil after you're done is always a pain, unless you have an oil recycling station in your area. Either way, let the oil cool. If you're going to save it (once-used oil is still fine to fry with again or to use for stir-frying), strain it, pour it into a jar, and refrigerate. If you're not going to save it, pour it into a jar and cover the jar tightly, or use a plastic container like a used yogurt container and secure the cap with tape, and throw it in the trash.

21 Poultry Dishes That Are Good Cold or at Room Temperature

Whether left over or prepared in advance, many simple chicken dishes are super at room temperature or straight from the fridge. Some personal favorites:

1. Broiled Boneless Chicken or Grilled Boneless Chicken (page 596)
2. Chicken Escabeche (page 598)
3. Chicken Teriyaki (page 601)
4. Poached Boneless Chicken Breasts or Thighs with Lemon Sauce (page 611)
5. Roast Chicken Parts with Olive Oil or Butter (page 615)
6. Chicken Adobo (page 616)
7. Simply Grilled or Broiled Chicken Parts (page 617)
8. Arroz con Pollo (pages 625)
9. My New Favorite Fried Chicken (page 628)
10. Simplest Whole Roast Chicken or any of its variations (page 633)
11. Roast Chicken with Garlicky Herb Butter (page 636)
12. White Cut Chicken (page 637)
13. Smoky Whole Chicken (page 640)
14. Chicken Under a Brick (page 641)
15. Grilled or Broiled Split Chicken (page 642)
16. Forty-Five-Minute Roast Turkey (page 646)
17. Roast Turkey Breast, on the Bone (page 650)
18. Fast "Roast" Duck, Chinese Style (pages 654)
19. Grilled or Broiled Cornish Hens with Sherry Vinegar (page 658)
20. Roast Quail with Honey, Cumin, and Orange Juice (page 660)
21. Grilled or Broiled Chicken Kebabs (see page 673)

My New Favorite Fried Chicken

MAKES: 4 servings | TIME: 2 to 24 hours, largely unattended

This is the easiest, most foolproof way I've ever found to fry chicken. The trick is a slightly lower temperature than you would normally use for deep-frying. Since the recipe is so basic, you've got a lot of room to play. I like to use all dark meat if everyone coming for dinner is agreeable. Vary the soak or the breading with ideas in the list at right; there's also a list of dipping sauces on page 630.

2	**cups buttermilk**
	Salt and pepper
3 to 4	**pounds bone-in chicken parts (1 whole chicken, cut up, or any combination of pieces)**
	Good-quality vegetable oil for deep-frying
2	**cups all-purpose flour**
	Lemon wedges for serving

1. Put the buttermilk in a large bowl or gallon zipper bag. Add several large pinches salt and some pepper and stir or shake to combine. Add the chicken and cover the bowl or seal the bag, squeezing out as much air as you can. Let it sit, refrigerated, for 1 to 24 hours.

2. When you're ready to cook, fit a wire rack on a rimmed baking sheet; line a platter with towels. Put 2 to 3 inches oil in a large pot over medium heat (see "Deep-Frying," page 22). For this recipe, you want the oil at about 315°F, so keep an eye on it. If you don't have a thermometer, heat the oil until a cube of bread sinks a bit before rising to the top and bubbling merrily. Just make sure the oil isn't too hot.

3. Put the flour in a large shallow bowl with some salt and at least 1 tablespoon pepper; stir to combine. Working with one piece at a time, remove the chicken from the marinade and dredge it, turning and tossing in the flour, until thickly coated. Transfer each piece to the wire rack.

4. Working in batches to avoid overcrowding or overflowing, carefully add a few pieces of the chicken to the oil. They should quickly rise to the top and bubble enthusiastically. Adjust the heat so the oil maintains a steady but not-too-crazy cooking pace. Cook, turning occasionally, until the meat is cooked but still juicy and the outside is deeply browned, 10 to 15 minutes. The chicken is done when an instant-read thermometer inserted into the thickest part reads between 155° and 165°F. Adjust the heat so the coating

Many More Ways to Spin Fried Chicken

Rub a spice mixture onto the chicken before marinating, or add it to the flour:

- Chili powder (to make your own, see page 32); or mix 2 tablespoons chili powder, 2 tablespoons ground cumin, 2 teaspoons ground coriander, and ½ teaspoon cayenne (optional)
- Curry powder (to make your own, see page 32)
- Garam masala (to make your own, see page 34)
- Jerk seasoning (to make your own, see page 34)
- Any ground mild, hot, or smoked dried chile
- Add 1 tablespoon fresh thyme to the flour mixture and heat 10 bay leaves in the cooking oil (when the oil comes up to temperature, remove the bay leaves).

Spike the buttermilk:

- Add 1 tablespoon or more any Chile Paste (pages 40–46).
- Replace 1 cup with a 14-ounce can coconut milk (or to make your own, see page 372).
- Go easy on the salt and whisk in ¼ cup any miso (the light ones are mildest).
- Add a few dashes soy sauce or fish sauce.
- Add up to 1 tablespoon ground spices like curry or chile powder.

Change the coating:

- Replace ½ cup of the flour with ½ cup cornmeal.
- Replace 1 cup of the flour with 1 cup bread crumbs (see page 801).

doesn't darken too quickly but the oil continues to bubble.

5. As the chicken pieces finish, transfer them to the towels to drain. Add a raw piece of chicken as you take out each cooked piece, until you're finished cooking. Serve at any temperature with salt, pepper, and lemon wedges.

---

10 SAUCES FOR FRIED CHICKEN

1. Any mustard (page 35)
2. Any herb sauce (page 52)
3. Any raw or cooked salsa (starting on page 55)
4. Soy Dipping Sauce and Marinade (page 64)
5. Blue Cheese Dressing and its variations (page 59)
6. Any chutney (starting on page 61)
7. Ginger-Scallion Sauce (page 64)
8. Any mayonnaise (page 69)
9. Real Ranch Dressing and its variations (page 71)
10. Barbecue Sauce (page 74) or any of its variations

Chicken MarkNuggets

MAKES: 4 servings | TIME: About 30 minutes

Dumb name, huh? I've been using it for years and haven't been sued yet. And these boneless bits of chicken are better than the fast-food kind, since you start with quality ingredients.

Other proteins you can use: shrimp, clams, squid, oysters.

1½ pounds boneless chicken (breasts, tenders, or thighs), blotted dry
1 cup all-purpose flour for dredging
2 eggs
2 cups bread crumbs (preferably fresh; see page 801) or panko for dredging
Salt and pepper
½ teaspoon cayenne
Good-quality vegetable oil for deep frying
Any of the sauces in "10 Sauces for Fried Chicken" (at left) for serving

1. Fit a rimmed baking sheet with a wire rack. Cut the chicken into 2-inch strips or pieces of about equal thickness. Put the flour, beaten eggs, and bread crumbs on separate plates or shallow bowls next to each other. Sprinkle the eggs with salt and pepper and the cayenne, and whisk with a fork to combine thoroughly.

2. Dredge the chicken a few pieces at a time in the flour, then dip in the eggs, then dredge in the bread crumbs. As you work, put the chicken on a baking sheet. When it's all breaded, transfer to the refrigerator to chill for at least 10 minutes and up to 3 hours. (At this point, you can freeze the chicken on the baking sheet and then transfer the frozen pieces to zipper bags or wrap in plastic; they'll keep for a month or 2.)

3. Heat the oven to 200°F. Put 2 to 3 inches oil in a large pot over medium-high heat; bring to 350°F (see "Deep-Frying," page 22). If you don't have a thermometer, heat the oil until a cube of bread sinks a bit before rising to the top and bubbling merrily. Just make sure the oil isn't too hot. When the oil is ready, turn the heat up a bit and add a few chicken pieces, regulating the heat so that there is a constant sizzle but no burning. Cook in batches as necessary, making sure not to crowd the pan.

4. Turn the chicken pieces as they brown. The total cooking time should be about 4 minutes. As pieces finish, transfer them to the wire rack to drain and keep warm in the oven. Serve as soon as all the pieces are cooked, with sauce for dipping.

 fast make ahead vegetarian

CORNMEAL CHICKEN MARKNUGGETS Substitute cornmeal for the bread crumbs.

SUPER-CRUNCHY PAN-FRIED CHICKEN MARKNUGGETS
A tad less messy: Omit the eggs and bread crumbs; instead of the cayenne, use 1 tablespoon any spice mixture from the list on page 628. Rub the chicken all over with a tablespoon rice vinegar or cider vinegar; sprinkle with salt, pepper, and the spice mixture; and rub again. Whisk the flour with about ½ cup warm water to make a paste about as thick as yogurt. Heat about ¼ inch oil in a skillet over medium-high heat. Coat the chicken in the batter and pan-fry in batches, turning and adding more oil as necessary to keep the pieces sizzling until they're browned on all sides. Drain and keep warm as described above.

THE BASICS OF WHOLE CHICKEN

There is no secret to making excellent whole roast chicken: Start with a good bird, cook it properly, and serve it promptly—and that's the trickiest part; the crisp skin and moist interior for which roast chicken is justly renowned are fleeting qualities. (Though of course leftovers are also wonderful.)

For the simplest take on whole roast chicken, see page 633. I suggest you take a few moments to cut off the flap that covers the inside cavity if it's still there. Refrigerate or freeze the fat for rendering (see page 622). You can also trim off the little pointed wing tips; they're good for stock. You can use a knife for these tasks, but kitchen scissors are easiest.

A word about trussing—tying—the bird: One or two pieces of string around the legs and wings keeps them in place, and makes the bird slightly easier to handle, and supposedly more attractive, though both of these points are disputable. Birds often come tied already. If not, sometimes I do it myself; sometimes I prefer to have more surface area exposed to crisp the skin.

I usually bake any stuffing separately in a greased, uncovered baking dish while I roast the bird. (Depending on the size of the dish and the recipe, the stuffing might be ready a little sooner, so keep an eye on it.) Try any of the stuffings starting on page 649, or see the list "5 Other Recipes You Can Use to Stuff Poultry" also on that page.

You don't need a rack to roast a chicken, though elevating the bird above the pan helps keep more skin crisp and prevents it from sticking. My cast-iron skillet method on page 633 needs no rack at all, and it works just fine. Or you can use an ordinary roasting pan; try the smallest roasting pan that will comfortably hold the bird, so you can concentrate the juices and keep them from burning. You'll need a larger pan if you want to add roast vegetables to the mix.

Quartering a Roast Chicken

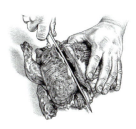 

STEP 1 Cut straight down on each side of the breastbone, following the shape of the carcass. Continue to cut down toward the back until you reach the joints holding the thighs and wings to the carcass. Remove the backbone from one half if you like and freeze it for stock.

STEP 2 With each half, cut between the breast and thigh to easily separate them.

Carving a Roast Chicken

STEP 1 Cut straight down on each side of the breastbone, following the shape of the carcass.

STEP 2 Continue to cut down toward the back until you reach the joints holding the thigh and wing to the carcass.

STEP 3 Cut through those joints to free the entire half of the bird.

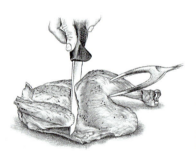

STEP 4 Separate the leg and breast sections by cutting through the skin that holds them together; hold the knife almost parallel to the cutting board, cut from the breast toward the leg, and you will easily find the right spot.

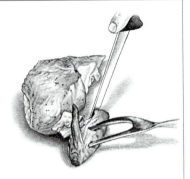

STEP 5 Separate the wing from the breast if you like.

STEP 6 Separate leg and thigh; the joint should offer little resistance once you find it.

F fast   **M** make ahead   **V** vegetarian

Simplest Whole Roast Chicken

MAKES: 4 servings | **TIME:** About 1 hour

Putting a whole chicken on a heated skillet cooks the thighs faster than the breasts, which are exposed only to the heat of the oven. So you get solid browning without drying out the breast meat. The recipe is also easy to vary.

If at any point during the cooking the pan juices begin to smoke, add a little water or wine (white or red, your choice) to the pan. This will reduce browning, however, so don't do it unless you must. I suggest serving the pan juices with the chicken, but if you prefer to make a more complicated pan sauce, see page 636.

1   **whole chicken (3 to 4 pounds), trimmed of excess fat**

3   **tablespoons olive oil**
    Salt and pepper
    A few sprigs fresh tarragon, rosemary, or thyme (optional)
5 or 6   **cloves garlic, peeled (optional)**
    Chopped fresh herbs for garnish

1. Put a cast-iron or other heavy ovenproof skillet on a rack in the lower third of the oven and heat the oven to 450°F. Rub the chicken with the oil, sprinkle it with salt and pepper, and put the herb sprigs inside the cavity if you're using them.

2. When both oven and pan are hot—start checking after about 15 minutes—carefully put the chicken, breast up, in the hot skillet; if you're using garlic, scatter it around the bird. Roast undisturbed for 40 minutes, then check for doneness; an instant-read thermometer inserted in the thickest part of a thigh reads between 155° and 165°F. Remove from the oven or continue roasting until it's done

3. Tip the pan to let the juices from the chicken's cavity flow into the pan; if they are red, roast for another

5 minutes. Transfer the chicken to a platter and let it rest for 5 to 10 minutes. If you like, pour the pan juices into a clear measuring cup, then pour or spoon off some of the fat. Discard the herb sprigs. Reheat the juices if necessary, quarter the chicken (see the illustrations on page 614), garnish with chopped herbs, and serve with the pan juices.

ROAST CHICKEN WITH CUMIN, HONEY, AND ORANGE JUICE Sweet and spiced: After about 20 minutes, spoon or brush over the chicken a mixture of 2 tablespoons fresh orange juice, 2 tablespoons honey, 1 teaspoon chopped garlic, 2 teaspoons ground cumin, and salt and pepper to taste.

ROAST CHICKEN WITH SOY SAUCE Chinese-style roast chicken, made easy: Replace the olive oil with good-quality vegetable oil. Whisk together ¼ cup soy sauce; 2 tablespoons honey; 1 tablespoon chopped garlic; 1 tablespoon grated or chopped fresh ginger, or 1 teaspoon ground ginger; and ¼ cup chopped scallion. When the skin is crisp and the chicken is cooked through, spoon or brush the glaze over the chicken and serve.

Varying Simplest Whole Roast Chicken

Choose one seasoning, one addition to the roasting pan, or one sauce to baste with. Or combine options at multiple steps.

SEASON THE BIRD

- **Lemon:** 3 tablespoons fresh lemon juice in addition to or instead of olive oil, and/or a halved lemon in the cavity.
- **Soy-Lime:** 3 tablespoons fresh lime juice, good-quality vegetable oil, ¼ cup soy sauce instead of the olive oil; or lime juice with chopped fresh chile or red chile flakes, chopped fresh cilantro to taste, and a table-spoon or two of oil.
- **Spiced Chicken:** Mix about 1 tablespoon ground spice with the olive oil; paprika is my first choice, but use any favorite like chile powder or Five-Spice (page 35).
- **Chile Rub:** 1–2 tablespoons Harissa or other Chile Paste (page 40).
- **Seasoned Butter:** A few tablespoons any Compound Butter (page 78) between the skin and the meat.

ADD TO THE ROASTING PAN

- **Wine Pan Sauce:** ½ cup white wine, 2 cloves garlic, crushed; baste with this a couple times during roasting.
- **Herbed Potatoes:** About 1½ pounds potatoes, cut into 1-inch chunks; 1 tablespoon chopped fresh thyme, rosemary, marjoram, oregano, or sage.
- **Roasted Aromatics:** 1½–2 pounds chopped mixed sturdy vegetables like fennel, carrots, celery, and/or onions.

- **Mushrooms:** 8 ounces fresh mushrooms, cut into chunks; a handful whole garlic cloves (don't bother to peel); 2 shallots, cut into chunks.
- **Roasted Root Vegetables:** 2 cups chopped any sturdy root vegetable like sweet potato, parsnip, or turnip; 1 cup cooked chickpeas (page 407).

BASTE WHILE ROASTING

- **Honey-Mustard Glaze:** 2 tablespoons to ⅓ cup mustard, 2 tablespoons honey; baste with this mixture a couple times during roasting.
- **Curry Baste:** Coat with good-quality vegetable oil instead of olive oil. Combine ½ cup coconut milk, 2 tablespoons curry powder; baste with this mixture a couple times during roasting.
- **Fresh Herb Finish:** ¼ cup olive oil, 2 tablespoons chopped fresh parsley, chervil, basil, or dill over the chicken. Baste after about 20 minutes; garnish with more chopped herbs.
- **Miso Glaze:** Miso Dipping Sauce or any of the variations (page 66); baste with this mixture a couple times during roasting.
- **Molasses Glaze:** ¼ cup Molasses Mustard (page 37); 2–3 tablespoons cider vinegar; salt and pepper. Baste after about 20 minutes.

Roast Chicken with Garlicky Herb Butter

MAKES: 4 servings | TIME: About 1 hour

A classic with the most important elements: a crisp-skinned chicken smacking of butter and herbs. This recipe is one of the few in which olive oil simply won't do; if you cannot or don't want to cook with butter, stick with Simplest Whole Roast Chicken (page 633).

8	tablespoons (1 stick) butter
3	tablespoons chopped fresh dill, tarragon, parsley, or chervil, or a combination
	Salt and pepper
1	whole chicken (3 to 4 pounds), trimmed of excess fat
6 to 10	cloves garlic, peeled

1. Heat the oven to 450°F. Use a fork or mini food processor to combine 4 tablespoons of the butter with 2 tablespoons of the herb(s), and salt and pepper. With your fingers, loosen the skin of the chicken wherever you can without tearing it and spread some of this herb butter between skin and meat. Put a little in the chicken cavity and spread the remainder on top of the breast. Sprinkle the outside of the bird with salt and pepper.

2. Put the remaining 4 tablespoons butter in a large ovenproof skillet (not cast-iron) or roasting pan and put the pan in the oven. When the butter melts and the foam subsides, add ½ cup water and the garlic. Put the chicken, breast down, on a wire rack in the pan. Roast for 20 minutes.

3. Baste the chicken with the pan juices, then turn it breast up. (If at any point the pan juices begin to stick to the pan, add a little more water.) Baste again, then again after 10 minutes. At this point the breast should be beginning to brown; if it isn't, roast for a few more minutes. Turn the heat down to 325°F, baste again, and roast until an instant-read thermometer inserted into the thickest part of a thigh reads between 155° and 165°F. Total roasting time will be under 1 hour.

4. Before removing the chicken from the pan, tip the pan to let the juices from the bird's cavity flow into the pan; if they are red, cook for another 5 minutes before checking again. Transfer the chicken to a platter and let it rest for about 5 minutes before carving.

5. Meanwhile, skim some of the fat from the pan drippings and put the roasting pan on a burner (or 2) over medium-high heat. If the pan looks dry, add a little more water and cook, stirring and scraping the bottom of the pan to loosen any solids that have stuck there; mash the garlic with the back of the spoon if you'd like. Stir in the remaining 1 tablespoon of the herb; serve the sauce with the chicken.

ROAST CHICKEN WITH MISO BUTTER A simply incredible way to season a bird: Omit the garlic and herbs. Let the

---

Flavor Under the Skin

Here's a terrific way to flavor the meat, rather than just the skin, of any poultry, especially when grilling or roasting. Simply loosen the skin a bit with your fingers; then rub a pinch of the seasonings underneath. Flavored butters, chopped fresh herbs or aromatics, or any of the spice blends on pages 27 to 35 will work well. Here are seven recipes that are easily adapted to this technique.

1. Roast Chicken Parts with Olive Oil or Butter (page 615)
2. Simply Grilled or Broiled Chicken Parts (page 617)
3. Roast Chicken with Garlicky Herb Butter (page 636)
4. Chicken Under a Brick (page 641)
5. Grilled or Broiled Split Chicken (page 642)
6. Forty-Five-Minute Roast Turkey (page 646)
7. Roast Turkey Breast, on the Bone (page 650)

 fast make ahead ⓥ vegetarian

butter come to room temperature, then use a fork to mix in ⅓ cup miso. Light miso will be milder; dark will be more robust. Proceed with the recipe, but go a little easy on the salt.

OTHER METHODS FOR COOKING WHOLE CHICKEN

Roast chicken isn't the only way to cook a whole bird. You can poach them (and crisp them up a bit afterward), grill them, or even smoke them. All of these methods give wonderful—though different—results.

I like poaching whole chicken—or call it boiling or simmering—since it's just about foolproof, infuses the chicken with flavor, creates stock that I can use in the final dish or elsewhere, and prepare in advance. Since you're not looking for crisp skin (if you are, just run the cooked bird under the broiler or put it on the grill for a few minutes), you can cook it with much less baby-sitting than other methods. This doesn't mean you can overcook it, however.

Grilling a whole bird isn't as hard as you might think; there's a recipe on page 640. And you can also grill split and butterflied birds with excellent results (page 642). With charcoal you need to pay only a little extra attention to maintain the heat of the fire, and move the bird now and then for even cooking. (For more about grilling in general, see page 21.)

White Cut Chicken

MAKES: 4 servings | TIME: 40 minutes, largely unattended

This elegant poached chicken dish is popular throughout China and in some Chinese restaurants here in the States. Almost always served at room temperature, it's tender and flavorful when served with nothing more than soy sauce, but it's even better with Ginger-Scallion Sauce (page 64). Strain the cooking liquid and save it for soup stock.

5 or 6 slices fresh ginger (don't bother to peel)
5 scallions, chopped
2 star anise pods
2 tablespoons salt
2 tablespoons sugar
1 whole chicken (3 to 4 pounds), trimmed of excess fat
Soy sauce for serving

1. Use a pot large enough to hold the chicken plus at least 2 quarts water. Combine the ginger, scallions, star anise, salt, and sugar in a large pot with 8 cups water. Bring to a boil over high heat. Submerge the chicken in the water, breast up, and bring the water back to a boil. Turn the heat to low, cover, and simmer for 20 minutes. Remove from the heat and let the chicken sit in the water for another 10 minutes or so, still covered; it is done when an instant-read thermometer inserted into the thickest part of a thigh reads between 155° and 165°F.

2. Remove the chicken from the pot and cool to room temperature. Cut into serving pieces (see page 632). Serve with soy sauce. Or cover and refrigerate until you're ready to serve.

Chicken Pot Pie

MAKES: 4 to 6 servings | TIME: About 2 hours

Extreme comfort food comes at a price, but don't let the extra steps put you off, since each component (the piecrust, the chicken and sauce, and the vegetables) can be done a day or two ahead and the whole assembled right before baking. (And the variation starts with already cooked chicken.) For vegetables I use the classics, though you can try other complementary trios, like parsnips, green beans, and shallots or rutabaga, celery, and leeks. Just make sure root vegetables are cut small.

1 whole chicken (3 to 4 pounds), trimmed of
   excess fat
2 onions, quartered
3 bay leaves
10 whole black peppercorns
   Salt and pepper
1 recipe Savory Tart Crust (page 870), chilled
2 tablespoons butter or olive oil, plus more for
   greasing the baking dish
1 cup pearl onions, peeled (frozen are fine; run
   under cold water to thaw a bit, then drain)
2 large or 4 small to medium carrots, chopped
2 tablespoons all-purpose flour
1 tablespoon chopped fresh sage or 1 teaspoon
   dried sage
½ cup cream
1 cup peas (frozen are fine; don't bother to thaw)
1 egg, beaten

1. Put the chicken and onions in a large pot with just enough water to cover. Bring to a boil over medium-high heat, then immediately reduce the heat to medium-low. Skim any foam that rises to the surface. Add the bay leaves, peppercorns, and a generous pinch salt and pepper. Simmer until the chicken is cooked through, about 45 minutes; it is done when an instant-read thermometer inserted into the thickest part of a thigh reads between 155° and 165°F.

2. Transfer the chicken to a shallow bowl to cool. Leave the cooking liquid in the pot. (This is a good time to make the dough if you haven't already done so.)

3. Remove the chicken meat from the bones; discard the skin. Chop or pull the meat into pieces and reserve. Return the carcass to the pot, breaking up the pieces if necessary so they're submerged; don't add any water. Bring the liquid back to a boil. Adjust the heat so it bubbles steadily and cook, stirring occasionally, until the color deepens and the liquid reduces an inch or 2, about 30 minutes. Strain into a large pot and discard the solids. Bring the liquid to a boil and reduce until you have about 1½ cups, 15 to 30 minutes, depending on how much you started with. (At this point, the chicken and cooking liquid may be stored separately in the refrigerator for up to 2 days.) If you're baking the pie now, heat the oven to 375°F and generously grease a 2-quart baking dish.

4. Put the butter or oil in a deep skillet over medium heat. When the butter is melted or the oil is hot, add the pearl onions and carrots and cook, stirring frequently, until they just begin to soften, about 5 minutes. Reduce the heat to medium-low and stir in the flour; continue cooking and stirring until it just turns tan. Add the sage and cook, stirring, for another minute. (At this point, you can refrigerate the vegetable-flour mixture for up to a day, and reheat just before proceeding.)

5. Add the reduced chicken-cooking liquid and the cream to the vegetable-flour mixture and turn the heat up to medium. Cook, stirring constantly and scraping the bottom of the pan, until the liquid begins to bubble and thicken, but don't let it come to a rolling boil. Taste and adjust the seasoning, turn off the heat, and stir in the chicken and peas. Transfer the mixture into the prepared baking dish. (At this point, you can cover and refrigerate the filling for up to a day; bring to room temperature before proceeding.)

6. Roll out the tart crust large enough to cover the dish. Lay it on top of the dish and flute it as for a piecrust (see page 868), or just drape it over the sides a little. Use a sharp knife to cut 3 or 4 vents in the top. Brush the top with the beaten egg. Bake until the crust is deeply golden and the filling is bubbling, 50 to 60 minutes. Serve hot.

FASTER CHICKEN POT PIE For when you have leftovers or pick up a cooked chicken: Skip Steps 1, 2, and 3 and start by bringing 4 cups chicken stock (to make your own, see page 176) to a boil. Reduce by about half. Meanwhile, skin, bone, and chop the cooked chicken. You should have about 3 cups meat, but if not, simply substitute more vegetables (chopped green beans are nice) to make up the difference. Proceed with the recipe from Step 4.

CHICKEN SHEPHERD'S PIE Omit the tart crust. In Step 6, spread 1 recipe Mashed Potatoes (page 329) on the top so there are no gaps. Omit the egg but dot with butter, if you like. Bake as directed.

F fast   **M** make ahead   **V** vegetarian

Chicken Pot Pie,
page 637

CHICKEN-N-BISCUIT PIE In place of the tart crust, roll out 1 recipe Buttermilk or Yogurt Biscuits (page 773). Either leave it large enough to fit over the entire baking dish, or cut into individual biscuits; in Step 6, use it to top the filling. Brush with the egg and bake as directed, only the topping will be ready in 20 to 30 minutes.

PHYLLO-TOPPED CHICKEN POT PIE In place of the tart crust, thaw phyllo dough and cut into 6 squares large enough to top the baking dish (omit the egg). Melt 4 tablespoons butter. In Step 6, put 1 sheet over the dish and brush with butter; repeat with the remaining sheets. Tuck the corners into the baking dish, cut vents, and bake as directed, only the topping will be ready in 20 to 30 minutes.

Smoky Whole Chicken

MAKES: 4 to 6 servings | **TIME:** About 1¼ hours

Yes, it can be done. As is often the case, I recommend indirect heat (see "Grilling over Fire," page 21) and using wood chips for extra flavor. This recipe is complete, but for a little more detail, see "Grilled (or Broiled) Chicken Parts," page 617.

- 1 **whole chicken (3 to 4 pounds), trimmed of excess fat**
- 2 **tablespoons olive oil**
  Salt and pepper
  Any of the seasonings from "Ideas for Seasoning Any Grilled or Broiled Chicken," page 621 (optional)
  Lemon wedges for serving (optional)

1. Prepare a charcoal or gas grill for hot indirect cooking; make sure the grates are clean If you like, soak some wood chips in water for a few minutes, then sprinkle them directly on the grate over the hotter part of the fire or put them in a foil container over the flames. Rub the chicken with the oil and sprinkle it with salt and pepper; if you're using a seasoning rub, now's the time to put it on.

2. Put the chicken on the cool side of the grill, breast up, and cook until some of the fat has been rendered, about 20 minutes. Turn it onto one of its sides. If at any point

Splitting, Butterflying, or Spatchcocking Chicken

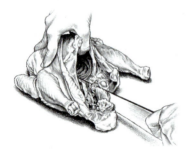

STEP 1 With the breast facing up, use a heavy knife to cut on one side of the backbone, from front to rear, carefully rocking as necessary. (To use kitchen scissors efficiently, turn the bird over.)

STEP 2 Cut on the other side of the backbone and remove it. Open the chicken out flat. Press down on the breast bone to flatten the chicken.

STEP 3 If you like, cut down through the breast bone to split the chicken into two halves.

 fast make ahead  vegetarian

the fire flares up, move the chicken to an even cooler part of the fire. Turn every 5 to 10 minutes until most of the fat has been rendered and the bird is browned and almost fully cooked at the bone, usually about 40 minutes; add more coals if necessary to keep the fire consistent. At this point, move the chicken directly over the fire to brown, turning frequently. If at any point the fire flares up, return the bird to the cool part of the grill.

3. When the chicken is done, it will be firm and brown all over, and an instant-read thermometer inserted into the thickest part of a thigh will read between 155° and 165°F. Remove it from the grill and let it rest for a few minutes before carving. Serve hot, warm, or at room temperature, with lemon wedges or any of the sauce suggestions from "Ideas for Seasoning Any Grilled or Broiled Chicken."

SPLIT CHICKEN

Cooking faster and easier to handle than whole chicken, split or butterflied—sometimes called *spatchcocked*—chicken is almost whole; the backbone is usually removed. It cooks nearly as quickly as cut-up chicken and retains more of its juice. Plus, it looks pretty spectacular. Split chicken is not always readily available in the supermarket, but it's easy to split a chicken at home; follow the illustrations on the previous page. And you may be able to ask the supermarket butcher to do it for you.

Almost any recipe can be adapted for split chicken; follow the directions here for cutting the bird, and season the chicken in any of the ways you would for sautéed, grilled, roasted, or broiled whole chicken or parts.

Chicken Under a Brick

MAKES: 4 servings | **TIME:** 45 minutes

The wonderful dish associated with Lucca, Italy, in which split chicken is weighted to flatten it, producing an evenly cooked, crisp, and moist bird with just a little heavy lifting. The Italians use the word for brick (*mattone*), but I usually weight the chicken with a cast-iron

pan and a couple of big rocks; handle the hot, heavy pan with two hands if you go this route.

I prefer rosemary here, which is traditional. But most herbs are also wonderful: Try savory or dill in similar quantity; parsley, basil, chervil, chives—use twice as much; or tarragon, oregano, marjoram, or thyme—use half as much.

- 1 **whole chicken (3 to 4 pounds), trimmed of excess fat**
- 1 **tablespoon chopped fresh rosemary or 1 teaspoon dried rosemary (plus 2 optional sprigs fresh rosemary, optional)**
- 2 **teaspoons salt**
- 1 **tablespoon chopped garlic**
- 2 **tablespoons olive oil**
  Lemon wedges for serving

1. Remove the backbone and split the chicken (see page 640). Heat the oven to 450°F. Mix the rosemary, salt, garlic, and 1 tablespoon of the olive oil and rub this all over the chicken. Tuck some of it under the skin as well.

2. Heat a large ovenproof skillet over medium-high heat for about 3 minutes. Press the rosemary sprigs, if you're using them, onto the skin of the chicken. Put the remaining olive oil in the pan and wait a minute for it to heat up. Put the chicken in the pan skin side down, along with any bits of rosemary and garlic that didn't stick. To press the chicken, cover another skillet or a flat pot cover with foil, put it over the bird, and weight it with a couple of bricks or rocks. The idea is to flatten the chicken by applying weight evenly over its surface.

3. Cook over medium-high heat until the chicken renders some fat, about 10 minutes. Transfer, still weighted, to the oven. Roast until the skin releases easily from the pan, about 15 minutes more. Take the rig from the oven and remove the weight(s). Turn the chicken over (it will now be skin side up) and return to the oven to roast until done, a final 10 minutes or so. To check for doneness, insert an instant-read thermometer into the thickest part of the thigh; it should read between 155° and 165°F. Cut into pieces and serve hot or at room temperature, with the lemon wedges.

Grilled or Broiled Split Chicken

MAKES: 4 servings | **TIME:** 40 to 60 minutes

Basically the same ingredients as in the preceding recipe, but cooked by different techniques. It's not essential to weight the bird when you grill it, although it still helps the meat to brown evenly. (It's impossible to weight it for broiling, of course.) A couple of bricks or rocks, wrapped in aluminum foil, will do the trick.

- 1 whole chicken (3 to 4 pounds), trimmed of excess fat
- 2 tablespoons chopped fresh parsley or 1 teaspoon dried parsley (or any of the herbs listed on page 615)
- 2 teaspoons salt
- 1 tablespoon chopped garlic
- 2 tablespoons olive oil
  Lemon wedges for serving
  Any of the sauce suggestions from "Ideas for Seasoning Any Grilled or Broiled Chicken" (page 621; optional)

1. Prepare a charcoal or gas grill for hot indirect cooking (make sure the grates are clean) or turn on the broiler and position the rack about 6 inches below the heat. If you like, soak some wood chips in water for a few minutes, then sprinkle them directly on the grate over the hotter part of the fire or put them in a foil container over the flames. Remove the backbone and split the chicken (see page 640). Mix the parsley, salt, garlic, and 1 tablespoon of the olive oil and rub this all over the chicken. Tuck some of it under the skin as well.

2. TO GRILL: Put the chicken on the cool side of the grill, skin side up and cover the grill. After some of the fat has been rendered, about 10 minutes, turn the chicken; if the fire flares up, move the chicken to an even cooler part of the fire or turn it so the skin side is up again. Cook, turning occasionally, until both sides are browned and the flesh is firm and cooked through about 30 minutes more, adding more coals if necessary. At this point, move the chicken directly over the fire to brown thoroughly, turning it frequently. If at any point the fire flares up, return the bird to the cool part of the grill.

TO BROIL: Line a roasting pan with foil to help cleanup if you like. Start with the skin side down and broil, making sure the bird doesn't burn, until browned, about 20 minutes. Turn and cook until the skin is brown and the juices run clear, another 10 to 15 minutes. If it needs a few more minutes, turn it skin side down again and cook until done, then turn the chicken skin side up again for a minute or so.

3. When the chicken is done, it will be firm and brown, and an instant-read thermometer inserted in the thickest part of a thigh will read between 155° and 165°F). Remove it from the grill or broiler and let it rest for a few minutes. Then drizzle with the remaining olive oil and serve hot, warm, or at room temperature, with lemon wedges or any of the sauce suggestions if you like.

TANDOORI CHICKEN You can marinate this for up to a day if you like: Omit the parsley, salt, garlic, and olive oil. In a blender or food processor, combine 1 chopped onion; 2 cloves garlic; a ½-inch piece fresh ginger; 1 tablespoon ground cumin; 1 teaspoon ground coriander; ¼ teaspoon cayenne, or to taste; 1 teaspoon salt; and 1 cup yogurt. Blend until smooth. Marinate the split chicken in this, covered and refrigerated, for 12 to 24 hours, turning occasionally. Scrape off most of the marinade before grilling.

JERK CHICKEN Pretty close to authentic, especially if you scatter pimento or other fruity wood chips over the fire. This paste has more fresh ingredients than the spice blend on page 34, but you can also mix 2 tablespoons of that with 2 tablespoons good-quality vegetable oil and use that to rub the bird: Omit the parsley, salt, garlic, and olive oil. In a food processor, combine 4 chopped scallions; 3 cloves garlic; a 2-inch piece ginger, chopped; 1 shallot, chopped; 1 habanero or Scotch bonnet chile, seeded; ¼ cup good-quality vegetable oil; 3 tablespoons fresh lime juice; 1 tablespoon honey, 1 tablespoon fresh thyme leaves; 1 tablespoon whole allspice berries. Sprinkle with salt and pepper. Let the machine run until a paste forms. Rub this onto the chicken as directed in Step 1.

THE BASICS OF WHOLE TURKEY

No matter how you feel about the bird the rest of the year, most Americans will inevitably eat turkey at least once during the fall. Properly cooked turkey is plain good eating; however, it can be a tricky bird to handle, especially given its size. The good news is that turkey parts are no more difficult to deal with than other cuts of meat. But let's start with the big birds.

TYPES OF TURKEY

Like chicken, there are several kinds of turkeys available, including standard, "wild," free range, self-basting (like Butterball), and kosher. Usually they're sold frozen, although increasingly you see them fresh around Thanksgiving, especially those raised locally. Here are my views on each.

STANDARD This often amazingly cheap bird is versatile and, well, standard. It is raised under the same (usually deplorable) conditions as standard chickens and so has the same environmental and ethical baggage attached. For many of us, though, it is the only option, and until something better comes along—like a consistently high-quality free-range bird—this is what we consume most often. If you choose this type of turkey, avoid the self-basting kind, which are full of unnecessary additives.

"WILD" True wild turkeys are thriving in many parts of the United States. But you're not going to get one to eat unless you (or a friend) shoot it yourself. The "wild" turkeys sold by mail-order houses and specialty stores are domesticated. They're quite expensive, not especially flavorful, and generally pretty tough. Try one out before you commit to making it your Thanksgiving bird.

FREE RANGE In theory a better bird than standard but in practice, wildly inconsistent and often outrageously expensive. In addition, many free-range turkeys are tougher than the standard variety and no more flavorful. Your best bet is to find a local source for free-range birds—or those similarly raised with room to roam outside—and, if it's good and reasonably priced, stick to it.

KOSHER Like kosher and halal chickens, marginally better in flavor and texture than standard birds, at about twice the price. Worth a try though. You can pretty much duplicate its better qualities by brining a standard bird; see "Is Brining Worth the Effort?" on page 633.

HERITAGE These are the turkey breeds that were raised before commercialized and industrial farming. They tend to have smaller breasts and be more flavorful, slightly chewier, and way more expensive. You have many options now, however, and generally if they're in your budget, this is the way to go. You can get them at farmers' markets, natural food stores, and directly from a producer, either online or at the farm.

FRESH VERSUS FROZEN TURKEY

Although more and more turkey parts are sold fresh, most of the whole birds are still frozen. Unless the turkey is of ultra-high quality, it doesn't make much difference. Frozen turkey is often put on sale at almost incomprehensibly low prices and offers the convenience (as long as you have a large freezer) of having the bird whenever you want it.

Of course, if your turkey is frozen, you must thaw it before cooking, and even small turkeys take quite a while. The easiest way to thaw a turkey is to let it sit in the refrigerator for two days before you plan to cook it. If you're in a hurry, thaw it by letting it sit in a sink or bowlful of cold water, changing the water occasionally; but you should still plan for it to take a whole day, or more for an especially large bird. This is one process you cannot rush.

Left to right: Corn Bread Stuffing with Oysters and Sausage, page 651; Cranberry Relish, page 74; Turkey Gravy, page 649; and Forty-Five-Minute Roast Turkey, page 646

ROASTING WHOLE TURKEY

This will sound like heresy: I suggest that you try to avoid roasting a bird larger than 12 pounds or so. Even that is way too big to mess around with turning this way and that. For many of us, just getting a pan big enough to hold the thing is an issue, as is figuring how to turn something that's huge and very hot.

So I either buy two smaller birds or cook another meat at the same time. I roast the turkey breast side up the whole time. And guess what? It works well, especially if you follow the high-heat method described here, which even results in moist and juicy breast meat.

Forty-Five-Minute Roast Turkey

MAKES: At least 10 servings | TIME: 45 minutes

This method is so quick it might inspire you to cook turkey more often. It is, after all, classic in sandwiches.

On Thanksgiving, however, when time and oven space are at a premium, butterflying a whole turkey is a boon to hosts. Split, flattened, and roasted at a high temperature, a 10-pound bird will be done in about 40 minutes. Really. It will also be more evenly browned, more evenly cooked (the legs are more exposed; the wings shield the breasts), and moister than birds cooked conventionally. But please take note: You *must* use a relatively small turkey. Please do not plan your most important meal of the year around trying this method with a 20-pound bird. It won't work.

    1   8- to 12-pound turkey
   10   or more cloves garlic, lightly crushed
        Several sprigs fresh sage or thyme, or several
        pinches dried
   ⅓   cup melted butter or olive oil
        Salt and pepper

1. Heat the oven to 450°F. Cut the backbone out of the turkey as you would a chicken (see page 640). Turn the bird over and press on it to flatten. Put

---

How to Carve a Roast Turkey

STEP 1 First remove the leg-thigh section by cutting straight down between the leg and carcass and through the joint holding the thigh to the carcass. Repeat on the other side and set aside.

STEP 2 The easiest option is to cut thick slices of white meat from the breast. To remove the breast first, see the illustrations on page 648.

STEP 3 Cut the wings from the carcass and carve the meat from the leg-thigh sections.

 F fast   **M** make ahead  **V** vegetarian

it breast up in a roasting pan that will just accommodate it; a slightly snug fit is okay. The wings should partially cover the breasts, and the legs should splay out a bit.

2. Tuck the garlic and herbs under the bird and in the nooks of the wings and legs. Drizzle with the butter and sprinkle liberally with salt and pepper.

3. Roast for 20 minutes, undisturbed. By this time the bird should be browning; remove it from the oven, baste with the pan juices, and return it to the oven. Reduce the heat to 400°F, or 350°F if it seems to be browning very quickly.

4. Begin to check the bird's temperature about 15 minutes later, or 10 minutes if the bird is on the small side. It is done when an instant-read thermometer inserted into the thickest part of a thigh reads between 155° and 165°F; check in a couple of places, without touching bone.

5. Let the bird rest for about 10 minutes before carving. Serve with the garlic cloves and pan juices, or make Turkey Gravy, page 649.) Or serve it at room temperature.

Classic Roast Turkey with Gravy

MAKES: At least 15 servings, plus leftovers | TIME: 3½ hours or more
Ⓜ

Cook the stuffing outside the bird (see page 649) to save yourself time, mess, and worrying about everything cooking through. Serve with Mashed Potatoes (page 329), Traditional Cranberry Sauce (page 74), and any seasonally appropriate vegetable side, and you've got a complete Thanksgiving dinner.

Turkey Timing

All these times are approximate, but in most cases, if your turkey is fully thawed and your oven is pretty accurate, the roasting will be close, though probably on the long-and-extremely-safe side. Remember, an instant-read thermometer inserted into the thickest part of the turkey's thigh should read between 155° and 165°F when the bird is ready to come out of the oven. Remember, too, that the bird must rest for at least 15 minutes before being carved, and the temperature will go up another 5°F or so during that time. (See my recommendations in "Chicken Safety and Doneness," page 593, which apply to turkey as well.)

THAWING

WEIGHT	THAWING TIME: REFRIGERATED	THAWING TIME: COLD WATER
6–8 pounds	18–24 hours	4–6 hours
8–12 pounds	24–36 hours	8–12 hours
12–18 pounds	36 hours+	12–16 hours
18 pounds+	48 hours+	18 hours+

ROASTING

WEIGHT	ROASTING TIME: UNSTUFFED	ROASTING TIME: STUFFED
8–12 pounds	2¾–3 hours	3–3½ hours
12–14 pounds	3–3¾ hours	3½–4 hours
14–18 pounds	3¾–4¼ hours	4–4¼ hours
18–20 pounds	4¼–4½ hours	4¼–4¾ hours
20–24 pounds	4½–5 hours	4¾–5¼ hours
24–30 pounds	5–5¼ hours	5¼–6¼ hours

1 12- to 18-pound turkey
8 tablespoons (1 stick) butter, softened, or a few
   tablespoons olive oil
   Salt and pepper
1 onion, cut into chunks
2 large carrots, cut into chunks
1 celery stalk, cut into chunks
   Stems from 1 bunch fresh parsley, tied together
   (optional)
   Turkey Gravy (recipe follows) for serving

1. Heat the oven to 500°F. Remove the giblets from the turkey; use them to make stuffing or stock if you like, or roast them with the bird to add to the gravy. Smear the bird all over with butter or brush it with oil, then sprinkle well with salt and pepper.

2. Put the turkey breast up on a rack in a large roasting pan. Add ½ cup water to the pan along with the turkey neck, giblets if you're using them, any other turkey trimmings, and the onion, carrots, celery, and parsley stems. Put the turkey in the oven legs first if possible.

3. Roast until the skin begins to brown, 20 to 30 minutes, then turn the heat down to 350°F. Continue to roast, checking and basting with the pan juices every 30 minutes or so; if the skin threatens to brown too much, put a piece of foil directly on the breast. (If the pan dries out and threatens to burn, add water about ½ cup at a time; keep at least a little liquid in the bottom of the pan at all times.) The turkey is done when an instant-read thermometer inserted into the thickest part of a thigh reads between 155° and 165°F, about 3 hours total for this size bird, not stuffed (see the chart on page 647 for other estimates). If when the turkey is nearly done, the top is not browned enough, turn the heat back up to 425°F for the last 20 to 30 minutes of cooking.

4. Remove the turkey from the oven. Take the bird off the rack and let it sit for about 20 minutes before carving, longer if you don't mind it at room temperature. Make the gravy while the bird rests.

Removing Roast Turkey Breasts

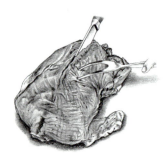

STEP 1 For more even slices of meat, you can remove the breast from the bone after cutting off the wings, thighs, and legs. Begin by slicing directly down along the side of the breast bone.

STEP 2 Keep the side of the blade pressed against the bone as you free the entire breast.

STEP 3 Slice the breasts crosswise as you would a boneless roast.

 fast    M make ahead   V vegetarian

Turkey Gravy

MAKES: 5 to 6 cups (enough for 12 servings) | **TIME:** 20 minutes, after roasting a turkey

"Gravy" is little more than thickened stock—essentially a reduction sauce (see page 80)—and when that stock comes from roasted turkey, it's pretty good stuff. It's no wonder people love it. Use the cornstarch if you like thicker gravy. Double or triple this recipe—or quadruple, if it comes to that—as needed.

Make the stock at least a couple days ahead. If you want to use turkey stock, then buy some extra parts; wings and dark meat work best.

> Giblets from Classic Roast Turkey (page 647; optional)
> Pan juices from Classic Roast Turkey, still in the roasting pan
> 6 cups stock (preferably turkey but chicken is fine; to make your own, see page 176)
> Salt and pepper
> 5 tablespoons butter (optional)
> ⅓ cup cornstarch (optional)

1. Remove any giblets from the bottom of the roasting pan. Chop and reserve them if you're adding them to the gravy or the stuffing. Pour or spoon off excess fat (that's a judgment call, but leave at least ¼ cup fat in there); leave as much of the bits of skin and bones and as much of the dark liquid on the bottom of the pan as possible. Put the roasting pan over two burners and turn the heat to high.

2. Add the stock and cook, stirring and scraping all the brown bits off the bottom of the pan, until the liquid has reduced by about one quarter, 5 to 10 minutes. (If you're not using cornstarch and want a thicker gravy, continue to reduce a little more.) Strain the liquid into a saucepan, discarding the solids.

3. Over medium heat, stir in the butter if you're using it and keep warm until ready to serve. If you're using cornstarch, mix it with ¼ cup cold water, then add to the simmering gravy with the giblets if you're using them, stirring constantly. The gravy should thicken almost immediately; if not, keep stirring. Serve hot.

STUFFINGS FOR TURKEY AND OTHER POULTRY

I tend to be pretty conservative with almost all aspects of turkey-making for feasts (just butter and woodsy herbs for me), and that includes the stuffing. So I keep the ingredients simple and strive to make the stuffing one of the less challenging aspects of the meal. Any stuffing you make from scratch is going to be infinitely better than the instant kind most people are used to, so you're way ahead of the game.

A few more thoughts about stuffing: You'll get better results by cooking stuffing separately from the bird. The turkey will cook more evenly; the textures of the stuffing will range from custardy to crisp around the edges.

If you still want to pack some stuffing in the bird, remember that the temperature of the stuffing needs to reach 165°F, just like the meat to kill any harmful bacteria. That means the turkey might actually be overdone—another good reason to cook them separately. Finally, don't skimp on the fat or the seasonings; lean, underseasoned stuffing is little more than mushy bread.

5 Other Recipes You Can Use to Stuff Poultry

1. Steamed Sticky Rice (page 430) or any of the variations
2. Rice Pilaf (page 434)
3. Quinoa with Roasted Corn (page 458)
4. Wild Rice Pilaf (and its variations page 467)
5. Wheat Berries with Candied Walnuts (page 468)

My Favorite Bread Stuffing

MAKES: About 6 cups (enough for an 8-inch pan) | TIME: 20 minutes, plus time to bake

This classic stuffing is based on a wonderful recipe by James Beard; it's amazing with butter, but check out the variations for some other options. Also, feel free to use whole-grain bread for more flavor. If you want to stuff a bird, plan on roasting the turkey about 30 minutes longer, and cook until the stuffing registers between 155° and 165°F on an instant-read thermometer.

½	**pound (2 sticks) butter, plus more for the pan**
1	**onion, chopped**
½	**cup pine nuts or chopped walnuts**
6 to 8	**cups fresh bread crumbs (see page 801)**
1	**tablespoon chopped fresh sage or 1 teaspoon dried sage**
½	**cup chopped scallions**
	Salt and pepper
½	**cup chopped fresh parsley leaves**
1	**cup chicken or vegetable stock (to make your own, see page 176 or 174), or as needed**

1. Heat the oven to 350°F. Grease an ovenproof glass or enamel baking dish. Put the butter in a large skillet or pot over medium heat. When it has melted, add the onion and cook, stirring, until it softens, about 5 minutes. Add the nuts and cook, stirring almost constantly, until they begin to brown, about 3 minutes.

2. Add the bread crumbs and sage and toss to mix. Turn the heat down to low. Add the scallions and sprinkle with salt and pepper. Toss again; taste and adjust the seasoning. Stir in the parsley. Turn off the heat. Add the stock a little at a time and stir until the mixture has the consistency of streusel and sticks together when you pinch it. (At this point, you can refrigerate the stuffing, well wrapped or in a covered container, for up to a day before proceeding.)

3. Transfer the stuffing to the prepared dish and bake until golden on top and cooked through, about 45 minutes. (Or you can cook it up to 3 days in advance and just warm it up right before dinner.)

THE BASICS OF TURKEY PARTS

It's easy to forget that turkey is raised fifty-two weeks a year. So turkey parts—legs, ground turkey, boneless breasts—are available everywhere.

All for the better: Whole turkey breast is quite good roasted, on or off the bone (see below and page 652). Turkey thighs make a nice change from the breast meat—or even chicken—and become reminiscent of pork when braised. And boneless turkey may in fact be slightly tastier than chicken cutlets; it can be treated exactly the same and used in every recipe in which you'd use boneless chicken (pages 596–612).

Roast Turkey Breast, on the Bone

MAKES: 6 to 12 or more servings | TIME: About 1 hour
 M

At 3 to 6 pounds, a turkey breast is a fine choice for a small party, and produces plenty of leftovers for sandwiches. The roasting itself is a breeze, and you can also use any of the additions from "Varying Simplest Whole Roast Chicken" on page 635. See the illustrations on page 648 for how to carve a turkey breast.

1	**3- to 6-pound turkey breast**
	About 3 tablespoons olive oil or melted butter for basting
	Salt and pepper

1. Heat the oven to 450°F. Put the turkey on a rack in a roasting pan, skin side up. Brush with oil and sprinkle with salt and pepper.

2. Roast for about 45 minutes, basting with the pan drippings every 15 minutes or so, then begin checking every few minutes with an instant-read thermometer. The turkey is ready when the thermometer reads between

My Favorite Stuffing, 6 Ways

Follow the directions for the main recipe, cooking the fat and aromatics in Step 1 and adding the bread and seasonings in Step 2.

NAME	FAT	AROMATICS	BREAD	SEASONINGS
Basic Stuffing	½ pound (2 sticks) butter	1 onion, chopped; 2 carrots, chopped; 2 celery stalks, chopped. Add ½ cup dry white wine when the vegetables are soft.	6 to 8 cups fresh bread crumbs (see page 801)	½ cup chopped toasted pecans (see page 309); 1 tablespoon chopped fresh sage or thyme (or 1 teaspoon dried)
Bread Stuffing with Giblets and Fruit	½ pound (2 sticks) butter	1 onion, chopped. Chop the raw gizzard, heart, and liver; add after the onion is soft, and cook until the giblets are no longer pink.	6 to 8 cups fresh bread crumbs (see page 801)	2 teaspoons fresh thyme or 1 teaspoon dried thyme; 1 finely crumbled bay leaf; 1½ cups chopped pitted prunes; 2 cups peeled, diced tart apples
Bread Stuffing with Sage and Chestnuts	½ pound (2 sticks) butter	1 onion, chopped. Add 1 pound Boiled Chestnuts (page 282), shelled, skinned, and chopped, and ½ cup dry white wine after the onion is soft; boil for 5 minutes.	6 to 8 cups fresh bread crumbs (see page 801)	1 tablespoon fresh sage (or 1 teaspoon dried), ¼ cup chopped fresh parsley
Bread Stuffing with Sausage	1 pound sausage (casings removed); cook until no longer pink; spoon off the fat	1 onion, chopped; 1 tablespoon chopped garlic	6 to 8 cups fresh bread crumbs (see page 801)	1 teaspoon ground cumin (optional); ¼ cup chopped fresh parsley
Corn Bread Stuffing with Oysters and Sausage	1 pound sausage (casings removed); cook until no longer pink; spoon off most of the fat	1 onion, chopped; 1 tablespoon chopped garlic	1 recipe Corn Bread (page 769), crumbled	1 to 2 dozen oysters, shucked, plus their liquid; ¼ cup chopped fresh parsley
Bacon-Nut Stuffing	1 pound slab or sliced bacon, chopped; cook until crisp; spoon off most of the fat	1 onion, chopped; 1 tablespoon chopped garlic. Add 1 cup dry white wine and 2 bay leaves when the onions are soft; boil for 5 minutes. Remove the bay leaves before proceeding.	6 to 8 cups fresh bread crumbs (see page 801)	½ cup toasted pine nuts or chopped walnuts; ¼ cup chopped fresh parsley

155° and 165°F. Let the turkey rest for 5 to 10 minutes before carving and serving hot or at room temperature (or refrigerate and slice for sandwiches and salads).

BASIC ROAST BONELESS TURKEY BREAST Heat the oven to 450°F. Put the turkey in a roasting pan (no need for a rack), brush all over with olive oil, and sprinkle

with salt and pepper. Roast, skin side up, for 25 to 30 minutes, until the turkey is almost done; it will be firm to the touch but not rubbery, white or very pale pink inside, and an instant-read thermometer inserted in the thickest part should read between 155° and 165°F.

Turkey Thighs in Almond Mole

MAKES: 6 to 8 servings | **TIME:** About 1½ hours, somewhat unattended

To this day, the most exciting turkey dish I've ever had comes from Oaxaca and involves mole. Many moles are quite intricate and take days to make. Others, like this almond-based example, are easy enough for a weeknight and, when it comes to producing a flavorful dish without too much trouble, very reliable. Serve with plain rice or warm tortillas.

2	dried ancho or other mild chiles
4	tablespoons good-quality vegetable oil
1	teaspoon chopped fresh chile like jalapeño or serrano, or to taste, or red chile flakes or cayenne, to taste
1	large white onion, chopped
1	cup almonds
	Salt and pepper
5	large cloves garlic, peeled, or more to taste
3 or 4	tomatoes, cored and chopped (about 3 cups; canned are fine)
½	teaspoon ground cinnamon
	Pinch ground cloves
1	tablespoon dry red wine or cider vinegar, or to taste
2	cups chicken stock (to make your own, see page 176), or as needed
3 or 4	small bone-in turkey thighs (about 4 pounds total)
	Slivered almonds for garnish (optional)

1. Soak the anchos in hot water to cover. When they're soft, after 15 to 30 minutes, drain them and remove their stems and seeds. Put 2 tablespoons of the oil in a large skillet over medium-high heat. Add the fresh chile and onions and cook, stirring occasionally, until the onions begins to soften, 3 to 5 minutes. Add the almonds, a sprinkle of salt, at least ½ teaspoon pepper, the garlic, tomatoes, cinnamon, cloves, ancho chiles, wine, and enough stock to keep moist and cook, stirring occasionally, until the tomatoes begin to break up, about 10 minutes.

2. Cool slightly, then purée in a blender. Taste and add more salt, pepper, or wine if you like. (You can let the sauce cool for several hours before puréeing, and/or refrigerate the purée for up to a day before continuing.)

3. Put the remaining 2 tablespoons oil in the skillet over medium-high heat. When it's hot, add the turkey, skin side down. Sprinkle with salt and pepper and a couple of minutes later (it's not important that it brown well), pour the sauce over it. Cover, adjust the heat so the sauce bubbles steadily, and cook, turning the pieces once or twice, until the thighs are very tender, about an hour.

4. Transfer the turkey to a cutting board, slice the meat from the bone in big pieces and return it to the sauce. Taste and adjust the seasoning. Garnish with slivered almonds if you like and serve hot.

THE BASICS OF DUCK AND GOOSE

These two birds have a lot in common: They're all dark meat that is rich and fatty—amazingly so if you're used to chicken—which means they must be treated differently from other birds. It also means they develop a beautifully crisp, dark skin. They're flavorful without being gamy. (I'm talking about domesticated ducks and geese. Wild ones are quite gamy—but they're also hard to come by.) Finally, their size is deceptive; they look big but there's only enough meat on the average 4- to 5-pound duck to serve two or three people.

Duck fat is a dream for cooking things like potatoes, eggs, grains, or pasta. If you simply roast the bird in an empty pan, you get a lot of gorgeous, clean fat that keeps for weeks in the refrigerator or months in the freezer. Ditto for goose. If you're serious about rendering some, see the section on page 622.

"Duck," by the way, usually means Pekin duck, the kind found at most supermarkets. It's usually sold "fresh" but in fact is shipped frozen and then thawed; truly fresh duck is rare. Increasingly, you can also easily find duck breasts or duck legs, which are incomparable when braised (page 657). But rarely do you see them both packaged together (that is, a cut-up whole duck). It's a shame, because duck parts cook well together, as you'll see if you try the following recipes. If you decide to use duck breasts alone for any of these recipes, just be

About Ground Chicken and Turkey

I don't generally cook with them, but ground chicken and turkey can be used in any recipe calling for ground meat, if that's your preference. What people like is exactly what I dislike: their low fat content. If that's your concern, then look for 5 percent or less on the label. Far better, in my opinion, is to grind your own and include some skin. (See "Do-It-Yourself Ground Meat" on page 686.)

A distinct advantage to grinding your own meat is that you can add seasonings during the final stages of processing, making your finished dishes that much more flavorful. If you choose to use a food processor, cut the meat, which should be very cold or even partially frozen, into chunks. Pulse in the machine until it reaches the texture you like.

In general, ground chicken and turkey are good substitutes for other ground meat where the meat will be cooked until well done, like Meatballs, Three Ways (page 127), Meat Loaf (page 688), Slow Simmered Beef Chili (page 403), Meat Sauce (page 495), Meaty Lasagne (page 502), and Pot Stickers or Steamed Dumplings (pages 124 and 126).

careful not to overcook them. And whole duck is always a showstopper.

Goose is nearly always sold frozen. The easiest way to thaw goose is to let it sit in the refrigerator for 2 days before you plan to cook it. If you're in a hurry, thaw it by letting it sit in cold water, changing the water occasionally; but you should still plan for it to take the better part of a day for a 10-pound bird.

Roast Duck

MAKES: 2 to 4 servings | TIME: About 1¼ hours

Duck is difficult to roast badly, so there are as many methods as cooks. Having tried many of them, I can say that the results are all about the same. I rely on this one, which is pretty simple and probably the easiest way to guarantee a beautifully browned, succulent bird.

Trying to stretch a duck to serve four is not easy, but if the four are not big on meat and you provide plenty of side dishes, it can be done.

> 1 whole duck (4 to 5 pounds), trimmed of excess fat
> Pepper
> ¼ cup soy sauce, or as needed

1. Heat the oven to 450°F. Discard the neck and giblets or keep them for another use; remove excess fat from the duck's cavity.
2. Put the duck breast down (wings up) on a rack in a roasting pan; add water to just below the rack. Sprinkle with pepper and brush with a little soy sauce.
3. Roast for 30 minutes, undisturbed. Prick the back all over with the point of a sharp knife, then turn the bird onto its back. Sprinkle with pepper and brush with soy sauce again. Add a little more water to the bottom of the pan if the juices are spattering—carefully; you don't want to get water on the duck).
4. Roast for 20 minutes, prick the breast all over with the point of a knife, and brush with soy sauce. Roast for

10 minutes and brush with soy sauce. Roast for another 5 or 10 minutes if necessary, until the duck is a glorious brown all over and an instant-read thermometer inserted into a thigh reads between 155° and 165°F. Let rest for 5 to 10 minutes before carving. Meanwhile, skim most of the fat from the pan drippings; serve the remaining juices with the duck.

ROAST DUCK WITH ORANGE MARMALADE-SAKE SAUCE
Easier than duck à l'orange, and better: Omit the soy sauce and season the duck all over with salt in Step 2. Roast the bird until it's done in Step 4, pricking it all over as directed. Melt 1 cup good-quality orange marmalade in a small saucepan. Brush the duck once with the marmalade, transfer the duck to a platter, and pour off the fat from the pan. Put the pan over two burners set for medium heat. Add 1 cup sake and cook, scraping up the browned bits until most of the liquid boils away. Add the pan drippings to the saucepan with the marmalade and heat until just bubbling. Carve the bird and serve it with the sauce.

Fast "Roast" Duck, Chinese Style

MAKES: 4 servings | TIME: About 1 hour

Producing the type of roast duck you see hanging in the windows of many Chinese restaurants is nearly impossible at home. But you can get similar results in less than an hour if you begin by cutting up the duck. With just a little attention, the duck will develop a beautiful mahogany skin that belies the amount of work you put into it.

> 1 whole duck (4 to 5 pounds) trimmed of excess fat and cut into 8 pieces (see page 614)
> Salt and pepper
> 2 tablespoons rice wine or dry sherry
> 3 tablespoons soy sauce
> ½ cup brown sugar
> One 3-inch cinnamon stick

5 or 6 slices fresh ginger
4 star anise pods
2 whole cloves
1 teaspoon coriander seeds

1. Put the duck, skin side down, in a 12-inch skillet over medium-high heat and sprinkle it liberally with salt and pepper. When the duck begins to sizzle, cover the skillet and turn the heat down to medium. After 15 minutes, turn the duck and sprinkle the skin side with salt and pepper. After 15 minutes more, uncover the skillet and turn the heat back to medium-high. Cook the duck, turning as necessary, so that it browns on both sides; this will take another 15 minutes or so.

2. Transfer the duck to a plate and pour off all but 1 tablespoon fat (if there are any solids, leave them in the pan). Over medium-high heat, add the rice wine and bring to a boil. Add the soy sauce and 2 tablespoons water and bring back to a boil; stir in the sugar, cinnamon, ginger, star anise, and cloves until the sugar melts. Once the sauce starts bubbling, return the duck to the skillet and cook, turning it frequently, until the sauce is very thick and the duck is well glazed, 5 to 10 minutes. Remove the duck, then scoop the whole spices out of the sauce. Spoon the sauce over the duck and serve.

Duck Confit

MAKES: 6 to 8 servings | **TIME:** About 24 hours, largely unattended

Confit—a word that's come to mean long, slow cooking in fat—is straightforward, though you might associate it with fancy food. You have a few choices for the fat: Render your own (see page 622), purchase duck fat from a specialty store or online, or use olive oil. The last solution is perfectly acceptable, though it won't leave you with the delicious leftover duck fat to use for cooking. Whatever you use, after making the confit, strain the fat and store it in an airtight container in the refrigerator for weeks or the freezer for months; it's the best for cooking eggs or potatoes, or tossing with pasta, egg noodles, or rice.

I like to eat duck confit with something sharp or acidic (or both) like a salad with frisée or radicchio; add a crumble of blue cheese and a handful of hazelnuts and I'm all set. Confit is also excellent sautéed with cooked white beans for a fast skillet cassoulet.

1 cup kosher salt
1 tablespoon pepper
2 tablespoons fresh thyme, chopped, or 1 tablespoon dried thyme
2 bay leaves, ground or finely crumbled
8 duck legs or 4 whole legs and thighs, rinsed and blotted dry
8 cups rendered duck fat or olive oil

1. Combine the salt, pepper, thyme, and bay leaves. Put the duck legs on a rimmed baking sheet, sprinkle with the salt mixture, and rub it into the duck all over. Wrap in plastic and cure in the refrigerator overnight or for at least 8 hours.

2. Put the fat or oil in a wide pot over medium heat. Meanwhile, rinse the salt from the legs and blot them dry. When the fat is melted and just barely sending up a bubble, carefully add the legs; use tongs to prevent splattering. Adjust the heat so the oil sends up bubbles every now and then. Cook the legs, undisturbed, until the meat pulls away from the bones and is very tender, about 2 hours. (At this point, you can let the confit cool, covered. Transfer it to a container, making sure the legs are covered with the fat, and refrigerate for up to a couple of weeks. Remove as much of the solid fat as you like before proceeding.)

3. To serve, heat the oven to 300°F. Remove the legs from the fat and let the excess fat drain off. Put a large ovenproof skillet over medium-high heat; when it's hot, add the duck pieces skin side down, and cook until the skin is browned and crisp, about 10 minutes; transfer the skillet to the oven and bake until completely golden brown, about 15 minutes. Serve hot, warm, or at room temperature.

Duck Confit, page 655

Crisp-Braised Duck Legs with Aromatic Vegetables

MAKES: 4 servings | TIME: About 2 hours, largely unattended

In a fraction of the time, you can get a lot of the same benefits as from confit: crisp skin, very tender meat, and as a bonus, delicious vegetables. Serve with bread or mashed potatoes to soak up the sauce.

    4 whole duck legs, trimmed of excess fat
       Salt and pepper
    3 carrots, chopped
    3 celery stalks, chopped
    1 large onion, chopped
    2 cups chicken or duck stock (to make your own,
       see page 176) or water

1. Heat the oven to 400°F. Put the duck legs, skin side down, in an ovenproof skillet large enough to accommodate all the ingredients comfortably; turn the heat to medium and cook, rotating (but not turning) the pieces as necessary to brown the skin thoroughly and evenly.

2. When the skin is deeply browned, turn the legs over and sear for 1 to 2 minutes, sprinkle with salt and pepper, and transfer to a plate. Pour or spoon out all but about 2 tablespoons of the fat. Add the carrots, celery, and onion, and sprinkle with salt and pepper. Cook over medium-high heat, stirring occasionally, until they begin to brown, about 10 minutes.

3. Return the legs to the pan, skin side up, and add the stock; it should come about halfway up the legs but not cover them. Turn the heat to high, bring to a boil, and transfer the skillet to the oven.

4. Cook for 30 minutes, then turn the heat to 350°F. Continue to cook, undisturbed, until the duck is tender and the liquid reduced, at least another 30 minutes and probably a bit longer. (At this point, you can turn the oven down to 200°F and hold the duck for up to another hour.) Skim any excess fat from the braising liquid and serve hot.

8 Poultry Dishes That Reheat Well

Prepared in advance or simply left over, most moist poultry dishes are fine reheated. These are some of the best—and be sure to check out their variations too.

1. Chicken Teriyaki (page 601)
2. Chicken Adobo (pages 616)
3. Chicken and Lentils (page 622)
4. Coq au Vin (page 624)
5. Turkey Thighs in Almond Mole (page 652)
6. Duck Confit (page 655)
7. Cornish Hens and Sauerkraut (page 659)
8. Pheasant Stewed with Dried Fruits (page 662)

Roast Goose

MAKES: 6 to 10 servings | TIME: About 3 hours

The rich, dense meat of roast goose is enormously satisfying and the skin makes the effort worth it, even if you can't feed many people per pound. One way to extend a goose is to bake some stuffing in a pan alongside it; for some ideas see pages 649 to 651. Stuffings with fruit work especially well with goose, since their acidity and sweetness help offset the richness. And since the pan drippings will be mostly fat—which you can strain and save to use as you would duck fat; see page 622—a compote, salsa, or relish are good sauce options.

    1 whole goose (8 to 10 pounds), trimmed of
       excess fat
       Salt and pepper

1. Heat the oven to 350°F. Prick the skin all over with a sharp fork, skewer, or thin-bladed knife; try not to hit the meat (the fat layer is usually about ¼ inch thick). Sprinkle with salt and pepper. Put the goose breast down on a rack in a roasting pan.

2. Roast for 20 minutes, prick the exposed skin again, then roast until it begins to brown, about 20 minutes longer. Turn the goose breast up, prick again, and baste with some of the accumulated pan juices (there will be plenty). Roast for another hour, pricking the skin and basting 2 or 3 times.

3. Unless the goose is already very brown, raise the heat to 400°F and continue to roast until the meat is done, about another 30 minutes. An instant-read thermometer inserted into a thigh will read about 165°F. At that point, all juices should run clear, and the leg bone should wiggle a little in its socket. Let rest for a few minutes, then carve as you would turkey (see page 646) and serve.

THE BASICS OF OTHER WHOLE BIRDS

Cornish hens, poussins, and guinea hens can all be cooked using any chicken recipe, as long as you adjust the time. That's a good thing, because for the most part they're more flavorful than the chickens you can get at a grocery store.

Look for small Cornish hens, just over 1 pound each. They serve one or two people each and are ideal for splitting before cooking. Poussins, which are essentially baby chickens, may be treated like Cornish hens but tend to be a little bigger. Both have a distinct advantage over chicken: Because they're so small you can grill them quickly, and they're unlikely to burn or dry out, even over direct heat.

Guinea hens are a variety of chicken, usually more flavorful. Buy them if you see them and roast them simply, as on page 633.

Grilled or Broiled Cornish Hens with Sherry Vinegar

MAKES: 2 to 4 servings | **TIME:** About 40 minutes

This sauce is super with any grilled poultry, from chicken to squab, and rabbit too, especially during warmer months. Once you split the hens, you can also cook them according to any recipe for split chicken (starting on page 641), reducing the cooking time by about a third.

Other protein you can use: split rabbit (see page 624).

- 2 **Cornish hens, about 1 pound each**
  Salt and pepper
- 1 **cup chicken or vegetable stock (to make your own, see page 176 or 174)**
- 2 **tablespoons sherry vinegar**
  Chopped fresh parsley for garnish

1. Prepare a charcoal or gas grill for hot indirect cooking (make sure the grates are clean) or turn on the broiler and position the rack about 6 inches below the heat. Remove the backbones from the hens by cutting along their length on both sides. Open the hens skin side up and flatten them gently with the heel of your hand. Sprinkle on all sides with salt and pepper.

2. While the grill or broiler is heating, bring the stock and backbones to a boil in a small saucepan. Simmer until reduced by about half, about 30 minutes. Remove the bones, stir in the vinegar and salt and pepper if necessary.

3. TO GRILL: Start the hens on the cool side of the grill, skin side up, and close the lid. Cook until the skin begins

Making a Quick Poultry Stock

See the soup chapter for full-fledged stock recipes, but remember that you can make a simple but flavorful stock from the trimmings of any bird: Combine the backbone, neck, wing tips, and any other scraps except the liver and heart in a small saucepan and add water to cover. Add 1 small onion (don't bother to peel it), quartered; 1 carrot, cut into chunks; and 1 celery stalk, cut into chunks, along with a pinch salt and a few peppercorns. Bring to a boil, turn the heat to low, cover partially, and cook for as little as 30 minutes if you're in a hurry to as much as 60 minutes. Strain the stock through a fine-mesh sieve, pressing on the solids to extract as much liquid as possible. Discard the solids.

 fast  make ahead vegetarian

to crisp, about 15 minutes. Cook 10 to 15 minutes more, moving and turning them over both sides of the fire to crisp the skin, until the juices run clear and the meat is no longer pink at the bones.

TO BROIL: Line a rimmed sheet pan with foil to help cleanup if you like. Put the birds on the pan skin side down and broil, watching carefully, until the meat and bones brown a bit, 10 to 15 minutes. Turn and broil the other side, another 10 to 15 minutes, being careful not to let the skin burn.

4. Toward the end of the cooking time—after about 15 minutes for grilling and about 20 minutes for broiling—baste the hens with the vinegar sauce. Serve hot or at room temperature, drizzled with the remaining sauce and garnished with parsley.

---

5 OTHER SAUCES THAT ARE GREAT BASTED ON AND SERVED WITH GRILLED OR BROILED CORNISH HENS

1. Chimichurri (page 52)
2. Soy Dipping Sauce and Marinade (page 64)
3. Compound Butter (page 78)
4. Any Five-Minute Drizzle Sauce (page 81)
5. Any Vinaigrette (page 188)

Cornish Hens and Sauerkraut

MAKES: 4 to 6 servings | TIME: About 2 hours

With so few ingredients, you need to get the good stuff. Steer clear of canned sauerkraut; instead, look for a bottled or vacuum-sealed brand that contains no more than cabbage, salt, and water. This preparation also works well with pheasant, chicken, and duck.

    4 **Cornish hens, about 1 pound each**
    4 **slices bacon, diced, or 3 tablespoons olive oil**
    2 **pounds sauerkraut**
    2 **whole cloves**
    1 **teaspoon juniper berries, crushed with the side of a knife**
    1 **sprig fresh thyme or a pinch dried thyme**
    1 **bay leaf**
    1 **cup dry white wine**
    1 **cup chicken stock (to make your own, see page 176) or water, as needed**
       Salt and pepper

1. Heat the oven to 300°F. Remove the backbones from the hens by cutting along their length on both sides. Separate the breast and leg quarters (see page 614).

2. Put the bacon in a large skillet over medium heat and cook until crisp, about 10 minutes; remove the bacon with a slotted spoon and reserve. Or heat the oil until it shimmers. Add the hen backbones to the bacon fat or olive oil and brown them on all sides. Meanwhile, rinse the sauerkraut in a colander; drain well.

3. When the hen pieces are browned, return the bacon to the skillet and add the sauerkraut, cloves, juniper berries, thyme, bay leaf, and wine. Cook over medium heat until about half of the wine has evaporated, about 10 minutes; transfer the skillet into the oven.

4. Bake, stirring occasionally and adding stock as needed to keep the sauerkraut moistened, until the legs are tender and the sauerkraut is lightly browned, about 30 minutes. Remove the skillet from the oven; remove and discard the bones, cloves, and bay leaf. Taste the sauce, adjust the seasoning, and serve hot or warm.

CORNISH HENS WITH CABBAGE A little fresher: Omit the sauerkraut, cloves, and juniper berries. After browning the birds in Step 2, remove them from the skillet and add 8 cups chopped cabbage, 1 cinnamon stick, and 1 tablespoon chopped garlic; sprinkle with salt and pepper. Cook, stirring often, until the cabbage has wilted, a minute or two. Add 2 cups wine, 2 bay leaves, and the thyme and stir to combine. Return the hens to the pan, and proceed with the recipe from Step 4. Remove the cinnamon stick and bay leaf before serving.

QUAIL

You probably don't think of quail as weekday fare. But you can roast quail, or fry, braise, grill, broil, or sauté them, and it's hard to go wrong and can take as little as 20 minutes. They only weigh about 4 ounces each, for crying out loud. (Which means you need two per serving.)

Quail basically looks like a tiny chicken, but it's got a strong flavor that minimizes the need to dress it up. Unlike chickens, quail are raised mostly if not entirely free range. This puts their flavor squarely between that of domesticated birds and truly wild birds like partridge, grouse, and woodcock, which have starkly gamy flavors.

You can cook them whole, but I like to semibone them before cooking—a technique you can use with any small bird and even with chicken—cutting straight down along the breastbone to produce a bird that's really easy to eat. (See the illustrations at right.) The bird's skin is so delicate that you may wind up with a quartered bird because there's nothing else holding breast and leg together, but that's easy enough to deal with.

It's nearly impossible to find quail fresh. But every major food wholesaler can supply them, so your super-market or butcher should be able to provide them on a couple of days' notice. The internet, of course, offers another alternative.

Roast Quail with Honey, Cumin, and Orange Juice

MAKES: 4 servings | TIME: About 40 minutes

Crisp skin with outstanding flavor in well under an hour—this is guaranteed to make you a quail fan.

- 8 quail
  Salt and pepper
- 2 tablespoons olive oil
- 2 tablespoons fresh orange juice
- 2 tablespoons honey
- 1 teaspoon minced garlic
- 1 tablespoon ground cumin

1. Heat the oven to 500°F. Sprinkle the quail all over with salt and pepper. Put them, breast up, in a roasting pan just large enough to accommodate them. Combine the oil, orange juice, honey, garlic, and cumin, and brush about half of this over the quail.

2. Roast for about 10 minutes, brush with the remaining baste, then continue to roast until done, about 10 minutes more; the juices should run clear. Serve the quail hot, with the pan juices, or warm or at room temperature.

SQUAB AND PHEASANT

Birds like these need not be strong-flavored to be distinctive, and in fact gaminess is becoming rare as these are farm raised more and more. Still, it's amazing how different in flavor they can be, even within species: Farm-raised pheasant are plump and mild-tasting, not unlike chickens; free-range birds are leaner and slightly gamy; and most truly wild specimens—which have darker skin, meat, and fat—have a powerful flavor.

Squab, pheasant, partridge, and quail (see at left), the most common game birds, are sometimes sold fresh, but more often they're frozen. You can cook them as you would any chicken dish, though I generally prefer them simply roasted, grilled, or broiled. Squab—in my opinion the most delicious bird there is—can be ordered by any butcher; each bird weighs about a pound and is so rich that it can legitimately serve two. Pheasant is fairly common and is often sold in rural areas where it is raised; it can also be ordered. Pheasant have tough, muscular legs that require longer cook-ing than their breasts. The answer, quite frequently, is to cook the legs and breasts separately. Domesticated pheasant, the most common kind, are much like chick-ens, weighing in at 2 pounds or more, and you check for doneness the same way.

Grilled or Broiled Squab, Vietnamese Style

MAKES: 4 to 8 servings | TIME: About 1 hour

This boning technique—leaving the wing intact to protect the breast against overcooking—can be used with any bird, including chicken. You can substitute quail (just split them in half) or even Cornish game hens; the results will be less flavorful, but less expensive too.

- 4 squab (about 1 pound each), trimmed of excess fat, innards removed
- 1 tablespoon olive oil or good-quality vegetable oil
- 1 tablespoon chopped garlic
- 2 tablespoons chopped shallot
- 2 teaspoons sugar
- ¼ cup fish sauce or soy sauce
- 1 teaspoon sesame oil
- ½ teaspoon pepper

1. Semibone the squab following the illustrations below.

2. Mix together the olive oil, garlic, shallot, sugar, fish sauce, sesame oil, and pepper. Pour into a heavy zipper bag or baking dish and add the squab. Marinate the squab for up to 2 hours in the refrigerator, or as little as 20 minutes if that's all you have time for. Meanwhile, prepare a charcoal or gas grill for hot direct cooking (make sure the grates are clean) or turn on the broiler and position the rack about 4 inches below the heat.

3. Remove the squab from the marinade, letting any excess drip off. Grill or broil the squab, turning once, until it's crisp outside and still pink and juicy inside, about 6 minutes per side. Serve hot.

Semiboning Squab and Quail

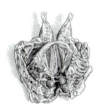

STEP 1 Put the bird on its back on a cutting board. Using a sharp boning knife or kitchen scissors, cut down alongside the backbone on both sides; remove it as you would butterfly a chicken (see page 640). Open the bird out, skin side up. Press down gently on the breast to flatten it a bit (you should hear the breastbone crack). Turn the bird over.

STEP 2 Use a sharp knife to cut underneath the cartilage or "flap" in the center of the bird and remove it. Use the same technique to cut through the "shoulder" joint on one side, where the wing meets the body. Carefully cut the meat away from under the rib cage. Remove the rib cage and wishbone.

STEP 3 Using your hands, pop out the "hip" joint and separate the thigh from the body, then cut through the skin, meat, and tendons with the knife. Repeat on the other half of the bird.

STEP 4 You will have a whole butterflied bird. Handle it gently, since the leg and breast quarters are held together by nothing more than skin. (To cut the bird into halves, cut straight through the center.) Discard the bones, or reserve to make stock.

Pheasant Stewed with Dried Fruits

MAKES: 2 to 4 servings | TIME: About 1 hour

Pheasant is like an extreme version of chicken, with tough legs that must be cooked for considerably longer than the tender breast. This easy sweet-and-sour recipe takes that into account. Use any dried fruit you like here. Serve on a bed of barley, orzo, or rice.

12   dried apricots
12   pitted prunes
2   tablespoons olive oil
1   pheasant (2 to 3 pounds), cut into serving pieces (see page 614)
     Salt and pepper
1   cup sliced onion
1   tablespoon chopped garlic
2   cups chicken, beef, or pheasant stock (to make your own, see page 176) or water
     Chopped fresh parsley for garnish

1. If the fruit is especially dry, soak it in warm water to cover for 10 to 20 minutes; if it's moist enough to eat, don't bother.

2. Put the oil in a large skillet or pot over medium-high heat. When it's hot, add the pheasant and sprinkle with salt and pepper. Cook, turning them once or twice and sprinkling with a little more salt and pepper, until the pieces brown all over, 5 to 10 minutes. As they finish, transfer them to a plate.

3. Turn the heat down to medium and add the onions to the oil in the skillet; cook, stirring occasionally, for 2 to 3 minutes. Add the garlic and cook for 30 seconds more. Add the stock and fruit (drain it first, if necessary). Turn the heat up to high and bring to a boil. Return the pheasant to the skillet, turn the heat down to low, and cover.

4. After 20 minutes, check the breast pieces with a sharp knife; when they are cooked through but still tender and juicy, transfer them to a warm plate; cover loosely with foil. Continue to cook the legs until tender, another 20 to 30 minutes.

5. If the sauce is watery, turn the heat to high and cook, stirring and scraping the bottom of the pan, until the liquid is reduced by about half. When done, return the breast pieces to the pan and reheat them. Garnish with parsley and serve.

 fast   make ahead   vegetarian

Meat

CHAPTER AT A GLANCE

The Basics of Buying and
Cooking Meat 664

The Basics of Beef 665

The Basics of Pork 689

The Basics of Lamb,
Goat, and Veal 706

The balance between meat, vegetables, and "starch" on our plates is what has changed most noticeably since I wrote the first edition of this book in 1997. Back then, animal protein was still considered the "center of the plate," accompanied by a spoonful of something colorful—or maybe a salad—and some kind of noodle, rice, or potato.

And while most Americans still enjoy big burgers, steaks, and chops for some meals, these days many people—me included—are consuming measurably less beef, pork, lamb, and veal overall. Now it's common to base our meals on vegetables and grains and then build in the meat. So sure, I'll still make a big beef roast or hearty lamb stew, only now I serve it with multiple sides and either feed a crowd or plan for leftovers.

The recipes in this chapter give you the same flexibility. The "Makes" line—which usually offers a range in the numbers of servings for roasts, steak, chops and other dishes without vegetables included—will let you easily adjust the proportion of meat to accompaniments: The lower end indicates bigger portions of 6 or more ounces; the higher number shows how many smaller 3- to 4-ounce servings to expect. In stir-fries and stews where other ingredients are included, the amount of meat is almost always on the small side of that range.

Then be sure to check out the "Other cuts and meats you can use" line in most recipes. In addition to the main recipes, variations, lists, and sidebars, these suggestions can expand your meat-cooking options to different proteins, including chicken, turkey, and seafood.

THE BASICS OF BUYING AND COOKING MEAT

They're both equally important. Let's start with what you do first (unless you raise your own).

BUYING MEAT

Having a lot of choice is both a blessing and a curse. I used to say "buying beef in a supermarket is a crap shoot," and it still can be. But there, next to the mass-produced meat, are also more high-quality, sustainably raised options than there were 20 years ago. So you can actually do well at a mainstream store. Better still, seek out a butcher who can guide you and handle special requests; they're definitely making a comeback. Buying directly from the people who raised the animal—at the farm, ranch, or a farmers' market—is eye opening, and I encourage anyone who can to try it at least once.

Wherever you decide to buy meat, and whether it's fresh or frozen, it should never look dry, discolored, or freezer burned. If it's not in a package, take a sniff—you shouldn't smell much. Avoid meat that's too lean, especially pork; it will never be juicy no matter how you cook it. There should be noticeable fat, but not so much that it needs much further trimming.

Buy what works best for your budget. The best meat tends to be the most expensive. If you want to eat high-quality meat without spending a fortune, take my advice: Think of meat as a treat and enjoy it in smaller portions, or eat it less often. Or buy the big expensive cuts when you want to celebrate or cook in bulk for leftovers and use the recipes here to help you make the most of them.

COOKING MEAT

Most meat tastes best when it's browned, a process that creates hundreds of flavor compounds. Dry heat techniques—grilling, broiling, pan-grilling, roasting, or sautéing, often with added fat—cause the outside of meat to sear and form the crust we call "browned." Thin, tender, relatively lean cuts require nothing more; with large, tough, or fatty cuts, low heat and slow cooking techniques like braising bring out their best.

 F fast M make ahead V vegetarian

When you're braising or stewing meat, browning before adding liquid will heighten the meaty flavors and improve the texture, but it isn't always essential—and it's unlikely that you'll be disappointed by the results if you skip that step. Don't get me wrong: I'm all for browning, but if I have to choose between finding another recipe and proceeding without the browning step, I'll sometimes pick the latter, and I'm rarely sorry.

Meat cooks best if it is at room temperature when it hits the heat. Thirty minutes to an hour at room temperature is all it takes; don't let it sit out much longer than that. Nor should you cook still-frozen meat. Instead, thaw it in the fridge over the course of a day or two. Second-best is to put the wrapped meat in a large container of cool water and change the water every 30 minutes or so. I don't recommend trying to thaw meat in the microwave (it semicooks) or on the counter-top (too long at room temperature isn't safe).

Once you choose a cooking technique, many cuts of meat from different animals—including poultry—are interchangeable. To help you make these substitutions, I've included suggestions immediately after the headnote.

THE BASICS OF BEEF

Cattle raised for meat are almost always neutered males, called steers. But there are really only two things you need to know to cook beef well: the cut, and whether it should be cooked fast or slow. Tender cuts like sirloin, tenderloin, and rib-eye are best quickly grilled or roasted and cooked rare. Tougher cuts like chuck, round, and brisket must be broken down with long cooking and moist heat; if you grill chuck, for example, or roast round, they will be chewy and you're sure to be disappointed. Braising a sirloin steak will be equally awful, and you'll waste money too.

The recipes that follow will point you toward specific cuts and possible substitutions. An overview of the major animal parts will put the details in context.

CHUCK The neck/shoulder area is muscular and has lots of connective tissue, which means it is flavorful and best suited to long, slow cooking, or grinding. Cuts from the chuck may be called shoulder roast or steak; arm roast or steak; blade, top blade, or underblade roast or steak; and eye roast. The steaks have decent flavor but are tough. Sliced boneless chuck meat, however, works perfectly for stir-frying.

RIB AND SHORT RIB Behind the chuck, ribs 6 through 12 comprise one of the most valuable parts of the steer; ribs 10 through 12 are considered the best in terms of marbling and size. Rib steaks or rib-eye steaks are as good as they come; rib roasts are the best beef to roast; and short ribs—pieces of the long rib bones cut into sections—are wonderful for braising.

Checking Meat for Doneness

You can test the doneness of all meat by touch, sight, or temperature. Just remember that when you remove it from the heat, it continues to cook as it rests or "reposes." Letting the meat rest a few minutes (five usually does the trick; figure a little longer for larger roasts) helps the meat relax and become juicy throughout. So figure the doneness will go up one step as the meat rests: Pull a steak at rare to eat it medium-rare, and so on.

Meat gets firmer as it becomes more well-done, and testing it by touch requires some practice to associate the degrees of firmness with the corresponding levels of doneness. Testing by sight is easy: Just nick the thickest part with a knife and peek in. A thermometer is the most reliable way to test doneness in cuts of meat at least an inch thick. Here are temperature ranges and visual cues:

125° to 130°F for rare (still quite red)
130° to 135°F for medium-rare (pinkish red)
135° to 145°F for medium (little or no pink)
145° to 155°F for well-done (no pink)

The United States Department of Agriculture recommends slightly higher temperatures for each level, and 140°F is the temperature for killing most of the bacteria and other pathogens common to meat. (See The Basics of Food Safety on page 3.)

LOIN OR SHORT LOIN Actually two highly valuable sections behind the rib, the top (shell) and the bottom (tenderloin). The tenderloin may be sold whole or cut into large lengths for elegant roasts, or cut against the grain into the small, thick steaks called filet mignon or the medallions toward the tip, named tournedos. Either way, the meat is supremely tender but not that flavorful or chewy, so it benefits from sauces. The shell, which extends alongside the tenderloin to the sirloin, yields some of the best and most popular steaks, especially the New York strip (also called shell steak, Kansas City strip, club steak, or strip loin steak). T-bone and porterhouse steaks (nearly identical) are part tenderloin (tender but not especially tasty) and part shell (not so tender, but much more flavorful). Delmonico steaks contain no tenderloin and are often boneless. The hanging tender steak (or hanger steak) also comes from the short loin.

SIRLOIN Behind the loin and the flank, the sirloin contains the rear end of the shell, which makes steaks of varying tenderness and usually lots of flavor. You just never quite know what you're getting unless you talk to the butcher. They may simply be labeled *sirloin*; if there's more detail, choose pin-bone. Identifications like top or bottom or butt or rump give you the location toward the round (see the illustration), where they start to get more chewy. The popular tri-tip roast comes from the sirloin too. You can cook sirloin like other roasts and steaks—and I like this cut quite a bit—but it's best sliced relatively thin before eating.

ROUND The rear end of the steer, usually used for ground meat, is also cut into steaks (top round, also called rump) and roasts (top or bottom round), which are almost always tough and never especially flavorful—they're too lean. For pot-roasting, look to chuck instead.

Major Parts of Beef

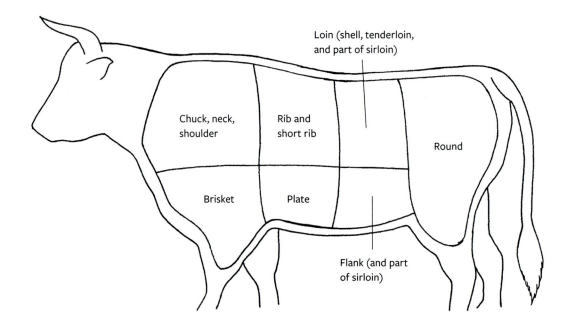

Loin (shell, tenderloin, and part of sirloin)

Chuck, neck, shoulder

Rib and short rib

Round

Brisket

Plate

Flank (and part of sirloin)

For oven-roasting or steaks, look to the rib, loin, or sirloin. Meat from the round is good for stir-frying, as long as it is thinly sliced.

Also from the rear end of the steer comes oxtail—rarely, if ever, from ox anymore—which is cross-cut and used for soups and stews. (And from the opposite end, another similar delicacy comes from the head—beef cheeks.)

FLANK Under the loin is the flank, a lean cut that can be made into flank steaks, which must be thinly sliced, always against the grain (crosswise), to avoid toughness. So-called London broil—which is usually cut from the flank, round, or sirloin—isn't technically a cut but rather a cooking method for a large steak; you still see it sold as a cut, though. Flank is good for stir-frying and broiling.

BRISKET Directly under the chuck, the brisket has good flavor but will never become what you call tender; even if you cook the daylights out of it, it will be chewy. This doesn't mean it's unpleasant; it's quite tasty, just chewy. It's often used for corned beef and pastrami.

In front of the brisket are the foreshank and shin, good for stew or soup meat.

PLATE Behind the brisket and under the rib, this is even tougher and harder to cook than brisket; it's often cured to make pastrami, but is sometimes sold as steaks, which have good flavor but are tough. Good for braising. Skirt steak, a long, narrow strip of meat from this section of the steer (actually the diaphragm), is fantastic grilled or pan-cooked, as long as you don't overcook it.

Steaks and Other Quick-Cooking Beef

Several cuts of beef are both tender and tasty enough to be cut as steaks and grilled or broiled without much fuss. Strip steaks, usually sold boneless, make the ideal individual steak. T-bone or porterhouse steaks are best cut thick to serve two or more people. Rib-eye steaks are also very tender and very flavorful and make good individual—or even shareable—steaks.

Steaks simply labeled "sirloin" and sold bone-in or boneless are riskier (see page 666), but they're usually quite flavorful; the worst that can happen is that they are on the chewy side. Ditto flank steak, which is guaranteed to be chewy but flavorful—so you slice it; no big deal.

Then there are the unusual cuts like flat iron, hanger, skirt, and tri-tip (cut from the sirloin roast of the same name). These are all fine alternatives if you can find them. Avoid chuck steak, though. It's meant for braising, not cooking like a true steak.

Many Ways to Cook Steak

MAKES: 2 to 4 servings | **TIME:** 10 to 40 minutes

Starting with a turn over a charcoal fire, as in the main recipe, and ending with the unorthodox reverse-sear method, here are the core techniques for cooking a

What Does "Grass-Fed" Mean?

Labeling definitions for organic and "natural" beef, pork, lamb, and veal are the same as they are for chicken (see pages 592–593). Some beef on the market, though, is "grass-fed," which means the animal ate pasture grasses for its entire life, as opposed to the more conventional American method of feeding—or "finishing"—cattle on a diet of soy, corn, and other grains in the final weeks before they go to market.

Grass-fed beef has different texture and flavor from the grain-finished beef you may be used to. Some studies show it's better nutritionally and less damaging to the environment. In my experience, grass-fed beef varies depending on the source and can be quite appealing when it's good. The government currently regulates this labeling, but like anything, quality will vary from producer to producer.

Grilled
Porterhouse Steak

well-browned steak with a juicy inside. Pick the one that suits your preferences, your equipment, the cut of steak, and your skills—and then try some of the others.

Other cuts and meats you can use: For more beef cuts, see "Steaks and Other Quick-Cooking Beef" (page 667); center-cut lamb or veal loin or rib chops, or shoulder chops or steaks; any pork chops.

> 2 beef strip, rib-eye, or other steaks, 8 ounces each, about 1 inch thick (preferably at room temperature)
> Salt and pepper

1. Prepare a charcoal grill for hot indirect cooking; make sure the grates are clean. If possible, the rack should be no more than 4 inches from the top of the coals.

2. Dry the steaks with towels and sprinkle with salt and pepper. Put them over the hot side of the fire and grill uncovered and undisturbed until they release from the grate, about 3 minutes. Turn, then grill another minute or 2.

3. Check for doneness; if you must, make a small slit and look. (With practice, you'll know by sight and touch.) Pull them off when they're a little less done than you ultimately want them. To cook the steaks further, move them to the cooler side of the grill and cook for another minute; check every minute after that. When they're done, sprinkle with more salt and pepper if you like and serve.

CHARCOAL-GRILLED PORTERHOUSE OR T-BONE STEAK

These bone-in combination tenderloin-and-strip-loin cuts are best when 1½ inches thick or thicker, weighing about 2 pounds, in which case they will serve 4 to 6 people after slicing: In Step 2, grill for 4 to 5 minutes per side, taking care not to burn the meat; the leaner tenderloin (the smaller of the two pieces on either side of the bone) is best very rare, so keep it toward the cooler part of the fire. Check for doneness. If not done yet, move the steaks to the cooler part of the grill and cook for another 2 to 3 minutes per side before checking again.

STEAKS ON A GAS GRILL

Works for either the main recipe or the first variation. Since you're covering the grill and trapping heat, the steaks will cook faster and will develop a charbroiled-style crust: Prepare a gas grill for hot indirect cooking; make sure the grates are clean. Season the steaks and put them over the fire as described in Step 2, then close the grill. After turning, check thin steaks for doneness after 1 minute, thick porterhouse or T-bones after 2 minutes.

PAN-GRILLED STEAK

A terrific option for steaks no more than 1 inch thick, provided you have a strong exhaust fan; otherwise, try the Reverse Sear option below: Heat a cast-iron or heavy steel skillet just large enough to hold the steaks over medium-high heat for 4 to 5 minutes; the pan should be smoking hot. Sprinkle in some coarse salt and add the steaks. Clouds of smoke will instantly appear; do not turn down the heat. The timing remains the same as for charcoal-grilled steaks. If you want pepper, add it after you turn the steaks for the last time.

BROILED STEAK

Also good for 1-inch-thick steaks: Turn on the broiler and position the rack about 4 inches below the heat; let it get fully hot. About 10 minutes before you're ready to cook, put a rimmed baking sheet on the rack. Season the steaks with salt and pepper and put them into the hot pan. Timing will depend on the heat of your broiler, so check for doneness frequently. The steak will sear on both sides without turning. Serve with any pan drippings poured on top if you like.

PAN-GRILLED, OVEN-ROASTED STEAK

An excellent method if you don't have a first-rate exhaust system or your steak is thicker than 1½ inches: Heat the oven to 500°F and set a rack in the lowest possible position. Heat a cast-iron or other sturdy ovenproof skillet large enough to hold the steaks over medium-high heat for 4 to 5 minutes; the pan should be really hot, just about smoking. Sprinkle the pan with coarse salt and put in the steaks. Carefully but immediately transfer the skillet to the oven. Roast the steaks, turning once and sprinkling with pepper; timing remains the same as for grilled steaks; thick steaks will take longer but check them frequently.

REVERSE-SEARED STEAK And for something totally different, a technique that works for the main recipe or any of the variations. (Even broiling: Either start with the low temperature or begin with the rack 6 inches from the heat source.) Basically, do the exact opposite of the directions above: On a charcoal or gas grill, start the steaks on the cooler side and cook, turning once, until they're much less done in the center than you want them but cooked on the outside, 3 to 5 minutes total for 1-inch steaks, a minute or 2 longer if thicker. Then move them to the hot side of the grill to brown both sides; it will only take a couple of minutes. If using a pan variation, start it over medium-low heat or in a 300°F oven and use the same timing before cranking up the heat for final browning.

---

5 UNEXPECTED SAUCES FOR STEAKS

1. Fresh Tomato or Fruit Salsa (page 55)
2. Blue Cheese Dressing (page 59)
3. Thai Chile Sauce (page 66)
4. Real Ranch Dressing or any of its variations (page 70)
5. Any Five-Minute Drizzle Sauce (page 81)

Grilled or Broiled Flank Steak

MAKES: 4 to 6 servings | **TIME:** About 40 minutes

I used to always marinate flank steak, not for tenderness—slicing it thin takes care of that—but for flavor. Now I prefer to sauce it afterwards. To season the meat with more than salt and pepper, before cooking rub on a tablespoon or two curry powder, chili powder, or any other spice mixture (to make your own, see pages 27–35).

Other cuts and meats you can use: sirloin; London broil cut; top round steak; skirt steak (which will cook a minute or two faster per side).

1½   pounds flank steak (2 large pieces work fine)
   Salt and pepper
   Olive oil as needed

1. Prepare a charcoal or gas grill for medium direct cooking (make sure the grates are clean), or turn on the broiler and position the rack no more than 4 inches below the heat. Put the steak on a rimmed baking sheet, sprinkle it all over with salt and pepper, and rub all over with olive oil.

2. TO GRILL: Put the steak directly over the fire and close the lid. Cook undisturbed until it releases easily, 2 to 4 minutes. Turn, close the lid again, then cook to one stage less than your desired doneness. If the steak is less than 1 inch thick this might only be a minute more; check thicker steaks every minute after that.

TO BROIL: Put the pan with the steak under the heat source and cook until it browns in places, 2 to 5 minutes, depending on how hot your broiler gets. Turn and cook to one stage less than your desired doneness. If the steak is less than 1 inch thick this might only be a minute more; check thicker steaks every minute after that.

3. When the steak is done, transfer it to a cutting board and let it rest for 5 minutes. Slice thin against the grain (crosswise) and serve with any accumulated juices.

GRILLED OR BROILED SKIRT STEAK Follow the directions above but reduce the cooking time per side by about half. (In other words, check early and often! This cut cooks in a flash.) And since the grain runs crosswise, you'll slice the meat lengthwise; so first cut the steak into manageable pieces.

GRILLED OR BROILED BUTTERFLIED LEG OF LAMB The irregular thickness of this boned, flank-steak-like cut ensures there are slices perfectly done for everyone's tastes, so be sure to keep some parts pretty rare: Prepare the grill for hot indirect cooking so you can move the meat (which is thicker) back and forth. If you're broiling, move the rack 4 to 6 inches below the heat source if you can. Cook as described in the main recipe, checking before turning at about 10 minutes.

After turning, start checking thinnest and thickest parts after 5 minutes, then every couple minutes thereafter. Total cooking time will be between 20 and 30 minutes.

Pepper Steak with Red Wine Sauce

MAKES: 4 servings | **TIME:** 15 minutes

Steak au poivre elegance—pan sauce included—in almost no time. For a little extra flavor, coat the steaks with the peppercorns an hour or so before cooking and let them sit at room temperature.

Other meats you can use: any bone-in pork, lamb, or veal chops; increase the total weight to 1½ to 2 pounds.

    4 tenderloin (filet mignon or tournedo), sirloin,
       strip, or boneless rib-eye steaks (4 to 6 ounces
       each), or 2 large steaks (the same kinds, 8 to
       12 ounces each); all cut about 1 inch thick
       Salt
    2 tablespoons black pepper (preferably coarse,
       either freshly ground or cracked with the flat
       side of a knife)
    3 tablespoons butter
    1 tablespoon chopped shallot
    1 cup fruity red wine

1. Heat a large skillet over medium heat for about 3 minutes. Sprinkle the steaks with salt, then rub in the pepper on both sides.
2. Put 2 tablespoons of the butter into the skillet; when the foam subsides, turn the heat up to medium-high and add the steaks. Cook, turning once, until they're one stage less cooked than you want them, about 3 minutes per side for medium-rare, a minute or so less for rare, more for medium.
3. Transfer the steaks to a platter and return the skillet to medium heat. Add the remaining butter and the shallot and cook, stirring occasionally, until the shallot softens, about 1 minute.

4. Add the wine, raise the heat to high, and scrape up any browned bits from the bottom of the pan. Let the liquid bubble away for a couple minutes, until reduced by about half. Pour any juices that have accumulated around the steaks into the sauce. Slice the steaks if you like or cut them into portions. Spoon the sauce over the steaks and serve.

SICHUAN STEAK WITH PLUM WINE SAUCE Substitute coarsely ground Sichuan peppercorns for the black pepper and plum wine for the red wine.

STEAK TERIYAKI Make a batch of Teriyaki Sauce (page 76). Use sirloin steaks, and just a sprinkle of pepper with the salt in Step 1. Omit the wine. Cook the steaks as directed and transfer them to the platter when they're ready. In Step 4, use the teriyaki sauce to deglaze the pan and make the sauce.

Stir-Fried Beef with Green Peppers and Black Beans

MAKES: 4 servings | **TIME:** 30 minutes

Start some rice or noodles to serve alongside before you even read the directions below. This stir-fry is fast. I like the way the slight bitterness of green peppers helps cut the richness of meat, so I often use them instead of red peppers in stir-fries. For many more ways to vary this recipe, see "Improvising Meat-and-Vegetable Stir-Fries" on page 672.

    1   pound boneless beef chuck or sirloin
    ¼   cup fermented black beans
    ¼   cup white wine, sake, or water
    3   tablespoons good-quality vegetable oil
    1½   pounds green bell peppers, cored, seeded, and
         sliced
    1   tablespoon chopped garlic
    1   tablespoon minced fresh ginger
    2   tablespoons soy sauce, plus more to taste
    2   scallions, chopped

Improvising Meat-and-Vegetable Stir-Fries

There are chicken, seafood, and vegetable stir-fry recipes on pages 603, 543, and 244. Use this graphic to help you make substitutions in the recipe on page 671. Be sure to slice any meat as thin as possible, and cut vegetables into uniform-size pieces.

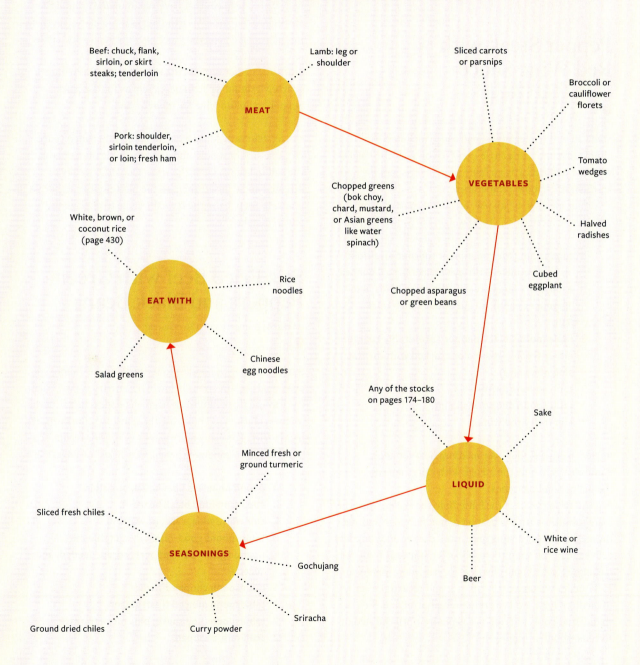

Beef: chuck, flank, sirloin, or skirt steaks; tenderloin

Lamb: leg or shoulder

Sliced carrots or parsnips

Broccoli or cauliflower florets

MEAT

Pork: shoulder, sirloin tenderloin, or loin; fresh ham

VEGETABLES

Tomato wedges

Halved radishes

Chopped greens (bok choy, chard, mustard, or Asian greens like water spinach)

Cubed eggplant

White, brown, or coconut rice (page 430)

Rice noodles

EAT WITH

Chopped asparagus or green beans

Salad greens

Chinese egg noodles

Any of the stocks on pages 174–180

Sake

Minced fresh or ground turmeric

LIQUID

Sliced fresh chiles

SEASONINGS

White or rice wine

Gochujang

Beer

Ground dried chiles

Curry powder

Sriracha

1. Put the beef in the freezer for 15 to 30 minutes while you prepare the other ingredients (this makes it easier to slice). Soak the black beans in the wine.

2. Put 1 tablespoon of the oil in a large skillet over high heat. When it's hot, add the bell peppers and cook, stirring only occasionally, until they brown in places and soften, 5 to 10 minutes. Transfer them to a bowl with a slotted spoon. Don't wipe out the pan and leave it off heat.

3. Slice the beef against the grain (crosswise) as thin as you can. Return the skillet to high heat and add another tablespoon of the oil. When it's hot, add half the beef and cook, stirring only once or twice, until browned all over. Transfer the beef to the bowl with the bell peppers and repeat with the remaining oil and beef.

4. Add the garlic and ginger to the skillet and cook, stirring, until fragrant, about 30 seconds. Add ⅓ cup water, the soaked beans and their liquid, and the soy sauce. Cook, stirring occasionally and scraping up any browned bits, until the liquid thickens, 3 to 5 minutes.

Return the bell peppers and beef to the skillet and toss until heated through and coated with sauce, just a minute or 2. Taste and adjust the seasoning, adding more soy sauce if you like. Serve garnished with the scallions.

Grilled Beef Kebabs with Lots of Vegetables

MAKES: 4 to 6 servings | **TIME:** 45 minutes

The classic, with a Mexican spin. The vegetables need a little more time to cook than the meat, so thread them on separate skewers. Like stir-fries, kebabs are made by assembling components, so they're also easy to change up; see "Varying Kebabs" below.

Varying Kebabs

Use the techniques for threading, marinating, and cooking in the recipe above. But vary the protein and marinade as described here. As long as you keep the vegetables on separate skewers and check the meat, poultry, or seafood frequently, anything is possible. Keep the protein pieces no more than 2 inches wide.

Beef: Sirloin and tenderloin are different (see page 666) but the best choices. You can also press ground beef into cylinders around the skewers.

Lamb: Shoulder (tender but fatty) and leg (leaner, with some potential for dryness) are both good. Don't overcook leg; it should still be pink inside.

Pork: Shoulder (again, tender but fatty) is ideal. Loin is a good second choice. Tenderloin can be okay, but don't overcook; it's best to pull it off the heat when it's still a little pink.

Chicken: Thighs are best by a long shot. Breast meat almost inevitably overcooks.

Ground meats: Beef, pork, lamb, chicken, and poultry all make excellent kebabs. Season the meat as you would for burgers then form them into long patties about 1-inch thick around the skewers and grill, avoiding too much handling,

until firm and done until no longer pink inside for pork and poultry, or slightly pink for lamb or beef if you'd like.

Fish (see page 566): 1½- to 2-inch chunks of sturdy fish like tuna, swordfish, halibut, and salmon are all good, as are whole shrimp and scallops. Fish will cook much faster than meat and chicken, so watch it carefully and start checking after 2 minutes.

Vegetables: See the chart on page 252 for some ideas about which vegetables and seasonings work best on the grill. Then cut them into chunks that you can easily thread on skewers and cook as described in the main recipe.

Marinades: Try any of the pestos or herb purées (pages 51–52), Peanut Sauce (page 75), Tahini Sauce (page 56) Teriyaki Sauce (page 76), or any of the miso sauces (pages 66–67).

Grilled Beef Kebabs
with Lots of Vegetables,
page 673

3   tablespoons olive oil
2   tablespoons fresh lime juice
1   tablespoon soy sauce
     Salt and pepper
2   tablespoons chopped fresh cilantro leaves, plus
     more for garnish
1   tablespoon minced garlic
4   onions, quartered
2   bell peppers (any color except green), cored,
     seeded, and cut into 1½-inch chunks
16   small button mushrooms, trimmed but left
     whole
1   pound cherry tomatoes
1½   pounds beef sirloin, cut into 1½- to 2-inch
     chunks
     Fresh Tomato Salsa (page 55; optional)

1. If you're using wooden skewers, soak them in warm water for about 30 minutes. Combine the oil, lime juice, soy, salt and pepper, cilantro, and garlic in a large bowl; pour about half of the marinade into a medium bowl. Toss the vegetables in the marinade in the large bowl and the meat in the other bowl; let them sit while the fire is getting ready.

2. Prepare a charcoal or gas grill for hot indirect cooking; make sure the grates are clean. Thread the vegetables and meat on separate skewers, leaving a little space between pieces.

3. Start the vegetables first on the cooler part of the grill. Cover and cook, turning once or twice until they begin to brown and become tender, 10 to 15 minutes. Then put the meat over the hottest part of the fire. Cover and cook until the meat browns and releases easily, about 2 minutes, then turn and repeat with the other side, careful not to overcook (cut into a couple of chunks after 5 minutes to see how they're doing).

4. Transfer the meat skewers to a platter as they're ready. If you like, move the vegetable kebabs directly over the fire to char in places; transfer to the platter when done. Serve the kebabs hot or at room temperature, on the skewers or slide the food off onto the platter. Pass the salsa on the side if you like.

ROASTED BEEF KEBABS When I can't grill, I prefer the even cooking—and less fuss—of a hot oven for kebabs. Heat the oven to 450°F and grease 2 rimmed baking sheets with some olive oil. Divide the kebabs among the pans and roast, turning them once or twice, until they're browned and as done as you like, 15 to 20 minutes. Remove them from the pan as they finish.

Roast Beef

Dry cooking in an oven does very little to tenderize big pieces of beef. So your choices are limited—you must start with tender cuts—but not all of them are super-expensive. And I serve lots of side dishes when I make a roast, so no one is tempted to eat a pound of meat; this makes the meat go a lot further.

Let's start with the most economical cuts.

ROUND ROASTS Cut from the hindquarter near the legs of the animal, these lean roasts are best slowly roasted and sliced as thin as you can, even if that means the pieces come out in shards or "shaved," which are tender and easy to eat. The common cuts are top round, bottom round, and eye of round (the cut used for deli roast beef).

SIRLOIN ROASTS Pleasantly chewy and quite flavorful. You just have to be sure not to overcook them, and then cut thin slices against the grain (crosswise). Tri-tip—so named for its triangular shape—is getting easier and easier to find, so I've included a recipe in this section. Other sirloin options include top sirloin roasts (large and "petite") and sirloin tip roast.

WHOLE STRIP This is boneless New York strip before it's cut into steaks. Very flavorful and rather expensive, but my second-favorite roast after prime rib. A whole strip roast weighs about 10 pounds and will serve 20 people or more, but you can ask for smaller pieces. This can easily be grilled in much the same way as the filet (see page 676).

PRIME RIB The piece of the steer that gives us rib-eye steaks is so well marbled that it's juicy even when no longer pink. For the best roast, get it cut to order from a butcher or well-serviced meat counter. Ask for the small end (the 7th through 12th ribs), with the short ribs removed; you want what's called a "short" roast. (You can cook those short ribs separately with any of the recipes on pages 679–683.) The butcher can take the meat off the bones, or you can cook the roast bone in and carve the whole thing (see the illustrations below); it's easy to cut the bones free after slicing if you don't want to serve them with the meat. Cooking the roast without the bones decreases the cooking time considerably, so be careful not to overcook.

FILET OF BEEF This is the whole tenderloin, wonderfully tender but not super-flavorful; you'll want a sauce with this. I prefer something more interesting but people like it for the ease of cooking and impressive presentation. You can also grill whole filet; it won't take more than 30 minutes using a combination of indirect and direct cooking.

BEEF ROASTS AND DONENESS

All beef is rare at 125°F (120°F for really rare). There are noticeable differences in meat color for each 5-degree difference in temperature. I'd never cook any beef beyond 155°F—only slightly pink after resting—and my preference is for much rarer. Large roasts will rise at least 5 degrees in temperature between the time you remove them from the oven and the time you carve them. Remember too: If you're at all in doubt, cut into the middle and peek.

Prime Rib Roast for a Small Crowd

MAKES: About 6 servings | **TIME:** About 1½ hours, largely unattended

The simplest roasting technique: high heat to sear the meat, lower heat to cook it through. If you want a crisp

exterior, turn the heat back to 450°F for a few minutes at the end of cooking; this won't affect the internal temperature too much. Try serving prime rib with Popovers (page 775). Leftover roast beef makes great sandwiches.

> 1 3-rib bone-in beef roast (about 5 pounds), trimmed of excess but not all fat
>   Salt and pepper
> 2 cloves garlic, peeled (optional)
> 1 cup red wine, beef stock (to make your own, see page 176), or water

1. Bring the meat to room temperature by removing it from the refrigerator at least an hour before cooking, but no more than 2. Heat the oven to 450°F.

2. Put the meat bone side down in a large roasting pan. Sprinkle it liberally all over with salt and pepper. If you like garlic, cut the cloves into slivers; use a paring knife to poke small holes in the meat, and insert the garlic into them.

3. Put the roast in the oven and cook, undisturbed, for 15 minutes. Turn the heat down to 350°F and continue to roast for about 45 minutes; check in several places with a meat thermometer. The meat is rare when no spot checks in at under 125°F (120°F if you and your guests like meat really rare); cook for another 5 or 10 minutes if

Carving Prime Rib

STEP 1 Cut close to the bone, between the ribs, for the first slice.

STEP 2 Unless you want huge portions, the second slice is boneless.

 f fast **M** make ahead **V** vegetarian

you like it better done, then check again, but in no case let the temperature of the meat go above 155°F.

4. Remove the meat from the oven. Pour off all but a few tablespoons of the fat and put the roasting pan on a burner over high heat. Add the wine and cook, stirring and scraping up any brown bits, until it is reduced by half, 5 to 10 minutes. Carve the roast (see at left) and serve, splashing a little of the sauce on the meat platter and passing the rest at the table.

PRIME RIB FOR A BIG CROWD With bigger roasts, 5 ribs or more, allow up to 2 hours to let the meat reach room temperature before cooking. In Step 2, use more garlic if you like. In Step 3, increase the initial browning time to 20 minutes. After that, the cooking time will be only marginally longer, but be sure to use an instant-read thermometer to check the meat in several different places. Increase the liquid in Step 4 to at least 2 cups.

BONELESS PRIME RIB Have the butcher remove the bones and tie the roast so that it is of roughly uniform thickness. Cook as directed, using a meat thermometer to gauge doneness; total weight won't matter much since there is no bone and the roast is relatively thin. A 3-pound boneless roast is almost certain to be done in less than an hour, so plan accordingly and watch it carefully; start checking a 5- or 6-pound roast at the 1-hour mark then every 5 minutes after that.

Roast Tri-Tip with Chimichurri

MAKES: 6 to 12 servings | **TIME:** At least 1½ hours, largely unattended

The triangular shape makes an unusual presentation. This roast isn't bland, but I like to serve it with the classic Latin American sauce chimichurri—both for the bright green color and piquant sharpness.

Other cuts and meats you can use: beef eye of round; veal loin.

1 recipe Chimichurri (page 52)
1 tri-tip roast (1½ to 3 pounds)
   Salt and pepper

1. Make the chimichurri up to a couple of hours before serving. Heat the oven to 450°F. Sprinkle the roast all over with salt and pepper and put it on a rimmed baking sheet or in a roasting pan so that the broadest side is on the bottom.

2. For small tri-tips roast for 15 minutes, then check with a meat thermometer or nick at the thickest point with a small knife and peek; cook large cuts for 20 minutes before checking. You want to pull it from the oven when it's one stage less done than you want it. (If

Grilling Large Cuts of Meat

This technique works for 2-pound or larger standing rib and strip loin roasts, lamb leg and shoulder, pork shoulder and loin, and large cuts of veal and game meat.

Prepare a charcoal, wood, or gas grill for hot indirect cooking as described on page 21. If your grill has a thermometer, shoot for around 450°F when the cover is closed. Sprinkle the meat liberally with salt and pepper on all sides. You can rub the outside with cut garlic cloves or season with any spice mixture (to make your own, see pages 27–35).

Put the roast on the cooler side of the grill, cover, and set a timer for 30 minutes. From that point on, your job is to monitor the meat's temperature, turn it once or twice if you'd like and, if you're using charcoal or wood, feed the fire to keep it alive. The target internal temperature for the meat is just over 120°F for rare or about 125°F for medium-rare; the meat's temperature will climb about 5 degrees after you take it off the grill. A 3-pound roast will take about 45 minutes; 5-pounders will be done in a little over an hour; if there are bones in the meat, it can take a few minutes longer. But timing will depend largely on the heat of the fire and the temperature of the meat when you began cooking it. Let the meat rest for at least 5 minutes before slicing and serving.

Roast Tri-Tip with
Chimichurri, page 677

the meat measures 125°F in a couple of places, it will end up rare to medium-rare.) If it's not ready, return it to the oven and check again in 5 minutes.

3. Let the meat rest for about 5 minutes before carving. Cut crosswise into slices about ½ inch thick and serve with the chimichurri.

ROAST STRIP LOIN WITH BLUE BUTTER You can roast anything from a 3- to a 10-pound (whole) strip; here the weight won't affect cooking time much, because there is no bone and the thickness is uniform: Instead of the chimichurri, combine 6 ounces blue cheese with 8 tablespoons (1 stick) softened butter, mashing them together with a fork. Cook the meat in a roasting pan as directed, with the fat cap up. Start checking the temperature after 40 minutes. Slice and serve with the blue butter.

ROAST TENDERLOIN WITH HOLLANDAISE You can ask your butcher to cut the size you want. Figure you'll get 3 to 4 moderate servings per pound: Cook as directed in the variation above, checking after 30 minutes. Instead of chimichurri or blue butter, while the roast cooks make Hollandaise Sauce (page 80), doubling the recipe if necessary to match the number of servings. Keep it warm on the stove in a water bath until you're ready to serve.

Braised Beef

The opposite of dry-heat grilling or roasting, braising—also known as stewing—involves slow and low cooking with liquid. This method tenderizes tough, fatty cuts like beef chuck, brisket, round, and rump, as well as short ribs, and specialty cuts like oxtails and beef cheeks. Cooking time varies depending on the size of the piece or pieces, the amount of fat marbling, and the way the meat was raised.

Don't try to rush by boiling the liquid; the meat will only become tough. It's better to save time by skipping the searing step. And if you make the dish in advance—or have leftovers—all the better: It will taste even better the next day and reheat just fine, even after refrigeration for days or freezing for months. When refrigerated, a layer of fat will rise to the surface, so as a bonus you can make the sauce less greasy by scraping it off with a spoon before reheating.

Beef Stew

MAKES: 4 to 6 servings | **TIME:** 1½ to 2 hours, largely unattended

Ⓜ

The main recipe covers the classic American version. The variations spin it around the globe. To avoid standing over the stove browning the meat in Step 1, heat the oven to 500°F and roast the seasoned pieces in a large roasting pan with 1 tablespoon of the oil, shaking the pan to turn the cubes once or twice, until brown all over, 15 to 20 minutes.

Other cuts and meats you can use: cubed beef brisket; pork shoulder or fresh ham (pork leg); leg of lamb or lamb shoulder.

 2 tablespoons olive oil
1½ to 2 pounds boneless beef chuck or round, cut into 1½-inch cubes
 Salt and pepper
 2 onions, cut into wedges
 2 tablespoons chopped garlic
 3 tablespoons all-purpose flour
 3 cups chicken, beef, or vegetable stock (to make your own, see pages 174–178) or water, plus more if needed
 2 bay leaves
 1 tablespoon fresh thyme leaves or 1 teaspoon dried
 1 pound waxy or all-purpose potatoes, peeled and cut into 1-inch chunks
 4 carrots, cut into 1-inch chunks
 1 cup fresh or frozen peas
 Fresh parsley leaves for garnish

1. Put the oil in a large pot over medium-high heat. When it's hot, add a few pieces of the meat, keeping enough space in between so they sizzle. Sprinkle with salt and pepper and cook, turning to brown well on all sides, about 10 minutes total. As they finish, transfer the pieces to a plate with a slotted spoon and add more to the pot; repeat until all the beef is browned. (If you used the oven to brown the meat, scrape the pan drippings into a large pot and pick up from here.)

2. Spoon off all but 2 tablespoons of the fat and lower the heat to medium. Add the onions. Cook, stirring, until softened and falling apart, about 10 minutes. Add the garlic and flour and cook, stirring, until they become golden, about 2 minutes. Add the stock, bay leaf, and thyme, and return the meat to the pot. Bring to a boil. Lower the heat so the stew bubbles gently, and cover. Cook, stirring once or twice, for about 1 hour.

3. The meat should be cooked but a still little tough. Put the potatoes and carrots on top; if they're not submerged, add a little more stock. Stir, return the liquid to a boil, then lower the heat and cover again. Cook until the meat and vegetables are tender, 30 to 45 minutes. Taste and adjust the seasoning. (At this point, you can refrigerate the stew for up to a couple of days or freeze it for up to a few months.)

4. If you're pleased with the stew's consistency, continue to cook it covered over low heat. If it's too soupy, remove the cover and raise the heat to high to reduce the sauce. Add the peas, adjust the heat to medium low, and cook just until they're warmed through, about 5 minutes. Remove and discard the bay leaf. Serve in shallow bowls, garnished with parsley.

CARBONNADE Beef braised in beer, Belgian style: In Step 2 omit the flour. Use 1½ cups full-bodied dark beer for the liquid. Omit the potatoes, carrots, and peas. Just before serving, stir in a tablespoon or 2 Dijon mustard. To serve, spoon the stew over buttered noodles or mashed potatoes.

BRAISED BEEF WITH CHILES AND LIME In Step 2, omit the bay leaf and thyme and add another tablespoon chopped garlic, 2 or 3 small dried hot red chiles or to taste, and the grated zest of 1 lime; use only 1½ cups liquid and omit the vegetables. When the meat is tender, finish the stew by adding the juice of 1 or 2 limes, to taste. Garnish with chopped fresh cilantro leaves and serve with warm corn tortillas or plain white rice.

BEEF STEW WITH TOMATOES AND DRIED MUSHROOMS Omit the carrots, potatoes, and peas. Reduce the stock to 1½ cups. Bring the stock to a boil in in a saucepan, turn off the heat, and add 2 ounces dried porcini mushrooms; let sit for 20 minutes before browning the meat. In Step 2, before adding the garlic, lift the mushrooms from the stock with a small strainer and add them to the pot. Cook, stirring, until they sizzle for a couple of minutes, then proceed. Carefully pour in the stock, leaving behind any sediment, and add one 28-ounce can whole tomatoes, juice and all. As the stew cooks, stir to break up the tomatoes a bit. Serve with pasta.

SORT-OF SAUERBRATEN Omit the potatoes and peas. In Step 2, as you cook the onions, add 2 chopped celery stalks, and a few juniper berries if you like. For the liquid, use 1 cup each stock or water, red wine, and red wine vinegar. Proceed, and serve over Spaetzle (page 518) or buttered egg noodles, garnished with fresh chopped dill.

BURGUNDY BEEF Americanized *Boeuf à la Bourguignonne*. The wine doesn't have to be from Burgundy; just use a fruity one you like to drink: Omit the olive oil, onions, potatoes, carrot, and peas. Before searing the meat in Step 1, cook 4 slices bacon, chopped, until crisp; remove from the pot with a slotted spoon and use the fat to brown the beef. After you spoon off the fat in Step 2, put 12 small button mushrooms and at least 12 peeled pearl onions (frozen are fine) in the pot and cook, stirring occasionally, until lightly browned, 5 to 10 minutes. For the liquid, use 1 cup stock or water and 2 cups red wine. Garnish with fresh chopped parsley and chives and serve with Mashed Potatoes (page 329) or tons of sliced baguette.

 F fast **M** make ahead **V** vegetarian

Beef Stroganoff with Mushrooms

MAKES: 4 to 6 servings | **TIME:** 30 minutes

I'm keeping this classic quick braise in this edition because it's easy and people love it—when it's good. It's one time you don't want to brown the meat before adding the liquid. Serve this over buttered egg noodles or white rice, or with soft, eggy bread like challah or brioche.

Other meats you can use: boneless veal or pork shoulder; veal round.

- 3 tablespoons butter
- 1 large onion, sliced
- 8 ounces cremini mushrooms, trimmed and sliced
  Salt and pepper
- 1½ pounds beef tenderloin or sirloin, cut into 1-inch pieces
- 1 tablespoon Dijon mustard
- 1 cup beef or chicken stock (to make your own, see page 176)
- 1 cup sour cream
  Chopped fresh dill or parsley for garnish

1. Put the butter in a large skillet over medium heat. When it foams, add the onions and mushrooms and sprinkle with salt and pepper. Cook, stirring occasionally, until they are soft but not browned, 10 to 15 minutes.
2. Add the beef and cook, stirring, for just a minute. Add the mustard and stock and adjust the heat so the liquid bubbles steadily. Cook, stirring occasionally until the meat is just cooked through but still tender, about 5 minutes.
3. Add the sour cream and stir until it heats through and forms a sauce, careful not to let it come to a boil. Taste, adjust the seasoning, garnish with dill, and serve.

Mustard-Braised Short Ribs

MAKES: 4 to 6 servings | **TIME:** About 3 hours, largely unattended

Braising bone-in meat is a game changer. The flavor is just incredible, and the marrow and connective tissue make the richest sauce ever. Browning short ribs will test your patience but after the initial work on the stove you do virtually nothing while they're in the oven, and the rewards are totally worth it. Serve with plain baked or boiled potatoes.

Other cuts and meats you can use: beef shank, shin, cheeks, or oxtails (cooking times will probably be a little longer for the fattier, bonier pieces).

- 2 tablespoons olive oil
- 3 pounds meaty beef short ribs, at least 2 inches long, cut between the bones
  Salt and pepper
- 1 large onion, chopped
- 1 tablespoon chopped garlic
- ½ cup dry red wine or water
- 2 cups chicken, beef, or vegetable stock (to make your own, see pages 174–178) or water, plus more if needed
- ¼ cup stone ground mustard
  Chopped fresh chives for garnish

1. Put the oil in a large pot over medium-high heat. When it's hot, add several short rib pieces (avoid crowding them) and cook, turning and sprinkling them with salt and pepper, until they're browned on all sides, 5 to 10 minutes. As they finish, transfer them to a plate and repeat with the remaining short ribs; you won't need to add any more fat, but don't rush this step.
2. Heat the oven to 300°F. Spoon off all but 2 tablespoons of the fat, and lower the heat to medium. Add the onion and garlic and sprinkle with salt and pepper. Cook, stirring occasionally, until soft, 5 to 10 minutes. Add the wine and raise the heat so it starts to bubble, scraping up any browned bits from the bottom of the pot.

Beef Stroganoff with Mushrooms, page 681

3. Stir in the stock and mustard and return the short ribs to the pot along with any juices. Bring to a boil, then lower the heat so it bubbles gently. Cover and transfer to the oven. Cook undisturbed for an hour.

4. Take a peek, stir, and stick a fork in the meat of a thick rib. The short ribs are ready when it slides in easily and virtually all the fat has melted from the bone. If they're not ready, return to the oven and continue to check every 30 minutes.

5. When the short ribs are ready, transfer them to a bowl with tongs. (At this point, you can refrigerate the meat and the sauce separately overnight. The next day, scrape most of the solid fat from the top of the liquid and proceed.) Skim as much fat off the surface as possible and return the sauce to a boil. Cook, stirring frequently, until it reduces and thickens; return the short ribs to the sauce to heat through, just a few minutes. Taste and adjust the seasonings, and serve, garnished with chives.

COFFEE-CHILE BRAISED SHORT RIBS Omit the mustard. Substitute brewed coffee for 1 cup of the stock. In Step 2, after the onion and garlic are soft, stir in 2 whole ancho chiles and 2 bay leaves. When the stew is ready, fish out the chiles and bay leaves, and if you like, remove the chile seeds and stems (if they're still intact) and return the flesh to the pot. Serve over plain white rice, garnished with cilantro.

BRAISED OXTAILS Instead of short ribs, use oxtails. These cook a little faster, so they'll probably be ready when you check at the hour mark in Step 3.

Pot Roasts

The difference between stews or braises and pot roasts is that in a pot roast, the meat is braised whole, in less liquid. Chuck, rump roast, and brisket are classic cuts for this treatment, though you can use shin, oxtails, or cheeks this way for a more stew-like dish; small whole pieces will cook faster than large ones, so just check earlier and more frequently.

When the meat is tender, it is done. Hold the roast—or slices—in the warm sauce for up to 10 minutes or so, not much more. Even though the sauce is wet and rich, when all the fat is cooked out of the meat, it dries out quickly.

All-American Pot Roast

MAKES: 4 to 8 servings | **TIME:** 2½ to 3 hours, largely unattended

Low heat is important here, as is cooking just until done; don't let the roast fall apart—that's a signal it's drying out.

- 1 boneless chuck or rump roast (2 to 3 pounds)
- 2 cloves garlic, slivered
  Salt and pepper
- 2 tablespoons olive oil
- 2 large onions, chopped
- 2 carrots, chopped
- 1 celery stalk, chopped
- 1 bay leaf
- ½ cup red wine or water
- 2 cups chicken, beef, or vegetable stock (to make your own, see pages 174–178) or water

1. If the roast has an irregular shape, tie it with twine to create more uniform thickness. Poke holes in several spots around the roast with a thin-bladed knife and insert the garlic slivers. Rub the roast all over with salt and pepper.

2. Put the oil in a large pot over medium-high heat. When it's hot, add the roast and brown it on all sides, taking your time and adjusting the heat so it browns but the fat does not burn, about 15 minutes. Transfer the roast to a platter. Add the onions, carrots, and celery to the pot, raise the heat so the vegetables sizzle, and cook, stirring frequently, until they're soft and brown in places, about 10 minutes.

3. Add the bay leaf and wine and cook, scraping the bottom of the pot with a wooden spoon, until the wine has just about evaporated, 3 to 5 minutes. Add about 1½ cups of the stock, return the roast to the pot, adjust the heat so the liquid bubbles gently, and cover.

4. Turn the roast every 20 minutes and add a little more liquid to maintain about 2 inches in the pot, then re-cover. The roast is ready when a fork pierces the meat without much resistance and the juices will run clear—1½ to 2½ hours, depending on the thickness of the roast. Be careful not to overcook.

5. Remove the roast and vegetables from the pot. Skim the fat from the surface of the liquid. Remove and discard the bay leaf. Turn the heat up to high and cook, stirring and scraping the bottom of the pan, until the liquid thickens and about 1 cup remains, about 5 minutes. Taste and adjust the seasoning. Slice the meat and serve it with the vegetables and pan juices.

ITALIAN-AMERICAN POT ROAST Instead of the bay leaf, use 2 sprigs fresh rosemary and insert the slivered garlic as described in Step 1. Cook 2 tablespoons chopped garlic with the onion in Step 2 and substitute one 28-ounce can whole tomatoes, with their liquid, for the carrots and celery; cook until the tomatoes begin to bubble then proceed with Step 3, adding only about ½ cup stock.

FIVE-SPICE POT ROAST Omit the bay leaf; chop the garlic instead of slivering it (you need 1 tablespoon). Skip inserting the garlic into the meat. Combine 2 teaspoons five-spice powder with 1½ teaspoons salt and ½ teaspoon pepper to rub into the meat in Step 1. Add the garlic and 1 tablespoon chopped ginger with the onions in Step 2. Substitute ¼ cup rice vinegar and ¼ cup water for the red wine. Replace ¼ cup of the stock with soy sauce.

Braised Beef Brisket

MAKES: 10 or more servings | **TIME:** About 3 hours, largely unattended

My go-to seasonings are quite basic, and I like to serve brisket the classic ways: over buttered egg noodles, with boiled potatoes, or in a sandwich on a crusty roll with mustard. The variation offers bolder spices and sweetish accompaniments.

Two technical points: Whole briskets are massive and are usually cut in two pieces—the flat and the point end. Go for the flat for braising. You can skip the initial browning if you're pressed for time or don't want to bother; the difference, in the end, will be minimal. And although it's tempting to "tear" brisket along the grain, it's better to slice it against the grain (crosswise); use a sharp carving knife and you will get beautiful, thin slices.

- 1 tablespoon good-quality vegetable oil or olive oil (optional)
- 1 flat end piece beef brisket (4 to 5 pounds) Salt and pepper
- 3 tablespoons butter
- 2 large onions, chopped
- 3 tablespoons tomato paste
- 1 teaspoon minced garlic
- 3 cups chicken, beef, or vegetable stock (to make your own, see pages 174–178) or water

1. Heat the oven to 325°F. If you choose to brown the brisket first, put the oil in a large pot over medium-high heat. (If not, skip to Step 2.) When it's hot add the brisket, fat side down, and sprinkle with salt and pepper. Cook until it browns and releases easily, about 5 minutes, then turn, season the fat side, and brown the other side. Transfer the brisket to a platter.

2. If you browned the brisket, remove the pot from the heat and spoon out the fat. Put the pot over medium heat and add the butter. When it foams, add the onions and cook, stirring, until golden and soft, 10 to 15 minutes. Add some salt and pepper, then stir in the tomato paste and garlic. Return the brisket to the pot fat side up along with any juices, add the stock, and cover.

3. Transfer the pot to the oven, and cook, turning the brisket about every 30 minutes, until a fork pierces it without much resistance, 2½ to 3 hours. If the sauce seems thin, transfer the brisket to a cutting board and boil the sauce down over high heat, scraping the bottom of a pan with a wooden spoon, until it thickens. Taste

Corned Beef with Cabbage
and Potatoes, page 686

the sauce and adjust the seasoning. Thinly slice the brisket against the grain, return it to the sauce along with any accumulated juices, and serve.

BRAISED BEEF BRISKET WITH SWEET POTATOES, CARROTS, DRIED FRUIT, AND LOTS OF GARLIC In Step 3, when the meat is somewhat tender but not quite done—after 1½ to 2 hours—add 1 pound sweet potatoes, peeled and cut into chunks, 2 carrots, cut into chunks, ½ cup dried apricots, ½ cup pitted prunes or other dried fruit, and 1 head garlic, peeled but with the cloves left whole. Continue to cook until all the fruits and vegetables are soft but not until they dissolve, 30 to 60 minutes. Serve, spreading the soft garlic on crusty bread.

Corned Beef with Cabbage and Potatoes

MAKES: 8 to 12 servings | **TIME:** 3 hours, largely unattended

This traditional New England boiled dinner is the ultimate one-pot meal. Even if you're not expecting a crowd, make this at least once a year, on Saint Patrick's Day (or any other day). Corned beef is brisket that's been cured and steeped in a spicy brine, and leftovers make unbeatable sandwiches on rye bread.

- 1 flat end piece corned beef (3 to 5 pounds)
- 1 bay leaf
- 1 head garlic, root end trimmed
- 1 tablespoon black peppercorns
- 1 tablespoon yellow mustard seeds
- 3 whole cloves
- 5 allspice berries or a pinch or 2 ground allspice
- 2 large onions, peeled and halved top to bottom
- 2 pounds small waxy potatoes
- 4 carrots, whole or cut into 1-inch chunks
- 1 small head green cabbage, cut into 8 to 12 wedges

1. Drain any liquid from the package of corned beef and put the meat in a large pot with the bay leaf, garlic, peppercorns, mustard seeds, cloves, allspice, and onions. Add enough water to cover by about 2 inches. Bring to a boil and skim off the foam that rises to the surface.

2. Lower the heat so that it bubbles gently. Cover and cook, turning the meat every 30 minutes or so, for about 2 hours. Pierce the thickest part with a thin-bladed knife; the meat is ready when the knife can be inserted to the middle without much resistance. If the meat is not done, continue cooking it, checking every 15 minutes. Heat the oven to 300°F.

3. Transfer the meat to a rimmed baking sheet, fat side up, and put it in the oven while the vegetables cook in the seasoned broth. Or wrap it in foil, put the broth into an airtight container, and refrigerate both for up to 2 days. Reheat the foil-wrapped meat at 300°F for about 30 minutes; unwrap and heat for about 15 minutes more. Skim any fat off the broth and pour the broth back into the pot (you can strain it if you'd like and discard the solids).

4. Add the potatoes to the broth in the pot along with about 2 cups water, and bring to a boil. Cook for about 5 minutes, then add the carrots and cabbage. Adjust the heat so the broth bubbles steadily, cover, and cook until the vegetables are tender, 10 to 15 minutes. Slice the

Do-It-Yourself Ground Meat

A few rules: First, buy relatively fatty meat. For beef that means chuck roast or well-marbled sirloin or round. Pork or lamb shoulder, or boneless chicken or turkey thighs—all the better with some skin—are other possibilities.

Assuming you have a standard size food processor, work in batches of no more than 2 pounds. Cut the meat into 1-inch chunks and pulse it with the metal blade a few times until it's chopped. Don't overprocess—you want chopped meat, not a purée; the finer you grind the meat, the more likely you'll be to pack it together too tightly and make the burgers, meatballs, or meat loaf tough and dry.

 F fast **M** make ahead **V** vegetarian

corned beef thin against the grain, and serve in shallow bowls with the vegetables and broth.

Ground Meat

The key to excellent burgers is starting with the right meat, which is why I encourage you to grind your own (see at left). When you buy meat labeled simply "ground beef," you have no idea what you're getting. It likely comes from anonymous cuts of several different animals, and is often ground in huge quantities, which increases the risk for spreading bacteria or pathogens.

Knowing the source and terms like ground sirloin, ground chuck, 85 percent or 90 percent lean, and so on helps you make better choices: You'll know at least what cut of beef has been ground up, and how much fat the meat contains. And that's important, since you need some fat to get a juicy burger, meat loaf, or meatball.

When shaping ground meat, handle it gently and minimally. And salt it aggressively; I start with a large pinch, cook a teeny bit to taste, and work up from there. There are more ideas for flavoring burgers at right.

My Classic Burger

MAKES: 4 to 6 servings | **TIME:** 40 minutes

A burger doesn't need much work, just attention to detail: not-too-lean meat, gentle handling, and quick cooking over high heat. And for goodness' sake, don't press on it with a spatula during cooking. It drives me crazy to see all the juice and fat go sputtering out.

Other cuts and meats you can use: See "Do-It-Yourself Ground Meat" on the previous page; anything other than beef and lamb will require a few more minutes per side to cook all the way through (make sure you cook pork and poultry until no longer pink inside).

1½ pounds not-too-lean sirloin or chuck, cut into 1-inch chunks, or 80% lean preground meat

½ small onion, peeled and cut into chunks, or minced if using preground meat
Salt and pepper
Buns or rolls, lettuce, tomato slices, and condiments for serving

1. If you're grinding your own meat, follow the directions on page 686, putting the onion chunks in the food processor at the same time as the meat. If you're using preground meat, put it in a bowl with the minced onion. Sprinkle the meat with salt and pepper and gently but thoroughly mix in the seasoning. Cook up a bite in the microwave or a skillet and adjust the seasoning if necessary—this step is worth it until you get the hang of how much salt to add.

13 Mix-and-Match Ideas for Flavoring Burgers

1. 2 tablespoons minced fresh parsley, basil, chives, chervil, or other herb
2. ½ teaspoon minced garlic or 1 clove roasted garlic
3. 1 tablespoon minced anchovies
4. 1 teaspoon minced or grated fresh ginger or ground ginger
5. 1 tablespoon soy, Worcestershire, or steak sauce
6. ¼ cup minced shallots or scallions
7. Tabasco or other hot sauce, to taste; start with ½ teaspoon
8. Up to 1 tablespoon curry powder, chili powder, or other spice mixture (to make your own, see pages 27–35)
9. Up to ½ cup grated or crumbled cheese like Parmesan, cheddar, blue, or feta
10. 1 cup cooked spinach or other greens, squeezed dry and chopped
11. 1 to 2 tablespoons ground dried porcini; or ¼ cup dried porcini, reconstituted and chopped
12. 1 dried mild chile like ancho, soaked until tender, seeds removed if you'd like, and minced
13. 1 tablespoon or more freshly grated horseradish or prepared horseradish

2. Handling the meat as little as possible to avoid compressing it, shape it lightly into 4 to 6 burgers, about 1 inch thick.

3. Prepare a charcoal or gas grill for hot direct cooking; make sure the grates are clean. When it's ready, put the burgers directly over the fire and cook about 3 minutes per side for very rare and another minute per side for each increasing stage of doneness, but no more than 10 minutes total unless you like hockey pucks. Serve on buns, dressed as you like.

MY CLASSIC BURGER IN A SKILLET The reverse-sear method (see page 670) is perfect here: After forming the burgers, put them in a dry skillet (preferably cast iron) over medium-low heat. Cook undisturbed until they begin to lose their pinkness around the edges and release from the pan, about 10 minutes. Turn and cook on the other side for 5 minutes. Now crank up the heat to high and finish cooking the burgers to your desired doneness, turning once to brown both sides, another 2 to 5 minutes total.

CHEESE-STUFFED BURGERS Works with either the main recipe or skillet variation. Especially good with smoked mozzarella or cheddar; try these with ground lamb: Omit the onion. Cut 4 ounces of any melting cheese into 4 to 6 pieces and form the meat into burgers around each piece; proceed with the recipe.

Meat Loaf

MAKES: 6 to 8 servings | TIME: About 1 hour, largely unattended

Free-form meat loaf has several advantages over one cooked in a loaf pan: It develops a lovely crust on three sides instead of just one, and the fat can drip off and be used for basting. Plus it's easy to shape however you want it, including into a "pie" to cut in wedges, patties, or meatballs; just cook it for less time. You can use all one kind of meat or a mixture of two or more that have complimentary flavors; veal, pork, and beef is the Italian classic, for example, but lamb and pork aren't a particularly good combination. If you go with all beef make sure it's no more than 80 percent lean or the meat loaf will be dry and crumbly.

Other proteins you can use: ground chicken or turkey, but not in combination with other meat.

½ cup bread crumbs (preferably fresh; see page 801)

½ cup milk

1 egg

2 pounds ground meat, like beef, veal, pork, or lamb, alone or in combination (see the headnote)

½ cup grated Parmesan cheese

1 small onion, minced

1 tablespoon minced garlic

1 tablespoon chopped fresh oregano or 1 teaspoon dried

Salt and pepper

3 slices bacon (optional but good, especially if the meat is lean)

1. Heat the oven to 350°F. Put the bread crumbs and milk in a large bowl and soak until the milk is absorbed, about 5 minutes. Beat in the egg.

2. Add the meat, cheese, onion, garlic, and oregano and sprinkle generously with salt and pepper. Gently but thoroughly combine everything with your hands or a spoon, mixing as little as possible. Cook up a bite in the microwave or a skillet, taste, and adjust the seasoning if necessary—this step is worth it until you get the hang of how much salt to add.

3. Shape the meat into an oval loaf on a rimmed baking sheet; top with the bacon if you like. Bake for 45 to 60 minutes, basting occasionally with the pan juices. When it's done, the meat loaf will be browned lightly and firm, and an instant-read thermometer inserted into the center will read 160°F. Let cool for a few minutes before slicing and serving.

MEAT LOAF WITH SPINACH Bring a large pot of water to a boil and salt it. Cook 10 ounces fresh spinach for

30 seconds, then drain it in a colander. Press out all the liquid with a spoon as it cools. Chop the spinach and season it with more salt plus some pepper and a pinch freshly grated nutmeg. In Step 1, increase the bread crumbs to 1 cup. In Step 2, incorporate the chopped spinach into the meat mixture and proceed.

THE BASICS OF PORK

For a while in the 1980s and '90s, all you could find was super-lean pork—part of the no-fat trend—which almost always cooked up dry and bland. And Americans were directed to cook pork to death. Thankfully all that's changed.

But buying the right cut of pork is still important, because like beef, some cuts require longer cooking time and lower heat to become tender and render their fat. The major cuts are relatively simple to understand.

SHOULDER The front leg; the most common cut is called Boston butt or picnic ham. Sometimes smoked, salted, or cured, like ham (the rear leg), but more often sold fresh. Fatty and usually delicious, this is among the best cuts to roast or cook in liquid because it remains moist and becomes tender. Hocks and trotters (feet) also come from the front legs. Pork steaks are sometimes cut from the shoulder.

LOIN Behind the shoulder, this part of the animal contains the ultra-lean tenderloin, which must be cooked only minimally to prevent it from drying out. The loin also produces steaks, roasts, and chops, boneless and bone-in. There are several names commonly used for loin roasts: rib end (from near the shoulder), loin or rump end (from the rear), and center loin, center-cut loin, or center-cut rib. The rear end is the leanest and mildest, the shoulder end fattier and most flavorful. All of these roasts may be cut into chops with the same characteristics. Back ribs and country-style ribs (which are not ribs at all) are also cut from the loin. So are one of my new favorites, pork sirloin steaks.

Grilling Pork Chops and Steaks

This is so simple you don't even need a recipe, and it works for chops 1- to 2-inches thick, bone-in or boneless: Prepare a charcoal or gas grill for medium indirect cooking; make sure the grates are clean. Sprinkle the chops with salt and pepper and cook directly over the fire, with the lid closed, until browned, 2 to 4 minutes per side. Move the chops to the cooler side of the grill and cook, covered again, until they're tender but still a little pink at the center, another 10 to 20 minutes total. Serve with any salsa (see pages 55–58 or 71–74) or Applesauce (page 364).

BELLY The cut that contains spareribs and bacon. Salted belly is salt pork; cured and smoked belly is American bacon. Uncured and almost entirely fat belly is popular as a sandwich or taco filling or simply roasted, sliced, and eaten as is.

HAM The rear legs, almost always cured and/or smoked (in any number of ways), sold whole, in pieces, or in slices. See "All About Ham" on page 704 for more details.

Chops and Other Quick-Cooking Pork

I'm out of the mainstream here since my favorite chops are from the shoulder; fortunately they're easier to find than they were 20 years ago—as are sirloin chops, which are also sold as steaks. Loin cuts—the bone-in center or rib chop and boneless loin chop—are more universally prized. Since they're from different parts of the pig, each looks and tastes a little different though they cook the same way, even with the bone still attached.

Some quick-cooking pork is like white-meat chicken: Overcooked, it's dry. That's why fattier sirloin and shoulder pieces are more forgiving. The recipes in this section give you options and direct you toward the techniques that ensure the meat stays juicy and tender.

Skillet Pork Chops

MAKES: 4 to 6 servings | TIME: 30 minutes

A basic sear-and-simmer technique that provides the foundation for all sorts of flavor combinations (see "Varying Skillet Pork Chops" on page 692).

Other cuts and proteins you can use: boneless pork sirloin chops, pork medallions cut from the tenderloin (which will cook more quickly); bone-in chicken thighs (which will require more cooking).

    4 bone-in shoulder or center-cut loin pork chops
       (about 1 inch thick; about 2 pounds total),
       trimmed of excess fat
       Salt and pepper
    2 tablespoons olive oil
    ½ cup dry white wine
    1 tablespoon chopped garlic
    1 tablespoon butter or more olive oil
    1 tablespoon cider vinegar
       Chopped fresh parsley for garnish

1. Sprinkle the chops with salt and pepper. Put the oil in a large skillet over medium-high heat. When it's hot, add the chops and raise the heat to high. Cook until they brown and release easily, about 2 minutes. Turn and brown the other side. Transfer the chops to a plate.

2. Reduce the heat to medium. Add the wine and garlic and cook, scraping the bottom of the pan, until the wine almost bubbles away, about 2 minutes. Return the chops to the pan and turn them once or twice in the pan juices. Add ½ cup water, adjust the heat so the liquid barely bubbles, cover, and cook until the chops are tender and slightly pink inside, but not dry, 5 to 10 minutes.

Major Cuts of Pork

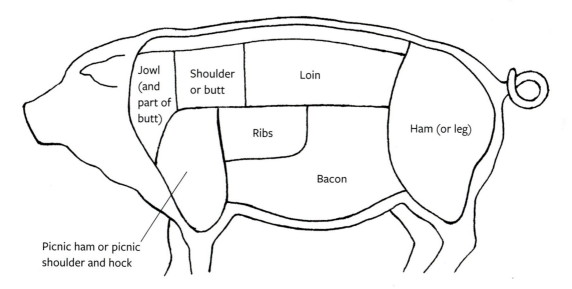

3. Transfer the chops to a platter. Stir the butter into the pan juices. Add the vinegar, taste, and adjust the seasoning. Pour the sauce over the chops, garnish with parsley, and serve.

Stir-Fried Pork with Bok Choy

MAKES: 4 servings | TIME: About 30 minutes

Any Asian green—like mizuna, tatsoi, or water spinach—can fill in for bok choy. So can other greens like arugula, watercress, chard, dandelion, and even romaine lettuce. For more ideas about varying and serving, see "Improvising Meat-and-Vegetable Stir-Fries" on page 672. When you're ready to cook, have all the ingredients ready.

Other cuts and proteins you can use: beef, preferably sirloin; lamb, preferably from the shoulder or leg; boneless chicken thighs.

1 recipe White Rice (page 430; optional)
1 pound boneless pork shoulder
1 pound bok choy, trimmed
4 scallions
2 tablespoons good-quality vegetable oil
2 tablespoons chopped garlic
2 tablespoons soy sauce, plus more if needed
2 tablespoons lemon juice

Varying Skillet Pork Chops

Think of this list as a mix-and-match free-for-all. Don't worry about what's "authentic" or traditional. Just combine the flavors you like.

CHANGE THE SEASONING

Replace the garlic with:

- 1 tablespoon chopped ginger
- ¼ cup chopped red onion or scallions
- 2 tablespoons chopped shallot
- 2 tablespoons chopped fresh rosemary, thyme, or oregano
- Fresh chopped red chile like serrano, to taste
- 1 tablespoon curry powder (to make your own, see page 32)

CHANGE THE LIQUID

Replace the water with:

- Chicken stock
- Canned tomatoes (whole, diced, or crushed)
- Sake
- Beer
- Dry red wine

- Dry or slightly sweet white wine
- Orange juice
- Apple cider
- Coconut milk
- Carrot Juice

CHANGE THE ADDITIONS

Replace the vinegar with:

- Dijon mustard
- Sriracha or other hot sauce
- Ketchup
- Soy sauce
- Fish sauce

CHANGE THE GARNISH

- Serve with lime or lemon wedges.
- Garnish with fresh chives, basil, or mint.
- Sprinkle with chopped toasted peanuts, hazelnuts, or cashews.

 F fast **M** make ahead **V** vegetarian

1. If you're making the rice, start it first. Put the pork in the freezer for 15 to 20 minutes while you prepare the other ingredients (this makes it easier to slice). Remove the leaves from the bok choy stems, chop both, and keep them separate. Slice the scallions, reserving the green parts for garnish.

2. Slice the pork as thin as you can. Cut the slices into strips about ¼ inch wide. Put a large skillet over high heat until it's smoking hot—don't walk away. Immediately add half the oil and all the pork. Cook until the pork browns and is easy to stir, about 2 minutes. Then toss a couple times until the meat loses all traces of pinkness, another minute or so. Transfer the pork to a bowl with a slotted spoon and lower the heat to medium.

3. Add the remaining oil to the skillet. Swirl it around, add the garlic, and stir once or twice. Cook until the garlic begins to color, about 30 seconds, then return the heat to high and add the bok choy stems and scallion whites. Stir frequently, until they soften, another minute or 2.

4. Add the bok choy leaves along with the pork and stir for 1 minute. Add the soy sauce, lemon juice, and ½ cup water. Cook, stirring for another minute, then turn off the heat. Taste and add more soy sauce if necessary. Garnish with the scallion greens and serve immediately, over the rice if you're using it.

Pork Sirloin Steaks with Fresh Orange Sauce

MAKES: 4 to 6 servings | **TIME:** 30 minutes

A two-pan technique that results in a tangy sauce. It's not complicated, though, and the results are restaurant worthy, especially if you serve the steaks with Potato Rösti (page 332).

Other proteins you can use: boneless pork chops, pork tenderloin medallions; beef sirloin steaks; lamb shoulder chops; boneless chicken thighs; salmon steaks.

1½ cups fresh orange juice
¼ teaspoon cayenne, or to taste
1 teaspoon ground cumin
1 shallot, minced
Salt and pepper
2 teaspoons grated orange zest
1 tablespoon chopped fresh oregano
1½ pounds boneless pork sirloin steaks (about 1 inch thick)
½ cup sweet wine like riesling, or water

1. Heat the oven to 450°F. Combine the orange juice, cayenne, cumin, and shallot in a small skillet or saucepan and bring to a boil. Cook, stirring, until it reduces to about 1 cup, about 10 minutes. Taste and adjust the seasoning, adding salt or a touch more cayenne if you like; cover and keep warm. Combine the orange zest with the oregano and some pepper in a small bowl.

2. Put an ovenproof skillet large enough to hold the pork in one layer over high heat. Sprinkle the pork with salt and pepper. When the pan is smoking hot, add the pork and cook until it browns and releases easily, 1 to 2 minutes. Turn the pork and carefully transfer the skillet to the oven.

3. Cook the pork until firm but not tough and still slightly pink in the center, about 10 minutes. Cut the pork into portions if you like and transfer it to a platter. Put the skillet over medium heat, add the wine, and cook, scraping up any browned bits, until it thickens; stir the pan drippings into the orange sauce. Spoon the sauce over the meat, then scatter over the oregano–orange zest mixture and serve.

PORK STEAKS WITH HONEY-SOY PAN SAUCE Perfect with Sticky Rice (page 430) or plain White Rice (page 430): Omit the cumin and cayenne. Instead of the orange juice, use ½ cup soy sauce, ¼ cup lemon juice, 3 tablespoons honey, and ½ cup water; use ginger instead of shallot and reduce the sauce to ¾ cup in Step 1. For the final topping, substitute lemon zest for the orange zest and 1 tablespoon (or more to taste) chopped fresh hot red chile like Thai for the oregano, and garnish with cilantro sprigs and chopped peanuts.

PORK STEAKS WITH BALSAMIC-PEPPER GLAZE Omit the cumin and cayenne. Instead of the orange juice use balsamic vinegar (this is the time to go with the inexpensive stuff) and season the sauce with lots of black pepper. Use garlic instead of the shallot. In Step 3, use red wine. For the final garnish, omit the orange zest–oregano mixture and scatter chopped fresh basil and sea salt over the steaks and sauce.

Roasted Pork Tenderloin with Lots of Herbs

MAKES: 6 to 8 servings | TIME: About 30 minutes, plus time to marinate

Fresh herbs—and lots of them—help keep the leanest of all pork cuts juicy. And the added fat in the herb mixture benefits the flavor, too. The cooking time is extremely short—and leftovers make fantastic sandwiches, though for dinner, I like to eat thick slices of tenderloin with Garlicky Mashed Potatoes (page 329) drizzled with Brown Butter (page 78) and the pan juices.

- ½ cup chopped fresh parsley or cilantro
- ¼ cup chopped basil or mint
- 3 tablespoons olive oil
  Salt and pepper
- 2 small or 1 large pork tenderloin (about 2 pounds)

1. Put the herbs in a small bowl with the olive oil and season generously with salt and pepper. Stir to combine, mashing with the back of the spoon to crush the herbs a bit.
2. Put the tenderloins on a rimmed baking sheet and rub the herb mixture all over. Let sit for up to 30 minutes before roasting, or cover and refrigerate for up to a day.
3. Heat the oven to 400°F. Transfer the pork to the oven and cook undisturbed until the meat loses its pinkness, 10 to 15 minutes.
4. Turn the pork, brush the top with any accumulated pan juices, and roast the other side the same way, another 10 to 20 minutes, depending on the thickness of the cut. For medium-rare, take the pork out of the oven when the internal temperature is no more than 145°F; for medium, let it go to 150°F, but no more than that. Let the pork sit for about 5 minutes before slicing as thin or thick as you like, and serve, drizzled with any remaining pan juices.

GRILLED OR BROILED PORK TENDERLOIN WITH HERB CRUST A little trick makes tenderloin quick and easy to cook perfectly with direct heat: Prepare a charcoal or gas grill for medium indirect cooking (make sure the grates are clean) or turn on the broiler and position the rack about 4 inches below the heat. Use a sharp knife to split the tenderloins lengthwise, almost all the way through, and open them like a book. Rub them all over with some olive oil and put them cut side down over the hot side of the grill, or cut side up under the broiler. Cover if grilling, and cook until browned, 3 to 5 minutes. Turn them onto the cooler side of the grill (or turn them in the pan and put them back under the broiler). Spread the herb mixture all over the cut side of the tenderloins. Cover, if grilling, or return to the broiler, and cook until the meat is done, 10 to 15 minutes on the grill or about 5 minutes in the broiler.

ROASTED, GRILLED, OR BROILED PORK TENDERLOIN WITH MISO CRUST The crust chars wonderfully: Instead of the herb mixture, combine ⅓ cup white, yellow, or red miso with 1 tablespoon sesame oil, 2 tablespoons good-quality vegetable oil, a little salt, and some pepper. Use this mixture to spread on the pork and cook as directed in either the main recipe or the preceding variation.

Pork Roasts

Both loin and shoulder cuts—bone-in or -out—make successful pork roasts. So does fresh ham, which when unsmoked is like the shoulder, only a little leaner.

Many people prefer a boneless loin roast, which is certainly less work when it comes to carving, but leaving the bone in usually results in juicier, more flavorful meat, and the added bulk and protection of the bone give you more flexibility in timing. And carving to accommodate bones isn't that difficult.

Loin roasts, with their lightly marbled interior and gorgeous exterior fat cap, are best cooked to medium-rare. (And the government finally agrees and lowered the safe temperature recommendation.) Shoulder requires longer, slower cooking to melt away the fat and tenderize the meat. The recipes here give you the cues you need to help determine doneness.

Roast Pork with Garlic and Rosemary

MAKES: 8 or more servings | TIME: 1½ to 2 hours, largely unattended

Roast pork at its most basic. If you want even more garlicky flavor, cut a clove of garlic into tiny slivers, and using a thin-bladed knife, insert them into the meat. You can do this a day or two in advance; if you do, rub the roast all over with salt as well and keep it refrigerated, covered loosely with a towel or wax paper.

　　Salt and pepper
2　tablespoons chopped fresh rosemary
1　tablespoon minced garlic
1　3- to 4-pound bone-in pork loin roast, one 2- to 3-pound boneless loin roast, or a similar-sized bone-in or boneless shoulder or fresh ham

1½　cups dry white wine, stock (to make your own, see pages 174–180), or water, plus more if necessary
2　tablespoons cold butter, cut into bits

1. Heat the oven to 450°F. Mix a generous sprinkle of salt and pepper with the rosemary and garlic and rub all over the roast. Fit a rack in the roasting pan and put the meat bone side down on the rack (or fat side down if it's boneless). Roast undisturbed for 15 minutes.

2. Turn over the roast and pour about ½ cup of the wine over the top; lower the heat to 325°F. Continue to roast, adding about ¼ cup liquid every 15 minutes or so; use the juices that accumulate on the bottom of the pan to baste the meat.

3. The roast is likely to take about 1½ hours total cooking time; start checking after 1¼ hours. When it is one stage less done than you want it—an instant-read thermometer will register 140°F for medium-rare—transfer the roast to a warm platter. Put the pan on the stove over 1 or 2 burners on medium-high heat. If there is a lot of liquid in it, let it bubble down to about ¾ cup, scraping the bottom with a wooden spoon to release any brown bits that have accumulated. If the pan is dry, add 1 cup more liquid and follow the same process. Turn off the heat and whisk in the butter. Slice the roast crosswise as thick as you like (between the bones if necessary) and serve with the sauce.

Roast Pork Shoulder, Puerto Rican Style

MAKES: 8 to 12 servings | TIME: At least 5 hours, largely unattended

I've adapted this recipe for traditional *pernil* a bit from the one generously shared with me more than twenty years ago by the family of my friend Peter Blasini. It remains among my favorite ways to cook pork shoulder, is a huge crowd pleaser, and is almost no work. The

variations in this edition now cover shredded pork and carnitas (for tacos and the like) and a candied version that has a haunting sweetness.

- 1 **small head garlic, cloves separated and peeled**
- 1 **onion, quartered**
- 1 **small red bell pepper, seeded (optional)**
- 1 **small dried hot red chile, or more to taste (optional)**
- 2 **tablespoons fresh oregano leaves or 1 tablespoon dried**
- 1 **tablespoon salt**
- 2 **teaspoons pepper**
- 2 **tablespoons good-quality vegetable oil**
- 2 **tablespoons sherry vinegar or red wine vinegar**
- 1 **4- to 7-pound bone-in pork shoulder or portion fresh ham, skin-on if you'd like**

1. Put the garlic, onion, bell pepper if you're using it, chile, oregano, salt, and pepper in a food processor. With the machine running, add the oil in a stream; stop to scrape down the sides as necessary. Or chop and combine everything on a cutting board and mix with the oil in a small bowl. Blend in the vinegar.

2. Rub this marinade into the pork well, getting it into every nook and cranny you can find. Put the meat on a rack in a roasting pan and let sit, uncovered, for 1 hour at room temperature or up to 24 hours in the refrigerator, loosely covered. (If refrigerating, take it out an hour before you're ready to cook.)

3. Heat the oven to 300°F. Roast the pork directly in the pan for at least 3 hours, turning it every 30 minutes or so and basting with the pan juices, until it's well-done to the bone and very tender, and the skin is crisp. This could take up to 5 hours for the largest roasts. The internal temperature should be at least 160°F but no more than 170°F. Let the pork rest for 10 to 15 minutes before cutting it; the meat should be so tender that cutting into uniform slices is almost impossible; rather, whack it up into chunks.

CANDIED ROAST PORK SHOULDER Ends up barely sweet with bits of crackled pork caramel: Omit the garlic, onion, bell pepper, chile, oregano, chile, and vinegar; instead combine ½ cup turbinado sugar with the salt, pepper, and oil in a small bowl. Rub this all over the roast. Don't refrigerate, but do let it sit out, uncovered, for an hour to come to room temperature before roasting as directed.

CARNITAS Crisp chunks of garlicky pork: Omit the garlic, onion, bell pepper, chile, oregano, chile, oil, and vinegar; instead season the meat with just the salt and pepper. Don't refrigerate, but do let it sit out, uncovered, for an hour to come to room temperature before roasting as directed. Transfer the roasted pork to a cutting board; set the roasting pan with the drippings aside. Spoon off all but ¼ cup of the fat from the roasting pan, leaving the drippings behind. Raise the oven to 425°F. When the pork is cool enough to handle, cut the meat from the bone in chunks of various sizes. Toss the meat in the pan drippings with 2 tablespoons chili powder, 1 tablespoon ground cumin, and ¼ cup chopped garlic. Roast, turning and scraping the bottom with a spatula, until the meat is sizzling and crisp, 15 to 20 minutes. Taste and add salt and pepper if you like, and serve with lime wedges.

SHREDDED PORK Use the marinade in the main recipe or seasoning in the first variation before roasting the meat as described. Transfer the finished pork to a cutting board; reserve the roasting pan with the drippings. When the meat is cool enough to handle, cut the skin (if there is any) and meat from the bones and shred it with your hands or two forks. Spoon off all but ¼ cup of the fat from the roasting pan, leaving the drippings behind. Toss the shredded meat in the pan drippings. Taste and add salt and pepper if you like. You can make the meat ahead to this point; cover with foil and warm in a 325°F oven for 20 to 30 minutes.

Slow-Roasted Spareribs

MAKES: 6 to 8 main-dish servings; more as an appetizer |
TIME: 2½ to 3½ hours, largely unattended

The foolproof way to cook ribs is with low heat for a long time, then crisp and sauce them. As the fat melts away slowly, it keeps the meat from drying out and allows the seasoning to do their job; the final blast forms a crust, sealing in juiciness. Whether you choose to use the oven or a grill matters only for smokiness. The recipe and variations have got you covered on both fronts with two flavor profiles, starting with the easiest method.

Other cuts you can use: baby back ribs (which are meatier and will cook in a little more than half the time).

- 2 racks St. Louis or center-cut pork spareribs (about 6 pounds total)
  Salt and pepper
- 1 recipe Barbecue Sauce (page 74)
  Hot sauce, optional

1. Heat the oven to 250°F. Put the ribs in a large rimmed baking sheet. Sprinkle salt and pepper all over and rub them into the meat.

2. Cook the ribs, turning every 30 minutes or so, until they release most of their fat and start to look meaty and dry, 2 to 3 hours depending on how fatty they are. You'll know they're ready when a fork slides in and out of the meat easily but the meat is not falling off the bones.

3. Remove from the oven; turn the heat up to 400°F. Spoon off all but a thin film of fat from the pan. When the ribs are cool enough to handle, cut between the bones to separate the ribs.

4. Brush the ribs generously on all sides with the sauce, and return them to the oven. Cook, turning the ribs every 5 minutes or so, until they become crisp and charred in places, 15 to 20 minutes. Serve hot or at room temperature with any remaining sauce (and hot sauce if you'd like) on the side.

SLOW-GRILLED SPARERIBS Prepare a charcoal or gas grill for low indirect cooking; make sure the grates are clean. You want the heat under the grill cover to be between 225° and 275°F. In Step 1, put the ribs on the cooler side of the grill, cover, and proceed with the recipe through Step 2, adding more coals to the fire as necessary to maintain the temperature. At the end of Step 2, intensify the fire to medium or high heat by adding more coals or turning up the burners. Skip to Step 4, leaving the racks of ribs intact; brush them with the sauce and put them over the hot side of the grill to finish.

CHAR SIU SLOW-ROASTED OR SLOW-GRILLED SPARERIBS Instead of the barbecue sauce, combine ¼ cup each hoisin and soy sauces and honey in a small bowl. Add 2 tablespoons rice wine or dry sherry, 1 tablespoon minced fresh ginger, and ½ teaspoon five-spice powder. Follow the recipe or variation, using this sauce to baste the ribs in Step 4.

Crown Roast of Pork

MAKES: About 12 servings | TIME: About 2½ hours, largely unattended

The granddaddy of celebration roasts, with a side of drama in the presentation. Even though like a turkey, crown roast is usually roasted with the center brimming with stuffing, I cook them separately for maximum crisping.

Other stuffings you can use: My Favorite Bread Stuffing or any of its variations (page 650).

- ½ pound (2 sticks) butter, plus more for greasing the baking dish
- ½ cup dried tart cherries or cranberries
- 1 tied crown roast of pork (14 to 16 ribs, 7 to 10 pounds)
  Salt and pepper
- 1 carrot, chopped

1 celery stalk, chopped

1 onion, cut into quarters, plus 1 onion, chopped

3 tablespoons olive oil

1 tablespoon chopped garlic

2 tablespoons fresh chopped sage or 2 teaspoons dried

6 cups bread crumbs (preferably fresh; see page 801)

1 cup white wine or water

1. Grease a 13 × 9-inch baking dish with some butter. Heat the oven to 450°F and move the racks so there's room for the stuffing either next to or below the roasting pan with the pork. Soak the cherries in hot water to cover. Sprinkle the roast with salt and pepper and put it on a rack in a roasting pan. Toss the carrot, celery, and quartered onion with 1 tablespoon of the olive oil, ¼ cup water, and some salt and pepper and scatter them in the pan.

2. Mix the remaining oil with half each of the garlic and sage. Rub this all over the roast. Cook for 20 minutes, then lower the heat to 325°F.

3. Meanwhile, melt the ½ pound butter in a large pot over medium heat. Add the chopped onion and cook, stirring, until soft, about 5 minutes. Drain the cherries, add them, and stir. Add the bread crumbs and the remaining garlic and sage, and sprinkle with salt and pepper. Toss with a large fork to combine. Put the stuffing in the prepared dish. When the roast has been baking for an hour, put the stuffing in the oven. Cook the stuffing until the top is crisp, then stir it; repeat this process while the roast finishes cooking.

4. Total cooking time for the roast will be 2 hours or a little longer. Check the temperature in several places with an instant-read thermometer; it should be about 140°F for medium-rare. When it's ready, transfer it to a cutting board and let rest while you make the sauce. If the stuffing is browned and heated through, lower the oven temperature to 200°F to keep it warm; if the stuffing looks dry, cover it with foil.

5. Pour or spoon off as much of the fat from the roasting pan as you can without losing any of the juices. Put

the roasting pan on the stove on 1 or 2 burners over medium-high heat. Add the wine and about ½ cup water and cook, stirring and scraping, until the liquid is reduced by about half, 5 to 10 minutes. Strain the sauce into a serving bowl or boat and press to extract the remaining liquid; discard the vegetables.

6. Pile the stuffing into the center of the roast if you like, to present at the table. Carve the roast between the bones and serve the meat and stuffing side by side, passing the sauce on the side.

Pork Stews and Braises

The shoulder is the best cut for braising. The fat melts during the long, wet cooking process. And while it is possible to overcook pork—even in liquid—until it becomes dry and stringy, the window of doneness when stewing or braising is big enough that you don't have to fret about overcooking when keeping the stew warm for a few minutes before serving.

Boneless shoulder roasts are fine for braising, and easier to deal with than bone-in cuts; just make sure they are cut into even-sized pieces or tied into a relatively uniform shape so that everything cooks evenly. And as with other braises, if you're pressed for time, you can skip the browning step with little loss of flavor.

Braised Pork with White Wine and Celery Root

MAKES: 4 to 6 servings | **TIME:** About 2 hours, largely unattended

Ⓜ

Since the last edition of this book, I've learned that a slightly sweet, fruity white wine is better than red wine for braising pork. This stew is so simple you can make it in a slow cooker since you need not brown the meat first (though there is some benefit in doing so; see the last variation). And the celery root almost totally falls apart, thickening the sauce and adding an amazing flavor. Serve over plain rice, millet or quinoa, or egg noodles.

Other proteins you can use: beef chuck or brisket (cooking time will be longer); bone-in or boneless chicken thighs; lamb shoulder.

Other vegetables you can use: parsnips, carrots, rutabaga, peeled all-purpose potatoes.

  1½   pounds boneless pork shoulder, trimmed of
        excess fat and cut into 2-inch chunks
   2   cups sweet white wine like riesling
   1   pound celery root, peeled and cut into 1-inch
        chunks
        About 10 cloves garlic, peeled
        Salt and pepper
        Chopped fresh parsley for garnish

1. Combine the pork, wine, celery root, and garlic in a large pot or slow cooker and sprinkle with salt and pepper. Add enough water so that the liquid barely covers the pork and vegetables. Bring to a boil, then adjust the heat so the mixture bubbles gently and cover. If you're using a slow cooker, just turn it to high and walk away.

2. Cook, stirring every 30 minutes or so (no need to stir if you're using a slow cooker), until the meat is fork-tender and just about falling apart, about 2 hours. Use a slotted spoon to transfer the meat and celery root to a bowl and turn the heat to high. If you're using a slow cooker, transfer the liquid to a saucepan. Reduce the liquid to about a cup. Taste and adjust the seasoning. Reheat the meat and vegetables in the sauce, and serve, garnished with the parsley.

BRAISED PORK WITH TOMATOES AND FENNEL
Substitute 1 28-ounce can crushed tomatoes for the wine; add water as described in Step 1. Instead of the celery root, trim 1 pound fennel bulbs and cut them into wedges; chop and add the stalks, and reserve the most tender fronds for garnish.

BRAISED PORK WITH COCONUT MILK AND CARROTS
Substitute coconut milk for the wine. Instead of the celery root, use carrots; in addition to the garlic, use 2 tablespoons chopped fresh ginger. Add 1 tablespoon curry powder to the stew in Step 1.

SEARED AND BRAISED PORK
Even more flavor with only a little extra work. Use this technique for any of the preceding variations or the main recipe: Heat 2 tablespoons oil in the large pot over medium-high heat. (Use olive oil for the main recipe and the tomato-fennel variation, good-quality vegetable oil for the coconut milk variation.) Add about half the pork and cook, turning occasionally, to thoroughly brown all sides. Repeat with the remaining pieces. When it's all browned, spoon out most of the fat and proceed with the recipe from the beginning.

Spicy Braised Pork with Vietnamese Flavors

MAKES: 8 to 12 servings | **TIME:** About 3 hours, largely unattended

Ⓜ

A pork pot roast that you cook once and eat for many meals. You can, of course, eat it hot immediately (with lots of rice or noodles and stir-fried vegetables), but I like to make it in advance, refrigerate it, and skim off the fat, then slice the meat and use it in one of three ways: reheated in the sauce, cold in banh mi–style sandwiches with pickled vegetables, or added to stir-fries (page 672) or rice or noodle bowls (page 527).

Other cuts and meats you can use: boneless pork shoulder, rolled and tied (you'll get more even slices); bone-in or boneless beef arm (chuck) roast.

   1   onion, halved and thinly sliced
   2   tablespoons chopped garlic
   2   tablespoons chopped ginger
1 or 2 fresh hot chiles like serrano or Thai, chopped,
        or 2 or 3 dried hot chiles

     ¼   cup soy sauce
     ¼   cup fish sauce
     1   tablespoon sugar
     2   star anise pods or 1 cinnamon stick
     2   bay leaves
3 to 4   pounds bone-in pork shoulder, in 1 or 2 pieces
     ¼   cup fresh lime juice
         Salt and pepper
         Fresh cilantro sprigs for garnish
         Chopped scallion for garnish

1. Combine the onion, garlic, ginger, chiles, soy and fish sauces, sugar, star anise, and bay leaves in a large pot with 2 cups water. Add the pork. Bring to a boil, then adjust the heat until it bubbles gently. Cook, covered, turning the pork every 30 minutes or so, until the pork is fork-tender, at least 2 hours. (At this point, you can refrigerate the meat and cooking liquid for a day or two before proceeding.)

2. Transfer the roast to a cutting board. Remove and discard the bay leaves from the cooking liquid. Skim off some fat and bring to a boil. Cook, stirring occasionally, until reduced to about 1 cup, 5 to 10 minutes. Add the lime juice, taste, then add plenty of pepper and some salt if necessary. Slice the meat as thick or thin as you like or break it into chunks, and add any juices from the cutting board to the sauce. Strain the sauce if you'd like and serve it alongside the pork, garnished with cilantro and scallions.

Braised Spareribs with Root Vegetables

MAKES: 4 servings | **TIME:** About 1½ hours, partially unattended

Ⓜ

Slowly cooking ribs this way delivers the best of both worlds: You get to enjoy the savory bones, while eating a delicious, old-fashioned, thick vegetable stew.

Other cuts and meats you can use: baby back or country-style ribs (both will become tender a little more quickly); beef short ribs (which will take longer to cook).

     2   tablespoons olive oil
     1   rack spareribs (preferably St. Louis style; about
         3 pounds), cut into individual ribs
         Salt and pepper
     1   large onion, halved and sliced
     6   cloves garlic, peeled and crushed with the flat
         side of a knife
     2   carrots, cut into large chunks
     2   turnips, cut into large chunks
     8   ounces all-purpose potatoes, peeled and halved
         or quartered
     3   bay leaves
     2   cups chicken stock (to make your own, see
         page 176) or water, plus more if needed
         Chopped fresh parsley for garnish

1. Put the oil in a large pot over medium-high heat. When it's hot, add the ribs, meatiest side down; sprinkle with salt and pepper. Cook, more or less undisturbed, adjusting the heat so the meat browns but doesn't burn, 5 to 10 minutes. If the pot is crowded, work in batches or just accept less browning, which in this instance is okay. Turn the ribs and brown the other side. Transfer the ribs to a platter.

2. Spoon off all but about 2 tablespoons fat and return the pot to medium-high heat. Add the onion and garlic and cook, stirring frequently and scraping up any browned bits, until the onion begins to soften, just a minute or 2. Add the carrots, turnips, potatoes, and bay leaves, sprinkle with salt and pepper, and stir to combine. Pour in the stock, then return the ribs to the pot, nestling them into the vegetables as much as possible. Add more stock or water if necessary so the liquid covers the vegetables but not much of the ribs.

3. Bring to a boil, then lower the heat so the liquid bubbles gently. Cover and cook, checking every 20 minutes or so to make sure the mixture doesn't dry out; if it starts to, add a little more liquid. The stew is ready when the ribs are fork-tender and the vegetables are falling apart, about 1 hour.

Braised Spareribs with Root Vegetables, page 701

4. Transfer the ribs to a shallow bowl. Remove and discard the bay leaves. If the sauce is soupy, turn the heat to high and cook, stirring occasionally, until the sauce is thick, mashing the vegetables a little if you like. (You can make the stew and refrigerate up to 2 days ahead; gently reheat before proceeding.) Serve the ribs and vegetables together or separately, garnished with the parsley.

BRAISED SPARERIBS WITH GREENS Instead of the carrots, turnips, and potatoes, use greens like green or red cabbage, collards, kale, or mustard greens—nothing too delicate. Slice the leaves and ribs crosswise into big ribbons. Add them to the pot after the onions and garlic soften in Step 2. Along with the greens, add 1 tablespoon juniper berries or 1 teaspoon fresh thyme leaves and 1 tablespoon caraway seeds and proceed with the recipe.

Pork Sausage and Ground Pork

It's the same deal with ground pork as ground beef: Make your own in a food processor if possible (see at left). Otherwise, buy coarsely ground pork with visible fat.

Homemade Breakfast (or Any Other Meal) Sausage

MAKES: 6 to 8 servings, 8 large or 16 small sausages | TIME: About an hour if grinding your own

It's so easy to make homemade sausage meat. You control the seasoning; the quantities below are on the light side. If you're not cooking for a crowd, wrap some of the raw sausages individually in parchment paper and freeze in an airtight container to have handy for future meals. You can even cook them from frozen.

 2 pounds pork shoulder, or preground pork
 2 teaspoons salt
 1 teaspoon pepper
 ¼ teaspoon freshly grated nutmeg
 ¼ teaspoon ground allspice
 1 tablespoon minced fresh sage or 1 teaspoon dried

1. Line a rimmed baking sheet with parchment. If you're grinding the pork yourself, cut the meat and fat into 1-inch cubes. Put about half of the meat and fat in a food processor and pulse until coarsely ground but not puréed. Transfer to a bowl and repeat with the remaining meat and fat.

2. Sprinkle with the salt, pepper, nutmeg, allspice, and sage and mix gently with your hands or two forks. Cook a pinch in the microwave or a small skillet until no longer pink. Taste it and adjust the seasonings. Without overworking it, shape the sausage mixture into large or small tubes or patties, transferring them to the prepared pan as you finish. Heat the oven to 200°F and fit a rimmed baking sheet with a wire rack.

3. Heat a large skillet over medium heat for 2 or 3 minutes, then add the sausages; work in two batches to avoid overcrowding. Cook undisturbed until they release easily from the pan, 3 to 5 minutes, then turn to brown and crisp the other side, rotating and turning them until they're brown and crisp all over, 10 to 15 minutes total. As they finish, transfer them to the pan with the wire rack and put them in the oven to keep warm. Repeat with the remaining sausages and serve hot.

ITALIAN-STYLE PORK SAUSAGE, HOT OR SWEET Replace the sage, nutmeg, and allspice with 1 tablespoon or more minced garlic and 1 tablespoon fennel seeds. Also add ¼ to ½ teaspoon cayenne or red chile flakes to make 'em hot.

All About Ham

Hams are not all the same. There's fresh ham, and then there are two basic "treated" hams, dry- or wet-cured. These treated hams are cured with salt; some are smoked, some not. Here are brief descriptions and cooking and serving directions for the major types.

Fresh ham refers to the rear leg of a pig and is neither cured nor smoked. You can substitute it in any recipe that calls for shoulder, though it's usually a little leaner, so it will cook faster and be a little chewier.

Dry-cured hams include the world's great hams, from Italian prosciutto to Spanish *jamón ibérico* to the best domestic country and prosciutto-style hams from Virginia, Kentucky, and Iowa. Small American producers are even making excellent prosciutto-style hams.

Dry-cured hams keep practically forever—if mold appears, just cut or scrub it away—and are meant to be sliced thin and eaten raw in small quantities, or chopped and used as an ingredient. Cut off a sliver and make a sandwich, put tiny pieces on crackers, cut paper-thin slices and eat them alone or with fruit. Or use a few small chunks in pasta sauce or as a seasoning in a pot of beans or stew.

To bake a whole country ham: This tames the saltiness and leaves you with a rare treat that's worth the effort. Get the producer or butcher to saw off the bottom of the leg, or be prepared to do that yourself. Scrub the outside with a brush under running water, then soak it in cold water to cover for 24 hours in the fridge, changing the water once or twice. Put it in a large pot, cover with fresh water, bring to a boil and add the aromatics and spices of your choice. Reduce the head to a steady bubble and cook, turning occasionally, until you can easily spear it with a large fork, about 2 hours. Heat the oven to 400°F. Put the ham on a rack in a roasting pan and pat it dry. Bake until the outer layer is crisp and brown, about 30 minutes. Let rest for 10 to 15 minutes before carving into thick or thin slices.

Wet-cured ham includes just about everything else, from the sweet, smoked American-style mail-order hams to the high-tech chemically cured hams you find at the supermarket. The best hams begin with a real brine of salt, water, and sugar and conclude with a long period of smoking. A high-tech cure begins with a chemically augmented injected brine and ends with a dose of liquid smoke. You can taste the difference.

To bake a wet-cured ham: All they require is reheating in a relatively low oven—300° to 350°F—until an instant read thermometer at the thickest part hits 165°F. This can take up to an hour or so, depending on whether the bone is in, how big the ham is, and how cold it was going in the oven. I like to cover it for the first 30 minutes or so to keep it juicy.

SUPER-SEASONED SAUSAGE Keep the nutmeg and allspice, but replace the sage with 1 tablespoon minced garlic, 1 teaspoon ground coriander, 1 teaspoon ground cumin, 1 teaspoon dried thyme, ¼ teaspoon ground cinnamon, and ¼ teaspoon cayenne.

SAUSAGES WITH PEPPERS AND ONION The best sandwich filling ever. After cooking the sausages, use the same skillet to make My Mom's Pan-Cooked Peppers and Onions on page 320. Use any color bell peppers you like. When they're ready, return the sausages to the pan and toss to coat and reheat.

Garlicky Pork Burgers

MAKES: 4 to 6 servings | **TIME:** 30 minutes

Pork makes juicy burgers whether you grill them or cook them on the stove in a skillet or grill pan. And they take to all sorts of seasonings; see the list on page 687 for some ideas. Serve them dressed on buns like beef burgers, or in rice or grain bowls. Or shape the mixture into a free-form meat loaf and bake as described in the recipe on page 688.

 fast   make ahead   V vegetarian

1½ pounds pork shoulder, cut into chunks, or preground pork

1 teaspoon salt

1 teaspoon pepper

2 tablespoons chopped garlic

1. Prepare a charcoal or gas grill for hot indirect cooking; make sure the grates are clean. If you'll be cooking on the stovetop, when you're ready to start cooking, heat a large skillet or grill pan over medium-high heat for 3 or 4 minutes; sprinkle its surface with coarse salt.

2. If you're grinding the meat yourself, put the meat, salt, pepper, and garlic in a food processor, in batches if your machine is small, and pulse until it's coarsely ground but not puréed. If using preground meat, gently mix in the seasonings. Cook up a bite in the microwave or a skillet and adjust the seasoning if necessary—this step is worth it. Handling the meat as little as possible to avoid compressing it, shape it lightly into 4 to 6 burgers, about 1 inch thick.

3. Put the burgers directly over the fire and cover, or put them in the hot pan. Cook until the bottoms are browned and release easily, 2 to 5 minutes. Turn and repeat on the other side. Move them to the cooler side of the grill and cover again or lower the heat under the pan to medium-low and cook until no longer pink inside, another 5 to 10 minutes. Serve right away.

LEMONGRASS PORK BURGERS It's especially important to cook-a-bit-and-taste for these to get the heat just right. Before adding the meat to the food processor, pulse into a paste 3 or 4 large shallots or 1 medium red onion; the garlic; 2 trimmed stalks lemongrass; 1 small fresh hot chile like jalapeño or Thai, or to taste, or a pinch red chile flakes or cayenne to taste; 1 tablespoon fish sauce; and 1 teaspoon sugar. Transfer the mixture to a bowl then grind the pork and stir gently to combine. Shape into burgers and cook as directed.

Major Cuts of Lamb

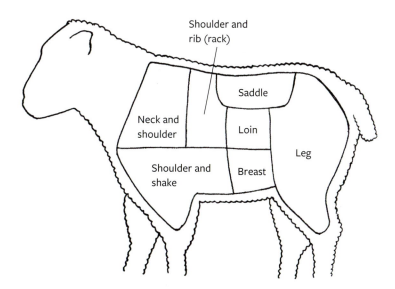

Shoulder and rib (rack)

Saddle

Neck and shoulder

Loin

Leg

Shoulder and shake

Breast

THE BASICS OF BACON

All bacon—with the exception of Canadian bacon—is cured and smoked pork belly. (Canadian bacon falls into the category of wet-cured hams.) You can also find cured, unsmoked pork parts like pancetta or guanciale, which are used as seasoning and for rendering their fat. These products aren't eaten on their own like American-style bacon, though I do use them as ingredients in some recipes in this book.

Choose slab bacon if you want to cook with cubes, or thick-cut bacon for nearly everything else. Doneness is a matter of taste; I like bacon still chewy, but many people prefer it crisp, almost burned. Always drain bacon on towels for a minute or 2 before serving it by itself; when you're using it in other dishes—where you want the fat for seasoning—that's not necessary.

---

3 WAYS TO COOK BACON

1. **Sautéing:** Start the bacon in a large, deep skillet over medium-high heat. When it begins to sizzle, separate the slices if you haven't done so already. Regulate the heat so the slices brown evenly without burning, turning them frequently. Total time will be 10 to 20 minutes, longer for large quantities; you may need to cook in batches.

2. **Microwaving:** The best method for three to six slices. Put the bacon on a triple layer of towels on a microwave-safe plate and cover with a double layer of towels. Microwave on high for 2 minutes, then check; move the pieces around a little and continue to microwave in 1-minute intervals until done. Total time will depend on the power of your microwave, but will be less than 5 minutes even in a small oven.

3. **Roasting:** Slow but easy and reliable, especially for large quantities. Heat the oven to 450°F. Put the bacon in a large roasting pan or rimmed baking sheet in a single layer and slide it into the oven. Roast, checking every 5 minutes or so and turning occasionally. If the pan starts smoking or the bacon is browning too quickly, lower the heat to 425°F. As the meat cooks, take out the extra fat by carefully tipping the pan a little and spooning it into a heatproof bowl. Turn the pieces as they brown and release from the pan. Total cooking time will be 20 to 30 minutes, depending on how much you cook and how you like it.

THE BASICS OF LAMB, GOAT, AND VEAL

By far the smallest of the common meat animals, lamb is flavorful, tender, and easy to cook. Sadly, it's not always easy to find. You may have to go to specialty stores, butcher shops, or farmers' markets.

Still, I try to encourage home cooks to serve lamb as often as I do, which is why there are so many recipes here. Several recipes in this chapter include veal variations, another meat that is hard to find (see page 713). Since goat is becoming more popular and easier to find—and is so similar to lamb in terms of cuts and cooking and eating characteristics—consider it a fine substitute for lamb in all cases.

Lamb and goat don't deserve their bad rap of being "gamey." Even though sheep and goats are easy to raise and herd, and can graze where other animals cannot, they aren't wild. And though they do take to assertive seasonings, the meat is delicious with just salt and pepper. Veal is milder, so I usually use a gentle hand with spices; herbs, however, enhance its slightly sweet, floral flavor.

Most lamb and goat is best cooked rare, though not quite as rare as beef. However, it also can be quite delicious medium and even well-done; this is especially true of the shoulder and chops taken from the shoulder—it has enough fat and flavor to handle it. As for the leg—with or without the bone—its odd shape means that if the thick center is cooked to rare, the thinner edges will

 fast    make ahead   vegetarian

be well-done. So for once, you can satisfy everyone. Goat is smaller so it will cook a little faster than lamb. Here are the main cuts:

SHOULDER Fatty and flavorful, ideal for roasting and stewing; good cut into chops as well. Chops cut from this area should always be cooked medium; large chunks or bone-in roasts are best slow-cooked to well-done.

SHANK Inexpensive ends from the legs are wonderful braised.

BREAST Usually cut into "riblets," which are spectacular slow-roasted or grilled.

RIBS Best known as rack of lamb, this section can also be cut into rib chops. Always good cooked rare to medium-rare.

LOIN This can be sold whole, as a saddle; it's a lovely roast. Or it can be cut into loin chops, which are fine. It can also be boned and cut into medallions.

LEG Sold whole or in halves, bone in or out; occasionally cut into steaks or cubed for shish kebab—you can't go wrong with any of these.

Grilled or Broiled Lamb Chops

MAKES: 4 servings | **TIME:** 20 minutes

Fast-cooking and barely in need of seasoning, lamb chops are a nice change from steaks. If you have a butcher or a responsive supermarket meat counter and fancy a treat, ask for double-rib chops, which are easier to cook to medium-rare. You can also do these in a skillet; see Many Ways to Cook Steak (page 667).

> 4 **double-rib or large shoulder lamb chops or 8 rib or loin lamb chops (about 2 pounds total)**
> **Salt and pepper**
> 1 **clove garlic, peeled (optional)**
> **Lemon wedges for serving**

1. Prepare a charcoal or gas grill for medium direct cooking (make sure the grates are clean) or turn on the broiler, position the rack about 4 inches below the heat source, and put a rimmed baking sheet in the oven to get hot. Sprinkle the lamb with salt and pepper. If you like, cut the garlic clove in half and rub it over the meat.

Carving a Leg of Lamb

STEP 1 To carve a leg of lamb, take a slice or two off the thick end and set aside.

STEP 2 Make a long slice parallel to the cutting board as close to the bone as is possible.

STEP 3 Cut thin slices from the top of the leg.

Broiled Lamb Chops,
page 707, with Baked
Sweet Potatoes, page 343

2. Grill the chops directly over the heat, or broil directly under the heat source, turning once, until they're browned on both sides, and done one stage before you ultimately want them. For single-thickness chops, allow no more than 2 or 3 minutes per side. With double chops, there is a greater margin for error, but the total cooking time will still be less than 10 minutes. Serve right away, with lemon wedges.

GRILLED OR BROILED LAMB CHOPS, ITALIAN STYLE

Using the food processor, purée 2 or more anchovy fillets, ½ cup fresh parsley leaves, 1 tablespoon each olive oil and fresh lemon juice, the garlic clove, and a good sprinkle of salt and pepper. Rub the chops all over with half of the mixture. If you have time, let them marinate for about an hour at room temperature. Proceed with the recipe, basting the chops frequently with the remaining herb mixture. Serve with any risotto (page 440).

Roast Leg of Lamb

MAKES: At least 6 servings | **TIME:** About 1½ hours, largely unattended

Leg of lamb is a near-ideal roast for six people or so—even with minimal seasoning, its flavor will power the meal and support lots of vegetable and grain sides. Buy the leg without the shank, which doesn't take that well to roasting, adds expense, and doesn't fit in most pans.

You can also buy half-legs of lamb; the butt half is preferable. Plan on cooking time for a 3- to 4-pound half-leg to be about two-thirds of what it is for a whole leg. Also consider a boneless leg, which you can buy or do yourself. Then tie and roast it as described in the variation here, or see the flank steak recipe on page 670 for how to cook a butterflied leg of lamb on the grill.

Other meat you can use: 1 or 2 goat legs or shoulders.

- 1 5- to 7-pound leg of lamb (preferably at room temperature)
- 2 teaspoons salt

- 1 teaspoon pepper
- 2 pounds waxy red or white potatoes, peeled and cut into 1½-inch chunks
- 4 carrots, cut into 1½-inch chunks
- 2 onions, quartered
- 1 cup chicken, beef, or vegetable stock (to make your own, see pages 174–178) or water, plus more if needed

1. Heat the oven to 425°F. Remove as much of the surface fat as possible from the lamb; rub the meat all over with the salt and pepper. Put it in a roasting pan and scatter the potatoes, carrots, and onions around it; moisten with ½ cup stock.

2. Roast the lamb for 30 minutes, then turn the heat down to 350°F. If the vegetables look dry, pour over another ½ cup stock.

3. After about 1 hour of roasting, check the internal temperature of the lamb in several places with an instant-read thermometer; you're looking for 130°F for medium-rare; 125°F for very rare. Continue to check every 10 minutes, adding a little more stock if necessary. Total cooking time will be less than 1½ hours. Let it rest for a few minutes before carving. Serve with the vegetables and pan juices.

ROAST LEG OF LAMB WITH THYME AND ORANGE Omit the vegetables and stock. Mix the salt and pepper with 3 tablespoons chopped fresh thyme, 1 tablespoon chopped garlic, and 1 tablespoon grated orange zest. Use a thin-bladed knife to cut small slits in the lamb. Push a bit of the herb mixture into them; rub the lamb all over with the rest. If you have time, let the lamb sit for an hour or more (refrigerate if it will be longer than an hour). Roast as directed in Step 2.

ROAST LEG OF LAMB WITH GARLIC AND CORIANDER SEEDS Include or omit the vegetables as you like. Mix the salt and pepper with 2 tablespoons crushed coriander seeds and 2 tablespoons chopped garlic. Use a thin-bladed knife to cut small slits in the lamb. Push a bit of the spice mixture into them; rub the lamb all over with the rest. If you have time, let the lamb sit for an hour or more (refrigerate if it will be much longer than an hour). Roast as directed in Step 2, omitting the stock if you chose to omit the vegetables. This roast is better closer to medium than to rare—pull it from the oven at about 135°F.

ROAST LEG OF LAMB WITH ANCHOVIES Omit the vegetables or not, as you like. Mix the salt and pepper with 2 tablespoons chopped fresh rosemary, 1 tablespoon chopped garlic, 3 or 4 minced anchovy fillets, and 2 tablespoons olive oil or oil from the anchovies. Use a thin-bladed knife to cut small slits in the lamb. Push a bit of the mixture into them; rub the lamb all over with the rest. If you have time, let the lamb sit for an hour or more (refrigerate if it will be longer than an hour). Roast as directed in Step 2, omitting the stock if you chose to omit the vegetables. When the meat is done, transfer it to a warm platter. Spoon or pour off most of the fat from the roasting pan and put the pan on 1 or 2 burners over medium-high heat. Add ½ cup red wine and ½ cup water and cook, scraping up the browned bits from the bottom of the pan, 1 to 2 minutes. Carve the lamb and serve with the sauce.

ROLLED AND TIED LEG OF LAMB ROAST You can buy one boned, rolled, and tied, but then you can't season the center, so you'll have to untie and retie it yourself. This works for the main recipe or any of the variations: Spread out a boneless butterflied leg of lamb in the roasting pan, and sprinkle all over with the salt and pepper; scatter chopped garlic on top. (If you're making one of the variations, spread most of the seasonings on top of the lamb.) Roll the meat tightly into a tube so that the grain runs lengthwise. Secure the roll with twine in several places, rub with the rest of the seasonings, then roast as directed with the vegetables and stock as in the main recipe or following any of the additions in the variations. It will take less time, so start checking after 30 minutes.

Lamb Stew with Cinnamon and Lemon

MAKES: 6 to 8 servings | TIME: 1½ to 2 hours, largely unattended

Wherever there is lamb, there is lamb stew. I give a few variations here, but this is a perfect place to start. Serve this with simply cooked rice, couscous, or other whole grain (pages 430 or 450–455), or flat bread. For my spin on an Irish version, make the beef stew on page 679, substituting boneless lamb shoulder for the beef. Whatever you do, leftovers freeze beautifully.

Other meats you can use: boneless pork shoulder; goat shoulder; beef chuck.

2	**tablespoons olive oil**
2	**pounds boneless lamb shoulder or 3 to 4 pounds bone-in lamb shoulder, cut into 2-inch chunks**
	Salt and pepper
1	**red onion, chopped**
1	**tablespoon minced garlic**
1	**teaspoon ground cinnamon**
2	**cup red wine or stock (to make your own, see pages 174–180)**
1	**lemon**
	Chopped fresh parsley for garnish

1. Put the olive oil in a large pot over medium-high heat. When it's hot, add some of the lamb in a single layer to avoid overcrowding and sprinkle with salt and pepper. Cook, turning as necessary to brown the pieces on all sides, 5 to 10 minutes. As the pieces finish, transfer them to a plate and repeat with the remaining lamb.
2. Spoon off all but 2 tablespoons of the fat, return the pot to medium heat, and add the onion and garlic. Cook, stirring occasionally, until they're soft, scraping up the browned bits from the bottom of the pot, 5 to 10 minutes. Add the cinnamon and stir until fragrant, less than a minute.
3. Add the wine, return the lamb to the pot along with any juices, and bring to a boil. While the stew is coming

to a boil, chop the lemon, rind and all, remove the seeds, and add the lemon to the pot. Adjust the heat so the stew bubbles gently, cover, and cook, stirring occasionally, until the lamb is fork-tender, 1 to 1½ hours. (At this point, you can cool the stew, cover, and refrigerate for up to a day before removing the surface fat, reheating, and proceeding.)

4. If the stew is soupy, raise the heat a bit and cook until the sauce thickens. Taste and adjust the seasoning, then garnish with parsley and serve.

LAMB STEW WITH MUSHROOMS Omit the lemon; replace the cinnamon with 2 tablespoons chopped fresh thyme. Soak 1 ounce dried porcini in 1 cup boiling water until soft, about 30 minutes. Trim and slice 8 ounces shiitake mushrooms and 8 ounces button mushrooms. When the porcini are ready, lift them from the water with a strainer; reserve the soaking liquid. In Step 2, before you add the onion and garlic, cook all the mushrooms, stirring occasionally, until they release their water and begin to brown, 5 to 10 minutes. Then proceed with the recipe. Carefully pour in the soaking water with the wine in Step 3, leaving behind any grit.

LAMB STEW WITH EGGPLANT OR GREEN BEANS The vegetables almost melt into the stew: Omit the cinnamon and lemon and increase the garlic to 2 tablespoons. Peel and cube 1 pound eggplant or trim 1 pound green beans. In Step 2, before cooking the onion and garlic, sauté the eggplant or green beans until they just begin to soften, about 3 minutes. Proceed with the recipe, replacing 1 cup of the wine with one 15-ounce can diced tomatoes. During cooking, add more wine or water if the stew looks dry. Garnish with chopped fresh dill.

LAMB STEW WITH WHITE BEANS This works with the main recipe or any of the variations, and best with beans you cook yourself (see page 390): Use 1 cup bean cooking liquid (or water) in place of the wine in Step 2. When the lamb is ready in Step 3, add 2 cups cooked or canned cannellini beans and continue to cook until heated through.

Ways to Use Game in These Recipes

Whether you can get your hands on truly wild game—caught by hunters—or some of the farm-raised "game" now available, cooking either is not very different from cooking other meats. Just one word of caution: Game tends to be very lean; wild animals run around a lot. So if you're grilling, searing, broiling, or sautéing, be extra careful not to overcook. And if you're braising, be sure to let the meat simmer long enough to get fully tender.

Here's a simple list of substitutions for cooking different kinds of game:

1. Use beef recipes for venison.
2. Use pork recipes for wild boar.
3. Use lamb recipes for goat (which is not exactly game but is still a specialty meat).
4. Use chicken recipes for rabbit (see page 624).

LAMB CURRY I like this finished with yogurt but you can also use coconut milk: Omit the cinnamon and lemon. Use good-quality vegetable oil to cook the lamb, and chicken stock or water for the liquid. In Step 2, add 2 tablespoons chopped fresh ginger with the onions and garlic and cook until they're soft. Stir in 2 tablespoons curry powder (to make your own, see page 32). When the lamb is tender in Step 3, stir in 1½ cups whole milk regular or Greek yogurt and reduce the heat so it never comes to a boil. Serve over basmati rice, garnished with chopped fresh cilantro and cashews or pistachios.

Lamb Shanks with Tomatoes and Olives

MAKES: 4 to 8 servings | **TIME:** About 3 hours, largely unattended

Lamb shanks are so satisfying, especially during cold weather. You can braise them on top of the stove or in the oven; I give both methods here. My favorite olives in this recipe are a mixture of the big green kind from southern Italy—castelvetranos, which are delicious but time consuming to pit—and kalamatas or the small dried olives from Morocco or Greece. And like most braised meat dishes, these shanks can be cooked in advance—up to a day or two ahead and refrigerated, up to a week or two and frozen.

Other cuts and proteins you can use: beef short ribs (which will also take a long time); chunks of lamb or pork shoulder (which will be faster) or beef chuck or brisket; bone-in chicken thighs (which will be much quicker).

- 1 tablespoon olive oil
- 4 lamb shanks (about 1 pound each)
  Salt and pepper
- 1 large onion, halved and sliced
- 1 tablespoon chopped garlic
- 1 tablespoon chopped fresh thyme or 1 teaspoon dried
- 1 cup chicken, beef, or vegetable stock (to make your own, see pages 174–178), white or red wine, water, or a combination
- 1 15-ounce can diced tomatoes
- 1½ cups olives, pitted
  Chopped fresh mint for garnish

1. Put the oil in a large pot over medium-high heat. When it's hot, add the shanks and cook, turning as they release and sprinkling with salt and pepper, until they're brown on all sides, about 10 minutes. You can also do the initial browning in the oven: Heat the oven to 425°F and roast the shanks, turning once or twice, until brown all over; this will take a little longer but will be some-what easier.

2. Transfer the shanks to a plate. Spoon off all but 2 tablespoons of fat from the pot, or put the oil in the pot if you roasted the lamb, and return the pot to medium heat. Add the onion and cook, stirring occasionally, until softened and golden, 5 to 10 minutes. Add the garlic and thyme and cook for another minute. Add the stock and tomatoes, sprinkle with salt and pepper, and stir. Return the shanks to the pot, bring to a boil, adjust the heat so the liquid bubbles gently, and cover.

3. Cook undisturbed for 30 minutes. Then turn the shanks and add the olives. Cover and continue to cook for at least another hour, turning occasionally, until the shanks are very tender and the meat is nearly falling from the bone; a fork or knife inserted into them will meet little resistance. (At this point, you can refrigerate the shanks for a day or 2, or freeze for up to 2 weeks. Skim excess fat from the top before reheating.) You can pull the meat from the bone and return it to the sauce or serve each person a whole shank. Either way, garnish with mint.

OSSO BUCO The classic accompaniments are either Polenta (page 460) or saffron risotto (page 440): Omit the olives. Instead of lamb, use 4 cut veal shanks, 8 to 12 ounces each. They'll take about the same amount of time to become tender, maybe a little more. When you cook the onion in Step 2, add 1 celery stalk and 1 carrot, both chopped. Proceed with the recipe. Instead of mint, garnish with fresh chopped parsley combined in equal parts with grated lemon zest.

Roast Rack of Lamb with Persillade

MAKES: 4 to 8 servings | **TIME:** 30 minutes

Lamb rack is expensive and luxurious, delicious, and shockingly easy to cook. And this traditional presen-tation continues to be the best. This cut is often sold frenched, with the meat and fat on and between the bones removed. It looks fancy, but it's not necessary. And if you like to chew on the bones, you might prefer the whole thing intact.

- 2 racks of lamb (about 2 pounds each)
- 2 tablespoons olive oil
- 1 cup bread crumbs (preferably fresh; see page 801)

½   cup chopped fresh parsley
2   teaspoons minced garlic
    Salt and pepper

1. Heat the oven to 500°F. If it hasn't been done already, trim the lamb of excess fat, but leave a layer of fat over the meat. If the racks haven't been frenched and you'd like to do it yourself (see the headnote), cut about halfway down along the bones; scrape off the meat and fat between them.
2. Combine the olive oil, bread crumbs, parsley, garlic, and a sprinkle of salt and pepper. Use this to coat the meat side of the racks, patting it firmly to adhere. Put the racks in a roasting pan coating side up. Roast for 20 minutes, then insert an instant-read meat thermometer straight through the meaty part. If it reads 125°F or more, remove the racks immediately for rare (which is what you really want). If it reads less, put the racks back for 5 minutes, no more. Remove from the oven and let sit for 5 minutes. Serve, separating the ribs by cutting down straight through them between the bones.

THE BASICS OF VEAL

Veal production spurred the original charges against inhumanely raised meat—many calves on factory farms were (and still are) tightly confined. And "milk-raised" veal (raised on formula, not its mother's milk) is still objectionable. But the good news is that it's easier than ever to find what the USDA calls "calf," which is also sold as "humanely raised" or "natural" veal. There is organic and free-range veal out there also, though mostly what you see in conventional supermarkets remains so-called milk-fed. With veal, as with other meat, the closer you get to traditional farming practices, the better.

Regardless of the kind of veal you buy, it will be quite lean. And even though veal is a young cow, its cuts are more similar to lamb than beef. Properly cooked, it will be quite tender. Chops and the rear leg—where medallions for cutlets and scaloppini are cut from—are best when some pinkness remains at its thickest part, but no redness. Stop cooking when the temperature reaches

135°F or a little more and you'll hit it right. Braised veal, like osso buco or shoulder meat for stews, must be cooked until well done and tender. However, this takes considerably less time than corresponding cuts of beef.

Grilled or Broiled Veal Chops

MAKES: 4 servings | **TIME:** 30 minutes

Excellent veal chops are a rare occurrence, so you will want to keep things simple and savor the meat. My favorite way is to rub the meat lightly with good olive oil, then give it the perfume of rosemary and garlic.

Other meats you can use: bone-in pork loin chops.

4   bone-in veal loin or rib chops (6 to 10 ounces each, 1 inch thick)
1   clove garlic, halved
3   tablespoons olive oil
1   tablespoon chopped fresh rosemary, plus an extra teaspoon if you like
    Salt and pepper

1. Prepare a charcoal or gas grill for hot direct cooking (make sure the grates are clean) or turn on the broiler and position the rack about 4 inches below the heat. As the fire heats, let the chops reach room temperature, if you haven't already done so.
2. Rub the chops all over with the garlic, then with 2 tablespoons of the oil. Mix most of the rosemary with some salt and pepper and rub this into the chops well.
3. Grill the chops over the fire or broil until they are lightly browned, 3 to 5 minutes. Turn, grill or broil for 4 minutes more. Figure 8 to 10 minutes total cooking time for a 1-inch-thick chop. Check for doneness—the center should be fairly pink but no longer red, and an instant-read thermometer should read 130°F or a little more. If the chops aren't done yet, cook for a minute or so more. Transfer to a platter or plates and let rest for about 5 minutes. Drizzle with the remaining oil, sprinkle with a tiny bit more rosemary, and serve.

Breakfast, Eggs, and Dairy

CHAPTER AT A GLANCE

The Two Fastest, Most Versatile Breakfasts 716

The Basics of Eggs 718

Essential Egg Recipes 720

Omelets, Frittatas, and Other Flat Omelets 730

Quiches, Custards, and Soufflés 734

French Toast, Pancakes, Waffles, Crêpes, and Doughnuts 738

Breakfast Cereals 748

The Basics of Dairy 751

Cheese 753

In some ways, this chapter is the most old-fashioned in the book. Eggs and dairy, porridge, pancakes, waffles, and the like—these are the iconic breakfast foods of a bygone era. Nowadays you might choose any food from elsewhere in the book as your first meal of the day: Compose a bowl of savory grains and vegetables, happily dive into last night's pasta leftovers, or dunk oatmeal cookies in your coffee.

Then again, traditional breakfast foods are utterly modern. It's perfectly fine to make the recipes here any time of the day. In fact it's become downright trendy to put an egg on everything—and I show you how to make them simply, many ways—or eat doughnuts for dessert. And this chapter also includes small projects like do-it-yourself fresh cheese, soufflés, and crêpes.

Ultimately, this chapter is the most flexible. Whether you decide go bacon-and-eggs for weekend brunch, sip a smoothie as an afternoon snack, or make French toast for dinner, these are the components of excellent meals. Add some homemade bread, crisp potatoes, and—if you're like me—a side of vegetables or a salad, and you can feed your family and friends quite well all day long.

The Two Fastest, Most Versatile Breakfasts

You've got to eat in the morning. (It's true: You will almost certainly feel better if you do.) And unless you love leftovers, that means whipping up a little something. Enter smoothies and toast, the easiest breakfasts I know, especially since you can make them with whatever's on hand.

Fruit Smoothie

MAKES: 1 serving (about 12 ounces) | **TIME:** 10 minutes

This is the recipe and variations that cover all the bases, including vegan breakfast if you go with the tofu option.

1 cup chopped fruit like peaches, mangoes, or pears, or whole berries (frozen is fine)
1 small banana, peeled and cut into chunks
½ cup yogurt or soft silken tofu
    Ice cubes as needed
    Fresh lemon or orange juice, or water (optional)

1. Put the fruit in a blender. Add the banana, yogurt, and 3 or 4 ice cubes; you might not need any if your fruit was frozen and the mixture is already slushy.

2. Purée until smooth. Add a little juice or water if you want a thinner consistency; add another couple ice cubes and blend briefly to crush them for a thicker smoothie. Serve right away.

GREEN SMOOTHIE Replace the fruit with 1 packed cup fresh greens like spinach or kale and instead of the banana, use half an avocado. A pinch of salt is good, too.

FRUIT AND VEGETABLE SMOOTHIE You can combine ½ cup chopped of each to get a little more sweetness in the mix; just remember that green plus orange or red comes out brown. Some pretty ideas: cucumber-peach or mango, beet-blueberry, banana-carrot. You get the idea.

COCONUT SMOOTHIE I love this with the banana and pineapple for the fruit: Instead of the yogurt use coconut milk. (This is one time it's okay to use the reduced-fat kind.) Add 2 tablespoons shredded coconut (either toasted, see page 372, or raw) at the same time.

NOT-TOO-SWEET CHOCOLATE SMOOTHIE With raspberries it's divine, but even pears or apples work

Top to bottom: Welsh Rarebit Toast, Fresh Cheese Toast, toast with mashed avocado (see "Topping Toast," page 718)

well for some background sweetness. Add 2 tablespoons cocoa powder to the blender along with the banana.

THE BASICS OF EGGS

Eggs are a near-ideal source of protein, minerals, and vitamins, and one of only a handful of foods with naturally occurring vitamin D. Although eggs have been vilified for their high cholesterol content (an egg contains around 200 milligrams), recent studies have questioned the link between dietary cholesterol that's found in food and blood cholesterol, the cholesterol produced by your body. So unless your doctor advises you against high-cholesterol foods, don't worry about it.

THE ANATOMY OF AN EGG

There are three main components to an egg: the shell, the white, and the yolk. The shell is made up of calcium carbonate and varies in color depending on the breed of hen. The white—or albumen—comprises about two-thirds of the egg, with over half of the egg's protein and minerals. The yolk contains all of the fat and zinc, the majority of the vitamins, and the remaining protein and minerals.

BUYING EGGS

It's now pretty easy to get locally raised eggs from small producers—either at the store, the farmers' market, or even from a neighbor or your own hens. I always recommend this option for quality and freshness.

Whether you buy eggs direct from the farmer or from a supermarket, they'll probably be sized, based on weight per dozen, to standards set by the United States Department of Agriculture: jumbo, extra-large, large, medium, small, and peewee. Extra-large and large eggs are most common, and most recipes, including mine, assume large eggs, though you can substitute extra-large

 fast make ahead vegetarian

with no ill consequences since the difference between them is only a quarter-ounce per egg.

Eggs from large-scale producers are also graded by the USDA. That doesn't mean that eggs without a stamp are inferior, only that they're from smaller farms. For what it's worth, the grades AA, A, and B are based on appearance, shape, and so-called character of the egg. The thicker and less runny the white, the rounder and "taller" the yolks, and the less blemished and properly shaped the shell, the higher the grade. AA and A are the most commonly available grades—B grade is most often used in commercial or institutional kitchens—and there is little difference between them.

Always check the sell-by date or packed-on date; ideally you want them as fresh as possible. Then take a quick peek inside the carton to make sure all the eggs are intact. After that, you have to crack open the egg to check quality clues—not something you can do in a supermarket. At home, you can look for these five signs of a fresh shelled egg:

- The white is thick and doesn't spread out much.

- The white is a bit cloudy. (This means that the naturally occurring carbon dioxide hasn't had time to fully escape from the egg after laying.)

- The yolk is firm and stands tall.

- The chalazae (the coiled cordlike attachments to the yolk) are prominent.

- There might be a small blood spot in the yolk, a small vein rupture common to the freshest eggs. If it bothers you, remove it with the tip of a knife.

UNDERSTANDING EGG LABELS

Some labels on egg cartons matter. Most of these have been in use for only a few years and fall into two categories: those that are associated with specific regulated programs and those that are used without oversight or enforcement. It's worth noting that no chickens are legally raised using hormones, so the label "raised without hormones" is meaningless for eggs—they all are, or are supposed to be.

Two labels are associated with a specific set of voluntary rules and regulations and monitored by third-party auditors so the assumption of truth is higher:

ORGANIC (CERTIFIED ORGANIC) The USDA Certified Organic stamp means the hens are raised without cages and with access to the outdoors; are fed organic, all-vegetarian diets; are raised without antibiotics, pesticides, or insecticides; and that the eggs aren't irradiated. Certified Organic is the only way to guarantee that your eggs were raised without antibiotics. A new term, Beyond Organic, is gaining recognition as being stricter than the USDA Certified Organic standards, though it isn't USDA regulated. But you probably won't see it in a grocery store.

CERTIFIED HUMANE, FREE FARMED, AND ANIMAL CARE CERTIFIED Technically separate, these all refer to the animals' living conditions, guaranteeing a minimum amount of space; access to fresh air, water, and food; and limited stress and/or noise, among other things. The certification is overseen by independent associations whose inspection regulations are approved by the USDA, but they are not part of a USDA regulatory program. Participation is voluntary. These eggs are not organic unless separately labeled so.

The following group are the labels the USDA allows producers to use on an honor system, without formal oversight or inspection:

FREE-RANGE (AKA FREE-ROAMING) Implies that the birds are not kept in cages and sometimes have outdoor access, though it can be just a door open at some point in the day. Free-range as defined by the USDA applies only to chickens used for meat and not egg layers, so there are no USDA standards for so-called free-range eggs.

CAGE-FREE The birds are not kept in cages, but no outdoor access is guaranteed.

NATURAL Probably the most abused and misunderstood label for eggs—and many other foods. In fact there are no standards for "natural" eggs. This label essentially means nothing.

OMEGA-3 ENRICHED These have nearly six times the amount of omega-3 fatty acids in standard eggs but look, cook, and taste no different. The hen's feed is supplemented with a mix of vitamins and omega-3 fatty acids. I'd recommend getting your omega-3s elsewhere, but these are hardly harmful.

VEGETARIAN FED No animal by-products are included in the feed. If it were true, "100% Vegetarian-Fed" would be a more secure assurance of feed quality, but unfortunately it's not regulated or enforced.

STORING EGGS

After laying, eggs are edible for weeks. So although a fresh egg will give you the most amazing fried or poached egg, you can use older eggs in baking and other recipes without worry; they just won't be quite as delicious. May as well eat them as fast as you can.

Eggs should be refrigerated to prolong freshness and minimize the growth of any harmful bacteria like salmonella. Don't store them in the door of the fridge, which is often too warm. (Some people, including me, prefer to store just-laid eggs at room temperature for a day or two, though it's not officially recommended.) Since the shells are porous, keep them away from strong-smelling foods. And you'll know when they're off: Bad eggs have an unmistakably foul aroma.

COOKING EGGS

Eggs are tolerant of a wide range of temperatures; the only real rule is not to overcook them or they will toughen. For example, for years I made my favorite scrambled eggs lovingly and leisurely, taking 40 minutes to do so (see The Best Scrambled Eggs, page 724). Then I discovered I could get just about the same texture by cooking them quickly, stirring constantly, and removing them from the heat the instant they threatened to overcook (see Everyday Scrambled Eggs, page 723). Both ways work fine; the first requires more patience, the second more attention.

Then there's the language of eggs. For example: Boiled eggs aren't really "boiled," because the water should never be at a real boil; all boiling does is bounce the eggs around the pot and crack the shells. Nor should eggs ever become completely hard; even "hard-boiled" eggs should have yolks that remain somewhat creamy, not chalky.

Using lower heat makes capturing ideal doneness a little easier. Fried eggs stay tender and become evenly firm over medium-to-low heat; boiled and poached eggs develop better texture and are less like to be damaged in water that bubbles only gently. But you can cook quickly and keep eggs tender and soft, as in real omelets (see page 730); again, it just takes attention.

The degree of doneness is only a matter of timing, and room-temperature eggs will cook in about a minute less than those straight from the refrigerator. If you're cooking more than one egg, make sure you use a saucepan big enough for the water to circulate freely. You'll also need to extend the cooking time to the maximum in each of the recipes in the following section.

Essential Egg Recipes

Beginning cooks can use this bundle of recipes as a way to learn basic egg-making skills, while those with more experience will learn why techniques work the way they do and how to pinpoint doneness. I start with the simplest egg-only preparations—which you can multiply for as many servings you like—and build through more involved dishes like Benedict and rancheros, then on to sections on omelets and other recipes that feature eggs.

 **F** fast **M** make ahead **V** vegetarian

Soft-Boiled Egg

MAKES: 1 serving | TIME: Less than 10 minutes

The egg lover's way to eat eggs, barely cooked but warm and comforting. Soft-boiled eggs are also dreamy stirred into a bowl of reheated leftover brown rice or a cup of broth.

1 or 2   eggs
         Salt and pepper

1. Fill a saucepan about two-thirds full of water and bring it to a gentle boil.
2. Use a spoon, slotted spoon, or spider to lower the egg into the gently boiling water. Adjust the heat so the water barely simmers, then cook for 3 to 4 minutes, the shorter time if you want the yolk completely runny and the white still slightly liquid, the longer if you want the white very soft but set.
3. Run the egg briefly under cold water, crack the shell, and scoop out the egg into a small bowl (or eat straight from the shell). Sprinkle with salt and pepper and serve.

MEDIUM-BOILED EGG Easier than poached, but similar: In Step 2 cook the eggs for 6 to 7 minutes; the shorter time guarantees a cooked but runny yolk but there may be some undercooked white.

Hard-Boiled Egg, My Usual Way

MAKES: 1 serving | TIME: About 15 minutes

Hard-cooked eggs are so convenient and versatile you may want to keep a few ready in the fridge at all times; they keep for a week. Just use a larger pot and more eggs. I think they're best when the yolks are just slightly undercooked and still jammy and the whites are just set.

Quickly chilling the eggs helps minimize the chance of a green ring forming around the yolk and can help you peel more easily, though sadly only older eggs peel reliably. See the variation for another approach.

1 or 2   eggs
         Salt and pepper

1. Fill a saucepan about two-thirds full of water and add the egg. Bring to a boil, then turn off the heat and cover. The average large to extra-large egg will be my idea of perfect (as described above) 6 minutes later, but see the variations for softer or harder results.
2. Plunge the egg into a bowl of ice water for a minute or so, or drain and run the pot under cold water, then refrigerate or crack and peel. Sprinkle with salt and pepper and serve.

SOFTER HARD-BOILED EGG Not quite runny yolks, but still pretty gooey. Stop steeping the egg at 5 minutes.

HARDER HARD-BOILED EGG For egg salad and other times you want to cut it. Stop steeping the egg at about 10 minutes.

HARD-BOILED EGG, ANOTHER WAY Some people swear by this method for easy peeling but you've got to make sure the eggs don't bobble around or they will crack. Bring the water to a boil without the egg in Step 1, then lower it into the water with a spoon and adjust the heat to a gentle but steady bubble. If you start counting the minute the eggs hit the water, the doneness timing is about the same as for the main recipe. Drain and chill as described in Step 2.

Fried Eggs

MAKES: 1 to 2 servings | TIME: 10 minutes

Correctly cooked, fried—or sunny-side-up—eggs are nearly as delicate as poached, with tender whites and a

Eggs in a Nest, or
Eggs in the Hole

barely cooked yolk. Low heat is the easiest way to get there, but with practice you'll be able to use higher heat and get the same results. Butter is the most luxurious fat for frying eggs; olive oil is also delicious, just different. Sesame oil is interesting, especially if you're frying an egg to put on top of Rice Porridge with Fresh Garnishes (page 155).

1 tablespoon butter or olive oil
2 to 4 eggs
Salt and pepper

1. Put a medium skillet over medium heat for about 1 minute. Add the butter or oil and swirl it around the pan. When the butter's foam subsides or the oil is hot, about a minute later, crack the eggs into the skillet. As soon as the whites lose their translucence—this takes only a minute—turn the heat to low and sprinkle the eggs with salt and pepper.

2. Cook until the whites are completely firm; the last place this happens is just around the yolk. If the egg has set up high, rather than spread out thin, there are two techniques to encourage it to finish cooking: The first is to cut through the uncooked parts of the white with a knife, allowing some of the uncooked liquid to sink through the cooked white and hit the surface of the pan, where it will cook immediately. Or cover the skillet and cook for a minute or 2 longer. Start checking after a few seconds by gently pressing on the yolk with your finger or nicking with a small knife; it can change dramatically in less than a minute. When the eggs are cooked to your preference of firmness lift them from the pan with a spatula and eat right away.

OVER-EASY EGGS This solves the challenge of cooking the top if you're willing to try the maneuver: In Step 2 when the eggs are solid enough to be lifted by a spatula, carefully turn them over to cook the other side until the yolk is as runny or set as you like.

EGGS IN A NEST OR EGGS IN THE HOLE You need to double the butter here and use a larger skillet: Use a biscuit cutter or drinking glass to cut a big hole out of the middle of 1 slice bread for each egg. After the butter is hot in Step 1, put the bread slices and the circles in the pan (separately) and crack the eggs into the holes. When the eggs start to firm up, carefully turn the bread slices and the circles over and cook the other side for a minute or 2, then serve.

---

5 SIMPLE IDEAS FOR FRIED EGGS

1. As the butter or oil heats, season it with a few fresh herb leaves or a smashed clove garlic.

2. First cook bacon in the skillet, then use the rendered fat to fry the eggs.

3. As the white sets, use a butter knife to fold its edges over the yolk, making a little package to protect the yolk from overcooking.

4. Add Worcestershire sauce or other liquid seasoning like soy or hot sauce to the white before it sets.

5. Cook ½-inch-thick tomato slices—either ripe or green tomatoes—alongside the eggs (increase the amount of butter slightly).

Everyday Scrambled Eggs

MAKES: 2 servings | **TIME:** 10 minutes

Very good scrambled eggs can be had in a hurry, provided you don't overcook them. Adding a little extra liquid helps prevent overcooking—and if that liquid is cream, it also lends a luxurious texture. A few drops of lemon juice will make them even more tender. The tradeoff is that they then taste a little less "eggy."

4 or 5 eggs
Salt and pepper
2 tablespoons milk or cream, or no more than a teaspoon lemon juice, or water (optional)
2 tablespoons butter or olive oil

1. Crack the eggs into a bowl and beat them just until the yolks and whites are combined. Season with salt and pepper and beat in the liquid if you're using it.

2. Put the butter or oil in a medium skillet over medium-high heat. When the butter is melted or the oil is hot, add the eggs. Cook, stirring frequently and scraping the sides of the pan (a silicone spatula or spoon is an excellent tool for this).

3. As the eggs begin to curdle, you may notice that some parts are drying out; whenever you see that, remove the pan from the heat and continue to stir until the cooking slows down a bit. Then return to the heat and continue cooking. The eggs are done when creamy, soft, and still a bit runny; do not overcook unless, of course, you intend to. Serve immediately.

SCRAMBLED EGGS WITH CHEESE Use virtually any kind of cheese you like except the ones that don't melt easily, like feta or queso fresco: As the eggs begin to set, stir in ½ cup grated cheese.

SCRAMBLED EGGS WITH FINE HERBS "Fines herbes" in French: Add about ½ teaspoon chopped fresh tarragon, 1 teaspoon chopped fresh chervil, and 1 tablespoon each chopped fresh parsley and chives to the eggs before beating, or anytime during cooking.

SCRAMBLED EGGS WITH BACON OR SAUSAGE Before making the eggs, cook up to 8 ounces chopped bacon or sausage in the pan, stirring occasionally until the pieces brown and crisp, 5 to 10 minutes. Drain off all but a tablespoon or 2 of the fat. Proceed with the recipe, heating and using the pan with the meat and fat to cook the eggs.

The Best Scrambled Eggs

MAKES: 2 servings | **TIME:** 40 minutes

There's only one way to get a truly silky texture: slow cooking. These are perfect for dinner or a lazy weekend brunch, because they're easily cooked while you prepare other ingredients.

4 or 5	**eggs**
	Salt and pepper
2	**tablespoons cream**
2	**tablespoons butter or olive oil**

1. Crack the eggs into a bowl and beat them just until the yolks and whites are combined. Season with salt and pepper and beat in the cream.

---

12 Simple Additions to Scrambled Eggs

Ingredients to add alone or in combination to any scrambled eggs, just as they start to set. Figure about ½ cup total except where otherwise noted:

1. Minced pickled jalapeño to taste
2. Sautéed mushrooms, onion, spinach, or other cooked vegetables, chopped
3. Chopped cooked shrimp or other seafood
4. 1 teaspoon chopped fresh stronger herbs like oregano, tarragon, or thyme or 1 tablespoon milder ones like parsley, chive, chervil, basil, or mint
5. Chopped smoked salmon or other smoked or cured fish
6. Chili (see page 403) or any cooked beans
7. Chopped salami or other smoked or cured meat
8. Up to 1 cup peeled, seeded, and diced tomato or ¼ cup reconstituted dried tomatoes (or even better, ½ cup Oven-Dried Tomatoes, page 348)
9. Tabasco, Worcestershire, or other prepared sauce, to taste
10. Minced scallions
11. Chopped Roasted Red Peppers (page 318)
12. Any cooked salsa (see pages 71–74), drained if it's quite moist

 fast make ahead vegetarian

2. Put a medium skillet over medium heat for about 1 minute. Add the butter or oil and swirl it around the pan. After the butter melts, but before it foams (or when the olive oil starts to look thin) turn the heat to low.

3. Add the eggs and cook over low heat, stirring occasionally with a wooden spoon. At first nothing will happen; after 10 minutes or so, the eggs will begin to form curds. Do not lose patience: Stir frequently, breaking up the curds as they form, until the mixture is a mass of soft curds. This will take 30 minutes or more. Serve right away.

Poached Eggs

MAKES: 1 or 2 servings | **TIME:** 10 minutes

Some technical notes: Ragged edges don't bother me so I rarely bother to trim the edges with scissors, as some cooks do. I also no longer bother trying to rein in the whites with vinegar, since I can taste it. To poach more than two eggs at once, use a bigger pan to avoid crowding. To make poached eggs in multiple batches, keep a second, large pot of water warm over very low heat. Make sure the temperature hovers between 145° and 150°F; as the eggs finish poaching, move them to the second pot of water and keep covered. Fish them all out with a slotted spoon when you're ready to serve.

    1   teaspoon salt
2 to 4   eggs

1. Bring 1 to 2 inches water to a boil in a small deep skillet, add the salt and lower the heat to the point where the water barely bubbles; if you measure it with an instant-read thermometer, the temperature is just under 200°F. One at a time, break the eggs into a shallow bowl or saucer and slip them into the water.

2. Cook for 3 to 5 minutes, just until the white is set and the yolk has filmed over. Remove with a slotted spoon and allow the water to drain off for a couple seconds. If you are eating the eggs right away, put them directly on the toast or what have you. If you like, drain them briefly

Are Runny Egg Yolks Safe?

The perfect egg—for me and many other enthusiasts—is soft and tender, with a liquid yolk. But salmonella outbreaks in eggs have happened over the last 20 years; I can't deny it. So if you or anyone you cook for is very old, very young, or has a compromised immune system—or if you are worried about eggs for any reason—you should rinse and dry them before using and cook them thoroughly: Salmonella is killed in eggs if their temperature is maintained at 160°F for 1 minute or 140°F for 5 minutes. At 160°F, egg yolks are firm; at 140°F, they're not.

Precooking eggs for recipes that call for raw eggs can be a little tricky, but it's useful for mayonnaise (page 69): Put the shelled eggs in a small metal or heatproof glass bowl set over a pot of bubbling water on the stove. You don't want the water to touch the bottom of the bowl. Use a whisk to stir and an instant-read thermometer to monitor their temperature. When they reach 140°F,

adjust the heat on the burner to maintain that temperature and keep stirring for 15 minutes. (This completely changes the flavor and texture, of course so they won't whip up into meringues or behave the same way in baked goods.)

Another alternative, when you want poached eggs with runny yolks but without the risk of salmonella, is to hold them in a water bath: Keep the cooked eggs in 150°F water for at least 5 minutes. See the headnote with the Poached Eggs recipe (above) for the details.

You can also use pasteurized eggs—you'll notice the difference—which are available both in and out of their shells. Dried egg whites can also give you peace of mind, with only a little sacrifice in flavor and performance for meringues and mousses. To use, you simply mix the powder with water (the proportions are on the package) and beat as you would fresh egg whites.

on towels before serving. Poached eggs are delicate, but they can be handled as long as you're careful.

Baked Eggs

MAKES: 1 to 2 servings | **TIME:** 30 minutes

 F V

There's something about the custardy texture of baked eggs (also called shirred) that can't be duplicated by other cooking methods. Bake them alone, or use leftover cooked meat or seafood, vegetables, grains, legumes, or sauce as the base before adding the egg. Or right before popping them in the oven, top the eggs with bread crumbs, grated cheese, or chopped fresh herbs. This is also one of the best ways to cook eggs for a crowd (see the variation).

> Butter or oil for greasing the cups
> 4 tablespoons cream (optional)
> 4 eggs
> Salt and pepper

1. Heat the oven to 375°F. Smear a bit of butter or oil in 4 custard cups or small ramekins. If you like, put up to a tablespoon of cream in the bottom of each (a nice touch). Break 1 egg into each cup, then put the cups on a baking sheet.
2. Bake for 10 to 15 minutes, until the egg yolks just begin to set and the whites are solidified. Because of the heat retained by the cups, these will continue to cook after you remove them from the oven, so it's best to undercook them slightly (the precise time, on the middle rack of a good oven, is 12 minutes). Sprinkle with salt and pepper and serve.

BAKED EGGS FOR A CROWD Serves 6 and some will be more well done than others, which is perfect for pleasing everyone at the table: Grease a 13 × 9-inch glass baking dish and drizzle in about ¾ cup cream if you'd like. Crack in a dozen eggs and bake as directed in Step 2.

Eggs Poached in Tomato Sauce

MAKES: 4 servings | **TIME:** 30 minutes

 F M V

I added a version of the Middle Eastern dish *shakshuka* to this edition since it's become a sensation over the last decade. No wonder: It's an easy, hearty, and versatile breakfast-for-dinner (or anytime) recipe. Tomato sauce Is the liquid for poaching the eggs, traditionally seasoned with cumin, paprika, and cayenne. But I like to make it with all different kinds of tomato sauces, or even creamed vegetables (see the variation). Since you can add the eggs one at a time and cook them to different donenesses, it's a great dish for pleasing everyone at the table. Serve this with plenty of bread, or even plain polenta (page 460) or grits (page 748), or any simply cooked whole grain (especially millet or couscous, pages 452 or 454).

> 1 recipe Fast Tomato Sauce, With or Without Pasta or any of the variations (page 478, without pasta)
> 8 eggs
> Salt and pepper

1. Prepare the sauce in a large skillet; you can do this up to a couple of days ahead if you like.
2. When you're ready to eat, take the eggs out of the fridge. Add 1 cup water to the sauce and bring to a boil. Crack the eggs one at a time into a small bowl or saucer and slide them into the sauce. Adjust the heat so the sauce bubbles gently. Cover and cook just until the whites are set and the yolks are as firm as you like them, 3 to 5 minutes for runny. For firmer eggs, cover the pan again and continue to cook another minute or 2. (The eggs that went in first will be the first ones done.) To serve, remove the eggs and some of the sauce with a large spoon.

EGGS POACHED IN TOMATO SAUCE WITH CHEESE After all the eggs are in the pan, scatter ½ cup crumbled feta

 fast make ahead vegetarian

EGGS POACHED IN CREAMED SOMETHING Instead of the tomato sauce, make a batch of Creamed Onions or any of the variations (page 316). In Step 1, add ½ cup more cream and ½ cup water. Never bring it to a boil; instead just keep it at a steady but gentle bubble and proceed with the recipe.

Eggs Benedict

MAKES: 4 servings | **TIME:** 30 minutes

The traditional way to make the quintessential brunch classic is with English muffins, Canadian bacon, and hollandaise sauce. But the formula is easy to vary by replacing any components. You can even make Benedict with scrambled or baked eggs instead of poached, which is obviously much easier for large gatherings. Check the chart that follows for ideas or improvise your own combinations. The only thing that requires last-minute attention is the eggs; everything else can be prepared ahead and kept warm.

1	recipe Hollandaise Sauce (page 80)
4	English muffins, split
2	tablespoons butter
8	slices Canadian bacon, about 8 ounces total
8	eggs
	Chopped fresh parsley for garnish (optional)
	Sweet or smoked paprika for garnish (optional)

1. Make or reheat the hollandaise, cover, and keep it warm over a double boiler or in a bowl set over a pot of simmering water. Toast the English muffins until golden; keep warm.

F fast   **M** make ahead   **V** vegetarian

2. Put a large skillet over medium-high heat. Add half of the butter. When it melts and begins to bubble, add half of the bacon. Cook until lightly browned and crisped, just a minute or 2, then turn and cook on the other side. Transfer to towels to drain and repeat with the remaining butter and bacon.

3. When you're ready to serve, poach the eggs following the directions for Poached Eggs (page 725). You may need to work in 2 batches and hold the finished eggs in warm water as described in the headnote. To assemble each Benedict, put the top and bottom of a muffin on each plate, split side up. Top each with a slice of bacon, an egg, and a spoonful of hollandaise. Garnish if you like and serve.

Huevos Rancheros

MAKES: 4 servings | TIME: 35 minutes

Another egg dish perfect for entertaining: Go bare-bones or add lots of sides and garnishes (do most of the prep in advance) and serve a festive brunch drink. Some possible additions might be sliced or crumbled cooked chorizo or other sausage, Radish Salsa (page 58), any guacamole (page 105), chopped fresh chiles, shredded lettuce, crema for drizzling, and lime wedges.

- ½ cup good-quality vegetable oil, plus more as needed
  Eight 6-inch corn tortillas
- 1 cup Refried Beans (page 393) or any soft, well-seasoned beans
- 2 tablespoons butter, lard, or bacon fat
- 8 eggs
  Salt and pepper
- 1 cup Salsa Roja or Salsa Verde (pages 71 and 73)
- ½ cup crumbled queso fresco or grated Monterey Jack or cheddar cheese
- ¼ cup chopped fresh cilantro for garnish

1. Heat the oven to 375°F. Line a baking sheet with towels. Heat ½ cup oil in a large skillet over medium heat. When it's hot, fry the tortillas 1 or 2 at a time until softened and heated through, about 3 seconds per side, making sure they don't brown or crisp. Add more oil as needed. As they finish, drain on the prepared baking sheet. Remove the skillet from the heat and carefully pour out the oil.

2. Remove the towels and put the tortillas into the baking sheet in a single layer. Spread each with about 2 tablespoons of the beans.

3. Put the butter in the skillet and return it to medium heat. When the butter foams, crack in the eggs. Cook until translucent, about 1 minute, then turn the heat to low and sprinkle with salt and pepper. Cook until a little less done than you like them, just a few minutes (or turn them for Over-Easy Eggs, see page 723). Separate the eggs with a spatula and carefully transfer 1 to each tortilla, then top with 2 tablespoons salsa and 1 tablespoon cheese each.

4. Bake until the cheese is melted, 3 to 5 minutes. Serve immediately, garnished with cilantro.

Breakfast Sandwiches, Burritos, and Tacos

At the risk of stating the obvious: Any eggs you make in a pan can be made into a hand-held breakfast, even better if it includes meat, cheese, and/or vegetables. First spread toasted bread or a roll with butter (or mayonnaise if you like) or gently warm corn or flour tortillas (see "Preparing Tortillas," page 811) and serve with salsa for last-minute dressing.

Omelets, Frittatas, and Other Flat Omelets

Omelets, folded or not, make excellent vehicles for other ingredients. The classic French omelet takes a little practice but is easy to master: Start with a nonstick pan or a well-seasoned cast-iron pan, and a silicone spatula; heat butter or oil well and keep the heat fairly high; and avoid overstuffing. Then fold it (see below and at right).

Or just leave it flat, as in a frittata or any other thick or thin free-form open-face omelet. Unlike their folded counterparts, these can be loaded up with all kinds of cheeses and cooked foods. They're so versatile—I make them for lunch, supper, and brunch, and for an appetizer, cut into small wedges or squares and served with toothpicks. Go ahead and make them in advance—they're just as good cold or at room temperature as they are warm.

Omelet

MAKES: 2 servings | TIME: 15 minutes

Omelets are ideal at breakfast, brunch, lunch, and dinner. This recipe is for a really basic omelet, cooked in one pan and shared. (For individual omelets, divide the ingredients in half and cook in batches.) But you can fill them with almost anything. The variations and list that follow range from classic—and simple—to a bit more complex; some are practically all-in-one meals.

    4 eggs
    2 tablespoons milk or cream (optional)
       Salt and pepper
    2 tablespoons plus 1 teaspoon butter or olive oil

1. Crack the eggs into a bowl, add the milk if you're using it, and beat just until the yolks and whites are combined. Season with salt and pepper.
2. Heat a medium skillet over medium-high heat for 1 minute. Add the 2 tablespoons butter or oil. When the butter foams or the oil is hot, swirl it around the pan until the butter foam subsides or the oil coats the pan, then pour in the egg mixture. Cook, undisturbed, for about 30 seconds, then use a rubber spatula to push the edges of the eggs toward the center. As you do this, tip the pan to allow the uncooked eggs in the center to reach the perimeter. Continue until the omelet is mostly cooked but still runny in the center, a total of about 3 minutes. Or if you prefer, cook it until the center firms up.
3. There are a couple of ways to proceed. You can fold the omelet in half (see below) or in thirds (see page at right), sliding it from the pan. Rub the top of the omelet with the remaining teaspoon butter or oil and serve.

TOMATO OMELET Before cooking the omelet, melt 1 tablespoon butter in a small saucepan over medium heat. Add 2 tablespoons chopped scallion or onion and cook for 30 seconds. Stir in 1 cup chopped tomato and cook for about 2 minutes. Sprinkle with salt, pepper and smoked paprika and keep warm. Just before finishing the omelet, spoon some of this sauce in a line down the center, fold in half or thirds, and serve.

DENVER OMELET Before cooking the omelet, melt 2 tablespoons butter in a small saucepan over medium heat. Add 2 tablespoons each of chopped onion and red bell pepper and cook for 30 seconds. Stir in ½ cup

Folding an Omelet in Half

STEP 1 First, hold the pan at a 45-degree angle so that half of the omelet slides onto the plate.

STEP 2 Gently increase the angle of the pan over the plate, allowing the omelet in the pan to fold over onto the first half.

F fast   **M** make ahead   **V** vegetarian

chopped cooked ham and cook for about 2 minutes. Sprinkle with salt and pepper and keep warm. Just before finishing the omelet, spoon the ham mixture in a line down the center, fold in half or thirds, and serve.

13 IDEAS FOR FILLING OMELETS

Cooked fillings, like vegetables or grains, should be warmed first; cheeses should be finely grated or crumbled so they melt or at least heat up quickly; other raw fillings should be chopped in small pieces to heat quickly. Mix and match any of the fillings, but keep the total quantity to about 1 cup.

1. Grated cheese (virtually any kind that melts at least a little), about 2 tablespoons per egg
2. About ½ cup sautéed mushrooms, onion, spinach, or leftover cooked vegetables (steamed, boiled, or sautéed; rinse with boiling water if necessary to remove unwanted flavors); chop them as finely as you like.
3. Tomato, peeled and seeded if you'd like and chopped (up to ½ cup per egg), drained of excess moisture
4. Cottage cheese or goat cheese, mixed with fresh chopped herbs if you like
5. Chopped ham, crisp-cooked bacon, or cooked sausage meat or other chopped meat
6. Marmalade, jam, or jelly; sprinkle the top of the omelet with a little sugar before serving if you like
7. 1 teaspoon chopped fresh stronger herbs like oregano, tarragon, or thyme or 1 tablespoon milder ones like parsley, chive, chervil, basil, or mint
8. Fruit like berries or peeled and grated apples, briefly cooked with butter, sugar, and cinnamon
9. About ¼ cup each cream cheese and smoked salmon cut into bits
10. Cooked seafood like shrimp, scallops, lobster, or crabmeat, shredded or minced
11. Chopped red bell pepper, mild chiles like New Mexico or poblano, or Roasted Red Pepper (page 318)
12. About ½ cup sautéed chopped onion or scallions
13. Mashed Potatoes (page 329) or other vegetables

Fresh Tomato and Cheese Frittata

MAKES: 4 servings | **TIME:** 30 minutes

The model for all sorts of vegetable fillings. See the variations and the list that follows for even more ideas. I give a range of eggs for when you might want more stuff, less eggs.

2	tablespoons olive oil
½	onion, sliced
	Salt and pepper
2	large ripe tomatoes, peeled and seeded if you'd like, chopped
6 to 8	eggs
½	cup grated Parmesan cheese

1. Heat the oven to 350°F or turn on the broiler. Put 1 tablespoon of the olive oil in a large skillet over medium-high heat. When it's hot, add the onion and cook, sprinkling with salt and pepper, until soft, about 5 minutes. Add the tomato and adjust the heat so the juices bubble. Cook, stirring occasionally until the pan is almost dry, another 5 to 10 minutes.
2. Meanwhile, beat the eggs in a bowl with some salt and pepper until the yolks and whites are just combined.

Folding an Omelet in Thirds

STEP 1 Using a large spatula, loosen one edge of the omelet; lift and fold about a third of it toward the center.

STEP 2 Now slide the spatula under the center of the omelet; lift and fold it over the opposite edge.

Pour the eggs over the vegetables, using a spoon if necessary to evenly distribute them. Sprinkle the cheese over the top and cook, undisturbed, until the eggs are barely set, 5 to 10 minutes.

3. Transfer the skillet to the oven and cook until the edges brown and puff but the center is still jiggly, about 5 minutes, or put it under the broiler for just a minute or 2. Cut into wedges or squares and serve hot, warm, or at room temperature.

FRITTATA WITH CRUMBLED SAUSAGE Substitute about 6 ounces crumbled sausage for the tomato; add it with the softened onion and cook, stirring until it's no longer pink, 5 to 10 minutes.

LEFTOVER PASTA, NOODLE, GRAINS, OR RICE FRITTATA
Omit the tomato and, if appropriate to the flavor profile, increase the Parmesan to 1 cup, or omit it. Figure you'll need about 2 cups cooked pasta, Asian noodles, grains, or rice. (It's fine if the leftovers have some sauce; if not, toss with melted butter or oil.) In Step 1, warm the pasta, noodles, grains, or rice in the oil after the onion is soft. In Step 2, if you're using the cheese, stir it into the eggs and proceed with the recipe.

---

12 ADDITIONS TO FRITTATE AND FLAT OMELETS

Just about any vegetable, herb, or cheese can be used in a flat omelet, alone or in combination. Figure up to ½ cup cooked filling per egg. If you're using leftover cooked vegetables, give them a quick flash in the pan with some oil or butter, then add the beaten eggs and cook as directed in the frittata recipe.

If you're starting with raw fresh vegetables, chop them into bite-sized pieces and cook in the pan with a tablespoon or 2 oil or butter until tender, or boil them separately in salted water until tender (page 16) and drain very well. For frozen vegetables, cook them in the butter or oil in pan until they're thawed and any water evaporates before adding the eggs.

1. Chopped steamed spinach or chard, mixed with a dash lemon juice and a pinch freshly grated nutmeg or sautéed in olive oil with minced garlic
2. Chopped or crumbled crisp bacon mixed with pan-fried apple and onion slices
3. Minced salami or ham, cooked crumbled sausage, flaked cooked or smoked fish
4. Sautéed onion, fresh tomato, and basil
5. Asparagus or other green vegetable, goat cheese, and basil
6. Cubed or sliced cooked eggplant and/or bell peppers (any way is good, but grilled is delicious)
7. Chopped or grated and quickly sautéed zucchini (see page 242)
8. Sautéed Mushrooms (page 306)
9. Caramelized Onions (page 315) and blue cheese
10. Leftover Mashed Potatoes (page 329)
11. Peeled, seeded, and diced tomatoes or Oven-Dried Tomatoes (page 348)
12. My Kind of Croutons and variations (page 801)

Spanish Tortilla

MAKES: 4 to 6 main-dish or 8 to 12 appetizer servings | **TIME:** About 40 minutes

I've been making this omelet since I first visited Spain decades ago. It's usually served as a tapa or on sandwiches (don't laugh! It's lovely), but it's also fine for breakfast. That's why I give a range of eggs, so you can decide how big you want to make it. Don't worry about using so much olive oil; a lot will be poured off and you can refrigerate it for sautéing vegetables later in the week.

1	cup olive oil
3 or 4	waxy potatoes (about 1¼ pounds), peeled and thinly sliced
1	medium onion, thinly sliced
	Salt and pepper
	Pinch smoked paprika (pimentón; optional)
6 to 8	eggs

F fast   **M** make ahead   **V** vegetarian

1. Put the oil in a large skillet over medium heat. About 3 minutes later, add a slice of potato; once bubbles appear, the oil is ready. Add all the potatoes and onion and sprinkle with salt and pepper, along with smoked paprika if you're using it. Turn the potato mixture in the oil with a wooden spoon and adjust the heat so that the oil bubbles gently.

2. Cook, turning the potato mixture gently every few minutes and adjusting the heat so the potatoes do not brown, until they are tender when pierced with the tip of a small knife, 5 to 10 minutes. Meanwhile, beat the eggs with some salt and pepper in a large bowl.

3. Drain the potato mixture in a colander, reserving the oil. Wipe out the skillet, return it to medium heat, and add 2 tablespoons of the reserved oil. Combine the potato mixture with the eggs and add to the skillet. As soon as the edges firm up (this will only take a minute or so), reduce the heat to medium-low and cook, undisturbed, until the eggs begin to set more toward the center, about 5 minutes.

4. Insert a rubber spatula all around the edges of the tortilla to make sure it's firm enough to move. Carefully slide it out of the pan onto a plate; the top will still be somewhat runny. Cover with another plate and, holding the plates tightly, invert them (see illustration, page 332).

5 Essential Breakfast Dishes Found Elsewhere in This Book

For some, breakfast is not complete without potatoes and/or sausage or bacon. Here's where to find all that:

1. For home-fried potatoes, I suggest you make Crisp Pan-Fried Potatoes (page 331), substituting butter for the olive oil if you like.
2. For hash browns, try Potato Rösti (page 332): Cook it slowly so the inside becomes tender before the outside burns.
3. For basic breakfast sausage, see page 703.
4. To cook bacon, see page 706.
5. For fruit salad, see page 210 and for macerated fruit, see page 363.

5. Add another tablespoon of the oil to the skillet and return it to medium heat. Use a spatula to gently push the tortilla off the plate, back into the skillet. Cook until the center no longer jiggles when you shake the pan, another 5 to 10 minutes, then slide the tortilla from the skillet to a clean plate. Or finish the cooking by putting the skillet in a preheated 350°F oven for about 10 minutes. Let the tortilla sit for 5 to 10 minutes before slicing. Serve warm or at room temperature.

Quiches, Custards, and Soufflés

Egg-based pies and custards are nearly universal to all cuisines, though the most familiar—quiches and soufflés—come from France. They're "fancier" than flat omelets: Cream or milk are components, and quiches have the added bonus of a pastry crust—though you can certainly go crustless (see page 734). Cheese is the best-known other filling component, but vegetables, meats, and herbs (including leftovers) can play a part and vary widely. Soufflés require a more deliberate hand in adding ingredients to maintain the signature poufiness.

Cheese Quiche

MAKES: 4 to 8 servings | TIME: About 1½ hours, somewhat unattended; less if you use a premade crust

The cheese dictates the flavor and texture. Go with a sharp hard cheese for intensity. Or choose a soft fresh cheese like goat or cream cheese, ricotta, or cottage cheese, and the quiche becomes mild and creamy. (Reduce the cream by about ½ cup to compensate.) Fresh herbs are a simple way to bring freshness to the custard filling; add ¼ cup chopped fresh basil, parsley, chives, chervil, cilantro, or dill, 1 teaspoon or so chopped fresh tarragon, thyme, or rosemary, or about 1 tablespoon chopped fresh marjoram or oregano.

- 1 recipe Flaky Piecrust (page 867), made without sugar, or Savory Tart Crust (page 870), fitted into a 9-inch deep-dish pie plate or 10-inch tart pan and chilled
- 6 eggs, at room temperature
- 2 cups grated Emmental, Gruyère, cheddar, or other flavorful melting cheese
- 2 cups heavy cream or half-and-half, heated gently just until warm
- ½ teaspoon salt
- ¼ teaspoon cayenne, or to taste

1. Heat the oven to 425°F and set the rack in the middle. Prebake the chilled crust as described on page 869 until the crust begins to brown, 10 to 12 minutes. Remove and let cool on a rack while you prepare the filling. Reduce the oven temperature to 325°F.

2. Combine the eggs, cheese, cream, salt, and cayenne in a large bowl and whisk until well blended. Put the pie plate on a baking sheet and pour the filling into the shell. Bake until the filling still jiggles just a little in the middle and is lightly browned on top, 30 to 40 minutes. Cool on a rack until warm or room temperature before cutting into wedges. (You can make this ahead, cover it with foil when cool, and refrigerate for up to several hours. Reheat, covered in a 350°F oven until hot.)

Onion Quiche

MAKES: 4 to 8 servings | **TIME:** About 1½ hours, somewhat unattended; less if you use a premade crust

You can substitute nearly any vegetable you like for the onions (see "How to Use Other Ingredients in Quiche or Baked Custard"), though this is an absolute classic and—when the onions are cooked until almost melted, as they are here—really lovely.

- 1 recipe Flaky Piecrust (page 867), made without sugar, or Savory Tart Crust (page 870), fitted into a 9-inch deep-dish pie plate or 10-inch tart pan and chilled
- 4 tablespoons (½ stick) butter or olive oil
- 6 cups thinly sliced onion (about 2 pounds) Salt and pepper
- 1 teaspoon fresh thyme leaves or ½ teaspoon dried
- 6 eggs, at room temperature
- 2 cups heavy cream, half-and-half, milk, or a combination, heated gently just until warm

1. Heat the oven to 425°F and set the rack in the middle. Prebake the chilled crust as described on page 869 until the crust begins to brown, 10 to 12 minutes. Remove and let cool on a rack while you prepare the filling. Reduce the oven temperature to 325°F.

2. Put the butter or oil in a large, deep skillet over medium heat; when the butter melts or the oil is hot, add the onion and some salt and pepper. Turn the heat up to medium-high and cook, stirring frequently, until the onions are very soft and lightly browned, at least 20 minutes and probably longer; adjust the heat so they don't brown too much or crisp up, but cook until the onions practically melt. Add the thyme, stir, turn off the heat, and cool slightly.

3. Combine the eggs and cream in a bowl, then add the onion mixture. Put the pie plate on a baking sheet and pour the filling into the shell. Bake until the filling still jiggles just a little in the middle and is lightly browned on top, 30 to 40 minutes. Cool on a rack until warm or room

Crustless Quiche

Consider this a cross between a frittata or tortilla and a custard baked in a water bath. It's great for weeknights or quick, elegant lunches. Grease a 9-inch deep-dish pie plate or 8- or 9-inch square or 2-quart oval baking dish and pour in the filling. Bake at 325°F until the center still jiggles a little when you shake the baking dish, 25 to 35 minutes.

 **F** fast **M** make ahead **V** vegetarian

temperature before cutting into wedges. (You can make this ahead, cover it with foil when cool, and refrigerate for up to several hours. Reheat, covered in a 350°F oven until hot.)

ONION QUICHE WITH BACON Omit the butter or oil. Chop 8 slices bacon and cook until crisp, 5 to 10 minutes. Remove the bacon with a slotted spoon and cook the onion in the bacon fat as described in Step 2. Scatter the bacon into the partially baked crust before adding the filling.

Silky Baked Custard

MAKES: 4 to 6 servings | **TIME:** 45 minutes

Custard at its most basic. You can toss in up to 1 cup cheese or 2 tablespoons chopped fresh herbs, especially chopped chives, chervil, or tarragon.

1	tablespoon butter
2	tablespoons minced shallot or onion
2	cups heavy cream or half-and-half
1	sprig fresh thyme (optional)
2	eggs plus 2 yolks
	Pinch cayenne
½	teaspoon salt

1. Put the butter in a medium saucepan over medium heat. When it melts, add the shallot and cook until soft, 3 to 5 minutes. Lower the heat a bit, pour in the cream, add the thyme if you're using it, and cook just until it begins to steam, a couple of minutes more. Remove from the heat and let cool to room temperature.

2. Heat the oven to 325°F and bring a kettle of water to a boil. Put the eggs, egg yolks, cayenne, and salt in a medium bowl and whisk or beat until blended. Remove the thyme if you used it. Gradually add the cream to the egg mixture, whisking constantly. Pour the custard into a 1-quart dish or into 4 to 6 small (6-ounce) ramekins or custard cups.

How to Use Other Ingredients in Quiche or Baked Custard

There are two ways to prepare vegetables before adding them to the egg mixture for quiches and custards. The first is to cook them in butter or oil like the onions in the Onion Quiche. Most vegetables won't take as long as onions; see Sautéed Vegetables on page 242 for a master recipe. Greens work best after they have been cooked in boiling salted water (see "Boiling, Parboiling, and Blanching Vegetables," page 237), drained, then chopped and squeezed dry. Either way, cool the vegetables before adding them to the custard, and limit the total quantity of extra ingredients—vegetables, cheese, nuts, whatever—to 2 cups for quiche and 1 cup for custard.

3. Put the baking dish or ramekins in a larger baking pan and pour in boiling water to within about 1 inch of the top of the dish or ramekins. Bake until the mixture is not quite set—it should jiggle a bit in the middle—25 to 35 minutes for ramekins, longer for a baking dish. Check the progress frequently since the window of doneness is small and cream sets up a little faster than milk. Remove from the water bath. Serve warm or at room temperature, or refrigerate and serve cold within a few hours of baking.

Cheese Soufflé

MAKES: 4 to 6 servings | **TIME:** About 1 hour

The word *soufflé* has the same root as the French word for breath; this is all about air. The only difficult thing is the timing: You have to eat this as soon as it's out of the oven. As long as you beat the egg whites correctly (the directions here and the illustrations on page 852 should be your guide), and fully but gently incorporate

Cheese Soufflé, page 735

them into the base, everything will be fine. Keep in mind that soufflés with cheese and vegetable purées won't become quite as lofty as those without, but won't fall as much either; in other words, they're more stable.

- 4 tablespoons (½ stick) butter, plus more for greasing
- ¼ cup all-purpose flour
- 1½ cups milk, warmed until hot to the touch (about 1 minute in an average microwave)
- 6 eggs, separated
  Salt and pepper
  Dash cayenne or ½ teaspoon dry mustard
- ½ cup freshly grated Parmesan cheese
- ½ cup grated cheddar, Manchego, Roquefort, Emmental, and/or other melting cheese

1. Grease a 2-quart soufflé or other deep baking dish with butter. (Hold off on this step if you're not going to bake the soufflés until later.)

2. Put 4 tablespoons butter in a medium saucepan over medium-low heat. When the foam subsides, stir in the flour and cook, stirring, until the mixture darkens, about 3 minutes. Turn the heat to low and whisk in the milk, a bit at a time, until the mixture is thick. Let cool for a few minutes, then beat in the egg yolks, sprinkle with salt and pepper, cayenne or mustard, and the cheeses. (At this point, you can cover the base tightly and refrigerate it for a couple of hours; bring it back to room temperature before continuing.)

3. When you're ready to bake the soufflé, heat the oven to 375°F and grease the baking dish if you haven't already. Use a stand or hand-held mixer or a whisk to beat the egg whites until stiff peaks (see page 852). Fold about one-third of the egg whites into the base. Use a rubber spatula to scoop the mixture from the bottom and fold it over the top; don't worry too much about deflating the whites at this point. Add the rest of the egg whites, using the same folding technique, but more gently. Incorporate the whites well into the base, but if light streaks of white remain, that's okay. If the batter goes flat, it's overmixed and your soufflé won't rise much; the results will be more like a puffy quiche so not a total disaster.

4. Transfer the batter to the prepared baking dish. Bake until the top is brown, the sides are firm, and the center is still quite moist, about 30 minutes. Use a thin skewer to check the interior; if it comes out quite wet, bake for another 5 minutes. If it is just a bit moist, the soufflé is done. Serve right away, spooned directly from the baking dish.

INDIVIDUAL CHEESE SOUFFLÉS Instead of using a single baking dish, put 4 to 6 buttered 1½- to 2-cup ramekins on a rimmed baking sheet. Divide the batter evenly among them in Step 4. The cooking time may be reduced by as much as half; start checking after 15 minutes.

Separating Eggs

STEP 1 To crack the egg, smack the side definitively—but not too aggressively—on a flat, hard surface, stopping your hand when you hear the shell crack.

STEP 2 The easiest way to separate eggs is to use the shell halves, pouring the yolk back and forth once or twice so that the white falls into a bowl. Be careful, however, not to allow any of the yolk to break and mix in with the whites or they will not inflate fully during beating.

French Toast, Pancakes, Waffles, Crêpes, and Doughnuts

Eggs play a supporting role in breakfast baking. And I say "baking" loosely, since French toast, pancakes, and crêpes are all made on the stove, waffles require a specially patterned iron, and the doughnuts here are fried.

French Toast

MAKES: 4 servings | **TIME:** 20 minutes

Originally a way to bring new life to stale bread—it's called *pain perdu* ("lost bread") in France—French toast can be made with virtually any fresh or stale bread, including quick breads and even tortillas. Rustic loaves require a bit more soaking to soften the crust and take longer to cook through, while hearty whole grain breads make more dense slices. I like them all, especially thick slices of eggy brioche or challah, which make a truly decadent French toast.

To vary the recipe: Use soy or other nondairy milk if you like, or for richer French toast, use half-and-half or heavy cream. Season with ground cardamom, cloves, allspice, nutmeg, or almond extract instead of the cinnamon or vanilla.

3	eggs
1	cup milk
⅛	teaspoon salt
2	tablespoons sugar (optional)
1	teaspoon vanilla extract or ground cinnamon (optional)
	Butter or good-quality vegetable oil for frying
8	slices good-quality bread, each about 1 inch thick

1. Heat the oven to 200°F if you want to serve all the slices at once. Put a large griddle or skillet over medium-low heat while you prepare the egg mixture.

2. Beat the eggs lightly in a wide, shallow bowl and stir in the milk, salt, and sugar and vanilla or cinnamon if you're using them.

3. Add about 1 teaspoon butter or oil to the griddle or skillet. When the butter is melted or the oil is hot, spread it over the surface. One at a time and working in batches if necessary, dip both sides of the bread slices in the batter and put them on the griddle. Cook until browned on each side, turning as necessary, no more than 10 minutes total; you may find that you can raise the heat a bit. Butter or oil the griddle between batches, if necessary. Serve right away or keep warm on a baking sheet in the oven for up to 30 minutes.

CARAMELIZED FRENCH TOAST A sugar coating melts and creates a lightly crunchy coating: Sprinkle or dredge the dipped bread with sugar. Proceed with the recipe. Serve immediately.

Maple Syrup

Maple syrup is made by boiling and evaporating sap from a specific kind of maple tree. It takes about 40 gallons of sap to make 1 gallon syrup, so it's not inexpensive. But the difference between real thing and colored and flavored sugar syrup is pronounced. Read the label: The ingredients should say "pure maple syrup" and nothing else. It might be from Canada or the United States, and it will be graded.

There is no longer so-called Grade B syrup. Everything is now all graded "A" and identified by four color classes—Golden, Amber, Dark, and Very Dark. The flavor gets stronger as the syrups get darker. But unless you prefer a milder flavor, there's no reason to buy anything but Dark or Very Dark.

 fast    make ahead   vegetarian

French Toast with Raw Fruit
Sauce, page 862

Aside from or in addition to the obvious maple syrup:

1. Sautéed apples, pears, bananas, or other fruit, or any fruit compote (pages 365 and 360)
2. Whipped Cream (page 854)
3. Maple Frosting (page 857)
4. Orange Glaze (page 857)
5. Creamy Caramel Sauce (page 860)
6. Fruit Sauce, Two Ways (page 862)

Everyday Pancakes

MAKES: 4 to 6 servings | TIME: 20 minutes

It's amazing how quickly you can whip up this batter, and you can keep it refrigerated for a couple of days before making the pancakes. You can also mix the dry ingredients to store indefinitely (this is, essentially, pancake mix); just add the eggs and milk when you're ready to cook.

  2 cups all-purpose flour
  2 teaspoons baking powder
  ½ teaspoon salt
  1 tablespoon sugar (optional)
  2 eggs
1½ to 2 cups milk
  2 tablespoons butter, melted and cooled (optional)
     Butter or good-quality vegetable oil for cooking

1. Combine the flour, baking powder, salt, and sugar if you're using it, in a large bowl. In a smaller bowl, beat the eggs with 1½ cups milk, then stir in the melted butter if you're using it. Gently stir this into the dry ingredients, mixing only enough to moisten the flour; don't worry about a few lumps. If the batter seems thick, add a little more milk.

2. When you're ready to cook, heat a griddle or large skillet over medium-low heat. Heat the oven to 200°F.

Use a little butter or oil each time you add batter, unless your skillet is truly nonstick. When the butter foam subsides or the oil shimmers, ladle batter onto the griddle or skillet, making any size pancakes you like. Adjust the heat as necessary; usually, the first batch will require higher heat than subsequent batches. The idea is to brown the bottom in 2 to 4 minutes without burning it. The pancakes are ready to turn when bubbles appear in the center and the bottoms are golden brown; they won't hold together well until that stage.

3. Cook until the second side is lightly browned, a couple of minutes more, and serve right away. Or hold on an ovenproof plate or baking sheet in the oven for up to 15 minutes.

Light and Fluffy Pancakes

MAKES: 4 to 6 servings | TIME: 20 to 30 minutes

Here the egg whites are whipped into a foam and folded into the batter, creating a cross between pancakes and a soufflé.

6 Tips for Perfect Pancakes

1. Use a nonstick griddle or skillet, or one of well-seasoned cast iron to minimize butter or oil.
2. Heat until a few drops of water skid across the surface before evaporating.
3. Ladle the pancakes onto the griddle with enough room in between for turning.
4. The edges of the pancake will set first; when bubbles appear in the center of the pancake and the bottom is golden brown, it's ready to flip.
5. Serve the pancakes immediately, if possible; that's when they are best.
6. Melt the butter and gently heat the maple syrup or whatever topping you're using (the microwave does a good job here).

1   cup milk
4   eggs, separated
1   cup all-purpose flour
⅛   teaspoon salt
1   tablespoon sugar
1½ teaspoons baking powder
    Butter or good-quality vegetable oil for cooking

1. Heat the oven to 200°F if you want to serve all the pancakes at the same time. Heat a griddle or large skillet over medium-low heat. Beat together the milk and egg yolks in a small bowl. Combine the flour, salt, sugar, and baking powder in a large bowl. Beat the egg whites with a whisk or stand or hand-held mixer until stiff peaks form.

2. Add the milk-yolk mixture to the dry ingredients and stir until combined but not overmixed, some lumps are okay. Gently fold in the egg whites; they should remain somewhat distinct in the batter.

3. Put about 1 teaspoon butter or oil on the griddle or in the skillet and when the butter melts or the oil is hot, spread it over the surface. Add batter by the heaping tablespoon, making sure to include some of the egg whites in each spoonful. Cook until lightly browned on the bottom, 3 to 5 minutes, then turn and cook until the second side is brown, a couple of minutes more. Serve immediately. Or hold on an ovenproof plate or baking sheet in the oven for up to 15 minutes.

Everyday Waffles

MAKES: 4 to 6 servings | **TIME:** 10 minutes, plus time to cook

If you've got buttermilk, sour cream, or yogurt, these are the most tender, spontaneous waffles you can make. Plain milk works too; see the first variation. The extra five minutes it takes to beat the egg whites separately is considered mandatory; the fluffiness factor is too powerful to deny.

2   cups all-purpose flour
½   teaspoon salt
2   tablespoons sugar
1½ teaspoons baking soda
1¾ cups buttermilk or 1½ cups sour cream or yogurt thinned with ¼ cup milk
2   eggs, separated
4   tablespoons (½ stick) butter, melted and cooled
½   teaspoon vanilla extract (optional)
    Good-quality vegetable oil for brushing the iron

1. Heat the oven to 200°F if you want to serve all the waffles at the same time. Combine the flour, salt, sugar, and baking soda in a large bowl. In another bowl, whisk together the buttermilk and egg yolks. Stir in the butter and the vanilla if you're using it.

Pancake Variations

Try these variations with either pancake recipe.

Buttermilk, Yogurt, Sour Cream, or Sour Milk Pancakes: Substitute one of these for the milk in either recipe (to sour your own milk, see page 751); use ½ teaspoon baking soda in place of the baking powder and proceed with the recipe. Thin the batter with a little milk if necessary.

Blueberry or Banana Pancakes: Use fresh or frozen (not thawed) blueberries; overripe bananas are my favorite: Just before cooking, stir the blueberries into the batter. For the bananas, slice them and press into the uncooked batter on top of the pancakes. Cook these pancakes over lower heat than you would other pancakes, as they burn more easily.

Whole Grain Pancakes: A bit denser in texture but with distinctive grain flavor: Substitute whole wheat, quinoa, amaranth, or teff flour or cornmeal, rolled oats, or a combination for up to 1 cup of the flour.

Lemon–Poppy Seed Pancakes: An especially good variation of the Light and Fluffy Pancakes: Substitute ½ teaspoon baking soda for the baking powder. When you add the milk, add 2 tablespoons freshly squeezed lemon juice, 2 teaspoons grated lemon zest, and 2 tablespoons poppy seeds.

 fast   make ahead   **V** vegetarian

2. Brush the waffle iron lightly with oil and heat it. Stir the wet ingredients into the dry. Beat the egg whites with a whisk or stand or hand-held mixer until they hold soft peaks. Fold them gently into the batter.

3. Spread enough batter onto the waffle iron to barely cover it; close the iron and cook until the waffle is done, 3 to 5 minutes, depending on your iron. Serve immediately or keep warm for a few minutes on a wire rack over a baking sheet in the oven.

WHOLE GRAIN WAFFLES Substitute up to 1 cup whole wheat or other whole grain flour, cornmeal, or rolled oats, or a combination, for 1 cup of the all-purpose flour.

Overnight Waffles

MAKES: 4 to 6 servings | TIME: 8 hours or more, largely unattended

With a distinctive yeasty flavor and a fluffy but chewy texture, these waffles are incredible. Eat them traditionally with butter and syrup for breakfast or use them like bread to serve with savory dishes like soups, stews, or fried chicken.

2	cups all-purpose flour
1	tablespoon sugar
2	teaspoons instant yeast
½	teaspoon salt
1½	cups milk
8	tablespoons (1 stick) butter, melted and cooled
½	teaspoon vanilla extract (optional)
	Good-quality vegetable oil for brushing the iron
2	eggs, separated

1. The night before you want to serve the waffles, combine the flour, sugar, yeast, and salt in a large bowl. Stir in the milk, then the butter and the vanilla if you're using it. The mixture will be creamy and loose. Cover with plastic wrap and set aside overnight or at least 8 hours at room temperature. (Of course, you can do this in the morning if you want waffles for supper.)

---

7 Waffle Variations

You can make these changes or additions to either of the two waffle recipes.

1. Add up to 2 teaspoons ground cinnamon or any curry powder (to make your own, see page 32).

2. Add up to 1 cup chopped nuts; Granola, My New Way (page 749) or customized (see page 751); or sweetened or unsweetened shredded coconut.

3. Add about 2 teaspoons minced or grated orange or lemon zest.

4. Add 1 cup grated mild cheese like Emmental, Gruyère, or cheddar, or ½ cup grated Parmesan.

5. Substitute rye flour, cornmeal, or another flour for up to half of the all-purpose flour.

6. Add up to 2 teaspoons minced fresh or candied ginger.

7. Add up to 1 cup puréed cooked sweet potatoes or winter squash and up to ⅛ teaspoon freshly grated nutmeg or ground cloves.

---

2. The batter will be bubbly and smell like bread dough. When you're ready to cook, heat the oven to 200°F. Brush the waffle iron lightly with oil and heat it. Separate the eggs and stir the yolks into the batter. Beat the whites until they hold soft peaks. Fold them gently into the batter.

3. Spread enough batter onto the waffle iron to barely cover it; cook until the waffle is done, usually 3 to 5 minutes, depending on your iron. Serve immediately or keep warm for a few minutes on a wire rack fitted into a rimmed baking sheet in the oven.

Buckwheat Crêpes, Sweet or Savory

MAKES: 8 to 12 crêpes, depending on the size | TIME: 40 minutes

Crêpes are the pancakes that eat like tortillas—thin and perfect for stuffing with sweet or savory fillings. They're perfect for breakfast, brunch, lunch, a light supper, or dessert, and the batter can be made a day ahead.

What more do you want? Well, they could be a little easier to cook: Use a nonstick or well-seasoned skillet. To turn, lift the edge with a spatula and use your fingers to pull it up off the pan, then put the other side down in the pan. But after a few tries—the first one or two crêpes almost never work, even for professionals—you'll get the knack. And there's plenty of batter to make up for the loss.

1 cup buckwheat flour
¼ cup all-purpose flour
2 eggs
½ cup milk, plus more if needed
2 tablespoons butter, melted and cooled
⅛ teaspoon salt
Butter for cooking
Filling of your choice (see at right)

1. Put the buckwheat and all-purpose flours in a large bowl with the eggs, milk, melted butter, and salt. Add 1 cup water and whisk until smooth. (You can do this in a blender if you like.) If the batter isn't quite pourable, add a little more water. Let the batter rest at room temperature for 1 hour or cover and refrigerate for up to 24 hours.

2. Heat the oven to 200°F. Put a large skillet (preferably nonstick or well-seasoned cast iron or steel) over medium heat and wait a couple of minutes; add a small pat of butter. When the butter melts, spread it over the surface. Stir the batter with a large spoon or ladle and pour about 2 tablespoons into the skillet. Swirl it around so that it forms a thin layer almost covering the bottom of the pan.

3. When the top of the crêpe is dry, after about 1 minute, turn it and cook the other side for 15 to 30 seconds. (The crêpe should brown only very slightly and not become at all crisp.) Bear in mind that the first crêpe almost never works, so discard it if necessary.

4. Repeat the process, adding butter to the skillet and adjusting the heat as needed, until all the batter is used up. Stack the crêpes on an ovenproof plate and hold in the oven, then fill and fold them all at once. Or better still, fill and fold each crêpe while it's still in the pan and serve as it's ready; if you want the filling warmed, keep the pan over low heat for a few minutes.

5. To fill and roll or fold crêpes: Put the filling over half the crêpe, fold over the other half to enclose it, then fold in half again. Or put the filling in the center of the bottom third and start rolling at the end with the filling.) Return to the skillet and warm gently to heat the filling if you like. Slide it onto a plate and serve.

---

6 FILLINGS OR TOPPINGS FOR SWEET CRÊPES

As simple as sugar and lemon juice, or any of the following:

1. Any jam, jelly, marmalade, or macerated fruit (see page 363)
2. Nutella or any nut butter, including peanut butter
3. Any peeled, seeded, pitted, or cored fresh fruit, cooked briefly with sugar to taste, butter if you like, and a little rum or cinnamon (see Sweet Sautéed Apples, page 365)
4. Crème fraîche, sour cream, or yogurt (sweetened, if you like)

 fast  make ahead vegetarian

Buckwheat Crêpes with ham and Gruyère, page 743

5. Brown Butter (page 78), sprinkled with ground cinnamon, cardamom, and/or cloves
6. Creamy Caramel Sauce (page 860); not too much

---

5 FILLINGS FOR SAVORY CRÊPES

Gruyère and ham are the most common fillings for savory crêpes, but of course there are other possibilities.

1. Any grated, thinly sliced, or crumbled cheese like Gruyère, Brie, soft goat, mozzarella, cheddar, or fresh cheese
2. Cooked, drained, and chopped vegetables, reheated in butter or oil per the directions on page 242; don't bother to chop vegetables whose shape is naturally suited to rolled crêpes, like asparagus spears
3. Any thick stew of vegetables, meat, chicken, or seafood
4. Silky Baked Custard (page 735), spooned into the crêpe
5. Cooked beans or lentils

Chocolate-Glazed Cake Doughnuts

MAKES: About 1 dozen doughnuts and holes | TIME: About 1 hour

These old-fashioned doughnuts are leavened with baking powder rather than yeast, which gives them a denser, more cakelike crumb and a satisfyingly crisp crust. This dough doesn't need to rest, making it a good choice for spontaneous breakfasts. If chocolate isn't your thing, try orange or one of the other glazes on pages 857–858, cinnamon sugar, or nothing at all.

1 recipe Chocolate Glaze (page 858; optional)
3½ cups all-purpose flour, plus more for rolling out the dough
1 tablespoon baking powder
1 teaspoon salt
¾ teaspoon freshly grated nutmeg (optional)
2 eggs
⅔ cups sugar
¾ cup milk
4 tablespoons (½ stick) butter, melted and cooled
Good-quality vegetable oil for frying, plus more for greasing

1. Make the glaze first if you're using it; have it ready in a shallow bowl.
2. Combine the flour, baking powder, salt, and the nutmeg if you're using it. In a separate bowl, beat the eggs and sugar until thick, then stir in the milk and melted butter. Add the flour mixture a little at a time, mixing first with a whisk and then switching to your hands once it gets too thick. The dough should be sticky but hold together; if it's too wet, add flour a tablespoon at a time until it comes together.
3. Transfer the dough to a well-floured surface and knead a few times. Roll it out to ½-inch thick; if it contracts as you roll, let it rest for a few minutes, then try again. Dip a doughnut cutter, a 3-inch cookie cutter, or the rim of a sturdy glass in flour to cut out the doughnuts; cut out the holes with a smaller cookie cutter or shot glass (save them and fry along with the doughnuts). Gather any scraps together, being careful not to overwork them, and repeat. Arrange the doughnuts on a floured or parchment paper–lined baking sheet and cover with a kitchen towel while you heat the oil.
4. Put 2 to 3 inches oil in a large pot over medium heat; bring it to 375°F. Line a large rimmed baking sheet with a wire rack.
5. Working in batches to avoid overcrowding, carefully add a few doughnuts to the oil. Cook until the bottoms are deep golden, about a minute, then turn them with a slotted spoon and cook on the other side for another minute. Doughnut holes cook faster, less than 30 seconds per side. As they finish, transfer the doughnuts to the prepared racks and repeat with the remaining dough, adjusting the heat as needed to keep the oil at 375°F.

6. When the doughnuts are cool enough to handle, stir the glaze, then dip the doughnuts in the glaze or drizzle it on. Serve as soon as possible.

Breakfast Cereals

No one says you have to buy cereal in a box or bag. You can make all of these whole-grain breakfasts in large quantities well in advance, even the cooked ones—refrigerate them for up a week and warm them by the bowl in the microwave. So nothing could be more convenient.

Buy your grains, if possible, in bulk at a natural food store, where they are liable to be fresher (and certainly cheaper) than the packaged stuff. And be sure to check out the recipes in the Grains chapter starting on page 425 to make satisfying savory breakfasts.

Oatmeal or Other Creamy Breakfast Cereal

MAKES: 2 servings | TIME: 15 minutes

You can cook any kind of rolled or flaked grain this way—try wheat, rye, quinoa, millet, kamut, or brown rice flakes. Please don't bother with quick-cooking or instant oats; the old-fashioned style takes barely 5 minutes more, and the flavor and texture are far better.

¼   teaspoon salt
1   cup rolled oats or other rolled or flaked grain
     Butter (optional)
     Sweetener like maple syrup, sugar, or honey, and/or milk or cream for serving

1. Combine 2¼ cups water, the salt, and the oats in a small saucepan over high heat. When the water boils, turn the heat down to low and cook, stirring, until the water is just absorbed, about 5 minutes. Add butter if you like, cover the pan, and turn off the heat.
2. Five minutes later, uncover the pan and stir. Add a sweetener and dairy if you like, and serve.

RICH OATMEAL OR OTHER CREAMY BREAKFAST CEREAL
Substitute whole milk for some or all of the water.

THICK OATMEAL OR OTHER CREAMY BREAKFAST CEREAL
Reduce the water or milk to 1¾ cups.

Grits

MAKES: 2 to 4 servings | TIME: 20 minutes

Grits are made from ground dried hominy (a form of corn; see page 464). And I cook them a little differently than I do polenta (made from straight dried corn; see page 460). The flavor difference is subtle. But grits are a Southern favorite, mostly served as a breakfast side with butter, or as a meal topped with something savory like Still the Simplest and Best Shrimp Dish (page 542).

2½   cups water, or half milk and half water
1   cup grits (preferably stone-ground)
      Salt and pepper
1   tablespoon butter, plus more to taste

1. Put the water or milk and water in a small saucepan and bring to a boil over medium-high heat. Turn the heat down to low and slowly stir or whisk in the grits. Beat with a wire whisk to eliminate lumps.
2. Turn the heat down to a minimum and cover the saucepan. Cook, stirring occasionally, until all the water is absorbed and the grits are creamy, 10 to 15 minutes. If the mixture becomes too thick, whisk in a bit more water. Sprinkle with salt and pepper, stir in butter, and serve.

CHEESY GRITS Omit the butter in Step 2, and add up to 4 ounces grated cheddar, Parmesan, or manchego cheese. Stir constantly until it melts.

SCRAPPLE Cook a double recipe of grits as directed; you can use cornmeal if you like. When the grits are just about done, stir in 1 to 2 cups chopped cooked bacon or sausage meat, along with 1 tablespoon minced fresh sage or 1 teaspoon dried sage. Continue to cook until the mixture is thick. Pack it into a greased small loaf pan, cover with plastic wrap, and refrigerate overnight. At breakfast time, cut into ½-inch-thick slices and pan-fry the slices in butter, oil, or bacon fat over medium heat until browned and crisp on both sides, about 3 minutes per side.

Granola, My New Way

MAKES: About 8 cups | TIME: 40 minutes

I've made granola many ways over the years—but always without oil since even a little tastes greasy to me. What's changed here is that I now give the oats a head start. It's even more foolproof to make and vary. Be sure to see the sidebar on page 750 for more ideas.

6 cups rolled oats (not quick-cooking or instant)

2 cups nuts or seeds or a combination (see the sidebar on page 751)

1 cup shredded coconut

1 teaspoon ground cinnamon, or to taste
Salt

½ to 1 cup honey or maple syrup, or to taste

1 cup raisins or chopped dried fruit

1. Heat the oven to 300°F. Spread the oats evenly on a rimmed baking sheet and bake, stirring occasionally, until they darken a little, about 20 minutes, Scatter the nuts on top and bake until they begin to toast, about 5 minutes. Scatter the coconut over the nuts and bake until golden, another 5 minutes.

2. Drizzle the honey over the granola and stir with a spatula to combine. Return the pan to the oven and bake, turning once or twice, until the granola is as brown as you like; the darker it gets without burning, the crunchier it will be.

3. Remove the pan from the oven and fold in the raisins. Cool in the pan on a rack, stirring once in a while until the granola reaches room temperature. Transfer to a sealed container and store in the refrigerator; it will keep indefinitely.

Granola, My New
Way, page 749

THE BASICS OF DAIRY

This section provides a good overview for all milk products, including alternatives to cow's milk and a recipe for how to make your own fresh cheese.

First, a word about sourcing dairy. Like all fresh foods, locally sourced cheese and milk are always the best choice. Fortunately you don't always need to go to a farmers' market to find them. Many supermarkets now carry products from nearby producers. If they don't, ask that they do. If you can find organic locally raised dairy foods, all the better.

Now for some of the technical information: Most dairy products stay freshest refrigerated in their original containers, ideally at 40°F or a little below. (The exceptions are many cheeses, which can be held at room temperature for hours.) Pour or cut off what you need, then immediately return the rest to the fridge. Never put unused milk or cream back in the carton or bottle, or it'll cause the whole batch to spoil faster. Store cheese and butter tightly wrapped in the refrigerator. You can freeze unsalted butter for a month or so without noticeably affecting its flavor, and salted butter somewhat longer, but don't freeze milk or cream.

Finally, some definitions:

MILK—WHOLE (3.25% FAT); REDUCED-FAT (2% FAT); LOW-FAT (1% FAT); FAT-FREE, SKIM, OR NONFAT (0% FAT) I prefer whole milk for cooking and baking. You can use reduced-fat (but not fat-free), but the results won't be as rich. If you can't tolerate cow's milk, then substitute grain, soy, or nut milks as you prefer.

BUTTERMILK This tangy, thick, and sometimes lumpy liquid isn't what it used to be: the liquid that remained after churning butter. Now it's made from milk of any fat content, cultured with lactic acid–producing bacteria, so it's more like thin yogurt than anything else. Use it for baking, flavoring mashed potatoes, or making cold sauces, dips, and dressings. If you ever see true old-fashioned buttermilk (called "traditional buttermilk"), grab it; the difference is amazing.

Customizing Granola

The components of granola fall into these categories. Use them to vary the main recipe as you like.

SWEETENERS

- Maple syrup
- Brown sugar
- Molasses
- Agave nectar or brown rice syrup

FLAVORINGS

- **Spices:** cinnamon, nutmeg, cloves, cardamom, anise, coriander, allspice
- Vanilla extract (mixed with the sweetener)
- Peanut butter, other nut butter, or tahini
- **Ginger:** fresh, ground, or candied
- Orange, lemon, or grapefruit zest

CRUNCH AND CHEW

- **Nuts:** peanuts, almonds, walnuts, pecans, pistachios, cashews, hazelnuts, macadamias
- **Seeds:** sesame, sunflower, flax
- **Dried fruits:** apricots, dates, cranberries, cherries, blueberries, apples, pineapple, pears, papaya, mango
- Chocolate or carob chips

For a quick and direct substitute, you can "sour" regular milk. Let 1¾ cups milk come to room temperature (or microwave it for 30 seconds or so). Stir in 2 tablespoons white vinegar and let the mixture sit until clabbered (thick and lumpy) about 10 minutes—you'll know.

CREAM You'll see all sorts of confusing labels for cream, but the kind you want is heavy cream, not whipping or light cream, without any additives or emulsifiers, and not ultrapasteurized (which takes longer to whip and has a distinctive, definitely cooked, flavor). Generally 1 cup cream whips up to about 2 cups. The fat content of heavy cream is 36 percent or more, while that of whipping cream ranges from 30 percent to 36 percent.

HALF-AND-HALF Half milk, half cream, with a fat content that can range anywhere from 10.5 percent to 18 percent. It's nice in soups or sauces when you don't need quite the richness of heavy cream, and you might already have it on hand for your morning coffee. But you could also mix your own.

SOUR CREAM A cream with some of the fat removed and cultured with lactic acid bacteria to make it thick and produce its characteristic tangy flavor. Sour cream can be tricky to cook with because it can curdle—though not as quickly as yogurt—so add it to other ingredients over very low heat. I don't recommend reduced-fat sour creams, but if you must, find one without a lot of added ingredients and stabilizers.

CRÈME FRAÎCHE Similar to sour cream in that it's cultured, only the cream contains more fat and the culture is milder. So it's less sour than sour cream and a little thinner, but rich and a decadent addition to many recipes and doesn't curdle when heated. Crème fraîche is easier to find these days than it used to be, but can be expensive. To make your own: Put 1 cup cream in a small glass bowl and stir in 2 tablespoons buttermilk or yogurt. Cover and let sit at room temperature until thickened, anywhere from 12 to 24 hours. Cover tightly, refrigerate, and use within a week or so.

YOGURT Cultured milk, made with bacteria that produce its unique flavor and texture. Look for "live, active cultures" or similar terminology on the label, and avoid any with gelatins, gums, or stabilizers. Yogurt is available in whole, low-fat, and nonfat versions, as well as all sorts of crazy flavors. But you can flavor yogurt yourself (see far right); you can also make it yourself (see at right). It can be warmed gently but not heated to the point it bubbles or it will curdle. In recipes, whole-milk yogurt always gives the richest results. You can substitute the thicker strained or Greek yogurt (see at right) in recipes though it will curdle the same way.

COTTAGE CHEESE The result of separating milk with a coagulant (see "The Basics of Making Fresh Cheese," page 756), cottage cheese is fresh milk curds with just a little whey. Like milk, it comes in whole, reduced-fat, and fat-free varieties. It's lumpier than other dairy products but if that bothers, you purée it to use like yogurt—delicious. To make your own, see page 758.

BUTTER Butter is fat, milk solids, and water; the supermarket standard is 80 percent fat, which means about 20 percent is water; higher-fat butter—sometimes labeled European—tends to be higher quality and better tasting. The only way to know the exact fat content is to read the nutritional label on the package. Always buy unsalted butter, also called sweet butter; keep what you need in an airtight container in the fridge and store extra sticks wrapped well in the freezer, to prolong freshness and avoid absorbing odors. Never use whipped butter in recipes, because its volume isn't the same as stick butter. Clarified butter—melted butter with the milk solids skimmed or poured off—can be heated to a higher temperature without burning.

UHT MILK Short for "ultra-high-temperature milk," this is the nonrefrigerated stuff you see in vacuum-sealed boxes on supermarket shelves. UHT is always dated and after opening, it keeps for a few days like fresh milk in the refrigerator. It's great to have some in the pantry.

Yogurt

MAKES: 1 quart | **TIME:** Overnight or longer, largely unattended

Though many excellent-quality yogurts are sold in stores, there is nothing quite like the flavor of homemade, especially when you use a super-fresh whole milk. And though yogurt is a little trickier to make than fresh cheese (see page 756)—mostly because the temperature must be controlled for a long time while it ferments—it's easy enough to get the hang of. Whole milk makes the richest yogurt, though you can use any kind of dairy milk you like. And once you make your first batch, reserve ½ cup so you have a starter for the next.

    4 cups milk
    ½ cup natural yogurt with active cultures, ideally
       at room temperature

1. Put the milk in a small to medium saucepan and bring it just to a boil; turn off the heat and cool to 110°–115°F; use an instant-read thermometer to be sure.

2. Whisk the yogurt into the milk. Put in a yogurt maker, a prewarmed thermos or a heated bowl (fill either with boiling water and let sit for a few minutes). Then wrap the bowl in a towel or blanket and set in a warm place, like near a heat source or in a sunny spot. The idea is to keep the mixture at about 100°F.

3. Do not disturb the mixture at all for at least 6 hours. Then carefully check by tilting the container to see whether the milk has thickened and become a little lumpy. If not, leave it alone for up to another 6 hours. When the mixture looks, tastes, and smells like thin yogurt, refrigerate in airtight containers and use within 1 week.

STRAINED YOGURT Most commonly known as Greek yogurt, though there are variations from other countries: After you make the yogurt, line a fine-meshed strainer with a coffee filter or several layers of cheesecloth. Put the strainer over a large bowl and pour in the yogurt. Let it drain in the refrigerator until it reaches the desired consistency, usually after 1 to 2 hours.

YOGURT CHEESE You can make this with store-bought yogurt too. There are even filters available specifically for this purpose: Instead of refrigerating the yogurt, put it in several layers of cheesecloth or a jelly bag and suspend it over the sink or a large bowl. Let drain for at least 6 hours, preferably longer, until the yogurt has a cream cheese–like consistency. (You can reserve and use the liquid—whey—in smoothies, soups, and sauces.) Store and use exactly as you would cream cheese.

---

8 IDEAS FOR FLAVORING PLAIN YOGURT

Start by adding just a little, then adjust to taste.

1. Honey
2. Maple syrup
3. Vanilla extract, with or without a sweetener
4. Chopped nuts
5. Preserves or jam
6. Any spice mixture (see pages 32–35)
7. Fresh or cooked salsa (pages 55–58 and 71–74)
8. Any chutney (pages 61–62)

Cheese

The variety of cheeses is staggering. They may be made from cow's, sheep's, or goat's milk (or for that matter, yak's, water buffalo's, or camel's), or a mixture; they may be fresh or aged—from as little as 30 days to as long as several years. This is what makes shopping for cheese so much fun.

For most of us, cooking with cheese or eating cheese as a snack or appetizer with crackers is far more common than eating a cheese course. But the principles that determine which cheese works best in which dishes—strength of flavor, firmness, graininess, the ability to crumble or melt—also work for eating cheese plain.

Store cheese in the warmest part of the refrigerator—a compartment in the door is probably best—preferably in a resealable container. Specialty cheese paper also works, as do wax or parchment paper; and even though almost everyone uses it, plastic wrap should be avoided as it doesn't allow the cheese to breathe, and can transfer its smell to the cheese.

A bit of white or green mold doesn't mean cheese has gone bad; just trim it off. In general, if a cheese smells

18 Cheesy Recipes Elsewhere in the Book

1. Blue Cheese Dressing (page 59)
2. Mornay (Cheese) Sauce (page 79)
3. Marinated Mozzarella (page 96)
4. Herbed Goat Cheese (page 100)
5. Cheese Fondue (page 118)
6. Spinach-Cheese Triangles (page 122)
7. Bean and Cheese Empanadas (page 126)
8. Chile Rellenos (page 319)
9. Risotto with Three Cheeses (page 441)
10. One-Pot Pasta with Butter and Parmesan (page 478)
11. Baked Macaroni and Cheese (page 499)
12. Meaty Lasagne (page 502)
13. Cheese Ravioli (page 513)
14. Cheese Tortellini (page 515)
15. Cheese Soufflé (page 735)
16. Grilled Cheese (page 804)
17. Cheese Quesadilla (page 814)
18. Pizza with Tomato Sauce and Mozzarella (page 819)

like anything other than ammonia or sulfur, it's fine. And take a little nibble; if it tastes fine to you, it is. But if a bloomy rind cheese (like brie or Camembert) develops a pinkish-red mold, throw it out. Beyond those caveats, follow your nose and trust your instincts.

Most cheese is best eaten at room temperature, which can take several hours for a piece of cheese taken right from the fridge; keep it covered with paper or a clean kitchen towel, or place it in a cheese dome until you're ready to serve it.

What follows is a rather idiosyncratic overview of the types of cheeses used in cooking; it is hardly comprehensive. It's meant to illustrate the ways that cheese can be incorporated into cooking, and those I use most often. I encourage you to experiment with other cheeses too.

ALL-PURPOSE CHEESES

These are kitchen workhorses that can be used in recipes in a multitude of ways, from tangy dips to rich pasta dishes, from pancakes to desserts.

GRATING CHEESES Parmesan is king (see "Parmesan, the Ultimate All-Purpose Cheese," page 755), but there's also pecorino Romano, Manchego, Grana Padano (the next closest thing to real Parmesan, and less expensive), dry Jack, and more. They can be sharp and strong, like Romano (which is also the saltiest), or mild enough to snack on, like Manchego. Use them grated in pasta sauces, to garnish and enrich all sorts of dishes, and in

combination with other dairy for delicious dips. You can hardly go wrong.

RICOTTA In between the best (found at specialty stores and some farmers markets) and the mass-produced kinds is the easy "ricotta" you make yourself (page 758). Wonderful spread on toast with a drizzle of olive oil or jam, or stirred into a sauce or grain dish to add richness, or used as a stuffing for pasta. Nice to have around, though it doesn't keep for more than a week, usually.

BLUE CHEESES Gorgonzola, Roquefort, Cabrales, other European blues, and American blue cheese like Maytag. Blue-veined cheeses, which intentionally cultivate flavorful but harmless molds, may be an acquired taste, but devotees (I'm one) crave them. Try sprinkling some strong blue cheese on plain cooked vegetables along with bread crumbs and running the whole thing under the broiler. Wonderful in sauces, dressings, and dips.

FETA Though many feta cheeses are now packed in airtight plastic, I prefer to buy those stored in brine. The flavor is fresh and milky, with salty rather than sharp notes, and the texture is dry and crumbly. If the feta you buy is too salty for you, rinse the cheese and pat it dry before using; next time, try a different variety. Use it crumbled into salads or grain dishes, or mashed with lemon juice and fresh herbs and spread on crostini or crackers.

 fast make ahead vegetarian

FRESH SOFT GOAT CHEESE Sometimes called *chèvre* (which is simply French for "goat"), this distinctive cheese is great used as part of creamy fillings and spreads or dolloped on top of a bowl of soup to be swirled in for a bit of tangy richness.

CREAM CHEESE Supermarket varieties only hint at the potential of cream cheese, which is tangy, rich, and creamy at its best.

FRESH MEXICAN-STYLE CHEESES: QUESO FRESCO, COTIJA Not brined, so less salty and milder than feta, but they crumble the same way and are used as a garnish on traditional tacos, enchiladas, salads, and soups.

MELTING CHEESES

The best melting cheeses melt smoothly; it's best to grate or slice them thin for quick, even melting. Use these types of cheeses to top dishes for a creamy finish, make into a grilled cheese sandwich, or use for quesadillas or other Mexican dishes like enchiladas (see page 759).

Parmesan, the Ultimate All-Purpose Cheese

I cannot emphasize how important it is to spring for the real thing—Parmigiano-Reggiano—which is produced only in Italy (and, in fact, only in a small part of the Emilia-Romagna region). Look for irregularly sized chunks with a waxy rind marked with the name in the distinctive pinhole-punched lettering. Parmesan has a complex, nutty flavor and a slightly grainy but almost buttery texture that goes with nearly everything.

You can grate it finely or coarsely, or "shave" it with a vegetable peeler. And don't throw away the rind; save rinds in your freezer so they're always handy. They are great for seasoning and enriching soups and stews; cook chunks of rind for 15 minutes or longer and they'll become soft enough to eat.

SWISS-STYLE CHEESES: GRUYÈRE, FONTINA, EMMENTAL ("SWISS"), RACLETTE, APPENZELLER, COMTÉ Though each of these is unique, I'm grouping them together here because they share a velvety texture when melted and a complex, nutty taste that makes them good choices for combining with other ingredients.

MONTEREY JACK, QUESO ASADERO, AND QUESO OAXACA Mild, with good body when melted, these rindless cheeses are perfect for Mexican food as a creamy counterpoint to assertive seasoning.

CHEDDAR I prefer sharp cheddar cheeses with at least a little bit of age on them, because they are more flavorful and melt better. Cheddars are also good cheeses for snacking, especially when combined with apples, dried fruit, nuts, and whole grain toast.

MOZZARELLA Freshly made mozzarella, which often comes packed in water, is quite different from the drier, slightly aged brick kind. Fresh mozzarella tastes like milk, only with a little tang, and should never be rubbery or stringy. It's a great cheese to melt on pizza or pasta—obviously—or to eat raw in salads or sandwiches.

CHEESES THAT KEEP THEIR SHAPE DURING COOKING

These cheeses have a high melting point and will soften rather than melt when heated. They can be thrown on the grill or fried or seared in a skillet, developing a delicious brown crust. In some cheeses, the interior will get creamy; in others it will retain its structure when heated through.

HALLOUMI A semihard brined cheese usually made from a combination of goat's and sheep's milk. It originated in Cyprus but is now made around the world and is particularly popular in Greece, Turkey, and the Middle East. It has a distinctive salty flavor.

PANEER A mild fresh cheese made from water buffalo's or cow's milk that is a staple in the cooking of India,

Pakistan, Nepal, and Bangladesh in dishes like saag paneer. Look for it in Indian food stores, or use Fresh Cheese, the Easy Way (at right).

QUESO DE FREÍR OR QUESO PARA FREÍR A firm, mild cow's milk cheese with a salty taste. It is popular throughout Central America and the Caribbean, usually prepared by slicing, then frying or pan-searing. Look for it in the supermarket where other Hispanic dairy products are sold; it may simply be labeled "Grilling Cheese."

KASSERI, KEFALOTYRI, AND GRAVIERA These Greek cheeses, made from a combination of sheep's, cow's, and/or goat's milk, are great choices for pan-searing.

THE BASICS OF MAKING FRESH CHEESE

Yes, you can make cheese, and I strongly urge you to give it a try. It's easy, fun, and everything you need is available at the supermarket. Best of all, the recipe requires virtually no practice; your very first batch will blow you away.

All cheese begins by separating curds (the milk solids) and whey (the watery liquid). Most commercially made cheeses rely on rennet—an enzyme from the stomach of cows (though there are vegetable rennets)—to curdle milk, but there are easier ways for the home cook; buttermilk, which acts as a mild-tasting and effective coagulant, is the best. The result is tender cheese with a pure, milky flavor, akin to the Indian staple paneer; true queso fresco, the fresh white cheese common in Mexico; the fromage blanc of France; or a dozen other products made around the world. To use fresh cheese, just cut it into slices or cubes or gently crumble it by hand or with two forks; it's too soft to grate. Fresh cheese will keep for 3 or 4 days in the fridge, though you may freeze it, tightly wrapped, for up to 3 months.

Fresh Cheese, the Easy Way

MAKES: 6 to 8 servings | **TIME:** 2 hours, largely unattended

The recipe—and all the variations except for the cream cheese—work with 1%, 2%, and whole milk, which of course makes the richest cheeses. If you live near a farm or have a good local source and can find super-fresh whole milk, you'll get the best flavor.

½ gallon milk
1 quart buttermilk
Salt (optional)

1. Put the milk in a large, heavy-bottomed pot over medium-high heat. Cook, stirring occasionally to keep it from scorching, until the milk bubbles up the sides of the pot, about 10 minutes.
2. Line a strainer or colander with a triple layer of cheesecloth or a clean piece of undyed cotton muslin and set it in the sink or over a bowl if you want to save the whey. Have a long piece of kitchen string ready.
3. Add the buttermilk to the boiling milk all at once and stir constantly until the mixture separates into curds and whey; this will take just a minute or so. It will look like cooked egg whites suspended in a slightly thick yellowish liquid. Remove from the heat and stir in a large pinch salt if you like.
4. Carefully pour the mixture through the strainer so that the curds collect in the cloth and the whey drains off (see page 753 for ideas how to use it). Gather up the corners of the cloth and twist the top to start shaping the curds into a ball. Run the bundle under cold water until it's cool enough to handle. Keep twisting and squeezing out the whey until the bundle feels firm and dry. Don't worry about handling it roughly; it can take it.
5. Tie the string around the top to hold it tight, then tie the string around the handle of a long spoon or a stick to suspend the cheese back over the pot or over a deep bowl to drain. Let it rest undisturbed until cool and set,

 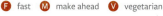

about 90 minutes. Untie the bundle, remove the cheese from the cloth, and serve immediately, or wrap in plastic and refrigerate for up to 3 days. Or freeze, wrapped well or in an airtight container, for up to 3 months.

FRESH COTTAGE CHEESE Incredible stuff; drain as dry or as moist as you like: Follow the recipe through Step 3. In Step 4, after you pour the curds and whey through the cheesecloth, leave the curds loose in the strainer until they've drained the amount of moisture you desire, anywhere from 30 to 60 minutes. Then scoop the curds into a container and store in the refrigerator for no more than a week.

SHORTCUT RICOTTA Also unbelievable, especially with top-quality milk, even though it's not made the traditional way: Reduce the amount of buttermilk to 2 cups and proceed with the recipe through Step 3. The mixture will look like thickened buttermilk. In Step 4, after you pour it through the cheesecloth, leave the ricotta in the strainer until it reaches the texture you like, anywhere from 30 to 60 minutes. Then scoop the ricotta into a container and store in the refrigerator for no more than a week.

BRINED FRESH CHEESE Like a mild feta: After the cheese has set, mix a brine of 2 tablespoons salt and 2 cups water in a jar or storage container. Submerge the cheese in the brine and refrigerate for at least 24 hours before eating.

---

4 WAYS TO FLAVOR FRESH CHEESE

In Step 4, after pouring the curds and whey into the cloth-lined strainer, immediately stir any of the following ingredients into the curds (up to the amount indicated) and proceed with the recipe.

1. Up to 2 tablespoons curry powder, chaat masala, or garam masala (to make your own, see pages 32–34)
2. Up to ¼ cup any Chile Paste (page 40)
3. Up to ¼ cup Traditional Pesto (page 51) or any of the herb purées on page 52
4. Up to ¼ cup finely chopped Roasted Red Peppers (page 318), pimientos, piquillos, or olives

Finishing Fresh Cheese

STEP 1 Pour the coagulated, lumpy mixture into a cheesecloth-lined strainer.

STEP 2 Twist and squeeze out excess moisture.

STEP 3 Hang from a wooden spoon or other implement over the pot, the sink, or a bowl.

 F fast **M** make ahead **V** vegetarian

Cheese Enchiladas

MAKES: 6 to 8 servings | TIME: About 1½ hours; less if you use premade sauce

Simple enough for a weeknight, especially if you have sauce already made. Use anything else you like to fill the enchiladas—along with or in place of the cheese—including simply seasoned cooked ground beef, Shredded Pork (page 697), sliced Roasted Red Peppers or chiles (page 318), or even roasted vegetables. Just don't overfill them.

    2 recipes (about 4 cups) Red Enchilada Sauce
       (page 73)
       Good-quality vegetable oil, for frying
   24 6-inch corn tortillas, plus more if any break
    3 cups shredded asadero or Monterey Jack
       cheese
    ½ cup crumbled queso fresco for garnish
    ½ cup chopped red onion or scallion for garnish
    ½ cup chopped fresh cilantro for garnish
       Lime wedges for garnish

1. Prepare the sauce if you haven't already. (You can cool the sauce, then refrigerate it for up to 3 days; reheat gently before proceeding.)

2. Heat the oven to 350°F. Spoon a thin layer of the sauce in a 13 × 9-inch baking dish. Put about ½ inch of the oil in a medium skillet over medium-high heat. When hot but not smoking, cook the tortillas one at a time until softened and pliable, about 10 seconds. Drain on towels. Add more oil to the pan as needed.

3. Sprinkle about 2 tablespoons of the asadero cheese down the center of a tortilla, roll it tightly, and put the tortilla in the prepared dish, seam side down. Repeat with all the tortillas and asadero. The tortillas should be packed in snugly against one another, in a single layer. Cover the top with some more sauce and bake until bubbly, 20 to 30 minutes. Reheat the remaining sauce. When the enchiladas come out of the oven, sprinkle them with the queso fresco, onion, and cilantro. Serve with lime wedges on the side and pass the sauce at the table.

CHEESE ENCHILADAS WITH GREEN SAUCE Also known as Enchiladas Suisas: Instead of the red sauce, prepare a double recipe of Green Enchilada Salsa (page 73). Increase the amount of asadero to 5 cups. Use the remaining 2 cups cheese to sprinkle on top of the enchiladas before baking. Garnish as in the main recipe.

CHICKEN ENCHILADAS Use either red or green sauce and omit the cheese from the filling. Prepare Grilled or Broiled Chicken with Cilantro and Lime (page 620). When it's cool enough to handle, remove and discard the skin, pull the meat from the bone, and break it into bite-sized pieces. You'll need about 3 packed cups meat. Use 2 tablespoons of the chicken to fill each tortilla. Bake and garnish as in the main recipe.

16 Iconic Mexican Dishes Elsewhere in the Book

Be sure to check out the salsa, spices, and dips sections of the book (or the Index) for seasonings and condiments.

1. Nachos (page 110)
2. Lightning-Quick Fish Soup, Mexican Style (page 116)
3. Tortilla Soup (page 165)
4. Quick-Pickled Vegetables, Mexican Style (page 229)
5. Chiles Rellenos (page 319)
6. Refried Beans (page 393)
7. Tamales (page 416)
8. Chipotle Pozole (page 469)

9. Naked Chicken Enchiladas (page 612)
10. Turkey Thighs in Almond Mole (page 652)
11. Huevos Rancheros (page 729)
12. Flour Tortillas (page 781)
13. Fish Tacos, Four Ways (page 811)
14. Cheese Quesadillas (page 814)
15. Fajitas Burritos (page 815)
16. Flan (Crème Caramel) (page 890)

Bread, Sandwiches, and Pizza

CHAPTER AT A GLANCE

The Basics of Flour 762

The Basics of Leavening 765

Quick Breads 767

Unleavened Flatbreads 777

The Basics of Yeast Bread 781

Sandwiches, Tacos, and Burritos 803

Pizza 816

More than any other act of cooking, baking—bread especially—will always symbolize love and warmth. Making bread at home, whether quickly with baking powder or slowly with yeast, has steadily returned to favor among home cooks over the last twenty years.

I'm thrilled to see the tide turn; when I last updated this chapter, it seemed almost necessary to apologize for the little bit of mess and attention baking requires. And though it's still true that there might be some dishes, the process is easy, and the time it takes can be bent to your own schedule (see page 783).

Basic information about key baking ingredients opens the chapter. After that, I start with beloved recipes like corn bread and biscuits that you can make on a weeknight or for weekend breakfast. They're called "quick breads" since they're easy to assemble and get an immediate blast of airiness from baking soda or baking powder (or both). This new edition includes some new twists and streamlining with variations, including a terrific stovetop bread that's a great entry point if you've never made bread before, as well as tortillas and other simple flatbreads.

The yeast bread recipes that follow build in complexity, though none are difficult or too time consuming. The six-thousand-year-old process hasn't changed much since 1859, when Louis Pasteur made the commercial production of standardized yeast possible; modern equipment and methods only make the work easier and more reliable. Making bread still feels magical, however, so I urge you to try Jim Lahey's popular No-Knead Bread—prepare yourself to be blown away and hooked on baking for life.

Even if you buy bread and tortillas, this chapter will inspire you to make classic and improvised sandwiches, tacos, burritos, and wraps. And of course, any discussion of bread must include everyone's favorite, pizza. Together these recipes provide the perfect foundation for using leftovers, packing office and school lunches, and getting easy suppers on the table fast.

THE BASICS OF FLOUR

The backbone of all baking is flour, which is ground (milled) from wheat and other grains. Though the milling determines how much of the grain is actually used and the texture of the flour, the type of grain and how it's grown also influence the characteristics of the final bread. So if you become an enthusiast, the source of the wheat will become important to you, too.

The standard wheat flour for baking in this country is all-purpose white, though as the interest in whole wheat and other whole grains increases, so does interest in flours milled from them, as well as flours made from nuts, beans, and even roots. I've included information about how to use some of these alternative flours here. They may be called "flour," but they don't have the same baking qualities those made from wheat—I get into that more in "The Magic of Gluten" on page 788—and they don't taste the same.

Here are the primary flours you'll need for baking the breads in this chapter, plus a few more if you might want to experiment further.

WHITE FLOURS

These are "regular" flours, the finely ground endosperm of the wheat kernel, without the bran or germ. (See page 426 for more on grain anatomy.) I use only unbleached flour; the bleaching process uses harsh chemicals and serves no purpose other than cosmetic.

ALL-PURPOSE FLOUR As the name implies, this is the most versatile flour. Since it's milled from a variety of different wheats, it has moderate protein—8 to 11 percent—so it works well in a range of applications, from pastry to noodles to bread. It may also be enriched

 fast · M make ahead · V vegetarian

with vitamins and nutrients in an attempt to compensate for those that are stripped through the removal of bran and germ.

BREAD FLOUR Bread flour is milled from hard varieties of wheat, so it has more protein than all-purpose flour—up to 14 percent—and therefore greater gluten strength. Many people choose it for elastic, easy-to-handle bread doughs that produce a chewy crumb and sturdy crust. Bread flour is sometimes "conditioned" with ascorbic acid, but even moderate quantities can make the finished dough taste slightly sour, so you're better off without it.

CAKE AND PASTRY FLOURS The low protein content of these flours (5 to 8 percent for cake, 8 to 9 percent for pastry) comes from milling all soft wheat varieties. The doughs and batters made from cake or pastry flour don't develop much elasticity, and result in a tender, delicate crumb in cakes and flaky pastries.

SELF-RISING FLOUR Also called "phosphated flour." This is essentially all-purpose flour plus salt and a leavening agent like baking powder, and has limited use for biscuits and quick breads but not yeast breads so I never use it.

WHOLE WHEAT FLOURS

Produced by milling all three components of the wheat kernel—the bran, the germ, and the endosperm. This give them more fiber and nutrients than white flour (up to 14 percent protein), as well as a pleasantly assertive flavor, especially in breads. But anything made with 100 percent whole wheat flour will be heavier and denser than with white flours, so I sometimes combine it with some white flour for lighter results. To incorporate whole wheat flour into a recipe without making other adjustments, replace half of the white flour with whole wheat, but expect the results to be heavier and less delicate, with more pronounced wheat flavor.

WHOLE WHEAT FLOUR When this is how the flour is labeled, think of it as all-purpose whole wheat flour. It

should say whether it's whole grain or 100% whole grain. If not, it's some lesser "extraction," meaning some of the bran and/or germ has been sifted out.

WHOLE WHEAT PASTRY FLOUR Milled from soft wheat and about 10 percent protein. Like its white counterpart, it produces a delicate crumb in cakes and pastries, but with the flavor and nutrition characteristics of whole wheat. The same rules apply here as to regular whole wheat flour: Substitute this for no more than 50 percent of the cake flour in any recipe.

WHITE WHOLE WHEAT FLOUR Similar to conventional whole wheat flour in baking performance and nutritional profile, this relatively new variety is milled from white wheat cultivars instead of red wheats. It has a relatively mild flavor, so it's perfect if you don't like the strong flavor of conventional whole wheat flour but want the nutritional advantage.

NON-WHEAT FLOURS

These are most common specialty flours that lack the ability to form gluten like wheat flours. For some guidance about how to substitute them (and others) in recipes, see the chart on page 764.

RYE FLOUR Milled from rye berries, a grass similar to, but different from, wheat. The darker the flour, the more bran is left, the stronger the flavor, and the higher the protein and fiber, which makes this a nice substitute for a small amount of the white flour in bread recipes. Since it has low gluten-forming ability, rye flour is almost always combined with white flour. But even if your ratio is high in wheat flour, baked goods made with rye flour tend to be moist, dense, deeply colored, and slightly (deliciously) sour tasting. Pumpernickel flour is dark whole grain rye; it makes a delicious addition to many breads.

CORNMEAL Ground dried corn, available in fine, medium, and coarse grinds and in yellow, white, and blue colors, depending on the corn. Stone-ground cornmeal—which is generally what you want—retains the hull and germ, so it's more nutritious and flavorful than common steel-ground cornmeal, though also more perishable; store it in the freezer. In yeast breads you can generally substitute up to 10 percent cornmeal for wheat flour without adjusting the recipe. But you will see corn bread recipes that are anywhere from 50 to 100 percent cornmeal.

Corn flour is another name for finely ground cornmeal (but be careful; in recipes written in the UK, it refers to cornstarch). To make corn flour, grind medium or coarse cornmeal in a food processor for a few minutes.

BUCKWHEAT FLOUR Milled buckwheat (the hulled, crushed kernels of which are called groats; see page 454), is gluten free and is graded dark, medium, and light, depending on how much hull remains after milling. As with rye flour, the darker the color, the stronger the flavor. Buckwheat flour is slightly sour; it's most commonly used in pancakes, waffles, blintzes, crêpes, muffins, and noodles. In yeast breads, it must be combined with a gluten-forming flour like all-purpose or bread flour.

RICE FLOUR Also available as rice powder, ground rice, sweet rice flour, and cream of rice, these are ground,

Substituting Flours in Baking

Use this chart as a quick reference for replacing a portion of the all-purpose or bread flour. You can mix and match, but don't go over the maximum percentage for any one flour; the results will be denser—but more flavorful—than the all-white flour counterpart. When in doubt about the volume to use, just put the estimated amount of alternative flour (or flours) in the measuring cup first, then fill the rest of the way with all-purpose flour and level it off.

FLOUR	PROPORTION TO USE IN RECIPES
Whole Wheat	Up to half
Rye	
-light	Up to half
-medium	Up to one-third
-dark or pumpernickel	Up to one-quarter
Cornmeal	Up to one-sixth
Buckwheat	Up to one-quarter
Rice (any kind of true rice flour)	One-quarter to one-third
Nut	One-quarter to one-third
Soy	Up to one-quarter
Spelt	All; then either decrease water by one-quarter or increase flour by one-quarter
Oat	One-quarter to one-third
Potato	One-quarter to one-third

 fast make ahead  vegetarian

sifted raw white (or sometimes brown) rice. Beware that the grind can range from fine to almost coarse. In Southeast Asia it's used to make noodles, pastries, and sweets and as a thickening agent and coating. Gluten free.

BROWN RICE FLOUR Milled from rice that has had only the outer hull removed. Higher in protein and fiber than white rice flour, brown rice flour adds a nutty flavor and slight color to baked goods. It has a grainy, gritty texture that yields a dry, fine crumb.

NUT FLOURS Made by finely grinding nuts, nut flours—also called nut meals—are gluten free and high in protein and fat. They work fine in quick breads or for breading vegetables or croquettes, but you must mix them with gluten-producing flours in yeast breads; generally you can substitute up to 30 percent nut flour for wheat flour in baking without making other adjustments.

Almond flour is the most widely available nut flour, with a consistency that resembles cornmeal. You'll also find coconut flour, hazelnut flour, and chestnut flour, which has a complex, slightly sweet flavor and is sometimes used to make pasta.

SPELT FLOUR A high-protein, low-gluten-forming flour. Spelt has a pleasant nutty flavor and is a good wheat substitute for people with low tolerance for wheat, though some people with wheat allergies are also allergic to spelt. You can find both white and whole grain spelt flour.

OAT FLOUR Oat flour produces baked goods that are moist, crumbly, and nutty tasting. You can grind your own coarse oat flour by giving rolled oats a whirl in the blender or food processor. For yeast breads, use no more than 30 percent oat flour and the rest higher-protein flour.

THE BASICS OF LEAVENING

Baking soda, baking powder, yeast, and natural starters like sourdough are all leaveners, which means they give baked goods lift (the word *leaven* means "lighten"). They all work the same way: by producing carbon dioxide bubbles that are trapped by the dough or batter's structure and expand to make it rise.

Baking soda and powder, typically used in quick breads, cookies, cakes, and the like, are chemical leaveners. Yeasts are living organisms that produce carbon dioxide as they feed on the sugar and starch in bread and pastry doughs; they can be store-bought, or cultivated in starters like sourdough.

The recipes here have been developed so you don't have to worry about how much to add, or make substitutions. This rundown will explain why you're using what, when.

BAKING SODA

Baking soda (sodium bicarbonate) produces carbon dioxide only in the presence of liquid and acid, usually an acidic liquid, like buttermilk, yogurt, or vinegar. Every recipe that uses baking soda must have an acidic component or it will not rise. And since baking soda releases all of its gas at once, it's usually best to add it with the flour, and to bake the batter as soon as possible after mixing. The exceptions are in denser foods like cookies, where you want more controlled rise, and when there's also baking powder in the recipe.

BAKING POWDER

Baking powder is simply baking soda with a dry acid added to it, along with starch that keeps the baking powder dry and therefore inert until it is added to a recipe. Since it already contains an acid, it doesn't require an acidic ingredient in the recipe. Double-acting powder is the most common; it usually contains both cream of tartar and slower-acting sodium aluminum sulfate, so it releases gas in two phases and allows you to let the batter or dough sit for a bit before baking. Single-acting powders generally contain cream of tartar as the acid, which is activated by moisture, so the batter must be baked immediately after mixing, just like those containing baking soda. Too much baking powder can give baked goods a bitter taste and,

Gluten-Free Baking

The gluten formed by proteins in wheat flour accomplishes a great deal: It adds structure, texture, moisture, and flavor; this combination can't be duplicated by anything else, at least not generally. (See page 788 for more on gluten.) For the people who can't digest gluten, there are now more nonwheat flours and starches available than ever before, including ready-made gluten-free blends, optimized to mimic flour's role in different types of baked goods. These are in some cases quite good, and offer quality control and unbeatable convenience since you can swap them cup for cup for wheat flour. It's also easy enough to make your own blends; see the chart that follows for some examples.

A word about xanthan gum: I'm in favor of eating only "real" food, with ingredients you can pronounce and recognize. But don't rule out this key component of gluten-free baking. Xanthan gum is a fine white powder that results when a specific microorganism digests sugar, typically from corn; it has no flavor or noticeable texture, and can mimic gluten, adding elasticity, thickness, and body, for a more cohesive dough that you can easily handle and shape. And you can now find it in supermarkets. Take care to use it in very small amounts; true to its name, too much will make food gummy. Ground chia or flaxseeds mixed with water are a good substitute, as are gelatin and eggs, but xanthan gum is the most convenient to use.

These mixes can be substituted for wheat flours in equal measure, but keep in mind that there is always some variation when it comes to substituting flours.

WHEAT FLOUR TO REPLACE	GLUTEN-FREE MIX INGREDIENTS	YIELD
All-Purpose	1½ cups brown rice flour ¾ cup potato flour ¼ cup tapioca flour 1 teaspoon xanthan gum (optional)	2½ cups
Pastry	1¾ cups white rice flour ¾ cup potato flour ¼ cup tapioca flour	2¾ cups
Bread*	1½ cups brown rice flour ¾ cup potato flour ¾ cup sweet rice flour 2½ teaspoons xanthan gum	About 3 cups
Cake	1½ cups brown rice flour ½ cup potato starch ¼ cup tapioca flour ½ teaspoon xanthan gum	2¼ cups

* Consider replacing 2 tablespoons of the water in the recipe with 1 egg white for extra protein to take the place of the gluten.

if the air bubbles grow too big and break, even cause them to collapse.

YEAST

All the recipes here are calibrated for the dried yeast known as instant yeast (also called fast-acting, fast-rising, rapid-rise, and bread machine yeast). Since you can add it directly to the dough without dissolving first in liquid, it's fast, reliable, and convenient.

Instant yeast has ascorbic acid added (and sometimes traces of other ingredients too); this helps the dough stretch easily and increases loaf volumes. In most

 fast make ahead  vegetarian

breads, you won't notice any difference in flavor. It keeps almost forever, refrigerated.

Other kinds of yeast are fresh yeast (also called cake or compressed yeast; it's usually sold in foil-wrapped cakes of 0.6 ounce and must be refrigerated) and active dry yeast. Active dry yeast is still relatively common and was used by most home bakers until instant yeast came along. It's fresh yeast that has been pressed and dried until the moisture level reaches about 8 percent. Unlike instant, active dry yeast must be rehydrated in 110°F water before it's added to the dry ingredients; below 105°F it will remain inert; above 115°F it will die. So it's more finicky than instant.

SOURDOUGH STARTERS

Even though this book contains no bread made with a sourdough starter, once you start baking yeast breads you might be interested enough to try one; my book *How to Bake Everything* contains several recipes and more information on making and maintaining a starter.

Also called *levain* or "mother dough," sourdough is a natural starter that does not necessarily rely on yeast—though I am among the home bakers who believe a bit of yeast helps build a reliable sourdough and improves the bread's flavor. The idea is to mix flour and water, add a pinch yeast if you like, and let it sit for a period of days; the starter will catch airborne wild yeasts and *Lactobacillus* bacteria. The slow fermentation creates a characteristic tang and deep flavor. Then you maintain this starter by feeding it with more flour and water regularly.

Quick Breads

Making quick bread is easy: You mix the dry ingredients, then the wet ingredients, combine the two, and bake. Banana bread, corn bread, and muffins all fall under this category. No special techniques or equipment needed; even the choice of baking pans is flexible.

The batter—it can't be called a dough, because it's pourable, not kneadable—is rich, usually containing eggs, butter, and milk, often with at least a little sugar or other sweetener. It's usually leavened with baking powder, or sometimes use baking soda, and there are times when a combination is best. The goal is a delicate, cake-like crumb, moist interior, and nicely browned and still-tender crust with a little chew but no real crunch. To achieve this you need fat, which contributes to flavor and tenderness, and minimal mixing.

Overmixing will make quick breads tough by developing too much gluten—the exact opposite of what you want to achieve with yeasted breads. So heed this advice: Combine dry and wet ingredients as quickly

Freezing Breads and Bread Dough

Breads freeze well at various stages of the process. Soft, moister breads—like most quick breads—should be wrapped in plastic and then foil before freezing. Thaw in the refrigerator if time allows and then remove the wrapping. Warming is optional: Reseal in the foil and put in a 300°F oven until heated through but not dry.

Toss whole crusty yeasted loaves into plastic bags, close them tightly, and put in the freezer. Use them as soon as possible, either by thawing on the countertop or in the fridge and then crisping, unwrapped, in a 350°F oven for 10 minutes or so, or by reheating them, still frozen and loosely wrapped in foil, in a 400°F oven for about 20 minutes.

You can also freeze unbaked yeast doughs. After the first rise or after shaping, wrap tightly in foil or plastic wrap and freeze for up to several weeks. Thaw in the refrigerator, then finish any additional shaping and/or rise at room temperature. Bake according to the recipe.

Griddled Olive Oil Salt Bread

as you can and don't beat or stir the batter any more than necessary. When you see no more dry bits of flour, the job is done; don't worry about remaining lumps.

As a general rule, quick breads are best eaten the day they're made. (The exceptions, like banana bread, tend to be moist and more like cake, so they'll keep a couple days.) It's fine to bake them a few hours in advance and, once cool, keep them wrapped in wax paper or foil. If you'd like to freeze them for later or save leftovers, see "Freezing Breads and Bread Dough" (page 767).

Griddled Olive Oil Salt Bread

MAKES: 4 to 8 servings | **TIME:** About 40 minutes

These crumpet-like rolls are the fastest way to get fresh warm bread on the table. The rich and flaky dough is easier to handle than biscuit dough and takes to all sorts of additions, like cheese (especially Parmesan), chopped olives, or chopped fresh herbs. Just knead them in with your hands after processing. The breads are terrific warm, but keep surprisingly well for a day or two, stored in an airtight container.

- 3 cups all-purpose flour, plus more if needed
- 1 tablespoon baking powder
- 1 teaspoon salt, preferably coarse or sea salt, plus more for sprinkling
- ⅓ cup olive oil, plus more for shaping and frying
- 1 cup warm water

1. Put the flour, baking powder, and salt in a food processor and turn the machine on. Pour the olive oil, then most of the water, through the feed tube and process for about 30 seconds. Stop the machine and remove the cover. The dough should be in a well-defined, barely sticky, easy-to-handle ball. If it is too dry, add the remaining water 1 tablespoon at a time; process for 5 or 10 seconds after each addition. If it is too wet, which is unlikely, add a tablespoon or 2 flour and pulse until just incorporated.

2. Divide the dough into 8 pieces. Grease your hands with a little oil and pat each piece into a patty no more than ½ inch thick.

3. Heat a griddle or large skillet over medium heat and add enough olive oil to thinly coat the bottom. When it's hot, add as many breads as will fit comfortably without crowding; you might have to work in batches. Cook, undisturbed, until they begin to brown on the bottom, 5 to 10 minutes. Turn and cook until the other side is crisp and golden and the inside is firm and no longer raw (peek with a sharp knife), a few minutes more. Sprinkle with salt and serve.

Corn Bread

MAKES: About 6 servings | **TIME:** About 45 minutes

You might call the main recipe a general American corn bread, slightly spartan, neither too sweet nor too cakey. From here the adjustments vary from region to region and cook to cook. For more intensely flavored renditions, see the variations here and the suggestions in "10 Additions to Virtually Any Quick Bread, Muffin, Biscuit, or Scone" (page 774).

- 2 tablespoons butter, melted, or olive oil, plus butter for greasing
- 1½ cups cornmeal
- ½ cup all-purpose flour
- 1 teaspoon baking soda
- 1 teaspoon salt
- 1 tablespoon sugar, more if you like sweet corn bread
- 1 egg
- 1¼ cups buttermilk or yogurt, plus more if needed

1. Heat the oven to 375°F. Butter a 9-inch square baking pan or ovenproof skillet.

2. Combine the cornmeal, flour, baking soda, salt, and sugar in a large bowl. Whisk the egg into the buttermilk in a small bowl. Stir the buttermilk mixture into the dry ingredients just enough to combine. If the batter is very dry and doesn't come together easily, add a few tablespoons more buttermilk, 1 tablespoon at a time, until it comes together.

3. Add the melted butter and stir until just incorporated; avoid overmixing. Pour the batter into the prepared pan and spread into an even layer. Bake for 24 to 30 minutes, until the top is lightly browned, the sides have pulled away from the pan, and a toothpick inserted into the center comes out clean. Cool for a few minutes, then cut into squares. Serve warm.

LIGHTER, RICHER CORN BREAD Use 4 tablespoons (½ stick) butter; do not use oil. Increase the sugar to ¼ cup. Use 2 eggs, separated; whisk the yolks into the buttermilk and beat the whites until stiff but not dry. Gently fold the whites into the prepared batter after the yolks and buttermilk have been incorporated. Bake as directed.

CORNY CORN BREAD Add 1 cup fresh or frozen corn kernels or about 1 cup creamed corn to the buttermilk mixture in Step 2.

BACON CORN BREAD First cook up to 4 slices chopped bacon in 1 tablespoon good-quality vegetable oil, bacon fat, or lard until crisp. Remove the bacon with a slotted spoon, leaving the fat behind. Pour off the fat in the pan, leaving behind a thin film; no need to butter the pan. Make the batter as directed, adding the crumbled bacon and using 2 tablespoons of fat instead of the butter in Step 3. Heat the pan before adding the batter and proceed with the recipe.

CORN MUFFINS To make the main recipe or any of the variations into muffins, grease a 12-cup muffin tin or line with paper or foil cups if you like. Divide the batter among the cups and bake for 20 to 25 minutes.

Banana Bread

MAKES: One 9-inch loaf | **TIME:** About 1¼ hours

The best banana bread is a balancing act: It requires a fair amount of fat to keep it moist and lighten the crumb, and just enough sweetness without overpowering the super-ripe fruit. This version—from my late dear friend Sherry—has fabulous crunch if you add the walnuts and coconut, which I usually do. Or try other nuts or chopped dried fruit or raisins. It keeps better than most quick breads, though it probably won't be around too long.

8	tablespoons (1 stick) butter, softened, plus more for greasing
2	cups all-purpose flour
½	teaspoon salt
1½	teaspoons baking powder
1	cup sugar
3	very ripe bananas
2	eggs
1	teaspoon vanilla extract
½	cup chopped walnuts (optional)
½	cup unsweetened shredded coconut (optional)

1. Heat the oven to 350°F. Grease a 9 × 5-inch loaf pan with butter.

2. Whisk together the flour, salt, baking powder, and sugar in a large bowl.

3. Mash the bananas with a fork in a medium bowl until very smooth. Mix in the butter. Beat in the eggs and vanilla until well combined. Stir this into the dry ingredients, just enough to combine everything. Gently fold in the nuts and coconut if you're using them.

4. Pour the batter into the prepared pan. Bake for 50 to 60 minutes, until the bread is golden brown and a toothpick inserted in the center comes out almost entirely clean. Cool on a wire rack for 15 minutes, then carefully turn the pan upside down to release the loaf. Serve warm or at room temperature. Or wrap in plastic and store at room temperature for up to 2 days.

HONEY WHOLE GRAIN BANANA BREAD Substitute 1¼ cups whole wheat flour and ¾ cup oat bran for the all-purpose flour. Reduce the sugar to ¾ cup, and add 1 teaspoon ground cinnamon. Add ¼ cup honey to the banana along with the butter in Step 3.

PUMPKIN BREAD Instead of the bananas, use 1 cup pumpkin purée (canned is fine). Whisk 1 teaspoon ground cinnamon, ¼ teaspoon freshly grated nutmeg, ¼ teaspoon ground ginger, and ⅛ teaspoon ground cloves into the dry ingredients.

BANANA OR PUMPKIN MUFFINS (HONEY WHOLE GRAIN OR NOT) To make the main recipe or any of the variations into muffins, grease a 12-cup muffin tin or line with paper or foil cups if you like. Divide the batter among the cups and bake for 20 to 25 minutes.

Muffins, Many Ways

MAKES: 12 medium or 8 large muffins | **TIME:** About 40 minutes

The only real difference between muffins and other quick breads is the pan you bake them in. Anything goes when it comes to varying this most basic master recipe, starting with the simple addition of a teaspoon vanilla (though I often prefer the simple flavor of butter). Or see "10 Additions to Virtually Any Quick Bread, Muffin, Biscuit, or Scone" (page 774) for more ways to spike the recipe.

    4 tablespoons (½ stick) butter, melted, plus more
       butter for the muffin tin
    2 cups all-purpose flour
    ½ cup sugar
    2 teaspoons baking powder
    ½ teaspoon salt
    1 egg
    1 cup milk, plus more if needed

1. Heat the oven to 375°F. Grease a 12-cup muffin tin or line it with paper or foil muffin cups if you like.
2. Combine the flour, sugar, baking powder, and salt in a large bowl. Beat together the egg, milk, and melted butter in a medium bowl. Make a well in the center of the dry ingredients and pour the wet ingredients into it. Use a large spoon or rubber spatula to combine the ingredients swiftly, stirring and folding rather than beating; stop as soon as all the dry ingredients are moistened. If the batter is very dry and doesn't come together easily, add another 1 to 2 tablespoons milk.
3. Spoon the batter into the muffin tins, filling them about two-thirds full and handling the batter as little as possible. (If you prefer bigger muffins, fill 8 cups almost to the top; pour ¼ cup water into each of the empty cups.) Bake until golden, firm, and a toothpick inserted in the center of a muffin comes out clean, 20 to 30 minutes, depending on the size of the muffins. Remove from the oven and let cool on a wire rack for 5 minutes before taking them out of the tin. Serve warm or keep in an airtight container for a day or so.

BRAN MUFFINS Compact, but not at all dense: Substitute 1 cup oat or wheat bran for 1 cup of the flour (you can use whole wheat flour for the remainder if you like). Use 2 eggs, and honey, molasses, or maple syrup (add it to the liquid ingredients) as the sweetener. Fold ¾ cup raisins into the prepared batter after mixing.

SOUR CREAM OR YOGURT MUFFINS Reduce the baking powder to 1 teaspoon and add ½ teaspoon baking soda to the dry ingredients. Substitute 1¼ cups sour cream or yogurt for the milk and cut the melted butter back to 1 tablespoon.

SPICE MUFFINS Add 1 teaspoon ground cinnamon, ½ teaspoon each ground allspice and ground ginger, and 1 pinch each ground cloves and mace or nutmeg to the dry ingredients; use 1 cup whole wheat flour in place of 1 cup of the all-purpose flour. Add ½ cup raisins, currants, or chopped dates or dried figs to the prepared batter if you like.

BLUEBERRY OR CRANBERRY MUFFINS Try substituting cornmeal for up to ½ cup of the flour. Add 1 teaspoon ground cinnamon to the dry ingredients. Stir 1 cup fresh or frozen blueberries or cranberries into the batter at the last minute. Blueberry muffins are good with ½ teaspoon grated lemon zest added to the batter along with the wet ingredients. Cranberry muffins are excellent with ½ cup chopped nuts and/or 1 tablespoon minced orange zest added to the prepared batter.

CHEESE AND CHIVE MUFFINS Reduce the melted butter to 2 tablespoons. Cut the sugar back to 1 tablespoon and increase the salt to 1 teaspoon. Add 1½ cups grated cheddar or Gruyère cheese and 2 tablespoons chopped fresh chives to the batter just before baking. Refrigerate any leftovers in an airtight container after a couple hours.

Coffee Cake

MAKES: At least 8 servings | **TIME:** About 1 hour

The classic breakfast or brunch cake, equally good for dessert or as a snack with a cup of tea.

- 8 tablespoons (1 stick) cold butter, plus softened butter for the pan
- 2 cups plus 3 tablespoons all-purpose flour
- 1¼ cups sugar
- 2 teaspoons ground cinnamon
- 1 cup chopped walnuts or pecans
- 2 teaspoons baking powder
- ½ teaspoon salt
- 1 egg
- ¾ cup milk

1. Heat the oven to 375°F. Grease a 9-inch square baking pan with softened butter.

2. For the streusel filling and topping, combine 3 tablespoons of the flour, ¾ cup of the sugar, 1 teaspoon of the cinnamon, and 3 tablespoons of the butter with the nuts; mix with your fingers until it's just coming together. Let it sit.

3. Cut the remaining 5 tablespoons butter into bits. Combine the remaining 2 cups of flour, the baking powder, salt, the remaining ½ cup of sugar, the remaining teaspoon cinnamon, and the butter in a separate bowl. Mix well with a fork until all the flour is coated with some of the butter. Or mix on low speed with a stand or hand-held mixer.

4. Beat in the egg (still on low speed if using a mixer), then the milk, and mix until just combined. Pour half the batter into the prepared pan and sprinkle about half the streusel over it. Pour in the remaining batter, then top with the remaining streusel. Bake until a toothpick inserted in the center comes out clean, about 30 minutes. Cool on a wire rack for at least 15 minutes before cutting. Best served warm, but not bad a day or two later, reheated.

CINNAMON-ORANGE COFFEE CAKE In Step 3 add 2 teaspoons grated orange zest with the egg and substitute ¼ cup orange juice for the same amount of milk.

COFFEE CAKE WITH CARDAMOM Use almonds for the nuts if you like, and use 1 teaspoon ground cardamom in Step 1 for the streusel and 1 teaspoon in the batter, in place of the cinnamon.

Buttermilk or Yogurt Biscuits

MAKES: 10 or more biscuits, depending on size | **TIME:** 20 to 30 minutes

Buttermilk is the classic biscuit but I also like them made with yogurt, which produces tender, flaky results with a tad more tang. If you have neither, make the all-baking powder variation. For an extra-soft crumb, use cake flour. Vary these biscuits with any of the ideas listed in "10 Additions to Any Quick Bread, Muffin, Biscuit, or Scone" (page 774). And a final suggestion:

Try to eat these as soon as possible after baking; they'll keep for a day but will never be as good as they are warm.

- 2 **cups all-purpose or cake flour, plus more for kneading**
- 1 **tablespoon baking powder**
- 1 **teaspoon baking soda**
- 1 **teaspoon salt**
- 5 **tablespoons cold butter, cut into ½-inch slices**
- ¾ **cup plus 2 tablespoons buttermilk or whole milk yogurt**

1. Heat the oven to 450°F. Combine the flour, baking powder, baking soda, and salt in a large bowl. Add the butter and work it into the flour mixture, breaking it into tiny pieces with your fingers until the mixture looks like coarse meal.

2. Add the buttermilk and stir just until the mixture comes together and forms a ball. Spread some flour (about ¼ cup) on a clean work surface and turn the dough out onto the flour. Knead the dough a few times, adding a little more flour to your hands only if the dough is very sticky.

3. Press the dough out ¾ inch thick and cut out 1½- to 2½-inch rounds with a biscuit cutter or a sturdy glass. Put the biscuits on an ungreased baking sheet. Press together the scraps, pat them out ¾ inch thick, and cut out more biscuits. Repeat once more if possible.

4. Bake for 5 to 10 minutes, depending on size, until the biscuits are golden brown. Transfer the biscuits to a wire rack and serve within 15 minutes. Or wrap in foil and keep in a 200°F oven for up to an hour.

BAKING POWDER BISCUITS Slightly different flavor, but with good texture: Increase the baking powder to 4 teaspoons and omit the soda. Use milk in place of buttermilk or yogurt.

10 Additions to Virtually Any Quick Bread, Muffin, Biscuit, or Scone

You can change up the recipes in this section simply by adding an ingredient—or two or three. Just use a little common sense so flavors and textures don't clash. I've given some guidance for the quantities, but again you've got to go by your taste and good judgment.

1. Spice mixtures like chili or curry powder (to make your own, see pages 27–35) or single spices like cumin, saffron, cardamom, or caraway seeds. Generally no more than 1 tablespoon, whole or ground as you like. Add to the dry ingredients.

2. Traditional Pesto (page 51) or any other herb purée page 52), ¼ to ½ cup. Drizzle it onto the batter once it's in the pan and use a knife to swirl it in like marble cake.

3. Minced or sliced pickled jalapeños, from 1 tablespoon to ¼ cup. Add with the liquid ingredients.

4. Grated cheese, either soft, melting, or hard types; from ½ to 1 cup. Add to the dry ingredients.

5. Molasses or honey, in place of some or all of the sugar (if there is any); use about half the volume. Add with the liquid ingredients.

6. Minced herbs, up to ¼ cup mild ones like mint, parsley, or cilantro; up to 2 tablespoons of strongly flavored ones like rosemary, oregano, or thyme. Add to the dry ingredients.

7. Sautéed onions, shallots, or leeks, about ½ cup. Add with the liquid ingredients. (If there is milk or other liquid, with this and other very savory additions, using stock for half the volume enhances the umami flavors.)

8. Chopped nuts or seeds, like almonds, pecans, or pumpkin, poppy, or sesame seeds, up to ½ cup. Add to the dry ingredients.

9. Dried cherries, blueberries, or cranberries or raisins; soak in a little warm water first and drain well. Up to 1 cup. Add to the finished batter or dough.

10. Grated citrus zest; about 1 tablespoon. Add to the dry ingredients.

 fast make ahead vegetarian

DROP BISCUITS These don't rise as much, but they're good and you'll save a step: Increase the buttermilk, yogurt, or milk to 1 cup and drop a couple heaping tablespoons of the dough onto a greased baking sheet like big cookies. Bake as directed.

SWEET POTATO OR WINTER SQUASH BISCUITS
Southern-style goodness; killer with My New Favorite Fried Chicken (page 628). Grease the baking sheet. Stir 1 cup puréed cooked sweet potato or winter squash into the butter-flour mixture. Add only enough yogurt or buttermilk to form the dough into a ball, usually between ½ and ¾ cup (if your sweet potatoes are very dry, you may need the larger amount). Roll the dough a little thinner, about ½ inch. Cut into biscuits as directed (you'll get a few more), and bake for 12 to 15 minutes.

processor and pulse to combine. Add the butter and pulse until the mixture resembles cornmeal.

2. Add the egg and just enough cream to form a slightly sticky dough. If it's too sticky, add a little flour, but very little; it should still stick a little to your hands.

3. Transfer the dough onto a lightly floured surface and knead once or twice, then press it into a ¾-inch-thick circle and cut 2-inch rounds with a biscuit cutter or sturdy glass. Put the scones on an ungreased baking sheet. Gently reshape the leftover dough and cut again. Brush the top of each scone with a bit of cream and sprinkle with a little of the remaining sugar.

4. Bake until the scones are golden brown and springy when gently pressed, 8 to 12 minutes. Serve right away, or within a couple of hours.

Scones

MAKES: 8 to 10 scones | **TIME:** 20 minutes

Scones are really just ultra-rich and flaky biscuits, with cream as the primary liquid ingredient and usually some mix-ins like the currants in the main recipe, or other sweet or savory additions.

> 2 **cups all-purpose or cake flour, plus more for kneading**
> ½ **teaspoon salt**
> 2 **teaspoons baking powder**
> 3 **tablespoons sugar**
> 5 **tablespoons cold butter, cut into pieces**
> 1 **egg**
> ½ to ¾ **cup cream, plus more for brushing**
> ⅓ **cup dried currants or raisins (or choose from the list of additions below)**

1. Heat the oven to 450°F. Put the flour, salt, baking powder, and 2 tablespoons of the sugar in a food

Popovers

MAKES: 6 to 12 popovers | **TIME:** About 45 minutes

Popovers, a one-bowl recipe that comes together in no time, are the classic accompaniment for Prime Rib Roast (page 676), though they're so easy and good—even after they've deflated—you'll want to make them all the time.

> 1 **tablespoon butter, melted, or good-quality vegetable oil, plus more for greasing the muffin tin**
> 2 **eggs**
> 1 **cup milk**
> 1 **teaspoon sugar**
> ½ **teaspoon salt**
> 1 **cup all-purpose flour**

1. Heat the oven to 425°F. Grease a 12-cup muffin tin or a 6- or 8-cup popover tin and put it in the oven while you make the batter.

Popovers

2. Beat together the eggs, milk, butter or oil, sugar, and salt until creamy. Beat in the flour a little bit at a time; the batter should be smooth.

3. Fill the cups at least halfway but no more than two-thirds; if the cups are large, this will make fewer than 12 popovers. Bake for 15 minutes, then reduce the heat to 350°F and continue baking for 15 minutes more, or until the popovers are puffed and browned. Do not check the popovers until they have baked for a total of 30 minutes. Remove from the pan and serve hot and still puffy, if possible.

Unleavened Flatbreads

These familiar and traditional breads prove that even without yeast, baking powder, or baking soda, flatbreads can be quite flaky and light. The easy-to-mix and handle doughs are shaped by pressing or rolling. It's not important that the resulting breads and crackers be perfect; they're delicious whether they come out oval, squarish, or like an amoeba. Once you free yourself of that stress, handling the dough becomes an utterly simple and fast task.

Crackers

MAKES: About 3 dozen | **TIME:** About 25 minutes

Homemade crackers are a snap to make, with lots of room for improvising. In any of these recipes, you can blend pretty much whatever you'd like—cheese, nuts, garlic, herbs, and/or spices, for starters—directly into the dough or replace up to half of the all-purpose flour with whole wheat, rye, or cornmeal. Or just before baking, dust the tops with coarse salt, poppy seeds, or spices.

You don't need any special equipment to make crackers, though a food processor speeds things up a bit. The success of a cracker depends on your ability to roll out the dough until it's quite thin, ⅛ inch or even less. Flour is your friend, but use only as much as you need to keep the dough from sticking.

> 1 cup all-purpose flour, plus more for kneading and rolling
> ½ teaspoon salt
> 2 tablespoons butter or good-quality vegetable oil

1. Heat the oven to 400°F with a large pizza stone on the center rack if you have one.

2. Put the flour, salt, and butter in a food processor and pulse until combined, or cut them together in a bowl with 2 knives or your fingertips. Add about ¼ cup water and continue to mix until the dough holds together but is not sticky, adding water 1 tablespoon at a time as needed.

3. Put a large piece of parchment paper on a clean work surface and dust lightly with flour. Turn out the dough onto the parchment and knead it a few times to make a smooth ball. Divide the dough in half and roll out each piece to ⅛ inch thick or even thinner—it can't be bigger than your baking sheet, but aim to get it about that size—turning it a few times to prevent sticking and sprinkling with more flour as needed. If it sticks, sweep a bench scraper under the dough to help lift it. If at any point the dough shrinks back, leave it alone to rest, uncovered, for a few minutes. Score lightly with a sharp knife or pizza cutter if you want to break the crackers into neat squares or rectangles after baking. Poke the surface all over with a fork if you like. Repeat with the other half to bake both pieces at one time or set it aside if you're baking in batches.

4. Transfer the parchment with the dough directly to a baking sheet or the pizza stone. Bake until the bottom is lightly browned, about 10 minutes, checking periodically to make sure the edges don't burn. Depending on your oven, the crackers may brown unevenly; you may want to trim or break off any darker parts along the edges and then let the rest finish. If the crackers brown before they've fully crisped up, crack the oven door, decrease the heat to 200°F, and continue baking until completely

dried out and crisp, another 5 minutes or so. Cool on the parchment on a wire rack, then carefully break the crackers apart. Serve at room temperature or store in an airtight container for up to a couple of days.

CREAM CRACKERS Rich and delicious, they really need nothing but a little salt on top: Increase the butter to 4 tablespoons (½ stick). Substitute milk or cream for the water. Sprinkle the unbaked dough with coarse salt.

PARMESAN CRACKERS Perfect with salads or grilled vegetables: In Step 1, add ½ cup grated Parmesan cheese along with the flour.

Chapati

MAKES: 4 servings (8 to 12 chapati) | TIME: At least 1 hour, partially unattended

In Indian cooking, chapati are made with a finely ground whole wheat flour (called *atta* or chapati flour) and then twice-cooked quickly—first on a dry griddle, then over an open flame—so that the dough traps steam and puffs up dramatically. This technique is simpler but makes a bread that is still unbelievably simple, nutritious, and delicious. Eat chapati with any food, Indian or not. They're best with stews and soups, especially their traditional accompaniment, Simplest Dal (page 409), and other bean dishes.

　2¼　**cups whole wheat flour**
　　1　**cup all-purpose flour, plus more for kneading and shaping**
　　1　**teaspoon salt**

1. Sift the flours and salt into a food processor or a large bowl. Discard any coarse bran that's left in the strainer or save it for another use.
2. With the machine running, pour in 1 cup warm water and process for about 30 seconds, then remove

the cover. The dough should be in a well-defined, barely sticky, easy-to-handle ball. If it is too dry, add more water 1 tablespoon at a time and process for 5 or 10 seconds after each addition. If wet, which is unlikely, add a tablespoon or 2 of flour and process briefly. If you're working by hand, add the water in intervals, stirring after each addition until combined, and continue to work the dough in the bowl until it pulls together.
3. Turn the dough out onto a lightly floured surface; knead a few times if you mixed it by hand until it smooths out. Cover and let rest for at least 30 minutes and up to 2 hours. (At this point, you can wrap the dough tightly in plastic and refrigerate for up to 1 day; bring to room temperature before proceeding.)
4. Divide the dough into 8 to 12 evenly sized pieces, depending on how thick you'd like the chapati. Using only enough flour to keep the dough from sticking, pat each piece into a 4-inch disk. Dust lightly with flour and put them on a baking sheet; cover them with plastic or a damp kitchen towel while you roll out the others. It's okay to overlap them a bit, but don't stack them.
5. Line a basket or serving plate with a cloth napkin and keep it handy. Put a griddle or heavy skillet over medium heat. When it's hot, roll out a disk until it's about ⅛ inch thick, dusting as necessary with flour; the shape doesn't matter (as long as it fits on the griddle or pan). Pat off

Scoring and Docking Crackers

STEP 1 Cut the dough in a grid pattern before baking.

STEP 2 Prick the dough with the tines of a fork to keep the dough from puffing as it bakes.

the excess flour and put the chapati on the griddle or pan, count to 15 or so, then use a spatula to turn it. Cook the other side until it starts to blister, char, and puff up a bit, about 1 minute. (Use this time to finish rolling out the next disk.) Turn and cook the first side again, until dark and toasty smelling. Transfer to the prepared basket, wrap loosely, and repeat until all are cooked. Serve right away.

GRILLED CHAPATI Rustic, smoky, and puffy—perfect for when you've already got a fire going and have some room on the grill: Prepare a charcoal or gas grill for medium direct heat and put the rack about 4 inches from the heat source. Clean and oil the grates well. If you have the space, take the disks outside for the final rolling. If not, roll all the chapati out, flour them well, and stack between layers of wax or parchment paper. Cook several at a time as described in Step 5, on the grill grate with the lid closed instead of the griddle.

---

4 WAYS TO VARY CHAPATI DOUGH

1. Replace up to ½ cup of the whole wheat flour with cornmeal, brown rice flour, or chickpea flour (*besan*).
2. Replace the all-purpose flour with whole wheat; the dough will be slightly more difficult to handle, but the results will be delicious.
3. Reduce the water to 1 cup and add ½ cup yogurt to the flour at the same time.
4. Brush the chapati with good-quality vegetable oil, coconut milk (to make your own, see page 372), or melted butter during cooking.

Paratha

MAKES: 4 servings (8 to 12 paratha) | **TIME:** At least an hour

Unlike chapati, this dough is enriched with butter or oil, which gives it a lovely flaky texture. (Use oil if you want the paratha to be vegan.) Like chapati, though, paratha must be eaten immediately after cooking: Line a basket or plate with a cloth napkin before starting, and as they finish, pile them up and wrap loosely.

You can also grill these; follow the directions in the variation for Grilled Chapati.

  1½ cups whole wheat flour
  1½ cups all-purpose flour, plus more for shaping
  1 teaspoon salt
     About 4 tablespoons (½ stick) butter, melted, or ¼ cup good-quality vegetable oil

1. Combine the flours and salt in a food processor. Turn the machine on and add ¾ cup water through the feed tube. Process for about 30 seconds, until the mixture forms a ball and is slightly sticky to the touch. If it's dry, add another tablespoon or 2 water and process for another 10 seconds. In the unlikely event that the mixture is too sticky, add flour 1 tablespoon at a time. Remove the dough and, using flour as necessary, shape into a ball; wrap in plastic and let rest for at least 20 minutes and up to several hours at room temperature. (At this point, you can wrap the dough tightly in plastic and refrigerate for up to 1 day or freeze for up to 1 week; bring back to room temperature before proceeding.)

2. Divide the dough into 8 to 12 pieces. Using flour as necessary, pat or roll each piece into a 4-inch disk and brush the top with butter or oil. Roll up like a cigar, then into a coil not unlike a cinnamon bun; let the coils sit until you finish all the pieces.

3. Line a basket or serving plate with a cloth napkin and keep it handy. Put a griddle or cast-iron skillet over medium heat. When it's hot, press one of the coils flat, then roll it out into a thin disk (about a size of a tortilla). Put in the pan and cook until lightly browned on one side, 3 to 5 minutes; brush the top with butter, turn, and brown on the second side, another few minutes. Transfer to the prepared basket, wrap loosely, and repeat until all are cooked. Serve right away.

Flour Tortillas

MAKES: 8 to 12 | **TIME:** About 1½ hours, partially unattended

Eating a freshly rolled tortilla straight from the skillet is a pleasure reserved for the home cook. Nothing about the process is difficult. You don't even need a tortilla press, although if you have one, here's a chance to use it.

- 1½ **cups all-purpose flour, plus more for kneading**
- ¼ **teaspoon salt**
- 2 **tablespoons good-quality vegetable oil**
   About ½ cup boiling water, or more as needed

1. In a large bowl or a food processor, mix together the flour and salt. Stir or pulse in the oil. Add the water slowly, a tablespoon or 2 at a time if you're mixing by hand or in a thin stream with the food processor running, until the dough holds together in a ball.

2. Transfer the dough to a lightly floured surface and knead until it becomes smooth and elastic, 4 to 5 minutes if you mixed by hand or about 1 minute if you used a food processor. Wrap the dough in plastic and let it rest at room temperature for at least 30 minutes or up to a couple of hours. (At this point, you can refrigerate it for up to a few days; bring it back to room temperature before proceeding.)

3. Divide the dough into 8 pieces if you're rolling by hand. On a lightly floured surface, slightly flatten each piece into a disk, then cover and let rest for a few minutes. When you're ready to cook the tortillas, use a heavy rolling pin to roll each disk as thin as possible into a circle at least 8 inches in diameter, stacking them between sheets of plastic wrap or wax paper as you work. To save time, you can continue to roll out the tortillas while the first pieces cook in Step 5.

4. If you're using a tortilla press, divide the dough into 12 pieces (you need less dough for each tortilla because it will get thinner). Shape each into a slightly flattened disk and let rest for a few minutes. Put a piece of plastic wrap or parchment paper on the inside of the press, add the dough, top with another piece of plastic or parchment, and close the press. Squeeze the clamp as hard as you can; if you'd like it thinner, rotate the dough and repeat.

5. Line a basket or serving plate with a clean kitchen towel or cloth napkin and keep it handy. Put a large skillet or griddle (preferably cast iron) over medium-high heat for 4 to 5 minutes. Cook the tortillas one at a time until brown spots begin to appear on the bottom, about 1 minute; turn and cook the other side for 1 minute more. Transfer to the prepared basket, wrap loosely, and repeat until all are cooked. Serve immediately, or let them cool, wrap tightly, and store in the fridge for a few days or in the freezer for up to a few months.

MOSTLY WHOLE WHEAT TORTILLAS Substitute 1 cup whole wheat flour for 1 cup of the all-purpose flour.

THE BASICS OF YEAST BREAD

You can make an amazing loaf of bread on your first try. Really. If you have a food processor, you can be pulling it from the oven 2 or 3 hours from now. You can make it even faster if you push. Or you can make it slower, with so little work that you'll be amazed. And in each of these cases it'll be good, very good, better than what is served to you in most restaurants.

Shaggy Versus Smooth Dough

STEP 1 Dough about halfway through the mixing process; note that it still looks quite shaggy.

STEP 2 When the dough is ready, it will be ball shaped and easy to handle.

EQUIPMENT

All you really need is a bowl, a wooden spoon, and an oven. Beyond that, here's what I have and what I recommend you acquire eventually, if not all at once.

A FOOD PROCESSOR If you're going to cook regularly, you want one anyway. What it does for bread making is remarkable: It turns the process of making dough from a laborious chore into a task that takes less than a minute of work. The hardest part is washing the work bowl afterward.

A STANDING MIXER A big investment and not mandatory, but if you're going to get into baking doughs that require kneading it's quite handy. Just be sure to get a good one.

A PIZZA STONE You buy one, shove it into your oven, and forget about it. It can stay there forever, won't hurt anything else you cook in there, and is essential for pizza and a good thing to have for bread.

AN INSTANT-READ THERMOMETER You should have one anyway (see page 10).

A SMALL STRAINER Good for dusting flour on top of loaves; not essential, but nice.

That's it. You don't even need bread pans, at least not for European-style breads; you will for sandwich loaves, of course. And you can live without all of the preceding items—and rely on an oven-proof pot with a lid—if you become an aficionado of Jim Lahey's No-Knead Bread (page 785).

INGREDIENTS

Again, baking at its most basic: All-purpose flour is good in most cases; bread flour in others; see pages 762–763 for details. A bit of rye or whole wheat adds flavor, variety, and some fiber. For these recipes you'll need instant yeast (see page 766). Water and salt, of course. And every now and then you might want a bit of olive oil, butter, and/or eggs.

MIXING AND KNEADING

Eventually you will learn to mix and knead and judge dough by sight and feel alone—really. For now, just follow the recipes and illustrations here, which offer sensory details.

Kneading—which can sometimes be skipped or minimized if you let time or a machine do the work— allows the flour-and-water mixture to develop gluten, the protein that gives bread structure, elasticity, and chewiness.

The best way to understand how dough changes during kneading is to feel it. In most of the recipes here, the dough starts out rough looking, what bakers call "shaggy." After the folding, stretching, and pressing actions of kneading—which usually involves adding more flour—the dough becomes smoother and more elastic, almost as if by magic. You can knead in a standing mixer with a dough hook attachment, or in the food processor with a plastic blade, but I encourage you to try at least a few loaves by hand.

Wetter doughs tend to have a looser interior crumb with open holes. They're also much harder to knead than firmer doughs, and in fact you don't want to over-handle them. This section encourages you to try a range of different styles and learn by experience.

Kneading Dough

STEP 1 Using as little flour as possible, press the lump of dough down with the heels of your hands.

STEP 2 Fold the dough back over itself, then repeatedly press and fold the dough for 5 to 6 minutes, until it becomes far less sticky and quite elastic, like a taut ball.

F fast   **M** make ahead   **V** vegetarian

LETTING THE DOUGH RISE

As the yeast feeds on the flour in the dough, it releases gases that are trapped and will cause the bread to rise. The dough is technically fermenting, also called "proofing." Time and temperature affect the rate of this process; the warmer the room, the more active the yeast. Within limits, slower rising is better; it allows flavor to develop and improves the final product in subtle but noticeable ways.

In most cases the dough rises one time in the bowl and another time after shaping. There are no precise times; dough is quite flexible. You can slow things down by refrigerating dough during the process, but I don't recommend trying to speed things up by letting it rise in a low oven. Just try to be patient—and observant.

SHAPING

You can make any shape—loaves, rolls, twists, and so on—with almost any bread dough, including pizza (see page 817). Just remember to lightly flour the work surface before putting the dough on it; you can use cornmeal if you prefer, which will add a little crunch.

BOULE Meaning "ball," the simplest shape; see the illustrations on page 784. To bake, turn the dough over onto a floured peel, wooden board, or flexible cutting board, slash it (see page 785), and slide it directly onto a pizza stone, or turn it onto a lightly oiled baking sheet, slash it, and put the sheet into the oven.

ROLLS To make rolls, simply divide the dough into 6 to 12 pieces and shape each as you would a boule. Treat them the same way from that point on, though baking time will obviously be shorter.

BAGUETTE These are easy with a little practice; see the illustrations on page 784. If you like, you can turn the shaped dough into a ring just by pinching the ends together. To help them keep their shape as they rise, create a *couche*—a baguette bed, essentially—by sprinkling a piece of heavy muslin or linen, a clean cotton (not terry) kitchen towel, or a large tablecloth folded into quarters lightly with flour. Arrange the baguettes on top, pulling the cloth between the loaves to hold them in place. Cover and let rise.

LOAF A loaf pan helps keep the crust tender for softer loaves like sandwich bread. See the illustrations on page 784.

SLASHING

Controlling the way steam escapes from the dough as it bakes helps the bread develop an even crumb and keep its shape. Most bakers slash the top of their dough just before baking. It's not essential, but it usually results in a more attractive loaf inside and out. Use a sharp knife or razor blade; for baguettes, make three or four crosswise cuts, each about ¼ inch deep. For boules, make a crosshatch or similar pattern. For rolls, just make an X.

BAKING

There are many ways to bake bread, each with a different outcome, and several are demonstrated in the following recipes. Use a covered pot, for example, and you create an oven within an oven to maximize the rise and ultimately develop a crisp crust—similar in effect to introducing steam during baking with a pan of water. Other loaves benefit from being baked directly on a heated pizza stone, which creates a crisp bottom crust. Some loaves—like braided Challah (page 793) or rolled Breadsticks (page 800) can be baked on baking sheets, while for others you'll want the structure of loaf pans.

Most bread is done when it makes a hollow sound when you thump it, or when an instant-read thermometer inserted in the center of the loaf reads between 200° and 210°F. If you're going to reheat or toast it, which is often the case, underbake the bread a bit and pull it from the oven at 190°F.

STORING BREAD

You can store unbaked dough, well wrapped in foil or plastic, in the freezer for several weeks. You can also store baked bread, wrapped in wax paper or

Shaping Boules and Rolls

STEP 1 To make a boule, shape the dough into a ball.

STEP 2 Continually tuck the dough under, toward the center of the bottom, stretching the top slightly so that the ball becomes smooth and taut. Pinch the seam at the bottom to smooth it over as much as possible.

STEP 3 Put the ball to rise in a bowl lined with a floured kitchen towel. Fold the towel over the top and let rise for at least 1 hour, preferably 2 or 3.

STEP 4 Shape rolls as you would a small boule, then roll them on a lightly floured surface.

Shaping Baguettes

STEP 1 Roll the dough into a log.

STEP 2 Pinch the seam shut.

STEP 3 Let the baguettes rise on a couche made from a folded kitchen towel or tablecloth.

Shaping a Sandwich Loaf

STEP 1 If the dough has risen in an oiled bowl, you need no flour; otherwise, work on a very lightly floured surface. Use the heel of your hand to form the dough into a rectangle.

STEP 2 Fold the long sides of the rectangle over to the middle.

STEP 3 Pinch the seam closed, pressing tightly with your fingers.

STEP 4 Fold under the ends of the loaf.

STEP 5 Use the back of your hand to press the loaf firmly into the pan.

F fast   **M** make ahead   **V** vegetarian

a towel—plastic makes the crust soggy—on the counter for up to a few days, especially if you like toast; large loaves containing some whole grain flour keep better than small ones baked with just white flour, because the whole grain contains some fat. And breads baked with added fat, like those on pages 791–794, keep well, too.

Baked bread can also be frozen; in this instance foil or plastic freezer bags are fine, because you'll need to reheat the bread anyway (see page 767).

Jim Lahey's No-Knead Bread

MAKES: 1 large loaf | **TIME:** Nearly 24 hours, almost completely unattended

This innovation—the word recipe does not do the technique justice—originally came from Jim Lahey, owner of Sullivan Street Bakery in New York City. Jim created a way for home cooks (and not only ones who are serious bakers) to nearly duplicate an artisan bakery loaf with a crackling crust, open-holed crumb, light texture, and fantastic flavor. All without kneading, fancy ingredients, or special equipment.

Since the method was first published in 2006, many people—including me—have tinkered with the formula. This is the original, simplest version. The only thing required is forethought. Ideally, you will start the dough about 24 hours before you plan to serve it. (If you want to know more about how the process works, see "The Science Behind No-Knead Bread," page 787). After all these years I still say with confidence the results will blow your mind.

　4　cups all-purpose or bread flour, plus more for dusting
　　　Scant ½ teaspoon instant yeast
　2　teaspoons salt
　　　Cornmeal, semolina, or wheat bran as needed (optional)

1. Combine the flour, yeast, and salt in a large bowl. Add 2 cups water (it should be about 70°F) and stir until blended. You'll have a shaggy, sticky dough; add a little more water if it seems dry. Cover the bowl with plastic wrap and let sit for about 18 hours at room temperature (a couple of hours less if your kitchen is warm; a couple more if it's cool). The dough is ready when its surface is dotted with bubbles.

2. Lightly flour a work surface, transfer the dough to it, and fold once or twice; it will be soft but not terribly sticky once dusted with flour. Cover loosely with plastic wrap and let rest for about 15 minutes.

3. Using just enough flour to keep the dough from sticking, gently and quickly shape the dough into a ball. Generously coat a clean cotton kitchen towel (not terry cloth) with cornmeal, or use a silicone baking mat; put the dough seam side down on the towel and dust with more flour or cornmeal. Cover with another cotton towel or plastic wrap and let rise for about 2 hours. When it's ready, the dough will be more than doubled in size and won't spring back readily when poked with your finger.

4. After the dough has been rising for about 1½ hours, put a 3- to 4-quart cast-iron, enamel, Pyrex, or ceramic pot, with its lid, in the oven and heat the oven to 450°F. When the dough is ready, carefully remove the pot from

Slashing the Dough

Slash the top of the shaped dough with a sharp knife or razor blade to allow steam to escape.

Jim Lahey's No-Knead
Bread, page 785

This bread puts time and moisture to work so you don't have to. The dough uses very little yeast, but compensates for that by fermenting very slowly, giving the yeast time to multiply on its own schedule. This delivers a more complex flavor than using more yeast and fermenting faster. The dough is extremely wet, more than 40 percent water, at the extreme high end of the possible range.

You couldn't knead this dough if you wanted to. The moisture content—combined with the long fermentation time—gives the gluten in the dough (see page 788 for more on that) an environment that lets it develop its distinctive elastic, weblike structure, which traps the carbon dioxide generated by the yeast as it feeds. The resulting crumb of the finished bread is well structured, with open holes.

By starting this very wet dough in a hot covered pot, you develop a crunchy yet chewy bakery-style crust, since the moist, enclosed environment of the pot is, in effect, the oven, and that oven has plenty of steam in it, which is necessary to create that kind of surface. Once uncovered, the crust hardens and browns and the bread is done. (And fear not: The dough does not stick to the pot, any more than it would to a heated bread stone.)

the oven, uncover it, and turn the dough over into the pot, seam side up. (Slide your hand under the towel and just turn the dough over into the pot; it's messy, and it probably won't fall in artfully, but it will straighten out as it bakes.) Cover with the lid and bake for 30 minutes. (If at any point the dough starts to smell scorched, lower the heat a bit.)

5. Remove the lid and bake for another 20 to 30 minutes, until the loaf is beautifully browned. The bread's internal temperature should be about 200°F when you insert an instant-read thermometer. Remove the bread from the pot with a spatula or tongs and cool on a wire rack for at least 30 minutes before slicing.

Rustic French Bread

MAKES: 1 boule | **TIME:** About 5 hours, largely unattended

This bread-making technique is more traditional than the previous recipe, and quite a bit faster. But you will be shaping the dough and creating steam in the oven, so there's a little more work involved. You could also mix and knead the dough by hand or in a stand mixer as described on page 791.

> 4 cups all-purpose or bread flour, plus more for kneading and shaping
> 1 teaspoon instant yeast

1. Put the flour in a food processor, add the salt and yeast, and turn the machine on. With the machine running, pour 1½ cups water through the feed tube in a steady stream. Process until the dough forms a sticky ball. If the dough begins sticking to the side of the bowl, you've added too much water; add more flour, 1 to 2 tablespoons at a time,

Baking No-Knead Bread

STEP 1 The trick is not to hesitate: Use the towel on which the dough rose to turn it over into the pot.

STEP 2 Use tongs to lift out the finished bread.

and keep going. If it's too dry, add water 1 tablespoon at a time and process for 5 or 10 seconds after each addition.

2. Put the dough into a large bowl, cover with plastic wrap, and let rise in a warm place until the dough doubles in size, 3 to 4 hours. The rising time will be shorter at warmer temperatures, a bit longer if your kitchen is chilly.

3. Dust a work surface with a little flour. Shape the dough into a boule (see page 784), sprinkling with flour as necessary but keeping it to a minimum. Line a colander or large bowl with a well-floured kitchen towel, put the dough on top, and cover with another towel (this keeps it from spreading too much). Let the dough rise until puffy, about 40 minutes.

4. Put an ovenproof skillet (preferably cast iron) on the floor or lowest rack of the oven and heat the oven to 450°F. If you'll be baking the dough on a pizza stone, put it on the rack above the skillet; if not, line a baking sheet with parchment paper.

5. Slash the top of the loaf once or twice with a razor blade or sharp knife (see page 785). If you're using a pizza stone, slide the boule, seam side down, onto a lightly floured peel or flexible cutting board; otherwise, put it on the prepared baking sheet. Use the peel or cutting board to transfer the boule to the stone or slide the baking sheet onto the rack above the heated skillet. Partially pull out the skillet and very carefully pour in 1 cup hot water (it will create a lot of steam). Quickly slide the skillet back in and immediately close the oven door.

6. Bake, rotating the bread or the baking sheet halfway through, until the crust is browned and the internal temperature reaches 200°F, or the loaf sounds hollow when tapped, 40 to 45 minutes. If it's browning already when you rotate the pan, lower the temperature to 425°F. At this stage if you want a shinier crust, you can remove the loaf, spray with a bit of water, and return it to the oven to finish. After baking, cool on a wire rack for at least an hour before slicing.

BAGUETTES OR FRENCH ROLLS Same dough, different shape: Follow the directions and illustrations on page 784. Go light on the flour when you're shaping the dough; a little friction makes rolling easier. Cover and let rise on a floured towel, then transfer to the pizza stone or baking sheet. Bake at 465°F for 20 to 25 minutes, until the internal temperature reaches 200°F. Cool for at least 20 minutes before serving.

The Magic of Gluten

Gluten is what gives different kinds of baked foods their characteristic textures. High-protein flours make dough sturdier and more elastic, allowing yeast breads to rise; low-protein flours produce the fine, tender crumb you want in desserts and quick breads.

To make gluten, it takes water and two individual proteins, glutenin and gliadin, both of which are abundant in wheat and present in some other grains, though usually in much lesser quantities. Since these proteins are even more accessible when the grains are ground, wheat flour allows greater gluten formation.

As you mix and knead wheat-based batters and doughs—or simply allow them to rest, as in Jim Lahey's No-Knead Bread, the gluten develops into a weblike structure that supports the flour's starch and other components, which in turn traps the carbon dioxide bubbles produced by yeast during fermentation or by other leaveners like baking powder (see page 765). This structure becomes permanent as the bread, cake, muffin, or cookie bakes and moisture evaporates, creating the nooks, crannies, and air pockets in the interior, or "crumb."

Significant gluten development is really desirable only in crusty, chewy breads, where you can use high-protein bread flour and work the dough vigorously. When you want a tender bread crumb, it's better to start with a relatively low-protein flour, like all-purpose or even cake flour, and take care not to knead the dough too much; if you overwork a delicate dough, it becomes tough.

 fast make ahead vegetarian

Everyday Sandwich
Bread, page 790

Everyday Sandwich Bread

MAKES: 1 large loaf | **TIME:** At least 3 hours, largely unattended

This is your classic loaf of white bread. Subtly sweet and rich with milk, with a perfectly tender and golden crust and slightly tight crumb, it's better than anything you can buy at the store. To get the dough to rise above the sides of the loaf pan (which is nice for looks but not essential), it helps to do the second rise (Step 5) in a warm place. In winter I break my usual rule and heat the oven as low as it will go, turn off the heat and let it cool back down a bit, let the dough rise in the oven for the first hour, then move the pan on top of the stove for the last 30 minutes while I preheat the oven for baking.

1¼	cups whole or 2% milk, plus more as needed
3½	cups all-purpose flour or bread flour, plus more for kneading and shaping
1	teaspoon salt
2¼	teaspoons (1 package) instant yeast
1	tablespoon sugar
2	tablespoons good-quality vegetable oil, plus more for greasing

1. Heat the milk in the microwave or in a pot on the stove until it reaches about 100°F, a little hotter than lukewarm.

2. To mix the dough in a standing mixer (helpful here because it's less likely than a food processor to overwork the wet dough), combine the flour, salt, yeast, sugar, oil, and milk in the mixer bowl. With a dough hook, mix on medium-low speed until the ingredients are combined, then on medium speed until the dough is tacky and smooth, 8 to 10 minutes. (Or mix and knead by hand as described on page 791; the dough will take about twice as long to get to this stage.)

To mix the dough in a food processor, pulse the dry ingredients together a few times to combine, then with the machine running add the oil and milk through the feed tube and process until the dough is a well-defined, barely sticky, easy-to-handle ball, about 30 seconds. Turn

it out onto a lightly floured work surface and knead (you shouldn't need much flour) until smooth, 4 or 5 minutes.

3. Grease a large bowl with oil. Shape the dough into a rough ball, put it in the bowl, turn it to coat all over with oil, and cover with plastic wrap. Let rest at room temperature until the dough has doubled in size, 2 hours or more.

4. Press down on the dough to deflate it. Dust the work surface with a little flour, turn the dough out onto it, cover with plastic wrap, and let rest for 15 minutes.

5. Grease a 9 × 5-inch loaf pan with oil. Shape the dough into a sandwich loaf (see page 784) and transfer it to the pan. Loosely cover with a clean kitchen towel or plastic wrap and let rise in a warm place (see the headnote) until the top of the dough expands to about an inch above the pan, about 1½ hours.

6. Heat the oven to 350°F. Brush or spray the top of the loaf lightly with water. Bake for 45 to 50 minutes, rotating the pan once, until the loaf falls easily from the pan and the bottom of the loaf sounds hollow when you tap it. (The internal temperature will be about 200°F.) Remove the loaf from the pan and cool completely on a wire rack before slicing.

50 PERCENT WHOLE WHEAT SANDWICH BREAD

Something more like what you get in the supermarket, though not quite as fluffy: Substitute 1¾ cups whole wheat flour for half of the flour. Use honey for the sweetener, increasing it to 2 tablespoons. Proceed as directed.

100 Percent Whole Wheat Bread

MAKES: 1 loaf | **TIME:** 15 to 29 hours, almost completely unattended

True whole wheat breads like this one—a variation of No-Knead Bread (page 785), baked in a loaf pan—are so sturdy they're often called "travel bread." The nutty flavor makes slices perfect for topping with pungent

cheeses, jams, or any bean or dairy spread, and the dough can accommodate all sorts of additional ingredients (see the list on page 774). You can also substitute rye, cornmeal, oat, or other whole grain flour for up to 1 cup of the wheat flour. For a softer, lighter loaf that's partially whole wheat, see the 50 Percent Whole Wheat Sandwich Bread variation on page 790.

    3   cups whole wheat flour
    2   teaspoons salt
    ½   teaspoon instant yeast
        Good-quality vegetable oil for greasing and
        brushing

1. Whisk the flour, salt, and yeast together in a large bowl. Add 1½ cups water and stir until blended; the dough should be very wet, almost like a batter; add more water if it's too thick. Cover the bowl with plastic wrap and let it rest in a warm place for about 12 hours, or in a cooler place (even the fridge) for up to 24 hours. The dough is ready when its surface is dotted with bubbles. The rising time will be shorter at warmer temperatures, a bit longer if your kitchen is chilly.

2. Grease a 9 × 5-inch loaf pan lightly with oil. Scoop the dough into the loaf pan and use a rubber spatula to gently spread it in evenly. Brush or drizzle the top with a little more oil. Cover with a clean kitchen towel and let rise until doubled in size, an hour or 2 depending on the warmth of your kitchen. (It won't reach the top of the pan, or will just barely.) When it's almost ready, heat the oven to 350°F.

3. Bake until the bottom of the loaf sounds hollow when you tap it or the internal temperature is about 200°F on an instant-read thermometer, about 45 minutes. Remove from the pan and cool completely on a wire rack before slicing.

Brioche

MAKES: 2 loaves | **TIME:** At least 3 hours, largely unattended

Brioche is the richest of all the breads in this section, loaded with butter and eggs, yet the result feels light and tender rather than like overkill. Bake it in standard loaf

---

Making Yeast Bread Dough by Hand or with a Standing Mixer

BY HAND

Combine half the flour with the salt and yeast in a large bowl and stir to blend. Add all of the water and any butter, oil, eggs, or other liquids, and stir with a wooden spoon until smooth. Add the remaining flour a bit at a time; when the mixture becomes too stiff to stir with a spoon, begin kneading (see "Kneading Dough," page 782), adding as little flour as possible—just enough to keep the dough from being a sticky mess. Knead until smooth but still tacky; the time will vary depending on the recipe.

WITH A STANDING MIXER

To make yeast bread—including pizza dough—with a standing mixer, the machine must be fairly powerful or it will stall. Combine half the flour with the salt, yeast, and all of the water, plus any butter, oil, eggs, or other liquids); beat until smooth using the paddle attachment. With the machine on slow speed, add the remaining flour a little at a time, until the mixture has become a sticky ball that pulls away from the sides of the bowl; switch to the dough hook if the paddle is getting bogged down. When the dough is smooth—after several more minutes in the mixer—knead by hand on a floured work surface for 1 minute, adding as little flour as possible, then follow the directions in the recipe rising and shaping.

pans for superb sandwiches and toast, or in a special fluted brioche pan if you'd like (don't worry about making the traditional fancy knob on top). Hand-shaped rolls are always an option; see the directions for shaping and baking rolls on pages 783 and 784). Leftover brioche makes yummy French Toast (page 738).

    4   cups all-purpose flour, plus more for shaping
    1   teaspoon salt
    ¼   cup sugar
    1½   teaspoons instant yeast
    8   tablespoons (1 stick) cold butter, cut into
         chunks, plus softened butter for greasing
    3   eggs plus 1 egg yolk
    ½   cup plus 2 tablespoons lukewarm milk

1. Combine the flour, salt, sugar, and yeast in a food processor and process for 5 seconds. Add the cold butter and the 3 whole eggs and process for 10 seconds. With the machine running, rapidly pour ½ cup of the milk and ⅓ cup water through the feed tube. Process for about 30 seconds, then remove the cover. The dough should be very sticky, almost like batter. If it is too dry, add water 1 tablespoon at a time and process for 5 or 10 seconds after each addition. If it is too wet, which is almost impossible, add another tablespoon or 2 flour and process briefly.

2. Grease a large bowl with softened butter and scrape the dough into it. Cover with plastic wrap and let rise until doubled in size, 2 to 3 hours. The rising time will be shorter at warmer temperatures, a bit longer if your kitchen is chilly.

3. Grease two 9 × 5-inch loaf pans. Press down on the dough to deflate it. Using just enough flour to enable you to handle it, divide the dough in half and shape it into 2 sandwich loaves (see page 784). Put the dough in the prepared pans, cover with plastic or clean kitchen towels, and let rise in a warm place until puffy, about 1 hour.

4. Heat the oven to 400°F. Mix the egg yolk with the remaining 2 tablespoons milk and brush the top of the loaves. Bake the brioche for about 30 minutes, until

nicely browned, the bottom sounds hollow when you tap it, and the interior temperature reaches 190°F on an instant-read thermometer. Let cool on a wire rack for 10 minutes in the pans, then remove to finish cooling directly on the rack—the bread will fall easily from the loaf pan.

COCOA SWIRL BREAD Not too sweet, but definitely chocolaty: Follow the directions through Step 2. Mix together ¼ cup cocoa powder and ½ cup sugar. After dividing the dough in Step 3, gently press each piece into a rectangle about 9 inches long and 1 inch thick. Sprinkle half the cocoa mixture evenly over each rectangle. Wet your hands and shake a few drops of water over all or spray lightly with water; you can also use milk. Use a fork to press the cocoa mixture into the dough a bit; it should be a light paste. Roll up the dough tightly, seal the seam well, and fit the dough seam side down into the prepared loaf pans. Proceed with the recipe.

POPPY SEED SWIRL BREAD An Old World treat made easy with prepared prune (dried plum) spread, which should be available in your supermarket: Follow the variation for Cocoa Swirl Bread, but instead of the cocoa-sugar mixture, combine ¾ cup prune paste with ¼ cup poppy seeds; spread over the rectangles of dough (no need to add any water). Roll and seal the loaves as directed in the first variation; proceed with the recipe.

CINNAMON BUNS Cinnamon bread in roll form: In Step 3, butter a 13 × 9-inch baking pan or dish. While the dough is rising for the first time, combine 2 tablespoons ground cinnamon with ¾ cup sugar in a small bowl. Press and roll all the dough into a large rectangle about 15 inches long and ¾-inch thick. (If the dough is very elastic, you may need to roll, let it rest for a few minutes, and roll again.) Sprinkle the cinnamon sugar evenly over all. Wet your hands and shake a few drops of water over all or spray lightly with water; use a fork to press the cinnamon sugar into the dough a bit; it should be a light paste. Roll up the dough lengthwise and seal the seam as well as you can. You'll have a long log. Slice it

 **F** fast   **M** make ahead   **V** vegetarian

crosswise into 15 pieces. Put them cut side up in the prepared baking pan in 3 rows of 5 buns. Proceed with the recipe, letting the buns rise until doubled in size, about an hour. Reduce the baking time to about 20 minutes; they should be lightly browned and spring back when gently pressed. Cool briefly in the pan on a wire rack. If you like, when the cinnamon buns cool down a bit, sprinkle them with confectioners' sugar or drizzle them with Vanilla Glaze (page 858). Or for sticky bun–style decadence, smear with Caramel–Cream Cheese Frosting (page 862) and sprinkle with chopped pecans. Serve warm, right from the pan.

Challah

MAKES: 1 large loaf | **TIME:** At least 3 hours, largely unattended

The traditional Sabbath bread of European Jews is rich, eggy, and very, very tender. It's not buttery like Brioche (page 791) and there's more dough to make a festive braided loaf, which is easier than you might think. However, unless you have a large food processor (one with at least an 11-cup work bowl), you will have to make this by hand or with a standing mixer (see page 791). Leftover challah makes excellent French Toast (page 738) and Bread Pudding (page 893).

- 5 **cups all-purpose flour, plus more for kneading and shaping**
- 2 **teaspoons salt**
- 2 **teaspoons instant yeast**
  A few threads saffron (optional)
- 1 **tablespoon honey or sugar**
- 3 **eggs plus 1 yolk**
- 1 **cups water or milk, lukewarm, plus more as needed**
  Good-quality vegetable oil or softened butter for greasing the bowl and baking sheet
- 1 **tablespoon poppy seeds (optional)**
  Coarse salt (optional)

1. Put the flour in a food processor. Add the salt, the yeast, and saffron if you're using it and process for 5 seconds. With the machine running, add the honey, whole eggs, and 1 cup of the water or milk through the feed tube. Process for about 30 seconds, then remove the cover. The dough should be in a well-defined, barely sticky, easy-to-handle ball. If it is too dry, add water or milk 1 tablespoon at a time and process for 5 or 10 seconds after each addition. If it is too wet, which is unlikely, add another tablespoon or 2 flour and process briefly. Turn the dough out onto a lightly floured surface and knead until it's smooth and elastic, just a few minutes.

2. Grease a large bowl. Shape the dough into a rough ball, put it in the bowl, and cover with plastic wrap or a damp kitchen towel. Let rise for at least 1½ hours, until nearly doubled in size. The rising time will be shorter at warmer temperatures, a bit longer if your kitchen is chilly.

3. Press down on the dough to deflate it. Cut it into 3 equal pieces and shape each into a ball. Let them rest on a lightly floured surface, covered, for about 15 minutes.

4. Roll each ball into a rope about 14 inches long and 1 inch thick. Braid them on a lightly greased baking sheet, as illustrated on page 794. Cover and let rest for 30 minutes while you heat the oven.

5. Heat the oven to 375°F. Beat the egg yolk with 1 teaspoon water and brush the top of the loaf with this mixture; sprinkle with poppy seeds and/or a little coarse salt if you're using them. Bake for 40 to 50 minutes, until the bottom of the loaf sounds hollow when you tap it and the internal temperature reaches about 195°F on

How Do I Get That Shiny Crust?

This is also essential to get coarse salt, seeds, and spices to stick to the top of loaves and rolls: Right before the bread goes into the oven, make an egg wash by beating 1 egg yolk with 1 tablespoon water. Lightly brush the top of the loaves or rolls with this egg wash, sprinkle whatever else on top if you'd like, and pop them into the oven.

an instant-read thermometer. Cool completely on a wire rack before slicing. Wrap any leftovers loosely in foil and eat within a couple days or use for toast.

Onion Rye Bread

MAKES: 1 large round or oval loaf | TIME: About 5 hours, largely unattended

Rye breads are known for being tricky, but not this one, especially if you use a food processor. The crumb is dense and there's a lot of flavor thanks to the unexpected additions of cornmeal and onion. It's awesome for corned beef or pastrami sandwiches and with cream cheese and smoked salmon.

1½ cups all-purpose or bread flour, plus more for kneading and shaping
1 cup rye flour
½ cup fine cornmeal, plus more for sprinkling
2 teaspoons instant yeast
1 tablespoon sugar, honey, or molasses
2 teaspoons salt
⅔ cup milk, lukewarm
½ cup minced onion
1 tablespoon plus 1 teaspoon caraway seeds
2 teaspoons good-quality vegetable oil, for greasing the bowl

1. Combine the flours, cornmeal, yeast, sugar, and salt in a food processor and process for 5 seconds. With the machine running, rapidly pour the milk and ¼ cup water

---

Making Challah

STEP 1 Cut the dough into three equal pieces.

STEP 2 Roll each piece into a rope about 14 inches long.

STEP 3 Lay the ropes next to each other and press one end together.

STEP 4 Braid, just as you would hair.

STEP 5 Continue to braid the pieces.

STEP 6 When you are finished braiding, use your fingers to tightly press the ends together.

F fast   M make ahead   V vegetarian

through the feed tube. Process for about 30 seconds, then remove the cover. The dough should be in a defined but shaggy ball, still quite sticky; you would not want to knead it by hand. If the dough is too dry, add water 1 tablespoon at a time and process for 5 or 10 seconds after each addition. If it is too wet, which is unlikely, add another tablespoon or 2 flour and process briefly. Turn the dough out onto a lightly floured counter, sprinkle evenly with the onion and 1 tablespoon of the caraway seeds, and knead them in by hand.

2. Put the oil in a large bowl and add the dough, turning it to coat all over, then cover with plastic wrap. Allow to double in size, 2 to 3 hours. The rising time will be shorter at warmer temperatures, a bit longer if your kitchen is chilly.

3. Turn the dough out onto a lightly floured surface and shape it into a boule (see page 784) or an oval loaf; it won't rise much in the oven, so don't make it too flat. If you're using a pizza stone, sprinkle a peel or flexible cutting board with cornmeal and lay the loaf on top; if not, sprinkle a baking sheet with cornmeal and put the loaf on it. Cover again and let rise until puffy, about 1 hour.

4. Put an ovenproof skillet (preferably cast iron) on the oven floor or the lowest rack and heat the oven to 450°F. If you're using a pizza stone, put it on the rack above the skillet.

5. Once you're ready to bake, slash the top with a sharp knife or razor blade (see page 785), brush the loaf with a little water, and sprinkle with the remaining 1 teaspoon caraway seeds. Use the peel or cutting board to transfer the loaf to the stone or slide the baking sheet onto the rack above the heated skillet. Partially pull out the skillet and very carefully pour in 1 cup hot water (it will create a lot of steam). Quickly slide the skillet back in and immediately close the oven door.

6. Bake for 15 minutes, then lower the heat to 350°F and bake for another 30 to 45 minutes, until the loaf is nicely browned, its bottom sounds hollow when you tap it, and the internal temperature is 210°F on an instant-read thermometer. Cool completely on a wire rack before slicing.

Black Bread

MAKES: 2 small loaves or 1 large loaf | **TIME:** 3 hours, largely unattended

This bread features a one-step mixing technique that keeps the process simple, and in return you get a full-flavored, fairly dense, almost-black Russian-style loaf that's perfect with hearty soups and stews or a wedge of sharp cheddar cheese, some pickles, and a smear of whole grain mustard.

½   cup wheat bran
2   cups all-purpose or bread flour, plus more for kneading and shaping
1   cup rye flour
1   cup whole wheat flour
2   tablespoons cocoa powder
2   tablespoons sugar
1   tablespoon instant yeast
2   teaspoons salt
4   tablespoons (½ stick) butter, softened, or ¼ cup good-quality vegetable oil, plus more for greasing
¼   cup molasses
2   tablespoons cider vinegar or fresh lemon juice
1¼ cups strong brewed coffee, lukewarm

1. Put the bran, flours, cocoa, sugar, yeast, and salt in a food processor and pulse for a few seconds to combine. Add the butter and molasses and pulse a few more times. With the machine running, pour the vinegar and 1 cup of the coffee through the feed tube. Process for about 30 seconds; the dough should be a well-defined, barely sticky, easy-to-handle ball. If it's too dry, add more coffee 1 tablespoon at a time and process for 5 or 10 seconds after each addition. If too wet, which is unlikely, add a tablespoon or 2 of flour and process briefly.

2. Grease a large bowl with butter or oil. Shape the dough into a rough ball, put it in the bowl, and cover with plastic wrap or a damp kitchen towel. Let rise until nearly doubled in bulk, 2 to 3 hours. The rising time will be shorter at warmer temperatures, a bit longer if your kitchen is chilly.

Black Bread,
page 795

3. Press down on the dough to deflate it. Shape it once again into a ball; let rest on a lightly floured work surface for about 15 minutes, covered lightly with plastic wrap. (You can make the dough ahead to this point, cover it, and refrigerate for several hours or overnight; return it to room temperature before proceeding.)

4. Using only enough flour to keep the dough from sticking to your hands and the work surface, knead the dough a few times. Shape it into one large oval loaf or divide it in half and make 2 smaller, round loaves. Grease a baking sheet. Put the loaf or loaves on the sheet. Cover again and let rise until the dough has plumped up again considerably, about an hour.

5. Heat the oven to 325°F. Bake for 55 to 60 minutes for a large loaf or 40 to 45 minutes for smaller ones, until the bottom sounds hollow when you tap it and the internal temperature is about 210°F on an instant-read thermometer. Carefully slide the loaf from the sheet and cool completely on a wire rack before slicing.

PUMPERNICKEL RAISIN BREAD Soak 1 cup raisins until soft in enough hot water or coffee to barely cover them. Drain well. Omit the bran and sure to use dark rye flour; increase the quantity to 1½ cups. In Step 4, knead the raisins into the dough along with 1 tablespoon caraway seeds.

BLACK BREAD WITH CHOCOLATE Lovely with a smear of cream cheese or sour cream: Coarsely chop a 4-ounce piece of dark chocolate into chunks. In Step 4, knead the chocolate into the dough.

15 Ingredients to Add to Any Plain Yeast Bread

Here are some ways to add flavor or texture to virtually any yeast bread. Add any of these ingredients along with the flour and yeast (before the water or other liquids):

1. **Spice blends:** 1 to 2 tablespoons, depending on their pungency, lightly toasted first in a dry pan (see pages 27–35 to make your own)
2. **Spice seeds, like caraway or cumin:** Up to 1 tablespoon, lightly toasted first in a dry pan
3. **Cooked whole grains:** Up to ½ cup
4. **Finely ground coffee or tea:** Up to ¼ cup
5. **Wheat germ:** Up to ¼ cup; lightly toast first in a dry pan if you like

Knead any of these ingredients into the dough during the final shaping:

1. **Chopped nuts or seeds, toasted if you like:** Up to 1 cup
2. **Chopped dried fruit (including dried tomatoes) or raisins:** Up to ½ cup
3. **Chopped pitted olives:** Up to ½ cup
4. **Chopped or crumbled bits of cooked ham, bacon, sausage, or pancetta, or prosciutto:** Up to ½ cup
5. **Grated hard or medium-hard cheese like Parmesan, Manchego, pepper Jack, or ricotta salata:** Up to 1 cup
6. **Bits of soft cheese like goat cheese, blue cheese or Gorgonzola, or cream cheese:** Up to ½ cup
7. **Minced fresh herbs:** Up to ¼ cup mild ones like parsley, mint, cilantro, dill, or chives; no more than 1 tablespoon strong ones like rosemary, sage, or oregano
8. **Minced fresh chile like jalapeño or Thai, hot red pepper flakes, or cayenne:** To taste
9. **Roasted Garlic (page 294), lightly mashed or coarsely chopped:** Up to ½ cup
10. **Caramelized Onions (page 315):** Up to ½ cup

Pita

MAKES: 6 to 12 pitas, depending on size | TIME: At least 2 hours, somewhat unattended

Supermarket pita (also called *pide*) is never the same as the chewy, slightly puffed rounds that are the standard flatbread of the Eastern Mediterranean. Luckily baking your own is a simple enough task; you've got a couple equipment options here, including a stovetop method that delivers a golden crisp crust.

You can make whole wheat pitas by simply substituting whole wheat flour for half the white flour.

- 3 **cups all-purpose or bread flour, plus more for kneading and shaping**
- 3 **tablespoons olive oil**
- 2 **teaspoons instant yeast**
- 2 **teaspoons kosher or coarse sea salt**
- ½ **teaspoon sugar**
   Good-quality vegetable oil, for baking (optional)
   Melted butter (optional)

1. Combine the flour, olive oil, yeast, salt, and sugar in a food processor. Turn the machine on and add 1 cup water through the feed tube. Process for about 30 seconds, adding more water a little at a time until the mixture forms a ball and is slightly sticky to the touch. If it's dry, add another tablespoon or 2 water and process for another 10 seconds. In the unlikely event that the mixture is too sticky, add flour a tablespoon at a time.

2. Turn the dough onto a floured work surface and knead by hand for a few seconds to form a smooth, round dough ball. Put the dough into a large bowl and cover with plastic wrap; let it rise until doubled in size, 1 to 2 hours. The rising time will be shorter at warmer temperatures, a bit longer if your kitchen is chilly.

3. When the dough is ready, press down on the dough to deflate it. Divide it into 6 to 12 pieces; roll each piece into a ball. Put each ball on a lightly floured work surface, sprinkle with a little flour, and cover with plastic wrap or a towel. Let rest until they puff slightly, about 20 minutes.

4. Roll each ball out to less than ¼ inch thick, using flour to prevent sticking as necessary. As you finish

 fast make ahead **V** vegetarian

rolling, spread the disks out on a floured work surface; keep them covered. When all the disks are rolled out, heat the oven to 350°F while the disks rest for at least 20 minutes. If you have a pizza stone, put it on the lowest rack in the oven; if not, lightly oil a baking sheet and put it on the center rack. Alternatively, lightly oil and wipe out a heavy skillet or griddle, preferably cast iron.

5. To bake on a stone, use a peel or a large spatula to slide the individual disks—as many as will fit comfortably—directly onto the stone. Or bake as many disks as will fit on the baking sheet without overlapping. To cook on the stovetop, put the skillet or griddle over medium-high heat; when the pan is very warm, add the dough. Whichever method you use, bake the pitas until lightly browned on one side, then turn and brown on the other side. Total baking time will be between 5 and 10 minutes, generally only 5 to 6, perhaps a bit less for stovetop baking.

6. As the pitas finish baking, transfer them to a wire rack. Repeat with the remaining disks of dough. If you're going to serve the pitas fairly soon, brush with melted butter. Otherwise, cool completely, then store in wax paper or plastic bags; reheat gently in a 200°F oven before serving.

Naan

MAKES: 12 naan | TIME: 2 to 3 hours, largely unattended

With their slightly sour flavor and ultra-soft texture, they're the perfect accompaniment to dal (page 409) or any Indian-style curry. (And you don't need a traditional tandoor oven to make them.) Using a little whole wheat flour along with all-purpose results in a slightly warmer, more savory flavor, but you could use all-purpose only.

    2   teaspoons instant yeast
    2   tablespoons milk, lukewarm
    2   tablespoons yogurt
    1   tablespoon sugar
    3½ cups unbleached all-purpose flour, plus more
        for kneading and shaping
    ½   cup whole wheat flour
    1   egg
    2   teaspoons salt
        Good-quality vegetable oil, for greasing the
        bowl
    4   tablespoons (½ stick) butter, melted and still
        warm

1. Stir together the yeast, milk, yogurt, and sugar in a bowl and set aside.

2. Combine the flours, egg, and salt in a food processor. Turn the machine on and add the yeast mixture through the feed tube. Process for about 30 seconds, adding 1½ cups water, a little at a time, until the dough forms a ball and is slightly sticky to the touch. If it is dry, add another tablespoon or 2 water and process for another 10 seconds. In the unlikely event that the mixture is too sticky, add flour a tablespoon at a time.

3. Turn the dough onto a floured work surface and knead by hand for a few seconds to form a smooth, round ball. Put the dough in a lightly oiled bowl and cover with plastic wrap; let rise until the dough doubles in size, 1 to 2 hours. (You can cut this rising time short if you are in a hurry, or you can let the dough rise in the refrigerator for up to 6 or 8 hours.)

4. Put a pizza stone or baking sheet on the lowest rack of your oven; heat the oven to 500°F. Press down on the dough to deflate it. Using as much flour as necessary to keep the dough from sticking to the work surface and your hands, roll it into a snake, then tear the snake into 12 equal-size balls. Let them rest for 10 minutes covered with plastic wrap or a damp kitchen towel.

5. Roll out one of the balls to an oval roughly 6 to 8 inches long and 3 to 4 inches wide. Open the oven door, grab a piece of dough, one hand on each end of the oval, give it a little tug with one hand to shape it into a teardrop, then toss it onto the baking sheet or stone. Close the oven door immediately. Turn the naan after 3 minutes. The naan is ready when it's puffed, mottled, and browned around the edges, 6 to 8 minutes total. You can bake as many naan as will comfortably fit at once.

6. Line a basket or serving plate with a clean kitchen towel or napkin. Brush the baked naan on one side with melted butter and wrap in the towel to keep them warm and pliable. Serve as soon as possible.

Breadsticks

MAKES: 50 to 100 sticks, depending on how you cut them | **TIME:** 1 day or so, largely unattended

In Piedmont—known as the breadstick capital of Italy—you would eat breadsticks without adornment. But I sometimes like to sprinkle them with poppy or sesame seeds or sea salt before baking. This recipe includes two different techniques for making breadsticks: one for rustic-looking hand-rolled ones, and another for more uniform results.

> 3 **cups all-purpose or bread flour, plus more for rolling**
> 2 **teaspoons instant yeast**
> 1 **teaspoon sugar**
> 2 **teaspoons salt**
> 2 **tablespoons olive oil, plus more for greasing the bowl**
> **Semolina flour or cornmeal for sprinkling the baking sheets**

1. Combine the flour, yeast, sugar, and salt in a food processor; pulse once or twice. Add the oil and pulse a couple of times. With the machine running, add 1 cup water through the feed tube. Continue to add water 1 tablespoon at a time until the mixture forms a ball. It should be a little shaggy and quite sticky.

2. Put a little oil in a bowl and transfer the dough ball to it, turning to coat it well. Cover with plastic wrap and let it rise for 1 hour in a warm place. Press down on the dough to deflate it. Reshape the ball, put it back in the bowl, cover again, and let rise in the refrigerator for several hours, preferably overnight.

3. Heat the oven to 400°F. Lightly grease 2 baking sheets with olive oil and sprinkle very lightly with semolina flour or cornmeal.

4. Cut the dough into 3 pieces; keep 2 covered while you work with the first. To roll by hand: On a well-floured surface, roll a piece of dough out as thin as possible into a rectangle about a foot long. Use a sharp knife or pizza cutter to cut the dough into roughly ¼-inch-thick strips; slightly smaller is better than slightly bigger.

5. To cut with a pasta machine: Roll out the dough to ¼ inch thick by hand. Put it through the machine at the thickest setting and cut it using the fettuccine cutter. Cut the strips into 1-foot lengths.

6. Transfer the strips to the baking sheets, spaced apart just a little, and brush with olive oil. Bake until crisp and golden, 10 to 20 minutes, then cool completely on the baking sheets on wire racks. Serve immediately or store in an airtight container for up to 1 week.

SESAME RICE BREADSTICKS Fun to serve with Chinese, Vietnamese, or Thai dishes: Replace 1 cup of the flour with brown rice flour. Use good quality vegetable oil for brushing then sprinkle the breadsticks with light or black sesame seeds before baking.

Two Essentials Made from Bread

Sure: You can buy bread crumbs and croutons—and pretty good ones at that—but if you like to eat bread, you're going to have leftovers. So sock extra odds and ends away in the freezer; thaw them out as needed. Then here's what you should do with them.

Fresh Bread Crumbs

MAKES: 3 to 4 cups | **TIME:** 10 minutes

The most common ways to use bread crumbs are in stuffing or as breading. They can also add a welcome crunch when incorporated into dishes as they cook or used for garnish. When you do need to use store-bought, panko crumbs are a good alternative.

About 8 ounces good-quality bread, preferably a day or 2 old

1. Tear the bread into pieces and put about half in a food processor. Pulse a few times, then let the machine run for a few seconds until coarsely chopped.

2. Remove and repeat with the remaining bread. Use immediately or store in an airtight container for up to a month.

TOASTED BREAD CRUMBS After grinding, spread the bread crumbs on a baking sheet. Bake in a 350°F oven, shaking the pan occasionally, until lightly browned, about 15 minutes; store these the same way as fresh. Alternatively, toast fresh bread crumbs just before using them.

FRIED BREAD CRUMBS These are delicious; seasoning sticks to them better than uncoated bread crumbs, but they don't keep as well, so use them immediately after frying: For every cup of bread crumbs, heat about 2 tablespoons olive oil in a large skillet. When it's hot, add the crumbs and cook, stirring occasionally, until lightly browned, about 5 minutes. Season with salt or any spice mixture (to make your own, see pages 27–35) and drain on towels; use immediately.

NUTTY BREAD CRUMBS Add ½ cup cashews, almonds, pistachios, or hazelnuts to the food processor along with the bread. The yield will be a little more than 4 cups. Toast or fry as in the previous variations if you'd like, or not.

My Kind of Croutons

MAKES: 4 servings | **TIME:** 15 minutes

There are times I make soup or a nice big salad just as an excuse to make and eat croutons. You know, the "real" kind that are basically small slices of toast. Or maybe big cubes that stay crunchy a long time (see the variations). Start with good bread—and that might be corn bread, whole grain, or cinnamon-raisin—and good olive oil and you'll also be a convert.

    ¼ cup or more olive oil, plus more if needed
    1 clove garlic, smashed (optional)
    4 (if large) to 12 (if small) ½-inch-thick slices
       good bread
       Salt and pepper

1. Put the oil and garlic if you're using it in a skillet large enough to accommodate the bread in one layer and turn the heat to medium. (If you don't have a big enough pan you may need to work in batches, although it's okay if the slices touch.) When the oil shimmers and the garlic sizzles, add the bread.

2. When the bread browns lightly on the bottom, turn to brown the other side; this will take 5 to 10 minutes total. If the pan dries out (which it likely will), add more olive oil. When the second side is browned, sprinkle with salt and pepper, and remove the croutons from the pan. (Leave the garlic behind.) Use right away, or let cool and store in an airtight container for up to 1 day.

CUBED CROUTONS I like the crust left on: Instead of slicing the bread, cut about 8 ounces from a whole loaf into ½-inch to 1-inch cubes. (Or if you already have slices, cut into squares.) In Step 1, cook them in the oil, tossing occasionally, sprinkling with salt and pepper, and adding more oil as needed, until lightly browned and crisp all over, 10 to 15 minutes.

Cubed Croutons,
page 801

HERBED CROUTONS Best with cubes: As the bread browns, stir in about ¼ cup finely minced parsley, dill, or chervil, or a combination.

HIGHLY SEASONED CROUTONS Season with plenty of pepper, along with about 1 teaspoon chili powder or curry powder (to make your own, see page 32) or store-bought ancho chile powder.

DRY-BAKED CROUTONS Perfect for large batches; when kept in an airtight container, these will stay crunchy for at least a week. Plus, there's no fat: Omit the oil and garlic. Use bread slices, as in the main recipe, or cubes as in the first variation. Heat the oven to 400°F. Spread the bread out on a rimmed baking sheet. Bake the croutons, undisturbed, until they begin to turn golden, about 15 minutes. Turn the slices or shake the pan to roll the cubes around a bit. Continue baking until they're the desired color, 5 to 15 minutes more. Sprinkle with salt and pepper, or other seasoning, if you like.

THE BASICS OF SANDWICHES

The recipes in this section, which includes wraps, are for what I'd call specific, slightly involved sandwiches. The ingredient lists, directions, and variations are straightforward, and you don't need much additional information. Beyond that, this introduction offers guidelines for improvising new sandwiches and improving your own standbys—even ones as simple as peanut butter and jelly.

CHOOSING THE RIGHT BREAD

Bread's role in a sandwich is more than as a holder and transporter of the filling. You want to be able to taste it, which means store-bought white is usually not the best choice. In fact, it might be the worst.

Sliced yeast breads, rolls, and all sorts of flatbreads and tortillas are often the best sandwich breads because they have the structure to support the filling, and a nice chewy texture. But some yeast breads simply aren't cut out for sandwiches; those with very hard or thick crusts can make sandwiches nearly impossible to eat, and breads with large holes just can't hold the filling.

Crumbly quick breads can sometimes work, but are best as open-face sandwiches with simple and small amounts of topping. (The charts below and on pages 805 and 808 give bread and filling pairing suggestions for different sandwiches.) Beyond the type of bread you use, there's what you do with it: Toasting, grilling, and broiling make bread crisp and tastier. You can also toast or grill many sandwiches after filling.

FILLINGS AND SPREADS

There are few rules for fillings and even fewer for spreads. When you're using sliced bread or rolls, the fillings should be sliced thin or cut small enough so you can bite into the sandwich easily, but not so small that the pieces fall out of the bread. In cases where the filling is in bits, turn to pliable flatbreads, pocket pitas, or tortillas to keep everything manageable.

Spreads should be full of flavor and provide some moisture and/or creaminess, so cheese spreads, soft

Top 8 Spreads for Sandwiches and Wraps

The classic sandwich spreads are mustard and mayonnaise (to make your own, see pages 37 and 69). Also consider:

1. Traditional Pesto or other herb sauces (pages 51–52)
2. Any fresh salsa (page 55–58)
3. Any chutney (pages 61–62)
4. Barbecue sauce (to make your own, see page 74)
5. Any of the dips or spreads in the Appetizers chapter (starting on page 99)
6. Vinaigrette and other salad dressings (pages 188–191)
7. Caramelized Onions (page 315)
8. Soft-boiled egg yolks (page 721)

cheeses, and vegetable and bean purées are ideal. Obviously you don't want anything so wet it sogs up the bread or wrapper. Many spreads can become the filling as well, like hummus; they make simple but tasty sandwiches that can easily be transformed into bite-sized hors d'oeuvres (see page 96).

Tuna Salad with Lemon and Olive Oil

MAKES: 4 sandwiches | **TIME:** 10 minutes

My alternative to the traditional tuna sandwich has loads of bright flavor from lemon zest and capers. If you use water-packed tuna, drain well and add another tablespoon or 2 olive oil. Try it with pitas.

2	5- to 6-ounce cans tuna (preferably packed in olive oil), drained
	Grated zest and juice of 1 lemon
1	small shallot or 3 scallions, minced
1 or 2	tablespoons capers, rinsed, drained, and chopped
½	cup chopped fresh parsley leaves
3	tablespoons olive oil
	Salt and pepper
4	leaves romaine lettuce, washed and dried
8	slices any bread

1. Mix the tuna with the lemon zest and juice, shallots, capers, parsley, and olive oil and sprinkle with some salt and pepper. (You can make the salad up to several hours ahead and refrigerate in an airtight container; or store leftovers the same way for up to a couple days.)

2. Toast the bread if you'd like. Make sandwiches with the tuna mixture, lettuce, and bread. Serve immediately.

TUNA SALAD WITH LIME AND CILANTRO Substitute the juice of 2 limes and the zest of 1 for the lemon and cilantro for the parsley; use the scallions and omit the capers.

TUNA SALAD WITH OLIVES Substitute ¼ cup Tapenade (page 109) or any chopped olives for the capers and use lemon juice to taste (you made decide to use none) at the end.

TUNA SALAD WITH MAYO Remarkably improved with homemade mayonnaise (page 69). Substitute ¼ cup or more mayonnaise for the olive oil; omit the lemon zest and juice if you like and try chopped pickles instead of the capers.

EGG SALAD WITH MAYO Instead of the tuna in the preceding variation, use 6 hard-boiled eggs (page 721). Chop them as fine or coarse as you like before combining with the mayonnaise. Add 1 tablespoon mustard (or more to taste) and pickles, capers, minced celery, or scallion, or a combination.

Grilled Cheese

MAKES: 1 sandwich | **TIME:** 10 minutes

The concept of griddling a sandwich isn't exclusive to one cuisine. And you don't need a fancy press to make a beautifully crisp and browned sandwich; the plate technique here does the job perfectly. Improve simple grilled cheese by adding your favorite dressing or using other fillings; see the following chart.

1	tablespoon butter, olive oil or good-quality vegetable oil
2	slices any bread
	Several slices (2 to 3 ounces) good melting cheese like Emmental, Gruyère, Jarlsberg, or cheddar

1. Put a small skillet over medium heat and add the butter or oil. Make a sandwich with the bread and cheese.

7 Other Grilled Sandwiches

For any of the griddled sandwiches below, use the technique in Grilled Cheese (left), smearing one slice of bread with the spread, filling as described, and cooking long enough to brown the bread and melt the cheese and heat the filling.

SANDWICH	BREAD	SPREAD	FILLING
Grilled Cheese and Onions	Any bread; whole wheat or multigrain is best	None	Several slices smoked cheddar or other smoked cheese, up to ¼ cup Caramelized Onions (page 315)
Tuna Melt	Any bread; try a sourdough	None	¼ to ½ cup any Tuna Salad (page 804), several slices good melting cheese like Emmental, Gruyère, Jarlsberg, or cheddar
Reuben	Rye bread	Russian dressing (an equal mix of ketchup and mayonnaise) or mustard	2 to 3 ounces sliced pastrami or corned beef, ¼ cup drained sauerkraut, several slices Swiss cheese
Cuban Sandwich	6- to 10-inch section of long Italian loaf or baguette	Mustard	3 ounces sliced roast pork, ham, and/or mortadella if you like, several slices Swiss cheese, thinly sliced dill pickle
Chicken-Pesto Panino	Ciabatta or similar crusty Italian-style bread	Traditional Pesto (page 51)	2 to 3 ounces sliced cooked chicken breast, several slices mozzarella cheese (preferably fresh), 2 or 3 thin slices ripe tomato
Monte Cristo	Sandwich Bread (page 790), Challah (page 793), or Brioche (page 791). Fill the sandwich with several slices Gruyère cheese, 2 ounces or so sliced country ham. Then soak the bread in an egg beaten with a little milk as in French toast before cooking.	A smear of Dijon mustard	To gild the lily, add a fried egg on top
Grilled Nut Butter and Kimchee Sandwich	Rustic French Bread (page 787) or Sandwich Bread (page 790)	Almond or any nut butter (spread on both pieces of bread)	¼ cup kimchee, drained well

2. When the butter melts or the oil is hot, put the sandwich in the skillet. Set a plate on top of the sandwich and weight the plate with whatever is at hand—a couple of cans of soup or a small but heavy pot cover, for example.

3. Cook until the bottom of the bread is browned lightly, 2 or 3 minutes. Turn, replace the plate and weight, and cook the other side. Eat immediately.

BROILED CHEESE FOR A CROWD Turn on the broiler and position the rack about 4 inches below the heat. Assemble up to 8 sandwiches per large rimmed baking sheet. Melt 1 tablespoon butter for each sandwich and brush the exposed sides of the bread generously. Broil, turning the sandwiches once, until the bread is toasted on both sides and the cheese is melted, 2 or 3 minutes per side.

Pan Bagnat with Tuna

MAKES: 4 servings | TIME: 1 hour, plus time to rest overnight

Marinated sandwiches—like this Provençal classic that translates to "bathed bread"—are some of the most beautiful sandwiches you've ever seen, and ideal for picnics: The longer they sit (within reason), the better they get. View this recipe as a general guideline; you can make the sandwich with whatever cooked food you have on hand, including leftover grilled fish or meat and leftover vegetables. Then dress it as described here.

1	medium zucchini, summer squash, or eggplant
	Salt and pepper
	Olive oil for brushing the vegetables, plus more for drizzling as needed
2	red bell peppers, or 2 jarred roasted red peppers
1	8- to 10-inch round loaf crusty bread
2	5- to 6-ounce cans (preferably packed in olive oil), not drained

1	teaspoon drained capers, or more to taste
6 to 8	pitted black or green olives
4 to 6	anchovy fillets, or more to taste
4	marinated artichoke hearts, quartered
2 or 3	slices ripe tomato
	Chopped fresh parsley or basil
	Juice of ½ lemon

1. Cut the zucchini lengthwise into ¼-inch slices. If time allows, put it in a colander and salt liberally; let sit for 30 to 45 minutes, then rinse and dry thoroughly, pressing to extract excess moisture. Meanwhile, prepare a charcoal or gas grill for medium indirect cooking (make sure the grates are clean) or turn on the broiler and position the rack about 4 inches below the heat.

2. Brush the zucchini with some olive oil and grill or broil until lightly browned on both sides, 5 to 7 minutes total. Grill or broil the red bell peppers until the skin blackens and blisters all around, about 5 minutes total. When the peppers are cool enough to handle, peel, core, and seed them; cut into strips. If you're using jarred peppers, drain and rinse them, and cut them into strips.

3. Cut the bread in half horizontally. Remove some of the crumb from each half to make the bread somewhat hollow. Then build the sandwich by first layering on the tuna and enough of its oil to moisten the bread without saturating. Follow with the bell pepper, zucchini, capers, olives, anchovies, artichoke hearts, tomato, and parsley or basil. Sprinkle with salt and pepper, drizzle the filling and the inside of the top piece of bread with enough of the remaining tuna oil (or some olive oil) to just moisten everything; sprinkle with lemon juice.

4. Close the sandwich; wrap well in aluminum foil. Put it on a plate, set another plate on top, and weight the second plate with rocks, bricks, a gallon jug of water—whatever is handy. Use a lot of weight, 5 pounds or more. Refrigerate overnight or for up to 24 hours. Unwrap, cut into wedges, and serve.

28 Perfect Hot and Cold Dishes for Filling Sandwiches

1. Deviled Eggs (page 91)
2. Tomato, Mozzarella, and Basil Salad (page 199)
3. Any chicken, meat, or seafood salad (pages 221–227)
4. Any of the burgers on pages 413, 443,547, 687, 688, 704, and 705
5. Deep Fried Seafood (page 540)
6. Seafood prepared by any of the master recipes on pages 534–538
7. Broiled Soft-Shell Crabs or Lobster (page 543), shelled
8. Chile Shrimp with Celery (page 545)
9. Gravlax (page 551)
10. Bare-Bones Crab Cakes (page 585)
11. Broiled or Grilled Boneless Chicken (page 596)
12. Grilled Chicken Escabeche (page 598)
13. Sautéed Chicken with Wine Sauce (page 609)
14. Eggplant Parmigiana (page 609)
15. Any Poached Boneless Chicken (pages 611–612)
16. Chicken MarkNuggets (page 630)
17. All the Many Ways to Cook Steak (page 667)
18. Roast Tenderloin with Hollandaise (page 679)
19. Braised Beef Brisket (page 684)
20. Corned Beef (page 686)
21. Meat Loaf (page 688)
22. Grilled or Broiled Pork Tenderloin with Herb Crust (page 694)
23. Any of the roast pork recipes on pages 695–698
24. Braised Pork with Vietnamese Flavors (page 697)
25. Baked Country Ham (page 704)
26. Homemade Breakfast (or Any Other Meal) Sausage (page 705)
27. Roast Leg of Lamb (page 709)
28. Grilled or Broiled Veal Chops (page 713)

Fish Sandwich with Chili-Lime Mayo

MAKES: 4 sandwiches | **TIME:** 30 minutes

I love fried fish sandwiches, but you can always broil or grill the fish without coating it if you prefer (see pages 534–535).

- ¼ cup mayonnaise (to make your own, see page 69)
- 2 tablespoons freshly squeezed lime juice
- 1 tablespoon chili powder (to make your own, see page 32)
- 1 teaspoon minced garlic
  Salt and pepper
- ¼ cup good-quality vegetable oil, plus more as needed
- 4 4-ounce fillets firm white fish like cod or halibut, or catfish, salmon, or mahi-mahi
- ¼ cup all-purpose flour
- 1 egg, beaten with 2 tablespoons water
- ¾ cup bread crumbs, preferably fresh (page 801)
- 4 rolls or 8 slices bread, toasted if you like
- 8 slices ripe tomato
- 2 cups shredded napa cabbage or iceberg lettuce
- ¼ cup chopped fresh cilantro leaves (optional)

1. Put the mayonnaise, lime juice, chili powder, garlic, and some salt and pepper in a small bowl and whisk until combined. Taste, adjust the seasoning, and let sit.

2. Put the oil in a large skillet over medium-high heat. Sprinkle the fish with salt and pepper, then dredge both sides in the flour, dip in the egg, and coat in the bread crumbs. When the oil is hot, add the fish and cook until golden brown on both sides, about 8 minutes total.

3. To assemble the sandwiches, spread the rolls with the chili-lime mayo, add the fillets (cut in half to fit on the bun as necessary), and top with tomato slices, cabbage, and cilantro if you're using it. Close and serve right away.

FRIED CHICKEN SANDWICH WITH RANCH DRESSING
You can stick with straight mayo if you like: Substitute Real Ranch Dressing (page 71) for the chili-lime mayo,

Wraps

The sandwich-burrito hybrid has become a standard. Because wraps are folded and rolled like a burrito (or simply roll up), they can hold items that would otherwise fall out of two pieces of bread or make a soggy mess of sandwich bread.

Any large, flat, flexible bread will work as a wrapping; flour tortillas and lavash are the most common, though you can also use pitas (split if they have pockets).

Lavash comes both soft (basically freshly baked) and as a hard cracker. Both can be used for wraps. To soften the cracker (large Ak-Maks, widely available, work here), run it lightly under water on both sides, put it in a plastic bag, seal it, and let it sit in a cool place or refrigerator until it's completely soft, about 3 hours.

You can fill a wrap with a dressed salad, sliced or ground cooked meat, cooked fish or shellfish, grains, legumes, stir-fried vegetables, or chopped raw vegetables and any condiment you can think of. Roll it up, tucking the ends in like a burrito (see the illustration on page 812). Eat whole, cut in half (it looks nice cut on a slight diagonal), or get multiple servings by slicing crosswise into thick rounds. This chart will get you going.

WRAP	WRAPPER	SPREAD AND/OR CONDIMENTS	FILLING
Caesar Wrap	Large white or whole wheat flour tortilla	Shaved or finely grated Parmesan	Caesar Salad (page 196), sliced grilled chicken or shrimp
Thai-Style Wrap	Large white or whole wheat flour tortilla	Peanut Sauce (page 75), chopped scallion, fresh cilantro (optional)	Stir-Fried Vegetables (page 244), with or without meat or tofu
Indian-Style Wrap	Lavash or softened Ak-Mak	Raita (page 59) or plain yogurt, any chutney (pages 61–64), fresh cilantro	Curry-Poached Chicken (page 612) or Simplest Dal (page 409)
Steak-and-Pepper Wrap	Lavash or softened Ak-Mak	Herbed Goat Cheese (page 100)	Steak slices (page 667), My Mom's Pan-Cooked Peppers and Onions (page 320)
Wrapped Omelet	Large white or whole wheat flour tortilla	Mayonnaise, spiked with hot sauce if you'd like	Any omelet or frittata (pages 730–732)

torn mixed greens for the cabbage, four 4-ounce boneless chicken tenders (or half-breasts) for the fish, and cornmeal for the bread crumbs.

THE BASICS OF TACOS AND BURRITOS

Hot sandwiches, tacos, and burritos have a lot in common besides the fact that you can eat them with your hands. Though warmed and soft or fried and crisp corn or flour tortillas take the place of the bread, the filling components should combine contrasting but complimentary flavors and textures.

KINDS OF TORTILLAS

What was once simply a choice between traditional corn and flour tortillas has grown to a dizzying array that includes flavors, colors, sizes, and even options touted as "low-carb" or gluten-free (which corn tortillas

Building Hot Sandwiches

Some of these are assembled from leftovers and heated; others begin with raw ingredients that are then cooked together in the sandwich (like grilled cheese). Once you get the hang of breaking sandwich-making into these components, you'll easily improvise your own concoctions. See the list on page for a head start with filling ideas.

SANDWICH	BREAD	SPREAD AND/OR CONDIMENTS	FILLING	COOKING
Broiled Roast Beef and Avocado Sandwich	Everyday Sandwich Bread (page 700) or Jim Lahey's No-Knead Bread (page 785)	Guacamole (page 105) or mashed or sliced avocado, or Aioli (page 70)	Sliced roast beef, Roasted Red Peppers or poblanos (page 318), sliced cheddar or Jack cheese	Toast the bread, layer the spread and fillings on 1 slice bread, broil until the cheese melts, add second piece bread.
Pita Sandwich Stuffed with Spicy Lamb and Onions	Pita (page 798)	Simplest Yogurt Sauce (page 59)	Ground lamb, chopped onion and garlic, pinch cinnamon; thinly sliced zucchini; tomato slices	Sauté lamb in olive oil with onion, garlic, and cinnamon. Warm pita in oven; assemble the sandwich.
Open-Face Ratatouille Sandwich with Melted Mozzarella	Jim Lahey's No-Knead Bread (page 785), or any Italian-style bread	Fresh basil leaves; drizzle of olive oil (optional)	Grilled Eggplant (page 252) or Sautéed Eggplant with Basil (page 290); Roasted Red Peppers (page 318) or tomato slices; sliced mozzarella	Grill or toast the bread if you like. Layer vegetables on bread, top with mozzarella, melt cheese under the broiler. Garnish with basil.
Grilled Chicken Breast Sandwich with Roasted Garlic and Mustard	Everyday Sandwich Bread (page 700) or Onion Rye Bread	Roasted Garlic (page 294), mashed, and grainy mustard	Grilled or roasted boneless chicken breast, Muenster or provolone cheese, arugula or raw spinach leaves	Melt cheese on the chicken in the last couple minutes cooking. Grill or broil bread, spread garlic and mustard on each slice, assemble.
North Carolina BBQ Sandwich	French Rolls (page 788), rolls made from brioche dough (see the headnote and recipe on page 791), or other airy rolls	Barbecue Sauce (page 74)	Roast Pork Shoulder (page 695) or Slow-Roasted Spareribs (page 698), bones removed; Spicy No-Mayo Coleslaw (page 203)	Wrap rolls in foil, warm in oven. Heat pork if necessary, then shred. Assemble sandwich, adding the slaw last.
Warm Goat Cheese Sandwich with Toasted Nuts	50 Percent Whole Wheat Sandwich Bread (page 790) or any multigrain bread	Plain soft goat cheese	Toasted chopped almonds, Roasted Red Peppers (page 318), arugula or raw spinach leaves	Spread goat cheese on both pieces of bread and broil until bubbly. Sprinkle with almonds and finish with greens.

F fast   M make ahead   V vegetarian

naturally are). The good news is that many supermarkets now offer local or regional tortillas along with national brands; you can even find good-quality hard taco shells. If you live near a place that makes them fresh, it's worth the trip to buy really good tortillas.

Flour tortillas are soft and subtle, almost neutral in flavor. When fresh, they are delicious and almost fluffy; if not, they're dull and rubbery. You'll find plain (the most useful), whole wheat, and flavored and colored ones (like spinach or tomato, which I avoid). Flour tortillas are almost always served and used soft, but are also fried crisp for quesadillas and some styles of burritos. Choose store-bought versions that are made with only a few ingredients, or make your own (page 781).

Corn tortillas—white, yellow, and sometimes blue—offer more texture and flavor since they're made from hulled corn. The best are dated and have a fresh corn taste, and are soft and pliable. Corn tortillas can be served either soft or crisp, depending on your taste, the freshness of the tortilla, and what you're making.

PREPARING TORTILLAS

Soft flour or corn tortillas should be served hot or warm. Warm them over direct heat, like a grill or the flame of a gas stove, turning them every few seconds, or on a dry skillet or griddle, turning once. To heat bigger batches, wrap 6 to 8 in foil and warm them in a 375°F oven for 5 to 10 minutes. Or enclose them in a damp kitchen towel and microwave for a minute or 2. Keep them hot in a tortilla holder (a shallow round container with a lid) or wrapped in a towel.

Both corn and flour tortillas fry up crisp and golden. There are two methods: Pan-fry in a skillet with shallow or deep hot oil, turning when the edges brown (you can mold it into a taco shape when it's still slightly soft and flexible). Or stuff with a filling, secure with toothpicks, and pan-fry in ¼ inch or so hot oil until both sides are golden. Drain the tortillas on towels for several seconds before serving.

FILLING TORTILLAS

Avoid the urge to overfill. For tacos, a couple of tablespoons in a 6-inch tortilla do the trick and leave room for garnishes. Burritos hold more, especially if you use those huge tortillas. Just make sure your first fold comfortably encloses the ingredients (see the illustrations on page 812).

Bits or small chunks of seasoned meat, chicken, and fish once were the most common taco and burrito fillings in America, though vegetable tacos are everywhere now. Grilled foods are my favorites, though broiled, pan-fried, deep-fried, and braised, or even microwaved fillings (see below) all have a place. I generally like things chopped up a bit. Beans and rice or other whole grains can make excellent fillings in small doses; just be sure to add a crisp raw garnish or salsa to vary the texture.

TOPPINGS

Homemade salsa improves tacos and burritos immeasurably; see pages 55–58 and 71–74. For texture—crunchy and/or creamy—try shredded lettuce or cabbage, chopped tomatoes, grated cheese or the more authentic crumbled queso fresco, sour cream or yogurt, and sliced avocados or Guacamole (page 105). Hot sauces are also a given. Serve everything in bowls on the table for everyone to add as desired.

Fish Tacos, Four Ways

MAKES: 4 servings | **TIME:** 20 minutes

Steamed fish is one time you can use the microwave with excellent results (or not). For other cooking methods, see the variations.

Other proteins you can use: shrimp, scallops, salmon (fillets or steaks), shelled split whole lobster; boneless white or dark meat chicken or turkey; pork loin. Poultry and pork will take a little longer to cook than seafood.

1 large onion, chopped
  2 jalapeño chiles, chopped
    About 1½ pounds thick white fish fillets like cod,
    red snapper, sea bass, grouper, or halibut
    Salt and pepper
12 to 16 6-inch corn tortillas
    Fresh salsa (to make your own, see pages 55–58
    and 71–74)
    Hot sauce or Chile Paste (page 40; optional)
    Sour cream, or crumbled queso fresco or other
    grated cheese (optional)
    Shredded cabbage, chopped tomato and
    cucumber, and cilantro sprigs (optional)
    Lime wedges

1. Put the onion and jalapeños in a large skillet with a tight-fitting lid or in a microwave-safe covered baking dish. Add 1 tablespoon water and the fish; sprinkle with salt and pepper. Cover and put over medium heat or in the microwave. Cook for about 6 minutes or microwave on high power until the fish is flaky; start checking after 3 minutes.
2. While the fish cooks, heat the tortillas. You can toast them in a skillet over medium heat, one at a time, turning them once until hot, a minute or so, wrap them in two equal batches in foil and warm them in a 375°F oven for 5 to 10 minutes, or enclose them in damp kitchen towels and microwave for a minute or 2.
3. To serve, fill the warm tortillas with a small portion of fish along with a bit of the onion and jalapeño. Top with salsa and, if you like, hot sauce, sour cream or cheese, and/or vegetables. Squeeze lime juice over all.

GRILLED FISH TACOS Omit the onion and jalapeño, or chop them up as another garnish. Brush the fish with olive oil and sprinkle with salt and pepper and, if you like, rub with chili powder (to make your own, see page 32). Let the fish rest while you prepare the grill, then follow the instructions for Grilled Seafood on page 535.

BROILED FISH TACOS Prepare the fish as described in the preceding variation, then follow the instructions for Broiled Thick Fillets or Steaks on page 534.

FRIED FISH TACOS You have a few choices, depending on whether you want deep-, shallow-, or oven-fried fish.

Rolling Burritos

STEP 1 Put the filling in the middle of the tortilla, slightly off center toward the edge closest to you.

STEP 2 Fold in the sides a little bit.

STEP 3 Roll up from the edge closest to you, tucking in the sides and the top edge to form a tight roll. Put the burrito seam side down on the plate or wrap the bottom half in foil or wax paper to help keep it together.

F fast   **M** make ahead   **V** vegetarian

Fish Tacos, page 811; pictured: microwaved, left, and grilled, right

Unusual Ideas for Filling Tacos and Burritos

Mix and match these recipes from elsewhere in the book, adding the usual lettuce or cabbage, tomatoes, cheese, avocadoes, and so on if you like.

FILLINGS	SALSAS, TOPPINGS, AND EXTRAS
Roasted Beans with Oil (page 88) and Yellow Rice (page 436)	Fresh Tomatillo Salsa (page 56), especially with crumbled queso fresco
Crisp Pan-Fried Potatoes (Home Fries; page 332) with crisp-fried slices of Spanish chorizo	Avocado-Tomatillo Salsa (page 56) and shredded iceberg or romaine lettuce
Baked Black Beans and Rice (page 410)	Radish Salsa (page 58)
Garlic Shrimp with Tomatoes and Cilantro (page 545)	Green Papaya Salsa (page 58)
Pan-Cooked Salmon (page 548)	Chipotle-Cherry Salsa (page 58)
Arroz con Pollo (page 627); remove the bones and shred or chop	Cabbage and Carrot Slaw, Mexican Style (page 205)
Smoky Whole Chicken (page 642); remove the bones and shred or chop	Citrus Salsa (page 57)
Grilled or Broiled Flank Steak (page 672)	Pan-Roasted Corn with Cherry Tomatoes (page 286) and Cilantro Sauce (page 52)
Carnitas (page 699) or Shredded Pork (page 699)	Oven-Roasted Plum Tomatoes (page 347) and Real Ranch Dressing (page 71); garnish with chopped fresh cilantro

Prepare the fish as described in the first variation, then follow the instructions for either Deep-Fried Seafood (page 538), Broiled Seafood (page 534), or Oven-"Fried" Fish Fillets (page 554). Substitute cornmeal for the flour in any of them if you like.

Cheese Quesadillas

MAKES: 4 main-dish or up to 12 appetizer servings | TIME: 30 minutes

As with tacos and other stuffed wrappers, the key to successful quesadillas is to resist overfilling them. Too much cheese makes them ooze all over the place; too many other ingredients, and the cheese can't hold the two tortillas together.

That said, few hot dishes make better—or easier—use of little bits of leftovers. (See the chart in "The Basics of Tacos and Burritos" on page 809 for ideas.) Any shredded or thinly sliced cooked meat is a fine addition to quesadillas too.

Good-quality vegetable oil for frying (optional)

8 8-inch flour tortillas (to make your own, see page 781)

2 cups grated melting cheese like Asadero, cheddar, or Jack, or a combination

½ cup chopped scallions

1 or 2 chopped fresh jalapeño chiles (optional)

1 cup any fresh (pages 55–58) or cooked salsa (pages 71–74) for serving

1. Heat the oven to 200°F and have a baking sheet or 2 handy. Put about 1 tablespoon oil, if you're using it, in a medium skillet over medium heat. When it's hot, put a tortilla in the skillet. Top with one-quarter of the cheese, scallions, and chiles if you're using them, then with another tortilla.

2. Cook, pressing with a spatula to help seal the tortilla, until the tortilla browns in places and the cheese begins to melt, 2 to 3 minutes. Carefully turn and cook the other side until the cheese is fully melted and both sides are toasted, another 2 to 3 minutes. Transfer to a baking sheet and keep warm in the oven while you repeat with the remaining ingredients. Cut into wedges and serve hot, passing the salsa at the table.

GRILLED QUESADILLAS Crisp, slightly smoky, and delicious: Prepare a gas or charcoal grill for medium direct cooking (make sure the grates are clean) and put the rack about 4 inches from the heat. Brush one side of a tortilla with oil and set it on the grill. Build the quesadilla as instructed in Step 1 and brush oil on the top tortilla. Continue with the recipe.

Tostadas

Like an open-face sandwich on toast, a tostada is a taco served on a flat fried or oven-crisped tortilla. I prefer the flavor and texture of corn tortillas, but you might like flour. For either, heat a thin film of good-quality vegetable oil in a skillet over medium heat and fry the tortillas on both sides, one at a time. Or spread them on baking sheets, brush with the oil on both sides and toast until golden in a 400°F oven.

The other main difference between a taco and a tostada is that for a tostada you want something to help the toppings stick to the tortilla. Refried or mashed beans are traditional, as are not-too-soupy braised meats. Finish with shredded cabbage or lettuce, grated or crumbled cheese, salsa, and guacamole or sour cream and serve as soon as possible.

Fajitas Burritos

MAKES: 4 servings | **TIME:** 30 minutes

You can keep those monster burritos, overstuffed with rice and beans. I'll fill mine with some simply seared meat and vegetables and a piquant sauce, and use excellent tortillas. Traditional fajitas are made with skirt steak, which you can certainly substitute for the flank steak if you can find it. (Since it's often thinner it might cook more quickly.) To expand to other proteins, here's my basic formula so everyone can fill their own.

- 1 pound Broiled or Grilled Boneless Chicken (page 596) or any variation, 1 pound Grilled or Broiled Flank Steak (page 670), or 1 pound Grilled Shrimp (page 535)
- 1 pound grilled or broiled mixed vegetables (see page 250)
- 1 cup sour cream
- 1 cup Guacamole (page 105)
- 1 cup any fresh (pages 55–58) or cooked salsa (pages 71–74)
- 2 cups shredded lettuce
- 2 tomatoes, chopped
- 4 large or 8 small flour tortillas (to make your own, see page 781)

1. Heat the chicken, meat, or shrimp and vegetables if needed, cut into small bite-size pieces, and keep them warm. Meanwhile, put the sour cream, guacamole, salsa, lettuce, and tomato in serving bowls.

2. Heat the tortillas until just warm and pliable: on a grill for about 15 seconds per side, in a medium skillet over medium-high heat for about 15 seconds per side, or all together wrapped in foil in a 375°F oven for about 10 minutes. Wrap them in a clean kitchen towel to stay warm. Serve the tortillas with all the fixings and let everyone fold their own burritos as shown on page 812.

THE BASICS OF PIZZA

Pizza dough is a simple bread dough made with flour, yeast, salt, and water, usually with olive oil for a little extra crunch and flavor. The toppings can be simple and traditional (thick tomato sauce and mozzarella) or unexpected and more involved (a white sauce with clams). Or anything in between.

PREPARING PIZZA DOUGH

A food processor makes pizza dough in a minute; that's how the recipe is written. If you prefer to use a mixer, see "Making Yeast Bread Dough by Hand or with a Standing Mixer," page 791. To mix and knead the dough by hand, start by combining the ingredients in a big bowl, then knead the dough on a floured work surface. In any case, start to finish, you can have pizza dough ready in about an hour. But to develop more flavor—and make this a do-ahead dish—let it rise and ferment in the refrigerator for 6 to 8 hours, even overnight.

SHAPING THE DOUGH

The romantic image of pizza makers spinning, stretching, and tossing the dough into a perfect circle is unrealistic. You'll get equally good results by laying the dough on a work surface and gently pressing it with opened fingertips until it dimples and slowly stretches into shape. (This is how professionals make focaccia; see at right.) Equally easy is to flatten the dough a bit, then roll it out.

In either case, patience is key; the crust is easier to shape and will have a better texture if you allow the dough to rest between steps as you work. Whenever you handle the dough, it becomes more elastic and more difficult to work; that's the gluten doing its thing.

THICK CRUST OR THIN?

You can make any size or thickness of pizza using the same recipe and technique. It all depends on how you divide and flatten the dough. Large, thin pizzas are the hardest to handle because they are more likely to tear during rolling or collapse when topped. I usually divide the dough into at least two pies, or three or four if they're going on the grill (see page 819).

No matter how thin you roll the crust, it will just about double in thickness during proofing and baking. (The temperature of your kitchen, the toppings, and even how you shape the dough will affect this.) You can increase the thickness of the crust somewhat by letting the dough rise for a few extra minutes after you shape it and before topping it, but don't let it puff up too much or your pizza will have big bubbles and sunken valleys.

THE TOPPINGS

Topping pizza is much like saucing pasta: Distinct, clean flavors are better than a mishmash of ingredients. You can stick to classic combinations: tomatoes, basil, and Parmesan; tomato sauce and mozzarella; or a little mozzarella with some crumbled sausage or sliced pepperoni. You can, of course, play around with different meats, seafood, poultry, vegetables, and cheeses. Just don't load up the "house special"—too many ingredients translate to muddled flavors, and if you smother the dough with toppings, it will steam as it bakes, turning a potentially crisp and light crust into a soggy mess.

BAKING

Pizza must be baked in a very hot oven, 500°F or even higher; professional pizza ovens run 700°F or more. The best way to cook pizza is directly on a pizza stone, which crisps up the bottom of the crust and dries it out perfectly. Pizza is also just fine baked on a flat baking sheet or one with a small rim. You want the oven—and the stone—thoroughly heated, so turn the oven on a good half hour before baking. And of course there's also pizza on the grill; see page 819.

The ideal pizza stone is a large rectangle; it should be unglazed and relatively thick. Once you've got the stone, you really need a peel. The wooden board with a handle that looks like a large square Ping-Pong paddle is good, but the metal ones that work like huge spatulas are even better. Sprinkle flour or cornmeal on top and you can shape and top the dough directly on the peel, then slide it right onto the stone. Or put parchment paper on the

 F fast   M make ahead   V vegetarian

peel and shape the pizza on that; transfer the whole thing to a stone and remove the paper after the crust forms, a few minutes into baking.

If you use a baking sheet to bake the pizza, grease it with a little olive oil to keep the dough from sticking, rather than dusting the surface with flour or cornmeal as you would a peel. Once you do that, just press the dough right onto the pan to shape it.

CUTTING AND SERVING

Pizzas with little or no cheese or other rich ingredients that might congeal when cooled are also good served at room temperature. You can cut pizza into wedges or into small squares, which are good if you're feeding a crowd or just prefer smaller pieces.

Pizza Dough

MAKES: Enough for 1 large or 2 or more small pies | **TIME:** 1 hour or more

You won't believe how simple it is to make pizza dough at home. And because the dough freezes very well, it's even practical to whip up a batch for one or two people and tuck the rest away for another day. To make this dough with a standing mixer or by hand, see page 791. If you'll be using it to make focaccia (page 822), add an extra tablespoon oil.

3 cups all-purpose or bread flour, plus more for kneading and shaping

2 teaspoons instant yeast

2 teaspoons coarse kosher or sea salt, plus more for sprinkling

2 tablespoons olive oil

1. In a food processor, combine the flour, yeast, and salt. Gradually add 1 cup water and the oil, pouring it through the feed tube with the machine running, until combined.

2. Continue to process, slowly adding ½ cup more water, until the dough forms a ball and is slightly sticky to the touch. If it is still dry, add another tablespoon or 2 water and process for another 10 seconds, but be careful not to overwet the dough. In the unlikely event that the mixture is too sticky, add flour a tablespoon at a time.

3. Once the dough comes together in a ball, turn it out onto a floured work surface and knead by hand for a few seconds to form a smooth, round dough ball. Put the dough in a large bowl and cover with plastic wrap; let rise until the dough doubles in size, 1 to 2 hours. (You can cut this rising

---

Shaping Dough for Pizza and Calzones

STEP 1 Stretch the dough with your hands. If at any point the dough becomes very resistant, cover and let it rest for a few minutes.

STEP 2 Press the dough out with your hands. Use a little flour or olive oil to keep it from sticking.

STEP 3 Alternatively, roll it out with a rolling pin; either method is effective.

STEP 4 To make a calzone; add your filling, fold the dough over onto itself, and pinch the seams closed.

time short if you're in a hurry, or you can let the dough rise more slowly, in the refrigerator, for up to 8 hours; let it come back to room temperature before proceeding.)

4. Proceed with any of the pizza recipes that follow. Or wrap the dough tightly in plastic wrap or a zipper bag and freeze for up to a month. Thaw in the bag or a covered bowl in the refrigerator or at room temperature; bring to room temperature before shaping.

WHOLE WHEAT PIZZA DOUGH With a nutty flavor and a little fiber: Use 1½ cups each whole wheat and either all-purpose or bread flour. You'll probably need to add closer to 1½ cups water, maybe even a little more.

CRUNCHIER PIZZA DOUGH This dough may be a little more difficult to handle, but it has a pleasant corn flavor and crunch: Substitute ½ cup fine cornmeal for ½ cup of the flour.

GLUTEN-FREE PIZZA DOUGH See "Gluten-Free Baking" on page 766 and substitute the all-purpose flour blend for the flour in this recipe.

White Pizza

MAKES: 1 large or 2 or more small pies | TIME: About 1 hour with premade dough

Pizza bianca—white pizza, pizza without sauce—is the mother of all pizzas. This may seem spare, but I urge you to try it and experiment with some of the possible additions and tweaks that follow, because it's among the best pizzas you'll ever eat.

> 1 recipe Pizza Dough (page 817)
> All-purpose flour for shaping the dough
> Olive oil as needed
> Kosher or coarse sea salt
> 1 tablespoon or more roughly chopped fresh rosemary leaves

1. If you have a pizza stone, put it on the lowest rack in the oven; otherwise put a rack in the middle of the oven. Heat the oven to 500°F. Form the dough into a ball for one big pizza or divide it into as many pieces as you like for smaller pizzas. Cover lightly with plastic wrap or a kitchen towel and let rest until the dough puffs slightly, about 20 minutes.

2. Roll or lightly press each dough ball into a flat round, as thin as you like, lightly flouring the work surface and the dough as necessary; use only as much flour as you need to. Let the rounds sit for a few minutes; this will relax the dough and make it easier to roll out. If you are using the pizza stone, shape the pizza on a peel, turning it occasionally and sprinkling it with flour as necessary. If you're using baking sheets, oil them, then shape each pizza directly on a prepared sheet.

3. Sprinkle the top(s) with salt and the chopped rosemary, and drizzle with a little olive oil. Slide the pizza onto the stone or slide a baking sheet onto the middle rack. Bake until the bottom is crisp and browned

and the top is bubbling, 6 to 12 minutes, depending on your oven and size of the pies. If you're baking more than one pizza, repeat with the next one after you remove the first from the oven. Let the pizza(s) cool on a wire rack for a few minutes before slicing. Serve hot or at room temperature; these will keep for a few hours.

MARGHERITA PIZZA The classic Neapolitan pizza: Top the pie(s) with sliced fresh tomato, olive oil, a little mozzarella cheese, preferably fresh, fresh basil leaves, salt, and grated Parmesan.

MARINARA PIZZA All tomatoes, no cheese: Top the pie(s) with sliced fresh tomato or Fast Tomato Sauce, With or Without Pasta (page 478), thinly sliced garlic, olive oil, and if you like, a few chopped black olives or whole capers.

WHITE PIZZA WITH PROSCIUTTO AND PARMESAN Omit the salt and rosemary. Instead you'll top each pizza with a few very thin slices prosciutto, a drizzle of olive oil, and some grated Parmesan cheese; wait to add the toppings until the crust is no longer doughy on top, 3 to 6 minutes. Garnish with chopped fresh parsley if you like.

WHITE PIZZA WITH CLAMS Also good with diced peeled lightly cooked shrimp or shelled lightly steamed mussels: Omit the rosemary. Top each pizza with a few freshly shucked littleneck clams and a drizzle of their juice, if you have it, a few very thin slivers of garlic, a little coarse salt, and some minced fresh parsley leaves.

Pizza with Tomato Sauce and Mozzarella

MAKES: 1 large or 2 or more small pies | **TIME:** About 1 hour with premade dough and sauce

Your basic American-style pizza. It's a little too loaded to grill as is so cut the sauce and topping quantities in half if you want to that. The good news is that the cheese helps unwieldy toppings like broccoli, bell peppers, or olives stick to the pie. For more variations, see "19 Ideas for Pizza Toppings," on page 821.

1 recipe Pizza Dough (page 817)
   All-purpose flour for shaping the dough
2 tablespoons olive oil, plus more as needed
   Up to 2 cups Fast Tomato Sauce (page 478) or other tomato sauce
2 cups grated mozzarella cheese
   Salt and pepper

Pizza on the Grill

Grilled pizza is fun to make, and easier than you'd think, especially if your grill has a cover. Wood fires are the trickiest to control, but impart a great flavor to the crust, gas grills are naturally the easiest, and charcoal lies somewhere in between.

You want a fire that is hot enough to brown the dough, but not so hot that it scorches it before the interior cooks; you should be able to hold your hand a few inches above the fire for 3 to 4 seconds. An ideal setup is indirect grilling (see "Grilling over Fire," page 21), where part of the grill is hot and part of it cool. On a gas grill, this means setting one side to "high" and the other to "low," or some similar arrangement; with a charcoal or wood-fired grill, build your fire on only one side. Use the hot side for the initial browning of the dough, the cooler side to heat the toppings.

Grill the dough on one side, just enough to firm it up and brown it a bit, then turn it (for small pizzas, use tongs; otherwise two spatulas or a spatula and your fingers do the trick) and add minimal toppings. Fully loaded grilled pizzas won't cook properly and will be impossible to handle. One way around this is to grill pizzas with one or two ingredients, then add more—like arugula, herbs, or an extra grating of cheese—after you remove them from the fire. A final drizzle of olive oil and sprinkle of salt before slicing are always welcome.

White Pizza with Prosciutto and Parmesan, page 819

19 Ideas for Pizza Toppings

Use the following ingredients, alone or in combination, on any of the pizzas in this section.

1. Lightly cooked crumbled sausage or chopped bacon
2. Thinly sliced salami, prosciutto, Spanish chorizo, or other cured meat
3. Small amounts of Gorgonzola or other blue cheese; gratings of Parmesan are almost always welcome
4. Dollops or dabs of fresh goat cheese or ricotta; first drain ricotta for a few minutes in a mesh sieve or on towels to draw out excess moisture
5. Minced raw or mashed Roasted Garlic (page 294)
6. Minced fresh chile like jalapeño or Thai, or red pepper flakes
7. Pitted black olives, especially the oil-cured kind (good in combination with caramelized onions and vinegar), or green olives
8. Canned anchovy fillets, with some of their oil
9. Reconstituted dried tomatoes or Oven-Dried Tomatoes (page 348)
10. Thinly sliced ripe tomatoes and basil, with olive oil and/or grated Parmesan, or peeled, seeded, and chopped tomatoes tossed with basil
11. Traditional Pesto or other herb purée (pages 51–52).
12. Sliced boiled waxy or all-purpose potatoes; great added to White Pizza (page 819)
13. Well-washed and dried tender greens, especially spicy ones like arugula and watercress, added after baking or grilling, when the heat from the crust will wilt them (this takes about a minute)
14. Sautéed spinach, asparagus, or broccoli raab
15. Roasted Red Peppers (page 318)
16. Grilled Eggplant (page 252) or Breaded and Fried Eggplant (page 288)
17. Slices of grilled zucchini (page 253)
18. Thinly sliced cremini or button mushrooms, tossed with a little olive oil, or Sautéed Mushrooms (page 306)
19. Any lightly cooked seafood, or well-drained canned clams or flaked canned tuna

1. If you have a pizza stone, put it on the lowest rack in the oven. Heat the oven to 500°F. Form the dough into a ball for one big pizza or divide it into as many pieces as you like for smaller pizzas; cover lightly with plastic wrap or a kitchen towel and let rest until the dough puffs slightly, about 20 minutes.

2. Roll or lightly press each dough ball into a flat round, as thin as you like, lightly flouring the work surface and the dough as necessary; use only as much flour as you need to. Let the rounds sit for a few minutes; this will relax the dough and make it easier to roll out. If you are using a pizza stone, shape the pizza on a peel, turning it occasionally and sprinkling it with flour as necessary. If you're using baking sheets, oil them, then shape each pizza directly on a prepared sheet.

3. Drizzle the rounds with the olive oil, then top them with a thin layer of tomato sauce and the cheese; sprinkle with salt and pepper. Slide the pizza onto the stone or slide a baking sheet onto the middle rack. Bake until the crust is crisp and the cheese melted, 8 to 12 minutes. If you're baking more than one pizza, repeat with the next one after you remove the first from the oven.

4. Let the pizza(s) cool on a wire rack for several minutes to set up the cheese before slicing. Serve hot.

PIZZA WITH TOMATO SAUCE AND FRESH MOZZARELLA

Since fresh mozz doesn't melt the same way as the commercial stuff, and because it's moist, slice it, don't grate it: Use less than 8 ounces fresh mozzarella—usually 1 medium ball packed in water. Drain well and slice thin. After you top with the oil and sauce, spread the cheese on top of the pizza; you will have gaps in between so the crust can breathe and crisp up. Proceed with the recipe. When the pizza comes out of the oven, sprinkle with chopped fresh basil or oregano if you like, and grated Parmesan.

PIZZA WITH TOMATO SAUCE, MOZZARELLA, AND SAUSAGE OR PEPPERONI Scatter 4 ounces or so crumbled and lightly cooked sausage or thinly sliced pepperoni over the cheese.

Pissaladière

MAKES: 4 main-dish or 8 appetizer servings | **TIME:** About 1½ hours with premade dough

The classic chewy-crusted Niçoise pizza, loaded with sweet, soft-cooked onions; salty olives and anchovies add contrast. Since there's no sauce and very few ingredients, be sure to simmer the onions very, very slowly so they become as spreadable as thick jam.

½	recipe Pizza Dough (page 817)
	All-purpose flour for shaping the dough
3	tablespoons olive oil, plus more for the baking sheet (optional)
1½	pounds onions, thinly sliced
	Salt and pepper
1	teaspoon fresh thyme leaves or ½ teaspoon dried
6 to 10	anchovy fillets (optional)
	About 12 black olives, pitted and halved (optional)
6 to 8	thin slices tomato (optional)

1. If you have a pizza stone, put it on the lowest rack in the oven. Heat the oven to 450°F. Knead the dough lightly. Put it on a lightly floured surface, sprinkle it with a little flour, and cover it with plastic wrap or a kitchen towel. Let it rest while you cook the onions.

2. Put the olive oil in large skillet over medium-high heat. When it's hot, add the onions, sprinkle with salt and pepper, and cook, stirring frequently, until the onions give up their liquid and become quite soft, at least 15 minutes; don't let them brown. When they are cooked, turn off the heat and stir in the thyme.

3. Pat or roll out the dough to thin rectangle or freeform shape about ¼ inch thick, using more flour as necessary. The process will be easier if you allow the dough to rest occasionally between rollings. If you are using a pizza stone, shape the dough on a peel, turning it occasionally and sprinkling it with flour as necessary. If you're using a baking sheet, oil it, then press the dough into a flat rectangle directly on the oiled sheet. Let the dough rest for 15 to 30 minutes, until it begins to puff ever so slightly.

4. Spread the dough with the onions and then decorate if you like with anchovies, olives, and/or tomato. Slide the pissaladière onto the stone or slide the baking sheet onto the middle rack. Bake until browned and crisp, 15 minutes or more; if the pizza is browning unevenly, rotate it back to front after about halfway through the cooking time. Serve hot or at room temperature.

Rosemary Focaccia

MAKES: 4 main-course or 8 appetizer or sandwich servings | **TIME:** About 1¾ hours with premade dough

Focaccia is like pizza, but a little easier to make since it's just pressed into the pan. You generally top it more minimally too unless you're making deep-dish pizza (see the variation); see "7 Other Ingredients for Topping Focaccia," page 824.

1	recipe Pizza Dough (page 817), made with an extra tablespoon olive oil
	All-purpose flour for shaping the dough
3	tablespoons olive oil
1	tablespoon chopped fresh rosemary leaves, plus more to taste
	Kosher or coarse sea salt

1. Lightly knead the dough, form it into a ball, and put it on a lightly floured surface. Sprinkle with a little more flour, cover with plastic wrap or a kitchen towel, and let it rest for 20 minutes.

Pissaladière

Turn Any Pizza into Calzone

One day I messed up sliding a pizza into the oven: Part of it folded onto itself on the pizza stone. I couldn't take it back out, and I couldn't bake it the way it was. So I finished the job, folding it over (and not too neatly), encasing the filling entirely in the dough. Voilà: accidental calzone.

Intentionally made calzone are even better, since the filling is neatly enclosed in the dough. Start with the pizza dough recipe on page 817 and divide it into 2 or 4 pieces before shaping. While you can fill calzone with any pizza toppings (see "19 Ideas for Pizza Toppings," page 821), they're best with cheese and something else rather than all cheese. The filling should be fairly dry, so skip the tomato sauce. Wet fillings will leak or make the dough soggy; that's why drained ricotta is an ideal base. Brush the tops with olive oil and bake the calzone on a baking sheet or directly on a pizza stone until golden on top and piping hot inside, 30 to 40 minutes, depending on how thick they are. Serve calzone with Fast Tomato Sauce (page 478) or any other tomato sauce for dipping or topping—or naked.

2. Use 1 tablespoon of the olive oil to grease a large rimmed baking sheet. Press the dough into a small rectangle and put it in the pan; let it relax there for a few minutes. Press and stretch the dough to the edges of the pan. If it resists, let it rest for a few minutes, then stretch it some more. Sometimes this takes a while, because the dough is so elastic. Don't fight it; just stretch, rest, then stretch again. Try not to tear the dough. Cover with a kitchen towel and let rise until the dough is somewhat puffy, at least 30 minutes.

3. Heat the oven to 425°F. Uncover the dough and dimple the surface all over with your fingertips. Drizzle with the remaining 2 tablespoons olive oil and sprinkle with the rosemary and plenty of salt.

4. Put the focaccia in the oven, lower the temperature to 375°F, and bake until the top is golden, 25 to 35 minutes. Transfer the pan to a wire rack to cool a little before removing the focaccia. Cut the focaccia into squares or triangles and serve as a side or a snack. Or slice squares in half horizontally and use to make sandwiches.

DEEP-DISH PIZZA, CHICAGO STYLE Make the focaccia through Step 3. In Step 4 bake the dough until it's just firm, about 10 minutes, then remove it from the oven. While the crust is baking, grate 2 cups mozzarella cheese and ½ cup Parmesan, and heat about 1½ cups Fast Tomato Sauce (page 478). Smear the pizza with a thin layer of sauce (you may have extra), sprinkle with the cheeses and any other ingredients you like), and bake for 20 to 25 minutes more, until hot and bubbly and browned on the bottom. For more toppings, see Pizza with Tomato Sauce and Mozzarella (page 819) and "19 Ideas for Pizza Toppings" (page 821).

7 OTHER INGREDIENTS FOR TOPPING FOCACCIA

1. Any other minced fresh herbs, or fresh chiles
2. Thinly sliced tomatoes, patted dry
3. Caramelized Onions (page 315)
4. Pitted black or green olives or Tapenade (page 109)
5. Grated Parmesan or other sharp cheese
6. Thin slices prosciutto
7. Thin slices peeled fruit like peaches, nectarines, apples, or plums, or halved grapes or cherries

 fast  make ahead vegetarian

Desserts

CHAPTER AT A GLANCE

The Basics of Sweeteners 826

The Basics of Butter and Other Baking Fats 827

The Basics of Chocolate 828

Cookies, Brownies, and Bars 829

Cakes 844

Frostings, Glazes, Soaks, and Sauces 854

Pies, Tarts, Cobblers, and Crisps 864

Puddings, Custards, and Mousses 886

Frozen Desserts 897

Two Simple Candies 904

My hope is that this book inspires you to cook *and* bake. The selection of desserts here are what I consider the modern classics, ranging from cookies and bars to simple pastry to puddings, and ice cream. With a little bit of everything in between. But you don't need to be a wizard to make desserts. Even though baking, with its special groups of ingredients and techniques, might be the most technical form of cooking, these recipes are as straightforward as in the rest of the book.

If you're a newcomer, I suggest you start with the ingredient information at the beginning of the chapter, and from there work through the cookie section or try a cobbler or crisp (pages 882 and 884). Then maybe Pound Cake (page 846) or Rich Chocolate Torte (page 853). Or just jump right in and make something like Vanilla Cream Pie made with graham cracker crust (page 875). And then if you skipped the yeast bread or pizza sections in the previous chapter, you'll probably want to go back and take a second look.

For more advanced baking, Apple Pie is rewarding and only a moderate challenge (page 871). Panna Cotta (page 888) and Ice Cream (page 897) are always impressive, as is anything that includes Chocolate Ganache (page 858). Trying the variations and ideas from the lists in this chapter will bring even more creativity to your Desserts. Before you begin, read through the ingredient basics that follow and you'll be ready to explore all the many options for customizing.

THE BASICS OF SWEETENERS

We crave desserts because they're sweet. Here's an overview of the ingredients that make them that way. (Note that I'm not including artificial sweeteners, since you can't really bake with them, no matter what you hear otherwise.)

GRANULATED SWEETENERS

The easiest to use, measure, and store because they're dry.

WHITE SUGAR The most common, highly refined from sugarcane or sugar beets. It's what I mean when recipes call for "sugar;" in that way it's akin to all-purpose flour. The grains are medium size and dissolve well when heated or combined with a relatively large amount of liquid.

The only other form of white sugar used in this chapter is confectioners' sugar (also called powdered, icing, or identified by the fineness of the particles as 10X, 6X, or 4X sugar). It's regular sugar ground to a fine powder, with cornstarch added to prevent caking, so it dissolves very easily and is often used for sifting over desserts: Put it in a small mesh sieve and tap the sides to "dust" on a thin layer.

BROWN SUGAR Brown sugar is simply white sugar with molasses added for a more complex taste and extra moisture. Generally dark brown sugar is more intense than light or golden brown sugar, but since the difference is subtle, I use them interchangeably. You can substitute brown sugar for white, as long as you remember the color and flavor will be different. Be sure to pack the cups down before leveling them off as you measure. Store double-sealed in airtight containers to keep it from hardening; if it does get hard, put the sugar in a microwave-safe bowl, top with a damp towel, and microwave it in 15-second intervals, just until it is loose again; use it immediately.

TURBINADO SUGAR Also called raw, Demerara, or muscovado sugar, these slightly different coarse gold or

F fast **M** make ahead **V** vegetarian

brown sweeteners are made exclusively from sugarcane. They taste less sweet than regular sugar and have a distinctive caramel flavor. You can make it fine enough to use as white sugar by whirring some in a coffee grinder. I like it best sprinkled on top of baked goods like scones and cookies to add a mildly sweet crunch.

LIQUID SWEETENERS

Though these aren't directly interchangeable with granulated sugars, they often can be substituted to bring different flavors to desserts. For maple syrup, see page 738.

HONEY Made, as you know, by bees. There are more than 300 varieties of honey in the United States alone, including orange blossom, clover, and eucalyptus, and they all taste at least a little bit different. But most commercial honeys are blends, so their flavor is more consistent—and they're often less exciting than those produced by a single source. All honey is about 25 percent sweeter than regular white sugar, so you use less of it to achieve the same sweetness. You can try replacing some of the sugar in your favorite recipe at a ratio of about 3:4 (if it calls for 1 cup sugar, you might use ⅓ cup honey to replace ½ cup of the sugar). But be careful: Remember that the color of honey will darken food slightly and causes cookies, for example, to spread more than cookies baked with sugar.

MOLASSES A heavy brown syrup produced during the sugar-making process. The first boiling produces light molasses, which can be used like honey; the second produces dark molasses, which is thick, full flavored, and not so sweet; the third produces blackstrap molasses, the darkest, thickest, most nutritious, and least useful of the bunch. Blackstrap isn't generally used for cooking and baking, but you can do it; if you do, it's best to blend it with light molasses or honey.

CORN SYRUP A thick, sticky sweetener processed from cornstarch. Light corn syrup is clarified; dark is flavored with caramel, which makes it sweeter and darker.

It's useful in making Caramels (page 906) and other candies and sauces (like Hot Fudge Sauce, page 859) but otherwise you can live without it.

THE BASICS OF BUTTER AND OTHER BAKING FATS

Butter is the most important ingredient in many desserts, since it combines two qualities not found in most other fats: good flavor and the ability to hold air when beaten.

I use unsalted butter exclusively, and that's what "butter" means in the recipes. If you do buy salted butter, you'll need to eliminate a small amount of the salt in recipes for sweet baked goods; there's almost always enough salt in the butter to compensate, but you can't really be sure, which is part of the problem.

Some liquid vegetable oils, like olive or nut oils, have good baking characteristics but an overly distinctive flavor; and since they lack the water in butter, they can't add the lift created by steam. That said, olive oil can be quite good, especially in cakes. If you're trying to avoid animal fats, you can try neutral-tasting good-quality vegetable oils (see page 184) instead of butter. In some recipes they'll work fine as long as you don't expect the exact same results; in others—especially where the butter is cold—liquid fat won't work at all.

Solid vegetable shortenings, including special baking blends made from tropical oils, are now available everywhere. As is coconut oil, also solid at room temperature. They can be handy for vegan baking, but I rarely use them since they don't perform as well as butter (and coconut oil has a pronounced flavor).

Pure lard, once the baking fat of choice, is finally back in style. Health-wise, it's equivalent to butter. When it's freshly rendered (by you, a pig farmer, or other small producer), it's fantastic in pie and tart crusts. (Stay away from the large-scale packaged stuff.) Use one part lard with three parts butter.

THE BASICS OF CHOCOLATE

I approach chocolate the same way I do cheese or wine: Mastering the types and nuances is a lifelong journey, so start with the best-quality you can afford and find without hassle. If the chocolate is delicious when you take a bite—and, in my recipes, by chocolate I usually mean dark chocolate—it's certainly good enough for baking. This is why I avoid chocolate chips and packaged chocolate sauces. It's simple enough to buy a good bar in a supermarket, then chunk, chop, or melt it as needed.

HOW TO BUY CHOCOLATE

The type of chocolate is determined by the percentage of cacao, the solids remaining from the beans after processing, to the amounts of other ingredients such as milk or sugar. Fortunately, this number now appears on the labels of most types of good-quality chocolate. This is a huge help since some of the common names are used interchangeably. It's now easier to read the label to know exactly what you're getting. The higher the percentage of solids, the less sweet the chocolate and the more intense the flavor, since there's less sugar in the formula. Here's a quick rundown of the lingo.

UNSWEETENED CHOCOLATE (BAKING CHOCOLATE, CHOCOLATE LIQUOR) A combination of cocoa solids and cocoa butter, and nothing else; 100% cacao. Unsweetened chocolate is too bitter to eat but is useful for baking, cooking, and home chocolate making.

DARK CHOCOLATE (BITTERSWEET, SEMISWEET, DARK, EXTRA DARK, EXTRA BITTERSWEET) This is the type of chocolate I use most often. The solid cacao content ranges from 35 to say 85% or so, with less than 12 percent milk solids. That's a big range, so look for an exact number—70% or higher if you like an intense, slight bitterness; less than 60% starts to taste like milk chocolate and higher verges into unsweetened

territory, but those might be what you want. Just having a high percentage of solids doesn't guarantee good quality, but it does mean there isn't a lot of room for fillers. Many good-quality dark chocolates snap when you break them and taste almost chalky if you're not used to them. But they coat your mouth evenly without any waxiness or grittiness; that's the cocoa butter at work.

SWEET CHOCOLATE With 15 to 34 percent cacao solids and no more than 12 percent milk solids. "Sweet chocolate" is the common name, though it's also sometimes called "dark chocolate" (even though I don't consider it in that category).

MILK CHOCOLATE If you like sweet, melt-in-your-mouth chocolate, this is it. It must contain a minimum of 10 percent cacao solids, 12 percent milk solids, and 3.39 percent milk fat. But don't skimp. Make sure it includes real ingredients (for example, real cocoa butter or cream, not vegetable oil) and tastes rich and almost buttery. Milk chocolate should be as nuanced as dark chocolate, with the flavors muted against a backdrop of creaminess.

WHITE CHOCOLATE White chocolate is technically not chocolate, but a confection made from cocoa butter. It must contain at least 20 percent cocoa butter, 14 percent milk solids, and 3.39 percent milk fat. It's a completely different ingredient, though you can almost always substitute white chocolate for dark or milk. Scan the label for ingredients: Cocoa butter should be first on the list. And taste before using it: The flavor should be subtle, not bland, and the feel never waxy or gritty.

COCOA POWDER After most of the cocoa butter is pressed out of the nibs, or separated from the chocolate liquor, the solids are finely ground into a powder. "Natural" cocoa powder—ground roasted cocoa beans and nothing else—is lighter brown and can have a more intense chocolate flavor and natural acidity.

 F fast **M** make ahead **V** vegetarian

"Dutched," "Dutch-process," or "alkalized" cocoa has been treated with an alkaline ingredient to reduce acidity and darken the color. Some manufacturers are combining both in one blend and many don't even identify the type on the label or online product information. As long as they're unsweetened, natural and Dutch-process cocoas are interchangeable in the recipes here.

STORING CHOCOLATE

There's no need to refrigerate chocolate, but you should keep it in a cool, dry place (the fridge is as good as any, as long as it's well wrapped). Stored properly, dark and white chocolate can last for at least a year; dark chocolate can even improve as it ages. However, milk chocolate doesn't keep nearly as long as dark chocolate—only a few weeks.

Sometimes chocolate develops a white or gray sheen or thin coating. Don't panic. The chocolate hasn't gone bad; it has bloomed, a condition caused by too much humidity or fluctuating temperatures, which cause the fat or sugar to come to the surface of the chocolate and crystallize. In either case the chocolate is still perfectly fine for cooking, as long as you're not making coated candy. It's also okay to eat bloomed chocolate out of hand, though it may be grainy.

COOKING WITH CHOCOLATE

Good-quality chocolate bars are fine for melting or chopping, but if you want big chunks or decorative shavings, buy a piece from a larger brick; specialty, baking, and some natural food stores sell chocolate like this. Chop it with a chef's knife on a cutting board. To make chocolate shavings, put the chocolate on a clean kitchen towel and carefully scrape of shards by pushing a small knife or a vegetable peeler away from you. It might take a couple of passes to get the hang of it (and you might prefer the more perilous motion of working toward you) but it's surprisingly easy.

Melting chocolate with liquids is tricky so in these recipes I either tell you how or call for melted chocolate on its own, then add other ingredients. Here's how:

Chop the chocolate; small pieces melt faster than big chunks. Put the pieces in the top of a double boiler, over simmering water, and stir until melted. Or microwave the chocolate for a minute or 2 on the lowest power, stopping to stir it frequently.

Cookies, Brownies, and Bars

Everyone loves these hand-held treats. They're generally so easy and quick that a batch of cookies or brownies can be coming out of the oven half an hour after inspiration hits.

Cookies fall into two basic categories: Drop, where you spoon the dough directly onto baking sheets, and sliced, rolled, or otherwise shaped cookies, which sometimes need to be chilled before shaping.

Making the batters and doughs for brownies and bars are similar to the techniques for cookies. But you bake them in one block before cooling and cutting. This makes them easier for constructing layers.

MIXING COOKIE DOUGH

Most of the recipes call for an electric mixer; hand-held or standing kinds will both work. Here's how to make adjustments if you don't have either.

To combine the ingredients by hand: Mix the flour, baking powder or baking soda, and salt (and any other dry ingredients like spices) together in a bowl. Cream the softened butter with a fork, then mash in the sugar until well blended. Stir in the vanilla and the egg, then about half the flour mixture. Add any milk or other liquid called for in the recipe, then the remaining flour.

To make the dough in a food processor: Put all the dry ingredients in the processor and pulse once or twice to combine. Cut chilled butter into bits, add to the machine, and process for about 10 seconds, until the butter and flour are well blended. Add any flavoring, egg, and milk or other liquid and pulse just enough to blend.

Creaming butter and sugar

BAKING COOKIES

Most ovens have hot spots that cause uneven baking. The solution is simple: Halfway through the estimated baking time, rotate the pans from back to front; if you're baking more than one sheet at the same time, exchange them from top to bottom as well.

STORING COOKIES

You'll probably eat all the cookies within a day or 2. Until then most store well in a closed container—like a cookie jar or tin—at room temperature. There are exceptions for crisp, soft, and decorated styles noted in the recipes. Soft and crisp cookies should be stored separately, or each type will lose its texture. To store cookies longer, put them in an airtight container. They also freeze successfully for a couple months; just make sure they're covered or wrapped very tightly. Even better is to shape the dough in a log, roll it in a couple of layers of plastic, and freeze. You can then slice directly from the freezer (30 minutes of thawing will make that job a little easier) and bake.

Chocolate Chunk Cookies

MAKES: 3 to 4 dozen | **TIME:** About 30 minutes

Dark chocolate—for me, the higher percentage of cacao, the better—delivers the traditional semisweet chip taste, only better. But try these with milk or even white chocolate sometime.

2	cups all-purpose flour
1	teaspoon salt
¾	teaspoon baking soda
½	pound (2 sticks) butter, softened
¾	cup granulated sugar
¾	cup packed brown sugar
2	eggs
1	teaspoon vanilla extract
8	ounces dark chocolate, chopped (about 1⅓ cups)

1. Heat the oven to 375°F.

2. Whisk the flour, salt, and baking soda and salt together in a medium bowl.

3. Use an electric mixer to cream the butter and granulated and brown sugars in a large bowl until light and fluffy. Add the eggs one at a time and beat until well blended, then mix in the vanilla. Add the dry ingredients to the creamed mixture and stir until just incorporated. Fold in the chocolate.

4. Drop tablespoon-size mounds of dough about 2 inches apart on ungreased baking sheets. Bake until lightly browned on the bottom, 8 to 10 minutes. Cool for about 2 minutes on the sheets before transferring the cookies to wire racks to finish cooling. Store in a covered container at room temperature for a day or 2.

CHOCOLATE–CHOCOLATE CHUNK COOKIES Be sure to use good chocolate here: Melt 2 ounces dark chocolate and add to the dough after combining the wet and dry ingredients.

WHITE CHOCOLATE–PISTACHIO COOKIES Trust me, better than macadamia nuts: Substitute 1 cup each chopped white chocolate (6 ounces) and chopped pistachios for the dark chocolate.

Left to right: Oatmeal-Something Cookies, page 834;
Gingersnaps, page 837; Nutty Biscotti, page 839;
and Chocolate Chunk Cookies, page 831

Oatmeal-Something Cookies

MAKES: 3 to 4 dozen | TIME: About 30 minutes

One of the advantages of oatmeal cookies is their flexibility: They're delicious both plain and loaded with all sorts of goodies from dried fruit to nuts. Toss in raisins, dried cranberries or cherries, chocolate chunks, coconut, crumbled shredded wheat cereal, even leftover cooked whole grains—the dough can handle up to 1½ cups total.

2	cups rolled oats
1½	cups all-purpose flour
1	teaspoon baking soda
2	teaspoons ground cinnamon
1	teaspoon salt
12	tablespoon (1½ sticks) butter, softened
½	cup granulated sugar
1	cup packed brown sugar
2	eggs
1	teaspoon vanilla extract
¼	cup milk
	Up to 1½ cups additions (see headnote; optional)

1. Heat the oven to 375°F.

2. Whisk the oats, flour, baking soda, cinnamon, and salt together in a medium bowl.

3. Use an electric mixer to cream the butter and granulated and brown sugars in a large bowl until light and fluffy. Add the eggs one at a time, beating after each addition, until just combined, then add the vanilla and mix to combine. Gradually add the dry ingredients and the milk to the creamed mixture, mixing on low speed. If you're adding anything else, stir it in now by hand.

4. Drop tablespoon-size mounds of dough onto ungreased baking sheets about 2 inches apart. Bake for 12 to 15 minutes, until lightly browned. Cool for about 2 minutes on the pans before transferring the cookies to wire racks to finish cooling. These will keep in a covered container for a day or 2.

LACY OATMEAL COOKIES No flour—and no additions in these, please: Melt the butter and combine it with the sugars, oats, and salt; beat in the eggs. Omit the flour, baking powder, milk, and vanilla; add the cinnamon if you like. Bake at 350°F on greased baking sheets for 8 to 10 minutes; let rest for a minute before transferring to wire racks with a thin-bladed spatula to finish cooling.

Sugar Cookies

MAKES: 3 to 4 dozen | TIME: 35 minutes, plus time to chill

Refrigerating this dough gives it a stiff consistency that's perfect for rolling and cutting out cookies—for any holiday (see the variation). But an easier method is to roll the dough into a log and then slice off rounds to shape nearly perfect circles. Generally, rolled cookies

 fast make ahead V vegetarian

are more crumbly and less chewy than drop cookies. But if you want these on the chewy side, underbake them by a couple of minutes, removing them from the oven while the center is still a little soft.

Serve as is or top with Vanilla Glaze (page 858) and sprinkles; smear with any frosting (pages 856–857) or Caramel–Cream Cheese Frosting (page 862); or simply drizzle with any glaze (pages 857–858), Caramel (page 860), or Chocolate Ganache (page 858). Depending on how gooey they are, you'll need to store them in a single layer or between sheets of wax paper, in a covered container.

2¾ cups all-purpose flour
1 teaspoon baking soda
½ teaspoon salt
½ pound (2 sticks) butter, softened
2 cups granulated sugar
1 egg
2 teaspoons vanilla extract
   Turbinado or other coarse sugar for rolling
   (optional)

1. Whisk the flour, baking soda, and salt together in a medium bowl.

2. Use an electric mixer to cream the butter and sugar in a large bowl until light and fluffy. Add the egg and vanilla and beat until light and fluffy, at least 2 minutes. Add the dry ingredients to the creamed mixture and stir just until a sandy dough forms. On sheets of plastic wrap, form the dough into 2 logs about 2 inches in diameter; wrap tightly and chill until firm, about 2 hours or overnight. (Or freeze for up to a couple months.)

3. Heat the oven 375°F. Unwrap the dough and roll each log in coarse sugar to coat fully if you like. Cut the dough into ¼-inch slices and put on ungreased baking sheets about 2 inches apart. Bake until the edges are starting to brown and the centers are set, 6 to 8 minutes. The cookies will still be very soft and almost seem not quite done when you take them out of the oven; be careful not to overbake. Cool for about a minute on the pans, then carefully transfer the cookies to wire racks to finish cooling. These will keep in an airtight container for a day or 2.

CHOCOLATE SUGAR COOKIES Decrease the flour to 2½ cups and add ¼ cup cocoa powder. Melt 3 ounces chopped chocolate (any kind) and stir it into the dough before forming the logs. Bake for a couple of minutes longer, 8 to 10 minutes.

BROWN SUGAR AND SALT COOKIES Use a nice sea salt or similar: Substitute brown sugar for the granulated sugar. Proceed with the recipe, but sprinkle each cookie with a tiny pinch flaky sea salt halfway through baking.

ROLLED SUGAR COOKIES The classic for decorating: Shape the dough into a disk instead of logs, wrap tightly in plastic, and chill as directed. To bake, cut the dough disk in half. Lightly flour a work surface and a rolling pin, then roll out the dough gently until about ¼ inch thick, adding flour as necessary and turning the dough to prevent sticking. Cut with any cookie cutter.

SANDWICH SUGAR COOKIES Make the main recipe or any the three previous variations and let the cookies cool completely. Smear 1 teaspoon of your favorite jam or frosting between 2 cookies.

BUTTER COOKIES Decrease the sugar to 1 cup and the vanilla to 1 teaspoon. Substitute 1 teaspoon baking powder for the baking soda. Drop the dough into tablespoon-size mounds on the sheets instead of shaping; bake as directed. If you like, sprinkle the tops of the just-baked cookies with a pinch coarse salt before cooling.

Peanut or Other Nut Butter Cookies

MAKES: 3 dozen | TIME: About 30 minutes

These cookies have chewy centers, crunchy edges, and big peanut flavor, all the more so if you add chopped nuts. Creamy or crunchy peanut butter is your call, but do make sure it's unsweetened.

    1   cup all-purpose flour
    ½   teaspoon baking soda
    ¼   teaspoon salt
    8   tablespoons (1 stick) butter, softened
    ½   cup granulated sugar
    1   cup packed light brown sugar
    1   cup peanut butter
    2   eggs
    1   teaspoon vanilla extract
    1   cup roasted peanuts or other nuts, chopped
        (optional)

1. Heat the oven to 350°F.

2. Whisk the flour, baking soda, and salt together in a medium bowl.

3. Use an electric mixer to cream the butter and granulated and brown sugars in a large bowl until light and fluffy, then beat in the peanut butter. Add the eggs and the vanilla. Add the dry ingredients and mix until just combined. If you're using them, fold in the peanuts.

4. Drop tablespoon-size mounds of dough onto ungreased baking sheets about 2 inches apart. Use the back of a fork to press lines into the tops of each cookie, rotating it to make a crosshatch pattern. If the fork gets too sticky, dip it in cold water. Bake for 8 to 10 minutes, until lightly browned. Cool for about 2 minutes on the sheets before transferring the cookies to wire racks to finish cooling. These will keep in a covered container for a day or 2.

FLOURLESS PEANUT OR OTHER NUT BUTTER COOKIES These have only 5 ingredients, so even if you aren't avoiding gluten, they're irresistibly convenient: Omit the flour, baking soda, salt, butter, and nuts. Increase the peanut butter to 2 cups and beat it with the sugars, eggs, and vanilla until fully combined. Bake as directed.

Gingersnaps

MAKES: 4 to 5 dozen | TIME: About 40 minutes, plus time to chill

Not too sweet—in fact, bordering on savory—these gingersnaps are crisp-chewy, the kind that stick in your teeth. Try these topped with Vanilla or Maple Frosting (page 856) or drizzled with Vanilla, Orange, or Lemon Glaze (page 857).

    3¼   cups flour
     1   heaping tablespoon ginger
     1   tablespoon cinnamon
     1   teaspoon salt
     2   sticks butter, softened
     1   cup molasses
     ½   cup granulated sugar
     ½   cup packed brown sugar
     1   teaspoon baking soda

1. Whisk the flour, ginger, cinnamon, and salt together in a large bowl.

2. Use an electric mixer to cream the butter, molasses, and sugars in a large bowl until smooth and fluffy. Gradually add the dry ingredients to the creamed mixture, beating well between additions. Dissolve the baking soda in 2 tablespoons hot water and beat into the dough.

3. Shape the dough into 2 logs about 1 to 2 inches in diameter, wrap in wax paper, and refrigerate for several hours or overnight. Or wrap very well in plastic and freeze for up to a couple months; you can proceed to Step 4 with still-frozen dough.

4. Heat the oven to 350°F. Slice the cookies as thin as you can and put on ungreased baking sheets. Bake until golden around the edges, about 10 minutes, watching carefully to prevent burning. Use a spatula to carefully transfer the warm cookies to wire racks to cool. Store in an airtight container at room temperature for up to several days.

MOLASSES-SPICE COOKIES Add ½ teaspoon freshly grated nutmeg, ¼ teaspoon ground allspice, and ⅛ teaspoon ground cloves along with the ginger and cinnamon.

GINGERBREAD PEOPLE Shape the dough into a disk and chill as directed. Remove from the refrigerator to soften while the oven heats. When the dough is slightly softened, roll it out on a lightly floured work surface as thin as possible; use a gingerbread person cutter, or even hand cut, if you're brave. Bake as directed, then cool. For softer cookies, remove the dough from the oven when the center is still puffy and soft, a couple minutes sooner. Decorate, if you like, with small candies and Vanilla Glaze (page 858). Store in a covered container (separated by layers of wax paper if they're decorated) at room temperature for up to several days.

Shortbread

MAKES: About 2 dozen | TIME: About 20 minutes, plus time to chill

This is a short dough, meaning it's made with lots of butter, so the cookies are very tender—and the cornstarch in confectioners' sugar makes them even more so—and very yummy. You can cut these, put them on a baking sheet, cover them, and freeze them for weeks before baking straight from the freezer (figure another 2 to 3 minutes if so). Or just chill the dough for about an hour and then slice and bake.

Try smearing these with Caramel–Cream Cheese Frosting (page 862) or drizzle with Orange Glaze (page 857), Chocolate Glaze (page 858), or a spoonful of jam.

    ½   pound (2 sticks) butter, softened
    ⅔   cup confectioners' sugar
     1   egg yolk
     2   cups all-purpose flour
     ½   teaspoon salt

1. Use an electric mixer to cream the butter and sugar on low speed in a large bowl, just until combined, about

30 seconds. Still on low speed, beat in the egg yolk, then the flour and salt, until the mixture barely holds together; this will take a few minutes. Take care to not overwork the dough.

2. Shape the dough on sheets of plastic wrap into 2 logs about 2 inches in diameter. Wrap the logs tightly in plastic and refrigerate until firm, at least 1 hour or overnight.

3. Heat the oven to 275°F. Slice the logs ¼ inch thick and put on ungreased baking sheets about 2 inches apart. Bake until just firm but still quite tender and not at all brown, 15 to 20 minutes. Cool for a minute on the sheets before transferring the cookies to wire racks to finish cooling. Store uncovered on a plate for no more than a day; or in an airtight container for a few more days at room temperature or in the freezer for up to a couple months.

WHOLE WHEAT SHORTBREAD A portion of whole wheat flour gives the shortbread a nice nutty flavor: Replace the all-purpose flour with whole wheat flour. Add another egg yolk. These are good sprinkled with crunchy sugar like turbinado or muscovado before baking.

LEMON SHORTBREAD Add 2 tablespoons grated lemon zest to the bowl with the butter and sugar before creaming. For an even stronger lemon flavor, drizzle the cooled cookies with Lemon Glaze (page 858). Or dust with confectioners' sugar.

CHEESE SHORTBREAD Use the food processor to make these puffy savory cookies, which are perfect for cocktail parties: Heat the oven to 400°F and lightly grease or line 2 baking sheets with parchment paper. Omit the confectioners' sugar and egg yolk. Reduce the butter to 8 tablespoons (1 stick) and the flour to 1½ cups; put them in a food processor along with 2 cups grated Gruyère, cheddar, or other semihard cheese, 1 egg, and the salt. Pulse the machine just until the mixture resembles a coarse meal; do not overprocess. Form the dough into 1-inch balls. Line the balls on the prepared baking sheets, leaving 2 inches between them. Slightly flatten each ball with your fingers. Bake until

the shortbreads brown, about 10 minutes. After cooling sprinkle with paprika if you like, and serve.

---

6 SIMPLE ADDITIONS FOR SHORTBREAD

Add these to the dough alone or in combination to vary the main recipe.

1. Grated orange or lemon zest, about 2 tablespoons. For more flavor, replace 2 tablespoons of the butter with 2 tablespoons fresh orange or lemon juice.

2. Minced fresh rosemary, thyme, or lavender leaves or dried flowers, about 1 teaspoon.

3. Chopped toasted pine nuts, ½ cup (nice with lemon zest or rosemary).

4. Ground cinnamon or ginger, 1 teaspoon.

5. Vanilla or almond extract, 1 teaspoon (especially good with nuts).

6. Melted dark chocolate, 1 ounce (about 3 tablespoons).

Vanilla Biscotti

MAKES: 3 to 4 dozen | **TIME:** About 1¼ hours

Who says biscotti have to be dunked in something to avoid breaking your teeth? These are nice and crunchy but not rock-hard; they're great on their own *and* ideal for serving with coffee. To add nuts or anything else, see the list that follows, or try your own stir-ins.

- 4 tablespoons (½ stick) butter, plus more for greasing
- 2 cups all-purpose flour, plus more for dusting and shaping
- 1 teaspoon baking powder
- ¼ teaspoon salt
- 1 cup sugar
- 2 eggs
- 1½ teaspoons vanilla extract

1. Heat the oven to 375°F. Grease a baking sheet with butter and dust it with flour; tap the sheet over the sink to remove excess flour.

2. Combine the flour, baking powder, and salt in a medium bowl.

3. Use an electric mixer to cream the butter and sugar in a large bowl until light and fluffy. Add the eggs one at a time, then the vanilla; beat until well blended. Add the dry ingredients to the creamed mixture a little at a time, beating until just combined.

4. On a well-floured surface, divide the dough in half and form each half into a loaf about 2 inches wide, 6 inches long, and 1 inch high, taking care to shape them as uniformly as possible so they bake evenly. You can lightly roll the tops with a rolling pin to smooth them out. Put the loaves a few inches apart on the prepared baking sheet and bake for 25 to 30 minutes, until they're golden and beginning to crack on top. (Use 2 baking sheets if the loaves will crowd each other.) Cool the logs on the sheet for a few minutes, then transfer them both to a wire rack. Lower the oven temperature to 250°F.

5. When the loaves are cool enough to handle, carefully move them to a cutting board and use a serrated knife to slice each diagonally into ½-inch-thick slices. Put the cookies back on the baking sheet, cut side down; it's okay if they are close to each other. Bake for 15 to 20 minutes, turning the biscotti halfway through baking, until they dry out. Transfer to wire racks to cool. These will keep crunchy in an airtight container for up to a week.

7 BISCOTTI VARIATIONS

Use these ideas alone or in combination.

1. **Spiced Biscotti:** Omit the vanilla. Add 1 teaspoon ground fennel or anise seeds or 1 teaspoon ground cinnamon to the dry ingredients.

2. **Nutty Biscotti:** Reduce the vanilla to ½ teaspoon. At the end of Step 3, fold in ¾ cup chopped toasted almonds, hazelnuts, walnuts, pecans, or pistachios, or whole toasted pine nuts, into the dough before shaping.

3. **Citrusy Biscotti:** Reduce the vanilla to ½ teaspoon. Mix 1 teaspoon minced lemon or orange zest into the dry ingredients.

4. **Chocolate-Frosted Biscotti:** Reduce the vanilla to ½ teaspoon. Melt 8 ounces dark chocolate with 3 tablespoons butter. Spread this mixture onto one flat surface of the biscotti when they are dry. Cool on a wire rack until the chocolate coating is firm.

5. **Ginger Biscotti:** Omit the vanilla. At the end of Step 3, fold in about ⅓ cup minced candied ginger.

6. **Fruit Biscotti:** At the end of Step 3, fold in about ½ cup dried fruit like raisins, cherries, or cranberries, or chopped dried apricots or figs.

7. **Chocolate Chunk Biscotti:** At the end of Step 3, fold in about ¾ cup chopped any chocolate.

Coconut Macaroons

MAKES: 2 to 4 dozen | **TIME:** About 20 minutes, plus time to chill

Easiest. Cookies. Ever. And quite versatile: Use up to 5 cups coconut for something lighter and chewier, or replace some or all of the coconut with nuts (see the variation). Unsweetened, untoasted, ground or finely shredded coconut is the only thing that works here. Fortunately it's commonly available; if all you can find are the ribbons, pulse them a few times in the food processor to get the right texture.

3 egg whites
1 cup sugar
3 cups unsweetened finely shredded coconut (see the headnote)
1 teaspoon vanilla extract
Pinch salt

1. Heat the oven to 350°F and line 2 baking sheets with parchment paper.

2. Lightly beat the egg whites with the sugar until frothy, then mix in the coconut, vanilla, and salt until the coconut is evenly coated.

3. Wet your hands and make small mounds of the mixture, each 1 to 2 tablespoons, about an inch apart on the prepared sheets. Bake until golden, about 15 minutes. Cool the macaroons on wire racks for at least 30 minutes before eating. These will keep in an airtight container for up to 3 days.

WALNUT OR OTHER NUT MACAROONS Super with chocolate chunks too: Substitute finely chopped walnuts for some or all of the coconut.

Brownies

MAKES: About 1 dozen | TIME: 30 to 40 minutes

Brownies and the other bars that follow start with cookie-ish batters, but unlike cookies they're baked in a single block, which makes them cakelike or fudgy. These are relatively thin, chewy, and dense, with a fudgy center and a chewy, crackly top. My kids taught me that brownies are better without nuts but you can add them if you like; see the list that follows.

The best ways to finish brownies: Top with Whipped Cream (page 854), drizzle with Clear or Creamy Caramel Sauce (page 860) or Vanilla Custard Sauce (page 864); or serve with a scoop of a surprisingly compatibly flavored ice cream like coconut or buttermilk (see the chart on page 902).

12	tablespoons (1½ sticks) butter, plus more for greasing (optional)
1	cup cocoa powder
½	cup all-purpose flour
	Pinch salt
1¼	cups sugar
2	eggs
1	teaspoon vanilla extract

1. Heat the oven to 325°F. Grease an 8- or 9-inch square baking pan with butter or line it with parchment paper.

2. Whisk the cocoa, flour, and salt together in a medium bowl. Melt the butter, then whisk in the sugar until combined. Let cool slightly. Beat the eggs and vanilla into the butter mixture, then stir in the dry ingredients until thoroughly combined.

3. Pour the batter into the prepared pan. Bake until just barely set in the middle; when you jiggle the pan you'll see some movement, about 20 minutes, (It's better to underbake brownies than overbake them.) Cool the pan on a wire rack until the brownies are almost completely cool before cutting. These will keep in an airtight container for no more than 1 day.

CREAM CHEESE SWIRL BROWNIES Beat together ½ cup (4 ounces) softened cream cheese and ½ cup sugar until fluffy; beat in 1 egg. Pour half the brownie batter into the pan and drop the cream cheese mixture evenly over it; top with the remaining batter. Use a knife to swirl the cream cheese into the brownies for a marbled effect. Increase the baking time by about 10 minutes.

8 SIMPLE IDEAS FOR BROWNIES

1. Add ¼ cup peanut butter or ½ to 1 cup chopped toasted nuts to the batter.

2. Add ½ to 1 cup chocolate chunks (any kind) to the batter.

3. Use ½ teaspoon almond or mint extract in addition to or in place of the vanilla.

4. Add ½ cup mashed banana to the batter.

5. Add ¼ cup bourbon, Scotch, or other whiskey to the batter; increase the flour by 1 tablespoon.

6. Add 2 tablespoons instant espresso powder along with the vanilla.

7. Stir ½ cup dried fruit, especially dried cherries, into the batter.

8. Frost the cooled brownies with Vanilla or Chocolate Frosting (page 856) before cutting.

 fast make ahead  vegetarian

Blondies

MAKES: About 1 dozen | **TIME:** 30 to 40 minutes

What you get when you take the chocolate out of brownies—a distinct and addictive butter flavor. Any of the "8 Simple Ideas for Brownies" listed on page 840 will work here too.

8	tablespoons (1 stick) butter, plus more for greasing
¾	cup sugar
1	egg
1	teaspoon vanilla extract
	Pinch salt
1	cup all-purpose flour

1. Heat the oven to 350°F. Grease an 8- or 9-inch square baking pan with butter or line it with parchment paper and butter the parchment.

2. Use an electric mixer to cream the butter and sugar in a large bowl until very smooth. Mix in the egg and vanilla, scraping down the sides of the bowl every now and then to fully incorporate them.

3. Add the salt, then gently fold in the flour. Spread in the prepared pan. Bake until barely set in the middle; when you jiggle the pan you'll see some movement, about 20 minutes. (It's better to underbake blondies than overbake them.) Cool the pan on a wire rack until the brownies are almost completely cool. These will keep in an airtight container for a few days.

BUTTERSCOTCH BLONDIES Instead of the granulated sugar, use 1 cup brown sugar.

MY MAGIC BARS So named because you can put almost anything in them; they're not at all like that '60s condensed-milk concoction: Add up to 1½ cups total shredded coconut; any kind of chocolate chunks, toffee or caramel chunks; roughly chopped nuts and/or dried fruit, alone or in combination. Stir the additions into the batter just before pouring into the pan.

APRICOT-ALMOND BARS Use ½ teaspoon almond extract instead of the vanilla. Reduce the sugar to ¼ cup and the flour to ¾ cup. Add 1 cup chopped dried apricots, ¼ cup apricot jam, and ½ cup finely chopped almonds to the batter along with the eggs.

Lemon Squares

MAKES: About 1 dozen | **TIME:** About 1 hour

People—especially me—just love these layered squares for their tart sweetness, delivered via a gooey top and sandy crust.

8	tablespoons (1 stick) butter, softened, plus more for greasing
1¾	cups granulated sugar
	Pinch salt
1	cup plus 3 tablespoons all-purpose flour
3	eggs
¼	cup fresh lemon juice
½	teaspoon baking soda
2	tablespoons grated lemon zest
	Confectioners' sugar, sifted, for dusting

1. Heat the oven to 350°F. Grease an 8- or 9-inch square baking pan with butter.

2. Use an electric mixer to cream the butter with ¼ cup of the granulated sugar and the salt until light and fluffy. Stir in 1 cup of the flour. (This mixture will be quite dry.) Press it into the pan and bake for 20 minutes, until it's just turning golden. Remove from the oven and cool slightly; leave the oven on.

3. Beat the eggs, lemon juice, and the remaining 1½ cups granulated sugar until lightened and thick. Mix in the remaining 3 tablespoons flour, the baking soda, and lemon zest. Pour over the crust. Bake until firm on the edges but still a jiggly in the middle, 25 to 30 minutes; don't overbake them. Cool completely in the pan on a wire rack, then dust with confectioners' sugar and cut into squares. These can be stored, covered, in the refrigerator for up to 2 days.

COCONUT-LIME BARS Make the crust as directed. Increase the sugar in the filling to 1¾ cups and substitute lime juice and zest for the lemon. Sprinkle ¾ cup unsweetened shredded coconut over the filling just before baking. Omit the confectioners' sugar.

JAM BARS Make the crust as directed. For the filling, reduce the sugar to ¾ cup and omit the flour and baking soda. Substitute ¼ cup of your favorite jam for the lemon juice and zest, beating it with the eggs and sugar.

Cakes

I like what you might consider rustic-style cakes. They're slightly more indulgent and delicate than muffins or banana bread and just as suitable for everyday eating. Before you start, a few important tips:

ABOUT INGREDIENTS

Use high-quality butter, eggs, chocolate, nuts, and extracts for the best cakes. They'll mix and bake better if they're at room temperature (unless otherwise stated). Cakes have a way of showcasing off-flavors,

On Sifting Dry Ingredients

Flour, once an inconsistent product, is now so fine that sifting is usually unnecessary. Nor is it necessary when mixing flour with other dry ingredients, like sugar, salt, or baking powder, although it's worth whisking those ingredients together with a fork or whisk just to eliminate any lumps. When you do need to sift—as in delicate cakes like Angel Food Cake or Rich Chocolate Torte (pages 847 and 853)—put the flour through an old-fashioned sifter or simply pass through a not-too-fine sieve. And of course this is an excellent technique for dusting cakes with a decorative flurry of confectioner's sugar or cocoa.

and if a component is stale or second-rate, that will pop to the fore. See pages 15 to 16 for how to measure ingredients.

ABOUT PAN SIZE

The recipes direct you toward the right pan, though you have some flexibility as long as you adjust the baking time accordingly. For example, the difference between an 8-inch and a 9-inch cake pan is 17 square inches—that's a large extra area over which to spread a batter. So a 9-inch cake will be thinner and take less time to bake. Tube pans—plain or fluted—or Bundt pans can be substituted for any recipe that makes two layers or one 13×9-inch rectangular pan; in this case the baking time will be a little longer, because the batter is deeper. And if you want to make more servings of a single-layer cake that is baked in an 8-or 9-inch square or round pan, double the recipe and bake it in a 13- by 9-inch pan or a Bundt pan.

GREASING AND FLOURING PANS

Often butter alone suffices, but here's how to add flour when necessary: Smear the butter all over the inside of the pan, dust with flour, then invert the pan and tap out the excess flour. To be doubly sure you won't leave part of the delicate cake behind, you can line the pan with parchment or wax paper before greasing.

FOR EVEN BAKING AND RISING

As with cookies, when you're baking cakes, rotate the pan(s) about halfway through baking so that different sections bake in different parts of the oven for equal times.

STORING CAKES

If you're not frosting the cake right away, wrap each layer tightly with plastic wrap and store at room temperature for up to 2 days, or double-wrap with plastic wrap and foil and store in the freezer for up to a few months. Once frosted, a cake can hold for a day if covered loosely with foil or put in a cake dome; those with custard, whipped cream, or curd should be refrigerated.

Yellow Cake, page 847, with
Chocolate Frosting, page 856

Unfrosted cakes can stay in the pan if you'd like. No cake—frosted or not—is ever again as tender and moist as it is the day you make it.

Pound Cake

MAKES: At least 8 servings | **TIME:** About 1½ hours

 M V

A classic cake whose name derives from its basic ingredients: a pound each butter, flour, sugar, and eggs. Here the formula is roughly cut in half to make one nice-size loaf, and a few extra ingredients are added to increase flavor and lighten the texture. I suggest using cake flour for extra tenderness; if you don't have it, the results with all-purpose will still be quite good.

Pound Cake is wonderful finished with any glaze (pages 857–858) or served with Fruit Sauce, Two Ways (page 862).

- ½ pound (2 sticks) butter, softened, plus more for greasing
- 2 cups cake flour or all-purpose flour
- 1½ teaspoons baking powder
- ½ teaspoon salt
- ½ teaspoon freshly grated nutmeg (optional but very nice)
- 1 cup sugar
- 5 eggs
- 2 teaspoons vanilla extract

1. Heat the oven to 325°F. Grease a 9 × 5-inch loaf pan with butter.

2. Whisk the flour, baking powder, salt, and nutmeg if you're using it together in a medium bowl.

3. Use an electric mixer to cream the butter in a large bowl until it's smooth. Add ¾ cup of the sugar and beat until it's well blended, then add the remaining sugar; beat until the mixture is light in color and fluffy. Beat in the eggs, one at a time. Add the vanilla and beat until blended.

4. Stir in the dry ingredients by hand just until the mixture is smooth and everything is incorporated; don't mix it too much and don't use the electric mixer.

5. Transfer the batter to the prepared pan and smooth the top with a rubber spatula. Bake until a toothpick inserted into the center comes out clean, about 1 hour. Let the cake cool in the pan for 5 to 10 minutes, then gently run a knife around the edges and remove the cake from the pan. Set the cake upright on a wire rack to finish cooling. Serve warm or at room temperature. When completely cool, store at room temperature, wrapped in plastic, for 3 days.

MARBLE CAKE A pound cake that's sure to impress: In a separate bowl, combine 3 tablespoons cocoa powder with 5 tablespoons sugar. At the end of Step 4, add about 1 cup of the batter and stir to blend. Put half the plain batter in the loaf pan; top with the cocoa batter, then the remaining plain batter. Using the handle of a wooden spoon or a spatula, move across the pan lengthwise, swirling the batters together with large strokes; repeat the movement in the opposite direction. Be careful not to overmix or the marbling effect will be lost.

POLENTA POUND CAKE Substitute 1 cup cornmeal for 1 cup of the flour.

YOGURT POUND CAKE Lighter, tangier, and even more moist, if possible: Substitute ¾ cup yogurt for half the butter.

6 WAYS TO VARY POUND CAKE

Combine any of these ideas. One of my favorites is almond flour with orange zest; lemon with poppy seeds is classic.

1. Use a vanilla bean in place of the vanilla extract (see "Using a Vanilla Bean," page 899).

 F fast   M make ahead   V vegetarian

2. Add 1 teaspoon grated or minced lemon, orange, lime, or grapefruit zest and 1 tablespoon citrus juice. Omit the vanilla extract.

3. Add 1 teaspoon of ground spices, like cinnamon, ginger, cardamom, nutmeg, allspice, or cloves (alone or in combination).

4. Substitute 1 cup any nut meal or flour for 1 cup of the flour; use all-purpose flour for the remaining cup.

5. Add 1 to 2 tablespoons minced candied ginger.

6. Add ¼ cup poppy or sesame seeds.

Yellow Cake

MAKES: At least 10 servings | **TIME:** About 1 hour, plus time to cool

This tender, delicate cake takes either vanilla or chocolate frosting beautifully. The recipe makes enough batter for either a 2- or 3-layer cake or a sheet cake; if making a sheet cake you can either frost it in the pan or turn it out onto a large board or platter and decorate the sides too. For individual servings, see "Making Cupcakes" on page 848.

10	tablespoons (1¼ sticks) butter, softened, plus more for greasing
2	cups cake flour or all-purpose flour, plus more for dusting the pans
2½	teaspoons baking powder
¼	teaspoon salt
1¼	cups sugar
8	egg yolks
2	teaspoons vanilla extract
¾	cup milk

1. Heat the oven to 350°F. Grease and flour the bottom and sides of two 9-inch or three 8-inch cake pans, or a 13 × 9-inch baking pan.

2. Whisk the flour, baking powder, and salt together in a medium bowl.

3. Use an electric mixer to cream the butter until smooth, then gradually add the sugar. Beat until light in color and fluffy, 3 or 4 minutes. Beat in the egg yolks one at a time, then the vanilla. Stir the dry ingredients to the creamed mixture by hand a little at a time, alternating with the milk. Stir just until smooth.

4. Turn the batter into the pan(s) and bake until a toothpick inserted into the center of the cakes comes out clean, 20 to 30 minutes, depending on the thickness of the batter. Let the cake(s) cool in the pan(s) for 5 minutes, then invert onto a wire rack to finish cooling.

5. Frost or glaze as you like (see the illustrations on page 857 and recipes on pages 856–857) and store loosely covered or in a cake dome for a couple days.

COCONUT CAKE Spectacular as a layer cake but easier as a sheet cake: Stir ½ cup shredded coconut into the batter along with the dry ingredients and the milk. If you're making a layer cake: Spread a layer of cooled Vanilla Pudding (page 887) or Lemon Curd (page 862) on the cooled bottom layer, then sprinkle with ½ cup shredded coconut. For a 3-layer cake repeat with the second cake layer, more pudding, and more coconut. Put on the top layer and frost with Vanilla Frosting (page 856). Press another 2 cups or more shredded coconut onto the top and sides.

Angel Food Cake

MAKES: At least 10 servings | **TIME:** About 1½ hours, plus time to cool

Angel food cake is made only with egg whites, no yolks and no butter or other fat. Spongy and light, with a delicately sweet flavor and a kind of "crust," the keys to success involve repeated sifting and the crazy upside-down cooling. The tube shape of the cake makes it ideal

for drizzling with a glaze (pages 857–858) or Chocolate Sauce (page 858). Or slice and serve with any fruit sauce (page 862) or macerated fruit (see page 363).

1 **cup cake flour**
½ **cup confectioners' sugar**
¼ **teaspoon salt**
9 **egg whites, at room temperature**
1 **teaspoon cream of tartar**
½ **cup granulated sugar**
1 **teaspoon vanilla extract**
¼ **teaspoon almond extract**

1. Heat the oven to 325°F.
2. Sift the flour, confectioners' sugar, and salt together into a medium bowl. Sift again.
3. Beat the egg whites until foamy. Add the cream of tartar and continue to beat until they hold soft peaks. Beat in the granulated sugar and the extracts; continue to beat until the peaks begin to stiffen.
4. Sift one-third of the dry ingredients over the egg whites and gradually and gently fold it in using

a rubber spatula. Repeat with the rest of the dry ingredients, adding them in two more increments, until incorporated. Scoop the batter into an ungreased 9- or 10-inch straight-sided tube pan. Bake until the cake is firm, springy, and well browned, 45 to 55 minutes.
5. Remove the pan from the oven, and invert the cake in the pan over the neck of a bottle to cool. When completely cooled, run a butter knife carefully around the sides of the cake and the tube and remove. Cool completely before slicing with a serrated knife or pulling apart with 2 forks. Angel food cake is best the day it's made; it becomes dry quickly, though it is wonderful toasted.

CHOCOLATE ANGEL FOOD CAKE Substitute ¼ cup cocoa powder for ¼ cup of the flour.

LEMON-SCENTED ANGEL FOOD CAKE Omit the almond extract. When you add the sugar and vanilla in Step 3, add 1 packed tablespoon grated lemon zest.

Serving Angel Food Cake

Slicing angel food cake with a knife can compress the soft interior; instead, use this technique: Insert two forks back to back, and use them to gently pull apart the cake into slices.

 fast   make ahead    vegetarian

Strawberry or Other Fruit Shortcakes

MAKES: 6 large or 12 small servings | TIME: About 1 hour, including baking the biscuits

Strawberries are the classic filling, but use any ripe and flavorful fruit like cherries, blueberries, peaches, or apricots, or a combination. In winter, try sliced Poached Pears (page 381).

1	recipe Buttermilk or Yogurt Biscuits (page 773; bake 12 biscuits)
4 to 5	cups ripe berries or sliced fruit
2	tablespoons sugar, or to taste
2	cups cream
½	teaspoon vanilla extract

1. Let the biscuits cool completely on a wire rack before proceeding; you don't want them to be hot, or the whipped cream will melt.

2. Meanwhile, wash and prepare the fruit as needed. Toss with 1 tablespoon of the sugar, or more or less to taste, and let sit while you whip the cream. Whip the cream until it holds soft peaks, then slowly add the remaining sugar and the vanilla and whip for until it forms peaks as soft or firm as you like, 1 or 2 minutes more.

3. Split the biscuits and fill them with cream and fruit. Serve right away.

Pineapple Upside-Down Cake

MAKES: At least 8 servings | TIME: About 1½ hours, plus time for cooling

A golden-ripe fresh pineapple is a must here so the fruit's sugary juices seep out and caramelize to create a rich, almost crunchy topping when the cake is inverted. You can cut the pineapple into rings (see the illustrations on page 382), slices of any size, or ½-inch cubes—whatever you prefer. Use a skillet rather than a cake pan if you want to maximize this browning effect.

8	tablespoons (1 stick) butter, softened
½	cup packed brown sugar
6	½-inch-thick slices peeled and cored fresh pineapple, or as much as will fit in the pan (see the headnote)
2	cups all-purpose flour
1	teaspoon baking soda
¼	teaspoon salt
1	cup buttermilk
2	eggs
½	cup granulated sugar
	Ice cream for serving (to make your own, see pages 897–904)

1. Heat the oven to 350°F. Over low heat, gently melt half of the butter in a 9- or 10-inch ovenproof skillet, then remove from the heat, or liberally grease a 9-inch round cake pan with half of the butter. Sprinkle the brown sugar evenly over the butter and arrange the pineapple slices in a single layer on top of the brown sugar.

2. Melt the remaining 4 tablespoons (½ stick) butter; set aside to cool slightly.

3. Whisk the flour, baking soda, and salt together in a large bowl. In a medium bowl, whisk the melted butter, buttermilk, eggs, and granulated sugar until foamy in a medium bowl. Gradually add the egg mixture to the dry ingredients and stir until well incorporated.

4. Carefully spread the batter over the pineapple, using a spatula to make sure it's evenly distributed. Bake until the top of the cake is golden brown and a toothpick inserted into the center comes out clean, 50 to 60 minutes. Let the cake cool in the pan on a wire rack for no longer than 5 minutes.

5. Run a knife around the edge of the pan. Put a serving plate on top of the pan and invert everything so the plate is on the bottom and the pan is on top. The cake should fall out onto the plate. If it sticks, turn it back right side up and run the knife along the edge again, then use a spatula to gently lift the cake and pineapple at the edge. Invert the cake again onto the plate and tap on the bottom of the pan. If any of the fruit sticks to the pan, don't worry; use a knife to remove the pieces and fill in any gaps on the top of the cake. Serve warm with ice cream.

PLUM UPSIDE-DOWN CAKE The sweet and savory pairing is an unusual twist on the classic: Substitute 4 or 5 ripe, sweet plums, pitted and cut into slices or chunks, for the pineapple. Sprinkle 1½ tablespoons minced fresh rosemary leaves over pan along with the brown sugar.

APPLE UPSIDE-DOWN CAKE Substitute 3 or 4 medium peeled, cored, and sliced apples for the pineapple. Add 1 teaspoon ground cinnamon to the dry ingredients if you like.

BERRY UPSIDE-DOWN CAKE Use 3 to 4 cups fresh berries like blackberries, blueberries, raspberries, or gooseberries in place of the pineapple, enough to cover the bottom of the pan in a single even layer. If you use strawberries, stem, core, and quarter them first.

Cheesecake

MAKES: At least 12 servings | **TIME:** About 2½ hours, plus time to chill

Everyone has a favorite cheesecake recipe, and this one is mine. I can live without crust, but if you can't, see the variation. I must have the sour cream topping, however.

	Butter for greasing
4	eggs
3	8-ounce packages cream cheese, softened
1¼	cups sugar
2	teaspoons vanilla extract
1	cup sour cream

1. Heat the oven to 325°F. Grease the bottom and sides of a 9-inch springform pan with butter. Line the bottom with a circle of parchment paper. Wrap the outside of the pan well with foil.

2. Use an electric mixer to beat the eggs until light. Add the cream cheese, 1 cup of the sugar, and 1 teaspoon of the vanilla, and beat until smooth.

3. Spread the batter in the prepared pan and put the pan in a larger baking pan that holds it comfortably. Pour enough warm water into the larger pan to come to within an inch of the top of the springform pan. Transfer carefully to the oven and bake until the cheesecake is just set and very lightly browned, about 1 hour. Remove the springform pan from the water bath. Turn the oven up to 450°F.

4. In a small bowl, combine the sour cream with the remaining ¼ cup sugar and 1 teaspoon vanilla; spread on the top of the cheesecake.

5. Return the cheesecake to the oven for 10 minutes, without the water bath; turn off the oven and let the cheesecake cool inside for 30 minutes before removing it. Run a knife around the edge of the cheesecake to prevent sticking to the pan, then let it cool completely on a wire rack. Cover with plastic wrap and refrigerate until well chilled before removing from the pan, slicing, and serving. This will keep in good shape, refrigerated, for several days.

CHEESECAKE WITH CRUST Press a double recipe of Graham Cracker Crust (page 871) into the bottom of the greased pan. Prick it all over with a fork and bake at 350°F until it's fragrant and set, 10 to 12 minutes. Cool completely before filling with the cheesecake batter and baking as directed.

RICOTTA CHEESECAKE Lighter texture; good with or without crust: Substitute 1½ pounds fresh ricotta for the cream cheese. Beat it with an electric mixer until lightened, then add the eggs. Increase the sugar in the batter to 1¼ cups. Add 1 tablespoon grated orange zest and use 1 tablespoon vanilla in the batter. Omit the sour cream topping.

Strawberry and Cherry
Shortcakes, page 849

How to Beat Egg Whites

Egg whites beaten until airy and stiff are the essential ingredient in many light and fluffy creations, like meringues, soufflés, and mousses. They're also used to lighten batters like Angel Food Cake (page 847) and Everyday Pancakes (page 740).

For equipment, at the most you'll need a mixer with a whisk attachment and a spotlessly clean metal or glass bowl; at the least, a big whisk, the bowl, and a well-rested arm. While a copper bowl will yield a sturdier foam, almost any type of metal or glass bowl will do. Avoid plastic, because its porous surface can retain fat, and fat interferes with the whites' ability to foam.

There are only a couple of potential pitfalls: The first is getting even the tiniest bit of yolk—or any fat—in the whites; even oil residue clinging to the sides of a bowl will ruin your whites' ability to whip up. If a bit of yolk does get in the whites, get it out or start with fresh whites.

The other mistake when whipping whites is to overbeat them. As with whipped cream, there are various stages. Soft peaks means the foam will just make a low peak with a tip that readily folds onto itself. Medium peaks will form a solid peak, still soft, with a tip that folds over but not onto itself. Stiff peaks have tips that

hardly bend; dragging your finger through the foam will leave a mark. When overbeaten, the foam will be clumpy and rough looking, and will leak water. Once egg whites are overwhipped, there's no repairing the damage; the foam is contains too much air, is too unstable, and will deflate when folding and baking. Start over with fresh egg whites.

Never add more than the tiniest pinch salt to the eggs; salt does add flavor, but it creates a less stable foam. Many people add cream of tartar with the belief that it helps stability, but I've never found it makes much difference, except in angel food cake.

On the other hand, whipping in sugar has both positive and negative aspects: It makes the process slower, but it also makes for a more stable foam when baked. Sugar helps egg whites retain moisture while baking, so they're less likely to fall and leak water; this is important for meringues and soufflés in particular. When you do add sugar, use confectioners' sugar, or superfine if you have it; both dissolve more quickly than granulated sugar. (Undissolved grains of sugar can cause syrupy beads to form on the surface of a meringue.) Add the sugar once the whites have formed medium peaks.

Beating Egg Whites

STEP 1 At the soft-peak stage, egg whites look soft, and when you remove the whisk or beaters, the tops fold over.

STEP 2 At the stiff-peak stage, the whites look stiff, and when you remove the whisk or beaters, the tops make distinct peaks. Do not beat beyond this point.

Folding in Whipped Cream or Egg Whites

STEP 1 To fold whipped cream or egg whites into a batter, first lighten the batter by stirring a couple of spoonfuls of cream or whites into it.

STEP 2 Then use a rubber spatula to gently fold in the rest of the cream or egg whites, scooping under the mixture and smoothing over the top.

 fast make ahead **V** vegetarian

Chocolate Cake

MAKES: At least 10 servings | TIME: About 1 hour, plus time to cool

The real deal. When the cake is cool, frost with Chocolate, Mocha, or Peanut Frosting (pages 856–857), or Caramel–Cream Cheese Frosting (page 862).

8	tablespoons (1 stick) butter, softened, plus more for greasing
2	cups cake flour or all-purpose flour, plus more for dusting
3	ounces dark chocolate, chopped (about ½ cup)
2	teaspoons baking powder
½	teaspoon baking soda
½	teaspoon salt
¾	cup sugar
2	eggs, separated,
1	teaspoon vanilla extract
1¼	cups milk

1. Heat the oven to 350°F. Grease and flour the bottom and sides of two 9-inch or three 8-inch cake pans, or a 13 × 9-inch baking pan.
2. Melt the chocolate in a small saucepan over very low heat or in a double boiler over hot—not boiling—water, stirring occasionally. When the chocolate is just about melted, remove from the heat and stir until smooth.
3. Whisk together the flour, baking powder, baking soda, and salt in a medium bowl.
4. Use an electric mixer to cream the butter until smooth. Gradually add the sugar and beat until light in color and fluffy, 3 to 4 minutes. Beat in the egg yolks, one at a time, then the vanilla, and finally the chocolate. Stir the dry ingredients into the chocolate mixture a little at a time, alternating with the milk. Stir just until smooth.
5. Wash and dry the beaters thoroughly, then beat the egg whites in a clean medium bowl until they hold soft peaks. Use a rubber spatula to fold them gently but thoroughly into the batter. Scoop it evenly into the prepared pan(s). Bake until a toothpick inserted into the center of the cakes comes out clean, 20 to 30 minutes depending on the thickness of the batter. Let the cake(s) cool in the pan for 5 minutes, then invert onto a wire rack to finish cooling.
6. Frost or glaze if you like (see the illustrations on page 857) and store at room temperature loosely wrapped or in a cake dome.

CHOCOLATE-CINNAMON CAKE Grind a cinnamon stick in a spice grinder for the best results: Substitute 2 teaspoons ground cinnamon for the vanilla extract.

DEVIL'S FOOD CAKE Substitute 1 cup sour cream or buttermilk for the regular milk; omit the baking powder and increase the baking soda to 1½ teaspoons. Baking time will be a few minutes less.

Rich Chocolate Torte

MAKES: 10 to 12 servings | TIME: About 1¼ hours, plus time to cool

For those of you keen on molten cakes (I'm ambivalent, to be honest) try this simple alternative. Then either dust it with confectioners' sugar, or gussy it up. Some of the best ways: Top with Whipped Cream (page 854) or serve with raspberry purée (see page 862) and/or Vanilla Custard Sauce (page 864) or Vanilla Custard Ice Cream (page 897). Or drizzle with Chocolate Glaze (page 858). To go truly decadent, split the cake into two layers, then fill and frost with Chocolate Ganache or Glaze (page 858).

	Butter for greasing
1	cup all-purpose flour, plus more for the pan
	Cocoa powder, for dusting the pan (optional)
½	teaspoon salt
6 to 7	ounces dark chocolate (at least 70% cacao)
5	eggs
2	teaspoons vanilla extract
¾	cup granulated sugar
	Confectioners' sugar for garnish (optional)

1. Heat the oven to 350°F. Butter a 9-inch layer cake pan. Cover the bottom with a circle of wax or parchment paper and butter the paper. Use a sieve to dust the pan with flour or cocoa powder, invert the pan over the sink, and tap to remove any excess.

2. Whisk the flour and salt together in a medium bowl. Melt the chocolate with ½ cup water in a double boiler, stirring occasionally. Remove from the heat and let cool.

3. In a large bowl, use an electric mixer to beat the eggs and vanilla until light. Gradually add the sugar, continuing to beat until the mixture is very thick, 8 to 12 minutes. Gently sift half the flour mixture over the egg mixture and stir it in, followed by the melted chocolate. Then sift and mix in the remaining flour, being careful not to overmix and deflate the eggs.

4. Pour the batter into the prepared pan. Bake until a toothpick inserted into the center of the cake comes out clean or with a few moist crumbs, 30 to 40 minutes. Let the cake cool in the pan for 5 minutes, then invert onto a wire rack to finish cooling. Dust the cake with confectioners' sugar if you like and serve small slices.

CHOCOLATE-HAZELNUT TORTE Substitute ¼ cup finely ground hazelnuts for ¼ cup of the flour. Stir ½ cup lightly toasted chopped hazelnuts (see page 309) into the batter just before pouring into the pan.

Frostings, Glazes, Soaks, and Sauces

You never *have* to add anything to cake, but as long as you've come this far, right? You can mix and match any of these recipes with others in the chapter. It's all fair game. Many of these are great accompaniments to cookies, ice cream, and other treats (or even pancakes or French toast). Some, like Lemon Curd (page 862) and Ganache (page 858) keep well for days in the fridge and make crowd-pleasing alternatives to jelly or preserves.

Whipped Cream

MAKES: About 2 cups, enough for 4 servings | TIME: 5 minutes

Whipping cream is so easy—even by hand, with a whisk and a bowl—please promise me you'll never buy the canned stuff. All you need is cold fresh cream with no additives, a clean metal or glass bowl, and a balloon whisk or a mixer fitted with the whisk attachment. See the following list for some flavoring ideas to add after the cream starts to take shape.

    1 **cup heavy cream**
       Up to ¼ cup sugar (optional)
       Flavoring (optional; see below)

1. In a large bowl, use a whisk or electric mixer to beat the cream to soft or stiff peaks, as desired (see the illustrations). If you're sweetening it, when soft peaks form, start sprinkling in the sugar 1 tablespoon at a time.

2. Fold in flavorings if you like and serve immediately. Or cover and refrigerate for up to 2 hours. If it starts to separate, whisk it lightly until it comes together again.

---

8 WAYS TO FLAVOR WHIPPED CREAM

1. Scrape the seeds from half a vanilla bean into the cream, or use 1 teaspoon good-quality vanilla extract.
2. Use honey instead of sugar.
3. Sprinkle and fold in ground cardamom, cinnamon, freshly grated nutmeg, or any finely ground sweet spice.
4. Add 1 to 2 tablespoons bourbon, brandy, Kahlúa, Grand Marnier, framboise, amaretto, or other liqueur.
5. Add about ½ teaspoon grated citrus zest.
6. Add ½ teaspoon finely grated or very finely minced fresh ginger.

F fast   M make ahead   V vegetarian

Rich Chocolate Torte,
page 853

7. Add a tablespoon or 2 sour cream, or crème fraiche or mascarpone, which will be tangier or thicker, respectively.
8. Add 1 to 2 teaspoons rose water or orange blossom water.

Vanilla Frosting

MAKES: Enough frosting and filling for one 8-inch 3-layer cake, one 9-inch 2-layer cake, or 2 dozen cupcakes | **TIME:** 10 minutes

There is no easier frosting—essentially American-style buttercream—and it's flexible enough to pair well with just about any cake, cupcake, or cookie. Cream is best here, but you can use milk for a little less richness.

    8 tablespoons (1 stick) butter, softened
    4 cups confectioners' sugar
    6 tablespoons cream or milk, plus more if needed
    2 teaspoons vanilla extract
       Pinch salt

1. Use an electric mixer to cream the butter in a large bowl. Gradually work in the sugar, alternating with the cream and beating well after each addition.
2. Stir in the vanilla and salt. If the frosting is too thick to spread, add a little more cream, a teaspoon at a time. If it's too thin (unlikely, but possible), refrigerate; it will thicken as the butter hardens.

CHOCOLATE FROSTING Before starting, melt 2 ounces chopped dark chocolate over very low heat in a double boiler; let cool to room temperature. Add it to the frosting in Step 1, after you've beaten in about half each of the sugar and cream.

MOCHA FROSTING An adult frosting: Add 1 ounce unsweetened chocolate, melted and cooled as in the preceding variation, to the frosting after adding about

Stages of Whipped Cream

SOFT PEAKS: Cream is thickened just enough so you can no longer pour it. When you dip beaters or a whisk into the bowl, the cream is not yet stiff enough to hold peaks; it just sort of flops over. But it doesn't take long from this stage to stiff peaks, so be sure to stop and check the consistency frequently.

STIFF PEAKS: Cream that stays on a spoon, slightly firm and stable. To assess the cream in the bowl, dip the beaters or whisk into the cream and pull up; the peak formed should stand upright with minimal drooping.

OVERBEATEN: If you beat whipped cream too much, it will start to look "clotted" or curdled. If this happens, try stirring in a little more cream by hand until smooth again.

 fast make ahead **V** vegetarian

half the sugar. Substitute 2 tablespoons very strong brewed coffee (espresso is best) for 2 tablespoons of the cream or milk.

LEMON OR ORANGE FROSTING This is very good made with half butter and half cream cheese, but it can also be made with all butter. Omit the cream. Reduce the vanilla to 1 teaspoon and add 1 teaspoon fresh lemon juice or 1 tablespoon fresh orange juice. Stir in 1 teaspoon grated or minced lemon zest or 1 tablespoon grated or minced orange zest.

MAPLE FROSTING Thinner than the usual frosting; use for cakes or spread on pancakes, waffles, and French toast: Substitute ½ cup maple syrup for 2 cups of the confectioners' sugar. Omit the vanilla. Proceed with the recipe, then refrigerate the frosting to solidify it somewhat before using.

PEANUT BUTTER FROSTING Perfect with chocolate cupcakes or sandwiched between oatmeal cookies: Substitute ¼ cup smooth peanut butter for 4 tablespoons of the butter. Proceed with the recipe; this may require extra cream to get it to the right consistency.

Orange Glaze

MAKES: About 3 cups, enough to drizzle on any cake or 2 dozen cupcakes | TIME: 10 minutes

I barely count this as a recipe: Put some confectioners' sugar in a bowl and stir in liquid until it's the consistency of maple syrup, or thicker if you want to spread it on or sandwich it between cookies.

Other citrus that you can use: tangerine, grapefruit, and blood orange all work well.

- ½ **cup fresh orange juice**
- 1 **tablespoon grated orange zest**
- ½ **teaspoon vanilla extract (optional)**
- 3 **cups confectioners' sugar, plus more if needed**
  Pinch salt

Frosting a Cake

STEP 1 Put the first layer rounded top down on a plate or cake stand. For a two-layer cake, spread about a third of the frosting on top, all the way to the edges. Use a table knife if you don't have an offset spatula. It's okay if the edges are a little messy; you'll smooth things out at the end.

STEP 2 Put the other layer on top, flat bottom down. Spread another third of the frosting on top.

STEP 3 Use the remaining frosting to cover the sides of the cake, scooping up any excess to add to the top. Smooth it if you like, or wiggle your hand a bit to make little peaks and swirls. For a three-layer cake, save about one-third for the sides and divide the remaining two-thirds of the frosting among the three layers.

Combine all the ingredients and beat until combined and smooth; it should be about the consistency of thick maple syrup—just pourable. For a thicker glaze, add more confectioners' sugar. Use immediately or store, covered, in the refrigerator for up to 2 weeks. Beat to recombine before using.

CREAMY ORANGE GLAZE Substitute ¼ cup cream for half of the orange juice. Add 3 tablespoons very soft butter if you like.

VANILLA GLAZE Substitute cream, milk, or a combination for the orange juice. Omit the zest and use only the vanilla extract, increasing it to 1 teaspoon if you like.

LEMON OR LIME GLAZE Substitute ¼ cup lemon or lime juice and ¼ cup water for the orange juice. Omit the vanilla.

MOCHA GLAZE Substitute ½ cup freshly brewed coffee for the orange juice. Add 1 ounce dark chocolate, melted and cooled, or 3 tablespoons cocoa powder. Omit the zest.

COCONUT GLAZE Omit the vanilla extract. Substitute coconut milk for the orange juice and ¼ cup shredded coconut for the zest. Or don't add any coconut to the glaze, but top the glazed item with toasted shredded coconut instead.

Chocolate Ganache

MAKES: About 1½ cups | **TIME:** 15 minutes

A luscious mixture of chocolate and cream that works as sauce, frosting, and so much more, depending on which consistency you use (see "4 More Ways to Vary and Use Chocolate Ganache" on page 859). You can substitute milk or white chocolate for dark chocolate; just decrease the cream to ¾ cup.

- 1 cup cream
- 8 ounces dark chocolate, chopped (about 1⅓ cups)

1. Put the cream in a small pot over low heat and heat it until it's steaming. Put the chocolate in a heatproof bowl, pour on the hot cream, and whisk until the chocolate is melted and incorporated into the cream.

2. Use right away as a sauce or coating; as it cools down, it will start to set and get stiffer and harder to spread but works well for other things (see the list that follows).

CHOCOLATE GLAZE Reduce the cream to ¾ cup. Add 6 tablespoons (¾ stick) butter, ½ cup confectioners' sugar (or more to taste), ½ teaspoon vanilla extract, and a tiny pinch salt. Proceed with the recipe, melting the butter in the cream and stirring the other ingredients into the chocolate along with the cream. Use immediately or store, covered, in the fridge for up to 4 days. Melt over very low heat or in a double boiler before using.

Chocolate Sauce

MAKES: About 1½ cups | **TIME:** 15 minutes

A rich chocolate sauce, more substantial than syrup but thinner than ganache, so it's perfect for drizzling into cold or hot milk, swirling into pudding or ice cream, or turning into hot fudge sauce (see the variation).

- 4 ounces dark chocolate, chopped (about ⅔ cup)
- 4 tablespoons (½ stick) butter
- ¼ cup sugar
  Pinch salt
- 1 teaspoon vanilla extract

1. Combine the chocolate, butter, sugar, salt, and ¼ cup water in a small saucepan over very low heat. Cook, stirring, until the chocolate melts and the mixture is smooth.

2. Remove from the heat and stir in the vanilla. Serve immediately, keep warm over hot water until you're ready to serve it, or refrigerate in an airtight container for up to a week and rewarm before using.

HOT FUDGE SAUCE This is chewy and fudgy when you put it on top of ice cream: At the end of Step 1, add ⅓ cup corn syrup. Bring to a boil, turn the heat to low, and cook for 5 to 10 minutes, until thick and shiny. Add the vanilla and serve hot. Or refrigerate in an airtight container for up to a week and reheat very gently before serving.

Simple Syrup

MAKES: 2 cups | **TIME:** 10 minutes

Simple syrup is aptly named. All it requires is sugar, water, and some stove time. The result is an easy way to add sweetness to sorbets, granitas, iced drinks and cocktails, and macerated fruit (see page 363). Or use it as a neutrally flavored way to add moisture to plain cake layers. See the sidebar on flavoring dessert sauces (page 860) for ways to vary simple syrup, too.

2   cups sugar

Combine the sugar with 2 cups water in a small saucepan; bring to a boil and cook until the sugar is dissolved, stirring occasionally. Set aside to cool to room temperature. Use immediately or store in a clean airtight container or jar in the fridge for up to 6 months.

Caramel Crackle

MAKES: About 1½ cups | **TIME:** 20 minutes

The most elementary sauce, candy, or candy coating comes from cooking sugar, which hardens when it cools. But beware: This gets extremely hot and can cause bad burns, so resist any temptation to stick your finger into the hot sugar or lick a coated spoon until you're absolutely sure it's cooled. You'll need a candy thermometer. The main recipe makes a crunchy caramel that works as a candy coating or decorative garnish; for caramel sauce, see the variations.

7 Ways to Flavor Ganache and Other Dessert Sauces

Here are some simple ways to flavor nearly any dessert sauce. Obviously, not all of these will work with every sauce, so match flavors accordingly. Add them to taste, starting with a small amount.

1. Ground spices like cinnamon, cardamom, allspice, nutmeg, and star anise.
2. Earl Grey tea: Steep in the hot cream for about 10 minutes, then strain out.
3. Freshly brewed espresso or instant espresso powder; try with any of the chocolate-based sauces.
4. Maple syrup.
5. Any nut butter; pair with Chocolate Sauce, page 858.
6. Citrus zest, grated or finely minced; orange is nice with ganache or Creamy Caramel Sauce, at right.
7. Candied ginger, minced, or very finely minced fresh ginger; add to the Fruit Sauce, Two Ways, page 862

2 cups sugar
   Pinch salt

1. If you plan on making candy-like crumbles or garnishes, line a large rimmed baking sheet (or 2) with wax paper. Combine the sugar and salt with 1 cup water in a large saucepan or deep skillet over medium-low heat. Cook until the sugar dissolves, without stirring but swirling the pan gently, 3 to 5 minutes.

2. The mixture will bubble and gradually darken; cook until it's caramel colored and the temperature measures 245°F on a candy or deep-frying thermometer, about 15 minutes; a small spoonful of it will form a firm ball when dropped into a glass of cold water, but the thermometer is an easier and surer test.

3. While the caramel is still hot, you can carefully pour or drizzle over whatever you like for a crunchy candy coating. Or drizzle onto wax paper to make decorative garnishes. Or spread it over the paper in a thin layer, and when it cools, pound it with a rolling pin to make a candy crumble for dusting.

CLEAR CARAMEL SAUCE Cook in a deep pot: After Step 2, remove from heat and carefully add ¼ cup water to the hot caramel (it will bubble up). Stir until it's incorporated. Add more water if needed to reach the desired consistency.

CREAMY CARAMEL SAUCE Substitute cream for the water in the previous variation and add 4 tablespoons (½ stick) butter and 1 teaspoon vanilla extract if you like at the same time; add more cream if it's too thick.

CARAMEL COFFEE SAUCE Substitute freshly brewed coffee or half coffee and half cream for the water or cream in the above variations.

BOOZY CARAMEL SAUCE Use the Creamy Caramel Sauce variation and add 2 to 3 tablespoons liqueur.

 fast   make ahead    vegetarian

Creamy Caramel Sauce

CARAMEL–CREAM CHEESE FROSTING Make the Clear Caramel Sauce variation and let it cool completely. Whip 1 pound softened cream cheese until fluffy. Drizzle in the caramel, whipping until it's thoroughly mixed; thin with a little milk or cream as needed.

Fruit Sauce, Two Ways

MAKES: About 2 cups | **TIME:** 5 to 10 minutes

I believe in options. The first fruit sauce, which is no work at all, gives you pure, straightforward flavor and a very saucy consistency; it works well with soft fruits and berries. The second, which is thicker, is more luxurious, and wonderful with apples and pears.

Raw Fruit Method

- 2 cups berries or other soft ripe fruit (peaches, cherries, nectarines, mangoes, citrus), picked over, washed and dried, peeled, pitted, and chopped as necessary
  Confectioners' sugar
  Fresh orange or lemon juice or fruity white wine (optional)

1. Purée the fruit in a blender. If you're using raspberries or blackberries, put the purée through a fine-meshed strainer to remove the seeds.

2. Add confectioners' sugar to taste. If necessary, thin with a little water, orange juice, lemon juice, or fruity white wine. Use immediately or refrigerate in an airtight container for up to 2 days.

Cooked Fruit Method

- 2 cups berries or other ripe fruit (apples, pears, bananas, peaches, cherries, nectarines, berries, mangoes, melons, citrus, pumpkins), picked over, washed and dried, pitted, and/or peeled as necessary

- ½ cup sugar
- 3 tablespoons butter

1. Chop the fruit or cut it in wedges. If you're using citrus, cut it into segments as shown on page 378.

2. Combine the sugar and butter with ½ cup water in a heavy-bottomed medium saucepan over medium-high heat. Cook, swirling the pan or stirring, until thick and syrupy but not colored, 3 to 5 minutes.

3. Toss in the fruit and cook over low heat until the fruit begins to break up and release its juices, about 2 minutes for berries, longer for other fruit; some fruits, like apples, may require the addition of a little more water. Press the fruit through a fine-meshed strainer or run it through a food mill to purée and remove skins (if you left them on) or seeds. Serve warm, or let cool to room temperature. This sauce keeps well, refrigerated in an airtight container, for up to a week.

Lemon Curd

MAKES: About 2 cups | **TIME:** 15 to 30 minutes

You may as well call it lemon pudding because you'll want to just eat it with a spoon. Instead smear it on morning toast, between layers of cake, or sandwiched between cookies for a midnight snack. (I'm looking at you, Gingersnaps, page 837.) And yes, you can also make this with other citrus.

- ¾ cup milk
- 3 tablespoons grated lemon zest
- ⅓ cup fresh lemon juice
- 4 egg yolks
- 8 tablespoons (1 stick) butter, softened
- 1 cup sugar

1. Whisk all the ingredients together in a medium saucepan. Cook over medium heat, whisking almost

Lemon Curd

constantly, until the mixture thickens and reaches between 175° and 180°F on an instant-read thermometer, about 5 minutes. Don't let it boil. (It will make a thick coating on the back of a spoon; see the illustration on page 887.)

2. Remove from the heat. While it's still hot, pour the curd through a fine-meshed strainer into a bowl and let cool a bit. Serve warm or chilled. Lemon curd will keep in an airtight container in the refrigerator for up to 3 days.

SHORTCUT LEMON MOUSSE Whip 1 cup cream as described on page 854 and fold in 1 cup chilled lemon curd. Leave some streaks if you like.

Vanilla Custard Sauce

MAKES: About 2 cups | **TIME:** 15 to 30 minutes

Crème anglaise is an excellent, classic sauce for cakes, tarts, poached fruit, cookie-dipping, and more. This one-pot method is simple and yields fine results. You can change the flavor easily; see "Infusing Liquids with Flavor" on page 900.

    1 vanilla bean, split, or 1 teaspoon vanilla extract
    2 cups milk
    4 egg yolks
    ½ cup sugar

1. If you're using the vanilla bean, heat the milk and the bean together in a small saucepan until the milk steams. Remove from heat, cover and let sit for 15 minutes. Remove the bean and scrape the seeds into the milk. If you're not using the bean, just heat the milk.

2. Once the milk has cooled back down to almost room temperature, add the egg yolks and sugar and whisk well to combine. Cook over medium heat, whisking almost constantly, until the mixture thickens and reaches

between 175° and 180°F on an instant-read thermometer. Don't let it boil. (It will make a thick coating on the back of a spoon; see the illustration on page 887.)

3. Remove from the heat. While it's still hot, strain the custard through a fine-meshed strainer into a bowl and let it cool a bit. Stir in the vanilla extract if you're using it. Serve the sauce warm or chilled. It keeps, tightly covered, in the refrigerator for up to 3 days.

Pies, Tarts, Cobblers, and Crisps

These fundamental American desserts were once made daily in many households, and no wonder: They combine common ingredients with easily mastered techniques for often dramatic and always satisfying results.

All have some form of crust, a universally loved treat that almost always depends on a fair amount of fat—usually butter—to make it light, flaky, and delicious. What distinguishes pies and tarts from cobblers and crisps is the composition of the crust, how it is formed, and whether it's on the top or bottom.

Though the technique for making pie and tart crusts must be learned, it is literally child's play. If you can roll out a Play-Doh pie, you can make a real one. If you don't feel up to the challenge, start with cobblers and crisps and work your way up.

Though dedicated pie makers do get better and better at producing flaky, flavorful, nicely shaped, and beautifully colored crusts, it need not take years of trial and error to get the technique right; in fact, you can make good crusts your first time out, and quickly.

MAKING AND RESTING THE DOUGH

The best crusts start with butter. (And maybe with some lard for extra flakiness, if you can get your hands on some that's freshly rendered.) Butter gives the crust a rich, delicious flavor and good color, and if you handle it right and avoid overworking, excellent texture.

Flaky Piecrust, page 867

Technique and flour turn that butter into something magical. It isn't difficult, especially with a food processor, despite what the purists might say. You can mix the dough by hand, of course, pinching the butter with flour between your fingers or using various utensils like a pastry blender or two forks. However you do it, the idea is to get small bits of butter coated in flour, which will make for a flaky and light crust.

When the dough is properly mixed, you will be able to see bits of butter in it. In fact, the less you handle it, the flakier it will be. Avoiding kneading keeps the gluten of the flour in check; unlike bread dough, these crusts should have tenderness, not chew.

Once you make a dough, let it rest in the refrigerator or freezer so the gluten relaxes. This also hardens the butter, which makes rolling easier and helps the crust hold its shape during baking to create a flaky crust. Once the dough is frozen, wrap it tightly, and tuck it away for weeks.

ROLLING THE DOUGH

Transforming dough from a ball or disk to a fairly uniform round crust, less than ¼ inch thick, involves a combination of patience and practice. Ideally you'll roll the dough out only once, because rerolling will toughen it. At first, though, you may need more than one try. Although rolling tart dough makes a more even and flat crust, it can just be pressed into the pan.

These tips will make rolling dough easier.

- Start with dough that is firm and slightly chilled but not hard or frozen. It should yield a bit to pressure, but your fingers shouldn't sink in; if they do, refrigerate or freeze for a while longer.

- Flour the work surface, the rolling pin, and the top of the dough to prevent sticking. Beginners should use flour liberally; as you get the hang of it, you'll use less and less.

Rolling Pie Dough

STEP 1 Roll with firm, steady, but not overly hard pressure, from the inside out, sprinkling with flour if necessary.

STEP 2 You can also roll between two sheets of parchment paper or plastic wrap, which is sometimes easier. If at any point during rolling the dough becomes sticky, refrigerate it for about 15 minutes.

STEP 3 Patch any holes with pieces of dough from the edges.

STEP 4 When the dough is ready, flour the dough and pin very lightly and pick up the dough using the rolling pin.

STEP 5 Drape it over the pie plate.

 fast make ahead  vegetarian

- Or if the dough isn't too sticky, you can sandwich it between two sheets of plastic wrap or parchment paper and roll it in there.

- Roll from the center of the disk outward, rotating the rolling pin and rotating the dough a quarter-turn from time to time to make sure it's evenly rolled. Apply even and firm but gentle pressure to the rolling pin.

- Fix any holes or tears with tiny pieces from the edges; add a dab of water to help seal the patches in place. Don't try to pinch the hole closed.

- If the dough becomes sticky or slick, slide it onto a baking sheet and stick it in the freezer for a few minutes.

- When the dough is rolled out, transfer it by draping it over the rolling pin and moving it into the plate. Or by peeling off the top piece of plastic wrap or parchment, inverting the crust over the plate to lay it in place, then removing the other piece.

- Press the dough firmly into the plate, working from the bottom up. Refrigerate for about an hour before filling; if you're in a hurry, freeze for about a half-hour.

Once the dough is in the pan, you can trim it and make the edge more attractive. Tarts typically have a simple edge; just use a knife to cut away excess dough. Fluted tart pans make a pretty, ruffled-looking edge without any extra work on your part.

Piecrusts, on the other hand, have more elaborate edges. Different pie makers prefer different techniques, some more complicated than others; see page 868.

BAKING THE CRUST

There are a couple of ways to go about it: either baking the whole pie, filling and all, or prebaking the bottom— or only—crust alone first ("blind baking"). Though it

adds a step, in many cases prebaking the crust gives better results.

When you're baking a filled pie, always put it on a baking sheet; this encourages bottom browning and prevents spillovers from charring your oven floor. If the edges of the crust start to get too dark, loosely wrap a ring of foil around them.

Flaky Piecrust

MAKES: 1 crust for a 9-inch pie | **TIME:** 20 minutes, plus time to chill

I've used this recipe and technique for years and always been pleased with the results; it may be basic, but piecrusts don't get much more flaky and flavorful. This is enough dough for a single-crusted pie; simply double the recipe for fruit pies where you need a bottom and top (or lattice) crust.

- 1 cup plus 2 tablespoons all-purpose flour, plus more for rolling
- 1 teaspoon sugar
- ½ teaspoon salt
- 8 tablespoons (1 stick) very cold butter, cut into about chunks
- 3 tablespoons ice water, plus more if necessary

1. Use a food processor to pulse the flour, sugar, and salt together. Add the butter and pulse until it is just barely blended with the flour, and the butter is broken down to the size of peas. If you prefer to make the dough by hand, combine the flour, sugar, salt, and butter in a large bowl. With your fingertips, 2 knives or forks, or a pastry cutter, work the butter pieces into the dry ingredients, being sure to incorporate all of the butter evenly, until the mixture has the texture of small peas.

2. Add 3 tablespoons ice water (not just cold water). Process for about 5 seconds or mix by hand with a wooden spoon, just until the dough beings to clump together, adding 1 to 2 tablespoons more ice water if necessary. Add a little more flour if you add too much water.

3. Press the dough into a disk about 1 inch thick. It's important not to overheat, overwork, or knead the dough; squeeze it with enough pressure to just hold it together. Wrap in plastic or put in a zipper bag, pushing out as much air as possible. Freeze the disk of dough for 10 minutes or refrigerate for at least 30 minutes before rolling. (You can make the dough to this point and refrigerate for up to a couple days or freeze for months. Thaw in the refrigerator overnight before proceeding.)

4. Dust a large pinch flour over a clean work surface. Put the dough on the work surface. Sprinkle a little more flour on top of the dough and dust the rolling pin with flour. (Too much flour will dry the dough; you can always sprinkle on a little more if the dough starts to stick.) Using firm but not too hard pressure on the pin, start rolling the dough from the center outward to form a circle. If the dough feels too hard or is cracking a lot, let it rest for a few minutes. As you roll, only add flour as needed to prevent it from sticking to the pin; lift, rotate, and turn the dough with a spatula to form an even circle.

5. When the dough circle is about 2 inches wider than the pie plate and less than ⅛ inch thick, it's ready. Roll the dough halfway onto the pin so it's easy to move, then center it over the pie plate and unroll it in place. Press the dough into the contours of the dish without squishing or stretching it; patch any tears with a small scrap of dough from the edge and seal with a drop of water. Trim any excess dough to about ½ inch all around.

6. If you're making a single-crust pie, tuck the edges under themselves so the dough is thicker on the rim than it is inside the plate; if you're making a double-crust pie, leave the edges untucked for now. Put the pie plate in the fridge until the crust feels cool to the touch before filling or prebaking (see page 869). For a top crust, make a second batch of dough, roll it the

Crimping the Crust

PINCHING METHOD: Pinch the edges of the dough between the side of your forefinger and your thumb.

KNUCKLE METHOD: Use the thumb and forefinger of one hand to hold the dough in place. Then press a knuckle from your other hand against the crust, pushing it into the space between your thumb and forefinger.

FORK METHOD: Press down with the tines of a fork along the edges of the dough.

F fast   **M** make ahead   **V** vegetarian

same way, and put in the fridge on a flour-dusted baking sheet.

SAVORY PIECRUST What you want for savory quiches, tarts, and pastries: Omit the sugar from the main recipe or any of the other variations.

WHOLE WHEAT PIECRUST Slightly nutty flavor, a deeper golden brown color; there's some sacrifice in texture, but it's a worthwhile trade-off: Substitute ½ cup whole wheat for ½ cup of the all-purpose flour. A bit more ice water may be necessary.

NUT PIECRUST Rich and delicious, especially with macadamias or pine nuts: Substitute ¼ cup finely chopped or ground nuts for ¼ cup of the all-purpose flour. Pulse a few extra times in the food processor before adding the butter in Step 1. Proceed with the recipe.

GENEROUS PIE SHELL For a 10-Inch or Larger Pie or a Deep-Dish Pie: Increase the flour to 1½ cups, salt to ¾ teaspoon, sugar to 1½ teaspoons, butter to 10 tablespoons (1¼ sticks), and the ice water to ¼ cup.

Sweet Tart Crust

MAKES: One 9-inch tart shell | **TIME:** About 15 minutes

Tart crust contains more butter than piecrust, plus an egg yolk, which makes it extra-rich and almost like shortbread—think of it as a large cookie. Be sure to check out the variations too.

- 8   tablespoons (1 stick) very cold butter, cut into small pieces, plus more for greasing
- 1¼   cups all-purpose flour, plus more for kneading and rolling
- ¼   cup confectioners' sugar
        Pinch salt
- 1   egg yolk
- 1   tablespoon ice water, plus more if necessary

1. Generously butter a 9-inch tart pan. Use a food processor to pulse together the flour, sugar, and salt. Add the butter and pulse until the mixture has the texture of cornmeal. If you're making the dough by hand, combine the flour, sugar, and salt in a large bowl, then use your fingertips, 2 knives or forks, or a pastry cutter to mash the butter into the dry ingredients.

Add the egg yolk and pulse to combine, or use a fork to incorporate it. Pulse in the ice water, adding a tablespoon more at a time if necessary, until the dough starts to form a ball. If you prefer to make the dough by hand, combine the flour, sugar, salt, and butter in a large bowl. With your fingertips, 2 knives or forks, or a pastry cutter, work the butter pieces into the dry ingredients, being sure to incorporate all of the butter evenly, until the mixture has the texture of small peas. Then stir in the egg yolk and ice water. Turn the dough out onto a lightly floured counter and knead it just until it's combined and smooth. (You can make the dough to this point and refrigerate for up to a couple days or freeze for months.)

2. To press the dough into the pan: Gently press the dough evenly into the tart pan, being sure to tuck it into the contours.

3. To roll out the dough: Form the dough into a disk, wrap it in plastic, and refrigerate until firm, at least 1 hour. Dust a clean work surface with a large pinch flour. Unwrap and put down the dough; sprinkle a bit more flour over it. Use a rolling pin to firmly and evenly roll out the dough, starting in the center and working outward, rotating the dough a quarter-turn from time to time to make an even circle. If the dough is too stiff, let it rest for a few minutes. Sprinkle a bit of flour on the dough and rolling pin as needed to prevent sticking. When the dough circle is about 2 inches wider than the tart pan and less than ⅛ inch thick, it's ready. Roll the dough up halfway onto the pin so it's easy to move, then center it over the tart pan and unroll it into place. Press the dough into the contours of the pan without squishing or stretching it.

4 Simple Variations to Any Pie or Tart Crust

1. Substitute up to ¼ cup ground whole seeds like sesame, poppy, sunflower, or pumpkin, or nuts for the same amount of the flour or crumbs.
2. Substitute up to ¼ cup finely shredded or ground coconut as above.
3. Add a pinch ground spices like cinnamon, ginger, allspice, star anise, anise, cardamom, or coriander, or freshly grated nutmeg.
4. Add up to 1 tablespoon grated citrus zest.

4. Trim the dough even with the top of the pan. Before filling or prebaking, put the tart pan in the fridge for about 30 minutes or freeze for at least 10 minutes, until the crust feels cool to the touch.

SAVORY TART CRUST What you want for savory tarts or for any type of sugarless tart crust: Omit the sugar. (All the other variations except the chocolate one can be made savory by omitting the sugar.)

NUTTY SWEET TART CRUST Substitute ½ cup ground nuts, like almonds, hazelnuts, walnuts, pecans, macadamias, or peanuts, for ½ cup of the flour. Decrease the sugar to 2 tablespoons. If your dough seems a bit dry, add a tablespoon or 2 more ice water to it when you're kneading.

CHOCOLATE TART CRUST An even richer-flavored crust; be sure it doesn't overwhelm the filling: Substitute ¼ cup Dutch process cocoa powder for ¼ cup of the flour.

SPICED TART CRUST For the main recipe or the variations; subtle is best: Add ¼ teaspoon ground cardamom or cinnamon, or ⅛ teaspoon ground allspice, black pepper, red chile, or star anise.

 fast make ahead vegetarian

Graham Cracker Crust

MAKES: One 8- to 10-inch pie | TIME: 20 minutes

There are times only a crumb crust will do: cheesecakes, for example. It's also a great option for cream, meringue, or even pumpkin pies. Crumb crusts, including the variations that follow, are almost always prebaked.

    3   tablespoons sugar
    1½ cups graham cracker crumbs (about 6 ounces)
    4   tablespoons (½ stick) butter, melted, plus more
        if needed

1. Combine the sugar with the graham cracker pieces in a bowl or food processor. (To make this without a food processor, put the crackers in a zipper bag, seal it, then roll over the bag as necessary with a rolling pin; transfer the crumbs to a bowl and proceed.) Slowly add the butter, processing or stirring until well blended. If the crumbs aren't all moistened, add a little bit more butter. Press the crumbs into the bottom and up the sides of the pie plate.

2. Heat the oven to 350°F. Bake the crust for 8 to 10 minutes, just until it begins to brown. Cool on a wire rack before filling; the crust will harden as it cools.

GINGERSNAP OR OTHER CRUMB CRUST Nearly any plain cookie works here: Reduce the butter by 1 or 2 tablespoons if the cookies are very buttery, and likewise reduce the sugar a bit if they're sweet. Substitute gingersnaps, vanilla or chocolate wafers, or any crisp cookies for the graham crackers. You can even use saltine or buttery crackers if you like.

Apple Pie

MAKES: One 9-inch pie (about 8 servings) | TIME: 1½ hours

It's hard to imagine autumn without apple pie. Whether for Thanksgiving dinner or a dessert that lasts all week,

this is the classic recipe you'll turn to again and again when the weather turns crisp. I usually don't use flour as a thickener, but this recipe is an exception. I also keep spices to a minimum since I'd rather taste the apples; you could double their quantity if you like a spicy pie, or see the list that follows for more seasoning ideas. Vanilla ice cream or whipped cream are classic accompaniments, though some enthusiasts swear by a slice of cheddar cheese on top.

    ¼   cup all-purpose flour
    ¾   cup sugar, plus more for sprinkling
    ½   teaspoon ground cinnamon
    ½   teaspoon freshly grated nutmeg
    ¼   teaspoon salt
    3   pounds firm, sweet apples like Honeycrisp, Pink
        Lady, or Northern Spy, peeled, cored, and sliced
        into wedges about ¼ inch thick
    1   tablespoon fresh lemon juice
    2   tablespoons butter, cut into pieces
    2   recipes Flaky Piecrust (page 867), bottom crust
        fitted into a 9-inch pie plate, top crust transferred
        to a rimless baking sheet, both chilled
    2   tablespoons butter, cut into bits
        Milk for brushing

Tips for Fruit Pies

- Keep the thickener to a minimum.
- Taste the fruit as you sweeten it, to use just the right amount of sugar. Some blueberries, which can be quite tart, will take relatively large amounts of sugar, but perfectly ripe peaches or pears need very little.
- Frozen fruit has improved greatly in recent years, although it tends to become watery as it thaws. If you increase both sugar and add a little thickener, frozen fruit can help keep you in pies through winter.
- Don't thaw or wash frozen fruit before baking, though if the pieces are large—like peach halves— they should be thawed enough to slice.

1. Heat the oven to 450°F. In a small bowl, whisk together the flour, sugar, cinnamon, nutmeg, and salt. In a large bowl, mix the apples and lemon juice. Add the dry ingredients to the apples and toss to coat.

2. Layer the apple mixture in the bottom crust (make sure to pour in any juices), making the pile a little higher in the center than at the sides, then dot with the butter. Cover with the top crust, press the edges of the 2 crusts together, then decorate the edges with a fork or your fingers as illustrated in page 868.

3. Put the pie on a baking sheet and brush the top lightly with milk and sprinkle with sugar. Use a sharp paring knife to cut two or three 2-inch-long slits in the top crust to allow steam to escape. Bake for 10 minutes. Reduce the heat to 350°F and bake until the pie is golden brown, another 40 to 50 minutes. Check on the pie when it has been baking for a total of 35 minutes and if the edges of the crust are browning too quickly, cover them loosely with pieces of foil to prevent burning. Cool on a wire rack before serving warm or at room temperature. Cover and store the leftovers at room temperature for up to 2 days; if there's still anything left after that, move it to the fridge for another couple days.

APPLE-PEAR PIE The essence of autumn: Add 1 tablespoon minced fresh ginger or 1 teaspoon ground ginger with the other spices. Use half apples and half pears. Add 2 tablespoons cornstarch or 3 tablespoons instant tapioca instead of the flour in Step 1.

DUTCH APPLE PIE Cream poured into the pie—does it get any better? Use 2 tablespoons cornstarch or 3 tablespoons instant tapioca instead of the flour in Step 1. Proceed as directed, making sure to cut a large vent hole in the center of the top crust. About 30 minutes into the baking time, pour ½ cup cream into the vent hole; finish baking as directed.

DEEP-DISH APPLE PIE WITH STREUSEL TOPPING Use the Generous Pie Shell (page 869) and a deep-dish pie plate. Increase all filling ingredients by one-third. Make the streusel topping from the coffee cake on page 773; scatter it over the top of the apples. Bake at 375°F for 45 to 60 minutes, until the center of the pie is bubbly and the streusel mixture and bottom crust are nicely browned.

---

7 EASY ADDITIONS TO APPLE PIE

1. ½ to 1 cup chopped nuts

2. Any sweet spice like minced fresh or candied ginger, or ground cardamom, allspice, or cloves, generally in small amounts

3. About 2 tablespoons bourbon or rum sprinkled over the filling

4. About 1 cup fresh or frozen cranberries; increase the sugar slightly

5. 1 cup or more pitted, cut stone fruit, like plums or cherries, or whole raspberries, blueberries, or blackberries; reduce the amount of apples accordingly

6. ½ to 1 cup dried fruit, like raisins, dried cherries, cranberries, pineapple, mangoes, or blueberries, or some dried apple slices to intensify the apple flavor

7. 1 tablespoon grated lemon zest

Peach or Other Stone Fruit Pie

MAKES: One 9-inch pie (about 8 servings) | **TIME:** About 1½ hours

Perfectly ripe fruit—peaches or otherwise—is crucial to success here. Ginger Ice Cream (page 902) is fantastic with this.

Other fruits to substitute: apricots, plums, sweet cherries, nectarines.

 **F** fast **M** make ahead **V** vegetarian

About 2 pounds peaches (6 to 10 peaches, depending on size)

1 tablespoon fresh lemon juice
   About ½ cup sugar, more if the peaches are not quite ripe, plus more for sprinkling

1½ tablespoons cornstarch or 2 tablespoons instant tapioca

¼ teaspoon ground cinnamon

⅛ teaspoon freshly grated nutmeg or ground allspice

2 recipes Flaky Piecrust (page 867), bottom crust fitted into a 9-inch pie plate, top crust transferred to a rimless baking sheet, both chilled

2 tablespoons butter, cut into bits
   Milk for brushing

1. Heat the oven to 450°F. Peel the peaches: Bring a large pot of water to a boil and drop the peaches into it, a couple at a time, for 10 to 30 seconds, until the skins loosen. Plunge into a bowl of ice water. Slip the skins off, using a paring knife to ease the process. Pit and slice the peaches, and toss with the lemon juice in a large bowl.

2. Mix together the sugar, cornstarch or tapioca, cinnamon, and nutmeg in a small bowl. Add to the peaches and toss to coat them. Pile into the pie shell, making the pile a little higher in the center than at the sides. Dot with the butter. Cover with the top crust (or make a lattice crust; see below). Crimp and decorate the edges with a fork or your fingers, using any of the methods illustrated on page 868.

3. Put the pie on a baking sheet and brush the top lightly with milk; sprinkle with sugar. Use a sharp paring knife to cut two or three 2-inch-long slits in the top crust; this will allow steam to escape. Bake for 10 minutes; reduce the heat to 350°F and bake for another 40 to 50 minutes or until the pie is golden brown. Check on the pie when it has been baking for a total of 35 minutes and if the edges of the crust are browning too quickly, cover them loosely with pieces of foil to prevent burning. Do not underbake. Cool on a wire rack before serving warm or at room temperature. Cover and store the leftovers at room

Making a Lattice Top

STEP 1 Begin by rolling out a piece of dough a couple of inches longer than the diameter of the pie plate and 5 to 6 inches wide. Cut enough strips to cover the pie as much as you like, depending on the width of each strip. Set half the strips in one direction on the pie.

STEP 2 Fold back half of the strips laid in one direction and add strips in the other direction.

STEP 3 Continue weaving the strips over the top of the pie.

STEP 4 When the weaving is completed, press the edges into the crust and trim.

Peach Pie, page 872

temperature for up to 2 days; if there's still anything left after that, move it to the fridge for another couple days.

PEACH AND BERRY PIE Blueberries are the classic choice: Add 1 cup fresh or frozen berries to the filling.

PEACH AND GINGER PIE Add 1 tablespoon minced fresh ginger or 1 teaspoon ground ginger to the filling.

PLUM PIE The small prune (Italian) plums that come into season in early autumn are especially good but any other plums work well: Use plums instead of peaches; no need to peel them.

CHERRY PIE Tart (aka sour) cherries are best for pie: Substitute 4 to 5 cups pitted sour cherries for the peaches; omit the lemon juice unless you're using sweet cherries. If you use frozen tart cherries, thaw them then drain well, and increase the thickener by 1 tablespoon.

Vanilla Cream Pie

MAKES: One 9-inch pie (about 8 servings) | **TIME:** About 1½ hours, plus time to chill

Okay, I top cream pies with meringue, and I'm not alone. Egg yolks are traditional and wonderful when making cream pie filling, which makes using their whites for the topping a natural choice. But you can put the "cream" back in a cream pie by topping it with whipped cream instead (see the last variation). Just don't put cream in the filling, which makes the custard too thick; do use whole milk.

1 recipe Flaky Piecrust (page 867) or Graham Cracker Crust (page 871), fitted into a 9-inch pie plate and chilled
¾ cup granulated sugar
2 tablespoons cornstarch
Salt

4 eggs, separated
2½ cups whole milk, or 2¼ cups low-fat milk mixed with ¼ cup cream
2 tablespoons butter, softened
Seeds scraped from 1 vanilla bean, or 2 teaspoons vanilla extract
¼ cup confectioners' sugar

1. Bake the flaky piecrust completely (see page 869) or bake the crumb crust as described in the recipe. Start the filling while the crust is in the oven. Cool the crust slightly on a wire rack, but leave the oven on at 350°F.

2. In a small saucepan, combine the granulated sugar, cornstarch, and a pinch salt. Mix the egg yolks, milk, and vanilla seeds together in a small bowl. Stir the wet ingredients into the dry ingredients and put the pot over medium heat. At first, whisk occasionally to eliminate lumps. Then whisk almost constantly until the mixture boils and thickens enough to coat the back of a spoon (see page 887), about 10 minutes. Remove from the heat, stir in the butter and the vanilla extract if you're using it, and set aside.

3. Make the meringue: Beat the egg whites with a pinch salt until foamy. Keep beating, gradually adding the confectioners' sugar, until the mixture is shiny and holds fairly stiff peaks.

4. Pour the filling into the crust. Cover with the meringue, making sure to spread the meringue all the way to the edges of the crust; this will keep it from shrinking. As you spread the meringue, make peaks and swirls if you like. Put the pie plate on a baking sheet to catch drips and bake for 10 to 15 minutes, until the meringue is lightly browned. Cool on a wire rack, then refrigerate for at least 2 hours. Serve cool.

COCONUT CREAM PIE A classic: Toast 1 cup unsweetened shredded coconut by placing it in a dry skillet over very low heat and cooking, shaking almost constantly, until it begins to brown, 3 to 5 minutes. Immediately remove from the pan and stir into the thickened filling. Add a drop almond extract to the meringue along with the

Vanilla Cream Pie,
page 875

confectioners' sugar. Top the meringue with ½ cup untoasted coconut before baking.

BANANA CREAM PIE Use the vanilla cream or the chocolate cream in the next variation: Stir 1 cup thinly sliced bananas into the filling just before pouring it into the baked pie shell.

CHOCOLATE CREAM PIE I like dark best: Add 2 ounces chopped or grated dark or white chocolate (about ⅓ cup) to the filling along with the butter.

VANILLA-ORANGE CREAM PIE Aka Creamsicle Pie: Substitute ½ cup fresh orange juice for ½ cup of the milk and add 1 tablespoon grated or finely minced orange zest; add both to the milk mixture in Step 2. Proceed with the recipe.

CREAM-TOPPED CREAM PIE This works for the main recipe or any of the other variations: Substitute 2 whole eggs for the yolks and proceed as directed. After pouring the filling into the prebaked shell, cover it directly with plastic wrap to prevent a skin from forming and refrigerate until cool. Just before serving, beat 1 cup cream with 2 tablespoons confectioners' sugar and ½ teaspoon vanilla or almond extract, brandy, or rum, until the cream holds stiff peaks. Spoon over the pie and serve.

Lemon Meringue Pie

MAKES: One 9-inch pie (about 8 servings) | **TIME:** About 1½ hours
Ⓜ Ⓥ

Marvel as your fork spears through three layers of texture: a toasted cloud of slightly sweet meringue, the rich tang of lemon custard, a shatter of crisp, buttery crust. As with Vanilla Cream Pie (page 875), you can replace the meringue topper with whipped cream; follow the variation for Cream-Topped Cream Pie (page 877).

1 recipe Flaky Piecrust (page 867) or 1 recipe Graham Cracker Crust (page 871), fitted or pressed into a 9-inch pie plate and chilled

1 cup granulated sugar

½ teaspoon salt

2 cups boiling water

4 eggs, separated

⅓ cup cornstarch

2 tablespoons butter, softened

2 teaspoons grated lemon zest

6 tablespoons fresh lemon juice

¼ cup confectioners' sugar

1. Bake the flaky piecrust completely (see page 869) or bake the crumb crust as described in the recipe; start the filling while the crust is in the oven. Cool the crust slightly on a wire rack, but leave the oven on at 350°F.

2. In a small saucepan, combine the granulated sugar, ¼ teaspoon of the salt, and the boiling water and cook, stirring frequently until the sugar dissolves, just a minute or 2; keep warm. Beat the egg yolks and cornstarch until smooth. Whisk about ½ cup of the sugar syrup into the egg yolks. Immediately stir the egg yolk mixture back into the syrup and bring to a boil, whisking constantly. Keep whisking and let it boil until just combined, less than a minute. Remove from the heat and add the butter. Stir in the lemon zest and juice and set aside to cool.

3. Make the meringue: Beat the egg whites with the remaining ¼ teaspoon salt until foamy. Keep beating, gradually adding the confectioners' sugar, until the mixture is shiny and holds stiff peaks.

4. Pour the filling into the crust. Cover with the meringue, making sure to spread it all the way to the edges of the crust to keep the meringue from shrinking. As you spread the meringue, make peaks and swirls if you like. Put the pie plate on a baking sheet to catch drips and bake for 10 to 15 minutes, until the meringue is lightly browned. Cool on a wire rack, then refrigerate for at least 2 hours. Serve cool and refrigerate the leftovers.

KEY LIME PIE Do this instead of Step 2: Omit the granulated sugar, salt, water, cornstarch, butter, and lemon zest and juice. Whisk the egg yolks in a bowl just until combined, then beat in one 14-ounce can sweetened condensed milk. Gradually whisk in ⅓ cup lime juice, a bit at a time (ideally Key lime, but normal lime is fine). Pour the filling into the warm crust and bake as directed. Make and bake the meringue topping as described in Step 3, or cool the pie completely and top with Whipped Cream (page 854).

Pecan or Walnut Pie

MAKES: One 9-inch pie (about 8 servings) | TIME: About 1½ hours

Ⓜ Ⓥ

Classic pecan pie contains not only sugar but also corn syrup. I've bucked tradition and made it without corn syrup, and I like it better. This way it's more of a custard pie, loaded with pecans—or walnuts if you'd rather. Toast the pecans first for the best flavor. Top with Vanilla Custard Ice Cream or Coffee Ice Cream (pages 897 or 902) and/or Whipped Cream (page 854).

1 recipe Flaky Piecrust (page 867), fitted into a 9-inch pie pan and chilled
2 cups pecan or walnut halves
5 eggs
1 cup granulated sugar
½ cup packed brown sugar
Pinch salt
6 tablespoons (¾ stick) butter, melted
1 tablespoon vanilla extract

1. Partially bake the crust (see page 869). Meanwhile, toast the pecans in a dry skillet, shaking and stirring, for about 5 minutes or until the pecans are toasted and fragrant. Cool the nuts and coarsely chop.
2. Start the filling while the crust is in the oven. In a medium saucepan, beat the eggs well until foamy. Beat

in the granulated and brown sugars, salt, and melted butter. Warm this mixture over medium-low heat, stirring occasionally, until hot to the touch; do not boil. When the crust is done, remove it from the oven and turn the oven up to 375°F.
3. Stir the vanilla and pecans into the filling. Put the pie plate on a baking sheet to catch drips. Pour the filling into the still-hot crust and bake for 30 to 40 minutes, until the mixture shakes like Jell-O but is still quite moist. Cool on a wire rack. Serve warm or at room temperature. Refrigerate the leftovers and eat within a couple days.

CHOCOLATE PECAN OR WALNUT PIE Before beginning Step 2, melt 2 ounces semisweet chocolate with 3 tablespoons butter until smooth. Let cool while you beat the eggs, sugars, and salt; omit the remaining butter. Combine the chocolate and egg mixtures and warm gently as in Step 2, then proceed as directed.

BUTTERSCOTCH PECAN OR HAZELNUT PIE Extra-sugary and caramelly, this is terrific with hazelnuts instead of the pecans: Use 4 eggs, 1 cup brown sugar, and add ¾ cup cream. Omit the granulated sugar. Add the cream with the sugar and butter in Step 2 and proceed as directed.

Pumpkin Pie

MAKES: One 9-inch pie (about 8 servings) | TIME: About 1½ hours

Ⓜ Ⓥ

I'll never understand why most people only eat this pie once a year, especially since there are so many ways to vary it. (Note how I ordered the crust options in the ingredient list—a cookie crumb crust is my preference.) Substitute cooked, puréed, and strained winter squash, sweet potatoes, or white beans (yes) for the pumpkin if you like. Top with Whipped Cream (page 854), naturally.

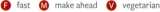

1 recipe Graham Cracker Crust (page 871) made with gingersnaps or graham crackers, or 1 recipe Flaky Piecrust (page 867), pressed or fitted into a 9-inch pie plate and chilled

3 eggs

½ cup sugar

½ teaspoon ground cinnamon

¼ teaspoon ground ginger

⅛ teaspoon freshly grated nutmeg

⅛ teaspoon ground allspice

¼ teaspoon salt

1½ cups canned or well-drained cooked fresh pumpkin purée

1 cup half-and-half, heavy cream, or whole milk

1. Bake the crumb crust as described in the recipe or partially bake the flaky piecrust (see page 869). Start the filling while the crust is in the oven. Cool the crust slightly on a wire rack, and turn the oven up to 375°F.

2. Use an electric mixer or whisk to beat the eggs with the sugar, then add the cinnamon, ginger, nutmeg, allspice, and salt. Mix in the pumpkin, then the half-and-half.

3. Put the pie plate with the crust on a baking sheet. Pour the filling into the crust all the way to the top. (You might have some left over, which you can cook on the stove over low heat, whisking, until it's steaming.) Bake for 45 to 55 minutes, until the filling is firm along the edges but still a bit wobbly at the center. Cool on a wire rack until it no longer jiggles. Slice into wedges and serve, or let cool, cover, and refrigerate for up to 2 days.

SWEET POTATO PIE A touch of orange makes it stand out: Substitute puréed sweet potato for the pumpkin and add 2 teaspoons grated or finely minced orange zest.

VEGAN PUMPKIN CUSTARD Tofu takes the place of the eggs and half-and-half with good results: Skip the crust. Substitute 1 pound silken or other soft tofu for the eggs

and half-and-half. Drain the tofu, purée it with the other ingredients, pour it into an oiled pie plate, and proceed with the recipe. Start checking after 30 minutes to avoid overbaking.

Fruit Galette

MAKES: 8 servings | **TIME:** About 1 hour, plus time to chill the crust

A free-form, rustic tart, filled and baked right on a baking sheet. Since I can use almost any kind of fruit and there's no stress in making a perfectly shaped crust, it's among the most useful desserts in my repertoire; it's perfect for beginners, always impressive, really delicious. Dust with confectioners' sugar or top with any ice cream (see pages 897–904) or Whipped Cream (page 854).

1 recipe Sweet Tart Crust (page 869), chilled until firm but not hard

2 pounds ripe stone fruit like peaches, apricots, plums, or nectarines, peeled, pitted, and sliced; or 2 pounds apples or pears, peeled, cored, and very thinly sliced; or about 3 cups berries

2 tablespoons butter, melted
Milk for brushing

1 tablespoon sugar

1. On a lightly floured piece of parchment paper on a flat surface, roll the crust out to a 10-inch round. Transfer the dough (still on the parchment) to a baking sheet and refrigerate for at least 15 minutes or until you're ready to assemble the galette.

2. Heat the oven to 425°F. Scatter the fruit on the dough, leaving a border about 2 inches wide. Brush or drizzle the fruit with the butter. Fold in the edges of the dough over the filling, pleating them in place. Brush the crust with milk, and dust everything with sugar.

3. Bake until the rim of the crust is golden brown and the fruit has softened, 25 to 30 minutes. Cool the galette to room temperature on the baking sheet on a wire rack before cutting into wedges and serving. Cover and store the leftovers at room temperature for up to 2 days; if there's still anything left after that, move it to the fridge for another couple days.

5 SIMPLE IDEAS FOR GALETTES

1. Put a layer of crushed almonds or walnuts under the fruit.
2. Brush the fruit with a combination of 2 tablespoons honey and 1 tablespoon melted butter.
3. Toss the fruit with 1 teaspoon or more ground cinnamon before putting it on the crust.
4. Sprinkle with a mixture of ½ teaspoon ground cinnamon and 2 tablespoons granulated, brown, or turbinado sugar after brushing with butter. (Don't use confectioners' sugar.)
5. Toss the fruit with 1 teaspoon or more minced candied ginger before putting it on the crust.

Making a Galette

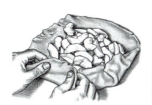 

STEP 1 To make a free-form tart, roll out the dough, then spread it with the topping to within 2 inches of the edge.

STEP 2 Fold the edges over, pleating them so they remain in place. Make a border around the entire circumference of the dough.

Fresh Berry Tart with Vanilla Pudding Filling

MAKES: One 8- to 10-inch tart (about 8 servings) | **TIME:** About 1½ hours, less with premade pudding

I prefer a berry tart topped with a "salad" of macerated berries rather than fussily arranged and glazed fruit. The other surprise here is vanilla pudding, which is a lot like traditional pastry cream. You won't need all of it, leaving you with some extra for snacking—or freezing and eating that way.

> 1 recipe Vanilla Pudding (page 887)
> 1 recipe Sweet Tart Crust (page 869), fitted into a tart pan and chilled
> ¼ cup sugar
> 3 cups strawberries, raspberries, blackberries, and/or blueberries, picked over, stemmed, and hulled if necessary

1. Make the pudding and chill thoroughly; you can do this up to a day ahead of assembling the tart. Prebake the crust (see "Prebaking Pie and Tart Crusts," page 869). While the crust bakes, toss the berries with the sugar in a bowl and let macerate in the refrigerator, stirring a couple of times to dissolve the sugar.

2. When the tart crust is cool, spread on a layer of pudding about ½ inch thick. Drain the berries, reserving the juice. Spoon the fruit on top of the pudding and serve with the reserved juice for drizzling if you like. This tart is best eaten within a day.

FRESH BERRY TART WITH CHOCOLATE Use milk, dark, or white chocolate: Instead of the pudding, spread a thin layer of melted chocolate, about 3 ounces, in the prebaked tart shell before adding the berries.

FRESH BLUEBERRY TART WITH LEMON CURD Instead of the pudding, use lemon curd; replace the mixed berries with just blueberries and macerate as described.

Tarte Tatin

MAKES: One 9-inch tart (about 8 servings) | TIME: About 1 hour

A classic French caramelized apple tart, turned upside down after baking. You need firm, super-crisp apples that keep their shape, and sometimes they still get quite soft. That's okay; it's more important to serve the tart soon out of the oven. The ideal is to prepare it just before serving the meal and bake it while you're eating. Top with Whipped Cream (page 854), Vanilla Custard Ice Cream (page 897), or Vanilla Custard Sauce (page 864).

- 6 Granny Smith or other tart, hard apples (about 2 pounds)
- 8 tablespoons (1 stick) butter, cut into pieces
- ¾ cup sugar
- 1 recipe Sweet Tart Crust (page 869), dough chilled but not rolled out

1. Heat the oven to 400°F. Peel, core, and quarter the apples. Press the butter into the bottom and up the sides of a heavy ovenproof 10-inch skillet (cast iron is good). Sprinkle the butter with the sugar. Press the apple quarters into the sugar, arranging them in concentric circles and making certain to pack them in tightly; they will shrink considerably during cooking.

2. Put the pan over medium-high heat. Cook until the butter-sugar mixture has turned deep, dark brown and the apples are just tender when pierced with a knife tip, 15 to 20 minutes; rotate the pan and give it a gentle shake if the apples are cooking unevenly. Meanwhile, roll out the dough just a little bigger than the pan. When the apples are ready, remove the pan from the heat. Lay the dough on top of the apples, bringing the dough to the edges of the pan to seal it. Prick the dough with a fork. Bake until the crust is golden brown, about 20 minutes.

3. Remove the tart from the oven and let it sit for 5 minutes. Shake the hot pan to loosen the apples stuck to the bottom of the skillet. Put a heatproof serving plate on top of the skillet and invert everything so the plate is on the bottom and the skillet is on top. (Take care not to burn yourself; the juices are hot.) Carefully lift off the skillet. If some apples stick to the bottom of the pan, patch them onto the top as best as you can. Serve right away, or at room temperature. Keep leftovers at room temperature for up to a day or 2.

CARAMELIZED PINEAPPLE TART You have to use fresh pineapple for this; canned won't do: Substitute slices of pineapple (roughly the size of apple quarters) for the apples.

CARAMELIZED PEACH OR PLUM TART Do this in the summer, when stone fruit are at their best: Substitute ripe, slightly soft pitted peaches or plums for the apples. In Step 1 let the butter and sugar cook alone in the skillet until syrupy but not too dark, about 5 minutes. Then remove from the heat and carefully add the fruit.

Blueberry Cobbler

MAKES: 6 to 8 servings | TIME: About 1 hour

My friend John Willoughby found this recipe in a Southern boardinghouse decades ago. The topping is somewhere between a biscuit and a cookie: fluffy, tender, buttery, and slightly sweet. I love this with blueberries, but you can make it with any fruit you like. Top with Buttermilk Ice Cream (page 902), Vanilla Custard Ice Cream (pages 897), or Whipped Cream (page 854).

- 8 tablespoons (1 stick) cold butter, plus more for greasing
- About 6 cups blueberries, rinsed and drained
- 1¼ cups sugar, or to taste
- 1 cup all-purpose flour
- 1 teaspoon baking powder
- Pinch salt
- 2 eggs
- ½ teaspoon vanilla extract
- 1 teaspoon grated lemon zest (optional)

Tarte Tatin

1. Heat the oven to 375°F. Lightly grease a 8- or 9-inch square baking pan with butter. Toss the blueberries in a medium bowl with ¼ cup of the sugar. Taste and add more sugar if you like. Put the berries in the prepared pan.

2. Cut up the butter into ¼-inch bits. Put the flour, baking powder, salt, and remaining sugar in a food processor and pulse once or twice to combine. Add the butter and process until the dough is just combined, only a few seconds; you should still see bits of butter. Transfer to a bowl and beat in the eggs, vanilla, and lemon zest if you're using it with a fork.

3. Drop the dough onto the blueberries, 1 heaping tablespoon at a time, spacing the mounds as evenly as you can; leave gaps in between them so the filling can vent steam as it bakes. Bake until the dough is just starting to brown and the blueberries are tender and bubbling, 35 to 45 minutes. Serve hot, warm, or at room temperature. Transfer any leftovers to a non-reactive container if necessary and refrigerate for up to a couple days.

Apple Crisp

MAKES: 6 to 8 servings | TIME: About 1 hour

The hardest part of making a crisp is preparing the fruit, and even that doesn't take much work or time You can use apples, pears, stone fruit (I love tart cherries in the summer), berries, or a combination. In any case, start with 6 cups fruit, somewhere between 2 and 3 pounds. If you use super-juicy fruits, like berries, toss them with a tablespoon flour, instant tapioca, or cornstarch before baking, or up to 2 tablespoons if you like the filling thick. With very tart fruits like rhubarb, increase the sugar.

>   5 tablespoons cold butter, plus more for greasing
>   6 cups peeled, cored, and sliced apples (2 to 3 pounds)

>   1 teaspoon ground cinnamon
>   Juice of ½ lemon
>   ⅔ cup packed brown sugar
>   ½ cup rolled oats (not instant)
>   ½ cup all-purpose flour
>   Pinch salt
>   ¼ cup chopped nuts (optional)
>   Vanilla Custard Ice Cream (page 897) or Whipped Cream (page 854) for serving (optional)

1. Heat the oven to 400°F. Cut the butter into ¼-inch bits and put in the fridge or freezer. Lightly butter a 9-inch square baking pan. Toss the apples with the cinnamon, lemon juice, and 1 tablespoon of the brown sugar in a large bowl. Spread them out in the prepared pan.

2. Put the butter, the remaining brown sugar, the oats, flour, salt, and nuts if you're using them in a food processor and pulse a few times to combine. Process continuously for a few seconds more, until everything is combined but not too finely ground. (To mix by hand in a bowl, mash everything together between your fingers.)

3. Crumble the topping evenly over the apples. Bake for 30 to 40 minutes, until the topping is browned and the apples are tender and bubbling. Serve hot, warm, or at room temperature, with ice cream or whipped cream if you like. Cover and store the leftovers at room temperature for up to a day; if there's still anything left after that, move it to the fridge for another couple days.

Baklava

MAKES: 4 dozen pieces | TIME: About 2½ hours, largely unattended, plus time to cool

Buttery and nutty, sticky-sweet and crunchy, this is one of the most wonderful, foolproof, impressive, and

Baklava

delicious desserts on the planet—and it feeds a crowd. Follow the nuanced directions in the recipe steps: They come from the food stylist at our photo shoot, Victoria Granof, channeled from learning at the elbow of her Turkish grandmother. The results are flakier than any you've ever had.

½ pound (2 sticks) butter, melted (and clarified if you'd like; see page 752)
1 pound shelled walnut halves, chopped (about 4 cups)
1 teaspoon ground cinnamon
At least 18 sheets store-bought phyllo dough, 14 × 9 inches (half a 1-pound package), thawed overnight in the fridge if frozen
1½ cups sugar
½ cup honey
2 teaspoons fresh lemon juice

1. Brush the bottom and sides of a 13 × 9-inch baking dish with butter. Finely chop the nuts, by hand or in a food processor, and combine them with the cinnamon.
2. Unfold the phyllo and cover the sheets with a damp kitchen towel while you work so they don't dry out.
3. Drape a phyllo sheet inside the prepared baking dish, brush it lightly with butter, then gently scrunch it with your fingers to create ripples and folds; repeat with another sheet. Tuck in the corners so the edges of the dough creep up the sides; this will keep the nuts from burning as the baklava bakes. Repeat with two more sheets to form the base layer.
4. Sprinkle 1 cup of the nuts in an even layer over the phyllo. Layer, brush, and scrunch another 2 sheets of phyllo on top the same way as in Step 1, then spread with another cup of the nuts. Repeat that pattern (2 sheets, butter, scrunch, nuts) two more times, until you've used all the nuts. Finally, top the baklava with 4 more layers of slightly scrunched phyllo, brushing with butter between each addition. (You will probably have some left over.) Brush generously with the remaining butter. At this point you can cover the pan and refrigerate for up to a day.

5. To bake, heat the oven to 300°F. Score the top of the baklava with a sharp knife, first lengthwise into 4 strips, then widthwise into 6 sections, and finally diagonally across the scored rectangles, to make 48 triangles. Bake until golden brown all over; start checking after 90 minutes but this will likely take almost 2 hours.
6. To make the syrup, combine the sugar, honey, and lemon juice in a saucepan with 1 cup water and bring to a boil. Stir to dissolve the sugar. Set aside to cool completely. (You can make this hours or a few days in advance and keep it refrigerated in an airtight container until you're ready to use it.)
7. When the baklava is still hot, cut all the way through the score marks in the top layer with a sharp, thin-bladed knife. Pour the syrup all over, tilting the pan so it really spreads. Cool to room temperature, then serve. Baklava keeps well in an airtight container at room temperature for several days.

Puddings, Custards, and Mousses

This bundle of recipes demonstrates a few of the different ways to thicken liquids and almost miraculously turn them in to rich, satisfying desserts. Gently cooked eggs lend a silken texture unmatched by anything else, though cornstarch, grains, bread, gelatin, and even fruit can also create luxurious desserts.

There's no trick to cooking eggs in the recipes that use them here, except to remember that overcooked eggs are essentially scrambled eggs, which is not what you want. You must cook eggs at relatively low heat, and just until they thicken, to keep them smooth and uniform. When cooking on top of the stove—as you will with most soft custards—this isn't much of a problem. But knowing when to remove custards and other egg-thickened desserts from the oven is trickier: By the time a custard appears to be set, it's almost always overcooked. You must make a leap of faith and remove it from the oven while the center is still wobbly.

Although it's not always essential, texture is almost always improved by baking custards in a water bath (also called a bain-marie). By moderating the temperature around the custard, the water bath makes for more even, slower cooking. The recipes explain how to rig one.

Mousses are ethereal puddings, lightened by whipped egg whites and/or cream. They always feel so elegant though they're really not difficult to make.

Vanilla Pudding

MAKES: 4 to 6 servings | TIME: About 20 minutes, plus time to chill

This is a soft stovetop pudding, not much more difficult to produce than the packaged "instant" variety. Top with Whipped Cream flavored with booze, cinnamon, or nutmeg if you like (page 854).

2½	cups half-and-half or whole milk
⅔	cup sugar
¼	teaspoon salt
3	tablespoons cornstarch
2	tablespoons butter, softened
1	teaspoon vanilla extract

1. Combine 2 cups of the half-and-half with the sugar and salt in a medium saucepan and cook over medium-low heat, stirring occasionally, until the mixture just begins to steam, 2 to 3 minutes.

2. Whisk the cornstarch with the remaining ½ cup half-and-half in a bowl until completely smooth. Stir this into the hot half-and-half and cook, stirring occasionally, until the mixture thickens and just starts to simmer, another 3 to 5 minutes. Reduce the heat to very low and continue to cook, stirring constantly, until the pudding thickens noticeably and starts to stick to the pan, 3 to 5 minutes more. Add the butter and stir until it melts completely. Stir in the vanilla.

3. Pour the pudding into a large heatproof glass serving bowl, or 4 to 6 small ramekins or heatproof glasses. Put plastic wrap directly on top of the pudding to prevent the formation of a skin, or leave it uncovered if you like that. Refrigerate until chilled, at least an hour, and serve within a day.

CHOCOLATE PUDDING In Step 2, add 2 ounces chopped dark chocolate to the thickened pudding.

BUTTERSCOTCH PUDDING The easy way: Substitute brown sugar for the granulated sugar and increase the salt to ¾ teaspoon.

BANANA PUDDING Use whole milk and reduce the sugar to ¼ cup. Peel 3 very ripe bananas, cut them into 1-inch chunks, and add them to the warm milk in Step 1. Steep for 20 minutes, then strain them out and return the milk to the pot. Proceed with the recipe.

Coating the Back of a Spoon

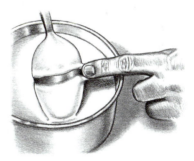

The easiest way to know when stovetop egg-based custards are done is to dip a tablespoon into the liquid and drag the tip of your finger across the back. If a good layer of liquid clings to the back of the spoon and your finger leaves a distinct trail, it's properly thickened. If the liquid just slides right off the spoon, or your finger trail is covered quickly by runny liquid, keep cooking and stirring.

SUPER-RICH PUDDING Substitute heavy cream for the half-and-half in the main recipe or any of the variations.

Panna Cotta

MAKES: 4 to 6 servings | TOTAL TIME: About 20 minutes, plus time to chill

The silken Italian favorite, cream thickened with gelatin and flavored with vanilla. I like the tangy buttermilk variation too. Lovely with a fruit sauce (page 862) or macerated fruit (see page 363).

Good-quality vegetable oil for greasing
3 cups heavy cream or 1½ cups heavy cream and 1½ cups half-and-half
1 ¼-ounce envelope (about 2½ teaspoons) unflavored gelatin
1 vanilla bean, or 1 teaspoon vanilla extract
½ cup sugar

1. Use a towel and a bit of oil to very lightly grease the insides of 4 large or 6 small custard cups.

2. Put 1 cup of the cream in a medium saucepan and sprinkle the gelatin evenly over it; let sit for 5 minutes to soften. Put the saucepan over low heat and whisk until the gelatin dissolves completely, 3 to 5 minutes.

3. Cut the vanilla bean in half lengthwise. Scrape out the seeds with a sharp knife; add the seeds and pod to the cream mixture, along with the sugar and the remaining cream. Increase the heat to medium and stir until the sugar has completely dissolved and steam rises from the pot, another 3 to 5 minutes. (If you're using vanilla extract, heat the cream, gelatin, and sugar until the sugar dissolves, then add the vanilla.) Let the panna cotta cool for a few minutes.

4. Remove the vanilla bean and pour the panna cotta into the custard cups. Chill until set, at least 4 hours (or up to a day). Serve in the cups, or run a thin knife along

the sides to loosen the panna cotta, dip the cups in hot water for about 10 seconds each; invert onto plates and serve.

BUTTERMILK PANNA COTTA Subtly tangy and especially wonderful with macerated fruit: Use 1½ cups heavy cream and 1½ cups buttermilk.

ALMOND PANNA COTTA Almond milk replaces the cream: Substitute unsweetened almond milk for the cream, almond extract for the vanilla, and 2 teaspoons powdered agar for the gelatin if you want to make this vegan. In Step 2, follow the directions for using vanilla extract. Proceed with the recipe.

TEMBLEQUE A Caribbean dessert made with coconut milk: Substitute coconut milk for the cream, and omit the vanilla. Soften and then dissolve the gelatin in ½ cup of the coconut milk, then add the remaining coconut milk and the sugar. Cook over medium heat, stirring constantly, just until the sugar dissolves. Unmold from the cups and dust with ground cinnamon just before serving.

Baked Custard

MAKES: 4 to 6 servings | TIME: About 50 minutes

True *pots de crème* use vanilla instead of cinnamon and nutmeg, spices that signal an all-American feel. So for a more traditional version, substitute 1½ teaspoons vanilla extract for the spices or steep a split vanilla bean in the milk in Step 1. Either way, finish with Whipped Cream (page 854) and/or fresh berries.

2 cups cream, whole milk, or a mix
2 whole eggs plus 2 yolks
¼ teaspoon salt
½ cup sugar, or more if you like things very sweet
½ teaspoon ground cinnamon
½ teaspoon freshly grated nutmeg

Panna Cotta

1. Heat the oven to 325°F and put a kettle of water on to boil. In a small saucepan over medium heat, warm the cream just until it begins to steam, 3 to 5 minutes. In a medium bowl, beat the eggs and yolks with the salt, sugar, cinnamon, and nutmeg until pale yellow and fairly thick, about 3 minutes with an electric mixer.

2. Gradually add one-third of the hot cream to the egg mixture, whisking constantly, then stir this mixture back into the remaining cream. Strain through a fine-meshed sieve and pour into six 4- to 6-ounce custard cups or a baking dish, then put the cups or dish in a larger baking pan. Pour the boiling water into the pan so that it comes about halfway up the sides of the cups or dish.

3. Bake until the custard is not quite set—it should wobble a little in the middle—30 to 40 minutes for individual cups and a little longer if you're using one large dish. Remove the pan from the oven and carefully take the cups or dish out of the water. Serve warm or at room temperature. Or cover and refrigerate until cold (they'll firm up more as they cool) and serve within a day.

CRÈME BRÛLÉE Add ½ cup more cream, omit the whole eggs, and use 6 egg yolks. Use flameproof cups or baking dish. Bake as directed, let cool, cover with plastic wrap, and chill for up to 2 days. Put an oven rack as close to the broiler heat source as the height of the cups or baking dish will allow. Sprinkle ½ cup sugar in a thin, even layer over the custards, then put them on a baking sheet and transfer the pan to under the broiler in the cold oven. Turn on the broiler and broil for 5 to 10 minutes, watching carefully and rotating the dishes as necessary: when the sugar bubbles and browns, it's ready. Let cool for a few minutes before serving. Or if you want to serve it cold, which is traditional, chill in the fridge for about 30 minutes (much longer than that and the brûléed sugar will get soggy). You can also do the brûlée with a propane torch. Same concept: Heat the sugar with the flame until it bubbles and browns.

FLAN (CRÈME CARAMEL) Here a layer of caramel is put on the bottom of the custard before baking: Put

1 cup sugar and ¼ cup water in a small saucepan. Turn the heat to low and cook, stirring occasionally, until the sugar melts and the syrup turns clear, then golden brown, about 15 minutes. Remove from the heat and immediately pour the caramel into the dish or custard cups. Carefully pour the strained custard into the dish or cups. Bake as directed. Cool on a wire rack until the bottom is barely warm. Or cover and refrigerate for up to a day. To serve, run a thin knife along the sides to loosen the custard, dip the dish or cups in boiling water for about 15 seconds (closer to a minute if cold from the fridge), then invert onto a plate or plates. Be sure to let all the caramel drip down over the custard.

CHOCOLATE CUSTARD Richer than Chocolate Pudding (page 887), but no more difficult to make: Substitute 1 teaspoon vanilla extract for the cinnamon and nutmeg. Melt 1 ounce chopped dark chocolate (or 2 ounces for an even more intense flavor) in a double boiler or a very small saucepan over very low heat, stirring almost constantly; cool slightly. Proceed with the recipe, stirring the chocolate into the beaten eggs before the cream.

LEMON CUSTARD You need more eggs to compensate for the added liquid and more sugar to compensate for the tartness here; as a result, this will serve 6 easily. In Step 2, increase the whole eggs to 3, the yolks to 4, and the sugar to ¾ cup. Add ½ cup strained fresh lemon juice and 1 tablespoon very finely minced lemon zest and proceed with the recipe.

5 MORE IDEAS FOR VANILLA PUDDING OR BAKED CUSTARD

1. Add 1 to 2 tablespoons minced candied ginger after straining.
2. Add ¼ cup or more shredded coconut after straining.

F fast   M make ahead   V vegetarian

3. Add about 1 teaspoon minced or grated orange zest after straining.
4. Put 1 to 2 tablespoons raspberries or other fruit, per serving, on the bottom underneath the custard after straining.
5. Before starting the recipe, infuse warm cream or milk with ½ cup coarsely ground coffee or 1 tablespoon matcha (powdered green tea) or other ingredients; see "Infusing Liquids with Flavor" (page 900); let stand for 10 minutes. Strain before proceeding.

Raspberry Fool

MAKES: 4 to 6 servings | **TIME:** 20 minutes

The easiest mousse ever and a perfect treatment for raspberries, which require no cooking at all to be tender. A fool can be made with any soft, ripe fruit—most you won't even need to strain after puréeing—in the same way.

- 3 cups fresh raspberries
- ½ cup confectioners' sugar, plus more if needed
- 1 cup cream, very cold
- 1 tablespoon granulated sugar

1. Purée about one-third of the raspberries in a blender with ¼ cup of the confectioners' sugar. Force the purée through a fine-meshed sieve to remove the seeds. Taste; the purée should be quite sweet. If not, add a little more sugar.

2. Set aside a few berries for garnish and roughly mash the remaining berries just until they're broken up. Toss with the remaining ¼ cup confectioners' sugar.

3. Beat the cream with the granulated sugar until it holds soft peaks. Beat in the raspberry purée, then fold in the sugared berries and any juices. Taste and add more confectioners' sugar if necessary. Garnish with the whole berries and serve immediately. Or cover and refrigerate for no more than 2 hours.

YOGURT RASPBERRY FOOL A lighter, tangier flavor to use with any fruit: Decrease the cream to ½ cup; whip it with the sugar, then fold in 1 cup plain yogurt.

Chocolate Mousse

MAKES: 6 servings | **TIME:** 20 minutes, plus time to chill

Always a real winner. And blazing quick to make—I've waited to prepare it after dinner and still served it before anyone got up from the table. It's also surprisingly easy to adapt to different diets—see the variations. You can spike it with rum, coffee, or other flavorings, but it's tough to improve on the intensity of the chocolate coming through the fluffy texture. Top with Whipped Cream (page 854) and shaved chocolate if you like.

- 4 ounces dark chocolate, chopped (about ⅔ cup)
- 2 tablespoons butter, softened
- 2 tablespoons rum, bourbon, Grand Marnier, or other liqueur (optional)
- 3 eggs, separated
- ½ teaspoon vanilla extract
- 2 tablespoons sugar
- ½ cup cream, very cold

1. Use a microwave on low power or a double boiler over low heat to melt the chocolate and butter, and the liqueur if you're using it. Check and stir the mixture frequently to prevent burning, then immediately remove from the heat and stir until smooth. Transfer to a large bowl and let sit until the bowl is cool enough to hold, then whisk in the egg yolks and vanilla.

Raspberry Fool, page 891

2. In a medium bowl, beat the egg whites with 1 tablespoon of the sugar until they hold stiff peaks. In a separate bowl, using clean beaters, beat the cream with the remaining 1 tablespoon sugar until it holds soft peaks.

3. Stir a couple of large spoonfuls of the egg whites into the chocolate mixture to lighten it, then fold in the remaining whites, using thorough but gentle strokes (see the illustrations on page 852). Fold in the whipped cream until combined, so there are no streaks of white. Cover and refrigerate until chilled. If you're in a hurry, divide the mousse among 4 to 6 cups; it will chill much faster. Serve within 1 day.

Dried Apricot Clafoutis

MAKES: 6 to 8 servings | **TIME:** About 45 minutes

This rustic dessert—essentially a large, sweet, eggy pancake baked over fruit—is incredibly simple and naturally sweet. The variations offer some fresh fruit ideas but you can go beyond; figure about 1 pound before trimming or pitting. Serve with a dollop of crème fraîche or even a drizzle of Chocolate Glaze (page 858).

1½	cups chopped dried apricots
1	cup rum or bourbon (optional)
	Butter for greasing
½	cup granulated sugar, plus 1 tablespoon for sprinkling
3	eggs
1½	cups cream, milk, or a mix
1	teaspoon vanilla extract
¼	teaspoon salt
¾	cup all-purpose flour
	Confectioners' sugar for garnish

1. Put the apricots in a bowl and pour over 2 cups warm water, pressing down to submerge the fruit. (Or substitute 1 cup warm water and the rum or bourbon.) Let sit until the apricots are soft and plump, about 30 minutes. Drain the fruit and squeeze dry.

2. Heat the oven to 375°F. Grease a 13 × 9-inch baking dish (or any similar shape that's big enough to hold the fruit in one layer) with butter and sprinkle it evenly with 1 tablespoon sugar. Lay the apricots in the dish.

3. Beat the eggs, then add the remaining ½ cup sugar and continue to beat until foamy and fairly thick, about 3 minutes. Stir in the cream, vanilla, and salt, then beat in the flour until just combined. (If you like, you can do this in a blender instead.)

4. Pour the batter over the fruit. Bake for about 30 minutes or until the clafoutis is nicely browned on top and a knife inserted into the center comes out clean. Sift confectioners' sugar over the top and serve warm or at room temperature.

CHERRY CLAFOUTIS This classic is a treat when cherries are in season: Instead of the apricots, use 1 pound sweet cherries, pitted and halved.

GRAPE CLAFOUTIS Same deal: Halve 1 pound large seedless grapes (red, green, or purple) and use them instead of the apricots.

Bread Pudding

MAKES: 6 servings | **TIME:** About 1 hour, largely unattended

Transforming stale bread into a popular dessert almost requires no recipe. I purposefully included no lists of possible substitutions or additions, since it's easier to just say: Start with different kinds of bread (whole wheat, challah, rye, or cinnamon raisin) or day-old pastry (Danish, cinnamon rolls, or muffins). Stir in chopped chocolate, nuts, or chopped dried fruit. Then top the finished pudding with plain or flavored Whipped Cream (page 854), a glaze (pages 857–858), or Vanilla Custard Sauce (page 864). Or if booze-spiked sauces are your thing, this is the place to use one.

Dried Apricot Clafoutis,
page 893

- 3 cups cream, milk, or a mix
- ½ cup plus 1 tablespoon sugar
- ¾ cup raisins
- 4 tablespoons (½ stick) butter, plus more for greasing
- 1½ teaspoons ground cinnamon
- ¼ teaspoon salt
- 8 slices white bread (preferably stale), crusts removed if they are very thick or dark
- 4 eggs

1. Heat the oven to 350°F. Combine the milk, ½ cup of the sugar, the raisins, butter, 1 teaspoon of the cinnamon, and the salt in a medium saucepan over medium-low heat, stirring occasionally, just until the butter melts.

2. Meanwhile, fill a kettle with water and bring it to a boil. Butter a loaf pan or 8- or 9-inch square baking dish.

3. Cut or tear the bread into bite-sized pieces—not too small. Put the bread in a large bowl, then pour the milk mixture over it and stir to submerge completely. Let it sit for a few minutes to soak up the liquid. Beat the eggs just to combine them, then stir into the soaking bread. Pour the pudding into the prepared pan dish. Mix together the remaining 1 tablespoon sugar and ½ teaspoon cinnamon and sprinkle over the top. Let sit for a few minutes for the bread to absorb the custard. Set the pan in a larger baking pan and pour in enough boiling water to come about halfway up the sides of the pan with the pudding.

4. Bake until a knife inserted in the center comes out clean or nearly so and the center is just a little wobbly, 45 to 60 minutes, If you want to brown the top, turn on the broiler, remove the pan from the water, and broil for about 30 seconds. Serve warm or cold. This keeps well for 2 days or more, covered and refrigerated.

CHOCOLATE BREAD PUDDING Omit the cinnamon and use only ¼ cup sugar. Replace the raisins in Step 1 with 3 ounces dark chocolate, chopped; heat until it's completely melted. For double chocolate, stir in another 3 ounces chopped chocolate after you add the milk mixture to the bread.

Rice Pudding

MAKES: At least 4 servings | **TIME:** About 2 hours, largely unattended

It's hard to believe so little rice thickens into pudding, but trust me. The only trick is patience. Once you buy in, make it your own: Try coconut, hazelnut, or almond milk instead of cow's milk. Consider the world of white rices: long-grains like basmati or jasmine will deliver the most delicate texture and fragrance, while short- or medium-grain rice like Arborio will be thicker and chewier, more like risotto.

- 4 cups whole milk
- ½ cup sugar
- ⅓ cup white rice (see headnote)
- ¼ teaspoon salt

1. Heat the oven to 300°F. Stir all the ingredients together in a 3- or 4-quart baking dish or large oven-proof saucepan. Bake uncovered for 30 minutes, then stir. Bake for 30 minutes more; at this point the rice may have started to swell and the milk should be developing a bubbly skin. Stir again to incorporate the skin into the milk.

2. Bake for 30 minutes more. The pudding is almost done when the rice predominates the mixture and the skin becomes more visible and darker. Stir the skin back into the pudding and return it to the oven. From now on, check every 10 minutes, stirring gently each time.

3. The pudding will be done before you think it's done. The rice should be really swollen and the milk thickened considerably but still pretty fluid; the pudding will thicken while it cools. Stir it once more, which helps release the rice's starch and thicken it even more. Serve warm or at room temperature, or cover with plastic wrap (press it directly on the pudding's surface if you want to prevent a skin from forming) and serve it cold within a couple days.

9 Rice Pudding Variations

VARIATION	SWEETENER	LIQUID	FLAVORINGS AND/OR GARNISH
Cinnamon-Raisin Rice Pudding	⅓ cup sugar, ½ cup raisins	4 cups milk	Add a 3-inch cinnamon stick before baking.
Vanilla Bean Rice Pudding	⅓ to ½ cup sugar, to taste	4 cups milk	Split a 1-inch piece of a vanilla bean lengthwise and add it before baking. When the pudding is ready, scrape the vanilla seeds into the pudding and stir.
Yogurt or Ricotta Rice Pudding	⅓ to ½ cup sugar, to taste	3 cups water	Stir in 2 cups yogurt or ricotta after the pudding has cooled for about 10 minutes.
Honey-Saffron Rice Pudding with Nuts and Golden Raisins	⅓ cup honey instead of the sugar	4 cups milk	Add a large pinch saffron threads in Step 1. After baking, stir in ¼ cup golden raisins and ¼ each chopped almonds and pistachios.
Hazelnut Rice Pudding	½ cup sugar	4 cups hazelnut milk or dairy milk	Garnish with chopped toasted hazelnuts.
Butterscotch Rice Pudding	½ cup brown sugar	4 cups milk, 8 tablespoons (1 stick) butter	Stir in about 2 tablespoons dark rum if you like after baking. Garnish with chopped toasted nuts.
Maple Rice Pudding	¾ cup maple syrup	3¼ cups milk	Garnish with freshly grated nutmeg or ground cinnamon, and chopped toasted nuts.
Mango Rice Pudding	⅓ cup sugar	3½ cups dairy milk or coconut milk	Stir in 1 cup mango purée (see page 862) after the pudding has cooled for at least 10 minutes.
Coconut Rice Pudding	⅓ cup sugar	4 cups coconut milk	Sprinkle with toasted shredded coconut (see page 372).

 fast make ahead vegetarian

Frozen Desserts

Even the simplest homemade ice creams will amaze you, because—despite the fact that it is stored in the freezer—ice cream is at its peak when it comes straight from the machine, at which point its temperature is just below freezing.

If you're going to get into homemade ice cream, you will need an ice cream machine. The best are the 1-quart-plus capacity machines with built-in refrigeration units; they weigh about 50 pounds, cost a few hundred dollars when new, and do all the work for you. But many good options—where you freeze a canister to chill the ice cream, then crank by hand or run a small motor to do the churning—cost less than $100.

The main recipe in this section is a custard-based ice cream sometimes called French ice cream. In the variation, cornstarch mimics the eggs well, so you can make eggless ice cream too. You can also make ice "cream" from nondairy milks, like coconut or nut milk. Sorbet and granita are other good nondairy options. They're all quite similar and can be varied multiple ways. Here's a review of the different types of other frozen desserts to help you understand the differences.

FROZEN YOGURT

Frozen yogurt is best when it remains true to its origins—which is to say that it should taste slightly sour. The recipe here will give you a fresh-but-tangy yogurt that you can flavor in the same ways as ice cream.

ICE MILK

Think of ice milk as either less-rich ice cream, or sorbet made with a little dairy. What you lose in texture and mouthfeel—it's a little crystalized, like sorbet—you gain in lightness.

SORBET

Typically (though not always) fruit based and dairy and egg free, sorbet is, at its core, about intensity of flavor. It can be made with just two to three ingredients, like fruit purée (the base), sugar, and sometimes a bit of water. The key to sorbets is to serve them fresh from the machine if at all possible. I'll even go so far as to suggest you let any uneaten sorbet thaw out in the fridge, then refreeze it in the ice cream maker a day or two later. Any fruit—or vegetable, for that matter—can serve as a sorbet base, as can chocolate, coffee, tea, and more. See "11 More Sorbet and Ice Milk Flavors" on page 903 for inspiration.

GRANITA

Granita has one huge advantage over other frozen desserts: You don't need a machine to make it. The crunchy flakes of intensely flavored ice are made by stirring and scraping a liquid as it freezes, which forms small ice crystals—like a good snow cone.

Vanilla Custard Ice Cream

MAKES: About 1 quart | **TIME:** About 30 minutes, plus time to chill and churn

The ultimate level of richness. A couple technical notes: To get you closer to a less rich ice milk, reduce the number of yolks to four or even three. The cornstarch variation has a surprising and wonderful texture, by the way; try it at least once. And for stir-in and flavoring ideas, see "5 More Simple Ideas for Ice Cream" (page 899) and the chart starting on page 902.

6	egg yolks
½	cup sugar
2	cups half-and-half
1	cup heavy cream
	Pinch salt
2	teaspoons vanilla extract

1. Combine the egg yolks and sugar in a large saucepan and use a whisk or electric mixer to beat them until thick and pale yellow, about 5 minutes.

Vanilla Custard Ice Cream, page 897, with Hot Fudge Sauce, page 859

2. Whisk the half-and-half, cream, and salt into the yolks until thoroughly combined. Put the saucepan over medium-low heat and cook, stirring constantly, until thick; if the custard ever starts to simmer, turn down the heat. It's ready when it coats the back of a spoon and a line drawn with your finger remains intact (see the illustration on page 887), this should take about 5 minutes.

3. Pour the custard through a fine-meshed strainer into a bowl and stir in the vanilla. Cover and refrigerate until it is completely cool, at least 2 hours and preferably overnight. Transfer to an ice cream maker and churn according to the manufacturer's directions.

4. Eat the ice cream right after churning or cover tightly and refrigerate for up to 20 minutes or so if you're not quite ready. After that, freeze it for up to several weeks; let it sit at room temperature or in the refrigerator until it can once again be easily scooped.

Using a Vanilla Bean

Real vanilla beans can make a tremendous difference in many desserts. But they're expensive, so you want to get as much flavor from each bean as possible.

If you're flavoring a warm liquid, heat a piece of bean in the liquid to infuse it. To add the seeds to a batter or other mixture, split the pod lengthwise and scrape out the seeds with the tip of a paring knife; add according to the recipe. The precious de-seeded pods—providing they've never been soaked—can find a second life buried in a jar of sugar to make vanilla sugar; added to a bottle of vanilla extract (or to make your own, added to a small jar of vodka or bourbon); or steeped with your next pot of tea or coffee.

STEP 1 To use a vanilla bean, split a whole bean or a piece in half lengthwise.

STEP 2 Scrape out the seeds.

SIMPLEST VANILLA ICE CREAM Substitute 2 tablespoons cornstarch for the egg yolks. In Step 1, whisk the cornstarch with 2 tablespoons of the half-and-half to make a slurry. In Step 2, put the remaining half-and-half, cream, sugar, and salt in the saucepan. Cook, whisking frequently, until the mixture begins to gently bubble; whisk in the slurry and proceed with the recipe.

VANILLA FROZEN YOGURT Instead of making a custard, whisk together 3½ cups plain yogurt, ¾ cup granulated or superfine sugar, and 1 teaspoon vanilla until combined. Chill for 30 minutes, then add any extra ingredients you like (see below) and churn in an ice cream maker according to the manufacturer's instructions.

5 MORE SIMPLE IDEAS FOR ICE CREAM

1. As soon as the ice cream is out of the machine, swirl in cold Chocolate Sauce (page 858), any Caramel Sauce (page 860), or any fruit purée (see page 862).

2. Stir in any nut butter, about ¼ cup per batch, before freezing; the churning will distribute it evenly.

3. Stir in up to ¾ cup chopped toasted nuts like almonds, walnuts, hazelnuts, pecans, peanuts, and/or macadamias, at any point after straining the custard.

4. Stir in ½ cup or more chopped or crushed candy or cookies after you remove the ice cream from the machine.

5. Stir in up to ¾ cup chopped fresh or cooked fruit—anything from raspberries, cherries, or mango to sautéed apples or poached pears—after you remove the ice cream from the machine.

Fresh Fruit Sorbet

MAKES: About 3 cups | **TIME:** 20 minutes, plus time to chill and churn

Berries, mangoes, peaches, apricots—the "soft" fruits—are all obvious and excellent candidates for this simple sorbet. But other fruits like melons, apples, and pears work well too. See the "More Sorbet and Ice Milk Flavors" chart that follows. This is one time I oversweeten a little, because the sweetness will be less apparent when the sorbet is frozen.

1 to 1½ pounds ripe fruit, washed, stemmed, peeled, pitted, and chopped as necessary (2½ cups)

½ cup granulated sugar, superfine sugar, or Simple Syrup (page 859), or more to taste

1 tablespoon fresh lemon juice, or more to taste

1. Purée the fruit in a blender with the sugar and lemon juice. Taste and add more of either if necessary. If you're using mango or seedy berries, strain the purée, stirring and pressing the mixture through a fine-meshed strainer with a rubber spatula to leave any fibers or seeds behind; be sure to scrape all the purée from the underside of the strainer.

> ## Infusing Liquids with Flavor
>
> You can infuse milk, cream, or almost any liquid with an ingredient when you want its flavor and aroma but not its body—a useful technique for flavoring the milk when making a custard. Infusing water is also a good way to flavor sorbets. Usually the flavoring agent is a spice, herb, or other highly aromatic ingredient like ginger, lemongrass, or green tea. It's just like making tea: Heat the liquid to boiling (or nearly so for milk), add the flavoring ingredient loose, in a tea ball, or wrapped in cheesecloth, and let it sit for 5 to 20 minutes, depending on the ingredient and how much flavor you want to infuse. Taste, and when the flavor is right, remove or strain out the ingredient.

2. Refrigerate until well-chilled. Churn in an ice cream maker according to the manufacturer's directions.

3. Eat the sorbet right after churning or cover tightly and refrigerate for up to 20 minutes or so if you're not quite ready. After that, freeze it for up to several weeks; let it sit at room temperature or in the refrigerator until it can once again be easily scooped.

FRUIT ICE MILK In terms of richness, somewhere in between sorbet and ice cream: Substitute 1 cup milk (or cream if you want it a little rich) for 1 cup of the fruit and omit the lemon juice.

Granita

MAKES: About 3 cups | **TIME:** About 2 hours

Granita is a no-special-equipment-needed, minimal-effort dessert that can be made of almost any juice or other liquid imaginable. Use any strongly flavored liquid, or any sorbet recipe or variation; figure about 2 cups total before freezing. Add a splash or 2 of vodka or rum to this or any other granita and it becomes a frozen cocktail.

2 cups soft ripe fruit like cherries, berries, mangoes, or melons, picked over, pitted, peeled, washed, and/or dried as necessary; or 2 cups fruit juice, coffee, or coconut milk (to make your own, see page 372)

Simple Syrup (page 859; optional)

Fresh lemon juice (optional)

1. Purée the fruit in a blender or food processor with a tablespoon or so of syrup; if you're not using it, add some water if necessary to get the machine going. Strain the purée if there are lots of seeds or fibers. You should end up with a little less than 2 cups purée, but don't stress about the exact quantity. Add lemon juice if you're using it, or Simple Syrup, either to taste.

(continued)

Mango Granita

10 More Ice Cream Flavors

The base ratio always remains the same: 6 egg yolks (or 2 tablespoons cornstarch) with 3 cups total liquid; only the type of liquid, the flavorings (substituting for the vanilla), and the sweetener change.

VARIATION	FLAVORING(S)	LIQUID	SWEETENER
Chocolate Ice Cream	5 ounces dark chocolate, chopped (melt into the hot liquid)	2 cups half-and-half or milk, 1 cup cream	½ cup sugar
Strawberry or Any Berry Ice Cream	1 cup berry purée, strained (see page 862, stir in in Step 4)	2 cups half-and-half or milk	½ cup sugar
Coffee Ice Cream	2 to 3 shots freshly brewed espresso; or ½ cup ground coffee (steep in hot liquid for 20 minutes; see page 900)	2 cups half-and-half or milk, 1 cup cream	½ cup sugar
Coconut Ice Cream	½ cup shredded coconut (toast in a dry skillet until lightly browned if you like; stir in in Step 4)	2 cups half-and-half, nondairy milk, or whole milk, 1 cup coconut milk	½ cup sugar
Pumpkin Ice Cream	1 cup canned or cooked fresh pumpkin purée, ½ teaspoon each ground cinnamon and ginger (add to the custard after straining)	2 cups half-and-half or milk, 1 cup cream	½ cup sugar
Maple-Nut Ice Cream	1 cup chopped toasted nuts. Stir in in Step 4	2 cups half-and-half or milk, 1 cup heavy cream	¾ cup maple syrup
Buttermilk Ice Cream	None	2 cups half-and-half or milk, 1 cup buttermilk	½ cup sugar
Banana Ice Cream	2 ripe bananas, sliced (steep in hot liquid for 20 minutes; see page 900)	2 cups half-and-half or milk, 1 cup cream	½ cup sugar
Ginger Ice Cream	2 tablespoons chopped fresh ginger (steep in hot liquid; see page 900), ½ cup minced candied ginger (add to the custard after straining)	2 cups half-and-half or milk, 1 cup cream	½ cup sugar
Green Tea Ice Cream	1 tablespoon matcha (powdered green tea) (add to the custard after straining); or leaf green tea (steep in hot liquid; see page 900)	2 cups half-and-half or milk, 1 cup cream	½ cup sugar

F fast   M make ahead   V vegetarian

11 More Sorbet and Ice Milk Flavors

You can make simple additions like spices, citrus zest, or chopped nuts, or substitute fresh juices for some or all of the puréed fruit. Or you can try one of these variations; the liquid option replaces the purée. To make any ice cream into ice milk, see the headnote on page 897.

VARIATION	FLAVORING(S)	LIQUID	SWEETENER
Orange, Tangerine, or Grapefruit Sorbet	1½ teaspoons grated zest; ½ teaspoon grated fresh ginger (optional)	2 cups fresh citrus juice	1 cup superfine sugar or Simple Syrup (page 859)
Lemon or Lime Sorbet	1½ teaspoons grated lemon or lime zest	1 cup fresh lemon or lime juice mixed with 1 cup water	2 cups Simple Syrup (page 859)
Raspberry or Strawberry–Red Wine Sorbet	1 cup raspberries or hulled strawberries	1 cup red wine (cook all ingredients for 10 minutes, then purée and strain)	1 cup Simple Syrup (page 859)
Vanilla-Pineapple Sorbet	1 vanilla bean (steep in hot Simple Syrup; see page 859)	2 cups pineapple purée (see page 862) or juice	1 cup Simple Syrup (page 859)
Papaya-Lime Sorbet	1½ teaspoons grated lime zest, 3 tablespoons fresh lime juice or to taste	2 cups papaya purée (see page 862)	½ cup superfine sugar or Simple Syrup (page 859)
Honeydew-Mint Sorbet	2 sprigs fresh mint (steep in hot Simple Syrup; see page 859), 2 tablespoons minced fresh mint leaves	2 cups honeydew purée (see page 862)	1 cup Simple Syrup (page 859)
Pear- or Apple-Ginger Sorbet	2 tablespoons chopped fresh ginger (steep in hot Simple Syrup; see page 859)	2 cups peeled, cored, chopped pears or apples, puréed with lemon juice	¾ cup Simple Syrup (page 859)
Lime-Basil Sorbet	1 sprig fresh basil (steep in hot Simple Syrup; see page 859), 2 tablespoons minced fresh basil leaves, 1½ teaspoons grated lime zest	1½ cups fresh lime juice	1½ cups Simple Syrup (page 859)
Orange-Cassis Sorbet	2 tablespoons minced candied orange zest or 1 tablespoon grated orange zest	1¾ cups fresh orange juice, ¼ cup cassis liqueur	½ cup superfine sugar or Simple Syrup (page 859)
Chocolate or Cherry-Chocolate Sorbet	¾ cup cocoa powder; 1 cup pitted, halved cherries if you like (add in Step 1 after straining)	2 cups boiling water (mix ½ cup water with the cocoa and sugar; then add remaining ingredients)	¾ cup superfine sugar or Simple Syrup (page 859)
Espresso Sorbet or Ice Milk	3 or 4 shots freshly brewed espresso; 2 tablespoons crushed chocolate-covered espresso beans (optional; add in Step 1 after straining)	2 cups water, nondairy or dairy milk, or cream	1 cup superfine sugar or Simple Syrup (page 859)

2. Pour into a large shallow metal pan or baking dish and freeze, using a fork to scrape and break up the ice every 30 minutes. It should be slushy and crunchy with ice crystals and completely frozen after about 2 hours. Serve right away or pack loosely in an airtight container and freeze for up to a week. When it becomes too hard, chop it into chunks with a mallet and pulse it just once or twice in a food processor.

---

6 GREAT GRANITAS

Use one of these as your base and sweeten it as you like.

1. **Pomegranate:** 2 cups bottled or fresh pomegranate juice; splash fresh lemon juice or 2 teaspoons grated lemon zest (optional)
2. **Orange, Tangerine, or Grapefruit:** 2 cups fresh juice, ½ teaspoon grated or finely minced zest
3. **Watermelon-Basil:** 2 cups chopped seeded watermelon, ¼ cup fresh basil leaves (purée together, then strain)
4. **Green Apple–Lime:** 1 cored, chopped Granny Smith apple (peeled if you like), ¼ cup fresh lime juice, ½ teaspoon grated or finely minced lime zest (purée together to minimize browning)
5. **Red Wine:** 1½ cups pinot noir, beaujolais, or other fruity wine, ½ cup water
6. **Apricot–Orange Blossom Water:** 2 cups pitted, chopped apricots, puréed, 1 teaspoon orange blossom water

Two Simple Candies

Candy making can be a major challenge, but these two recipes are rewarding and easy. If you're going to tackle candy making, even the simple kind, it's worth buying a candy thermometer, one that concentrates on the range between 230°F and 300°F, where sugar works its crystalline magic. You can judge the stage of cooked sugar by dropping a bit of it into a glass of cold water but the thermometer is far easier and more reliable.

Peanut Brittle

MAKES: About 1 pound | **TIME:** About 20 minutes, plus time to cool

If you've never made peanut brittle, you will not believe how simple it is.

> Butter for greasing
> 2 cups sugar
> 2 cups roasted peanuts (salted or unsalted)
> Pinch salt if you're using unsalted peanuts

1. Grease a rimmed baking sheet with butter. Put it on the counter close to the stove.

2. Put the sugar and ⅓ cup water in a medium saucepan over low heat. Cook, without stirring, until the sugar dissolves and becomes a nutty caramel color but is not yet dark brown, 5 to 10 minutes; swirl the pan if the sugar is cooking unevenly. If there's sugar clinging to the sides of the pan, use a pastry brush dipped in water to wash it back down. Watch carefully, as sugar has a tendency to burn the second you turn your back on it.

3. Stir in the peanuts and the salt if you're using it until combined. Remove from the heat and immediately pour the candy onto the prepared baking sheet and tilt the pan if it's not spreading fast enough to coat the bottom. Let cool at room temperature. To make even squares, score the brittle with a sharp knife once it's solidified slightly but before it has hardened, then cut when completely cooled. Otherwise, break it into pieces when cool. Store in a covered container at room temperature indefinitely.

POPCORN BRITTLE Omit the peanuts. Pop about ¼ cup popcorn kernels; you should have about 4 cups popcorn. Put the popcorn in a large heatproof bowl and pour the caramel over it. Toss to coat, working quickly so the sugar doesn't harden, and immediately spread the mixture on the prepared baking sheet, using a greased piece of parchment paper to press it into a thin and even layer if necessary.

 fast  make ahead vegetarian

Caramels

MAKES: More than 1 pound | TIME: About 20 minutes, plus time to cool

Creamy and dreamy, caramels keep for weeks.

4	tablespoons (½ stick) butter, plus more for greasing
1½	cups cream
2	cups sugar
½	cup light corn syrup
	Pinch salt
1½	teaspoons vanilla extract

1. Line an 8- or 9-inch square baking pan with enough parchment or wax paper to hang over the sides, then lightly grease the paper with butter.

2. Clip a candy thermometer to the side of a medium saucepan, making sure it doesn't touch the bottom of the pan. Cook the cream over medium-low heat until it just starts to steam. Add the sugar, corn syrup, butter, and salt all at once. Cook, stirring frequently, until the sugar dissolves. Bring to a boil and cook until it reaches 245°F (firm ball stage).

3. Remove from the heat, stir in the vanilla, and pour into the prepared pan. Let cool to room temperature. Use the parchment to lift the block of caramel out of the pan and use a sharp knife to cut it into small squares, dipping it in hot water once or twice between strokes. Wrap each square in a small piece of parchment or wax paper (this is a good project to do with kids). These keep for weeks but are best eaten fresh.

CHOCOLATE CARAMELS Omit the butter if you like. Chop 4 ounces dark chocolate. Add it to the cream with the other ingredients; stir almost constantly until it melts and the sugar dissolves. Proceed with the recipe.

CHEWY CARAMELS A bit of baking soda adds air bubbles that make a lighter and chewier caramel: Increase the cream to 1¾ cups. Add 1 teaspoon baking soda along with the vanilla.

 fast make ahead V vegetarian

More Ways to Navigate the Book

For a book this size, a big index is the most comprehensive tool for finding recipes, variations, ingredient, lists, and other features; it starts on page 911. Here are a handful of key lists that point you to the how-to illustrations, the recipes I consider essential, some of my favorite variations and lists—"hidden gems"—and a short list of one-dish, one-pot "all-in-one" meals.

How-To Illustrations

Cooking Basics
Using a Steel · 6
Using a Chef's Knife · 14
Chopping · 14
Slicing · 14
Using a Mandoline · 15
Making Julienne · 16
Using a Paring Knife · 16
Measuring Dry Ingredients · 17
Ways to Rig a Steamer · 20

Spices, Herbs, Sauces, and Condiments
Removing Leaves from Thyme · 51

Appetizers and Snacks
Sealing Wontons · 115
Shaping Summer Rolls and Egg Rolls · 116
Filling and Forming Samosas · 117
Folding Spinach-Cheese Triangles · 122
Stuffing and Sealing Pot Stickers · 124

Soups
Using an Immersion Blender · 140

Salads
Rinsing Salad Greens · 194

Vegetables and Fruit
Preparing Whole Artichokes · 258
Quartering Artichokes · 259
Preparing Asparagus · 262
Preparing Avocados · 264
Coring and Shredding Cabbage · 275
Chopping a Carrot · 276
Prepping Celery · 279
Preparing Chestnuts · 282
Preparing Corn · 283
Preparing Cucumbers · 287
Preparing Fennel · 293
Crushing and Peeling Garlic · 294
Preparing Leafy Greens with Thick Ribs · 300
Preparing Leeks · 302
Chopping Onions · 314
Stringing a Pod Pea · 317
Chiles Rellenos · 319
Preparing Peppers · 320
Preparing Plantains · 323
Turning Potato Rösti or Any Large Vegetable Pancake · 332

Folding Vegetables in Parchment · 340
Preparing Tomatoes · 345
Peeling Winter Squash · 349
How to Stuff Vegetables · 356
Coring an Apple · 364
Preparing Strawberries · 370
Peeling and Pitting a Mango, Version I · 376
Peeling and Pitting a Mango, Version II · 377
Cutting Citrus Segments (Supremes) or Wheels · 378
Preparing a Pineapple, Two Ways · 382

Beans
Shaping Bean Burgers · 413
Squeezing Tofu · 418

Rice and Other Grains
Rolling and Cutting Sushi Rolls · 447
Forming Tamales · 463

Pasta, Noodles, and Dumplings
Basic Pasta-Making Techniques · 503
Using a Manual Pasta Machine · 504

Cutting Pasta · 504
Making Dumpling or Wonton Skins and Egg Roll Wrappers · 509
Making Cannelloni · 512
Making Tortellini · 514
Making Gnocchi · 516
Making Spaetzle or Passatelli · 519

Seafood
Preparing Shrimp · 542
Skinning a Fillet · 548
Removing Pin Bones · 549
Filleting Fish · 553
Cutting Fish Steaks · 554
Scaling Fish · 571
Removing Fins · 571
Removing Gills · 571
Removing Heads and Tails · 571
Shucking Clams · 574
Removing a Mussel Beard · 575
Shucking Oysters · 576
How to Eat Crab · 583
Preparing Lobster for Cooking · 584
How to Eat Lobster · 586
Cleaning Squid · 589

(continued)

Poultry

Sectioning and Boning Chicken
Legs · 597
Boning Chicken Breasts · 597
Butchering Chicken · 614
Quartering a Roast
Chicken · 631
Carving a Roast Chicken · 632
Splitting, Butterflying, or
Spatchcocking
Chicken · 640
How to Carve a Roast
Turkey · 646
Removing Roast Turkey
Breasts · 648
Semiboning Squab and
Quail · 661

Meat

Major Parts of Beef · 666
Carving Prime Rib · 676
Major Cuts of Pork · 691
Major Cuts of Lamb · 705
Carving a Leg of Lamb · 707

Breakfast, Eggs, and Dairy

Folding an Omelet in Half · 730
Folding an Omelet in
Thirds · 731
Separating Eggs · 737
Finishing Fresh Cheese · 758

Bread, Sandwiches, and Pizza

Scoring and Docking
Crackers · 779
Shaggy Versus Smooth
Dough · 781
Kneading Dough · 782
Shaping Boules and Rolls · 784
Shaping Baguettes · 784
Shaping a Sandwich Loaf · 784
Slashing the Dough · 785
Baking No-Knead Bread · 787
Making Challah · 794
Rolling Burritos · 812
Shaping Dough for Pizza and
Calzones · 817

Desserts

Serving Angle Food Cake · 848
Beating Egg Whites · 852
Folding in Whipped Cream or
Egg Whites · 852
Stages of Whipped Cream · 856
Frosting a Cake · 857
Rolling Pie Dough · 866
Crimping the Crust · 868
Making a Lattice Top · 873
Making a Galette · 881
Coating the Back of a
Spoon · 887
Using a Vanilla Bean · 899

61 Essential Recipes

Even if at first a few of them might not seem like it, these will become the foundation of your cooking—the go-to dishes and components you can eat all sorts of different ways.

1. Traditional Pesto (page 51)
2. Fresh Tomato or Fruit
   Salsa (page 55)
3. Soy Dipping Sauce and
   Marinade (page 64)
4. Homemade Mayonnaise
   (page 69)
5. Bruschetta (page 95)
6. Hummus (page 103)
7. Meatballs, Three Ways
   (page 127)
8. Minestrone (page 147)
9. Universal Bean Soup
   (page 151)
10. Chicken Soup, Many Ways
    (page 164)
11. Vegetable Stock
    (page 174)
12. Vinaigrette (page 188)
13. Chopped Salad (page 197)
14. Tabbouleh (page 217)
15. Quick-Pickled Vegetables
    (page 228)
16. Boiled or Steamed
    Vegetables (page 238)
17. Stir-Fried Vegetables
    (page 244)
18. Roasted Vegetables or
    Fruits (page 247)
19. Sautéed Eggplant with Basil
    (page 290)
20. Flash-Cooked Kale or
    Collards with Lemon Juice
    (page 300)
21. Sautéed Mushrooms
    (page 306)
22. Mashed Potatoes
    (page 329)
23. Baked Sweet Potatoes
    (page 343)
24. Roasted Whole Winter
    Squash (page 349)
25. Applesauce (page 364)
26. Simply Cooked Beans
    (page 390)
27. Baked Tofu (page 419)
28. Rice Pilaf (page 434)
29. Risotto, Five Ways
    (page 440)
30. Cooking Grains, the Easy
    Way (page 450)
31. Polenta (page 460)
32. One-Pot Pasta with Butter
    and Parmesan (page 478)
33. Fast Tomato Sauce,
    with or Without Pasta
    (page 478)
34. Spaghetti with Meat Sauce
    (page 495)
35. Baked Ziti with Mushrooms
    (page 499)
36. Cold Noodles with Sesame
    or Peanut Sauce
    (page 522)
37. Broiled Seafood (page 534)
38. Still the Simplest and Best
    Shrimp Dish (page 542)
39. Broiled Boneless Chicken
    (page 596)
40. Roast Chicken Parts
    with Olive Oil or Butter
    (page 615)
41. My New Favorite Fried
    Chicken (page 628)
42. Classic Roast Turkey, with
    Gravy (page 647)
43. Many Ways to Cook Steak
    (page 667)
44. Beef Stew (page 679)
45. Skillet Pork Chops
    (page 691)
46. Roast Pork with Garlic and
    Rosemary (page 695)
47. The Best Scrambled Eggs
    (page 724)
48. Eggs Poached in Tomato
    Sauce (page 726)
49. Fresh Tomato and Cheese
    Frittata (page 731)
50. French Toast (page 738)
51. Granola, My New Way
    (page 749)
52. Corn Bread (page 769)
53. Jim Lahey's No-Knead
    Bread (page 785)
54. Fish Tacos, Four Ways
    (page 811)
55. Pizza with Tomato Sauce
    and Mozzarella
    (page 819)
56. Chocolate Chunk Cookies
    (page 831)
57. Brownies (page 840)
58. Pound Cake (page 846)
59. Chocolate Ganache
    (page 858)
60. Fruit Galette (page 879)
61. Vanilla Pudding (page 887)

40 Hidden Gems

Tucked away among the recipe variations, lists, and tables are some of the most interesting dishes in the book. I hope this list inspires you to pay even more attention to the extras that follow the main recipes.

1. Vietnamese-Style Chile Paste (page 45)
2. Zhug (page 52)
3. Blue Cheese Dressing (page 59)
4. Green Chile Salsa (page 73)
5. Roasted Beans with Oil (page 88)
6. Miso Caramelized Nuts (page 88)
7. Un-Avocado Guacamole (page 105)
8. Lime-Garlic-Coconut Soup (page 137)
9. Lightning-Quick Fish Soup, French Style (page 161)
10. Greek Salad, Simplified (page 196)
11. Quick-Pickled Corn Coins with Sichuan Peppercorns (page 229)
12. Seaweed and Celery Stir-Fry (page 246)
13. Shredded Gingered Carrots (page 276)
14. Caramelized Shallots (page 315)
15. Braised and Glazed Brussels Sprouts (page 336)
16. Crisp Kimchi Pancakes (page 355)
17. White Beans and Sausage (page 402)
18. Chickpea Chili with Lamb (page 406)
19. Indian-Style Split Pea Fritters (page 416)
20. 10 More Rice or Other Grain Pilafs (page 436)
21. Sort-of-Sichuan Noodles with Clams (page 492)
22. 17 Dishes to Toss with Asian Noodles (page 526)
23. Fish Steamed over Something (page 558)
24. Grilled Chicken Escabeche (page 598)
25. Stir-Fried Tofu with Ketchup (page 605)
26. Eggplant Parmigiana (page 609)
27. Oil-Poached Chicken (page 612)
28. Grilled or Broiled Butterflied Leg of Lamb (page 670)
29. Five Spice Pot Roast (page 684)
30. Candied Roast Pork Shoulder (page 697)
31. Leftover Pasta, Noodle, Grain, or Rice Frittata (page 732)
32. 16 Iconic Mexican Dishes Elsewhere in the Book (page 759)
33. Pumpkin Bread (page 771)
34. Black Bread with Chocolate (page 797)
35. Broiled Cheese for a Crowd (page 806)
36. 28 Perfect Hot or Cold Dishes for Filling Sandwiches (page 808)
37. Flourless Peanut or Other Nut Butter Cookies (page 836)
38. Cheese Shortbread (page 838)
39. Shortcut Lemon Mousse (page 864)
40. Rice Pudding (page 895)

27 All-in-Ones

Vegetables and meat, dairy, eggs, grains, or beans, together in one pot or pan. There might be a little pasta or rice thrown in; if not, just serve these with bread or simply cooked noodles or grains and you have dinner, streamlined.

1. Minestrone (page 147)
2. Rice Porridge with Fresh Garnishes (page 157)
3. Pho-Style Noodle Soup with Pork (page 161)
4. Beef and Vegetable Soup (page 168)
5. Hot and Sour Soup (page 168)
6. Warm Spicy Greens with Bacon and Eggs (page 199)
7. Grilled Beef Salad with Mint (page 223)
8. 10 More Fish, Chicken, or Meat Salads (page 224)
9. Tomatoes Stuffed with Sausage and Rice (page 356)
10. Stewed Chickpeas with Eggplant or Zucchini (page 400)
11. Vegetable Chili (page 406)
12. Braised Tofu with Eggplant and Shiitakes (page 422)
13. Fried Rice with Shrimp and Pork (page 444)
14. Grits Gratin with Arugula and Garlic (page 462)
15. Chipotle Pozole (page 469)
16. One-Pot Pasta with Chicken and Fennel (page 480)
17. Pasta with Broccoli Raab, Cauliflower, Broccoli, Greens, or Asparagus and Sausage (page 485)
18. Vegetarian Lasagne (page 502)
19. Glass Noodles with Vegetables and Meat (page 524)
20. Shrimp and Scallion Stir-Fry (page 543)
21. Fish Steamed over Summer Vegetables (page 555)
22. Stir-Fried Chicken with Broccoli or Cauliflower (page 603)
23. Stir-Fried Beef with Green Peppers (page 671)
24. Grilled Beef Kebabs with Lots of Vegetables (page 673)
25. Corned Beef with Cabbage and Potatoes (page 685)
26. Braised Pork with Tomatoes and Fennel (page 700)
27. Lamb Stew with Eggplant or Green Beans (page 711)

Converting Measurements

Essential Conversions

VOLUME TO VOLUME

3 teaspoons	1 tablespoon
4 tablespoons	¼ cup
5 tablespoons plus 1 teaspoon	⅓ cup
4 ounces	½ cup
8 ounces	1 cup
1 cup	½ pint
2 cups	1 pint
2 pints	1 quart
4 quarts	1 gallon

VOLUME TO WEIGHT

¼ cup liquid or fat	2 ounces
½ cup liquid or fat	4 ounces
1 cup liquid or fat	8 ounces
2 cups liquid or fat	1 pound
1 cup sugar	7 ounces
1 cup flour	5 ounces

Metric Approximations

MEASUREMENTS

¼ teaspoon	1.25 milliliters
½ teaspoon	2.5 milliliters
1 teaspoon	5 milliliters
1 tablespoon	15 milliliters
1 fluid ounce	30 milliliters
¼ cup	60 milliliters
⅓ cup	80 milliliters
½ cup	120 milliliters
1 cup	240 milliliters
1 pint (2 cups)	480 milliliters
1 quart (4 cups)	960 milliliters (0.96 liter)
1 gallon (4 quarts)	3.94 liters
1 ounce (weight)	28 grams
¼ pound (4 ounces)	114 grams
1 pound (16 ounces)	454 grams
2.2 pounds	1 kilogram (1,000 grams)
1 inch	2.5 centimeters

OVEN TEMPERATURES

Description	°Fahrenheit	°Celsius
Cool	200	90
Very slow	250	120
Slow	300–325	150–160
Moderately slow	325–350	160–180
Moderate	350–375	180–190
Moderately hot	375–400	190–200
Hot	400–450	200–230
Very hot	450–500	230–260

Index

Note: Page references in *italics* indicate photographs and illustrations.

A

Adzuki beans, 387
Afghan style
    peaches, pickled, 231
    winter squash, 352
Aïoli, 70
All-American pot roast, 683
All-purpose flour, 762–763, 766
Allspice, 28
Almond(s)
    about, 310
    apricot-, bars, 843
    broccoli or cauliflower, crunchy,
        with raisins, saffron, and, 269,
        270
    meatballs, Spanish-style, 127
    mole, turkey thighs in, 652
    panna cotta, 888
Alsatian mac and cheese, 419
Aluminum, about, 9
Amaranth, 452
Amchoor, 28
Anaheim chile, 41
Anasazi beans, 387
Ancho chiles, 41
Anchovies
    about, 5
    broccoli raab with, 272
    -caper vinaigrette, 191
    deviled eggs with, 93
    mayonnaise, 70
    roast leg of lamb with, 710
    spread, 103
    tahini sauce, 59
Angel food cake, 847, *848*
    about, *848*
    chocolate, 848
    lemon-scented, 848
Animal care certified eggs, 719
Anise seeds, 28
Annatto, 28
Anything-scented peas, 317
Appenzeller cheese, 755

Appetizers and snacks, 85–133. *See also*
    Dips and spreads
    about, 86–87
    crudités, 102
    finger food ideas, 96
    fish, poultry, and meat dishes as, 130
    lettuce cups and wraps, 121
    party food, 118–133
        bean and cheese empanadas, 126
        ceviche, 132
        cheese fondue, 118, *119*
        chicken or pork satay, 130, *131*
        chicken wings, 127, *129*
        meatballs, three ways, 127
        pot stickers, 124, *124*, *125*
        spinach-cheese triangles, 122, *122*
        stuffed grape leaves, 120
        stuffed mushrooms, 120
        Vietnamese summer rolls, 123
    quick bites, 87–99
        bruschetta, 95
        caramelized spiced nuts, 88, *89*
        chickpea flatbread, 97
        deviled eggs, 91, *92*
        deviled eggs, 9 more ways, *92*, *93*
        edamame (or any bean) in their
            shells, 90
        cheese and marinade combinations,
            97
        marinated celery and carrots,
            Chinese style, *94*, 95
        marinated mozzarella, 96
        marinated olives, 91
        popcorn, 90
        roasted nuts with oil or butter, 87
        shrimp cocktail, *98*, *99*
    sit-down dishes as, 130
    sizzled starters, 109–118
        about, 109–110
        fried tortilla chips, 110
        fried wontons or egg rolls, 115, *115*,
            116
        nachos, 110

    nachos, 8 ideas for topping, 111
    plantain chips, 111
    potato-filled samosas, 116, *117*
    vegetable fritters, 114
    sprinkles for tortilla, pita, plantain,
        vegetable chips, 110
    tempura, 112, *113*
    tempura, 10 excellent dipping sauces
        for, 115
    vegetable fritters, 111
    30 sit-down dishes as, 132
Apple(s)
    about, 364, *364*, 366
    applesauce, 364
    applesauce, seasonings for, 365
    baked, 365, *368*
    baked, 7 ideas for, 367
    cider vinegar, 187
    crisp, 884
    -ginger sorbet, 903
    pie, 871
        deep-dish, with streusel topping, 872
        Dutch, 872
        -pear, 872
        7 easy additions to, 872
    roasted slices, savory, 248
    slaw, 205
    sweet sautéed, 365
    sweet sautéed, savory, 365
    upside-down cake, 850
    wheat berry salad with, and walnuts,
        217
Appliances, about, 12
Apricot(s)
    about, 367
    -almond bars, 843
    rice salad with dried, 217
Aromatic poached fish, 565
Arroz con pollo, 625
Arroz con pollo, 7 ingredients to add, 626
Artichoke(s)
    about, *258*, 258–259, *259*
    dip, 107, *108*

Artichoke(s), *continued*
   dip, parmesan, 108
   fish steamed over, 558
   grilled, 252
   hearts
      braised, 261
      braised, stir-ins for, 262
      braised, with ham, wine, and lemon, 261
      braised, with potatoes, 261
      roasted, 261
   and herbs in parchment, 341
   Jerusalem, about, 298
   Jerusalem, crisp-cooked, 298
   in shaved vegetable salad, 206
   steamed, 259, *260*
Arugula
   classic creamy dip, 100
   corn salad with, 201
   grits gratin with arugula and garlic, 462, *465*
   pesto, 52
Arugula, about, 192
Asafetida, 28
Asian greens and bok choy, about, 265–267
Asian style. *See also* Noodles, Asian
   dumplings
      wrappers, 509, *509*
   eggplant, curried, 292
   skimmers and spiders for, 11
Asparagus
   about, 262, *262*
   boiled, 263
   gratin, with gruyère, 256
   grilled, 252
   microwaved, 263
   pasta with, 484
   in shaved vegetable salad, 206
   shrimp and, stir-fry, 543
   steamed, 10 ways, 263
   steamed asparagus spears, 262
   stir-fried, 246
Avocado(s)
   about, 263, *264*
   beef and, salad, 224
   corn salad with, 201
   -cucumber salsa, 58
   guacamole, 105
      -crab spread or dip, 105
      crunchy corn, 105
      with fruit, 105
      "guacasalsa," 105
   sandwich, broiled roast beef and, 810
   -tomatillo salsa, 56

   for topping toast, 717, 718
   vinaigrette, 191

B
Baby bok choy, 265
Bacon
   about, 706
   black beans orange-glazed with, 395
   Brussels sprouts sautéed with, 272
   caramelized onions with, 315
   corn bread, 770
   fried rice with, 445
   lentil soup with, 154
   -nut stuffing, 651
   onion quiche with, 735
   pan-fried whole trout, with red onions and, *572, 573*
   pasta all'amatriciana, 498
   pasta carbonara, 498
   ranch dressing, 71
   scrambled eggs with, 724
   scrapple, 749
   seared baby bok choy with bacon vinaigrette, 267
   3 ways to cook, 706
   vinaigrette, 190
   warm spicy greens with, and eggs, *198*, 199
Baguettes, about, *784, 788*
Baked apples, 365, *368*
Baked apples, 7 ideas for, 367
Baked beans, 400
   black beans and rice, 410, *411*
   with cracker crumb crust, 400
   7 ideas for, 401
   vegetarian, 400
Baked custard, 888
Baked custard, 5 more ideas for, 890
Baked eggs, 726
Baked eggs, for a crowd, 726
Baked potatoes, 325
Baked samosas, 118
Baked sweet potatoes, 343
Baked tofu, 419
Baked tortilla chips, 110
Baked vegetables
   fennel, in orange juice, 293
   potatoes, mashed, 329
Baking, about, 20–21
Baking fats, about, 827
Baking powder
   about, 4, 765–766
   biscuits, 774
Baking sheets, about, 8
Baking soda, about, 4, 765

Baklava, 884
Balloon whisks, about, 11
Balsamic vinegar, 186
Banana peppers, 41
Banana(s)
   about, 367
   banana cream pie, 877
   bread, 770
   bread, honey whole grain, 771
   broiled or grilled, 361
   ice cream, 902
   muffins, 771
   pudding, 887
   roasted, 369
   sautéed, 369
Barbecue sauce, 75
   bourbon, 75
   chipotle, 75
   curry, 75
   Korean-style, 75
   mustardy, 75
Bare-bones crab cakes, 585
Barley
   hulled, 455
   pearled, 453
   soup
      chicken and, 155
      mushroom-, more traditional, 155
      mushroom-, my new way, 154
Bars
   apricot-almond, 843
   coconut-lime, 844
   jam, 844
   my magic, 843
   10 that kids can help make, 834
Basic roast boneless turkey breast, 652
Basic steamed cauliflower, 278
Basil. *See also* Pesto
   about, 47
   bruschetta with, and tomatoes, 96
   farro with cherry tomatoes, leeks, and, 467
   fried, farfalle with mascarpone and, 492
   purée, 52
   salad, with tomato, mozzarella, 199
   sautéed eggplant with, 290
   sautéed eggplant with, and chiles, 290
   stuffing, broiled or grilled scallops with, *578, 579*
   Thai-style chicken stir-fried with chiles and, 606
   tomato-, vinaigrette, 190
Bay leaves
   about, 47
   in baked potatoes, 326

Bean(s), 385–423. *See also* Lentils; Tofu
    about, 4, 386–390
        additions to, 394
        calculating how much to make, 386
        cooked, storing, 390
        cooking in machines, 393
        fresh and frozen shell beans, 401
        mashed, 402
        methods for, 394
        serving, 390
    baked, 400
        with cracker crumb crust, 400
        7 ideas for, 401
        vegetarian, 400
    bean dip
        cheesy, 104
        creamy, 104
        and salsa, 104
        variations, 104
    black
        about, 387
        baked, and rice, 410, *411*
        in bean dip, 104
        chicken, stir-fried with, 606
        chile and black bean paste, 45
        chili, and pork, 406
        fermented, flash-cooked kale or
            collards with, 300
        fermented, in shrimp and cabbage
            stir-fry, 545
        orange-glazed, 395
        purée with chipotles, 392
        salad, spicy, 214
        sauce, quick-braised fish in, 570
        soup, smoky, 152
        soup, smoky, from scratch, 152
        stir-fried beef with green peppers
            and, 671
    burgers, fritters, and griddle cakes,
        413–416
    and cheese empanadas, 126
    cooked or canned, 392–400
    dip, 103
    dried, 389–390
        buying and storing, 386
        cooking, 389
        preparing, 389
    edamame in their shells, 90
    fava
        about, 387
        in bean dip, 104
        greens and pasta combos, 397
        and mint salad with pecorino, 215,
            216
        one-pot pasta with, 480

    fish steamed over, 558
    greens and pasta combos, 397
    lima
        in bean dip, 104
        greens and pasta combos, 397
    oven-baked or stovetop mixed
        vegetables with, 354
    pasta
        with creamy, sauce, 490
        27 dishes to toss with, 485
    in pots, 392–410
    rice and, 410–412
    roasted, with oil, 88
    salads
        basic, 212
        fava bean and mint, with pecorino,
            215
        10 variations on, 214
        warm chickpea, with arugula, 213
    salsa, 57
    simply cooked, 390, *391*
    simply cooked, flavoring, 390
    soups
        pasta e fagioli, 148, *149*
        ribolitta, 148
        smoky black bean, 152
        universal, 151, *153*
        universal, additions to, 152
    and tomatoes, 396
    and tomatoes, rich and elegant, 398
    white
        in bean dip, 104
        with cabbage, pasta, and prosciutto,
            396
        lamb stew with, 711
        purée, 392
        ribolitta, 148
        salad, tabbouleh style, 214
        and sausage and kale, 402
        and shrimp, 402
        Tuscan style, 402
Bean sprout(s)
    about, 264
    bean sprout fritters, 114
    griddlecakes, 416
    stir-fried, 246
Bean threads, about, 520
Béchamel sauce, 79
Béchamel sauce, baked chard in, 256
Beef
    about, 664–666, *666*, 667–675
        buying, 664
        checking for doneness, 665
        cooking, 664–665
        "grass-fed," 667

    grilling large cuts, 677
    major parts of, 665–667, *666*
    and barley soup, 138
    beef roasts, about doneness, 676
    braised, 679–683
        about, 679
        mustard-, short ribs, 681
        stew, 679
        stew with tomatoes and dried
            mushrooms, 680
        stroganoff with mushrooms, 681,
            682
    chili, fast, 405
    chili, slow-simmered, 403, *404*
    game substituted for, 711
    ground, 687–689
        about, 687
        burgers, my classic, 687
        burgers, 13 mix-and-match ideas for
            flavoring, 687
        do-it-yourself, 686
        meat loaf, 688
    ground meat, 687–689
    pot roasts, 683–687
        about, 683
        all-American, 683
        braised brisket, 684
        corned beef with cabbage and
            potatoes, 685, 686
    roast, 675–679
    roast beef
        about, 675–676, *676*
        prime, roast for a small crowd, 676
        tri-tip with chimichurri, 677, *678*
    salads
        and avocado, 224
        grilled, with mint, 223
    soup
        and mushroom, 168
        and vegetable, 168, *169*
        and vegetable, spicy, 168
    steaks and other quick-cooking
        and-pepper wrap, 809
        charcoal-grilled porterhouse or
            t-bone, 669
        5 unexpected sauces for steaks, 670
        flank steak, grilled or broiled, 670
        on a gas grill, 669
        grilled porterhouse, 668
        kebabs, grilled with lots of
            vegetables, 673, *674*
        kebabs, varying, 673
        many ways to cook, 667–669
        pan-grilled, 669
        pan-grilled, oven-roasted, 669

Beef, *continued*
  steaks and other quick-cooking
    pepper steak with red wine sauce,
      671
    reverse-seared, 670
    stir-fried, improvising, 672
    stir-fried, with green peppers and
      black beans, 671
  stock, 176, *177*
Beef-filled samosas, 117
Beet(s)
  about, 264
  baked in foil, 264
  classic creamy dip, 100
  and horseradish dip, 100
  rösti
    carrot and onion, 265
    with parmesan, 265
    with rosemary, 265, *266*
  in shaved vegetable salad, 206
  in vegetable chips, 111
Bell peppers
  about, 41, 320
  pan-cooked with paprika, 322
  pan-cooked with vinegar, 322
  sausages with onions and, 704
  spiced, in parchment, 341
  stuffed, 358
Bell peppers, red
  my mom's pan-cooked peppers and
    onions, 320, *321*
  roasted, 318
    on the grill, 318
    10 things to do with, 318
Belly (pork), about, 689
Berry(ies). *See also* Cranberry(ies)
  about, 370, *370*
  blueberry
    cobbler, 882
    muffins, 773
    tart, lemon curd and fresh, 881
  ice cream, 902
  peach and, pie, 875
  raspberry
    fool, 891, *892*
    fool, yogurt, 891
    sorbet, 903
  raspberry fool, 891, *892*
  strawberry
    ice cream, 902
    -red wine sorbet, 903
    shortcakes, or other fruit, 849,
      851
  tarts
    fresh, with chocolate, 881

fresh, with vanilla pudding filling,
  880, 881
fresh blueberry, with lemon curd,
  881
  upside-down cake, 850
  yogurt raspberry fool, 891
Best scrambled eggs, 724
Beurre noisette sauce, 79
Biscotti
  nutty, *832–833*
  7 variations, 839
  vanilla, 838
Biscuits
  baking powder, 774
  buttermilk or yogurt, 773
  chicken-n-, pie, 640
  drop, 775
  sweet potato or winter squash, 775
  10 additions to, 774
Black beans
  about, 387
  baked, and rice, 410, *411*
  in bean dip, 104
  chicken, stir-fried with, 606
  chile and black bean paste, 45
  chili, and pork, 406
  fermented, flash-cooked kale or collards
    with, 300
  fermented, in shrimp and cabbage
    stir-fry, 545
  orange-glazed, 395
  purée with chipotles, 392
  salad, spicy, 214
  sauce, quick-braised fish in, 570
  soup, smoky, 152
  soup, smoky, from scratch, 152
  stir-fried beef with green peppers and,
    671
Black bread, 795, *796*
  with chocolate, 797
  pumpernickel raisin, 797
Black-eyed peas
  about, 387
  in bean dip, 104
  salad, curried, 214
Blanching technique, 237–238
Blender Hollandaise, 80
Blenders, about, 12
Blondies, 843
  butterscotch, 843
  my magic bars, 843
Blueberry(ies)
  cobbler, 882
  muffins, 773
  tart, lemon curd and fresh, 881

Blue cheese
  about, 754
  dressing, 59
Boiled potatoes, 325
Boiled seafood
  crab or lobster, 584
  spicy crab or lobster, 585
Boiled vegetables
  about
    crisp-tender, 240
    shocking, 238, *239*
  asparagus, 263
  asparagus, 10 ways, 263
  chestnuts, 282
"Boiled water," 137, *139*
  lime-garlic-coconut, 137
  roasted garlic soup, 137
  tomato-garlic soup, 137
Boiling, about, 16–17
Bok choy
  about, 265–267
  cold, and ginger salad, 207
  fried rice with, 445
  seared
    with bacon vinaigrette, 267
    with black vinegar, 267
    with chile vinaigrette, 267
  shrimp and water chestnuts, stir-fry,
    544, 545
Boneless chicken
  breaded cutlets, 608
  breaded cutlets, 6 more ways, 609
  naked enchiladas, *610*
  in packages with orange, 612
  poached, 611
    breasts or thighs, 611
    breasts or thighs, 5 ways, 612
    breasts or thighs, with lemon sauce,
      611
    8 more additions to liquid for, 611–612
Boneless chicken, baked, 601
  herb-, 602
  with tomatoes, 601
  with tomatoes, 4 ways, 602
Boneless chicken, grilled or broiled, 596
  about, 596
  boneless, about, *597*
  escabeche, 598
  grilled, 598
  pounding, 598
  10 ways, 599
  teriyaki, *600*, 601
Boneless chicken, sautéed, 605
  with wine sauce, 607
  with wine sauce, 12 simple spins on, 608

Boneless chicken, stir-fried, 603
    with broccoli or cauliflower, 603
    with cabbage, *604*, 605
    with ketchup, 605
    6 ways, 606
    teriyaki, 601
    13 simple additions, 603–604
Boneless prime rib, 677
Boniato, 348
Boozy caramel sauce, 860
Bouillabaisse, 162
Boules, about, *784*
Bourbon barbecue sauce, 75
Bowls, about, 10
Braised and glazed radishes, turnips, or
        other root vegetable, 334, *335*
Braised artichoke hearts, 261
Braised beef
    burgundy, 680
    carbonnade, 680
    with chiles and limes, 680
    mustard-, short ribs, 681
    sort-of-sauerbraten, 680
    stew, 679
    stew with tomatoes and dried
        mushrooms, 680
    stroganoff with mushrooms, 681, *682*
    with tomatoes and dried mushrooms,
        680
Braised endive, escarole, or radicchio with
        prosciutto, 292
Braised pork. *See* Pork
Braised vegetables
    about, 247
        celery, oven-, 294
        endive, escarole, radicchio with
            prosciutto, 292
        endive with orange juice, 292
        leeks au gratin, *254*
        tomato gratin, *254*
    artichoke hearts, 261
Braising, about, 21
Bran muffins, 771
Brazil nuts, about, 310
Bread, 761–824. *See also* French toast;
        Stuffing
    about
        flours, 762–765
        flours, substituting, 764
        gluten-free, 766
        leavening, 765–767
    essentials made from, 800
        crumbs, fresh, 801
        my kind of croutons, 801
    freezing dough and, 767

grilled bread salad, 221
pizza, 816–824
pudding, 893
pudding, chocolate, 895
quick, 767–777
sandwiches, 803–809
tacos and burritos, 809–815
toast
    fresh cheese, 717
    toppings for, 718
    Welsh rarebit, *717*
tomato and, soup, 145
unleavened flatbreads, 777–781
yeast, 781–800
Bread, yeast
    about, *781*, 781–785, *782*, *784*, *785*
    black, 795, *796*
    breadsticks, 800
    breadsticks, sesame rice, 800
    brioche, 791
    challah, 793, *794*
    essentials from. *See also* Croutons
        croutons, my kind of, 801, *802*
        crumbs, fresh, 801
    15 ingredients to add to, 797
    gluten for, 788
    by hand vs. standing mixer, 791
    making time for, 798
    naan, 799
    no-knead
        about, 787
        Jim Lahey's, 785, *786*
        science behind, 787
    100 percent whole wheat bread, 790
    onion rye, 794
    pita, 798
    rustic French, 787
    sandwich
        about, 784, 803
        everyday, 789, 790
        50 percent whole wheat, 790
    shiny crust for, 793
Breaded and fried eggplant (or any other
        vegetable), 288, 289
Breaded and fried eggplant (or any other
        vegetable), 3 ways to vary, 290
Breaded chicken cutlets, 608
Breaded chicken cutlets, 6 more ways, 609
Breaded seafood. *See* Seafood
Bread flour, 763, 766
Breads, quick
    about, 768–769
    banana, 770
    buttermilk or yogurt biscuits, 773
    coffee cake, 772, 773

corn, 769
griddled olive oil salt, 768, 769
muffins, many ways, 771
popovers, 775, *776*
scones, 775
10 additions to, 774
Breakfast, 715–759
    cereals, 748–756
        granola, my new way, 749, *750*
        grits, 748
        oatmeal or other creamy, 748
    dairy. *See also* Cheese
        about, 751–752
        cheese, about, 753–756
        cheese, fresh, 756–759
        yogurt, 752
    eggs. *See also* Egg(s)
        about, 718–721
        essential recipes, 721–729
        omelets, frittatas, and other flat
            omelets, 730–733
        quiches, custards, soufflés, 733–737
    fastest, versatile
        fruit smoothie, 716–717
        toast, 717, 718
    5 essential dishes for, 733
    French toast, pancakes, waffles, crêpes,
        doughnuts, 738–748
    homemade, (or any other meal)
        sausage, 703
    maple syrup for, 738
Breast (lamb), about, 707
Brined fresh cheese, 758
Brining, 633
Brioche, 791
    cinnamon buns, 792
    cocoa swirl bread, 792
    poppy seed swirl bread, 792
Brisket
    about, 667
    braised, 684
    braised, with sweet potatoes, carrots,
        dried fruit, and lots of garlic, 686
Broccoli
    about, 268–269
    with chicken, stir-fried, 603
    crunchy, 269
        almonds, raisins, and saffron, 269
        with garlic, vinegar, and capers, 269
        with onion and olives, 269
    fritters, 114
    pasta with, 484
    puréed, 241
    stir-fried, with shiitakes, gingery, 246
    tofu braised with, 423

Broccolini, about, 268–269
Broccoli raab
    about, 268–269
    with anchovies, 272
    with garlic and pecorino, 272
    pasta with, 484
    with sausage and grapes, 269
Broiled cheese for a crowd, 806
Broiled chicken. *See* Boneless chicken,
    grilled or broiled; Chicken parts
Broiled fish tacos, 812
Broiled flank steak, 670
Broiled jícama with chile-lime glaze, 299
Broiled seafood, 534
    octopus, 534
    scallops, 534
    scallops, with basil stuffing, *578, 579*
    shrimp or squid, 534
    soft-shell crabs or lobsters, 534
    thick fish fillets or steaks, 534
    whole fish, 534
Broiled tofu, 419
Broiled vegetables
    about, 250
    broiled vegetable gratin, 251
    broiled vegetable gratin, rich, 255
    vegetable gratins, 256
Broiling, about, 21
Broth, noodles in, 157. *See also* Soups
Brownies, 840, *841*
    blondies, 843
    cream cheese swirl, 840
    8 simple ideas for, 840
    lemon squares, *842, 843*
Brown rice, about, 430
Brown rice flour, 765
Brown sauce, 79
Brown sugar
    about, 826
    cookies, 836
Bruschetta, 95
    with parmesan, 96
    with tomatoes and basil, 96
    toppings for, 96
Brushes, about, 11
Brussels sprouts
    about, 272
    braised and glazed, 336
    roasted, with garlic, 248
    sautéed, with bacon, 272
    sautéed, with caramelized onions, 273
    sautéed, with hazelnuts, 273
Buckwheat
    buckwheat crêpes, sweet or savory,
        743

buckwheat crêpes with ham and
        gruyère, *745*
    flour, about, 764
    flour, in fresh pasta, 505
    groats, 454
Buffet appetizers, serving, 86
Bulgur
    about, 452
    basic, 457
    pilaf with lentils, 458
    pilaf with vermicelli, 458
    pilaf with vermicelli and hot sausage, 458
Burdock
    about, 273
    quick-braised, and carrots, 273
Burgers
    bean
        about, *413*
        and-cheese, 415
        and-spinach, 415
        simplest, 413
    beef
        cheese-stuffed, 688
        my classic, 687
        my classic, in a skillet, 688
        13 mix-and-match ideas for flavoring,
            687
    pork burgers, garlicky, 704
    pork burgers, lemongrass, 705
    rice for, 443
    shrimp, 547
Burritos
    about, 809–811, *812*
    eggs in, 729
    fajitas, 815
    fillings for, 814
Butter
    about, 5, 752
    about, for baking, 827
    -basted, seared scallops with pan sauce,
        577
    blue, strip loin with, 679
    brown, skate or other fish with honey,
        capers and, 562
    buttered cabbage, 274
    celery root, pan-roasted, with rosemary
        butter, 280
    celery root, pan-roasted with hazelnut
        butter, 280
    compound, 78
    cookies, 836
    creaming, *830, 831*
    leeks braised in oil or butter, 302
    nuts, sautéed, 87
    nuts, spiced, 87

one-pot pasta with parmesan and, 478,
        479
    pesto with, 51
    popcorn, salty-sweet, 90
    roast chicken parts with, 615
    roast chicken with garlicky herb, 636
    roast chicken with miso, 636
    salmon roasted in, 549
    sauce, 76
        additions to, 78
        beurre noisette, 79
        black, 78
        brown, 77, 78
    sautéed soft-shell crabs, four ways, 587
Buttermilk
    about, 751
    biscuits, 773
    chicken salad with corn bread, 224
    ice cream, 902
    mashed potatoes, 329
    panna cotta, 888
Butternut squash
    braised and glazed, 334
    curried, in parchment, 341
    gnocchi, 518
    grain-fried, 288
    pasta, pansotti, 510
    puréed, 241
    wheat berries with candied walnuts
        and, 469
Butterscotch
    blondies, 843
    pecan or hazelnut pie, 878
    pudding, 887
    rice pudding, 896

C
Cabbage. *See also* Kimchee/ Kimchi
    about, 274, *275*
    boneless chicken, stir-fried, *604, 605*
    buttered, 274
    buttered, spiked, 274
    chicken stir-fried with, 606
    Chinese noodle soup with, and ginger,
        158
    coleslaw, spicy no-mayo, 203
    corned beef with potatoes and, *685, 686*
    fermented black beans and shrimp, stir-
        fry, 545
    grilled or broiled Cornish hens with
        sherry vinegar with, 659
    mustardy, 274
    sauerkraut
        with cabbage, 275
        and Cornish hens, 658

with juniper berries, 275
with juniper berries and ham, 275
stuffed, 358
white beans with, pasta, and prosciutto, 396
Cacio e pepe, one-pot, 480
Caesar salad, 196
Caesar salad, with chicken, shrimp, or vegetables, 196
Caesar wrap, 809
Cage-free eggs, 719
Cake flour, 763, 766
Cake(s)
about, 844
beating egg whites for, 852, *852*
pans for, 9
sifting dry ingredients for, 844
angel food, 847, *848*
about, 848
chocolate, 848
lemon-scented, 848
cheesecake, 850
with crust, 850
ricotta, 850
chocolate, 853
angel food, 848
cinnamon, 853
devil's food, 853
hazelnut, 854
torte, hazelnut, 854
torte, rich, 853, *855*
coffee, *772*, 773
with cardamom, 773
cinnamon-orange, 773
cupcakes, making, 848
frosting for
about, 854, *857*
caramel–cream cheese frosting, 862
chocolate, *845*, 856
ganache, 858
ganache, 4 more ways, 859
ganache, 7 ways to flavor, 860
lemon or orange, 857
maple, 857
mocha, 856
peanut butter, 857
vanilla, 856
glaze for
about, 854
chocolate, 858
coconut, 858
creamy orange, 858
lemon or lime, 858
mocha, 858
orange, 857

simple syrup, 859
vanilla, 858
pound, 846
marble, 846
polenta, 846
6 variations, 846
yogurt, 846
sauce for
caramel, creamy, *861*
caramel crackle, 860
chocolate, 858
fruit, two ways, 862
lemon curd, *863*
vanilla custard, 864
shortcakes, strawberry or other fruit, 849, *851*
upside-down
apple, 850
berry, 850
pineapple, 849
plum, 850
whipped cream for, 854, *856*
yellow, *845*, 847
California peppers, 41
Calzones
about, *817*
turning pizza into, 824
Candies
about, 904
caramels, 906
chewy caramels, 906
chocolate caramels, 906
peanut brittle, 904, *905*
popcorn brittle, 904
Canned cannellini cassoulet, 405
Canned fish, 567
Cannellini beans
about, 387
cassoulet, canned, 405
salad with balsamic dressing, 214
Capers
about, 5
anchovy-, vinaigrette, 191
deviled eggs with, 93
lemon- sauce, 82
skate or other fish with brown butter, honey, and, 562
Caramel crackle, 860
Caramel fish fillets, 559
Caramelized onion dip, 100
Caramelized onions, 315
Caramelized onions, lentil soup with, 154
Caramelized shallots, 315
Caramelized spiced nuts, 88, *89*
fiery, 88

miso, 88
rosemary, 88
Caramel(s)
candies, 906
chewy, 906
chocolate, 906
sauce
boozy, 860
clear, 860
coffee, 860
–cream cheese frosting, 862
creamy, 860, *861*
Caraway, 28
Carbonnade, 680
Cardamom
about, 28
coffee cake with, 773
Cardoons. *See also* Artichokes
about, *258*, 258–259
creamed, 316
"Carpaccio"-style vegetables, 95
Carrots
about, 275–276, *276*
braised and glazed, 334
braised brisket with sweet potatoes, dried fruit, lots of garlic, and, 686
braised pork with coconut milk and, 700
and burdock, quick-braised, 273
in coleslaw, 205
miso-, sauce with citrus, 67
miso-, sauce with ginger, 67
puréed, 241
quinoa with, 460
roasted, with cumin, 248
rösti, 265
shredded
with chiles and chives, 276, *277*
cumin, with golden raisins, 276
curried, 276
gingered, 276
whole wheat pasta with, 490
Cascabel peppers, 41
Cashews
about, 310
shrimp and, stir-fry, 545
Cassava
about, 348
puréed, 241
Cassoulet
authentic, 407
cannellini beans, canned, 405
Cast iron, seasoning, 7
Cauliflower
about, 278
with chicken, stir-fried, 603

Cauliflower, *continued*
  crunchy, 269
    with almonds, raisins, and saffron, 269, *270*
    with garlic, vinegar, and capers, 269
    with onion and olives, 269, *271*
  fritters, 114
  Manchurian-style, 278
  Manchurian-style, roasted, 279
  millet-, mash, 466
  pasta with, 484
  puréed, 241
  roasted, with raisins and vinaigrette, 248
  steamed, basic, 278
Celery
  about, 279, *279*
  chile shrimp stir-fry with, 545
  fritters, 114
  oven-braised, 294
  -parsley-parmesan salad, 201
  puréed soup, 142
  radish-mint salad, 201
  seeds, 28
  in shaved vegetable salad, 206
  stir-fried, 246
Celery root
  about, 279
  bean purée with, 392
  braised pork with white wine and, 699
  pan-roasted
    and croutons, 280
    with hazelnut butter, 280
    with rosemary butter, 280
Ceramic, about, 9
Cereals
  granola, my new way, 749, *750*
  grits, 748
  oatmeal or other creamy, 748
Ceviche, 132
  poke, 133
  sashimi, 133
Chaat masala, 34
Challah, 793
  about, *794*
  shiny crust for, 793
Chapati, 779
  4 ways to vary dough for, 780
  grilled, 780
Charcoal-grilled porterhouse or t-bone, 669
Charcoal-grilled porterhouse steak, 669
Chard
  about, 280
  gratin, baked chard in béchamel, 256

  with olives and feta, 282
  with oranges and shallots, 280, *281*
Char siu slow-roasted or slow-grilled spareribs, 698
Chayote
  about, 340
  cheesy chayote fritters, 114
Cheese(s). *See also* Cream cheese
  about, 753–756
    all-purpose, 754
    all-purpose, parmesan as, 755
    graters for, 10
  appenzeller ("Swiss"), 755
  bean and, empanadas, 126
  bean dip, 104
  blue
    about, 754
    dressing, 59
  burgers, bean-and, 415
  chayote fritters, 114
  cheddar, about, 755
  cheesecake, 850
    with crust, 850
    ricotta, 850
  and chive muffins, 773
  chorizo and, empanadas, 127
  comté, 755
  cookies, shortbread, 838
  corn chowder, 147
  cottage
    about, 752
    fresh, 758
  creamed corn with, 284
  eggs
    frittata, fresh tomato and, 731
    poached, with cheese, 726
    quiche, 733
    scrambled, 724
    soufflé, 737
  18 recipes with, 754
  enchiladas, 759
  enchiladas with green sauce, 759
  feta
    about, 754
    chard with olives and, 282
    corn salad with, and mint, 201
    deviled eggs with, 93
    kale or collards, flash-cooked with, 300
    marinated, 97
  5 marinade combinations for, 97
  fondue, 118, *119*
  fondue, flavor added to, 118–120
  fresh
    about, 756, *758*
    brined, 758

    cottage, 758
    the easy way, 756
    the easy way, *757*
    4 ways to flavor, 758
    ricotta, shortcut, 758
  goat
    anchovy spread, 101
    flavorful cream cheese spread, 100
    fresh soft, about, 755
    herbed, 100, *101*
    honied, 100
    marinated, 97
    rosemary-honey, 100
    sandwich, warm, with toasted nuts, 810
    -stuffed figs, 100
  gorgonzola, pasta with fried sage and, 491
  graviera, 756
  grits, 749
  halloumi, 755
  kasseri, 756
  kefalotyri, 756
  mascarpone, farfalle with fried basil and, 492
  Mexican salsa, 57
  millet-cauliflower mash, 467
  Monterey Jack, 755
  mornay sauce, 79
  mozzarella
    fresh, pizza, with tomato sauce and, 821
    marinated, 96
    open-face ratatouille sandwich with melted, 810
    pizza, with tomato sauce, and sausage or pepperoni, 821
    pizza, with tomato sauce and, 819
    salad, with tomato and basil, 199
  paneer
    about, 755
    marinated, 97
  parmesan
    about, 5
    as all-purpose, 755
    artichoke dip, 109
    bean purée with, 392
    broiled or grilled boneless chicken with, 599
    bruschetta or crostini with, 96
    celery-parsley salad, 201
    chicken, not-quite, 612
    cold escarole salad with garlic, 207
    crackers, 779
    deviled eggs, 93

-herb, oven "fried" chicken, 616
one-pot pasta with butter and, 478,
    479
popcorn, 90
ranch dressing, 71
rice pilaf, 437
vinaigrette, 190
white pizza with prosciutto and, 819,
    820
quesadillas, 814
queso de freír, 756
raclette, 755
ravioli, 513
ravioli, mushroom-, 513
ricotta
    about, 754
    baked ziti with, 499
    cheesecake, 850
    marinated ricotta salata, 97
    one-pot pasta with butter and, 478
    ravioli, and herb, 513
    ravioli, spinach-, 512
    rice pudding, 896
    shortcut, fresh, 758
sandwiches
    broiled, 806
    grilled, 804
    grilled, and onions, 805
spinach-triangles, 122, *122*
-stuffed burgers, 688
stuffed tomatoes with, 359
three, risotto with, 441
toast
    fresh, *717*
    Welsh rarebit, *717*
tortellini, 515
vegetable gratins, 256
yogurt, 753
Cherimoyas, 370
Cherries
    about, 370
    chipotle-, salsa, 58
    jubilee, 372
    in port, sweet or savory, 372
    stewed, sweet and savory, 370, *371*
    stewed, sweet or savory, 370
Cherry(ies)
    -chocolate sorbet, 903
    clafoutis, 893
    pie, 875
    shortcakes, 849, *851*
Chervil, 47
Chestnut(s)
    about, 282, *282*
    boiled, 282

bread stuffing with, 651
grilled or roasted, 283
pasta, pansotti, 512
puréed, 241
wild rice with, 468
Chewy caramels, 906
Chicken. *See also* Boneless chicken,
    grilled or broiled; Chicken, whole;
    Chicken parts
about, 592–594, *597*
    boneless (skinless), 594–596
    butchering, *614*
    customizing recipes for, 595
    fat, rendering, 622
    fresh vs. frozen, 593
    quartering, *631*
    safety and doneness, 593–594
    size and age, 593
    types of, 592–593
curry fried rice, 445
enchiladas, 759
fried
    many more ways, 628
    Marknuggets, 630
    Marknuggets, cornmeal, 631
    Marknuggets, super-crunchy
        pan-fried, 631
    my new favorite, 628, *629*
    10 sauces for, 630
ground, 653
jambalaya, 439
-n-biscuit pie, 640
one-pot pasta with fennel and,
    480
paella, 435, 436
paella, and chorizo, 436
parmigiana, 609
-pesto panino, 805
pot pie, 637, *639*
    phyllo-topped, 640
pot pie, faster, 638
pounding, 598
rabbit, substituted for, 711
roasted, about, *631*, *632*
salads
    buttermilk, with corn bread, 224
    Caesar, 197
    curried, 224
    and daikon, 224
    grilled, with lemongrass, 225
    with olive oil and fresh herbs, 221,
        222
    traditional, 223
sandwiches
    fried, with ranch dressing, 808

grilled breast, with roasted garlic and
    mustard, 810
satay, 130, *131*
split, *640*, 641
split chicken, grilled or broiled, 642
stewed chickpeas with seared, 398
with stir-fried vegetables, 246
stock, quickest, 176
tagine, chickpea and, 400
tofu braised with, and eggplant, 423
whole wheat pasta with browned, 490
wings, 127, *128*
    grilled, 129
    honey mustard, 129
    lemon-garlic, 129
    sauces for, 130
    smoky chile lime, 129
    special case of, 618
    spicy peanut, 129
Chicken, whole
about, 631, *633*, 640
under a brick, 641
brining, 633
methods other than roasting, 637
roasted
    about, *632*
    about, carving, *632*
    about, quartering, *631*
    with cumin, honey, and orange, 635
    flavor under skin for, 636
    with garlicky herb butter, 636
    simplest, *632*, *633*
    simplest, varying, *634*, 635
    with soy sauce, 635
    white cut, 637
smoky, 640
split, grilled or broiled, 642
Chicken parts
about, 613
braised, 622
    arroz con pollo, 625
    biryani, 626
    coq au vin, 624
    and lentils, 622, *623*
breasts
    poached, 611
    poached, 8 more additions to liquid
        for, 612
    poached, 5 ways, 612
    poached, with lemon sauce, 611
fried, about, 627
grilled or broiled
    Japanese style, 618
    seasoning ideas, 621
    simply, 9 ways, 620

Chicken parts, *continued*
    simply grilled, *619*
    Thai style, 621
    Vietnamese style, 622
  roasted, 613
    adobo, 616
    with olive oil or butter, 615
    with olive oil or butter, unleashed, 615
    oven "fried," 616
    oven "fried," parmesan-herb, 616
    oven "fried," sesame, 616
  thighs
    broiled or grilled, 598
    poached, 611
    poached, 8 more additions to liquid for, 612
    poached, 5 ways, 612
    poached, with lemon sauce, 611
Chicken soup
  and barley, 155
  with butter dumplings, 166
  chipotle, 165
  many ways, 164
  with matzo balls, 166
  and noodles in broth, 158
  with passatelli, 166
  with rice, Chinese style, 165
  with rice, Mexican style, 165
  stock, quickest, 176
  Thai style, 165, *167*
  tortilla, 165, *167*
  with vegetables, 165
Chickpea(s)
  about, 387
  chicken and, 624
  chili with lamb, 406
  flatbread, 97
  greens and pasta combos, 397
  pasta and, in broth, 158
  pasta with garlic, oil, and, 477
  salad with chutney, 214
  stewed, with seared chicken, 398
  warm salad, with arugula, 213
Chicory, about, 192, 292
Chile(s)
  about, 39–40
  braised beef with limes and, 680
  chicken stir-fried with orange and, 606
  chicken wings, smoky, 129
  Chilean salsa, 57
  coffee-, braised short ribs, 683
  corn and noodle salad with, 201
  de arbol, 41
  fried rice with, 445

  -garlic salsa, super-hot, 73
  green chile salsa, 56
  -lime glaze, broiled jícama with, 299
  macaroni and cheese with, 501
  mayonnaise, 70
  paste, 40
    and black bean, 45
    chile-garlic, 45
    chipotle, 45
    -garlic paste, 45
    harissa, 45
    Indian-style, 45
    Mexican-style, 45
    nine ways, 40
    7 uses for, 45
    Thai-style, 45
    Vietnamese-style, 45
  poblano, pan-roasted corn with, 286
  rellenos, 319, *319*
    with corn and pumpkin seeds, 320
    grilled, 320
    with meat or poultry stuffing, 320
  sautéed cooked grains with, 456
  sautéed eggplant with basil and, 290
  -scallion sauce, 64
  shredded carrots with, and chives, 276, 277
  shrimp stir-fry, with celery, 545
  squid with, and greens, 588
  tahini sauce, 59
  Thai, sauce, 66
  Thai-style chicken stir-fried with basil and, 606
Chili
  beef, fast, 405
  beef, slow-simmered, 403, *404*
  5 more, slow or fast, 406
Chili powder
  about, 32
  fish sandwich with, -lime mayo, 808
Chimichurri, 52
Chinese black vinegar, 187
Chinese cabbage. *See* Bok choy
Chinese mustard, 38
Chinese style
  chicken soup with rice, 165
  egg noodles, about, 520
  fast "roast" duck, 654
  lightning-quick fish soup, 161
  marinated celery and carrots, 94, 95
  noodle soup with cabbage and ginger, 158
  restaurant-style greens, 268
  restaurant-style greens, with thickened soy sauce, 268

  vegetables, 95
  wheat noodles, about, 520
Chipotle pepper(s)
  about, 42
  barbecue sauce, 75
  black beans orange-glazed with, 396
  black beans purée with, 392
  -cherry salsa, 58
  chicken soup, 165
  paste, 45
  pozole, 469, *470*, 471, 481
    with pumpkin seeds, 471
    10 garnishes for, 481
Chive(s)
  about, 47
  and cheese muffins, 773
  shredded carrots with chiles and, 276, *277*
  sour cream- sauce, halibut steaks with, 566
Chocolate
  black bread with, 797
  bread pudding, 895
  cake glaze, 858
  cakes, 853
    angel food, 848
    cinnamon, 853
    devil's food, 853
    torte, rich, 853, *855*
  caramels, 906
  cocoa swirl bread, 792
  cookies
    chocolate-, chunk, 831
    chunk, 831, *833*
    sugar, 836
    white, -pistachio, 831
  custard, 890
  doughnuts, -glazed cake, 738, 746, *747*
  fresh berry tart with, 881
  frosting, *845*, 856
  fruit smoothie, not-too-sweet, 716
  ice cream, 902
  mocha frosting, 856
  mocha glaze, 858
  mousse, 891
  pie, cream, 877
  pie, pecan or walnut, 878
  pudding, 887
  sauce, 858
  sorbet, 903
  tart crust, 870
Chocolate custard, 890
Chocolate-glazed cake doughnuts, 746, *747*

Chopped salad, 197
 with coconut, 197
 with peanut dressing, 197
 Southwest style, 197
 12 other ingredients for, 197
Chopping, about, 13, *14*
Chorizo
 and cheese empanadas, 127
 chicken paella with, 436
 smoked, chickpeas in, 407
Chowder
 clam chowder, no-holds-barred, 162
 clam or fish, Manhattan, 164
 corn, 145
  cheesy, 147
  roasted, 147
Chuck (beef), about, 665
Chutney
 chickpea salad with, 214
 cilantro-mint, 62
 cilantro-mint, creamy, 62
 coconut, 61
 dried fruit and nut, 62, *63*
 hot or mild pepper, 62
 raw onion, 61
 real garlicky nut, 64
Cider vinegar, 187
Cilantro
 about, 47
 chutney, -mint, 62
 edamame with fresh tomatoes and
  cilantro, 398, *399*
 garlic shrimp with tomatoes and, 543
 purée, 52
 rice pilaf with, *432–433*
 sauce, 52
Cinnamon
 about, 29
 chocolate cake, 853
 cinnamon buns, 792
 lamb stew with lemon and, 710
 -orange coffee cake, 773
 pears poached with, 381
 -rice pudding, 896
Citrus
 about, *378*
 broiled or grilled, 361, *362*
 with chicken, grilled or broiled, 620
 grapefruit
  about, 374
  rice salad with, and pistachios, 217
  sorbet, 903
 key lime pie, 878
 lemon
  about, 5, 375

cake glaze, 858
-caper sauce, 82
with chicken and herbs, grilled or
 broiled, 620
collard greens, flash-cooked with,
 300
cookies, shortbread, 838
cookies, squares, *842, 843*
curd, 862, *863*
curd, fresh blueberry tart, 881
custard, 890
frosting, 857
-garlic wings, 130
lamb stew with cinnamon and, 710
lentil soup with, and dill, 154
meringue pie, 877
one-pot pasta with zucchini and, 480
preserved, 375
roasted artichoke hearts with ham,
 wine, and lemon, 261
sautéed fish with pan sauce, 537
-scented angel food cake, 848
shortcut mousse, 864
sorbet, 903
tuna salad with olive oil and, 804
vinaigrette, 190
lime
 about, 5, 375
 braised beef with chiles and, 680
 chicken wings, smoky, 129
 chile-, glaze, broiled jícama with, 299
 coconut-, bars, 844
 fish sandwich with chili-, mayo, 808
 -garlic-coconut soup, 137
 key lime pie, 878
 papaya-, sorbet, 903
 sorbet, 903
 sorbet, -basil, 903
 vinaigrette, 190
lime leaves, 48
mandarins, 378
marinated olives with, 91
miso-, dipping sauce, 67
miso-carrot sauce with, 67
orange
 boneless chicken in packages with,
  612
 cake glaze, 857
 cake glaze, creamy, 858
 chard with, and shallots, *281*
 chicken stir-fried with chiles and,
  606
 -cinnamon coffee cake, 773
 fennel salad with, *204, 205*
 fresh pasta, 508

frosting, 857
-glazed black beans, 395
juice, braised endive with, 292
juice, quail roasted with honey,
 cumin, and, 660
orange-cassis sorbet, 903
roast chicken with cumin, honey,
 and, 635
roast leg of lamb with thyme and, 710
salads with, 205
-scented quinoa with shallots, 460
sorbet, 903
vanilla-, cream pie, 877
-pickled ginger, 296
salsa, 57
tangerines, about, 378
tangerine sorbet, 903
Clams
 about, 574–575
 about, shucking, 574
 baked, with wasabi bread crumbs, 580
 with corn, creamed, 284
 grilled seafood, 536
 linguine with, 492
  with mussels, 492
  and pesto, 492
  red clam sauce, 492
  sort-of-Sichuan noodles with, 492,
   493
 Manhattan chowder, 164
 pan-roasted, 537
 steamed, 579
 steamed, 6 ways to vary, 581
 white pizza with, 819
Classic creamy dip
 beet and horseradish, 100
 caramelized, 100
 five ways, 99
 smoked salmon or trout, 100
 watercress or arugula, 100
Classic roast turkey with gravy, 647
Clear caramel sauce, 860
Cloves, 29
Cobblers
 about, 864–866
 blueberry, 883
Cocoa powder, 828
Cocoa swirl bread, 792
Coconut
 about, 372
 baked, rice and kidney beans, 412
 cake, 847
 cake glaze, 858
 chickpeas in broth, 407
 chopped salad with, 197

Coconut, *continued*
  chutney, 61
  coconut milk, 372
  cream pie, 875
  curried, eggplant with potatoes,
    291
  curry, shrimp stir-fry with, 545
  -curry vinaigrette, 191
  -fried plantains, 288
  fruit smoothie, 716
  ice cream, 902
  -lime bars, 844
  lime-garlic-, soup, 137
  macaroons, 839
  milk, 372, *373*
    about, 5
    braised pork with carrots and,
      700
  oil, 185
  rice, 430
  rice pudding, 896
  tahini sauce, 59
  tembleque, 888
  toasting, 372
Coffee
  caramel sauce, 860
  -chile braised short ribs, 683
  espresso sorbet or ice milk, 903
  grinders for, 12
  ice cream, 902
  mocha frosting, 856
  mocha glaze, 858
Coffee cake, *772, 773*
  with cardamom, 773
  cinnamon-orange, 773
Colanders, about, 10
Cold cooked and dressed greens, 206
Cold mustard sauce, 70
Collard greens
  about, 299–300, *300*
  flash-cooked
    with fermented black beans, 300
    with feta and tomato, 300
    with lemon juice, 300
  with peanut sauce, 301
  with pot liquor, 307
  with tahini, 301
  with yogurt, 301
Comté cheese, 755
Condiments. *See also* Ketchup; Mustard;
  Sauce(s)
  about, 5, 24–25
  flavored oils, 53–55
  fresh (uncooked) sauces, 55–67
  mayonnaise, 67–71

Cookies. *See also* Bars
  about, 829–830
  biscotti
    vanilla, 838
  chocolate chunk, 831, *833*
  coconut macaroons, 839
  gingersnaps, *832–833*, 837
  nutty biscotti, *832–833*
  oatmeal-something, *832*, 834
  peanut or other nut butter, 836
  sheets for, 9
  shortbread, 837
  6 tips for improvising, 835
  sugar, 834
  10 that kids can help make, 834
Cooking basics, 2–22
  appliances and electric gadgets, 12
  cutting techniques, 13–15, *14–16*
  equipment, 3–6
  food safety, 3
  heat, importance of and cooking
    techniques, 16–22, *18–20*
  ingredients, organic, 2
  ingredients, stocking kitchen with, 4–5
  ingredients to buy, 2
  knives, *6*, 6–7, *14*
  measuring techniques, 15, *17*
  ovenware, 12–13
  pots and pans, 7, *8–9*
  repurposing leftovers, 22
  seasoning cast iron, 7
  techniques for individual foods. *See*
    individual types of foods
  tools, 10–11
Copper, about, 9
Coq au vin, 624
Coriander
  about, 29
  roast leg of lamb with garlic and, 710
Coring, about, 15
Corn
  about, 283, *283*
  chile rellenos with, and pumpkin seeds,
    320
  chowder, 145
    cheesy, 147
    roasted, 147
  cornstarch, about, 4
  creamed, 284, *285*
    with cheese, 284
    with clams or seafood, 284
    with onion, 284
  crunchy, guacamole, 105
  fritters, 114
  grain dishes

    grits gratin with arugula and garlic,
      462, *465*
    hominy, about, 455
    hominy, beans with tomatillos and,
      397
    hominy, creamed, 469
    hominy, creamed, and kale, 469
    polenta, 461
    polenta, 14 dishes to serve on top
      of, 461
    pozole, chipotle, 469, *470*
    pozole, chipotle, 10 garnishes for, 481
    tamales, 461
    tamales, about, *463*
    tamales, 10 dishes for tamale fillings,
      462
  grilled, 252
  grits
    breakfast, 748
    breakfast, cheesy, 749
    breakfast, scrapple, 749
    gratin with arugula and garlic, 462,
      465
  muffins, 770
  pan-roasted
    with cherry tomatoes, 286
    with poblano chiles, 286
    with stewed tomatoes, 286
  pasta with zucchini, tomatoes, and, 488
  puréed, 241
  quick-pickled coins, with Sichuan
    peppercorns, 229
  roasted, quinoa with, 458
  salad, with avocado, 201
  salsa, 56
  sort-of-steamed, on the cob, 283
  10 flavorings for, 284
Corn bread, 769
  bacon, 770
  corny, 770
  lighter, richer, 770
  salad, 221
  stuffing with oysters and sausage, 644,
    651
Corned beef with cabbage and potatoes,
  685, 686
Cornish hens
  about, 658
  grilled or broiled, with sherry vinegar,
    658
  and sauerkraut, 658
Cornmeal
  about, 4, 453, 763–764
  chicken, Marknuggets, 631
  polenta pound cake, 846

Corn syrup, 827
Cottage cheese
  about, 752
  fresh, 758
Couscous, about, 452
Crab(s)
  about, 580–582, *583*
  about, cleaning soft-shell, 582
  boiled or steamed, 584
  cakes, bare-bones, 585
  deviled eggs with, 93
  9 things to serve with, 585
  one-pot pasta with, 480
  soft-shell, broiled, 534
  soft-shell, sautéed, four ways, 587
Cracked wheat, 454
Cracked wheat with mustard, 466
Cracker(s), 777, *778*
  cream, 779
  crumb crust, baked beans with, 401
  parmesan, 779
Cranberry beans
  about, 387
  greens and pasta combos, 397
Cranberry(ies)
  about, 374
  muffins, 773
  relish, 644
Crawfish boil, Louisiana style, 545
Cream
  about, 751
  crackers, 779
Cream cheese
  about, 755
  frosting, caramel–, 862
  swirl brownies, 841
Creamed corn, 284, *285*
Creamed onions, 316
Creamed soups
  about, 142
  mushroom, 140
  mushroom, robust, 140
Creamed vegetables
  cardoons, 316
  onions, 316
  scallions, whole, 316
  spinach, 316
Cream pie(s)
  banana, 877
  chocolate, 877
  coconut, 875
  -topped, 877
  vanilla, 875
  vanilla-orange, 877
Creamy bean dip, 104

Creamy caramel sauce, 860
Creamy vinaigrette, 190
Crème brûlée, 890
Crème fraîche, 752
Crêpes
  buckwheat
    sweet or savory, 743
  5 fillings for, savory, 746
Crisp-cooked Jerusalem artichokes, 298
Crisp pan-fried potatoes, 331
Crisps
  about, 864–866
  apple, 884
Crisp sautéed leeks, 303
Crisp sesame fish fillets, 568
Crisp vegetable pancakes, Korean style, 355
Crostini, 95
  with parmesan, 96
  with tomatoes and basil, 96
  toppings for, 96
Croutons
  celery root and, pan-roasted, 280
  cubed, 801, *802*
  dry-baked, 803
  herbed, 803
  highly seasoned, 803
  my kind of, 801
  olives sautéed with, 314
  tofu, 419
Crudités, 102
Crunchier pizza dough, 818
Crunchy broccoli or cauliflower, 269
Crunchy corn guacamole, 105
Crustless quiche, about, 734
Cuban sandwich, 805
Cubed croutons, 801, *802*
Cucumber(s)
  about, 286–287, *287*
  avocado-, salsa, 58
  celery-mint salad, 201
  farro salad with, 218
  raita, 59, *60*
  in salads, 205
  Thai style salsa, 58
Cumin
  about, 29
  in carrot slaw, 205
  quail roasted with honey, orange juice, and, 660
  roast chicken with honey, orange, and, 635
Cupcakes, 848
Cups, ceramic, 9

Currants
  about, 374
  pasta with radicchio, pine-nuts, and, 495
  rice pilaf with, 436
  spinach with, and nuts, 339
Curried coconut eggplant with potatoes, 291
Curried deviled eggs, 93
Curried fish, 560, *561*
Curried fish, Thai-style or green, 560
Curry dishes
  barbecue sauce, 75
  broiled or grilled boneless chicken, 599
  broth, steamed clams or mussels with, 581
  chicken
    fried rice, 445
    grilled, 620
    poached, 612
  coconut, shrimp stir-fry with, 545
  coconut-, vinaigrette, 191
  lamb, 711
  red curry paste, about, 46
  Thai-style chicken, baked, 602
  vinaigrette, *189*
  winter squash, 350, *351*
Curry leaf, about, 47
Curry powder, 32, *33*
Custard(s,) dessert
  about, 886, 887
  baked, 888
  chocolate, 890
  crème brûlée, 890
  5 more ideas for, 890
  flan, 890
  lemon, 890
  panna cotta, 888, *889*
    almond, 888
    buttermilk, 888
  sauce, vanilla, 864
  tembleque, 888
Custards, silly baked, 735
Cutting boards, about, 10
Cutting techniques, 13–15, *14–16*

D

Dairy. *See also* Cheese
  about, 751–752
  yogurt, 752
  yogurt pound cake, 846
Dal
  about, 409
  with daikon, 410

Dal, *continued*
  with potatoes or other root vegetables, 410
  simplest, 409
Dandelion greens, about, 192, 307
Dark chocolate, 828
Dashi, 179
  dipping sauce, 76
  5 ways to use, 180
  7 quick additions to, 76
Dates, about, 374
Deep-dish apple pie with streusel topping, 872
Deep-dish pizza, Chicago style, 824
Deep-fried fish with twice-fried ginger, garlic, or shallots, 562
Deep-fried seafood, 539
  spiced or herbed, 541
  with thicker crust, 541
Deep-frying, about, 22
Deglazing, for sauces, 80
Denver omelet, 730
Desserts, 825–906. *See also* Brownies; Cake(s); Cookies; Custard(s), desserts; Frozen desserts; Pie(s); Tart(s)
  baklava, 884
  bars
    apricot-almond, 843
    coconut-lime, 844
    jam, 844
    my magic, 843
    10 that kids can help make, 834
  butter and fats, about, 827
  candies
    about, 904
    caramels, 906
    chewy caramels, 906
    chocolate caramels, 906
    peanut brittle, 904, *905*
    popcorn brittle, 904
  chocolate, about, 828–829
  cobblers
    about, 864–866
    blueberry, 883
  crisps
    about, 864–866
    apple, 884
  infusing liquids with flavor, 900
  sweeteners, about, 826–827
Deviled eggs, 91, *92*
  with anchovies and capers, 93
  curried deviled eggs, 93
  with feta, 93
  herb-stuffed eggs, 93

jalapeño deviled eggs, 93
miso deviled eggs, 93
parmesan deviled eggs, 93
pesto deviled eggs, 93
with shrimp, lobster, or crab, 93
smoky deviled eggs, 93
variations, *92, 93*
Devil's food cake, 853
Dijon-style mustard, 38
Dill
  about, 47
  green beans with yogurt and, 298
  lentil soup with lemon and, 154
  pesto, 51
  purée, 52
  sauce, with cold poached salmon or trout, 551, *551*
  seeds, 29
Dips and spreads
  about, 99
  artichoke dip, 107, *108*
    parmesan, 108
  bean dip, 103
    bean and salsa, 104
    cheesy, 104
    creamy, 104
    variations, 104
  classic creamy dip, 99
    beet and horseradish, 100
    caramelized, 100
    smoked salmon or trout, 100
    watercress or arugula, 100
  for crudités, 102
  eggplant dip, grilled or roasted, 105, *105*
  goat cheese
    anchovy spread, 101
    flavorful cream cheese spread, 100
    herbed, 100, *101*
    honied, 100
    rosemary-honey, 100
    -stuffed figs, 100
  guacamole, 105
    avocado-crab spread or dip, 105
    crunchy corn, 105
    with fruit, 105
    "guacasalsa," 105
    un-avocado guacamole, 105
  hummus, 103
    herbed, 103
    miso, 103
    spicy, 103
  7 ways to use, 107
  tapenade, 109
  ways to use, 107
Double boilers, about, 8

Dried apricot clafoutis, 893, *894*
Dried chiles, 39–40
Dried fruit(s)
  about, 5, 369
  braised brisket with sweet potatoes, carrots, lots of garlic, and, 686
  and nut chutney, 62, *63*
  oven-drying, 360
  pheasant stewed with, 662
  vinaigrette, 191
  wild rice with, 468
Dried tomato tapenade, 109
Drizzle sauce, five-minute, 81
Drop biscuits, 775
Dry-pan eggplant, 287
Dry-roasted nuts, 88
Duck
  about, 653
  confit, 655, *656*
  crisp-braised legs with aromatic vegetables, 657
  fast "roast," Chinese style, 654
  roast, 654
  salad with dried cherries, 224
  stock, 176
Dumplings, steamed, 126
Durum wheat flour, in fresh pasta, 505
Dutch apple pie, 872

E
Edamame
  about, 398
  in bean dip, 104
  edamame in their shells, 90
    shell beans, edamame-style, 90
    spicy stir-fried, 90
  flavor boosters for, 91
  with fresh tomatoes and cilantro, 398, *399*
Egg drop soup, 138
Eggless pasta, fresh, 508
Eggplant
  about, 287
  baba ghanoush, 107
  breaded and fried, 288, *289*
  breaded and fried, variations, 290
  curried, Southeast Asian style, 292
  curried, with potatoes, 291
  dip, grilled or roasted, 105, 106
  dry-pan, 287
  fried, pasta with, 486, *487*
  fritters, 114
  grilled, 252
  grilled or roasted eggplant dip, 105, *105*
  lamb stew with, 711

parmigiana, 609
puréed, 241
ratatouille, open-face sandwich with melted mozzarella, 810
ratatouille, oven-baked, 352, *353*
roasted, pasta with, 486
sautéed
   additions for, 291
   with basil, 290
   with basil and chiles, 290
   with greens, 290
   with walnuts, 290
stewed chickpeas with, 400
stuffed, 358
tofu braised with, 422, *423*
Egg rolls. *See* Fried wontons or egg rolls
Egg(s). *See also* Custards, dessert
about, 5
beating whites of, 852, *852*
custard
   about, 733
   silky baked, 735
deviled, 91, *92*
   with anchovies and capers, 93
   curried deviled eggs, 93
   with feta, 93
   herb-stuffed eggs, 93
   jalapeño deviled eggs, 93
   miso deviled eggs, 93
   parmesan deviled eggs, 93
   pesto deviled eggs, 93
   with shrimp, lobster, or crab, 93
   smoky deviled eggs, 93
   variations, *92*, 93
essential recipes
   baked, 726
   Benedict, mix-and-match, 728
   fried, 721
   hard-boiled, my usual way, 721
   huevos rancheros, 729
   medium-boiled, 721
   in a nest, *722*
   over-easy, 723
   poached, 725
   poached, in creamed something, 728
   poached in tomato sauce, 726, *727*
   scrambled, best, 724
   scrambled, everyday, 723
   soft-boiled, 721
fresh pasta, 505, *506*
fried rice with fried, 445
frittatas
   about, 730
   with crumbled sausage, 732

fresh tomato and cheese, 731
leftover pasta, noodle, grains, or rice, 732
12 additions to, 732
quiche
   about, 733
   cheese, 733
   crustless, 734
   and custard, ingredients to use in, 735
   onion, 734
   onion, with bacon, 735
runny egg yolks and safety, 725
salad with mayo, 804
sandwiches, burritos, tacos with, 729
soufflé
   about, 733, *737*
   cheese, 735, *736*
   cheese, individual, 737
   warm spicy greens with bacon and, *198*, *199*
Einkorn, 454
Electric gadgets, about, 12
Electric mixers, about, 12
Emmental ("Swiss") cheese, 755
Emulsification, demystifying, 188
Enchiladas
   cheese, 759
   cheese with green sauce, 759
   chicken, 759
Endive
   about, 192, 292
   braised, with prosciutto, 292
   salad with nut oil vinaigrette, 194
Enriching, of sauces, 80
Equipment, about, 3–6
Escabeche
   chicken, 598
   fish, 564
Escarole
   about, 292
   braised, with prosciutto, 292
   cold, and garlic, parmesan salad, 207
Espresso, sorbet or ice milk, 903
Everyday pancakes, 740, *741*
Everyday sandwich bread, *789*, 790
Everyday scrambled eggs, 723
Everyday waffles, 742

F

Fajitas burritos, 815
Falafel, *414*, 415
Family-style appetizers, serving, 86
Farfalle, whole wheat, with roasted sweet potatoes, 488, *489*

Farfalle, with mascarpone and fried basil, 492
Farro
   about, 454
   with leeks, cherry tomatoes, and basil, 467
   salad with cucumber and yogurt-dill dressing, 218
Fast "roast" duck, Chinese style, 654
Fat, rendering, 622
Fattoush, *220*, 221
Fava bean(s)
   about, 387
   in bean dip, 104
   greens and pasta combos, 397
   and mint salad with pecorino, 215, *216*
   one-pot pasta with, 480
Fennel
   about, 292, *293*
   baked in orange juice, 293
   baked in stock, 293
   fish steamed over, *556*, 558
   one-pot pasta with chicken and, 480
   with onions and vinegar, 294
   pork, braised with tomatoes and, 700
   salad, with orange, *204*, 205
   seeds, 29
   spicy chicken, baked, 602
   steamed, in parchment, 341
Fenugreek, 29
Feta cheese
   about, 754
   chard with olives and, 282
   corn salad with, and mint, 201
   deviled eggs with, 93
   kale or collards, flash-cooked with, 300
   marinated, 97
Fettucine alfredo, one-pot, 480
Fiery caramelized nuts, 88
50 percent whole wheat sandwich bread, 790
Figs
   about, 374
   broiled or grilled, 361, *362*
Filet of beef, about, 676
Fine herbs, scrambled eggs with, 724
Finger foods, ideas for, 96. *See also* Appetizers and snacks
Fish
   about
      canned, 567
      11 dishes to serve on greens, 227
      simply cooked, seasoning, 539
   adding to vegetable dishes, 257
   anchovies

Fish, *continued*
    about, 5
    broccoli raab with, 272
    -caper vinaigrette, 191
    deviled eggs with, 93
    mayonnaise, 70
    roast leg of lamb with, 710
    spread, 103
    tahini sauce, 59
in appetizers and snacks, 130
cakes, bare-bones, 587
chowder, 162
lightning-quick soup, 161, *163*
monkfish, about, 559
salads, Niçoise, 225
salmon
    about, 547–548, *548, 549*
    cold poached, with dill sauce, *550,*
        551
    gravlax, 551
    pan-cooked, 548
    pan-cooked, 10 sauces for, 549
    roasted in butter, 549
sandwiches, with chili-lime mayo, 808
sashimi, 133
sauce, about, 5
sauce, vinaigrette, *189,* 191
sautéed, with lemony pan sauce, 537
soup, lightning-quick, 161, *163*
stock, 178
tacos
    broiled, 812
    four ways, 811, *813*
    fried, 812
    grilled, 812, *813*
thick fillets and steaks
    about, 552–553, *553, 554*
    aromatic poached, 565
    baked in foil, 554
    broiled, 534
    caramel fillets, 559
    curried, 560
    deep-fried, with twice-fried ginger,
        garlic, or shallots, 562
    escabeche, 564
    fritters, 564
    halibut, with creamy saffron sauce,
        566
    kebabs, 566
    mackerel simmered in soy sauce,
        563
    oven-"fried" fillets, 555
    pan-roasted tuna or other, 567
    skate or other fish with brown butter,
        honey, and capers, 562

steamed over autumn vegetables,
    556, 558
steamed over fennel, *556,* 558
steamed over something, variations,
    558
steamed over summer vegetables,
    555, *556,* 558
thick fillets or steaks
    sautéed, with lemony pan sauce,
        538
thin fillets
    about, 567
    broiled, *533*
    crisp sesame, 568
    sardines on the grill, 573
    10 other recipes for, 569
tilapia, about, 568
trout
    about, 547–548, *548, 549*
    cold poached, with dill sauce, 551
    dip, smokes, 100
    whole, with bacon and red onions,
        pan-fried, *572, 573*
whole, 569
    about, 571
    broiled, 534
    grilled, 536
    poached, 565
    quick-braised, in black bean sauce,
        570
    roasted, 537
    trout with bacon and red onions,
        pan-fried, *572, 573*
Five-minute drizzle sauce, 81
    miso five-minute, 81
    sesame-soy five-minute, 81
Five-spice pot roast, 684
Five-spice powder, 35
Flageolets, 387
Flageolets, greens and pasta combos,
    397
Flaky piecrust, *865, 867*
Flan, 890
Flank (beef), about, 667
Flank steak, grilled or broiled, 670
Flash-cooked kale or collards with lemon
    juice, 300
Flatbreads. *See also* Tortillas
    about, 777, *779*
    chapati, 779
    crackers, 777, *778*
    cream, 779
    parmesan, 779
    flour tortillas, 781
    paratha, 780

Flavored oil(s), 53
    about, 52–53
    11 combinations, 53
Flavorful cream cheese spread, 100
Flaxseed
    about, 310
Flourless peanut or other nut butter
    cookies, 836
Flour(s)
    about, 4
    baking
        about, 763
        gluten, magic of, 788
        gluten-free, 766
        non-wheat, 763–764
        nut, 765
        oat, 765
        pastry, 763, 766
        rice, 764–765
        self-rising, 763
        sifting, 844
        spelt, 765
        white, 762–763
    fresh pasta, 505
    gluten-free pizza dough, 818
    tortillas, 781
Focaccia
    rosemary, 822
    other ingredients for topping,
        824
Foil-wrapped packages
    beet baked in, 264
    chicken in, with orange, 612
    fish baked in, 554
Fontina, 755
Food processors, about, 12
Food safety, about, 3
Forty-five-minute roast turkey, 646
Free farmed certified eggs, 719
Freekeh, 454
Free range chicken, 593
Free-range eggs, 719
French fries, 333
French style
    bread, rustic, 787
    green sauce, 70
    lightning-quick fish soup, 161
    rolls, about, 788
    steamed clams or mussels, 581
French toast, 738
    caramelized, 738
    with raw fruit sauce, 739
    6 toppings for, 740
Fresh berry tart with vanilla pudding
    filling, *880, 881*

Fresh bread crumbs, 801
  fried, 801
  nutty, 801
  toasted, 801
Fresh cheese
  about, *758*
  brined, 758
  cottage, 758
  the easy way, 756, *757*
  4 ways to flavor, 758
  ricotta, shortcut, 758
  toast, *717*
Fresh (uncooked) sauces
  tomato or fruit, *54*, 55
  tomato or fruit, puréed, *54*, 55
Fresno peppers, 42
Fried bread crumbs, 801
Fried chicken sandwich with ranch
    dressing, 808
Fried eggs
  about, 721
  5 simple ideas for, 723
Fried fish tacos, 812
Fried okra, 288
Fried onion rings, streamlined, 288
Fried plantains, 323, *324*
Fried tortilla chips, 110
  baked tortilla chips, 110
  fried or baked pita chips, 110
  sprinkles for, 110
Fried vegetables, 255–257
  battered and, 255
  breading, variations, 290
  7 dipping sauces for, 257
Fried wontons or egg rolls, 115
  sealing and shaping, *115–116*
  vegetarian, 116
Frittata(s)
  about, 730
  with crumbled sausage, 732
  fresh tomato and cheese, 731
  leftover pasta, noodle, grains, or rice,
    732
  12 additions to, 732
Fritters
  bean, 413
    black-eyed pea, 415
    falafel, *414*, 415
    split pea, Indian style, 416
  fish, 564
  fish, Indian-style, 565
  7 more vegetables for, 114
Frosting. *See also* Glaze, cakes
  about, 854, *857*
  caramel–cream cheese frosting, 862

chocolate, *845*, 856
  ganache, 858
    4 more ways, 859
    7 ways to flavor, 860
  lemon or orange, 857
  maple, 857
  mocha, 856
  peanut butter, 857
  vanilla, 856
Frozen desserts
  about, 897
  granita, 900
    about, 897
    mango, *901*
    6 great, 904
  ice cream
    banana, 902
    buttermilk, 902
    chocolate, 902
    coconut, 902
    coffee, 902
    5 simple ideas for, 899
    ginger, 902
    green tea, 902
    maple-nut, 902
    pumpkin, 902
    strawberry or any berry, 902
  sauce, hot fudge, 859, *898*
  sorbet
    chocolate or cherry-chocolate, 903
    espresso, 903
    fresh fruit, 900
    honeydew-mint, 903
    lemon or lime, 903
    lime-basil, 903
    orange, tangerine, or grapefruit, 903
    orange-cassis, 903
    papaya-lime, 903
    pear- or apple-ginger, 903
    raspberry or strawberry-red wine,
     903
    10 more flavors, 903
    vanilla-pineapple, 903
Fruit(s). *See also individual names of fruits*
  about, 234, 363
    buying and handling fresh produce,
     234–236
    refrigerating, 235
  buying and handling, 234–236
  cooking techniques, 247–250, 359–363
  drying. *See* Dried fruits
  fried, 363
  fruit smoothie, 716–717
    chocolate, not-too-sweet, 716
    coconut, 716

    green, 716
    and vegetable, 716
  galette
    about, *881*
    5 simple, 881
    fruit, 879
  grilled or broiled
    about, 363
    9 sweet and savory ways, 361
  guacamole with, 105
  ice milk, 900
  long-lasting, 5
  macerating and seasoning, 363
  pickling, 228
  pies
    apple, 871
    peach or other stone fruit, 872,
     874
    tips for, 871
  raw, French toast with, *739*
  roasted, 247–250, *247*, 360
  salads
    green papaya salad, 210, *211*
    mixed, 211
  sauce, two ways, 862
  sautéed, 360
  shortcakes, strawberry or other, 849,
    851
  sorbet, fresh, 900
  stewed, 360
  summer fruit salsa, 58
  tarts
    caramelized peach or plum, 882
    caramelized pineapple, 882
    tarte tatin, 882, *883*
Fuchsia pasta, 508
Fusilli and roasted garlic soup, 158

G
Gai lan, 265
Galette(s)
  about, *881*
  5 simple ideas, 881
  fruit, 879
Game, grilling large cuts, 677
Ganache, 858
  4 more ways, 859
  7 ways to flavor, 860
Garam masala
  about, 34
  rice pilaf with, *433*
Garlic
  about, 294, *294*
  aïoli, 70
  bean purée with, 392

Garlic, *continued*
braised brisket with sweet potatoes, carrots, dried fruit, and lots of, 686
broccoli raab with, and pecorino, 272
chile-, salsa, super-hot, 73
chile-garlic paste, 45
cold escarole, and parmesan salad, 207
deep-fried fish with, 562
grits gratin with, 462, *465*
lemon-, wings, 130
in mashed potatoes, 329
nut chutney, 64
pasta with oil and, 476
pork burgers, 705
roast chicken with, herb butter, 636
roasted, 294, *295*
  8 ways to use, 295, 296
  faster, 295
  grilled chicken breast sandwich with mustard and, 810
  teriyaki, 76
  vinaigrette, 190
roast leg of lamb with coriander seeds and, 710
in sautéed ripe plantains, 323
shrimp, with tomatoes and cilantro, 543
soup
  fideo, 158, *159*
  fusilli and, 158
  lime-garlic-coconut, 137
  roasted, 137
  tomato-, 137, 145
spicy greens with, 307, *308*
Gazpacho
chunky, 150
fast and simple, 150
7 more ways, 150
Generous pie shell, 869
Gigante beans, 387
Ginger
about, 29, 296
Chinese noodle soup with cabbage and, 158
citrus-pickled, 296
cold bok choy and, salad, 207
fried rice with, 445
gingerbread people, 837
gingersnap piecrust, 871
gingersnaps, *832–833*, 837
ice cream, 902
peach and, pie, 875
pear- or apple- sorbet, 903
pears poached with, 381

quinoa with ground pork, soy sauce, and, 460
reduction sauce, 82
-scallion sauce, 64
seared scallops with pan sauce with, 577
spicy greens with, 307
sweet potatoes, fish steamed over, 558
twice-fried, deep-fried fish with, 562
vinaigrette, 190
Glass cookware, about, 9
Glass noodles with vegetables and meat, 524, *525*
Glaze
cakes
  about, 854
  chocolate, 858
  coconut, 858
  creamy orange, 858
  lemon or lime, 858
  mocha, 858
  orange, 857
  simple syrup, 859
  vanilla, 858
Glazed vegetables, 247
Gluten, magic of, 788
Gluten-free baking, about, 766
Gluten-free pizza dough, 818
Gnudi with noodles, 518
Goat
about, 706–707
lamb recipes substituted with, 711
Goat cheese
anchovy spread, 101
flavorful cream cheese spread, 100
fresh soft, about, 755
herbed, 100, *101*
honied, 100
marinated, 97
rosemary-honey, 100
sandwich, warm, with toasted nuts, 810
-stuffed figs, 100
"Good-quality vegetable oil," 184
Goose
about, 653
roast, 657
Graham cracker crust, 871
Grain-fried butternut squash, 288
Grain(s). *See also* Rice
about, 4, 426–427, 450, 452–455
  8 ways to enhance, 450, 452–456
beef and barley soup, 138
breakfast. *See also* Cereals
  cooked, 12 ideas for, 749
bulgur

basic, 457
pilaf with vermicelli, 458
corn-based
about, 464
grits gratin with arugula and garlic, 462, *465*
hominy, about, 455
hominy, beans with tomatillos and, 397
hominy, creamed, 469
hominy, creamed, and kale, 469
polenta, 461
polenta, 14 dishes to serve on top of, 461
pozole, chipotle, 469, *470*
pozole, chipotle, 10 garnishes for, 481
tamales, 461
tamales, about, *463*
tamales, 10 dishes for tamale fillings, 462
couscous
Israeli, pilaf with black olives, 457
simple white or whole wheat, 450, 452–456
16 dishes to serve over, 457
cracked wheat with mustard, 466
farro with leeks, cherry tomatoes, and basil, 467
kasha, 463
about, 453
with browned onions, 463
with mushrooms, 464
varnishkes, 466
leftover, in frittata, 732
millet-cauliflower mash, 466
pilaf
bulgur with vermicelli, 458
Israeli couscous, with black olives, 457
10 more, 436–437
wild rice, 467
quinoa and sweet potato salad, 219
quinoa with roasted corn, 458, *459*
salads
about, 215
farro, with cucumber and yogurt-dill dressing, 218
fattoush, *220*, 221
quinoa and sweet potato, 219
rice, with dried apricots, 217
tabbouleh, 217
sautéed cooked, 450
with chiles, 456
with toasted spice, 456
17 dishes for leftovers, 435

soups
    creamy, with fresh garnishes, 157
    mushroom and, 155
    mushroom-barley, my new way, 154
    rice porridge with fresh garnishes, 155, *156*
    10 unexpected combinations, 157
    wheat berries with candied walnuts, 468
Grainy mustard, *36, 37*
Granita, 900
    about, 897
    mango, *901*
    6 great, 904
Granola
    customizing, 751
    my new way, 749, *750*
    12 ideas for, 749
Granulated sweeteners, 826
Grapefruit(s)
    about, 374
    rice salad with, and pistachios, 217
    sorbet, 903
Grape leaves
    lamb-stuffed, 122
    stuffed, 120
Grape(s)
    about, 374
    broccoli raab with sausage and, 269
    broccoli raab with sausage and grapes, 269
    clafoutis, 893
Gratins
    corn, 284
    corn grits, with arugula and garlic, 462, 465
    large dishes for, 8
Gratins, vegetable
    asparagus or green bean and gruyère, 256
    baked chard in Béchamel, 256
    leeks, braised, 256
    potatoes, scalloped, 256
    spinach or greens, 256
    summer squash and salsa, 256
    sweet potato, 256
    tomato, 256
    winter squash, 256
Graviera cheese, 756
Gravlax, 551
Great Northern beans, 388
Greek salad, simplified, 196
Green beans
    about, 297
    gratin, with gruyère, 256

lamb stew with, 711
slow-cooked, 297
slow-cooked, with bacon, 298
tofu braised with, 423
with yogurt and dill, 298
Green chile salsa, *56*, 73
Green curried fish, 560
Green enchilada salsa, 73
Green goddess ranch dressing, 71
Green olive mojo, 52
Green olive tapenade, 109
Green papaya salsa, Thai style, 58
Green rice pilaf, 436
Green(s)
    about, 240, 307
    beans and, 403
    beans and pasta combos, 397
    beet greens, about, 264
    bok choy and Asian greens, about, 265–267
    canned beans with, 403
    chicken stir-fried with, 606
    fritters, 114
    gratin, 256
    pasta with, 484
    restaurant-style, 268
    restaurant-style, with thickened soy sauce, 268
    salads
        about, 192, *194, 195*
        Caesar, 196
        chopped, 196
        simple, *194*
        warm spicy, with bacon and eggs, *196, 199*
    sautéed eggplant with, 290
    smoothie, 716
    spareribs braised with, 703
    spicy, with double garlic, 307, *308*
    spicy, with double ginger, 307
    squid with chiles and, 588
Green sauce, cheese enchiladas with, 759
Green sauce, French style, 70
Green tea ice cream, 902
Green tomatoes
    pan-fried, *346, 347*
    salsa, 56
Griddlecakes
    bean, 416
    bean sprouts, 416
    6 sauces for, 417
    10 additions to, 416
Griddled olive oil salt bread, *768, 769*

Grilled beef
    about, 689
    flank steak, 670
Grilled chicken. *See* Boneless chicken, grilled or broiled; Chicken parts
Grilled chiles rellenos, 320
Grilled fish tacos, 812, *813*
Grilled or broiled Cornish hens with sherry vinegar, 658
    with cabbage, 659
    5 sauces for, 658
Grilled or roasted eggplant dip, 105, *106*
Grilled porterhouse steak, *668*
Grilled quesadillas, 815
Grilled sandwiches
    cheese, 804
    7 other, 805
Grilled seafood, 535
    clams or mussels, 536
    octopus, 536
    oysters, two ways, 536
    scallops, 535
    scallops, with basil stuffing, *578, 579*
    shrimp or squid, 535
    whole fish, 536
Grilled tofu, 419
Grilled vegetables, 250–255, *251*
    artichokes, 252
    asparagus, 252
    corn, 252
    eggplant, 252
    leeks vinaigrette, 252
    mushrooms
        miso-marinated, 252
    onions, 253
    peppers, 252
    potatoes, 253
    radicchio, balsamic, 253
    squash or zucchini, 253
    sweet potatoes, 253
    winter squash, 253
Grilled wings, 129
Grilling, about
    over fire, 21
    pork, 689
    utensils for, 11
Grits
    breakfast, 748
        cheesy, 749
        scrapple, 749
    gratin with arugula and garlic, 462, *465*
Ground chicken and turkey, about, 653
Gruyère
    about, 755
    buckwheat crêpes with ham and, *745*

Guacamole, 105
    avocado-crab spread or dip, 105
    crunchy corn, 105
    with fruit, 105
    "guacasalsa," 105
    un-avocado guacamole, 105
"Guacasalsa," 105
Guajillo peppers, 42
Gyoza (vegetarian pot stickers), 126

H

Habanero peppers, dried, 42
Halal chicken, 593
Half-and-half, 752
Halibut steaks
    with creamy saffron sauce, 566
    with sour-cream-chive sauce, 566
Halloumi cheese, 755
Ham
    about, 689, 704
    buckwheat crêpes with gruyère and, *745*
    roasted artichoke hearts with ham,
        wine, and lemon, 261
    sauerkraut with juniper berries and, 275
    soup, split pea and, 138
Hard-boiled egg, my usual way, 721
Harissa
    lentil soup with, 154
    paste, 45
Hazelnut(s)
    about, 310
    Brussels sprouts sautéed with, 273
    celery root, pan-roasted with hazelnut
        butter, 280
    chocolate torte, 854
    pie
        butterscotch, 878
        chocolate, 878
    rice pudding, 896
Heat, importance of and cooking
    techniques, 16–22, *18–20*
Heirloom vegetables, 347
Herb(s) and herbed dishes
    about, 24–25, 46–51
    -baked chicken, 602
    with chicken and lemon, grilled or
        broiled, 620
    croutons, 803
    deep-fried seafood, 541
    fine, scrambled eggs with, 724
    fresh, about, 5
    fresh pasta, 508
    gnocchi, 517
    goat cheese, 100, *101*
    hummus, 103

miso-, dipping sauce, 67
-parmesan, oven "fried" chicken, 616
pasta with garlic, oil, and, 477
pesto, purées, and sauces, 51–52
pilaf, 436
roast chicken with garlicky herb butter,
    636
salmon roasted with, 551
sauces, creamy, fish with, 562
simple green salad with, 194
spaetzle, 519
-stuffed eggs, 93
summer squash and, in parchment,
    341
vinaigrette, *189*, 190
Highly seasoned croutons, 803
Hollandaise sauce, 80
    blender, 80
    tenderloin with, 679
Homemade breakfast (or any other meal)
    sausage, 703
Homemade mayonnaise, 69
Hominy
    about, 455
    beans with tomatillos and, 397
    creamed, 469
    creamed, and kale, 469
Honey
    about, 827
    banana bread, whole grain, 771
    goat cheese, 100
    goat cheese, rosemary-, 100
    mustard chicken wings, 129
    mustard vinaigrette, 190
    quail roasted with cumin, orange juice,
        and, 660
    roast chicken with cumin, orange, and,
        635
    -saffron rice pudding with nuts and
        golden raisins, 896
    skate or other fish with brown butter,
        capers, and, 562
Honeydew-mint sorbet, 903
Honied goat cheese, 100
Hoppin' John, 412
Horseradish
    about, 298
    classic creamy dip, 100
Hot-and-sour soup, 168
    with shrimp, 171
    vegetarian, 170
Hot fudge sauce, 859, 898
Huevos rancheros, 729
Hulled barley, 455
Humane certified eggs, 719

Hummus, 103
    herbed, 103
    miso, 103
    spicy, 103

I

Ice cream
    banana, 902
    buttermilk, 902
    chocolate, 902
    coconut, 902
    coffee, 902
    5 simple ideas for, 899
    frozen desserts
        10 more flavors, 902
        vanilla, *898*
        vanilla, simplest, 899
        vanilla custard, 897
    ginger, 902
    green tea, 902
    maple-nut, 902
    pumpkin, 902
    strawberry or any berry, 902
    10 more flavors, 902
    vanilla, *898*
    vanilla, simplest, 899
    vanilla custard, 897
Ice milk
    about, 897
    espresso, 903
    fruit, 900
Immersion blenders, *140*
Indian style
    chile paste, 45
    fish fritters, 565
    mulligatawny, 148, *149*
    spicy vegetables, mixed, 354
    split pea fritters, 416
    wrap, 809
Ingredients. *See also individual names of foods*
    buying, 2
    organic, 2
    stocking kitchen with, 4–5
Instant-read thermometers, about, 10
Israeli style
    couscous pilaf with black olives, 457
    couscous pilaf with spinach, 457
Italian-American style
    meaty lasagne, 502
    pot roast, 684
Italian style
    lamb chops, grilled or broiled, 709
    with peppers and onion, 704
    pork sausage, hot or sweet, 703
    super-seasoned, 704

J

Jalapeño deviled eggs, 93
Jalapeño peppers, about, 42
Jam bars, 844
Japanese style
   grilled or broiled chicken, 618
   shrimp and rice, 546
Jerk chicken, 642
   grilled or broiled, 620
   grilled or broiled, shortcut, 620
Jerk seasoning, 34
Jerusalem artichokes
   about, 298
   crisp-cooked, 298
Jícama
   about, 299
   broiled with chile-lime glaze, 299
   salsa, 56
   simple salad, 200
Jim Lahey's no-knead, 785, 786
Joël Robuchon mashed potatoes, 329
Julienne, about, 15, 16
Juniper berries
   about, 30
   sauerkraut with, 275
   sauerkraut with ham, 275

K

Kale
   about, 299–300, 300
   creamed hominy and, 469
   flash-cooked
      with fermented black beans, 300
      with feta and tomato, 300
      with lemon juice, 300
   with peanut sauce, 301
   stuffed, 358
   with tahini, 301
   warm spicy greens with bacon and eggs, 199
   white beans and sausage with, 402
   with yogurt, 301
Kamut, 455
Kasha
   about, 453
   with browned onions, 463
   with mushrooms, 464
   varnishkes, 466
Kasseri cheese, 756
Kebabs
   beef, grilled with lots of vegetables, 673, 674
   beef, varying, 673
   fish, 566
Kefalotyri cheese, 756

Ketchup
   boneless chicken, stir-fried, 605
   tofu, stir-fried, 605
Key lime pie, 878
Kidney beans
   about, 388
   greens and pasta combos, 397
Kimchee/kimchi
   pancakes, crisp, 355
   potato pancakes with scallions and, 332
   rice pilaf, 437
   sandwich, grilled nut butter and, 805
   shortcut, 229
Kitchen scissors, about, 11
Kitchen towels, about, 10
Kiwis, about, 375
Knives, about, 6, 6–7, 14, 16
Kohlrabi
   about, 301
   in shaved vegetable salad, 206
Korean style
   barbecue sauce, 75
   vegetable pancakes, crisp, 355
   vegetable pancakes with seafood, 356
Kosher chicken, 593
Kosher pickles, the right way, 230
Kumquats, about, 375

L

Lacy oatmeal cookies, 834
Lamb
   about, 706–707
      carving, 707
      cuts of, 705, 707
      grilling large cuts, 677
   chickpea chili with, 406
   chops, grilled or broiled, 707
   chops, grilled or broiled, Italian style, 709
   curry, 711
   -filled samosas, 117
   game substituted for, 711
   osso buco, 712
   pita sandwich stuffed with onions and spicy, 810
   roast leg of, 709
      with anchovies, 710
      with garlic and coriander seeds, 709
      rolled and tied, 710
      with thyme and orange, 709
   roast rack of, with persillade, 712
   shanks with tomatoes and olives, 711
   soup, North African style, 171
   stew
      with cinnamon and lemon, 710

      with eggplant or green beans, 711
      with mushrooms, 711
      with white beans, 711
   stock, 176
   -stuffed grape leaves, 122
Last-minute crisp pan-fried potatoes, 332
Latkes, 332
Lavender, 48
Leavening, about, 4, 765–766, 830, 831
Leeks
   about, 301, 302
   braised
      au gratin, 254
      with mustard, 303
      in oil or butter, 302
      with olives, 303
      in red wine, 303
      with tomato, 303
   braised in oil or butter, 302
   crisp sautéed, 303
   crisp spiced, 303
   farro with cherry tomatoes, basil, and, 467
   fried rice with, 445
   gratin, braised, 256
   grilled, vinaigrette, 252
   soup, potato and, 138
Leftovers, repurposing, 22
Leg (lamb), about, 707, 707
Lemongrass, 48
Lemongrass pork burgers, 705
Lemon(s)
   about, 5, 375
   cake glaze, 858
   -caper sauce, 82
   with chicken and herbs, grilled or broiled, 620
   collard greens, flash-cooked with, 300
   cookies
      shortbread, 838
      squares, 842, 843
   curd, 862, 863
   curd, fresh blueberry tart, 881
   custard, 890
   frosting, 857
   -garlic wings, 130
   lamb stew with cinnamon and, 710
   lentil soup with, and dill, 154
   meringue pie, 877
   one-pot pasta with zucchini and, 480
   preserved, 375
   roasted artichoke hearts with ham, wine, and lemon, 261
   sautéed fish with pan sauce, 537
   -scented angel food cake, 848

shortcut mousse, 864
sorbet, 903
tuna salad with olive oil and, 804
vinaigrette, 190
Lentil(s)
about, 388, 408
bulgur pilaf with, 458
chicken and, 622, *623*
dal
about, 409
with daikon, 410
with potatoes or other root
vegetables, 410
simplest, 409
-filled samosas, 118
greens and pasta combos, 397
with lardons, 409
Moroccan style, 408
with parsnips and nutmeg, 409
red, in bean dip, 104
with roasted winter squash, 409
salad, lemony, 214
salad with herbs, 214
six ways, 408
soup, six ways, 152
Spanish style, 408
21 main-course dishes, 417
Lettuce cups and wraps, 121
Lettuces, about, 192
Light and fluffy pancakes, 740
Lighter, richer corn bread, 770
Lightning-quick fish soup, 161, *163*
Lima beans
in bean dip, 104
greens and pasta combos, 397
Lime leaves, 48
Lime(s)
about, 5, 375
braised beef with chiles and, 680
chicken wings, smoky, 129
chile-, glaze, broiled jícama with, 299
coconut-, bars, 844
fish sandwich with chili-, mayo, 808
-garlic-coconut soup, 137
key lime pie, 878
papaya-, sorbet, 903
sorbet, 903
sorbet, -basil, 903
vinaigrette, 190
Linguine. *See* Pasta, linguine
Liquids, infusing with flavor, 900
Liquid sweeteners, 827
Liquor. *See also* Wine
boozy caramel sauce, 860
bourbon barbecue sauce, 75

Loaf pans, about, 8
Lobster
about, 580, 583–584, *584*
about, eating, *586*
boiled or steamed, 584
broiled, 534
deviled eggs with, 93
9 things to serve with, 585
salad, 223
stock, 179
Loin (beef), about, 666
Loin (lamb), about, 707
Loin (pork), about, 689
Long beans. *See* Green beans
Louisiana-style shrimp or crawfish boil,
with vegetables, 545
Lychees, about, 377
Lyonnaise, salad, 199

M
Macadamia nuts, about, 310
Mace, 30
Mackerel simmered in soy sauce, 563
Malanga, 348
Malt vinegar, 186
Manchurian-style cauliflower, 278
Mandarins, about, 378
Mandolines, about, 11, *15*
Mango(es)
about, *376–377*, 377
broiled or grilled, 361
quick-pickled, 229
rice pudding, 896
Manhattan clam or fish chowder, 164
Maple syrup
about, 738
frosting, 857
ice cream, maple-nut, 902
rice pudding, 896
smoky glaze, with grilled or broiled
chicken, 620
Marble cake, 846
Margherita pizza, 819
Marinara pizza, 819
Marinated celery and carrots, Chinese
style, *94*, 95
"carpaccio"-style vegetables, 95
other vegetables in, 95
Marinated feta, 97
Marinated goat cheese, 97
Marinated mozzarella, 96
Marinated olives, 91
Marinated olives, with citrus, 91
Marinated paneer, 97
Marinated queso fresco, 97

Marinated ricotta salata, 97
Marjoram, 48
Mashed potatoes, *328*, 329
Mayonnaise
about, 67–68, *68*
chili-lime, fish sandwich with, 808
egg salad with, 804
homemade, 69
13 sauces to make with, 70
tuna salad with, 804
Measuring techniques, about, 15, *17*
Meat, 663–713. *See also* Beef
about, 664–666
buying, 664
checking for doneness, 665
cooking, 664–665
"grass-fed," 667
about, checking for doneness, 665
adding to vegetable dishes, 257
in appetizers and snacks, 130
beef
about, 665–667, *666*
braised, 679–683
ground meat, 687–689
pot roasts, 683–687
roasted, 675–679
steaks and other quick-cooking,
667–675
chiles rellenos with, 320
8 dishes to serve on greens, 225
glass noodles with vegetables and, *524*,
525
goat, about, 706
grilling large cuts, 677
ham, about, 704
lamb
about, *705*, 706, *707*
chops, grilled or broiled, 707
roast leg of, 709
roast rack of, with persillade, 712
shanks with tomatoes and olives, 711
stew with cinnamon and lemon, 710
lasagne, 502
lasagne, Italian-American style, 502
loaf, 688
loaf with spinach, 688
pilaf with, 437
pork
about, 689, *691*
chops and other quick-cooking,
689–695
roasts, 695–699
sausage and ground,
703–705, *703–706*
slow-roasted spareribs, 698

stews and braises, 699–703
    stews and braises, about, 699
rice porridge with, 157
sauces, 495, *497*
sauces, dishes that work as, 494
soup, 166–171
steamed clams or mussels with, 581
stir-fried noodles with, and vegetables, 524
with stir-fried vegetables, 246
tortellini, 514
using game in recipes, 711
veal
    about, 706, 713
    chops, grilled or broiled, 713
Meatballs, 127
    skewered, Vietnamese-style, 127
    skewered and grilled meatballs, three ways, 127
    spaghetti and, 496
    Spanish-style almond, 127
Meat soups
    beef and vegetable, 168, *169*
    hot-and-sour, 168
    lamb, North African style, 171
    19 whole-meal, 170
Mediterranean style
    chicken, broiled or grilled, 599
    seafood salad, *226, 227*
Medium-boiled egg, 721
Melons, about, 377
Mesclun, about, 192
Mexican style
    cheese enchiladas, 759
    cheese salsa, 57
    chicken soup with rice, 165
    chile paste, 45
    coleslaw, 205
    lightning-quick fish soup, 161
    quick-pickled vegetables, 229
    16 iconic dishes, 759
Microwaved vegetables
    about, 237
    asparagus, 263
    asparagus, 10 ways, 263
Microwave ovens, about, 12
Milk, about, 751
Milk chocolate, 828
Millet
    about, 454
    -cauliflower mash, 466
    -cauliflower mash, cheesy, 467
Minestrone, 147
Minestrone, 5 more takes on, 148
Mint

about, 48
cilantro-, chutney, 62
corn salad with feta and, 201
fava bean and, salad with pecorino, 215, *216*
pesto, 51
purée, 52
radish-celery salad, 201
tahini sauce, 59
Miso
    about, 5
    -baked tofu, 419
    broiled or grilled boneless chicken with, 599
    caramelized nuts, 88
    -carrot, with ginger, 67
    deviled eggs, 93
    dipping sauce, 67
        -carrot, with citrus, 67
        -herb, 67
        -soy, 67
    five-minute drizzle sauce, 81
    hummus, 103
    mayonnaise, 70
    roast chicken with, butter, 636
    root vegetables, braised and glazed with, 334
    salmon roasted with, butter, 551
    salmon salad with snow peas, 224
    seaweed salad, 210
    soup, 138
    stuffing, broiled or grilled scallops with, 579
    vinaigrette, 191
Mitts, about, 10
Mixers, about, 12
Mixing bowls, about, 10
Mocha frosting, 856
Mocha glaze, 858
Molasses
    about, 827
    -spice cookies, 837
Monkfish, about, 559
Monte Cristo, 805
Monterey Jack cheese, 755
Mornay (cheese) sauce, 79
Mostly whole wheat tortillas, 781
Mousse
    about, 886
    chocolate, 891
    lemon, shortcut, 864
    raspberry fool, 891, *892*
    yogurt raspberry fool, 891, *892*
Mozzarella
    marinated, 96

    open-face ratatouille sandwich with melted, 810
    pizza
        fresh, with tomato sauce and, 821
        with tomato sauce, and sausage or pepperoni, 821
        with tomato sauce and, 819
    salad, with tomato and basil, 199
Muffins
    banana and pumpkin (honey whole grain or not), 771
    blueberry or cranberry, 773
    bran, 771
    cheese and chive, 773
    corn, 770
    many ways, 771
    sour cream or yogurt, 771
    spice, 771
    10 additions to, 774
    tins for, 9
Mulligatawny, 148, *149*
Multicookers, about, 12
Mung beans, 388
Mushroom(s)
    about, 303–304
    baked ziti with, 499
    beef stroganoff with, 681, *682*
    -cheese ravioli, 513
    chicken stir-fried with, 606
    dried
        about, 4
        beef stew with tomatoes and, 680
        reconstituting, 304
    fresh and dried, pasta with, 486
    grilled, miso-marinated, 252
    kasha with, 464
    lamb stew with, 711
    one-pot pasta with, 480
    pasta with, 485
    reduction sauce, 82
    rice pilaf with, 436
    risotto, 441
    sautéed, *305*, 306
    sautéed, dry style, *305*, 306
    sautéed, 8 additions to, *305, 306*
    in shaved vegetable salad, 206
    shiitakes
        cold soba noodles with, 522
        in parchment, 343
        sautéed, with soy sauce, 306
        seaweed "shake," 35
        stir-fried broccoli and, gingery, 246
        tofu braised with, 422, *423*
    soup
        beef and, 168

Mushroom(s), *continued*
    cream of, 140
    mushroom and other grain soup, 155
    mushroom-barley, more traditional, 155
    mushroom-barley, my new way, 154
    stock, 174
    stuffed, 120
    stuffed, 10 more ideas, 120
Mussels
    about, 574–575, *575*
    grilled seafood, 536
    pan-roasted, 537
    steamed, 579
    steamed, 6 ways to vary, 581
Mustard
    about, 35–36, 38
    barbecue sauce, 75
    -braised short ribs, 681
    broiled or grilled boneless chicken with, 599
    cabbage, mustardy, 274
    with chicken, grilled or broiled, 620
    cracked wheat with, 466
    grainy, *36, 37*
    grainy, 14 ways to flavor, 37–38
    grilled chicken breast sandwich with roasted garlic and, 810
    honey mustard chicken wings, 129
    leeks braised with, 303
    sauce, cold, 70
    vinaigrette, 190
Mustard greens, 307
My classic burger, 687
My classic burger, in a skillet, 688
My favorite bread stuffing, 650
My favorite bread stuffing, 6 ways, 650
My kind of croutons, 801, 803. *See also* Croutons
My magic bars, 843
My mom's pan-cooked peppers and onions, 320, *321*
My new favorite fried chicken, 628, *629*
My new favorite fried chicken, more ways to spin, 628

N
Naan, 799
Nachos, 110
Nachos, 8 ideas for toppings, 111
Naked chicken enchiladas, *610*, 612
Natural chicken, 592
Natural eggs, 720
Navy beans, 388

Nectarines
    about, 379–381
    broiled or grilled, 361
New Mexico peppers, 42
Nigella, 30
Non-wheat flours, 763–764
Noodles
    about, 4
    leftover, in frittata, 732
    rice-'n'-, 436
    salads
        corn, with chile, 201
Noodles, Asian
    about, 519–522
    bowls, improvising, 527
    cold
        with sesame or peanut sauce, 522
        spicy, with pork, 522
    18 dishes to toss with, 526
    soba noodles
        about, 520
        cold, with dipping sauce, *521, 522*
        cold, with shiitakes, 522
    stir-fried
        glass noodles with vegetables and meat, 524, *525*
        with meat and vegetables, 524
        pad Thai, 523
    udon, about, 520
    udon, stir-fried, 524
Noodle soups, 157–161
    in broth, 157
    chicken and, in broth, 158
    garlic fideo, 158, *159*
    pho-style, 160
Nori chips, *337*, 338
North African style
    lamb soup, 171
    spiced broiled or grilled boneless chicken, 599
North Carolina BBQ sandwich, 810
Not-quite chicken parmesan, 612
Not-too-sweet chocolate smoothie, 716
Nut(s). *See also* Peanut(s); Pecan(s)
    about, 5, 307–308, 310–311
    almond
        about, 310
        apricot-, bars, 843
        broccoli or cauliflower, crunchy, with raisins, saffron, and, 269, *270*
        meatballs, Spanish-style, 127
        mole, turkey thighs in, 652
        panna cotta, 888
        bacon-, stuffing, 651
        baklava, 884

    cashews
        about, 310
        shrimp and, stir-fry, 545
    chutney, dried fruit and, 62, *63*
    chutney, real garlicky, 64
    cookies
        nutty biscotti, *832–833*
        peanuts or other nut butter, 836
        peanuts or other nut butter, flourless, 836
        white chocolate-pistachio, 831
    crisp, -crusted fish, 569
    flours, 309
    fresh bread crumbs, 801
    hazelnut
        about, 310
        Brussels sprouts sautéed with, 273
        celery root, pan-roasted with hazelnut butter, 280
        chocolate torte, 854
        pie, butterscotch, 878
        pie, chocolate, 878
        rice pudding, 896
    honey-saffron rice pudding with golden raisins and, 896
    macadamia, 310
    macaroons, walnut or other, 840
    maple-, ice cream, 902
    nut butters
        grilled sandwich and kimchee, 805
        10 ways to season, 309
    oils, 185
        nutty vinaigrette, 191
        vinaigrette, 191
    pasta with garlic, oil, and, 478
    pecan
        about, 311
        pie, 878
        pie, butterscotch, 878
        pie, chocolate, 878
    piecrust, 869
    pistachios
        about, 311
        rice salad with grapefruit and, 217
    roasted nuts with oil or butter, 87
        dry-roasted, 88
        roasted beans with oil, 88
        roasted pumpkin, squash, or sunflower seeds, 88
        sautéed buttered, 87
        spiced buttered, 87
    sauce, 79
    Spanish-style almond meatballs, 127
    spinach with currants and, 339
    sweet tart crust, 870

warm goat cheese sandwich with toasted, 810
Nut sauce, 79
Nutty sweet tart crust, 870

O
Oat flour, 765
Oatmeal, 748
  cookies
    lacy, 834
    -something, *832*, 834
  rich, 748
  thick, 748
  12 ideas for, 749
Oats
  about, 453
  rolled, about, 452
Octopus
  about, 588
  broiled, 534
  grilled, 536
  with tomatoes and red wine, 590
Oil
  about, 183, 185–186
  heating, and smoke points, 183
  leeks braised in oil or butter, 302
  olive, 184
    griddled bread, *768, 769*
    roast chicken parts with, 615
    stovetop mixed vegetables with, 354
    tuna salad with lemon and, 804
  pasta with garlic and, 476
  -poached chicken, 612
  types
    about, 4
Okra
  about, 312
  fried, 288
  gumbo
    with roux, 312
    with seafood, 313
    with spicy sausage, 312
    vegetarian, 312
Olive oil
  about, 184
  griddled bread, *768, 769*
  roast chicken parts with, 615
  stovetop mixed vegetables with, 354
  tuna salad with lemon and, 804
Olives
  about, 313
  chard with, and feta, 282
  edamame with tomatoes and, 398
  green olive mojo, 52
  green olive tapenade, 109

Israeli couscous pilaf with black, 457
lamb shanks with tomatoes and, 711
leeks braised with, 303
marinated olives, 91
  with citrus, 91
in salads, 205
sautéed, 313
  with croutons, 314
  with tomatoes, 314
tuna salad with, 804
Omega-3 enriched eggs, 720
Omelet(s), 730
  about, 730, *730, 731*
  Denver, 730
  Spanish tortilla, 732
  13 ideas for filling omelets, 731
  tomato, 730
    fresh, and cheese, 731
  wrapped, 809
One-pot pasta, a-little-less simple, 480
One-pot pasta with butter and parmesan, *478, 479*
Onion(s)
  about, 314–315, *314–315*
  caramelized, 315
    with bacon or pancetta, 315
    Brussels sprouts sautéed with, 273
    sweet-and-sour, 315
    sweeter, 315
    10 uses for, 316
  creamed, 316
  creamed corn with, 284
  egg dishes
    quiche, 734
    quiche, with bacon, 735
  fennel with, and vinegar, 294
  fried onion rings, streamlined, 288
  fried rice with, 445
  grilled, 253
  grilled cheese and, sandwich, 805
  kasha with browned, 463
  my mom's pan-cooked peppers and, 320, *321*
  pita sandwich stuffed with spicy lamb and, 810
  raw onion chutney, 61
  red
    pan-fried whole trout, with bacon and, *572, 573*
    in salad, with orange, 205
  roasted halves, 248
  rösti, 265
  rye bread, 794
  sausages with peppers and, 704

soup, 145
stuffed, *357*, 358
Open-face ratatouille sandwich with melted mozzarella, 810
Orange(s)
  about, 378
  boneless chicken in packages with, 612
  cake glaze, 857
  cake glaze, creamy, 858
  -cassis sorbet, 903
  chard with, and shallots, 280, *281*
  chicken stir-fried with chiles and, 606
  -cinnamon coffee cake, 773
  fennel salad with, *204*, 205
  fresh pasta, 508
  frosting, 857
  -glazed black beans, 395
  juice, braised endive with, 292
  juice, quail roasted with honey, cumin, and, 660
  roast chicken with cumin, honey, and, 635
  roast leg of lamb with thyme and, 710
  salads with, 205
  -scented quinoa with shallots, 460
  sorbet, 903
  vanilla-, cream pie, 877
Oregano, 48
Organic (certified) eggs, 719
Organic chicken, 593
Organic foods, about, 2
Orzo and fresh herb soup with yogurt, 148
Osso buco, 712
Oven-baked ratatouille, 352, *353*
Oven "fried" chicken, 616
Oven "fried" chicken, parmesan-herb, 616
Oven-"fried" fish
  fillets, 555
  6 ways to vary, 555
  sticks or nuggets, 555
Oven-roasted plum tomatoes, 347
Oven-roasted potatoes, 329
Oven thermometers, about, 9
Ovenware, about, 8, 12–13
Over-easy eggs, 723
Overnight waffles, 743
Oxtails, braised, 683
Oysters
  about, 574, 575
  about, shucking, 575
  corn bread stuffing with, and sausage, *644*, 651
  grilled, two ways, 536
  pan-roasted, 537
  sautéed, lemony pan sauce, 538
  sautéed with cream, 538

P

Pad Thai, 523
Pad Thai, vegetarian, 524
Pakoras
    dipping sauces for, 115
    recipe for, 114
Pan bagnat with tuna, 806, *807*
Pancakes
    breakfast
        everyday, 740, *741*
        light and fluffy, 740
        6 tips for, 740
        variations, 742
    variations, 742
    vegetable
        kimchi, crisp, 355
        Korean style, crisp, 355
        Korean style, seafood and, 356
        zucchini, 343
Pancetta
    caramelized onions with, 315
    pasta with pecorino and, 496
Pan-cooked salmon, 548
Pan-cooked salmon, 10 sauces for, 549
Paneer
    about, 755
    marinated, 97
Pan-fried green or red tomatoes, *346*, 347
Pan-frying, about, 21
Pan-grilled steak, 669
Pan-grilled steak, oven-roasted, 669
Panna cotta, 888, *889*
    almond, 888
    buttermilk, 888
Pan-roasted celery root with rosemary
        butter, 280
Pan-roasted corn with cherry tomatoes,
        286
Pan-roasted fish
    tuna or other steaks, 567
    tuna or other steaks, sesame-crusted,
        567
Papaya(s)
    about, 379
    green papaya salad, 210, *211*
    green salsa, Thai style, 58
    -lime sorbet, 903
    quick-pickled, 229
    salsa, 57
Paprika
    about, 30, 42
    bell peppers, pan-cooked with, 322
Parboiling
    in butter or oil, 242
    technique, 237–238

Parchment, *340*, 340–343
Paring, about, 15, *16*
Parmesan cheese
    about, 5
    as all-purpose, 755
    artichoke dip, 109
    bean purée with, 392
    broiled or grilled boneless chicken with,
        599
    bruschetta or crostini with, 96
    celery-parsley salad, 201
    chicken, not-quite, 612
    cold escarole salad with garlic, 207
    crackers, 779
    deviled eggs, 93
    -herb, oven "fried" chicken, 616
    one-pot pasta with butter and, 478, *479*
    popcorn, 90
    ranch dressing, 71
    rice pilaf, 437
    vinaigrette, 190
    white pizza with prosciutto and, 819, *820*
Parmigiana
    chicken, 609
    eggplant, 609
Parsley
    about, 49
    celery-parmesan salad, 201
    purée, 52
Parsnip(s)
    about, 317–318
    puréed, 241
    white bean and, purée, 392
Party food. *See* Appetizers and snacks
Pasilla, 42
Pass-along appetizers, serving, 87
Passatelli, *519*
Passatelli, chicken soup with, 166
Passion fruit, about, 379
Pasta, 473–527. *See also* Noodles
    about, 4, 474–476
        calculating portions, 475
        choosing shapes, 475
        cooking, 474
        cut, 476
        draining, saucing, tossing, 475
        long, 476
    all'amatriciana, 498
    Asian noodles, 519–527
    baked, 499–503
    beans and greens combos, 397
    bulgur pilaf with vermicelli, 458
    cannelloni
        about, *512*
        spinach-cheese, 514

carbonara, 498
with dairy, eggs, seafood, or meat,
        491–498
    14 dishes that work as sauces, 494
    with meat sauce, 495, *497*
    with pancetta and pecorino, 496
    with pesto, 491
    with sardines, 495
    with sausage, 498
dumplings, 515–519
    gnudi with noodles, 518
    spaetzle, 518, *519*
    vegetarian ravioli nudi, 518
farfalle
    with mascarpone and fried basil, 492
    whole wheat, with roasted sweet
        potatoes, 488, *489*
fresh, 503–509
    about, 503, *503–504*
    Chinese-style egg noodles, 508
    eggless, 508
    egg pasta, 505, *506*
    5 other flavors for, 508
    flours in, 505
    free-form, 507
    fuchsia, 508
    herbed, 508
    orange, 508
    pizzocheri, 507
    saucing and tossing, 510
    spinach, 508
gnocchi
    about, 515–516, *516*
    herb, 517
    potato, 517
    spinach, 518
    sweet potato or butternut squash,
        518
    "twice-cooked," 517
kasha varnishkes, 466
lasagne
    meaty, 502
leftover, in frittata, 732
linguine
    with clams, 492, *493*
    with raw tomato sauce, 482, *483*
macaroni and cheese, 499, *500*
    Alsatian mac and cheese, 419
    with chiles, 501
    rich, 501
    shortcut, 501
    6 great combos, 501–502
manual machines for, 11
pansotti
    stuffed, butternut squash, 510

stuffed, chestnut, 510
stuffed, sweet potato, 510
penne with tomato-shrimp sauce, 494
ravioli
  cheese, 513
  mushroom-cheese, 513
  ricotta and herb, 513
  spinach, 513
  spinach-ricotta, 512
simplest, 476–482
  fast tomato sauce, 478
  15 additions to, 477
  with garlic and oil, 476
  one-pot, a-little-less simple, 480
  one-pot, with butter and parmesan, 478, 479
spaghetti and meatballs, 496
stuffed, 509–515
  about, 509–510, 512, 514
  meat tortellini, 513
  28 dishes for, 513
tortellini
  about, 514
  cheese, 515
  meat, 514
  seafood, 515
with vegetables or beans, 482–490
  broccoli raab, 484
  corn, zucchini, and tomatoes, 488
  with creamy bean sauce, 490
  fried eggplant, 486
  mushrooms, 485
  27 vegetable and legume dishes to toss with, 485
white beans with cabbage, and prosciutto, 396
whole wheat, about, 490
ziti
  baked, with mushrooms, 499
  baked, with ricotta, 499
  baked, with sausage, 499
  with creamy gorgonzola sauce and fried sage, 491
Pasta e fagioli, 148, 149
Pasta soup
  and chickpeas in broth, 158
  Chinese, with cabbage and ginger, 158
  fusilli and roasted garlic soup, 158
  orzo and fresh herb soup with yogurt, 158
  and pesto, 158
Pastry flour, 763, 766
Pattypan squash, 340
Peach(es)
  about, 379–381

broiled or grilled, 361
caramelized, tart, 882
pickled, Afghan style, 231
pie
  and berry, 875
  and ginger, 875
  or other stone fruit, 872, 874
Peanut(s)
  about, 310
  chicken wings, spicy, 129
  oil, 184
  peanut butter
    cookies, 836
    cookies, flourless, 836
    frosting, 857
  peanut dressing, chopped salad with, 197
  sauce, 75
    with chicken, grilled or broiled, 620
    cold Asian noodles with, 522
    collards or kale with, 301
    Southern-style, 75
Pearled barley, 453
Pear(s)
  about, 379, 381
  apple-, pie, 872
  -ginger sorbet, 903
  poached
    cinnamon, 381
    with ginger and star anise, 381
    with vanilla, 380, 381
    with wine or port syrup, 381
  poached, with vanilla, 380, 381
Pea(s)
  about, 317, 317
  anything-scented, 317
  with bacon, lettuce, and mint, 318
  dried, 388
  farro salad with, 218
  15 flavors for, 318
  puréed, 241
  shoots, 318
  snow
    in shrimp stir-fry, 543
  split, and ham soup, 138
Pecan(s)
  about, 311
  pie, 878
    butterscotch, 878
    chocolate, 878
Pecorino
  broccoli raab with garlic and, 272
  fava bean and mint salad with, 215, 216
  pasta with pancetta and, 496

Peelers, about, 10
Peeling, about, 15
Pepitas, salsa, 56
Pepper(s). See also individual types of peppers
  about, 39–40, 318
  chutney, hot or mild, 62
  grilled, 252
  puréed, 241
Pepper (seasoning), about, 4, 26–27
Pepper steak with red wine sauce, 671
Persillade, roast rack of lamb with, 712
Persimmons, about, 381–382
Pesto
  arugula, 52
  with butter, 51
  chicken-, panino, 805
  deviled eggs, 93
  mint or dill, 51
  pasta and, soup, 158
  pistou, 148
  spaghetti with, 491
  traditional, 50, 51
Pheasant
  about, 659, 660
  stewed with dried fruits, 662
Pho-style noodle soup, 160
Phyllo-topped chicken pot pie, 640
Pickled ginger, 296
Piecrust, 869
  about, 866, 866–867, 868, 873
  flaky, 865, 867
  4 simple variations, 870
  generous pie shell, 869
  gingersnap, 871
  graham cracker, 871
  nut, 869
  prebaking, 869
  savory, 869
  tart crust
    chocolate, 870
    nutty sweet, 870
    savory, 870
    spiced, 870
    sweet, 869
Pie(s). See also Piecrust
  about, 864–866
  cream
    banana, 877
    chocolate, 877
    coconut, 875
    -topped, 877
    vanilla, 875
    vanilla-orange, 877

Pie(s), *continued*
  fruit
    apple, 871
    peach or other stone fruit, 872, *874*
    tips for, 871
  galette, fruit, 879
  lemon meringue, 877
  pecan, 878
    butterscotch, 878
    chocolate, 878
  pecan or walnut, 878
  plates for, 8
  pumpkin, 878
Pigeon peas, 388
Pimiento, 42
Pineapple
  about, 382, *382*
  broiled or grilled, 361
  cake, upside-down, 849
  caramelized, tart, 882
  vanilla-, sorbet, 903
Pine nuts
  about, 311
  pasta with radicchio, currants, and, 495
  rice pilaf with, 436
Pink beans
  about, 388
  in bean dip, 104
Pinto beans, 388
Piquín peppers, 43
Pissaladière, 822, *823*
Pistachios
  about, 311
  rice salad with grapefruit and, 217
Pistou, 148
Pita, 798
  crust, stuck-pot rice with, 440
  sandwich stuffed with spicy lamb and
    onions, 810
Pita chips
  fried or baked, 110
    sprinkles for, 110
  nachos, 110
Pizza
  about, 816–817, *817*
  deep-dish, Chicago style, 824
  dough, 817
    crunchier, 818
    gluten-free, 818
    whole wheat, 818
  4 tips for foolproof toppings, 818
  on the grill, 819
  margherita, 819
  marinara, 819
  19 ideas for toppings, 821

  pissaladière, 822, *823*
  rosemary focaccia, 822
  stones, peels, cutters for, 11
  with tomato sauce, mozzarella, and
    sausage or pepperoni, 821
  with tomato sauce and fresh
    mozzarella, 821
  with tomato sauce and mozzarella, 819
  turning into calzone, 824
  white, 818
    with clams, 819
    with prosciutto and parmesan, 819,
      820
Pizzocheri, 507
Plantain(s)
  about, 322, *323*
  chips, 111
  coconut-fried, 288
  fried, 323, *324*
  sautéed ripe, 322
  sautéed ripe, garlicky, 323
Plate (beef), about, 667
Plated-portion appetizers, serving, 87
Plum(s)
  about, 382–383
  broiled or grilled, 361
  caramelized, tart, 882
  pie, 875
  upside-down cake, 850
Poached boneless chicken
  breasts or thighs, 611
  breasts or thighs, with lemon sauce, 611
  chickens or thighs
    5 ways, 612
  8 more additions to liquid for, 611–612
Poached eggs, 725
  in creamed something, 728
  in tomato sauce, 726, *727*
  in tomato sauce with cheese, 726
Poached fish
  aromatic, 565
  4 liquids for, 565
  whole, 565
Poached pears
  cinnamon, 381
  with ginger and star anise, 381
  with vanilla, *380*, 381
  with wine or port syrup, 381
Poblano peppers, 43
Poke, 133
Polenta, 461
  14 dishes to serve on top of, 461
  with fresh corn, 461
  grilled or fried, 461
  pound cake, 846

Pomegranate
  about, 383
  molasses vinaigrette, 191
Popcorn, 90
  brittle, 904
  flavor boosters for, 91
  parmesan, 90
  salty-sweet buttered, 90
Popovers, 775, 776
Poppy seeds, about, 30
Poppy seed swirl bread, 792
Pork
  about, grilling, 689
  about cuts of, 689, *691*
  and black bean chili, 406
  black beans orange-glazed with, 395
  chops and other quick-cooking,
    689–695
    about, 689
    roasted, tenderloin with lots of herbs,
      694
    sirloin steaks with fresh orange juice,
      693
    skillet chops, *690*, 691
    skillet chops, varying, 692
    stir-fried, with bok choy, 692
  edamame with fresh tomatoes and
    ground, 398
  fried rice with, 444
  game substituted for, 711
  grilling large cuts, 677
  ground, quinoa with ginger, and soy
    sauce, 460
  rice noodle soup with, 161
  roasts, 695–699
    crown, 698
    with garlic and rosemary, 695
    shoulder, Puerto Rican style, 695, *696*
    slow-roasted spareribs, 698
  salad
    with green beans, spicy, 224
    and mango salad, 224
  satay, 130
  sausage and ground, 703–705, *703–706*
    burgers, garlicky, 704
    sausage, homemade breakfast (or any
      other meal), 703
  shredded, empanadas, 127
  slow-roasted spareribs, 698
  spicy, cold Asian noodles with, 522
  spicy ground, tofu braised with, 423
  stews and braises
    about, 699
    braised, spicy, with Vietnamese
      flavors, 700

braised, with white wine and celery root, 699

braised spareribs with root vegetables, 701, *702*

stock, 176

Portions. *See individual types of foods*

Potato(es)

about, 325

baked, 325

bay- or rosemary-scented, 326

salted, 326

16 toppings for, 326

twice-, 15 fillings for, 327

boiled, 325, 326

chips, 333

corned beef with cabbage and, *685*, 686

crust, stuck-pot rice with, 439

curried coconut eggplant with, 291

dal with, 410

fish steamed over, 558

French fries, 333

fried

crisp pan-fried, 331

crisp pan-fried, Spanish style, 332

last-minute crisp pan-, 332

oven-roasted "fries," 331

gnocchi, 517

gratin, scalloped, 256

grilled, 253

latkes, 332

latkes, garnishes for, 333

mashed, *328*, *329*

baked, 329

buttermilk, 329

flavors for, 330

garlicky, 329

Joël Robuchon, 329

"smashed" baked, 329

vegetables to mash with, 330

mashers for, 11

oven-roasted, 329

oven-roasted hash browns, 331

pancakes with scallions and kimchi, 332

roasted artichoke hearts with, 261

salads

additions for, 209

with mustard vinaigrette, 207, *208*

soup, leek and, 138

steamed, 327

stir-fried, curried, 246

using in recipes, 325

Potato-filled samosas, 116

baked, 118

beef- or lamb-filled samosas, 117

filling and forming, *117*

lentil-filled samosas, 117

Potato rösti, 332, *332*

Potato rösti, 8 garnishes for, 332

Pot holders, about, 10

Pot liquor, collard greens with, 307

Pot roast

about, 683

all-American, 683

five-spice, 684

Italian-American, 684

Pots and pans, about, 7, 8–9

Pot stickers, 124, *125*

steamed dumplings, 126

stuffing and sealing, *125*

vegetarian pot stickers or gyoza, 126

Poultry, 591–662. *See also* Chicken; Turkey

adding to vegetable dishes, 257

in appetizers and snacks, 130

chiles rellenos with, 320

Cornish hens

about, 659

grilled or broiled, with sherry vinegar, 658

and sauerkraut, 658

customizing recipes for, 595

ground chicken and turkey, 591–662

guinea hens, about, 658

pasta

dishes that work as sauces for, 494

pheasant, about, 659, *661*

pheasant, stewed with dried fruits, 662

poussins

about, 658

quail, about, 659

quail, roasted with honey, cumin, and orange juice, 660

reheating, 657

squab, about, 659, *661*

squab, grilled or broiled, Vietnamese style, 661

stock, quick, 658

12 dishes for greens, 223

21 dishes at cold or room temperature, 627

Pound cake, 846

marble, 846

polenta, 846

6 variations, 846

yogurt, 846

Pozole

chipotle, 469, *470*

chipotle, 10 garnishes for, 481

chipotle, with pumpkin seeds, 471

Preserved lemons, 375

Pressure cookers, about, 12

Prime rib, about, 676

Prime rib roast

for a big crowd, 677

boneless, 677

carving, *676*

for a small crowd, 676

Prosciutto

braised endive, escarole, or radicchio with, 292

white beans with cabbage, pasta and, 396

white pizza with parmesan and, 819, *820*

Puddings

about, 886

bread, 893

chocolate bread, 895

dried apricot clafoutis, 893, *894*

fresh berry tart with vanilla, filling, *880*, 881

rice, 895

rice, 9 variations, 896

super-rich pudding, 888

vanilla, 887

Pumpernickel raisin bread, 797

Pumpkin

bread, 771

ice cream, 902

muffins, 771

pie, 878

puréed, 241

Pumpkin seeds

about, 311

chile rellenos with corn and, 320

chipotle pozole with, 471

Puréed soups

about, 142

combinations for, 142

vegetable, with peas and mint, *143*

Puréed vegetables, 240–242

broccoli, 241

butternut squash, 241

carrots, 241

cauliflower, 241

chestnuts, 241

corn, 241

eggplant, 241

parsnips, turnips, or rutabagas, 241

peas, 241

peppers, chile or bell, 241

rich, 242

winter squash, 241

Q

Quail
  about, 659, *661*
  roasted with honey, cumin, and orange
    juice, 660
Queso asadero, 755
Queso de freír cheese, 756
Queso fresco, marinated, 97
Queso Oaxaca, 755
Quiche(s)
  about, 733
  cheese, 733
  crustless, 734
  onion, 734
Quick-braised burdock and carrots, 273
Quick-braised fish in black bean sauce
  fillets, 570
  whole, 570
Quick-pickled vegetables, 228
  corn coins with Sichuan peppercorns,
    229
  mango or papaya, 229
  Mexican-style, 229
  relish, 229
  spicy, 229
Quince, about, 383
Quinoa
  about, 453
  with carrots, 460
  with ground pork, ginger, and soy sauce,
    460
  orange-scented, with shallots, 460
  with roasted corn, 458, *459*
  and sweet potato salad, 219

R

Rabbit
  chicken recipes substituted with,
    711
  cooking, 624
Raclette cheese, 755
Radicchio
  about, 292
  braised, with prosciutto, 292
  grilled, balsamic, 253
  pasta with pine nuts, currants, and,
    495
Radish(es)
  about, 334
  braised and glazed, 334, *335*
  salads
    -celery-mint, 201
  salsa, 58
  simple salad, 200
Rainbow chard, 280

Raisin(s)
  bread, pumpernickel, 797
  honey-saffron rice pudding with nuts
    and golden, 896
Raita (cucumber yogurt sauce), 59, *60*
Ramekins, ceramic, 9
Ramen, about, 520
Raspberry(ies)
  fool, 891, *892*
  fool, yogurt, 891
  sorbet, 903
Ratatouille
  open-face sandwich with melted
    mozzarella, 810
  oven-baked, 352, *353*
Real ranch dressing, 71
  bacon, 71
  green goddess, 71
  parmesan, 71
Red beans and rice, 412
Red chile flakes, 43
Red curry paste, 46
Red enchilada sauce, 73
Red rice pilaf, 436
Red slaw, 205
Reduction sauce, 81
  about, 80
  flavors for, 81–82
  ginger, 82
  lemon-caper, 82
  mushroom, 82
Red wine
  leeks braised in, 303
  octopus with tomatoes and, 590
  sauce, pepper steak, 671
  seared scallops with pan sauce with,
    577
  strawberry-, sorbet, 903
  vinegar, 186
Refried beans, 393
Refried beans, 8 additions to, 393
Rémoulade, 70
Restaurant-style greens, 268
Restaurant-style greens, with thickened
  soy sauce, 268
Reuben, 805
Reverse-seared steak, 670
Rhubarb, about, 383
Rib (beef), about, 665
Ribolitta, 148
Ribs (lamb), about, 707
Rice, 425–471
  about, 4, 425–430
    brown vs. white, 427
  beans and

baked black beans, 410, *411*
  hoppin' John, 412
  red beans and rice, 412
chicken and, 624
  arroz con pollo, 625
  arroz con pollo, 7 ingredients to add,
    626
  paella, 435
15 30-second ways to jazz up white, 431
flour, 764–765
fried, 443–444
  5 tips for, 446
  14 additions or substitutions, 446
  with shrimp and pork, 444
  simplest, 444
  6 simple variations, 445
griddle cakes and burgers from, 443
leftover, in frittata, 732
main-dish recipes with, 440
noodle soup with pork, 161
pilaf, 432–433, *434*
  baked, 434
  with cilantro, *432–433*
  with garam masala, *433*
  10 more, 436–437
porridge
  with fresh garnishes, 155, *156*
  with meat, 157
  with vegetables, 155
pudding, 895
risotto, 440, *442*
  alla Milanese, 441
  five ways, 440
  fried rice balls, 441
  mushroom, 441
  with seafood, 441
  with three cheeses, 441
salad with dried apricots, 217
sesame breadsticks, 800
17 dishes for leftovers, 435
shrimp and, Japanese style, 546
shrimp jambalaya, 437, *439*
16 stir-in for, 434
sticks/vermicelli, about, 520
sticky, souped-up, 430
sticky, steamed, 430
stuck-pot, with potato crust, 439
stuffed tomatoes with, 359
sushi, 447
  about, 447, *447*
  rolls, 448, *449*
  rolls, 10 fillings for, 448–450
tomatoes stuffed with sausage and, 356
vinegar, 186
white, 430

Rich chocolate torte, 853, *855*
Rich spinach pie, 339
Ricotta
    about, 754
    baked ziti with, 499
    cheesecake, 850
    marinated ricotta salata, 97
    one-pot pasta with butter and, 478
    ravioli
        and herb, 513
        spinach-, 512
    rice pudding, 896
    shortcut, fresh, 758
Roast beef
    about, 675–676, *677*
    broiled, and avocado sandwich, 810
    prime rib roast for a small crowd,
        676
    strip loin with blue butter, 679
    tenderloin with Hollandaise, 679
    tri-tip with chimichurri, *677, 678*
Roasted bananas, 369
Roasted fruits, 247–250, *249*, 360
Roasted garlic, 294, *295*
    8 ways to use, 296
    soup, 137
    teriyaki, 76
    vinaigrette, 190
Roasted nuts with oil or butter, 87
    dry-roasted nuts, 88
    flavor boosters for, 91
    roasted beans with oil, 88
    roasted pumpkin, squash, or sunflower
        seeds, 88
    sautéed buttered nuts, 87
    spiced buttered nuts, 87
Roasted pepper(s)
    red, 318
    vinaigrette, 191
Roasted seafood, 536
    pan-roasted clams, mussels, oysters,
        537
    scallops, 537
    shrimp or squid, 537
    whole fish, 537
Roasted vegetables, 247–250, *249*
    apple slices, savory, 248
    artichoke hearts, 261
        with ham, wine, and lemon, 261
        with potatoes, 261
    Brussels sprouts with garlic, 248
    carrots with cumin, 248
    cauliflower with raisins and vinaigrette,
        248
    onion halves, 248

    oven-roasted potatoes, 329
    scallions, 248
    winter squash slices, 248
Roasted whole winter squash, 349
Roast goose, 657
Roasting, about, 20
Roasting pans, about, 8
Rolled oats, about, 452
Rolled sugar cookies, 836
Rolling pins, about, 11
Rolls
    about, *784*
    French, about, 788
Root vegetables. *See also individual types of*
        root vegetables
    braised spareribs with, 701, *702*
    dal with, 410
    in shaved vegetable salad, 206
Rosemary
    about, 49
    in baked potatoes, 326
    broiled or grilled boneless chicken with,
        599
    caramelized nuts, 88
    celery root, pan-roasted, with rosemary
        butter, 280
    focaccia, 822
    goat cheese, -honey, 100
Rosemary focaccia, 822
Rösti
    beets
        carrot and onion, 265
        with parmesan, 265
        with rosemary, 265
    carrots, 265
    onion, 265
    potato, 332, *332*
    potato, 8 garnishes for, 332
Round (beef), about, 666
Round roasts, about, 675
Rustic French bread, 787
Rutabagas
    about, 346
    puréed, 241
Rye
    bread, onion, 794
    flour, 763
    whole, 455

S
Safety, about, 3
Saffron
    about, 30
    honey-, rice pudding with nuts and
        golden raisins, 896

    mayonnaise, 70
    sauce, halibut steaks with, 566
Sage
    about, 49
    bread stuffing with, and chestnuts, 651
    fried, pasta with creamy gorgonzola
        sauce and, 491
Saimin, about, 520
Sake-simmered fish, 563
Salad dressings. *See also* Salad(s)
    5 more, 188
    oil for, 182–183, 184–185
    vinaigrette
        about, 187–188
        curry, *189*
        fish sauce, *189*
        herb, *189*
    vinegar for, 183–188
Salad(s), 181–231
    bean, 212–215
    buying, preparing, storing greens for,
        193
    chicken, meat, or fish, 221–228
    composed, 205
    egg, with mayo, 804
    fruit, 210–212
    grain, 215–221
    green, 192–199
    oil, about, 181–185
    oil, vinegar, 183, 186–187
    pickling fruits and vegetables, 228–231
    salade Niçoise, 225
    salt for, 203
    17 picnic-perfect, 219
    spinners for, 11
    tuna, with lemon and olive oil, 804
    vegetable, 199–210
    vinaigrette dressings, 187–191
Salmon
    about, 547–548, *548, 549*
    cold poached, with dill sauce, *550, 551*
    dip, smokes, 100
    gravlax, 551
    pan-cooked, 548
    pan-cooked, 10 sauces for, 549
    roasted in butter, 549
    roasted with herbs, 551
    roasted with miso butter, 551
    salads
        miso, with snow peas, 224
Salsa
    avocado-cucumber, 58
    avocado-tomatillo, 56
    bean, 57
    Chilean, 57

Salsa, *continued*
  chile-garlic, super-hot, 73
  chipotle-cherry, 58
  citrus, 57
  corn, 56
  cucumber, Thai style, 58
  green chile, 56, 73
  green enchilada, 73
  green papaya, Thai style, 58
  green tomato, 56
  "guacasalsa," 105
  jícama, 56
  Mexican cheese, 57
  papaya, 57
  pepita, 56
  radish, 58
  roja, 71, 72
  roja, charred, 73
  summer fruit, 58
  summer squash and, gratin, 256
  tomatillo, 56
  tomatillos
    avocado-, salsa, 56
  tomatillos, fresh, 56
  verde, 73
  watermelon, Thai style, 58
Salt
  about, 4, 26–27
  bread
    griddled olive oil, *768*, *769*
  brining with, 633
  for salads, 203
  seasoning, 32
Salty-sweet buttered popcorn, 90
Samosas
  beef- or lamb-filled, 117
  filling and forming, *117*
  lentil-filled samosas, 117
  potato-filled, 116
Sandwiches
  about, 803–804
  bread for
    about, *784*, 803
    everyday, *789*, *790*
    50 percent whole wheat, 790
  eggs in, 729
  fillings, about, 803–804
  fish, with chili-lime mayo, 808
  grilled, 7 other, 805
  grilled cheese, 804
  hot, building, 810
  top 8 spreads for wraps and, 803
  tuna
    pan bagnat with, 806, *807*
    salad with lemon and olive oil, 804

28 perfect hot and cold dishes for
    filling, 808
  wraps, 809
Sandwich sugar cookies, 836
Sardines
  fresh, pasta with, 495
  on the grill, 573
  pasta with, 495
Sashimi, 133
Satay
  chicken, 130, *131*
  pork, 130
Sauce, desserts
  caramel
    boozy, 860
    clear, 860
    coffee, 860
    –cream cheese frosting, 862
    creamy, 860, *861*
  chocolate, 858
  fruit, two ways, 862
  hot fudge, 859, *898*
  lemon curd, *863*
  vanilla custard, 864
Saucepans, about, 8
Sauce(s). *See also* Tomatoes, sauce; Wine
  about, 24–25
  about pan sauces, 80
  barbecue, 75
    bourbon, 75
    chipotle, 75
    curry, 75
    Korean-style, 75
    mustardy, 75
  Béchamel, 79
  Béchamel, baked chard in, 256
  butter, 76
    additions to, 78
    beurre noisette, 79
    black, 78
    black bean, quick-braised fish in, 570
    brown, 77, 78
  chimichurri, 52
  chimichurri, roast tri-top with, 677
  cooked, 71–83
  creamy bean, pasta with, 490
  creamy gorgonzola, and fried sage, for
    pasta, 491
  drizzle, five-minute, 81
  drizzle, ten-minute, 81
  5 unexpected sauces for steaks, 670
  for griddlecakes, 417
  Hollandaise, 80
    blender, 80
    tenderloin with, 679

lemon
  -caper sauce, 82
  chicken in, 611
  fish sautéed with, 537
  oysters sautéed in, 538
  sautéed fish with, 537
miso, 67
  -carrot, with citrus, 67
  dipping sauce, 67
  -herb, 67
  -soy, 67
mornay, 79
persillade, roast rack of lamb with, 712
for poultry
  almond mole, turkey thighs in, 652
  for Cornish hens, 658
raw fruit, French toast with, *739*
reduction, 81
reduction, about, 80
reduction, flavors for, 81–82
reduction, ginger, 82
reduction, lemon-caper, 82
reduction, mushroom, 82
relish
  cranberry, *644*
  quick-pickled, 229
saffron, halibut steaks with, 566
7 dipping sauces for battered and fried
    vegetables, 257
soy
  about, 4
  -baked tofu, 419
  cherry tomato salad with, 200
  mackerel simmered in, 563
  mayonnaise, 70
  miso-, dipping sauce, 67
  quinoa with ground pork, ginger,
    and, 460
  restaurant-style greens, with
    thickened, 268
  roast chicken with, 635
  sautéed shiitakes with, 306
  seared scallops with pan sauce with,
    577
  sesame-, five-minute drizzle, 81
  steamed clams or mussels, 581
tahini, 56
  anchovy, 59
  chile, 59
  coconut, 59
  minty, 59
  yogurt, 59
10 excellent dipping sauces for tempura,
    115
10 for fried chicken, 630

thickening, 82
white (velouté), 79
Sauerkraut
    with cabbage, 275
    and Cornish hens, 658
    with juniper berries, 275
    with juniper berries and ham, 275
Sausage
    baked ziti with, 499
    bread stuffing with, 651
    broccoli raab with sausage and grapes,
        269
    bulgur pilaf with vermicelli and hot, 458
    corn bread stuffing with oysters and,
        644, 651
    crumbled, frittata, 732
    homemade breakfast (or any other
        meal), 703
    Italian-style, hot or sweet, 703
    jambalaya, 439
    pasta with, 498
        and greens, 498
    pasta with vegetables and, 484
    pizza with tomato sauce, mozzarella,
        and, 824
    scrambled eggs with, 724
    spicy, okra gumbo with, 312
    tomatoes stuffed with, and rice, 356
    white beans and kale with, 402
Sautéed bananas, 369
Sautéed boneless chicken, 605
    with cream sauce, 608
    with wine sauce, 607
    with wine sauce, 12 simple spins on,
        607
Sautéed Brussels sprouts with bacon,
    272
Sautéed buttered nuts, 87
Sautéed eggplant with basil, 290
Sautéed fish with lemony pan sauce, 537
Sautéed fish with lemony pan sauce, thick
    fillets, 538
Sautéed olives, 313
Sautéed ripe plantains, 322
Sautéed soft-shell crabs, four ways, 587
    breaded, 587
    buttery, 587
    simplest, 587
Sautéed vegetables, 243. See also Braised
    vegetables
    about, 240–242
    eggplant
        additions for, 291
        with basil, 290
        with basil and chiles, 290

with greens, 290
with walnuts, 290
mushrooms, 305, 306
    dry style, 305, 306
    8 additions to, 305, 306
    shiitakes with soy sauce, 306
Sautéing, about, 17–18
Savory crêpes
    buckwheat
        sweet or, 743
    buckwheat, with ham and gruyère,
        745
    5 fillings for, 746
Savory piecrust, 869
Savory sweet sautéed apples or other fruit,
    365
Savory tart crust, 870
Scales, about, 12
Scallions
    chile-, sauce, 64
    creamed, whole, 316
    ginger-, sauce, 64
    potato pancakes with, and kimchi, 332
    purée, shrimp and, stir-fry, 543
    roasted, 248
    shrimp and, stir-fry, 543, 544
Scallops
    about, 574
    broiled, 534
    broiled or grilled with basil stuffing,
        578, 579
    ceviche, 132
    grilled, 535
    roasted, 537
    seared, with pan sauce, 577
Scarlet runner beans, 388
Scissors, about, 11
Scones, 775
Scones, 10 additions to, 774
Scrambled eggs
    with bacon or sausage, 724
    best, 724
    with cheese, 724
    everyday, 723
    with fine herbs, 724
    12 simple additions to, 724
Scrapple, 749
Seafood, 529–590. See also Fish; individual
    types of shellfish
    about, 530–532, 588
    on a bed, 560
    buying, 530–531
    broiled, 534
    ceviche, 132
    with corn, creamed, 284

deep-fried, 538
11 dishes to serve on greens, 227
14 dishes that work as sauces for, 494
grilled, 535
Korean-style vegetable pancakes with,
    356
okra gumbo with, 313
portion sizes, 532
preparing, 531–532
risotto with, 441
roasted, 536
salads, Mediterranean style, 227
seasoning simply cooked fish, 539
simmering in tomato sauce, 536
6 ways to serve simply cooked, 535
soup, 161–164
    bouillabaisse, 162
    clam chowder, no-holds-barred,
        162
    lightning-quick fish, 161, 163
    squid paella, 437
    sustainability, 531
    tortellini, 515
Seared and braised pork, 700
Seared baby bok choy with bacon
    vinaigrette, 267
Seared scallops with pan sauce, 577
    butter-basted, 577
    with cherry tomatoes, 577
    with ginger and soy, 577
    with red wine, 577
    with white wine, 577
Seasoning, of sauces, 80
Seasoning salt, 32
Seaweed
    about, 336–337
    nori chips, 337, 338
    "shake," 35
    stir-fried, 246
Seeds. See also Sesame
    about, 5, 307–308, 310–311
    anise, 28
    caraway, 28
    celery, 28
    dill, 29
    poppy, 30
    poppy seed swirl bread, 792
    pumpkin
        about, 311
        chile rellenos with corn and, 320
        chipotle pozole with, 471
    sunflower, 311
Self-rising flour, 763
Semolina flour, in fresh pasta, 505
Serrano peppers, 43

Sesame
    cold Asian noodles with, 522
    crisp, fish fillets, 568
    -crust, pan-roasted tuna with, 567
    oil, 5, 184
    oven "fried" chicken, 616
    rice breadsticks, 800
    seaweed salad, 209
    seaweed salad, additions to, 210
    seeds, 31
    simple green salad, watercress and, 194
    -soy five-minute drizzle sauce, 81
Shallots
    about, 338
    caramelized, 315
    chard with oranges and, 280, 281
    deep-fried fish with, 562
    fried rice with, 445
    quinoa orange-scented with, 460
    sauce, 79
Shallot sauce, 79
Shanghai bok choy, 265
Shank (lamb), about, 707
Shaved vegetable salads, 206
Shellfish. See individual types of shellfish
Sherry vinegar, 186
Shiitake mushroom(s)
    cold soba noodles with, 522
    in parchment, 343
    sautéed, with soy sauce, 306
    seaweed "shake," 35
    stir-fried broccoli and, gingery, 246
    tofu braised with, 422, 423
Shishito peppers, 43
Shiso, 49
Shortbread, 837
    cheese, 838
    lemon, 838
    6 simple additions for, 838
    whole wheat, 838
Shortcut kimchi, 229
Shortcut lemon mousse, 864
Short ribs
    about, 665
    coffee-chile braised, 683
    mustard-braised, 681
Shoulder (lamb), about, 707
Shoulder (pork), about, 689
Shredded carrots with chiles and chives, 276, 277
Shredded-pork empanadas, 127
Shrimp
    about, 541–542, 542
    broiled, 534
    burgers or sliders, 547

deviled eggs with, 93
fried rice with, 444
garlic, with tomatoes and cilantro, 543
grilled, 535
one-pot pasta with, 480
or crawfish boil, Louisiana style, 545
paella, 437, 438
peel-and-eat, steamed, 580
penne with tomato-, sauce, 494
and rice, Japanese style, 546
roasted, 537
salads
    Caesar, 197
    grilled, with chile and basil, 225
    pesto, 224
scampi, 542
smoky, 542
soup, hot-and-sour, 171
still the simplest and best, 542
stir-fries
    and asparagus, 543
    and bok choy, with water chestnuts, 544, 545
    and cabbage, with fermented black beans, 545
    and cashews, 545
    chile, with celery, 545
    with coconut curry, 545
    with fermented black beans, 545
    and scallion, 543, 544
    with scallion purée, 543
    and snow peas, 543
    with vegetables, 246
stock, 179
summer squash and, in parchment, 341
and white beans, 402
Shrimp cocktail, 98, 99
Shrimp cocktail, Louie, 99
Sichuan peppercorns, quick-pickled corn coins with, 229
Sichuan steak with plum wine sauce, 671
Silky baked custard, 735
Simple green salad, 194
    endive, with nut oil vinaigrette, 194
    15 ideas for, 194
    with fresh herbs, 194
    Greek salad, simplified, 196
    watercress and sesame, 194
Simplest dal, 409
Simplest fried rice, 444
Simplest yogurt sauce, 59
    additions to, 59
    uses for, 61
Simple syrup, 859
Simply cooked beans, 390, 391

Simply cooked beans, flavoring, 390
Simply grilled chicken parts, 619
Sirloin (beef), about, 666
Sirloin roasts, about, 675
Skate or other fish with brown butter, honey, and capers, 562
Skewered, Vietnamese-style meatballs, 127
Skewered and grilled meatballs, three ways, 127
Skewers, about, 11
Skillet pork chops, 690, 691
Skillets, about, 8
Slicing, about, 14, 15
Sliders, shrimp, 547
Slow-cooked green beans, 297
Slow-grilled spareribs, 698
Slow-roasted spareribs, 698
Slow-simmered beef chili, 403, 404
Smoked salmon
    farro salad with, 218
    or trout dip, 100
Smoky black bean soup, 152
Smoky chile lime chicken wings, 129
Smoky deviled eggs, 93
Smoky shrimp, 542
Smoky whole chicken, 641
Soba noodles
    about, 520
    cold, with dipping sauce, 521, 522
    cold, with shiitakes, 522
Sofrito, salsa, 73
Soft-boiled egg, 721
Somen, about, 520
Sorbet
    about, 897
    chocolate or cherry-chocolate, 903
    espresso, 903
    fresh fruit, 900
    honeydew-mint, 903
    lemon or lime, 903
    lime-basil, 903
    orange, tangerine, or grapefruit, 903
    orange-cassis, 903
    papaya-lime, 903
    pear- or apple-ginger, 903
    raspberry or strawberry-red wine, 903
    vanilla-pineapple, 903
Sorghum, 455
Sorrel, about, 338
Sort-of-sauerbraten, 680
Sort-of-steamed corn on the cob, 283
Soufflé
    about, 733
    cheese, 735, 736

Soup(s), 135–180
  about building, 136–137
  bean, 151–154
    pasta e fagioli, 148, *149*
    ribolitta, 148
    smoky black bean, 152
    universal, 151, *153*
    universal, additions to, 152
  chicken
    and barley, 155
    with butter dumplings, 166
    chipotle, 165
    many ways, 164
    with matzo balls, 166
    with passatelli, 166
    with rice, Chinese style, 165
    with rice, Mexican style, 165
    stock, quickest, 176
    Thai style, 165, *167*
    tortilla, 165, *167*
    with vegetables, 165
  chowder
    clam chowder, no-holds-barred, 162
    clam or fish, Manhattan, 164
    corn, 145
    corn, cheesy, 147
    corn, roasted, 147
  creamed
    about, 142
    mushroom, 140
    mushroom, robust, 140
  creaming and puréeing, 142
  on the fly, 141
  grain, 154–157
  hot-and-sour, 168
    with shrimp, 171
    vegetarian, 170
  meat, 166–171
    beef and vegetable, 168, *169*
    hot-and-sour, 168
    lamb, North African style, 171
    19 whole-meal, 170
  minestrone, 147
  minestrone, 5 more takes on, 148
  noodle
    in broth, 157
    chicken and, in broth, 158
    garlic fideo, 158, *159*
    pho-style, 160
  seafood, 161–164
  stock, 171–180
  thickening, 146
  vegetable, 137–151

Sour cream
  -chive sauce, halibut steaks with, 566
  muffins, 771
Sourdough starters, 767
"Sour" regular milk, 751
Southwest style
  chopped salad, 197
  millet and sweet potato salad, 219
Soybeans, about, 388
Soy dipping sauce and marinade, 64, 65
  sesame-, 64
  sweet-and-sour, 64
  tahini, 64
Soy nuts, about, 311
Soy sauce
  about, 4
  -baked tofu, 419
  cherry tomato salad with, 200
  mackerel simmered in, 563
  mayonnaise, 70
  miso-, dipping sauce, 67
  quinoa with ground pork, ginger, and, 460
  restaurant-style greens, with thickened, 268
  roast chicken with, 635
  sautéed shiitakes with, 306
  seared scallops with pan sauce with, 577
  sesame-, five-minute drizzle, 81
  steamed clams or mussels, 581
Soy vinaigrette, 190
Spaetzle, 518, *519*
Spaghetti and meatballs, 496
Spanish style
  almond meatballs, 127
  chicken, baked, 602
  potatoes, crisp pan-fried, 332
  tortilla omelet, 732
Spareribs
  braised, with greens, 703
  braised, with root vegetables, 701, *702*
  char siu slow-roasted or slow-grilled, 698
  slow-grilled, 698
  slow-roasted, 698
Spazote, 48
Spelt, about, 455
Spelt flour, 765
Spiced broiled or grilled boneless chicken, 599
Spiced buttered nuts, 87
Spiced deep-fried seafood, 541
Spiced lentil soup, 154
Spiced mayonnaise, 70

Spiced tart crust, 870
Spice muffins, 771
Spices. See also *individual types of spices*
  about, 4, 24–27
  grinders for, 12
  mixtures, 27–32
  salt and pepper, about, 26–27
  toasting and grinding, 27
Spicy beef and vegetable soup, 168
Spicy greens with double garlic, 307, *308*
Spicy hummus, 103
Spicy no-mayo coleslaw, 203
Spicy peanut chicken wings, 129
Spicy stir-fried edamame, 90
Spinach
  about, 338–339
  burgers, bean-and, 415
  -cheese triangles, 122
  -cheese triangles, folding, *122*
  creamed, 316
  with currants and nuts, 339
  -feta pie, 340
  fresh pasta, 508
  gnocchi, 518
  gratin, 256
  Israeli couscous pilaf with, 457
  one-pot pasta with butter and, 478
  with oven-roasted tomatoes, 339
  pie, rich, 339
  ravioli, 513
  ravioli, -ricotta, 512
  sushi-style, 339
  warm spicy greens with bacon and eggs, 199
Split pea(s)
  fritters, Indian style, 416
  and ham soup, 138
Spoons and spatulas, about, 10
Squab
  about, 659, 660, *661*
  grilled or broiled, Vietnamese style, 661
Square pans, about, 8
Squash
  acorn, stuffed, 358
  butternut
    braised and glazed, 334
    curried, in parchment, 341
    gnocchi, 518
    grain-fried, 288
    pasta, pansotti, 510
    puréed, 241
    wheat berries with candied walnuts and, 469

Squash, *continued*
  chayote
    about, 340
    cheesy chayote fritters, 114
  grilled, 253
  pattypan, 340
  pumpkin
    bread, 771
    ice cream, 902
    muffins, 771
    pie, 878
    puréed, 241
  pumpkin seeds
    about, 311
    chile rellenos with corn and, 320
    chipotle pozole with, 471
  summer
    about, 340
    and herbs in parchment, 341
    and salsa gratin, 256
    and shrimp in parchment, 341
  winter
    about, 349, *349*
    Afghan style, 352
    biscuits, 775
    curry, 350, *351*
    gratin, 256
    grilled, 253
    with mirin, 352
    puréed, 241
    roasted, pieces in the shell, 350, *351*
    roasted, whole wheat pasta with, 490
    roasted, wild rice with, 468
    roasted slices, 248
    roasted whole, 349
    Thai style, 352
    whole, steamed, 350
  zucchini
    about, 340
    grilled, 253
    lemony, one-pot pasta with, 480
    pancakes, 343
    pasta with corn, tomatoes, and, 488
    in shaved vegetable salad, 206
    stewed chickpeas with, 400
    stuffed, 358
Squid
  about, 588, *589*
  broiled, 534
  with chiles and greens, 588
  grilled, 535
  one-pot pasta with, 480
  paella, 437
  roasted, 537
  tomato-, sauce, penne with, 494

Stainless-steel spoons and spatulas, about, 10
Star anise
  about, 31
  pears poached with, 381
Star fruit, about, 383
Steak
  teriyaki, 671
Steaks, fish. *See* Fish, thick fillets and steaks
Steak(s)
  about, 667
  and-pepper wrap, 809
  charcoal-grilled porterhouse or t-bone, 669
  5 unexpected sauces for steaks, 670
  flank steak, grilled or broiled, 670
  on a gas grill, 669
  grilled porterhouse, 668
  kebabs, grilled with lots of vegetables, 673, *674*
  kebabs, varying, 673
  many ways to cook, 667–669
  pan-grilled, 669
  pan-grilled, oven-roasted, 669
  pepper, with red wine sauce, 671
  pepper steak with red wine sauce, 671
  reverse-seared, 670
  Sichuan style, with plum wine sauce, 671
  stir-fried, improvising, 672
  stir-fried, with green peppers and black beans, 671
Steamed artichokes, 259, *260*
Steamed asparagus spears, 262
Steamed dumplings, 126
Steamed seafood
  clams or mussels, 579
  clams or mussels, 6 ways, 581
  crab or lobster, 584
  crabs or king crab legs, 585
  shrimp, 580
Steamed sticky rice, 430
Steamed sticky rice, souped-up, 430
Steamed vegetables
  about, 237–240
  artichokes, 259, *260*
  asparagus, 10 ways, 263
  cauliflower, basic, 278
  corn
    sort-of-steamed, 283
  crisp-tender, 240
  fennel, 341
  potatoes, 327
  shocking, 238, *239*

  sweet potatoes, 344
  winter squash, whole, 350
Steaming and steaming baskets, about, 11, 17, *20*
Stew
  beef, 679
  lamb
    with cinnamon and lemon, 710
    with eggplant or green beans, 711
    with mushrooms, 711
    with white beans, 711
Stewed cherries, sweet or savory, 370, *371*
Stewed chickpeas with seared chicken, 398
Stewed tomatillos and tomatoes, 344
Still the simplest and best shrimp dish, 542
Stir-fried beef, improvising, 672
Stir-fried beef with green peppers and black beans, 671
Stir-fried noodles. *See* Noodles, Asian
Stir-fried shrimp and scallion, 543, *544*
Stir-fried tofu
  with snow peas or sugar snap peas, 420, *421*
  10 additions to, 422
Stir-fried vegetables, 244–247
  asparagus, *245*, 246
  bean sprouts, 246
  broccoli and shiitakes, gingery, 246
  curried stir-fried potatoes, *245*
  improvising, 672
  potatoes, curried, 246
  seaweed and celery, 246
  shrimp, chicken, meat and, 246
  tofu and, 246
  Vietnamese style, 247
Stir-frying, about, 20
Stock
  about, 171–174
  beef, pork, lamb, or veal, 176, *177*
  canned or packaged, about, 4
  chicken, quickest, 176
  darker and richer, 178
  dashi, 179
  dashi, 5 ways to use, 180
  fennel baked in, 293
  fish, 180
  poultry, quick, 658
  6 quick, 173
  6 variations, 179
  vegetable, 174, *175*
  water vs., 136
Stockpots, about, 8
Storing foods. *See individual types of foods*

Stovetop mixed vegetables with olive oil, 354
Stracciatella, 138
Strainers, about, 10
Strawberry(ies)
    about, 370, *370*
    ice cream, 902
    -red wine sorbet, 903
    shortcakes, or other fruit, 849, *851*
String beans. *See* Green beans
Strip loin with blue butter, 679
Stuffed grape leaves, 120
Stuffed grape leaves, lamb-stuffed, 122
Stuffed vegetables
    acorn squash, 358
    cabbage or kale, 358
    eggplant, 358
    onions, *357*, 358
    peppers, 358
    tomatoes
        quick, 359
        with rice and cheese, 359
        with sausage and rice, 356
    zucchini, 358
Stuffing
    broiled or grilled scallops with, *578*, *579*
    for poultry
        corn bread with oysters and sausage, *644*, 651
        5 other recipes to use as, 649
        my favorite bread, 650
Sugar
    about, 826–827
    cookies, 834
        brown, and salt, 836
        chocolate, 836
        rolled, 836
        sandwich, 836
    creaming, *830*, 831
Sumac, 31
Summer fruit salsa, 58
Summer squash
    about, 340
    and herbs in parchment, 341
    and salsa gratin, 256
    and shrimp in parchment, 341
Summertime fresh tomato soup, 144
Sunflower seeds, about, 311
Super-crunchy pan-fried chicken Marknuggets, 631
Super-rich pudding, 888
Sushi
    bowls, improvising, 451
    rice, 447
        about, 447, *447*

rolls, 448, *449*
    rolls, 10 fillings for, 448–450
    sushi-style spinach, 339
Sweet-and-sour caramelized onions, 315
Sweet chocolate, 828
Sweet crêpes
    buckwheat
        or savory, 743
    6 fillings or toppings for, 744
Sweeteners, about, 5, 826–827
Sweeter caramelized onions, 315
Sweet peppers
    about, 40
    red, roasted, vinaigrette, 191
    stir-fried beef, with black beans and, 671
Sweet potato(es)
    about, 343
    baked, 343
    biscuits, 775
    boiled or steamed, 344
    braised brisket with carrots, dried fruit, lots of garlic, and, 686
    gingered, fish steamed over, 558
    gnocchi, 518
    gratin, 256
    grilled, 253
    mashed, 344
    pasta, pansotti, 512
    quinoa and, salad, 219
    roasted, whole wheat farfalle with, 488, *489*
Sweet sautéed apples or other fruit, 365
Sweet sautéed apples or other fruit, savory, 365
Sweet tart crust, 869
Swiss chard, 280
"Swiss" (emmental) cheese, 755

T
Tabbouleh, 217
Tacos
    about, 809–811
    eggs in, 729
    fillings for, 814
    fish, four ways, 811, *813*
    tostadas, 815
Tahini
    collard greens with, 301
    sauce, 56
        anchovy, 59
        chile, 59
        coconut, 59
        minty, 59
        yogurt, 59

Tamales, 461
    about, *463*
    one big naked, 462
    10 dishes for tamale fillings, 462
Tandoori chicken, 642
Tangerine(s)
    about, 378
    sorbet, 903
Tapenade, 109
    dried tomato, 109
    green olive, 109
Taro, 348
Tarragon
    about, 49
    corn salad with, 201
Tartar sauce, 70
Tart(s)
    about, 864–866
    crust
        about, *866*, 866–867, *868*, *873*
        chocolate, 870
        4 simple variations, 870
        graham cracker, 871
        nutty sweet, 870
        prebaking, 869
        savory, 870
        spiced, 870
        sweet, 869
    fresh berry
        with chocolate, 881
        with vanilla pudding filling, *880*, 881
    fresh blueberry with lemon curd, 881
    fruit galette, 879
    tarte tatin, 882, *883*
Tatsoi, 265
T-bone, charcoal-grilled porterhouse, 669
T-bone steak, 669
Techniques for individual foods. *See individual types of foods*
Teff, 453
Tembleque, 888
Tempeh
    about, 418
    chili, 406
Tempura, 112, *113*
    dipping sauces for, 115
    eggless vegetable tempura, 114
    pakoras, 114
Ten-minute drizzle sauce, 81
Teriyaki, 76
    chicken, *600*, 601
    chicken, grilled, *600*, 601
    chicken, stir-fried, 601
    roasted garlic, 76
    steak, 671

Thai basil
    broiled or grilled scallops with, 579
Thai peppers
    about, 43
        chile paste, 45
    giant, 43
Thai style
    broiled or grilled boneless chicken with, 599
    chicken, grilled or broiled, 621
    chicken soup, 165, *167*
    chile sauce, 66
    curried fish, 560
    curry chicken, baked, 602
    8 additions to mixed spicy vegetables, 355
    lightning-quick fish soup, 161, *163*
    mixed spicy vegetables, 354
    salsa
        cucumber, 58
        green papaya, 58
        watermelon, 58
    steamed clams or mussels, 581
    winter squash, 352
    wrap, 809
Thanksgiving side dishes, 652
Thermometers, about, 9, 10
Thousand Island sauce, 70
Three-bean salad, 214
Three-day pickles, 230
Thyme, 49, *51*
    broiled or grilled boneless chicken with, 599
    roast leg of lamb with orange and, 710
Tilapia, about, 568
Timers, about, 10
Toast
    fresh cheese, *717*
    toppings for, 718
    Welsh rarebit, *717*
Toasted bread crumbs, 801
Tofu. *See also* Tempeh
    about, *417*, 417–418
    baked, 419
    baked, miso-, 419
    baked, soy-, 419
    barbecue- or -teriyaki-glazed, 420
    braised-
        with chicken and eggplant, 423
        with eggplant and shiitakes, 422
        with shiitakes and broccoli, 423
        with shiitakes and green beans, 423
        with spicy ground pork, 423
    chili, 406
    croutons or sticks, 419

15 sauces for, 420
    grilled or broiled, 419
    skins/noodles, about, 520
    stir-fried, 10 additions to, 422
    stir-fried, with snow peas or sugar snap peas, 420, *421*
    with stir-fried vegetables, 246
    stir-fried with ketchup, 605
Tomatillos
    about, 344
    avocado-tomatillo salsa, 56
    beans with hominy and, 397
    fresh salsa, 56
    stewed, and tomatoes, 344
Tomato(es)
    about, 345, *345*
    -basil vinaigrette, 190
    beans and, 396
    beef stew with dried mushrooms and, 680
    braised, gratin, *254*
    bruschetta with, and basil, 96
    cherry
        farro with leeks, basil and, 467
        oven-roasted, whole, 348
        pan-roasted corn with, 286
        seared scallops with pan sauce with, 577
    chicken
        boneless, baked with, 601
        spiced, poached, 612
    dried, tapenade, 109
    edamame with fresh, and cilantro, 398, *399*
    egg dishes
        fresh, and cheese frittata, 731
        omelet, 730
        omelet, and cheese, 731
    everyday, oven-roasted, 348
    flash-cooked kale or collards with feta and, 300
    garlic shrimp with, and cilantro, 543
    gratin, 256
    and herbs in parchment, 341
    lamb shanks with olives and, 711
    leeks braised with, 303
    octopus with, red wine, 590
    oven-dried, 348
    oven-roasted, spinach with, 339
    oven-roasted plum, 347
    pan-fried green and/or red, *346*, 347
    pasta with corn, zucchini, and, 488
    pizza
        with sauce, mozzarella, and sausage or pepperoni, 824

with sauce and mozzarella, 819
    with sauce and mozzarella, fresh, 821
    plum
        oven-roasted, 347
        oven-roasted, canned, 348
    pork, braised with fennel and, 700
    rice salad with, 217
    salads, 200
        cherry tomato, with soy sauce, 200
        mozzarella, and basil, 199
    sauces
        fast, with or without pasta, 478
        fresh raw tomato sauce, linguine with, 482, *483*
        fresh (uncooked), 54, 55
        poached eggs, with cheese, 726
        poached eggs in, 726, 727
        seafood simmered in, 536
        -shrimp, penne with, 494
        16 spins on, 481–482
    soup, 144
        and bread, 145
        -garlic, 145
        gazpacho, chunky, 150
        gazpacho, fast and simple, 150
        gazpacho, 7 more ways, 150
        smooth, 145
        summertime fresh, 144
        tomato-garlic, 137
        wintertime, 144
    steamed clams or mussels with, 581
    stewed
        pan-roasted corn with, 286
    stewed tomatillos and, 344
    stuffed, quick, 359
    stuffed, with rice and cheese, 359
    stuffed with sausage and rice, 356
    tabbouleh with, 218
Tools for cooking, about, 10–11
Tortilla(s)
    about, 809–810
    chicken soup, 165, *167*
    flour, 781
    mostly whole wheat, 781
    nachos, 110
    Spanish omelet, 732
    tortilla chips
        baked, 110
        fried, 110
        sprinkles for, 110
Tostadas, 815
Traditional cranberry sauce, 74
    firm or jelly, 74
    relish, 74

Tropical tubers, 348
Trout
about, 547–548, *548*, *549*
cold poached, with dill sauce, 551
dip, smokes, 100
whole, with bacon and red onions, pan-fried, *572*, 573
Tuna
pan-roasted, 567
pan-roasted, sesame-crusted, 567
poke, 133
salad
with lemon and olive oil, 804
with mayo, 804
with olives, 804
sandwiches
melt, 805
pan bagnat with, 806, *807*
tomato-, sauce, penne with, 495
Turbinado sugar, 826–827
Turkey
basic roast boneless breast, 652
gravy, *644*, 649
classic roast, with, 647
ground, 653
parts
about, 650
roast breast, on the bone, 650
thighs in almond mole, 652
red beans with smoked, and rice, 413
stock, 176
stuffing
5 recipes for, 649
my favorite, 6 ways, 651
my favorite bread, 650
Thanksgiving side dishes for, 652
whole
about, 643, 648
classic, with gravy, 647
forty-five minute roast, *644–645*, 646
roasting, about, 646, *646*
timing, 647
Turkish-style baked chicken, 602
Turmeric, 31
Turnip greens, 307
Turnips
about, 346
braised and glazed, 334, *335*
puréed, 241
puréed soup, 142
Tuscan-style white beans, 402
Twice-baked potatoes, 327
Twice-baked potatoes, 15 fillings for, 327
"Twice-cooked" gnocchi, 517

U

Udon, about, 520
Udon, stir-fried, 524
UHT (ultra-high-temperature) milk, 752
Un-avocado guacamole, 105
Universal bean soup, 151, *153*
Universal bean soup, additions to, 152
Unleavened flatbreads. *See* Flatbreads
Unsweetened chocolate, 828
Urad beans, 388

V

Vanilla
bean, rice pudding, 896
beans, 31
beans, about, *899*
biscotti, 838
cake glaze, 858
cream pie, 875
custard sauce, 864
fresh berry tart with, pudding filling, *880*, 881
frosting, 856
frozen yogurt, *899*
ice cream, *898*
custard, 897
simplest, 899
-orange cream pie, 877
pears poached with, *380*, 381
-pineapple sorbet, 903
pudding, 887
Veal
about, 706–707, 713
chops, grilled or broiled, 713
grilling large cuts, 677
stock, 176
Vegan red beans and rice, 413
Vegetable fritters, 111
variations, 114
Vegetable(s). *See also individual names of vegetables*
about, 234, 235–237
blanching, 237–238
boiling, 237–240
braising and glazing, 247
buying and handling fresh produce, 234–236
crisp-tender, 238
freezing, 237
jazzing up, 251
microwaving, 237
parboiling, 237–238, 242
refrigerating, 235
roasting, 247
sautéing, 240–242
shocking, 238
steaming, 237, 242
stir-frying, 242–247
aromatic, about, 4
autumn, fish steamed over, 556, 558
beef and, soup, 168, *169*
boiled. *See* Boiled vegetables
broiled. *See* Broiled vegetables
buying and handling, 234–236
chicken soup with, 165
chili, 406
crisp-braised duck legs with aromatic, 657
dip, grilled or roasted, 107
folding, in parchment, *340*
frozen, about, 5
frozen, fried rice with, 445
fruit and, smoothie, 716
glass noodles with, and meat, 524, *525*
glazed, 247
heirloom, 347
long-lasting, 5
Louisiana-style shrimp or crawfish boil with, 545
mixed
about, 352
crisp kimchi pancakes, 355
crisp vegetable pancakes, Korean style, 355
oven-baked ratatouille, 352, *353*
seafood and, Korean style, 356
spicy, additions, 354
spicy, Thai-style, 354
parboiling in butter or oil, 242
peelers for, 10
pickling, 228
kosher pickles, the right way, 230
quick-pickled, 228
shortcut kimchi, 229
three-day pickles, 230
puréed. *See* Puréed vegetables
roasted. *See* Roasted vegetables
root or tuber
braised and glazed, 334, *335*
braised and glazed, with miso, 334
braised and glazed carrots, 334
rutabagas, 348
turnips, 348
sautéed. *See* Sautéed vegetables
soups. *See* Vegetable soup
spring, fish steamed over, 558
steamed. *See* Steamed vegetables
stir-fried. *See* Stir-fried vegetables
stir-fried, improvising, 672
stir-fried noodles with, and meat, 524

Vegetable(s), *continued*
    summer, fish steamed over, 555, *556*,
        558
    27 dishes to toss with pasta, 485
Vegetable salads
    Caesar salad, 196
    cherry tomato, with soy sauce,
        200
    corn, with avocado, 201
    8 shaved, 206
    fennel and orange, *204*, *205*
    simple radish or jícama, 200
    spicy no-mayo coleslaw, 203
    tomato, mozzarella, and basil, 199
Vegetable soup
    "boiled water," 137, *139*
    creaming and puréeing, 142
    4-ingredient soups, 138
    frozen vegetables in, 148
    immersion blenders for, *140*
    minestrone, 147
    puréed, without cream, 140
    rice porridge with, 155
    soups to serve cold, 151
    thickening, 146
Vegetarian recipes, finding with icons,
    viii
Vegetarian fed eggs, 720
Velouté (white) sauce, 79
Vichyssoise, 142
Vietnamese style
    braised pork, spicy, 700
    broiled or grilled boneless chicken with,
        599
    chicken parts, grilled or broiled,
        622
    chile paste, 45
    skewered meatballs, 127
    squab, grilled or broiled, 661
    stir-fried vegetables, 247
    summer rolls, 123
Vinaigrette
    about, 187–188
    in a jar, 188
    salads
        potato, with mustard, 207, *208*
    21 variations on, 190–191
    uses for, 66
Vinegar
    about, 4, 183–188
    bell peppers, pan-cooked with, 322
    fennel with onions and, 294
    sherry
        Cornish hens, grilled or broiled with,
            658

W

Waffles
    everyday, 742
    5 tips for, 744
    overnight, 743
    7 variations, 743
    whole grain, 743
Walnuts
    about, 311
    candied, wheat berries with, 468
    macaroons, 840
    sautéed eggplant with, 290
    wheat berry salad with apples and,
        217
Warm goat cheese sandwich with toasted
    nuts, 810
Warm spicy greens with bacon and eggs,
    198, 199
    BLT salad, 199
    kale salad, 199
    salad Lyonnaise, 199
    spinach salad, 199
Wasabi, 38
    bread crumbs, baked clams with, 580
    mayonnaise, 70
Water chestnuts
    about, 349
    shrimp and bok choy, stir-fry, *544*,
        545
Watercress
    about, 192
    classic creamy dip, 100
    farro and, salad, 218
    or arugula dip, 100
    simple green salad, 194
Watermelon
    broiled or grilled, 361
    pickled rind, 231
    salsa, Thai style, 58
Wax beans. *See* Green beans
Welsh rarebit toast, 717
Wheat berry(ies)
    about, 455
    with candied walnuts, 468
    with candied walnuts and butternut
        squash, 469
    salad with apples and walnuts, 217
Whipped cream, 854
    about, *852*, 856
    8 ways to flavor, 854
Whisks, about, 11
White beans
    in bean dip, 104
    with cabbage, pasta, and prosciutto, 396
    lamb stew with, 711

    purée, 392
    ribollita, 148
    salad, tabbouleh style, 214
    and sausage and kale, 402
    and shrimp, 402
    Tuscan style, 402
White chili, 406
White chocolate cookies, 828
White chocolate cookies, -pistachio, 831
White cut chicken, 637
White flours, 762–763
White pizza, 818
    with clams, 819
    with prosciutto and parmesan, 819
White rice, 430
White sugar, 826
White (velouté) sauce, 79
White vinegar, 187
Whole fish. *See* Fish, whole
Whole grain bread, quick, banana or
    pumpkin, 771
Whole grain waffles, 743
Whole rye, 455
Whole strip roast beef, about, 675
Whole wheat
    bread, 50 percent, 790
    bread, 100 percent, 790
    cookies
        shortbread, 838
    flour
        about, 763
        in fresh pasta, 505
        pastry, 763
        white whole wheat, 763
    pasta
        about, 490
        with browned chicken, 490
        with carrots, 490
        farfalle with roasted sweet potatoes,
            488, *489*
        with roasted winter squash, 490
    piecrust, 869
    pizza dough, 818
Wild rice
    about, 454, 468
    with chestnuts, 468
    with dried fruit, 468
    pilaf, 467
    with roasted winter squash, 468
Wine
    about, 5
    beef burgundy, 680
    cherries in port, sweet or savory, 372
    coq au vin, 624
    dijon-style mustard, 38

mirin, winter squash with, 352
orange-cassis sorbet, 903
pears poached with, or port syrup, 381
plum wine sauce, Sichuan style steak with, 671
red
    leeks braised in, 303
    octopus with tomatoes and, 590
    sauce, pepper steak, 671
    seared scallops with pan sauce with, 577
    strawberry-, sorbet, 903
    vinegar, 186
roasted artichoke hearts with ham, lemon, and, 261
sake-simmered fish, 563
sauce, boneless chicken sautéed with, 607
vinegars, 186
white
    braised pork with celery root and, 699
    seared scallops with pan sauce with, 577
Winter squash
    about, 349, *349*
    Afghan style, 352
    biscuits, 775
    curry, 350, *351*
    gratin, 256
    grilled, 253

with mirin, 352
puréed, 241
roasted
    pieces in the shell, 350, *351*
    slices, 248
    whole, 349
    whole wheat pasta with, 490
    wild rice with, 468
Thai style, 352
whole, steamed, 350
Wintertime tomato soup, 144
Wire racks, about, 9
Wonton soup, 138
Wooden spoons and spatulas, about, 10
Wraps
    Caesar, 809
    fillings, about, 803–804
    Indian-style, 809
    omelet, 809
    steak-and-pepper, 809
    Thai-style, 809
    top 8 spreads for sandwiches and, 803

Y
Yams
    about, 343
    noodles, 530
    noodles/shirataki, about, 520
    in vegetable chips, 111
Yeast, about, 766–767
Yellow cake, *845*, 847

Yellow rice pilaf, 436
Yellow split peas, in bean dip, 104
Yogurt
    about, 752
    biscuits, 773
    cheese, 753
    collards or kale with, 301
    8 ideas for flavoring, 753
    frozen, about, 897
    green beans with, and dill, 298
    muffins, 771
    orzo and fresh herb soup with, 158
    pound cake, 846
    raita, 59, *60*
    raspberry fool, 891
    rice pudding, 896
    simplest sauce, 59
    strained, 753
    tahini sauce, 59

Z
Zhug purée, 52
Zucchini
    about, 340
    grilled, 253
    lemony, one-pot pasta with, 480
    pancakes, 343
    pasta with corn, tomatoes, and, 488
    in shaved vegetable salad, 206
    stewed chickpeas with, 400
    stuffed, 358

KEEP COOKING WITH

How to Cook *Everything*®

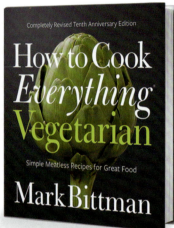

Completely Revised Tenth Anniversary Edition

How to Cook *Everything*® **Vegetarian**

Simple Meatless Recipes for Great Food

Mark Bittman

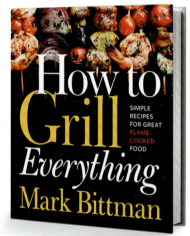

How to **Grill** *Everything*

SIMPLE RECIPES FOR GREAT **FLAME-COOKED** FOOD

Mark Bittman

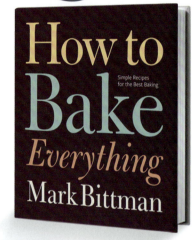

How to **Bake**

Simple Recipes for the Best Baking

Everything

Mark Bittman

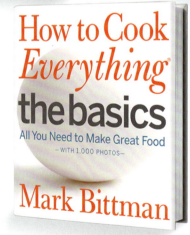

How to Cook *Everything*®

the basics

All You Need to Make Great Food

—WITH 1,000 PHOTOS—

Mark Bittman

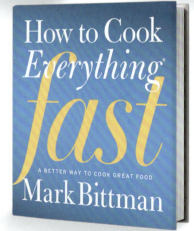

How to Cook *Everything*®

fast

A BETTER WAY TO COOK GREAT FOOD

Mark Bittman

△▽○
HMH

hmhbooks.com   markbittman.com

"Your big red cookbook has been my bible since college and it completely transformed how I approached cooking. It has made me a confident, flexible, and happy cook for my family (my kids say I make better food than a restaurant, and it's true, thanks to your books). Thanks for doing what you do."

—BAYLEY FREEMAN, QUANTICO, VA

"I'm a PhD student in pure math and just wanted to say how mathematical your cookbook is! You pick a few key axioms and concepts and then vary them to create an amazing variety. I've loved learning how to cook from your book. Thanks for such a concise and elegant book—truly beautiful."

—SAMUEL STEWART, MINNEAPOLIS, MN

"Your book *How to Cook Everything* has helped my family to eat decently while on a tight budget. We make the weekly menu based on what's in season, and your recipes (with many suggestions and improvisations) are always a life- and dinner-saver. Three cheers for the great work and thanks for everything."

—ANNA MARTINO, SÃO PAULO, BRAZIL

"Thank you for all your years of guidance to all of us (especially me) and making me a better cook in my kitchen and for my family."

—CHUCK DALLDORF, FRIDAY HARBOR, WA

"Your recipes have made my life easier, reduced the tension around shopping, prep time, and cleanup, and saved our family money because we eat out less often. I'm not exaggerating when I say you have significantly improved my quality of life and the health of my marriage (not kidding). Thank you, thank you, thank you."

—LYNN GARCIA, AUSTIN, TX